THE
ALL ENGLAND
LAW REPORTS

1979

Volume I

Editor
PETER HUTCHESSON
Barrister, New Zealand

Assistant Editor
BROOK WATSON
Barrister, New South Wales

Consulting Editor
WENDY SHOCKETT
of Gray's Inn, Barrister

London
BUTTERWORTHS

ENGLAND: BUTTERWORTH & CO. (PUBLISHERS) LTD.
LONDON: 88 Kingsway, London WC2 6AB
AUSTRALIA: BUTTERWORTHS PTY. LTD.
SYDNEY: 271–273 Lane Cove Road, North Ryde, NSW 2113
Also at Melbourne, Brisbane, Adelaide and Perth
CANADA: BUTTERWORTH & CO. (CANADA) LTD.
TORONTO: 2265 Midland Avenue, Scarborough, MIP 4SI
NEW ZEALAND: BUTTERWORTHS OF NEW ZEALAND LTD.
WELLINGTON: 33–35 Cumberland Place, Wellington
SOUTH AFRICA: BUTTERWORTH & CO. (SOUTH AFRICA) (PTY.) LTD.
DURBAN: 152–154 Gale Street, Durban
USA: BUTTERWORTH & CO. (PUBLISHERS) INC.
BOSTON: 10 Tower Office Park, Woburn, Mass. 01801

©

Butterworth & Co (Publishers) Ltd

1979

Reprinted 1982

ISBN 0 406 85123 9

Printed in Great Britain by Thomson Litho Ltd, East Kilbride, Scotland

House of Lords

The Lord High Chancellor: Lord Elwyn-Jones

Lords of Appeal in Ordinary

Lord Wilberforce
Lord Diplock
Viscount Dilhorne
Lord Salmon
Lord Edmund-Davies

Lord Fraser of Tullybelton
Lord Russell of Killowen
Lord Keith of Kinkel
Lord Scarman

Court of Appeal

The Lord High Chancellor

The Lord Chief Justice of England: Lord Widgery

The Master of The Rolls: Lord Denning

The President of the Family Division: Sir George Gillespie Baker

Lords Justices of Appeal

Sir John Megaw
Sir Denys Burton Buckley
Sir John Frederick Eustace Stephenson
Sir Alan Stewart Orr
Sir Eustace Wentworth Roskill
Sir Frederick Horace Lawton
Sir Roger Fray Greenwood Ormrod
Sir Patrick Reginald Evelyn Browne
Sir Geoffrey Dawson Lane

Sir Reginald William Goff
Sir Nigel Cyprian Bridge
Sir Sebag Shaw
Sir George Stanley Waller
Sir James Roualeyn Hovell-Thurlow
Cumming-Bruce
Sir Edward Walter Eveleigh
Sir Henry Vivian Brandon
Sir Sydney William Templeman

Chancery Division

The Lord High Chancellor

The Vice-Chancellor: Sir Robert Edgar Megarry

Sir John Patrick Graham
Sir Peter Harry Batson Woodroffe Foster
Sir John Norman Keates Whitford
Sir John Anson Brightman
Sir Ernest Irvine Goulding
Sir Raymond Henry Walton
Sir Peter Raymond Oliver

Sir Michael John Fox
Sir Christopher John Slade
Sir Nicolas Christopher Henry Browne-Wilkinson
Sir John Evelyn Vinelott
(appointed 4th December 1978)

Queen's Bench Division

The Lord Chief Justice of England

Sir Aubrey Melford Steed Stevenson
(retired 23rd April 1979)
Sir Gerald Alfred Thesiger
(retired 31st December 1978)
Sir Alan Abraham Mocatta
Sir John Thompson
Sir Helenus Patrick Joseph Milmo
Sir Joseph Donaldson Cantley
Sir Hugh Eames Park
Sir Stephen Chapman
Sir John Ramsay Willis
Sir Graham Russell Swanwick
Sir Patrick McCarthy O'Connor
Sir John Francis Donaldson
Sir Bernard Caulfield
Sir Hilary Gwynne Talbot
Sir William Lloyd Mars-Jones
Sir Ralph Kilner Brown
Sir Phillip Wien
Sir Peter Henry Rowley Bristow
Sir Hugh Harry Valentine Forbes
Sir Desmond James Conrad Ackner
Sir William Hugh Griffiths
Sir Robert Hugh Mais
Sir Neil Lawson
Sir David Powell Croom-Johnson

Sir Tasker Watkins VC
Sir John Raymond Phillips
Sir Leslie Kenneth Edward Boreham
Sir John Douglas May
Sir Michael Robert Emanuel Kerr
Sir Alfred William Michael Davies
Sir John Dexter Stocker
Sir Kenneth George Illtyd Jones
Sir Haydn Tudor Evans
Sir Peter Richard Pain
Sir Kenneth Graham Jupp
Sir Robert Lionel Archibald Goff
Sir Stephen Brown
Sir Gordon Slynn
Sir Roger Jocelyn Parker
Sir Ralph Brian Gibson
Sir Walter Derek Thornley Hodgson
Sir Anthony John Leslie Lloyd
Sir Frederick Maurice Drake
Sir Brian Thomas Neill
Sir Roderick Philip Smith
Sir Michael John Mustill
Sir Barry Cross Sheen
Sir David Bruce McNeill
(appointed 10th January 1979)

Family Division

The President of the Family Division

Sir Reginald Withers Payne
Sir John Brinsmead Latey
Dame Elizabeth Kathleen Lane
(retired 9th January 1979)
Sir Robin Horace Walford Dunn
Sir Alfred Kenneth Hollings
Sir John Lewis Arnold
Sir Charles Trevor Reeve
Sir Francis Brooks Purchas
Dame Rose Heilbron

Sir Brian Drex Bush
Sir Alfred John Balcombe
Sir John Kember Wood
Sir James Peter Comyn
Sir Ronald Gough Waterhouse
Sir John Gervase Kensington Sheldon
Sir Thomas Michael Eastham
Dame Margaret Myfanwy Wood Booth
(appointed 10th January 1979)

CITATION

These reports are cited thus:

[1979] 1 All ER

REFERENCES

These reports contain references, which follow after the headnotes, to the following major works of legal reference described in the manner indicated below.

Halsbury's Laws of England

The reference 35 Halsbury's Laws (3rd Edn) 366, para 524, refers to paragraph 524 on page 366 of volume 35 of the third edition, and the reference 26 Halsbury's Laws (4th Edn) para 577 refers to paragraph 577 on page 296 of volume 26 of the fourth edition of Halsbury's Laws of England.

Halsbury's Statutes of England

The reference 5 Halsbury's Statutes (3rd Edn) 302 refers to page 302 of volume 5 of the third edition of Halsbury's Statutes of England.

English and Empire Digest

References are to the replacement volumes (including reissue volumes) of the Digest, and to the continuation volumes of the replacement volumes.

The reference 44 Digest (Repl) 144, 1240, refers to case number 1240 on page 144 of Digest Replacement Volume 44.

The reference Digest (Cont Vol D) 571, 678b, refers to case number 678b on page 571 of Digest Continuation Volume D.

The reference 28(1) Digest (Reissue) 167, 507, refers to case number 507 on page 167 of Digest Replacement Volume 28(1) Reissue.

Halsbury's Statutory Instruments

The reference 12 Halsbury's Statutory Instruments (Third Reissue) 125 refers to page 125 of the third reissue of volume 12 of Halsbury's Statutory Instruments; references to subsequent reissues are similar.

CORRIGENDUM

[1978] 2 All ER

p 904. **Re H (a minor) (wardship: jurisdiction).** Line c2: delete the line commencing 'to have the writ set aside . . .'

Cases reported in volume 1

R v National Insurance Commissioner, ex parte Stratton

QUEEN'S BENCH DIVISION

LORD WIDGERY CJ, MELFORD STEVENSON AND CANTLEY JJ

13th MARCH, 21st APRIL 1978

National insurance – Unemployment benefit – Disqualification for benefit – Payment in lieu of remuneration which would have been received – Royal Air Force officer made redundant – Officer receiving capital sum on redundancy under special government scheme – Capital sum assessed on loss of prospects, loss of higher pension etc and including unspecified element for loss of remuneration – Whether capital sum a 'payment . . . in lieu . . . of the remuneration which he would have received' – Whether officer entitled to unemployment benefit – Social Security (Unemployment, Sickness and Invalidity Benefit) Regulations 1975 (SI 1975 No 564), reg 7(1)(d).

The applicant, an officer with a permanent commission in the Royal Air Force, was made redundant. He was not entitled to compensation under the Redundancy Payments Act 1965 since that Act did not apply to members of the armed services but instead he received a tax-free capital sum under a government scheme for members of the armed services who were made redundant. The capital sum was assessed by taking into account the applicant's period of service, the period he could have expected to serve, his loss of prospects, his loss of a higher rate of pension from longer service and the difficulties he might encounter in starting a civilian career. After leaving the air force the applicant was unemployed and applied for unemployment benefit. The Chief National Insurance Commissioner held that he was not entitled to unemployment benefit because the capital payment he had received was 'a payment . . . in lieu . . . of the remuneration which he would have received', within reg 7(1)(d)[a] of the Social Security (Unemployment, Sickness and Invalidity Benefit) Regulations 1975, which therefore disqualified him from entitlement to unemployment benefit for a period of up to one year after the termination of his employment. The applicant applied for an order of certiorari to quash the commissioner's decision.

Held – Although compensation for curtailment of a service career contained an element of payment in lieu of possible loss of remuneration, the extent to which it did so was speculative and unascertainable, and on the true construction of reg 7(1)(d) of the 1975 regulations the inclusion of an unspecified element of lost remuneration was irrelevant in deciding whether a capital payment received by a redundant employee was a payment in lieu of remuneration. The officer was therefore entitled to unemployment benefit and an order of certiorari would issue to quash the commissioner's decision (see p 4 *b c e f* and *h* to p 5 *b*, post).

Notes

For unemployment and sickness benefit, see Supplement to 27 Halsbury's Laws (3rd Edn) 726–733, paras 1320–1326.

For the Social Security Act 1975, s 14, see 45 Halsbury's Statutes (3rd Edn) 1092.

Motion for certiorari

Derrick Ross Stratton ('the applicant') applied for an order of certiorari to remove into the

---

a Regulation 7(1), so far as material, is set out at p. 2 *f*, post

High Court and quash a decision of the Chief National Insurance Commissioner made on 3rd November 1977 that the applicant was not entitled to unemployment benefit following *a* his compulsory early retirement from his employment as an officer in the Royal Air Force, because of his receipt of a special capital payment on termination of his service. The facts are set out in the judgment of Cantley J.

Harry Woolf and *Ian Glick* for the applicant.
David Latham for the commissioner.

b

Cur adv vult

21st April. The following judgments were read.

CANTLEY J (delivering the first judgment at the invitation of Lord Widgery CJ). *c* Counsel moves on behalf of Derek Ross Stratton ('the applicant') for an order of certiorari to quash a decision of the Chief National Insurance Commissioner dated 3rd November 1977. The applicant was a squadron leader with a permanent commission in the Royal Air Force and he received what is called a special capital payment on termination of his employment by reason of compulsory redundancy in 1975. The commissioner held that by reason of the terms of reg 7(1)(d) of the Social Security (Unemployment, Sickness and *d* Invalidity Benefit) Regulations 1975[1] ('the Social Security Regulations') this payment disqualified the applicant from entitlement to unemployment benefit for a period of one year from the date when his employment with the Royal Air Force was terminated.

On becoming unemployed the applicant was subject to the provisions of the Social Security Regulations, entitled by virtue of s 14 of the Social Security Act 1975 to receive unemployment benefit for every day of unemployment except the first three. *e*

Regulation 7(1)(d) of the Social Security Regulations provides as follows:

'... a day shall not be treated as a day of unemployment if it is a day in respect of which a person receives a payment (whether or not a payment made in pursuance of a legally enforceable obligation) in lieu either of notice or of the remuneration which he would have received for that day had his employment not been terminated, so however that this sub-paragraph shall not apply to any day which does not fall within *f* the period of one year from the date on which the employment of that person terminated.'

As a member of the armed forces the applicant had no legal right to notice or to payment in lieu of notice. As a matter of grace and in accordance with an understandably considerate policy of giving as much help as possible towards establishing displaced officers in civilian *g* life the applicant was given a long advance notice or warning of the date when he would have to leave the service. It is conceded that his special capital payment was not a payment in lieu of notice. The only question which arises in the present proceedings is whether his subsequent period of unemployment was a period in respect of which he received a payment in lieu of the remuneration which he would have received for that period had his employment not been terminated. *h*

On leaving the service the applicant was not entitled to a payment under the Redundancy Payments Act 1965. If he had been the present question would not have arisen because it has been for some time accepted that these statutory redundancy payments are not within reg 7(1)(d) of the Social Security Regulations. However, the 1975 Act does not apply to members of the armed services and as redundancy is redundancy in whatever sphere of employment it arises it was necessary as a matter of justice and decency to make special *j* provision for members of the armed services whom it was decided to make redundant in 1975. An appropriate scheme was accordingly prepared.

---

1   SI 1975 No 564

The scheme was described as follows in Annex H of the Government Statement on
a Defence Estimates, a white paper presented to Parliament in March 1975[1]:

'1. The compensation to be paid to United Kingdom personnel who are made
redundant is described below. As in past redundancy programmes, it will take
account of the curtailment of their expected Service careers (to which they are
committed by binding engagements), their loss of prospects, the higher rates of
pension which they might have earned had they served longer and the difficulties
b they may face in starting new careers in civilian life.

'2. For officers serving on permanent commissions who are prematurely retired
... compensation will take the form of a tax-free lump-sum payment or Special
Capital Payment, graduated according to length of service given and the length of
time for which, but for redundancy, the individual could have expected still to serve
before normal retirement. A Special Capital Payment equivalent to 18 months'
c military salary will be paid to those who at the time of redundancy would still have
had more than five years to go before normal retirement, and who have already given
at least 13 years' qualifying service in the case of officers ... The Special Capital
Payment will be smaller for those who have less than five years still to go or have
already served for more than 12 years but less than 13 ...

'4. Those who have given less than twelve years' qualifying service at the time of
d redundancy will ... receive a Special Capital Payment graduated according to length
of service and rising to 19 months' military salary for those with eleven years'
qualifying service, together with any other terminal benefits to which the service they
have given would normally entitle them.'

On 19th March 1975 a standing instruction was issued by command of the Ministry of
Defence to give effect to the scheme and it dealt in detail with the calculation of the special
e capital payments for officers of the Royal Air Force. They were in three categories set out
in para 4 of this instruction as follows. (i) Officers with at least 13 years' qualifying service
are to receive a number of months pay graduated according to the number of uncompleted
years of service to normal retiring age. The applicant was in this category and had four
years and three months of uncompleted service. At the bottom of the category is the
officer with one uncompleted year. He is to receive three months pay. At the top is the
f officer with five or more years of uncompleted service. He is to receive 18 months' pay.
(ii) Officers with 12 but less than 13 years' service are to receive 15 months' pay. (iii)
Officers with less than 12 years' completed service. Their payment is graduated according
to the number of years of completed service. At the top is the officer with 11 years. He
gets 19 months' pay. At the bottom is the officer with one year. He gets one month's pay.

What is the nature of this payment? It is not to be ascertained from the method of
g calculation. The amount is calculated on uncompleted years of service in the case of
officers with 13 or more years of completed service. It is calculated on years of completed
service in cases of officers with 12 or less years of completed service. After each calculation
the result is the special capital payment intended to satisfy the purposes set out in the white
paper to which I have referred. It is a composite payment to take account of four factors:
(i) curtailment of an expected service career; (ii) loss of prospects; (iii) loss of higher rates
h of pension from longer service; and (iv) the difficulties facing a man whose career is cut
short and who has to find some other employment as a late starter.

As is said in the Command Paper, Compensation for Premature Retirement from the
Armed Forces[2], 'These factors are, in many cases, not susceptible of precise evaluation and
the relative weighting to be given to each is a matter of judgment.'

Curtailment of a career involves far more than loss of the money which would be
j earned. A man does not usually join the armed services in order to become rich. If he is
fortunate enough to get alternative employment his earnings in civilian life may replace
or exceed his service pay but the alternative employment may not offer the features which

---

1 Cmnd 5976
2 Cmnd 231 (1957)

appeal to him in the service. He has lost a way of life. Moreover, curtailment of a career may involve frustration of a natural and otherwise attainable ambition or deprive a man of achievement or status which he values. If his career is cut short midway after he has established himself in his chosen profession he will be lucky indeed if time and opportunity allow him to take up some new employment which can be called a career and which will give him the same satisfaction even though it provides him with an equivalent income for the remainder of his working life.

In none of the government or service documents which have been referred to in this case is there any express reference to this payment as being made in lieu of remuneration which would have been received in the service had the employment not been terminated. I accept that, at least by implication, loss or possible loss of such remuneration is an element taken into account, but it is quite impossible to quantify it. The loss may not even occur. An officer who was going to be made redundant was given long notice of the date and was also offered advice and training to help him in resettlement in civilian life. It was at least within the contemplation of the parties that the officer might secure alternative employment and suffer no loss of remuneration and no unemployment. In such a case it is quite clear from what is stated in the documents that he would still be entitled to retain the whole of his special capital payment unless he was re-engaged in the armed services or employed in the civil or foreign service.

In the case of the man who receives 12 months' pay and is unemployed for a year after redundancy it cannot be right to treat each month's pay which is included in the computation of the payment as a payment in lieu of the remuneration he would have received during that month had his employment not been terminated. That would result in his receiving nothing at all for the other factors in respect of which he has been promised he will be compensated. The payment is a composite payment and in so far as it contains an element of payment in lieu of remuneration the extent of that element is speculative and unascertainable.

The commissioner has held that compensation for curtailment of the expected service career contains an element of payment in lieu of remuneration. I would not dissent from that although as I have said its extent is speculative and unascertainable. He goes on to say, citing a previous decision of the commissioners, that the presence of such an element in a payment which is composite and made for a variety of considerations suffices to bring the regulations into play. I would respectfully dissent from that, at least as a principle of general application covering the present case. He goes on logically to hold that this element in the special capital payment is intended to compensate for and to be referable to remuneration which would have been earned for all the days in the period following termination or curtailment up to the date when the career would have ended in normal retirement.

If this construction of the effect of reg 7(1)(d) is correct the effect in the case of the man who gets three months, or one month's pay and is then unemployed for 12 months would not only be grotesque, it would be shameful. It is quite impossible to suppose that the authorities who devised this scheme could have stooped to such a trick. I am not at all surprised that the view I have formed on the construction of the regulation leaves their honour unsullied even by suspicion.

In my view the conception of an unspecified element of remuneration is irrelevant to the proper construction of reg 7(1)(d). The regulation speaks not of elements but of 'a payment in lieu of [which I translate as "in the place of"] the remuneration he would have received'. It is common enough in life and was well known before the Redundancy Payments Act 1965 for an employee whose employment is prematurely determined to receive from his employer a payment in lieu of the remuneration he would have received for some specified period, whether measured in days or weeks and whether paid under legal or moral obligation or out of compassion. There is in my view no need and certainly no legal compulsion to construe the phrase in reg 7(1)(d) as if it said 'receives an element of payment in lieu of the remuneration he would have received', particularly when the element is indefinite and unascertainable and will in some cases be insignificant.

a I would grant the order which is asked for.

MELFORD STEVENSON J. I agree.

LORD WIDGERY CJ. I agree also.

Order of certiorari granted.

b Solicitors: *Treasury Solicitor*; *Solicitor, Department of Health and Social Security*.

Lea Josse   Barrister.

c
Cheryl Investments Ltd v Saldanha
Royal Life Saving Society v Page

COURT OF APPEAL, CIVIL DIVISION

d LORD DENNING MR, GEOFFREY LANE AND EVELEIGH LJJ

2nd, 3rd, 4th, 24th MAY 1978

Landlord and tenant – Business premises – Occupation of residential tenancy for business purposes – Test of occupation for business purposes – Business activity on premises required to be a significant purpose of the occupation – Occupation where business activity is merely incidental to the residential
e *occupation contrasted with occupation where substantial volume of tenant's business carried on from residential flat – Landlord and Tenant Act 1954, s 23(1).*

In the first case, the landlords, in December 1975, let to the tenant a residential flat consisting of a bed-sittingroom, bathroom and toilet and an entrance hall with a cooker in it. The tenant was a partner in a business which did not have trade premises and which the
f partners carried on from their respective homes. The tenant installed a telephone in the flat, and placed office equipment consisting of a table, a typewriter, files and a lot of paper in the entrance hall. Notepaper headed with the name of the business gave as the telephone number of the business that of the flat. The tenant issued business statements on the notepaper from the flat and had frequent visitors to the flat carrying brief cases. There was evidence that a considerable volume of trade was carried on from the flat. In
g February 1977 the landlords gave the tenant notice to quit but the tenant claimed the protection of the Rent Acts. The landlords brought proceedings for possession in the county court claiming, inter alia, that the tenancy was not a regulated tenancy under the Rent Acts but was a business tenancy since the tenant occupied the flat 'for the purposes of a business carried on by him', within s 23(1)[a] of the Landlord and Tenant Act 1954. The judge declined to make a declaration to that effect and the landlords appealed.
h In the second case, the residue of a lease of a maisonette constructed as a separate dwelling was assigned to the tenant in 1963. The tenant was a medical practitioner who had his consulting rooms nearby and who took the lease in order to live in the maisonette as his home. However, he wished to see patients at the maisonette occasionally and obtained the landlords' consent to do so. He occupied the maisonette as his home, but entered the address of both his consulting rooms and the maisonette in the Medical
j Directory and printed the telephone numbers for both addresses on the separate notepaper

---

a   Section 23(1) provides: 'Subject to the provisions of this Act, this Part of this Act applies to any tenancy where the property comprised in the tenancy is or includes premises which are occupied by the tenant and are so occupied for the purposes of a business carried on by him or for those and other purposes.'

he had for each address. In fact the only professional use he made of the maisonette was to see a patient there once or twice a year in an emergency. In 1976 the landlords gave him *a* notice to quit the maisonette under Part II of the 1954 Act. The tenant did not comply with the notice, and the landlords brought proceedings in the county court for possession. The tenant contended that the maisonette was his residence and that he was entitled to the protection of the Rent Acts. The landlords contended that the tenancy was a business tenancy. The judge dismissed the claim for possession holding that the tenancy was not a business tenancy, within s 23(1) of the 1954 Act. The landlords appealed.   *b*

Held – (i) Premises were occupied by a tenant 'for the purposes of a business carried on by him', within s 23(1) of the 1954 Act, only where the business activity on the premises was a significant purpose of the occupation of the premises or part of the reason for the occupation. Where, therefore, the business activity was merely incidental to residential occupation of the premises, and did not amount to a significant use of them, the premises *c* were not occupied 'for the purposes of a business' (see p 9 *f g*, p 11 *h*, p 13 *g* to *j* and p 15 *j* to p 16 *a*, post); dictum of Lord Morris of Borth-y-Gest in *Sweet v Parsley* [1969] 1 All ER at 355 applied.

(ii) In the first case, therefore, although the tenant was occupying the flat as his dwelling as well as for the purposes of his business, the occupation for the purposes of his business *d* was, in all the circumstances, a significant purpose of the occupation and could not be dismissed as de minimis. It followed that at the expiry of the notice to quit the tenant was occupying the flat 'for the purposes of a business carried on by him', within s 23(1). The landlords were therefore entitled to the declaration claimed and the appeal would be allowed (see p 11 *f* to *h*, p 12 *d* to *f* and p 15 *b* to *d* and *h j*).

(iii) In the second case, however, there was only one significant purpose for which the *e* tenant occupied the maisonette, namely for residential purposes, because his mere intention at the commencement of the tenancy to use the maisonette occasionally for professional purposes, and the obtaining of consent to do so, did not alter the residential character of the occupation, and his subsequent user of the maisonette for professional purposes was not, in the circumstances, a significant user but was merely incidental to his residential occupation. Accordingly, his tenancy was not a business tenancy, within s 23(1) *f* of the 1954 Act, but was a regulated tenancy protected by the Rent Acts. It followed that the appeal in the second case would be dismissed (see p 10 *f g*, p 15 *f* to *h* and p 16 *a*, post).

Per Geoffrey Lane LJ. To come within s 23(1) the business occupation must exist both at the time the contractual tenancy comes to an end and at the date of service of the notice of termination under s 25 of the 1954 Act (see p 13 *c d*, post).

g

Notes
For tenancies to which the Landlord and Tenant Act 1954, Part II, applies, see 23 Halsbury's Laws (3rd Edn) 885, para 1707, and for cases on the subject, see 31(2) Digest (Reissue) 940–943, 7708–7716.

For the Landlord and Tenant Act 1954, s 23, see 18 Halsbury's Statutes (3rd Edn) 555.

h

Cases referred to in judgments
Appah v Parncliffe Investments Ltd [1964] 1 All ER 838, [1964] 1 WLR 1064, CA, 31(1) Digest (Reissue) 226, *1841*.

Palser v Grinling, Property Holding Co Ltd v Mischeff [1948] 1 All ER 1, [1948] AC 291, [1948] LJR 600, HL, 31(2) Digest (Reissue) 1017, 8072.

Sweet v Parsley [1969] 1 All ER 347, [1970] AC 132, [1969] 2 WLR 470, 133 JP 188, 53 Cr *j* App R 221, HL, Digest (Cont Vol C) 671, *243bda*.

Vickery v Martin [1944] 2 All ER 167, [1944] KB 679, 113 LJKB 552, 171 LT 89, CA, 31(2) Digest (Reissue) 1014, 8053.

Wolfe v Hogan [1949] 1 All ER 570, [1949] 2 KB 194, CA, 31(2) Digest (Reissue) 1002, 7988.

Cases also cited

a *Abernethie v AM & J Kleiman Ltd* [1969] 2 All ER 790, [1970] 1 QB 10, CA.
Bagettes Ltd v GP Estates Co Ltd [1956] 1 All ER 729, [1956] Ch 290, CA.
Caplan (I & H) Ltd v Caplan (No 2) [1963] 2 All ER 930, [1963] 1 WLR 1247.
Horford Investments Ltd v Lambert [1974] 1 All ER 131, [1973] 3 WLR 872, CA.
Lewis v MTC (Cars) Ltd [1975] 1 All ER 874, [1975] 1 WLR 457, CA.
Lewis v Weldcrest Ltd [1978] 3 All ER 1226, [1978] 1 WLR 1107, CA.
b *Teasdale v Walker* [1958] 3 All ER 307, [1958] 1 WLR 1076, CA.
Town Investments Ltd v Department of the Environment [1977] 1 All ER 813, [1978] AC 359, HL; *rvsg* [1976] 3 All ER 479, [1976] 1 WLR 1126, CA.
Turner & Bell (trading as Avro Luxury Coaches) v Searles (Stanford-le-Hope) Ltd (1977) 33 P & CR 208.

c
Appeals

Cheryl Investments Ltd v Saldanha

By amended particulars of claim the plaintiffs, Cheryl Investments Ltd, the owners of premises comprising flat 6, Essex House, 47 Beaufort Gardens, London SW3, pleaded, inter alia, that the defendant, Roland Saldanha, at all material times occupied the premises partly d for the purposes of a business carried on by him, within Part II of the Landlord and Tenant Act 1954, and that by reason thereof his tenancy of the premises was subject to the 1954 Act, and sought a declaration that the tenancy was so subject. On 10th October 1977 Mr S A Goldstein, sitting as a deputy circuit judge at West London County Court, inter alia, dismissed the claim for the declaration. Cheryl Investments Ltd appealed on the ground that the judge misdirected himself and was wrong in law in holding that the tenancy was e not subject to Part II of the 1954 Act in that the defendant occupied the premises partly for the purposes of a business carried on by him, within s 23 of the 1954 Act, and conducted from the premises, on his own admission, not less than 30 per cent of that business. The facts are set out in the judgment of Lord Denning MR.

f
Royal Life Saving Society v Page

By particulars of claim dated 6th October 1977 the plaintiffs, The Royal Life Saving Society ('the society'), the leasehold owners of premises known as the Maisonette, situated on the third and fourth floors at 14 Devonshire Street, London, pleaded that the defendant, Dr Ernest Donald Page, was the tenant of the premises under an assignment dated 30th July 1963 of the residue of an underlease granted in 1960, that his tenancy had been determined g by a notice to quit dated 30th April 1976 served on him by the society, that he was not entitled to the benefit of the Rent Acts because the premises were governed by Part II of the Landlord and Tenant Act 1954, but that he had failed to apply to the court for the grant of a new tenancy. Accordingly the society claimed possession of the premises, £600 arrears of rent and mesne profits. On 5th December 1977, his Honour Judge Clapham, sitting at Bloomsbury and St Marylebone County Court, dismissed the society's claim for h possession. The society appealed. The grounds of the appeal were (1) that the judge misdirected himself in assuming that the frequency of occasions when Dr Page saw clients in consultation on the premises decided the purposes for which the premises were occupied, (2) that the judge made an erroneous inference from the fact that the society offered to make a joint application with Dr Page to the rent officer and (3) that the judge misdirected himself in holding that Dr Page had not represented that he practised at the premises. The j facts are set out in the judgment of Lord Denning MR.

John Stuart Colyer QC and *P de la Piquerie* for Cheryl Investments Ltd
Andrew Walker for Mr Saldanha
John Stuart Colyer QC and *David Parry* for the society
Charles Falconer for Dr Page

Cur adv vult

24th May. The following judgments were read.   *a*

LORD DENNING MR. Here we have a topsy-turvy situation. Two landlords contend
that their tenants are 'business tenants' and entitled to have their tenancies continued
under the statute in that behalf, whereas the tenants contend that they are not so entitled
at all. The reason for this oddity is because, if the tenants are not 'business tenants', their   *b*
tenancies are 'regulated tenancies' and they are protected by the Rent Acts. The protection
under the Rent Acts is much better for the tenants than the protection under the business
statute. So the landlords seek to chase them out of the Rent Acts and put them into the
'Business Acts'.

The statutes on this subject cannot properly be understood except in the light of their
history. I will, therefore, sketch it in broad outline, taking by way of illustration a   *c*
situation which used to be very common. It is where a shopkeeper lives over the shop, or
a doctor has his consulting room in his house. For over 35 years from 1920 onwards such
a person was protected by the Rent Acts, not only in respect of the amount of rent, but also
from eviction. The Acts distinctly declared that the application of them 'to any house or
part of a house shall not be excluded by reason only that part of the premises is used as a
shop or office or for business, trade or professional purposes': see s 12(2) proviso (ii) of the   *d*
1920 Act[1]. This protection was carried so far that when a lady ran a guest house as a
business and had her own bedroom and sitting-room there, entirely ancillary to the
business, she was protected by the Rent Acts: see *Vickery v Martin*[2].

This protection was continued until 1957. There was no break in 1954; for, although
the Landlord and Tenant Act 1954, Part II (which I will call 'the Business Tenancy Act')
gave rights to tenants of business premises, it did not apply to tenancies which were   *e*
protected by the Rent Acts: see s 43(1)(c) of the 1954 Act.

But in 1957 there was a fundamental change. By the Rent Act 1957 most houses were
decontrolled. Thenceforward the shopkeeper who lived over the shop, and the doctor who
had his consulting room in his house, were no longer protected by the Rent Acts. They
were only protected by the Business Tenancy Act: see the Rent Act 1957, s 11(7), Sch 4, para
11.   *f*

In 1965 there was another fundamental change. By the Rent Act 1965 Parliament
restored protection for the tenants of dwelling-houses who lived at home away from the
business. But this time Parliament did not give this protection to the shopkeeper or the
doctor who lived over the shop or the consulting room. Parliament left them to the
protection of the Business Tenancy Act. From 1965 onwards Parliament divided tenancies
into two separate and distinct categories: 'regulated tenancies' and 'business tenancies'.   *g*
Every tenancy had to be placed into one category or the other. 'Regulated tenancies' were
dwelling-houses protected by the Rent Acts. 'Business tenancies' were premises protected
by the Business Tenancy Act. This dichotomy was made by s 1(3) and (6) and Sch 1, paras
1(1) and 3, of the Rent Act 1965, and has been continued by the Rent Acts 1968 and 1977:
see s 9(5) of the 1968 Act and s 24(3) of the 1977 Act.

The result is this. If a house is let as a separate dwelling (without being occupied in   *h*
whole or in part for business purposes) it is a 'regulated tenancy'. But, if it is occupied by
the tenant 'for the purposes of a business carried on by him or for those and other purposes'
it is a 'business tenancy': see s 23(1) of the Business Tenancy Act. It cannot be both.

It is of the first importance now to be able to place a tenancy into the correct category,
because the two categories are very different animals.

Regulated tenancy   *i*
    When a tenancy is a 'regulated tenancy' the tenant is protected by the Rent Acts. So long

---

1   Increase of Rent and Mortgage Interest (Restrictions) Act 1920
2   [1944] 2 All ER 167, [1944] KB 679

as the contractual tenancy continues, the tenant is a 'protected tenant'. He is protected in
a respect of the rent he can be charged. As soon as the contractual tenancy is determined by
effluxion of time or expiry of notice to quit, he becomes a 'statutory tenant'. This is a
privilege which is personal to him, and, after he dies, to his widow or a member of the
family residing with him. He cannot assign it to anyone else. His residence there must be
continuous. If he ceases to reside thus, he loses his right as statutory tenant; and he cannot
revive it by going in again. It is so personal that, if the tenant is a limited company, it has
b no right to continue the tenancy after the contractual tenancy has come to an end.

Business tenancy
This is altogether different. During the contractual tenancy, the tenant is there under
the terms of the contract. But, once the contractual tenancy comes to an end (by effluxion
of time or notice to quit) there is automatically a continuation of the tenancy for an
c indefinite time in the future unless and until it is terminated in accordance with the
statute. There has to be at least six months' notice, and not more than 12 months' notice.
Until it is so terminated, the relations of the parties are governed by the terms of the
contract of tenancy. This 'continuation tenancy' is nothing like a 'statutory tenancy'. It is
not a personal privilege of the tenant. It is a piece of property which he can assign or
dispose of to a third person, provided that it was not prohibited by the terms of the
d contract. And he can give it up on proffering notice to the landlord.

The application of the statute
There was much discussion before us as to the meaning of the Business Tenancy Act (I
use those words because I think 'Landlord and Tenant Act 1954, Part II' is a little confusing),
especially the word 'purposes' in s 23(1); and the time or times at which those 'purposes'
e had to exist; and the effect of a change by the tenant in the use to which he put the
property. Could he take himself in or out of the Act at his option? I found all these
matters so confusing that I do not propose to attempt a solution today. I am only going to
take four simple illustrations to show how the statute works; for they will suffice for our
present cases.
f First, take the case where a professional man is the tenant of two premises: one his office
where he works; the other his flat, conveniently near, where he has his home. He has then
a 'business tenancy' of his office; and a 'regulated tenancy' of his home. This remains the
situation even though he takes papers home and works on them at evenings or weekends
and occasionally sees a client at home. He cannot in such a case be said to be occupying his
flat 'for the purposes of' his profession. He is occupying it for the purpose of his home,
even though he incidentally does some work there: see *Sweet v Parsley*[1] by Lord Morris of
g Borth-y-Gest.
Second, take the case where a professional man takes a tenancy of one house for the very
purpose of carrying on his profession in one room and of residing in the rest of the house
with his family, like the doctor who has a consulting room in his house. He has not then
a 'regulated tenancy' at all. His tenancy is a 'business tenancy' and nothing else. He is
clearly occupying part of the house 'for the purposes of' his profession, as *one* purpose; and
h the other part for the purpose of his dwelling as *another* purpose. Each purpose is
significant. Neither is merely incidental to the other.
Third, suppose now that the first man decides to give up his office and to do all his work
from his home, there being nothing in the tenancy of his home to prevent him doing it.
In that case he becomes in the same position as the second man. He ceases to have a
'regulated tenancy' of his home. He has only a 'business tenancy' of it.
j Fourth, suppose now that the second man decides to give up his office at home and to
take a tenancy of an office elsewhere so as to carry on his profession elsewhere. He then has
a 'business tenancy' of his new premises. But he does not get a 'regulated tenancy' of his

1 [1969] 1 All ER 347 at 355, [1970] AC 132 at 155

original home, even though he occupies it now only as his home, because it was never let to him as a separate dwelling, unless the landlord agrees to the change.

Those illustrations point to the solution of the present two cases.

a

Royal Life Saving Society v Page

Number 14 Devonshire Street is a house with four floors. It is owned by the Howard de Walden Marylebone Estate. In 1945 they let it on a long lease to the Royal Life Saving Society ('the Society') for 64½ years. The society occupy most of the house themselves; but in 1960 they let the top two floors as a maisonette to a Mr Gut. It was for 14 years at a rent of £600 a year. There was a covenant prohibiting assignment without the landlord's consent. There was no restriction on the use which the tenant made of the premises. But it would appear that the maisonette was constructed for use as a separate dwelling, and that the letting was 'as a separate dwelling' within the tests laid down in *Wolfe v Hogan*[1].

b

In 1963 the tenant, Mr Gut, made arrangements to assign the lease to Dr Ernest Donald Page. He was a medical practitioner who had his consulting rooms at 52 Harley Street. His major appointment was medical adviser to Selfridges and he did clinics there five days a week. He took this maisonette in Devonshire Street so that he could live there as his home. But he thought that in the future he might possibly want to use it occasionally so as to see patients there. So, when he took the assignment, he asked for consent to do so. Such consent was readily given by the society (his immediate landlords) and by the Howard de Walden Estate (the head landlords). It was a consent to carry on his profession in the maisonette. After the assignment he moved in and occupied it as his home. He put both addresses (Harley Street and Devonshire Street) in the Medical Directory. He had separate notepaper for each address and put both telephone numbers on each. This was, of course, so that anyone who wished to telephone him could get him at one or other place. But he did very little professional work at the maisonette. Over the whole period of the tenancy, he had only seen about one patient a year there. The last patient was in distress 18 months ago. He summarised the position in one sentence: 'Harley Street is my professional address, and the other is my home.'

c

d

e

On those facts it is quite clear that 14 Devonshire Street was let as a separate dwelling and occupied by Dr Page as a separate dwelling. There was only one significant purpose for which he occupied it. It was for his home. He carried on his profession elsewhere in Harley Street. His purpose is evidenced by his actual use of it. Such user as he made in Devonshire Street for his profession was not a significant user. It was only incidental to his use of it as his home. He comes within my first illustration. He is, therefore, protected by the Rent Acts as a 'regulated tenancy'.

f

The society later on alleged that he was a business tenant and gave him notice to terminate under the Business Tenancy Act. He was quite right to ignore it. He is entitled to stay on as a statutory tenant under the Rent Acts. I agree with the judge, and would dismiss the appeal.

g

Cheryl Investments Ltd v Saldanha

Beaufort Gardens is a fine London square, in which there were in former times large houses occupied by well-to-do families and their servants. These houses have long since been converted into apartment houses. In particular 46/47 Beaufort Gardens have been turned into 25 separate apartments. These are owned by a property company called Cheryl Investments Ltd, which is run by a Mr Welcoop. In December 1975 the company advertised these apartments in the Evening Standard, in these words: 'Knightsbridge. Essex House, near Harrods, serviced flats and flatlets. Doubles from 20 guineas, Flats from 27 guineas. Short-long lets.'

h

Mr Roland Saldanha answered the advertisement. He had been living in Weybridge, but he wanted a permanent residence in the centre of London. He was shown one of these flats which he liked. It had a large double room with twin beds in it, a bathroom and a toilet. It had no separate kitchen, but there was an entrance hall with a cooker in it which

j

---

1   [1949] 1 All ER 570 at 575, [1949] 2 KB 194 at 204–205, per Denning LJ

a could be used as a kitchen. The company provided the furniture and service in the shape of a maid to clean it and change towels, etc. It took her half an hour a day. The charge was £36·75 a week, plus 5 per cent surcharge.

His stay there turned out to be very unhappy with quarrels between him and the landlords. Eventually on 9th February 1977 the company gave him notice to quit on 26th March 1977. He claimed the protection of the Rent Acts. He said: 'I am a fully fledged tenant entitled to full protection under the Rent Acts.' The company took proceedings in b the county court claiming that he was not a tenant but a licensee. They relied on *Appah v Parncliffe Investments Ltd*[1]. But the judge held that he was a tenant and that the amount in respect of attendance did not form a substantial part of the whole rent: see s 7 of the Rent Act 1977 and *Palser v Grinling*[2]. So the judge decided those points in favour of Mr Saldanha, and there is no appeal on them.

But on the day of the trial, 27th September 1977, after previous notice, the company c amended their particulars of claim so as to assert that Mr Saldanha occupied the flat for business purposes and was, therefore, not entitled to the protection of the Rent Acts, and a declaration accordingly. The judge rejected this claim. It is from this decision that the company appeal to this court.

Now on this point the evidence was this: Mr Saldanha is an accountant by profession. He is a partner in a firm called Best Marine Enterprises. They carry on the business of d importing sea foods from India and processing them in Scotland. The firm has no trade premises. The two partners carry on the business from their own homes. The other partner works at his home at Basildon. Mr Saldanha works at the flat in Beaufort Gardens, and goes from there out to visit clients. When he went into the flat, he had a telephone specially installed for his own use, with the number 589 0232. He put a table in the hall. He had a typewriter there, files and lots of paper. 'The usual office equipment', said the e manageress. He had frequent visitors carrying brief cases. He had notepaper printed:

'Best Marine Enterprises. Importers of Quality Sea-foods. Telephone 589 0232 [that is the number I have just mentioned]. P.O. Box. 211, Knightsbridge, London, S.W.3.'

He issued business statements on that very notepaper. A copy of one was found by the f maid in a wastepaper basket showing that the firm had imported goods at a total cost of £49,903·30 and sold them for £58,152·35. The maid (whose evidence the judge explicitly accepted in preference to his) said: 'I presumed Mr Saldanha conducted business there.'

On that evidence I should have thought it plain that Mr Saldanha was occupying this flat, not only as his dwelling, but also for the purpose of a business carried on by him in partnership with another. When he took the flat it was, no doubt, let to him as a separate g dwelling. It was obviously a residential flat with just one large room with twin beds in it. No one can doubt that it was constructed for use as a dwelling and let to him as such within *Wolfe v Hogan*[3]. But as soon as he equipped it for the purposes of his business of importing sea foods, with telephone, table and printed notepaper, and afterwards used it by receiving business calls there, seeing customers there and issuing business statements from there, it is plain that he was occupying it 'for the purposes of a business carried on by h him'. This was a significant purpose for which he was occupying the flat, as well as a dwelling. It was his only home, and he was carrying on his business from it. It comes within my second illustration.

He did it all surreptitiously. He tried to keep all knowledge of it from the landlord; but that does not alter the fact that, once discovered, it means that his was a 'business tenancy' within s 23 of the Business Tenancy Act. Some may say: 'This is a very strange result. It j means that he can alter the nature of his tenancy surreptitiously without the consent of his landlord, and thus get a statutory continuation of it with all the consequences that this

---

1   [1964] 1 All ER 838, [1964] 1 WLR 1064
2   [1948] 1 All ER 1, [1948] AC 291
3   [1949] 1 All ER 570 at 575, [1949] 2 KB 194 at 204–205, per Denning LJ

entails for the landlord.' That is true; but I see no escape from the words of the Acts. Section 40 of the Business Tenancy Act clearly contemplates that the landlord may *a* sometimes be quite unaware of the purposes for which a tenant is occupying the premises. It enables a landlord to serve a notice on the tenant so as to find out. But, strange as the result may be, it does open a way to the landlord by which he can get possession. He can give notice of termination to the tenant and oppose any grant of a new tenancy on the ground that he has surreptitiously without the consent of the landlord changed the use of the holding: see s 30(1)(c) of the 1954 Act. I should have thought that the landlord might *b* well be successful. It places him in a better position to evict the tenant than if the tenancy was a 'regulated tenancy' protected under the Rent Acts.

The judge took a different view. He said:

'I think he [Mr Saldanha] is carrying on some business on the premises, but of a nominal kind, and not worth even considering. It is, in my view, de minimis. It amounts to having a few files at home and making a few telephone calls from home.' *c*

It is to be noticed that the judge is there speaking of the actual 'use' made of the premises: whereas the statute requires us to look at 'the purposes' for which he is occupying it. A professional man may occupy premises for the 'purposes' of seeing clients, but he may make little 'use' of them because no clients come to see him. On the evidence it seems to me that Mr Saldanha is in the same position as the man in my second illustration. He has *d* only one home, the flat in Beaufort Gardens, and he is occupying it, not only for the purpose of his home, but also for the purpose of a business carried on by him: and that was a significant purpose. It cannot be dismissed by invoking the maxim de minimis non curat lex. That maxim must not be too easily invoked. A man cannot excuse himself from a breach of contract by saying that it did no damage. Nor is it permissible for a man sued in tort to say: 'It was only a little wrong and did only a little damage.' So here, I do not *e* think the 'purpose' of Mr Saldanha can be excused by saying: 'It was only little used.'

I would ask: what is the alternative? It could only be that Mr Saldanha would be protected by the Rent Acts and be able to stay there, using the flat for business purposes as much as he liked.

On the case of Mr Saldanha, therefore, I take a different view from the judge. I think that at the expiry of the notice to quit Mr Saldanha was occupying this flat for the purposes *f* of a business carried on by him. So the landlords are entitled to a declaration to that effect. I would allow the appeal in this case.

GEOFFREY LANE LJ. The Landlord and Tenant Act 1954, Part II, appears on its face to have been enacted for the benefit of tenants, in particular business and professional tenants. It provides among other things that under the proper circumstances such tenants *g* may obtain security of tenure, may apply to the court for a new tenancy or for compensation where no new tenancy is granted.

It therefore comes as a surprise to find in these two cases that it is the landlord who is contending that the 1954 Act applies to the tenancy and the tenant in each case who is contending that it does not. It is clear that in certain circumstances the protection given to the tenant by Part II of the 1954 Act is weaker than that provided by the Rent Acts and *h* that there may be advantages to the landlord in a finding that the premises are occupied by a tenant 'for the purposes of a business carried on by him or for [the purpose of a business carried on by him] and [for] other purposes': see s 23(1) of the 1954 Act.

There are two separate matters to be decided. First, what is the point of time at which for the purpose of the present two cases the requirements of s 23(1) of the 1954 Act must be shown to be fulfilled? Secondly, what do those requirements mean? *j*

To answer the first question, it is necessary to look at the difference in effect between the 1954 Act on the one hand and the Rent Acts on the other. A tenancy to which Part II of the 1954 Act applies does not generally speaking come to an end when the contractual term expires. By s 24, unless the parties take the proper steps in accordance with the terms of Part II of the Act, the contractual tenancy is continued. Thus, where there is a tenancy for a term of years certain and no steps are taken under the 1954 Act to terminate at the end

a of the term, the statute willy-nilly causes the tenancy agreement to stay alive. Where, however, the premises are subject to the Rent Acts and not the 1954 Act, at the end of the term the contractual relationship between the parties comes to an end and thereafter the tenant assumes a different status, one regulated by statute. Once that has happened it seems clear that the contractual tenancy cannot be revived (other than by a fresh agreement between the parties) whether or not the tenant starts to occupy for purposes of a business.

b Thus the first date on which the provisions of s 23(1) of the 1954 Act must be shown to exist is the date on which the contractual tenancy came to an end.

If the tenant continues the 'business occupation' (if it may be called that) thereafter, no further difficulty arises. What is the situation, however, if between the end of the contractual tenancy and the service of notice of determination by the landlord the business occupation ceases? Section 25 provides that the landlord 'may terminate a tenancy to

c which this Part of this Act applies by a notice given to the tenant in the prescribed form specifying the date at which the tenancy is to come to an end . . .' If at the time the notice is served the business occupation has ceased, there is no 'tenancy to which this Part of [the] Act applies', and nothing on which a s 25 notice by the landlord can bite. It seems therefore that the business occupation must exist both at the time the contractual tenancy comes to an end and at the date of service of the notice of determination. It is necessary to

d point out, however, that in neither of the two cases with which we are concerned was there any change of purpose between the term date and the service of notice of determination. In each case the question is, was there or was there not a s 23(1) business occupation at the time the contractual tenancy ended?

We have had lengthy and learned submissions made to us as to the various possible interpretations of s 23. It is, perhaps, unecessary to deal with them in detail. One possible

e way of discovering what was in the mind of Parliament in choosing the words they did is to look at the earlier legislation and compare the wording of the similar section. That is s 17(1) of the Landlord and Tenant Act 1927. It runs as follows: 'The holdings to which this Part of this Act applies are any premises held under a lease . . . and used wholly or partly for carrying on thereat any trade or business . . .' The similarity of phraseology is obvious, and the draftsmen of the 1954 Act must have had s 17 of the 1927 Act in mind.

f Any difference in wording may be assumed to be deliberate and considered. 'Used wholly or partly for carrying on thereat any . . . business' has become 'occupied by the tenant and are so occupied for the purposes of a business carried on by him or for those and other purposes'. In one sense the new words are wider and in another they are narrower than the old. Wider, because it is no longer necessary that the business should be carried on at the premises, and narrower, because, as it seems to me, 'occupied for the purposes of a business'

g may entail something more than 'used . . . partly for carrying on thereat any . . . business'. It might be possible to use premises for carrying on thereat a trade or business without occupying them for the purpose of a business. It is obviously a very fine distinction, but the words in s 23 seem to have been used in an attempt to make it absolutely clear that activities on the premises which are merely incidental to residential occupation do not bring the premises within the section although they may properly be described as using

h them for carrying on a trade or business. The businessman, for example, who takes work home in the evening which he does in a study set aside for the purpose may very well be using the premises partly for carrying on thereat a business, but he could scarcely be said to be occupying the premises for the purposes of a business, any more than the person who watches the television regularly every evening can be said to be occupying his house for the purpose of watching television. It is only if the activity is part of the reason for, part of his

j aim and object in occupying the house that the section will apply. Lord Morris of Borth-y-Gest expressed the concept clearly when dealing with the meaning of the words of s 5 of the Dangerous Drugs Act 1965 in *Sweet v Parsley*[1]:

---

1   [1969] 1 All ER 347 at 355, [1970] AC 132 at 154–155

'It seems to me, therefore, that the words "premises . . . used for the purpose of smoking cannabis" are not happily chosen if they were intended to denote premises *a* in which at any time cannabis is smoked. In my opinion, the words "premises used for any such purpose . . ." denote a purpose which is other than quite incidental or casual or fortuitous; they denote a purpose which is or has become either a significant one or a recognised one though certainly not necessarily an only one.'

As is so often the case in matters of this kind it will in the end come down to a question of *b* degree, and borderline cases will produce their usual difficulties.

It so happens that the two appeals which we for the purposes of convenience are dealing with together provide good illustrations of the principles involved, one on one side of the line, one on the other.

The facts in *Cheryl Investments Ltd v Saldanha* were as follows. The premises were what was called a 'self-catering flat' let to the tenant in December 1975 at a rent of 35 guineas a *c* week plus a 5 per cent surcharge to cover increases in the cost of services provided, which consisted of cleaning and providing linen and so on. The landlords duly determined that tenancy by notice to quit in February 1977. On 21st March 1977 the tenant applied to the rent officer for the determination of a fair rent. The landlords' claim had originally been based on the allegation that the interest created was a licence and not a tenancy, or in the alternative that the attendance and services provided constituted a substantial proportion *d* of the whole rent and accordingly the agreement was subject to s 7 of the Rent Act 1977 and that the tenancy was not protected. It is enough to say that the judge found in favour of the tenant on both these aspects of the case. There is no appeal against these findings.

By a last minute amendment, however, the landlords alleged and sought to prove that the tenant at all material times occupied the premises 'partly for the purposes of a business carried on by him', and so came within the 1954 Act. They asked for a declaration *e* accordingly. The learned judge on this point also found in favour of the tenant and it is this finding alone which is the subject of appeal.

There is no doubt that the landlords at the time of the original agreement had no intention of creating 'a business occupation', whatever may have been the tenant's aims. The flat was in effect a bed-sittingroom with separate bathroom and water closet and an entrance hall with an electric cooker in it. The resident manageress gave evidence that it *f* was used as an office; that there was a typewriter and a number of files; that the tenant had many visitors during the day. It was however on the evidence given by the tenant himself that the landlords chiefly relied. He, the tenant, said that he had paid to have the telephone connected to the flat and that the files were to do with his business. He said that this business was called Best Marine Enterprises; it was a partnership between himself and one other man. The head office was in Basildon, which was the home of his partner. A *g* document was put to him with a 'Best Marine Enterprises' letterhead setting set out in typed form calculations of the profit made on two business ventures which amounted in all to over £8,000. He agreed that the headed notepaper was that of his business but suggested that the current letterheads were different. The interesting features of this document however were, first, that the tenant's telephone number at the flat was printed alongside the heading 'Best Marine Enterprises', and that the address given for the business *h* is not a Basildon address, as one might have expected, but a post-office box in Knightsbridge, SW3, the same postal district as that of the flat.

The judge dealt with the matter as follows:

'There was a last ditch effort put forward by the landlords that the tenant used these *j* premises partly for business purposes. An amendment was made and not opposed by counsel for the tenant. I think he is carrying on some business at the premises, but of a nominal kind and not worth even considering. It is in my view de minimis. It amounts to having a few files at home and making a few telephone calls from home. He called it 20 per cent to 30 per cent but that is 20 per cent or 30 per cent of very little. I am satisfied that the main business is carried on elsewhere, other than at home. As I say, this was a very half-hearted, last ditch attempt by the landlords.'

That is a view of the facts which must be treated with respect. There were enquiries made of the judge as to what he had meant by his references to 20 per cent to 30 per cent. The judge agreed that the evidence was that the tenant had said that he carried on 20 per cent to 30 per cent of his business at the flat. It seems to me that the result of all this evidence was to show that almost the whole of the business of Best Marine Enterprises was being carried on from the flat. The volume of trade was obviously considerable. There was little to suggest that there was any other place from which the business was being conducted. In my judgment the tenant came squarely within the words of s 23 of the 1954 Act. This was a good example of how a situation which may have started as an ordinary residential occupancy can develop to the point where one, if not the principal, purpose for the tenant occupying the flat is the business purpose. If he had to stop the business activity he would most likely have to leave the flat.

The judge was understandably, but I think unduly, influenced by the lateness of the amendment and the fact that the argument based on the allegation of a business occupancy was no doubt subsidiary to the landlords' other two contentions. So far as this case is concerned, I would allow the appeal.

The facts in *Royal Life Saving Society v Page* are very different. The premises are on the third and fourth floors at 14 Devonshire Street. The landlords are the owners of the head lease. They leased the premises to one Emile Gut in 1960 and by a deed of 1963 Gut assigned the residue of the term to the tenant, Dr Page. The landlords served notice to quit on the tenant in April 1976 expiring in November 1976, and contend that the tenant is not entitled to the protection of the Rent Acts because Part II of the 1954 Act applies to the premises. The facts on which they base this contention are these. The tenant is a medical practitioner. He agreed that at the time of the assignment of the lease to him he obtained from the landlords a licence to use the front room for professional purposes. He said that he obtained that licence as a precaution for the future, but that he had never seen any patients in that room. The only professional use he had made of the premises was 'to see, once or twice, a patient in the lounge in an emergency'. The judge accepted that evidence as truthful and correct. The landlords, however, sought to argue that certain other matters showed that the tenant was occupying the premises for purposes of his profession. It seems to me, without going into the details of the evidence, that the landlords had signally failed to show that the judge was wrong in his assessment of the evidence. He accepted the word of the tenant and that, in the circumstances of this case, was the end of the matter.

No doubt the tenant at the outset was minded to use the premises for the purpose of his profession, hence the request for a licence, but in fact he never did so. A mere intention unaccompanied by any action putting into effect that intention is not enough. Accordingly it seems plain to me that the requirements of s 23 of the 1954 Act are not fulfilled and that the landlords in this case must fail. The occupation was at the outset purely residential and nothing ever happened to alter its character. The judge was right in holding that the premises were subject to the Rent Act 1977 and in dismissing the landlords' claim.

In this case, therefore, I would dismiss the appeal. In each case I reach the same conclusion as Lord Denning MR.

EVELEIGH LJ. I agree that the appeal in the case of Roland Saldanha should be allowed, I think, for the reasons given in the judgments just delivered, that he was at all times occupying for business purposes.

Again, for the reasons just given, I think that Dr Page was at no time occupying for business purposes.

In these circumstances it becomes unnecessary to say at what particular time it has to be shown that s 23 applies.

Appeal of Cheryl Investments Ltd allowed. Declaration accordingly.

Appeal of Royal Life Saving Society dismissed. Leave to appeal to the House of Lords refused.

Solicitors: *Rees, Kon, Freeman & Co* (for Cheryl Investments Ltd); *Dawson & Co* (for the society); *Eric Hauser & Co* (for Mr Saldanha); *Monro, Pennefather & Co* (for Dr Page).

Sumra Green   Barrister.

International Factors Ltd v Rodriguez

COURT OF APPEAL, CIVIL DIVISION
BUCKLEY, BRIDGE LJJ AND SIR DAVID CAIRNS
8th, 9th MAY 1978

Conversion – Possession – Right to immediate possession – Factoring agreement – Debts assigned by company to plaintiffs – Cheques made payable to company to be held in trust for plaintiffs and handed over immediately to plaintiffs – Director of company paying cheques into company's bank account – Plaintiffs suing director for conversion – Whether plaintiffs entitled to sue – Whether plaintiffs having right to immediate possession – Whether director entitled to set up plaintiff's right of action against debtors as a defence.

In 1973 the plaintiffs and a company entered into a factoring agreement whereby the plaintiffs agreed to purchase all the company's book debts and the company agreed to assign them to the plaintiffs for 98½ per cent of the full amount of the debts. Under the agreement all the company's invoices were to be endorsed with a statement indicating that the debt concerned was assigned to the plaintiffs. In the case of each debt the company was to execute an assignment to the plaintiffs and notify each debtor when it was completed. Clause 11(e) of the agreement provided: 'If any payment in respect of an assigned debt is paid direct to the [company] then the [company] shall hold the same in trust for the [plaintiffs]. The [company] shall in that event immediately after receipt of any such payment hand to the [plaintiffs] the identical cash cheque or bill of exchange and if it be necessary for such cheque or bill of exchange to be endorsed to the [plaintiffs] to enable the [plaintiffs] to receive payment the [company] shall endorse the same over to the [plaintiffs].' In 1974 four cheques, totalling £11,370·69, were sent to the company by debtors in discharge of debts which were subject to the agreement. The company was in financial difficulties and the defendant, one of its directors, arranged for the cheques to be paid into the company's bank account. He knew that what he was doing was contrary to the company's agreement with the plaintiffs and that the cheques should have been handed direct to the plaintiffs. The plaintiffs brought an action against him for conversion of the cheques and claimed £11,370·69 as damages. The judge held that the payment of the cheques into the company's bank account amounted to conversion, that the defendant was personally liable for that conversion and that the measure of damages was the face value of the cheques (ie £11,370·69). The defendant appealed, contending, inter alia, (i) that the plaintiffs were not entitled to sue in conversion because they did not have a proprietary right to the cheques, (ii) that he could not be liable in conversion unless the company itself was guilty of conversion and unless he, as an officer of the company, was vicariously liable for conversion, and (iii) that, in any event, the plaintiffs had not suffered any damage because they had a cause of action against the original debtors which was not affected by reason of the cheques having been paid into the company's bank account instead of having been handed to the plaintiffs.

Held – The appeal would be dismissed for the following reasons—
   (i) The plaintiffs were entitled to sue in conversion because cl 11(e) of the agreement gave them a right to immediate possession of the cheques since it imposed on the company an obligation to hand over immediately to the plaintiffs any cheque which came into its possession and (per Bridge LJ and Sir David Cairns) it created in their favour a trust which arose as soon as the cheques were received by the company (see p 20 *e f h* and p 21 *c d* and *h* to p 22 *h*, post).
   (ii) The defendant was the primary tortfeasor because it was he who had misapplied the cheques by disposing of them in a manner which conflicted with the plaintiffs' rights in respect of them, and it was accordingly no defence for him that he had acted on behalf of the company (see p 19 *d*, p 21 *a b h* and p 22 *d* to *g*, post).

(iii) Furthermore the defendant was not entitled to set up against the plaintiffs' claim the contention that they had a cause of action against the debtors (see p 21 g h, post).   *a*

Notes

For the law of conversion, see 38 Halsbury's Laws (3rd Edn) 775–781, paras 1286–1293, and for cases in the subject, see 46 Digest (Repl) 458–465, 86–135.

Cases referred to in judgments   *b*

Bute (Marquess) v Barclays Bank Ltd [1954] 3 All ER 365, [1955] 1 QB 202, [1954] 3 WLR 741, 46 Digest (Repl) 490, 381.

Fairline Shipping Corpn v Adamson [1974] 2 All ER 967, [1975] 1 QB 180, [1974] 2 WLR 824, [1974] 1 Lloyd's Rep 133, 36(1) Digest (Reissue) 38, 114.

Healey v Healey [1915] 1 KB 938, 84 LJKB 1454, 113 LT 694, 27(1) Digest (Reissue) 300, 2246.   *c*

Jarvis v Williams [1955] 1 All ER 108, [1955] 1 WLR 71, CA, 46 Digest (Repl) 489, 371.

Performing Right Society Ltd v Ciryl Theatrical Syndicate Ltd [1923] 2 KB 146; rvsd on other grounds [1924] 1 KB 1, CA, 51 Digest (Repl) 579, 2110.

Appeal

The defendant, Roy A Rodriguez, appealed against the decision of Mr John Newey QC,   *d* sitting as a deputy judge of the High Court, on 20th May 1977, whereby it was ordered that the defendant should pay to the plaintiffs, International Factors Ltd, £11,370·69 by way of damages for conversion together with interest thereon. The facts are set out in the judgment of Sir David Cairns.

Alan Steinfeld for the defendant.
Neil Butter QC and *Geoffrey Conlin* for the plaintiffs.   *e*

SIR DAVID CAIRNS delivered the first judgment at the invitation of Buckley LJ. This is an appeal from a judgment of Mr John Newey QC, sitting as a deputy judge of the Queen's Bench Division. He gave judgment for the plaintiffs in the action for the sum of £11,370·69 plus interest, a total of something over £14,000. There are two issues on the   *f* appeal, both of them issues of law. The defendant adduced no evidence at the trial and the learned judge found all the facts to be as deposed to by the plaintiffs' witnesses.

The defendant was a director of a company now in liquidation; I shall refer to it simply as 'the company'. Its business was the manufacture of loudspeakers and other components for hi-fi equipment. The defendant was also a guarantor of the company's bank account.

On 7th April 1973 an agreement under seal was entered into between the plaintiffs and   *g* the company. The plaintiffs carry on the business of discounting debts, and the agreement was in a standard form of what is called a factoring agreement. By it the plaintiffs agreed to purchase from the company all the book debts of the company and the company agreed to sell them to the plaintiffs for the sum of 98½ per cent of the full amount of the debts. The detailed machinery is of course set out in the agreement. It was contended in the court below that that machinery had not been complied with, but that argument has not been   *h* pursued in this court.

The machinery involved that in order to ensure that the plaintiffs received the amount of the debts, all the company's invoices were to be endorsed with a statement indicating that the debt flowing from the invoice was assigned to the plaintiffs, and then the practice was for the company in the case of each debt to execute an assignment to the plaintiffs and to give express notice to every debtor as soon as the assignment had been completed. There   *j* was an express provision in the agreement that if any debtor paid the company by cheque the company was to hand over that cheque immediately to the plaintiffs.

In June and July 1974, four cheques were sent by debtors to the company, the total amount of the four cheques being the sum which I have mentioned, £11,370·69. Those payments were made in purported discharge of debts for goods supplied, but it is now

accepted that those were debts which had been assigned to the plaintiffs and the learned
judge found that all the machinery laid down in the agreement had been duly complied
with. As I have already indicated, there is now no issue about that. But what happened was
that instead of the cheques being handed straight to the plaintiffs as they should have been,
they were all paid into the company's bank account and, as the learned judge found and as
is now no longer in issue, this was done on the instructions of the defendant himself, who
was largely responsible for the running of the company, which at that time was in
considerable financial difficulties, and he knew perfectly well that what he was doing was
contrary to the agreement with the plaintiffs.

That this was a breach of contract by the company is obvious. It is also obvious that a
cause of action in contract would not lie by the plaintiffs against the defendant, who as an
individual was not a party to the contract. The learned judge however found that a cause
of action in tort, in conversion, was established against the defendant, and he based his
judgment on three propositions: first, that a director is liable for torts committed by him
in connection with the affairs of a company; he cited as authority for that proposition
Performing Right Society v Ciryl Theatrical Syndicate Ltd[1] and *Fairline Shipping Corpn v
Adamson*[2]. It is not now in dispute that the learned judge was right up to that point.

Counsel for the defendant, in this court, has interpreted the learned judge's judgment as
meaning that the tort was primarily a tort of the company and that the defendant became
liable as the person who was instrumental in committing the tort on behalf of the
company. I do not so read the judgment; I read it as meaning that the defendant himself
was here the primary tortfeasor, and the fact that he was acting on behalf of the company
is no defence to him.

There now come two propositions which are challenged. The first is that the learned
judge held that payment of the cheques into the company's bank account was a conversion
of the cheque. The second is that having so found and having held that the defendant was
liable for that conversion, he went on to hold that the measure of damages was the face
value of the cheques.

As to whether this was a conversion, counsel for the defendant says that the plaintiffs
here had no more than a contractual right to receive these cheques; they had no proprietary
right so as to enable them to sue in conversion. On the issue of damages, counsel's
proposition is that in this case, because the debts had been assigned, because notice of the
assignment had been given to the debtors, their payment of the debts to the company did
not discharge them from liability; that accordingly the plaintiffs are in a position to recover
the full amount of those debts from the original debtors and that their damages should be
limited to any trouble, inconvenience and expense to which they might be put in
recovering the debts from the debtors and, no doubt, to any amount that proved to be
irrecoverable if it so happened that any of the debtors were not able to pay.

I do not find it necessary to go any further into the provisions of the agreement of 7th
April 1973, except to refer to one vital clause; that is the clause numbered 11(e), which
provides as follows:

'If any payment in respect of an assigned debt is paid direct to the Supplier [the
supplier being the company] then the Supplier shall hold the same in trust for the
Factor [the factor being the plaintiffs]. The Supplier shall in that event immediately
after receipt of any such payment hand to the Factor the identical cash cheque or bill
of exchange and if it be necessary for such cheque or bill of exchange to be endorsed
to the Factor to enable the Factor to receive payment the Supplier shall endorse the
same over to the Factor.'

In support of his contention that here the plaintiffs were not entitled to sue in conversion,
counsel relies first on a passage in Clerk and Lindsell on The Law of Torts[3] indicating that

---

1   [1924] 1 KB 1
2   [1974] 2 All ER 967, [1975] 1 QB 180
3   14th Edn (1975), para 1108

to have a right to sue in conversion the plaintiff must have a right to possession, that a mere contractual right is not sufficient, but that a cestui que trust would have a right to sue for *a* conversion of property the legal ownership of which was in a bare trustee.

It is clear law that a contractual right to have goods handed to him by another person is not in itself sufficient to clothe the person who has that right with power to sue in conversion. That was the decision of this court in *Jarvis v Williams*[1]. The headnote of that case reads as follows[2]:

'In January, 1948, J. delivered bathroom fittings to W. at P.'s request. P. did not pay *b* for them and in September, 1949, it was agreed, between J. and P., that J. should take back the goods, collecting them from W. at P.'s expense. W., however, refused to deliver up the goods to J. J. claimed in detinue against W. for the return of the goods. *Held*, that J. could not maintain an action in detinue against W. since the property in the goods, which had passed to P. on delivery to W. at P.'s request, had remained vested in P., notwithstanding the agreement that J. should recover the goods.' *c*

Evershed MR, giving the leading judgment, said, after citing passages from the judgment in the court below[3]:

'I take that to mean that the contractural right which Jarvis had vis-à-vis Paterson to go and collect goods from Paterson's agent was a right of a sufficient character to enable Jarvis to bring an action in detinue against the agent of the owner of the *d* property in these goods. But, with all respect to the learned county court judge, I am unable to accept that as a good proposition of law.'

So a contractural right is not sufficient.

In my view, however, there was here something more than a contractural right. Clause 11(e) of the agreement provided both that the supplier was to hold any debt paid direct to *e* the supplier in trust for the factor, that is, the company was to hold in trust for the plantiffs, and immediately after receipt of a cheque, in the case of payment by cheque, to hand over that cheque to the company. Taking together the trust which was thereby set up and the obligation immediately on receipt to hand over the cheque to the plaintiffs, I am satisfied that the plaintiffs had here a sufficient proprietary right to sue in conversion.

For the proposition that a person with an equitable title to goods can sue in conversion, *f* assistance is derived from the decision of Shearman J in *Healey v Healey*[4]. That was a case where by a marriage settlement a husband assigned to trustees certain chattels on trust to allow them to be used by the wife during her life. The wife brought an action against the husband for wrongful detention of the chattels and it was held that the action could be maintained by the wife without joining the trustees of the settlement as parties. It is perhaps curious that that is the only decision that counsel has been able to discover of a *g* cestui que trust being entitled to sue in conversion, but it seems to me that since the fusion of law and equity that is sound law.

It was contended on behalf of the defendant that no trust arose here until some further act had been done by the company after receipt of the money. In my view that is wrong. The effect of cl 11(e) was that as soon as one of these cheques came into the possession of the company there arose a trust for the plaintiffs along with the obligation of *h* immediately handing over the cheque itself to the plaintiffs. It is further contended that *Healey v Healey*[4] is no authority for the proposition that the trustee himself can be sued in conversion. It would be surprising to me if the trustee could not be sued in conversion; certainly before the Theft Act 1968 there was a specific crime of conversion by trustee;

j

---

1 [1955] 1 All ER 108, [1955] 1 WLR 71
2 [1955] 1 WLR 71
3 [1955] 1 All ER 108 at 111, [1955] 1 WLR 71 at 74
4 [1915] 1 KB 938

probably under the Theft Act a disposal for his own purposes of goods held in trust by the
trustee would constitute theft, and I find it difficult to suppose that a trustee making away
for his own benefit with trust property, or for the benefit of some person other than the
equitable owner of it, would not be liable in conversion. But however that may be, the
defendant himself was not the trustee; the defendant himself disposed of the cheques in
such a way as to take them away from the plaintiffs, who were entitled to have them, and
put them into the company's bank account; that was a disposition which I am quite
satisfied amounted to a conversion.

The learned judge in the court below derived assistance in reaching his decision from the
judgment of McNair J in *Marquis of Bute v Barclays Bank Ltd*[1]. That was a case of conversion
of certain warrants by a farm manager, who had received the warrants in connection with
his occupation as farm manager, with the intention that the money should go to his
employer, the Marquis of Bute; the defendant used the warrants for his own purposes and
it was held that, notwithstanding the fact that the warrants were made out in the name of
the defendant, his act constituted a conversion of them. That decision is of some assistance
to the plaintiffs in this case, inasmuch as it shows that the fact that the cheques were made
out in favour of the company is no sufficient answer to the claim of the plaintiffs that they
were the persons who owned the cheques in equity and were entitled to have them handed
directly to them. I am accordingly satisfied that conversion was established here.

So far as damages are concerned, in my view the general position in relation to the
conversion of a cheque is that the conversion gives the person entitled to the cheque a right
to damages measured by the face value of the cheque; that, as the learned judge stated in
his judgment, has been established by a whole series of cases in some of which the
defendants were banks. The damages may, of course, be mitigated by special circumstances;
for example, to take the case which counsel for the defendant suggested to us, if the cheque
were stopped before payment into his bank by the wrongdoer and a fresh cheque given in
substitution for it which was duly met. But it would be for the defendant to establish that
there were circumstances of that kind which relieved him of his full liability in damages.

It is said here that the plaintiffs are not shown to have suffered any damage, certainly are
not shown to have suffered the amount of damages which they claim, because they still
have a right of action against the debtors. That seems to me to be no ground on which the
defendant can escape from paying damages in full. The position simply is that assuming,
as I will, that there is a right of action against the debtors, a plaintiff who has two causes of
action cannot be met when he makes a claim against one defendant by the answer: 'Oh no;
you've suffered nothing by my tort because you have a cause of action against somebody
else.' That clearly cannot be right. To take an example, if X wrongfully converted Y's
motor car and handed it to Z, an auctioneer, who innocently sold it, Y could recover full
damages from Z and it would be no answer to his claim to say that he had an equal claim
against X. This is an a fortiori case, because here it is the defendant who is the wrongdoer,
and in my judgment he cannot set up against the plaintiffs' claim to the full value of the
cheques the contention that the plaintiffs could call on the debtors to pay over again for
goods that they have already paid for, though unfortunately they made the mistake of
paying them to the wrong person at the time.

I am quite satisfied that the learned judge here was right both as to liability and as to
damages and I would dismiss the appeal.

BRIDGE LJ. I agree.

BUCKLEY LJ. I agree. On the first point that has been discussed by Sir David Cairns in
his judgment, the question of the status of the plaintiffs to sue the defendant in conversion,
it seems to me to be inescapable that under cl 11(e) of the agreement the plaintiffs had a
right to immediate possession of any cheque which might come into the possession of the

---

1 [1954] 3 All ER 365, [1955] 1 QB 202

company as the result of a debt which had been assigned to the plaintiffs being mistakenly paid to the company. Clause 11(e) not only provides that if any payment in respect of an *a* assigned debt is paid directly to the company, then the company shall hold the same in trust for the plaintiffs, but it goes on to provide specifically that the company shall in that event, immediately after receipt of any such payment, hand to the plaintiffs the identical cash, cheque or bill of exchange, and if necessary for such cheque, bill or bill of exchange to be endorsed to the plaintiffs to enable the plaintiffs to receive payment, the company, shall endorse the same over to the plaintiffs.   *b*

It is manifest on the terms of that sub-clause of the agreement that the intention of the parties was that the cheque itself, if payment was by cheque, should be handed on, endorsed if necessary, to the plaintiffs and that confers on the plaintiffs, as it seems to me, an immediate right to possession of any such cheque quite sufficient to support a cause of action in conversion against anyone who wrongfully deals with the cheque in any other manner. The payment of the cheque into the company's bank account was a wrongful *c* application of the cheque in direct conflict with the requirements of that sub-clause of the contract, and the fact that the company would have been accountable to the plaintiffs for the proceeds of the cheque does not in my judgment make that application any less wrong.

Counsel for the defendant, in a well presented argument, has argued that it cannot be a conversion to pay the cheque into the company's account the company being, under the terms of this clause of the agreement, a trustee of the proceeds of the cheque for the benefit *d* of the plaintiffs; but in my judgment that cannot be an answer to a claim in conversion when the clearest possible indication is contained in the contract between the parties that the cheque shall not be paid into the company's own account but shall be handed over in specie to the plaintiffs in order that they may have the benefit of it and be able to negotiate it or deal with it in any way they choose at their own discretion.

Accordingly, whether or not an enforceable trust would attach immediately on the *e* payment of any debt direct to the company by cheque, whether or not an immediate trust would attach to such a cheque, I think that there is a contractual right here for the plaintiffs to demand immediate delivery of the cheque to them, and that that is a sufficient right to possession to give them a status to sue in conversion. On the findings of the learned judge the defendant was personally responsible for the payment of each of the four cheques to which this case relates into the company's account, and in those circumstances the right *f* conclusion appears to me to be that it was the defendant who misapplied the cheque and who is liable for conversion. Counsel for the defendant has suggested that he could only be made liable in conversion if the company itself was guilty of conversion and so he, as an officer of the company, could be made vicariously responsible for conversion. In my view that is the wrong approach; the cheque was physically in the possession or under the control of the defendant, it was he who applied it wrongly in a manner in conflict with the *g* right of the plaintiffs, and in my judgment it was he who was guilty of conversion as a primary participant and not merely as a secondary participant in the transaction.

Accordingly, I fully agree with the view expressed by Sir David Cairns in the judgment which he has delivered, that in this case the plaintiffs are entitled to recover against the defendant for conversion. I also agree with what Sir David Cairns has said about the measure of damages, and I consequently agree that this appeal should be dismissed. *h*

Appeal dismissed.

Solicitors: *Raymond Dobson & Co*, Chichester (for the defendant); *Sidney Pearlman & Greene* (for the plaintiffs).

j

J H Fazan Esq   Barrister.

Tucker (Inspector of Taxes) v Granada Motorway Services Ltd

COURT OF APPEAL, CIVIL DIVISION
STAMP, ORR LJJ AND SIR DAVID CAIRNS
13th, 14th JUNE 1978

Income tax – Deduction in computing profits – Capital or revenue expenditure – Payment to secure improvement in asset – Payment to secure modification of rent obligation in lease – Modification necessary to enable taxpayer to trade profitably – Modification resulting in reduction of revenue expenses – Whether capital or revenue expenditure.

In 1965 the Minister of Transport ('the landlord') granted to a company a lease of a motorway service area for a term of 50 years from 16th October 1964. The rent payable under the lease consisted of two elements: a fixed rent of £15,000 per annum, to be paid by equal quarterly payments in advance, and an additional rent consisting of a percentage of the previous year's gross takings, derived from the provision of services, such as the supply of petrol and catering, which the company had agreed to provide under the lease. The gross takings included the amount of tobacco duty concealed in the selling price of tobacco and thus as tobacco duty increased the amount payable as additional rent increased while the company's ratio of profit to turnover decreased and it found it difficult to operate the service area profitably. Negotiations to amend the lease ensued and eventually the landlord offered to exclude for the residue of the term the amount of the tobacco duty from the gross takings for the purpose of calculating the additional rent, provided that the company paid the landlord a lump sum, equal to six times the amount of additional rent due on tobacco duty for the year ending 31st July 1973. The company accepted that offer and in August 1974 paid the landlord a lump sum of £122,220. Thereafter the additional rent paid by the company was calculated on gross takings exclusive of tobacco duty. The company claimed that the payment of the £122,220 to the landlord was deductible in computing its taxable profits for the accounting period ended 30th September 1974 since it was a payment made to get rid of an annual charge against revenue in the future. The Special Commissioners upheld that claim. On appeal Templeman J[a] held that the lease was a fixed capital asset and the lump sum paid to reduce the rent payable under the lease was therefore a lump sum paid to secure an improvement in a fixed capital asset and as such was capital expenditure, notwithstanding that the improvement had been necessary to enable the company to continue its trade and had resulted in a reduction of its revenue expenses, and accordingly was not deductible in computing the taxable profits of the company. The company appealed.

Held – The lease was part of the fixed capital of the company's business, and by reducing the rent payable for the whole of the remainder of the term the lump sum payment had created a more favourable lease for the company than it had had before in the same manner as if it had surrendered the existing lease in return for a new lease at the reduced rent on payment of a premium of £122,220. By increasing the value of part of the company's fixed capital the payment had procured an advantage which endured for the benefit of trade in the way that fixed capital endured, and was therefore not deductible in computing the company's taxable profits. Accordingly the appeal would be dismissed (see p 26 a to d and f, p 28 b c and h to p 29 a, post).

Dictum of Rowlatt J in *Anglo-Persian Oil Co Ltd v Dale (Inspector of Taxes)* (1932) 16 Tax Cas at 262 applied.

Per Stamp and Orr LJJ. In determining whether a payment is of a capital or revenue nature, the questions to be asked are whether the payment brings some asset or advantage

---

a [1977] 3 All ER 865, [1977] STC 353

into existence and whether it is an enduring asset and advantage, ie enduring in the same way that fixed capital endures, and not whether it is made with a view to bringing into *a* existence some asset or advantage for the enduring benefit of the trade (see p 28 *a to c*, post). Decision of Templeman J [1977] 3 All ER 865 affirmed.

Notes

For items ranking as capital expenditure, see 23 Halsbury's Laws (4th Edn) para 302, and for cases on the subject, see 28(1) Digest (Reissue) 180–196, 538–608.   *b*

Cases referred to in judgments

Anglo-Persian Oil Co Ltd v Dale (Inspector of Taxes) (1931) 16 Tax Cas 253; *affd* [1932] 1 KB 124, [1931] All ER Rep 725, 16 Tax Cas 253, 10 ATC 149, 100 LJKB 504, 145 LT 529, CA, 28(1) Digest (Reissue) 185, 563.

British Insulated and Helsby Cables Ltd v Atherton [1926] AC 205, [1925] All ER Rep 623, 4 *c* ATC 47, 95 LJKB 336, 134 LT 289, sub nom *Atherton v British Insulated and Helsby Cables Ltd* 10 Tax Cas 155, HL; *affg* [1925] 1 KB 421, 10 Tax Cas 155, CA, 28(1) Digest (Reissue) 211, 627.

Comr of Taxes v Nchanga Consolidated Copper Mines Ltd [1964] 1 All ER 208, [1964] AC 948, [1964] 2 WLR 339, 43 ATC 20, [1964] TR 25, PC, 28(1) Digest (Reissue) 204, *677.

Green (Inspector of Taxes) v Cravens Railway Carriage & Wagon Co Ltd, Inland Revenue Comrs *d* *v Cravens Railway Carriage & Wagon Co Ltd* (1951) 32 Tax Cas 359, [1951] TR 377, 30 ATC 361, 45 R & IT 63, 28(1) Digest (Reissue) 153, 485.

Hancock (Surveyor of Taxes) v General Reversionary & Investment Co Ltd [1919] 1 KB 25, 88 LJKB 248, 119 LT 737, 35 TLR 11, sub nom *Hancock (Surveyor of Taxes) v General Reversionary & Investment Co Ltd, General Reversionary & Investment Co Ltd v Hancock (Surveyor of Taxes)* 7 Tax Cas 358, 28(1) Digest (Reissue) 207, 619.   *e*

Inland Revenue Comrs v Carron Co 1968 SC (HL) 47, 45 Tax Cas 18, 47 ATC 192, [1968] TR 173, HL, 28(1) Digest (Reissue) 196, 608.

Appeal

In 1965 the Minister of Transport granted to Granada Motorway Services Ltd ('the company') a lease of a motorway service area for a term of 50 years from 16th October *f* 1964. The rent payable under the lease consisted of a fixed rent of £15,000 per annum, to be paid by equal quarterly payments in advance, and an additional rent calculated as a percentage of the previous year's gross takings, derived from the provision of those services, such as the supply of petrol and catering, which the company had agreed to provide under the lease. The gross takings included the amount of tobacco duty concealed in the selling price of tobacco. Thus as tobacco duty increased the amount payable as *g* additional rent increased but the company's ratio of profit to turnover decreased and it found it difficult to operate the service area profitably. Negotiations to amend the lease ensued and eventually the Minister offered to exclude, during the residue of the term, the amount of tobacco duty from the gross takings for the purpose of calculating the additional rent, provided that the company paid the Minister a lump sum, equal to six times the amount of additional rent due on tobacco duty relating to the year ending 31st July *h* 1973. The company accepted that offer and in August 1974 paid the Minister £122,220. Since then the additional rent paid by the company under the lease had been calculated on gross takings exclusive of tobacco duty. The Commissioners for the Special Purposes of the Income Tax Acts upheld the company's claim that the payment of £122,220 to the Minister was a payment of a revenue nature and accordingly deductible in computing its taxable profits for the accounting period ended 30th September 1974, holding that the *j* £122,220 was paid to ensure the more economical and profitable running of the company's trade and not to dispose of or to acquire a capital asset. On the Crown declaring its dissatisfaction with the determination the commissioners stated a case[1] for the opinion of

---

1   The case stated is set out at [1977] 3 All ER 866–869

the High Court. On 6th July 1977 Templeman J[1] allowed the appeal. The company appealed to the Court of Appeal.

Peter Rees QC and *Richard Fitzgerald* for the company
Stewart Bates QC and *Brian Davenport* for the Crown

STAMP LJ. In this appeal the relevant facts are clearly and concisely stated in the report of the case in the court below[1], and I need not repeat them. The court is also indebted to the judge for his clear analysis of the authorities relied on in the court below, to which counsel appearing for the company in this court could hardly take exception. I say 'hardly' because there were one or two phrases in the judge's summary of the case of which he did express some disapproval.

Counsel for the company, in opening this appeal, submitted that the authorities show that a payment made by a trader once and for all is only to be regarded as a capital payment and so not deductible in computing the profits of the trade if it is not only made once and for all but also with a view to bringing into existence an asset or advantage for the enduring benefit of the taxpayer's trade in such a way that fixed capital endures. Leaving aside for the moment the speech of Lord Wilberforce in *Inland Revenue Comrs v Carron Co*[2], I would accept that the result of the cases is as propounded by counsel for the company. That was the way that Rowlatt J put the matter in *Anglo-Persian Oil Co Ltd v Dale*[3] in the court of first instance. Rowlatt J there, after remarking that it had been argued that the expenditure there in question was capital expenditure because it secured an enduring benefit by getting rid of an onerous contract, remarked that that was not to state the material thing and was completely inconclusive. He went on to say[4]:

'I think I know where that phrase comes from, and that is from the speech of Lord Cave in the case of *Atherton v. British Insulated & Helsby Cables, Ltd.*[5], where he said this: "when an expenditure is made, not only once and for all, but with a view to bringing into existence an asset or advantage for the enduring benefit of a trade", then it is capital. But the fallacy is in the use of the word "enduring". What Lord Cave is quite clearly speaking of is a benefit which endures in a way that fixed capital endures; not a benefit that endures in the sense that for a good number of years it relieves you of a revenue payment. It means a thing which endures in the way that fixed capital endures. It is not always an actual asset, but it endures in the way that getting rid of a lease or getting rid of onerous capital assets or something of that sort as we have had in the cases, endures. I think that the Commissioners, with great respect, have been misled by the way in which they have taken "enduring" to mean merely something which extends over a number of years. I do not quite understand how the view that they appear to have taken is consistent with the numerous cases such as *Hancock's* case[6] or any of the others.'

Then he went on to say[4]:

'That is how it strikes me on that footing. There is no sort of question so far of any question of fact. I do not question what they say about the facts, or claim a jurisdiction to question that it was an enduring benefit by getting rid of an onerous contract. All that I say is that it does not go far enough. When I look at the facts, so far, all I see is one thing, that it is getting rid of a payment which falls to be charged to the revenue account every year, namely payment of commissions to people who run the business.'

---

1   [1977] 3 All ER 865, [1977] 1 WLR 1411, [1977] STC 353
2   1968 SC (HL) 47, 45 Tax Cas 18
3   (1931) 16 Tax Cas 253
4   16 Tax Cas 253 at 262
5   [1926] AC 205 at 213, [1925] All ER Rep 623 at 629, 10 Tax Cas 155 at 192
6   [1919] 1 KB 25, 88 LJKB 248, 7 Tax Cas 358

In the instant case the lease was clearly part of the fixed capital of the company's business. If the company had paid a premium to obtain it, the payment of the premium *a* would have been a capital payment as one made not only once and for all, but also with a view to bringing into existence 'an asset or advantage for the enduring benefit of the taxpayer's trade', namely the lease. It would have been of enduring benefit partly because it would have operated to reduce the annual rent which would no doubt have been payable had not the premium been demanded and paid. The payment here in question reduced the future payment of the rent during the whole period of the residue of the term of the *b* lease. It operated to relieve the company of the burden of the covenants for payment of rent contained in the lease and it operated to relieve it from those payments throughout the whole period of the lease. As a result, it seems to me beyond peradventure that the company had a more favourable lease than it had before, and I can see no difference in principle between the transaction which in fact took place and one whereunder the same result would have been achieved by the surrender of the lease and the granting of a new *c* lease at the reduced rent for a premium of £122,220. Inasmuch as the £122,220 in fact operates to increase the value to the company of the lease which is part of its fixed capital, the advantage procured cannot in my judgment be said to endure for the benefit of the trade otherwise than, and I quote the words of Rowlatt J, 'in the way that fixed capital endures'.

Counsel for the company submitted in this court, as he did in the court below, that the *d* payment of the money reduced the burden of recurrent business expenses which happened to be in the form of rent chargeable against revenue similar to the reduction obtained in the *Anglo-Persian* case[1], and that the payment was made with that end in view. It is no doubt correct that the purpose was to reduce the burden of recurrent business expenses and if it had been made to obtain variation of the terms of a trading contract in a way to benefit the company, it might have been treated as a regular revenue payment, because it would *e* not have brought into existence an advantage enduring in the way that fixed capital endures. I cannot, however, accept the conclusion that the fact that the advantage here was a variation in the terms of the lease making the lease less onerous than it was, and the fact that the lease was part of the fixed capital of the business and not a trading contract, makes no difference. Unlike a payment made merely to obtain better trading terms, here the payment operated to improve the terms under which the trader occupied the fixed asset *f* and so could not do otherwise than endure for benefit of trade in the way the lease itself, which was fixed capital, endures.

Counsel for the company relied on a passage in the speech of Lord Wilberforce in *Inland Revenue Comrs v Carron Co*[2], where Lord Wilberforce used language suggesting at first glance that a payment to be a capital payment must have the characteristics that it produces a recognisable capital asset, but at the end of his speech[3], Lord Wilberforce recognised that *g* the capital asset may be of a negative character:

'. . . an extension perhaps of, but not an exception to, the principle that, in some sense or other, an asset of a capital nature, tangible or intangible, positive or negative, must be shown to be acquired.'

He uses the word 'asset' to comprehend an advantage of a negative character which is not *h* recognised in the sense that it could be identified. Lord Reid remarked in that same case that what matters is the nature of the advantage for which the money was spent. Here, of course, a reduction of the amount payable for the improvement by the taxpayer of the terms of the fixed asset is the advantage. Lord Guest, I think, uses similar language. It can hardly be doubted that to spend £10,000 improving the company's premises in a physical way produces no recognisable or identifiable new asset, but it can hardly be doubted that

---

1   [1932] 1 KB 124, [1931] All ER Rep 725, 16 Tax Cas 253
2   1968 SC (HL) 47, 45 Tax Cas 18
3   1968 SC (HL) 47 at 65, 45 Tax Cas 18 at 75

it is a capital payment and I cannot think that Lord Wilberforce would have, for a moment,
a thought otherwise.
The way in which the case was put and the reasons the judge gave in the court below, I
find convincing. The judge said[1]:

'The authorities show that payment of a lump sum which reduces a burden on
revenue, albeit a burden which would otherwise extend over a long period, is an
income expense if the reduction is the direct and only consequence of the payment.
b But where a lump sum is paid to acquire, dispose of, improve or modify a fixed capital
asset, the lump sum payment is capital expenditure although, as a result of dealing
with the capital asset, the future revenue expense of the taxpayer is reduced. In the
present case, the revenue expense of the taxpayer company has been lower because the
rent payable under the lease is lower. That lower rent is a characteristic of the
modified fixed capital asset, namely the lease, and enures for the benefit of the tenant
c under the lease irrespective of his trade and for the benefit of any mortgagee,
liquidator, assignee or other person who at any time takes an interest under the lease.'

Counsel for the company made some verbal criticism of that part of the learned judge's
judgment and pointed out that the lease was in fact not assignable. Nevertheless, in my
judgment, the sense of the learned judge's words was clear, and I borrow his language to
d express all that I can say on the matter. The learned judge added[2]:

'Counsel for the taxpayer company said that there was no evidence that the payment
of £122,220 and the reduction in rent improved the fixed capital asset by increasing
the value of the lease. But the object and effect of the transaction was to make the
lease less onerous and therefore less negative or more positive in value. It is not
necessary to produce a valuation before and after. It is sufficient that the lump sum
e of £122,220 procured an improvement in the terms of the lease which enured to the
benefit of anyone interested in the lease and thus procured an improvement in a fixed
capital asset of the taxpayer company.'

Again, subject to the point made by counsel for the company that the lease was not
assignable, I find that is convincing.
f Counsel for the company emphasised that the payment here was to reduce the variable
rent based on sales and not a fixed rent. That is so, but with respect I cannot see that this
affects the principle of the matter in any way.
Counsel for the Crown has referred us to *Comr of Taxes v Nchanga Consolidated Copper
Mines Ltd*[3] where it was pointed out that, in the context of the question whether the sum
there in question was to be regarded as a capital or revenue payment, phrases such as
g 'enduring benefit' and 'capital structure' are descriptive rather than definitive. I quote
from that authority[3]:

'For example, while it is certainly important that in *Atherton's* case[4] expenditure
that did secure an enduring benefit for a company's business was spoken of as being
for that reason a capital expenditure, it would be a misuse of that authority to suppose
h that it gives any warrant for the idea that securing a benefit for the business is prima
facie capital expenditure, so long as the benefit is not so transitory as to have no
endurance at all. The present case is one in which the advantage obtained was
conditioned to last for not more than twelve months, the very period adopted for the
ascertainment of each successive profit balance, and in their lordships' opinion its
essential facts are so unlike those of the *Atherton* case[4] that no useful analogy can be
j constructed between them.'

---

1   [1977] 3 All ER 865 at 873, [1977] 1 WLR 1411 at 1416, [1977] STC 353 at 361
2   [1977] 3 All ER 865 at 873–874, [1977] 1 WLR 1411 at 1417, [1977] STC 353 at 361–362
3   [1964] 1 All ER 208 at 212, [1964] AC 948 at 959
4   [1926] AC 205, [1925] All ER Rep 623, 10 Tax Cas 155

I would also refer to the passage[1] in that authority where the Privy Council comments on the undesirability of determining the nature of a payment by the motive or the object of the payer. In that connection I would remark that, so far as the Special Commissioners in the instant case decided the case on the ground that the payment was in their view not made with a view to bringing into existence some asset or advantage for the enduring benefit of the trade, they misdirected themselves. The questions that ought to have been asked were whether the payment did bring some asset or advantage into existence, and whether it was an enduring asset and advantage, ie enduring in the same way that fixed capital endures.

I would dismiss this appeal.

ORR LJ. I agree.

SIR DAVID CAIRNS. I have found this a difficult case.

The finding in the case stated that the purpose of the payment was to discharge the company's obligation to pay additional rent was a pure finding of fact. The further finding that the payment was not made with a view to bringing into existence some asset or advantage to the enduring benefit of the trade was also a finding of fact, subject to the question of law of what in this context constitutes an asset or advantage for the enduring benefit of the trade.

There can be no doubt that the Special Commissioners were using that phrase in the sense in which it was explained in *Anglo-Persian Oil Co v Dale* by Rowlatt J[2] and by Romer LJ[3]. For my part, I find it difficult to say that the Special Commissioners misinterpreted or misapplied the words. I am mindful of the warning given by Romer LJ that the commissioners should decide the question as a question of fact applying Lord Cave's test[4]. That, it seems to me, was exactly what the Special Commissioners did here.

I think it is clear from almost all the authorities from *British Insulated and Helsby Cables Ltd v Atherton*[5] to *Green v Cravens Railway Carriage Co*[6] (a decision of Donovan J) that the proper test is the purpose and not the effect of the payment. Although here the effect was to increase the value of the lease, I should have been surprised if the Special Commissioners had found that the company's purpose was to obtain such an increase in value, and they did not so find.

It may be, however, having regard to what was said by Lord Radcliffe in *Comr of Taxes v Nchanga Consolidated Copper Mines Ltd*[7], that Lord Cave's test cannot now be treated as it was treated by the Court of Appeal in the *Anglo-Persian Oil* case[8] and by Donovan J in *Green's* case[6] as applicable to every situation, so it may be that the Special Commissioners erred in confining their consideration to that test, and it may be that if they had made a different approach they might have come to a different conclusion.

While still not entirely persuaded that the Special Commissioners were wrong in their decision, I am not now confident that they were right. I am loath to differ from the

1   [1964] 1 All ER 208 at 211, [1964] AC 948 at 958
2   (1931) 16 Tax Cas 253 at 262
3   [1932] 1 KB 124 at 146, [1931] All ER Rep 725 at 735, 16 Tax Cas 253 at 274
4   See *British Insulated and Helsby Cables Ltd v Atherton* [1926] AC 205, [1925] All ER Rep 623, 10 Tax Cas 155
5   [1926] AC 205, [1925] All ER Rep 623, 10 Tax Cas 155
6   (1951) 32 Tax Cas 359
7   [1964] 1 All ER 208, [1964] AC 948
8   [1932] 1 KB 124, [1931] All ER Rep 725, 16 Tax Cas 253

conclusion reached by both Stamp and Orr LJJ, whose experience in this field is far greater than my own, that Templeman J's decision was right and should be upheld. Therefore I too would dismiss this appeal.

Appeal dismissed. Leave to appeal to the House of Lords granted.

Solicitors: *Turner & Peacock* (for the company); *Solicitor of Inland Revenue.*

A S Virdi Esq   Barrister.

Marks v Warren

CHANCERY DIVISION
BROWNE-WILKINSON J
15th MAY 1978

Landlord and tenant – Covenant against parting with possession without consent – Breach – Tenant assigning tenancy without landlord's consent – No restriction on assignment in terms – Whether tenant in breach of covenant not to part with possession without consent.

A landlord and tenant entered a tenancy agreement which provided, inter alia, that the tenant was 'not to underlet or part with possession of the premises without the Landlords previous consent in writing which [shall] not be unreasonably witheld'. The tenant assigned the tenancy to the plaintiff without first obtaining the landlord's consent. The plaintiff later decided that he did not wish to accept the assignment and brought an action against the tenant claiming repayment of the amount he had paid the tenant for the assignment. The question whether the tenant required the landlord's prior consent before assigning was tried as a preliminary issue, the tenant contending that the omission of any specific restriction on assignment in the agreement meant that the tenant was free to assign without the landlord's consent.

Held – Although a landlord was required to express any restriction on alienation of the premises by the tenant in clear terms, a covenant not to assign, underlet or part with possession involved three separate covenants which were not mutually exclusive, and a breach of one could constitute a breach of another. Since the assignment by the tenant necessarily involved a parting with possession of the premises and since that fell within the ordinary normal meaning of the words of the covenant, it followed that the assignment constituted a breach of covenant unless the landlord's consent had been obtained or unreasonably withheld notwithstanding that there was no express restriction on assigning the premises (see p 30 g to p 31 a and e to g, post).

Russell v Beecham [1923] All ER Rep 318 applied.

Notes

For covenants between landlord and tenant against assignment or underletting and parting with possession, see 23 Halsbury's Laws (3rd Edn) 629–632, paras 1333, 1334, 1336, and for cases on the subject, see 31(2) Digest (Reissue) 676–686, 5546–5631.

Cases referred to in judgment

Doyle and O'Hara's Contract, Re [1899] 1 IR 113, 31(2) Digest (Reissue) 691, *1982.
Russell v Beecham [1924] 1KB 525, [1923] All ER Rep 318, 93 LJKB 441, 130 LT 570, CA, 32(2) Digest (Reissue) 682, 5596.

Procedure summons

By a writ issued on 5th January 1978 the plaintiff, Graham Simon Marks, brought an action *a*
against the defendant, Guy Howard Warren, claiming (i) rescission of an agreement made
on 3rd November 1977 whereby the tenant agreed to assign the tenancy of 2 Bullfinch
Cottages, Hurstpierpoint, Sussex to the plaintiff for the sum of £3,250, and (ii) repayment
of the sum of £3,250 together with interest. By a summons issued on 21st February 1978
the tenant sought (i) specific performance of the agreement, pursuant to RSC Ord 86, or
alternatively interlocutory judgment for specific performance, pursuant to RSC Ord 14, *b*
(ii) the sum of £150 for fixtures and fittings purchased by the plaintiff, and (iii) a
declaration that the plaintiff was liable to idemnify the tenant for rent paid by the tenant
to the landlord. The facts are set out in the judgment.

Paul Hampton for the plaintiff.
Romie Tager for the defendant.   *c*

BROWNE-WILKINSON J. I have to construe a covenant in a tenancy agreement
which reads as follows:

> 'THE TENANT agrees with the Landlord as follows . . . not to underlet or part with
> possession of the premises without the Landlords previous consent in writing which
> shall not be unreasonably withheld.'   *d*

In the statement of the parties at the beginning of the agreement Mr Warren is defined as
'"the Tenant" which expression where the context admits includes the person deriving title
under him'.

The question which I am asked to decide as a preliminary point of law is whether an
assignment by Mr Warren, the original tenant, to another party, in this case the plaintiff, *e*
did or did not require the consent of the landlord previously to be obtained. It will be
noted that the covenant is in slightly unusual form, in that it does not in terms expressly
preclude assignment but only underletting or parting with possession. It is said that in this
particular case the assignment of this cottage by the defendant to the plaintiff was intended
to be for the occupation of the plaintiff, and therefore although physical occupation was
not intended to change until 30th November 1977 (that is to say, one month after the date *f*
of the assignment) the act of assigning must necessarily have involved a breach of the
covenant not to part with possession. Therefore, it is said that the consent of the landlord
was required.

In my judgment, on the facts of this particular case, it is clear that what was involved in
this assignment did necessarily involve a parting with possession, and I do not think
counsel for the defendant really disagreed with that as being the normal meaning of the *g*
words read out of context. What he argues in this case is that covenants against assigning,
underletting and parting with possession have a very long and very well known legal
history and are to be construed on the basis that if one of the limbs of the covenant is
omitted its omission is to be treated as a significant factor. He says, and in my judgment
quite rightly on the authorities, that if a landlord wishes to restrict the free alienation by
his tenant of the estate that has been granted to him, the burden lies on the landlord to *h*
express that restriction in clear terms, so that there can be no doubt as to what the
restriction consists of, especially as the penalty for a breach is forfeiture. As I say, I think
that proposition is well founded and is supported by the approach of the Court of Appeal
in *Russell v Beecham*[1].

But that does not, in my judgment, mean that one has to distort the ordinary meaning
of words so as to depart from their ordinary meaning. Here the parting with possession *j*
which is involved falls within the obvious meaning of the words. There is no reason to
treat, as counsel for the defendant suggests I must, each of the limbs of a covenant not to
assign, not to underlet and not to part with possession as being three mutually exclusive

---

1   [1924] 1 KB 525, [1923] All ER Rep 318

areas. They are, as he points out, to be treated as three separate covenants; but it does not follow that an act which would constitute a breach of one of those covenants may not also constitute a breach of another of those covenants. He has not shown me any authority to that effect.

It is an open question, which I do not need to resolve, whether a covenant against underletting alone precludes an assignment. Woodfall on Landlord and Tenant[1] states that it does. But in my judgment the decision of the Irish Court of Appeal in *Re Doyle and O'Hara's Contract*[2] shows that it is by no means a concluded question and it very much depends on the actual words used in each covenant. But when it comes to the words 'part with possession' in my judgment the decision of the Court of Appeal in *Russell v Beecham*[3], which I have already referred to, strongly suggests that a covenant against parting with possession does preclude not only parting with possession simpliciter, without any underletting or assigning, but also a parting with possession under an underletting and, in my judgment, under an assignment. In that case the covenant was that the tenant should not 'assign or part with this lease or the premises hereby demised or any part thereof', and the tenant sublet the premises. On the basis of that subletting the landlord claimed there had been a breach of the covenant. It is to be noted that there was no express covenant against subletting the premises. It was alleged that by subletting he was in breach of a covenant not to part with the premises, or a part thereof. Bankes and Atkin LJJ decided on the meaning of those words in that document that the covenant not to 'part with the premises ... demised or any part thereof' meant an outright parting with the whole interest; it did not mean the same as parting with the possession thereof. The whole of the argument in that case revolved round that question, it being assumed that, if on its true construction it was a covenant against parting with possession of the premises, the underletting would itself have constituted a breach. In my judgment that emerges clearly from the words of Bankes LJ[4]: 'Apart from authority I do not think anybody would deny that this letting to Grice was a parting with possession and a breach of a covenant not to part with possession of the demised premises.' He also dealt with the matter further[5], where it is clear that his decision turned solely on the construction of those words. In my judgment, that indicates that a covenant which omits the covenant against underletting, but which precludes a parting with possession, precludes underletting, because it constitutes a parting with possession. In my judgment, it is against counsel's submission for the defendant that they are to be treated as mutually exclusive categories.

So in this case it seems to me that the assignment by the defendant to the plaintiff necessarily involved a parting with possession, and, therefore, as it falls within the fair, ordinary, normal meaning of the words, undistorted and unstrained, it constituted a breach of the covenant, unless the landlord's permission was obtained or unreasonably withheld.

Judgment for the plaintiff.

Solicitors: *Brecher & Co* (for the plaintiff); *Frere Cholmeley & Co* (for the defendant).

Hazel Hartman   Barrister.

1   27th Edn (1968), vol 1, para 1219
2   [1899] 1 IR 113
3   [1924] 1 KB 525, [1923] All ER 318
4   [1924] 1 KB 525 at 531–532, cf [1923] All ER Rep 318 at 321
5   [1924] 1 KB 525 at 534, [1923] All ER Rep 318 at 322

Re Aro Co Ltd

CHANCERY DIVISION
OLIVER J
16th, 17th, 18th MAY, 14th JUNE 1978

Company – Winding-up – Stay of pending proceedings – Stay of proceedings where creditor not a secured creditor at commencement of winding-up – Action in rem against ship – Ship only asset of company in liquidation – Writ in action issued but not served before commencement of winding-up – Plaintiff applying for leave to continue action – Whether plaintiff a secured creditor – Whether mere issue of writ in rem constituting plaintiff a secured creditor – Companies Act 1948, s 231.

The only asset of a company was a ship. The applicants, who were claiming damages from the company in respect of a cargo carried by the ship, issued a writ in rem against the ship. Before the writ was served and the ship could be arrested, the company was ordered to be wound up. In the winding-up the applicants applied, under s 231[a] of the Companies Act 1948, for leave to proceed with the action, notwithstanding the winding-up, on the ground that the issue of the writ in rem prior to the commencement of the winding-up had been sufficient to constitute the applicants as secured creditors of the company so that leave to proceed with the action should be granted in accordance with the principles which were applicable by the court in granting leave under s 231.

Held – The mere issue of a writ in rem against a ship by a plaintiff did not invoke the jurisdiction of the Admiralty Court, since that jurisdiction was not invoked until service of the writ on the ship, and therefore the mere issue of the writ in rem did not constitute the plaintiff a secured creditor of the owners of the ship, for the plaintiff's claim remained inchoate and unperfected until the writ was served. It followed that the applicants were unsecured creditors at the commencement of the winding-up, and that leave to proceed with the action could not be granted since to grant leave would enable the applicants to perfect their security and to achieve priority over other unsecured creditors of the company, which was contrary to the principles governing the grant of leave under s 231 of the 1948 Act. Accordingly the application would be dismissed (see p 47 *e g* and *j* to p 48 *a*, post).

Dicta of Lord Denning MR and of Megaw LJ in *The Banco* [1971] 1 All ER at 533–534, 537–538 and *The Berny* [1978] 1 All ER 1065 applied.

The Cella (1888) 13 PD 82 and *The Monica S* [1967] 3 All ER 740 considered.

Notes
For the power in a liquidation to stay pending proceedings, see 7 Halsbury's Laws (4th Edn) paras 1044, 1359, and for cases on the subject, see 10 Digest (Reissue) 1098–1100, 6744–6761.

For actions in rem, see 1 Halsbury's Laws (4th Edn) para 311.

For the Companies Act 1948, s 231, see 5 Halsbury's Statutes (3rd Edn) 299.

Cases referred to in judgment
Anglo-Baltic and Mediterranean Bank v Barber & Co [1924] 2 KB 410, [1924] All ER Rep 226, 93 LJKB 1135, 132 LT 1, [1924] B & CR 224, CA, 10 Digest (Reissue) 1170, 7284.

Banco, The [1971] 1 All ER 524, [1971] P 137, [1971] 2 WLR 335, [1971] 1 Lloyd's Rep 49, CA, Digest (Cont Vol D) 5, 766a.

Beldis, The [1936] P 51, [1935] All ER Rep 760, 106 LJP 22, 154 LT 680, 18 Asp MLC 598, CA, 1 Digest (Repl) 121, 69.

Berny, The [1978] 1 All ER 1065, [1978] 2 WLR 387, [1977] 2 Lloyd's Rep 533.

Berry (Herbert) Associates Ltd, Re [1978] 1 All ER 161, [1977] 1 WLR 1437, HL.

---

a   Section 231 is set out at p 35 *a b*, post

Cella, The (1888) 13 PD 82, 57 LJP 55, 59 LT 125, 6 Asp MLC 293, CA, 1 Digest (Repl) 191,
a 767.
Colorado, The [1923] P 102, [1923] All ER Rep 531, 92 LJP 100, 128 LT 759, 16 Asp MLC
145, CA, 42 Digest (Repl) 660, *4122.*
Constellation, The [1965] 3 All ER 873, [1966] 1 WLR 272, [1965] 2 Lloyd's Rep 538, 10
Digest (Reissue) 1000, *6765.*
Croshaw v Lyndhurst Ship Co [1897] 2 Ch 154, 66 LJ Ch 576, 76 LT 553, 10 Digest (Reissue)
b 1080, *6623.*
Great Ship Co Ltd, Re, Parry's Case (1863) 4 De GJ & Sm 63, 3 New Rep 181, 33 LJ Ch 245,
9 LT 432, 10 Jur NS 3, 46 ER 839, LJJ, 10 Digest (Reissue) 1102, *6775.*
Heinrich Bjorn, The (1885) 10 PD 44, 54 LJP 33, 52 LT 560, 5 Asp MLC 391, *affd* sub nom
The Henrich Björn (1886) 11 App Cas 270, HL, 1 Digest (Repl) 120, *67.*
James W Elwell, The [1921] P 351, 90 LJP 132, 8 Ll L Rep 115, 1 Digest (Repl) 191, *766.*
c *London and Devon Biscuit Co, Re* (1871) LR 12 Eq 190, 40 LJ Ch 574, 24 LT 650, 10 Digest
(Reissue) 1101, *6769.*
Monica S, The [1967] 3 All ER 740, [1968] P 741, [1968] 2 WLR 431, [1967] 2 Lloyd's Rep
113, Digest (Cont Vol C) 1079, *215a.*
Oak Pits Colliery Co, Re (1882) 21 Ch D 322, [1881–5] All ER Rep 1157, 51 LJ Ch 768, 42
LT 7, CA, 10 Digest (Reissue) 1109, *6826.*
d *Pacific, The* (1864) Brown & Lush 243, 3 New Rep 709, 33 LJPM & A 120, 10 LT 541, 10
Jur NS 1110, 2 Mar LC 21, 1 Digest (Repl) 147, *344.*
Pieve Superiore, The, Giovanni Dapueto v James Wyllie & Co (1874) LR 5 PC 482, 43 LJ Adm
20, 30 LT 887, 2 Asp MLC 319, 1 Digest (Repl) 172, *568.*
Roundwood Colliery Co, Re [1897] 1 Ch 373, [1895–9] All ER Rep 530, 66 LJ Ch 186, 75 LT
641, CA, 10 Digest (Reissue) 1101, *6772.*
e *Stanhope Silkstone Collieries Co, Re* (1879) 11 Ch D 160, 48 LJ Ch 409, 40 LT 204, CA, 10
Digest (Reissue) 1080, *6621.*
Thurso New Gas Co, Re (1889) 42 Ch D 486, 61 LT 351, 10 Digest (Reissue) 1152, *7171.*
Two Ellens, The (1872) LR 4 PC 161, 8 Moo PCCNS 398, 41 LJ Adm 33, 26 LT 1, 1 Asp MLC
308, 17 ER 361, 1 Digest (Repl) 151, *374.*
Volant, The (1842) 1 Wm Rob 383, 5 LT 185, 525, 6 Jur 540, 1 Digest (Repl) 163, *507.*
f *Vron Colliery Co, Re* (1882) 20 Ch D 442, 51 LJ Ch 389, CA, 10 Digest (Reissue) 940, *5516.*
Wanzer Ltd, Re [1891] 1 Ch 305, 60 LJ Ch 492, 10 Digest (Reissue) 1101, *6766.*
Zafiro, The [1959] 2 All ER 537, [1960] P 1, [1959] 3 WLR 123, [1959] 1 Lloyd's Rep 359,
1 Digest (Repl) 151, *378.*

Cases also cited

g *Commercial Bank Corpn of India and the East, Smith Fleming & Co's Case, Gledstanes & Co's Case*
(1866) 1 Ch App 538.
Lloyd & Co (David), Re, Lloyd v David Lloyd & Co (1877) 6 Ch D 339, CA.

Summonses

Texaco Export Inc ('Texaco') issued a summons dated 7th February 1978 in the liquidation
h of Aro Co Ltd ('the company'), an unregistered company ordered to be compulsorily
wound-up on 16th January 1978, for an order that notwithstanding the winding-up
Texaco should be given leave pursuant to s 231 of the Companies Act 1948 to continue
actions (i) in rem against a vessel owned by the company and (ii) in personam against the
company itself, in respect of a claim for damage to a cargo carried by the vessel, which had
been commenced by Texaco prior to the winding-up. By a cross-summons dated 3rd April
j 1978, Guy Thomas Ernest Parsons, the liquidator of the company, sought the determination
of the court whether (i) the actions in rem and in personam were actions or proceedings
against the company for the purposes of s 231 of the 1948 Act, (ii) Texaco by reason of the
issue of the writ in the action in rem and the entry of a caveat under RSC Ord 75, r 14, were
entitled to payment of any damages awarded to them out of any fund arising from the sale
of the vessel in priority to the liquidator's claims, (iii) Texaco would be entitled to keep the

benefit of such a payment notwithstanding s 325 of the 1948 Act and (iv) Texaco should be given leave under s 231 to continue the action in rem and the action in personam. The *a* facts are set out in the judgment.

N J M Teare for Texaco.
David Grace and *David A S Richards* for the liquidator.

b

Cur adv vult

14th June.   **OLIVER J** read the following judgment: The matter which calls for decision in this case arises out of cross-summonses issued in the liquidation of an unregistered company which was on 16th January 1978 ordered to be compulsorily wound-up. The company is a Liberian shipping company which was incorporated on 8th March 1968. Its *c* principal place of business was in Piraeus and it had no place of business in the United Kingdom. Its only asset is the vessel Aro. That is a motor tanker of about 10,000 light displacement tons and it has, since 1975, been laid up in the Blackwater river for lack of employment. It is not an asset of great value. I have been told that the only likely purchaser is a purchaser for scrap and that the vessel is unlikely to raise more than about $US 300,000.   *d*

The company was wound up on the petition of Oceanus Mutual Underwriting Association (Bermuda) Ltd, a protection and indemnity club ('the P & I club') to whom there was an admitted indebtedness in respect of calls for a sum of $US134,912·37. In addition, there are three other principal claims. First, there is a debt owed to Shell Co (Hellas) Ltd ('Shell') amounting to $US147,598·40 for fuel supplied. Secondly, there is a debt of £106,000 claimed as due to a company called Petrolaro SA in respect of *e* disbursements, management fees and expenses. Thirdly, there is the claim of the present applicants, Texaco Export Inc ('Texaco'), for damage to a cargo of oil carried by the vessel in September 1974. That is an unliquidated claim but is estimated to amount to about $US60,000. In addition there is a small claim by the Admiralty marshal for expenses arising out of the arrest of the vessel in the circumstances to which I shall now have to allude.   *f*

Prior to the winding-up order a number of actions were commenced against the company. On 3rd March 1977, Shell issued a writ in rem in the Admiralty Court in respect of their debt, and on 7th May 1977 that writ was served on the vessel and she was arrested. On 4th May 1977 the P & I club commenced an action against the company in the Commercial Court in respect of its debt and in that action it obtained an injunction restraining the company from removing the vessel from the jurisdiction. The P & I club *g* has made no claim in rem against the vessel. Texaco too had a claim in respect of which a writ in rem was an appropriate remedy, under the provisions of s 1(1)(g) and (h) of the Administration of Justice Act 1956, and on 29th July 1977 such a writ was issued in respect of their claim in damages. That writ has not been served, nor has the vessel been arrested by Texaco. A caveat in the Admiralty registry was lodged by Texaco on the same day as the issue of the writ with the result that if Shell lifted its arrest the vessel would still be unable *h* to be moved without notice to Texaco.

The petition was presented on 29th November 1977. On 5th December 1977 the Official Receiver was appointed provisional liquidator. As I have already mentioned the winding-up order was made on 16th January 1978, and on 17th March 1978 the present liquidator was appointed. A caveat has a life of only six months, and in the meantime, on 15th February 1978 Texaco had applied to the registrar for leave to lodge a new caveat. Leave to do that was granted but without prejudice to the liquidator's contentions on this summons. Also by consent, and similarly without prejudice, Texaco was given leave to renew its writ on 28th April 1978.

Although various questions are raised by the liquidator's summons the essential question which I have to decide is that which is raised by Texaco's summons, namely whether leave

should now be given pursuant to s 231 of the Companies Act 1948 for Texaco to continue
a the action which it had commenced prior to the winding-up. That section provides:

> 'When a winding-up order has been made or a provisional liquidator has been
> appointed, no action or proceeding shall be proceeded with or commenced against the
> company except by leave of the court and subject to such terms as the court may
> impose.'

b For the purposes of these cross-summonses Texaco has been prepared to concede that an
action in rem against the company's ship is an action against the company for the purpose
of the section, and that point, which is raised in terms by the liquidator's summons, has not
been argued before me.

The principles on which the court will grant leave to continue proceedings commenced
before the liquidation are tolerably clear and are not in issue between the parties in the
c instant case. The underlying principle in a winding-up, whether of a registered or, as here,
an unregistered company, is that the assets available in the liquidation shall be distributed
pari passu, a principle implicit in a compulsory winding-up but expressly applied in the
case of a voluntary winding-up by s 302 of the 1948 Act. Putting the matter broadly,
therefore, a creditor who has not already obtained a priority over other creditors by
obtaining some proprietary or possessory interest in some asset of the company before the
d commencement of the winding-up will not be permitted, after winding-up, to continue a
proceeding which will result in his achieving such a priority, except in exceptional
circumstances. There may, for instance, be cases where the process of investigating
disputed questions of fact may more suitably be conducted in a pending action rather than
in the winding-up. But even here leave will normally be given only on terms restricting
the plaintiff's right, if successful, to enforce judgment against the company's assets: see for
e instance *Re Thurso New Gas Co*[1] per Kay J.

There are exceptions, no doubt, to the general rule, but it is not contended that any of
those applies in the present case, and counsel for Texaco takes his stand on the argument
that, by commencing an action in rem, he puts himself in the position, for the purposes of
the principles on which the court's jurisdiction to grant leave is exercised, of a secured
creditor.

f Before turning to a consideration of the peculiarities and effects of an action in rem, it
is perhaps useful to look at the principles which govern executions and other similar
processes against a company's property, for these illustrate the wider principle of pari passu
distribution to which I have already referred. So far as concerns such processes put in force
after the winding-up, these are specifically avoided by s 228 of the 1948 Act, which is in the
following terms:

g > '(1) Where any company registered in England is being wound up by the court, any
> attachment, sequestration, distress or execution put in force against the estate or
> effects of the company after the commencement of the winding up shall be void to all
> intents.'

The company in this case is not a company registered in England, but under s 404 of the
h 1948 Act the provisions as to the winding-up of unregistered companies are expressed to
be in addition to and not in restriction of those relating to registered companies, and the
same principles must, I think, apply by analogy. Despite the express terms of the section
which declares the process to be void, it is clear that the section is to be read together with
s 231, and there are numerous authorities governing the principles on which the court will
permit a creditor who has instituted a process of the type described in s 228 to retain the
j benefit of such process in priority to the other creditors of the company. Examples as to
execution are *Re Vron Colliery Co*[2] and *Re Thurso New Gas Co*[3]; as to attachment of debts,

---

1   (1889) 42 Ch D 486 at 490–491
2   (1882) 20 Ch D 442
3   42 Ch D 486

Anglo-Baltic and Mediterranean Bank v Barber & Co[1]; and as to distress by landlords, *Re Oak Pits Colliery Co*[2] and *Re Roundwood Colliery Co*[3].

In all the cases the critical matter is the stage which the process has reached at the commencement of the winding-up. The authorities make it clear that what is required before the court will grant leave to continue is not the mere initiation of the procedural steps which will lead to the creditor obtaining a security for his debt, but the actual creation of that security. Thus, a distress is not put in force until the goods are seized (see for instance the recent case of *Re Herbert Berry Associates Ltd*[4]), and an execution is not put in force until the writ of fi fa is actually executed by the sheriff's seizure of the goods (*Re London & Devon Biscuit Co*[5]). A good illustration is *Croshaw v Lyndhurst Ship Co*[6], where a judgment creditor had before the winding-up obtained an order for the appointment of a receiver by way of equitable execution but no order had been made for actual payment to the receiver. It was held that the court ought not under s 87 of the Companies Act 1862 (that is the predecessor of the present s 231) to permit further proceedings under the order. Stirling J observed that the order created no security. He said[7]:

'It is simply an uncompleted process to obtain payment of money. It is not a charge, because there is no order upon the executors to pay the money. If they did not choose to pay it to the receiver they could not be attached for disobeying the order. It is true that by proper proceedings an order for payment could be obtained against them. It would be almost as of course, and, unless they could give some good reason for not paying the receiver, they would probably have to pay the costs of the application. But still the property is not yet the judgment creditors'; it was short of that; they had not acquired an equitable interest in the property as distinguished from a right to get it by a process which was not yet complete . . . Then what is their position? They are in the position of judgment creditors who have recovered judgment and are attempting to obtain payment or satisfaction out of the assets of the debtor. In that state of things I have to consider what effect the winding-up of the mortgagor company has upon their rights. Now, as is well known, that question is governed by two sections of the Companies Act, 1862, namely, ss. 87 and 163. [I pause to interpolate that s 163 is the predecessor section to s 228 of the 1948 Act.] It has been held that these two sections are to be read together, and that, notwithstanding the strong language of s. 163, there are cases in which a judgment creditor who at the commencement of the winding-up had not actually realised his execution by a sale may nevertheless be allowed to proceed with his execution by leave of the Court under s. 87. It is now well settled that the Court has a discretion as to whether it will allow proceedings which have reached a certain point to go further or no. That was laid down in *In re Great Ship Co*.[8], which has been followed in many subsequent decisions. As to the exercise of this discretion the general rule which has been laid down amounts to this: that where as regards execution creditors the sheriff has at the date of the commencement of the winding-up actually seized goods belonging to the company, but has not sold them, the Court will, in the absence of special circumstances, allow the execution to be proceeded with, and the goods to be sold and realized. On the other hand, if the writ has merely reached the hands of the sheriff and he has not seized, the Court has held that it will not allow the proceedings to go further—again in the absence of special circumstances. An illustration of this is to be

1   [1924] 2 KB 410
2   (1882) 21 Ch D 322
3   [1897] 1 Ch 373, [1895–9] All ER Rep 530
4   [1978] 1 All ER 161, [1977] 1 WLR, 1437
5   (1871) LR 12 Eq 190
6   [1897] 2 Ch 154
7   [1897] 2 Ch 154 at 160–161
8   (1863) 4 De GJ & Sm 63

a

found in *In re London and Devon Biscuit Co.*[1], before Malins V.-C. Another illustration is to be found in the case of *In re Stanhope Silkstone Collieries Co.*[2], which relates to the effect of a garnishee order. There a judgment creditor had obtained a garnishee order nisi to attach the debts of the debtor, but had not at the commencement of the winding-up served the order on the garnishee, and it was held that the creditor had not become a secured creditor at the commencement of the winding-up, and that leave could not be given to proceed further.'

b   And then finally he concluded[3]:

'Something more has to be done to make the process effective. That being so, no further steps after the winding-up proceedings can be taken without the leave of the Court to make that order effectual. Ought that leave to be given? The rule of the Court is that where the execution is incomplete, and there has been no seizure or anything equivalent to it, the Court does not give leave to proceed further, except under special circumstances.'

So the question which I have to decide, and there is really no conflict between the parties as to this, is, does the mere issue of a writ in rem against a ship owned by a company in liquidation (assuming the writ to be regularly issued, of course) constitute the plaintiff in the action thus constituted a secured creditor of the company so that, in accordance with the general principle to which I have already referred, he should be granted leave to proceed with his action and take the benefit of any judgment which he obtains in the action in priority to the claims of other unsecured creditors?

The argument has centred on the peculiar nature of an action in rem as itself giving rise, so it is claimed, to a species of security as a result of the special procedures available in the Admiralty Court. Counsel have been good enough to give me an instructive review of the Admiralty practice so far as relevant to the present question, and, without pretending to too great a degree of accuracy it may, as I understand it, be summarised thus. The action in rem is an action against the vessel itself and continues as such even though it may also be an action in personam against the owners or may become one if they appear and contest the claim. Once an action in rem has been instituted, the vessel can, assuming it to be within the jurisdiction, be taken into the custody of the court by arrest, and for that purpose the plaintiff has to obtain a warrant of arrest which he can only do by swearing an affidavit. In effecting an arrest, he makes himself responsible for the expenses of the Admiralty marshal. Once taken into the custody of the court, the vessel may be appraised and sold either pendente lite or at the termination of the suit, and it is no longer capable of being used by the owner unless and until he provides security which enables it to be released. It may be arrested at the suit of more than one plaintiff, but each arresting party makes himself responsible pro tanto for the costs of the Admiralty marshal and, once the vessel has been arrested at the suit of one plaintiff, other claimants, whether or not they have commenced proceedings by issuing writs, may protect their position by entering a caveat under RSC Ord 75, r 14, in which event the vessel will not be released without notice enabling them to commence proceedings or, if they have already commenced them, to proceed to arrest. Thus, the effect of arrest is that the vessel itself remains in the custody of the court until released and save to the extent that the owners satisfy any claimant otherwise, it can be sold under the order of the court free from all liens and charges and its proceeds distributed amongst all those claimants who have proceeded and obtained judgment in rem in accordance with their respective priorities.

The right to invoke the Admiralty jurisdiction was formerly restricted to those having maritime liens, but it has been since extended by a series of statutes from 1840 to the present day and is now regulated by Part I of the Administration of Justice Act 1956, s 1(1)

---

1   (1871) LR 12 Eq 190
2   [1879] 11 Ch D 160
3   [1897] 2 Ch 154 at 162–163

of which confers jurisdiction to hear a large number of specified types of claim which include, in paras (g) and (h) claims, such as Texaco's in the present action, for loss or damage *a* to goods carried in a ship or claims arising out of an agreement for the carriage of goods in a ship. Under s 3(1), subject to certain restrictions as regards the residence of the defendant or the place where the claim arose, the Admiralty jurisdiction may be invoked by an action in personam, but it may also be invoked by an action in rem and the type of action with which I am concerned in the instant case is one regulated by s 3(4), the material parts of which I had better read. It is in these terms: *b*

> 'In the case of any such claim as is mentioned in paragraphs (d) to (r) of subsection (1) of section 1 of this Act, being a claim arising in connection with a ship, where the person who would be liable on the claim in an action in personam was, when the cause of action arose, the owner or charterer of, or in possession or in control of, the ship, the Admiralty jurisdiction of the High Court . . . may (whether the claim gives rise to a maritime lien on the ship or not) be invoked by an action in rem against— *c* (a) that ship, if at the time when the action is brought it is beneficially owned as respects all the shares therein by that person; or (b) any other ship which, at the time when the action is brought, is beneficially owned as aforesaid.'

This section has a critical importance to counsel for Texaco's argument, because of the provisions of paras (a) and (b) of the subsection. It has been clearly established by the *d* decision of Brandon J in *The Monica S*[1], that, once an action in rem has been commenced under this section against the person who was at the time of the issue of the writ the owner of the ship, it can be proceeded with despite any subsequent change in the ownership of the vessel, even if that change has taken place before the writ is served and, a fortiori, before the ship is arrested. Thus, once the writ is issued against a vessel as to which it can be established that, at the time of the issue of the proceedings, it was owned by a person *e* against whom the cause of action in personam lay, that cause of action can be prosecuted against the vessel into whosesoever hands it comes and it can be arrested and sold under the Admiralty procedure to meet the claim.

It is this which, counsel for Texaco claims, constitutes Texaco a secured creditor in the instant case. A claimant who merely enters a caveat secures a protection only against the vessel being released without notice to him, but he may find himself barred from claiming *f* in rem against the vessel if, before he commences his proceedings, a change of ownership takes place. He who issues a writ, however, whether he serves it or not, has taken a further and crucial step along the road because he has fixed the vessel as the target of his claim no matter what changes of ownership subsequently take place, and has put himself in a position where he has an accrued right of arrest. If, therefore, the corporate owner of the vessel subsequently goes into liquidation, the liquidator is equally subject to the security *g* conferred by the accrued right of arrest and the plaintiff is properly described as a secured creditor who ought to be permitted to proceed to retain the priority which he has already achieved by issuing his proceedings.

That the actual arrest of a vessel puts the arresting plaintiff in the position of a secured creditor is not disputed in the instant case, but I am not sure that to speak of a person as a secured creditor because he has 'an accrued right of arrest' does not, to some extent, beg the *h* question, if 'accrued' is taken to mean 'indefeasible'. A plaintiff in any sort of action has a right to put in motion the procedural steps which are open to him under the rules and practice of the court in which he sues, but subject, in the case of a corporate defendant which goes into liquidation, to the provisions of the Companies Act 1948 and the winding-up rules. The right to arrest a ship is merely one of the procedural steps which it is open to the plaintiff to take, just as it is open to a judgment creditor in an action in personam to *j* secure his judgment by execution, garnishee proceedings, or charging order or equitable execution. Yet it is clear that in the ordinary case of the action in personam, the creditor

---

1   [1967] 3 All ER 740, [1968] P 741

is not entitled for the purposes of s 231 of the 1948 Act to be considered a secured creditor
unless and until he has perfected his process. Up to that moment his rights are inchoate
and are liable to be defeated by a winding-up intervening between institution and
perfection. Does it make any difference that the plaintiff has, by issuing a writ in rem for
the purpose of invoking the Admiralty jurisdiction, put himself in a position to perfect his
claim against anyone into whose hands the vessel may subsequently come? Counsel for
Texaco suggests that it does and he points out, quite rightly, that if for instance, an action
in rem has been commenced but no arrest has taken place before the winding-up and the
vessel is subsequently sold by the liquidator, the plaintiff in that action would be perfectly
entitled to pursue his action against the vessel in the hands of the purchaser from the
liquidator and to arrest the vessel in his hands. It is only by an invocation of the Admiralty
procedure that the vessel can be sold free from his right to pursue it. If, therefore, his right
to follow and sue the vessel is unaffected where no arrest has taken place, why should the
exercise of that right be inhibited simply because someone else has chosen to arrest the
vessel so that it may be appraised and sold under the Admiralty jurisdiction?

Some support for counsel for Texaco's concept of the plaintiff in rem as a secured creditor
can be derived from the authorities, although cases prior to the Supreme Court of
Judicature Act 1875 have to be treated with a certain degree of caution, because, decided
as they were at a time when the institution of proceedings and the warrant of arrest were
substantially contemporaneous, it was not usually necessary or material to draw any clear
distinction between the two events.

In *The Heinrich Bjorn*[1], the Court of Appeal (subsequently upheld by the House of Lords[2])
held that the Court of Admiralty Act 1840, which enabled the necessaries man to proceed
in rem did not create a maritime lien for necessaries. There is, at the end of the judgment,
what might be taken to be a suggestion that the bringing of the action itself creates a
security. Fry LJ[3], who delivered the judgment of the court, said that although the statute
had enabled the necessaries man to enforce his claim in the Admiralty Court 'and as one
means has given him a right to arrest the ship, it has given him no maritime lien, and
consequently no right against the ship *till action brought*' the emphasis is mine. But I doubt
whether much can be made to turn on this, for it is clear from an earlier passage in the
judgment that what the court had in mind was the arrest of the ship and not the mere
institution of the suit. Fry LJ said[4]:

> 'But, on the contrary, the arrest of a vessel under the statute is only one of several
> possible alternative proceedings ad fundandam jurisdictionem; no right in the ship or
> against the ship is created at any time before the arrest; it has no relation back to any
> earlier period; it is available only against the property of the person who owes the debt
> for necessaries; and the arrest need not be of the ship in question, but may be of any
> property of the defendant within the realm. [I should pause to mention that that last
> clause was subsequently disapproved[5].] The two proceedings, therefore, though
> approaching one another in form, are different in substance: in the one case the arrest
> is to give effect to a pre-existent lien, in the other, the arrest is only one of several
> alternative modes of procedure, because, to use the language of Dr. Lushington in *The
> Volant*[6], "it offers the greatest security for obtaining substantial justice in furnishing
> a security for prompt and immediate payment".'

More closely in point is the decision of the Court of Appeal in *The Cella*[7], which was a case
of competing rights in a liquidation. The facts are not altogether clearly set out in the

1   (1885) 10 PD 44
2   (1886) 11 App Cas 270
3   10 PD 44 at 61
4   10 PD 44 at 54
5   *The Beldis* [1936] P 51, [1935] All ER Rep 760
6   (1842) 1 Wm Rob 383
7   (1888) 13 PD 82

report. The plaintiff had commenced an action in rem in June 1885 whilst the vessel was already under arrest in another action. In the plaintiff's action a mortgagee of the ship had *a* intervened and an agreement was made between him and the plaintiff which was embodied in an order which released the vessel forthwith on the intervener undertaking to pay to the plaintiff whatever the plaintiff would have recovered after satisfying prior incumbrances if the arrest had continued. The company which owned the vessel was wound up two months later. The report does not state that the plaintiff had actually himself arrested the vessel in his action, but if he had not it is a little difficult to see how the *b* court could have made, in that action, an order for its release, and the argument of the plaintiff's counsel, which was based on an incumbrance having been created in favour of 'a claimant who seizes a ship', suggests that the plaintiff himself had arrested. Certainly this was the footing on which the court seems to have approached the case, but there is a passage in the judgment of Sir James Hannen P at first instance[1] which gives some support for the concept of the mere commencement of proceedings as itself creating a security. He *c* said[2]:

> 'At the time that undertaking was given the plaintiff had a lien on the ship by virtue of the proceedings he had instituted against it. It was not, indeed, a maritime lien, which arises at the moment the claim comes into existence, but it was a security arising at the commencement of this action in rem. This distinction appears to me to be fully recognised by the judgments in the cases of *The Two Ellens*[3], *The Pieve* *d* *Superiore*[4], and *The Heinrich Björn*[5]. The right of the plaintiff as against Wood must be determined by the rights which the plaintiff had against the ship at the time she was released, and the subsequent history of the ship and of the owners is irrelevant for the purpose of this inquiry.'

On appeal, however, the emphasis was put rather on the arrest as the critical event. Lord *e* Esher MR said[6]:

> 'Now the jurisdiction given to the Admiralty Division by the Act in question can, as I have said, be exercised by an action in rem, that is to say, upon the production of a proper affidavit, a warrant of arrest is issued and under it the marshal may seize the ship, and the Court will adjudicate upon it. Possession is taken by the marshal in order that the ship may be sold, and that the rights of the plaintiff may be satisfied out *f* of the ship. These rights must exist before the ship is seized, for the Court adjudicates upon the ship on the ground that it had jurisdiction to seize it and realize it for the plaintiff, on account of something which happened before the seizure, which in this case was repairing her. Even without the cases cited for the plaintiff, it would seem to me to be clear that whatever may be the judgment of the Court it must take effect from the time of the writ. The judge is to enforce the writ, and to determine the *g* rights of the parties at the time the writ is served. That is so, as it seems to me, in every action. But in every action we may have bankruptcy and I know not what intervening, so that when judgment is given it cannot be effectually carried out. But if the money be in court, or the Court has possession of the res, it can give effect to its judgment as if it had been delivered the moment after it took possession of the res. It is contrary to the principle of these cases and to justice that the rights of the parties *h* should depend not upon any act of theirs but upon the amount of business which the Court has to do. Therefore the judgment in regard to a thing or to money which is in the hands of the Court, must be taken to have been delivered the moment the thing or the money came into the possession of the Court. In addition to the two cases cited

1   (1888) 13 PD 82
2   13 PD 82 at 85
3   (1872) LR 4 PC 161
4   (1874) LR 5 PC 482
5   (1886) 11 App Cas 270
6   13 PD 82 at 86–87

j

for the plaintiff, there are also the Admiralty cases of *The Two Ellens*[1], *The Pieve Superiore*[2], and *The Heinrich Björn*[3], which are undoubtedly based on the same rule as the two bankruptcy cases, and they shew that though there may be no maritime lien, yet the moment that the arrest takes place, the ship is held by the Court as a security for whatever may be adjudged by it to be due to the claimant.'

Fry LJ said[4]:

'It appears to me that so long as 1842 Dr. Lushington, in *The Volant*[5], explained the principle upon which the Court proceeds, when he said that "an arrest offers the greatest security for obtaining substantial justice, in furnishing a security for prompt and immediate payment." The arrest enables the Court to keep the property as security to answer the judgment, and unaffected by chance events which may happen between the arrest and the judgment. That is Dr. Lushington's decision, and I think it is a right one . . . Lastly, it is in conformity with what has been the uniform practice of the Admiralty Court—that the effect of the arrest is to provide security for the plaintiff for the sum which he claims.'

Finally, Lopes LJ said[4]:

'From the moment of the arrest the ship is held by the Court to abide the result of the action, and the rights of the parties must be determined by the state of things at the time of the institution of the action, and cannot be altered by anything which takes place subsequently.'

Counsel for Texaco would, I think, seek to place the main emphasis on the statement of Lord Esher MR that the judgment is to take effect from the time of the writ, and the statement of Lopes LJ that the rights of the parties must be determined by the state of things at the institution of the action. I doubt, however, whether too much can be made of this. No doubt, once arrest has taken place, the court holds the res as security for whatever claim the plaintiff has asserted by the writ, but the court there was concerned I think to meet the argument that the plaintiff had in some way disabled himself from relying on his security by subsequently proceeding to a judgment in personam in another action, rather than to define the precise point of time at which the security arose.

In *The Zafiro*[6], which was another liquidation case, the question was whether a vessel having been arrested by the plaintiffs before the commencement of a voluntary winding-up of the owner company but after notice that such a winding-up was imminent, the plaintiff's action ought to be permitted to continue, the contention being that the arrest constituted an execution within s 325 of the 1948 Act. That section prevents the execution creditor from retaining the benefit of his execution unless he has completed it by sale prior to the commencement of the winding-up, subject to a dispensing power in the court. Hewson J rejected that contention and held that the plaintiffs, having arrested the vessel prior to the commencement of the winding-up, were secured creditors and should not be restrained from proceeding with their action. In his judgment, the emphasis was placed on the arrest as the critical factor, but since both the writ and the arrest occurred on the same day and prior to the winding-up, there was no particular reason to distinguish between them. He said[7]:

'I agree with [counsel's] submission that if the issue of the writ and arrest had preceded the notice I, at all events, would have exercised my discretion in favour of

1   (1872) LR 4 PC 161
2   (1874) LR 5 PC 482
3   (1886) 11 App Cas 270
4   (1888) 13 PD 82 at 88
5   (1842) 1 Wm Rob 383
6   [1959] 2 All ER 537, [1960] P 1
7   [1959] 2 All ER 537 at 542, [1960] P 1 at 11

the necessaries man. I agree with that submission, for this reason, that, by arresting without having notice of the meeting he would have made himself a secured creditor under a statutory lien.'

After citing *The Cella*[1], he said[2]: 'As I see it, *The Cella*[1] is still good law, and arrest in such cases creates a statutory lien, making the holder a secured creditor.'

In considering the application of s 325, Hewson J distinguished between execution, which follows judgment, and arrest, and said[3]:

'. . . it will be seen that the execution follows either a judgment or an order for the payment of money. The arrest of a ship in an action in rem is the means whereby, among other things, a necessaries man obtains security for a debt of a special character without a judgment or order for payment of money. It is a right given to him by the legislature, a right the scope of which, in my view, has recently been extended by the Administration of Justice Act, 1956, s. 1(1)(m), and possibly also by s. 1(1)(p). . . Counsel for the defendants very strongly argued that an arrest such as this could be regarded as an anticipatory execution. Arrest, as I see it, is the means, given by law, whereby security is obtained for a debt of a special character, and, by so arresting, the necessaries man becomes a secured creditor. It seems to me (and I accept what counsel for the defendants says) that the wording of some of the sections, to which I have referred, in the Companies Act, 1948, is very inapt when applied to certain Admiralty matters; but I see no reason why I should extend the meaning of the word "execution" to include a writ in rem in the circumstances that we have to consider in this case. Execution, in my view, succeeds, and does not precede, judgment, whereas in arrest there is no existing judgment on which to execute.'

The authorities were extensively and helpfully reviewed in the judgment of Brandon J in *The Monica S*[4]. This is an important case from the point of view of counsel for Texaco because, first of all, it establishes quite clearly his central proposition that the effect of the issue of a writ in rem is to enable the plaintiff to proceed against the vessel in the hands of subsequent owners, provided that, at the date of issue, it was owned by the person against whom the cause of action in personam subsisted, and secondly because of the references to 'a statutory right in rem' sometimes referred to as 'a statutory lien'. Counsel for Texaco particularly relies on the following passages in the judgment of Brandon J[5]:

'Like HEWSON, J., I prefer the expression "statutory right of action in rem" to the expression "statutory lien", for it seems to me to be the more accurate description of the right in question. The expression "statutory lien" is, however, a convenient one if it is used to mean no more than an irrevocably accrued statutory right of action in rem. Using the expression in that sense, it seems to me that it is common ground that a statutory lien does attach to the res at some time, and the only question is when. Is it on action brought or is it on arrest? Whichever time for the event is correct, the result of the event is, from a practical point of view, the same, namely, to charge the res with the claim, subject to prosecution of the action to judgment and to priorities. If this is in effect to create a substantive right, as counsel for Tankoil argues, then such creation is something which occurs, even on his contention as to the law, at the time of arrest. If it can occur then, I do not see, as a matter of principle, why it should not occur earlier, at date of action brought.'

Then he said[6]:

---

1 (1888) 13 PD 82
2 [1959] 2 All ER 537 at 543, [1960] P 1 at 13
3 [1959] 2 All ER 537 at 544, [1960] P 1 at 14–15
4 [1967] 3 All ER 740, [1968] P 741
5 [1967] 3 All ER 740 at 758, [1968] P 741 at 768–769
6 [1967] 3 All ER 740 at 760–761, [1968] P 741 at 773

> *a* '. . . I see no reason, as a matter of construction of the [Administration of Justice Act 1956], for implying a further provision that, in cases where the claim does not give rise to a maritime lien, if there is a change of ownership after action brought but before service or arrest, the right which is given to proceed in rem against the ship is thereupon to lapse. As I said earlier, the jurisdiction which is invoked by an action in rem, whether under s. 3 (2), (3) or (4), is the jurisdiction to hear and determine the questions and claims listed in s. 1 (1). I see no reason why, once a plaintiff has properly
> *b* invoked that jurisdiction by bringing an action in rem, whether under s. 3 (2), (3) or (4), he should not, despite a subsequent change of ownership of the res, be able to prosecute it through all its stages, up to and including judgment against the res, and payment of the amount of the judgment out of the proceeds.'

c I should perhaps mention that the references there to invocation of the Admiralty procedure may perhaps require some modification in the light of subsequent authorities to which I will have to refer a little later.

It has, however, to be remembered that what Brandon J was considering in that case was the effect on a pending action of a change of ownership. He did not have before him, and indeed expressly said so, the question of the status of the plaintiff as a secured creditor in a liquidation. He said[1]:

> *d* 'There are, as it seems to me, three main classes of case in which the time when a statutory right of action becomes effective may be important. The first class of case is where there is a transfer of ownership either before or after an action is begun. In that class of case the question is whether the right can be exercised at all against the res in the hands of its new owner. The second class of case is where there is another competing right of action in rem, for instance under a mortgage. The question then
> *e* is not as to the existence of the right, but as to its priority in relation to the competing claim. The third class of case is where the owner of the res goes bankrupt, or, if it is a company, goes into liquidation. The question then is whether the person claiming the statutory right of action in rem is to be treated as a secured creditor or not. These three classes of case, although they have something in common, are not the same. Accordingly, while it may be that the questions raised by all three classes of case can
> *f* be solved by the application of the same or similar principles, it cannot be assumed that this is necessarily so.'

It should also be noted that Brandon J was careful to distinguish the right to obtain security and the actual obtaining of security. In reviewing the decision of Dr Lushington P in *The Pacific*[2], Brandon J said[3]:

> *g* 'In one passage Dr. LUSHINGTON says the material man has no security till institution of suit. In a second passage he says that, at the date of registration of the mortgage, the plaintiffs have not instituted a suit, and, therefore, had no lien on the ship. In a third passage, he says security was obtained on arrest. I do not think that the third of these passages need be regarded as in conflict with the other two. Taken together, the passages are consistent with the view that, by instituting the cause, the necessaries
> *h* man acquired the right to arrest and thereby obtain security for his claim; and that, by arresting immediately after institution of the cause, he did in fact obtain such security. So interpreted, the judgment appears to treat institution of cause as the time when the claim attaches.'

He adverts to this distinction again in connection with the judgment of Sir Montague
j E Smith in *The Pieve Superiore*[4], and said[5]:

---

1   [1967] 3 All ER 740 at 745, [1968] P 741 at 748–749
2   (1864) Brown & Lush 243
3   [1967] 3 All ER 740 at 747, [1968] P 741 at 751
4   (1874) LR 5 PC 482
5   [1967] 3 All ER 740 at 749, [1968] P 741 at 754

'When Sir Montague E. Smith said that the arrest could not avail against any valid charges on the ship or against a bona fide purchaser, it is not clear that he was referring *a* to charges in existence, on a sale which had occurred, at any time before arrest. He may equally well have meant charges in existence, or a sale which had occurred, at any time before institution of the cause. The distinction was not material on the facts and, like other judges in other cases, he may well not have been applying his mind to it. Further, when he said that the object of the statute was only to found a jurisdiction against the owner who was liable for the damage, and to give the security of the ship *b* from the time of arrest, he may well have meant no more than that the person against whom the cause had to be instituted was the carrier who would have been liable in personam, and that arrest following institution of a cause was the method by which security was, from a practical point of view, obtained. It is, I think, important, when considering this passage, and other passages in later judgments on the same lines, to keep clearly in mind the distinction between having a right to arrest a ship in order *c* to obtain security for a claim, and the actual exercise of that right by arrest. It is the arrest which actually gives the claimant security; but a necessary preliminary to arrest is the acquisition, by the institution of a cause in rem, of the right to arrest.'

He then quoted[1] this passage from the speech of Lord Watson in the House of Lords in *The Henrich Björn*[2]:

d

'We have been informed that under the recent practice of the Admiralty court the remedy is also given to creditors of the shipowner for maritime debts which are not secured by lien; and in that case the attachment of the ship, by process of the court, has the effect of giving the creditor a legal nexus over the proprietary interest of his debtor, as from the date of the attachment. The position of a creditor who has a proper maritime lien differs from that of a creditor in an unsecured claim in this *e* respect—that the former, unless he has forfeited the right by his own lâches, can proceed against the ship notwithstanding any change in her ownership, whereas the latter cannot have an action in rem unless at the time of its institution the res is the property of his debtor.'

As to this, Brandon J accepted the contention of counsel for the plaintiff that when Lord *f* Watson referred to the 'legal nexus' over the proprietary interest of the defendant he was directing himself not to the time when the right to obtain the security accrued but to the time from which the security when obtained took effect. For the purposes of the instant case, counsel for Texaco has to establish that the distinction between the right to obtain security and the actual obtaining of it is immaterial in a consideration of whether the plaintiff can be said to be a secured creditor, and he is entitled to rely on this further passage from Brandon J's judgment where, in reviewing *The Cella*[3], he said[4]:

g

'. . . since the order to wind up the company was made after the agreement for release the plaintiff was, as against the liquidator, in the position of a secured creditor. I recognise that Lord Esher, M.R., and Fry, L.J., laid great stress on arrest as conferring on the plaintiff the status of secured creditor, and it may be that, in that connection, they were treating service of the plaintiff's writ on the ship when already under arrest *h* by the master as equivalent to a notional arrest by the plaintiff. It does not seem to me, however, that it is necessarily right to infer from this stress laid on arrest, that these two judges were of opinion that, if the owning company had been ordered to be wound up after the plaintiff had issued his writ but before he had served it, he would have had no right to proceed with the action. Those were not the facts of the case before them, and I do not think they were applying their minds to such a question. *j*

---

1   [1967] 3 All ER 740 at 751, [1968] P 741 at 757
2   (1886) 11 App Cas 270 at 277
3   (1888) 13 PD 82
4   [1967] 3 All ER 740 at 754–755, [1968] P 741 at 763

Such an opinion does not, in any case, seem to have been held by Lopes, L.J. He said
a that, from arrest, the court holds the ship to abide the result of the action, and that the
rights of the parties must be determined by the state of things at the time of the
institution of the action, and cannot be altered by anything which takes place
subsequently. This describes the legal position after arrest, but it seems to me to be
consistent with the view that, once a writ has been issued, there is an accrued right to
arrest and thereby establish that position.'

b However, Brandon J was again at pains to point out that the considerations governing
the case before him did not necessarily apply to other classes of case which he had
previously mentioned. He said[1]:

'It may be, however, as I have indicated earlier, that the questions arising in the
three classes of case (change of ownership, priorities, and bankruptcy or liquidation)
c do not necessarily fall to be answered in the same way. In that connexion, it is to be
observed that the authorities most favourable to arrest as the critical time are
authorities on liquidation (*The Cella*[2], *The Zafiro*[3]) or priorities (*The James W.
Elwell*[4], *The Colorado*[5]). Since the present case is a change of ownership case, it may be
that I should be guided in the main by those authorities in which change of ownership
arose on the facts or was at least expressly discussed.'

d I think, therefore, that whilst counsel for Texaco derives some support for his argument
from *The Monica S*[6] that case cannot be regarded as an authority which necessarily governs
the question which has fallen for decision in the instant case, as to which Brandon J was
careful to say that different considerations might apply. It establishes no doubt the accrued
right of arrest and its effect so far as concerns the person against whom the action once
brought may be continued, but it does so without directly adverting to any limitations
e subject to which the accrual takes place or to the status of the plaintiff as a secured creditor
in a liquidation of the owner company, and it does draw a clear distinction between the
right to obtain security and the actual obtaining of security.

I have also been referred to the decision of Hewson J in *The Constellation*[7], but I find it of
only limited assistance. It was a case where a compulsory winding-up order had been made
on a petition which preceded the issue of a number of writs in rem, although the actual
f order was subsequent to the writ. The registrar had given leave for the action to continue
and the question which arose was whether the vessel could be appraised and sold having
regard to the provisions of s 228 of the 1948 Act. Since some of the claims appear to have
been claims in respect of maritime liens and there is no indication in the report of the
nature of the other claims, nor of the basis on which leave to continue the action was given,
it does not really assist in the present context.

g There are, however, two further authorities which have in my judgment an important
bearing on the instant case. It was held by the Court of Appeal in *The Banco*[8] that where
s 3(4) of the 1956 Act refers to the jurisdiction of the Admiralty Court being invoked by
an action in rem against:

'(a) that ship, if at the time when the action is brought it is beneficially owned as
h respects all the shares therein by that person; or (b) any other ship which, at the time
when the action is brought, is beneficially owned as aforesaid,'

the word 'or' is a true alternative and does not permit the prosecution of an action against

1 [1967] 3 All ER 740 at 759, [1968] P 741 at 770–771
2 (1888) 13 PD 82
j 3 [1959] 2 All ER 537, [1960] P 1
4 [1921] P 351
5 [1923] P 102, [1923] All ER Rep 531
6 [1967] 3 All ER 740, [1968] P 741
7 [1965] 3 All ER 873, [1966] 1 WLR 272
8 [1971] 1 All ER 524, [1971] P 137

more than one vessel. The case is important because, although it was probably not essential
to the decision, as Brandon J subsequently held in *The Berny*[1], the court reviewed the   *a*
Admiralty practice of issuing writs against a number of ships in the same ownership or
joining a number of ships as defendants to the same writ. Lord Denning MR said[2]:

> 'All this seems clear save for a point of practice which counsel for the plaintiffs
> raised before us. He said that, ever since the 1956 Act, the practice had been to issue
> a writ at once against *all* the ships owned by the defendant: and to serve it on the *one*
> ship considered the most worthwhile when it came within the jurisdiction. Counsel   *b*
> said that if under s 3(4) the jurisdiction in rem can only be invoked against one ship,
> it means that the action can only be *brought* against one ship, and the writ can only be
> *issued* against one ship: and that once it is invoked against one ship, it cannot be
> invoked against any other ship . . . I can see the force of this point, but I think that
> counsel for the defendants gave the right answer. When a plaintiff brings an action
> in rem, the jurisdiction is invoked not when the writ is issued, but when it is served   *c*
> on the ship and the warrant of arrest is executed. The reason is because it is an action
> in rem against the very thing itself, and does not take effect until the thing is
> arrested. This means that the practice is right. The plaintiff is entitled, as soon as his
> cause of action arises, to issue his writ in rem against the offending ship and all other
> ships which at that time, ie at the date of issue of the writ, belong to the same
> owner. That saves his time. Then he can wait until he finds the *one* ship which he   *d*
> thinks most suitable to arrest. Then he will serve her and execute a warrant of arrest
> against her. That having been done, he cannot go against the other ships and should
> strike them out of the writ.'

Then Megaw LJ said[3]:

> 'There remains one matter which was the subject of much learned and interesting   *e*
> argument. Since the 1956 Act, we are told, the practice in the Admiralty Court,
> where the jurisdiction in rem under s 3(4) of the Act has been relevant, has been that
> a writ in rem may be, and not infrequently is, issued naming more than one vessel
> alleged to be owned by the defendant. In no case, however, until the present case in
> July 1970, has any plaintiff attempted to make use of such a multiple writ by
> proceeding to the arrest thereunder of more than one vessel. A plaintiff by issuing the   *f*
> writ in that form has, at least so it was hoped, had his tackle in order. He has been
> ready for any contingency. He does not have to wait in order to see which vessel
> belonging to the plaintiffs will arrive in this country; and then, perhaps, in a hurry at
> the last minute, take out his writ naming that vessel. He does not, perhaps, feel
> subject to the same urgency to arrest the first vessel belonging to the defendant which
> happens to arrive within the jurisdiction. He may decide to hold his hand, hoping   *g*
> that a more valuable vessel, among those named in his writ, will arrive thereafter,
> giving him better security for his claim. When the plaintiff does decide to strike, he
> amends his writ by deleting the names of all the other vessels, and proceeds with
> service on, and the obtaining and execution of a warrant of arrest of, the chosen vessel,
> the name of which has now, by amendment, become the only name in the writ . . .
> It is said that the jurisdiction is "invoked" when the writ in rem is issued. Hence, if   *h*
> the defendants' construction of s 3(4) be correct, it would be contrary to the terms of
> the statute if a writ were to be issued naming more than one vessel. If the premise is
> right, I think that the conclusion must follow . . . However, I do not think that the
> premise is right. I do not accept that the Admiralty jurisdiction is invoked in an
> action in rem against a vessel merely by the issue of a writ which contains, inter alia,
> the name of that ship. I agree with counsel for the defendants that, for the purposes   *j*

---

1   [1978] 1 All ER 1065, [1978] 2 WLR 387
2   [1971] 1 All ER 524 at 533–534, [1971] P 137 at 153
3   [1971] 1 All ER 524 at 537–538, [1971] P 137 at 158–159

of this subsection, the jurisdiction is not invoked merely by the issue of the writ. That may be the start of the invocation, but the invocation is not complete until the writ is served, or, it may be, deemed to have been served, as a result of the entry of appearance by the defendant before service is effected. Moreover, it is to be observed that s 3(4) states: "... the Admiralty jurisdiction ... may ... be invoked by an action *in rem against that ship* ...". In my view, whatever might be the technicalities otherwise, the jurisdiction cannot properly be said to be invoked "against that ship" (or, equally, of course, "against ... any other ship") merely because a writ has been issued which names that ship amongst others, but which cannot lawfully be served upon that ship until something further is done to the writ itself, namely its amendment. If the jurisdiction can be said to have been invoked at all, it is not "against that ship". I do not think that there is anything in this procedural technicality which can, or should, affect the decision of the question before the court.'

The views expressed there were adopted and applied by Brandon J in *The Berny*[1] as a matter of direct decision. I should perhaps also mention *Re Wanzer*[2], which is relied on by counsel for Texaco. That was a case of sequestration which was permitted to continue by the court, but I do not think that it really helps counsel in the present context because the decision appears to have been based on the view taken of Scots law that the landlord sequestrating in that case was, under Scots law, already a secured creditor for the rent which was due to him.

I have not found the question which I am called on to decide at all an easy one, nor have the difficulties been ameliorated by my unfamiliarity with the waters through which counsel have been good enough to pilot me; but it seems to me that if it be right that the plaintiff who has issued a writ in rem has not yet invoked the jurisdiction of the Admiralty Court and does not do so until he serves his writ, it is really not possible to describe him in any real sense as a secured creditor. Take, for instance, the case of a company which owns a number of vessels. The plaintiff issues a writ claiming against them all, and then before he elects to proceed against any particular vessel, the company is wound up. To what does his security extend? Counsel for Texaco's answer is that it extends to whichever ship the plaintiff may care to select. But that cannot, in my judgment, be right. It seems to me that in such a case any security which the plaintiff may be able to obtain necessarily remains inchoate until he amends his writ by striking out the names of those vessels against which he does not require to proceed and perfecting the security for his claim by serving and arresting.

In a case such as the present, which is concerned with comparing rights in a liquidation, the authorities to which I have referred seem to me to point to the arrest as being the event which perfects and crystallises the security, although it is unnecessary in this case to decide as between service simpliciter and service and arrest. A claim is, in my judgment, no less inchoate and unperfected where the plaintiff contents himself simply with issuing his writ against one vessel only. It is true that he thus puts himself in a position where he can proceed against the one vessel named in his writ regardless of who owns it at the time when he chooses to serve his proceedings, but subject to this he is really in no different position from the creditor with a claim in rem who has not issued proceedings at all, or who has merely entered a caveat after an arrest of the vessel in someone else's action. As it seems to me, the legal nexus between the creditor and the res claimed as security cannot thus easily be established.

To give a plaintiff who has done no more than Texaco has done in this case leave to proceed with the action despite the winding-up would be to enable Texaco, at present an unsecured creditor, to perfect that which, at the date of the winding-up, was imperfect, and to achieve a priority over other unsecured creditors. That, as I understand the principles

---

1   [1978] 1 All ER 1065, [1978] 2 WLR 387
2   [1891] 1 Ch 305

on which the court acts in giving leave under s 231, is something which will not be permitted and I must accordingly decline to grant the relief sought on Texaco's summons. *a*

Texaco's summons dismissed; leave for action to proceed in personam granted; leave to appeal granted. No order in liquidator's summons.

Solicitors: *William A Crump & Son* (for Texaco); *Bentleys, Stokes & Lowless* (for the liquidator).

b

Evelyn M C Budd Barrister.

R v Vivian

c

COURT OF APPEAL, CRIMINAL DIVISION
BROWNE LJ, TALBOT AND MICHAEL DAVIES JJ
22nd AUGUST 1978

Sentence – Compensation – Order – Principles applicable in making order – Compensation order not to be made unless the sum claimed by the victim for the damage is agreed or proved – Powers of Criminal Courts Act 1973, s 35(1). *d*

The appellant was convicted of the offence of taking and driving away a motor car, and of driving it recklessly. Whilst driving the car he collided with another car and damaged it. At the trial the owner of the damaged car stated that he had received an estimate for its repair which amounted to £209. The appellant asserted that that estimate was excessive *e* because the damaged car was very old and had defects before the collision. The judge, in addition to sentencing the appellant to terms of imprisonment for the offences, made a compensation order against him, under s 35(1)[a] of the Powers of Criminal Courts Act 1973, in the sum of £100. The appellant appealed against the order.

Held – A compensation order under s 35(1) of the 1973 Act should not be made unless the *f* sum claimed by the victim as compensation for damage resulting from the offence was either agreed or had been proved. Since there was neither agreement on nor proof of the amount which the owner of the damaged car was entitled to claim, a compensation order ought not to have been made. Accordingly the order would be quashed (see p 50 g, post).
R v Inwood (1974) 60 Cr App R 70 applied.

Notes *g*

For compensation orders, see 11 Halsbury's Laws (4th Edn) para 804, and for cases on the subject, see 14(2) Digest (Reissue) 861–864, 7455–7491.

For the Powers of Criminal Courts Act 1973, s 35, see 43 Halsbury's Statutes (3rd Edn) 331.

Cases referred to in judgment *h*

R v Inwood (1974) 60 Cr App R 70, CA, 14(2) Digest (Reissue) 863, 7471.
R v Miller [1976] Crim LR 694, CA.

Appeal

On 7th April 1978 at the Crown Court at Snaresbrook before Mr R D Grey, sitting as a *j* deputy circuit judge, the appellant, Paul Vivian, pleaded guilty to the following offences: taking a motor vehicle without authority (counts 1 and 4), theft (counts 2 and 5), attempting to obtain property by deception (count 3) and reckless driving (count 7). He

---

a Section 35(1) is set out at p 50 *b*, post

was sentenced to concurrent terms of nine months' imprisonment on counts 1 to 5 and to
a one month's imprisonment on count 7. In addition he was disqualified for 12 months on
count 7 and ordered to pay £100 compensation to the owner of the car the subject-matter
of counts 4 and 7. He appealed against the making of the compensation order on the
following grounds: that such an order to pay the £100 compensation to the owner of the
car in a manner determined by the court after the appellant's release from prison was
wrong in principle and/or manifestly excessive in that (1) although the appellant had
b pleaded guilty to, inter alia, count 4 of the indictment, he disputed that he was responsible
for all the damage which it was alleged he had done to the car; (2) there was in fact no
admissible evidence before the court that the damage would cost £209·96 to repair in that
the estimate deposed to by the owner of the car was inadmissible as being hearsay evidence
and in any event the figure given was not accepted as being an accurate estimate of the cost
of repair; (3) there was no evidence that the appellant had any means to discharge the order
c on his release from prison having been sentenced to nine months' imprisonment; (4) the
order actually made was imprecise in that it left the details of the manner of payment to
be decided after the appellant's release from prison; and (5) the order might prove to be
counter-productive in that on his release from prison the appellant might be tempted into
crime in order to discharge it. The facts appear in the judgment.

d John Landaw (who did not appear below) for the appellant.

TALBOT J delivered the following judgment of the court: This is an appeal by leave of
the single judge in respect of an order made on 7th April 1978 at Snaresbrook Crown
Court, when the appellant pleaded guilty to a number of offences: taking a motor car
without authority (counts 1 and 4), theft (counts 2 and 5), attempting to obtain property
by deception (count 3) and reckless driving (count 7). He was sentenced, in all, for those
e offences to a sentence of nine months' imprisonment and disqualified for 12 months. In
addition he was ordered to pay the sum of £100 compensation, and it is in respect of that
order that this appeal has proceeded. There is no appeal in respect of the sentence of
imprisonment.

    The appellant committed these offences in October and November 1977, and in one of
them (count 4), on 17th November 1977, he took and drove away a Ford Corsair car. He
f drove it to a road in Wanstead and then abandoned it. Two days later, on 19th November,
he went and picked it up again and drove it (count 7). He was seen by police officers who
then gave chase. The appellant drove at great speed and drove recklessly, as he was
subsequently found guilty of, and he finally collided with a car which was immediately in
front of him. The result was that this Ford Corsair, belonging to a Mr Moulden, suffered
some damage and it was in respect of that damage that the deputy circuit judge ordered
g this sum of £100 compensation.

    The evidence as to that appears in the transcript, where the following exchange between
the judge and counsel for the prosecution took place:

> 'The deputy circuit judge. It is Mr Moulden, is it not, who owns the car which was
> damaged? Has the insurance company reimbursed him, do you know, or do not you
> **h** know? Counsel. I cannot answer that question, your Honour. The officer in the case
> does not know. ". . . I saw my car which was damaged . . . I have received an estimate
> for the repairs of the car which total £209·96 . . ." excluding VAT, and other expenses
> were £14·20.'

Counsel was quoting from a statement made by Mr Moulden, and that was the only
evidence.
j   When it came to sentencing, the deputy circuit judge ordered the £100 compensation
in these words:

> 'So far as compensation is concerned I will make a compensation order for £100 in
> view of what your counsel told me, and how that it is to be paid will be decided when
> you come out of prison.'

We are told by counsel now appearing for the appellant that the sum in fact was much disputed by the appellant who claimed that the estimate of £209 was excessive, as it was a very old car, and had a defective clutch, and in any event he was not entirely responsible. Compensation in these circumstances can be ordered under the Powers of Criminal Courts Act 1973, s 35(1), which reads:

'Subject to the provisions of this part of this Act, a court by or before which a person is convicted of an offence, in addition to dealing with him in any other way, may, on application or otherwise, make an order (in this Act referred to as "a compensation order") requiring him to pay compensation for any personal injury, loss or damage resulting from that offence or any other offence which is taken into consideration by the court in determining sentence.'

This question of compensation and the principles which should be applied have come before the court on previous occasions and I refer to *R v Inwood*[1] and in particular to what was said by Scarman LJ giving the judgment of the court. He said[2]:

'Compensation orders were not introduced into our law to enable the convicted to buy themselves out of the penalties for crime. Compensation orders were introduced into our law as a convenient and rapid means of avoiding the expense of resort to civil litigation when the criminal clearly has means which would enable the compensation to be paid. One has to bear in mind that there is always the possibility of a victim taking civil proceedings, if he be so advised. Compensation orders should certainly not be used when there is any doubt as to the liability to compensate, nor should they be used when there is a real doubt as to whether the convicted man can find the compensation.'

In addition this matter again came before this court in *R v Miller*[3], a brief report of which appears in the Criminal Law Review, where all the principles were set out and the second principle set out by James LJ, who gave the judgment of the court, was: '. . . an order should only be made where the legal position was quite clear.'

It is the submission of counsel in this case that the position was far from clear. There was a mere estimate contained in a statement of the owner of the motor car, which was quoted by counsel for the prosecution. The position furthermore, as I have said, was disputed by the appellant. The deputy circuit judge then appears to have taken a figure less than the estimate, on the basis, one would suppose, that that probably would be a safe figure to order for compensation.

The view of this court is that no order for compensation should be made unless the sum claimed by way of compensation is either agreed or has been proved. Neither of those circumstances obtain in this particular case. Therefore this court has reached the conclusion that in the absence of agreement or evidence as to the correct amount which could be claimed for the damage to the motor car, no order for compensation should have been made and it will be quashed.

Order quashed.

Solicitor: *Registrar of Criminal Appeals.*

N P Metcalfe Esq   Barrister.

---

1   (1974) 60 Cr App R 70
2   60 Cr App R 70 at 73
3   [1976] Crim L R 694

Re Freeston's Charity

COURT OF APPEAL, CIVIL DIVISION
BUCKLEY, GOFF LJJ AND SIR DAVID CAIRNS
24th, 25th JANUARY 1978

University – Trust – Scheme for administering university or college trusts – Fund held on trust to pay moiety of income for benefit of each of two beneficiaries – College trustee of fund and one of the beneficiaries – Whether college entitled to divide fund into a number of distinct trusts having separate endowments – Universities and Colleges (Trusts) Act 1943, s 2(1)(a)(b).

Charity – Charitable trust – Alteration of beneficial interests – Acquiescence by beneficiaries in alteration – Trust for benefit of charitable foundation – Minister of Education requesting division of trust fund into moieties for foundation and other beneficiary – Whether acquiescence of governors of foundation having effect of validating division – Whether Minister's request binding on governors and amounting to acquiescence.

A university college was the sole trustee of a charitable trust established in the 16th century for the benefit, inter alia, of the college and a school. By an agreement made in 1891 between the college and the Charity Commissioners compromising a claim by the college to the whole of the income of the trust fund, the fund was to be held by the college on trust to divide the income into moieties, one for the college and the other for the school. In 1893 the commissioners settled a scheme for the organisation of the school based on the agreement and providing for the college to account to the school for the trust income. Thereafter the college duly divided the net income of the fund between itself and the school. In about 1948 the college desired to make a scheme under s 2(1)[a] of the Universities and Colleges (Trusts) Act 1943 to amalgamate for the purposes of investment and administration all the trusts of which it was trustee. The scheme as originally drawn included the whole of the trust fund, which at that date consisted solely of fixed income securities. When the scheme was submitted for approval the Minister of Education claimed jurisdiction, because the fund was partly applicable for a school, and requested, in a letter dated 21st January 1950, that a moiety of the endowment be excluded from the scheme, but stated that he was willing to agree to the division of the endowments into two parts, one part to be retained in the scheme, and the other to be excluded. Thereafter the college divided the capital of the fund in half and included one half in the scheme and excluded the other half ('the excluded moiety'). The scheme stated that it applied, inter alia, to 'one moiety only' of the trust. The scheme was approved in December 1950. Thereafter the college paid to the school governors the net income from the excluded moiety and retained for itself the net income of the moiety administered within the scheme. The excluded moiety remained invested in fixed income securities because, so the college said, the Minister had so directed, whereas the college invested the moiety within the scheme in equities with the consequence that the income from it grew and increasingly exceeded the income from the excluded moiety. The college regularly accounted to the school governors, in accordance with the 1893 scheme, and the governors were aware of the discrepancy in the income from the two moieties. In November 1958 the school governors required more money to run the school and requested the college to increase the grant made to the school from the fund. The college refused and explained that the Minister was responsible for the division of the fund into moieties and for the investment of the school's moiety in fixed income securities and that nothing could be done to put the matter right without his consent. The college heard nothing more from the school governors until December 1967 when they wrote claiming that the college had not had power to divide the fund into moieties, that the school was entitled to one moiety of the

---

a   Section 2(1), so far as material, is set out at p 56 a to d, post

income of the whole fund and not merely to the income of one moiety, and that the college should account for the underpayment to the school since 1950 resulting from the wrongful *a* division, amounting to some £10,000. The college denied that the division had been wrongful. The school governors brought proceedings claiming a declaration that at all times they were entitled to one-half of the net income of the whole fund. Fox J[b] granted the declaration on the ground that the division made in 1950 had effected a variation of the trusts of the fund, that s 2(1) of the 1943 Act did not authorise the variation and that the school governors could not be held to have acquiesced in the variation. The college *b* appealed, contending that the division did not amount to a variation of the trusts, but that if it did the variation was authorised by the 1943 Act and the scheme made under it, and, furthermore, that the school governors had acquiesced in the division of the fund.

Held – The appeal would be dismissed for the following reasons—   *c*

(i) The division of the fund in 1950 into moieties, one to provide the income to which the school was entitled and the other to provide the income to which the college was entitled, had altered the beneficial interests under the trust, for an interest in half the income of an undivided fund, which was what the trust established by the 1891 agreement provided for, was quite different from an interest in the whole income of a divided part of the fund, which was what the division made in 1950 had provided for (see p 60 *b c*, p 63 *d* *c d* and p 64 *b*, post); *Macculloch v Anderson* [1904] AC 55 applied.

(ii) Moreover, the college was not authorised by the 1943 Act to alter the beneficial interests, for, on the true construction of s 2(1)(*a*) and (*b*) of that Act, only the capital fund of a trust, treated as a single fund, could be the subject of a scheme under s 2(1) and the college was not empowered by s 2(1) to sever the trusts of the fund relating to the application of the income and to bring into the scheme a severed part only of those *e* trusts. Furthermore, the exceptions from the scheme permitted by s 2(1)(*b*) only permitted exclusion from the scheme of part of the assets for the purpose of administration, and did not empower alteration of the beneficial interests in the fund. Accordingly, neither the Act nor the scheme made under it justified the purported alteration by the college of the beneficial interests in the fund, and the school remained entitled to half the income of the whole fund, ie to half the income of the moiety of the fund within the scheme and to half *f* the income of the excluded moiety (see p 61 *e* to *h*, p 63 *c* to *g* and p 64 *b*, post).

(iii) The college had failed to establish such acquiescence by the school governors in the division of the fund as would preclude them from asserting their true rights in the fund, for, having regard to all the circumstances, including the fact that the governors were not aware of their legal right to object to the division, as the college had told them in 1958 that they had no right to object and the matter lay with the Minister, there was not sufficient *g* evidence to raise an equity based on acquiescence against the governors. Even assuming that the Minister's letter of 21st January 1950 amounted to agreement by him that after the division of the fund the school should have an interest only in the moiety excluded from the scheme, the Minister was not entitled to bind the school, and the college could not rely on that letter as constituting acquiescence (see p 61 *j*, p 62 *d e* and *h* to p 63 *d* and *j* to p 64 *b*, post); *Holder v Holder* [1968] 1 All ER 665 applied.   *h*

Decision of Fox J [1978] 1 All ER 481 affirmed.

Notes

For schemes by a university or college for the unification of trusts, see 15 Halsbury's Laws (4th Edn) para 285.   *j*

For the doctrine of acquiescence, see 16 Halsbury's Laws (4th Edn) para 1473.

For the Universities and Colleges (Trusts) Act 1943, s 2, see 11 Halsbury's Statutes (3rd Edn) 115.

---

b   [1978] 1 All ER 481

Cases referred to in judgments

a   *Holder v Holder* [1968] 1 All ER 665, [1968] Ch 353, [1968] 2 WLR 237, CA: *rvsg in part* [1966] 2 All ER 116, [1966] 3 WLR 229, Digest (Cont Vol C) 1042, 2881a.

   Macculloch v Anderson [1904] AC 55, HL, 49 Digest (Repl) 688, 6486.

   Pauling's Settlement Trusts, Re, Younghusband v Coutts & Co [1961] 3 All ER 713, [1962] 1 WLR 86; *rvsd* [1963] 3 All ER 1, [1964] Ch 303, [1963] 3 WLR 742, CA, 47 Digest (Repl) 513, 4656.

b   *Willmott v Barber* (1880) 15 Ch D 96, 49 LJ Ch 792, 43 LT 95; *on appeal* 17 Ch D 772, CA, 44 Digest (Repl) 55, 409.

Cases also cited

   Cairncross v Lorimer (1860) 3 LT 130, [1843–60] All ER Rep 174, HL.

   Crabb v Arun District Council [1975] 3 All ER 865, [1976] Ch 179, CA.

c   *Newcastle-upon-Tyne Corpn v Attorney-General* (1845) 12 Cl & Fin 402, HL.

   Ramsden v Dyson (1866) LR 1 HL 129, HL.

   Thomas, Re, Thomas v Thompson [1930] 1 Ch 194, [1929] All ER Rep 129.

Appeal

This was an appeal by the defendants, the Master and Fellows of University College, Oxford
d ('the college') against the judgment of Fox J[1] given on 4th March 1977 holding in favour
of the plaintiff, Alfred Maurice Smith, the representative of the board of governors ('the
school governors') of Normanton School ('the school') that the college had altered the
beneficial interests under a charitable trust for the benefit of the college and the school, that
s 2(1) of the Universities and Colleges (Trusts) Act 1943 did not authorise the college to
alter the beneficial interests, and that it could not be said that the school governors had not
e acquiesced in the alteration since only the Attorney-General was competent to agree a
variation of the trusts. The facts are set out in the judgment of Goff LJ.

   Paul V Baker QC and *Nicholas Patten* for the college.

   John P Brookes for the school governors.

   Andrew Morritt QC for the Attorney-General.

f

GOFF LJ delivered the first judgment at the invitation of Buckley LJ. This is an appeal
against a judgment given by Fox J[1] on 4th March 1977. The appellants are the Master and
Fellows of University College, Oxford ('the college') and the respondents are, first, Alfred
Maurice Smith, who is one of the board of governors ('the school governors') of Normanton
School ('the school') (he was appointed by Fox J to represent the governors and he appears
g before us in that capacity) and, secondly, the Attorney-General.

   The case arises out of certain charitable trusts created by John Freeston in the 16th
century. By the trust as originally framed, the income of the trust property was assessed
at the precise amount of £63 6s 8d per annum, and was divided in specific amounts
between certain charitable purposes. These included £20 for the college for finding and
maintaining a fellow and two scholars, and £10 for the schoolmaster of the school. Save
h for one holding of consols, the trust estate in 1891 consisted of divers parcels of real
property. In part on the creation of the trust and in part shortly afterwards, the whole trust
estate and property came to be vested in the college as sole trustees and they have remained
such ever since.

   The school appears to have had a chequered history. In the 1880s the newly formed
school board directed it to be closed and directed that the pupils be sent to the board's
j school. The master refused to recognise this and declined to leave the school house, though
whether thereafter he had any pupils or not does not appear. But by this time the income
of the trust property had grown very substantially and there was a considerable surplus of
income over the £63 6s 8d. The college claimed to be entitled to the surplus for their

---

1   [1978] 1 All ER 481

general purposes. The Charity Commissioners objected to this claim, and as appears from a letter dated 19th December 1887, the Charity Commissioners contended that the school was entitled to share in this surplus. Negotiations ensued between the Charity Commissioners and the college, and an agreement was reached between them that the surplus should be divided equally between the college and the school. What occurred appears from a letter of 16th July 1891 written by the Charity Commissioners to the Master of University College, which reads:

> 'By the direction of the Charity Commissioners, I send for the confidential consideration of yourself and the fellows of the college six copies of the draft scheme for the regulation of the above-named charities under the Endowed Schools Acts and for carrying out the agreement between the college and the commissioners as to the augmentation of the income of the Normanton Grammar School and the Freeston Almshouses.'

There is also a reference to this matter in a long report before us, where it is said:

> 'After negotiations extending over some years the college offered a compromise which was accepted by the Charity Commissioners, and the scheme drafted upon that basis was approved by the Lord President of the Committee of Council on Education on the 16th February, and by Her Majesty in Council on the 16th May 1893.'

It appears that by that agreement certain fixed sums larger than those originally provided were directed to be paid for the benefit of beneficiaries other than the college and the school and the surplus was to be equally divided between the two last named bodies.

Having arrived at that agreement with the college, the Charity Commissioners settled a scheme dated 16th May 1893 for the organisation of the school. I need not go any further into the history of the charity. By this scheme the school was put on a proper basis, and it is true that the scheme was dealing only with the half of the income which was to be paid to the school; but it was quite clearly based on the agreement which had been reached between the Charity Commissioners and the college. That scheme is headed:

> 'In the Matter of the GRAMMAR SCHOOL, in the PARISH OF NORMANTON, in the West Riding of the County of York; in the Matter of the Charities of JOHN FREESTON, under a Deed dated the 17th September 1592, and his Will dated the 26th November 1594, for a Grammar School at Normanton aforesaid, and for the Alms Houses next mentioned, and for other purposes . . .'

Clause 1 provided:

> 'The parts of the above-named endowments applicable for purposes not educational . . . (b) in lieu of the sum of £23.8s.0d. per annum heretofor paid to the Trustees of the said almshouses by the Master and Fellows of University College, Oxford, herein-after called the College—(i) a capital sum of £150 to be paid as soon as conveniently may be [for repairing the almshouses]; (ii) a yearly sum of £76 to be paid by the College to the [trustees of the almshouses] in respect of each year from 1st January 1890.'

Clause 2 reads as follows:

> 'The endowments to be applied for the benefit of Normanton Grammar School, herein-after called the Foundation, under this scheme, are as follows:—(1) The schoolhouse and master's house . . . (2) Out of the income, including profits derived from minerals or timber, of the property specified in the schedule hereto, being the property subject to the trusts of the above-mentioned Deed and Will of the said John Freeston, or one of them, now vested in the College . . .'

I pause there to observe that the schedule contains the whole of the then trust estate, so that cl 2 is providing for the payment out of the income of the whole trust fund, and its provisions are, under (a) certain transitional directions which ceased in 1897; and (b) 'in respect of each year from the 1st January 1897, one-half of the net income', that is to say one half of the net income of the whole trust estate, 'remaining after payment of the expenses of management of property and business and of the said yearly sums of £76 and £4', which sums were afterwards commuted; and '(4) any existing endowment from other sources (if any) of the School or Schoolmaster.'

Then cl 4 provided that the payment by the college of the sums thereinbefore specified (1) for the benefit of the almshouses, and—

'(2) for the benefit of Wakefield Grammar School and the Foundation (being the proportions determined by the Charity Commissioners to be applicable to non-educational and educational purposes respectively) is hereby declared to be in full discharge of all payments or obligations which under the said Deed and Will of the said John Freeston, or either of them, are or would but for this Scheme be payable by or enforceable against the College.'

Clause 6 reads: 'Subject as herein provided, the Foundation shall be administered by a Governing Body, herein-after called the Governors . . .' and then follow detailed provisions for the appointment of governors.

Then in cl 24 it was provided:

'Until the completion of the full number of Governors, or the expiration of the first three calendar months, or further time, if any, allowed under this clause, from the date of this Scheme, the present Governing Body, so far as relates to the endowment of the Foundation, shall remain unaltered and shall retain such powers as will enable them to administer the same in the meantime under this Scheme . . .'

There is no evidence that the time was extended. It would therefore seem that the old governors ceased to exist for any purpose, and the government of the school and of the foundation, so far, if at all, as they were different, was vested in the one body of governors set up by this scheme.

Before passing from the scheme, I would refer back to cl 19:

'The College shall in every year make out and render to the Charity Commissioners such accounts as shall be required by them of the receipts and outgoings in respect of the property subject to the trusts of the Deed and Will of the said John Freeston, or either of them, now vested in the College, and shall also, on rendering such accounts to the said Commissioners, send a copy of the same to the Governors.'

Clause 27 made provision for bringing in a girls' school when the funds of the foundation should permit, and that in fact happened; and there was a provision that the governing body and three women appointed by them should govern the girls' school.

From that time forth the school was placed on a proper footing. It came to include a boys' and a girls' school, and it is perfectly clear from what I have read that whatever doubt or ambiguity there might have been before, the whole of the trust estate was thenceforth held, subject to certain payments which were afterwards commuted, on trusts as to one moiety of the income of the whole for the college and the other moiety for the school. Thereafter the college duly divided the net income between the governors of the school and themselves.

In or about 1948 the college desired to make a scheme under the powers conferred by the Universities and Colleges (Trusts) Act 1943, and in his affidavit Lord Redcliffe-Maud[1] says:

'The object of the scheme was to amalgamate for the purposes of investment and administration the many trusts of which the college was trustee and which for the most part had as their objects the provision of fellowships, scholarships and prizes at the college. As originally drawn, the scheme included the whole of the investments then subject to the trusts established by John Freeston and modified by the 1893 scheme.'

---

1   Master of the college from 1963 to 1976

It will be convenient at this stage to refer to the 1943 Act. I need not set it out at any very great length, but s 1 specifies the universities and colleges to which the Act is to apply, and there is no doubt that it includes the college. Section 2(1) provides:

'A university or college may make a scheme providing, in relation to that university or college, as the case may be, for the following matters:—(a) for the application of the scheme to such trusts as may be specified therein, being trusts which are administered by the university or college or which are administered by other trustees for purposes connected with the university or college and are included in the scheme with the consent of those trustees; (b) for enabling all the property held by the university or college on any trust to which the scheme applies, with such exceptions as may be specified in the scheme, to be administered by the university or college as a single fund (hereinafter referred to as "the Fund")... (e) for valuing the Fund and determining the shares of the various trusts therein; (f) for distributing the income of the Fund in accordance with the said shares, and for enabling, in the case of any trust, advances of capital to be made out of the Fund, up to an amount not exceeding the share of that trust, for any purpose for which capital is authorised by the terms of the trust to be advanced...'

Further sub-clauses provide for reserves and for authorising trustees in whom funds subject to the scheme are vested, to convey them to the college; and para (k) is 'for any incidental, consequential and supplementary matters for which the university or college considers it expedient to provide.' There is nothing there about varying the beneficial interest in any trust which is brought into the scheme. Section 3(4) provides:

'A scheme approved under this section shall have effect notwithstanding any instrument (including an Act of Parliament) relating to any trust to which the scheme applies.'

This scheme was submitted to the Privy Council on 15th October 1949. The Minister objected that half the endowment was subject to his jurisdiction, and I shall read the letter dated 21st January 1950, which was written on his behalf to the estates bursar of the college. In that letter it was stated:

'As you are aware, the endowments of the older Universities and their Colleges are exempt from the Minister's jurisdiction by virtue of Section 62 of the Charitable Trusts Act, 1853. However, in the case of endowments of which an Oxford College is the Trustee, but which are applicable for the benefit of scholars from a particular school or locality, the endowment is regarded by the Court as being primarily the endowment of the school or locality in question and, therefore, the exempting provisions of Section 62 do not apply to that endowment [and then a certain case was cited as authority for that proposition, and the letter continues:] Accordingly, the Minister must ask the College to exclude from any scheme which they make under the Universities and Colleges (Trusts) Act 1943, any scholarship endowments of which the College happen to be the Trustees, the benefits of which are confined to a particular school or locality. It appears, therefore, that Major Fletcher's Close Scholarship Fund should be so excluded. With regard to the Freeston Trust, the Minister must also request exclusion, but as a moiety of the endowment is for the corporate revenues of the College, the Minister would be quite willing to agree to the division of the endowments into two parts, one part to be retained in the scheme...'

In consequence of that the college decided to bring half the capital into the scheme and omit the other half. By this time the whole trust property had come to be invested in fixed income securities, and so the college divided every individual holding into exact halves. This scheme was approved by Order in Council on 8th December 1950.

Paragraph 1 of the scheme is headed 'Application of Scheme' and reads: 'This Scheme applies to the trusts shortly specified in the First Schedule hereto (Clause 15) being trusts all administered by the College itself.' The first schedule, referred to as cl 15, has as its first

item: 'Name of Trust, John Freeston (one moiety only)' and under 'Brief Purposes of Trust',
a 'Payment of three Freeston Close Scholarships from one moiety'.

Paragraph 2 in the body of the scheme is headed: 'Property included in Scheme: the Fund', and it reads:

> *b*
> 'All the property held by the College (or by the Minister of Agriculture and Fisheries on its behalf) on or after 31st December, 1948, and the said specified trusts shall be administered by the College as a single Fund (which with all additions thereto is hereinafter called the Fund) except that the assets specified in the Second Schedule hereto (Clause 16) shall be excluded from the Fund and the Scheme. The property included (or represented by assets included) in the Fund (as such property existed on 31st December, 1948) is specified in the Third Schedule hereto (Clause 17) and the said Second and Third schedules show to which of the trusts specified in the First Schedule
> *c*
> hereto the said assets and property were respectively attributable on the 31st December, 1948 . . .'

Schedule 2 contains half of each and every one of the investments forming the trust fund, and Schedule 3 also contains half of each and every one of such investments. The description 'John Freeston (one moiety only)' is not very apt because obviously one cannot
d have a moiety of a trust but I think that must mean that the trust referred to was the trust so far as it provided for the payment of a moiety of the income to the college.

Thereafter the college paid the school governors the net income of the investments representing the excluded half and retained the net income of the share of the income of the scheme fund allocated to the Freeston trust. It appears that there were one or two changes of investment of the excluded moiety, but very few. The whole remained in fixed
e income securities and the income was virtually static. The fund under the scheme, however, was invested in equities, and so the income of the scheme moiety grew. In fact, during the first two years the college received slightly less than the school, but thereafter increasingly more, and there is a list which shows this quite clearly and gives the figures from 1948 to 1969. The college regularly accounted to the school governors as they were required to do under the provisions of the scheme of 1893 which I have read. These
f accounts show the position exactly and, as the judge found and I repeat, there is no question whatsoever of any kind of suppression by the college.

The documents include the account for the year ending 31st December 1949, which was before the scheme. The accounts for the year ending 31st December 1951, after the scheme, clearly show the division between the two, and the school in that year received £1,125 against the college's £1,113. All the accounts were in the same form. There is a
g specimen for the year ending 31st December 1969, which again clearly shows the division, but in that year the school received £1,179, as it did in most years, and the college £2,821.

From 1950 onwards it seems to have been accepted that the divisional education officer should act as clerk to the school governors, and on 1st May 1957 the governors specifically appointed Mr J W Davies, who was the new divisional education officer, to be clerk.

On 26th June 1953 the two schools, boys' and girls', became aided schools under s 15(2)
h of the Education Act 1944 and on 24th January 1956 an order of the county council directed that they should continue to be governed by a single board of governors. At about that time some confusion appears to have arisen in the minds of the governors as to whether there were not two boards of governors, those of the foundation under the scheme and those of the school, but I am satisfied that there was only one. At all events, those who purported to act as either board were substantially the same persons, if not identical.

j After the scheme of 1950, matters went on without complaint by anybody until 28th November 1958, when Mr Davies (he, it will be remembered, was the clerk to the governors) wrote to the estates bursar of the college, stating that in connection with the schools becoming aided schools, difficulties were being experienced because it was necessary for the governors to provide capital sums as a contribution to the necessary improvements to the schools, which would involve expending most of their other capital, and then they would not have enough income to go on making the contributions to yearly expenses which would be required if they were to remain aided schools, and he said:

'I am therefore writing to you to ask if there is any possibility of the grant from the Freeston Trust being increased to assist the Governors and to avoid the necessity of the Governors having to surrender the status of Aided Schools.'

To that the college replied in a very important letter of 8th December 1958, in which they said: 'Until 1950 no distinction was made, in terms of investment, between the College and the [school].' Then they went on to deal with the establishment of the 1950 scheme and the Minister's objection to the inclusion of the whole, and the letter continued:

'The college therefore had no choice but to divide the capital of the Freeston Trust into two equal parts. One half was placed in the Trust Fund and invested in equities. The other half, the revenue from which goes to the [school], remained in gilt edged as directed by the Minister of Education. It is this division which is now responsible for the fact that the College's income is now substantially higher than that which goes to the School. This is a matter for regret but the Ministry of Education is entirely responsible for the present situation—yours is not, of course, the only Trust that suffered. The capital of the Trust was in effect divided equally in 1950. The old principle of straight forward division of income between the School and the College was thereby brought to an end. The best course for the Governors might be to raise this whole question with the Ministry of Education. I am sure that the College would, if the Ministry were to allow it, be very happy to take the School's capital into its own Trust Fund and return to the old principle of equality of income. At the present time, however, such a course is impossible.'

That reply of 8th December 1958 was submitted to a meeting of the school governors on 11th December 1958.

As far as the college was concerned, the matter remained quiescent from then on until 1967, when, no doubt, because of the struggle the governors were having in trying to maintain the aided status of the schools, the matter was taken up again in a letter dated 13th December 1967 from the clerk of the governors to the college bursar. That was a covering letter enclosing a copy of a letter which he had written to the Department of Education and Science. It said:

'Amongst other benefits the Foundation was given "in respect of each year from the 1st January, 1897, one half of the net income remaining after payment of the expenses of management of property and business" and after payment of two small yearly sums to Almshouses at Warmfield and Wakefield Grammar School. No subsequent Scheme of the Charity Commission has given the College power to do other than pay one half of the net income of the Freeston Trust to the Foundation. The Ministry of Education now claim jurisdiction over "the educational endowment of the Freeston Trust" which apparently they believe includes the power to direct a division of the capital of the Trust into two parts and to say how there should be invested that moiety in which the Foundation Governors are interested. The Foundation Governors have never given, or been asked to give, their consent to any division of capital assets or any transposition of investments. In 1950 the College decided to establish a trust fund whose investments would be primarily in equities and this was done after consultation with the Ministry of Education who directed that the College should exclude from any such proposal the John Freeston Trust but expressed agreement "to the division of the endowments into two parts, one part to be retained in the Scheme". Neither the College nor the Ministry gave the Foundation Governors any information about this agreement until some eight years later when the College declared that it was impossible to "return to the old principle of equality of income". The Ministry deny that any direction was given to the College that the investment of any part of the John Freeston Trust should be retained in gilt edge stock and point out that since the

Trustee Investments Act 1961 the College has had power to invest part of the trust
capital in equities but has not apparently exercised that power ... Whatever may be
the respective duties and powers of the College and the Ministry the pupils of
Normanton Grammar School have suffered as a consequence of action taken without
reference to their local trustees who claim that neither the University College nor the
Ministry of Education have power to do that which one of the bodies did and the
other approved. Accordingly, in whatever form the College, as trustees, have invested
the Freeston Trust property, or any part of it, they ought in the opinion of the
Foundation Governors to account to them for one half of the net proceeds of all the
invested funds.'

Then the letter goes on to say that it would appear that over the 17 years they had been
underpaid something in the neighbourhood of £10,000, and continues:

'The Governors feel that this failure of trust should be made good by a return to the
practice of equality of division of income from a single fund and that this should be
made retrospective to 1950 when, in error, the College purported to depart, and the
Ministry believed it was empowered to authorise a departure, from the principle laid
down by the Scheme of 1893.'

So from that time the position adopted by the school governors was made clear.

The college maintained that their application of income since the 1950 scheme was
correct, and eventually these proceedings were brought by an originating summons dated
29th May 1970, by which the governors claimed:

'(1) A declaration that notwithstanding a purported division into two funds
(purported to have been effected in or about the year 1950) of the assets then held by
the first named Defendants [that is, the college] as trustees of the above-mentioned
charity the Governors for the time being of the Foundation known as Normanton
Grammar School are and have at all times since the said purported division been
entitled as such Governors to one half of the net income of all the assets from time to
time held by the first named Defendants as trustees of the said charity',

and then they ask for accounts and other consequential relief, including accounts right
back to 1950.

The college submitted that what they had done did not amount to a variation of the
trusts, and that if it did they were authorised to do that and had done it by the Universities
and Colleges (Trusts) Act 1943; and alternatively that if they were otherwise wrong, the
Minister had, by his claim in 1950 to jurisdiction over half the fund and his objection to
the inclusion of the whole fund in the scheme, and the governors had by inaction with full
knowledge of all the facts, at least after 1958 if not before, acquiesced in what the college
had done, so that the school could no longer complain, nor could anyone on their behalf.

Fox J held that the college had varied the trusts and that they were not authorised to do
so by the Act. He found that the only relevant part of s 2(1) of the Act was para (k), 'for any
incidental, consequential and supplementary matters for which the university or college
considers it expedient to provide'. He held that varying the trusts could not be regarded
as 'incidental, consequential or supplementary' to a scheme under the Act for placing the
trust property into a common fund with property subject to other trusts. He pointed out[1]
that under that subsection what was done had to be in truth 'incidental, consequential or
supplementary'; it was not a case of making such provisions as the college might think
'incidental, consequential or supplementary'.

So far as acquiescence is concerned, the judge held that it was not competent for anyone
other than the Attorney-General to agree to vary the trusts, and therefore there could not
be any effective acquiescence.

He therefore decided in favour of the school governors, but in all the circumstances he
considered that the college ought only to be made accountable for six years' income; that

---

1   [1978] 1 All ER 481 at 489, [1978] 1 WLR 120 at 128

is, as from 3rd January 1971. He ordered accounts accordingly and there is no appeal or cross-appeal concerning that direction, that is to say, the college do not submit that if they are wrong they ought not to account for so long a period, and the school do not say that if the college are liable they ought to account for any longer period.

I now turn to consider the several points which arise in this case. Counsel submits on behalf of the college that what they did was to appropriate one moiety of the fund to answer by its income the share of income which they held in trust for the school, and one moiety to answer the share of income which they were entitled to retain for themselves. He must, of course, put his case that way, for if all they did was to bring one moiety under the investment provisions of the fund and leave the other moiety to the ordinary Trustee Act provisions, it would follow that the school would be entitled still to half the income of each moiety. He says, however, that such an appropriation did not alter the beneficial interests under the trust; he says that they remain income interests. I am wholly unable to accept that argument, since it is manifest that an interest in half the income of an undivided fund is quite different from the whole income of a divided part of that fund.

If any authority for that proposition be required, I think it is to be found quite clearly in all the speeches in *Macculloch v Anderson*[1], where a testator directed that the income of his property should be divided between his children; that in the event of any child dying leaving issue, his or her share of the income should be paid to the issue, and if a child left no issue the deceased's child's share should be divided among the survivors; and he finally directed that on the death of all his children his estate should be wound up and converted into money and divided among the children of his sons and daughters per stirpes. Four children survived; one died unmarried; a second died in 1880, survived by the appellant, his child, and the other two were still alive and had families. The appellant claimed payment of one-third of the corpus of the testator's estate. It was held that he was not entitled to have it, and, whilst it is true that to some extent their Lordships relied on the indication that there was to be a division of the whole on the death of the last survivor, to my mind the speeches make it abundantly plain that they considered that it would be impossible to pay out that one third share because it would alter the income interests. Lord Halsbury LC said[2]:

'The testator has intended that the estate should be kept together, and that until the period of distribution which he has himself ordained to be that which the will discloses, there should be the payment of the income to each of the persons entitled.'

Lord Shand made the position clear beyond doubt in this regard. He said[3]: 'If the appellant's view were to receive effect, the surviving daughters of the testator might be prejudiced pecuniarily in their testamentary rights during their lifetime', and that could only be because they would be prejudiced in their right during their lifetime to receive a share of the income of the whole fund.

Lord Davey said[3]:

'I think it is clear that the testator intended that the estate should remain in globo till the event which he points out—namely, the death of all his children; and that in the meantime, and until then, the income of the whole of the estate should be divided in third shares, in the events which have happened, between the beneficiaries.'

Counsel for the college next argued that such a transaction as we are considering could be effected under s 57 of the Trustee Act 1925, but the court cannot act under that section if what it is asked to do would vary the trusts, and therefore this cannot be varying the beneficial interests. But that does not seem to me to carry him anywhere either. The first enquiry would be whether it does or does not vary the beneficial interests and if one comes,

---

1 [1904] AC 55
2 [1904] AC 55 at 60
3 [1904] AC 55 at 61

as in my judgment one must come, to the conclusion that it does, then it would be a case where the court could not authorise it under that section.

He also sought to make something of the informality, or possible irregularity, of the proceedings in 1893, for he said, rightly, that the Charity Commissioners' scheme dealt only with the school's moiety and the division into moieties was the result of an agreement between the college and the Charity Commissioners. But I cannot see how he can derive any assistance from that, and it does not lie in his mouth to take the point. It is perfectly clear that with the consent of the college and by way of compromise of the claim which they were making to the whole, the trust was recognised as being a trust to divide the whole income in moieties. Therefore, as it seems to me, in order to succeed the college must find justification for varying the beneficial trusts, or they must establish a case in acquiescence.

I turn back, therefore, to the Universities and Colleges (Trusts) Act 1943 and in particular to s 2(1), which says that the scheme may provide, inter alia, for the following matters: '(a) for the application of the scheme to such trusts as may be specified therein . . .' As I have already said, the wording of the scheme is not very apt, but in my view whether one reads it as referring to the whole trust or part of the trust only, one arrives at the same result. If there were anything in the scheme which purported to effect an appropriation and to limit the college on the one hand to the income of the moiety in the fund and the school on the other to the income of the moiety outside it, it might be that, the scheme having been approved, that would now be binding by virtue of s 3(4), but there is no such provision. Then s 2(1)(b) is—

> 'for enabling all the property held by the university or college on any trust to which the scheme applies, with such exceptions as may be specified in the scheme, to be administered by the university or college as a single fund . . .'

So it is quite clear that what the Act is dealing with is the capital of the fund subject to the trust, and, whether or not one treats the trust to which the scheme applies as the share of income to be retained by the college or the trust to divide the income, still the property held on that trust within the meaning of s 2(1)(b) is the whole of the capital. Only half was brought into the scheme and that was in order because s 2(1)(b) allows exceptions, but that, as it seems to me, simply left one half of the assets within the scheme to be administered accordingly and the other half outside, not subject to the scheme, but there was nothing whatever to affect the beneficial interests in either half. Therefore, as it seems to me, the position remained that the college were entitled to half the income of that part of the trust fund which they put in the scheme and half that which they left out, and the school likewise to half of each. There is no provision in the scheme which, as I see it, purports to change the nature of the beneficial interests in the trust, and no power of appropriation given to the college which, had it been there, might have enabled them to make an appropriation which would affect the beneficial interests.

In my judgment, therefore, there is nothing in the Act or the scheme made under it to justify the purported alteration of the beneficial interest by the college.

I turn then to the question of acquiescence. As far as the Minister is concerned, I think his letter is not in this respect very clear, because all he said was:

> 'With regard to the Freeston Trust, the Minister must also request exclusion, but as a moiety of the endowment is for the corporate revenues of the college, the Minister would be quite willing to agree to the division of the endowments into two parts, one part to be retained in the scheme.'

He certainly does not say anything there at all about the beneficial interests affecting the whole or either part being altered, but assuming that it is inherent in what he was saying that he was agreeing that after the division the school should be interested only in the excluded half, he was not entitled to act on behalf of the school so as to bind it, and in my judgment the college cannot rely on that.

So far as the school governors are concerned, it is clear that they did not themselves do anything to induce the college to leave half the investments out of the scheme. But the case made against them is that afterwards, with full knowledge of the facts, they, by their inaction, encouraged the college to leave matters where they were, and if they had known earlier that the governors objected, the college might have applied for a supplemental scheme to bring the other half into the fund. They say that the college, if it now has to treat both moieties of the capital as subject to the overriding income trust, will be prejudiced because it has lost the opportunity of bringing the other half into the fund by a supplemental scheme. For some reason which has not been explained, it left the other half wholly in fixed income securities, whereas it might have invested at any rate part in equities. But, be that as it may, it seems to me that the college have failed to make out their case of acquiescence.

If the matter rested simply as it was laid down by Fry J in the very well known case of *Willmott v Barber*[1], it would be manifest that the college could not succeed, because they could not satisfy the third of the conditions in which in these circumstances Fry J said the court could interfere. He said[2]:

'Thirdly, the defendant, the possessor of the legal right, must know of the existence of his own right which is inconsistent with the right claimed by the plaintiff. If he does not know of it he is in the same position as the plaintiff, and the doctrine of acquiescence is founded upon conduct with a knowledge of your legal rights.'

Whilst it is clear from the facts which I have rehearsed that the governors were informed, at any rate in 1958, exactly what was happening, there is nothing to show that they knew their legal right to object. On the contrary, the college wrote and said that nothing could be done without the consent of the Minister to put the matter right.

But it does not rest there, because the position was reviewed by this court in *Holder v Holder*[3]. There each member of the court held that the true view of the matter was that one had to have regard to all the circumstances of the case, and that the third proposition laid down by Fry J[2] was not absolutely binding. Thus, Harman LJ said[4]:

'Like the judge, I should desire to follow the conclusion of WILBERFORCE, J., who reviewed the authorities in *Re Pauling's Settlement Trusts, Younghusband v. Coutts & Co.*[5] and this passage was mentioned without dissent in the same case in the Court of Appeal[6]: "The result of these authorities appears to me to be that the court has to consider all the circumstances in which the concurrence of the cestui qui trust was given with a view to seeing whether it is fair and equitable that, having given his concurrence, he should afterwards turn round and sue the trustees: that, subject to this, it is not necessary that he should know that what he is concurring in is a breach of trust, provided that he fully understands what he is concurring in, and that it is not necessary that he should himself have directly benefited by the breach of trust." There is, therefore, no hard and fast rule that ignorance of a legal right is a bar, but the whole of the circumstances must be looked at to see whether it is just that the complaining beneficiary should succeed against the trustee.'

In *Holder v Holder*[3] the claimant had actually received £2,000 out of the proceeds of the sale to which he was objecting.

So we have to look at all the circumstances, but even so, the fact that the governors did

---

1   (1880) 15 Ch D 96
2   15 Ch D 96 at 105
3   [1968] 1 All ER 665, [1968] Ch 353
4   [1968] 1 All ER 665 at 673, [1968] Ch 353 at 394
5   [1961] 3 All ER 713 at 730, [1962] 1 WLR 86 at 108
6   [1963] 3 All ER 1, [1964] Ch 303

not know of their legal rights and indeed, by the letter which I have read, were told that they had no right to object, is undoubtedly a factor which must be taken into account.

Then I consider also that the result of what has been done is not that the school has received a benefit, but that it has in truth received far less income than it ought to have received. Looking at all the circumstances of this case, in my judgment there is not sufficient to raise any equity against the governors to preclude them from asserting the true rights of the school.

It is said that even if there were, still that could not bind the Attorney-General and he would be entitled to take the point. Having regard to the conclusion which I have reached, and not having heard argument from counsel for the Attorney-General, I refrain from saying anything about this point because it is unnecessary to do so.

For the reasons which I have given, I would dismiss this appeal.

SIR DAVID CAIRNS. I entirely agree with the judgment which has been delivered by Goff LJ. I too would dismiss the appeal for the reasons which he has given.

BUCKLEY LJ. I also agree with the judgment which has been delivered. I would only add a short observation on the construction and effect of the Universities and Colleges (Trusts) Act 1943, as applicable to this case.

Section 2(1)(b) of that Act makes it clear that any trust to which a scheme under the Act is made applicable must be a trust of a capital fund. It follows that only such trusts are appropriate to fall within s 2(1)(a), and the words 'such trusts' in that sub-paragraph must be construed as limited to trusts of that nature. They are consequently not apt to apply to trusts declared only in respect of a part of the income of a trust fund. Accordingly, in my opinion the section does not empower a university or college to sever a part of the trusts of a charitable fund relating only to the application of a part of the income of that fund and treat that part of the trusts of the fund alone as brought into the scheme under the Act, leaving any trusts for other charitable purposes affecting that charitable fund standing alone as severed charitable trusts.

Where the fund is held in its entirety on trusts which comprise trusts for the application of the income of the fund for a number of charitable purposes in specified sums or proportions, it seems to me that that trust fund must be treated as a single trust for the purposes of the section. This does not mean that all the assets of the fund must be brought into the scheme, for s 2(1)(b) permits any part of the trust property to be excluded from the scheme. It does however mean that the university or college cannot dismember the trust, converting it into a number of severed and distinct trusts having separate endowments.

The Minister, in the letter to which Goff LJ has referred in the judgment which he has delivered, does not appear to have proposed such a dismembering of the Freeston trust fund, but merely the exclusion from the scheme of half of the capital of that trust fund. Apart from the rather ambiguous description of the fund in the first schedule to the scheme which the college made under the Act, where it is described as 'Name of trust, John Freeston (one moiety only); Brief Purposes of Trust, payment of three Freeston Close Scholarships from one moiety', what the scheme seems to have achieved is precisely what I have said, the inclusion in the scheme, and therefore in the pooling arrangements provided by the scheme, of half the capital of the trust fund and the express exclusion from the scheme of the other half of the capital of the trust fund, and it would not be appropriate for the scheme to have excluded the latter half unless the fund to which the framers of the scheme were intending to refer was the whole capital of the Freeston trust fund, out of the income of which half was to be paid to the school and the other half retained by the college. In my judgment the scheme did not in any way affect the beneficial interests under the trusts of the Freeston charity as they subsisted at the time when the scheme was made.

On the point about acquiescence, I only desire to say this with regard to the position of the Minister of Education: it is, I think, quite fallacious to suppose that he was acting in any way on behalf of, or as representing, the governors of the school. He was, I think, quite clearly acting in what he conceived to be the proper performance of his duties as an administrative authority having jurisdiction over educational charities under the Charitable Trusts Acts 1853–1925, and in my judgment nothing which he did or said is to be imputed to the governors in any way.

With regard to the conduct of the governors themselves in not protesting earlier that they were not receiving an equal half of the whole of the income of the trust fund, I entirely agree with what has been said by Goff LJ and do not wish to add anything further on that part of the case.

For the reasons which Goff LJ has elaborated in the judgment which he has delivered, I also agree that this appeal should be dismissed.

Appeal dismissed.

Solicitors: *Levinson, Gray & Collins,* agents for *Linnell & Murphy & Taylor & Co,* Oxford (for the college); *Hickmans* (for the school governors); *Treasury Solicitor.*

J H Fazan Esq   Barrister.

a
Ottley v Morris (Inspector of Taxes)

CHANCERY DIVISION
FOX J
21st, 22nd June 1978

b
Income tax – Appeal – Commissioners – Adjournment of appeal – Taxpayer appealing to commissioners against assessments – Crown alleging fraud, wilful default or neglect by taxpayer – Taxpayer asking for adjournment of appeal – Commissioners refusing to adjourn appeal and hearing appeal in taxpayer's absence – Commissioners finding that taxpayer had been fraudulent – Whether commissioners should have adjourned appeal – Whether injustice caused to taxpayer.

c
The taxpayer appealed against assessments to income tax, but when the appeals came on for hearing before the General Commissioners the taxpayer did not appear and neither was he represented. The commissioners had before them a letter from him requesting an adjournment on the ground that he had consulted leading counsel. The Crown opposed the application for the adjournment. The commissioners refused the application and d proceeded to hear the appeals. At the hearing the Crown alleged fraud or wilful default under s 36 of the Taxes Management Act 1970 or, alternatively, neglect under s 37 of the 1970 Act. The commissioners found that the taxpayer was guilty of fraud in the years 1963 to 1969 and confirmed the assessments apart from those for the years 1968–69 and 1969–70, which they varied. The taxpayer appealed contending that it was contrary to natural justice for the commissioners to have refused an adjournment.

e
Held – The adjournment of proceedings was, prima facie, a matter within the discretion of the commissioners and the court would be slow to interfere with their decision in that regard. However, taking into account the fact that the taxpayer was being charged with fraud and that there was a wide range of matters on which the taxpayer's evidence could have been of paramount importance, it was clear that the refusal of the adjournment had f prevented the taxpayer from putting his case and might have caused him serious injustice. In those circumstances the appeal would be allowed and the case remitted to be heard by different commissioners (see p 68 *j*, p 69 *d* to *g* and p 70 *c* and *g h* post).
Rose v Humbles (Inspector of Taxes) [1970] 2 All ER 519 followed.

Notes
For adjournment of hearing of appeals to the commissioners, see 23 Halsbury's Laws (4th g Edn) para 1594, and for cases on the subject, see 28 (1) Digest (Reissue) 561, 2056–2058.
For adjournment of proceedings before a judicial tribunal in the interests of natural justice, see 1 Halsbury's Laws (4th Edn) para 76.

Cases referred to in judgment
Maxwell v Keun [1928] 1 KB 645, [1927] All ER Rep 335, 97 LJKB 305, 138 LT 310, CA, h 30 Digest (Reissue) 169, 32.
Noble v Wilkinson (Inspector of Taxes) (1958) 38 Tax Cas 135, [1958] TR 233, 37 ATC 307, 51 R & IT 544, 28(1) Digest (Reissue) 561, 2057.
Rose v Humbles (Inspector of Taxes) [1970] 2 All ER 519, [1970] 1 WLR 1061, 48 Tax Cas 103, [1970] TR 61, 49 ATC 54, 28(1) Digest (Reissue) 561, 2058.

j **Cases also cited**
Hudson v Humbles (Inspector of Taxes) (1965) 42 Tax Cas 380.
James v Pope (Inspector of Taxes) (1972) 48 Tax Cas 142.
Johnson v Scott (Inspector of Taxes) p 476, ante, CA.
Nicholson v Morris (Inspector of Taxes) [1977] STC 162, CA.
Wellington v Reynolds (Inspector of Taxes) (1962) 40 Tax Cas 209.

Case stated

1. At a meeting of the Commissioners for the General Purposes of the Income Tax for *a* the Bolton and Bury Districts in the county of Greater Manchester held on 16th June 1977 an appeal by the taxpayer against assessments to income tax was set down for hearing. He appealed against the following assessments, (a) to income tax under Sch D, Case I:

	Trade as butcher
Year of assessment	Profits £
1963–64	283
1964–65	183
1965–66	277
1966–67	1,936
1967–68	315
1968–69	1,000
1969–70	1,000
1970–71	439
1971–72	854
1972–73	1,446
1973–74	3,266
1974–75	2,700
1975–76	1,800

(b) to income tax under Sch D, Case III

Year of assessment	Interest £
1965–66	52
1966–67	83
1967–68	83
1968–69	200
1969–70	260
1970–71	273
1971–72	292
1972–73	291
1973–74	628
1974–75	772

2. The taxpayer did not appear and was not represented. There was however a letter before the commissioners from the taxpayer dated 14th June 1977 requesting an *g* adjournment on the grounds that he had taken the advice of Queen's Counsel.

3. The inspector opposed the application for adjournment giving the following reasons: (i) The back duty enquiry resulting in the assessments before the commissioners had begun almost three years earlier, on 18th July 1974. (ii) The taxpayer had during that time the benefit of professional advice. The services of those professional advisers had since been dispensed with. (iii) All the outstanding appeals had been before the commissioners at *h* their meeting on 17th May 1977. At that meeting the commissioners had already granted the taxpayer an adjournment until 16th June 1977. (iv) The request for adjournment had only been received by the clerk on the afternoon before the meeting of 16th June. The commissioners had heard that their clerk and the inspector had then gone to some length by way of telephone calls and messages left at the taxpayer's home to stress the necessity of the taxpayer appearing at the commissioners' meeting. (v) Neither the inspector nor the *j* clerk had received any communication from anyone currently acting for the taxpayer.

4. The commissioners decided not to grant the taxpayer an adjournment and proceeded with the hearing.

5. The questions for their determination were: (i) whether there had been fraud or wilful default within the meaning of s 36 of the Taxes Management Act 1970 committed

by or on behalf of the taxpayer or alternatively whether there had been neglect on the part
a of the taxpayer or his agents within the meaning of s 37 of the 1970 Act, (ii) subject to (i),
above, which, if any, of the assessments (a) of profits as a butcher and/or (b) of interest
should be confirmed and in what amounts.

6. The commissioners found the following facts admitted or proved. (i) The taxpayer
was a married man with five children and lived at 17 Smith Lane, Bromley Cross. (ii) The
taxpayer had commenced business as a butcher at 210 Halliwell Road, Bolton on 15th
b January 1954. (iii) The shop premises had been modernised, were well kept and in a
thriving shopping area. (iv) The taxpayer's wife had been employed by the taxpayer as a
shop assistant from the year ending January 1958. (v) Certified accounts had been prepared
by Anson L Bentley & Co for all the years under appeal. The figures shown were accepted
originally as the basis for Sch D assessments. (vi) Extensive back duty enquiries had been
conducted by the inspector and information had been gathered from the taxpayer's
c accounts, his agents and his wife; the taxpayer himself had not given any direct oral
information during the enquiry. (vii) A mortgage on the taxpayer's private residence was
redeemed in 1965 by a payment of £1,873 5s to the Borough Building Society. (viii) An
account with Lombard North Central Ltd was opened on 1st July 1965 in the name of the
taxpayer's wife. The deposits in the accounts were as follows:

d
1st July 1965	opening deposit	£1,317 18s
21st July 1967	deposit	£2,000
23rd June 1972	deposit	£1,500
27th October 1973	deposit	£500

e The most probable source of the initial deposit was the proceeds of sale of certain land at
Abram owned jointly by the taxpayer and his wife. (ix) The taxpayer's income tax returns
for the years 1966–67 to 1974–75 inclusive had been incorrect in that they failed to disclose
the interest arising on the taxpayer's wife's account with Lombard North Central Ltd.
(x) The taxpayer's wife's housekeeping allowance was £24–£25 per week, in addition to
her wages. (xi) A capital, income and expenditure statement prepared by the inspector
f demonstrated that the taxpayer must have received an income in the years under
assessment greater than that declared in his income tax returns.

7. The inspector contended: (i) that on the facts found the taxpayer had committed
fraud or wilful default within the meaning of s 36 of the 1970 Act. (ii) alternatively that
the taxpayer had been guilty of neglect within the meaning of s 37 of the 1970 Act; (iii)
that the assessments before the commissioners therefore had been correctly made; (iv) that
all the assessments appealed against should therefore be confirmed or determined in the
g amounts corresponding with the deficiencies disclosed by the capital, income and
expenditure statement.

8. The commissioners' findings and decision were that they confirmed the further
assessments for the years 1963–64 to 1967–68 inclusive and for the years 1970–71 to 1974–
75 inclusive. The assessments for the year 1968–69 were determined at £2,387 profits and
£164 interest, 1969–70 at £365 profits and £220 interest. The assessments for 1975–76
h were determined at £3,003 profits minus capital allowances of £659 and £744 national
insurance contributions. They also held that the figures for 1963–69 had been fraudulently
understated.

9. The taxpayer through his solicitors on 27th June 1977 expressed his dissatisfaction
with the determination of the appeal and required the commissioners to state a case
j pursuant to s 56 of the 1970 Act.

10. The question for the opinion of the court was whether on the facts the commissioners
came to a correct decision in law.

Michael Mark for the taxpayer.
Brian Davenport for the Crown.

FOX J. This is an appeal by the taxpayer against a decision of the General Commissioners for the Bolton and Bury Districts of Manchester concerning assessments made on him (a) *a* under Sch D, Case I, for the years 1963–64 to 1975–76 inclusive in respect of profits as a butcher, and (b) under Sch D, Case III, in respect of interest from a deposit account. The taxpayer did not appear before the commissioners, and was not represented. The hearing was on 16th June 1977. The commissioners at that hearing had before them a letter from the taxpayer dated 14th June, in the following terms: 'Please defer the hearing for Thursday June 16th. I have taken the advice of a Queen's Counsel to deal with this diabolical *b* situation.' The inspector opposed the application for an adjournment for the following reasons: (1) the case resulted from a back duty enquiry which had begun in July 1974; (2) during that time the taxpayer had had professional advice, but had now dispensed with the services of those advisers; (3) all the appeals had been before the commissioners on 17th May 1977, when the taxpayer was given an adjournment until 16th June; and (4) the request had been received by the clerk only on the afternoon before the hearing. The *c* commissioners were told that their clerk and the inspector had gone to some length by way of phone calls and messages left at the taxpayer's house to stress the importance of his attending the hearing; (5) neither the inspector nor the clerk had had any communication from anyone currently acting for the taxpayer.

The commissioners refused the application for an adjournment and proceeded to hear the appeals. Evidence for the Crown was given by the inspector. There were two issues, *d* in essence, before the commissioners, which were these: first, whether there had been fraud or wilful default by the taxpayer, or, alternatively, neglect by him; secondly, subject to that, whether any of the assessments should be confirmed, and, if so, in what amounts. The commissioners found that the taxpayer was a married man with five children, that he had carried on business as a butcher in Bolton since 1954 and that the shop premises were modernised, well kept and in a good shopping area. The taxpayer's wife had worked in the *e* shop.

The commissioners found that a mortgage on the taxpayer's house was redeemed in 1965 by a payment of about £1,800 to the building society, and, also, that an account with Lombard North Central Ltd was opened on 1st July 1965, in the name of the taxpayer's wife, and that the deposits in that account were as follows: on 1st July 1965, an opening deposit of £1,317; on 21st July 1967, a deposit of £2,000; on 23rd June 1972, a deposit of *f* £1,500 and on 27th October 1973, a deposit of £500. The commissioners found that the most probable source of the initial deposit was the proceeds of sale of land owned jointly by the taxpayer and his wife. The commissioners found, further, that the taxpayer's tax returns for 1966–67 to 1974–75 did not disclose interest on the deposit account. The commissioners held that a capital income and expenditure statement prepared by the inspector showed that the taxpayer must have received an income in the years under *g* assessment greater than that declared.

So far as the Case I assessments are concerned, the profits returned by the taxpayer for the relevant years, that is 1963–64 to 1975–76, varied between about £1,000 a year and just over £2,000. The average was about £1,000 a year. The additional assessments raised by the inspector amounted to about £12,000. So far as Case III is concerned, assessments for 1965–66 to 1974–75 of amounts ranging from £52 in 1965–66 to £772 in 1974–75 were *h* raised. The commissioners in effect confirmed the assessments and, in addition, found that the taxpayer was guilty of fraud in the years 1963 to 1969. The taxpayer now appeals to this court and contends that it was contrary to natural justice for the commissioners to have refused an adjournment on 16th June, and he asks for the case to be remitted.

Prima facie, the adjournment of a proceeding is a matter within the discretion of the tribunal, and is a matter which will not be interfered with by an appellate court. But, if the *j* discretion has been exercised in such a way as to cause what can properly be regarded as an injustice to a party, then the proper course for an appellate court to take is to ensure that the matter is further heard: see *Rose v Humbles (Inspector of Taxes)*[1]. In that case, the General

---

1   [1970] 2 All ER 519, [1970] 1 WLR 1061, 48 Tax Cas 103

Commissioners had refused an adjournment to enable the taxpayer, who was ill, to give
a evidence. The nature of the case put forward by the taxpayer was that his funds were
derived from betting transactions. Buckley J decided that the case was one in which the
commissioners ought to have granted an adjournment, and that the failure to do so
resulted in the taxpayer suffering a substantial injustice. The case was therefore remitted
to be heard by different commissioners.

In *Maxwell v Keun*[1] Atkin LJ put the matter thus:

b   'I quite agree the Court of Appeal ought to be very slow indeed to interfere with the
discretion of the learned judge on such a question as an adjournment of a trial, and it
very seldom does do so; but, on the other hand, if it appears that the result of the order
made below is to defeat the rights of the parties altogether, and to do that which the
Court of Appeal is satisfied would be an injustice to one or other of the parties, then
the Court has power to review such an order, and it is, to my mind, its duty to do so.'

c
Under s 56(6) of the Taxes Management Act 1970 the courts have power to determine
only a question or questions of law arising on the case stated, but in *Rose v Humbles (Inspector
of Taxes)*[2] it was decided that the question whether or not an adjournment should have
been granted is such a question. The essential matter, I think, is whether the taxpayer
suffered such an injustice by reason of the refusal of an adjournment that the decision
d should not be allowed to stand. I am certainly of the view that the court should be slow
indeed to interfere with a decision of commissioners as to the adjournment of an appeal
before them, but I have come to the conclusion that the taxpayer here may have suffered
a substantial injustice in the circumstances of the present case, and that in the rather special
circumstances of the case it would be right to remit the matter to the commissioners.

My reasons for that conclusion are as follows. First, the taxpayer was being charged with
e fraud. The right of a person against whom such an allegation is made to have full
opportunity to resist it cannot be lightly set aside. On any issue of fraud in this case, the
taxpayer's own evidence could obviously be crucial. The commissioners, without hearing
the taxpayer, held that the allegation of fraud was established. No doubt an adjournment
would have caused some inconvenience to the Crown, but the Crown's only witness was
the inspector himself, and he conducted the case himself. I think that the possibility of an
f injustice by refusing an adjournment far outweighed such inconvenience as would have
arisen, or might have arisen, by granting it.

Secondly, it does not appear that the commissioners ever directed their minds at all to
the nature of the case against the taxpayer. It does not appear that they considered that a
case of fraud was being raised against him, or that the evidence on which the inspector was
relying depended to some substantial extent on estimates of the taxpayer's expenditure,
g which is obviously a matter on which the taxpayer's own evidence would be of major
importance.

Thirdly, while it is true that there had already been an adjournment on 17th May and
that a back duty enquiry had been proceeding for some three years, those facts, stated by
themselves, give a rather misleading impression of the position. Most of the assessments
appealed against were in fact made only in February 1977. As to the first adjournment,
h that was granted in May 1977, and the circumstances were peculiar. Although it was made
in accordance with the request of the taxpayer, it seems from what counsel for the Crown
has told me (in answer to a question from me) that it was or may have been due as much
to the fact that one of the commissioners was disqualified from sitting (by reason of the fact
that he had authorised the issue of assessments out of time in the same case) as to the
taxpayer's request.

j Fourthly, the case was concerned with a litigant in person. Notwithstanding the
reference in the letter of 14th June to obtaining the advice of leading counsel, the letter
itself suggests, as indeed does the submission of the inspector, that the taxpayer was at that

1   [1928] 1 KB 645 at 653, [1927] All ER Rep 335 at 338–339
2   [1970] 2 All ER 519, [1970] 1 WLR 1061, 48 Tax Cas 103

point acting in person; and I understand from counsel who appears for him that that was in fact so.

Fifthly, while on the face of it the taxpayer was acting very casually in simply writing a letter and not attending before the commissioners, it seems that the taxpayer sought the first adjournment by writing a letter, and he may very well have thought that that was an appropriate course to adopt in June and that personal attendance was not necessary. There is nothing in the facts to suggest that at the time of the May adjournment he was warned that no further time would be given. Counsel for the Crown points out that in *Noble v Wilkinson (Inspector of Taxes)*[1] where there was evidence that the commissioners had a practice whereby they accepted letters requesting adjournments Wynn-Parry J held that it did not follow that they would adopt that practice in every case. That is of course quite correct, but in *Noble v Wilkinson (Inspector of Taxes)*[1] the taxpayer was represented by a solicitor and was not acting in person. As to the fact that messages were left at the taxpayer's house, counsel's instructions are that the taxpayer did not receive them.

Sixthly, quite apart from any question of fraud there is a wide range of matters on which the taxpayer's evidence could be of paramount importance. As I have mentioned, the inspector tendered a capital, income and expenditure statement designed to show that the taxpayer's expenditure in the relevant years was well in excess of what he had returned as his income. The commissioners held that the statement demonstrated that the taxpayer *must* have received income in those years in excess of what he had returned. I say no more than that such conclusion is challenged by the taxpayer, since the statement includes many figures which, admittedly, are estimates only, and the taxpayer seeks to challenge many of those figures for themselves.

There is one further matter which I ought to mention. The statement shows the taxpayer as receiving a disability pension, which was indeed the case. It was a disability pension on account of war wounds, which is in fact tax-free. The statement shows it as being £81 a year from 1963 to 1973. In fact, the taxpayer says that the pension was £98, rising to about £200 per annum during the later years, and that this reduces the deficit between expenditure and known income in those years. As to the deposit account, that was in the name of the taxpayer's wife. It is admitted that it existed, and it is admitted that the taxpayer must be assessed, certainly on the past six years. But it is the taxpayer's case that the source of this account was largely moneys received by his wife from her parents of which he was unaware. There are, therefore, numerous matters which the taxpayer challenges in the inspector's statement and on which his evidence is quite obviously of importance.

In all the circumstances, it seems to me that the refusal of an adjournment prevented the taxpayer from putting his case and may have caused him serious injustice. Apart from the consequences in terms of tax, the finding of fraud is a matter of much personal importance to anybody. I think that in the circumstances the commissioners should have granted an adjournment. It could have been for a short time, and it could have been made plain that no further time would be given. That, I think, would have secured substantial justice in the matter without any real prejudice to the Crown. I therefore remit the case, apart from the assessments which are not now in dispute, to be heard by different commissioners.

Appeal allowed. No order as to costs.

Solicitors: *Beer, Dunnet & Maislish* (for the taxpayer); *Solicitor of Inland Revenue.*

Rengan Krishnan Esq Barrister.

---

1 (1958) 38 Tax Cas 135

Tolley v Morris

COURT OF APPEAL, CIVIL DIVISION
STEPHENSON AND ORR LJJ
2nd, 12th MAY 1978

Practice – Dismissal of action for want of prosecution – Inordinate delay without excuse – Infant plaintiff having right to bring second action within extended limitation period even if first action dismissed – Whether right to bring second action within extended period precluding court from dismissing action for want of prosecution – Limitation Act 1939, s 22(1).

On 21st May 1964 the plaintiff, an infant, who was then aged two, was severely injured in a road accident. On 3rd May 1967, within the three years' limitation period applicable, under s 2A of the Limitation Act 1939, to claims in negligence for personal injuries, her father issued a writ against the defendant claiming damages in respect of the plaintiff's injuries. The writ was served on 20th April 1968. Thereafter, through no fault of the plaintiff or her father, no further steps in the action were taken until 19th April 1977 when new solicitors instructed by the plaintiff gave notice of intention to proceed with the action. A statement of claim was served on 19th August. On 22nd September the defendant applied to have the action dismissed for want of prosecution, and on 8th November the district registrar dismissed the action. The plaintiff further appealed to a judge who upheld the registrar's decision. The plaintiff appealed contending that even though, as was conceded, there had been inordinate and inexcusable delay in prosecuting the action which had prejudiced the defendant, the plaintiff's legal right under the extended period of limitation conferred on infants by s 22[a] of the 1939 Act to issue a fresh writ precluded dismissal of her action for want of prosecution. The defendant contended that, where an infant, by her parent, had in fact brought an action for damages for personal injury within the original three years' limitation period prescribed by s 2A of the 1939 Act, the plaintiff could not avoid dismissal of the action for want of prosecution where there had been inordinate and inexcusable delay merely because of the extended period of limitation conferred by s 22, for that extension had been granted to protect an infant from its own or its parent's ignorance of the law, but in the instant case the plaintiff's father had known the law and had acted on it by bringing the action within the three years' limitation period.

Held – The rule that where a plaintiff had a legal right to issue a fresh writ his action should not be dismissed for want of prosecution save in exceptional circumstances applied to an infant plaintiff's legal right to issue a writ within the extended period of limitation conferred by s 22, and inaction, however long and outrageous, was not an exceptional circumstance warranting dismissal of the action within the limitation period. Accordingly, the court was required to take into consideration the fact that the plaintiff had a right to bring an action within the extended limitation period when considering whether to dismiss her action for want of prosecution after the original three years' limitation period had expired. It followed that the appeal would be allowed and that the action would be permitted to continue (see p 77 *d* to *f* and p 78 *c d*, post).

Birkett v James [1977] 2 All ER 801 applied.

Dicta of Lord Denning MR, Geoffrey Lane and Eveleigh LJJ in *Biss v Lambeth, Southwark and Lewisham Health Authority* [1978] 2 All ER at 131–132, 134 and 134–135 explained.

Notes

For the dismissal of actions for want of prosecution, see 30 Halsbury's Laws (3rd Edn) 410, para 771.

For the Limitation Act 1939, s 22, see 19 Halsbury's Statutes (3rd Edn) 81.

For the Limitation Act 1975, s 2, see 45 ibid 853.

---

a   Section 22, so far as material, is set out at p 72 *h* to p 73 *b*, post

Cases referred to in judgments

Birkett v James [1977] 2 All ER 801, [1978] AC 297, [1977] 3 WLR 38, HL.

Biss v Lambeth, Southwark and Lewisham Health Authority [1978] 2 All ER 125, [1978] 1 WLR 382, CA.

Spring Grove Services Ltd v Deane (1972) 116 Sol Jo 844, [1972] Court of Appeal Transcript 251.

Interlocutory appeal

This was an appeal by the plaintiff, Lynne Marie Tolley, an infant, against the order of Dunn J made on 27th January 1978 dismissing her appeal against an order of the district registrar at Yeovil whereby he dismissed for want of prosecution the plaintiff's action, brought by her father and next friend, Alan Frederick Tolley, against the defendant, George Arthur Morris, for damages for personal injuries sustained by the plaintiff in a road accident. The facts are set out in the judgment of Stephenson LJ.

William Phillips for the plaintiff.
Michael Turner QC and *Jeremy Griggs* for the defendant.

Cur adv vult

12th May. The following judgments were read.

STEPHENSON LJ. The plaintiff was born on 12th November 1961, so she is still an infant, 16 years old. She will not cease to be under the disability of infancy until 12th November 1979. On 21st May 1964 she suffered brain damage when, walking with her mother along a footpath in Ilchester, Somerset, she was struck by the defendant's motor car. Unfortunately, her injuries were so serious that she may never be able to live a normal independent life.

On 3rd May 1967 a writ was issued by her father and next friend claiming damages for negligence in respect of her injuries. It was served on 20th April 1968. But it was not until 19th July 1977 that the second firm of solicitors to act for her and her father gave notice of intention to proceed with the action and not until 19th August 1977 that the statement of claim in the action was served. Understandably, its service was followed on 22nd September 1977 by a summons to dismiss the action for want of prosecution. Understandably also, the Yeovil district registrar dismissed the action on 8th November 1977 and Dunn J on 27th January 1978 dismissed an appeal from his decision. But the judge gave leave to appeal, and that too is understandable when it is appreciated that what is in question here is the relationship between *Birkett v James*[1] and the Limitation Act 1975, a relationship which has been considered by this court in *Biss v Lambeth, Southwark and Lewisham Health Authority*[2] and, in particular the impact of the earlier case on s 2 of the 1975 Act, which appears not yet to have been considered in any reported case. In other words, can the infant plaintiff bring another action if this action is dismissed, and, if she can, is that a conclusive reason why this action should not be dismissed?

Section 22 of the Limitation Act 1939, as amended by ss 2(2) and 8(3) of the Law Reform (Limitation of Actions, &c) Act 1954, provided:

'(1) If on the date when any right of action accrued for which a period of limitation is prescribed by this Act, the person to whom it accrued was under a disability, the action may be brought at any time before the expiration of six years from the date when the person ceased to be under a disability or died, whichever event first

---

1   [1977] 2 All ER 801, [1978] AC 297
2   [1978] 2 All ER 125, [1978] 1 WLR 382

occurred, notwithstanding that the period of limitation has expired . . . [I omit the proviso to sub-s (1).]

'(2) In the case of actions for damages for negligence, nuisance or breach of duty (whether the duty exists by virtue of a contract or of provision made by or under a statute or independently of any contract or any such provision) where the damages claimed by the plaintiff for the negligence, nuisance or breach of duty consist of or include damages in respect of personal injuries to any person—(a) the preceding provisions of this section shall have effect as if for the words "six years" there were substituted the words "three years"; and (b) this section shall not apply unless the plaintiff proves that the person under the disability was not, at the time when the right of action accrued to him, in the custody of a parent.'

The district registrar dismissed the action on the ground that the plaintiff would not be able to prove that she was not in the custody of a parent at the time of the accident. But he, admittedly, erred because that last provision has been repealed by ss 2(2), 4(5) of and Sch 2 to the 1975 Act. I am not surprised that the registrar, having seen that this restraint on extending an infant's period of limitation survived its 1954 transplant from sub-s (1) to sub-s (2) of s 22 of the 1939 Act, missed its removal from what was left of the section in the course of the bewilderingly complicated treatment applied to the 1939 Act by the legislative surgery of 1975. The judge did not fall into that error. He was asked by counsel for the defendants to apply by analogy the reasoning of Lord Denning MR in Biss's case[1], then only reported in The Times newspaper, and did so in the following sentences taken from an agreed note, not approved by the judge, of his judgment:

'There are various considerations which have been taken into account by the court in exercising the discretion authoritatively laid down in Birkett v James[2] but in my judgment I accept the approach of Lord Denning MR that the House of Lords was directing its attention to the case where there was a specific limitation by the 1975 Act. By reason of the provisions of the 1975 Act cases of infants and other persons under disability, that is mental illness, are not now the subject of such strict periods of limitation as I think the House of Lords had in mind in Birkett v James[2]. I therefore accept the view of Lord Denning MR about there being much prejudice to the defendant, like the sword of Damocles, not knowing when he will be brought to trial in a case he had regarded as closed. A time comes when a defendant is to have peace of mind and is to be able to regard the incident as closed. The circumstances of Biss v Lambeth, Southwark and Lewisham Health Authority[1] are closer to this case than Birkett v James[2] and, in so far as there is a conflict, I feel I should follow Biss[1]. In exercising my discretion, I bear in mind that the public policy is to have some finality in litigation. Having regard to the very long delay in this case, the accident in 1964 nearly 14 years ago, the delay far exceeded the delay which occurred in the cases referred to today. With regard to the plaintiff, if Birkett v James[2] was followed in its letter, the plaintiff could delay taking action for another four years, by which time it will be 1982. It seems to me a case in which I should exercise my discretion and dismiss the action for want of prosecution.'

This becomes intelligible by reference to the 1975 Act. Section 1 of the 1975 Act first prescribes time limits by inserting additional provisions after s 2 of the 1939 Act as amended by the 1954 Act, including, for actions for damages for negligence in respect of personal injuries, a time limit of three years (a) from the date on which the cause of action accrued, or (b) the date (if later) of the plaintiff's knowledge: see the inserted s 2A(1) and

1 [1978] 2 All ER 125, [1978] 1 WLR 382
2 [1977] 2 All ER 801, [1978] AC 297

(4). Then s 1 of the 1975 Act gives the court a revolutionary power to override time limits if it appears to the court that it would be equitable to allow an action to proceed having regard to various matters: see the inserted s 2D. Next, s 2 of the 1975 Act provides:

> '(1) At the end of section 22 of the Limitation Act 1939 (persons under disability: time limit of 6 years from end of disability) there shall be inserted the following subsections:—"(2) If the action is one to which section 2A ... of this Act applies subsection (1) of this section shall have effect as if for the words '6 years' there were substituted the words '3 years'..."
>
> '(2) The provisions of this section are in substitution for the subsection (2) added to section 22 by the Law Reform (Limitation of Actions &c.) Act 1954...'

The effect of that substitution is to abolish the need for a plaintiff under a disability to prove that he was not, at the time when the right of action accrued to him, in the custody of a parent. It follows that an infant now has the extended period of limitation conferred by s 22 of the 1939 Act, as amended, which enables him or her to bring an action for personal injuries within three years from ceasing to be under the disability of infancy, ie from attaining his or her 18th birthday, whether or not in the custody of a parent at the time when the injuries were inflicted. So it was submitted to the judge and to this court that this plaintiff may, if her action is dismissed, bring another action any time up to the end of three years from 12th November 1979, that is up to 12th November 1982, which is 18 years from the date of her accident and the accrual of her cause of action and another five years from the registrar's dismissal of her first action.

Counsel, in his able argument for the plaintiff, concedes that there has been inordinate and inexcusable delay (through no fault of the infant plaintiff or her father) in allowing the action to go to sleep for ten years after the service of the writ and that that delay has caused serious additional prejudice to the defendant in that all records and statements regarding the accident have been destroyed, though the plaintiff's present solicitors have a copy of the accident report and the defendant's solicitors or insurers have managed with difficulty to trace him. But counsel for the plaintiff submits that the judge was wrong to apply the observations of Lord Denning MR in *Biss's* case[1] to this case, failed to distinguish the provisions of s 2D inserted by the 1975 Act to which they were directed and the position of Mrs Biss from the provisions of s 2A and the position of the infant plaintiff in this case, and should have applied to this case the unanimous direction of the House of Lords in *Birkett v James*[2] that where the plaintiff has a legal right to issue a fresh writ because the limitation period has not yet expired, his action should not be dismissed save in most exceptional cases. Lord Diplock (with whose speech Lord Simon of Glaisdale, Lord Edmund-Davies and Lord Russell of Killowen agreed) put the matter in this way[3]:

> 'There may be exceptional cases, of which *Spring Grove Services Ltd v Deane*[4] (to which I shall be referring later) may be an example, where the plaintiff's conduct in the previous proceedings has induced the defendant to do something which will create more difficulties for him in presenting his case at the trial than he would have had if the previous proceedings had never been started. In such a case it may well be that the court, in the exercise of its inherent jurisdiction, should stay the second proceedings on the ground that, taken as a whole, the plaintiff's conduct amounts to an abuse of the process of the court. But such exceptional cases apart, where all that the plaintiff has done has been to let the previous action go to sleep, the court in my opinion would have no power to prevent him starting a fresh action within the limitation period and proceeding with it with all proper diligence notwithstanding that his previous action had been dismissed for want of prosecution. If this be so, it

---

1   [1978] 2 All ER 125, [1978] 1 WLR 382
2   [1977] 2 All ER 801, [1978] AC 297
3   [1977] 2 All ER 801 at 806–807, [1978] AC 297 at 320–321
4   (1972) 116 Sol Jo 844

follows that to dismiss an action for want of prosecution before the limitation period has expired does not, save in the exceptional kind of case to which I have referred, benefit the defendant or improve his chances of obtaining a fair trial; it has the opposite tendency.'

Lord Diplock also said[1]:

'For my part, for reasons that I have already stated, I am of opinion that the fact that the limitation period has not yet expired must always be a matter of great weight in determining whether to exercise the discretion to dismiss an action for want of prosecution where no question of contumelious default on the part of the plaintiff is involved; and in cases where it is likely that if the action were dismissed the plaintiff would avail himself of his legal right to issue a fresh writ, the non-expiry of the limitation period is generally a conclusive reason for not dismissing the action that is already pending.'

Lord Salmon said[2]:

'I agree with my noble and learned friend, Lord Diplock, that if an action is dismissed for want of prosecution or even for the contumelious failure to comply with a peremptory order before the limitation period has elapsed, this would not empower the court to strike out a writ for the same cause of action subsequently issued within the limitation period. The fact that the plaintiff or his solicitor has behaved badly in the first action does not make him into a vexatious litigant barred from bringing any further proceedings without permission of the court. Nor does the dismissal of the first action without any decision on the merits constitute res judicata. If the plaintiff had not brought the first action at all but had delayed (as he was legally entitled to do) until the last day of the limitation period before issuing his writ, the defendant would have been in no better position than if the first action had never been brought. Indeed his position would have been worse because the first action at least gave him some information concerning the plaintiff's claim which he would not otherwise have obtained until after the issue of the second writ. In my view, the second action could not be dismissed as an abuse of the process of the court whatever inexcusable delay there may have been in the conduct of the first action. It follows therefore that the reasons given in the judgments in *Spring Grove Services Ltd v Deane*[3] cannot be supported although the decision itself may well be justified on the grounds of estoppel. It seems from the report that the plaintiffs had informed the defendant that they had abandoned their claim and relying on that statement the defendants' solicitors failed to keep in touch with an important witness whom they would have been unable to call at the trial had the action been allowed to continue to trial.'

Lord Edmund-Davies made similar comments on *Spring Grove Services v Deane*[3] and continued[4]:

'Putting aside cases where the plaintiff has so misled the defendant that it might be wrong to allow him to sue afresh, I hold that a plaintiff is free to issue within the limitation period a further writ claiming the same relief and based on the same grounds as an earlier writ dismissed for want of prosecution . . .'

In *Biss's* case[5] Lord Denning MR made this comment on *Birkett v James*[6]:

---

1   [1977] 2 All ER 801 at 808, [1978] AC 297 at 322
2   [1977] 2 All ER 801 at 813, [1978] AC 297 at 328–329
3   (1972) 116 Sol Jo 844
4   [1977] 2 All ER 801 at 817, [1978] AC 297 at 334
5   [1978] 2 All ER 125 at 131–132, [1978] 1 WLR 382 at 390
6   [1977] 2 All ER 801, [1978] AC 297

'In addition, it seems to me that in *Birkett v James*[1] the House of Lords only had in mind actions that were commenced within the old periods of limitation, that is, six years for breach of contract, and three years for personal injuries. They had not in mind actions like the present for personal injuries which under the recent legislation can be started more than three years after the accrual of the cause of action. It was the Limitation Act 1963 which first enabled some actions for personal injuries to be started after three years, but that did not give the plaintiff a legal right to do so. He could only start an action after the three years if the court gave him leave to do so: see s 1(1)(a). I know that in practice the court nearly always did give him leave, but still he had to get it. That Act is now replaced by the Limitation Act 1975, under which leave is no longer required. That Act now applies to this action here, because it is retrospective: see s 3(1). But even this 1975 Act does not give the plaintiff an unqualified legal right to start an action after three years. It depends on his state of knowledge: see s 2A(4)(b); or on whether it is equitable: see s 2D(1); and those are matters to be thrashed out later. He can issue his writ after three years, and then apply to the court to allow the action to proceed, notwithstanding that more than three years have elapsed ... If the House of Lords in *Birkett v James*[1] had had the 1975 Act in mind (which applies to all actions now pending for personal injuries), I cannot help feeling that they would have said that in all cases when the plaintiff seeks to take advantage of the 1975 Act the court can look at the totality of the delay and see whether the defendant was seriously prejudiced by it.'

It is clear to my mind from the full report of *Biss's* case[2] that counsel for the plaintiff is right in contending that what Lord Denning MR was there mainly considering were the provisions of the new s 2D inserted by the 1975 Act into the 1939 Act, which give the court power to override the time limits if it appears equitable.

This is borne out by what Geoffrey Lane and Eveleigh LJJ said; the one pointed out that[3]—

'A plaintiff who issues a writ outside the normal limitation period under the terms of either the 1963 Act or the 1975 Act has only a defeasible right to continue the action. That right will ultimately depend on the decision of the judge at the trial';

and the other said that[4]—

'The plaintiff may be able to issue another writ if this action is dismissed but she has no right to insist that the action should proceed, because she is outside the time limit imposed by the Limitation Act 1975 ... [and] is in the position of having to ask the court's discretion for her action to proceed ...'

This (he submits) is not the plaintiff's position. She has an absolute right, not, like Mrs Biss, a defeasible right, to issue a fresh writ and no judge has any discretion to stay or dismiss a fresh action begun before November 1982. So to dismiss this action would be a fruitless exercise.

Counsel for the defendant agrees that it would be open to the plaintiff to bring a fresh action at any time before that date if she had not brought this action; but, as she has brought this action within the three years' period of limitation, he submits that she has no right to bring a further action within the extended period of limitation granted by s 22 of the 1939 Act as amended. That extension was granted to infants to protect them from the consequences of their ignorance of the law and their parents' ignorance of the law; but this infant's parents have known the law and acted on it and she is thereby confined to this

---

1   [1977] 2 All ER 801, [1978] AC 297
2   [1978] 2 All ER 125, [1978] 1 WLR 382
3   [1978] 2 All ER 125 at 134, [1978] 1 WLR 382 at 393
4   [1978] 2 All ER 125 at 134–135, [1978] 1 WLR 382 at 393

action and cannot, by threatening a fresh action, avoid the consequences of prejudicing the fair trial of this one by inordinate and inexcusable delay.

Counsel for the defendant further submitted that it does no violence to the language of Parliament to hold that, when a person under a disability has in fact brought an action within the statutory period of limitation provided by s 2, the opportunity to extend it, provided by s 22, no longer exists. Furthermore, it does no violence to the language of what I have read from the speeches of their Lordships in *Birkett v James*[1] to read it as applying only to the likelihood of actions brought within what I may call an original period of limitation under Part I of the 1939 Act, not an extended period of limitation under Part II of that Act. Alternatively, counsel for the defendant argued that, if the observations of their Lordships did state a rule which applied to fresh writs within an extended period of limitation, even if that was not a subject-matter which they had had in mind, nevertheless this case came within the exception which they allowed. So a fresh action would be struck out at close of pleadings, if not before. Finally, if the application to strike out this action had been made in 1974 or at any time before the 1975 Act came into force, it would have been successful on the ground relied on by the registrar, for the plaintiff would have been in the custody of a parent on 21st May 1964 and that would then have defeated her right to the extended period of limitation.

Their Lordships in *Birkett v James*[1] may not have had in mind the novel powers to extend and override time limits recently conferred on the court by the 1975 Act; but I would assume that they gave their guidance not in entire forgetfulness of the extensions of time limits which had been provided by Part II of the 1939 Act for nearly 40 years.

In my judgment, the facts of this case bring it within the rule laid down for our guidance in *Birkett v James*[1] and not within the exception. I can find nothing in the provisions of the Limitation Acts or in the spirit or letter of the speeches in *Birkett v James*[1] to exclude from consideration the fresh action which s 22 of the 1939 Act gives the infant plaintiff a legal right to bring. She, not the court, has the right to decide whether to bring another action if this is dismissed. Her legal advisers have allowed it a longer sleep than usual and naturally lulled the defendant into thinking it would never be roused from slumber. But inaction, however long and outrageous, is not within the exceptional cases envisaged in *Birkett v James*[1]. Counsel for the plaintiff called attention to what would have been the position if a sleep of ten uninterrupted years had preceded any legal action whatever, and he submitted, in my opinion unanswerably, that the plaintiff could not then have been driven from the seat of judgment, though the defendant would then have been even more seriously prejudiced. He also pointed out that Lord Edmund-Davies had referred in *Birkett v James*[2] to one even longer statutory period of limitation than is available to the plaintiff: 30 years limitation in the Nuclear Installations Act 1965, s 15(1). And the report of the argument in *Birkett v James*[3] shows that their Lordships were expressly asked to bear much longer periods of limitation in mind and the difficulties which they would cause for defendants if the plaintiff's argument on this point were accepted.

Lastly, counsel for the plaintiff successfully countered counsel for the defendant's submission that this action would have been dismissed in 1974 or before the 1975 Act was passed, by calling our attention to the terms of s 3 of the 1975 Act in which transitional provisions apply the Act retrospectively:

'(1) The provisions of this Act shall have effect in relation to causes of action which accrued before, as well as causes of action which accrue after, the commencement of

---

1   [1977] 2 All ER 801, [1978] AC 297
2   [1977] 2 All ER 801 at 816, [1978] AC 297 at 332
3   [1978] AC 297 at 310–312

this Act, and shall have effect in relation to any cause of action which accrued before the commencement of this Act notwithstanding that an action in respect thereof has been commenced and is pending at the commencement of this Act.

'(2) For the purposes of this section an action shall not be taken to be pending at any time if a final order or judgment has been made or given therein, notwithstanding that an appeal is pending or that the time for appealing has not expired . . .'

This action was pending at the commencement of the Act and no final order or judgment would have been made or given therein by dismissing it then because there would have been no decision on the merits. So the provisions of the 1975 Act would have had effect in relation to the plaintiff's earlier cause of action, including the provision which abolished the requirement that she must not be in a parent's custody at the time when it accrued to her.

For these reasons I am in respectful disagreement with the decision of the judge. I am satisfied that the protection given by the legislature to infants against the incompetence, or malevolence, of those who have the care of their interests ought not to be whittled away by depriving this infant plaintiff, even where her parents have done their best to protect her interests, of her statutory right to sue when she comes of age (if she is mentally capable of doing so); and as she has that right it would be idle, and no help to the defendant, to dismiss this action. I would, therefore, allow the appeal and let the action go on, however difficult it may be to try it fairly after so long a lapse of time.

ORR LJ. I agree.

Appeal allowed. Leave to appeal to the House of Lords refused.

Solicitors: *Ward, Bowie*, agents for *David C Law & Co*, Sheffield (for the plaintiff); *Alms & Young*, Taunton (for the defendant).

L I Zysman Esq   Barrister.

Minton v Minton

HOUSE OF LORDS

LORD WILBERFORCE, VISCOUNT DILHORNE, LORD FRASER OF TULLYBELTON, LORD RUSSELL OF KILLOWEN AND LORD SCARMAN

16th, 17th OCTOBER, 23rd NOVEMBER 1978

Divorce – Financial provision – Jurisdiction to vary consent order incorporating terms agreed between spouses – Whether a consent order which incorporates terms agreed between spouses a final order – Matrimonial Causes Act 1973, s 23(1).

In November 1971 the wife obtained a decree nisi of divorce on the ground of the irretrievable breakdown of her marriage by reason of the husband's adultery. Her petition had included a prayer for financial provision, and in December 1971 she applied to the court for, inter alia, periodical payments and a lump sum for herself, and transfer of the matrimonial home to her. By the time of the decree absolute, in December 1972, the husband and wife had reached agreement on a final settlement of the financial and property questions between them. On 16th January 1973 the husband signed two draft documents containing the terms which they had agreed. By one of the documents it was provided that the matrimonial home should be conveyed by the husband to the wife, that on completion of the conveyance the wife should pay the husband a stated sum in full and final settlement of his beneficial interest in the home, that until the home was conveyed to the wife the husband should pay her the nominal maintenance of 5p per year, that those payments should cease on completion of the conveyance, and that there should be no order for a lump sum payment to the wife. The husband also signed a collateral agreement which included a statement that on completion of the conveyance the wife would sign and hand to him a document stating that she waived and relinquished all claims to maintenance. On 22nd January a county court judge, on the wife's application, made a consent order in the terms of the two draft documents, and the order thus incorporated the provisions in the documents as to the wife's maintenance, but it did not include or refer to the collateral agreement. The husband complied with the order and conveyed the matrimonial home to the wife, and on completion of the conveyance the order for the nominal periodical payments came to an end. The wife became dissatisfied with the financial provision made for her, and on 10th November 1976 applied to another county court judge for an order varying the maintenance payable under the consent order of 22nd January 1973. The judge dismissed the application for want of jurisdiction. The wife appealed contending that notwithstanding the consent order the court had jurisdiction, under s 23(1)[a] of the Matrimonial Causes Act 1973, to entertain a fresh application by her for maintenance.

Held – On the true construction of s 23(1) of the 1973 Act the court was empowered, in a proper case, to make a final order for a spouse's financial provision, and where the court had made a final order it had no jurisdiction to make any subsequent order for financial provision (except where the order was capable of variation under s 31 of the 1973 Act). Where, therefore, on an application for financial provision in the terms of an agreement made between the spouses, the court dealt with the application on its merits and either made an order dismissing the application by consent on terms recited in the court's order or made a consent order incorporating the financial provisions agreed on by the spouses, the court had no jurisdiction to make any subsequent order for financial provision since, in the case of each form of order, the substance of the transaction was a final settlement of the issue of financial provision approved by the court. Moreover, it was inconsistent with the principle of 'the clean break' after divorce (ie the principle that after a marital

---

a   Section 23(1) is set out at p 83 *b* to *e*, post

breakdown the financial and property issues should be settled once and for all to avoid bitterness) if the court's order could be regarded as final only if it dismissed the application for financial provision. It followed that the judge had been right to conclude that he had no jurisdiction to vary the consent order, and the appeal would therefore be dismissed (see p 81 *a b d* and *g h*, p 87 *b c* and *f* to *h* and p 88 *a* to *c*, post).

L v L [1961] 3 All ER 834 approved.

Hyman v Hyman [1929] All ER Rep 245 explained.

M v M [1967] 1 All ER 870 considered.

Per Viscount Dilhorne. The principle of 'the clean break' is of great importance, and the development of any practice whereby, in a case in which the court is satisfied that adequate or generous provision has been consented to, the court nevertheless, in case something happens in the future, makes an order for payment of a nominal amount so as to retain jurisdiction to increase the provision made is to be deprecated (see p 81 *c d*, post).

Notes

For waiver and dismissal of claims for financial provision and property adjustment, see 13 Halsbury's Laws (4th Edn) para 1158.

For the Matrimonial Causes Act 1973, s 23, see 43 Halsbury's Statutes (3rd Edn) 564.

Cases referred to in opinions

Barnard v Barnard (1961) 105 Sol Jo 441, CA, 27(2) Digest (Reissue) 838, 6672.

Burton v Burton and Gibbons (1964) 108 Sol Jo 584.

Carpenter v Carpenter (1976) 6 Fam Law 110, [1976] Court of Appeal Transcript 65A.

Fisher v Fisher [1942] 1 All ER 438, [1942] P 101, 111 LJP 28, 166 LT 225, CA, 27(2) Digest (Reissue) 858, 6833.

Hyman v Hyman [1929] AC 601, [1929] All ER Rep 245, 98 LJP 81, 141 LT 329, 93 JP 209, 27 LGR 379, HL, 27(1) Digest (Reissue) 274, 2030.

Kitchin v Kitchin [1952] VLR 143.

L v L [1961] 3 All ER 834, [1962] P 101 [1961] 3 WLR 1182, CA, 27(2) Digest (Reissue) 830, 6630.

M v M (No 1), E v E and R, B v B and T, B v B and D, M v M (No 2), W v W (No 2) [1967] 1 All ER 870, [1967] P 313, [1967] 2 WLR 1333, 27(1) Digest (Reissue) 510, 3686.

Mills v Mills [1940] 2 All ER 254, [1940] P 124, 109 LJP 86, 163 LT 272, CA, 27(2) Digest (Reissue) 829, 6626.

R v R (No 2) (1967) 111 Sol Jo 926.

Russell v Russell [1956] 1 All ER 466, [1956] P 283, [1956] 2 WLR 544, 120 JP 140, CA, 27(2) Digest (Reissue) 1015, 8130.

Shaw v Shaw (1965) 66 SR (NSW) 30.

Shott v Shott [1952] 1 All ER 735, CA, 27(2) Digest (Reissue) 825, 6606.

Sidney v Sidney (1867) 36 LJP & M 73, HL, 27(2) Digest (Reissue) 863, 6871.

Appeal

This was an appeal by Margaret Jean Minton ('the wife'), pursuant to leave of the House of Lords granted on 16th February 1978, against a decision of the Court of Appeal (Stamp and Orr LJJ) dated 23rd November 1977 dismissing her appeal from an order made by his Honour Judge Macdonald in the Bournemouth County Court on 19th August 1977 whereby he dismissed for want of jurisdiction an application by the wife to vary a consent order made by his Honour Judge King in the same court on 22nd January 1973 which was in the terms of an agreement between the wife and her former husband, Raymond Claude Minton, in respect of, inter alia, the wife's maintenance. The facts are set out in the opinion of Lord Scarman.

Joseph Jackson QC and *James Pavry* for the wife.
Anthony Ewbank QC and *Michael Norman* for the husband.

Their Lordships took time for consideration.

23rd November. The following opinions were delivered.

LORD WILBERFORCE. My Lords, I have had the benefit of reading in advance a print of the speech to be delivered by my noble and learned friend, Lord Scarman. I agree with it and would dismiss the appeal.

VISCOUNT DILHORNE. My Lords, I have had the advantage of reading in draft the speech of my noble and learned friend, Lord Scarman.

I agree with it and only desire to stress the desirability of the court being able to achieve finality as to the financial provisions made for a spouse after the breakdown of a marriage. A man may be prepared to consent to an order being made in favour of his former wife which made more provision for her than that to which he would be prepared to agree if faced with the possibility of later being required to pay more and to consent on the basis of finality to provide more than the court might have ordered but for his consent. The principle of 'the clean break', to which my noble and learned friend refers, I regard as of great importance, and I would deprecate a practice developing where, in a case in which the court is satisfied that adequate or generous provision has been consented to, the court nevertheless, in case something happened in the future, made an order for payment of a nominal amount so as to retain jurisdiction to increase the provision made. A court should have power to make a final order for provision for a spouse. It has in my opinion that power and in a proper case it should be exercised.

LORD FRASER OF TULLYBELTON. My Lords, I have had the advantage of reading in draft the speech prepared by my noble and learned friend, Lord Scarman, and I agree with it.

I only wish to add a comment on the question of public policy mentioned by my noble and learned friend in the last paragraph of his speech. I respectfully agree that there are great advantages in the finality of a 'clean break'. But it is easy to envisage an exceptional case in which a totally unforeseeable change in the circumstances of one of the former spouses occurs soon after a final court order has been made disposing of the financial issues between them. Such a change might render the order so inappropriate as to appear harsh and unjust. The change might be for better, as by unexpected inheritance of property, or for worse, as by a sudden serious illness. To cover such exceptional cases it would, in my view, be desirable that the jurisdiction of the court to vary any order should invariably be preserved as a matter of general law. It seems unsatisfactory that this jurisdiction should only be preserved in cases when the court anticipates the possible need for subsequent variation of its order, and provides for it by the device of making a nominal order. But I do not think that the legislation as it stands is capable of being construed so as to lead to the result that I regard as preferable.

I would dismiss the appeal.

LORD RUSSELL OF KILLOWEN. My Lords, I have had the advantage of reading in draft the speech of my noble and learned friend, Lord Scarman. I agree with it, and with the proposal that this appeal be dismissed.

LORD SCARMAN. My Lords, this is an appeal from an order of the Court of Appeal dismissing an appeal from an order made by his Honour Judge Macdonald sitting in the Bournemouth County Court whereby he dismissed for want of jurisdiction the application by the appellant for an order that the respondent, her ex-husband, should provide her with reasonable maintenance by way of periodical payments. The question for your Lordships' House is whether the wife, as I shall call the appellant, is precluded by an earlier consent order of the court from invoking the jurisdiction of the court. The answer depends on the view taken by your Lordships as to the extent of the jurisdiction conferred on the court by s 23(1) of the Matrimonial Causes Act 1973.

The parties were married in 1952. They had five children, four of whom survive. In November 1971 the wife obtained (on a supplemental petition dated 27th October 1971) a decree nisi of divorce on the ground that her marriage had broken down irretrievably by reason of her husband's adultery. She was granted the custody of the children. She had included in her petition a prayer for financial provision for herself and the children by way of periodical payments, secured provision, lump sum or sums, as might be just. After decree nisi she made further claims, so that the application, which ultimately fell to be considered by the court, was one dated 22nd December 1971.

In this application she sought specifically: (1) periodical payments for herself during joint lives, (2) a lump sum, for herself, (3) that the matrimonial home be transferred to her, (4) periodical payments in respect of the children, (5) continuation after the decree absolute of a land charge registered under the Matrimonial Homes Act 1967. Interim orders pending suit, with which your Lordships are not concerned, were made.

The decree was not made absolute until 13th December 1972. No doubt it was delayed because the wife was anxious to get her, and the children's, maintenance settled before the final act of dissolution of marriage. By December 1972 the parties were very near to, if they had not already agreed on, a final settlement of financial and property questions as between themselves. On 16th January 1973 the husband signed three documents, which contained the terms agreed between them, and covered maintenance for the children as well as the wife. No question arises in this appeal as to the provision for the children, for whom it is recognised that the husband has a continuing responsibility, and the court a continuing jurisdiction (until they reach the age of 18) to make such orders as it thinks appropriate.

Two of the documents were drafted in the form of consent orders. The third was expressed to be an agreement 'collateral to and conditional upon the necessary court orders being made as per draft "consent orders"'.

Your Lordships are concerned with only one of the two documents drafted as consent orders. This document, omitting immaterial matter, is in the following terms:

'By consent it is ordered that:—

'(1) The matrimonial home . . . in which both the [wife] and the [husband] have beneficial interests, be conveyed by the [husband] to the [wife] within 28 days of this order . . .

'(2) The [wife] do pay to the [husband], on completion of the Conveyance, the sum of £10,000·00, in full and final settlement of, and to extinguish the [husband's] said beneficial interest in the said matrimonial home.

'(3) The [husband] do transfer to the [wife] all such furniture furnishings, fixtures and fittings in the said matrimonial home as may belong to him on the date of completion . . .

'(5) The [wife] shall have no claims to any interest beneficial or otherwise in respect of any properties, other than the said matrimonial home, as are or may have been owned by the [husband].

'(6) The [husband] do pay to the [wife] maintenance at the rate of 5p per year until the matrimonial home is conveyed to her such payments to cease on completion of the Conveyance.

'(7) No order for any lump sum payments to be made in respect of the [wife].'

The collateral agreement included the following clause:

'(3) The [wife] to hand to the [husband] on completion a document duly signed in the following form:—I Margaret Joan Minton hereby waive and relinquish any or all claims in respect of maintenance from my former husband Raymond Claude Minton from the date hereof.'

On 22nd January 1973 his Honour Judge King, sitting in the Bournemouth County Court, made, on the wife's application, a consent order in the terms of the two drafts agreed by the parties. The order thus incorporated the provisions set out above. It did not, however, include cl 3 of the collateral agreement or make any reference to it.

The husband complied with the order, and on conveyance of the matrimonial home the nominal order for periodical payments to the wife came to an end. The wife, however, became dissatisfied and ultimately applied to the county court on 10th November 1976 for an order 'varying' the periodical payments payable under the order of 22nd January 1973 in respect of herself and the children. On 19th August 1977 his Honour Judge Macdonald, sitting at Bournemouth, varied the order in respect of the children but, as I have already mentioned, dismissed for want of jurisdiction the wife's application in respect of herself.

It is submitted on behalf of the wife that notwithstanding the consent order of 22nd January 1973 the court has jurisdiction to entertain a fresh application by the wife for a periodical payments order. Section 23(1) of the 1973 Act provides:

'On granting a decree of divorce, a decree of nullity of marriage or a decree of judicial separation or at any time thereafter (whether, in the case of a decree of divorce or of nullity of marriage, before or after the decree is made absolute), the court may make any one or more of the following orders, that is to say—(a) an order that either party to the marriage shall make to the other such periodical payments, for such term, as may be specified in the order; (b) an order that either party to the marriage shall secure to the other to the satisfaction of the court such periodical payments, for such term, as may be so specified; (c) an order that either party to the marriage shall pay to the other such lump sum or sums as may be so specified; (d) an order that a party to the marriage shall make to such person as may be specified in the order for the benefit of a child of the family, or to such a child, such periodical payments, for such term, as may be so specified; (e) an order that a party to the marriage shall secure to such person as may be so specified for the benefit of such a child, or to such a child, to the satisfaction of the court, such periodical payments, for such term, as may be so specified; (f) an order that a party to the marriage shall pay to such person as may be so specified for the benefit of such a child, or to such a child, such lump sum as may be so specified; subject, however, in the case of an order under paragraph (d), (e) or (f) above, to the restrictions imposed by section 29(1) and (3) below on the making of financial provision orders in favour of children who have attained the age of eighteen.'

The subsection is the latest of a sequence of statutory provisions creating and extending the jurisdiction of the court to make maintenance orders for the support of an ex-spouse. In 1857 Parliament made judicial divorce available, and conferred on the court power, on a decree of dissolution, to order that the husband make secured provision for the wife: see the Matrimonial Causes Act 1857, s 32. The maintenance jurisdiction of the court was extended and modified by later Acts, which were consolidated and re-enacted in s 190 of the Supreme Court of Judicature (Consolidation) Act 1925. Subsection (1) of that section provided that 'the court may, if it thinks fit, on any decree for divorce or nullity of marriage, order' that the husband make secured provision for the wife, and sub-s (2) that 'in any case as aforesaid the court may, if it thinks fit, by order . . . direct' the husband to pay the wife for her maintenance periodical sums during joint lives. The jurisdiction, was, therefore, conditional on the grant of a decree. In *Sidney v Sidney*[1] Lord Cranworth, in your Lordships' House, described the jurisdiction in these terms: 'till the decree was pronounced, no such question [ie whether to order secured provision] could be gone into'.

It was not long before the courts had to consider the question whether the jurisdiction was limited to the time of making the decree or extended thereafter, and, if so, for how long. The judges began by construing 'on' as meaning 'on or shortly after'; later they extended its meaning so that the jurisdiction could be exercised 'on or within a reasonable time thereafter': see *Fisher v Fisher*[2] and *Shott v Shott*[3].

Such were the limitations on the jurisdiction until 1958. Section 1 of the Matrimonial Causes (Property and Maintenance) Act 1958 provided that the power of the court to make maintenance orders after decree of divorce, nullity of marriage or judicial separation 'shall

1   (1867) 36 LJP & M 73 at 74
2   [1942] 1 All ER 438, [1942] P 101
3   [1952] 1 All ER 735

be exercisable either on pronouncing such a decree or at any time thereafter'. The making of a decree thus remained the essential condition for the exercise of the jurisdiction; but, once there was a decree, the jurisdiction was now without a time limit. The passage of time might influence the exercise of the court's discretion, but it could not destroy the jurisdiction. Section 23(1) of the 1973 Act re-enacts the jurisdiction as formulated in the 1958 Act.

In *L v L*[1] the Court of Appeal (Willmer and Davies LJJ) had to consider the nature of the jurisdiction as extended by the 1958 Act. In that case the wife agreed to accept a lump sum in full satisfaction of all present and future rights of maintenance for herself. The husband took out a consent summons and the court's order, after reciting the agreement, declared that 'by consent it is ordered that the petitioner's application for maintenance . . . be dismissed'. Three years later the wife made a fresh maintenance application. The Court of Appeal held that the 1958 Act did not give the court jurisdiction to entertain a fresh application by a wife who had, in pursuance of an agreement sanctioned by the court, received an agreed sum and had her application dismissed.

L v L[1] was, of course, a decision on s 190 of the 1925 Act as amended by the 1958 Act. Nevertheless, it remains a decision of critical importance, for, so far as the jurisdiction of the court is concerned, s 23(1) repeats the provisions of the 1958 Act.

The wife's counsel has attacked the decision in a number of ways. First, he submits that the Court of Appeal misunderstood the case law and practice before 1958. The submission has no foundation. The court was faced with a history of case law in which neither counsel nor the court could find a single case, prior to 1958, of the court assuming jurisdiction to award maintenance on a second application where the original application had been dismissed: see per Willmer LJ[2]. Counsel for the wife in the present case has had no greater success. Instead, he endeavours to make good his submission by an argument to the effect that this House in *Sidney v Sidney*[3] treated the words of s 32 of the 1857 Act, 'on such a decree', simply as a precondition, and not a limitation, on the court's jurisdiction. And he seeks to attribute the absence of any cases of a second application after dismissal of the first not to lack of jurisdiction to entertain such an application but to the time limit set to the jurisdiction by judicial decision. It is not, however, possible to use *Sidney v Sidney*[3] as supporting a submission that there is no limit to the court's jurisdiction. The House of Lords had no occasion in that case to consider the extent of the court's jurisdiction, and their decision did not touch the point now being considered. And counsel's point on the cases derives no support from what the judges in fact said as to the extent of their jurisdiction. For instance, in *Mills v Mills*[4] (a decision of the Court of Appeal which established the practice of the court in making consent orders), Greene MR said:

> '. . . the proper—and, indeed, the only—method of preserving some right in the wife, in such circumstances, was to provide what I have called a peg upon which subsequent applications could be hung. Such a peg could be provided by making an order for periodic maintenance, in a nominal sum, which order would remain in force and would be susceptible of variation if the circumstances called for it. In the absence of such a peg, however, no future order could be made . . . Once the order is discharged, the jurisdiction of the court disappears.'

With all respect for the research and ingenuity displayed by counsel in presenting his argument, I think Willmer LJ in *L v L*[5] summed up accurately the pre-1958 law when he said:

---

1   [1961] 3 All ER 834, [1962] P 101
2   [1961] 3 All ER 834 at 839, [1962] P 101 at 117
3   (1867) 36 LJP & M 73
4   [1940] 2 All ER 254 at 260–261, [1940] P 124 at 133–134
5   [1961] 3 All ER 834 at 838, [1962] P 101 at 117

'In my judgment, once an application for maintenance has been dismissed by the court, jurisidiction does not exist to entertain a fresh application. I entertain no doubt that this was the position on the law as it stood before the Act of 1958.'

Counsel's second challenge is more profound. He submits that the Court of Appeal in *L v L*[1] should have held themselves bound by the public policy recognised by this House in *Hyman v Hyman*[2] to declare that the court has jurisdiction to entertain a fresh application for maintenance notwithstanding that the applicant had consented to the dismissal of an earlier application or the discharge of an earlier order. The Court of Appeal dealt specifically with the point. Willmer LJ[3] accepted as well established the proposition, for which *Hyman v Hyman*[2] is usually cited, that the jurisdiction to award maintenance cannot be ousted by any private agreement between the parties. But he said it was 'otherwise when the agreement is brought before the court and an order of the court is made giving effect to its terms'[4]. And he quoted with approval an observation of Jenkins LJ in *Russell v Russell*[5] that 'The principle in *Hyman v Hyman*[2], be it remembered, is satisfied by any bargain which is brought before the court for approval and approved by the court'. Willmer LJ was, if I may say so with respect, plainly right in his approach to *Hyman v Hyman*[2]. Lord Hailsham LC put the principle of that decision into these words[6]:

'However this may be, it is sufficient for the decision of the present case to hold, as I do, that the power of the Court to make provision for a wife on the dissolution of her marriage is a necessary incident of the power to decree such a dissolution, conferred not merely in the interests of the wife, but of the public, and that the wife cannot by her own covenant preclude herself from invoking the jurisdiction of the Court or preclude the Court from the exercise of that jurisdiction.'

Hyman v Hyman[2] was concerned only with the effect of an agreement which purported to oust the jurisdiction of the court. It is no authority as to the extent of the court's jurisdiction. That question must depend on the true construction of the statute conferring the jurisdiction.

It is because this jurisdiction depends on the statute that I do not think it necessary to trouble your Lordships with a consideration of the Australian cases to which counsel referred in the course of his argument, notably *Kitchin v Kitchin*[7] and *Shaw v Shaw*[8]. They turned on the interpretation of Australian statutes, whereas the House is concerned with the language of s 23(1) of the 1973 English Act.

Lastly counsel referred to a number of dicta and decisions of the English courts which appear to conflict with the decision in *L v L*[1]. My Lords, I find it strange that this conflict should have arisen; but, having arisen, it must now be resolved.

Barnard v Barnard[9] was a decision of the Court of Appeal (Ormerod, Willmer and Danckwerts LJJ) given on 9th May 1961. It, therefore, preceded *L v L*[1], which was decided by the Court of Appeal on 23rd October 1961. It does not appear to have been cited in *L v L*[1], nor does Willmer LJ appear to have recollected it. I do not find this surprising. *Barnard v Barnard*[9] was no more than a motion for leave to appeal. After pronouncing a decree nisi of divorce, the trial judge had made a nominal maintenance order in favour of the wife at the rate of a shilling a year. The husband sought leave to appeal. In announcing

---

1   [1961] 3 All ER 834, [1962] P 101
2   [1929] AC 601, [1929] All ER Rep 245
3   [1961] 3 All ER 834 at 839, [1962] P 101 at 118
4   [1961] 3 All ER 834 at 839, [1962] P 101 at 119
5   [1956] P 283 at 295, cf [1956] 1 All ER 466 at 470
6   [1929] AC 601 at 614, [1929] All ER Rep 245 at 251
7   [1952] VLR 143
8   (1965) 66 SR (NSW) 30
9   (1961) 105 Sol Jo 441

the court's refusal to give leave, Ormerod LJ is reported to have said that the practical effect of the 1958 Act was that a nominal order for maintenance no longer served any useful purpose. Counsel has urged on your Lordships that Ormerod LJ must have taken the view that the amendment made to the jurisdiction by the 1958 Act had the effect of enabling the court to make a maintenance order notwithstanding an earlier application had been dismissed. It does not, however, follow that he (or his brothers) must have taken that view. His observation may have been intended to refer to a situation in which the court had made no order, that is to say, had not exercised jurisdiction. But, if he meant what counsel says he meant, an observation made on dismissing a motion for leave to appeal is no more than a dictum (with which the other members of the court may or may not have agreed). I have no hesitation in preferring the reasoned judgments in *L v L*[1], 'two-judge' court though it was. Accordingly, *Barnard v Barnard*[2] is not to be treated, in my judgment, as an authority on the interpretation of s 190 of the 1925 Act, as amended by s 1 of the 1958 Act.

In *Burton v Burton and Gibbons*[3] Ormrod J, and in *R v R (No 2)*[4] Karminski J, also expressed the view that since the 1958 Act dismissal of a maintenance application would not preclude a subsequent application. In neither report is there to be found any reference to *L v L*[1]. However, in the unreported case of *Carpenter v Carpenter*[5] the Court of Appeal did follow *L v L*[1], Ormrod LJ himself saying (albeit reluctantly): 'We have to accept on the authority of *L v L*[1] . . . that once a claim for periodical payments has been dismissed . . . the court no longer has any jurisdiction.'

In the series of cases known as *M v M*[6] Simon P gave guidance to the judges and the profession as to the exercise of the discretion conferred on the court by s 5(2) of the Matrimonial Causes Act 1965. The subsection replaced sub-ss (2) and (3) of s 4 of the Matrimonial Causes Act 1963, a section which reduced collusion from an absolute to a discretionary bar to divorce. The court was placed under a duty to enquire whether collusion existed, and provision was made for the court to take into consideration 'any agreement or arrangement made or proposed to be made between the parties'. The 1963 Act was a major step forward towards the promotion of conciliation and harmony between people whose marriages had foundered, and the elimination of marital bitterness. But, faced with collusion, the courts had to know how to exercise their discretion to allow the parties, who had colluded, to proceed to divorce. In the course of his judgment Simon P offered guidance as to the way in which the courts should approach agreements between spouses as to maintenance. He observed[7]:

> 'When I do dismiss a wife's claim for maintenance, it is intended as an indication to a judge dealing subsequently with an application by the wife for leave to make a claim for maintenance out of time or to a registrar dealing subsequently with a wife's claim for maintenance that I have been satisfied either that the wife's conduct has been such that it would be unjust that her husband should be ordered to provide maintenance for her or that her support has been adequately and reasonably provided for in some other way. Even so, the tribunal dealing with the matter subsequently is not concluded by my order; it is intended as no more than an indication of the view I have come to on the material before me.'

But, in considering *W v W (No 2)*[8] (the last of the series) Simon P 'was not prepared to countenance the dismissal of the wife's claim to maintenance' and approved an agreed

1   [1961] 3 All ER 834, [1962] P 101
2   (1961) 105 Sol Jo 441
3   (1964) 108 Sol Jo 584
4   (1967) 111 Sol Jo 926
5   (1976) 6 Fam Law 110
6   [1967] 1 All ER 870, [1967] P 313
7   [1967] 1 All ER 870 at 872, [1967] P 313 at 317
8   [1967] 1 All ER 870 at 877, [1967] P 313 at 325

nominal order. Why, one may ask, trouble to make such an order if the court had jurisdiction to make a second order after the dismissal of her first application?

In M v M[1] Simon P was not required to construe the 1958 Act (as then re-enacted in the 1965 Act). He was concerned to give guidance where parties who had made a collusive agreement were seeking a divorce. His problem was to indicate the circumstances in which the court could approve a collusive bargain. The inconsistency in the two passages of his judgment to which I have referred is an indication how peripheral the point was in the context of that series of cases. For myself, I do not read M v M[1] as helping your Lordships towards a proper construction of s 23(1) of the 1973 Act.

My Lords, I have come to the conclusion that L v L[2] was correctly decided. When one turns to the 1973 Act itself, one finds not only the jurisdictional language of the 1958 Act repeated in s 23(1) but a strong indication as to the intention of Parliament in the significantly different language formulating the jurisdiction of the court to order maintenance for children. Subsection (4) provides:

> 'The power of the court under subsection (1) or (2)(a) above to make an order in favour of a child of the family shall be exercisable from time to time; and where the court makes an order in favour of a child under subsection (2)(b) above, it may from time to time, subject to the restrictions mentioned in subsection (1) above, make a further order in his favour of any of the kinds mentioned in subsection (1)(d), (e) or (f) above.'

Thus, when the section is conferring jurisdiction in respect of children of the family, it expressly provides that orders may be made 'from time to time'. Had Parliament, when re-enacting s 1 of the 1958 Act, wished to overrule L v L[2], it could have added to sub-s (1) the words 'from time to time'. When Parliament wished to make it clear that no previous dismissal of an application or discharge or termination of an order could displace the court's power to make maintenance orders in favour of children, it added, by sub-s (4), the words 'from time to time' to the words 'at any time thereafter' which it had used in sub-s (1). No plainer indication could be given of the intention of Parliament.

For these reasons I conclude that s 23(1) of the 1973 Act does not empower the court to make a second or subsequent maintenance order after an earlier application has been dismissed. Counsel for the wife, however, submits that the present is not a case of dismissal: an order was made which included periodical payments and a property transfer order. As I understand his argument, he again invokes the public policy, which he says is to be derived from Hyman v Hyman[3], that it is in the interest of the public as well as the spouse that the court, having made an order, should have a continuing jurisdiction to make another. Thus he seeks to draw a distinction between a dismissal and an order. I agree with him that on its proper construction the consent order in this case is more than a dismissal. It contains an express provision for a limited period of maintenance (the nominal order until conveyance) and a provision for the transfer of the home.

The short answer to the point, however, is that on the true construction of s 23(1) the court does not have the jurisdiction. Once an application has been dealt with on its merits, the court has no future jurisdiction save where there is a continuing order capable of variation or discharge under s 31 of the 1973 Act. But the specious reliance on public policy calls for an answer. There are two principles which inform the modern legislation. One is the public interest that spouses, to the extent that their means permit, should provide for themselves and their children. But the other, of equal importance, is the principle of 'the clean break'. The law now encourages spouses to avoid bitterness after family breakdown and to settle their money and property problems. An object of the modern law is to encourage the parties to put the past behind them and to begin a new life

---

1 [1967] 1 All ER 870, [1967] P 313
2 [1961] 3 All ER 834, [1962] P 101
3 [1929] AC 601, [1929] All ER Rep 245

which is not overshadowed by the relationship which has broken down. It would be inconsistent with this principle if the court could not make, as between the spouses, a genuinely final order unless it was prepared to dismiss the application. The present case is a good illustration. The court having made an order giving effect to a comprehensive settlement of all financial and property issues as between spouses, it would be a strange application of the principle of the clean break if, notwithstanding the order, the court could make a future order on a subsequent application made by the wife after the husband had complied with all his obligations. The difference between a dismissal of an application by consent on terms recited or referred to in the order, which the courts have recognised as effectual since 1940 (if not earlier), and an order whose terms incorporate the parties' agreement is a mere formality. The substance of the transaction in each case is a final settlement, as between the parties, approved by the court. My Lords, I would not deny the court power, where it thinks it just, to achieve finality as between spouses (children are a different matter) unless compelled to do so by clear enactment. Your Lordships are under no such compulsion; on the contrary, s 23(1) is perfectly clear: it permits the court to achieve finality, if it thinks it appropriate, practical and just.

I would, therefore, dismiss this appeal.

Appeal dismissed.

Solicitors: *Church, Adams, Tatham & Co*, agents for *G A Mooring Aldridge & Brownlee*, Bournemouth (for the wife); *Lovell, Son & Pitfield*, agents for *Williams, Thompson & Co*, Christchurch, Dorset (for the husband).

Mary Rose Plummer   Barrister.

Keogh v Gordon

QUEEN'S BENCH DIVISION

LORD WIDGERY CJ, BOREHAM AND DRAKE JJ

18th APRIL 1978

Value added tax – Return – Responsibility for making return – Taxpayer registered for value added tax – Taxpayer ceasing to trade but remaining registered – Taxpayer failing to make return – Return if submitted would have shown nil liability – Whether taxpayer required to make return – Value Added Tax (General) Regulations 1975 (SI 1975 No 2204), reg 51(4).

A person registered for value added tax must, while he remains registered, furnish a return, pursuant to reg 51(1)[a] of the Value Added Tax (General) Regulations 1975, showing the amount of tax payable by or to him, notwithstanding that he may have ceased trading and that any return he would make would be a nil return (see p 91 *j* to p 92 *b*, post).

Notes

For the duty on a taxpayer to submit a return for the purposes of value added tax, see 12 Halsbury's Laws (4th Edn) para 952.

As from 1st January 1978 the Value Added Tax (General) Regulations 1975 have been replaced by the Value Added Tax (General) Regulations 1977.

Case stated

This was an appeal by the Crown by way of case stated by the justices for the county of Dyfed, in respect of their adjudication as a magistrates' court sitting at Llanelli.

On 2nd September 1976 an information was preferred by the Crown against the respondent, John Graham Gordon, that, being registered for the purpose of value added tax under the Finance Act 1972, he failed to comply with reg 51 of the Value Added Tax (General) Regulations 1975[1], by failing to furnish to the Controller, Customs and Excise, Value Added Tax Central Unit, Southend-on-Sea, not later than 27th May 1976, a return for the period from 1st October 1975 until 31st December 1975, in the form prescribed by the regulations, contrary to s 38(7) of the 1972 Act.

The justices heard the information on 11th October 1976, and found the following facts: (a) the respondent was a haulage contractor and was registered on 11th June 1975 by the Commissioners of Customs and Excise for the purpose of value added tax; (b) the commissioners, by a letter sent to the respondent, dated 18th May 1976, directed that, under reg 51(1)(c) of the 1975 regulations, the respondent furnish a return for the period 1st October 1975 to 31st December 1975 by 27th May 1976; (c) the required return was not made by the respondent; (d) the respondent on 28th July 1975 ceased work as a haulage contractor as the two vehicles he operated were taken by the liquidator of a company which provided loads for the respondent and the liquidator claimed the vehicles as the property of the company; (e) the respondent did not inform the commissioners of the changed circumstances and that he had ceased to trade; (f) at the date of the hearing the registration of the respondent had not been cancelled and the Crown was only aware of the fact that the respondent had ceased trading at the hearing of the case.

It was contended by the Crown that, for the respondent to comply with the law, he would have had to furnish a nil return for the required period by 27th May 1976.

---

a   Regulation 51(1), so far as material, provides: 'Every registered person shall, on the [prescribed form], furnish the controller with a return showing the amount of tax payable by or to him in respect of each period of 3 months ending on dates notified in the certificate of registration issued to him, or otherwise, and containing full information in respect of all other matters specified in the said form; and shall furnish such a return not later than the last day of the week next following the end of the period to which it relates . . .'

1   SI 1975 No 2204

It was contended by the respondent that as he had ceased to trade before the date of the relevant period of the required return the form of return stated in the information was not applicable.

The justices were of the opinion that on 28th July 1975 the respondent was a person who ceased to be liable to be registered and in accordance with reg 4 of the 1975 regulations he should have notified the commissioners of the changed circumstances so that his registration could be cancelled. Failure to do so within 21 days made the respondent liable to a penalty in accordance with s 38(7) of the 1972 Act. There was no specific provision in the 1972 Act or the 1975 regulations for a nil return. A nil return in the prescribed form of return (Form 4 in Sch 1 to the 1975 regulations) would have been meaningless. The 1975 regulations specifically provided for the action to be taken when a person ceased to trade and therefore ceased to be liable to be registered, since, by reg 51(4), a final return was required to be furnished in substitution for the normal return but the requirement to make the final return only became operative after the effective date of cancellation of the registration.

The justices were therefore of the opinion (i) that the respondent was not required to make a return for the period from 1st October 1975 until 31st December 1975, as on 28th July he had ceased trading, but that he was required to make a final return after his registration had been cancelled, (ii) that, having regard to reg 51(4) and the form of return prescribed in the 1975 regulations, a nil return was not a requirement of the legislation in a case where the registered person had ceased to trade. Accordingly the justices dismissed the information.

The question for the opinion of the High Court was whether the justices were right in law in determining that a nil return was not a legal requirement in the circumstances.

Harry Woolf and *Valerie Pearlman* for the Crown.
The respondent did not appear.

BOREHAM J delivered the first judgment at the invitation of Lord Widgery CJ. This is an appeal by way of case stated from the justices for the county of Dyfed sitting at Llanelli on 11th October 1976.

On that date the respondent appeared before the justices charged with an offence under s 38(7) of the Finance Act 1972. The particulars of that offence were that, being registered for the purpose of value added tax under the provisions of the 1972 Act, he failed to comply with reg 51 of the Value Added Tax (General) Regulations 1975 by failing to furnish to the Controller, Customs and Excise, Value Added Tax Central Unit, a return for the period from 1st October 1975 until 31st December 1975.

The 1972 Act was the Act which established the new value added tax. Counsel for the Crown, who has taken us through various sections of the 1972 Act, contends that in the main the responsibility for assessment, collection and application is put on the persons who are liable to pay the tax. In s 4 of the 1972 Act it is provided:

'(1) A person who makes or intends to make taxable supplies is a taxable person while he is or is required to be registered under this Part of this Act.

'(2) Schedule 1 to this Act shall have effect with respect to the registration of persons under this Part of this Act.'

By reg 3(1) of the 1975 regulations it is provided:

'Any person who is required under paragraphs 3, 5 or 6 of Schedule 1 to the Act to notify the Commissioners of his liability to be registered or who requests to be registered under paragraph 7 or 11(*b*) of the said Schedule shall do so on [a certain form].'

By reg 4 of the 1975 regulations it is provided that every registered person, with certain exceptions, shall, within 21 days after certain changes or after any changes of a certain character have been made either in respect of name, constitution or ownership of the business, notify the commissioners in writing of such change or event.

In other words, said counsel, it is the duty of the taxpayer or the taxable person in effect to take the initiative in many of the matters and procedures relating to value added tax. In particular, it is provided by reg 51(1) that every registered person shall on a particular form, which is described, furnish the controller with a return showing the amount of tax payable by or to him in respect of each three monthly period, provided that (and I paraphrase) power lies with the commissioners, in particular, where they are satisfied that in order to meet the circumstances of any particular case it is necessary to vary the length of any period or the date on which any period begins or ends or the date on which any return is to be furnished, to direct or allow a registered person to furnish returns accordingly. In other words, prima facie three monthly returns are required, but the dates may be varied, extended or amended by direction of the commissioners. By reg 51(2) it is provided that any person to whom the commissioners give any direction in pursuance of the proviso to the previous paragraph shall comply therewith.

The facts which the justices found are in substance these. First, the respondent was a haulage contractor and was registered on 11th June 1975 by the commissioners for the purpose of value added tax. Secondly, by a letter dated 18th May 1976 and sent to the respondent he was directed under reg 51(1)(c), which I have just paraphrased, to furnish a return for the period 1st October 1975 to 31st December 1975, and to furnish that return by 27th May 1976. In fact the return was not made by the respondent.

The justices also found (and this no doubt is the reason why the return was not made) that the respondent on 28th July 1975 had ceased work as a haulage contractor because the vehicles which he operated were taken by the liquidator of a company who claimed the vehicles as the property of that company. The respondent had not informed the commissioners of the changed circumstances or that he had ceased to trade. Indeed at the date of the hearing the registration of the respondent as a taxable person had not been cancelled, and the Crown was only aware of the fact that the respondent had ceased trading at the hearing of the case.

On those facts and taking into account the provisions to which reference has already been made, the justices came to the conclusion, seemingly on the ground that a nil return would have been made by the respondent had he complied with the commissioners' direction, that a nil return was something that was not envisaged by the 1975 regulations or indeed appropriate to the form that was laid down in Sch 1 to the regulations. Therefore, the justices came to the conclusion that there was no legal requirement on the respondent to make the return and that he was, therefore, not guilty of the offence with which he had been charged.

Counsel now contends that in that conclusion the justices were wrong. He contends, first, that the opening words in reg 51(1), 'Every registered person shall', mean exactly what they say, namely that so long as a person stays on the register he is in fact a registered person, even though he may, if he takes the appropriate steps, have himself removed from the register on various grounds, and in particular on the ground that he has ceased to trade. But, as I have said, counsel's contention is that so long as he stays on the register so his obligation to comply with the directions of the commissioners is maintained.

He points to the fact that in reg 51(4) the language is different, and there the reference is to any person who ceases to be liable to be registered; in other words, a distinction is drawn. Whereas it might be said in the present circumstances that the respondent if he had ceased trading in July 1975 had ceased to be liable to be registered, nevertheless he remained in fact registered.

For my part I would see no escape from the conclusion that the opening words of reg 51(1) in fact mean exactly what they say, that every registered person shall comply with the requirements of that regulation. The respondent was at the time the direction was sent to him a registered person. The direction was a valid direction under reg 51(1)(c). The respondent failed to comply with it though he was on the register, and, in my judgment, inevitably he was guilty of an offence under s 38(7) of the 1972 Act.

For my part I would send the case back to the justices with an order that on the facts that they found there should be a conviction.

DRAKE J. I agree.

LORD WIDGERY CJ. I agree also.

Appeal allowed; case remitted to justices.

Solicitors: *Solicitor, Customs and Excise.*

Jacqueline Charles   Barrister.

D v B (otherwise D) (child: surname)

COURT OF APPEAL, CIVIL DIVISION

STAMP AND ORMROD LJJ

24th, 25th MAY 1978

Minor – Change of surname – Unborn child – Husband and wife separating before birth – Wife adopting new surname by deed poll – Deed poll not enrolled – Birth of child registered in wife's adopted name – Whether judge entitled to direct mother to execute fresh deed poll and alter entry in registry to ensure child known by father's name – Births and Deaths Registration Act 1953, s 29(3) – Registration of Births, Deaths and Marriages Regulations 1968 (SI 1968 No 2049), reg 18(3).

Register of births – Correction of error in entry – Mother registering child in different surname without father's consent – Whether father able to require alteration of register – Whether intention of one parent that child be known by name entered in register sufficient to establish that 'it is intended' that child should be so known – Births and Deaths Registration Act 1953, s 29(3) – Registration of Births, Deaths and Marriages Regulations 1968 (SI 1968 No 2049), reg 18(3).

The father and the mother were married in 1970. Early in 1975, when the mother had formed an attachment with another man, B, she became pregnant by the father. In September 1975 she left the father to live with B and had lived with him ever since. On leaving the father the mother executed a deed poll by which she assumed B's surname for herself and any child of hers. The deed did not comply with the requirements of the Enrolment of Deeds (Change of Name) Regulations 1949, but no attempt was made to enrol it. In November 1975 she gave birth to the father's child. She entered the child in the register of births in the surname of B but declared in the entry that the father was the child's natural father. The father and mother were divorced in November 1976. The mother refused the father access to the child. The father applied to the court for access, and in the application applied for an order that the child should be known by his surname and not that of B, and that the mother should alter the entry in the register of births and take any other steps which the court directed. In December 1976 the judge[a] directed the mother to amend the deed poll and the register of births to ensure that they showed the child's surname as that of the father. The judge also ordered that until the child attained the age of 18 the mother should not cause or permit it to be known by any other surname than that of the father, without the father's consent or the court's order. The mother did not execute a fresh deed poll, and refused to sign a statutory declaration submitted to her

a   [1977] 3 All ER 751

for signature by the father for the purpose of altering the entry in the register. The father applied to the judge for further directions on the manner of effecting reregistration of the child's birth. The mother applied for variation of the order made in December 1976. By an order made in April 1978 the judge directed the mother to execute a statutory declaration to effect alteration of the entry in the register of births, and a fresh deed poll, within 14 days, and threatened committal proceedings against her should she disobey those directions. The mother appealed seeking to set aside that order and to vary the order made in December 1976.

Held – The appeal would be allowed for the following reasons—

(i) Since at common law a surname was merely the name by which a person was generally known, and the effect of a deed poll to alter a person's surname was merely evidential and had no other effect, the mother could not be required to execute a fresh deed poll. Furthermore, the mother's deed poll was not in any way vitiated by her failure to comply with the 1949 regulations, since (a) compliance with those regulations was required only where it was intended to enrol the deed, (b) the effect of a deed poll was the same whether or not it was enrolled and (c) there were no regulations governing the execution of deeds poll; the sole effect of the failure to comply with the 1949 regulations was that the deed could not be enrolled. Accordingly the direction in the April 1978 order to execute a fresh deed poll was unenforceable (see p 97 a to c and e to g, p 99 f, p 100 j and p 101 a to c, post).

(ii) Since the surname entered by the mother in the register was the surname by which, at the date of the registration, 'it [was] intended' the child should be known, within reg 18(3)[b] of the Registration of Births, Deaths and Marriages Regulations 1968, and since it was not necessary that both parents should intend that the child should be known by that surname for there to be the requisite intention, it followed that there had been no 'error' in the entry, within s 29(3)[c] of the Births and Deaths Registration Act 1953, which could be corrected by a statutory declaration under s 29(3). Accordingly the direction to execute a statutory declaration to alter the entry in the register of births was also unenforceable (see p 98 h to p 99 a and f, p 100 j and p 101 a to c, post).

(iii) Furthermore, it was in the child's best interests for the future that it should be known by the surname of B, and not by the father's surname, for it was human, sensible and practical that the child should be known by the surname of the family unit to which it belonged; and so long as the father and child knew one another and, in due course, the child recognised that the father was his natural parent the name by which the child was known was of little importance. Accordingly the order requiring the child to be known by the father's surname until he was 18 should be varied (see p 100 d e h j and p 101 a to c, post).

Decision of Lane J [1977] 3 All ER 751 varied.

Notes

For change of surname, see 29 Halsbury's Laws (3rd Edn) 394, paras 784, 785, and for cases on the subject, see 35 Digest (Repl) 787–788, 33–38.

For correction and alteration of a register of birth, see 32 Halsbury's Laws (3rd Edn) 474, para 802.

For the Births and Deaths Registration Act 1953, s 29, see 27 Halsbury's Statutes (3rd Edn) 1042.

Cases cited

D (minors), Re [1973] 3 All ER 1001, [1973] Fam 209, DC.
T (otherwise H) (an infant), Re [1962] 3 All ER 970, [1963] Ch 238.
W G, Re [1976] Court of Appeal Transcript 164.
Y v Y (child: surname) [1973] 2 All ER 574, [1973] Fam 147.

---

b   Regulation 18(3) is set out at p 98 f g, post
c   Section 29(3) is set out at p 98 d e, post

Appeal

The mother appealed against an order of Lane J made on 10th April 1978 directing her to execute a statutory declaration altering an entry in the register of births, and a deed poll, to ensure that her child was known by the father's surname and not by the name of another man, B. By the appeal the mother asked for an order (i) that the child's name should remain on the register of births as B, (ii) that the child should henceforth be known as B, and (iii) that the directions to execute the statutory declaration and the deed poll be revoked. The grounds of the appeal were (1) that the judge was wrong in law in holding that it was not in the child's interests that his name should remain, and/or that he should be known as, B; (2) that the judge misdirected herself in that she (i) failed to have sufficient regard to the fact that the mother was expecting another child in about June 1978 which would be known by her new surname of B, (ii) held that there was no advantage to the child being known by the name B, (iii) held that it was important to the relationship between the father and the child that the father's surname should be preserved, (iv) failed to have sufficient regard to the fact that the father was enjoying regular and satisfactory access to the child, and (v) attached more weight to the father's wishes than to the paramount interest of the child. The facts are set out in the judgment of Ormrod LJ.

I H Davies for the mother.
John E A Samuels for the father.
Shirley Ritchie for the Official Solicitor as guardian ad litem.

ORMROD LJ delivered the first judgment on the invitation of Stamp LJ. This is an appeal from an order which was made on 10th April 1978 by Lane J in a case which has caused a great deal of difficulty and trouble. It is a singularly unfortunate case. The difficulties arise because an issue of substance, not in itself of any great complexity, has become entangled with formalistic considerations which have led to a great deal of litigation.

The human situation between these two parties, the father and the mother, is such as to lead inevitably to severe emotional reactions by each side. That each should feel very strongly about the situation is all too easy to understand. The tragedy is that these feelings have been exacerbated to a point which is almost unbearable by, as I think, purely formalistic considerations which have led to this litigation.

The substantive issue in the case was whether or not the father should have access to a very young boy. The formalistic issues rotate round the question of the name by which this boy is to be known, and it is a great pity that these issues have come to overshadow the real issue of substance, which in fact has been resolved by an earlier decision of the judge.

The judge's order which is under appeal should be read in full in so far as the operative parts are concerned. The order is:

'1. That the [mother] do within 14 days of today execute the statutory declaration in the unamended form [contained in a certain exhibit] to the affidavit of [the father];
'2. That the [mother] do within the said period execute a fresh deed poll in such terms as will be necessary to cancel a deed poll executed by her in September 1975;
'3. That the [mother] be on notice that if she neglects to obey the above directions by the time therein limited, she will be liable to process of execution for the purpose of compelling her to obey the same . . .'

and then there is a stay pending a possible appeal.

The inclusion of the third paragraph in the order is most unusual. It was put in, I think it right to say, at the express direction of the judge and it constitutes the plainest possible threat to the mother; a threat of committal proceedings in the event that she does not obey the two directions. That, of course, inevitably provoked her to take every possible step that is open to her to challenge those directions, and, in the view that I have formed, she was fully entitled to challenge them both. But it does indicate the relationship between these parties that by April 1978 it was necessary, or thought to be necessary, for the father to be

adopting that sort of attitude towards the mother with the result which, in my experience,
a always follows. Committal proceedings in family disputes are almost always disastrous
and in this case, of course, they would be futile.

The facts of the case can be stated even more shortly than usual because they have been
dealt with in much more detail by the judge in her judgment[1]. These are the essential
facts. The father and the mother were married in July 1970. They were both 22 at the
time. The father is now a lawyer, and I do not specify any further than that, and the
b mother is a school teacher. For almost the first five years of the marriage there were no
children, but a child was conceived early in 1975. Before that the marriage had run into
difficulties, the details of which are quite unknown to us and are irrelevant to any question
we have to consider. All that is relevant is that by the autumn of 1974 the mother had
formed an attachment to the man to whom she is now married and it is common ground
that that association had not reached the sexual stage until the spring of 1975. Some
c attempt had been made by the father to effect a reconciliation with his wife and those steps
may or may not have progressed. What is clear is that sexual intercourse took place
between the father and the mother early in 1975 as a result of which a child was conceived,
and the child is the subject of these present proceedings. He is called M and he was born
on 23rd November 1975.

At a time when it is not clear whether the mother knew or did not know that she was
d pregnant, she resumed the association with Mr B, and for the first time had intercourse
with him. Then her pregnancy became apparent and, of course, a situation of the most
acute difficulty inevitably arose for all three adults. It was plainly an emotional situation
of the utmost intensity for all. The mother made the decision in the course of the summer
1975 that her marriage was at an end, that it was not capable of being repaired, and so she
took the decision to set up house with Mr B and steps were taken to find accommodation,
e and when the accommodation was found she left her husband, by now, of course, six
months or so pregnant, and thereafter she and Mr B have lived together.

Almost immediately after she left, which was in September 1975, she executed a deed
poll changing her name from D to B. The deed poll is, of course, in the usual form. By this
time, as the correspondence between herself and her husband clearly indicates, both sides
were under great stress and in a very confused state of mind as to what the future was to
f be. It is easy to understand the father's desperate anxiety that he was going to lose the
child, his only child, which may have been conceived, perhaps, with considerable difficulty,
one does not know. Equally it is extremely easy to understand the mother's feelings that
this child was going to be born into a new family which she and B were establishing; the
father would have little or no contact with this child, and to her, as she mentioned in at
least one letter, adoption by her and B seemed to be a sensible solution. It is easy to
g understand that the father would take a very different view of it. So the situation became
increasingly difficult.

When the child was born the mother felt that it would be better if the father did not see
the child or attempt to develop any relationship with the child. The father, understandably,
took exactly the opposite view. So the battle lines were drawn, and the only issue of
substance, in my judgment, in this case is which of them was right in relation to the
h question of access.

The father, unfortunately, perhaps because he was a lawyer, took great exception to the
fact that the mother intended the child to be known by the name of B, and it is at this point
that the first unusual fact arises in this case, because when the child was born the mother,
who was the informant, registered the child in a very unusual way. It is necessary to look
at the actual birth certificate. The birth was registered in the sub-district of Cambridge and
j the date and place of birth of the child is given as 'Twenty-third November 1975.
Maternity Hospital, Cambridge.' In space 2, 'Name and surname' of child, the entry is
'[MB] Male'. Then in space 4, under the heading 'Father', appears '[JD]' and his place of
birth and occupation are given. In space 7, under the heading 'Mother', appears '[DB]

---

1   [1977] 3 All ER 751, [1977] Fam 145

otherwise [DD]' and her place and birth and her maiden name are given, and she signs it as the informant mother in the name of DB.

An enormous amount of effort has been expended in this case on the question as to whether or not that entry in the register of births first should and secondly could be amended. It is necessary at this point, I think, to say that the form of registration is wholly irrelevant to any real issue in this case, because the real issues are human issues and not legal ones. It is unfortunate that so much effort has been put into trying to resolve the legal issues.

It will be necessary, unfortunately, in this case to look rather closely into these legal issues, and the reason for that, in my view, is this: that unless we can disentangle the formalistic aspects of this case from the substantive aspect this family is never going to have any peace at all. Fortunately, as a result of some further instructions which counsel for the father received just before the court rose last night, the father felt able to make a constructive contribution to the solution of these problems that must have come as a very agreeable surprise to the mother. It is to be hoped that from now on the issues between these two parents can be resolved in real terms and not in formalistic ones. It is necessary, however, in view of the history of this litigation, to deal with the matter in some detail.

The matter began immediately after the parties were divorced, and, just to complete the record, the decree nisi was pronounced on 19th November 1976 and on 13th December the matter came first before Lane J. She had two main issues to resolve: the first, as I have already mentioned, was the substantive issue of access, which she resolved in favour of the father, the mother taking the line, which I can understand perfectly well, just as I can understand the father's line, that it would be better if the father did not attempt to play any role in this child's life. It was inevitable that B should be the father figure in this child's life, that was unavoidable, and the mother thought it would only complicate the issue if there was another male adult involved in this child's life from an early age. Whether she was right about that or not is a matter of opinion. The father was clearly entitled to put his case, and put it as forcibly as he could to the court, to point out the advantages which he felt the child would enjoy by establishing contact with him from an early stage, and, as I have already said, the judge resolved that issue in his favour.

But right in the forefront of his mind in 1976 was this issue of the registration of the child's birth. The first paragraph of the notice of application dated 10th June and amended on 26th November asked for an order that—

> 'the child of the family, now known as [MB], be henceforth known as [MD] and that the [mother] do concur in an application to the Superintendent Registrar of the Registration District of Cambridge to make such alteration to the Register of Births as may give effect to the said change of name and/or that the [mother] do take such other steps to ensure that the said child is known as [MD] as the court may direct.
>
> '2. The [father] be afforded reasonable access to the said child of the family, to be defined by the court.
>
> '3. The [mother] and/or [B] may be ordered to pay the costs of this application.
>
> '4. That the court should consider whether the arrangements for the said child are satisfactory or the best that can be devised in the circumstances',

and fifthly asking for an order that custody of the child should be given jointly to the father and the mother, the intention being, of course, that care and control should be with the mother.

The first question is whether or not the order of the judge, made originally in December 1976 and reaffirmed in her recent order of April 1978, was an order which the court was competent to make, namely the order directing the mother to take all the necessary steps to alter the deed poll and to effect a change in the register of births. The person who appears to have appreciated the legal difficulties best, curiously enough, in this case is the mother herself.

So far as the deed poll is concerned, we asked at an early stage in the hearing of this appeal what change it was suggested the mother could make in the deed poll, and how she

was supposed to do it. I emphasise that the order is a mandatory order on her, combined
a with the threat of enforcement proceedings, to execute a fresh deed poll in such terms as
would be necessary to cancel the deed poll executed in September 1975. What she was
supposed to do under that term of the order was quite unclear from the order itself and in
fact counsel for the father himself was unable to suggest any answer to the question what
she was required to do. The answer is she can do nothing. Her present name is B, but in
order to keep one's mind clear it is, perhaps, worth observing that the name B is hers purely
b by convention, she has married Mr B and it is the normal convention in this country, but
it is no more than that, that she takes the name B and is thereafter known as B. The deed
poll had simply stated that that was how she wished to be known before her remarriage.
It is common ground that a surname in common law is simply the name by which a person
is generally known, and the effect of a deed poll is merely evidential: it has no more effect
than that. This part of the order is unenforceable and, therefore, should not have been
c made.
      The judge may have been misled by certain matters which were referred to in this
respect at the earlier hearing. In the report of the judgment in the Family Division there
is a long reference by the judge to some regulations, which are entitled the Enrolment of
Deeds (Change of Name) (Amendment) Regulations 1974[1] and the judge quoted
extensively from these regulations. The upshot of them is that a woman cannot *enrol* a
d deed poll relating to change of name unless she complies with the requirements of those
regulations, and among other requirements are that the deed should state whether she is
single, married, widowed or divorced, that she must produce her marriage certificate and
show that notice of her intention to apply for enrolment of the deed has been given to her
husband, and that she is required to demonstrate that either he has consented or that there
is good reason why his consent should be dispensed with. No doubt the judge felt that
e since the mother had complied with none of those formalities, this deed poll could be
amended or disposed of, in some unspecified way as being contrary to the regulations. But
that, with respect, is a complete misunderstanding. There are no regulations governing
the *execution* of deeds poll. The regulations only apply to the enrolment of such deeds poll,
and the purpose of enrolment is only evidential and formal. A deed poll is just as effective
or ineffective whether it is enrolled or not; the only point of enrolment is that it will
f provide unquestionable proof, if proof is required, of the execution of the deed, and no
more. So that the deed poll in this case is not vitiated in any way by failure to comply with
those enrolment regulations. It simply means that the deed cannot be enrolled. The
regulations in fact go on to provide that no deed poll which purports to change the name
of a child can be enrolled without the specific consent of the Master of the Rolls. Quite
clearly no attempt was made in this case, and no attempt was required to be made, to enrol
g that deed poll and so there is no more to be said about this aspect of the case. There is
nothing that the mother can do to comply with that part of the order.
      The other part of the order relating to the entry of the child's birth in the register of
births and deaths is more complicated. There are only two provisions in the Births and
Deaths Registration Act 1953 relating to effecting changes in the register. It is necessary
to look, first of all, at s 1 which simply provides that the birth of every child born in
h England and Wales shall be registered in accordance with the 1953 Act. Section 2 provides
that in the case of every birth it shall be the duty of the father and mother of the child to
give to the registrar information and particulars required to be registered concerning the
birth, and to sign the register. But that is subject to a proviso that the giving of information
and the signing of the register by any one qualified informant shall act as a discharge of any
duty under this section of every other qualified informant. So that either parent can give
j the necessary information and sign the register.
      Then there is a provision in s 13 relating to the alteration of the name of the child.
Section 13 (1) provides:

---

1   SI 1974 No 1937. These regulations amended the Enrolment of Deeds (Change of Name)
    Regulations 1949 (SI 1949 No 316)

'Where, before the expiration of twelve months from the date of registration of the birth of any child, the name by which it was registered is altered or, if it was registered without a name, a name is given to the child, the registrar ... upon delivery to him at any time of a certificate in the prescribed form ... shall, without any erasure of the original entry, forthwith enter in the register the name mentioned in the certificate as having been given to the child ...'

It is not necessary to examine s 13 in detail because the period of 12 months had elapsed in any event before the judge's order was made. Moreover, whether that section relates to changing the surname of the child is a matter which, in my opinion, might require further consideration. But since it does not arise in this case I say no more about it.

The only other section which gives any power at all to correct an entry in a register of births or deaths is s 29, and the form of this section is important. Subsection (1) reads:

'No alteration shall be made in any register of live-births, still-births or deaths except as authorised by this or any other Act.'

Subsection (2) deals with clerical errors. Subsection (3) deals with errors of fact and reads thus:

'An error of fact or substance in such register may be corrected by entry in the margin (without any alteration of the original entry) by the officer having the custody of the register, upon production to him by that person of a statutory declaration setting forth the nature of the error and the true facts of the case made by two qualified informants of the birth or death with reference to which the error has been made, or in default of two qualified informants, then by two credible persons having knowledge of the truth of the case.'

It will be observed that it is essential to the operation of this subsection that there should have been an error, and that the statutory declaration should set forth the nature of the error and the true facts of the case. The question then arises whether there was any error in the entry of this child's birth in the register at Cambridge.

The only error that can be suggested is an error relating to the surname of the child. But when one comes to look at the statutory regulations, the Registration of Births, Deaths and Marriages Regulations 1968[1], one finds that the requirement is that so far as the surname of the child is concerned, the entry shall represent the 'name by which the child is intended to be known'. It is reg 18 (3) which is the relevant one. It reads:

'With respect to space 2 (Name and surname) the surname to be entered shall be the surname by which at the date of the registration of the birth it is intended that the child shall be known and, if a name is not given, the registrar shall enter the surname preceded by a horizontal line.'

It may be surprising to some, certainly it was a surprise to me, to find that definition of 'surname' in the regulations. Here, of course, it is perfectly plain that the mother, when she registered this child's birth, did intend that the child should be known by the name of B. It seems, therefore, clear to me that there was no 'error' by her. She may have acted in a way of which many people would disapprove and in a way which may be, in moral terms, open to criticism, but so far as making an error is concerned, it seems to me to be plain that she made no error at all.

It was suggested that the words 'it is intended' should refer to the intention of both parents, but, speaking for myself, I find it very difficult to extract that construction from the relevant provisions. So I think the mother was entitled to take the point which she took herself, that there was no error on her part and that, consequently, she was in extreme difficulty in complying with the order of the court to make a statutory declaration in the

---

1   SI 1968 No 2049

necessary terms. In fact when a statutory declaration was submitted to her by the father's
a solicitors for her signature in compliance with the judge's order of December 1976 she
amended it. The draft statutory declaration reads:

> '5. At the date when the birth of the said child was so registered as aforesaid, I the
> said [DB], wrongly believed that I was entitled to register the surname of [M] as [B].
> I now know that the surname should have been registered as [D],
>   '6. In consequence of the above circumstances, the entry on the said Register is
b > wrong and the correct entry of the said child's name should be [MD]. And we the said
> [DB] and the said [JD] make this solemn declaration conscientiously believing the
> same to be true and by virtue of the provisions of the Statutory Declarations Act 1835.'

The mother, receiving that draft, amended it by striking out in para 5 the word
'wrongly' before 'believed', so that it now read 'I the said [DB] believed that I was entitled
c to register the surname of [M] as [B]', and then she struck out the words 'have been' so that
it now read 'I now know that the surname should be registered as [D]', and in para 6 she
deleted the words 'conscientiously believing the same to be true and' presumably because
she did not conscientiously believe the same to be true.

Of course, in its amended form the declaration was useless for effecting the purpose of
amending the register and that led to the second round of this dispute. What then
d happened was that the father's solicitors took out a summons asking for further directions
as to the manner of effecting the reregistration of the child's birth, and the mother issued
a cross-summons asking for a variation of the judge's order in relation to the certificate of
the register of births and the deed poll. Those were the two matters which came on before
Lane J on 10th April 1978. It was agreed that the mother's summons should be heard first
asking for the variation, and it is right to say that this point was not taken before the
e judge. Nor is it taken in the notice of appeal. But since the threat of committal is overt in
this case, this court has felt bound to examine all aspects of this order, first of all from the
jurisdictional point of view and secondly to see whether it was in fact possible for the
mother to comply with it. She was thought to be being recalcitrant over the matter, but
the view I have formed is that her view was right that she could not properly execute or
sign the necessary statutory declaration. That, of course, reduces those two paragraphs of
f the order of 10th April to nothing, so that in respect of those two parts of the order, in my
judgment, the mother is entitled to succeed on this appeal.

The judge did not in fact deal with the remainder of the mother's summons in which
she was seeking a variation of what one might call the substantive part of the earlier order
of the judge, that is, in relation to the practical questions relating to this child's name as
opposed to the legal ones. The original order had required that—
g

> 'Until the child attains the age of 18 years the mother do not cause or permit the
> said child to be known by any other surname than that of the father without the
> written consent of the father or further order of the court.'

This part of the order was also subject to the mother's application in April 1978 for a
h variation. She was asking the judge to reconsider that part of the order; in other words,
what was she to do about this child's name? The judge did not deal with that in her order
because, having made the order I have already recited, it followed that she was not prepared
to vary that part of the 13th December 1976 order, but we have to deal with it because that
issue is raised in the notice of appeal.

I am sure everyone understands that the question of the surname of a child is a matter
j of great emotional significance, particularly to fathers. If the name is lost, in a sense, the
child is lost. That strong patrilineal feeling we all to some extent share. But this has to be
kept within the bounds of common sense, in my judgment. It is not very realistic to be
litigating over how a child of 2½ should be called, so far as its surname is concerned. A
child at that age is quite unaware of its surname, even though it will acquire later on, fairly
quickly perhaps, some idea of what his name or her name is. But what matters is whether

the child identifies with the father in human terms. I suspect that children are much better at distinguishing between reality and formality than adults. If the child knows that D is his father, he may be confused later on if he is known by the name B, but I would doubt it. He is certain to be confused if everybody insists on calling him D when very nearly all the people he lives with are called B. But this is, as one appreciates all too clearly, a very sensitive issue. Fathers feel very sensitive about it. Mothers feel that it is a plague on a day-to-day basis: they have to explain to schools, people have to make special notes in records, and so on, about the name. The matter is one which, in my judgment, ought to be capable of being resolved by two sensible adults who bear in mind that they are dealing with a child, and a child who sooner or later, and probably sooner, will make some decisions for himself in the matter. Pressure, I would have thought, is more likely to produce unwanted results than anything else.

I cannot help reiterating the Official Solicitor's advice in this case, at the conclusion of his report which was prepared for the hearing in December. At the very end of the Official Solicitor's report, which had recommended, I should say, that access between the child and the father should be started at the earliest moment, although at that time the child was very young indeed, the report concludes with these words:

> 'For [the child] to be known as [D] when his mother and [Mr B] are called [B] could cause him some embarrassment particularly when he attends school. The mother and [Mr B] might well have children of their own and this in itself could cause some distress insofar as [the child] will be the only one in the family unit with a different surname. In the circumstances, should the Court decide that the father should have access to [the child], and the Official Solicitor recommends that he should, the father might consider that it would be in [the child's] best interests for the future not to insist on his being known by his real surname of [D].'

If I may say so with great respect to the Official Solicitor, that passage seems to me the best statement of good sense that I have read in this context for a long time. It seems to me human, sensible and practical. Any other solution seems to me inhuman, impracticable and bound to lead to trouble. The one thing that one should try to avoid in these cases is giving hostages to fortune, weapons to parties to quarrel with when the real issue between them is something quite other.

Nothing is more depressing than to have a mother brought back to the court over some infringement of this requirement, such as registering the child in a particular play group under the name B when it ought to be D. Fortunately, at the end of the day, the father, I think, has realised that substantive issues are what matter to children and formal issues can be left to look after themselves. If they are forgotten about nobody will worry about them. I can understand the father, in the early stages of this case, taking steps about the registration and, indeed, steps about the deed poll, because it must have seemed, in the autumn of 1976, as if the mother had laid her plans pretty well. She had changed her own name to B by deed poll so that she could say, 'Now I am properly known as B', and she had registered the child in the name of B so that she could say, 'But the child's real name is B', and one can understand that the father's tactics should direct an attack on those two points. It is bad enough for him that both of them have proved abortive. But neither of them is real. What is real is that the father and the child should know one another, that the child should, in course of time, come to recognise the fact that D is his natural father, and so long as that is understood names are really of little importance, and they only become important when they become a casus belli between the parents.

Having said that, I can only hope that from now on these young people, and they are still quite young, under 30, will direct their attention to the issues about this child which matter and not about formalistic things that do not much matter. A vast amount of money has been spent on this case which is little short of a disaster and should have been avoided, and could have been avoided, by a little good sense.

I would, therefore, allow the appeal. Just what form the order should take is not very easy. So far as the first two points are concerned, that is the deed poll point and the register of births point, all that will be necessary is to delete those two paragraphs of the order, which will in effect eliminate the order appealed against. But some order will have to be made, and it will be a question of deciding the appropriate form, to deal with the variation of the December 1976 order in relation to the practical use of names, and perhaps that is a matter which can be left for discussion later. I would therefore allow the appeal and substitute an order in such form as proves to be appropriate.

STAMP LJ. I agree. Out of respect to the judge in the court below, because we are differing, I would have delivered a judgment of my own, but having heard the way Ormrod LJ has put it I do not wish to do so. I entirely agree and would now invite submissions on the order as to which Ormrod LJ spoke.

Appeal allowed; order of 10th April 1978 discharged; by consent order of 13th December 1976 varied to enable the child henceforth to be known under the name B.

Solicitors: *Penningtons*, agents for *Wild, Hewitson & Shaw*, Cambridge (for the mother); *Jaques & Co* (for the father); *Treasury Solicitor*.

Avtar S Virdi Esq   Barrister.

Walkley v Precision Forgings Ltd

COURT OF APPEAL, CIVIL DIVISION
MEGAW, SHAW AND WALLER LJJ
22nd, 23rd MAY, 20th JUNE 1978

Limitation of action – Court's power to override time limit in personal injury or fatal accident claim – Whether plaintiff barred from commencing second action and seeking court's discretion to override time limit where plaintiff's first action liable to be dismissed for want of prosecution – Whether criteria for exercise of discretion to override time limit different from criteria for exercise of discretion to dismiss action for want of prosecution – Limitation Act 1939, s 2D(1) (as inserted by the Limitation Act 1975, s 1).

In 1969 the plaintiff, who was then employed by the defendants as a grinder, became aware that he had contracted a disease which could have been caused by the grinding machinery with which he worked. In November 1970 solicitors instructed by his union wrote to the defendants claiming damages on behalf of the plaintiff. The defendants denied liability. In October 1971 the solicitors issued a writ against the defendants claiming damages in respect of the disease on the ground of negligence or breach of statutory duty ('the first action'). No statement of claim was served and in due course the solicitors advised the plaintiff that his claim could not succeed. In October 1972 the plaintiff consulted a second firm of solicitors who wrote to the defendants asserting that they were liable for the plaintiff's disease The defendants' solicitors replied that they intended to apply to dismiss the action for want of prosecution if it were proceeded with. No further steps were taken in the first action but it was not discontinued. In or shortly after 1974 the plaintiff instructed a third firm of solicitors who took counsel's opinion and in April 1976 obtained an engineer's report, in consequence of which they advised him that his claim had a reasonable chance of success. On 6th December 1976, after the expiry of the period of limitation for the claim, those solicitors issued a writ ('the second writ') asserting the same cause of action as was asserted in the writ in the first action. The second writ and a statement of claim were served in February 1977 whereupon the defendants applied to a master to have them struck out. The master granted the application. The plaintiff appealed to a judge. He conceded before the judge that there had been inordinate and inexcusable delay in the conduct of the first action and that if proceeded with, it would be dismissed for want of prosecution. The judge allowed the appeal and restored the second action on the ground that as the plaintiff's conduct in respect of the first action had not been contumelious the court should exercise its discretion under s 2D[a] of the Limitation Act 1939 to allow the second action to proceed, notwithstanding that the first action if proceeded with would be dismissed for want of prosecution. The defendants appealed contending that it was not open to the court to hold that it was 'equitable', within s 2D(1), to allow the second action to proceed when the first action, having regard to the plaintiff's excessive and inexcusable delay, would be dismissed for want of prosecution.

Held – (i) Where a plaintiff brought a second action in respect of the same matter which gave rise to the first action brought by him, and the first action had been or was likely to be dismissed for want of prosecution, the plaintiff was entitled to ask the court to exercise its discretion under s 2D(1) of the 1939 Act to allow the second action to proceed, provided his conduct in respect of the first action had not been contumelious, notwithstanding the dismissal or likelihood of dismissal of the first action, for the criteria set out in s 2D for the exercise of that discretion were not identical to the criteria for the exercise of the discretion to dismiss an action for want of prosecution. Accordingly, even if an order were to be

---

a   Section 2D, so far as material, is set out at p 110 *g h* and p 111 *a* to *d*, post

made dismissing the first action for want of prosecution that would not be conclusive of whether it was equitable for the court to allow the second action to proceed, although the conduct of the first action and its effect on the fair trial of the second action and on prejudice to the defendants would be relevant in determining the issue under s 2D(1) (see p 106 e and h, p 107 d to h, p 108 j, p 109 c to e and g and p 110 b, post); *Birkett v James* [1977] 2 All ER 801 applied.

(ii) (Waller LJ dissenting) Since the plaintiff did not concede that all the evidence relevant to the determination of the issue under s 2D(1) was before the court, the court should not determine that issue even though the evidence which was before it indicated that the issue would be decided against the plaintiff. It followed that the appeal would be dismissed (see p 108 c d and p 109 h, post).

Per Shaw LJ. Since the 1975 Act does not lay down any specific procedure whereby the statutory power under s 2D of the 1939 Act is to be invoked, it would seem that the question can be raised at any appropriate stage of the litigation in respect of which the statutory power is invoked. The question may await the actual trial of the substantive issues in the action. More generally, in order to preclude undue prolongation of an action which it may not be equitable to permit to proceed, and to limit the burden of costs which may be imposed on a defendant, a summons by him to stay the action would serve to initiate the investigation contemplated by s 2D. In a clear case the action may thus be summarily terminated (see p 109 f g, post).

Notes

For the court's power to override the limitation period in personal injury actions, see Supplement to 24 Halsbury's Laws (3rd Edn) para 381.4.

For the Limitation Act 1939, s 2D, as inserted by the Limitation Act 1975, s 1, see 45 Halsbury's Statutes (3rd Edn) 850.

Cases referred to in judgments

Allen v Sir Alfred McAlpine & Sons Ltd, Bostic v Bermondsey and Southwark Group Hospital Management Committee, Sternberg v Hammond [1968] 1 All ER 543, [1968] 2 QB 229, [1968] 2 WLR 366, CA, Digest (Cont Vol C) 1091, 2262b.

Birkett v James [1977] 2 All ER 801, [1978] AC 297, [1977] 3 WLR 38, HL.

Biss v Lambeth, Southwark and Lewisham Health Authority [1978] 2 All ER 125, [1978] 1 WLR 382, CA.

Firman v Ellis [1978] 2 All ER 851, [1978] 3 WLR 1, CA.

Hess v Labouchere (1898) 14 TLR 350, CA, 51 Digest (Repl) 574, 2071.

Cases also cited

Spring Grove Services Ltd v Deane (1972) 116 Sol Jo 844, [1972] Court of Appeal Transcript 251.

Tolley v Morris p 71, ante, CA.

Interlocutory appeal

By an order dated 1st June 1977 Master Lubbock ordered that a writ and action issued and brought by the plaintiff, Anthony Walkley, against the defendants, Precision Forgings Ltd, should be struck out and dismissed on the ground that the action was brought in the same matter as a previous action pending between the same parties, and was therefore frivolous and vexatious and an abuse of the process of the court. The plaintiff appealed and on 20th April 1978 Swanwick J allowed the appeal and rescinded the master's order on the plaintiff undertaking to discontinue the prior action. The defendants appealed seeking restoration of the master's order. The facts are set out in the judgment of Megaw LJ.

Ronald Walker for the defendants.
Anthony Scrivener QC and *Christopher Carling* for the plaintiff.

Cur adv vult

20th June. The following judgments were read.

MEGAW LJ. This appeal from an order of Swanwick J dated 20th April 1978 raises a question as to the principle laid down by the House of Lords in *Birkett v James*[1] against the background of the provisions of the Limitation Act 1975.

The plaintiff was employed as a grinder by the defendants at their Cwmbran Works from 1966 until 1970 or 1971. In the autumn of 1966 he became aware that he had contracted a disease affecting the circulation of blood in the fingers known as Raynaud's Phenomenon. It is, or may be, caused by vibration such as may be created by the use of certain machine tools. The plaintiff consulted his union. They told him that their legal department did not think that a claim for damages could be established; but they passed the case to solicitors ('the first solicitors'). They wrote to the defendants in November 1970 claiming that the defendants were liable for damages in respect of the plaintiff's disease. In June 1971 the defendants' insurers denied liability. On 7th October 1971 the first solicitors issued a writ, thus bringing into being what may be called 'the first action'.

The indorsement on the writ was:

> 'The Plaintiff's claim is for damages for personal injury sustained by the Plaintiff in the course of his employment by the Defendants at their premises at Cwmbran, Monmouthshire, on or about December 1968 and caused by the negligence and/or breach of statutory duty of the Defendants.'

It is beyond dispute that what was being asserted was the claim in respect of the Raynaud's Phenomenon suffered by the plaintiff. An appearance was entered promptly. No statement of claim was served within the limit of time prescribed by RSC Ord 18, r 1 (14 days from entry of appearance). By April 1978 it had still not been served. It was by then some 6½ years out of time.

The first solicitors, having investigated the claim and taken counsel's opinion, told the plaintiff that he did not have a good claim. (This is deposed to in an affidavit of the plaintiff.)

The first action went to sleep, so far as the defendants knew, from October 1971 until June 1973. Meanwhile, in October 1972, the plaintiff had consulted another firm of solicitors ('the second solicitors'). On 15th June 1973 they wrote to the defendants asserting the defendants' liability in respect of the Raynaud's Phenomenon claim. On 1st August 1973 the defendants' solicitors wrote saying that, if it was the plaintiff's intention to proceed with the claim, a summons to dismiss for want of prosecution would be issued. There was no reply. Again, so far as the defendants knew, the action simply went to sleep. And it remained asleep for a further 3½ years, until February 1977. By that time more than seven years had passed since the plaintiff had become aware of his illness, more than six years since the first solicitors on his behalf had asserted that the defendants were liable, and more than five years since the writ had been issued. No single further step had been taken in the action.

The plaintiff's affidavit does not disclose when or in what circumstances he ceased to retain the second solicitors. But his affidavit says that, at some unspecified date (whether in or after 1974), he instructed yet another firm of solicitors ('the third solicitors') who have acted for him since. A civil aid certificate was issued in August 1975.

The plaintiff's affidavit asserts that the third solicitors 'took counsel's opinion and in April 1976 obtained a full and careful engineer's report'; and he says that he has been advised that his claim 'has a reasonable chance of success'. On 6th December 1976 another writ ('the second writ') was issued commencing the second action. The indorsement of the writ asserts a breach of duty on the part of the defendants 'from 10th November 1966 until in or about 1971', causing the plaintiff's Raynaud's Phenomenon. There is no doubt that this is the selfsame cause of action as was asserted in the first writ. The first action was not discontinued. The second writ and an accompanying statement of claim were served on the defendants on 23rd February 1977.

---

1 [1977] 2 All ER 801, [1978] AC 297

Meanwhile, as appears from the affidavits on behalf of the defendants, the defendants'
a　solicitors had returned all the papers to the defendants' insurers in July 1974. The
defendants no longer occupy the premises at Cwmbran. The relevant grinding machines
would be difficult to identify and the precise working conditions could not now be
simulated. The defendants' works manager has died. The senior group medical officer is
believed to have died. If he is still alive his whereabouts are unknown. His evidence, it is
said, would have been invaluable.

b　　In the court below it was conceded on behalf of the plaintiff that, if the plaintiff had
attempted to continue his first action, that action would have been dismissed for want of
prosecution (though it was contended that such dismissal would not result in a fresh action
being an abuse of the process of the court). It was therefore conceded that there had been
inordinate and inexcusable delay in the conduct of the first action, which delay had
resulted in the likelihood either that there could not be a fair trial of the action or that the
c　defendants would suffer serious prejudice if the action were to be tried. In this court,
counsel for the plaintiff, who did not appear in the court below, sought leave to alter that
concession, while not challenging that it had been made previously in the terms which are
set out above. The alteration sought was to substitute for 'that action would have been
dismissed' the words 'there would have been a definite liability that that action would have
been struck out'. I do not think that the precise formulation of the concession matters. I
d　have no doubt that, subject only to the possible effect of the Limitation Act 1975, the first
action would properly have been dismissed for want of prosecution.

The defendants, having been served with the writ and statement of claim in the second
action, entered a conditional appearance and promptly applied for an order, under the
inherent jurisdiction of the court and under RSC Ord 18, r 19, that the second action be
struck out and/or dismissed.

e　Master Lubbock on 1st June 1977 ordered that the second writ be struck out and the
second action dismissed. The plaintiff appealed. The appeal was not heard until 20th
April 1978, when Swanwick J allowed the appeal. He rescinded the master's order and
thus restored the second action to life, the plaintiff undertaking to discontinue the first
action. Proceedings in the second action were stayed until the plaintiff should have paid
the defendants' cost in the first action. (The plaintiff did not have legal aid in respect of the
f　first action.) The judge gave leave to appeal to this court.

The failure to discontinue the first action despite the issue and service of the second writ
may have been an oversight or it may have been an attempt to have the best of both
worlds. It must, surely, ordinarily be an abuse of the process of the court for the same
plaintiff to have two actions in existence simultaneously against the same defendant in
respect of the same cause of action. In some cases that might be an important matter. For
g　by RSC Ord 21, r 3(1), in those cases in which the leave of the court is required for a
discontinuance, the court may order the action to be discontinued 'on such terms as to
costs, the bringing of a subsequent action or otherwise as it thinks just'. In *Hess v
Labouchere*[1], it was said by A L Smith LJ that 'Generally, in allowing a plaintiff to discontinue
his action, the Court would consider whether they should not make it a condition that he
should not be at liberty to bring another action'. If the intended discontinuance is for the
h　purpose of avoiding the dismissal of the action for want of prosecution (as in the present
case), it would seem not improbable that the court would think it just to impose that
condition. It would hardly seem to be a valid objection to the exercise of this rule-given
discretion that the normal period of limitation for the bringing of the action had not yet
expired. This question did not arise, at least directly, in *Birkett v James*[2] (though counsel for
the defendants in argument referred to RSC Ord 21, r 3). In that case the plaintiff had not
j　started a second action, and his submission was that the first action should be allowed to
continue. In the present case also, though for a different reason, the question of the court

1　(1898) 14 TLR 350
2　[1977] 2 All ER 801, [1978] AC 297

imposing such a term as a condition of granting leave to discontinue does not arise. It does not arise because RSC Ord 21, r 2(1), provides that an action may be discontinued *without* *a* *leave* 'at any time not later than 14 days after service of the defence'. In the present case no defence has been served. That is no fault of the defendants. It is because the plaintiff, in breach of the rules, never served his statement of claim. So, curiously, the plaintiff, as a result of the wording of the rules, is in a stronger position than he would have been in if he had complied with the rules as to service of a statement of claim, resulting in the service of a defence. That is an odd and unsatisfactory state of affairs. But there it is. By RSC Ord *b* 21, r 4, where leave is not required, no condition can be imposed by the court as to the bringing (or rather the not bringing) of another action. RSC Ord 21, r 5, makes provision as to the costs of a discontinued action, but no more than that. Therefore, on the particular facts of the present case, the failure by the plaintiff to discontinue his first action (though I should have thought that it, by itself, justified the master's order) now falls to be treated as a technicality, which was regularised by the undertaking, required by Swanwick J's *c* order, to discontinue, belatedly, the first action.

At first sight it seems remarkable that the plaintiff's commencement of a second action, after he has already begun a previous action in respect of the identical cause of action and after he has conducted that first action with such excessive and inexcusable delay as to make it unlikely that there can now be a fair trial in respect of that cause of action, should not amount to an abuse of the process of the court. But in *Birkett v James*[1] it was held that, *d* in the absence of special circumstances, such as conduct on the part of the plaintiff which could be called 'contumelious', an action should not be dismissed for want of prosecution before the limitation period for the bringing of such an action had expired. That is because the plaintiff could properly and effectively frustrate the intended effect of such a dismissal by the simple process of issuing a fresh writ; and, save in cases of contumeliousness, the fresh action could not properly be struck out, stayed or dismissed as being an abuse of the *e* process of the court. In the present case, no question of contumelious behaviour on the part of the plaintiff arises. It is clear from *Birkett v James*[1] that it does not avail a defendant, who seeks to have an action dismissed for want of prosecution before the normal period of limitation has run, to be able to show that as a result of the plaintiff's delay a fair trial is impossible or that the defendant is likely to be seriously prejudiced. Parliament has prescribed a period of time within which an action may be brought. It is not for the courts *f* to treat the plaintiff as being prejudiced in any way in his legal right to pursue his action merely because he has taken the fullest advantage of the prescribed period and so has not issued his writ until the last day. If that makes a fair trial impossible, it is the defendant's misfortune.

Birkett v James[1] was not concerned with a claim for personal injuries. Therefore the Limitation Act 1975 was not relevant. In *Biss v Lambeth, Southwark and Lewisham Health* *g* *Authority*[2] Lord Denning MR and Geoffrey Lane LJ made it clear, and Eveleigh LJ concurred in their reasoning, that their Lordships in deciding *Birkett v James*[1] were not considering, and had no occasion to consider, questions as to the potential indefinite extension, by the Limitation Acts 1963 and 1975, of the primary fixed periods of limitation laid down by the Limitation Act 1939.

Nevertheless, though *Birkett v James*[1] is not a direct authority governing the present case, *h* the principle of that decision must be applied, if it be applicable having regard to the Limitation Act 1975.

By the Limitation Act 1975 Parliament has prescribed in the new s 2A of the 1939 Act that the limitation period for an action for negligence involving personal injuries shall, subject to the new s 2D, be three years from the date on which the cause of action accrued or the date (if later) of the plaintiff's knowledge, as defined in the following subsections of *j*

1	[1977] 2 All ER 801, [1978] AC 297
2	[1978] 2 All ER 125 at 131 and 133, [1978] 1 WLR 382 at 390 and 392

s 2A. That is what may be called the primary period of limitation. But by s 2D an action is not to be defeated as being out of time if the court in its discretion thinks it equitable that the action should be allowed to proceed, notwithstanding that the writ has been issued after the expiration of the s 2A period.

If on the true interpretation of the 1975 Act it could be said that s 2D can have no application to a second action, where a first action, started in time by the issue of a writ within the primary period of limitation, has been discontinued or dismissed, then the answer to the question raised by the present appeal would be simple. Section 2D would have no application. There would be nothing in the *Birkett v James*[1] principle which would apply. But that simple answer cannot, as I see it, be given in this case. It was not submitted by counsel for the defendants that s 2D can be construed as having no application to a case where a first writ has been issued within the primary period and that first action has been discontinued or dismissed. The second action is still 'an action' within the words of s 2D(1). It may be rare, in such a case, that a plaintiff could persuade the court that the requirements of s 2D are satisfied in favour of the plaintiff. But, though it may be rare, it cannot be said that it is impossible.

Counsel for the plaintiff does not contend that in a case like the present the court would not have been entitled to dismiss the first action, on the application of the defendants, for want of prosecution. In that respect, the present case differs from *Birkett v James*[1]. But he says that the effect of such an order, if made, cannot be to debar the plaintiff from the right given to him by Parliament by s 2D to issue a fresh writ and to have it determined, if the defendants raise the issue, at the proper time and place and by the proper procedure, whether 'it would be equitable to allow the action to proceed' by reference to the criteria set out in s 2D. Those criteria, he contends, are not identical with the criteria which are relevant for the court's decision in the exercise of its discretion in an application to dismiss for want of prosecution. For example, s 2D(1)(*a*) requires the court to take into account prejudice to the plaintiff, whereas in a dismissal for want of prosecution prejudice to the plaintiff is not a relevant factor. Counsel for the plaintiff suggests that there are other differences also, as to the factors relevant for the exercise of the respective discretions. Thus, he says, an order of the court to dismiss for want of prosecution, even though properly made, is not conclusive against the plaintiff in respect of the proper exercise of the court's discretion under s 2D. Many of the relevant considerations are the same, but not all.

Counsel for the defendants submits that it is absurd to suggest that a court could hold that it is 'equitable' to allow the second action to proceed where a court has already held, or would, if asked, properly hold that the excessive and inexcusable delay in the first action (being based on the same cause of action as in the second action) has made a fair trial impossible. That is a cogent argument. But it appears, as I have already said, that the application of the principle of *Birkett v James*[1] may prevent an action from being dismissed for want of prosecution even though a fair trial may be no longer possible.

I have come to the conclusion, with regret, that the submissions for the plaintiff are right. (I say 'with regret' because I think the probable result, if my conclusion is right, will be at least substantially to lessen the benefit to litigants in general which has been achieved by *Allen v Sir Alfred McAlpine & Sons Ltd*[2] prior to the Limitation Act 1975.) The plaintiff is entitled to have the question whether his second action should be allowed to proceed tested under s 2D of the Limitation Act 1939 by reference to the criteria therein set out. Of course, when the court decides that matter, the conduct of the first action and its effect on the prospects of a fair trial and of prejudice to the defendants will be relevant, possible vitally relevant, matters in the assessment whether it is equitable that the second action should proceed.

Counsel for the plaintiff submitted that the effect of a decision in the plaintiff's favour would make very little practical difference to the defendants; and, if there were to be

---

1   [1977] 2 All ER 801, [1978] AC 297
2   [1968] 1 All ER 543, [1968] 2 QB 229

future cases of the same nature, it would not involve any substantial additional delay or expense to the defendants, as compared with an application to dismiss for want of prosecution. Counsel for the plaintiff suggested that RSC Ord 33, r 3, could be used to secure a prompt decision of the s 2D issue as a preliminary issue; and that, in so far as counsel for the defendants was justified in his submission that substantially the same considerations were involved in an application for dismissal for want of prosecution and in a s 2D issue, there would be no more difficulty, delay or expense in regard to the evidence, if the matter were to be dealt with as a s 2D issue. I express no view on that procedural matter, other than to say that, if the procedure does not at present exist for a prompt determination of a s 2D issue, in a case like the present, as a preliminary issue, justice requires that such a procedure should be provided.

Counsel for the defendants submitted that, even if the plaintiff were entitled to have the matter considered by reference to s 2D, on the facts in evidence in this case the answer under s 2D is so clear that this court is entitled, and ought, to hold that it itself can decide that issue; and that decision can be only one way. Counsel for the plaintiff was not prepared, on his instructions, to concede that all relevant evidence for the determination of an issue under s 2D was before this court. In the face of that statement by counsel on his instructions, I do not think we are entitled to hold that the plaintiff is, beyond the possibility of any real argument, bound to fail on the issue under s 2D. As that issue may have to be decided by another court, it is undesirable that I should say more than that.

Accordingly, I think that Swanwick J reached the right conclusion and I would dismiss the appeal.

SHAW LJ. The history of the proceedings instituted by the plaintiff has been fully recounted in the judgment already given by Megaw LJ. It is unnecessary to recapitulate any part of it. I would only draw attention to the fact that as long ago as November 1970 the defendants were put on notice that the plaintiff was asserting a claim for compensation arising from an industrial disease contracted in the course of his employment by the defendants. Whatever path events might have taken thereafter, the defendants were then in a position to arm and array themselves against such a claim should it be persisted in and pursued. This fact might not, of itself, avail the plaintiff if he were thereafter guilty of contumelious or intentional default or of inordinate and inexcusable delay which resulted in serious prejudice to the defendants. It might, however, render the likelihood of such prejudice less real, at any rate in regard to a claim of the nature put forward by the plaintiff. This seems to me a consideration which justifies counsel for the plaintiff in qualifying the concession made before the judge in chambers to which Megaw LJ has referred. The effect of the views expressed in *Birkett v James*[1] is that the disciplinary principle which found expression in *Allen v Sir Alfred McAlpine & Sons Ltd*[2] may be in some degree indirectly muted by statutory provision.

The basic problem in the present appeal is what is the proper approach to the question whether or not an action commenced after the expiry of the primary period of limitation should be allowed to proceed. It seems to me inescapable that the answer must be sought in the provisions of the Limitation Act 1975 which create and define the 'court's power to override time limits'. Those provisions impinge on the common law powers of the courts to dismiss an action for want of prosecution and make an impact corresponding to that which the statutory period of limitation made on the opinions expressed in *Birkett v James*[1].

There is no suggestion in the present case that the plaintiff has been guilty of conduct which could be described as contumelious or that he has disobeyed any order of the court. So far from flouting its jurisdiction he seeks to invoke it. It is true that he has, for one reason or another, allowed his primary opportunity of pursuing his claim to go by

---

1 [1977] 2 All ER 801, [1978] AC 297
2 [1968] 1 All ER 543, [1968] 2 QB 229

default. In the circumstances the respective merits of the parties have never been touched
on, for they have not fallen to be considered or weighed on one side or the other. Counsel
for the defendants has contended that it is too late for such niceties and that the plaintiff
has, in effect, put himself out of court. The argument is in a practical sense a powerful one
but it is not, in relation to a claim of this nature, consonant with the provisions of s 2 of the
Limitation Act 1939, as amended by s 1 of the Limitation Act 1975. By what is now s 2A
of the 1939 Act the event from which the period of limitation begins to run is not
necessarily the date of accrual of the cause of action. It may instead be the later event of the
plaintiff's knowledge. In addition s 2D gives the court power to override the normal
prescribed limits 'if it appears to the court that it would be equitable to allow an action to
proceed' having regard to the considerations defined in sub-s (1)(a) and (b). These are (so far
as material to an action such as that instituted by the plaintiff), first, the degree to which
the provisions of s 2A prejudice the plaintiff and, secondly, the degree to which the exercise
of the power to override the normal time limits will operate to the detriment of the
defendant. The process of deciding whether it would be equitable to allow the action to
proceed thus involves weighing what the plaintiff will lose of what might otherwise be his
right if he is shut out by the application of the normal period of limitation against the
general prejudice to the defendant if he is exposed to liability by the relaxation of the
ordinary period of limitation. These broad considerations are to be regarded in relation to
(inter alia) the factors particularised in sub-s (3) of s 2D. We have not got before us the
materials to apply this process.

These factors are not, of course, unrelated to those taken into account by the court in
exercising its common law or inherent jurisdiction to dismiss an action for want of
prosecution. Nonetheless the emphasis on the potential detriment to a plaintiff if he were
deprived of his right of action is not specifically called into question as it is under s 2D. In
my judgment it follows that where a plaintiff seeks to rely on the exercise of the power
conferred by the section he is entitled to a hearing within the prescriptions of the statutory
code enacted by it.

The 1975 Act does not lay down any specific procedure whereby the statutory power
under s 2D is to be invoked and considered in relation to an action instituted by a writ
issued after the expiry of the primary period of limitation. It would seem, therefore, that
the question can be raised at any appropriate stage of the litigation so commenced. It may
await the actual trial of the substantive issues in the action; indeed it may in some
situations be so intimately and inextricably bound up with them as to make any summary
resolution of the question impracticable. More generally, in order to preclude any undue
prolongation of an action which it may not be equitable to permit to proceed and in
seeking to limit the burden of costs which may be imposed on a defendant, a summons by
him to stay the action would serve to initiate the investigation contemplated by s 2D. In
a clear case the action may be thus summarily terminated. In my opinion, by parity of
reasoning with the ratio in *Birkett v James*[1], the statutory opportunity conferred by s 2D to
institute proceedings and, subject to the provisions of that section, to pursue them must be
accorded to a plaintiff who issues a writ after the expiry of the primary period of limitation.

It follows that in my judgment the order of Swanwick J was the right order in the
circumstances of this case and I would dismiss the appeal.

WALLER LJ. I do not repeat the facts which have already been fully set out in the
judgment of Megaw LJ.

There can be no doubt that in the claim for this cause of action there has been inordinate
delay and that the defendants have been seriously prejudiced by that delay. I say this
because the first action was liable to be dismissed. The plaintiff claims, however, that by
virtue of s 2D of the Limitation Act 1939, as added by the Limitation Act 1975, he is

---

1   [1977] 2 All ER 801, [1978] AC 297

entitled to bring this claim because that section introduced new principles. He submits he
could have issued a writ even though there had been no previous proceedings, and the fact
of the issue of the previous writ was in his favour and not against him because it means that
the defendants at least were notified of the claim many years ago.

If a plaintiff who has started an action has instructed two firms of solicitors, one of whom
was retained for a period of 18 months and the other of whom for a period of about 12
months, and the plaintiff has been advised that he has no case, it is surprising, to say the
least, that he should be permitted to start another action for the same cause of action five
years after the first writ or two years after the second firm had ceased to act. If, however,
s 2D compels it in this case, then the action must be allowed to proceed.

The principles on which the court acts in cases where it is sought to strike out claims
under RSC Ord 18, r 19, have been fully considered by this court in *Allen v Sir Alfred
McAlpine & Sons Ltd*[1] and by the House of Lords in *Birkett v James*[2]. The latter case made
it clear that, unless there had been disobedience of a peremptory order, mere delay within
the statutory period of limitation would not be a ground for striking out. Counsel for the
plaintiff submits that, although the statutory period under s 2A has expired, since the court
has a discretion under s 2D to extend that period, and although there has been prejudice to
the defendants, s 2D requires the court to look at all the circumstances of the case and
enumerates some circumstances which may change the balance in favour of the plaintiff.
Further, he submits that this question is not for this court to consider because he might
wish to put other matters before the court. He further submits that it is not for this court
to consider on a question of striking out.

Taking the second part of his submission first, the papers before us show that there has
been an unusual amount of evidence put before the court which could only be relevant on
this issue. Further, in *Firman v Ellis*[3] it appears that the Court of Appeal was considering
this question on an application to strike out. I do not doubt that the substance of the
plaintiff's case is before us. I therefore go on to consider whether it could possibly be
argued that it would be equitable to allow this action to proceed.

It is at this point that I find myself disagreeing with the judgments already delivered.
I have already expressed the view that it would be surprising if the court were compelled
to allow this action to proceed. The defendants have come before the court in order to have
this action, which is admittedly prejudicial to them, dismissed. The limitation period
prescribed by s 2A has expired. It is for the plaintiff to show that it would be equitable to
allow the action to proceed.

Section 2D of the Limitation Act 1939 gives the court power to override time limits in
certain circumstances, and it provides:

'(1) If it appears to the court that it would be equitable to allow an action to proceed
having regard to the degree to which—(a) the provisions of section 2A or 2B of this Act
prejudice the plaintiff or any person whom he represents, and (b) any decision of the
court under this subsection would prejudice the defendant or any person whom he
represents, the court may direct that those provisions shall not apply to the action
. . .'

Then sub-s (3) says: 'In acting under this section the court shall have regard to all the
circumstances of the case and in particular . . .', and then the subsection sets out six separate
considerations. I deal with them one at a time in relation to this case.

'(a) the length of, and the reasons for, the delay on the part of the plaintiff.' In my
judgment this cannot possibly avail the plaintiff. He was aware of his claim at an early
stage and the delay can only be for one of two reasons: (1) that he was trying to find
somebody who would enable him to conduct the claim, his union and one firm of solicitors
having advised him that there was no case and another firm having been instructed for a

1   [1968] 1 All ER 543, [1968] 2 QB 229
2   [1977] 2 All ER 801, [1978] AC 297
3   [1978] 2 All ER 851, [1978] 3 WLR 1

period of twelve months not having then pursued the claim further; or (2) that he had allowed the whole matter to go to sleep until, many years later, he decided to revive it. In either of those cases they do not avail the plaintiff at all.

'(b) the extent to which, having regard to the delay, the evidence adduced or likely to be adduced by the plaintiff or the defendant is or is likely to be less cogent than if the action had been brought within the time allowed . . .' Again, this cannot possibly avail the plaintiff because it is clear that the more time goes by the more difficult it will be for either side to produce a case. The fact that they had notice of the claim in 1970 does not avail the defendants because they have filed away their papers as long ago as July 1974, the then works manager, who would be an important witness, has died, and their group medical officer, another important witness, is also believed to have died.

'(c) the conduct of the defendant after the cause of action arose . . .' In this case there can be nothing said against the conduct of the defendant and that does not avail the plaintiff.

'(d) the duration of any disability of the plaintiff arising after the date of the accrual of the cause of action.' That is not a matter which is of assistance in this case since the plaintiff at all times was of full age and sound mind (see s 31(2) and (3) of the 1939 Act).

'(e) the extent to which the plaintiff acted promptly and reasonably once he knew whether or not the act or omission of the defendant . . . might be capable . . . of giving rise to an action for damages.' This again does not assist because the plaintiff did act promptly in the first place.

'(f) the steps, if any, taken by the plaintiff to obtain medical, legal or other expert advice and the nature of any such advice he may have received.' Counsel for the plaintiff submits that he may, under this paragraph, be able to argue that it would be equitable to allow the plaintiff to proceed, and draws attention to the fact that there is now a consulting engineer's report. In my judgment this is fallacious. The plaintiff had consulted his union at the time and he had then consulted two firms of solicitors. I am prepared to assume that he had not previously obtained an engineer's report. If that was anybody's fault (and I do not suggest it was) it was certainly not the defendants'. I am unable to see how a consulting engineer's report made in 1975 can possibly avail the plaintiff. The factory is no longer occupied by the defendants and it would not be possible to identify the grinding machine on which the plaintiff worked. It inevitably follows that the consulting engineer's report cannot be based on a visit to the factory and can only be an expression of opinion based on information provided six years after the event by the plaintiff.

There may be cases where it would be right for the question arising under s 2D to be directed to be decided on summons before a judge. But where there is already admittedly much prejudice to the defendants it is in my opinion important that the question whether or not it is equitable to allow the case to proceed should if possible be decided at the earliest possible stage. All the evidence which has been put before the court is directed to this very issue and could be to no other. I regard it as unarguable that a consulting engineer's report, based as I have mentioned, could possibly make it equitable for the plaintiff to proceed after this delay. I am of opinion that it would not be equitable to allow this action to proceed. I would allow this appeal.

Appeal dismissed. Leave to appeal to the House of Lords granted.

Solicitors: *Hextall, Erskine & Co*, agents for *Cartwrights*, Bristol (for the defendants); *B M Birnberg & Co* (for the plaintiff).

Mary Rose Plummer   Barrister.

Practice Direction

FAMILY DIVISION

Practice – Matrimonial causes – Trial – Directions for trial – Defended causes – Pre-trial review – Registrar to ascertain true state of case and give directions for its disposal – Parties to be represented at pre-trial review by legal advisers conversant with case – Personal attendance of parties desirable – RSC Ord 25, Ord 34, r 5(3) – Matrimonial Causes Rules 1977 (SI 1977 No 344), rr 33(4) proviso, 46(4).

1. The proviso to r 33(4) of the Matrimonial Causes Rules 1977[1] enables a registrar to treat a request for directions for trial in a defended cause as a summons for directions under RSC Ord 25. In that event, the registrar is required to give the parties notice of a date, time and place at which the request will be considered (a 'pre-trial review'). The provisions of RSC Ord 34, r 5(3) (which provide for the parties to furnish the court with any information it may require as to the state of readiness of the case for trial) are applied to defended matrimonial causes by r 46(4) of the 1977 rules.

2. As from the beginning of the Hilary Term 1979 every request for directions for trial relating to a defended matrimonial cause proceeding in the Principal Registry will be referred to a registrar for a pre-trial review appointment to be fixed. Appointments are likely to be fixed for hearing from February onwards.

3. The prime objective behind the pre-trial review procedure is to enable the registrar to ascertain the true state of the case and to give such directions as are necessary for its 'just, expeditious and economic disposal'. In practice in those district registries where the system of pre-trial review has been applied to matrimonial causes, it has been found that under the registrar's guidance the parties are often able to compose their differences, or to drop unsubstantial charges and defences, and to concentrate on the main issues in dispute. Experience in the district registries has shown that, following pre-trial review, many cases proceed undefended under the special procedure, with consent orders as to financial provision or in respect of the custody of, or to access to, the children. Where contested issues remain, the registrar is able to give directions to facilitate their expeditious determination at the subsequent hearing before the judge.

4. To avoid possible adjournments and delay it is especially important that the parties are represented on a pre-trial review hearing by their legal advisers who are fully conversant with the facts of the case, including counsel if he has been so instructed. The personal attendance of the parties on the review hearing is normally desirable.

This practice note is issued with the approval of the President of the Family Division.

R L BAYNE-POWELL
19th December 1978   Senior Registrar.

---

1   SI 1977 No 344

Box Parish Council v Lacey

a

COURT OF APPEAL, CIVIL DIVISION
STAMP, ORMROD AND BRIDGE LJJ
21st, 22nd FEBRUARY, 24th MAY 1978

b   Commons – Registration – Common land and rights of common – Waste land of a manor – Requirements to constitute waste land of a manor – Waste land formerly part of manor severed from manor many years before date of registration – Whether waste land 'of a manor' – Whether waste land required to form part of a manor at date of registration or sufficient that it was formerly part of a manor – Commons Registration Act 1965, s 22(1).

c   The registrability as common land under s 1(1)[a] of the Commons Registration Act 1965 of waste land 'of a manor', within para (b) of the definition of 'common land' in s 22(1)[b] of that Act, depends on whether at the date of registration the land still forms part of the manor, since it is not sufficient that at the date of registration the land is merely waste land, which was formerly, but is no longer, part of that manor (see p 115 h to p 116 a and j to p 117 a, post).

d   Dictum of Foster J in Re Yateley Common, Hampshire, Arnold v Dodd [1977] 1 All ER at 517 and Re Chewton Common, Christchurch, Borough of Christchurch v Milligan [1977] 3 All ER 509 overruled.

Notes

For common and commonable lands, see 6 Halsbury's Laws (4th Edn) para 506, and for cases on the subject, see 11 Digest (Reissue) 27–37, 351–510.

e   For waste land of a manor, see 6 Halsbury's Laws (4th Edn) paras 510, 756, and for cases on the subject, see 11 Digest (Reissue) 23, 282–285.

For the Commons Registration Act 1965, s 22, see 3 Halsbury's Statutes (3rd Edn) 933.

Cases referred to in judgment

f
Attorney-General v Hanmer (1858) 27 LJ Ch 837, 31 LTOS 379, 22 JP 543, 4 Jur NS 751, 11 Digest (Reissue) 23, 283.

Chewton Common, Christchurch, Re, Borough of Christchurch v Milligan [1977] 3 All ER 509, [1977] 1 WLR 1242.

Doe d Clayton v Williams (1843) 11 M & W 803, 12 LJ Ex 429, 1 LTOS 316, 152 ER 1029, 13 Digest (Reissue) 9, 50.

Yateley Common, Hampshire, Re, Arnold v Dodd [1977] 1 All ER 505, [1977] 1 WLR 840.

g
,
Appeal

By a decision dated 17th January 1977 the chief commons commissioner, G D Squibb QC, refused to confirm the registration as common land, under the Commons Registration Act 1965, of land known as Box Hill Common, Box, Wiltshire, owned by George Thomas Lacey, on the ground that it was not waste land of a manor, within para (b) of the definition *h* of 'common land' in s 22(1) of the 1965 Act. Box Parish Council ('the parish council') appealed by case stated. By a judgment given on 13th October 1977 Foster J allowed the appeal and confirmed the registration of the land as common land. Mr Lacey appealed. The grounds of the appeal were that the judge erred in law in holding that the land was waste land of a manor, within s 22(1), although it had been severed from the manor of Box for many years and had not since then formed part of any manor, and that the decision in Re *j*   Chewton Common, Christchurch, Borough of Christchurch v Milligan[1], which the judge followed,

---

a   Section 1, so far as material, is set out at p 114 d, post
b   Section 22(1), so far as material, is set out at p 114 f, post
1   [1977] 3 All ER 509

was wrong in law and should be overruled. The facts are set out in the judgment of the court.

David Rowell for Mr Lacey.
John Bradburn for the parish council.

Cur adv vult

24th May. **STAMP LJ** read the following judgment of the court: This is an appeal by Mr George Thomas Lacey, who owns the land in question, from an order of Foster J made on 13th October 1977. By that order Foster J allowed an appeal by the Box (Wiltshire) Parish Council by way of case stated from a decision of the chief commons commissioner dated 17th January 1977 and confirmed, as the chief commissioner had refused to do, the registration of the land known as Box Hill Common, Box, Wiltshire, as common land under the Commons Registration Act 1965.

The question turns on whether the land was or was not 'common land' within the meaning of the 1965 Act at the date of its registration. That in turn depends on the construction of the interpretation section contained in the 1965 Act.

Section 1(1) of the 1965 Act provides for the registration of '(*a*) *land* . . . which is common land or a town or village green; (*b*) *rights of common* over such land; and (*c*) *persons* claiming to be, or found to be owners of such land . . .' Section 1(2) goes on to provide:

'. . . (*a*) no land capable of being registered under the Act shall be deemed to be common land or a town or village green unless it is so registered; and (*b*) no rights of common shall be exercisable over any such land unless they are registered either under the Act or under the Land Registration Acts 1925 and 1936.'

Before reciting the relevant facts it is convenient to refer to s 22(1) of the 1965 Act, which is the interpretation section, and which provides that:

'In this Act, unless the context otherwise requires,—"common land" means:—(*a*) land subject to rights of common (as defined in this Act) whether those rights are exercisable at all times or only during limited periods; (*b*) waste land of a manor not subject to rights of common; but does not include a town or village green or any land which forms part of a highway . . .'

The facts, so far as material for the purposes of determining the question which arises, are these. The land was formerly waste land of the manor of Box of which members of the Northey family were successively lords of the manor. It appears, however, that under the will of one Edward William Northey, a clergyman who died on 21st October 1914, and who was not lord of the manor, the land passed to his eldest son, who in 1924 sold it to a Mr Neate. So, long before 1922, the land and the lordship had been severed. The chief commons commissioner found as a fact that the land was 'open, uncultivated, and unoccupied', which was one of the descriptions of 'waste land' used by Watson B in *Attorney-General v Hanmer*[1], but that the land was not at the time of the registration 'subject to rights of common' as defined in the 1965 Act and so did not fall within para (*a*) of the definition in s 22(1).

Those being the facts, the whole question is whether, notwithstanding that the land had long since ceased to be part of the manor of Box, it still was at the date of the registration 'waste land of a manor not subject to rights of common' within the meaning of para (*b*) of the definition in s 22(1).

The judge in the court below, following the decision of Slade J in *Re Chewton Common*[2] and an earlier dictum in *Re Yateley Common*[3], held that so long as waste land was at some

1   (1858) 27 LJ Ch 837
2   [1977] 3 All ER 509, [1977] 1 WLR 1242
3   [1977] 1 All ER 505 at 517, [1977] 1 WLR 840 at 853

time in the past waste land of a manor it need not at the date of the registration still be
owned by the lord of the manor in order to fall within para (b) of the definition in s 22(1).
Slade J in *Re Chewton Common*[1] reasoned thus:

> 'In my judgment the phrase "waste land of a manor", used in relation to a particular
> piece of land in the context of a statute passed some forty years after copyhold tenure
> had been abolished, does not as a matter of legal language by any means necessarily
> import that the ownership of the land still rests with the lord of the relevant manor.
> The phrase in such a context is equally consistent with the sense that the land is waste
> land which, as a matter of history, was once waste land of a manor in the days when
> copyhold tenure still existed. Though the phrase has a strong retrospective flavour,
> now that manors in the pre-1926 sense no longer exist, I can see no sensible reason
> why the legislature in 1965 should have chosen to render the registrability or
> otherwise of waste land as "common land" dependent on whether immediately before
> 1st January 1926 the lordship of the relevant manor and the land itself were still
> united. Likewise I can see no good reason why Parliament should have chosen to
> make registrability dependent on whether, at the date of registration, the waste land
> still happens to be owned by the lord of the manor of which, historically, it had once
> formed part. To hold that it did would involve the conclusion that the lord of a manor
> could remove waste land of that manor not subject to rights entirely out of the ambit
> of the Act by the simple device of conveying the lordship to another person, while
> retaining the land, or vice versa.'

The judge added a little later in his judgment that he could not think that the legislature,
in using the phrase 'waste land of a manor', was intending the registrability or otherwise
of waste land as 'common land' to depend on such accidents as this.

If, however, one adopts the construction favoured by Slade and Foster JJ one is faced with
a similar improbability, for one asks the rhetorical question: why should Parliament have
chosen to make registrability dependent on whether the waste land had at some remote
date in the past been part or parcel of a manor?

The legislature must be taken to intend what is expressed and to use words in their
proper sense; and in the absence of anything in the relevant legislation to suggest another
construction, the language of the definition, with all respect to those who thought
otherwise, presents no difficulty.

Although copyholds were enfranchised by the effect of the Law of Property Act 1922,
the lord of the manor retained rights in respect of mines and minerals and franchises and
sporting rights. And the waste land of the manor was no less waste land of the manor after
the enfranchisement than it was before. If then one reads into s 1(1)(a) of the 1965 Act para
(b) of the definition in s 22(1), the relevant words of s 1(1) become 'there shall be registered
... land in England or Wales which *is* waste land of a manor not subject to rights of
common ...', and one has a provision which is surely without ambiguity as connoting
which *is* waste land of the manor at the date of registration. And as a matter of English the
phrase 'waste land of a manor not subject to rights of common' will hardly tolerate a
construction which will comprehend land which has long since ceased to be in any way
connected with a manor. The definition is expressed in a single phrase, not two phrases,
and it being accepted that in order to satisfy the definition the land must be 'waste land' at
the date of registration, it is inescapable that it must likewise be 'of the manor' at the date
of registration. It is to be emphasised that s 1(1) of the 1965 Act is in the present tense and
requires, by the effect of para (a) of that subsection, that land in England or Wales 'which
is common land or a town or village green' shall be registered, which points clearly to the
conclusion that in order to see whether a particular piece of land is registrable one must
have regard to its present characteristics. Accordingly, when one comes to para (b) of the
definition in s 22(1), all the characteristics there specified must be satisfied at the time of

---

1   [1977] 3 All ER 509 at 514–515, [1977] 1 WLR 1242 at 1249

registration and it would do violence to the language to hold it enough that the land is presently waste land and now or formerly 'of the manor'.   *a*

The court had its attention called to the several Acts of Parliament passed in comparatively recent times which have been concerned with rights of common, and more particularly the Metropolitan Commons Act 1876, the Urban Spaces Act 1906, s 193 of the Law of Property Act 1925 and the National Parks and Access to Countryside Act 1949, and counsel for the parish council pointed out the concern which Parliament has shown for giving to the public access over common lands. It was urged that the 1965 Act requiring   *b* registration, so it is to be surmised, was designed to prepare the way for further similar legislation. That may be so, but about that it is not necessary to speculate, for the 1965 Act clearly achieved other purposes. Once the registers are complete the 1965 Act should, by the effect of s 1(2), providing that no land capable of being registered under the Act shall be deemed to be common land and/or a town or village green unless it is so registered and that no rights of common shall be exercisable over any such land unless they are registered   *c* either under the 1965 Act or under the Land Registration Acts 1925 and 1936, bring to an end the unhappy history of disputes and litigation regarding such matters involving, as it did, expensive and difficult enquiries into the past. Furthermore, by the effect of s 10 of the 1965 Act, the registration of any land as common land or of any rights of common over such land is to be conclusive evidence of the matters registered as at the day of registration except where the registration is provisional only. And so there is another valuable provision,   *d* valuable to all who are concerned to know what rights exist over particular land.

What does clearly appear from the 1965 Act is that the legislature was concerned that the owner of any land which was registrable should be ascertained and the owner registered: see s 4 of the 1965 Act. It is also apparent that the legislature was concerned that where the owner could not be identified the local authority should 'take such steps for the protection of the land against unlawful interference as could be taken by an owner in possession of the   *e* land' and should be empowered to institute proceedings for any offence committed in respect of the land: see s 9 of the 1965 Act. These provisions perhaps provide the reason, for which Slade J searched in vain, why the legislature should have chosen registrability or otherwise of waste land to depend on whether it was still 'of the manor'. By 1965 upwards of 40 years had elapsed since the abolition of copyhold tenure and, as was pointed out in the course of the argument in this court, a situation had arisen when the lordship of a manor   *f* often carried with it nothing but a box of ancient deeds. There must by then have been many cases where the lord of the manor no longer lived in the vicinity of the manor and had disappeared. One knows only too well in this age of cars, caravans and campers, what happens where land, and more particularly waste land, is not looked after. And when the owner cannot be found the local authority may be in a difficulty in securing the protection of the waste land and compliance with its requirements. One may hazard a guess that this   *g* is why the legislature did elect to render the registration or otherwise of waste land as common land dependent on whether the lord of the manor still owned the land. But whether that be so or not, the argument based on the presumed intention of Parliament cannot avail against the clear expression of that intention.

Nor are we encouraged to adopt a construction of the relevant phrase which is not its natural construction by the consideration to which Slade J called attention, that unless you   *h* put a gloss on the words of para (b) of the definition in s 22(1) the lord of the manor could avoid registration. Section 13 of the 1965 Act provides for amendment of the register where land ceases to be common land, so where there are no rights of common and the land is registrable only because it is 'waste land of a manor' the lord of the manor can, as counsel for the parish council very properly called to our attention, in any event enclose and occupy the land and so avoid the registration.   *j*

Where, as here, the so-called waste land had more than 50 years before the 1965 Act ceased to have any connection at all with the manor of Box, it would be a misuse of language to describe it as waste land 'of the manor' of Box. Nor would you expect such land having none of the characteristics of common land except that it is open, uncultivated and unoccupied to be within the purview of 'An Act to provide for the registration of common *a*   land . . .' Unless, therefore, it is necessary to do so in order to give a sensible effect to the 1965 Act, we would reject the construction sought to be put on the definition on behalf of the parish council and adopted by the judge in the court below.

We have to add this, as we understand the decision of the chief commons commissioner an attempt was made before him to show that the definition would have no sensible effect unless a gloss be put on it. Issue appears to have been joined on the question whether there could strictly ever be 'waste land' of a reputed manor, and the chief commons commissioner

b   expressed the view that all manors are now reputed manors. On this basis the definition could never operate, and the chief commons commissioner got over this difficulty by finding that there could be waste land of a reputed manor. As authority for this proposition he cited *Doe d Clayton v Williams*[1]. Following the hearing of the appeal, the members of this court examined the facts and the judgment of Lord Abinger in *Doe d Clayton v Williams*[1] and we came to the conclusion that that case is not authority for the conclusion

c   at which the chief commons commissioner arrived. This being so, we asked counsel whether they would like an opportunity of further argument in court or would care to make written submissions on the point. They chose to take the latter course and we have had the advantage of most careful and learned submissions from both counsel. Among other things it was pointed out that the word 'manor' had been used in conveyancing statutes ever since the Conveyancing Act 1881 to include reputed manors, and that ever

d   since then a conveyance of a manor 'shall be deemed to include and shall by virtue of this Act operate to convey, with the manor, all . . . wastes . . . whatsoever, to the manor appertaining or reputed to appertain, or at the time of the conveyance demised, occupied, or enjoyed with the same, or reputed or known as part, parcel, or member thereof'. The relevant sections of the 1881 Act, namely ss 2(2)(iv) and 6(3), and the provisions of the 1925 legislation which replaced them, are, no doubt, of no direct application to the problem, but

e   they afford support for the view that, when 80 years later in 1965 the legislature used the simple phrase 'waste land of a manor not subject to rights of common' without further defining it, it was not drawing a distinction between manors and reputed manors and was using the expression 'waste land of a manor' to comprehend waste land of the lord of a reputed manor. So read the difficulty which the chief commons commissioner sought to overcome by reference to *Doe d Clayton v Williams*[1] does not arise. The appeal will be

f   allowed.

Appeal allowed. Leave to appeal to the House of Lords granted.

Solicitors: *Collyer-Bristow & Co*, agents for *Goughs*, Corsham (for Mr Lacey); *Simmons & Simmons* (for the parish council).

g

Avtar S Virdi Esq   Barrister.

---

1   (1843) 11 M & W 803

Belmont Finance Corporation Ltd v Williams Furniture Ltd and others

COURT OF APPEAL, CIVIL DIVISION
BUCKLEY, ORR AND GOFF LJJ
10th, 11th, 14th, 15th, 16th, 17th, 18th FEBRUARY 1977

Company – Conspiracy – Conspiracy by company's directors to enable purchase of company's shares with financial assistance from company – Whether directors' knowledge of illegality of transaction to be imputed to company – Whether company a co-conspirator with directors – Whether company entitled to sue directors – Companies Act 1948, s 54(1).

Pleading – Constructive trust – Knowledge of fraudulent or dishonest breach of trust required to be pleaded in clear and unequivocal terms – Whether allegation that defendant was aware or ought to have been aware of facts which showed a dishonest breach of trust sufficient – Whether defendant's knowledge of dishonesty of that breach of trust required to be pleaded – RSC Ord 18, r 15(1).

The first defendant owned all the shares in the second defendant which in turn owned all the shares of the plaintiff company, Belmont. The third to sixth defendants were the shareholders of another company, Maximum. The seventh and eighth defendants were directors of Belmont. The third to sixth defendants wished to purchase Belmont and on 3rd October 1963 they agreed to sell their shares in Maximum to Belmont for £500,000 and to purchase the share capital of Belmont from the second defendant for £489,000. At a board meeting of Belmont on 11th October at which the third to sixth defendants were also present, the seventh and eighth defendants, being a majority of Belmont's directors present, resolved that Belmont should implement the agreement of 3rd October and the transaction was completed later that day. Subsequently Belmont went into liquidation and its receiver commenced an action on behalf of Belmont against all the defendants alleging (i) that the value of Maximum's shares was only £60,000 and not £500,000, (ii) that the price of £500,000 for Maximum had been arrived at to enable the third to sixth defendants to purchase Belmont's share capital with money provided by Belmont, in contravention of s 54(1)[a] of the Companies Act 1948, (iii) that the defendants were 'aware or ought to have been aware' that the third to sixth defendants were unable to purchase Belmont's shares unless they obtained financial assistance from Belmont by its purchase of Maximum's shares at an inflated price, and, in the statement of claim, (iv) that the defendants had wrongfully conspired together to carry into effect the sale and purchase of Belmont's share capital in contravention of s 54(1) of the 1948 Act. Belmont claimed damages for conspiracy. At the trial Belmont also sought to claim that the defendants were liable as constructive trustees in respect of the misapplication of Belmont's assets by the seventh and eighth defendants in breach of their duties as directors of Belmont. The judge dismissed the action on the grounds (i) that Belmont was a party to the alleged conspiracy since it was a party to the agreement of 3rd October, and as a conspirator it could not sue its co-conspirators, and (ii) that, as the statement of claim did not allege that the defendants had knowledge that the seventh and eighth defendants' breach of trust was fraudulent or dishonest, it was not open to Belmont to claim relief against them as constructive trustees. Belmont appealed contending that it was not a party to the conspiracy because it did not have knowledge of the illegality of the agreement of 3rd October, that it was unnecessary to plead knowledge of fraud or dishonesty to found a claim based on breach of a constructive trust but was sufficient to plead knowing participation in a misfeasance

---

a   Section 54(1), so far as material, provides: 'Subject as provided in this section, it shall not be lawful for a company to give, whether directly or indirectly, and whether by means of a loan, guarantee, the provision of security or otherwise, any financial assistance for the purpose of or in connection with a purchase or subscription made or to be made by any person of or for any shares in the company, or, where the company is a subsidiary company, in its holding company . . .'

or breach of trust, and that, in any event, the facts as pleaded showed that the transaction in question was dishonest.

Held – (i) Having regard to the facts that s 54 of the 1948 Act was designed to protect a company where its shares were dealt with in breach of that section and that Belmont was a victim of the alleged conspiracy and since the essence of the agreement of 3rd October was to deprive it of a large part of its assets, the seventh and eighth defendants' knowledge that the agreement was illegal was not to be imputed to Belmont merely because those defendants were directors of Belmont. Accordingly, because Belmont did not have the necessary knowledge of the agreement's illegality, it was not a party to the conspiracy. However, even if Belmont had had knowledge of the illegality of the agreement of 3rd October it was not barred from claiming against the defendants because that agreement, although part of the means of implementing the conspiracy, was not in itself the conspiracy alleged since what had been alleged in the statement of claim was a prior conspiracy to enter into the transactions effected by the agreement. It followed that the judge had been wrong to dismiss the action (see p 125 g to j, p 126 a b, p 127 d to h, p 132 e, p 133 a b and f g and p 136 f, post); dicta of Viscount Dilhorne in *Churchill v Walton* [1967] 1 All ER at 503 and of Lord Denning MR in *Wallersteiner v Moir* [1974] 3 All ER at 239 applied; *Oram v Hutt* [1911–13] All ER Rep 376 considered.

(ii) The judge was, however, justified in holding that it was not open to Belmont on the pleadings as they stood to claim that there was a constructive trust, for in order to claim that a person was liable as a constructive trustee it was necessary to plead clearly and unequivocally that he had known that the breach of trust in respect of which it was sought to make him liable was 'fraudulent' or 'dishonest'. Although the statement of claim had pleaded all the facts necessary to show a dishonest breach of trust on the part of the seventh and eighth defendants, it had not, merely by pleading that the defendants were aware or ought to have been aware of those facts, clearly and unequivocally pleaded knowledge on their part of the dishonesty of that breach of trust and (per Goff LJ) it failed to comply with RSC Ord 18, r 15(1)[b], in that it did not specify the remedy or relief claimed in so far as it was based on a constructive trust (see p 130 c e and h to p 131 a and d e, p 132 d e, p 135 f to h and p 136 c and g, post); *Barnes v Addy* (1874) LR 9 Ch App 244 and *Davy v Garrett* (1878) 7 Ch D 473 applied; dictum of Ungoed-Thomas J in *Selangor United Rubber Estates Ltd v Cradock (No 3)* [1968] 2 All ER at 1105 disapproved.

Per Buckley LJ. (i) Although RSC Ord 18, r 15(1), requires that the statement of claim must state specifically the relief or remedy which the plaintiff claims, and a statement of claim must therefore specify at least one form of relief which the plaintiff claims, yet, on proof of the necessary facts the court is not confined to granting that particular form of relief but has jurisdiction to grant any relief that it thinks appropriate to the facts as proved. However, if a party seeks to raise in the course of the trial a new claim which has not been adumbrated in his pleading, the court should not give such relief without offering the opposing party an opportunity for an adjournment (see p 131 f and p 132 a b, post).

(ii) If the party sought to be made liable as a constructive trustee wilfully shuts his eyes to dishonesty, or wilfully or recklessly fails to make such enquiries as an honest and reasonable man would make, he may be found to have involved himself in the fraudulent character of the design, but otherwise, he should not be held to be affected by constructive notice (see p 130 f g, post).

Notes

For the ingredients of the tort of conspiracy, see 37 Halsbury's Laws (3rd Edn) 128, para 222.

For the provision of financial assistance by a company for the purchase of its own shares, see 7 Halsbury's Laws (4th Edn) para 208, and for cases on the subject, see 9 Digest (Reissue) 403–405, 2378–2379.

---

b   Rule 15(1) is set out at p 129 d, post.

For constructive trusts and the necessity for notice of the misappropriation of the trust property, see 38 Halsbury's Laws (3rd Edn) 855, 856, 859, paras 1440, 1441, 1447, and for cases on the subject, see 47 Digest (Repl) 180–192, 1493–1609.

For pleading fraud, see 30 Halsbury's Laws (3rd Edn) 17, para 36.

For the Companies Act 1948, s 54, see 5 Halsbury's Statutes (3rd Edn) 163.

Cases referred to in judgments

Alabaster v Harness [1895] 1 QB 339, [1891–4] All ER Rep 817, 64 LJQB 76, 71 LT 740, CA; *affg* [1894] 2 QB 897, 1 Digest (Repl) 96, 713.

Barnes v Addy (1874) LR 9 Ch App 244, 43 LJ Ch 513, 30 LT 4, LC & LJJ, 47 Digest (Repl) 191, 1593.

Bodenham v Hoskins (1852) 21 LJ Ch 864, [1843–60] All ER Rep 692, 19 LTOS 294; *affd* 2 De G M & G 903, LJJ, 1 Digest (Repl) 655, 2280.

Cargill v Bower (1878) 10 Ch D 502, 47 LJ Ch 649, 38 LT 779, 50 Digest (Repl) 118, 993.

Carl-Zeiss-Stiftung v Herbert Smith & Co (a firm) (No 2) [1969] 2 All ER 367, [1969] 2 Ch 276, [1969] 2 WLR 427, [1969] RPC 316, CA, Digest (Cont Vol C) 1040, 814a.

Churchill v Walton [1967] 1 All ER 497, [1967] 2 AC 224, [1967] 2 WLR 682, 131 JP 277, 51 Cr App R 212, HL, 14(1) Digest (Reissue) 126, 842.

Competitive Insurance Co Ltd v Davies Investments Ltd [1975] 3 All ER 254, [1975] 1 WLR 1240, Digest (Cont Vol D) 1011, 1554a.

Crofter Hand Woven Harris Tweed Co Ltd v Veitch [1942] 1 All ER 142, [1942] AC 435, 111 LJPC 17, 166 LT 172, HL, 45 Digest (Repl) 534, 1175.

Davy v Garrett (1878) 7 Ch D 473, 47 LJ Ch 218, 38 LT 77, CA, 50 Digest (Repl) 157, 1358.

Essex Aero Ltd v Cross [1961] Court of Appeal Transcript 388.

Karak Rubber Co Ltd v Burden (No 2) [1972] 1 All ER 1210, [1972] 1 WLR 602, [1972] 1 Lloyd's Rep 73, Digest (Cont Vol D) 53, 428b.

Lawrance v Lord Norreys (1890) 15 App Cas 210, [1886–90] All ER Rep 858, 59 LJ Ch 681, 62 LT 706, 54 JP 708, HL, 50 Digest (Repl) 21, 165.

Oram v Hutt [1914] 1 Ch 98, [1911–13] All ER Rep 376, 83 LJ Ch 161, 110 LT 187, 78 JP 51, CA, *affg* [1913] 1 Ch 259, 82 LJ Ch 152, 108 LT 410, 1 Digest (Repl) 82, 620.

Selangor United Rubber Estates Ltd v Cradock [1964] 3 All ER 709, [1965] Ch 896, [1965] 2 WLR 67, 50 Digest (Repl) 197, 1648.

Selangor United Rubber Estates Ltd v Cradock (a bankrupt) (No 3) [1968] 2 All ER 1073, [1968] 1 WLR 1555, [1968] 2 Lloyd's Rep 289, 9 Digest (Reissue) 403, 2379.

Sterman v E W & W J Moore Ltd (a firm) [1970] 1 All ER 581, [1970] 1 QB 596, [1970] 2 WLR 386, CA, 50 Digest (Repl) 1083, 1281a.

Wallersteiner v Moir, Moir v Wallersteiner [1974] 3 All ER 217, [1974] 1 WLR 991, CA, Digest (Cont Vol D) 1042, 1455b.

Interlocutory appeal

The plaintiff, Belmont Finance Corpn Ltd, by a receiver appointed out of court under debentures issued by the company, brought an action against the defendants, Williams Furniture Ltd (formerly Easterns Ltd), City Industrial Finance Ltd, James Peter Grosscurth, Andreas Demetri, Kenneth Maund, John Sinclair Copeland, Archie Spector and Frank Victor Smith, claiming (i) a declaration that a transaction effected by an agreement dated 3rd October 1963 made between the first three defendants and the plaintiff was unlawful and void under s 54 of the Companies Act 1948, (ii) damages and (iii) all necessary accounts and enquiries. Further and in the alternative the plaintiff claimed against the seventh and eighth defendants a declaration that they were guilty of misfeasance and breach of trust in relation to the plaintiff, as its directors, in procuring the plaintiff to enter into an unlawful agreement, and/or in procuring the purchase by the plaintiff of certain shares at a price which to the knowledge of those defendants was greatly in excess of the true value of the shares, and compensation for such misfeasance and breach of trust.

The third defendant, Mr Grosscurth, was a bankrupt and did not enter an appearance to the action. Shortly before the trial the plaintiff reached a compromise with the fifth defendant, Mr Maund. Early in 1970 the action was discontinued against the eighth defendant, Mr Smith, on compassionate grounds. At the trial of the action the plaintiff asserted that on the pleadings in the statement of claim it was entitled to claim additional relief against all defendants, on the basis of constructive trust.

On 30th July 1976 Foster J, at the close of the plaintiff's case, dismissed the action on the grounds that there was no case to answer on the claim for conspiracy, and that it was not open to the plaintiff, on the case as pleaded, to claim relief on the basis of constructive trust. The plaintiff appealed. The facts are set out in the judgment of Buckley LJ.

Michael Miller QC and *M J Roth* for the plaintiff.
Nicolas Browne-Wilkinson QC and *Brian Parker* for the first and second defendants.
Nicholas Stewart for the fourth and sixth defendants.
Gerald Godfrey QC and *Ian McCulloch* for the seventh defendant.

BUCKLEY LJ. On 30th July 1976 Foster J dismissed this action at the close of the plaintiff's case on the submission of the defendants that there was no case to answer in relation to an alleged conspiracy and that it was not open to the plaintiff on the statement of claim to seek relief on the basis of constructive trust.

The facts are these. Before the transaction out of which the action arose took place, the second defendant, a wholly-owned subsidiary of the first defendant, owned all the issued shares of the plaintiff; the third, fourth, fifth and sixth defendants owned between them all the shares in a company called Maximum Finance Ltd (to which I shall refer as 'Maximum'); another company, called Cityfields Properties Ltd, was a wholly-owned subsidiary of Maximum; the seventh and eighth defendants were at all relevant times directors of the plaintiff.

The third, fourth, fifth and sixth defendants wished to acquire the share capital of the plaintiff; for this purpose they required finance. The form which the transaction took was in essence this, that under a written agreement of 3rd October 1963, the third, fourth, fifth and sixth defendants sold all their shares in Maximum to the plaintiff at the price of £500,000 and bought all the issued shares of the plaintiff from the second defendant for £489,000. If the share capital of Maximum was worth £500,000, there would have been nothing wrong with this, but the plaintiff asserts that the shares of Maximum were not worth more than about £60,000, and that to the extent that the plaintiff did not get value for money it was giving the third, fourth, fifth and sixth defendants financial aid for the purchase of its own shares, in contravention of s 54 of the Companies Act 1948.

The action is brought in the name of the plaintiff by a receiver appointed out of court under debentures issued by the plaintiff. The plaintiff is now in compulsory liquidation and the receiver has prosecuted the action under the direction of the Companies Court.

On account of the way in which the case went, the judge has heard the evidence of the plaintiff's side only; he has heard no evidence of, or on behalf of, any defendant. He made no findings of fact; in view of his judgment it was unnecessary for him to do so. He dealt with the case on the plaintiff's pleading, and on that alone he held that since the agreement is alleged to have formed part of the alleged conspiracy, and since the plaintiff was a party to the agreement, the plaintiff was a conspirator. So he held that the claim in conspiracy failed in limine on the ground that one party to a conspiracy to do an unlawful act cannot sue a co-conspirator in relation to that act. He also held that on the statement of claim it was not open to the plaintiff to claim relief against the defendants on a basis of constructive trust.

It is common ground that for the purposes of this appeal we must assume that the plaintiff will be able to establish all the allegations in its statement of claim. When considering the statement of claim, two questions have to be kept in mind. First, on the allegations contained in it, was the judge right in holding that the plaintiff could not maintain its claim to relief on the basis that the defendants had conspired to the damage of the plaintiff? Secondly, on those same allegations and having regard to the form of the indorsement on the writ and the prayer for relief in the statement of claim, is the plaintiff entitled to any relief on the basis of constructive trust? The plaintiff asks us to hold that the judge was wrong in holding that the plaintiff could not succeed on the conspiracy point and in holding that the constructive trust point was not open to the plaintiff on the statement of claim. If he was right on the latter point, the plaintiff says that the judge should have allowed an amendment of the statement of claim, which in fact he refused.

The indorsement on the writ is in precisely the same form as the claim to relief in the statement of claim, to which I shall come in due course. The statement of claim pleads the agreement which I have mentioned, the effect of which was as follows. By the agreement (a) the third defendant agreed to sell and the plaintiff agreed to buy all the issued share capital of Maximum for £500,000; that is cl 2. (b) Such sale was to be completed on 11th October 1963; that is cl 3. (c) Subject to and on the completion of that sale, the second defendant agreed to sell and the third defendant to buy all the share capital of the plaintiff for £489,000 (cl 4) subject to adjustment as provided by cl 5. (d) The last-mentioned sale was to be completed immediately after the completion of the sale of the share capital of Maximum; that is cl 6. (I pause there to say, in parenthesis, that it is important to notice the close relationship between the two transactions, the purchase of the plaintiff's share capital being conditional on the sale of the Maximum shares having been completed, and itself to follow immediately after the completion of the sale of the Maximum shares.) (e) On completion of the sale of the share capital to the plaintiff the second defendant agreed to subscribe at par for 230,000 5 per cent redeemable preference shares of £1 each in the plaintiff, and to reconstitute the board of the plaintiff in accordance with nominations by the third defendant; and the third defendant agreed to subscribe at par for 20,000 5 per cent redeemable preference shares and 50,000 ordinary shares, all of £1 each, of the plaintiff; that is cl 2. There then follow some provisions of a subsidiary character, which I need not read; then (f) by cl 13 the third defendant warranted the correctness of the balance sheets of Maximum and Cityfield Properties Ltd, and certain ancillary matters designed to ensure that those balance sheets should substantially represent the state of those two companies at the completion of the sale of the share capital to Maximum. (g) The third defendant further warranted that the aggregate net profits before tax of Maximum and its subsidiaries for the period 22nd May 1962 to 31st May 1968 should not be less than £500,000; that is cl 13(h)(i). (h) Such last-mentioned warranty was to be secured by a deposit of the whole listed share capital of a company called Rentahome Ltd; that is cl 13(h)(ii). (i) The first and second defendants gave the third defendants certain warranties relating to the plaintiff and certain indemnities; that is cl 14. (j) The first defendant guaranteed to the third defendant the second defendant's due performance of the agreement. That agreement is incorporated by reference into the statement of claim.

The statement of claim proceeds to contain the following allegations. I do not read them in the language of the pleader, but in an abbreviated form, with the exception of certain paragraphs towards the end. It is alleged (a) that the fourth, fifth and sixth defendants were associates of the first defendant and active participants in negotiating and procuring the agreement; para 5. (b) That the seventh and eighth defendants and another were at all material times until 11th October 1963 directors of the plaintiff; para 6. (c) That the terms of the agreement were approved at a board meeting of the plaintiff on 3rd October 1963, which was attended by the seventh defendant and one other director of the plaintiff; para 8. (d) That at a board meeting of the plaintiff held at noon on 11th October 1963, at which the seventh and eighth defendants and another director of the plaintiff were present as directors, it was resolved that the plaintiff should purchase from the third, fourth and fifth defendants the issued share capital of Maximum for £500,000; para 9. (e) That the purchase was completed at that board meeting; para 9 (A). (f) That the board meeting was attended by the third, fourth, fifth and sixth defendants, by an accountant employed by the first defendant and its secretary and by the third defendant's solicitor; para 9 (B). (g) That on or about 11th October 1963 the second defendant resolved to sell the issued share capital of the plaintiff to the third defendant or as he should direct and that that transaction was completed on 11th October 1963, the 200,000 issued shares in the plaintiff company being transferred as to 116,668 to the third defendant, as to 41,666 to the fourth defendant and as to 41,666 to the fifth defendant; para 9 (A). (h) That at a further board meeting of the

plaintiff held in the afternoon of 11th October 1963, at which the same persons were
present as were present at the board meeting held at noon on that day, the rest of the terms
of the agreement were completed; paras 10 and 10(A). (i) That the initial negotiations for
the third defendant's purchase of the shares of the plaintiff were conducted between the
third defendant and one Lipert, then chairman of the second defendant, in the course of
which the third defendant wrote to the said Lipert a letter, from which I read this passage:
'. . . my present intention is to arrange the consideration for the purchase of [the plaintiff]
from [the plaintiff's] own resources and this I propose to accomplish by selling to [the
plaintiff] the whole of the issued share capital of Rentahome.' (j) That later, in the course
of negotiations, the third defendant wrote to one James, who was by then the chairman of
the first and second defendants, a letter, from which I read this passage:

> 'I am sorry that it has taken me so long to write to you with firm proposals for the
> mechanics of the purchase of [the plaintiff], following the news that I am unable to
> sell shares in Rentahome Limited because of the consequences of the Finance Act,
> 1962. Following our recent meeting, I have given considerable thought to your very
> helpful suggestions, but I have come to the conclusion that it would be more
> convenient for the transaction to proceed as follows: (1) that you or your associates
> should lend me by way of bridging finance, the amount required for completion say
> £480,000. (2) That I personally should purchase from [the second defendant] the
> Share Capital of [the plaintiff] for say £480,000. (3) That [the second defendant]
> should subscribe at par for £230,000 of Redeemable Preference Shares in [the
> plaintiff]. (4) That [the plaintiff] should purchase from me the whole of the Share
> Capital of Maximum Finance Limited for £500,000 (this will avoid me showing a
> large loan in [the plaintiff's] Accounts and deal with the Section 54 difficulty). (5)
> That I will repay the bridging loan of £480,000 and my costs out of the proceeds of
> sale of Maximum Finance.'

(k) That in the event the transaction proceeded on the basis of the agreement without any
bridging finance; para 16. There then come four very important paragraphs, which I shall
read in their entirety:

> '(17) The value of the entire share capital of Maximum Finance Ltd. was
> considerably less than the said sum of £500,000 as is borne out by its balance sheets
> and profit and loss accounts as at the 31st May 1963, 31st August 1963 and 31st
> August 1964. The said sum of £500,000 had been arrived at in order to enable [the
> third, fourth and fifth defendants] to purchase the plaintiff company's shares with
> money provided by it in contravention of Section 54 of the Companies Act 1948. A
> receiver and manager of Maximum Finance Ltd. was appointed on the 1st December
> 1966. The Statement of Affairs as at the 2nd December 1966 discloses a deficiency as
> regards creditors in the sum of £176,269.
> '(18) The defendants and each of them were at all material times aware or ought to
> have been aware of the fact that the [third, fourth and fifth defendants] were unable
> to purchase the share capital of [the plaintiff] unless they obtained financial assistance
> from [the plaintiff] through the purchase by it of their shares in Maximum Finance
> Ltd. at an inflated price [and then there is a reference to not being able to give
> particulars until after discovery].
> '(19) The defendants wrongfully conspired together to carry into effect the said sale
> and purchase of the entire share capital of the plaintiff company in contravention of
> the provisions of Section 54 of the Companies Act 1948 [and then it states what is to
> be found in that section].
> '(20) Further and in the alternative [the seventh and eighth defendants] are guilty
> of misfeasance and breach of trust in their capacities as directors of [the plaintiff] in
> procuring it to enter into the Agreement in contravention of Section 54 of the said
> Act.'

Paragraph 22 pleads damage and gives particulars from which it appears that the value which is put by the pleader on the entire share capital of Maximum is £60,038; the damages claimed is the difference between £500,000 and that sum of £60,038.

The relief claimed was in these terms:

'The plaintiff company's claim is against all the defendants for (1) a declaration that the transaction effected by the agreement dated the 3rd October 1963 and made between [the third defendant] of the first part, [the plaintiff] of the second part, [the second defendant] of the third part and [the first defendant] of the fourth part was unlawful and void under the provisions of Section 54 of the Companies Act 1948. (2) Damages with interest thereon from the 11th October 1963 to payment or judgment under the Law Reform (Miscellaneous Provisions) Act 1934. (3) All necessary accounts and inquiries.'

Then:

'Further and in the alternative against [the seventh and eighth defendants] for (4) A declaration that the said defendants and each of them were guilty of misfeasance and breach of trust in relation to the plaintiff company as directors in procuring the plaintiff company to enter into the said unlawful agreement dated the 3rd October 1963.

'(5) Alternatively a declaration that the said defendants and each of them were guilty of misfeasance and breach of trust in relation to the plaintiff company as directors in procuring the purchase by the plaintiff company of the entire share capital in Maximum Finance Limited at a price of £500,000 which was to the knowledge of the defendants greatly in excess of the true value of such shares.

'(6) An order that all necessary accounts and inquiries may be taken and made for ascertaining what sums the said [seventh and eighth defendants] are liable to contribute to the assets of the plaintiff company by way of compensation for such misfeasance and breach of trust in procuring the plaintiff company to enter into the said agreement dated the 3rd October 1963 and/or for the purchase of the said shares in Maximum Finance Limited.

'(7) An order that the said [seventh and eighth defendants] do jointly and severally contribute to the assets of the plaintiff company and do pay to the plaintiff all such sums as they may be found liable to contribute to such assets on taking and making such accounts and inquiries as aforesaid with interest on such sums from the 11th October 1963 to payment or judgment under the Law Reform (Miscellaneous Provisions) Act 1934.'

Then: 'Against all the defendants for: (8) Costs; (9) Further or Other Relief.'

I shall deal first with the conspiracy claim. The plaintiff's argument is to the following effect. On the allegations in the statement of claim, the agreement was illegal, and they say that an agreement between two or more persons to effect any unlawful purpose, with knowledge of all the facts which are necessary ingredients of illegality, is a conspiracy; and we were referred to *Crofter Hand Woven Harris Tweed Co Ltd v Veitch*[1] and *Churchill v Walton*[2]. The agreement was carried out, and damaged the plaintiff.

In the course of the argument in this court counsel for the first and second defendants conceded that the plaintiff is entitled in this appeal to succeed on the conspiracy point, unless it is debarred from doing so on the ground that it was a party to the conspiracy, which was the ground that was relied on by the judge.

The plaintiff points out that the agreement was resolved on by a board of which the seventh and eighth defendants constituted the majority, and that they were the two directors who countersigned the plaintiff's seal on the agreement, and that they are sued as two of the conspirators. It is conceded by counsel for the plaintiff that a company may be held to be a participant in a criminal conspiracy, and that the illegality attending a

---

1   [1942] 1 All ER 142, [1942] AC 435
2   [1967] 1 All ER 497, [1967] 2 AC 224

conspiracy cannot relieve the company on the ground that such an agreement may be ultra vires; but he says that to establish a conspiracy to which the plaintiff was a party, having as its object the doing of an illegal act, it must be shown that the company must be treated as knowing all the facts relevant to the illegality; he relies on *Churchill v Walton*[1], to which I have already referred.

The plaintiff in its reply denies being a party to the conspiracy and, says counsel for the plaintiff, it would be for the defendants to allege the necessary knowledge on the part of the plaintiff. But he further submits that even if the plaintiff should be regarded as a party to the conspiracy, this would not debar the plaintiff from relief; and he relies on *Oram v Hutt*[2].

The defendants' argument on this part of the case was to the following effect: that no party to an illegal contract can sue any other party to it on the contract. Here, counsel for the first and second defendants says that the plaintiff relies on the agreement to establish the conspiracy; that the conspiracy involved the agreement, and he refers to para 19 of the statement of claim, which I have read, and to the particulars given under it. These were particulars given in response to a request for particulars of the allegation that the defendants wrongfully conspired together, specifying all facts and matters relied on in support of this allegation, and the answer to that request is in the following terms:

'The best particulars which the plaintiff can give of overt acts of the parties to the said conspiracy are the negotiations which took place between the defendants and/or their respective solicitors and/or their duly appointed agents both at meetings between two or more of them and through the correspondence disclosed in this action, and the entry by the parties into the agreement on the 3rd October 1963 the completion thereof on the 11th October 1963 as alleged in the re-re-amended statement of claim and the concurrence in the agreement by [the fourth, fifth and sixth defendants] as evidenced in the correspondence.'

So, submits counsel for the first and second defendants, the plaintiff cannot seek relief in respect of the transactions there agreed on, that is to say, agreed on in the agreement; one joint tortfeasor cannot sue another for damages suffered by the plaintiff tortfeasor in consequence of the tort. But I feel impelled to ask: can the plaintiff sensibly be regarded as a party to the conspiracy, and in law ought it to be regarded as a party to the conspiracy? Section 54 of the Companies Act 1948 is designed for the protection of the relevant company whose shares are dealt with in breach of the section; that was so held in *Wallersteiner v Moir*[3].

In the present case the object of the alleged conspiracy was to deprive the plaintiff of over £400,000 worth of its assets, assuming always, of course, that the plaintiff succeeds in establishing that allegation. The plaintiff was the party at which the conspiracy was aimed. It seems to me that it would be very strange that it should also be one of the conspirators. The majority of the board which committed the plaintiff to carry out the project consisted of two of the alleged conspirators.

The judge said that the plaintiff was a vital party to the agreement, and it could not be said that the other parties were conspirators but not the plaintiff. With deference to the judge, who I think probably had very much less reference to authority in the course of the argument before him than we have had in this court, that view seems to me to be too simplistic a view, and not to probe far enough into the true circumstances of the case.

On the footing that the directors of the plaintiff who were present at the board meeting on 11th October 1963 knew that the sale of the Maximum shares was at an inflated value, and that such value was inflated for the purpose of enabling the third, fourth, fifth and sixth defendants to buy the share capital of the plaintiff, those directors must be taken to have known that the transaction was illegal under s 54. It may emerge at a trial that the facts are not as alleged in the statement of claim, but if the allegations in the statement of

1   [1967] 1 All ER 497, [1967] 2 AC 224
2   [1914] 1 Ch 98, [1911–13] All ER Rep 376
3   [1974] 3 All ER 217, [1974] 1 WLR 991

claim are made good, the directors of the plaintiff must then have known that the transaction was an illegal transaction. But in my view such knowledge should not be imputed to the plaintiff, for the essence of the arrangement was to deprive it improperly of a large part of its assets. As I have said, the plaintiff was a victim of the conspiracy. I think it would be irrational to treat the directors, who were allegedly parties to the conspiracy, notionally as having transmitted this knowledge to the plaintiff; and indeed it is a well-recognised exception from the general rule that a principal is affected by notice received by his agent that, if the agent is acting in fraud of his principal and the matter of which he has notice is relevant to the fraud, that knowledge is not to be imputed to the principal. So in my opinion the plaintiff should not be regarded as a party to the conspiracy, on the ground of lack of the necessary guilty knowledge.

Even though the plaintiff was to be supposed to be aware of the illegality, would this disentitle it to relief against co-conspirators? In *Oram v Hutt*[1], which I have already mentioned, the plaintiff was a member of a trade union and he sued, as a member of the trade union, to obtain relief for the union itself, which was an unincorporated body. The union had passed a resolution that it would indemnify any official of the union who took legal proceedings against one of the members of the union, called McNicholas, for defamation, and in reliance on that indemnity Mr Johnson, who was the general secretary of the union, sued Mr McNicholas for damages for defamation. He was successful and recovered damages. The union paid the solicitor who acted for Mr Johnson £775. Mr Oram, the plaintiff, sued for a declaration that the payment was ultra vires and asked for an order for the repayment of the money to the union. The matter came before Swinfen Eady J at first instance, who held[2] that the union had no power to authorise its officers to take proceedings for slander at the expense of the union and that the payment made in respect of the costs of Mr Johnson's action were invalid on the ground that they offended against the law of maintenance. He took the further subsidiary view that the acts of the union were ultra vires, inasmuch as the rules of the union did not specifically provide for the step that was taken; and he made a declaration and an order for the repayment of the £775 paid to Mr Johnson's solicitors.

In this court Lord Parker of Waddington dealt with the matter in this way[3]:

'The first question for decision, therefore, is whether the agreement by the association to indemnify any of its officers who took proceedings against McNicholas for libel was void on the ground of maintenance. In my opinion Swinfen Eady J. was bound and this Court is bound to hold this agreement void unless this case can be distinguished from the case of *Alabaster* v. *Harness*[4].'

He then discussed *Alabaster v Harness*[4] and came to the conclusion that the case then before the court could not be distinguished from that case, and he went on to say[5]: 'The question remains whether the payments in question were justified on any other ground.' He discussed that and he came to the conclusion that they were not, and in the result he said: 'I have come to the conclusion therefore that the appeal must be dismissed.'

Lord Sumner, who was also sitting in this court on that case, held that the law of maintenance affected the case and that the transactions were illegal on that ground, and he also agreed with Swinfen Eady J.

Warrington J, who was the third member of the court, said[6]:

'If the transaction amounted to maintenance on the part of the association, then the payment in question was made in pursuance of an illegal contract, and, in my opinion, it is impossible to hold that to make such a payment can be within the wide

---

1   [1914] 1 Ch 98, [1911–13] All ER Rep 376
2   [1913] 1 Ch 259
3   [1914] 1 Ch 98 at 104, [1911–13] All ER Rep 376 at 378
4   [1894] 2 QB 897; affd [1895] 1 QB 339, [1891–4] All ER Rep 817
5   [1914] 1 Ch 98 at 105, [1911–13] All ER Rep 376 at 378
6   [1914] 1 Ch 98 at 109, [1911–13] All ER Rep 376 at 380–381

a   powers of the association. I think, therefore, that the judgment of the learned judge was right and that this appeal fails.'

Counsel for the plaintiff put that case forward as authority for the proposition that the illegality of the agreement did not debar the union from relief, and he asked rhetorically: 'Why should having been a party to the agreement here debar the plaintiff from relief?'

Counsel for the first and second defendants has emphasised that in *Oram v Hutt*[1] the court came to the conclusion that the payments by the union were ultra vires payments; b   consequently no title to the property in the sum of £775 passed when the payment was made, all parties to the agreement being aware of the circumstances, the solicitor being also the solicitor to the union and Mr Johnson being its general secretary, and that accordingly the union did not have to rely on the illegal contract in any way for the purpose of making a case for recovery of the money; it relied on its own legal ownership of the money, which had never been determined as a result of the payment to Mr Johnson or his solicitors. He c   said that that case is unlike the present one because, as he contends, the claim in conspiracy in the case before us is founded on the illegal agreement and the plaintiff was a party to that agreement and to its being carried into effect.

I think one must look with some care at what is alleged to have been the conspiracy. I have read para 19 of the statement of claim, which asserts that the defendants wrongfully conspired to carry into effect the sale and purchase of the share capital to the plaintiff. The d   sale and purchase of the share capital of the plaintiff is to be found in the agreement, that is, the agreement for the sale and the agreement for the purchase, and as I read this paragraph the allegation is that antecedent to the agreement being entered into the conspirators conspired, the effect of the conspiracy being that they would enter into the agreement; and when one comes to look at the particulars delivered under para 19 one finds that there are relied on as overt acts of the parties to the conspiracy the negotiations e   and the correspondence which took place before the agreement was entered into, the entry into the agreement and its completion. I cannot understand how the negotiations could be overt acts of the conspiracy unless the conspiracy existed before those negotiations took place because, as I understand it, an overt act establishing the existence of a conspiracy is an overt act which shows that the agreement which is alleged to be conspiratorial has already been made. The entering into of the agreement of 3rd October 1963 is referred to in these f   particulars, as I read them, as part of the implementation of the conspiracy, not as itself constituting the conspiracy, and in the same way the completion of that agreement is part of the implementation.

So for my part I do not feel able to accept the contention of counsel for the first and second defendants that the conspiracy here is founded on the illegal agreement. It is quite true that the illegal agreement was part and parcel of the implementation, but it seems to g   me that the allegation of a conspiracy relates to something different.

The plaintiff, not being shown to have knowledge of the facts relevant to the illegality of the agreement, is not in my judgment debarred from suing the defendants for damages for the conspiracy, because the plaintiff is not shown to have been a party to the conspiracy or to guilty knowledge about the illegality of the transaction which was to be carried out under the agreement. On these grounds it seems to me that it is mistaken to regard the h   plaintiff as being in law party to the conspiracy. I feel glad to be able to reach that decision because, for reasons that I indicated at the beginning of this section of my judgment, it seems to me to be completely unreal to regard the plaintiff as party to the conspiracy. Accordingly, in my judgment, the judge was wrong in dismissing the action on that ground.

I come now to the subject of constructive trust. It should be realised that the claim in j   constructive trust came into the case only during the hearing before the judge. That arose in this way. The pleadings were framed in the way I have indicated and the case came before the judge with the statement of claim in that form. Shortly before the trial opened,

1   [1914] 1 Ch 98, [1911–13] All ER Rep 376

the plaintiff had reached a compromise with the fifth defendant, Mr Kenneth Maund, and the action was settled as far as he was concerned. The other defendants became aware of this when the trial opened and they asked to be allowed to know the terms of the settlement with Mr Maund, which ultimately they received, I think on about the second or third day of the trial. There was then a request by all the defendants before the court for an adjournment so that they could amend their pleadings to plead that the settlement with Mr Maund operated as a release of all the other alleged conspirators from any liability on the alleged conspiracy. Those amendments will be found now incorporated in the pleadings.

We have not been concerned with that question at all; it has not yet been judicially considered in any way. The reason for that is that during the adjournment the plaintiff's advisers gave notice of the fact that they would raise not only a claim for damages for conspiracy, but also a claim asserting that the defendants are liable as constructive trustees. The settlement with Mr Maund would not affect the viability of that claim in any way; so if the plaintiff is allowed to bring in, or to pursue, the claim of constructive trust there was no immediate purpose in pursuing the question of whether the settlement with Mr Maund had released the other defendants from their liability under the alleged conspiracy, because the facts relied on by the plaintiff in support of the constructive trust claim are the same, or substantially the same, as the facts relied on in the conspiracy claim.

But it is of some importance to realise that when the parties were preparing for trial, and indeed when the case came before the trial judge and for the first few days of the trial, the only claim before him was the claim in damages for conspiracy. Counsel for the plaintiff asserts that on the facts pleaded in the statement of claim, although there is no reference in it to constructive trusteeship, the plaintiff is entitled to relief on that footing against all the defendants before the court. I should perhaps have said that not all the original defendants were before the court: the third defendant is a bankrupt and is in default of appearance; Mr Maund, as I say, has been disposed of by compromise; and early in 1970 the action was discontinued against the eighth defendant, who I understand was a man of little substance and we were told that the proceedings were discontinued against him on compassionate grounds. But the claim in constructive trust is asserted against all the other defendants.

Counsel for the plaintiff contends that the statement of claim does not need any amendment, accountability on the footing of a constructive trust flowing as a legal result from the pleaded facts. He says that on those facts, particularly paras 17, 18 and 19 of the statement of claim, if proved, the court ought to find the plaintiff entitled to damages for conspiracy, and grant to the plaintiff any other relief to which, on those facts, it can show that it is entitled, particularly by way of account against all the participants in the conspiracy, because, he says, the legal consequences of the facts are to bring home to the participants in the conspiracy participation in a transaction which involved misapplying the plaintiff's assets in breach of trust, that is to say, in breach of the duties of the directors of the plaintiff and in breach of s 54 of the 1948 Act, and he emphasises that that section creates a criminal liability; he does that to emphasise the undesirable nature of the transaction.

Distinguishing the decision of Pennycuick J in *Selangor United Rubber Estates Ltd v Cradock*[1], counsel for the plaintiff says that the plaintiff does not in this case rely on any duty owed to him by the first and second defendants in his claim against those defendants as constructive trustees, but on the fact that in consequence of their conduct those two defendants are accountable on the basis of constructive trusteeship and therefore, he says, an allegation of the particular relationship giving rise to accountability is not necessary.

The plaintiff founds this part of its case on the statement of principle of Lord Selborne LC in *Barnes v Addy*[2] to the effect that anyone who assists with knowledge a dishonest or fraudulent design on the part of trustees is liable to be treated as a constructive trustee. Counsel for the plaintiff says that there is no need to plead fraud, and that knowing

---

1   [1964] 3 All ER 709, [1965] Ch 896
2   (1874) LR 9 Ch App 244 at 251–252

participation in a misfeasance or breach of trust ought to be held as a sufficient basis to claim liability on the footing of constructive trusteeship particularly if, as in the present case, the action complained of is of a criminal character directed to depriving the plaintiff of assets; he says that such an act must be sufficiently dishonest for the purposes of the doctrine. He admits that this is an extension of the rule as formulated by Lord Selborne LC; but he says that it is an extension which this court ought to make. He says moreover that there are here in fact sufficient facts pleaded to demonstrate that the transaction here in question was truly a dishonest transaction. Moreover, he says that the statement of claim shows that the second defendant and the third defendant received moneys of the plaintiff, or money which for the present purpose sufficiently represents the plaintiff's money, in circumstances which would support a claim of constructive trusteeship under the other head mentioned by Lord Selborne LC, which relates to cases in which the defendant has received and has become accountable for some part of the trust property. That, shortly, and I hope not too inadequately, describes the nature of the plaintiff's argument.

The defendants have relied to a great extent on the rules of court relating to pleadings. They have referred us to RSC Ord 6, r 2, which relates to the indorsement of the claim on the writ and statement of claim, which is required to contain a concise statement of the nature of the claim made or the relief or remedy required.

Counsel for the first and second defendants also referred us to RSC Ord 18, r 15 (1) and (2), which is in these terms:

'(1) A statement of claim must state specifically the relief or remedy which the plaintiff claims; but costs need not be specifically claimed.

'(2) A statement of claim must not contain any allegation or claim in respect of a cause of action unless that cause of action is mentioned in the writ or arises from facts which are the same as, or include or form part of, facts giving rise to a cause of action so mentioned; but, subject to that, a plaintiff may in his statement of claim alter, modify or extend any claim made by him in the indorsement on the writ without amending the indorsement.'

That second paragraph contemplates that, where two kinds of relief are sought arising out of common facts or facts which are to some extent common, those claims to relief may be combined in the statement of claim.

We were referred by counsel for the seventh defendant to RSC Ord 20, r 5(5), which provides:

'An amendment may be allowed under paragraph (2) notwithstanding that the effect of the amendment will be to add or substitute a new cause of action if the new cause of action arises out of the same facts or substantially the same facts as the cause of action in respect of which relief has already been claimed in the action by the party applying for leave to make the amendment.'

It appears to me that in that paragraph the rules committee must have been using the expression 'cause of action' as referring to a type of relief claimed rather than to pleaded facts.

The defendants argue that an account cannot be claimed as the plaintiff here seeks to claim an account on the basis of constructive trusteeship, without pleading the circumstances which give rise to the accountability; and they say that if the plaintiff relies on alternative causes of action, or intends to claim alternative relief based on facts which are to some extent, or even entirely, the same, each must be stated in the pleadings; and they say that the facts alleged in the present case in the statement of claim are insufficient to support a claim to constructive trusteeship, because an agreement to do an illegal act may be entered into in circumstances which involve no dishonesty: the parties may not have recognised the illegality of the act, even though they may have known all the facts which in truth make the act illegal. For example the transaction may have been embarked on and carried out under mistaken advice given in good faith by properly instructed advisers.

Counsel drew our attention to the requirements of RSC Ord 18, r 12, relating to the particularity with which misrepresentations, fraud, breach of trust, wilful default or undue influence should be pleaded, and to the notes in the Supreme Court Practice[1] which relate to that subject, and also to the note[2] which explains the functions of particulars in pleadings, and they have contended that if any fraud is intended to be pleaded by the statement of claim, this is only done by way of inference. They referred us to two authorities, *Davy v Garratt*[3], where Thesiger LJ said that fraud should not be inferred, and to *Lawrance v Lord Norreys*[4], where Lord Watson made a rather similar observation. They raised the question whether constructive knowledge that trust moneys were being wrongly applied was sufficient to render a defendant liable as a constructive trustee where he had not in fact received any of the trust moneys or any moneys sufficiently representing the trust moneys. I hope that gives a sufficient indication of the nature of the defendants' argument on this part of the case.

I think two questions need to be considered. First, is it necessary when a person is sought to be charged as a constructive trustee that the design of which he is alleged to have had knowledge should be a fraudulent and dishonest design? For this purpose I do not myself see that any distinction is to be drawn between the words 'fraudulent' and 'dishonest'; I think they mean the same thing, and to use the two of them together does not add to the extent of dishonesty required. The second question is: if this is necessary, does the statement of claim here allege dishonesty with sufficient particularity?

The plaintiff has contended that in every case the court should consider whether the conduct in question was so unsatisfactory, whether it can be strictly described as fraudulent or dishonest in law, as to make accountability on the footing of constructive trust equitably just. This, as I have said, is admitted to constitute an extension of the rule as formulated by Lord Selborne LC[5]. That formulation has stood for more than 100 years. To depart from it now would, I think, introduce an undesirable degree of uncertainty to the law, because if dishonesty is not to be the criterion, what degree of unethical conduct is to be sufficient? I think we should adhere to the formula used by Lord Selborne LC[5]. So in my judgment the design must be shown to be a dishonest one, that is to say, a fraudulent one.

The knowledge of that design on the part of the parties sought to be made liable may be actual knowledge. If he wilfully shuts his eyes to dishonesty, or wilfully or recklessly fails to make such enquiries as an honest and reasonable man would make, he may be found to have involved himself in the fraudulent character of the design, or at any rate to be disentitled to rely on lack of actual knowledge of the design as a defence. But otherwise, as it seems to me, he should not be held to be affected by constructive notice. It is not strictly necessary, I think, for us to decide that point on this appeal; I express that opinion merely as my view at the present stage without intending to lay it down as a final decision.

In the present case, do the facts alleged in the statement of claim suffice to bring home to the defendants or any of them a charge that (a) the object of the alleged conspiracy was a dishonest one and (b) that they actually knew, or must be taken to have known, that it was so?

An allegation of dishonesty must be pleaded clearly and with particularity. That is laid down by the rules and it is a well-recognised rule of practice. This does not import that the word 'fraud' or the word 'dishonesty' must necessarily be used: see *Davy v Garratt*[3], which I have already mentioned, per Thesiger LJ. The facts alleged may sufficiently demonstrate that dishonesty is allegedly involved, but where the facts are complicated this may not be so clear, and in such a case it is incumbent on the pleader to make it clear when dishonesty

---

1   (1976), vol 1, p 281 et seq
2   Ibid p 281, para 18/12/2
3   (1878) 7 Ch D 473 at 489
4   (1890) 15 App Cas 210 at 221, [1886–90] All ER Rep 858 at 864
5   (1874) LR 9 Ch App 244 at 251–252

is alleged. If he uses language which is equivocal, rendering it doubtful whether he is in fact relying on the alleged dishonesty of the transaction, this will be fatal; the allegation of its dishonest nature will not have been pleaded with sufficient clarity.

The facts that are asserted here are that the defendants and each of them were at all material times aware, or ought to have been aware, of the fact that the third, fourth and fifth defendants were unable to purchase the share capital of the plaintiff unless they obtained financial assistance from the plaintiff through the purchase by it of their shares in Maximum at an inflated price. That must be read in conjunction with the allegation in para 17 that the said sum of £500,000 had been arrived at in order to enable the third, fourth and fifth defendants to purchase the plaintiff's shares with money provided by it in contravention of s 54 of the Companies Act 1948. The allegation of the conspiracy is an allegation that the parties conspired to carry into effect the sale and purchase of the share capital of the plaintiff in contravention of s 54, and all the defendants were, in one capacity or another, parties to the agreement of 3rd October. They were well aware of everything to be found in that agreement, and I drew attention earlier to the very intimate connection in that agreement between the sale of the shares of Maximum and the sale of the plaintiff's shares.

The alleged design, namely to procure that the plaintiff should pay £500,000 for property worth about £60,000 in order to enable the third, fourth, fifth and sixth defendants to buy the share capital from the plaintiff, which they could not otherwise do, was in my judgment clearly dishonest if the alleged inflation of the price was actually known, but not otherwise. Paragraph 18 does not allege exclusively actual knowledge; it says that the defendants were aware, or ought to have been aware. It seems to me therefore that the plaintiff does not unequivocally assert that the fact that the price was an inflated one was known to the defendants or any of them, although it is open to him on the pleadings to prove that this was so. The pleading does not demonstrate that the plaintiff relies on dishonesty as an essential element of his cause of action. So in my opinion this statement of claim does not unequivocally and clearly indicate that the plaintiff is proposing to assert that the transaction was a dishonest one.

RSC Ord 18, r 15 (1), requires that the statement of claim must state specifically the relief or remedy which the plaintiff claims. A statement of claim must therefore specify at least one form of relief which the plaintiff claims, but on proof of the necessary facts the court is not I think confined to granting that particular or precise form of relief. We were referred to the Supreme Court of Judicature (Consolidation) Act 1925, ss 40 and 43, the first of which has the marginal note 'Equities appearing incidentally'. It says that the court or judge—

'shall take notice of all equitable estates, titles and rights, and all equitable duties and liabilities appearing incidentally in the course of any cause or matter, in the same manner in which the Court of Chancery would formerly have taken notice of those matters in any suit or proceeding duly instituted therein.'

The marginal note to s 43 reads: 'Determination of matter completely and finally.' The section is as follows:

'The High Court and the Court of Appeal respectively, in the exercise of the jurisdiction vested in them by this Act, shall, in any cause or matter pending before the court, grant, either absolutely or on such terms and conditions as the court thinks just, all such remedies whatsoever as any of the parties thereto may appear to be entitled to in respect of any legal or equitable claim properly brought forward by them in the cause or matter, so that, as far as possible, all matters in controversy between the parties may be completely and finally determined, and all multiplicity of legal proceedings concerning any of those matters avoided.'

It is clear that a plaintiff cannot claim relief which is inconsistent with the relief that he has explicitly claimed; the authority for that is *Cargill v Bower*[1]. But it appears to me that the court must have jurisdiction to grant any relief that it thinks appropriate to the facts as proved; but if a party seeks to raise a new claim, which has not been adumbrated in his pleading, in the course of the trial, in my opinion the court should not give relief of that kind, at any rate without offering the opposing party an opportunity for an adjournment, and giving them an opportunity to say whether they have been taken by surprise, or have been prejudiced by the fact that that particular form of relief had not been explicitly claimed earlier.

In the present case the absence of any claim in constructive trust, which was introduced, as I have said, at a late stage, has greatly added, it seems to me, to the likelihood of confusion about whether the statement of claim contains any sufficiently clear allegation of fraud and dishonesty; and indeed whether the plaintiff was intending to rely on any allegations of fraud and dishonesty at all. Dishonesty was not a necessary ingredient of the claim of conspiracy; all that would be necessary to support that claim would be actual, or possibly imputed, knowledge of the facts which rendered the transaction an illegal one. 'Crime' and 'fraud' are not synonymous: a criminal act may well be committed without any fraud or dishonesty.

In the present case, as it seems to me, there is no sufficiently clear allegation of dishonesty to be found in this statement of claim; and if it is to be raised it must be raised by amendment, and I understand that an application for amendment is to be made later.

For these reasons I think the judge was justified in saying that a claim in constructive trust was not one which was open to the plaintiff on the pleading as it stands. As I say, the learned judge refused leave to amend; I have said nothing about that because we have to hear argument about it later. For my part I think the judge was wrong on the conspiracy point, but right, to the extent that I have indicated, on the constructive trust point.

ORR LJ. I entirely agree with the judgment that has just been delivered by Buckley LJ and only wish to add a few words.

As to the circumstances in which a person may be held liable as a constructive trustee, the statement of Lord Selborne LC in *Barnes v Addy*[2] has, as Buckley LJ has pointed out, stood for over 100 years. I agree with his view that it would be wrong to extend the principle there stated and it might be productive of uncertainty in the law to do so.

As to the obligation to plead fraud, the notes in the Supreme Court Practice[3] to RSC Ord 18, r 12, state as follows: 'Fraudulent conduct must be distinctly alleged and as distinctly proved and it is not allowable to leave fraud to be inferred from the facts.' That statement is fully justified by the passage to which Buckley LJ has referred in the judgment of Thesiger LJ in *Davy v Garratt*[4] and in my judgment these requirements were plainly not satisfied in the present case.

I would only add that, where fraud has not been sufficiently pleaded, it is in my judgment no answer to say that if it had been sufficiently pleaded no further evidence would have been called for the defence. The presence or absence of a charge of fraud may, as it seems to me, affect the whole manner in which a defence is conducted.

I agree with the order proposed by Buckley LJ.

GOFF LJ. I would like to preface this judgment by pointing out that so far as the conspiracy question is concerned, we are dealing with a point of law on a particular pleading, and so far as the question of constructive trust is concerned we are dealing with a pleading point. It is, therefore, necessary that we should proceed on the footing that all the facts alleged in the statement of claim have been, or will be, proved; but in fairness to the defendants I should state that they deny that they joined in any conspiracy and they

1   (1878) 10 Ch D 502
2   (1874) LR 9 Ch App 244 at 251–252
3   (1976), vol 1, p 286, para 18/12/11
4   (1878) 7 Ch D 473 at 489

deny that they were dishonest or party to any dishonesty. Whether that denial is well
founded or not is a matter which will have to be investigated at the trial.

On the question whether the plea that the plaintiff cannot proceed on conspiracy because
it became a party to the unlawful act, or to the conspiracy, by becoming a party to the
agreement of 3rd October 1963, I entirely agree with the conclusion reached by Buckley
LJ and with his reasons. I would add only a few points of my own in amplification.

First, the agreement of 3rd October 1963 was not per se unlawful. It was the other facts
alleged concerning it, the fact that the purchase by the plaintiff was at an inflated price and
that that price was arrived at, not for any purpose of the plaintiff, which indeed it injured,
but to assist the third defendant, and to put him in a position to buy the shares in the
plaintiff which made the agreement illegal. In my judgment, therefore, the plaintiff
cannot on any showing be a party to that conspiracy and debarred from maintaining its
action unless it knew those facts.

This is shown by *Churchill v Walton*[1], to which Buckley LJ has referred, and I would read
just two passages from the speech of Viscount Dilhorne in that case. He said[2]:

> 'In answer to the question posed by the Court of Criminal Appeal in this case, I
> would say that mens rea is only an essential ingredient in conspiracy insofar as there
> must be an intention to be a party to an agreement to do an unlawful act; that
> knowledge of the law on the part of the accused is immaterial, and that knowledge of
> the facts is only material insofar as such knowledge throws a light on what was
> agreed.'

Then his Lordship said:

> 'The question is "What did they agree to do?" If what they agreed to do was, on the
> facts known to them, an unlawful act, they are guilty of conspiracy and cannot excuse
> themselves by saying that, owing to their ignorance of the law, they did not realise
> that such an act was a crime. If, on the facts known to them, what they agreed to do
> was lawful, they are not rendered artificially guilty by the existence of other facts, not
> known to them, giving a different and criminal quality to the act agreed on.'

I agree with Buckley LJ that it is not possible to impute to the plaintiff the knowledge
of the sixth and seventh defendants. It was suggested in reply that Mr James was somehow
in a different position, but I cannot see myself how that affects the matter. If he was
innocent, it carries it no further; if he had knowledge of the improper purpose of the
conspirators, I do not see how his knowledge either could be imputed to the plaintiff,
seeing that he was the chairman of the second defendants, who were one of the conspirators.

Finally, in support of what Buckley LJ has said, I would wish to cite two short passages
from *Wallersteiner v Moir*[3]. The first passage is in the judgment of Lord Denning MR,
where he said[4]:

> 'In *Essex Aero Ltd v Cross*[5] Harman LJ said: ". . . the section was not enacted for the
> company's protection but for that of its creditors . . . the company cannot enforce it".
> I do not agree. I think the section was passed so as to protect the company from
> having its assets misused. If it is broken there is a civil remedy by way of an action for
> damages.'

Scarman LJ spoke to the same effect, saying[6]:

> 'There was, on these facts, a breach of duty by Dr Wallersteiner as a director. The
> companies were, also, in breach of the section. But the maxim "potior est conditio

1 [1967] 1 All ER 497, [1967] AC 224
2 [1967] 1 All ER 497 at 503, [1967] AC 224 at 237
3 [1974] 3 All ER 217, [1974] 1 WLR 991
4 [1974] 3 All ER 217 at 239, [1974] 1 WLR 991 at 1014
5 [1961] Court of Appeal Transcript 388
6 [1974] 3 All ER 217 at 255, [1974] 1 WLR 991 at 1032–1033

defendentis" is of no avail to Dr Wallersteiner, for the section must have been enacted to protect company funds and the interests of shareholders as well as creditors. I do not agree with the dictum of Harman LJ in *Essex Aero Ltd v Cross*[1] to the effect that the section was enacted not for the company's protection but for that of its creditors.'

Turning to the other point, the question as to constructive trust, Foster J took many objections. We have heard argument on them, though in the end the matter came to be focussed, rightly, on the question of fraudulent breach of trust. I think I ought to refer to them and to say a few words about them.

Foster J said:

'There is not one word in the statement of claim that the second defendant is a trustee, that it was in breach of trust, that it received the moneys knowing the moneys belonged to [the plaintiff], or even that the moneys which it did receive did in fact belong to [the plaintiff].'

He cited a passage from the judgment in *Selangor United Rubber Estates Ltd v Cradock (No 3)*[2], which includes these words: 'There are thus three elements: (1) assistance by the stranger, (2) with knowledge, (3) in a dishonest and fraudulent design on the part of the trustees'; and then his Lordship said: 'These passages show the various allegations which have to be made and proved. In the statement of claim none of these things are even alleged, let alone proved.'

I am not able to agree with any of those objections, except the last, '(3) in a dishonest and fraudulent design on the part of the trustees'. In my judgment it was neither necessary nor proper to plead that the second defendants were trustees or that they had committed a breach of trust; that is not the basis on which it is sought to make them liable. Further, this is not a tracing action, and therefore in my judgment it is enough to show that the moneys received by the second defendant sufficiently represented the plaintiff's money: see the *Selangor* case[3].

As a matter of pleading, paras 9(A) and 9(B) of the statement of claim, and the agreement of 3rd October 1963 showing, as Buckley LJ has pointed out, the direct and immediate connection between the purchase by the plaintiff of the shares in Maximum and the purchase by the third defendant of the shares in the plaintiff do, so far as the question is one of fact, in my judgment sufficiently allege that the moneys represented the moneys of the plaintiff in the case of the second defendant; whilst, so far as concerns the third defendant, he received payment direct from the plaintiff. It is not now alleged that actual receipt of moneys can be advanced on the pleadings as they stand, without amendment against any other of the defendants.

In my view the allegations in the statement of claim as a whole clearly plead participation in any breach of trust committed by the directors; and in my judgment para 18 is a sufficient pleading of knowledge on the part of all the defendants, whether the true standard be actual knowledge or constructive notice.

It seems to me, therefore, that there are three questions which we have to decide: first, is it necessary to prove that the alleged breaches of trust by the directors were fraudulent or dishonest (and I agree with Buckley LJ that the two things really mean one and the same); secondly, if so, is that sufficiently pleaded; and thirdly, was it necessary to specify, either in the body of the statement of claim or in the prayer, the claim for relief on the footing of constructive trusteeship?

On the first point counsel for the plaintiff, in support of his argument that it is permissible to extend the principle of *Barnes v Addy*[4], relied on two passages in the *Selangor* case[5]. The first is where Ungoed-Thomas J said:

---

1   [1961] Court of Appeal Transcript 388
2   [1968] 2 All ER 1073 at 1096, [1968] 1 WLR 1555 at 1580
3   [1968] 2 All ER 1073 at 1123, [1968] 1 WLR 1555 at 1614
4   (1874) LR 9 Ch App 244
5   [1968] 2 All ER 1073 at 1097, 1105, [1968] 1 WLR 1555 at 1582, 1591

'It seems to me imperative to grasp and keep constantly in mind that the second category of constructive trusteeship (which is the only category with which we are concerned) is nothing more than a formula for equitable relief. The court of equity says that the defendant shall be liable in equity, as though he were a trustee. He is made liable in equity as a trustee by the imposition of construction of the court of equity. This is done because in accordance with equitable principles applied by the court of equity it is equitable that he should be held liable as though he were a trustee. Trusteeship and constructive trusteeship are equitable conceptions.'

In the second passage, which was introduced by the judge saying, 'I come to the third element, dishonest and fraudulent design on the part of the trustees', Ungoed-Thomas J said:

'It seems to me unnecessary and, indeed, undesirable to attempt to define "dishonest and fraudulent design", since a definition in vacuo, without the advantage of all the circumstances that might occur in cases that might come before the court, might be to restrict their scope by definition without regard to, and in ignorance of, circumstances which would patently come within them. The words themselves are not terms of art and are not taken from a statute or other document demanding construction. They are used in a judgment as the expression and indication of an equitable principle and not in a document as constituting or demanding verbal application and, therefore, definition. They are to be understood "according to the plain principles of a court of equity", to which Sir Richard Kindersley, V.-C., referred [in *Bodenham v Hoskins*[1]], and these principles, in this context at any rate, are just plain, ordinary commonsense. I accept that "dishonest and fraudulent", so understood, is certainly conduct which is morally reprehensible; but what is morally reprehensible is best left open to identification and not to be confined by definition.'

If and so far as Ungoed-Thomas J intended, as I think he did, to say that it is not necessary that the breach of trust in respect of which it is sought to make the defendant liable as a constructive trustee should be fraudulent or dishonest, I respectfully cannot accept that view. I agree that it would be dangerous and wrong to depart from the safe path of the principle as stated by Lord Selborne LC[2] to the uncharted sea of something not innocent (and counsel for the plaintiff conceded that mere innocence would not do) but still short of dishonesty.

In my judgment, therefore, it was necessary in this case to plead, and of course in due course to prove, that the breach of trust by the directors was dishonest.

I turn then to the second question, which is whether fraud or dishonesty has been sufficiently pleaded. I accept counsel for the plaintiff's submission that the statement of claim, when carefully analysed, does plead all the facts necessary to constitute a fraudulent breach of trust, namely a deliberate design to misapply the plaintiff's money in buying shares at an inflated price to place a third party in funds to buy the shares in the plaintiff, a design known to the directors and to all the participants in it. However, in my judgment this pleading is defective so far as fraud is concerned, because it does not make it clear that the pleader means to charge fraud, because he says in para 18 that the defendants and each of them were at all material times aware, or ought to have been aware; and the latter part is, as counsel for the plaintiff was constrained to admit, consistent with innocence.

I am unable to accept the submission that this should be construed as a charge of fraud, with an alternative claim to relief in the event of his failing to prove it; on the contrary, it seems to me to reflect what has been his attitude throughout, namely 'I do not have to charge fraud'. This passage and the general tenor of the statement of claim as a whole, taken in conjunction with the absence of any claim to relief specifically on the basis of a constructive trust, even if that be not a breach of the rules itself, in my judgment makes the

1   (1852) 21 LJ Ch 864 at 873, [1843–60] All ER Rep 692 at 697
2   *Barnes v Addy* (1874) LR 9 Ch App 244 at 251–252

pleading embarrassing and prevents it from showing the defendants what case they have to answer.

So far as the point on the relief claimed is concerned, it is said that the writ itself was defective under RSC Ord 6, r 2, because it did not state the nature of the claim or the relief or remedy required, and reliance was placed on *Sterman v E W & W J Moore Ltd (a firm)*[1] as showing that a mere general claim for damages, accounts and enquiries is insufficient. However, in my judgment the writ was valid and regular, since it claimed a declaration that the transaction effected by the agreement of 3rd October 1963 was unlawful and void. In my judgment that being so, it was competent under RSC Ord 18, r 15 (2), for the plaintiff to serve a statement of claim pleading a case of conspiracy or constructive trust or both, because such cases depend on, or include, the same facts as are required to support the cause of action for the declaration claimed in the writ. Indeed, apart from the special point that the plaintiff, it was said, could not sue for conspiracy because it was itself a party, of which we have already disposed, it was not suggested that the statement of claim was bad so far as it alleged conspiracy.

Nevertheless, in my judgment the pleading failed to comply with RSC Ord 18, r 15 (1), in that it did not specify the remedy or relief claimed, so far as based on constructive trust.

Finally, whilst wilfully shutting one's eyes to the obvious, or wilfully refraining from enquiry because it may be embarrassing is, I have no doubt, sufficient to make a person who participates in a fraudulent breach of trust without actually receiving the trust moneys, or moneys representing the same, liable as a constructive trustee, there remains the question whether constructive notice in what has been conveniently described as the 's 199' sense, will suffice.

Ungoed-Thomas J, in the *Selangor* case[2] held that it would, and Brightman J in *Karak Rubber Co Ltd v Burden (No 2)*[3] followed that decision.

But in *Carl-Zeiss-Stiftung v Herbert Smith & Co (No 2)*[4] Sachs and Edmund Davies LJJ threw great doubt on this. In *Competitive Insurance Co Ltd v Davies Investments Ltd*[5], which was in many respects a different case, but touched on similar ground, I took the view that constructive notice of the s 199 type would not be sufficient, and I adhere to that view. It is, however, as Buckley LJ has said, unnecessary for us to decide that particular matter; it can be left to the trial judge, who may not in the end have to decide it, either because it may turn out that the defendants had actual knowledge, or because there may be insufficient proof to establish constructive notice.

For the reasons that both Buckley and Orr LJJ have given, which I entirely accept, and for those which I have sought to express myself, I agree that Foster J was wrong in ruling that the plaintiff company could not maintain its claim in conspiracy, but that he was right in holding that they could not proceed on a claim based on constructive trust without amendment.

18th February. Order in terms of the judgment of 17th February. Leave to plaintiff on the exceptional facts of the case to amend the statement of claim to plead fraud or dishonesty. Leave to all defendants to appeal to the House of Lords.

Solicitors: *Sidney Pearlman & Greene* (for the plaintiff); *Freshfields* (for the first and second defendants); *Gentle Mathias & Co* (for the fourth and sixth defendants); *Arram, Fairfield & Co* (for the seventh defendant).

Mary Rose Plummer   Barrister.

1   [1970] 1 All ER 581, [1970] 1 QB 596
2   [1968] 2 All ER 1073, [1968] 1 WLR 1555
3   [1972] 1 All ER 1210 at 1241, [1972] 1 WLR 602 at 639
4   [1969] 2 All ER 367 at 379–380, 381–382, [1969] 2 Ch 276 at 298–299, 301
5   [1975] 3 All ER 254 at 263, [1975] 1 WLR 1240 at 1250

Fookes v Slaytor

COURT OF APPEAL, CIVIL DIVISION
STAMP, ORR LJJ AND SIR DAVID CAIRNS
9th JUNE 1978

Negligence – Contributory negligence – Apportionment of liability – Jurisdiction – Defence of contributory negligence not pleaded – Whether court can apportion liability in absence of such a plea.

On a dark night a motor vehicle driven by the plaintiff ran into the rear of an unlighted articulated vehicle parked by the roadside. As a result the plaintiff sustained personal injuries. He brought an action for damages against the driver of the articulated vehicle, claiming that he had been negligent. The defendant filed no defence even though ordered to do so by the court, and was accordingly debarred from defending the action. He was given notice of the date and time of the hearing of the action but did not attend. The judge found that the plaintiff was one-third to blame for the accident and reduced the damages accordingly. The plaintiff appealed contending that the judge was not entitled to do so because contributory negligence had not been pleaded.

Held – The defence of contributory negligence was only available if it was pleaded. It followed that in the absence of a pleading by the defendant of contributory negligence the judge had no jurisdiction to make a finding of such negligence on the part of the plaintiff. Accordingly the appeal would be allowed and the plaintiff awarded the full amount of the damages (see p 140 *f* to *h* and p 141 *a* to *c*, post).

Dann v Hamilton [1939] 1 All ER 59, *Slater v Clay Cross Co Ltd* [1956] 2 All ER 625 and *Taylor v Simon Carves Ltd* 1958 SLT (Sh Ct) 23 considered.

Notes
For contributory negligence, see 28 Halsbury's Laws (3rd Edn) 87–95, paras 92–99, and for cases on the subject, see 36(1) Digest (Reissue) 269–302, 1084–1216.

Cases referred to in judgments
Dann v Hamilton [1939] 1 All ER 59, [1939] 1 KB 509, 108 LJKB 255, 160 LT 433, 36(1) Digest (Reissue) 250, 976.
Slater v Clay Cross Co Ltd [1956] 2 All ER 625, [1956] 2 QB 264, [1956] 3 WLR 232, CA, 36(1) Digest (Reissue) 2, 81.
Taylor v Simon Carves Ltd 1958 SLT (Sh Ct) 23, 74 Sh Ct Rep 41.

Appeal
The plaintiff, Robin Fookes, appealed against an order of his Honour Judge McDonnell made at Lambeth County Court on 27th June 1977, whereby in an action against the defendant, Christopher Slaytor, for damages for negligence, it was directed that two-thirds of the plaintiff's claim should be allowed and that judgment should be entered for the plaintiff in the sum of £398·66. The facts are set out in the judgment of Sir David Cairns.

Alan Jeffreys for the plaintiff.
The defendant did not appear.

SIR DAVID CAIRNS delivered the first judgment at the invitation of Stamp LJ. This is an appeal from a judgment of his Honour Judge McDonnell given in Lambeth County Court on 27th June 1977. It was a judgment delivered in an action arising out of a collision between two motor vehicles. The plaintiff, the driver of one of the vehicles, had suffered personal injuries. He claimed damages for negligence and the judge awarded damages in the sum of £398·66 with the appropriate costs. He had found that the full amount which would be required to compensate the plaintiff for his suffering and his special damage would be the sum of £598, but he went on to find that the plaintiff was guilty of negligence which contributed to the accident and therefore reduced the damages by one-third. The plaintiff appeals, contending that the judge had no jurisdiction to make that reduction in the damages.

The circumstances were these. The accident took place on 21st November 1974. Driving a motor vehicle in a London street, the plaintiff came into collision with the rear of the trailer of an articulated vehicle which was parked by the side of the road. It was during the hours of darkness, the weather was bad and the articulated vehicle was unlighted.

The plaintiff commenced his action against the driver and the owners of the articulated vehicle. The owners filed a defence alleging that the driver of their vehicle was not acting as their servant or agent at the time. The driver filed no defence. The plaintiff then issued notice of discontinuance against the owners. At that stage the driver had not delivered a defence. An application was made to the registrar for an order for the delivery of a defence by him within a stated time and the registrar ordered that he should deliver a defence within seven days and if he failed to do so he should be debarred from defending. He did not deliver any defence. He was therefore debarred from defending. He was given notice of the date and time of the hearing in the county court but he did not attend. The plaintiff gave evidence describing the accident as well as he could, having regard to the fact that he suffered from retrograde amnesia, and further gave evidence of the nature of his injuries. That evidence was supported by a doctor's report. It was contended by counsel, who appeared in that court for the plaintiff and has appeared for him in this court, that in those circumstances the judge was not entitled to reduce the damages on the grounds of contributory negligence, because no such matter was in issue, the defendant having delivered no defence and having been debarred from defending. The judge did not accept that contention. There is no indication in his judgment as to the view he took about it. It is implied that he rejected it because he simply said:

'I reach the conclusion that the plaintiff must have been contributorily negligent and that the blame for the accident should be apportioned as to one-third to the plaintiff and two-thirds to the defendant.'

There appears to be no direct English authority on the question of whether in the absence of a pleading of contributory negligence the court has jurisdiction to make a finding that there was such negligence on the part of the plaintiff. Contributory negligence is dealt with, so far as the statute law is concerned, in the Law Reform (Contributory Negligence) Act 1945, s 1(1), which provides:

'Where any person suffers damage as the result partly of his own fault and partly of the fault of any other person or persons, a claim in respect of that damage shall not be defeated by reason of the fault of the person suffering the damage, but the damages recoverable in respect thereof shall be reduced to such extent as the court thinks just and equitable having regard to the claimant's share in the responsibility for the damage . . .'

That leaves open the question of whether the court can only make a finding of contributory negligence if there is a plea to that effect. The nearest case that the researches of counsel have been able to discover is the Scottish decision in *Taylor v Simon Carves Ltd*[1], a decision of the sheriff-substitute sitting at the sheriff court of the Lothians and Peebles at Edinburgh. The headnote reads as follows:

'In a jury trial arising out of an accident to a workman, his employers' counsel intimated, prior to opening his case, that he was not insisting in a plea of contributory negligence. The plea was not thereafter mentioned by counsel or the presiding judge. The jury, after retiring, requested guidance from the Court, since they were of the view that both parties were to blame for the accident. *Held*, that the jury must be directed that if they found the defenders to blame for the accident they should pay no regard to any fault on the part of the pursuer.'

In the course of his judgment, or what was described in the report as a note added to the final interlocutor, the sheriff-substitute said[1]:

'Alternatively the defenders' counsel argued that in terms of section 1(1) of the Law Reform (Contributory Negligence) Act, 1945, the Court was entitled if not, indeed bound to propone a question or questions relating to joint fault and to direct the jury with regard to apportionment of liability. Section 1(1) provides that "Where any person suffers damage as the result partly of his own fault and partly of any other person, a claim in respect of that damage" is not defeated "but the damages recoverable in respect thereof shall" be apportioned. It was contended that the subsection was peremptory and meant that if in any case it was found that a person suffered damage as the result of joint fault the damages recoverable must be apportioned and that the section covered the peculiar circumstances of this case. It was said that in an action of damages tried by a jury in the Court of Session the presiding judge had allowed contributory negligence to go to the jury although not pleaded. No report of such a case was referred to and the circumstances in which this was done were not explained. I had to decide the point on a reading of the subsection as applied to the peculiar circumstances of this case. In my view the defenders' contention is not well founded. The primary purpose of the Act was to alter the law whereby a claim was defeated if contributory negligence was established and to substitute, in such cases, an apportionment of liability. But if contributory negligence is not in issue between the parties then, in my opinion, the Act cannot apply. The "claim" is not a claim in respect of damages resulting from joint fault.'

That Scottish authority, though not of course in any way binding on this court, is directly on the point and is in favour of the proposition on which the plaintiff relies here.

Two English authorities have been mentioned by counsel for the plaintiff which perhaps throw a little light on the problem. The first is *Dann v Hamilton*[2], a decision of Asquith J. The headnote reads[3]:

'The plaintiff, knowing that the driver of a motor-car was under the influence of drink and that, consequently, the chances of accident were thereby substantially increased, nevertheless, being under no compulsion either of necessity or otherwise, chose to travel by the car. She was injured in an accident caused by the drunkenness of the driver, in which the driver was killed. In an action against the personal representative of the driver, the defendant raised the defence of volenti non fit

1   1958 SLT (Sh Ct) 23
2   [1939] 1 All ER 59, [1939] 1 KB 509
3   [1939] 1 KB 509

injuria:—*Held*, that, except perhaps in extreme cases, the maxim does not apply to the tort of negligence so as to preclude from remedy a person who has knowingly and voluntarily accepted the risks which may arise from the driver of a car being under the influence of drink, and has been injured in consequence, and that the plaintiff was entitled to recover, the case not being one of the extreme type referred to.'

It will be observed that the defence raised there was the defence of volenti non fit injuria, and that it was on that matter and not on any point of pleading that the decision was reached, but the paragraph which has some relevance for present purposes is where Asquith J said[1]:

'As a matter of strict pleading, it seems that the plea *volenti* is a denial of any duty at all, and, therefore, of any breach of duty, and an admission of negligence cannot strictly be combined with the plea. The plea *volenti* differs in this respect from a plea of contributory negligence, which is not raised in this case.'

There was some discussion in academic circles as to the correctness of that decision and the matter was alluded to in *Slater v Clay Cross Co Ltd*[2]. It was again a case where what was being discussed was the defence of volenti non fit injuria. It becomes relevant in a rather curious way, because Denning LJ[3] giving the first judgment, referred to a note which Lord Asquith had written for the Law Quarterly Review[4] in which he referred to criticisms that had been made of his judgment in *Dann v Hamilton* and said[5]:

'The criticisms . . . were to the effect that even if the volenti doctrine did not apply, there was here a cast iron defence on the ground of contributory negligence. I have since had the pleadings and my notes exhumed, and they very clearly confirm my recollection that contributory negligence was not pleaded. Not merely so, but my notes show that I encouraged counsel for the defence to ask for leave to amend by adding this plea, but he would not be drawn: why, I have no idea. As the case has been a good deal canvassed on the opposite assumption, I hope you will not grudge the space for this not unimportant corrigendum.'

Denning LJ went on to say, having decided that the doctrine of volenti did not apply[6]: 'In so far as he suggested that the plea of contributory negligence might have been available, I agree with him.' I think by implication Denning LJ was saying in effect there that the plea of contributory negligence would be available if, and only if, it was pleaded.

It appears to me that, with all respect to Judge McDonnell, it was not right in this case to treat the matter as if there were a plea of contributory negligence before the court. That seems to me to be the rule in relation to procedure. The opposite view would mean that a plaintiff in any case where contributory negligence might possibly arise, even though it was not pleaded, would have to come to court armed with evidence that might be available to him to rebut any allegation of contributory negligence raised at the trial. It is true that in the ordinary case it would not be likely to involve anything beyond the evidence he would be giving to establish negligence on the part of the defendant, but circumstances are reasonably conceivable in which it might be.

In my view, this appeal should succeed and the judgment should be amended by increasing the amount of damages to £598 with the appropriate costs.

---

1   [1939] 1 All ER 59 at 60, [1939] 1 KB 509 at 512
2   [1956] 2 All ER 625, [1956] 2 QB 264
3   [1956] 2 All ER 625 at 627–628, [1956] 2 QB 264 at 270
4   (1953) 69 LQR 317
5   [1939] 1 All ER 59, [1939] 1 KB 509
6   [1956] 2 All ER 625 at 628, [1956] 2 QB 264 at 271

ORR LJ. I agree and would only add in fairness to the judge that he did not have the advantage this court has had of considering the authorities to which we have been referred and which, understandably, counsel had not taken to the county court.

I would allow this appeal for the reasons given by Sir David Cairns, being reasons of principle, of authority and also of practical convenience.

STAMP LJ. I entirely agree with what Sir David Cairns and Orr LJ have said. I find that the language of the sheriff-substitute is as applicable to the instant case as it was to that case, and convincing. The action here, like the action there, was not an action for damages resulting from the negligence of both parties, but an action for damages resulting from the negligence of the defendant. There was no allegation that the plaintiff had been negligent. In my view it was wrong for the learned judge to make a finding against him of negligence.

I would also sympathise with the judge who, of course, did not have the advantages we have had of having the authorities referred to. I would allow this appeal.

Appeal allowed. Amount of damages awarded to plaintiff in court below increased to £598.

Solicitors: *Russell Jones & Walker* (for the plaintiff).

Avtar S Virdi Esq Barrister.

Nothman v London Borough of Barnet

HOUSE OF LORDS

LORD DIPLOCK, LORD SALMON, LORD EDMUND-DAVIES, LORD FRASER OF TULLYBELTON AND LORD
RUSSELL OF KILLOWEN

13th NOVEMBER, 13th DECEMBER 1978

*Unfair dismissal – Right not to be unfairly dismissed – Restriction on right where employee reaches
normal retiring age or specified age – Conjunctive or disjunctive requirement – Employee over
specified age but under normal retiring age – Whether employee entitled to remedy only if under
normal retiring age and under specified age – Whether employee over specified age but under
normal retiring age entitled to remedy – Trade Union and Labour Relations Act 1974, Sch 1, para
10(b).*

The respondent was a woman teacher employed by a local education authority under a
contract of employment which provided for her automatic retirement at the age of 65. At
the age of 61 she was dismissed on the ground that she was unable to perform her duties
satisfactorily. She made a complaint to an industrial tribunal alleging that she had been
unfairly dismissed. The tribunal held that it had no jurisdiction to entertain her claim
because she was a woman over the age of 60 and therefore barred by para 10(b)[a] of Sch 1 to
the Trade Union and Labour Relations Act 1974 from making a complaint of unfair
dismissal. The respondent appealed to the Employment Appeal Tribunal which upheld
the industrial tribunal's decision on the ground that, under the terms of para 10(b), a
double barrier was imposed, so that a person was barred from having a remedy for unfair
dismissal if he or she had reached either normal retiring age for his or her employment or
the age specified in para 10(b) (ie 60 in the case of a woman), whichever was the earlier. On
appeal, the Court of Appeal[b] held that the expression 'normal retiring age' in para 10(b) was
to be construed as meaning the age at which an employee was obliged to retire by the terms
of his or her contract of employment and that para 10(b) was to be construed as meaning
that a woman was barred from having a remedy for unfair dismissal if she had reached the
normal retiring age or, where there was no normal retiring age, she had reached the age of
60. The court held that, as the respondent had not reached the normal retiring age
specified in her contract, she was not barred from making a claim for unfair dismissal. The
education authority appealed to the House of Lords.

Held (Lord Diplock and Lord Fraser of Tullybelton dissenting) – On the ordinary and
natural construction of the words used, para 10(b) of Sch 1 to the 1974 Act was capable of
meaning that the right to claim for unfair dismissal was limited by reference to a person's
age only where there was no normal retiring age and there would otherwise have been no
age limit, and there was no good reason to prefer an alternative meaning which could work
injustice in cases such as that of the respondent. Paragraph 10(b) accordingly stated two
different age limits for different classes of claimants, one limit for those who had a normal
retiring age fixed by their conditions of service and a specified age for those who did not,
and an employee who was under the normal retiring age stated in his or her contract of
employment was entitled to make a claim for unfair dismissal even though he or she was
over the age specified in para 10(b). Since the respondent was under the normal retiring
age in the undertaking in which she was employed she was not precluded by para 10(b)
from making a claim for unfair dismissal. The appeal would therefore be dismissed (see
p 145 h j, p 146 b to d and g h, p 147 a f and j to p 148 b, p 150 e and g h and p 151 d,
post).

Decision of the Court of Appeal [1978] 1 All ER 1243 affirmed.

---

a   Paragraph 10 is set out at p 150 a to c, post
b   [1978] 1 All ER 1243

Notes

For an employee's exclusion from compensation for unfair dismissal because of age, see 16 Halsbury's Laws (4th Edn) para 620.

For the Trade Union and Labour Relations Act 1974, Sch 1, para 10, see 44 Halsbury's Statutes (3rd Edn) 1794.

As from 1st November 1978 para 10 of Sch 1 to the 1974 Act has been replaced by s 64(1) of the Employment Protection (Consolidation) Act 1978.

Cases referred to in opinions

Ord v Maidstone and District Hospital Management Committee [1974] 2 All ER 343, [1974] ICR 369, NIRC, Digest (Cont Vol D) 976, 1524cc.

Thompson v Goold & Co [1910] AC 409, 79 LJKB 905, 103 LT 81, HL, 34 Digest (Repl) 652, 4494.

Appeal

The London Borough of Barnet ('the council') appealed against a decision of the Court of Appeal[1] (Lord Denning MR, Lawton and Eveleigh LJJ) dated 2nd November 1977 allowing an appeal by the respondent, Miriam Nothman, against a decision of the Employment Appeal Tribunal[2] (Kilner Brown J and Mr J G C Milligan) dated 25th July 1977 dismissing her appeal against a decision of an industrial tribunal (chairman Mr J L Maxted) sitting in London North on 26th January 1977 whereby the tribunal determined that they had no jurisdiction to hear the respondent's complaint of unfair dismissal against the appellant. The facts are set out in the opinion of Lord Salmon.

Sir Frank Layfield QC and *David Wolley* for the council.
Miss Notham appeared in person.

Their Lordships took time for consideration.

f 13th December. The following opinions were delivered.

LORD DIPLOCK. My Lords, I have read in advance the speech to be delivered by my noble and learned friend, Lord Fraser of Tullybelton. I share with him the misfortune of differing from the majority of your Lordships and from the members of the Court of Appeal as to the meaning to be ascribed to the short and simple phrase that falls to be construed in this appeal. Like him and Kilner Brown J, I think that the words are clear and free from ambiguity and that the result of giving to them their ordinary meaning and grammatical effect leads to a result that is neither absurd nor unjust. It would be possible to expand, though without thereby improving, my noble and learned friend's reasons for holding the view that we share; but, since whatever meaning commends itself to three of your Lordships can alone be the right one, I will not waste print and paper in doing so.

LORD SALMON. My Lords, Miss Miriam Nothman was appointed by the Barnet London Borough Council as a full-time teacher of mathematics at Copthall School with effect from 1st September 1974. She was then 59 years of age. Her conditions of employment included a provision that her employment would terminate automatically at the end of the term during which she reached her 65th birthday. This was the normal retiring age alike for all full-time men and women teachers at that school.

---

1   [1978] 1 All ER 1243, [1978] 1 WLR 220
2   [1978] 1 WLR 220 at 221

In a case such as this, most teachers, especially those of Miss Nothman's age, would have hoped and expected to stay on at the school until reaching the retiring age. And this was certainly Miss Nothman's ambition.

Prior to 1971, employers were legally entitled to dismiss their employees providing that the relevant facts and the express or implied terms of the relevant contract of employment empowered them to do so. If, however, an employer wrongfully dismissed an employee, the employee could have brought an action only to recover damages for wrongful dismissal but not to obtain an order or a recommendation that he or she should be reinstated. The Industrial Relations Act 1971 was a remarkable piece of social legislation. Parliament recognised that even if the employer had the right, in strict law, to dismiss the employee there were circumstances in which it would be unfair for the employer to exercise that right. And so the concept of unfair dismissal was born. The 1971 Act laid down in detail what constituted unfair dismissal (ss 23 and 24). It gave the employee, in certain circumstances, the right not to be unfairly dismissed and, if so dismissed, the right of obtaining a remedy by complaining to an industrial tribunal (ss 22 and 28). If the industrial tribunal found the complaint to be justified and considered that it would be practicable and fair for the employee to be reinstated the tribunal could make a recommendation to that effect. Where the tribunal found that the employee's complaint of unfair dismissal was well founded, but did not make a recommendation for reinstatement or did make such a recommendation which was not complied with, the tribunal had to make an award of compensation to be paid by the employer in respect of the unfair dismissal (s 106). The general principles relating to the assessment of compensation were elaborately set out in ss 116 and 118.

The Industrial Relations Act 1971 was repealed by the Trade Union and Labour Relations Act 1974 which, so far as relevant to this appeal, came into force on 16th September 1974 and, amongst other things, reproduced all the provisions of the 1971 Act. The council dismissed Miss Nothman from her employment as from 31st December 1976 on the alleged ground that she was unable satisfactorily to carry out her duties. At the time of her dismissal she was 61 years of age. Not unnaturally she felt very hurt by this slur on her professional skill, and she had a genuine sense of grievance about the way in which she had been treated. Accordingly, she brought a claim before the industrial tribunal affirming that she had been unfairly dismissed. Her concern was to clear her professional reputation against the allegation of incompetence and to be reinstated so that she might continue to carry out, until she reached retiring age, the work in which she was greatly interested and which she believed would be of help to her pupils. This was of much greater importance to her than the financial loss she had suffered by what she was sure amounted to unfair dismissal.

Miss Nothman's claim was dismissed by the industrial tribunal on a preliminary objection raised by the council, and the question whether or not she had been unfairly dismissed did not arise for decision.

The council contended that even if she had been unfairly dismissed she was unable, in law, to complain because she was a woman over 60 years of age. Her appeal to the Employment Appeal Tribunal was dismissed. Both tribunals considered that their decisions worked a grave injustice but that the law made it impossible to arrive at any other decision. Miss Nothman appealed successfully to the Court of Appeal and the council now appeal to your Lordships' House on the ground that the decision of the Court of Appeal was wrong in law.

This appeal turns on the true construction of paras 4 and 10 of Sch 1 to the 1974 Act which replaced and re-enacted ss 22 and 28 respectively of the 1971 Act. The two paragraphs so far as relevant read as follows:

'*Right of employee not to be unfairly dismissed*
'[*Section 22*]
'4.—(1) In every employment to which this paragraph applies every employee shall have the right not to be unfairly dismissed by his employer, and the remedy of

an employee so dismissed for breach of that right shall be by way of complaint to an industrial tribunal under Part III of this Schedule, and not otherwise.

'(2) This paragraph applies to every employment except in so far as its application is excluded by or under any provision of this Schedule.'

'Qualifying period and upper age limit
[Section 28]

'10 ... paragraph 4 above does not apply to the dismissal of an employee from any employment if the employee—(a) was not continuously employed for a period of not less than 26 weeks ending with the effective date of termination, or (b) on or before the effective date of termination attained the age which, in the undertaking in which he was employed, was the normal retiring age for an employee holding the position which he held, or, if a man, attained the age of sixty-five, or, if a woman, attained the age of sixty ...'

Paragraph 4 gives every employee the right not to be unfairly dismissed by an employer, and enacts that the remedy for an employee so dismissed shall be by way of complaint to an industrial tribunal. That right is, however, expressed in para 4 as being subject, amongst other things, to its exclusion by either of the two exceptions set out in para 10. The first exception lays down the minimum duration of an employee's employment before he can complain of unfair dismissal, and is irrelevant to this appeal. The second exception, on which everything depends, lays down the maximum ages of an employee beyond which, in certain circumstances, a claim for unfair dismissal cannot be entertained.

When an employee reaches the age which, in the undertaking in which he is employed, is the normal retiring age for an employee holding the position which he held, his employment may be terminated on his reaching that age. No claim could reasonably be entertained for his alleged unfair dismissal on or after that date. On the other hand I can discover no reason to justify why before that date arrives the employee should be deprived of his right not to be unfairly dismissed. There are, as the legislature no doubt realised, very many occupations in which there is a normal retiring age at which the employee to whom it applies normally retires. That, in my view, is why the legislature put in the forefront of para 10(b) the normal retiring age as the age beyond which a claim for unfair dismissal should not be entertained.

There are, however, also many occupations in which the conditions of employment specify no normal retiring age. Clearly it might have appeared unjust if employees in such occupations retained their rights to claim compensation for unfair dismissal indefinitely, whilst so many in other occupations enjoyed their rights only up to the normal retiring age set out in the contract of employment. In cases where there is no contractual retiring age the employee more often than not retires when he reaches pensionable age under social security legislation, very often at the age of 65 for men and 60 for women. That is why, in my opinion, the second part of para 10(b) was framed as it is.

I do not agree that para 10(b) erects a number of barriers under or over each of which every employee must successfully scramble in order to preserve his rights in respect of unfair dismissal. In my opinion para 10(b) sets up only one barrier to be overcome by the class of employee whose conditions of employment specify a normal retiring age, and another and entirely different barrier to be overcome by the class of employee whose conditions of employment specify no retiring age. The first class of employee preserves the right to claim in respect of unfair dismissal only if it is established that that dismissal took effect before the normal retiring age specified in the conditions of employment had been reached. The second class of employee preserves the right to claim in respect of unfair dismissal only if he or she establishes that that dismissal took effect before the employee, if a man, had reached the age of 65 years or, if a woman, 60 years.

Paragraph 10(b) is, in my opinion, inelegantly drafted; and, although it may be capable of bearing the meaning attributed to it by the Employment Appeal Tribunal, to my mind much the more likely meaning for it to bear is the meaning attributed to it by the Court of Appeal.

It is well settled that, in the absence of clear necessity, it is wrong to read into a statute words which are not there: *Thompson v Goold & Co*[1]. It seems to me, however, to be difficult if not impossible to attribute to para 10(b) the meaning for which the council contend without tacking on to the end of it the words 'whichever is the earlier'. On the other hand, the meaning for which Miss Nothman respondent contends can be attributed to that paragraph without adding any words to it at all. Indeed, I think that it might well be otiose to insert the words 'where there is no normal retiring age' between the first and second parts of para 10(b). Clearly, in cases in which no normal retiring age is specified in the conditions of employment, the first part of para 10(b) could not apply; and that would automatically bring the second part of the paragraph into operation. I agree with Eveleigh LJ about the sense in which the word 'or' is used in para 10(b) and that that paragraph sets up two different upper age limits for basically different classes of people, one for those who have a normal retiring age fixed by their conditions of service and the other for those who do not.

If a woman's conditions of employment provide that her retiring age shall be 65, I can find no sensible or just excuse nor any words in para 10(b) to deprive her of her rights to compensation should she be unfairly dismissed by her employers after she reaches the age of 60 but before she attains the age of 65. Before the unfair dismissal she would probably have planned and arranged her life on the basis that she would continue in her employment until she retired. To be unfairly dismissed before that time, say when she was 61 years old, must surely be a cruel blow. Her plans for her future would be overturned. The chance of finding fresh employment would be minimal and her pension would probably be diminished.

I cannot accept that any of the statutes which define 'pensionable age' as meaning 65 for a man and 60 for a woman are relevant or can afford any justification for Miss Nothman being deprived of the rights to which I have referred. Nor do these statutes affect the status of employees, but only their pension rights. Nor, in my view, is the Redundancy Payments Act 1965 relevant to any issue raised by the appeal. Section 2(1) of that Act provides:

'An employee shall not be entitled to a redundancy payment if immediately before the relevant date the employee—(a) if a man, has attained the age of sixty-five, or (b) if a woman, has attained the age of sixty.'

The right to compensation for unfair dismissal and the right to redundancy payments are different in kind. A dismissal on account of redundancy often occurs without any fault on the part of the employer. Not so in the case of unfair dismissal; and there is no excuse for overlooking or ignoring Miss Nothman's unfair dismissal because it took place after her 60th birthday but before her normal retiring age.

In my view therefore, the language of paras 4 and 10(b) should, for the reasons I have stated, be given what I believe to be their ordinary and natural meaning.

My Lords, I would, accordingly, dismiss the appeal.

LORD EDMUND-DAVIES. My Lords, I take the facts calling for consideration in this appeal from the speech of my noble and learned friend, Lord Salmon. At the outset I should state that I am in entire agreement with it and with his conclusion that the appeal should be dismissed.

Both the industrial tribunal and the Employment Appeal Tribunal arrived with manifest reluctance at the conclusion that they had no jurisdiction to entertain Miss Nothman's complaint of unfair dismissal. It is, I think, a striking fact that, whereas Kilner Brown J held that the 'remarkable lucidity' of para 4 of Sch 1 to the Trade Union and Labour Relations Act 1974 rendered inconceivable 'any alternative to the obvious conclusion' that

---

1   [1910] AC 409

her claim must fail[1], the Court of Appeal were unanimous in arriving at the opposite conclusion.

The point is, as I think, largely one of first impression and, despite strong submissions to the contrary to which I have naturally paid the closest attention, I have found myself unable to depart from my original tentative view that the appeal could well fail. I should make clear, however, that I have found it impossible to approach the matter on the basis that, as Lawton LJ put it[2]:

> 'Paragraph 10 of Sch 1 to the Trade Union and Labour Relations Act 1974 takes away an employee's right to complain of unfair dismissal. That which is taken away must be clearly identified. If there is any doubt as to what should be taken away, that which is doubtful should be left within the right given by para 4.'

But para 4 (re-enacting s 22 of the Industrial Relations Act 1971) did not confer an unqualified right on all employees not to be unfairly dismissed. On the contrary, sub-para (2) thereof expressly provides: 'This paragraph applies to every employment except in so far as its application is excluded by or under any provision of this Schedule.' Accordingly, the construction of para 10 should not, in my judgment, proceed on any other basis than that it was incumbent on Miss Nothman (unaided by any sort of presumption in her favour) to establish that she fell within the classes of employees entitled to claim.

In the course of his admirably clear submission, counsel for the council laid stress on what he described as the anomalous result which would follow were Miss Nothman's right to claim be upheld. By way of establishing this anomaly, he referred your Lordships to what he submitted was 'cognate legislation', pointing out that in several statutes 'pensionable age' was defined as meaning 65 in the case of a man and 60 in the case of a woman: see the National Insurance Act 1946, s 78, the National Insurance Act 1965, s 114, and the Social Security Act 1975, s 27. He also stressed that the Redundancy Payments Act 1965, s 2, provided:

> '(1) An employee shall not be entitled to a redundancy payment if immediately before the relevant date the employee—(a) if a man, has attained the age of sixty-five, or (b) if a woman, has attained the age of sixty . . .'

My Lords, I have to say that I see no reason in law or in good sense why the fact that an employee has attained pensionable age should also involve that from that date onwards he must in all circumstances be debarred from claiming that he was unfairly dismissed. And it has to be observed that in the case of a claim for redundancy, which has some similarity to one for unfair dismissal, the Redundancy Payments Act 1965 Act makes it perfectly clear that none can be entertained after the ages of 65 or 60 have been attained, but makes no mention of the 'normal retiring age', a phrase which is apparently to be found only in the 1974 Act. Had the legislature intended to create a similar automatic bar against claiming unfair dismissal, nothing would have been easier than to adopt the clear and laconic language of the Redundancy Payments Act 1965. But, for reasons best known to Parliament, they seemingly desired to treat differently employment where there is a normal retiring age. It may be said that employees in such circumstances acquire a 'status' of their own and one quite independent of what in the course of argument was called the 'status of pensioners'. Again, had Parliament intended that the attainment of 60/65 would be a bar even where normal retiring age had not (as in the present case) been attained, nothing would have been easier than to insert in para 10 of Sch 1 to the Act a provision that employees not entitled to claim unfair dismissal include those who '. . . have reached the age of 65 (men) or 60 (women), or the normal retiring age for their employment, *whichever is the earlier*', which, incidentally was the view expressed in the Local Authority Community Service Advisory Board (LACSAB) handbook regarding the effect of para 10. Without some such words, for my part I do not think it possible to adopt the construction which has

---

1   [1978] 1 WLR 220 at 224
2   [1978] 1 All ER 1243 at 1248, [1978] 1 WLR 220 at 229

appealed to the minority of your Lordships. On the other hand, I respectfully differ from Lord Denning MR in thinking that the insertion of words like 'where there is no retiring age' after the second 'or' in sub-para (b) of para 10 is called for if Miss Nothman's claim to be heard is to be upheld. On the contrary, I am with Lawton LJ in holding that the wording as it stands is sufficient for that purpose. Where there is a normal retiring age in the employment and it has been attained, the employee has no right to claim unfair dismissal; but, if it has not been, he has a right to have his claim heard. Such, in my judgment, is the effect of the statutory provision and it follows from the established facts that the industrial tribunal has jurisdiction to entertain Miss Nothman's claim and should now proceed to hear and determine it.

I therefore concur in holding that the appeal should be dismissed.

LORD FRASER OF TULLYBELTON. My Lords, I have the misfortune to differ from the majority of my noble and learned friends in this appeal. The difference relates only to the construction of the single word 'or' where it occurs for the third time in para 10 of Sch 1 to the Trade Union and Labour Relations Act 1974, and I propose to state my view quite shortly.

The 1974 Act re-enacted, with minor amendments which are not material to this appeal, certain provisions of the Industrial Relations Act 1971. The re-enacted provisions are set out in Sch 1 to the 1974 Act. One of the important re-enacted provisions was that set out in para 4(1) of Sch 1, giving every employee a right not to be 'unfairly dismissed' by his employer, but the right was given only 'in every employment to which this paragraph applies'. Paragraph 4(2) provides that the paragraph applies to every employment 'except in so far as its application is excluded by or under any provision of this Schedule'. Excluding provisions are found in paras 9 and 10 of the schedule, but they are not in my opinion to be regarded as taking away a right previously granted by para 4. Rather they lay down limits within which, as para 4 itself warned the reader, that paragraph is to apply. Accordingly para 10, which is the relevant one for this appeal, should in my opinion receive effect according to the natural and ordinary meaning of its words, without any particular expectation of what limit it is likely to impose, and without any special strictness.

Read in this way, para 10 seems to me quite clearly to state four tests or barriers, any one of which, if not surmounted or avoided, will prevent an employee being able to claim compensation for unfair dismissal. If he 'was not continuously employed for a period of not less than 26 weeks' then he fails at the first barrier because he has not worked for the qualifying period, as provided by sub-para (a). Sub-paragraph (b) of para 10 specifies the other three barriers, each of which fixes an upper age limit at which an employee, even if qualified by a long enough period of service, will be disqualified from claiming. He will be disqualified if he has attained 'the normal retiring age for an employee holding the position which he held, or, if a man, attained the age of sixty-five, or, if a woman, attained the age of sixty'. (I have italicised the critical word 'or'.) If one reads the sub-paragraph without any preconceptions, it seems to me, as it did to Kilner Brown J in the Employment Appeal Tribunal, clear beyond argument that an employee will be disqualified either if he has attained the normal retiring age or if he has attained the age of 65 (for a man) or 60 (for a woman). (I agree with my noble and learned friend, Lord Russell of Killowen, that the distinction between men and women in the last part of sub-para (b) is irrelevant to the question now under consideration, which has nothing to do with sex discrimination.) Of course the meaning could have been made even clearer by adding some such words as 'whichever shall first occur', just as the other meaning contended for could have been made clear by inserting at the appropriate place words such as 'or if there is no normal retiring age', but the fact that either of these things could have been done is irrelevant. We have to construe the paragraph as it stands. And in my opinion there is no doubt about the primary meaning of the words.

If that meaning led to a result that was absurd or unjust, I would look for some other possible meaning, but that is not the position. Throughout the class of modern social legislation which includes the 1974 Act, Parliament has consistently treated persons who have attained the age of 65 for a man, or 60 for a woman, as having a different status, in connection with pensions and employment rights, from that of younger persons. That appears from many modern Acts such as the National Insurance Act 1946, s 78(1), the National Insurance Act 1965, s 114(1), and the Social Security Act 1975, s 27(1), all of which define 'pensionable age' as meaning 65 for a man and 60 for a woman. It also appears from the provisions for tapering off the amount of 'basic award' of compensation for unfair dismissal to employees aged 64 for a man, and 59 for a woman, under the Employment Protection Act 1975, s 74(6) and (7). The most relevant provision for the present purpose is in the Redundancy Payments Act 1965, s 2(1), which provides as follows:

'An employee shall not be entitled to a redundancy payment if immediately before the relevant date the employee—(a) if a man, has attained the age of sixty-five, or (b) if a woman, has attained the age of sixty.'

Having regard to what I think is the policy repeatedly applied by Parliament in this field, it is impossible for this House in its judicial capacity to say that that policy is absurd or unjust.

For these reasons I agree with the judgment of the Employment Appeal Tribunal and I would have allowed this appeal.

LORD RUSSELL OF KILLOWEN. My Lords, the question in this appeal is whether the respondent, Miss Nothman, a teacher employed by the appellant council, whose employment was terminated before she reached the normal retiring age, is debarred from claiming that she was unfairly dismissed under the provisions of the Trade Union and Labour Relations Act 1974 because before the termination of her contract of employment she had attained the age of 60. It is a short point of construction of the statute, though the differences of judicial opinion show that it is not an easy one. We are not concerned with the question whether she was unfairly dismissed. We are only concerned with a question of jurisdiction, whether there is jurisdiction to entertain a claim by her based on unfair dismissal.

The concept of unfair dismissal was first introduced in the Industrial Relations Act 1971. The concept and remedies based on it are purely statutory and not contractual. The relevant sections of the 1971 Act are re-enacted in Sch 1 to the 1974 Act, with amendments that are not relevant to this appeal. The fact that this is a re-enactment throws no light on the point of construction: there were no reported decisions on the point between the two statutes that could shed any light on the intention of the legislature in 1974. We were referred to *Ord v Maidstone and District Hospital Management Committee*[1] (Donaldson P), but it did not involve the point.

Paragraph 4 of Sch 1 to the 1974 Act reads as follows:

'Right of employee not to be unfairly dismissed
'[Section 22]

'4.—(1) In every employment to which this paragraph applies every employee shall have the right not to be unfairly dismissed by his employer, and the remedy of an employee so dismissed for breach of that right shall be by way of complaint to an industrial tribunal under Part III of this Schedule, and not otherwise.

'(2) This paragraph applies to every employment except in so far as its application is excluded by or under any provision of this Schedule.'

---

1   [1974] 2 All ER 343

Paragraph 10 of that schedule reads as follows:

'Qualifying period and upper age limit
'[Section 28]

'10. Subject to paragraph 11 below, paragraph 4 above does not apply to the dismissal of an employee from any employment if the employee—(a) was not continuously employed for a period of not less than 26 weeks ending with the effective date of termination, or (b) on or before the effective date of termination attained the age which, in the undertaking in which he was employed, was the normal retiring age for an employee holding the position which he held, or, if a man, attained the age of sixty-five, or, if a woman, attained the age of sixty; but this paragraph shall have effect in a case where the effective date of termination falls within the period of six months beginning with the commencement of this Schedule as if the reference in sub-paragraph (a) to 26 weeks were a reference to 52 weeks.'

The sections referred to in the cross-headings are the sections of the 1971 Act from which the paragraphs derive.

For completeness, I mention that para 9 lists various categories of employment to which para 4 does not apply, and para 11 empowers the Secretary of State by order made by statutory instrument to add to or vary any of the provisions of para 10, subject to approval of the draft by resolution of each House.

On analysis the question for solution depends on the alternative which is envisaged by the 'or' in the phrase 'or, if a man'. Is it the equivalent of 'or in any event', so that in effect you are to read straight through the paragraph and find three occasions or circumstances in which an employee cannot claim unfair dismissal on termination of his employment, being (i) the brevity of his employment, (ii) the passing of his normal retiring age and (iii) the attainment of the age stated? This Kilner Brown J considered was the clear answer, which no change in drafting could have made clearer. Or is it the equivalent of 'or if there be no normal retiring age in a particular case'?

In my opinion the language is patent of either meaning and I prefer the latter.

Now it is true that that part of para 10(b) that deals with normal retiring age does not state positively that there shall be a right to claim up to normal retiring age: its form is to say there shall be no claim after normal retiring age. But it is to be borne in mind that the subject-matter is unfair dismissal; and I would not expect Parliament to provide that, in a case where the normal retiring age is over the age of 65 or 60 (as the case may be), the employee should be required to submit to unfair dismissal when his employment expectations and way of life would be based on the reasonable assumption that it would continue to the normal retiring age, if there were one. The contrary view limits the operation of the reference to normal retiring age to cases in which the normal retiring age is under 65 (man) or 60 (woman), and I discover no reason for this.

I prefer the construction by which the reference to the specific ages is inserted to constitute a limit on the right to claim in cases where there is no normal retiring age, where there would otherwise be no time limit.

Reference was made to other statutes in which these specific ages for men and women were selected for the acquisition of pension rights, and in particular to the fact that for redundancy payment rights they are made the cut-off points. I am not persuaded by these references. Of course they are part of a general pattern into which para 10(b) fits if there is no normal retiring age; but I do not think they help to solve the particular problem in which the leading feature is the attainment of the normal retiring age. Nor am I persuaded by them to adopt and apply to the present problem a legislative scheme to transfer employees at these ages from a status of employees to a status of persons entitled to social security or pension benefits.

Kilner Brown J considered that the drafting of these provisions could not have been clearer. I cannot agree. That the council's contention is correct could have been made abundantly clear by adding the words 'whichever be the earlier', or, as I think, by re-casting sub-para (*b*) into a sub-para (*b*) and sub-para (*c*). That the respondent's contention is correct could have been made abundantly clear by inserting between 'or' and 'if a man' the words 'if there be no normal retiring age'. Unfortunately neither was done. If the conclusion of the majority of your Lordships is not acceptable to both Houses no doubt the matter will be made clear by a statutory instrument under para 11 of Sch 1.

I must, my Lords, say that I do not support part of the approach of Lawton LJ in arriving at the same conclusion. He started on the assumption that a right was given by para 4 and scrutinised para 10 as a provision taking away that right. With respect I do not think that is right. Paragraph 4 only applies if it is not excluded, and paras 4 and 10 must be read together.

I must also say that I do not find that any guidance is to be derived from the word 'limit' in the singular in the cross-heading to para 10, 'promoted' from a marginal note to s 28 of the 1971 Act.

Further I must say that in reaching my conclusion I place no reliance on, and indeed disclaim, the sweeping comments of Lord Denning MR below[1].

Finally let me say that this case has nothing whatever to do with sex discrimination. If there be sex discrimination it is built into para 10 on either construction, and the point of construction would be exactly the same if the age mentioned in para 10 had been 60 for both man and woman.

For these reasons, my Lords, I would dismiss this appeal with costs.

Appeal dismissed.

Solicitors: *Ernest M Bennett*, Hendon.

Mary Rose Plummer   Barrister.

---

1   [1978] 1 All ER 1243 at 1246–1247, [1978] 1 WLR 220 at 228

Clarks of Hove Ltd v Bakers' Union

COURT OF APPEAL, CIVIL DIVISION

STEPHENSON, ROSKILL and GEOFFREY LANE LJJ

12th, 13th JULY 1978

Redundancy – Employer's duty to consult appropriate trade union on proposed redundancies – Special circumstances rendering it not reasonably practicable to comply with duty – Company deciding to cease trading because of insolvency – Whether circumstances of insolvency amounting to 'special circumstances' rendering it impracticable for employer to consult union on redundancies – Employment Protection Act 1975, s 99(8).

The employers were a company trading as bakers and confectioners. In 1976 they were in serious financial difficulties but, up to the day before they ceased trading, they were hoping that they could carry on by selling some of their assets. In the event they were unable to do so and ceased trading, making 368 of their 380 employees immediately redundant. No consultation took place with the employees' union about the possibility of redundancies before the decision to cease trading was made. In consequence, once the decision had been made, the employers failed to comply with s 99(3)[a] of the Employment Protection Act 1975 by consulting the union about the redundancies at least 90 days before the first of the dismissals took effect. The union made a complaint, under s 101[b] of the 1975 Act, to an industrial tribunal which made a protective award of 49 days' remuneration in respect of the employees, holding that although it had not been reasonably practicable for the employers to consult the union there had been no 'special circumstances', within s 99(8) of the 1975 Act, which had rendered it impracticable for them to do so and which would have protected the employers. The employers appealed to the Employment Appeal Tribunal, contending that their sudden insolvency was a special circumstance which made it impracticable for them to consult the union, and that therefore they were protected by s 99(8). The tribunal[c] upheld the appeal on the ground that, although insolvency by itself was not a special circumstance, the situation in which the insolvency occurred might be. The tribunal adjudged that the industrial tribunal had not considered the situation in which the employers' insolvency had occurred and remitted the case to them for reappraisal. The employers appealed on the ground that if there were special circumstances the Employment Appeal Tribunal ought simply to have allowed the appeal. The union cross-appealed, contending that the industrial tribunal's order ought to be allowed to stand.

Held – An event had to be out of the ordinary or uncommon in order to be a 'special circumstance', within s 99(8) of the 1975 Act, thereby relieving an employer from the duty to consult the appropriate trade union on proposed redundancies. Insolvency in itself was not a special circumstance, but whether a particular insolvency amounted to a special circumstance depended on the cause of that insolvency. The industrial tribunal, in deciding that the cause of the employer's insolvency was the gradual running down of the company and that that was not an uncommon, exceptional or extraordinary event, had applied the correct test and there were no grounds for questioning its award. The award would therefore be restored, the union's cross-appeal allowed and the employers' appeal allowed in part (see p 159 e to j and p 160 b to d and g to j, post).

Decision of the Employment Appeal Tribunal [1978] 2 All ER 15 reversed.

Notes

For an employer's duty to consult trade union on redundancies, see 16 Halsbury's Laws (4th Edn) para 654: 1.

---

a   Section 99, so far as material, is set out at p 153 *j* to p 154 *c*, post
b   Section 101, so far as material, is set out at p 154 *d* to *g*, post
c   [1978] 2 All ER 15

For the Employment Protection Act 1975, ss 99, 101, see 45 Halsbury's Statutes (3rd Edn) 2412, 2415.

Cases referred to in judgments

National Union of Dyers, Bleachers and Textile Workers v Job Beaumont & Son Ltd (28th October 1976) unreported, Leeds industrial tribunal.
Whittall v Kirby [1946] 2 All ER 552, [1947] KB 194, [1947] LJR 234, 175 LT 449, 111 JP 1, 45 LGR 8, DC, 45 Digest (Repl) 123, *433*.

Case also cited

Hinchcliffe v Crabtree [1970] 1 All ER 1239, [1970] Ch 626.

Appeal

Clarks of Hove Ltd ('the employers') appealed against the judgment of the Employment Appeal Tribunal[1] (Kilner Brown J, Mr M L Clement-Jones and Mr S C Marley) given on 30th May 1977 allowing their appeal against the decision of an industrial tribunal sitting at Brighton (chairman Mr G I A D Draper) on 14th January 1977 which had upheld a complaint made by the Bakers' Union ('the union') under s 101(1) of the Employment Protection Act 1975 on behalf of its members employed by the employers. By their judgment the Employment Appeal Tribunal ordered that the case be remitted to the industrial tribunal for further consideration. The ground of the employers' appeal was that the Employment Appeal Tribunal having found that the industrial tribunal had wrongly interpreted the words 'special circumstances' in s 99(8) of the 1975 Act ought to have wholly allowed the employers' appeal. The union cross-appealed on the ground that the Employment Appeal Tribunal had wrongly interpreted the words 'special circumstances' and should have affirmed the industrial tribunal's decision. The facts are set out in the judgment of Geoffrey Lane LJ.

Anthony Grabiner for the employers.
Patrick Talbot for the union.
Michael Howard as amicus curiae.

GEOFFREY LANE LJ delivered the first judgment at the invitation of Stephenson LJ. This is an appeal by the employers from a decision of the Employment Appeal Tribunal[1] dated 30th May 1977, by which that Tribunal remitted the case to the industrial tribunal for what they called reappraisal. There is also a cross-appeal by the union, that is, the Bakers' Union. The employers say that the Employment Appeal Tribunal should have simply allowed the appeal and not remitted it for reappraisal. They submit that the EAT, as I will call it, should have quashed the order of the industrial tribunal. The union, on the other hand, submits that the EAT should have dismissed the appeal and left the order of the industrial tribunal as it was to stand.

The circumstances of the case are these. The employers are Clarks of Hove Ltd. There is no dispute that on Sunday, 24th October 1976, without any prior warning, they terminated the employment of nearly all their workforce, that is to say, some 368 of the 380 employees, and on that day the company ceased to trade. The union thereupon applied for a protective award, as it is called, under the terms of the Employment Protection Act 1975, and it is necessary now to read the relevant provisions of that Act in order to set the scene against which these events have been played out. The first material section is s. 99, and it reads as follows:

'(1) An employer proposing to dismiss as redundant an employee of a description in respect of which an independent trade union is recognised by him shall consult

---

1   [1978] 2 All ER 15, [1978] 1 WLR 563

representatives of that trade union about the dismissal in accordance with the following provisions of this section.'

No dispute arises at this stage as to whether the necessary independent trade union existed. The next relevant subsection is sub-s (3), which reads as follows:

'The consultation required by this section shall begin at the earliest opportunity, and shall in any event begin (a) where the employer is proposing to dismiss as redundant 100 or more employees at one establishment within a period of 90 days or less, at least 90 days before the first of those dismissals takes effect . . .'

The rest of the subsection is immaterial. Indeed, the next material provision in s 99 is the one around which most of the argument in this case has taken place, and that is s 99(8), which reads as follows:

'If in any case there are special circumstances which render it not reasonably practicable for the employer to comply with any of the requirements of subsections (3), (5) or (7) above, the employer shall take all such steps towards compliance with that requirement as are reasonably practicable in those circumstances.'

Section 100 imposes on the employer a corresponding duty, in those circumstances, to notify the Secretary of State, in writing, of the proposal to dismiss in similar circumstances to those in s 99. Section 101 reads as follows:

'(1) An appropriate trade union may present a complaint to an industrial tribunal on the ground that an employer has dismissed as redundant or is proposing to dismiss as redundant one or more employees and has not complied with any of the requirements of section 99 above.

'(2) If on a complaint under this section a question arises as to the matters referred to in section 99(8) above, it shall be for the employer to show—(a) that there were special circumstances which rendered it not reasonably practicable for him to comply with any requirement of section 99 above; and (b) that he took all such steps towards compliance with that requirement as were reasonably practicable in those circumstances.

'(3) Where the tribunal finds a complaint under subsection (1) above well-founded it shall make a declaration to that effect and may also make a protective award in accordance with subsection (4) below.

'(4) A protective award is an award that in respect of such descriptions of employees as may be specified in the award, being employees who have been dismissed, or whom it is proposed to dismiss, as redundant, and in respect of whose dismissal or proposed dismissal the employer has failed to comply with any requirement of section 99 above, the employer shall pay remuneration for a protected period.'

and the subsections then go on to describe the meaning of 'protected period' and the limitations which are imposed on the length of such period.

It is to be noted that, so far as the employer's duty to give notice to the Secretary of State is concerned, under s 105(1) there is a penalty imposed, or may be imposed, if that is not complied with. Section 105(1) reads as follows:

'If an employer fails to give notice to the Secretary of State in accordance with section 100 above, he shall be liable on summary conviction to a fine not exceeding £400.'

So that there are two forms of what may loosely be described as 'penalty'. If the employer fails to comply with his duties to notify the union he may find himself faced with the necessity of paying a protective award; if he fails to comply with his duty to notify the Secretary of State he may, on summary conviction, be fined up to a sum of £400.

The employers conceded that they failed to consult the union in this case, but they contend, and they contended before the industrial tribunal and the EAT, that there were special circumstances which rendered it not reasonably practicable for them to comply, and that there were no steps, they submitted, towards compliance with the requirement which were reasonably practicable in the circumstances.

Clarks of Hove Ltd came into existence as a limited company of that name in April 1974. In a different form it had been a family concern for very many years and had been trading as bakers and confectioners since about 1887. But from 1974 onwards, after incorporation, it is plain that there have been many financial rearrangements. It is unnecessary to go into them in any detail at all. It is sufficient to say that by about midsummer 1976, or very soon after, and certainly by early autumn of that year, the employers were in serious financial trouble. Amongst other things it seems that the company required about £100,000 by 20th October in order to meet their obligation to pay the purchase price of a factory and fresh food bakery which they were engaged in buying. The Eagle Star Insurance Co had agreed to advance some £75,000 on first mortgage, and a Mr Pike advanced £20,000 in August 1976 and had, as security, a charge on the book debts of the employers. That amount of £20,000 was required by the employers to pay the deposit.

But by early September it is quite clear that the employer's deposit account had been exhausted, they were trying desperately to raise money by the sale of their shops, which were mostly, if not entirely, held under lease, and also to raise money by borrowing from suppliers and anybody else who would oblige. It was hoped that Mr Pike would provide still more capital. There is no doubt that he was interested because he instructed his auditors to investigate the affairs of the employers and to prepare a report. The auditors did that, and the draft of that report was eventually shown to Mr Keen, who was the director of the employers most concerned with these affairs, but it seems it was not shown to him until about 14th October 1976, ten days before the final crash came. That report from Mr Pike's auditors was indeed a gloomy document. It is set out in part, that is, the material part, in the judgment of the industrial tribunal. I will read three extracts from it which indicate the stage at which things had arrived by this time:

'After a preliminary review it was disclosed that the company is heading towards a liquidity crisis resulting from substantial trading losses. [That is a euphemism for insolvency.] Steps are therefore being taken to dispose of the retail shops to generate working capital and to enable the management to concentrate on making the frozen confectionery business viable. In the absence of detailed information it is difficult to make any assessment of the profitability of the shops but it is believed that, at best, they are only breaking even ... The company has been let down by its financial controls and it is therefore necessary to strengthen the management team by the inclusion of a finance director ... The situation is rapidly deteriorating and the company will probably be unable to continue trading unless the shops are sold and additional working capital is made available immediately to finance the frozen confectionery business on a profitable basis. If the company is not able to meet its debts on the due date it will, of course, result in its liquidation. In this event the creditors of the company are unlikely to be paid in full.'

It was clear, at that stage, that things were very, very serious indeed. The last hope was that a group called the James Warren Group would buy some of the employers' shops and so provide the cash to tide them over at least for a moment or two. But a message came from that group on Sunday, 24th October 1976, round about midday, which made it clear that that last hope was now a forlorn one and the group was not interested in buying the shops or providing the money. It was at that point that it dawned on the directors of the company that the shutters would have to be put up, and it was at that moment, in fact, as the industrial tribunal eventually found, that the notice was posted up on the board dismissing the employees with whom we are concerned. Indeed, if they had gone on trading in those circumstances it is quite plain that they might have been in severe and criminal difficulties under the Companies Act 1948 in due course.

A receiver was appointed by the National Westminster Bank, which was a debenture holder, on 27th October, that is three days later, and it is plain that even if the employers had not dismissed the employees the receiver would have had to have done the same on the 27th, when he was appointed. There will, it seems be little left for the unsecured creditors from the assets of this concern.

That is necessarily a truncated version of events, but it does, perhaps, set the scene sufficiently to enable one to turn now to the findings of the industrial tribunal, which are at the root of this case. I should read them in full:

'20. Once the timing of the proposal had been so determined the only way for the [employers] to comply with the requirements of s 99 of the 1975 Act was to defer dismissals for redundancy for 90 days from 24th October. The financial position known to the directors made that course not reasonably practicable, if not impossible. There was no money to continue trading or to meet the wages and salaries of the labour force for that period. The failure to consult the union, as required by s 99(3), (5) and (7), is not denied by the [employers], but they contend that there were "special circumstances" which rendered it not reasonably practicable for them to comply with s 99. Although the dismissals had already taken effect when the receiver was appointed by the National Westminster Bank on 27th October 1976, there can be little doubt but that he would have had to make the same decision as to dismissals.

'21. We find that on 24th October it was not reasonably practicable for the [employers] to comply with the requirements of s 99 at the time they were proposing to dismiss their staff for redundancy. Further, that from the nature of the situation on that day there were no steps towards compliance with s 99(3), (5), and (7) that were reasonably practicable for them to take. The proposal and its execution were simultaneous. We are not concerned here with the moment when the [employers] ought to have considered proposals to dismiss their staff for redundancy, but the moment when in fact they did so propose.

'22. It therefore becomes necessary in this case to determine whether the [employers] have satisfied us that there were "special circumstances which rendered it not reasonably practicable" for them to meet the requirements of consultation under s 99. The circumstances relied on by the [employers] are those of the company's admitted insolvency, which the [employers] contend was not mainly, or substantially, the fault of the [employers]. We do not think it is necessary for the purpose of determining the existence of "special circumstances" to assess the degree of the company's culpability in arriving at the state of a large scale insolvency by 24th October. We are of the view that in the insolvency itself and the facts which led up to it, there was nothing uncommon or "special" which rendered it not reasonably practicable for the [employers] to comply with s 99. It is, unfortunately, a not infrequent occurrence, born of a culmination of causes, some avoidable and some not. We find that the insolvency and the factors which led to it and which occasioned dismissals for redundancy and the failure to consult the union, were not "special circumstances". There were circumstances which rendered it not practicable to meet the requirements of s 99(3), (5) and (7), but such circumstances were not "special". The failure to find new capital from a sale of assets or from a loan advanced on its undertaking or assets was, in one sense, the immediate cause of the insolvency, but neither of these failures nor the way in which the company had been run, amounted to "special circumstances".

'23. We have found some guidance as to "special circumstances", an expression not defined in the legislation, from a case decided by the Leeds industrial tribunal, *National Union of Dyers, Bleachers & Textile Workers v Job Beaumont & Son Ltd (in liquidation)*[1]. There the facts that led to the insolvency, a failure to be alerted, currently, to increasing losses, were described by the tribunal as "not uncommon". In this case [this is perhaps the material part of the judgment] we are satisfied that Mr Keen and his co-director did know of the true state of their business from about early September

---

1 (28th October 1976) unreported

1976, if not earlier, but that they had failed to face up to financial reality in thinking that all would come well and capital would be raised in the end. We consider that, as in the case above cited, more experienced and astute businessmen would have responded at some date well before 24th October and anticipated the events of that day. Such failure, even allowing for difficult and competitive trading and dilatory presentation of the company accounts, does not amount, in our view, to "special circumstances" for the purposes of ss 99(8) and 101(2) of the 1975 Act. The hope that money will be raised by sale of assets or loan on the security of the assets to meet high overheads and wages, and to reduce a large indebtedness, it not a "special circumstance" any more than is the failure of that hope to materialise. The essence of "special" in the context of ss 99 and 101 is something out of the ordinary run of events, and, in this context, commercial and financial events, such as a destruction of the plant, a general trading boycott, or the sudden withdrawal of supplies from the main supplier. What happened here cannot, we think, properly be designated as "special circumstances" for the purposes of s 99(8) or of s 101(2). Insolvency, per se, we do not take to be a "special circumstance" for the purpose of those provisions. The events disclosed in evidence that led up to the insolvency are not "special circumstances" nor do they make that insolvency a "special circumstance". We take "special circumstances", as used in ss 99 and 101, to mean those events which are not ordinary but are exceptional or out of the ordinary to an extent that rendered it not reasonably practicable for the [employers] to consult the union in the manner set out in s 99.'

In the upshot the industrial tribunal found that the complaint made under s 101 was well founded, and they decreed that there should be a protective award of 49 days' remuneration.

That brings me to the decision of the EAT. It was, as Kilner Brown J points out, a majority decision, and perhaps some of the difficulties which one finds on reading this decision spring from that fact, because it is certainly true that there are many passages in the judgment of the EAT which are not easy to understand. The matter of lack of unanimity is dealt with as follows[1]:

'Had we been unanimous it would have been a clear case in which we should not have shirked our responsibility and should ourselves have substituted a decision if we felt the evidence was clear. However, we are quite open about this, we are not unanimous. In an important case like this where we do not find unanimity it is much better for the industrial tribunal which took so much trouble in this case, to reconsider their decision along the lines of the guidance which we propose to give. The reappraisal requires an assessment of the witnesses which we are not able to embark on.'

Speaking for myself, it is not altogether clear what that means. It seems to contain a suggestion that the industrial tribunal should reconsider the facts, but the facts were already fully and lucidly set out in the judgment of the industrial tribunal. Be that as it may, one now turns to that part of the same judgment which seems to contain the nub of the decision. It reads as follows[2]:

'This case turns in the end on what is the meaning of "special circumstances". The word "special" has acquired a significance in various statutes. One turns, simply for the sake of analysis and by way of analogy, to the use of the term "special" in breaches of the Road Traffic Acts involving disqualification from holding a driver's licence. In that area it has been laid down that "special" reasons have to be special to the facts of the case. In that area various categories of persons have been, and still are, excluded from relying on the exclusion granted to a person who is in breach of the law and is rightly to be disqualified, by a claim that the class of person or type of function gives rise to a special reason. Regrettably, in our view, and in this respect all three of us are

1   [1978] 2 All ER 15 at 16, [1978] 1 WLR 563 at 564
2   [1978] 2 All ER 15 at 18, [1978] 1 WLR 563 at 566–567

unanimous, the approach of the industrial tribunal to the interpretation was far too generalised. The reason for that, we think, is to be found in their reliance on the decision of a Leeds industrial tribunal in *National Union of Dyers, Bleachers and Textile Workers v Job Beaumont & Son Ltd (in liquidation)*[1]. Broadly speaking what that case said, and broadly speaking what the industrial tribunal in this case said, was that insolvency on its own is not a special circumstance. Of course it is not. Nobody ever suggested that it was. What was said in the *National Union of Dyers* case[1], apparently, and seems to have been said in this case also, is that employers who are in the process of going into liquidation should not avoid the implications of the 1975 Act. In broad general terms, by way of generalisation, insolvency is normally something which is foreseeable. It is perfectly obvious in a number of cases that an employer can be faulted, if he ultimately goes bankrupt and does not say to the appropriate trade union, "The writing is on the wall. We may have to close down. We have got to start consulting and see what we can do about redundancies." Or, as Mr Barry for the union has put it one might have a sensible employer and a sensible trade union official getting together to see if it was necessary to close down the business altogether, if it was possible to reorganise, and matters of that kind. Unfortunately this is precisely where, in our unanimous judgment, this industrial tribunal fell into error. They did not, in our view, apply the fact of insolvency to the special circumstances of this case. The special circumstances of this case were that maybe the employers were too optimistic, maybe they were unrealistic, but at least, as the industrial tribunal found, they were genuinely hoping right up to the last minute, Sunday midday, 24th October, that they could carry on trading.'

That passage, again, is not altogether clear, and it is pointed out by counsel before us that if, as appears to be the case, the EAT were there saying that there were special circumstances in this case, then they had no business to be remitting the case to the industrial tribunal; they should simply have allowed the appeal simpliciter.

The way in which counsel for the employers (who has dealt with this case, if I may say so, with great skill and great tact and delicacy) seeks to deal with that decision of the EAT is this. He agrees with them respectfully that the industrial tribunal were wrong, but he says, as I have indicated already, that if special circumstances did exist here then the industrial tribunal's decision should have been reversed and his side, the employers, should have won the day there and then. On the other hand, he agrees with counsel for the union that there are many features of judgment which provide great difficulty, and he is obviously reluctant to rely too greatly on the conclusions reached by the EAT. The way he puts his case is this. Since the decision to cease to trade was made at the very same moment as the dismissal took place it was not reasonably practicable to comply with the provision with regard to consultation. There was no money to meet further wages for that day, let alone for 90 days in the future. It was found as a fact by the industrial tribunal that the employers, albeit unwisely, or even negligently, failed to foresee the obvious, yet nevertheless they did not realise the inevitable until it happened, and have therefore, he submits, shown that there were circumstances, and that those circumstances were special.

Where, as here, the employer has admittedly failed to give the requisite 90 days' notice the burden is clearly imposed on him, by the statute, to show that there were special circumstances which made it not reasonably practicable for him to comply with the provisions of the 1975 Act, and also that he took steps towards compliance with the requirements, such steps as were reasonably practicable in the circumstances. There are, it is clear, these three stages. (1) Were there special circumstances? If so, (2), did they render compliance with s 99 not reasonably practicable? And, if so, (3), did the employer take all such steps towards compliance with s 99 as were reasonably practicable in the circumstances?

If the employer succeeds in discharging the burden under those three heads, what is the

---

1   (28th October 1976) unreported

result? Does it mean that the industrial tribunal should not make a declaration at all that s 101 has been broken, or does it mean simply that no protective award should be made, or that a reduced protective award should be made? In other words, do the special circumstances act as a defence, or do they act merely in mitigation of the penalty? I think that arguments based on the special reasons or special circumstances in the Road Traffic Acts are unhelpful. The circumstances are so wholly different in this area compared with the road traffic area that any comparison would, in my judgment, be more misleading than helpful. It may not, in the end, matter very much whether it is a defence or a mitigation; but it seems to me that it would be unjust were an adverse declaration to be made against an employer who had proved, on the balance of probabilities, that he had done everything that was reasonably practicable to comply with s 99 and that special circumstances existed in his case. If he does succeed in that effort, succeeds in proving the matters required as I have indicated, then that, to my mind, provides him with a defence, and thereafter there can be no question of a protective award being made against him.

What, then, is meant by 'special circumstances'? Here we come to the crux of the case. In this aspect, also, decisions under the Road Traffic Acts appear to me to be unhelpful. The decisions are too well known to need reference. The basis of them all is probably *Whittall v Kirby*[1]:

> 'A "special reason" . . . is one which is special to the facts of the particular case, that is, special to the facts which constitute the offence . . . A circumstance peculiar to the offender . . . as distinguished from the offence is not a "special reason". . .'

In so far as that means that the special circumstance must be relevant to the issue then that would apply equally here, but in these circumstances, the Employment Protection Act 1975, it seems to me that the way in which the phrase was interpreted by the industrial tribunal is correct. What they said, in effect, was this, that insolvency is, on its own, neither here nor there. It may be a special circumstance, it may not be a special circumstance. It will depend entirely on the cause of the insolvency whether the circumstances can be described as special or not. If, for example, sudden disaster strikes a company, making it necessary to close the concern, then plainly that would be a matter which was capable of being a special circumstance; and that is so whether the disaster is physical or financial. If the insolvency, however, was merely due to a gradual run-down of the company, as it was in this case, then those are facts on which the industrial tribunal can come to the conclusion that the circumstances were not special. In other words, to be special the event must be something out of the ordinary, something uncommon; and that is the meaning of the word 'special' in the context of this Act.

Accordingly it seems to me that the industrial tribunal approached the matter in precisely the correct way. They distilled the problem which they had to decide down to its essence, and they asked themselves this question: do these circumstances, which undoubtedly caused the summary dismissal and the failure to consult the union as required by s 99, amount to special circumstances?; and they went on, again correctly, as it seems to me, to point out that insolvency simpliciter is neutral, it is not on its own a special circumstance. Whether it is or is not will depend on the causes of the insolvency. They define 'special' as being something out of the ordinary run of events, such as, for example, a general trading boycott, that is the passage which I have already read. Here, again, I think they were right.

There was ample evidence on which, on these correct bases, they could come to the conclusion which they did. But whether one would have reached the same conclusion oneself is another matter and is an irrelevant consideration.

For my part, I do not think that the criticisms levelled at the industrial tribunal by the EAT are in any way justified. It is not right to say, as the EAT did in the passage which I read[2] 'Unfortunately this is precisely where . . . this industrial tribunal fell into error. They

---

1   [1946] 2 All ER 552 at 555, [1947] KB 194 at 201
2   [1978] 2 All ER 15 at 18, [1978] 1 WLR 563 at 567

did not . . . apply the fact of insolvency to the special circumstances of this case', and so on. If that is intended to mean that the industrial tribunal did not go behind the insolvency to discover what caused it and to enquire whether those causes amounted to special circumstances, it is simply not correct. That is exactly what the industrial tribunal did in a full and careful analysis of the situation. If it means that there were, in the view of the EAT, special circumstances, as they say twice, then they should, and I have said it twice already, have allowed the appeal.

I would allow the employers' appeal in part and I would allow the cross-appeal of the union for these reasons, and I would restore the order of the industrial tribunal accordingly.

ROSKILL LJ. I entirely agree with the judgment which Geoffrey Lane LJ has just delivered. I hope that counsel for the employers will not think me unappreciative of the quality of his argument, which, if he will allow me to say so, loses none of its merits by its lack of ultimate success, if I deal very briefly with a few of the points which have been put forward.

For the reasons Geoffrey Lane LJ has given it seems to me, with great respect, that the EAT were wrong in remitting this matter for decision to the industrial tribunal, and this appeal and cross-appeal present the curious feature that neither counsel seeks to support that which the EAT did. The EAT refused leave to appeal, but we have found it necessary to give leave to appeal to the employers on the one hand and, on the other hand, to give leave to the union to cross-appeal out of time. I agree with Geoffrey Lane LJ that the cross-appeal must wholly succeed and the appeal must succeed, though only in part.

Essentially, to my mind, the issue was whether the industrial tribunal were right or wrong in their approach to the question whether the employers established the existence of 'special circumstances' for the purpose of ss 99 and 101 of the Employment Protection Act 1975. Geoffrey Lane LJ has referred to the nub of their conclusion being contained in para 23 of their quite admirably reasoned decision. I do not think it is possible to fault the last sentence in para 23, where they say:

> 'We take "special circumstances", as used in ss 99 and 101, to mean those events which are not ordinary but are exceptional or out of the ordinary to an extent that rendered it not reasonably practicable for the [employers] to consult the union in the manner set out in s 99.'

To my mind the position in a case of this kind is this. So long as the facts found by the tribunal of fact, which is the industrial tribunal, are capable of amounting to special circumstances it is a question of fact for the industrial tribunal whether those facts do, in their view, so amount to special circumstances.

In considering this matter in this case the industrial tribunal said, as a conclusion of fact, that this insolvency (and I emphasise the use of the definite article in para 22, and again in para 23) did not amount to special circumstances. That was a matter of fact for them. I can see no matter of law here. With all respect, I do not think that the EAT ought to have interfered. The reasoning of the industrial tribunal cannot be faulted save on one unimportant point. It is common ground between counsel that they misunderstood the position dealt with in para 24 under s 332 of the Companies Act 1948. But I do not regard that as in any way material.

I would therefore agree with Geoffrey Lane LJ that the appeal should be allowed in part and the cross-appeal allowed.

STEPHENSON LJ. I agree with both judgments and have nothing of my own to add.

Appeal allowed in part; cross-appeal allowed.

Solicitors: *Wilde, Sapte & Co* (for the employers); *Donne, Mileham & Haddock,* Brighton (for the union); *Treasury Solicitor.*

L I Zysman Esq   Barrister.

Melwood Units Pty Ltd v Commissioner of Main Roads

PRIVY COUNCIL
LORD WILBERFORCE, LORD HAILSHAM OF ST MARYLEBONE, LORD SIMON OF GLAISDALE, LORD RUSSELL OF KILLOWEN AND LORD KEITH OF KINKEL
7th, 8th, 9th, 13th MARCH, 23rd MAY 1978

Compulsory purchase – Compensation – Assessment – Development scheme – Land purchased by owner for development – Part of land compulsorily purchased before owner able to develop it – Whether compensation to be assessed by reference to price originally paid by owner or by reference to value land would have had if developed according to owner's original intention.

In December 1964 the appellant bought some 37 acres of residential land on the outskirts of Brisbane at an average price of $7,700 per acre for the purpose of developing a drive-in shopping centre. When he purchased the land the appellant was aware of proposals to build an expressway through the central strip of the land. In January 1965 he sought planning permission for the development. In April he was granted planning permission to develop about 25 acres of land north of the proposed expressway ('the north land') as a drive-in shopping centre with ancillary parking space. But for the expressway project and its impact on the 37 acres he would have been granted planning permission to develop the whole area for that purpose. In September the respondent acquiring authority compulsorily acquired the central strip of about 4 acres of the appellant's land for the expressway project and thereby severed the north land from the 7 acres or so of land lying south of the proposed expressway ('the south land'). In June 1966 the appellant sold the north land for development as a shopping centre at an average price of $40,000 per acre. Had the appellant obtained planning permission to develop the whole area as a shopping centre there would have been a market available to the appellant at the date of the compulsory acquisition for the whole 37 acres for that purpose and the purchaser to whom he sold the north land would have been one of the hypothetical purchasers in the market for the land. In October the appellant filed a claim in the Land Court for compensation totalling $280,000 for the value of the land compulsorily acquired and loss due to severance of the south land. Being dissatisfied with the conclusions of the Land Court the appellant appealed to the Land Appeal Court. In assessing compensation the Land Appeal Court took into consideration the fact that when the appellant had bought the land he had known that because of the expressway project there was no prospect of him getting planning permission to develop the whole 37 acres as a drive-in shopping centre. It valued the whole 37 acres at the date of compulsory acquisition at $9,250 per acre and rejected as irrelevant to the assessment the fact that in June 1966 the north land had been sold for $40,000 an acre. The appellant appealed on a case stated to the Full Court of the Supreme Court of Queensland and thence to the Privy Council contending that the Land Appeal Court was in error and mistaken in law in arriving at its valuation.

Held – The Land Appeal Court had erred in principle and therefore in law in arriving at its valuation because—

(i) The principle that a landowner could not claim compensation to the extent to which the value of his land was enhanced by the very scheme of which the land compulsorily acquired formed an integral part operated also in reverse, so that an acquiring authority could not by its project of acquisition destroy the potential of land for development and then acquire and sever on the basis that the destroyed potential had never existed. Accordingly in assessing compensation for the acquired land and for loss due to severance of the south land any diminution in the potential value of the whole of the 37 acres for development as a drive-in shopping centre attributable to the expressway project should have been disregarded, notwithstanding that planning permission had not been given for the whole 37 acres and would not have been given because of the expressway project. Even though the appellant, when he had bought the land, had known of the expressway project, the diminution in potential value was still to be disregarded since a person buying land bought it with the right to compensation for compulsory acquisition and severance. However, the fact that the appellant had considered that the north land alone could be a viable area for the drive-in shopping centre might, in itself, be a factor in determining for that purpose the value per acre of the compulsorily acquired land and the south land in comparison with the value per acre of the north land (see p 163 f to h, p 164 j to p 165 d and h j, post).

(ii) In assessing values for the purpose of compulsory acquisition a tribunal was not required to close its mind to transactions subsequent to the date of acquisition which might be relevant or of assistance. Accordingly the Land Appeal Court was wrong in principle and in law to reject from consideration the fact that the appellant had in June 1966 sold the north land for an average price of $40,000 per acre, since that figure was the only figure of the value of adjacent land available at the date of assessment to a person wishing to develop the land for its 'highest and best use' (see p 163 f to h, p 165 ef and p 166 g h, post).

Notes

For potential value and assumption of planning permission in the assessment of compensation on compulsory acquisition, see 8 Halsbury's Laws (4th Edn) paras 258–261, and for cases on the subject, see 11 Digest (Reissue) 129–142, 166–185.

For market value as the measure of value, see 8 Halsbury's Laws (4th Edn) paras 287–295.

Cases referred to in judgment

Pointe Gourde Quarrying and Transport Co Ltd v Sub-Intendent of Crown Lands [1947] AC 565, PC, 11 Digest (Reissue) 139, *237.
Spencer v The Commonwealth (1907) 5 CLR 418.
Woollams v The Minister (1957) 2 LGRA 338.

Appeal

Melwood Units Pty Ltd, by leave granted by the Full Court of the Supreme Court of Queensland on 30th July 1976, appealed against the judgment and order of the Full Court (Wanstall SPJ, Matthews and Dunn JJ) given on 23rd June 1976 whereby the Full Court on appeal to it on a case stated from the Land Appeal Court of Queensland ordered that the determination made by the Land Appeal Court on 4th December 1972 of the appellant's claim for compensation for the compulsory resumption by the respondent, the Commissioner of Main Roads, on 11th September 1965, of an irregular central strip of the appellant's property in Brisbane and severance and injurious affection of other adjoining property of the appellant's should be set aside and that the Land Appeal Court should make a fresh determination of the proper compensation. The facts are set out in the judgment of the Board.

Kenneth H Gifford QC (of the Queensland Bar) and *Nicholas Phillips* for the appellant.
J M Macrossan QC, W C Lee QC (both of the Queensland Bar) and *J G C Phillips* for the respondent.

LORD RUSSELL OF KILLOWEN. This appeal from the Full Court of the Supreme Court of Queensland arises in connection with a claim for compensation by the appellant for the compulsory resumption by the respondent on 11th September 1965 of an irregular central strip of the appellant's property in Brisbane, and for severance and injurious affection of other property of the appellant adjoining that strip to the south. The strip was to be the site of part of an expressway project from Brisbane to Combabah. The project for the expressway had reached a stage of detailed planning by the end of 1962, so that it was then a reasonable assumption that the central strip of the appellant's land would in due course form part of the site of the expressway and be resumed for that purpose.

In December 1964 the appellant exercised a series of earlier options and thus obtained a contractual right to acquire from five separate owners a total area of some 37 acres, at an average price of some $7,700 an acre. This area was bounded on the north by Logan Road and Kessels Road, on the west by Wadley Street and other land, on the south by Doone Street and on the east by other land. The area was irregular in shape. The projected expressway site which was subsequently resumed in September 1965 embraced two areas of the appellant's land, one triangular and one a parallelogram, totalling slightly over 4 acres. An effect of the resumption was to sever from the northern part of the appellant's land (some 25 acres) that part of that land lying to the south of the parallelogram (backing on Doone Street), some 7 acres. The total area of the land acquired by the appellant is conveniently referred to as 'the 37 acres'. That part lying to the north of the resumed land is referred to as the 25 acres and as 'the north land' and that part lying to the south of the resumed land as 'the south land'.

The appellant having in June 1966 sold the north land filed in October 1966 in the Land Court a claim for compensation totalling some $280,000 for the value of the resumed land and loss due to severance of the south land. Being dissatisfied with the conclusion of the Land Court the appellant appealed to the Land Appeal Court, which appeal involves a rehearing. The Land Appeal Court delivered a judgment on 4th December 1972, arriving at a figure of compensation of $83,000 odd made up as to $42,000 odd from the value of the resumed land and $40,000 odd as loss to the south land due to severance. Neither side was satisfied with this outcome. Appeal from the Land Appeal Court to the Supreme Court is by way of case stated. The Land Appeal Court was asked to state a case, and did so after the lapse of some considerable time. The case stated appended as part of it the judgment which the Land Appeal Court had delivered so that there is considerable overlap between the former and the latter. The case stated concluded with a series of questions, some expressed to be posed at the request of the appellant and some at the request of the respondent. As to two questions the Full Court answered that the Land Appeal Court, in connection with its inspection of the land on its own, had infringed the principles of natural justice and on that ground set aside the determination of compensation and remitted the matter for determination of the appellant's claim according to law. Their Lordships are not concerned with that or with any questions other than questions (a), (b) and (e) stated in the case, and relettered (a), (b) and (c)[1] in the order of the Supreme Court giving leave to appeal to Her Majesty in Council. The details of those questions are best understood after a fuller statement of the facts of this case. Suffice it for the present to say that the Full Court declined to answer them on the ground, to state it shortly, that an error in arriving at a valuation could only be a question of fact and could not involve a question of law. Neither the appellant nor the respondent supported that proposition and in their Lordships' opinion it is erroneous. If it should appear that the Land Appeal Court ignored a principle of assessment of compensation for compulsory acquisition (ie resumption) such as for example that commonly known as the *Pointe Gourde* principle[2], that in their Lordships' opinion would be an error in law. So also if the Land Appeal Court rejected as wholly irrelevant to assessment of compensation a transaction which prima facie afforded some evidence of value and rejected it for reasons which were not rational, that in their Lordships' opinion would be an error in law. And as will be seen it is on those lines that the appellant contends that the Land Appeal Court erred in this case.

To return to the narrative. The 37 acres, at the time when by contract in December 1964 the appellant acquired them, could not be used under the relevant planning law otherwise than for residential purposes unless a permit was obtained under that law for another use. The appellant sought planning permission in January 1965 for development

---

1   See p 167 *h* to p 168 *c*, post
2   See *Pointe Gourde Quarrying and Transport Co Ltd v Sub-Intendent of Crown Lands* [1947] AC 565

of the area as a drive-in shopping centre with ancillary parking space, the latter an obvious essential to such a project. The application was in terms applicable to the whole 37 acres but having regard to the impact of the expressway project, the course of which was indeed shown on the plans accompanying the application, it is now accepted that the application was rightly treated as an application for the 25 acres of north land and any consequential permit was also so limited.

On 23rd February 1965 the appellant was informed by letter from the Brisbane City Council that the Greater Brisbane Town Planning Committee had decided to recommend the drive-in shopping centre in principle to the registration board. That board was the decision-making body on applications for planning permissions such as this. On 15th April 1965 the appellant was informed by letter by Brisbane City Council that its registration board 'has granted the necessary permission, in principle, to use land [describing it in detail] and to erect buildings on such land for the purpose of a Drive-in Shopping Centre'. The letter concluded by pointing out that the approval gave permission to use and erect buildings on 'only that part of the land north of the proposed arterial road, as determined by the Main Roads Department'. The permission was expressed to be subject to a long list of conditions, of the kind that might be expected in a permission in principle or outline permission. The first condition was that a plan of the proposed layout satisfactory to the board be submitted showing, inter alia, facilities within the site for loading and unloading and for parking of not less than 2,500 vehicles.

Their Lordships can have no doubt that from the viewpoint of value of the 25 acres of the north land this permission in principle was the vital event, and that when, as happened in December 1965, the registration board reiterated its approval on the basis of a layout plan submitted in accordance with the first condition of the April permission this would not have significantly added to the value of those 25 acres of north land in the hands of the appellant. On this occasion their Lordships observe that substantially the same long list of conditions was attached as was attached to the April 1965 permission.

The Land Appeal Court referred to certain evidence set out in the case as 'uncontradicted and unchallenged'. Their Lordships add to the many occasions on which appellate courts have deplored the practice in cases stated of rehearsing evidence rather than directly finding facts. But in the relevant respects their Lordships conclude that the rehearsal of the uncontradicted and unchallenged evidence, as such, is tantamount to a finding of fact of the contents of that evidence. The following are what their Lordships, on that basis, accept as findings of fact: first, that but for the expressway project and its impact on the 37 acres an application to develop the whole area for a drive-in shopping centre with ancillary parking area would have been granted by the registration board, including the resumed land and south land; second, that had that been done there would have been a market available to the appellant for the whole 37 acres for that purpose. Moreover, it is clear that David Jones Ltd would have been one of the, perhaps limited, number of hypothetical purchasers in the market at the resumption date for the 37 acre area for that purpose. David Jones Ltd in June 1966 bought the 25 acres of north land for an average price of approximately $40,000 an acre.

This purchase appears to their Lordships to be a highly relevant piece of evidence for the evaluation of compensation in this case when it is considered in the context of the assumed findings of fact already mentioned. Their Lordships by no means say that it follows that David Jones Ltd as a notional purchaser, willing to buy the whole 37 acres, as a shopping centre plus ancillary parking, would have paid for the extra 12 acres (ie the resumed land and the south land) at the same rate per acre; the extra 12 acres would have been parking area more remote from the assumed actual buying area, though avoiding in part a need for a nearer and more expensive vertical car park building.

Their Lordships consider now various aspects of the Land Appeal Court decision in order to see whether they show an error in law. The Land Appeal Court purports to premise its assessment on the fact that the appellant was aware when it bought that because of the respondent's road project there was no prospect of a drive-in shopping centre other than on the 25 acre north land. In so far as this indicates a view that, as a consequence, the value of the resumed land and the loss by severance of the south land is to be based on the hypothesis that they never had a potential as part of a 37 acre drive-in shopping centre, it discloses in their Lordships' opinion an error in law.   Under the *Pointe Gourde* principle[1] the landowner cannot claim compensation to the extent to which the value of his land is enhanced by the very scheme of which the resumption forms an integral part; that principle in their Lordships' opinion also operates in reverse.   A resuming authority cannot by its project of resumption destroy the potential of the whole 37 acres for development as a drive-in shopping centre, and then resume and sever on the basis that that destroyed potential had never existed.   Moreover, in their Lordships' opinion the principle remains applicable in a case such as the present, notwithstanding that planning permission had not been given for the whole 37 acres and would not have been given, when the lack of such permission was manifestly due to the expressway project, and it is established that, without the expressway project, such planning permission would have been given for the whole 37 acres.   To hold otherwise in this case would enable the acquiring authority to inflict by its project the same injustice at one remove.

Further, as to the premise of the Land Appeal Court above mentioned, if it is meant thereby that, because the appellant bought the land with knowledge he should not, on some principle, be allowed compensation except on the basis of what he knew, this would be doubly wrong: a person buying land buys with it the right to compensation for resumption and severance.

In their Lordships' opinion the only light cast on the matter by the appellant's knowledge of the expressway project is that he considered that the north land alone could be a viable area for a drive-in shopping centre, and this in itself might be a factor in determining the value per acre of the resumed land and south land for that purpose in comparison with the value per acre of the north land.

Although there are strong indications of departure from principle on the above lines by the Land Appeal Court, when it comes to the estimate of value of the resumed land and loss by severance of the south land it might be arguable that ultimately, and in apparent contradiction of its 'premise', it adjusted to the principles stated above.   Its approach to valuation (which was for a different reason, later stated, in their Lordships' view erroneous in principle and therefore in law) was to take the whole 37 acres at the price of $7,700 per acre payable by the appellant in December 1964 as residential area value, add something for an assumed inflationary increase in value as such at 10% per annum for nine months to resumption date, and then add a further sum of about $1,000 per acre for the market potential generated by the April 1965 permit, a total of $9,250 per acre.   This figure was applied to the resumed area and as the basis for assessment of loss due to severance, and did not distinguish (apparently) between the potential of the three different zones of the 37 acres.   If this were so, and the passage is in some respects obscure, it would mean that the Land Appeal Court was not discounting as a result of the expressway project the value as part of a drive-in shopping centre of the resumed and south land, and were not infringing the reverse *Pointe Gourde* principle[1].   On the other hand, the Land Appeal Court in discussing *Woollams v The Minister*[2] pointed out that that decision was based on a section of the relevant New South Wales statute which, so to speak, embraced both the *Pointe Gourde* principle[1] and its reverse operation, and distinguished the relevant operative section of the Main Roads Acts 1920 to 1952 as only forbidding consideration of *increase* in value attributable to the relevant project.   This suggests that the Land Appeal Court thought that effect could be given to a decrease in value so attributable, which as their Lordships have indicated would be wrong in principle and in law.   In their Lordships' opinion it is a part of the common law deriving as a matter of principle from the nature of compensation for resumption or compulsory acquisition, that neither relevantly attributable appreciation nor depreciation in value is to be regarded in the assessment of land compensation.   The

1   [1947] AC 565
2   (1957) 2 LGRA 338

relevant New South Wales section merely reflects the law, as did s 9 of the Land Compensation Act 1961 in England, and the absence of the reverse of the medal in the relevant section of the Queensland Main Roads Acts is not to be taken as altering the law.

Immediately after that passage in the judgment of the Land Appeal Court, it says this:

> 'Apart from that, however, there is no evidence before us that, prior to the resumption, foreknowledge of the proposed expressway had a depressing effect on land values in the neighbourhood of the resumed land.'

Their Lordships venture to think that this overlooks the true question, which is whether such foreknowledge had a depressing effect on the development potential of the resumed and south land.

Having been left in some uncertainty on the question of departure in principle on the lines above mentioned, their Lordships turn to the second alleged error in principle and law. It has already been noted that the Land Appeal Court worked forward to a figure of $9,250 per acre as a value basis at the resumption date of September 1965. But David Jones Ltd in June 1966 bought the north land of 25 acres for the purpose of a drive-in shopping centre at a price of about $40,000 per acre. While it may well be that this average price should not be attributed without qualification to every part of the 25 acres, however important the more southerly part as a parking facility (which facility David Jones Ltd later found desirable to increase), this was the only tangible evidence of the value of land in this area for that purpose, and in respect of which there would have been availability of planning permission and demand from David Jones Ltd for the whole 37 acres. This was wholly rejected by the Land Appeal Court as irrelevant to the assessment of the value to the appellant of the resumed land and the assessment of loss due to the severance of the south land. What was the reason for this rejection, which led to an alternative build up which attributed no more than about $1,000 per acre to the commercial potential, a figure in support of which no evidence is referred to by the Land Appeal Court? The Land Appeal Court considered that by September 1965 (the date of resumption) the fact that in April 1965 there had been permission in principle for the relevant use would have become fairly widely known by September 1965. Their Lordships fail to see the relevance of this: the only relevant knowledge would be that of a narrow market of potential purchasers for the given purpose, who would be assumed to know of the April permission. Having attributed to this general knowledge some particular rise in the value of 'the land' beyond the December 1964 values the Land Appeal Court thought the price paid in June 1966 by David Jones Ltd (which as their Lordships have remarked was not less than an average $40,000 per acre for the 25 acre north land) not to be a reliable guide to the value of the resumed land at the date of resumption in September 1965. Now it is plain that in assessing values for the purpose of compensation for resumption on compulsory acquisition a tribunal is not required to close its mind to transactions subsequent to the date of resumption: they may well be relevant or of assistance to a greater or lesser degree, and in the instant case the figure paid by David Jones Ltd was the only figure available at the date of assessment of the value of the adjacent land to a person wishing to develop the land for its 'highest and best use'. Why then did the Land Appeal Court reject any consideration of this transaction in its evaluation? The first reason stated by the Land Appeal Court is that at the date of resumption planning permission had only been granted (in April) in principle, and then subject to a long list of conditions. But the December 1965 permission was subject to substantially the same conditions, and David Jones Ltd agreed to buy at an average price of $40,000 per acre nevertheless; and the Land Appeal Court considered that after the April permission in principle rezoning was virtually ensured. Moreover, the Land Appeal Court did not seek to attribute to the December 1965 planning permission the startling increase to an average price of $40,000 per acre.

The other reason for rejection of the David Jones figure as not relevant was that a witness for the appellant had advanced a figure based not only on the David Jones purchase price from the appellant but also on the price per acre of adjacent land, which David Jones Ltd paid in 1969 and 1970 as a desirable adjunct to its expected expansion of the drive-in

shopping centre, which opened in 1970. The Land Appeal Court referred to the
'circumstances surrounding' all three purchases by David Jones Ltd in 1966, 1969 and 1970
as preventing them complying, for relevance to valuation, with the requirements of
Spencer v The Commonwealth[1]. Counsel for the respondent suggested that in relation to the
1969 and 1970 purchases the 'circumstances surrounding' were the pressure to buy exerted
by the fact of being committed to the major 1966 purchase. That may be so, and the price
per acre paid in 1969 and 1970 may not consequently be a reliable guideline in this case,
though the acquisition may in part incidentally stress the value to such a project of parking
space. But no suggestion was advanced to suggest that the 1966 average price per acre was
not some guideline except that David Jones Ltd had been for some time in negotiation in
relation to the 25 acre site. If this, as their Lordships must suppose in default of any other
suggestion, was the reason for total rejection from consideration of the average price for the
relevant purpose of some $40,000 an acre (quite apart from additional benefits on the sale
to associated companies of the appellant) it was a rejection of evidence, and indeed the only
relevant evidence, of value which no properly instructed valuation tribunal should have
made, and was therefore an error in principle and of law. Their Lordships do not of course
say that the average price paid in June 1966 per acre for the 25 acres is necessarily to be
applied for compensation purposes to the rest of the 37 acres. Maybe some value is to be
attributed to the more definitive planning permit of December 1965. Maybe the south
land, or the more southerly parts of it, as being more remote as a parking area from the
actual shopping centre in the north land, would have been of less value per acre to a
hypothetical purchaser such as David Jones Ltd, although no doubt the alternative cost of
building vertical car parks (mentioned by the Land Appeal Court) would have been a
material consideration. But taking for example the resumed land there does not seem any
justification for ignoring a value of the immediately adjacent north land at an arm's length
sale in June 1966 of well over $31,000 per acre above inflated residential use value and
deciding on a comparable figure only nine months earlier of about $1,000 per acre. The
slight extra distance from the actual proposed shopping buildings coupled with the
December permit can scarcely be justification for a difference of $30,000 per acre. In
making these value contrasts their Lordships are not to be thought to overlook the fact that
$40,000 is an average figure and that it may be that the value per acre of the land for the
stated purpose diminishes with its increasing remoteness in a southerly direction from the
proposed site of the shopping area in the northern part of the north land.

Their Lordships have indicated the respects in which in their opinion the Land Appeal
Court erred in principle and therefore in law; and it might well be that this opinion would
suffice as a direction to the Land Appeal Court when it comes to reconsider the question of
value to the appellant of the resumed land and loss to the appellant as a consequence of
severance of the south land, on the remission ordered by the Full Court of the Supreme
Court of Queensland. And any answers given by their Lordships to the questions posed
will be interpreted in the light of the opinions here expressed.

Nevertheless it is as well to set out the questions referred to in the order giving leave to
appeal, being some of those extracted from the case stated. These were as follows:

'(a) Was the Land Appeal Court in error or mistaken in law in the method which
it adopted for assessing the value of the resumed land?

'(b) Was the Land Appeal Court in error or mistaken in law in assessing the value
of the resumed land and the effect of severance—(i) by reference to the facts that—(A)
at the time when the contracts for the purchase of the [appellant's] land were signed
in December, 1964 [the appellant] knew about the proposed location of the expressway
proposal? (B) at all relevant times from 1962 at the latest [the appellant] was aware that
the only land available to it for the drive-in regional shopping centre was the northern
land and that at no time did [the appellant] have any reasonable expectation of
receiving a permit to use the southern area for purposes of a drive-in regional

---

1 (1907) 5 CLR 418

shopping centre? (c) the centre line of the expressway proposal through the resumed land and in its vicinity was finally fixed in 1962? ... (ii) by reference to the market value of the [appellant's] land unaffected by proposals for its use as a drive-in regional shopping centre? (iii) by excluding from consideration the sale of the northern land by [the appellant] to David Jones Limited and the payments by David Jones Limited to other companies within the Hooker group of companies of which [the appellant] was a member?

'(c) Having regard to the evidence set out in paragraphs 17, 18, 20, 32 and 46 of the case stated should the Land Appeal Court have assessed compensation on the basis that but for the resumption—(i) a town planning consent would or would probably have been granted by Brisbane City Council by its registration board for the whole of the [appellant's] land to be developed as a drive-in shopping centre? (ii) the resumed land and the severance area would have been used for the purpose of a drive-in regional shopping centre?'

Taken by themselves the answers to these questions, on the basis of their Lordships' opinion, would be: (a) Yes, to some extent; (b) (i) (A) Yes, if it did, (B) Yes, if it did, (c) Yes, if it did, (ii) Yes, if it did; (iii) Yes, as to the direct payment at the average rate of about $40,000 per acre; (c) (i) Yes, (ii) Yes.

These answers by themselves may not serve any very useful purpose. The appellant at the hearing of this appeal reformulated the proper answers to the questions as follows: (a) (i) Yes; (ii) In assessing the value of the appellant's land (including the resumed land and the southern severance) the Land Appeal Court should (A) leave out of account any diminution in value attributable to the proposal for the expressway and (B) ascertain the highest and best use of the land on the basis that, there being for this purpose no expressway proposal, planning permission would have been obtainable for the use of the resumed land and of the southern severance as part of the drive-in regional shopping centre; (iii) neither the reasons given nor the material contained in the Land Appeal Court's reasons for judgment and in the case stated preclude the purchase by David Jones Ltd in 1966 from complying with the test in *Spencer v The Commonwealth*[1]; (iv) in assessing compensation for severance and injurious affection the Land Appeal Court should have regard to the existence of the expressway; (b) and (c) need not then be answered having regard to the answer to (a).

Their Lordships do not regard these answers, when read in the light of their opinions, as really being different save by way of formulation, and are prepared to adopt them.

Their Lordships are of opinion that the Full Court of the Supreme Court, in declining to answer certain of the questions posed, were for the reasons already stated in this opinion in error, and should in their order have remitted the case to the Land Appeal Court not only on the matters referred to in its order but also on the matters referred to in, and on the basis of, this opinion. The order of the Full Court of the Supreme Court must be varied accordingly and the appeal allowed, so that the Land Appeal Court shall on the reconsideration of the question of compensation have regard both to the order of the Full Court and to this opinion. In all the circumstances their Lordships are not minded to interfere with the order for costs in the Full Court but are of opinion that the respondent should pay to the appellant its costs of this appeal. Their Lordships will humbly advise Her Majesty accordingly.

Appeal allowed.

Solicitors: *Maxwell Batley & Co* (for the appellant); *Freshfields* (for the respondent).

Mary Rose Plummer   Barrister.

---

1   (1907) 5 CLR 418

Spindlow v Spindlow

COURT OF APPEAL, CIVIL DIVISION
STAMP, LAWTON AND ORMROD LJJ
16th MAY 1978

Injunction – Exclusion of party from matrimonial home – County court – Relationship between man and woman breaking down – Parties unmarried – Whether jurisdiction to exclude man from parties' home if he had not been violent – Whether jurisdiction to restrain man from molesting woman and children if no evidence of molestation – Domestic Violence and Matrimonial Proceedings Act 1976, s 1(1)(a)(b)(c).

The appellant and the respondent, an unmarried couple, were joint tenants of a council house. They had one child aged about 18 months and the respondent had a three year old child by a former marriage. The parties and the two children lived together as a family until the relationship broke down. The respondent left the house with the children and went to stay with friends in very congested conditions. The respondent applied to the county court for an order under s 1ᵃ of the Domestic Violence and Matrimonial Proceedings Act 1976 excluding the appellant from the house, and stated in evidence that she was not prepared to return to live with the appellant under any circumstances or to return to the house if he remained there and that she would rather put the children into the care of the local authority. The judge found that there had been no serious violence or adverse conduct on the appellant's part towards the respondent or the children, but that the parties' relationship had definitely come to an end. He held that the fair, just, reasonable and practicable solution in the interests of the children was to exclude the appellant from the house. The judge accordingly made orders restraining the appellant from molesting the respondent or the children and excluding him from the house. The appellant appealed contending that the orders ought not to have been made if there was no finding against him of violence or adverse conduct.

Held – (i) In the case of an unmarried couple living in the same house whose relationship had broken down, the county court had a general and unfettered discretion under s 1(1)(c) of the 1976 Act, as applied by s 1(2), to exclude one party from the house occupied by the couple, even though there had been no violence or molestation by the excluded party. However, having regard to the fact that for the purposes of s 1 of the 1976 Act unmarried couples were to be treated in the same way as married couples, the discretion was to be exercised according to the same principles on which the High Court exercised the similar jurisdiction to eject a spouse from the matrimonial home, namely that the court should be primarily concerned with the welfare of the children and the provision of a home for them. Accordingly, since the respondent was best able to provide a home for the children, the judge had been right to order the exclusion of the appellant from the house (see p 172 c to p 173 a and f g, p 174 f to h and p 175 a, post); *Bassett v Bassett* [1975] 1 All ER 513 and *Davis v Johnson* [1978] 1 All ER 1132 applied.

(ii) (per Stamp and Lawton LJJ) Before an injunction could be granted under s 1(1)(a) or (b) restraining one party from molesting the other party or the children there had to be evidence of molestation and since there was no real evidence of molestation by the appellant the injunction restraining him from molesting the respondent or the children would be discharged and to that extent the appeal would be allowed (see p 174 a b and p 175 a, post).

---

a Section 1, so far as material, is set out at p 171 *f g*, post

Notes

For the jurisdiction of the county court to grant matrimonial injunctions, see Supplement to 13 Halsbury's Laws (4th Edn) para 1228A.

For the Domestic Violence and Matrimonial Proceedings Act 1976, s 1, see 46 Halsbury's Statutes (3rd Edn) 714.

Cases referred to in judgments

Bassett v Bassett [1975] 1 All ER 513, [1975] Fam 76, [1975] 2 WLR 270, CA, Digest (Cont Vol D) 434, 7555c.

Davis v Johnson [1978] 1 All ER 1132, [1978] 2 WLR 553, HL.

Appeal

The appellant, Christopher Francis Spindlow, appealed against an order of his Honour Judge Stock QC made at Basingstoke County Court on 14th April 1978 whereby Mr Spindlow was restrained (i) from molesting the respondent, Jacci Spindlow, and her two children, and (ii) from remaining in the premises known as 1 Renoir Close, Basingstoke. The facts are set out in the judgment of Ormrod LJ.

Richard Gordon for Mr Spindlow.
Richard Crabb for Mrs Spindlow.

ORMROD LJ delivered the first judgment at the invitation of Stamp LJ. This is an appeal from an order which was made by his Honour Judge Stock QC on 14th April 1978 at Basingstoke County Court under the Domestic Violence and Matrimonial Proceedings Act 1976. Under his order, he ordered the appellant, Mr Spindlow, to leave what had been the joint home of himself and a lady known as Mrs Spindlow and two children at 1 Renoir Close, Basingstoke. The judge had an affidavit before him of Mrs Spindlow and heard oral evidence from Mr Spindlow and Mrs Spindlow, and he gave a fairly detailed judgment. He concluded, first, that it was a difficult case; and he noted it was a case in which there had not been any considerable physical violence. There was one occasion when Mr Spindlow pushed Mrs Spindlow onto a settee. The judge also said it was alleged that he shouted at her and said he would smack the child Nicola, who was a child of Mrs Spindlow aged four, I think, and not of Mr Spindlow. The judge did not think he had shown any violence or ill will to that child. It was said, also, he was an extremely jealous man. The judge thought that that allegation had been exaggerated to some extent, but Mr Spindlow himself agreed that he was a jealous character.

On 18th March Mrs Spindlow left, with the children, to live with friends in very congested conditions, which could not possibly continue for any length of time. She and her two children were sharing one room in a friend's house, and the house obviously was overcrowded in those circumstances. It is true that Mr Spindlow himself had no immediately alternative accommodation. It is possible he might have been able to stay with his mother for a time, or find other temporary accommodation.

Mrs Spindlow took the line that she was not on any account prepared to return to live with Mr Spindlow again, nor was she prepared to go back to the house if he were in it. She said rather than that she would go to the local authority and put the children into care. The judge thought that she meant it. He said:

> 'I have to consider the effect if I do not make the order. Either the children will be put in care or [Mrs Spindlow] will go back to 1 Renoir Close in spite of what is said. Although [Mr Spindlow] is in my view not guilty of any great violence, I think, if she did go back, the pressures of life are extremely serious and make a severe impact on these children. I do not think it is practicable for these four to live under one roof. They agree the relationship is at an end. She says he shouts at the children; I think that is exaggerated. If the children lived under these conditions tension would immediately build up and do them harm. A very difficult case; if [Mr Spindlow] is

not excluded either the children would be put in care—not in their interest—or
alternatively an attempt would be made to resume cohabitation with a separate
existence. I do not think that in practice living separate lives [that is, in the same
house] would work. It would only do the children harm. [Mr Spindlow] suggests
that they should come back and live separately. This would not be permitted
physically and [Mrs Spindlow] is not prepared to try.'

He then pointed out again that this was not a case of a battered wife or battered children.
In the circumstances he regarded it as in the interests of the children that he should make
an order excluding Mr Spindlow from the house, and he thought that the most fair, just,
reasonable and practicable solution he could come to.

The short facts are these. These parties started to live together in October 1976. Mrs
Spindlow has one child by her former marriage called Nicola, who was born in October
1974, and has another child by Mr Spindlow, who was born on 5th January 1977. As a
result of their forming a family consisting of themselves and Nicola they were allotted the
house at 1 Renoir Close by the council. It is perfectly obvious that the basis on which the
council allotted them this accommodation was that they had one child, and another was on
the way. For whatever reason, in March of this year the relationship between them came
to an end. Therefore the problem arises as to what is to be done so far as living
arrangements are concerned in the new situation. Counsel, who has said everything that
could be said on behalf of Mr Spindlow, has argued that this is not the class of case which
was contemplated by Parliament when it passed the Domestic Violence and Matrimonial
Proceedings Act 1976, s 1. That is the section, which has been the subject of a great deal
of litigation, which finally reached the House of Lords in *Davis v Johnson*[1]. But before
going to the report of that case in the House of Lords it is as well to look at the Act itself.
In the first place counsel for Mr Spindlow relies on the short title of the Act, where the
word 'Violence' appears, but as was pointed out by Lawton LJ in argument, in the long title
reference to violence relates only to police powers. When one comes to look at the two
sections, ss 1 and 2, one finds that s 1 gives the county court an unfettered discretion to
grant an injunction containing one or more of the following provisions:

'. . . (a) a provision restraining the other party to the marriage from molesting the
applicant; (b) a provision restraining the other party from molesting a child living
with the applicant; (c) a provision excluding the other party from the matrimonial
home or a part of the matrimonial home or from a specified area in which the
matrimonial home is included . . .'

and it is para (c) that is relevant to this case. Then sub-s (2) provides:

'Subsection (1) above shall apply to a man and a woman who are living with each
other in the same household as husband and wife as it applies to the parties to a
marriage and any reference to the matrimonial home shall be construed accordingly.'

But when one looks at s 2, which deals with the attachment to an injunction of a power of
arrest, one finds, at the end of sub-s (1), that that subsection is qualified by the words:

'. . . if he [that is, the judge] is satisfied that the other party has caused actual bodily
harm to the applicant or, as the case may be, to the child concerned and considers that
he is likely to do so again . . .'

So that s 2 is expressly qualified by a reference to violence. Section 1 is not so qualified. So
that it would be, on ordinary principles, surprising if it were right to construe s 1 as if it,
too, were subject to a similar qualification in relation to violence. That is the substantial
point on which counsel for Mr Spindlow has to rely in support of this appeal: he has to say
that s 1 should be read as though it were subject to some qualifying words importing
violence, or some adverse conduct of that kind.

1   [1978] 1 All ER 1132, [1978] 2 WLR 553

He supports his argument by reference to the speeches in *Davis v Johnson*[1]. It is true that there are passages, particularly in Lord Salmon's speech, which indicate that in Lord Salmon's view violence is an essential factor in the jurisdiction under the 1976 Act; but the other speeches contain very little to support that, and it is essential to bear in mind that their Lordships were not considering the limits of the jurisdiction of the county court to make an order excluding one party from the home. They were concerned with quite other things, and the fact that various observations were made by way of illustration of the sort of things that might or might not lead to an order under s 1 does not conclude the matter at all. This is the first time since *Davis v Johnson*[1] that this court has had to interpret the section in the light of that decision of the House of Lords, but without, of course, being bound by the dicta that appear there.

One thing that is plain, in my judgment, as a result of *Davis v Johnson*[1], is that the court must apply s 1 of the 1976 Act to persons who are living together, although unmarried, in exactly the same way as the section would be applied to married persons. There is no doubt, as counsel for Mr Spindlow concedes, that had these two parties been married, and had there been a divorce petition on the file, the court would have had jurisdiction, in the circumstances of this case, to make an order excluding Mr Spindlow from the home. That is clear from *Bassett v Bassett*[2], which dealt with the position as between husband and wife. This court has stressed many times that the court is primarily concerned in husband and wife cases of this kind with the welfare of the children. The High Court itself could make such an order under its powers in wardship proceedings if the interests of the children required it.

There is, therefore, no difficulty at all about jurisdiction, so far as the High Court is concerned, whether the parties are married or unmarried. There is no difficulty, as I see it, in the county court if a petition for divorce is on the file. This section of the 1976 Act fills in the gap which arises in the county court where there are no divorce proceedings on the file, and therefore no suit which is pending to which an injunction can be attached. It gives the court power to grant an injunction without there being any other proceedings on foot. It is true that it can be said to be intended primarily as an emergency type of proceeding, and so it is; but, then, so are ex parte and interim injunction proceedings. So, as I see it, the discretion under s 1 is completely general and unfettered except by the application of ordinary common sense to the circumstances before the court.

What is the position here? All the facts are relevant. The first is that these parties became joint tenants of the council accommodation only because they were living together as man and wife and there was one child and one child on the way. So that the allocation to these two adults of this house was directly dependent on the fact that there were children to be considered; and so it was clearly intended by the local authority to be a home for children. If the adults' relationship breaks down, as it has in this case, it is not very profitable to consider why. The fact of the matter is that it has broken down to the extent, as in *Bassett v Bassett*[2], when a young woman takes her two children and goes off and lives not just for a night or two but for quite a time in thoroughly difficult and uncomfortable conditions and says that nothing will induce her to return to live with the man. In those circumstances the court has to deal with the situation as it finds it, that is, that the relationship between the adults has wholly broken down and suitable arrangements have to be made primarily for housing the children. If there were no children here, if they were two independent adults, they could be left to get on with it, and the court might very well say, 'It is up to her. If she chooses to walk out and put herself into an uncomfortable position that is her affair'. But where there are two small children, that is not the position. Somebody has got to provide a home for these small children. Clearly the only person who can do it is Mrs

---

1 [1978] 1 All ER 1132, [1978] 2 WLR 553
2 [1975] 1 All ER 513, [1975] Fam 76

Spindlow in the circumstances of this case. So she and the two children must be provided with a home. If it is clear, as it was clear to the judge, that she is not prepared to go back and share her home with Mr Spindlow there is only one solution, namely that she must go back to the house and he must leave. It is all the more striking in this case that, if any other order were made, the absurd situation would arise that the local authority would have a single man living in a three-bedroom house on his own, with a woman and two children to house in other accommodation, all at public expense. The position is the more absurd because the local authority is in a position to terminate Mr Spindlow's tenancy of this house at a month's notice. They are not in any legal difficulty about the Rent Act or anything of that kind, though it is true that they are inhibited by general feelings of not wishing to be unkind or rough or tough on their tenants. One can understand that the housing department may well feel some reluctance to act against Mr Spindlow unless they have support from the court.

If this case is looked at rationally it is essentially a housing matter, housing for the children, and it should be looked at, in my judgment, mainly in that light. Parliament has, as it were, put onto the court the responsibility for making the decision, which was previously left with the housing authority. Now that the court has jurisdiction it may be more convenient and better that the court should adjudicate rather than that some administrative adjudication should be made. However, I am not to be taken as saying that exactly the same considerations would apply where the house, perhaps, is owned by one of the unmarried pair or one of the unmarried pair is a protected tenant of the property and has really substantial property rights in his house. It is clear from *Davis v Johnson*[1] that in such cases the right way to operate s 1 of the 1976 Act may be to use it on a temporary basis, not interfering unduly with the property rights but making temporary adjustments pending alternative arrangements being made. But in the present context, where it is a council house and the council are going to have to house these people, that kind of consideration does not really apply at all.

So I come back to my conclusion that the effect of the 1976 Act, combined with the decision of the House of Lords in *Davis v Johnson*[1], is for all practical purposes to equate a couple living together, with children, either their own or children of either of them, with the position of a married couple with children; and the court, in my view, should approach these cases with common sense in exactly the same way. It is said, of course, and it always is, that if this view is right a malicious girl with a child or children could oust her man friend from the house by merely walking out and putting up a bogus case. That may be the logical conclusion. But it is no good taking up a great deal of time talking in terms of blame or conduct. What we have to deal with is the reality of the situation, which is that two children are in need of a home and without one. That is the basis of my judgment, and I think the judge arrived at the same conclusion in this case, and I would dismiss this appeal.

LAWTON LJ. I agree with the judgment delivered by Ormrod LJ. I have only a few comments to add.

In my opinion, in the words of Lord Dilhorne in *Davis v Johnson*[2]:

'Our task is to give effect to the intention of Parliament if that can be seen from the language of the statute [ie the Domestic Violence and Matrimonial Proceedings Act 1976]. Here the language is clear and unambiguous and Parliament's intention apparent. Unmarried persons living together in the same household as husband and wife are for the purposes of s 1(1) to be treated as if they were married.'

I turn now to the wording of s 1 of the 1976 Act. In my judgment it is clear what was intended by sub-s (1): the jurisdiction of the county court to grant injunctions was to be

---

1   [1978] 1 All ER 1132, [1978] 2 WLR 553
2   [1978] 1 All ER 1132 at 1145, [1978] 2 WLR 553 at 568

extended in specified ways with the object of bringing it into line with the jurisdiction of
the High Court. The subsection provided in para (a) that a county court could grant an
injunction containing a provision restraining the other party to the marriage from
molesting the applicant, and in para (b) a provision restraining the other party from
molesting a child living with the applicant. It is clear from the wording of those two
paragraphs that before an injunction could be granted there would have to be some
evidence of molestation. There was not satisfactory evidence that Mr Spindlow had
molested Mrs Spindlow. It follows that no injunction in this respect should have been
granted. It is interesting, however, to note that in para (c) there is no reference to
molestation. There is to be power in the county court, akin to the jurisdiction of the High
Court, to insert into an injunction a provision excluding the other party from the
matrimonial home, or a part of the matrimonial home, or from a specified area in which
the matrimonial home is included. The question in this case is whether the High Court
would have had power, in the circumstances of this case, to make an injunction in the
terms of sub-s (1)(c). In the course of argument counsel for Mr Spindlow accepted that, in
the High Court, in the case of spouses with children, there would have been power for the
court, without any evidence of violence or molestation, to make an order of a kind akin to
para (c) if it was in the interests of the children. That power was considered by this court
in *Bassett v Basset*[1]. I refer to the judgment of Ormrod LJ in that case where he said:

> 'My conclusion is that the court, when it is dealing with these cases [his Lordship
> had in mind cases involving children], particularly where it is clear that the marriage
> has already broken down, should think essentially in terms of homes, especially for
> the children, and then consider the balance of hardship as I have indicated, being
> careful not to underestimate the difficulties which even single men have these days in
> finding somewhere to live, bearing in mind that the break will have to be made in the
> relatively near future and that property rights as between the spouses are of
> comparatively minor importance.'

Once it is accepted, as it now has to be, having regard to the judgment of the House of
Lords in *Davis v Johnson*[2], that unmarried couples are to be treated in the same way as
married couples for the purposes of s 1 of the 1976 Act, it seems to me clear that the county
court judge did have the jurisdiction which he purported to exercise. There was evidence
before him that the relationship had broken down, and once again, if I may rely on what
Ormrod LJ said in *Bassett v Bassett*[1], the woman in this case walked out taking the two
young children with her. There was no evidence that she was going off with another man;
there was no evidence that she was immature and running back to her mother. She must
have had some reason for leaving, albeit, as the judge found, it was not based on any
violence shown to her by the man. But, as the relationship has broken down, something
has got to be done about finding a home for the children.

For the reasons that Ormrod LJ has already given it seems to me right that the judge
should have made the order which he did.

STAMP LJ. I, too, agree with all that Ormrod LJ has said in the instant case. We should,
I think, do a great disservice to the administration of the law if we concluded that a county
court judge, in relation to s 1(1)(c) of the Domestic Violence and Matrimonial Proceedings
Act 1976, ought to exercise the jurisdiction as between man and mistress in a way different
from what he would do if the case came before him as between husband and wife on
precisely the same facts.

As a matter of construction of s 1, I can see no reason for drawing any such distinction.
It would be anomalous if, on precisely the same facts, the interests of the children in the
former case were less well protected than they would be if the parents were married.

---

1   [1975] 1 All ER 513 at 519, [1975] Fam 76 at 84
2   [1978] 1 All ER 1132, [1978] 2 WLR 553

I, too, would dismiss the appeal as regards so much of the order as excluded Mr Spindlow from the matrimonial home, but would discharge so much of the order as related to molestation, because there was, as I understand it, no real evidence of molestation.

Appeal dismissed.

Solicitors: *Lamb, Brooks & Bullock*, Basingstoke (for Mr Spindlow); *Morris & Hodges*, Basingstoke (for Mrs Spindlow).

Avtar S Virdi Esq Barrister.

Joyce v Joyce

CHANCERY DIVISION

MEGARRY V-C

11th, 12th, 13th APRIL 1978

Practice – Dismissal of action for want of prosecution – Delay – Inordinate delay without excuse – No steps taken by plaintiff for two years after close of pleadings – Summons to dismiss action for want of prosecution – Second action brought based on same cause of action – Summons to dismiss second action as abuse of process of court – Application of doctrine of laches – Burden of proof – Whether dismissal of first action futile in light of second action – Whether second action abuse of process of court.

The plaintiff and the defendant were the sole shareholders and directors of a private company. On 21st January 1974 the plaintiff issued a writ against the defendant claiming (i) specific performance of an alleged oral agreement, made on or about 1st January 1971, whereby the defendant agreed to sell his shares in the company to the plaintiff for £7,000, and/or (ii) damages for breach of contract. The plaintiff served a statement of claim on 19th September 1974 in which he alleged that the purchase price for the shares had been paid to the defendant by the end of September 1971. The defendant served a defence on 4th February 1975 in which he denied that he had ever agreed to sell his shares to the plaintiff and contended that the money which had been paid to him represented his part of the company's profits. On 8th September 1975 the plaintiff served a request for further and better particulars. Nothing further happened until 4th April 1977 when the defendant applied by summons to have the action dismissed for want of prosecution. However, the defendant died on 13th May and the hearing of the summons was adjourned. On 12th September letters of administration were granted to his widow and on 19th October an order to carry on was made, with her as the defendant. On 16th March 1978 the plaintiff issued a writ claiming (i) a declaration that he was absolutely and beneficially entitled to the disputed shares, or, alternatively, (ii) repayment of the money on the grounds that it had been paid for no consideration, or under a mistake of fact and for a consideration which had wholly failed. On 10th April the defendant applied by summons for an order to strike out the second action as being an abuse of the process of the court. The summonses in respect of the first and second actions were heard together. At the hearing the plaintiff accepted that he had been guilty of inordinate and inexcusable delay in respect of the first action but contended that the second action made it futile to dismiss the first action and that in the circumstances neither the doctrine of laches nor any fixed period of limitation applied.

Held – (i) In a case to which laches rather than any fixed period of limitation applied, it was for the plaintiff to establish that it would be futile to strike out the first action in view of the existence of the second action, and for that purpose he had to show that in the second action there was a prima facie case of his being able to overcome the doctrine of laches. The plaintiff had failed to do that and accordingly, since there had been inordinate delay, the first action would be dismissed for want of prosecution (see p 179 h to p 180 b, post); *Birkett v James* [1977] 2 All ER 801 applied; *Crofton v Ormsby* (1806) 2 Sch & Lef 583 and *Williams v Greatrex* [1956] 3 All ER 705 considered.

(ii) The plaintiff would face severe difficulties in respect of the second action but it would nonetheless be allowed to continue because (a) the fact that the first action was dismissed did not necessarily involve holding that the proprietary claim in the second action would be barred by laches, (b) the evidence did not show that the money claim was bound to fail, and (c) in any event, the defendant had not established that the second action would constitute a plain and obvious abuse of the process of the court. It followed that the summons in respect of the second action would be dismissed (see p 180 e to p 181 b, post); *Birkett v James* [1977] 2 All ER 801 applied.

Notes

For dismissal of actions for want of prosecution, see 30 Halsbury's Laws (3rd Edn) 410, para 771.

For striking out actions as an abuse of the process of the court, see ibid 407, para 767, and for cases on the subject, see 50 Digest (Repl) 83–95, 686–781.

Cases referred to in judgment

Birkett v James [1977] 2 All ER 801, [1978] AC 297, [1977] 3 WLR 38, HL.

Biss v Lambeth, Southwark and Lewisham Area Health Authority [1978] 2 All ER 125, [1978] 1 WLR 382, CA.

Crofton v Ormsby (1806) 2 Sch & Lef 583, 31(1) Digest (Reissue) 300, *884.

Tito v Waddell (No 2) [1977] 3 All ER 129, [1977] Ch 106, [1977] 2 WLR 496.

Williams v Greatrex [1956] 3 All ER 705, [1957] 1 WLR 31, CA, 44 Digest (Repl) 114, 939.

Summonses

By a writ issued on 21st January 1974 the plaintiff, Francis Xavier Joyce, brought an action against the defendant, Thomas Joyce, claiming, inter alia, (i) specific performance of an oral agreement made on or about 1st January 1971 between the plaintiff and the defendant whereby the defendant agreed to sell to the plaintiff 320 shares of £1 each in F & T Joyce Ltd ('the company') for £7,000, and (ii) damages in addition to or in lieu of specific performance. The statement of claim was served on 19th September 1974. In it the plaintiff alleged that the purchase money for the shares was paid to the defendant by the end of September 1971. The defence was served on 4th February 1975. The defendant denied that he had ever agreed to sell his shares to the plaintiff and contended that part of the £7,000 paid to him represented money owed to him by the company (£3,604·78) and the balance (£3,395·22) represented, or was believed by him to represent, money payable to him as his part of the company's profits. On 8th September the plaintiff served a request for further and better particulars. Nothing further happened until 4th April 1977 when the defendant applied by summons for an order, either under the court's inherent jurisdiction or under RSC Ord 25, r 1, dismissing the action for want of prosecution. The defendant died on 13th May and the hearing of the summons was adjourned. On 12th September letters of administration were granted to his widow, Mary Joyce, and on 19th October an order to carry on the action was made, with her as the defendant. On 16th March 1978 the plaintiff issued a writ claiming (i) a declaration that he was absolutely and beneficially entitled to the disputed shares, or, alternatively, (ii) repayment of £3,395·22 together with interest thereon pursuant to the Law Reform (Miscellaneous Provisions) Act 1934 from 20th September 1971 until payment. On 10th April the defendant applied by summons for an order, either under the court's inherent jurisdiction or under RSC Ord 18, r 19, to strike out the second action as an abuse of the process of the court. The facts are set out in the judgment.

Charles Purle for the plaintiff.
Jonathan Winegarten for the defendant.

MEGARRY V-C. I have before me two summonses taken out by the defendant in two actions which relate to the same transactions. They involve some consideration of how the recent decision of the House of Lords in *Birkett v James*[1] applies in cases where the action which the defendant seeks to strike out for want of prosecution involves claims in equity that are subject to the doctrine of laches instead of claims at law which are subject to a fixed period of limitation. The first summons is in an action for specific performance and damages commenced on 21st January 1974; and this summons seeks the dismissal of the action, either under the inherent jurisdiction or under RSC Ord 25, r 1, for want of prosecution. The action is based on an alleged oral agreement made on or about 1st January 1971 whereby the original defendant agreed to sell his 320 shares in a private company to the plaintiff for £7,000. According to the plaintiff, a little over half this sum, £3,604·78, was to consist of the payment of money already owed by the company to the defendant, and the remaining £3,395·22 was to be money paid by the plaintiff to the defendant. £500 in cash and £2,000 by cheque were in fact paid on or about 4th January 1971, and the remaining £4,500 was paid by cheque on or about 20th September 1971. The plaintiff and the defendant were the only two directors of the company, which had been formed in 1963, and the other 480 shares have at all times been held by the plaintiff. The plaintiff alleges, and the defendant denies, that on or about 1st January 1971 the defendant resigned as director, and the plaintiff's wife was appointed director in his place. The defendant also denies that he ever agreed to sell his shares to the plaintiff, and he contends that the £3,395·22 that the plaintiff says was the payment for the shares was instead his (the defendant's) share of the company's profit, or so he believed.

As I have said, the writ in this action was issued on 21st January 1974 and the statement of claim followed on 19th September 1974. The defence was served on 4th February 1975, and apart from a request for further and better particulars of the defence served on 8th September 1975, nothing further happened until the defendant's summons to dismiss the action for want of prosecution was issued on 4th April 1977. That was over two years after the pleadings had closed in February 1975. The affidavit in support of the summons, sworn on 5th May 1977, showed that the defendant was seriously ill; and in fact he died on 13th May 1977, four days before the return day for the summons. The hearing of the summons was accordingly adjourned. On 12th September 1977 letters of administration were granted to the defendant's widow, and on 19th October 1977 an order to carry on was made, with the widow as the present defendant. I shall use the term 'the defendant' for whichever is the relevant defendant at the time of which I speak.

Now in those circumstances counsel for the plaintiff very properly accepted that he was unable to resist the contention of counsel for the defendant that the plaintiff had been guilty of inordinate and inexcusable delay which gave rise to a substantial risk that it would not be possible to have a fair trial, or was likely to have caused serious prejudice to the defendant. Since the action was based on an alleged oral agreement which the original defendant denied, the death of the original defendant was plainly something which seriously prejudiced the defence. Although statements by him might well be admissible under the Civil Evidence Act 1968, he could not be cross-examined. Further, he would not be available to provide material for cross-examining the plaintiff about an oral agreement which the plaintiff alleged that the defendant had made well over seven years ago. True, the defence may well be aided by the tendency to require clear evidence to establish a claim against the estate of a deceased person, but that at most will mitigate the difficulties of the

---

1   [1977] 2 All ER 801, [1978] AC 297

defence. There is also the prejudice to the successive defendants in having the action hanging over their heads for so long: see *Biss v Lambeth, Southwark and Lewisham Area Health Authority*[1]. Thus far, there is clearly a strong case for striking out the action for want of prosecution. But that has to be considered against the decision in *Birkett v James*[2]. There, the House of Lords laid it down that apart from contumelious conduct by the plaintiff, an action ought not to be dismissed for want of prosecution while the plaintiff was still within time to commence a fresh action, for to do so would only aggravate the delay and increase the costs.

I pause there. The statement of claim alleges that it was an implied term of the alleged oral agreement that the defendant should execute and deliver to the plaintiff within a reasonable time all requisite stock transfers to perfect the plaintiff's title to the shares. Allow 28 days as a reasonable time for this, and the six years' period of limitation for breach of contract had expired by February 1977. For over a year it has been too late for the plaintiff to issue a writ for anything to which the six years' period applies. But, of course, the action is not merely an action for damages, but is primarily an action for the equitable relief of specific performance, with a claim for damages which counsel for the plaintiff says is a claim not at common law but under Lord Cairns's Act[3].

With that, I turn to the second action. This was commenced on 16th March 1978; and the defendant's summons is to strike this out under RSC Ord 18, r 19, and the inherent jurisdiction as being an abuse of the process of the court. The claim is, first, for a declaration that the plaintiff is absolutely and beneficially entitled to the disputed 320 shares. Counsel for the plaintiff accepts that this in substance is only a repetition of the claim for specific performance in the first action, though of course a declaration of beneficial ownership, unlike an order for specific performance, does not require the defendant to execute any transfer or the like. Alternatively, there is a claim for the £3,395·22 as having been paid to the defendant for no consideration or under a mistake of fact and for a consideration which has wholly failed. The money claim, says the plaintiff, was concealed by the fraud of the defendant within s 26(*b*) of the Limitation Act 1939 until on or about 29th September 1972, when the defendant had first alleged that he had never agreed to sell his shares to the plaintiff. 29th September 1972 is, of course, within the period of six years before the writ was issued in the second action. In that way, the plaintiff seeks to show that the money claim is not barred by limitation.

Fraudulent concealment is not alleged in respect of the claim for a declaration. What is said in respect of that claim is in effect that no period of limitation applies in respect of the assertion of a proprietary right in equity, at all events when the plaintiff who claims that right can show that he has paid all that is due in respect of it, and that the defendant has been excluded from all benefit. Here, the legal title to the shares has admittedly remained vested in the defendant at all material dates; but since the balance of the money was paid in September 1971, the plaintiff has done all that he was required to do under the contract, and he has been in effective control of the company, since the defendant has not attempted to assert any rights in respect of the bare legal ownership of the shares. In such circumstances, says counsel for the plaintiff, no fixed period of limitation applies, nor does any doctrine of laches. It would be open to the plaintiff to bring proceedings to assert his proprietary rights in the shares five or, for that matter, 50 years after the transaction which gave him that right. Accordingly, neither his proprietary claim to a declaration nor, by virtue of fraudulent concealment, his money claim, is barred, even though the writ was issued some seven years after the breach of contract. What follows from that, said counsel, was that the first action ought not to be struck out for want of prosecution, for even if the plaintiff is no longer in a position to issue a fresh writ for precisely the same relief, he has in fact issued another writ which covers much the same ground as that in the first action. Counsel accepted that the first action must be dismissed unless to do so would be futile by

---

1　[1978] 2 All ER 125, [1978] 1 WLR 382
2　[1977] 2 All ER 801, [1978] AC 297
3　Chancery Amendment Act 1858

reason of the existence of the second action; but he said that the second action did in fact make it futile to dismiss the first action.

In support of his contention that his proprietary claim could not be said to have been barred by laches, counsel for the plaintiff cited a line of cases beginning with *Crofton v Ormsby*[1] and ending with *Williams v Greatrex*[2]. In those cases, a significant factor, as it seems to me, is that the transaction which had brought the proprietary interest into being was not in issue. In the present case, of course, it has from the outset been in issue whether or not the alleged oral agreement was ever made. If it was not, the plaintiff has no proprietary interest. I can readily understand that if, by an undisputed transaction, the plaintiff has both the equitable interest and possession of the property, and all that he lacks is the bare legal ownership, his prolonged failure to get in the legal title will not normally be treated as laches that will bar his claim. In *Crofton v Ormsby*[3], on which counsel for the plaintiff relied, Lord Redesdale LC said that:

> 'The whole laches here consists in the not clothing an equitable estate with a legal title, and that by a party in possession. Now I do not conceive that this is that species of laches, which will prevail against the equitable title; if I should hold it so, it would tend to overset a great deal of property in this country, where parties often continue to hold under an equitable contract for 40 or 50 years, without clothing it with the legal title.'

Now in the present case the shares still stand in the name of the defendant. The plaintiff is not in possession of them, and has not obtained what he says he contracted to buy to any greater extent than is involved in the defendant not taking steps to enforce the rights that the shares confer. The plaintiff has, of course, paid the money; but far from it being possible to say that he has fully carried out his side of an admitted contract, the very existence of that contract is in dispute. In such a case, I think that the principle excluding laches has no application. Inactivity when you have everything save the bare legal title under an undisputed contract is one thing, inactivity when the contract is disputed and you lack more than the bare legal title, is another. Furthermore, I think that the doctrine in question was directed not to whether an equitable cause of action would be barred, but to whether the particular remedy of specific performance would be refused. Accordingly, I reject the contention that laches has no application to the proprietary claim in the second action.

Counsel's claim that the plaintiff's 1974 action should not be struck out for want of prosecution was based not only on the existence of the 1978 action but also on his contention that there was nothing to prevent him from issuing another writ today claiming the same relief as in the 1974 action: for he contended that no fixed period of limitation applied, and that laches could not be said to bar his claim to specific performance. I do not think that this can be right. What he is saying is that laches would not bar a claim made in April 1978 for the specific performance of an oral contract made in January 1971 and fully performed by the plaintiff in September 1971, when the defendant who has throughout denied the existence of the contract died in May 1977. I accept, of course, that the operation of the doctrine of laches is often less clear-cut than the operation of statutory periods of limitation, but I think that some common sense must be used. In applying *Birkett v James*[4] to cases that are subject to laches rather than any fixed period of limitation, I think that it is for the plaintiff to demonstrate the futility of striking out the earlier action; and to do this he must at least show that in the second action there is a prima facie case for his being able to overcome the difficulties resulting from the doctrine of laches. In this case the plaintiff has wholly failed to persuade me of this. Certainly the plaintiff has been very far from showing himself to be 'ready, desirous, prompt and eager'.

1   (1806) 2 Sch & Lef 583
2   [1956] 3 All ER 705, [1957] 1 WLR 31
3   2 Sch & Lef 583 at 603
4   [1977] 2 All ER 801, [1978] AC 297

The result is therefore as follows. First, the plaintiff has failed to show that he could issue another writ for the same relief that would not be defeated by the doctrine of laches. *a* Second, the writ that he has issued covers something of the same ground, but although it seeks different relief, it faces what seem to me to be considerable difficulties in relation to the elapse of time. Third, I cannot see that it would be futile to dismiss the first action for want of prosecution, for although the defendant would still be exposed to the claims in the second action, those claims face greater difficulties than did the claims in the first action. In other words, the defendant is better off in facing only the second action and not having *b* to meet the first. Fourth, if the second action is ignored, this is a plain case for dismissing the first action for want of prosecution; and when the second action is taken into account, there is nothing in it which suffices to defeat the claim to have the first action dismissed. I therefore dismiss the first action for want of prosecution.

That brings me to the summons to strike out the second action as being an abuse of the process of the court. The essence of counsel's submission for the defendant on this was that *c* the circumstances of delay and consequent prejudice to the defendant which sufficed for the dismissal of the first action for want of prosecution must amount to laches which would defeat the second action so far as the proprietary claim was concerned. It was therefore, at any rate quoad that claim, an abuse of the process of the court to bring the second action. As for the money claim, this was barred by the six years' period of limitation, and the attempt to get round this by the claim of fraudulent concealment was *d* hopeless, since there was nothing approaching fraudulent concealment in the case. When it was pointed out to counsel for the defendant that the courts had construed s 26(b) of the Limitation Act 1939 in such a way that it was not necessary to establish anything resembling fraud or concealment in the ordinary sense of those words, and that 'any unconscionable failure to reveal is enough' (*Tito v Waddell (No 2)*[1]), his submissions on the point became somewhat less confident. *e*

In considering this contention, it must be remembered that the application is based on there being an abuse of the process of the court. This postulates that there should be a sufficiently improper use of the machinery of the court to constitute an abuse. Further, the power to strike out cases on this ground will only be used in plain and obvious cases; doubts and uncertainties and reservations are not enough. *Birkett v James*[2] has now made it clear that it is not an abuse of the process of the court if a plaintiff who is in peril of *f* having his action dismissed for want of prosecution thereupon commences, before he is statute-barred, a new action for the same relief[3]. Has counsel for the defendant made out a sufficient case for the peremptory remedy of striking out the second action here as being an abuse of the process of the court?

In my judgment the answer is No. Plainly there are difficulties for the plaintiff in pursuing the second action; and it may well be that the difficulties may properly be *g* described as great difficulties. But an action is not to be struck out as being an abuse of the process of the court merely because the plaintiff appears to have great difficulties in his path. I think counsel for the defendant was inclined to contend, without quite putting it this way, that to hold that the first action should be dismissed for want of prosecution necessarily involved holding that at any rate the proprietary claim was barred by laches, not exactly as res judicata but by some sort of cousin of res judicata. Plainly there are some *h* elements in common between the circumstances which justify dismissing the first action for want of prosecution and the circumstances which amount to the laches which may prove a good defence in the second action: but I do not think that they are by any means the same. The doctrine of laches is of some complexity, and I certainly do not think that I could hold, merely on affidavit evidence, that the want of prosecution in the circumstances of this case amounts to laches which would bar the proprietary claim. There is also the *j*

1　[1977] 3 All ER 129 at 244, [1977] Ch 106 at 245
2　[1977] 2 All ER 801, [1978] AC 297
3　[1977] 2 All ER 801 at 808, 813, 817–818, [1978] AC 297 at 322, 328, 333–334

money claim; and on the material before me I can see no grounds for saying that this is bound to fail.

In any case, I cannot see what abuse of the process of the court there is. If it were an abuse of the process of the court to commence any action in which the plaintiff faced severe difficulties, actions which in the end would have limped into port would be lost with all hands, with many other actions, long before trial. The jurisdiction to strike actions out as an abuse of the process of the court must not be exercised on the basis so familiar under RSC Ord 14. In my judgment, there is no abuse of the process of the court here, and so I dismiss the summons in the second action. In doing this, I rule only on the case that has been argued before me, relating to abuse of the process of the court; I decide nothing on any other possible step that the defendant might have taken or may take hereafter.

First action dismissed for want of prosecution; summons in respect of second action dismissed.

Solicitors: *Rising & Ravenscroft* (for the plaintiff); *Penningtons* (for the defendant).

Hazel Hartman   Barrister.

Hopper v Hopper

COURT OF APPEAL, CIVIL DIVISION

STAMP, LAWTON AND ORMROD LJJ

22nd MAY 1978

Injunction – Exclusion of party from matrimonial home – County court – Time limit on operation of injunction – Remedy essentially short term pending other arrangements for accommodation being made by applicant or steps being taken to clarify matrimonial status – Remedy not to operate as permanent substitute for property adjustment order if applicant has no intention of proceeding to divorce or judicial separation – Domestic Violence and Matrimonial Proceedings Act 1976, s 1.

A matrimonial injunction granted by a county court under s 1[a] of the Domestic Violence and Matrimonial Proceedings Act 1976 is to be regarded as essentially a short term remedy. If an application be made under the 1976 Act alone with no intention of proceeding to divorce, or no immediate intention of proceeding to judicial separation, any injunction granted will, to all intent and purposes, operate as a substitute for an adjustment of property order under the Matrimonial Causes Act 1973. A court which feels it right to make an order under the 1976 Act should always have clearly in mind that it is dealing with the problem on a short term basis and that any injunction which is granted should be expressly limited in some way or it should be made perfectly clear to both parties that the protection of the injunction will be withdrawn after the lapse of a reasonable time, that

---

a   Section 1 provides:
  '(1) Without prejudice to the jurisdiction of the High Court, on an application by a party to a marriage a county court shall have jurisdiction to grant an injunction containing one or more of the following provisions, namely,—(a) a provision restraining the other party to the marriage from molesting the applicant; (b) a provision restraining the other party from molesting a child living with the applicant; (c) a provision excluding the other party from the matrimonial home or a part of the matrimonial home or from a specified area in which the matrimonial home is included; (d) a provision requiring the other party to permit the applicant to enter and remain in the matrimonial home or a part of the matrimonial home; whether or not any other relief is sought in the proceedings.
  '(2) Subsection (1) above shall apply to a man and a woman who are living with each other in the same household as husband and wife as it applies to the parties to a marriage and any reference to the matrimonial home shall be construed accordingly.'

being time enough to enable the wife to make other arrangements for her accommodation or, in the case of a married woman, to take steps to get her matrimonial status clarified and to enable the court to exercise its powers to make a property adjustment order (see p 184 c to f and h to p 185 b, post).

Dicta of Lord Salmon and of Lord Scarman in *Davis v Johnson* [1978] 1 All ER at 1151–1152, 1157 applied.

Notes

For the jurisdiction of the county court to grant matrimonial injunctions, see Supplement to 13 Halsbury's Laws (4th Edn) para 1228A.

For the Domestic Violence and Matrimonial Proceedings Act 1976, s 1, see 46 Halsbury's Statutes (3rd Edn) 714.

Case referred to in judgments

Davis v Johnson [1978] 1 All ER 1132, [1978] 2 WLR 553, HL.

Appeal

Jacqueline Hopper ('the wife') appealed from an order of his Honour Judge Hartley made at Leeds County Court on 15th May 1978 restraining Arthur Barry Hopper ('the husband'), from remaining in the matrimonial home at 1 Maltby Court, Leeds after 4 pm on 12th June 1978. The grounds of the appeal were that the husband should have been ordered to vacate the matrimonial home within 24 hours of the service of the order on him. The husband cross-appealed on the ground that no order should have been made against him at all. The facts are set out in the judgment of Stamp LJ.

Andrew Kershaw for the wife
Rodney Grant for the husband

STAMP LJ. This is an appeal from an order of his Honour Judge Hartley made on 15th May 1978 at Leeds whereby a husband was restrained from remaining in the matrimonial home at 1 Maltby Court, Leeds, after 4 pm on 12th June 1978. The wife appeals saying that 24 hours would have been quite long enough for the husband to remain in the matrimonial home and find alternative accommodation, and there is a cross-appeal by the husband in which he submits that there ought not to have been an order made against him at all.

The parties married on 11th May 1977, but they had been living together certainly since November of the previous year. They had throughout been living in Leeds. The wife's mother and her sister and brother-in-law also live in the neighbourhood. The wife had a child by a former marriage, a girl, who was born on 29th June 1965. So she is going to be 13 next month.

The wife, in her affidavit in support of the application to the judge, which was made under the Domestic Violence and Matrimonial Proceedings Act 1976, asserted that in October 1977 the husband started to gamble heavily and came home drunk almost every day. He would, she said, swear at her, and if she complained he would threaten to put her out of the house. In January 1978 the situation became so bad that she left home and went back to her mother, and stayed there for three days, so she says, but she returned on an undertaking or promise by her husband to behave better in the future. She says he did not behave any better, and again on 6th February she left, on this occasion for two nights. Again she was persuaded to go back, but she says that he remained drunk two or three times a week and was abusive and threatening when drunk. On 6th May there was an episode, a rather serious episode, in the course of which there was a fight in the car in which the parties were going home after a Saturday evening spent at a club. The wife as a result took refuge with her sister, who lives fairly near. She complains both of bruises on her face and upper arm and in other places. She says that the episode in the car was preceded by heavy drinking throughout the evening and that he made a comment regarding the mother's daughter to which, if it is true, if he made this comment, she justifiably took great exception and she flounced out of the room in which they were. Then later when they got into the car to go home he, so she alleges, started hitting her as he drove along the road. He hit her very hard. As a result there was a minor accident. When they got home again he started hitting her, and as a result she left home and sought refuge, as I have said, with her sister. A few minutes later, I suppose, her brother-in-law went and fetched the daughter and the daughter joined the wife.

The account given by the husband is altogether different, both regarding the marriage itself and the episode on Saturday, 6th May, to that of the wife. He alleges that the marriage was a perfectly happy one, although he concedes that the wife did leave on a day in January and again, I think for a night, in February. The wife, as I think I have said, accused him of gambling. He admits that he does gamble, but says that he did so very successfully and was able out of the proceeds of his gambling to provide his wife with a high standard of living, including fur coats, diamond rings and the like. He admitted arguments. He complained about his wife's quick temper. He complained that she was dominated by her mother. He gives a different account of the remark which triggered off the row on the Saturday evening, and a wholly different account of the journey home in the car, in the course of which he says that she attacked him and he had to beat her off as he was driving along. He agrees there was an accident. He concedes that he behaved very badly when they got home and that the police were sent for and he was arrested and charged with assault on his wife. The matter has not yet been heard.

The judge had the oral evidence of the wife and of her sister and that of the husband himself. There were, as I have said, differences of testimony in the affidavits and one has not got the means, as the judge had, of deciding where the truth lies. It was, however, the wife's evidence that she is now living with her sister in uncomfortable conditions, because her sister lives in a two bedroomed house in which there are also living the sister's husband and two children. She, she complains, has to sleep on the floor.

On behalf of the wife counsel stressed that it was really the daughter who was suffering very severely as a result of the judge not turning the husband out of the house sooner in that she is now living in very cramped conditions and has to sleep on a camp bed; a situation made very much worse by the fact that the unfortunate child has been suffering from, or is recovering from, a broken arm. However, I was glad to observe that the girl is now well enough to go back to school. I cannot think that the harm that may be done to this girl by having to sleep on a camp bed with a broken arm after being in hospital can possibly outweigh the undesirability of driving her stepfather out of the home at very short notice.

The judge, as I have said, had the opportunity of seeing both parties in the witness box. It may be that some judges would have given the husband a shorter time to leave the house, and others might, perhaps, have given him a longer time. But it is not a matter with which this court can, in my judgment, possibly think of interfering. The appeal of the wife is, in my judgment, a quite hopeless appeal and a thorough waste of public money.

There is more substance in the cross-appeal by which the husband seeks to have the order discharged. But, again, the judge saw and heard the witnesses and I am not persuaded that he was wrong in making an exclusion order. I cannot, however, leave matters quite there. The order was an order excluding the husband from the house for an indefinite period. The facts of this case are unusual. In view of the shortness of the marriage there can be no divorce proceedings for some two years, and unless the wife takes proceedings for judicial separation, the husband will not in the meantime be in a position, and indeed may not be in a position for five years, to apply for a property adjustment order. There is a dispute as to who is the owner of the house, but it is in circumstances such as these that I quote the answer to the question which was raised in one of the recent cases under the 1976 Act: how long ought a man to be excluded from the home under the Act? I would refer to the answers which were given in the House of Lords by Lord Salmon, Lord Scarman and Lord Dilhorne. Lord Salmon in *Davis v Johnson*[1] said this:

'. . . for how long? It is a pity that the Act did not regulate the period in which he could be deprived of occupation and his former mistress allowed to enjoy it [that, of course, was a case between lover and mistress and not husband and wife]. It is hoped that Parliament may consider amending the Act by specifying such a period, or, perhaps better still, laying down principles on which its duration may be calculated. In the meantime the period is entirely in the discretion of a multitude of county court judges and, there being nothing in the statute to guide them in the exercise of that discretion, it might be exercised with a considerable amount of discrepancy. I am sure, however, that those exercising the discretion will understand that to make a final order for a maximum period would probably convert it into a minimum period. I would hesitantly express the view that the best course would be to make an order for say a month with liberty for both parties to apply. Much depends on the circumstances of each case, but I find it difficult to believe that it could ever be fair, save in most exceptional circumstances, to keep a man out of his own flat or house for more than a few months.'

Lord Scarman said this[2]:

'Thirdly, and most importantly, the grant of the order is in the discretion of the county court judge. It is for him to decide whether, and for how long, it is necessary for the protection of the applicant or her child. Normally he will make the order "until further order", each party having the right to apply to the court for its discharge or modification. The remedy is available to deal with an emergency; it is, therefore, as my noble and learned friend, Lord Salmon, has said, a species of first aid. The order must be discontinued as soon as it is clear, on the application of either or both family partners, that it is no longer needed.'

Then there is a passage from Lord Dilhorne's speech[3] where he says that the purpose of the Act was 'the provision of immediate relief not permanent resolution of a situation arising on the break-up of a marriage or an association where the parties though unmarried had been living as if they were'.

It will, of course, be open to the husband to apply in the instant case for the discharge of the order, and I think it right, before parting from this case, to point out that the wife may be well advised to either petition for judicial separation, or to find alternative accommodation, or she might, perhaps, even consider the reconciliation which the husband offers her.

I would dismiss both the appeal and the cross-appeal.

LAWTON LJ. I agree with Stamp LJ's judgment and have nothing to add.

ORMROD LJ. I entirely agree and would only wish, since this is the first time this kind of case has come before the court since *Davis v Johnson*[4], to emphasise the theme which runs through all the speeches in the House of Lords in *Davis v Johnson*[4] in relation to this particular matter. That is that the Domestic Violence and Matrimonial Proceedings Act 1976 is to be regarded as a short term remedy essentially. Of course in a case where parties have been married, and married for a long time, and the marriage has broken down an application under the 1976 Act is, to all intents and purposes, equivalent to an application for an interim injunction in divorce proceedings. So the principles are clear in that direction. But if the application be made under the 1976 Act alone with no intention of

1   [1978] 1 All ER 1132 at 1151–1152, [1978] 2 WLR 553 at 576
2   [1978] 1 All ER 1132 at 1157, [1978] 2 WLR 553 at 582
3   [1978] 1 All ER 1132 at 1146, [1978] 2 WLR 553 at 569
4   [1978] 1 All ER 1132, [1978] 2 WLR 553

proceeding to divorce, or no immediate intention of proceeding to judicial separation, then the 1976 Act will, to all intents and purposes, operate as a substitute for an adjustment of property order under the Matrimonial Causes Act 1973. Courts who feel it right to make orders under s 1 of the 1976 Act should, in my judgment, always have clearly in mind that they are dealing with the problem on a short term basis and that the injunctions which are granted should be either expressly limited in some way or it should be made perfectly clear to both parties that the protection of the injunction will be withdrawn after the lapse of a reasonable time, the reasonable time being time enough to enable the wife to make other arrangements for her accommodation or to take steps, in the case of a married woman, to get her matrimonial status clarified, and to enable the court to exercise its powers to make property adjustment orders. If that is not done the 1976 Act will become a means of oppressing some people severely. Therefore, all courts making orders under this Act should, I think, have clearly in their mind the nature of the order that they are making. In this particular case I would anticipate that if the wife takes no steps, as Stamp LJ has suggested, either to try and find somewhere else to live or to get the marriage dissolved, and gets on with it so that the husband can apply for a property adjustment order, or she can do so, then she will find that this injunction is discharged and she will find herself back in the position she was in before it was made.

In those circumstances, I agree that the appeal and the cross-appeal should be dismissed.

Appeal dismissed. Cross-appeal dismissed.

Solicitors: *Spencer & Fisch*, Leeds (for the wife); *J Levi & Co*, Leeds (for the husband).

Avtar S Virdi Esq   Barrister.

Malhotra v Choudhury

COURT OF APPEAL, CIVIL DIVISION
STEPHENSON AND CUMMING-BRUCE LJJ
18th, 19th, 20th, 21st OCTOBER 1977

Sale of land – Damages for breach of contract – Inability to show good title – Vendor unwilling to use best endeavours to obtain good title – Whether damages for vendor's breach of contract should be limited to costs of investigating title.

Sale of land – Damages for breach of contract – Damages in substitution for specific performance – Date of assessment – Whether damages to be assessed as at date of hearing of action – Effect of plaintiff's delay in bringing proceedings.

The plaintiff was one of two partners in a medical practice of which the senior resided at a property comprising a house and a surgery. On the retirement of the senior partner the plaintiff agreed to take the defendant into the practice as junior partner, and the senior partner agreed to sell the property to the defendant and his wife. The partnership deed, made on 19th May 1972, two weeks after the contract for the sale of the property, provided, inter alia, that if the defendant ceased to be a partner, he would offer to sell the house and surgery to the plaintiff at a fair market price, to be fixed, in the absence of agreement, by a valuer. On 1st August the property was conveyed to the defendant and his wife as joint tenants. At the date of the partnership deed the plaintiff was practising from the surgery at the property and thereafter both he and the defendant practised from the surgery. The partnership was not successful, and on 30th March 1973 the plaintiff gave written notice to the defendant to dissolve it, and also gave notice that he wished to exercise the option requiring the defendant to offer the property to him for sale. The defendant asserted that in the events which had happened the option was not exercisable, and refused to sell the property to the plaintiff. In September 1973 the plaintiff commenced an action claiming, inter alia, specific performance of the option. By his defence the defendant denied that the plaintiff was entitled to specific performance and in an affidavit in support stated that the property was the home of his wife and himself, that it was vested in both of them, that the surgery was an integral part of the property, and that on termination of the partnership he intended to practise from the surgery on his own. On 28th October 1973 a judge held that the plaintiff had properly exercised the option and ordered specific performance of it. He also ordered that the defendant should give a valuer access to the property and deliver up all the deeds relating to it, that there should be an enquiry into title and that the plaintiff should be given vacant possession of the property. On the defendant's appeal, the Court of Appeal struck out the order for specific performance because the defendant's wife was a joint tenant of the property and might resist an order for sale and refuse to agree to any conveyance, but the court affirmed the rest of the judge's order. The defendant did not comply with that part of the order which was affirmed and the plaintiff took out a summons to proceed seeking the title deeds, access to the property and an enquiry as to title. On 8th November 1974 the defendant's wife swore an affidavit in the action stating that she refused to agree to any sale of the property to the plaintiff. The plaintiff took no further steps in the action between April 1975 and January 1977 when he issued a notice of motion asking for damages at common law for breach of the contract constituted by the option. The defendant admitted breach of the option but contested the measure of the damages payable. The judge, while finding that the defendant had not shown any enthusiasm for carrying out the court's order to show title, also found that there was uncontradicted evidence that the defendant was unable to make a good title because of his wife's refusal to consent to a sale and no evidence that he had persuaded her to refuse to consent, and held that because the defendant was unable to make a good title the damages recoverable by the plaintiff were limited to the costs of investigating the title to the property and any costs connected with obtaining a valuation. The plaintiff appealed seeking substantial damages under the general principles applicable to a breach of contract.

Held – The appeal would be allowed for the following reasons—

(i) The rule that where a vendor of land was unable to make a good title the damages recoverable by his purchaser for breach of the contract were limited to his expenses incurred in investigating title and did not include damages for the loss of his bargain was an exceptional rule which only applied if the vendor was unable, through no default of his own, to carry out his contractual duty to make a good title. To obtain the benefit of the rule the vendor was required to prove that he had used his best endeavours to make a good title. Bad faith on his part, even without actual fraud, was sufficient to exclude the rule, and unwillingness to use his best endeavours to make a good title constituted bad faith. The statement that the defendant's wife refused to consent to a sale did not indicate that the defendant had tried to persuade her to consent and, in the absence of any other evidence to that effect, it was to be inferred that the defendant had not used his best endeavours to persuade his wife to agree to the sale and that he was therefore guilty of bad faith. It followed that the plaintiff was entitled to substantial damages (see p 199 c to h, p 200 e to h, p 201 b to d, p 203 d to g, p 204 a to d and g and p 208 a, post); Bain v Fothergill [1874–80] All ER Rep 83 distinguished; Day v Singleton [1899] 2 Ch 320, Keen v Mear [1920] All ER Rep 147 and dictum of Salter J in Braybrooks v Whaley [1919] 1 KB at 441–442 applied.

(ii) Damages awarded in substitution for an order for specific performance of a contract of sale of real property were to be assessed by reference to the value of the property at the date of the judgment and not at the date of breach of the contract. However, as there had been delay by the plaintiff since 1975 in bringing the proceedings to a conclusion, the date for valuing the property would be moved back one year from the date of the judgment in October 1977 to October 1976. Furthermore, since the parties must have contemplated that if the plaintiff exercised the option, he would use the surgery for his practice, the damages in substitution for specific performance of the option should include such loss in the plaintiff's medical practice as had flowed in the past, or would flow in the future, from the defendant's failure to sell the house and surgery to the plaintiff (see p 204 c d, p 206 c d and j to p 207 d and h j and p 208 a, post); Wroth v Tyler [1973] 1 All ER 897 applied.

Notes

For the damages which a purchaser of land may recover for breach of the contract of sale, see 12 Halsbury's Laws (4th Edn) para 1183, and for cases on the subject, see 40 Digest (Repl) 284–291, 2358–2439.

For the Chancery Amendment Act 1858, s 2, see 25 Halsbury's Statutes (3rd Edn) 703.

Cases referred to in judgments

Bain v Fothergill (1874) LR 7 HL 158, [1874–80] All ER Rep 83, 43 LJ Ex 243, 31 LT 387, 39 JP 228, HL; affg (1870) LR 6 Exch 59, Ex Ch, 40 Digest (Repl) 287, 2392.

Braybrooks v Whaley [1919] 1 KB 435, 88 LJKB 577, 120 LT 281, DC, 40 Digest (Repl) 286, 2374.

Day v Singleton [1899] 2 Ch 320, 68 LJ Ch 593, 81 LT 306, CA, 31(2) Digest (Reissue) 700, 5723.

Engel v Fitch (1869) LR 4 QB 659, 10 B & S 738, 38 LJQB 304, Ex Ch; affg (1867) LR 3 QB 314, 40 Digest (Repl) 285, 2369.

Flureau v Thornhill (1776) 2 Wm Bl 1078, [1775–1802] All ER Rep 91, 96 ER 635, 40 Digest (Repl) 146, 1116.

General and Finance Facilities Ltd v Cooks Cars (Romford) Ltd [1963] 2 All ER 314, [1963] 1 WLR 644, CA, 46 Digest (Repl) 524, 678.

Grant v Dawkins [1973] 3 All ER 897, [1973] 1 WLR 1406, 27 P & CR 158, Digest (Cont Vol D) 856, 837b.

Hopkins v Grazebrook (1826) 6 B & C 31, 9 Dow & Ry KB 22, 5 LJOSKB 65, 108 ER 364, 40 Digest (Repl) 286, 2375.

Keen v Mear [1920] 2 Ch 574, [1920] All ER Rep 147, 89 LJ Ch 513, 124 LT 19, 40 Digest
(Repl) 285, 2368.

Leeds Industrial Co-operative Society Ltd v Slack [1924] AC 851, [1924] All ER Rep 259, 93 LJ
Ch 436, 131 LT 710, HL; *rvsg sub nom Slack v Leeds Industrial Co-operative Society Ltd*
[1923] 1 Ch 431, CA; *subsequent proceedings sub nom Slack v Leeds Industrial Co-operative
Society Ltd* [1924] 2 Ch 475, CA, 28(2) Digest (Reissue) 1012, 396.

Rosenthal v Alderton and Sons Ltd [1946] 1 All ER 583, [1946] KB 374, 115 LJKB 215, 174
LT 214, CA, 46 Digest (Repl) 515, 605.

Rudd v Lascelles [1900] 1 Ch 815, 69 LJ Ch 396, 82 LT 256, 44 Digest (Repl) 165, 1445.

Sachs v Miklos [1948] 1 All ER 67, [1948] 2 KB 23, [1948] LJR 1012, CA, 3 Digest (Repl) 115,
361.

Watts v Spence [1975] 2 All ER 528, [1976] Ch 165, [1975] 2 WLR 1039, 29 P & CR 501,
Digest (Cont Vol D) 805, 2309a.

Wroth v Tyler [1973] 1 All ER 897, [1974] Ch 30, [1973] 2 WLR 405, 25 P & CR 138, Digest
(Cont Vol D) 855, 837a.

Appeal

On 21st September 1973 the plaintiff, Dr Prem Krishnan Malhotra, issued a writ against
the defendant, Dr Jagodinda Kumra Choudhury, claiming, inter alia, (i) a declaration that
the medical partnership between them, constituted by a deed of partnership dated 19th
May 1972, be wound up, and (ii) specific performance of an agreement, constituted by an
option in the deed, for the sale by the defendant to the plaintiff of property comprising a
house and surgery, known as Novar, 37 Butt Hill, Kippax, Yorkshire. A statement of claim
claiming, inter alia, the same relief was issued on 1st October 1973. By his defence the
defendant denied that the plaintiff was entitled to exercise the option. The plaintiff also
issued on 21st September 1973, a notice of motion seeking, inter alia, an injunction to
restrain the defendant from preventing the plaintiff from having access to or use of the
surgery at Novar. On 28th October 1973, Blackett-Ord V-C held that the option had been
properly exercised by the plaintiff, and ordered specific performance of the option. He also
ordered that access to Novar should be given to a valuer, that there should be an enquiry
into title, delivery of all the deeds relating to Novar and that vacant possession should be
given to the plaintiff. Furthermore, he continued an undertaking by the defendant to
allow the plaintiff to use the surgery. On the defendant's appeal the Court of Appeal, on
4th June 1974, struck out the order for specific performance, on the ground that Novar was
jointly owned by the defendant and his wife and she might resist an order for sale and
refuse to concur in a conveyance, but affirmed the rest of Blackett-Ord V-C's order. The
defendant failed to comply with the part of the order which was affirmed. By a notice of
motion in the action issued on 21st January 1977 the plaintiff sought damages at common
law for breach of the agreement constituted by the exercise of the option and an enquiry
as to the damages. On 29th March Blackett-Ord V-C ordered that the plaintiff was entitled
to damages but that under the rule in *Bain v Fothergill* [1] they were to be limited to the costs
of investigating the title to Novar and to any costs connected with obtaining a valuation of
the property. The plaintiff appealed seeking an order that he was entitled to damages
ascertained according to the general principles of law applicable to damages for breach of
contract. The facts are set out in the judgment of Stephenson LJ.

Matthew Caswell for the plaintiff.
John Behrens for the defendant.

STEPHENSON LJ. This is an appeal from a decision of Blackett-Ord V-C dated 29th
March 1977. The appeal is concerned with a dispute between two doctors practising in
Kippax, Swillington, West Yorkshire.

---

1 (1874) LR 7 HL 158, [1874–80] All ER Rep 83

In 1972 Dr Choudhury, the defendant, gave Dr Malhotra, the plaintiff, an option to purchase the house and surgery called Novar, 37 Butt Hill, Kippax; but he has not conveyed that house and surgery to the plaintiff and still lives in it himself, practises from it and will not even allow the plaintiff to use it.

The house was built for a Dr Mathieson in 1933. In 1969 Dr Mathieson took into his medical practice as junior partner the plaintiff and he gave him an option to purchase Novar at the market price if and when he retired. We are not concerned with the terms of that option. Thereafter the plaintiff bought himself a house in the neighbouring village of Swillington, where the partners in this practice had, with others, a surgery, at a National Health Service clinic. So the plaintiff did not need Novar and did not exercise his option to purchase it from Dr Mathieson when Dr Mathieson retired in 1972.

In that year the plaintiff took the defendant into the practice and into partnership as junior partner. It is not disputed that at that time Dr Mathieson and the plaintiff saw both the defendant and his wife, but there is a dispute as to what was said when they met.

It is not disputed that in 1972 three legal documents were executed. First of all on 5th May contracts for the sale of Novar by Dr Mathieson to the defendant and his wife for £9,000 were exchanged; 'exchanged' by the same solicitor acting for both vendor and purchaser. A fortnight later, on 19th May, the plaintiff and defendant entered into a deed of partnership containing, among more common form provisions, in cl 22 an option in favour of the plaintiff to purchase Novar in certain circumstances. Finally on 1st August a conveyance of the property to the defendant and his wife was executed for the price of £9,000 raised entirely on a mortgage from the Halifax Building Society.

Unfortunately the partnership did not work. On 30th March 1973 the plaintiff, through his solicitors, gave the defendant a written notice. The relevant parts of it are in these terms:

> '. . . we do hereby give you formal notice of the dissolution of the partnership to take effect on the expiry of six months from the day of your receipt of this letter. We would add that if you wish to have the termination take effect at an earlier date Dr. Malhotra would be prepared to agree to this.'

Later in the letter comes this notice:

> '*House and Surgery at Novar Kippax.* We refer you to clause 22 of the deed of partnership whereby upon dissolution of your partnership with Dr. Malhotra you are required to offer to sell the house and surgery to Dr. Malhotra. We hereby give you notice that Dr. Malhotra does require you to offer the same to him for sale. We hope that a figure for fair market price will be agreed; otherwise Dr. Malhotra will rely on the provisions contained in this clause for fixing the same.'

The partnership deed was made between the plaintiff giving his address in Swillington and the defendant giving an address in Amersham, Buckinghamshire, from which he came with his wife and children to live in Novar. By cl 1:

> 'The Partners hereby mutually agree to become Partners in the Medical Practice hitherto carried on by Dr. Malhotra with Dr. Mathieson in Kippax Swillington and District in the West Riding of the County of York as from the Seventeenth day of July One thousand nine hundred and seventy two until determination as hereinafter provided and upon the terms hereinafter expressed.'

By cl 3:

> 'Each Partner shall provide and maintain himself in a dwellinghouse suitable for his share of the Practice and pay the whole costs thereof, including surgeries, consulting rooms and waiting rooms at such dwellinghouse . . .'

By cl 18:

> 'Either Partner may retire from the Partnership upon giving to the other six

months previous notice in writing of his intention so to do. Upon such retirement the Partner so retiring shall be entitled to receive his share of the profits up to the time of such retirement.'

There follows cl 19 which provides for what shall happen if the partnership is determined apart from retirement under cl 18; and it may be determined by, among other things, either partner 'giving notice to the other of his intention so to do if such other partner be guilty of gross neglect . . . or any breach of these articles' and so on. The notice to which I have referred purported to be given not under cl 19 but under cl 18 which I have just read. By cl 20:

'The Partners hereby mutually agree that if one Partner ceases to be bound by this Agreement the party so ceasing to be bound shall not for a period of three years from the date on which he so ceases to be bound practise within a distance of five miles from any premises at which the times [sic] of such cesser the Partnership practice is being carried on.'

Then I come to cl 22:

'If Dr. Choudhury shall cease to be a Partner under any of the provisions hereof, or while remaining a Partner cease to reside at Novar, Kippax he will further offer to sell such house, surgeries and grounds to Dr. Malhotra at a fair market price (to be fixed in the absence of agreement by a valuer) (to be appointed by Hartley & Worstenholme Solicitors Castleford) and Dr. Malhotra shall have one month from the date of such offer in which to accept and if he does not so accept shall be deemed to have refused.'

That partnership deed containing cl 22 was signed, sealed and delivered by both parties in the presence of the same Castleford solicitors. There followed the conveyance of the 1st August, and it is only necessary to refer to the fact that in cl 2(a) there is an express trust to sell:

'The Purchasers shall hold the said property upon trust to sell the same with power to postpone the sale thereof and shall stand possessed of the net proceeds of sale and of other money applicable as capital and the net rents and profits thereof until sale upon trust for themselves as joint tenants.'

The break-up of the partnership and the service of the notice of 30th March 1973 led to the first dispute which has brought these two doctors to court. It was a dispute whether the option was exercisable against the defendant on the true construction of cl 22, in the events which had happened. The defendant said it was not. But on 6th November 1973 Blackett-Ord V-C decided against him and held that the option was exercisable, and that decision was affirmed by this court on 4th June 1974, with one variation to which I shall refer later.

The defendant's attitude to this purported exercise of the option is relevant to the present dispute which divides the parties and which came before Blackett-Ord V-C much later. So I must go into the history of the matter between 30th March 1973 and the present dispute in 1977.

The plaintiff's solicitors naturally wished to go ahead with the exercise of the option, the valuation of the property and so on. But the defendant refused from the start and, as the judge rightly found, showed a marked lack of enthusiasm in carrying out the order of the court after it was made; indeed it is not too much to say that he obstructed it at every turn. On 3rd May 1973 his solicitors wrote to the plaintiff's solicitors as follows:

'With regard to the house and Surgery at Novar Kippax as your client is aware our client has spent considerable sums of money in renovating and making the property suitable for his own and his families [sic] personal occupation and it is felt that your client has terminated the partnership to enable him to endeavour to get hold of this property.'

That shows his attitude before the matter was taken to court and in that attitude he persisted.

On 24th May his solicitors wrote:

'Our Client is not bound by the option conferred by Clause 22 as he has not ceased to be a partner under any of the provisions of the Agreement. As we have considered the Notice you have given is an effective notice under Clause 18 of the partnership Deed.'

On the 30th of the same month the defendant's solicitors wrote to the plaintiff's solicitors:

'With regard to the house "Novar" the question of negotiations for the sale of this property to your Client does not arise as our Client has not given Notice of Retirement. We contend that as your Client has exercised his right to resign your Client is not entitled to invoke Clause 22 of the Partnership Deeds [sic]. We observe that you intend writing to Messrs. Hartley & Worstenholme asking them to appoint a Valuer to fix a fair market price. As Messrs. Hartley & Worstenholme prepared the partnership Deed no doubt they will consider the Notice served by your Client prior to appointing a Valuer on your behalf.'

The next month the plaintiff's solicitors tried to get hold of the title deeds of the property and they wrote on 15th June:

'We have, as promised, asked Messrs. Hartley and Worstenholme to appoint a valuer and they have today written us and we enclose a copy of their letter for your information. We are today writing Mr. Dickinson and hope to receive a copy of his valuation shortly. Perhaps in the meantime you could be obtaining your client's title deeds in order to deliver a full abstract of title to us so that we may draft the conveyance.'

It was in consequence of that letter that the defendant's solicitors wrote two letters on 18th June. In the first they referred the plaintiff's solicitors to their own letter of 30th May, which I have read, as having 'set out our views quite clearly and in view of this cannot understand your further action in the matter'. On the same day they also wrote to Mr Dickinson saying:

'We understand from A. Maurice Smith & Co. that they have written to ask you to make a valuation of the above property. We act for Doctor Choudhury the owner of the property and he has no intention of selling to A. Maurice Smith's client.'

On 13th July the plaintiff's solicitors, presumably because they had had brought to their attention, or remembered, that the defendant's wife was a party to the contract and to the conveyance, wrote to her: 'Re: "Novar" 37 Butt Hill, Kippax, Yorkshire', they said they were acting for the plaintiff and they drew her attention to cl 22. They enclosed a copy of the notice of 30th March 1973 and said:

'Please take notice that it is Dr. Malhotra's intention to exercise this option in conformity with the terms set out in the said clause 22. As we understand that "Novar" is held in the joint names of Dr. Choudhury and yourself we are sending you this letter on behalf of our client Dr. Malhotra so that you may be fully apprised of the position and take note thereof.'

They were of course not the solicitors who had been acting for the parties in the making of the contract and the executing of the conveyance. To that letter the plaintiff's solicitors received no reply. Two months later, on 13th September, they wrote to the defendant's solicitors again:

'We and our client are even more disturbed by the recent circular that your client has been distributing to the patients on his panel in the Kippax and Swillington areas. The circular appears to us to be gravely misleading as to Dr. Malhotra's plans and seems to us to prejudice the outcome of the legal action for possession of "Novar" which will presumably commence at the very beginning of October next. Our position at the present time is as follows:— (a) There is a legally enforceable option to purchase "Novar" embodied in the partnership deed which is binding upon your client. The option has been registered against your client and his wife at H.M. Land Charges Registry. Our client has given due notice in the dissolution of the partnership of his intention to exercise such option on the 1st of October next. Accordingly there is a legally binding contract of sale of "Novar" between your client and ours. (b) As from the 1st October we have precise instructions to proceed to acquire "Novar" if necessary by an action for specific performance in the Chancery Division of the High Court as early in October as the legal process will allow. (c) We cannot tolerate the position set out in your client's circular which in our opinion clearly prejudices the subject matter of the option.'

The circular was in these terms, apparently circulated in the preceding month, August, while the plaintiff's solicitors were waiting for a reply from the defendant's wife:

'The above member(s) of your family is/are my patients and I am writing to advise you that as from 30th September 1973 the partnership of Malhotra and Choudhury will cease and I will continue to practise alone from the Surgery at my home, 37 Butt Hill, Kippax and also from Swillington at The Clinic, Hill Crest Close, daily . . .'

On 18th September, the defendant's solicitors replied to that letter of complaint with a warning:

'With regard to the third paragraph of your letter, in our opinion, our client has no legal obligations in respect of the house and the option contained in the Partnership Deed will not become operative . . . With regard to the points raised we reply as follows:— (a) We do not agree that there is a legally binding contract for the sale of "Novar". (b) As stated above you must take such action as you feel is necessary. (c) Our client's circular was quite clear to the effect that he was to continue in practice as there appear to be rumours circulating that he was retiring from the Practise [sic].'

That defence, if it can be so called, led to the writ in the action which is the subject of the order under appeal. On 21st September 1973 the plaintiff issued his writ against the defendant, claiming—

'1. A declaration that the affairs of a medical partnership between the Plaintiff and the Defendant constituted by a Deed of Partnership dated the 19th May 1972 between the Plaintiff of the one part and the Defendant of the other part may be wound up.

'2. For the purposes aforesaid all necessary accounts and inquiries to be taken and made.

'3. A receiver.

'4. An injunction to restrain the Defendant from denying the Plaintiff the use of and access to the partnership surgery at the house known as "Novar" 37 Butt Hill Kippax in the County of York until the affairs of the said partnership shall have been fully wound up.

'5. Specific performance of an agreement whereby the Defendant agreed to sell and the Plaintiff agreed to purchase the said house "Novar".

'6. For the purposes aforesaid all necessary orders and directions.

'7. Costs.

'8 Such further or other relief as to the Court may seem fit.'

Contemporaneous with that writ, the plaintiff issued a notice of motion on 21st September, moving the court for—

'(1) An order that [Dr Mathieson] or some other fit and proper person may be appointed to collect get in and receive the debts now due and owing and other assets property or effects belonging to the partnership of medical practice carried on between the Plaintiff and Defendant in Swillington and in Kippax in the County of York

'(2) An injunction to restrain the Defendant by himself servants agents or otherwise from preventing the Plaintiff from having access to or the use of the surgery at "Novar" . . .'

In support of that notice of motion was filed the first of the plaintiff's affidavits. [His Lordship referred to the plaintiff's affidavit and to the statement of claim, which claimed the same relief as in the writ. His Lordship stated that on 3rd October 1973 the plaintiff took out a summons under RSC Ord 86 seeking specific performance of the agreement to sell Novar to him; and that on 6th October the defendant filed his defence to the action in which he disputed the plaintiff's right to an injunction or to specific performance of the option. His Lordship continued:] In sub-para (e) of para 3(c) of his affidavit the defendant states: '"Novar" is the home of my wife and myself vested in us both, and the surgery is an integral part of the house, and as soon as the partnership between the Plaintiff and I should end, I have intended and do now intend to practise from the property on my own. Neither the partnership nor the Plaintiff can have any right to use the surgery after such date, and I certainly do not intend to allow the Plaintiff so to use the surgery.'

It will be clear from what I have read from the correspondence, the pleadings and the evidence, that in none of them is there on the defendant's side a mention of his wife's position, except the statement in the sub-paragraph of the affidavit which I have just read, that Novar is the home of his wife and himself vested in them both. He is saying that it is the plaintiff and not he who has repudiated the partnership. He admits refusing to sell and refusing to allow the plaintiff to use the surgery; but his defence to the claims in the action, including the claim for specific performance of the option, is based on his construction of cl 22 and his view that he was not legally bound to offer Novar to the plaintiff for sale at all. His wife has only been brought into the matter at all by a letter written to her by the plaintiff's solicitors, a letter which, as I have pointed out, she did not answer and nobody answered on her behalf.

As I have said the defendant's view of his legal obligation, namely that it did not exist, was rejected by Blackett-Ord V-C and the Court of Appeal agreed. Blackett-Ord V-C ordered, on 28th October (his order was perfected on 6th November), first, that the defendant should give Mr Dickinson, the valuer, access to the property for the purpose of valuing it, then an enquiry whether a good title could be made to the property, then that the defendant deliver to the plaintiff all the deeds in writing and give the plaintiff vacant possession; and he continued the defendant's undertaking to allow the plaintiff to use the surgery. The order directed that the agreement dated 19th May 1972 ought to be specifically performed and carried into execution.

When the matter came before the Court of Appeal, it was appreciated that although the case was one in which, in the ordinary way, specific performance would be ordered, there was a bar to specific performance being in fact ordered, namely the possibility that the defendant's joint-tenant of the property might resist any order for sale and might refuse to concur in any conveyance of Novar to the plaintiff. So that part of Blackett-Ord V-C's order was struck out and the court declared that the option contained in cl 22 of the deed of partnership dated 15th May 1972 had been validly exercised by the plaintiff. Otherwise the order and directions which Blackett-Ord V-C had given were affirmed and repeated by the Court of Appeal.

Naturally the first thing the plaintiff's solicitors did after the decision of the Court of Appeal was to ask the defendant's solicitors for an abstract of title and for inspection of the property by Mr Dickinson, the valuer. They did that by a letter dated 5th June. To that they got no reply. This is the beginning of the period in which Blackett-Ord V-C noted the defendant's lack of enthusiasm to carry out the terms of the Court of Appeal's order. So the plaintiff's solicitors wrote again on 16th July 1974. They said:

'Our client is hoping to take an annual fortnight's holiday away from the practice in early August next. Would you please confirm that you agree with us that the mutual undertakings given by our respective clients to the Court will enable Dr. Malhotra to have his new junior partner, Dr. Smith, practise in Dr. Malhotra's place as normal at the Kippax surgery.'

They pointed out that if the defendant did not agree to that, they would have to go back to the court for fresh directions to cover not merely Dr Malhotra's use of the surgery on the defendant's undertaking, but that of his locum tenens as well.

On 19th July the defendant's solicitors replied to that letter in these terms:

'Dr Choudhury states that from an ethics point of view he has no objection to Dr Smith carrying on in Dr Malhotra's absence but has discussed this matter with his wife and his wife is quite adamant that she is not prepared to allow Dr Smith into the precincts of the property. She states she has been very patient in this matter and has allowed Dr Malhotra to continue practising there even though relationships have been very very strained over the past year Mrs Choudhury feels she must now insist on her rights. We have discussed the matter with Dr Choudhury and he states that obviously his wife is quite adamant in her views on this matter and she will not agree to Dr Smith taking the Surgery.'

That led the plaintiff's solicitors to take out a summons to proceed under RSC Ord 44. They wanted the title deeds to the property, they wanted access to the surgery for Dr Smith, the locum tenens, and they wanted enquiry as to the title and a valuation of the defendant's interest which was obviously an undivided half share of the equitable beneficial interest in the property.

The plaintiff's solicitors after taking out that summons wrote to the defendant's solicitors on 11th October asking for these things and complaining of needless delays and prevarications and on 28th October the defendant's solicitors replied: 'We have been unable to deal with the question of the Abstract of Title as we have not been able to obtain Mrs Choudhury's authority to forward this to you . . .' and they indicated that it might be necessary for Mrs Choudhury to be separately represented.

By the time the summons to proceed came on, Mrs Choudhury had sworn an affidavit, on 8th November, and that is of course a document of considerable importance. It was a short affidavit. Like many of the documents copied in this case it is not easy to read. It simply said:

'1. I am the wife of the Defendant herein. 2. I have read the affidavit sworn herein by my husband. I do refuse to agree or concur to any sale of the property to the Plaintiff. 3. I object to the Plaintiff or any locum tenens having any access to or use of the property most strongly as a disturbing influence on my home and want it stopped.'

The summons was supported by an affidavit of a Mr Smith, exhibiting correspondence, some of which I have read, and the result was an order of 3rd January 1975, made it is to be noted in this partnership action, 'That the inquiry as to title [of Novar] may proceed . . . That for the purposes aforesaid such directions are made, namely:— . . . That the Defendant produce all deeds and documents of title . . . that the Defendant and his wife do attend for cross-examination on the adjourned hearing before the District Registrar . . . That inquiry be made as to the value of the Defendant's interest in the said "Novar" . . . That direct notice of the judgment and order herein be served on [the defendant's wife].' So there was an order in these proceedings that the defendant and his wife should attend for cross-examination and, as the defendant's wife had sworn an affidavit in these proceedings, there can be no doubt that there was power to order her to attend for cross-examination. But that order was never carried out: neither the defendant nor his wife, to say nothing of any other witness, was ever cross-examined on affidavit nor was any oral evidence ever given in this or any other litigation between the parties. On 9th January the order was duly served in accordance with the registrar's directions on the defendant's wife.

[His Lordship referred to correspondence between the parties in which offers were made on the plaintiff's behalf to accept a conveyance of the defendant's equitable interest in his undivided half share in Novar or a conveyance of the surgery part only of the property, to a consent order made by agreement between the plaintiff and the defendant, on 28th April 1975, allowing a locum tenens to use the surgery at Novar whilst the plaintiff was on holiday, and to a summons issued by the plaintiff under s 30 of the Law of Property Act 1925, against the defendant and his wife, seeking execution of the trust for sale on which they held Novar and an immediate sale. His Lordship then read affidavits filed in the s 30 proceedings. Those included a second affidavit sworn by the defendant's wife in which she deposed that she believed that the plaintiff's concern to exercise the option was to secure the provision of suitable accommodation for himself and his family and averred 'that my sole concern in not giving title to Novar is that the same should remain the family home for myself and our children'. The defendant, also, filed an affidavit in the s 30 proceedings in which he stated: 'My wife refused to concur in any sale of Novar because it is our matrimonial home and the home of our children, on which we have expended much money and effort, and which is now an ideal home, and she does not want to move . . . In the circumstances, I cannot make title to Novar. . .' His Lordship continued:] One matter which is omitted from the defendant's affidavit is any statement that he had ever tried to persuade his wife to concur in his honouring his promise to offer this property for sale to the plaintiff and to concur in a conveyance of it to the plaintiff. On the contrary he indicates that he and his wife have expended much money and effort on an ideal matrimonial home for them both and their children. I do not think it is putting it too strongly to say that that seems to be the affidavit of a man who is on his wife's side in this matter.

These s 30 proceedings are in a state of suspended animation. They were not started till the beginning of 1976 and they are in the background to those proceedings which started at the beginning of the following year, 1977, in the action which had started as long ago as September 1973.

It has been submitted to us on behalf of the plaintiff that it was for the defendant himself to have taken out the summons under s 30 and that if he had done so there would have been no difficulty in an immediate execution of the trust and sale of Novar to the plaintiff, because there would have been no breach of trust involved in it or any other such consideration as frequently makes it inequitable or unjust for a court to enforce a trust for the sale of a matrimonial home housing a divorced wife and children. I shall say something about that later. The fact is that it is the plaintiff who has started s 30 proceedings and not pursued them so far.

On 21st January 1977 the plaintiff went back to move the court in his original action against the defendant Dr Choudhury alone, and in this action asked for damages at common law for breach of the contract constituted by the option. That is the plain effect of the notice of motion. He asks that—

'(1) [the Defendant] may be ordered to pay to the Plaintiff damages for breach of the contract constituted by the option secured by the Plaintiff as the same is referred to in the Order of this Court made on the 6th day of November 1973 as varied by the Order of the Court of Appeal made on the 4th day of June 1974.

'(2) for the purpose of ascertaining the measure of damages as aforesaid inquiries be made as the same are set out and directed in the Schedule hereto.'

Then he asks for costs.

I read the schedule: '(a) An inquiry what was the value of the property known as [Novar] . . . as on the 4th day of June 1974.' It is agreed, if this appeal succeeds, that the registrar should make that inquiry. '(b) An inquiry what is the value of [Novar] as on the 31st day of January 1977.' There is a dispute about that. '(c) For the purpose of the foregoing inquiries a direction that in the event of Geoffrey Dickinson FRICS FRVA . . . being refused admission into [Novar] the estimates of the values as aforesaid of the said Geoffrey Dickinson be received as evidence of the same.' There is no dispute about this if the appeal succeeds. '(d) An inquiry what loss has been sustained by the Plaintiff to his medical practice by reason of the said breach of contract.' There is a dispute about this. Enquiry (e) is no longer asked for. '(f) A direction that the damages herein ordered to be paid by the Defendant shall be certified as the aggregate of the following, namely (i) the difference between the value found upon inquiry (b) less the value found upon inquiry (a) if the former value be greater than the latter (ii) the greater of the two sums found under inquiries (d) and (e) respectively'; (i) depends on the earlier enquiries and (ii) in any event would have to be modified. That was the matter which came before Blackett-Ord V-C in February and March. It was a dispute as to damages.

The notice of motion was supported by an affidavit of a Mr Edington of which I need read very little. He is a partner in the firm of solicitors instructed by the plaintiff and he deposes in para 5 of his affidavit:

'The fact that the Plaintiff is being denied due performance by the Defendant of the contract for sale will inevitably result in a detriment to the Plaintiff's practice and a corresponding gain to the Defendant's practice. I am informed and verily believe that such detriment and gain in the context of the history of this matter is very substantial.'

In para 6 he says, after referring to the spurning of the offers to which I have already referred, 'The Defendant says that his wife would not agree to this.' Counsel have not been able to say where Mr Edington got that from. It is not in evidence and it cannot come from anything except an inference from the evidence in the material to which I have already referred.

The same is true I think of what he next says:

'To our suggestion that the Defendant as one of two trustees for sale can at least endeavour to execute the trust for sale and thereby to honour his bargain the Defendant and his wife have retorted that they are happily married so that the trust for sale is not enforceable; and there is implied in this that it would be truly a waste of time as well as imprudent for the Plaintiff to call for a conveyance to him of the Defendant's half interest in the property. Further I verily believe that if the Plaintiff were to call for such a conveyance the same will be resisted by the Defendant's wife and by the Defendant.'

He says that he is instructed by the plaintiff to state that 'even at this stage he is prepared to take a conveyance of the property upon the terms ordered by the Court were the Defendant to procure good title thereto'.

It seems to me that Mr Edington is drawing inferences from the evidence in matters of which he can have no first hand knowledge, and his evidence has to be considered in that light.

The notice of motion, supported by that affidavit, led the defendant into swearing and filing a fourth affidavit accepting the letter which I have already read, of 31st January 1975, and referring to the fact that he is not preventing Mr Dickinson from entering the house, but Mrs Choudhury is. In this fourth affidavit he does not accept Mr Edington's allegations or that they relate to matters within his personal knowledge. He says: 'It is true that Novar is jointly owned by my wife and I. There are at present proceedings before this Court by the Plaintiff for an order for sale of Novar under the provisions of section 30 of the Law of Property Act 1925.' He denies that he has consistently refused admission to the valuer.

In para 6 he says: 'I do not accept that there has been any detriment at all to the Plaintiff as a result of my not being able to complete the sale of Novar in accordance with the Order of the Court because of my wife's half share.' He asserts that in all the circumstances the plaintiff is not entitled to claim damages for breach of contract and the motion is misconceived.

The motion came on for hearing before Blackett-Ord V-C on that material on 7th and 21st February and 28th March 1977, and on 29th March he gave his judgment and made the order under appeal. His order declared that:

'... the Plaintiff is entitled to damages, such damages to be limited to the costs incurred investigating title of the property known as "Novar" and the costs (if any) in connection with attempts to value the said property in accordance with the Order of the Court of Appeal dated the 4th day of June 1974 AND it is directed that the District Registrar do determine the amount of damages (if any) to be paid by the Defendant to the Plaintiff [no order for costs was made except taxation of the defendant's costs under the Legal Aid Act] AND it is ordered that the undertaking given by the Defendant through his Counsel on the 26th day of September 1973 do continue until the 29th day of June 1977 after which date the said undertaking be discharged.'

That order was not satisfactory to the plaintiff because it limits the amount of damages to those recoverable under what is known as the rule in *Bain v Fothergill*[1] and deprives him, he says, of the substantial damages to which, if the case does not come within that rule, he would be entitled. The defendant seeks to support the judgment of Blackett-Ord V-C on the ground set out in the respondent's notice.

Blackett-Ord V-C's judgment applied this exceptional and anomalous rule. He set out the history of the matter in his judgment. He pointed out that the defendant had refused to admit that the option had been validly exercised, and had refused not on the ground that his wife was concerned. He pointed out that the defendant had been less than enthusiastic in carrying out the order of the court made in 1973 and affirmed in 1974. He read from the defendant's short affidavit of 29th June 1976 and he referred to Mrs Choudhury's shorter affidavit simply saying that she refused to sell and stated that that was sworn, like the defendant's affidavit, in subsequent proceedings brought by the plaintiff under s 30. If by shorter he means the shorter of her two affidavits and not shorter than her husband's affidavit, he would appear to be in error because he would then be referring to an affidavit which was sworn not in the proceedings under s 30 but in the 1973 proceedings.

However that error does not seem to matter, because it is perfectly plain that by consent of everybody the affidavits of the parties in both sets of proceedings were treated as evidence in these proceedings. Blackett-Ord V-C goes on to say, quite rightly, that the breach of the contract to offer Novar to the plaintiff was not denied but the contest of the present motion had been as to the measure of damages. He then gave a correct exposition, as one would expect, of the principle laid down in *Bain v Fothergill*[1] and applied to this case, 'that the damages recoverable by Dr Malhotra are substantially limited to the costs he has been put to in connection with the contract and the investigation of the title, and he cannot claim general damages'; and he went on to cite the observations of Lord Chelmsford in *Bain v Fothergill*[2]:

'. . . I think the rule as to the limits within which damages may be recovered upon the breach of a contract for the sale of a real estate must be taken to be without exception. If a person enters into a contract for the sale of a real estate knowing that he has no title to it, nor any means of acquiring it, the purchaser cannot recover damages beyond the expenses he has incurred by an action for the breach of the contract; he can only obtain other damages by an action for deceit.'

He cites that passage[2] of Lord Chelmsford's speech in which Lord Chelmsford referred to the rule being without exception and invited, as Blackett-Ord V-C put it, a party who seeks to get round and out of the rule to obtain his damages by an action for deceit. He points out that that invitation is not one which has been taken up on this occasion, and he goes on to say:

'But the rule is an anomalous one and is not to be extended. It is limited to defects of title, the original reason for it having been, it is said, the complications involved in showing title to land under English law. There is many a slip, the vendor can enter

---

1   (1874) LR 7 HL 158, [1874–80] All ER Rep 83
2   LR 7 HL 158 at 207, [1874–80] All ER 83 Rep at 87

into a contract and then the purchasers' researches into the title may show that unknown to himself the vendor cannot sell what he has contracted to sell. So the rule is limited to defect of title and it does not excuse a vendor from doing his best to show title.'

He then distinguished the decision of Megarry J in *Wroth v Tyler*[1] because of the different chronological order of the contract broken and the contract to convey in the two cases, and proceeded:

'Now as regards the second point that I mentioned, the duty of the vendor to use his best endeavours to carry out his contractual obligations, the defendant says on oath that his wife refuses to consent and Mrs Choudhury, his wife, says the same. They have not been cross-examined on their affidavits and I must I think accept that Mrs Choudhury will not consent whatever within reason the defendant may do to try to compel her to. There is no suggestion anywhere in the evidence that the defendant has tried to persuade his wife not to consent and the case is therefore different from *Day v Singleton*[2] where the property for sale was leasehold, the consent of the lessors to the assignment was required, and the vendor induced the lessors to withhold their consent. So although, as I have said, the defendant has not shown any enthusiasm for accepting the judgment of the court, the position in my judgment on the evidence is that he cannot show title and prima facie therefore the damages for which he is liable are limited by the rule in *Bain v Fothergill*[3].'

Having distinguished *Day v Singleton*[2] in that way, he then went on to consider an allegation of representation and held that there had been no representation by the defendant that he had or could make a good title. He said of the solicitor acting for both partners:

'. . . his left hand did not know what his right hand was doing on what it seems on the facts as they have come out, but I acquit the defendant of any intention at that time of seeking to defeat the option in the partnership deed by the ingenious expedient of vesting half the property in his wife, and the option itself cannot I think be treated as a representation, otherwise every contract would imply a representation and every vendor would be warranting his title.'

So he distinguished Graham J's decision in *Watts v Spence*[4].

Then he went on to deal with the equitable interest of the defendant in this property and held that he was not entitled on an authority[5] cited in *Watts v Spence*[4] and followed by Graham J in that case, to grant part specific performance. So he held that the rule in *Bain v Fothergill*[3] applied. Hence this appeal.

Counsel for the plaintiff has abandoned his appeal against Blackett-Ord V-C's finding that there was no misrepresentation. On the evidence such a finding seems to have been plainly right and I say no more about it. Nor do I find it necessary, on the view I take of this case, to consider whether Blackett-Ord V-C was right in rejecting part specific performance. Nor again do I consider the other interesting submissions which counsel for the plaintiff has put before us. I have to consider whether this rule, laid down in *Flureau v Thornhill*[6] in 1775 (that is when Lord Chelmsford said[7] it was laid down) and affirmed by

---

1   [1973] 1 All ER 897, [1974] Ch 30
2   [1899] 2 Ch 320
3   (1874) LR 7 HL 158, [1874–80] All ER Rep 83
4   [1975] 2 All ER 528, [1976] Ch 165
5   *Rudd v Lascelles* [1900] 1 Ch 815
6   (1776) 2 Wm Bl 1078, [1775–1802] All ER Rep 91
7   LR 7 HL 158 at 200, [1874–80] All ER Rep 83 at 85

the House of Lords in 1874 in *Bain v Fothergill*[1], applies in 1977 to a case as different as possible from those two cases.

It follows from the excerpts which I have read from Blackett-Ord V-C's judgment that this is not a case where the owner's difficulties in discovering whether he had a perfectly good title could excuse him. The defendant knew all along what his title was to Novar and that he shared it with his wife. Yet a fortnight after entering into a contract binding his wife, he granted an option which he clearly knew could not be enforced against him without her concurrence. As I have tried to point out, there is not a word in any of his affidavits to explain how he came to do that.

Blackett-Ord V-C decided this case I think on the ground that, no fraud being alleged or proved, he had to accept that the uncontradicted evidence, as there had in fact been none of the ordered cross-examination on the affidavits of the defendant and his wife, went so far as to prove that the defendant had tried to make good his title by asking his wife to concur in selling but had failed or perhaps, it is not clear which view Blackett-Ord V-C held, that if he had tried his wife would nonetheless have refused her concurrence.

This seems to me, with all respect to Blackett-Ord V-C, to ignore first of all the duty of the vendor, to which he refers, to use his best endeavours to carry out his contractual obligations, in this case by obtaining his wife's consent, and secondly the absence of any evidence that he did use those endeavours. Further it seems to me to ignore the inevitable inference from the evidence which was given, that the failure of the defendant to convey Novar to the plaintiff was due not to his inability to do so but to his unwillingness to do so by obtaining his wife's consent. I do not find it necessary to consider whether he should have gone as far as to convey his half share or to try to get his wife's consent to conveying the surgery alone, or whether he should have himself applied to the court under s 30 to execute the trust for sale and enforce an immediate sale against the wishes of his co-tenant.

But I conclude from my study of the authorities to which we have been referred that to come within this anomalous exception a vendor must prove his inability to carry out his contractual obligations. And if the evidence leaves the court in the position where the right inference is that inability is not proved, then, even where there is no allegation of the duty to use his best endeavours to carry out his contractual obligations and of a breach of that duty, as in this case, it is open to the court to hold that the ordinary principle of damages, putting a victim of a breach of contract in the position in which he would have been if the contract had been performed, applies to the exclusion of the anomalous exception created in *Flureau v Thornhill*[2] and *Bain v Fothergill*[1].

I am not saying that this matter should not be pleaded or that there may not be cases in which, the duty and the breach of it not being pleaded, the court would be bound to reach the same conclusion as Blackett-Ord V-C reached in this case. What I do say is that in the circumstances of this case, the affidavits standing as pleadings and all the material that was before Blackett-Ord V-C being taken into account, the fact that in a partnership action followed by a notice of motion as to damages there was no pleaded allegation to this effect does not prevent the court from considering whether the duty has been discharged.

If I am right, want of enthusiasm in carrying out the order of the Court of Appeal, if it extended to inhibiting the defendant from trying to obtain his wife's consent to something which obviously he himself would not lightly wish to come about, would be passivity, not a wilful act but an omission, fatal to a claim to rely on the exceptional rule in *Bain v Fothergill*[1] because what is required by the rule is proof of activity. Blackett-Ord V-C seems to me, if I may respectfully say so, first of all to have attached too much importance to the language of Lord Chelmsford in *Bain v Fothergill*[1], and too little to other matters which appear from the report of that case and in particular the speech of Lord Hatherley[3], and also

---

1   (1874) LR 7 HL 158, [1874–80] All ER Rep 83
2   (1776) 2 Wm Bl 1078, [1775–1802] All ER Rep 91
3   LR 7 HL 158 at 208, [1874–80] All ER Rep 83 at 87

to have been misled by the headnote to the decision of this court in *Day v Singleton*[1].

It is quite true that in *Flureau v Thornhill*[2] the rule laid down by De Grey CJ was that—

> 'Upon a contract for a purchase, if the title proves bad, and the vendor is (without fraud) incapable of making a good one, I do not think that the purchaser can be entitled to any damages for the fancied goodness of the bargain, which he supposes he has lost.'

Those words are to be found quoted in the speech of Lord Chelmsford in *Bain v Fothergill*[3], which ends[4] with a reference to 'any fraud or wilful act' on the part of vendors preventing them performing their contract.

But, as counsel for the plaintiff pointed out, the question which the judges were summoned by their Lordships to answer and which was proposed for their consideration was[5] 'Whether, upon a contract for the sale of real estate, where the vendor, *without his default* [my emphasis], is unable to make a good title, the purchaser is by law entitled to recover damages for the loss of his bargain?' That is the question which was answered in the judgment of Pollock B[6], which was also the judgment of Kelly CB, Keating and Brett JJ[7], and the question as it was stated by both Denman J[7] and Pigott B[8]. I note this is the way in which the rule is stated in Williams on Contract of Sale of Land[9], cited by Megarry J in *Wroth v Tyler*[10]:

> 'Where the breach of contract is occasioned by the vendor's inability, *without his own fault* [my emphasis], to show a good title, the purchaser is entitled to recover as damages his deposit, if any, with interest, and his expenses incurred in connection with the agreement, but not more than nominal damages for the loss of his bargain.'

It is not necessary to decide how far the words 'without his default' go, if I am right in thinking that inability without default is what one has to consider as attracting the rule in *Bain v Fothergill*[11].

There may be cases in which there has been no lack of bona fides, yet the rule in *Bain v Fothergill*[11] has been excluded. I would not however venture to suggest that anything less than lack of good faith could exclude the rule. But it seems from later decisions that fraud, in the full sense of that word such as would found an action for deceit, may not be necessary to exclude the rule. No doubt Blackett-Ord V-C had in mind that fraud must be strictly alleged and proved in all ordinary circumstances. But in my judgment, unwillingness to use best endeavours to carry out a contractual promise is bad faith, and for there to be bad faith which takes the case out of this exceptional rule it is not necessary that there should be either a deliberate attempt to prevent title being made good or anything more than the unwillingness which I find it inevitable to infer in this case. If a man makes a promise and does not use his best endeavours to keep it, it cannot take much and, in my judgment, may not need more to make him guilty of bad faith and to entitle the victim of his bad faith to his full share of damages to compensate him for what he has lost by reason of that breach of contract and bad faith.

Apart from the nature of the question which was proposed to the judges in *Bain v*

---

1   [1899] 2 Ch 320
2   (1776) 2 Wm Bl 1078, [1775–1802] All ER Rep 91 at 91–92
3   (1874) LR 7 HL 158 at 201, [1874–80] All ER Rep 83 at 85
4   LR 7 HL 158 at 208, [1874–80] All ER Rep 83 at 87
5   LR 7 HL 158 at 170, [1874–80] All ER Rep 83 at 84
6   LR 7 HL 158 at 170
7   LR 7 HL 158 at 176
8   LR 7 HL 158 at 193
9   (1930) p 128
10 [1973] 1 All ER 897 at 916, [1974] Ch 30 at 53
11 LR 7 HL 158, [1874–80] All ER Rep 83

Fothergill[1], I would also call attention to the speech of Lord Hatherley, in which he says[2],
after referring to *Engel v Fitch*[3] to which we were also referred:

'The vendor in that case was bound by his contract, as every vendor is bound by his
contract, to do all that he could to complete the conveyance. Whenever it is a matter
of conveyancing, and not a matter of title, it is the duty of the vendor to do everything
that he is enabled to do by force of his own interest, and also by force of the interest
of others whom he can compel to concur in the conveyance.'

I confess that I have not found it easy, perhaps as a common lawyer I may be forgiven,
to define or apply a distinction between matters of title and matters of conveyance which
comes easily to minds better versed in equity; but I venture to think that, whether the
defect is a real defect of title or a mere matter of conveyance, a vendor is equally bound to
use his best efforts either to cure the defect in title or to remedy the matter of the
impediment which is a matter of conveyance. I hope I may be forgiven also for referring
in that connection to a case which was not cited to us, *Keen v Mear*[4], where Russell J seems
to have treated it as plain law that one of two co-owners must have been acting perfectly
bona fide in selling property, which belonged to him and the co-owner, to another without
the consent of the co-owner and must satisfy the court not only of his perfect good faith but
also that he has done his best to get his co-owner's consent to the sale to which he has
without his authority agreed for his case to fall within the rule in *Flureau v Thornhill*[5] and
Bain v Fothergill.[1]

But as it seems to me, if I am right in this, the authority of this court which counsel for
the plaintiff relied on is really conclusive of this case. I refer to *Day v Singleton*[6]. The
headnote is in these terms:

'A purchaser of leasehold property, which the vendor cannot assign without a
licence from his lessor is entitled to damages (beyond return of the deposit, with
interest and expenses) for loss of his bargain by reason of the vendor's omission to do
his best to procure such licence. A vendor agreed with a purchaser for the sale of a
leasehold hotel, subject to the consent of the lessor being obtained to the assignment
of the lease, and the purchaser paid a deposit on his purchase-money. The vendor
died without having completed his contract, and the purchaser then brought an
action against his legal personal representative for specific performance. The
defendant, being desirous of freeing the vendor's estate from the action, induced the
lessor to refuse his consent to the assignment, which the lessor accordingly did, and
the purchaser thus lost his bargain. Thereupon the purchaser amended his action by
claiming damages and return of the deposit:— *Held*, that the plaintiff was entitled,
not only to the return of his deposit, with interest and costs of investigating title, but
also to the damages he had sustained by the loss of his bargain through the omission
of the defendant to obtain the lessor's consent.'

That case turned on a letter written by the solicitors for the vendor's personal representative,
of which Romer J, the trial judge, had taken what Lindley MR, giving the judgment of
himself and Rigby LJ in the Court of Appeal, described[7] as a very charitable view. Romer
J had thought that the letter was not an inducement to the lessors to withhold their consent
to the assignment to the plaintiff Day.

In the Court of Appeal, Sir Francis Jeune took the view[8] that the letter was an

---

1   (1874) LR 7 HL 158, [1874–80] All ER Rep 83
2   LR 7 HL 158 at 209, [1874–80] All ER Rep 83 at 88
3   (1867) LR 3 QB 314, LR 4 QB 659
4   [1920] 2 Ch 574 at 581, [1920] All ER Rep 147 at 152
5   (1776) 2 Wm BL 1078, [1775–1802] All E R Rep 91
6   [1899] 2 Ch 320
7   [1899] 2 Ch 320 at 328
8   [1899] 2 Ch 320 at 330–331

inducement, and that view is embodied in the headnote which I have just read and which
I respectfully suggest may have misled Blackett-Ord V-C. But a reading of the majority   *a*
judgment of Lindley MR indicates, I think, that the headnote does not accurately represent
the decision of the Court of Appeal, because as I understand that majority judgment it was
a decision that, even on the charitable view which Romer J took of the letter, *Bain v
Fothergill*[1] did not apply.

It is plain from the report[2] that there was in that case (unlike this) an amendment to
allege that Singleton, the personal representative of Dunn, the vendor—   *b*

> 'instead of doing his best to obtain the consent of the lessors to the assignment to
> him, the plaintiff, and in breach of his duty towards him, the plaintiff, endeavoured
> to induce and did induce the lessors to refuse to consent to an assignment to him, the
> plaintiff.'

But in giving the majority judgment, Lindley MR said[3]:
                                                                                          c
> 'The question raised by this appeal is whether a purchaser of leasehold property
> which the vendor cannot assign without a licence from his lessor is entitled to
> damages (beyond the return of the deposit with interest, and expenses) by reason of
> the vendor's omission to do his best to procure such licence.'

That was the question. It is *not* stated to be whether the purchaser was entitled to those *d*
damages by reason of the vendor's inducing the lessor not to give his consent to give the
licence. He stated[4] that 'It was Singleton's business, as Dunn's representative, to obtain that
consent if he could', and that 'Singleton never asked the lessors to accept Day as their tenant
without a bar, and consequently it would be for him, Singleton, to shew that if he had
asked them they would have refused'.

Lindley MR also pointed out[5] that the first question submitted to the judges in *Bain v* *e*
Fothergill[1], as I have said, used the words 'without his default, is unable to make a good
title', and added:

> 'Lord Chelmsford's speech is addressed to that question; and his observations on
> fraud are part of his comment on *Hopkins v. Grazebrook*[6], which had decided that the
> exceptional rule laid down in *Flureau v. Thornhill*[7] did not apply where the vendor
> knew that he had not a good title, although he believed he could get one, and had in   *f*
> fact an equitable title. Neither Lord Chelmsford's speech nor Lord Hatherley's is an
> authority for the application of that exceptional rule to the case of a vendor who can
> make good title but will not, or will not do what he can do and ought to do in order
> to obtain one. Such a case is, however, covered by *Engel v. Fitch*[8], which was to a
> certain extent based on *Hopkins v. Grazebrook*[6], and was much commented on in, but
> not overruled by, *Bain v. Fothergill*[1].'   *g*

Now I need not refer further to Sir Francis Jeune's judgment which, as I have said,
appears responsible for the form of the headnote, except to say this, that he did agree[9], as
I read his judgment, with the statement of the duty contained in the judgment of Lindley

                                                                                          h

---

1   (1874) LR 7 HL 158, [1874–80] All ER Rep 83
2   [1899] 2 Ch 320 at 323
3   [1899] 2 Ch 320 at 327
4   [1899] 2 Ch 320 at 327, 328
5   [1899] 2 Ch 320 at 328–329
6   (1826) 6 B & C 31
7   (1776) 2 Wm Bl 1078, [1775–1802] All ER Rep 91
8   (1867) LR 3 QB 314, LR 4 QB 659
9   [1899] 2 Ch 320 at 332

j

MR[1] and he agreed[2] that *Bain v Fothergill*[3] did not conflict with this view of the duty of the
vendor. He stated[4] that 'it is the duty of a vendor to make a good title for his purchaser if
he can, and certainly not to do anything to impair or spoil such title'.

That decision of this court is of course binding on us both as a decision and in what it says
that *Bain v Fothergill*[3] did or did not decide. It was followed by a Divisional Court in
Braybrooks v Whaley[5] where the facts were very different, but where I think it is relevant to
read what Salter J said. That was a case in which the mortgagor in possession called
attention to the fact that the mortgagee seeking to convey the premises to another had not
taken the statutory steps required by the Courts (Emergency Powers) Act 1914 to eject
him, and in following the decision in *Day v Singleton*[6] Salter J giving the second judgment
of the court said[7]:

> 'With regard to the suggestion that the application [for leave under the Act] would
> have failed on the merits I think that where it is alleged that damage has been caused
> to a person by reason of the wrongful omission of another to take some step which it
> was his duty to take, the onus rests upon the person in default, if he alleges that the
> step must have failed, to prove it. That, I think, is supported by the observations of
> Lindley M.R. in *Day v. Singleton*[8], where he said: "Singleton never asked the lessors to
> accept Day as their tenant without a bar, and consequently it would be for him,
> Singleton, to shew that if he had asked them they would have refused."'

In my judgment those authorities show that it is for the vendor seeking to excuse his
admitted breach of contract to show that it was inability and not unwillingness that has
prevented him from carrying out his contract if he wishes to limit his damages to those
obtainable under *Bain v Fothergill*[3]; compare the observations of Cockburn CJ in *Engel v
Fitch*[9].

If that is right, what is the effect of the evidence, the uncontradicted evidence, of the
defendant and his wife in this case? Accepting all his and her denials, rejecting in so far as
they conflict with these denials the evidence of the plaintiff and of Dr Mathieson, where is
there any evidence that the defendant tried to persuade his wife to consent to conveying
Novar to the plaintiff? The striking thing is that the defendant never says so. In one letter
his solicitors say that he discussed with his wife admitting Dr Smith to the surgery but she
was adamant, and in another that she was preventing Mr Dickinson from entering and was
adamant in refusing to convey. But nowhere is there on affidavit any statement to assert
that he tried to obtain his wife's consent to sell Novar. There is simply his statement and
her statement that she refused to give it, which might mean that she refused the request
from her husband or might simply mean that she refused the request from the plaintiff or
his solicitors.

I would go on to add that it may well be that the reason why he never swears in any
affidavit that he did ask his wife to consent is the excellent reason that if he had sworn so
it would have been perjury because in fact he never did ask her. His inclination, as counsel
for the plaintiff has pointed out, is obviously in line with his denial, so long maintained,
that he was under any legal liability to honour this option, namely to agree with her that
they should remain with their children in the home which they had got so cheap and on
which they had spent so much in improvements together with this convenient surgery.

1   [1899] 2 Ch 320 at 327
2   [1899] 2 Ch 320 at 333
3   (1874) LR 7 HL 158, [1874–80] All ER Rep 83
4   [1899] 2 Ch 320 at 332–333
5   [1919] 1 KB 435
6   [1899] 2 Ch 320
7   [1919] 1 KB 435 at 441–442
8   [1899] 2 Ch 320 at 328
9   (1867) LR 3 QB 314 at 333

There is, on the authorities, a plain duty, in my judgment, to try for consent in a case like this, whether it is a matter of conveyancing or a defect of title which you seek to remove. *a* There is evidence that the wife refused, from which, in other circumstances, a request by the defendant might be assumed. But, on the evidence in this case and on consideration of the matters to which I have referred, it would be impossible to presume such a request, still less any persistent or persuasive requests. So prima facie there is a failure by him in his duty to the plaintiff and he was in default. It is his unwillingness and not his inability which caused the failure to convey and the plaintiff is entitled to the damages caused by *b* that failure, even though in the circumstances of this case that is not a matter of any positive pleading or allegation.

There is no evidence in this case that the defendant was mistakenly expecting his wife to sign when he signed the partnership deed, including cl 22. Blackett-Ord V-C, in my judgment, had to be satisfied on the evidence that the defendant did act in good faith and did his best to induce his wife to concur in the sale of Novar to the plaintiff. In my *c* judgment, it would be wrong to be so satisfied and to apply *Bain v Fothergill* [1].

I accordingly regard the plaintiff as entitled to substantial damages. I understand that Cumming-Bruce LJ agrees with me. I agree with what he is going to say, both as to how those damages should be measured and how the registrar should be directed to assess them. We are much obliged to counsel for the assistance they have given us. I would allow the appeal.   *d*

CUMMING-BRUCE LJ. I agree with all that has fallen from Stephenson LJ. In particular it appears to me that Blackett-Ord V-C manifestly was misled by the headnote to *Day v Singleton* [2] when one considers the terms of his judgment, where he relies on the fact that Mrs Choudhury will not consent, whatever the defendant may do to try to compel her. There is no suggestion anywhere in the evidence that the defendant had tried to *e* persuade his wife not to consent. So the case is different from *Day v Singleton* [2]. That ratio of Blackett-Ord V-C is not consistent with the ratio of Lindley MR and Rigby LJ in *Day v Singleton* [2]. Indeed a scrutiny of Lindley MR's observations [3] show that it was present to the minds of the majority that their decision had the effect that the measure of damages was going to vary according to whether the defendant had tried and failed as compared to whether the third party had been resolutely recalcitrant without any attempt to change his *f* mind. For the reasons stated by Stephenson LJ, it is quite clear that on the ratio of *Day v Singleton* [2] the vendor who seeks to avail himself of the protection afforded by what is described as the rule in *Bain v Fothergill* [1] must go to the length of satisfying the court that he has done all that he reasonably can to mitigate the effects of his breach of contract by trying to remove such fault on the title as appears.

I turn to damages. The plaintiff is entitled to such damages as are properly to be assessed *g* without the restriction placed by the application of the *Bain v Fothergill* [1] rule. Though at one stage counsel for the defendant was presenting submissions covering a wider field in relation to damages, the issues between the parties are now accepted on both sides to be the following. (1) Are the damages awarded in substitution for a decree of specific performance to be assessed by reference to the value of the house at the date of the declaration and order of the Court of Appeal on 4th June 1974 or by reference to its value at the date of judgment *h* of this court on 21st October 1977? (2) Are the damages to include such loss in the plaintiff's medical practice as the plaintiff may prove to flow in the past or in the future

j

1   (1874) LR 7 HL 158, [1874–80] All ER Rep 83
2   [1899] 2 Ch 320
3   [1899] 2 Ch 320 at 329

from the failure of the defendant to deliver up the house and surgery? (3) Is the assessment

a of damages to be reduced by reason of the failure of the plaintiff to mitigate his damage, in particular by reason of the plaintiff's delay in the conduct of his legal proceedings during a period when the price of real property was rising such that the plaintiff increased the damages by his own delay?

Counsel for the plaintiff submits that when the court holds that where on the facts the contractual right of the plaintiff is such that specific performance may be ordered, if having

b regard to equitable principles it is appropriate to do so, but damages are awarded in substitution for specific performance, the value of the res will be assessed at date of judgment, and the plaintiff is entitled to the difference between the value at the date of contract, in this case by concession advanced to June 1974, and date of judgment. He relies on the decision of Megarry J in *Wroth v Tyler*[1] and of Goff J in *Grant v Dawkins*[2].

Counsel for the defendant seeks to distinguish *Wroth v Tyler*[1] on the facts and further

c submits that the decision was wrong and should not be followed. Though there are many differences between the facts in *Wroth v Tyler*[1] and the instant case, there is, in my view, no distinction relevant to the problem common to this case and *Wroth v Tyler*[1], that is, are damages awarded in substitution for an order of specific performance to be assessed at the date of breach of contract or at the date of judgment?

There is no authority binding on this court directly on the point. It is therefore

d necessary to consider the question in the light of general principles, having regard to the words of s 2 of the Chancery Amendment Act 1858, the substance of which remains in force in spite of repeal of parts of that Act by the Statute Law Revision and Civil Procedure Act 1883 (see *Leeds Industrial Co-operative Society Ltd v Slack*[3]).

Counsel for the defendant submits that, if the approach of Blackett-Ord V-C is right, it will produce the anomaly that damages in substitution for an order for specific performance

e could be, and in a period of rising price level will be, higher than damages at common law. He submits that at common law the underlying principle has always been to restore the injured party to the position he would have been in had the contract been performed, but that the courts have evolved rules which are now binding and which determine the way in which the general principle of restitutio in integrum should be applied. One such rule is that damages fall to be assessed at the date of breach and that rule applies even

f though by the date of judgment changes in price levels may have rendered such assessment no guide to the plaintiff's true loss.

So, when the court comes to the task of assessing damages in substitution for an order of specific performance, a court of equity, he submits, should follow the law and address itself to finding the proper substitute, having regard to those rules which the common law has evolved in order to restore the plaintiff to the position in which he would have been had

g the contract not been broken. Counsel for the defendant distinguishes the decision in *Leeds Industrial Co-operative Society Ltd v Slack*[3] on the ground that that was a case for damages in substitution for a quia timet injunction and so damages were awarded once for all to compensate for the future loss.

I cannot accept that these criticisms are valid. I would be content to adopt with respect the reasoning and conclusions of Megarry J in *Wroth v Tyler*[1]. The equitable remedy of

h specific performance has features markedly different from damages at common law for breach of contract. But there is an analogy at common law to the equitable remedy of specific performance. This is to be found in the action in detinue. The remedies available

j

1   [1973] 1 All ER 897, [1974] Ch 30
2   [1973] 3 All ER 897, [1973] 1 WLR 1406
3   [1924] AC 851, [1924] All ER Rep 259

in that action are well summarised in the note[1] to RSC Ord 13, r 3, and are explained by Diplock LJ in *General and Finance Facilities Ltd v Cooks Cars (Romford) Ltd*[2].

As Diplock LJ explained[3], the action in detinue partakes of the nature of an action in rem in which the plaintiff seeks specific restitution of his chattel. In that action, where an order for a writ of specific delivery can be made, the plaintiff has always been entitled instead to claim its value in money assessed at date of judgment.

That distinguishes the remedy of damages in detinue from damages for conversion and the dictum to the contrary in the judgment of Lord Goddard LJ in *Sachs v Miklos*[4] is unnecessary, is too wide and is based on the headnote in *Rosenthal v Alderton & Sons Ltd*[5] which is not in accordance with the last paragraph of the judgment in that case.

Thus, where the common law is concerned with the remedy of specific restitution of a chattel, it does seek to restore the plaintiff as completely as money can to the position he would be in if he had the chattel delivered up on the date of judgment. To this end the value of the chattel is assessed at the date of judgment and not the date of breach.

So I am satisfied that equity is following the law if in relation to an award of damages in substitution for an order for specific performance of a contract of sale of real property, it awards damages assessing the value of the realty at date of judgment and not the date of breach. Had Blackett-Ord V-C been referred to the cases of the common law remedy of specific restitution in detinue, he would not have had to contrast obedience to s 2 of Lord Cairns's Act[6] with the principle that equity follows the law.

The plaintiff seeks, as an element in his damages in substitution for specific performance, compensation for the loss sustained to his medical practice by reason of the breach of contract in failing to sell him the house with the surgery. Counsel for the defendant submits that that damage is too remote. He submits that on a proper construction of the option clause, the parties did not contemplate such a type of loss flowing from a failure to sell the house. He points to cl 3 whereby each party convenanted to provide and maintain himself in a dwelling-house suitable for his share of the practice and to pay the whole costs thereof, including surgeries, consulting rooms and waiting rooms at such dwelling-house. And in cl 20 of the partnership deed it is provided that, if one partner ceases to be bound by the agreement, the party so ceasing to be bound shall not, for a period of three years from the date on which he so ceases, practise within a distance of five miles from any premises at which at the time of such cesser the partnership practice is being carried on, but there is no reference to the particular premises specified in the option clause.

By cl 22 (that imposes the obligation on the defendant to sell the house) it is provided that he will offer to sell such house, surgeries and grounds at a fair market price.

Accepting that no finding of fact should be made inconsistent with the evidence of the defendant in respect of any matter on which the defendant has given unchallenged evidence, there still remains the clear background accepted by both sides to the effect that when the defendant entered into the partnership deed and became a partner to the plaintiff, the plaintiff was at the time practising from the surgery at Novar, that from the time when the partnership came into existence the two partners practised from that surgery although they also practised from a National Health Service clinic in another village. Further the option clause appears as one clause in a partnership agreement which is wholly concerned in setting out the terms by which the two partners shall carry on medical practice. The option clause dealing with the sale of Novar is one of the clauses which provides for the practice and opportunities of practice of each of the partners after cessation of the partnership or dissolution thereof.

In that context it appears to me that the parties must have contemplated that, if the

---

1 Supreme Court Practice (1976), vol 1, p 118, para 13/3/2
2 [1963] 2 All ER 314, [1963] 1 WLR 644
3 [1963] 2 All ER 314 at 318, [1963] 1 WLR 648 at 650
4 [1948] 1 All ER 67 at 69, [1948] 2 KB 23 at 38–39
5 [1946] 1 All ER 583, [1946] KB 374
6 Chancery Amendment Act 1858

plaintiff decided to exercise his option, he would exercise his option with the intent to use the surgery for the purpose for which it had been built and for which it had been used from the date of the partnership deed.

Thus if and in so far as the plaintiff is able to prove, on enquiry, that he has sustained loss in his professional practice, which has a sufficient nexus with the inability of the plaintiff to practise from the surgery at Novar, such loss is a proper ingredient of the damages and should be added to such figure as is arrived at by taking the value of the house at the date of judgment and assessing the difference between that value and the value on 4th June 1974 which by concession is accepted as the starting date.

It is perhaps unnecessary for me to emphasise that there is a distinction between loss of practice sustained by the plaintiff caused by his inability to practise from the surgery at Novar and loss sustained by the plaintiff in his practice as a consequence of the competition of the defendant. In so far as the plaintiff has sustained damage by reason of the competition of the defendant, that is a matter which, unless covered by restrictive covenant, is not an element for which the plaintiff can claim. He is entitled to such loss as can reasonably be inferred to have flowed from the fact that for such period as may be proved he was unable to practise from Novar. I use the past tense. If the plaintiff could prove on the balance of probabilities that as a result of being kept out of Novar in the future there was likely to be a quantifiable diminution in his practice income, damages awarded in substitution for specific performance would include such figure as appeared right to capitalise that future loss. But again as the loss will flow from the lack of use of the surgery, as compared to the competition of the defendant or other doctors, it is a matter of common sense that with every month that passes, assuming that the plaintiff is practising at Kippax, it is likely that such goodwill, if that is the right phrase, as is adherent to the Novar surgery, will progressively diminish as patients gradually get used to following the plaintiff to whatever lair he may have established for himself. We are told he has established himself in a lair 25 yards from the defendant's premises.

So I come to the third issue in dispute which is the question of delay. Counsel have agreed that they would prefer this court to determine whether the plaintiff's delay in bringing these proceedings to a conclusion should be taken into account by way of reducing the damages to which he is entitled on the ground that during the time the plaintiff has been dragging his heels through the law courts, if he has been dragging them, the price level of real property has been steadily moving upwards; and so if, for example, 12 months passed by which could have been avoided by greater exertion on the part of the plaintiff or his legal advisers the damages have been enhanced by that very delay.

I do not think at this juncture it is necessary for me (I certainly would be very reluctant to do it) to begin a careful examination of every step in the proceedings stating the dates of every affidavit or summons and exhibiting expressly the intervals of time that have passed before the next step in the action. Suffice it to say, the plaintiff undoubtedly was engulfed in tactical and legal problems of substantial difficulty, as is evidenced by the fact the unfortunate plaintiff is now having the privilege of paying for a second appearance of his legal advisers in the Court of Appeal.

Nonetheless, when all is said and done, it is unfair to the defendant that the deliberation with which the plaintiff moved from the middle of 1975 until he issued the present proceedings in January 1977 should be allowed to enhance the damage which the defendant has to pay the plaintiff if the price level of real property has risen during that period. For my part I would think that justice is done between them by holding that the plaintiff did not sufficiently mitigate his damage by proceeding with greater celerity in the various and difficult legal convolutions that he has been forced to undergo. The right order is that, for purposes of valuation of Novar, and the loss sustained by the plaintiff by the failure of the defendant to honour the contract for sale, the terminal date by reason of delay should be moved back from 20th October 1977 to 20th October 1976. Therefore the task of the assessment of damages is to arrive at the value on 4th June 1974 and the value in October 1976 and to award the plaintiff as one of the items in his damages the difference between these two sums.

STEPHENSON LJ. The appeal will be allowed. We set aside the whole of the order of
Blackett-Ord V-C and order enquiries as in the schedule as amended.   *a*

Appeal allowed.

Solicitors: *Maurice Smith & Co*, Castleford (for the plaintiff); *Willey Hargrave & Co*, Garforth
(for the defendant).

b

L I Zysman Esq   Barrister.

R v Leyland Magistrates, ex parte Hawthorn

QUEEN'S BENCH DIVISION
LORD WIDGERY CJ, MAY AND TUDOR EVANS JJ
24th JULY 1978

Certiorari – Justices – Natural justice – Prosecution not disclosing material evidence to defence – Prosecution not disclosing to defence before trial names of witnesses not proposed to be called at trial – Defendant convicted – Whether defendant denied fair trial – Whether certiorari available if justices not in error.

The applicant was convicted by justices for driving without due care and attention. Subsequently the applicant's solicitors received from the police the names of two further witnesses who had not been called as witnesses at the trial. The applicant sought an order of certiorari to quash his conviction on the ground that the failure of the police to notify him of the existence of the witnesses before the trial as they should have done amounted to a breach of the rules of natural justice.

Held – Although certiorari would not lie to quash the decision of the justices in order to introduce fresh evidence, the failure of the prosecution to notify the applicant of the existence of the two witnesses had prevented the justices from giving the applicant a fair trial, and, notwithstanding that the justices had not themselves been in error, certiorari would nevertheless go to quash the conviction (see p 210 *d* to *f* and p 211 *a* to *c*, post).

Notes
For the purposes for which certiorari is granted, see 11 Halsbury's Laws (4th Edn) para 1528, 1529, and for cases on the subject, see 16 Digest (Repl) 466–485, 2862–3038.

Case referred to in judgments
R v West Sussex Quarter Sessions, ex parte Albert and Maud Johnson Trust Ltd [1973] 3 All ER 289, [1974] 1 QB 24, [1973] 3 WLR 149, 137 JP 784, 71 LGR 379, CA, Digest (Cont Vol D) 268, 2897a.

Cases also cited
Dallison v Caffery [1964] 2 All ER 610, [1965] 1 QB 348, CA.
R v Bryant (1946) 31 Cr App R 146, CCA.
R v Gillyard (1848) 12 QB 527, 116 ER 965.
R v Leicester Recorder [1947] 1 All ER 928, [1947] KB 726, DC.

Motion for certiorari
This was an application by Paul Robert Hawthorn for an order of certiorari to bring up and quash his conviction on 16th March 1977 by justices sitting at Leyland in the County of Lancaster for the offence of driving a motor car on 9th August 1976 without due care and attention contrary to s 3 of the Road Traffic Act 1972. The facts are set out in the judgment of Lord Widgery CJ.

Michael Kershaw for the applicant.
Graham Boal for the prosecutor.

LORD WIDGERY CJ. In these proceedings counsel moves on behalf of the applicant for an order of certiorari to remove into this court for the purpose of its being quashed a conviction for an offence of driving a motor car without due care and attention, contrary to s 3 of the Road Traffic Act 1972, on 9th August 1976. The conviction was recorded by the justices of the peace in and for the county of Lancaster sitting at Leyland on 16th March 1977.

The facts on which this case depends can be stated in a very short space of time. The applicant was driving a motor car on a road when he came into collision with a motor car travelling in the opposite direction. It was obviously one of those cases where both cars were too near the centre of the road for comfort, and one of them must have been a little over the centre of the road. Who it was that had that unenviable position occupied much of the time at the trial,

However, the matter was tried eventually and a conviction was entered of driving without due care and attention. When all the tumult and shouting had died down and the papers were being sorted out to be put away, the applicant's solicitors received from the police authority the names and addresses of two further witnesses who had come to the police but whom the police did not seek to call. The police had not, as they undoubtedly should have done, notified the defence of the existence of these additional witnesses. Now the applicant has the names and addresses of those witnesses, and also has a brief statement of evidence which they could give, and in each instance that evidence might be helpful to the applicant as tending to show that it was not his car which was over the centre line of the road when the collision took place.

Counsel for the applicant has referred us to a number of authorities. He has pointed out that it is not enough from his point of view merely to say that additional evidence has come to light since the trial and ask for the matter to be reviewed on that basis.

It was decided not so very long ago in the Court of Appeal that there is no room for the use of certiorari to quash a decision in order to introduce fresh evidence. The case in question is *R v West Sussex Quarter Sessions, ex parte Albert and Maud Johnson Trust Ltd*[1].

Accordingly, counsel recognises he cannot simply say, 'I want certiorari to quash this conviction so that I may call fresh evidence next time'. He agrees that in order to get this matter on its feet he has to say that his client was deprived of the benefit of the rules of natural justice by not having had acceded to him by the prosecution the elementary right to be notified of additional witnesses who are known to the prosecution but whom the prosecution do not intend to call.

No one can doubt the importance of this case and the desire which, I think, everyone would feel to get this matter within the scope of certiorari, because the hardship, and indeed injustice, done to this applicant is there for all to see. But the problem is largely a technical one to see whether the remedy of certiorari can be employed in this case notwithstanding its limitations.

In Halsbury's Laws of England[2] this is said of the capacity of the court to order certiorari against justices:

> 'An order of certiorari is the appropriate remedy where the jurisdiction of justices is impugned, or where a conviction or order has been obtained by collusion, or, it would seem, by fraud, or where an error appears on the face of the proceedings, or where there has been a failure to comply with the statutory requirements that the defendant be asked whether he pleads guilty or not guilty. The issue of the order of certiorari in such a case is discretionary.'

Nothing is there said about breach of the rules of natural justice. There is no doubt that an application can be made by certiorari to set aside an order on the basis that the tribunal failed to observe the rules of natural justice. Certainly if it were the fault of the justices that this additional evidentiary information was not passed on, no difficulty would arise. But the problem, and one can put it in a sentence, is that certiorari in respect of breach of the rules of natural justice is primarily a remedy sought on account of an error of the tribunal, and here, of course, we are not concerned with an error of the tribunal: we are concerned with an error of the police prosecutors. Consequently, amongst the arguments to which

---

1   [1973] 3 All ER 289, [1974] 1 QB 24
2   11 Halsbury's Laws (4th Edn) para 1529

we have listened an argument has been that this is not a certiorari case at all on any of the accepted grounds.

We have given this careful thought over the short adjournment because it is a difficult case in that the consequences of the decision either way have their unattractive features. However, if fraud, collusion, perjury and such like matters not affecting the tribunal themselves justify an application for certiorari to quash the conviction, if all those matters are to have that effect, then we cannot say that the failure of the prosecutor which in this case has prevented the tribunal from giving the defendant a fair trial should not rank in the same category.

We have come to the conclusion that there was here a clear denial of natural justice. Fully recognising the fact that the blame falls on the prosecutor and not on the tribunal, we think that it is a matter which should result in the conviction being quashed. In my judgment, that is the result to which we should adhere.

MAY J. I agree.

TUDOR EVANS J. I agree.

Certiorari granted.

Solicitors: *James Chapman & Co*, Manchester (for the applicant); *Brian Hill*, Preston (for the prosecution).

Sepala Munasinghe Esq   Barrister.

Parkes v Secretary of State for the Environment and another

COURT OF APPEAL, CIVIL DIVISION
LORD DENNING MR, GEOFFREY LANE AND EVELEIGH LJJ
9th MAY 1978

Town and country planning – Discontinuance order made in respect of use of land for storing and sorting scrap material – Whether storing and sorting of scrap material a 'use' of the land or an 'operation' on it – Town and Country Planning Act 1971, ss 51(1)(g), 290.

P stored and sorted scrap material on land which was situated in a district renowned for its great natural beauty. The local planning authority considered that his use of the land in that way was detrimental to the amenities of the district and made an order, under s 51(1)(a)[a] of the Town and Country Planning Act 1971, requiring him to discontinue that use of the land. The order was confirmed by the Secretary of State for the Environment. P appealed contending that the order was ultra vires because the storing and sorting of scrap material amounted to 'operations' on the land and, under s 290[b] of the 1971 Act, a 'use' in relation to land did not include 'the use of land for the carrying out of any building or other operations thereon'. The judge allowed the appeal. On appeal by the Secretary of State,

Held – The word 'operations' in s 290 of the 1971 Act meant operations which resulted in a physical alteration to the land itself of some degree of permanence, whereas the word 'use'

---

a   Section 51(1), so far as material, is set out at p 212 *g h*, post
b   Section 290, so far as material, is set out at p 213 *d*, post

comprised activities which were done in, alongside or on the land and which did not
interfere with its actual physical characteristics. Because the storing and sorting of scrap
materials did not alter the actual physical characteristics of the land it was therefore a 'use'
of land and not an 'operation' on it. It followed that the discontinuance order had been
validly made and the appeal would be allowed (see p 213 *h* to p 214 *b* and *f g* and p 215 *a
b*, post).

Notes

For discontinuance orders, see 37 Halsbury's Laws (3rd Edn) 392, 396, paras 496–502.

    For the Town and Country Planning Act 1971, ss 51, 290, see 41 Halsbury's Statutes (3rd
Edn) 1646, 1903.

Case referred to in judgments

Coleshill and District Investment Co Ltd v Minister of Housing and Local Government [1969] 2 All
    ER 525, [1969] 1 WLR 746, 133 JP 385, 20 P & CR 679, HL, Digest (Cont Vol C) 961,
    11b.

Appeal

This was an appeal by the Secretary of State for the Environment against the judgment of
Forbes J given on 11th January 1978 whereby he allowed an appeal by Kenneth Parkes
against the Milldam Mine Discontinuance Order 1976, made by the Peak Park Planning
Board on 10th August 1976 and confirmed by the Secretary of State for the Environment
on 5th October 1977, and quashed that order. The facts are set out in the judgment of
Lord Denning MR.

Harry Woolf for the Secretary of State for the Environment.
Mr Parkes did not appear.

LORD DENNING MR. In the Peak National Park, high up near Great Hucklow in the
Derbyshire Dales, there is an area of great landscape beauty. But it is spoilt in one part by
an ugly heap of waste. It is near an old lead mine called Milldam Mine. There are old and
rusty pieces of equipment strewn over the site. There is a dilapidated old shed. There are
derelict stationary engines, and all sorts of old scrap. It has been there for 30 years or so.
Living there are a Mr Parkes and his sister Miss Parkes. They want to carry on this old scrap
heap. They sort the scrap there and store it there.

    The Peak National Park authority, wishing to preserve the amenities of the park, want
to get rid of this heap of waste. They seek to put into force s 51 of the Town and Country
Planning Act 1971. It enables the planning authority to order the discontinuance of a
use. If such an order is made and the use discontinued, the persons concerned (in this case
Mr Parkes and his sister) are entitled to compensation. Section 51(1) says:

> 'If it appears to a local planning authority that it is expedient in the interests of the
> proper planning of their area (including the interests of the amenity), regard being
> had to the development plan and to any other material considerations—(*a*) that any
> use of land should be discontinued, or that any conditions should be imposed on the
> continuance of a use of land; or (*b*) that any building or works should be altered or
> removed, the local planning authority may by order require the discontinuance of
> that use . . .'

Section 170 provides compensation for any person damaged by a discontinuation order.

    In the case of this waste heap a discontinuation order was made. An inquiry was held
by an inspector. His conclusion was:

> '. . . it seems to me that the storage of scrap and scrap materials is a land use which
> can be identified as such, and does not involve operations affecting the physical
> characteristics of the land. This use of the land falls within the compass of Section 51
> of the 1971 Act . . .'

So he recommended that the order be confirmed. The minister did confirm it.

a   Mr Parkes objected to the order. He applied to quash it. Forbes J did quash the order. The minister appeals to this court.

The issue depends on the meaning of the word 'use' in s 51(1)(a) of the 1971 Act. Forbes J drew a distinction between carrying out 'operations' on land and making a 'use' of land. The local authority had no power, he said, to stop 'operations' being carried out on land. It only had power to stop the 'use' of the land. The judge acknowledged that 'the deposit

b   of refuse or waste materials on land' was a use of it, because it is so described in s 22(3)(b) of the 1971 Act. But the judge said that in this case there was something more than the mere deposit of refuse or waste material, because Mr Parkes not only stored the scrap there. He sorted it into separate heaps or piles of material, according to the size or nature of the bits of scrap. In that way he processed the scrap there. The judge said that, if the scrap was ancillary to the processing, the whole thing would be the carrying out of

c   'operations' on the land, and, being 'operations', it was not the 'use' of the land. So no discontinuation order could be made. The result was that Mr Parkes could carry on there indefinitely.

The judge then gave a restricted meaning to the word 'use'. He was led to this view by the definition in s 290 of the 1971 Act. It says, '"use", in relation to land, does not include the use of land for the carrying out of any building or other operations thereon'. That led

d   the judge back to the definition of 'building operations'. It says that '"building operations" includes rebuilding operations, structural alterations of or additions to buildings, and other operations normally undertaken by a person carrying on business as a builder'. Then returning to the definition of 'use', the judge said that 'building operations' were excluded from 'use' and so also were 'other operations thereon'. By that line of reasoning the judge held that any operations of any kind were excluded from 'use'. So he held that the sorting

e   and processing of scrap material were excluded as being 'other operations thereon'.

The department are most concerned by the judge's interpretation of the word 'use'. I am not surprised, because it makes a serious gap in planning law. I wish we could have argument on both sides. But we had none on Mr Parkes's side. He conducted his own case in the court below. Unfortunately we have not had the benefit of his presence here today. But we have considered as well as we can the arguments which could be submitted

f   on his behalf. As a result I am afraid that I take a different view from the judge. I think that the 1971 Act divides 'development' into two halves. Section 22 says: '. . ."development" . . . means the carrying out of building, engineering, mining or other operations in, on, over or under land [that is one half] or the making of any material change in the use of any buildings or other land', and that is the other half. These two halves are found again in s 45(4). It says that a planning permission can be revoked—

g   '(a) where the permission relates to the carrying out of building or other operations, at any time before those operations have been completed; (b) where the permission relates to a change of the use of any land, at any time before the change has taken place . . .'

The two halves are found again in s 51(1)(a) and (b) respectively.

h   Looking at these various sections it seems to me that the first half, 'operations', comprises activities which result in some physical alteration to the land, which has some degree of permanence to the land itself, whereas the second half, 'use', comprises activities which are done in, alongside or on the land but do not interfere with the actual physical characteristics of the land. We were referred to *Coleshill and District Investment Co Ltd v Minister of Housing and Local Government*[1] when the House of Lords considered whether demolition of a

j   structure could be 'development'. There are interesting observations on the construction of these sections but none that affects our present case.

Coming back to the present case, it seems to me, with all respect to the judge, that the storing, sorting and processing of scrap on land amounts to a 'use' of land. There is no

---

1   [1969] 2 All ER 525, [1969] 1 WLR 746

physical alteration to the land. It is an activity on the land which is clearly a use of the land well within the definition. So an order can be made, and was properly made, for the discontinuance of the use.

I would therefore allow the appeal, remembering that the 1971 Act does provide for compensation for a person who is affected by such an order as this. So I would allow the appeal accordingly.

GEOFFREY LANE LJ. I agree. The local authority seek to apply the provisions of s 51(1) of the Town and Country Planning Act 1971, the material part of which reads as follows:

> 'If it appears to a local planning authority that it is expedient in the interests of the proper planning of their area (including the interests of amenity), regard being had to the development plan and to any other material considerations—(a) that any use of land should be discontinued, or that any conditions should be imposed on the continuance of a use of land . . . the local planning authority may by order require the discontinuance of that use . . .'

Here the local authority consider, and understandably consider, that the use of part of the Derbyshire Dales as a scrap heap or a place for sorting scrap metal is detrimental to the amenities of the Peak District. They failed before the judge by reason of the definition in s 290 of the 1971 Act of the word 'use', a negative definition reading as follows: ' "use", in relation to land, does not include the use of land for the carrying out of any building or other operations thereon.' It is clear, as the learned judge in his judgment points out, that that definition cannot be applied literally because, if any operations on the land are excluded from the meaning of the word 'use', then this part of the 1971 Act loses its efficacy entirely and might as well not have been passed. Consequently, some restriction must be placed on the apparent prima facie meanings of that definition section.

It seems to me in the particular circumstances of this case that it is unnecessary to decide what particular restriction needs to be applied, whether it is that of the ejusdem generis rule or the noscitur a sociis rule or whether one should simply read into that definition the word 'similar' so it would read ' "use", in relation to land, does not include the use of land for the carrying out of any building or similar operations thereon'. Whatever restriction one applies, on the facts of this particular case it is perfectly plain that the storing and sorting of scrap metal comes within s 51(1)(a).

I agree with the way in which Lord Denning MR has pointed out the pattern that runs through this Act, which is to be observed in ss 22, 45 and 51, and I agree respectfully with the way in which he applied that pattern to the decision in this case. As I say, whatever restriction one imposes necessarily on that definition section, the result is the same, and I respectfully disagree with the conclusion reached by Forbes J, and I too would allow this appeal.

EVELEIGH LJ. Without further argument on the point, I would not readily agree with the first submission of counsel for the Secretary of State to the effect that the definition of 'use' in s 290 should be read as shorthand and in its proper form would include the words of s 2(1) of the 1971 Act, namely 'the carrying out of building, engineering, mining or other operations in, on, over or under land'. If that was the intention of the legislature, it seems to me that the definition section itself could easily say so. In my view, for example, 'mining operations' may be within the definition of 'use' or may not depending on whether they are constructional or productive. Regulation 3 of the Town and Country Planning (Minerals) Regulations 1971[1] to which counsel for the Secretary of State has drawn our attention, reads as follows: 'For the purposes of those provisions, "use" in relation to the development of land does not include the use of land by the carrying out of mining operations . . .', and that provision would not have been necessary if the wider

---

1   SI 1971 No 756

a definition, for which counsel for the Secretary of State primarily contended, applied. However, I agree that 'operations' should not be given the wide meaning given to it by the judge. In my opinion the word means operations with the same kind of purpose as building operations, that is to say, to add to or to alter the condition or the state or the quality of the land, usually no doubt with the future or the continuing use of the land in mind.

I too would allow this appeal.

b *Appeal allowed.*

Solicitors: *Treasury Solicitor.*

Gavin Gore-Andrews Esq   Barrister.

c

Tuck and others v National Freight Corporation

COURT OF APPEAL, CIVIL DIVISION

d LORD DENNING MR, GEOFFREY LANE AND EVELEIGH LJJ
27th, 28th, 31st OCTOBER, 6th DECEMBER 1977

HOUSE OF LORDS
LORD WILBERFORCE, VISCOUNT DILHORNE, LORD FRASER OF TULLYBELTON, LORD RUSSELL OF KILLOWEN AND LORD SCARMAN
e 23rd, 24th, 25th OCTOBER, 23rd NOVEMBER 1978

British Transport Commission – Transferred undertaking – Compensation to employee – Worsening of employee's position – Right to compensation on worsening of position – Basis on which worsening of position to be assessed – Whether by comparison with employee's position with new employer since transfer or with his position if he had not been transferred – British Transport (Compensation to
f Employees) Regulations 1970 (SI 1970 No 187), reg 13(1).

The claimants were employed by the British Railways Board. Under the provisions of the Transport Act 1968 the claimants were transferred on 1st January 1969 to two subsidiary companies of the National Freight Corpn ('the NFC'), established under the 1968 Act. They had periodic increases in their salaries as they would have had if they had remained
g as employees of the board. They alleged however that between 14th October 1972 and 14th October 1974 the board's employees received a higher or faster rate of increase in pay than the employees of the NFC's subsidiaries. The claimants claimed that as transferred employees they were entitled to compensation, under reg 13(1)[a] of the British Transport (Compensation to Employees) Regulations 1970, on the ground that their position as employees had worsened causing them loss or injury and that the 'worsening of [their]
h position ... [was] properly attributable' to their transfer of employment from the board to the NFC. The NFC, as the compensating authority, rejected the claim, taking the view that reg 13(1)(a) only provided for compensation in the event of any worsening in an employee's position within his new employment and therefore any worsening of the claimants' position had to be assessed by comparing the claimants' position as employees of the NFC's subsidiaries on 14th October 1972 with their position as such employees on 14th October
j 1974, and that on that basis there had been no worsening of their position. The claimants made a complaint to an industrial tribunal which upheld the NFC's decision. On appeal by the claimants, the High Court[b] allowed their appeal, holding that reg 13(1)(a) was to be

---

a   Regulation 13(1), so far as material, is set out at p 220*f*, post.
b   [1978] 1 All ER 1266

construed as meaning that any worsening of their position was to be assessed by comparing their position since they had been transferred with their position if they had not been *a* transferred, and remitted the case to the industrial tribunal to decide whether the claimants' position had worsened and if so whether by reason of that fact they had suffered any loss or injury which was properly attributable to the transfer, within the meaning of s 135(1) of the 1968 Act and reg 13(1)(a) of the 1970 regulations. On appeal by the NFC, the Court of Appeal[c] upheld that construction of reg 13(1)(a) and dismissed the appeal on the ground that the worsening of the claimants' position was properly attributable to the transfer and *b* since the amount of the loss suffered by the claimants had not been disputed no remission to the tribunal was necessary. The NFC appealed to the House of Lords.

Held – (Lord Wilberforce and Viscount Dilhorne dissenting) – On the natural meaning of the phrase 'worsening of his position' in s 135(1) of the 1968 Act and reg 13(1)(a) of the 1970 regulations a claimant was only entitled to compensation under the statute and regulations if there had been a deterioration in the terms and conditions of his employment *c* such as to make his own position within his present employment with the NFC worse than it had been at some previous time during that employment, and there was nothing in the phrase to suggest a comparison with the position of any other employee or with the position in which the claimant himself might have been had he continued in his former employment. Since the claimants had not shown any such worsening of their position the appeal would be allowed (see p 233 e to g, p 234 a to c, p 235 a and g to j, p 236 a, p 239 a *d* c d and h and p 240 a, post).

Decisions of Donaldson J [1978] 1 All ER 1266 and of the Court of Appeal p 217, post, reversed.

Notes

For compensation to employees of the British Transport Commission, see 31 Halsbury's Laws (3rd Edn) 518, 519, paras 760, 761. *e*

For the Transport Act 1968, s 135, see 26 Halsbury's Statutes (3rd Edn) 1179.

Cases referred to in judgments and opinions

Borman v London and North Eastern Railway Co (1942) 167 LT 30, 58 TLR 153; *affd* [1942] 1 All ER 671, 167 LT 30, 58 TLR 277, CA, 38 Digest (Repl) 388, 550.

Minister of Pensions v Chennell [1946] 2 All ER 719, [1947] KB 250, [1947] LJR 700, 176 LT *f* 164, 17 Digest (Reissue) 547, 346.

Parker and Great Western Railway Co, Re Arbitration between [1944] 1 All ER 400, sub nom *Parker v Great Western Railway Co* 170 LT 284, 60 TLR 300, CA, 38 Digest (Repl) 296, 65.

Pegler v Great Western Railway Co (1946) 62 TLR 474; *affd* [1947] 1 All ER 355, 63 TLR 178, CA; *affd* sub nom *Pegler v Railway Executive* [1948] 1 All ER 559, [1948] AC 332, *g* [1948] LJR 939, HL, 38 Digest (Repl) 388, 551.

Appeal

The National Freight Corpn ('the NFC') appealed against the judgment of Donaldson J dated 8th July 1977[1] which (i) allowed an appeal by the claimants, William Henry Tuck, John Francis Moody and Stanley Arthur Wray, against the decision of an industrial tribunal (chairman J S Rumbold QC) sitting in London on 15th March 1977 dismissing the *h* claimants' appeals under reg 42 of the British Transport (Compensation to Employees) Regulations 1970[2] against the decision of the NFC as the compensating authority under the regulations not to award the claimants compensation under reg 12 of the regulations, and (ii) ordered the claimants' claim to be remitted to the industrial tribunal for it to consider under reg 13(1)(a) of the regulations whether the claimants' position had worsened and, if so, whether by reason of that fact they had suffered any loss or injury attributable to the *j* happening of the relevant event (ie their transfer from the British Railways Board to the

---

c   Page 217, post
1   [1978] 1 All ER 1266
2   SI 1970 No 187

NFC). The claimants cross-appealed contending that the judgment of Donaldson J should be varied by setting aside that part of his order which ordered that their claims should be remitted to the industrial tribunal for it to consider whether their position had worsened and whether they had suffered loss. The facts are set out in the judgment of Lord Denning MR.

Jon Harvey QC and *Andrew Thompson* for the NFC.
Ronald Waterhouse QC and *Alexander Irvine* for the claimants.

Cur adv vult.

6th December 1977. The following judgments were read.

LORD DENNING MR. This is a test case. Three men ('the claimants') claim compensation. They say they were employed by the British Railways Board ('British Rail') until 31st December 1968 and were then transferred compulsorily to new road companies. At first they were no worse off. Their wages in the new companies were just as good as if they had remained in British Rail. But then later on they became worse off. The men who had stayed with British Rail got increases in their wages. They went higher than the men who had been transferred to the new companies. The transferred men claim compensation for this worsening of their position.

The details of the three are these.

Mr Tuck started with the railways nearly 40 years ago. He was working as a clerk in the division which deals with road-vans collecting goods, and so forth. On 31st December 1968 he was transferred to National Carriers Ltd. He remained with them in the same grade. But from October 1972 the wages of the clerks with British Rail went up, and his did not. In the two years from October 1972 to October 1974 he got £125·03 less than he would have done if he had stayed with British Rail.

Mr Wray started with the railways 43 years ago. He, too, was transferred to National Carriers Ltd on 31st December 1968. He was promoted to a higher grade on 7th October 1969. For the two years from October 1972 to October 1974 he got £175·39 less than he would if he had stayed with British Rail.

Mr Moody started with the railways 27 years ago. He was transferred to Freightliners Ltd on 31st December 1968. He was promoted twice to higher grades. For the same two years, October 1972 to October 1974, he got £920·96 less.

We are told that there are many there with long service who have similar claims. If they are admitted, they will come to a very big sum. So the unions have taken up these cases.

The legal position

Many Acts of Parliament have grappled with the problem of transport by rail and road. Up to the end of 1968 there was the British Railways Board, which was constituted under the Transport Act 1962. It organised its undertaking in three divisions: (1) the 'railways division' which operated the railway system proper, carrying goods and passengers by rail; (2) the 'freightliner division' which operated a road system by which containers were carried by lorries on roads; (3) the 'rail sundries division' which operated the system by which goods of all kinds were carried to and from railway stations and depots.

The railway division had a monopoly of rail transport in England. But the other two divisions had only 5 per cent of the road transport in England.

In 1968 Parliament decided that there should be a complete reorganisation. The railways division was to be continued as British Rail. But the other two divisions were to be 'hived off' and to be run completely separately by two new concerns. The freightliners division was to be run by Freightliners Ltd. The rail sundries was to be run by National Carriers Ltd. Those two new concerns were to be subsidiaries of a new public authority called the National Freight Corpn ('the NFC') which was to hold 51 % of the securities of Freightliners Ltd and 100 per cent of the securities of National Carriers Ltd.

On 30th December 1968 those two new companies were formed. On 31st December those two companies took over all the property, rights and liabilities of the previous two divisions respectively. On 1st January 1969 the NFC acquired the securities in the two new companies.

On 31st December 1968, by the Transport Act 1968, s 5(3), the employees of the two previous divisions (the freightliner division and the rail sundries division) were automatically transferred to the two new companies (Freightliners Ltd and National Carriers Ltd). But this only applied to those employees who were 'wholly or mainly employed' for the purpose of the two previous divisions respectively. If any employee was so 'wholly or mainly employed' he was automatically transferred to the new company, together with all the rights and liabilities under his contract of service: see s 4(2) of the 1968 Act. The transfer took place without his consent. Each employee was given an option by which he could within three months say he would like to return to British Rail. In that event he would receive a list of any vacancies and could apply for one, but without any promise of getting it.

In respect of all those employees who were thus compulsorily transferred, the 1968 Act provided that compensation should be paid to them, if they should suffer any loss by reason of the transfer. The provisions for compensation followed the wording of many previous statutes and regulations in similar situations, such as the amalgamation of the railway companies under the Railways Act 1921 (Sch 3), the reorganisation under the British Transport Commission under the Transport Act 1947 (s 101), and later under the British Railways Board under the Transport Act 1962 (s 81(1)). In every one of those amalgamations or reorganisations, the statute provided that compensation should be paid to any employee in these oft repeated words: '. . . who suffers any loss of employment, or loss or diminution of emoluments or pension rights, or worsening of his position' in consequence of the transfer or which is properly attributable to the transfer.

Diminution of emoluments

That formula was adopted in the days when sterling was a stable currency: and I have no doubt that 'loss of emoluments' or 'diminution of emoluments' was reckoned in terms of sterling at the date of the transfer, without regard to subsequent inflation of currency. Thus in 1968 a man's wages might be £20 a week. If they dropped in 1970 to £18 a week, he would suffer a 'diminution of emoluments'. If they increased in 1970 to £22 a week, he would not suffer a diminution in emoluments, even though in 1970, owing to inflation, £22 did not in real terms represent as much as £20 did in 1968.

Worsening of position

Any injustice on that account is, however, remedied by the general words 'worsening of his position'. Those words require a comparison to be made between the position of the man as he *is* since the transfer, with what his position *would have been* if he had not been transferred. Thus, when a man with his previous company could have continued working until age 65, but under the new company he had to retire at age 60, it was held that his position was worsened by the transfer and he was entitled to compensation: see *Re Arbitration between Parker and Great Western Railway Co*[1]. And where a man's seniority in his previous company was reckoned from his date of joining as a boy, whereas it was reckoned in his new company from his becoming qualified as a skilled man, his position was worsened by the transfer: see *Pegler v Great Western Railway Co*[2].

So in these present days of inflation, if a man's wages for his work would have increased by inflation from £20 to £30 in his previous company but he is down-graded in the new company and receives £25 in his new company, his position is worsened by reason of the transfer. He is only getting £25, whereas if he had not been transferred, he would have got £30.

1   [1944] 1 All ER 400
2   [1948] 1 All ER 559, [1948] AC 332

Counsel for the NFC asked us to hold that 'worsening of his position' only applied to his worsening in his new company. The comparison should be, he said, only between his position in the new company at the date of the transfer and his subsequent position in the new company. That argument was accepted by the industrial tribunal, but I do not think it is correct. I find myself in agreement with Donaldson J on this point. I think 'worsening of position' involves a comparison between his position as it *is* and as it *would have been* if he had not been transferred. It applies to cases where, owing to the transfer, a man may become redundant, or be down-graded, or sent to a new place to work, or lose seniority, or have to retire earlier, and so forth, all of which makes his position worse than it would have been if he had not been compulsorily transferred.

'Properly attributable'

But there is another requirement to be satisfied. The 1968 Act says in s 135 that, in order to be entitled to compensation, the worsening of position must be 'properly attributable to the happening of' the relevant event. In the present case the relevant event is the transfer of the man from British Rail to the new company. If the new company, soon after the transfer, decided to effect economies or eliminate overmanning, which the old company would not have done, the worsening might well be said to be properly attributable to the transfer. But if some years pass and there is a depression in business which forces the new company to economise, then the worsening will not be due to the transfer but to the supervening depression in business: see *Borman v London and North Eastern Railway Co*[1]. In this particular statute, there is a special provision that, if there is a worsening in position owing to a reorganisation directed by a Minister, that can be the subject of compensation: see s 135(1)(b). In every case the question is whether the 'worsening of his position' is 'properly attributable' to the relevant event, in this case, to the compulsory transfer of the man from British Rail to the new company.

Application to the present case

There are many men in the new companies who are new entrants. They were never with the old railways or British Rail. They clearly have no claim to compensation under the 1968 Act.

In 1971 the trade unions took an important step in support of all the men in the new companies. They claimed that all of them, both old-timers and new entrants, should be paid wages which were broadly equivalent to the like grades in British Rail. In short, they should keep pace with the railway men. This claim was submitted to arbitration in accordance with s 137 of the 1968 Act. The arbitrator was Mr A R Swannack. He made a report[2] in which he said that the 'fundamental plank' in the unions' claim was that the pay of the men in the new companies should be comparable with that of the men in the railways. After full consideration the arbitrator rejected the claim. He pointed out that the wages of the railway men were negotiable by British Rail and that the new road companies had no part in them. He said that 'no company could (or should) be expected to be committed to settlements made outside its own control'. The new companies stressed their serious financial position. They pointed out that they operated in a fiercely competitive market. Reporting in October 1972, the arbitrator said:

> '... I have concluded that comparability with British Rail has become less relevant and that this divergence is likely to increase, especially in the case of National Carriers Limited.'

The result of that arbitration was that all the men in the new companies were paid alike, both new entrants and old-timers. It was less than the wages of comparable grades in British Rail.

---

1   (1942) 58 TLR 153
2   Recommended Award for Settlement of Dispute between National Carriers Ltd, Freightliners Ltd and Transport Salaried Staffs' Association (9th October 1972)

Now the unions have taken up the case of the old-timers. Their position has worsened since the transfer. They are worse off than they would have been if they had stayed with British Rail. But, is this worsening 'properly attributable' to the transfer? The simple facts are that an increase in the pay of the railwaymen is due to these factors. British Rail have a monopoly of transport by railway. The trade unions are powerful and demand big increases in wages for the railway staff, and have succeeded in getting them. The failure of the new road companies to make any comparable increase is due to these factors. The new road companies have no monopoly of road transport. They operate in a fiercely competitive market. They simply cannot pay their way if they have to pay wages equal to those of the railwaymen. They have to economise in every possible way.

On those facts it seems to me that, when it came to October 1972, the increase in the railwaymen's pay over the roadmen's pay was attributable to those new factors, and not to the transfer in December 1968. The transfer was not a cause at all but only part of the circumstances in or on which the cause operated: see *Minister of Pensions v Chennell*[1]. That was the view of the industrial tribunal. They said:

'The transfer giving rise to the relevant event in the present context is, we think, to be regarded as no more than a historical event. In our view the events which have occurred post-1969, giving rise to the differentials which now concern us, constitute a break in the claim of causation. The consequence is that any "worsening" there might have been is not "properly attributable" to the relevant event.'

I agree with the tribunal, and for that reason would allow the appeal. I would hold that the claimants are not entitled to compensation.

GEOFFREY LANE LJ. There is no necessity for me to repeat the facts of this case, which have already been summarised. In essence there are two problems to be decided. Both turn on the interpretation of reg 13(1) of the British Transport (Compensation to Employees) Regulations 1970, which reads as follows:

'Without prejudice to any other requirement of these regulations, the conditions for the payment of long term compensation to any person are that—(a) he has, before or not later than 10 years after the date of the relevant event, suffered loss of employment or loss or diminution of emoluments or worsening of his position, being loss, diminution or worsening (as the case may be) which is properly attributable to the happening of the relevant event . . .'

The first problem is the meaning of the expression 'worsening of his position'. With what is the comparison to be made? Does it mean that his position at the time of the claim is worse than it would have been had he stayed with the British Railways Board ('British Rail'), as the claimants contend, or does it mean that his position at the time of the claim must be shown to be worse than his position was at the time when he was moved from British Rail to his employment with National Carriers Ltd or Freightliners Ltd, as the case may be, as the NFC contend? Donaldson J decided this point in favour of the claimants, and I agree with him.

There is no need to go any further than the opening words of reg 13(1)(a). The conditions for the payment of long term compensation to any person are that he had '(a) . . . before . . . or not later than 10 years after the date of the relevant event, suffered . . . worsening . . .'

The relevant date is the date of transfer (1st January 1969) and at that time the only matter with which a comparison *could* be made was his position as an officer employed by British Rail. That is sufficient to dispose of the NFC's argument on this point.

There is no doubt that if this is the proper comparison each of the three claimants with whom we are here concerned has suffered a worsening of his position and financial loss.

1   [1946] 2 All ER 719 at 721–722, [1947] KB 250 at 254–256

Mr Tuck £125·03, Mr Wray £175·39, and Mr Moody £920·96. These figures are, as I understand it, not in dispute.

Can it be said that the worsening of their respective positions is 'properly attributable to the happening of the relevant event'? This is the second problem. The learned judge did not deal with this point, taking the view, it seems, that there was not an adequate basis of fact on which he could reach a conclusion. What he did was to remit the claim to the industrial tribunal for it to consider whether the claimants' positions as officers had worsened and, if so, whether that was attributable to the relevant event. It is true that the industrial tribunal did not find as a fact that any of these claimants had suffered any particular sum by way of loss or injury. It was not necessary for them to do so, deciding as they did that on their interpretation of the regulation there could have been no worsening of the claimants' position.

It has however not been disputed before this court that the claimants have each of them suffered the diminution of earnings mentioned compared with their opposite numbers in British Rail. In other words, had they remained as employees of British Rail they would have been that much the better off.

The NFC complain in their notice of appeal that the judge erred in holding that such worsening of position was or was capable of being properly attributable to the transfer of the claimants from British Rail, or alternatively that he failed adequately to consider the words 'properly attributable' in the regulation. We must therefore enquire whether the worsening of position is 'properly attributable to the relevant event', that is to say to the transfer of the employees to National Carriers Ltd or Freightliners Ltd. We are not enquiring why British Rail employees' wages have increased, or why those of the National Carriers Ltd or Freightliners Ltd have not increased or have not increased so quickly. No doubt the increase in British Rail wages took place at least partly because their unions were in a stronger position to exert pressure. No doubt National Carriers Ltd and Freightliners Ltd wages did not increase so much at least partly because their union was in a weaker position to exert pressure. The question is, was the worsening of the position of the transferred employees properly attributable to the fact of their transfer? I think it was. If they had stayed with British Rail, they would have been earning that much more. The fact that British Rail employees owe their favourable position to the strength of their union seems to me to be irrelevant. 'Attributable to' is a wider expression than 'caused by'. It embraces a number of possible causes. It is largely a matter of first impression, but it seems to me that it is an inescapable fact that the transfer of the men from British Rail to National Carriers Ltd or Freightliners Ltd was one of the factors, if not the principal factor, which contributed to the worsening of the men's position. Accordingly that worsening can properly be described as attributable to the transfer. The rise in British Rail wages was (for purposes of argument) attributable to union strength. The failure of National Carriers Ltd and Freightliners Ltd wages to rise similarly was (for purposes of argument) attributable to union weakness. The difference in wages between those men who stayed with British Rail and those who were seconded was attributable to the fact that they had been so seconded. I would so hold. The judge was right in his interpretation of the words 'worsening of his position'. By virtue of the way in which the appeal was presented to this court it is unnecessary to remit the matter to the tribunal for further findings. In my judgment the claimants are entitled to succeed.

EVELEIGH LJ. I will first try to deal with the arguments of the appellants ('NFC'). They were advanced to support the NFC's basic interpretation of the regulations. They do, however, also give an idea of the setting in which the words 'properly attributable' fall to be considered. The NFC contend that the regulations were made after the transfer so that those responsible for the regulations knew the position and would not in effect wish to impose a heavy burden on the NFC. However, the wording of reg 13 is not an innovation by the Minister but a repetition of the words of the Transport Act 1968 itself contained in s 135. The Minister has no discretion but to compensate people to whom Parliament was giving compensation.

Secondly, they say that diminution or worsening is referring to deterioration within the NFC itself. In my opinion however, the very wording of the regulation is against this for the words 'before' and 'on' are used. Moreover, when the intention is to compensate people who reluctantly leave one employer and are transferred to another, I can see no reason for refusing to look at the prevailing conditions in their original service. The NFC say that the new conditions which were ultimately worked out were virtually the same as they had in British Rail and therefore comparison within the new Freight Corporation would be starting from a basis arrived at by comparison with British Rail. This argument must assume that s 135 itself was drafted on the understanding that the terms of service in the NFC had already been established. There is nothing in the 1968 Act to suggest this. Here again, the NFC's fallacy lies in beginning the story with the regulations in this respect instead of with the Act.

Thirdly, they say that the claimants' contention will result in inequalities, irregularities and consequently discontent. Assume we accept the contention that comparisons should be made within the NFC itself. A former British Rail employee is employed for the moment, let us say, at the same wage as another NFC employee. Next year the NFC reduces the wages of that grade. The NFC concede that compensation is payable to the British Rail ex-employee. Yet such compensation could not be claimed by an employee who did not come from one of the old named organisations. Thus there is inequality. I suspect that there must be inequality in any event right from the start. I very much doubt if the Pickford's people had the same free facilities on British Rail as the British Rail employees took with them when they were transferred.

Fourthly, it is said that the scheme would be more expensive if construed according to the claimants' contention. This argument is based on conditions known to exist today. Bearing in mind that the regulations are dated 1970, how could one say at that time that the claimants' interpretation would be more expensive than that now put forward by the NFC. Let us assume that there were a corresponding reduction in wages in the NFC and British Rail. If the comparison is with British Rail, then the men transferred to the NFC would have no claim at all. If, however, the comparison is to be made within the NFC itself they might have a claim and find themselves better off than the men in British Rail. They would keep any rise within the NFC even though other employees of the NFC suffered a diminution in wages and even though British Rail employees also suffered a similar or greater loss. In these inflationary days it seems strange to talk of reductions in earnings, but I have done so because the NFC have contended that the diminution or worsening of the position is to be compared with a previous raise or condition in the NFC.

I found these peripheral arguments unattractive. We have to construe a statutory instrument and I prefer to do so by looking at it.

Regulation 5. This regulation is relied on by the NFC who say that the specific reference to emoluments 'which he would have enjoyed had he continued in his former employment' shows that such a comparison would not apply but for the specific words. They argue that in consequence the comparison under reg 13 cannot be a comparison within the British Rail service because there is no specific mention of it. I think that this is misconceived. Regulation 5 is dealing with a person who having been employed by British Rail is then in national service. The intention is that he should be able to resume his service (it may be with British Rail (initially)) and to suffer no loss as a result of having been called to the country's service. If a person returned and went straight to the NFC after the transfer under the 1968 Act, questions might arise as to what comparable employment should be taken in assessing his compensation. Should it be that which he held when he left for national service? Should it be the position which he would have held had he never gone on national service? This question could arise for example where there are automatic increments after so many years' service and the date for automatic increase occurs when the employee is on national service. Questions could arise whether or not a place in the hierarchy should be preserved with automatic promotion. I regard reg 5 as dealing with these situations. If, however, we give the NFC's construction to reg 13, the result would be that a person who returned from national service would, in the light of the facts of the present case, be considerably better off than a fellow British Rail employee who remained with British Rail until the date of the changeover and then was transferred to the NFC. The latter would be entitled only to a comparison within the NFC while the former would be entitled to a comparison with a British Rail employee on today's rates of pay. I can understand the legislature wishing to preserve the position of national servicemen but I cannot impute to it an intention to give them a *preference* over their former fellow employees.

I regard reg 5 as assisting the arguments of the claimants. It points to the conclusion that after the changeover the British Rail employees are not to be worse off than they would have been had they remained in British Rail employment. I regard the comparison with British Rail conditions as the natural one to make and I do not attach any value to the NFC's argument that this would be unduly costly for the NFC. That argument proceeds with hindsight. The use of the phrase 'before, on, or not later than 10 years after the date of the relevant event' emphasises to my mind that the standard of comparison is the position in British Rail.

The question then arises whether that comparison is to be made only at the date of the takeover or with conditions in British Rail at the time of the loss. The reference to 'not later than 10 years' is a strong pointer in my opinion to the latter choice. It seems to me an empty concession to make if one says that should you be worse off in ten years' time than you were with British Rail on the date of the changeover we will compensate you. Even before the effects of inflation were so strongly felt, no one could envisage a smaller wage packet in ten years' time. It is true that other conditions of employment might have changed, but the idea of comparing something today with something in ten years' time does not appeal to me. I believe that the words 'which he would have enjoyed had he continued in his former employment' are applicable under reg 13 as well as reg 5 but there is no need to introduce them specifically in reg 13 in the case of a person who has not been away on national service.

I would like to test the NFC's contention by considering the words in reg 13, 'which is properly attributable to the happening of the relevant event' (that is to say, to the changeover). If after three years at a given wage the employee suffers a reduction in wages, the NFC say that he will be entitled to the difference between his previous wage with the NFC and the new wage. Of course it would be necessary to show that the reduction was attributable to the relevant event. I find it very difficult indeed to show how a reduction in wages within the NFC (that is to say, a comparison between the lower wage and the previous higher wage within the NFC) can be attributable to the changeover. I cannot easily envisage how the changeover can be responsible for the NFC paying an employee less than it itself previously paid. On the other hand, it is not difficult to see that the changeover may be responsible for diminution in wages as compared with British Rail.

These arguments then provide a setting in which the words 'properly attributable to' fall to be considered. In my opinion the words 'properly attributable to' are wider than the words 'caused by'. Seeking to interpret them, we should bear in mind that the general scheme of compensation seems to be based on an intention to see that as far as reasonably possible no man should be worse off by having a new employer. That means that he should not be worse off than his counterpart who stayed with his old employer. Clearly, however, he is not to be compensated if the worsening of his position is due to something unconnected with the changeover, for example, if a new lorry were to be introduced to carry more goods and in consequence fewer drivers were needed, a loss of employment or overtime resulting from this situation could not be attributed to the changeover. If a new system of documentation were introduced which cut down the work considerably so that fewer clerks were required, again I do not think that this would be attributable to the changeover. When, however, the wages of British Rail go up and those of the NFC stand still, prima facie at any rate a workman with the NFC is worse off because he is employed by the NFC and not by British Rail. The fact that British Rail have been prompted to make an increase because of union pressure does not in my opinion alter the situation. If the claimants had remained with British Rail they would have benefited from the change in the rate of pay. The only reason they have not benefited is because they no longer work for British Rail. They have been given another employer. In my opinion, therefore, their claim should be allowed.

I would dismiss this appeal.

Appeal dismissed. Cross-appeal allowed. Direction that claimants entitled to compensation. Leave to appeal to the House of Lords.

Mary Rose Plummer   Barrister.

Appeal
The NFC appealed to the House of Lords.

Jon Harvey QC and *Andrew Thompson* for the NFC.
Alexander Irvine QC and *C Carr* for the claimants.

Their Lordships took time for consideration.

23rd November. The following opinions were delivered.

LORD WILBERFORCE. My Lords, the three claimants, now respondents in this appeal, for many years before the passing of the Transport Act 1968 were employed by the British Railways Board ('British Rail'). British Rail was then organised in three divisions, the railways division, the freightliner division and the rail sundries division. The claimants were in one or other of these: Mr Wray and Mr Tuck in rail sundries, Mr Moody in freightliner; but as the divisions had no separate legal existence, each man's employer was British Rail. In 1968 it was decided to 'hive off' British Rail's road transport activities into two bodies separated from it. By some complicated arrangements, which I do not think it necessary to go through, the assets and liabilities of British Rail relating to the freightliner and rail sundries divisions were on the vesting day (1st January 1969) transferred to two new companies called Freightliners Ltd and National Carriers Ltd which in turn were subsidiaries of a new public authority independent of British Rail and called the National Freight Corporation ('the NFC'). On this vesting taking place the claimants on 1st January 1969 automatically and involuntarily ceased to be employed by British Rail and became employees either of Freightliners Ltd or National Carriers Ltd. A large number of other employees of British Rail were similarly transferred.

When employees are involuntarily transferred from one employment to another, it has long been accepted that they must be protected against possible prejudice or loss. So Parliament has prescribed in a series of Acts, from the Railways Act 1921, through the Transport Act 1947 and the Transport Act 1962, and in regulations made thereunder, that compensation should be paid where appropriate and has set up mechanisms for assessing it. Similar legislation has been passed in relation to local government reorganisation. The departmental regulations dealing with this matter have grown in complexity and are now mildly labyrinthine, but the present cases, in my opinion, can and ought to be decided on broad principle rather than by use of the microscope. The critical provisions, for the present purpose, are to be found in s 135 of the Transport Act 1968 and in reg 13 of the regulations[1] made under it.

Section 135 (relevantly) provides:

> '(1) The Minister shall by regulations require the payment by such person as may be determined by or under the regulations, in such cases and to such extent as may be so determined, of compensation to or in respect of any person who is on the date of the happening of any of the following events, namely—(a) a transfer of any property, rights or liabilities under section 4, 5 . . . of this Act . . . and who suffers any loss of employment, or loss or diminution of emoluments or pension rights, or worsening of his position, which is properly attributable to the happening of that event.'

[1] The British Transport (Compensation to Employees) Regulations 1970, SI 1970 No 187

It is not disputed that the 'event' which applies to the claimants was the vesting which occurred as I have mentioned on 1st January 1969 by virtue of ss 4 and 5 of the 1968 Act. The regulations added some important qualifications. First they imposed a condition for the receipt of 'long-term compensation' (which is what the claimants claim) that a claimant must have been continuously engaged in relevant employment (ie by British Rail or the appropriate new subsidiary company) for at least eight years prior to the date of the loss, and secondly that compensation might be claimed for any loss occurring up to ten years after the vesting.

The vital provision in this appeal is reg 13(1)(a), but I quote reg 12 first:

'12. The compensating authority shall, subject to the provisions of these regulations, pay long-term compensation to any person to whom these regulations apply and who satisfies the conditions set out in regulation 13 and this Part of these regulations shall apply to that person.

'13. (1) Without prejudice to any other requirement of these regulations, the conditions for the payment of long-term compensation to any person are that—(a) he has, before, on, or not later than 10 years after the date of the relevant event, suffered loss of employment or loss or diminution of emoluments or worsening of his position, being loss, diminution or worsening (as the case may be) which is properly attributable to the happening of the relevant event . . .'

The claimants put their case on the words 'worsening of his position'. They say that between 1972 and 1974 a divergence developed between their rates of pay and those of comparable employees by British Rail which resulted in their being left behind. A table was put in which dealt separately with each claimant showing his grade and, where appropriate, any promotion. Then in parallel columns there were set out the remuneration received by the claimants on various dates (as pay rates were reviewed) and the remuneration 'If with BRB'. In each case, as one would expect, the claimant was receiving more, in money terms, than he was getting in 1968, but in each case the amount shown in the column 'If with BRB' was higher than this. On this the compensating authority (in fact the NFC) was asked to decide that the position of the claimants had been worsened, and on that basis to assess compensation. Your Lordships are not concerned with any question of quantum (this would have to be dealt with by the compensating authority) but only with the question of principle, whether the claimants can show a 'worsening of position' properly attributable to the relevant event and on what basis this should be reflected in compensation.

I consider first the words 'worsening of position'. Obviously they invite a comparison, the question is: with what? There are two (and I think only two) rival contentions.

The submission of the claimants is that the comparison should be of their rate of pay at the date when the loss is said to arise with the rate of pay which they would have been receiving at that date if they had remained employees of British Rail. This does not mean simply that you take an employee of British Rail of the same grade and ascertain his present pay: the process is more complicated than that. First it must not be assumed that a claimant who has been promoted with the NFC (as two of these claimants have) would necessarily have received the same promotion at the same time if he had remained with British Rail: he might or might not and his chances must be estimated. Secondly, the comparison cannot simply be with an employee of the existing board, for if the employee had remained with British Rail, so would the division in which he was employed. So the comparison must be with an employee of British Rail assumed to be still containing that employee's division. This approach was christened by the claimants' counsel as the dynamic approach presumably because the comparandum is movable and not fixed.

The NFC's submission is that the comparison is made with what the employee was receiving on the relevant date, ie the date of transfer. It is only a worsening within the NFC and its subsidiaries which counts, and the reference date is in all cases (of the kind we are considering) 1st January 1969. The claimant's counsel called this the static approach because the comparandum is always the same, fixed at 1st January 1969.

My Lords, to my mind there can be little doubt which of these represented the intention of Parliament. These men, and thousands of others, were being compulsorily transferred from employment with British Rail which they had served for many years and with which they probably expected to remain for most of their working life to a new company which was part of the NFC: *from* a monopoly undertaking not obliged to pay its way, where employees were supported by strong unions able to obtain pay settlements which the government would in all probability have to underwrite, *to* a new and different body obliged to operate as a company engaged in commercial enterprise operating in an intensely competitive field with only 5% of the business, one in which union pressure would inevitably be less effective. What protection, one may ask, would an employee so transferred ask and Parliament wish to confer? Surely one which left the employee, at least for a period which was fixed at ten years, in as good a position as he would have been if he had not been transferred. Compare this with the alternative. The offer would be merely to guarantee that his position would be no worse than at the date of transfer, as regards remuneration a completely empty promise unless one supposes a possible decline in remuneration. The NFC suggested that Parliament had in mind such 'worsening' as a reduction in the date of retirement. Perhaps that is so, but to leave the much greater interest in pay out of the calculation, which is what the argument effectively does, cannot in my opinion have been intended. And, with Eveleigh LJ, I totally fail to see how such a 'worsening' as this agreement suggests, ie a worsening within the NFC whether it occurred early or late in the ten year period, could ever be properly attributable to the transfer, words which themselves point clearly to a comparison being made with a pre-transfer situation. Still less can I see how, on the NFC's argument, a worsening of position could occur 'on' or 'before' the transfer, as contemplated by reg 13(1)(*a*) since there would be nothing to compare the man's new position with except his new position.

The arguments in favour of the NFC's alternative really rest, in the end, on two foundations, convenience and parity of treatment. To apply the claimants' method involves, it is said, speculative calculations of impossible difficulty, compounded many thousand times. It would require a high degree of inconvenience to deter me from what seemed to me, on the language, the true meaning of the 1968 Act and regulations. I am certainly not persuaded that this exists.

The compensatory authority is the NFC with an appeal to an industrial tribunal, bodies with intimate knowledge of the wages structure, industrial practice and normal expectations as to promotion. It appears in fact that the grading structure on both sides of the division is similar, and at the time of the Swannack Report[1] the staff was interchangeable. Problems which appear to a court, particularly to an appeal court, as nightmarish and insoluble are part of the normal and daily work of bodies on, or close to, the ground, and I see that the regulations (eg reg 14) in other places require equally complex calculations and assume that they can be carried out.

As regards parity, it is said that the claimants' argument would create discontent and anomaly by providing for better wages treatment of ex-British Rail employees than for new men taken into the NFC. Wages bargaining within the NFC would thus be impossible. There are two answers to this. First the claimants' contention does not involve any disparity *as to wages* within the NFC at all. It assumes equal treatment, but gives compensation for that treatment to those transferred from British Rail. Secondly, the 'privileged' class is a limited one. It can only be entered by men with at least eight years continuous service; and there is a period of ten years within which the worsening must occur. None of this makes wage bargaining unworkable, and all that needs justification is a measure of different treatment for those forced into the NFC as compared with those who join voluntarily. Many industries contain within them groups of employees who for some reason continue to enjoy advantages not extended to others: an example is the well-known 'red circling' cases.

---

1   Recommended Award for Settlement of Dispute between National Carriers Ltd, Freightliners Ltd and Transport Salaried Staffs' Association (9th October 1972)

My Lords, there are other small indications in the regulations which can be relied on to support the claimants' case, others which are said, less convincingly to my mind, to support the NFC. I rest my decision on the broader grounds I have stated. I am happy to find that all four learned judges who have considered this case are of the same opinion.

There remains the question of proper attributability which, as all questions relating to causation and similar concepts, is one of considerable difficulty. I think that two things can be said. First, the expression is certainly not identical with 'caused by'. Secondly, it is not identical with having (the relevant event as) a sine qua non. There must be some nexus or linkage less exclusive than the one but stronger than the other. If there is no causal link whatever between the event and the worsening, if the latter is caused exclusively by something else, the claimant does not succeed. Examples were given in the Court of Appeal of technical or managerial changes having no connection with the relevant event, producing a 'worsening' which would not be properly attributable to the transfer. No doubt many difficult cases can be imagined.

What, positively, the words mean can be well illustrated from the judgment of Lord Denning MR, dissenting on this point. He distinguishes between action taken by the new company which would not have been taken by the old company, in which case there might be attributability, and action forced on new and old company alike by economic conditions in which case there would not. I agree and I only venture to differ when he applies this analysis to the present situation. He points out, as I have done, the different position as between British Rail and the road companies, the one a monopoly with unions in a position of power, the other operating competitively and obliged to economise. The divergence in pay which occurred was, he says, due to these 'new' factors, and not to the transfer; the transfer was not a cause but only part of the history. I see much force in this and the argument is one of great difficulty. I have however arrived with diffidence at the opposite conclusion. The transferred men started with parity of pay as compared with British Rail. Thereafter it diverged. Any divergence must be due to some cause, some decision, otherwise it would not occur. So this cause or decision cannot be something which breaks the nexus of attributability. Otherwise there could be no case in which compensation could be given. If the relevant words were 'caused by' it might be said that the divergence was not caused, or not caused only, by the transfer, but I do not see why the divergence should not be properly attributable to the transfer. The transfer, in other words, was a factor, together no doubt with others, in bringing about the divergence; it had a causative, though not a uniquely causative, effect. The transfer from the monopoly body to a competitive commercial body was, as I see it, both a cause of the worsening, and precisely that against which protection was desired and intended. No other factors than (i) the transfer and (ii) decisions as to wage rates taken by British Rail and the NFC are said to exist.

On this basis, in my opinion, the worsening was properly attributable to the transfer. I would therefore dismiss the appeal and remit the case to the NFC as compensating authority to calculate the compensation payable in each case in the light of this opinion.

Since writing it I have had the benefit of reading in advance the opinion of my noble and learned friend, Viscount Dilhorne. I desire to say that I agree entirely with it as to points I have not dealt with and generally.

VISCOUNT DILHORNE. My Lords, the Transport Act 1968 by s 4 provided for the transfer of various assets of the National Freight Corpn ('the NFC') constituted by s 1 of the Act, and by s 5 for the transfer to and vesting in the two companies formed pursuant to that section, Freightliners Ltd and National Carriers Ltd, of all the property, rights and liabilities of the British Railways Board ('British Rail') in relation to the road transport activities of which British Rail was, by the Act, required to divest itself. Those rights and liabilities included its right and liabilities under contracts of employment with the consequence that, on the vesting taking place, those who prior thereto were employees of British Rail engaged in these road transport operations were made by the Act employees of one or other of those companies.

The Act also made provision for the redistribution of activities between the NFC and

British Rail and the Scottish Transport Group (ss 7 and 8) and for the transfer of certain property, rights and liabilities between British Rail, the National Bus Co and the Scottish Transport Group, and for changes in the manner in which the carrying on of the activities of British Rail or the NFC was organised.

The changes made by the Act necessarily involved many changes of employment. Changes which the Act gave power to make might also involve many changes of employment with the consequence that not only employees of British Rail but employees of other bodies might find themselves suddenly transferred to new employment.

It is against this background that s 135 of the Act has to be considered. The main question to be decided in this appeal is whether by that section the government and Parliament intended to enable some provision to be made to protect those compulsorily transferred from loss or worsening of their position compared with what it would have been if they had continued in their former employment, or whether the intention was to secure that they should not suffer loss of emoluments or pension rights compared with those they enjoyed at the commencement of their new employment or at some time during that employment or a worsening of their position compared with then.

I have no hesitation in concluding that it was the former. With the use of a few more words in the section and in the regulations made under it, the intention could have been made clear beyond argument. True it is if one was able to look at Hansard or the notes on clauses with which Ministers in charge of Bills are provided that might make the intention clearer but one would have to look at what was said at every stage of the passage of the Bill through both Houses of Parliament and the notes on clauses would only help if no change was made in the drafting of the clause during the Bill's passage.

Speaking for myself I do not feel any need for such aids. It is, I think, to be expected that any government and Parliament would seek to make provision to enable those compulsorily deprived of their employment and transferred to new employment to receive compensation should they suffer in consequence. Since 1921 steps have from time to time been taken to secure that.

Section 135 enables regulations to be made for the payment of compensation 'in such cases and to such extent as may be determined' to any person who is on the date of the happening of any of the events specified in the section or who was before that date in any employment to which the regulations apply and 'who suffers any loss of employment, or loss of diminution of emoluments or pension rights, or worsening of his position, which is properly attributable to the happening of that event'.

The events specified are all events brought about by or made pursuant to the exercise of the powers given by the Act. Any loss or worsening of position attributable to the event could, by virtue of this section, be made by regulations the subject of compensation. In every case it is employment or conditions of employment that must be affected by the change made by or pursuant to the Act.

No difficulty arises with regard to the meaning of 'loss of employment ... properly attributable to the happening of that event'. To determine whether there is a loss or diminution of emoluments or pension rights or worsening of position involves a comparison. With what is the comparison to be made? According to the NFC and the industrial tribunal it is with the emoluments and pension rights enjoyed and the position held at the commencement of or during the new employment. Parliament and the draftsmen may have thought that it was so obvious that the comparison was to be between the old and the new employment that it was unnecessary to state it. If that was thought, the history of this litigation and the division of opinion in this House shows that it was not correct. Quite apart from the improbability of Parliament intending to provide for comparison between conditions enjoyed at the outset or in the course of the new employment with those later enjoyed in that employment, I feel no doubt that the intention was that comparison should be made between conditions enjoyed in the new employment and those in the former employment.

I find it difficult to visualise a case where loss or diminution of emoluments or pension rights or worsening of position compared with the emoluments, pension rights and position enjoyed at the commencement or in the course of the new employment could be attributable to changes brought about by the Act itself. Of course changes made after 1968 in the exercise of powers conferred by the Act might lead to the emoluments and the pension rights being less and the position being worse than at the commencement of or later in the new employment, but it is to my mind inconceivable that Parliament should have intended one comparison to be made when the change of employment brought about by the Act, and another when the alleged loss or worsening of position occurs, it may be years after the passing of the Act, in consequence of changes made in the exercise of powers given by the Act.

When I turn to the massive regulations made in the exercise of the power given by s 135, I find that those regulations provide for comparison between the former and the new employment.

Part II of the British Transport (Compensation to Employees) Regulations 1970 defines those to whom compensation may be payable and reg 5 in that part makes special provision for those who would have been employed by a nationalised transport body or its subsidiary or by an existing operator immediately before 'the first material date' as defined in the schedule to the regulations but for being engaged on national service as defined by those regulations. If he is not given or offered re-employment in his former office or in any reasonably comparable office when his national service has ceased, he is entitled to have his case considered for payment of compensation for loss of employment and (if appropriate) for loss or diminution of pension rights and (reg 5(1)(b))—

> 'in a case where, in consequence of any such event, he is so re-employed with diminished emoluments, or with loss or diminution of pension rights or worsening of his position as compared with the emoluments, pension rights or position which he would have enjoyed had he continued in his former employment, to have his case considered for payment of compensation for diminution of emoluments, or for loss or diminution of pensions rights, or for worsening of his position (as the case may warrant).'

The definition regulation, reg 2, of the regulations, does not attach any meaning to the words 'worsening of position', but here one finds a clear statement showing with what emoluments, pension rights and position the comparison is to be made. They are all to be compared with those 'he would have enjoyed had he continued in his former employment'. His 'former employment' must mean the employment from which he had been transferred. It cannot mean employment by the employer who re-employed him. In the case of a national serviceman who had been employed by British Rail and who was re-employed, say, by National Carriers Ltd, it must mean employment by British Rail.

Unless the context otherwise requires, and I can find no case in which it does, the same meaning should be given to diminution of emoluments and to loss or diminution of pension rights or worsening of position, whenever they appear in the regulations. In every case the same comparison requires to be made.

Part III of the regulations provides for the payment of resettlement compensation in respect of their loss of employment to those who have been continuously employed for three years before loss of their employment. Subject to certain conditions Part IV, with which this appeal is concerned, provides for the payment of long-term compensation to those who have been continuously engaged for eight years before suffering loss of employment, loss or diminution of emoluments, or worsening of position 'properly attributable to the happening of the relevant event', ie to a change made by the Act itself or to the later exercise of the powers given by it. Part V provides for retirement compensation and payments on death in respect of the loss or diminution of pension rights by those continuously employed for eight years before the loss. Each of these parts provides that the compensation shall be payable to a person who 'before, on, or not later than 10 years after the date of the relevant event' suffers the loss or, in the case of long-term compensation, the worsening of position.

So the regulations provide for the payment of compensation under Parts IV and V to those who were in their former employment and new employment for eight years before the relevant event or before suffering the loss and they are given some protection against suffering loss during the period of ten years after the happening of the relevant event.

In the case of the claimants, the relevant event was the transfer of all the property, rights and liabilities of British Rail to Freightliners Ltd and National Carriers Ltd by virtue of s 5 of the Act. As I have said this included rights and liabilities under contracts of employment. For ten years thereafter the claimants could claim long-term compensation if they could satisfy the conditions laid down in Part IV. They had to show a loss of employment or loss or diminution of emoluments, or worsening of their position attributable to the transfer of their employment. They satisfied the condition of eight years' employment before the alleged attributable loss.

If the NFC is right, a man who but for national service would have been employed by British Rail on the happening of the relevant event and who was re-employed by, say, National Carriers Ltd would be entitled to have his case considered if he established a loss of emoluments or worsening of his position, compared with what he would have enjoyed if he had continued in his former employment, but could only obtain long-term compensation if, even though he showed that he would have got more if he had remained with British Rail, he can show that he has suffered a loss or diminution of emoluments or worsening of his position as compared with what he enjoyed at the commencement of or at some time during his employment by National Carriers Ltd. This in my opinion cannot be right.

Every possible argument was advanced by counsel for the NFC. It was said that to assess what would have been enjoyed in the former employment had it continued involved a hypothetical exercise of great difficulty. As British Rail had divested itself of these road transport activities, it was not possible to say what would have been the emoluments and position the claimants would have enjoyed had British Rail continued to employ them in these activities. I am not convinced that this is so for it may be that there are clerical officers now employed by British Rail on very similar work to that on which the claimants were engaged and it may be too that their promotion depended on length of service. Even if the exercise is hypothetical, I am not convinced that it cannot be made.

It was also said that, if the regulations had the effect which in my opinion they have, the resulting liability on the NFC would be of such a character as to render it impossible for that corporation, which has to be competitive, to discharge its statutory duties and obligations. We were repeatedly reminded of the daunting prospect which faced the NFC.

It may be that the Minister when making these regulations and Parliament when it approved them, while desiring to protect employees from adverse consequences due to changes made in their employment by or under the Act, did not appreciate the full extent of the burden being placed on the corporation, but, however that may be, I am glad to find myself in agreement with Lord Denning MR, Geoffrey Lane and Eveleigh LJJ and Donaldson J as to the interpretation to be placed on reg 13(1)(a).

No compensation is payable unless the loss or worsening of position is 'properly attributable to the happening of the relevant event', in this case the transfer of property, rights and liabilities of British Rail to Freightliners Ltd and National Carriers Ltd. It is difficult to attach any precise meaning to the words 'properly attributable' and it is, I think, regrettable that such imprecise language was used in s 135 and in the regulations. 'Attributable to' means, in my opinion, the same as 'due to' and 'in consequence of' and it is to be noted that in reg 5 the words used are 'in consequence of' and not 'attributable to'. Something is either 'attributable to' or it is not and I must confess my inability to attach any significance to the word 'properly' preceding the words 'attributable to'.

The claimants claim that between 1972 and 1974 their position worsened compared with what it would have been if their employment with British Rail had continued. It will be for them to establish their claim; it would be for them to show, if they claimed in respect of loss of employment, that their employment would not have been lost if they had remained with British Rail, and, if claiming loss or diminution of emoluments or pension rights or worsening of position, what their emoluments, pension rights and position would have been if they had continued in that employment. Mr Wray and Mr Moody gained promotion in their new employment. It should not be assumed that if they had remained with British Rail they would have gained promotion. Equally, it should not be assumed that Mr Tuck, who was not promoted in his new employment, would not have been promoted by British Rail.

If on a comparison with what they would have enjoyed if their employment had not been transferred, a loss or worsening of position is shown, then the question to be decided is a question of fact. Was it attributable to their transfer of employment?

The claimants claim that owing to the pressure of unions concerned with British Rail employees the wages of those employees have risen more than those in their new employment with the consequence that they have suffered a loss of emoluments and a worsening of their position compared with what it would have been had they remained with British Rail.

In my view one is not concerned about the reasons for the increase of the emoluments of employees of British Rail. The fact, if it be the fact, that it was brought about by union pressure does not render the claimants' loss of emoluments or worsening of position, if established, not attributable to their being transferred to the two companies. If such a loss or worsening is established, it would not have occurred but for that, and while in some cases great difficulty may arise in determining attributability, in the present case, if such a loss or worsening is established, in my opinion it was beyond doubt due to, in consequence of and attributable to that transfer. As Eveleigh LJ said[1]: 'The only reason they have not benefited is because they no longer work for British Rail.'

For these reasons I would dismiss the appeal and remit the case to the industrial tribunal for them to determine whether any such loss of emoluments or worsening of position occurred and, if so, to quantify it.

LORD FRASER OF TULLYBELTON. My Lords, this appeal concerns the construction of the British Transport (Compensation to Employees) Regulations 1970 made under the Transport Act 1968. That Act provided, inter alia, for the establishment of a new public authority, the present appellant ('the NFC'), to be responsible for the road haulage side of an integrated system for carriage of goods by road and rail. Those parts of the undertaking of the British Railways Board ('British Rail') that were concerned with road haulage were to be hived off and transferred to the NFC through subsidiary companies, and persons employed wholly or mainly in the hived-off parts of the undertaking were also to be transferred. Thereafter the responsibility of British Rail would be confined mainly to railway transport. The shares of other nationalised road haulage companies were also to be transferred to the NFC. The Minister of Transport, acting in accordance with s 135 of the 1968 Act, made the compensation regulations under which compensation is payable in certain events to certain classes of persons who suffer loss or worsening of their position which is properly attributable to certain 'relevant events' directed or authorised by the Act.

The respondents ('the claimants') are former employees of British Rail who were transferred from that employment under s 5 of the 1968 Act. They claim that they are entitled to compensation under the regulations on the ground that (as they allege) they have suffered worsening of their positions properly attributable to their transfer. There is no dispute that they were transferred from the employment of British Rail or that the transfers were relevant events. The two issues that arise are (1) whether the claimants have suffered worsening of their position in the sense of the regulations and (2) if so, whether it was properly attributable to the relevant event. The claims were rejected by the NFC and on appeal by the industrial tribunal, which decided both issues against the claimants. Before Donaldson J the claimants succeeded on both issues and his decision was affirmed by the Court of Appeal (Lord Denning MR, Geoffrey Lane and Eveleigh LJJ) by a majority (Lord Denning MR dissenting on the issue of attributability).

---

1   See p 224, ante

The machinery for transferring property under the 1968 Act was somewhat elaborate. The first stage was that British Rail separated from the remainder of their undertaking those parts concerned with road haulage. This stage was to be completed not later than two days before the appointed day. Stage 2 (also to be completed not later than two days before the appointed day) was for British Rail to secure the formation of two wholly-owned subsidiary companies ('the road companies'). One of these is now Freightliners Ltd and the other National Carriers Ltd. At stage 3 (which was to take place on the day before the appointed day) all the property, rights and liabilities comprised in the separated parts of British Rail's undertaking were to be transferred to and vested in the appropriate road company. Finally, in stage 4, on the appointed day there were to be transferred to the NFC 51 per cent of the shares in Freightliners Ltd and all the shares in National Carriers Ltd. These arrangements were duly carried out. The appointed day was 1st January 1969. It was the transfer of property, rights and liabilities under stage 3 that carried with it the contracts of employment of British Rail employees wholly or mainly engaged in the hived-off parts of its undertaking: see para 2 of Sch 4 to the 1968 Act. Since 31st December 1968 the claimants have been employed by the road companies, Mr Tuck and Mr Wray by National Carriers Ltd and Mr Moody by Freightliners Ltd. Until October 1972 each of the claimants received the same emoluments from the road companies as employees in the same grades were receiving from British Rail, but in October employees in British Rail got an increase in wages while employees in the road companies got either a smaller increase or no increase. In the two-year period from 14th October 1972 to 14th October 1974, there were further increases in the claimants' rates of pay, and Mr Moody was promoted to a higher grade, but each of the claimants received less pay than he would have done if he had been in the corresponding grade employed by British Rail. They claim that the difference is a loss representing worsening of their position, and that it is attributable to their transfer. The amounts claimed are, by Mr Tuck, £125·03, by Mr Wray, £175·39 and, by Mr Moody, £920·96. These amounts are not admitted by the NFC.

Section 135 of the Transport Act 1968, so far as immediately relevant, is as follows:

'(1) The Minister shall by regulations require the payment by such person as may be determined by or under the regulations, in such cases and to such extent as may be so determined, of compensation to or in respect of any person who is on the date of the happening of any of the following events, namely—(a) a transfer of any property, rights or liabilities under section 4, 5 . . . of this Act; or (b) any change in the manner in which the carrying on of the activities of the Railways Board or the Freight Corporation is organised made—(i) in pursuance of a direction under section 6(1) or 45(5) of this Act . . . or who has before that date been, in any employment so determined and who suffers any loss of employment, or loss or diminution of emoluments or pension rights, or worsening of his position, which is properly attributable to the happening of that event . . .'

The regulations made in accordance with that section provided for three different kinds of compensation. The relevant kind here is long-term compensation, which is an annual sum payable until the normal retiring age or death (reg 15). The regulations have a long interpretation regulation (reg 2) which provides (reg 2(1)) that 'emoluments' means all the obvious kinds of cash payments as well as the money value of travel privileges etc—

'but does not include payments for travelling, subsistence, accommodation, engagement of assistance or other expenses in the course of employment or over-time or other payments of a temporary nature . . .'

The other regulations directly relevant are as follows:

'3. These regulations shall apply to any person who suffers attributable loss and who—(a) was employed immediately before the first material date on a full-time basis, as an officer of a nationalised transport body or a subsidiary of such a body or as an officer of an existing operator, or (*b*) would have been so employed at that time but for any national service on which he was then engaged . . .

'12. The compensating authority shall, subject to the provisions of these regulations, pay long-term compensation to any person to whom these regulations apply and who satisfies the conditions set out in regulation 13 and this Part of these regulations shall apply to that person.

'13.—(1) Without prejudice to any other requirement of these regulations, the conditions for the payment of long-term compensation to any person are that—(*a*) he has, before, on, or not later than 10 years after the date of the relevant event, suffered loss of employment or loss or diminution of emoluments or worsening of his position, being loss, diminution or worsening (as the case may be) which is properly attributable to the happening of the relevant event . . .'

The 'relevant events' are set out in Sch 1 to the regulations, under ten paragraphs. The present claims arise under the first paragraph which includes transfer of property, rights or liabilities under s 5 of the Act.

The claimants have been selected as typical of many members of the Transport Salaried Staffs' Association who have been compulsorily transferred from employment with British Rail to the hived-off road companies. Their cases are thus test cases for a large number of others.

The worsening that the claimants allege is not in respect that their emoluments or conditions of service have ever been reduced or made worse than they were. On the contrary, their rates of pay were increased during the two-year period from October 1972 to October 1974. Their claim is that during the two-year period the increase in their emoluments was less than it would have been if they had been employed by British Rail. The question thus raised is whether the worsening is to be judged by comparison with rates of pay in British Rail.

'Worsening' evidently requires a comparison of some sort. The most natural comparison is between the state of something now and its state at an earlier time. A person's position was worsened if it is worse now than it was last year. The comparison may, of course, be with something else; a man's position may be said to have worsened compared with someone else's or compared with what it would have been if he had been in another job. If comparison of that sort is intended, I would generally expect that to be stated expressly, though no doubt it can be implied if the indications are clear enough. Neither s 135 of the Act nor reg 13(1) contains any express statement that that sort of comparison is to be made and the real question in this appeal is whether it is to be implied from the Act and from the regulations as a whole. I do not think it is.

So far as reg 13(1)(*a*) itself is concerned, all the other kinds of loss specified, loss of employment and loss or diminution of emoluments, relate only to the person's actual employment or emoluments. 'Worsening of *his* position' also clearly refers to his own position and does not appear to suggest comparison with the position of anyone else or with the position in which he himself might have been. The arguments in favour of making such a comparison fall into two groups. The first, and in my opinion the more attractive, group depends on general considerations as to the purpose of the Act. Parliament (it was said) evidently intended to give protection to the employees of British Rail and other concerns who were being compulsorily transferred under the Act to other employers, and it must therefore have intended 'worsening' to be measured by comparison with what an employee's position would have been if he had not been transferred. This argument derives most of its force from what, in my opinion, is an undue emphasis on the relevant event that applied in this particular case, transfer to a new employer. But neither s 135 of the Act nor the regulations apply only to employees who are transferred (whether compulsorily or otherwise): see reg 3. They provide for compensation in other events which have nothing to do with transfer. Thus in para 8 of Sch 1 the relevant event is reorganisation of the activities of British Rail or the NFC (presumably affecting mainly employees of these bodies who remain in their employment after the reorganisation) and in para 10 it is revocation by the Transport Executive of consent to a road service licence of a bus operator. I can see no reason why worsening attributable to relevant events of these kinds should mean anything other than worsening of the actual position.

It is said that the comparatively long period of ten years for which the protection is to continue is significant because no one in 1968 would have envisaged a smaller wage packet in ten years' time. But reg 13(1)(a) does expressly envisage that very thing by providing for compensation for diminution of emoluments. Worsening of position must refer to something other than diminution of emoluments and it must be, or at least must include, something which is not pecuniary loss (see reg 13(4)). In my view it means worsening of an employee's conditions of employment, for instance by a change in his retiring age, or in the basis of payment of travelling, subsistence or other expenses which are expressly 'not included' in the definition of emoluments in reg 2. So read, the protection seems to me to have content and to be of value to the employee.

Against these general considerations, there are others which, in my opinion, point in favour of what I regard as the natural meaning of worsening. In the first place, if the comparison was with what the claimant's position would have been, it would require several speculative assumptions to be made. These would include: (a) an assumption that each claimant would have remained in the employment of British Rail and would have been promoted to a higher grade within British Rail at exactly the same time as he was promoted in one of the road companies; (b) an assumption that if British Rail had retained their interest in road haulage they would have paid the same rates of wages to each grade of employee as they have paid since they hived off their road haulage divisions. The latter assumption seems to me unjustifiable having regard to the fiercely competitive market in which the road companies work and to their obligation under the Act to behave as if they were engaged in a commercial enterprise, in contrast to the quasi-monopoly position of British Rail. The claims as presented appear to be framed on the basis that the proper comparison is with the rates of pay actually prevailing in British Rail at the date of the alleged loss. But I do not think that can be right. If any comparison with conditions in British Rail is to be made at all, it should be with the rates that would have prevailed at the date of the alleged loss under British Rail constituted as it was before its road divisions were hived off. How these rates in a notional body that no longer exists are to be calculated I do not know.

Second, the proposed comparison, if it could be made at all, would be extremely laborious. It would have to be a continual running comparison of emoluments in each grade adapted to the particular circumstances of each employee qualified for compensation. Not all employees who are transferred from British Rail are qualified; only those with at least eight years continuous service up immediately before the date of the attributable loss are qualified: see reg 13(1)(c). Even so, the comparison would require much trouble.

Third, if the claimants are right, the result would be that the labour costs of the road companies would be, to some extent, uncontrollable by negotiations between those companies and the trade unions. In so far as the companies succeeded in negotiating wage rates lower than those prevailing in British Rail they would have to compensate their qualified employees in respect of the difference in rates so far as it was attributable to their transfer. The compensation would not in any event exceed two-thirds of the difference (reg 15(2)), but it might amount to a considerable sum in total. The importance of this matter is in my opinion not so much in the amount of money involved as in its effect in withdrawing a substantial part of the companies' costs from negotiation between the companies and the trade unions. It will also have the result that there would in effect be two different rates of pay for the same job: ordinary employees would receive the negotiated rates of pay while transferred employees who are qualified for compensation would in addition receive compensation. That would not seem to be conducive to good industrial relations and might be said to run counter to the careful provisions in s 137 of the Act for securing good industrial relations.

On balance these general considerations tend in my opinion to indicate that the word
a 'worsening' in reg 13 is used in its natural sense.

The second group consists of arguments based on the context in the regulations. The
most immediately relevant of these, and one that impressed Donaldson J and Eveleigh LJ
is in the word 'on' near the beginning of reg 13(1)(a). The argument, as I understand it, is
that the word 'on' shows that the worsening could take place at the moment of transfer and
therefore that the comparison may be between conditions under the road companies and
b conditions under British Rail. I do not think that is a correct analysis of the situation. I
think counsel for the NFC was right in submitting that an employee will be transferred
from British Rail to one of the road companies with his contract of employment as
previously existing under British Rail, and that any worsening that takes place 'on' transfer
would really involve a comparison between his position after the loss and his position
under the road companies at the first moment immediately after transfer. Whether that
c is right or not, the argument does not tend to support the contention of the claimants that,
if the comparison is to be made after the transfer, it is to be made with the conditions
prevailing in British Rail at the time of the loss.

Much reliance was placed on reg 5 which deals with the position of a former employee
of British Rail who was engaged in national service at the date when the Act was passed and
who within two months after ceasing to be so engaged gives notice that he is available for
d employment. He is entitled, if in consequence of the transfer he is re-employed 'with
diminished emoluments. . . or worsening of his position as compared with the emoluments
. . . or position *which he would have enjoyed had he continued in his former employment*', to have
his case considered for compensation. But it is not clear whether the hypothesis is that the
returning ex-serviceman had continued in his former employment until the date of the
loss or until the date when he would have been transferred. I think the latter was probably
e intended, because his former employment might have ceased to exist as from the date of
the transfer, and it would not be available for comparison thereafter. The object of reg 5
(1)(b) seems to be to provide compensation for any loss or worsening caused by interruption
of the employment; the comparison is between the actual position of an ex-serviceman
who is '*re-employed* in his former office or in any reasonably comparable office' and the
position he would have enjoyed 'had he *continued* in his former employment'. Interruption
f is avoided if (as I think) the hypothesis is that he continued in his former employment until
the date of the transfer and thereafter in some comparable employment to which he was
transferred. That would destroy the argument for the claimants. Even if it is wrong, I
would not regard this provision for the special case of re-employed ex-service employees as
affecting the construction of the more general case under reg 13(1)(a).

I agree with the view of my noble and learned friend, Lord Russell of Killowen, on the
g importance of reg 13(4)(a). No other provision in the regulations seems to me significant
as bearing on the proper construction of reg 13(1)(a).

The result is that in my opinion the industrial tribunal came to the right decision on the
first point and that the second point does not arise.

I would allow the appeal, and order that the claimants pay the NFC's costs in this House
and in the courts below.

h

LORD RUSSELL OF KILLOWEN. My Lords, I had prepared in outline a speech in
which I concluded that this appeal should be allowed. Since then I have had the advantage
of studying in draft the speeches of my noble and learned friends, Lord Fraser of
Tullybelton and Lord Scarman. I agree with their reasons for allowing the appeal, and do
j not trouble your Lordships with repetition. I would however add one point. Regulation
13(4)(a), in laying down the basis for calculation of compensation for worsening of position,
provides that the pecuniary value of the loss or injury suffered by reason of his position
being worsened 'shall be expressed in terms of his net emoluments immediately before his
position was worsened'. This basis seems to me to be quite inconsistent with the concept

that merely being outstripped by someone who might possibly be regarded as an 'opposite number' in British Rail's employment is a worsening of position.

I would allow the appeal.

LORD SCARMAN. My Lords, in this appeal the House is required to give a meaning to the words 'any . . . worsening of his position' in the context of s 135 of the Transport Act 1968, a section which provides for the payment of compensation to employees who have suffered loss properly attributable to certain events in the reorganisation of the nationalised transport industry effected by the Act. The statute offers no definition of the words in question: it leaves interpretation to the judges, without giving them any express indication as to the policy the words are intended to fulfil. The Minister has made regulations under the section: the British Transport (Compensation to Employees) Regulations 1970. Prominent among them is reg 2, three pages of interpretation. You will find in those pages of interpretation many explanations of the simple and the obvious, eg the meaning of 'emoluments', 'officer', 'office', many repetitions of interpretations already given by the Act (compare s 159(1) of the Act with the regulation), but not a word as to the meaning to be given to the critically important phrase 'any . . . worsening of his position'.

My Lords, I protest. I happen to take a different view from some of your Lordships as to the meaning of the words. I have no idea whether I, or they, have correctly divined the intention of Parliament. Perhaps none of us has succeeded in doing so. Yet the Minister and his departmental advisers must have known what they were trying to achieve. Whether or not they let Parliament into their confidence we, sitting judicially, are not permitted to know, or, if we happen to know, to notice. In the result your Lordships' House has spent the best part of three days chasing through the regulations in search of such faint clues to the intention of Parliament's enacted words as the ingenuity and industry of learned men, counsel and their advisers, have been able to expose. It is verging on the ridiculous that we should be searching the tangle in the regulations dealing with peripheral matters, eg the application of reg 5 to national servicemen (I wonder how many employees of British Rail were national servicemen in 1968) and the limitation provision (reg 13(1)(d)(iii)), in the hope of finding a clue to what Parliament intended to enact by s 135(1) of the Act. Indeed, I doubt whether the search is legitimate. Are we to adopt a Minister's view of the meaning of the Act? Is the Minister, or his departmental draftsman, to tell the courts what are the grounds of compensation which Parliament has established by statute?

My Lords, this case lays bare one of the fundamental weaknesses of English law. The way we draft and the way we interpret statutes do not always serve the interests of justice.

First, the drafting problem. Over the last hundred years the pattern of our statutes has been one of increasing elaboration and complexity. Parliament has required the draftsman to do what he can to cover all eventualities. The policy behind this style of drafting is to make the statute 'judge-proof'. Detailed provisions are thought to reduce the risk of a judicial interpretation contrary to the intention of Parliament. Most, but by no means all, English statutes are drafted this way. If it is done consistently and well, the theory is that the judges should need no help outside the context of the statute to interpret the statute as intended by Parliament. No extraneous aids to interpretation (the 'travaux préparatoires' of European legal systems, the 'record' in the United States of America) should be needed; nothing ought to be required of the judges other than a literal interpretation with such flexibility as the context permits or demands, and 'context' is itself a term describing a verbal environment. The words of the statute are, on this view, the self-sufficient ark of the covenant. But the difficulties inherent in this technique are twofold: (1) it is beyond human wisdom to foresee all eventualities, (2) it is impossible to adopt this pattern of drafting for all statutes, or for every provision of a statute. The Act illustrates both difficulties. Elaborate and detailed in its general pattern, it contains sections such as s 135(1) which uses terms vague, imprecise and general, without offering any definition of, or guide to, their meaning. The subsection speaks of 'worsening of position', 'properly

attributable'; but their meanings are left to the judges to determine without any express
a help offered by the statute.

Now the interpretation problem. Under English law the judges are confined, with a few
exceptions, to the words of the statute in their statutory context. Extraneous aids are not
to be used, save to determine the mischief being remedied: no 'travaux préparatoires' may,
as a general rule, be studied, and certainly not the record of proceedings in Parliament.
But, if Parliament chooses to use language that is general to the point of ambiguity, ought
b not judges to be allowed the aid of, for example, official reports or the record of proceedings
at the committee stage of the Bill to determine the intention of Parliament? Take this
case. With what is the employee's position to be compared for the purpose of determining
whether it has worsened? The silence of the legislature is deafening. And the regulations,
discretion being the better part of departmental valour, echo the statute's silence, their
draftsman content to repeat, without attributing meaning to, the phrase. Yet, hidden
c away in a departmental file there are, no doubt, the 'notes on clauses' which the Minister
used when taking the Bill through Parliament. How useful they would be! Not, of course,
decisive but an invaluable guide, and, I would think, a sounder guide than post-statute
regulations, since they are prepared as the Minister's brief for the purpose of conducting
the legislation through Parliament. Indeed, in some cases (this is, I think, one) proceedings
in Parliament, particularly the committee stage, could be very helpful. The Law
d Commissions of England and Wales and Scotland exposed these weaknesses in our law in
their joint Report on the Interpretation of Statutes[1] and prepared a draft Bill to give effect
to their recommendations, but nothing has been done.

Diffidently, for reasons which I hope I have made clear, I now approach the task of
construing the subsection. It places a duty on the Minister to provide by regulations for
compensation to be payable to certain persons who suffer loss of employment, loss or
e diminution of emoluments or pension rights or worsening of position, which is properly
attributable to the happening of any of the events specified in the subsection. To be
entitled to compensation a person must have been, before the happening of the event, in
an employment which is to be specified (the subsection uses the ambiguous word
'determined', but in the context it is clear what is meant) by the Minister in his
regulations. Note that, whereas the Minister may 'determine' the cases in which, and the
f extent to which, compensation may be paid, Parliament in the subsection has laid down
the grounds of compensation.

The subsection is silent as to the comparison required to be made in order to determine
whether a person has suffered any worsening of his position. The appellant, the National
Freight Corpn ('the NFC), contends that the person's existing position is to be compared
with his previous terms and conditions of employment (including benefits arising from
g custom and practice as well as from his contract of service). It is only if a person can show
that there has been a worsening in his own terms and conditions that he can show a cause
of claim. The Act, it is submitted, confines the comparison to the emoluments and other
benefits of the person's own employment.

According to the NFC, a claimant, therefore has to prove: (1) a worsening of his position,
so ascertained, (2) that the worsening is properly attributable to the happening of the
h event. If this contention be correct, the claimants must fail. They cannot point to any
worsening of position, if the comparison has to be made in the context of their own terms
and conditions of employment. Subject to inflation (which, if it has worsened their
position, cannot be said to be 'properly attributable' to any of the events specified in the
subsection), the claimants are better off now than they were at the date of their transfer
from British Rail and as well off as they have ever been since transfer.

j Before turning to the claimants' submission it may be helpful at this stage to note what,
as I understand it, the NFC does *not* submit. It is not its case that the comparison has to be
between the claimants' position at the date of the relevant event (ie, in this case, transfer
from British Rail on 31st December 1968) and their existing position, though this is a

---

1   HC Papers 1968–69 No 256 (Law Com No 21, Scots Law Com No 11)

possible way, I recognise, of interpreting the subsection. The NFC's case, as set out in its decision as compensating authority given on 26th July 1976 and upheld on appeal by the industrial tribunal, is that comparison has to be made between the claimants' position as it existed between 14th October 1972 and 14th October 1974, the period of alleged worsening of position, and their position immediately before that period of worsening: The claimants are not, therefore, pegged to a comparison with their position as at date of transfer. If they can prove a subsequent worsening of position compared with their previous position as employees of the NFC, they are entitled to compensation even though they remain, after the worsening, better off than they were at date of transfer, provided always they can prove that the worsening of which they complain was properly attributable to the relevant event (in this case their transfer from British Rail). There are, therefore, not two but three contentions being considered by your Lordships: (1) that the proper comparison is that for which the NFC contends, and which found favour with the compensating authority and the industrial tribunal; (2) that the proper comparison is between the employee's existing position and his position at the date of the relevant event; (3) that the proper comparison is that for which the claimants contend. The claimants can succeed only if they can make good their contention. On either of the other two views, they have suffered no worsening of position.

The NFC's submission commended itself to the industrial tribunal. In the course of an admirably formulated statement of reasons the tribunal summed up its view on the point in these words:

> 'Worsening involves deterioration. In the present case there has been no worsening or deterioration in the terms of employment. As far as we can see there has on the other hand been an amelioration in such terms whether by way of regrading or salary increase, or both. What has happened we are given to understand is that the [claimants] have not got on as far, or as fast, as they might have done had they remained in the employ of the British Railways Board. With the greatest respect to [counsel for the claimants'] skilful argument that seems to us to be something very different from a "worsening" in the context with which we have to deal. Our view on this point, if correct, is, of course, enough to dispose of the appeals which must accordingly fail.'

The claimants' contention, which was accepted by Donaldson J and all three members of the Court of Appeal, was that the correct comparison was not with the past but with what would have been the claimants' position today had they not been transferred from British Rail. It is common ground that since the date of the relevant event (their transfer from British Rail on 31st December 1968: s 5(3) of the 1968 Act and the Transport Act 1968 (Commencement No 1) Order 1968[1], Sch 2) British Rail employees have had more success with their wage settlements than employees of the NFC and its subsidiaries, Freightliners Ltd and National Carriers Ltd, into whose service the claimants were transferred. The argument runs as follows. Before the event, the claimants had the benefit of working for British Rail whose largely monopolistic position enabled them, when faced with strong union pressure, to negotiate wage settlements which an enterprise having to survive commercially in a fiercely competitive market could not afford. The NFC and its subsidiaries operate in such a market and have to act 'as if they were a company engaged in a commercial enterprise': see s 134(2) of the Act. They have not, therefore, been able to afford 'rail-type' wage settlements (see the 'Swannack' arbitration report of 9th October 1972[2], and, in particular, the opening paragraph of 'Synopsis of Evidence', 'Recommended Award', 'Future Action'). It must, it is argued, have been Parliament's intention that employees, who, whether they liked it or not, were losing as a result of the 1968 reorganisation of nationalised transport their protected position within British Rail,

---

1   SI 1968 No 1822
2   Recommended Award for Settlement of Dispute between National Carriers Ltd, Freightliners Ltd and Transport Salaried Staffs' Association, pp 2, 11 et seq, 15 et seq

should be compensated if the loss of this protection led to a worsening of their position compared with what it would have been if they had continued with British Rail.

I have come to the conclusion that Parliament did not intend the comparison for which the claimants contend. The comparison is, I believe, between a claimant's existing position and the emoluments and benefits he has previously enjoyed, ie the NFC's contention. The claimants' contention is plausible in the present case only because the relevant event in their case is a transfer from British Rail to another employer. But the subsection contemplates events other than such a transfer as giving rise to a claim for compensation. A person, who remains in the employment of British Rail but who can show a worsening of position attributable to a direction given under s 6(1) or s 45(5) of the Act, has a right to compensation: see s 135 (1)(b); so also has a British Rail employee whose position is worsened by an order of the Minister under para 5(4) of Sch 16 to the Act: see s 135(1)(c). A person employed by 'an existing operator', ie one who provides an area bus service, who, while remaining in the operator's employment, finds his position worsened by a passenger transport executive's revocation of the operator's licence, has a right to compensation: see s 135(1)(d). In none of these cases is the event, which gives rise to the entitlement, a transfer from one employer to another. The likelihood is that the claimant will remain with his pre-event employer, but the reorganisation has worsened his position. The comparison has, therefore, to be with the employee's terms and conditions of service before he was affected by the direction, order, or revocation. Although not conclusive, the specification by the subsection of these 'events' as giving rise in appropriate cases to compensation casts doubt on the basis of comparison for which the claimants contend.

Three other matters, none of them conclusive, point the same way. First, loss of employment, loss or diminution of emoluments or pension rights, can only be determined by contrasting a claimant's present employment position with his past position. It would be odd, though, I concede, not impossible, that Parliament, without saying what it was doing, should tack onto these grounds of compensation one which requires the compensating authority to look beyond the employment of the claimant, and to ascertain an entitlement to compensation on the basis of a comparison which was totally inappropriate in the context of the preceding grounds for compensation.

Secondly, s 137 of the Act provides that the new authorities (which include the NFC) are to ensure that there exists adequate machinery for negotiating with the appropriate unions terms and conditions of employment and for consultation with staff. The section envisages employees, through their unions, negotiating with the new authorities wage and other related settlements. If the future is left to such negotiation, I ask myself why it is necessary so to construe s 135(1) of the Act as to give former employees of British Rail a right to compensation if, through their unions, they agree less favourable terms than British Rail is persuaded to give its employees.

Thirdly, if one is to compare the employee's position under the NFC with what it would have been had he remained with British Rail, the proper comparable must be, as my noble and learned friend, Lord Fraser of Tullybelton, has pointed out, not the British Rail which as from 1st January 1969 has been divested of its freightliner and rail sundries activities, but a notional British Rail assumed to be still engaged in these activities. How can any such meaningful comparison be made? As counsel for the NFC commented, such an exercise would be piling hypothesis on hypothesis.

For these reasons I would allow the appeal. The claimants have not shown any worsening of their position. That being so, it is not necessary to consider whether the worsening of which they complain was 'properly attributable' to the happening of the relevant event, and I say nothing on the point.

My Lords, I am profoundly disturbed by the division of judicial opinion in this case. Four judges below and two of your Lordships have reached one conclusion. The industrial tribunal and three of your Lordships have reached another. The fault, however, lies with Parliament legislating vaguely and imprecisely against a legal background which confines the attention of the judges to the words and context of the statute.

Finally, I have, in preparing this opinion, refrained from relying on the regulations. For the reasons given by my noble and learned friends, Lord Fraser of Tullybelton and Lord Russell of Killowen, I believe them to be consistent with the interpretation I would put on the subsection. But, whether they are or are not, I prefer to base my opinion on the words of the statute.

I agree with the order as to costs proposed by my noble and learned friend, Lord Fraser of Tullybelton.

Appeal allowed.

Solicitors: *J S Seager* (for the NFC); *Russell Jones & Walker* (for the claimants).

Mary Rose Plummer   Barrister.

Swordheath Properties Ltd v Tabet and others

COURT OF APPEAL, CIVIL DIVISION
MEGAW, BROWNE AND WALLER LJJ
28th NOVEMBER 1978

Damages – Trespass to land – Residential property – Trespasser remaining on residential property – Whether owner required to prove property would have been let if trespasser had not been there – Measure of damages for trespass.

Where a person remains as a trespasser on residential property the owner is entitled to damages for the trespass without bringing evidence that he could or would have let the property to someone else if the trespasser had not been there. The measure of damages will be the value to the trespasser of the use of the property for the period during which he has trespassed, which in a normal case will be the ordinary letting value of the property (see p 242 *g h* and p 243 *a*, post).

Whitwham v Westminster Brymbo Coal and Coke Co [1896] 2 Ch 538 and *Penarth Dock Engineering Co Ltd v Pounds* [1963] 1 Lloyd's Rep 359 applied.

Notes

For the measure of damages for trespass to land, see 12 Halsbury's Laws (4th Edn) para 1170.

Cases referred to in judgments

Penarth Dock Engineering Co v Pounds [1963] 1 Lloyd's Rep 359.
Whitwham v Westminster Brymbo Coal and Coke Co [1896] 2 Ch 538, 65 LJ Ch 741, 74 LT 804, CA, 33 Digest (Repl) 854, 1094.

Appeal

This was an appeal by the plaintiffs, Swordheath Properties Ltd, against the judgment of his Honour Judge Solomon given in the West London County Court on 19th January 1978 and amended on 23rd February 1978 whereby he ordered the defendants, Tabet (male), Hugh M McGuane, Waterman Jones (feme sole), Heald (male) and Wendy Rose Spriggs, to give the plaintiffs possession of residential premises known as Flat 3, 2 Finborough Road, London SW10, and the first defendant to pay the plaintiffs the sum of £110·68 for rent and mesne profits, but dismissed the plaintiffs' claim against the second, third and fifth defendants for damages for trespass to the demised premises. The third and fifth defendants were in fact the same person, ie Miss Spriggs. The facts are set out in the judgment of Megaw LJ.

P de la Piquerie for the plaintiffs.
The defendants did not appear.

MEGAW LJ. This is an appeal brought by Swordheath Properties Ltd, who are the owners of a residential property known as Flat 3, 2 Finborough Road, London SW10. The action was brought in the West London County Court, where it was heard by his Honour Judge Solomon, who gave judgment in the action on 19th January 1978.

The relevant facts, as found by the judge, were these. The plaintiffs had let flat 3 to the first defendant, a gentleman called Mr Tabet, for a fixed term, beginning in April 1976 and ending on 4th July 1976. The first defendant, with the permission of the plaintiffs, introduced, to live in the flat as a licensee, a gentleman called Mr Hugh M McGuane, who was the second defendant in the action. The second defendant in his turn introduced, to live in the flat as a licensee, the fifth defendant, Miss Spriggs. There seems to have been some confusion there, because she was also joined in the action, under another name, as the third defendant, but in fact she is one and the same person.

The first defendant left flat 3 before the expiry of his fixed term, that is, before 4th July 1976. He therefore never became a statutory tenant. The second defendant's right as a licensee and the fifth defendant's right as a licensee came to an end, as a matter of law, when the first defendant's right thus came to an end by his leaving the premises.

The plaintiffs then brought their claim in possession against all the defendants. So far as the first defendant is concerned, he had already left the premises before 4th July 1976, so the plaintiffs were not concerned to get an order for possession against him. He was ordered to pay £110·68 for arrears of rent. But so far as concerns the second and fifth defendants they were continuing to reside in the flat and therefore the plaintiffs were anxious to obtain possession against them; and they claimed also damages for trespass for the period from 4th July 1976. The fourth defendant can be forgotten. He, it appears, was sued in error. It is accepted that he never was occupying the flat at all.

By their defence the second and fifth defendants raised two issues, both of which were decided against them and in favour of the plaintiffs by Judge Solomon. The two issues were: first, that the second defendant had achieved the status of a tenant by reason of payment of rent by him; and, second, it was contended that the plaintiffs were estopped from denying the existence of a tenancy. Both those issues, as I say, were decided in favour of the plaintiffs by the judge. There is no appeal against those findings or the decision of the judge on those defences on the part of any of the defendants. The judge, however, held that, though the plaintiffs were entitled to an order for possession against both the second and the fifth defendants, they were not entitled to any damages for trespass against them. It is against that part of the judge's decision that the plaintiffs appeal.

The plaintiffs in this court are represented by counsel. None of the defendants has appeared. The only two who would be affected by the appeal are the second and the fifth defendants. Counsel for the plaintiffs has read to us a letter from their solicitors, dated 25th October 1978, in which it is indicated that they do not propose to attend or be represented in order to present opposition to the appeal, though they do not consent to the appeal being allowed. Counsel for the plaintiff, therefore, has had to pursue his appeal and to show this court, if he can, that the judge was wrong in his decision.

The judge based his decision that there was no valid claim for damages on the ground that the plaintiffs had failed to adduce any evidence that they would have been able to relet the demised premises from the date from which damages for trespass were claimed, namely, 5th July 1976; and it was, indeed, the fact that the plaintiffs did not adduce any evidence that they could or would have relet the demised premises had they not been in the occupation of the two defendants on and after that date.

The judge referred to evidence which had been given by a witness, Mr Andrew Sadleir, on behalf of the plaintiffs, to the effect that the plaintiffs 'would not have offered the demised premises to anyone other than a person known to the plaintiffs whom the plaintiffs trusted'. The judge then posed the question: 'Could the plaintiffs have found such a person to accept a tenancy of the demised premises either on 5th July 1976, or thereafter?' That question the judge answered: 'I do not know. There was no evidence about it.' So he went on to hold that there was—

> 'a special situation of the plaintiffs' own making. In the absence of evidence I am bound to hold that the plaintiffs have failed to prove that as a consequence of the conduct of the second and fifth defendants they suffered damage.'

Accordingly, while he made the order for possession forthwith, he dismissed that part of the claim which asked for damages.

Counsel for the plaintiffs submits that the judge was wrong. There is indeed, curiously, no authority which directly deals with this question in relation to trespass on residential property. But counsel for the plaintiffs has referred us to a passage in Halsbury's Laws of England[1] where the authors of the title Damages say:

> 'Where the defendant has by trespass made use of the plaintiff's land, the plaintiff is entitled to receive by way of damages such sum as should reasonably be paid for the use. It is immaterial that the plaintiff was not in fact thereby impeded or prevented from himself using his own land either because he did not wish to do so or for any other reason.'

Then in a footnote various authorities are cited in support of that passage in the text. The first authority cited is *Whitwham v Westminster Brymbo Coal and Coke Co*[2]. That is a case which was decided by a Court of Appeal consisting of Lindley, Lopes and Rigby LJJ. It appears to me that the judgments, at any rate, of Lindley and Rigby LJJ fully support the proposition which is set out in Halsbury in the passage which I have read.

If further authority were needed, counsel for the plaintiffs has referred us to a decision of Lord Denning MR (sitting as an additional judge of the Queen's Bench Division) in *Penarth Dock Engineering Co Ltd v Pounds*[3]. In his decision in that case, so far as the question of damages arose, Lord Denning MR had no hesitation in saying that the plaintiffs, even though they would not themselves have made use, bringing in financial return, of the dock in respect of which the trespass was committed, were nevertheless entitled to damages for that trespass, calculated by reference to the proper value to the trespassers of the use of the property on which they had trespassed, for the period during which they had trespassed.

It appears to me to be clear, both as a matter of principle and of authority, that in a case of this sort the plaintiff, when he has established that the defendant has remained on as a trespasser in residential property, is entitled, without bringing evidence that he could or would have let the property to someone else in the absence of the trespassing defendant, to have as damages for the trespass the value of the property as it would fairly be calculated; and, in the absence of anything special in the particular case it would be the ordinary letting value of the property that would determine the amount of damages.

In the present case, therefore, it appears to me that this appeal falls to be allowed and that the plaintiffs ought to have, not merely judgment for possession, but also damages for trespass for whatever would have been the appropriate amount (on which, no doubt, we can have information from counsel) as being the proper letting value of the property from 5th July 1976 to the date of the judgment in the West London County Court.

---

1   12 Halsbury's Laws (4th Edn) para 1170
2   [1896] 2 Ch 538
3   [1963] 1 Lloyd's Rep 359

BROWNE LJ. I entirely agree; and have nothing to add.

WALLER LJ. I also agree.

Appeal allowed. Judgment below varied. Judgment to be entered for plaintiffs against second and fifth defendants for possession and for £1,276·11 as damages for trespass.

Solicitors: *Harold Stern & Co* (for the plaintiffs).

Mary Rose Plummer Barrister.

Newbury District Council v Secretary of State for the Environment and others

COURT OF APPEAL, CIVIL DIVISION

LORD DENNING MR, LAWTON AND BROWNE LJJ

14th, 15th, 16th, 19th, 20th, 21st JUNE, 13th JULY 1978

Town and country planning – Change of use – Conditions attached to permission for change of use – Permission for temporary change of use of existing building – Condition attached that building be removed at the end of period of permission – Whether condition valid – Town and Country Planning Act 1971, s 29(1).

Town and country planning – Development – Use classes – Repository – Use of building to store civil defence vehicles and synthetic rubber – Whether used as 'repository' – Town and Country Planning (Use Classes) Order 1972 (SI 1972 No 1385), Sch, class X.

In 1941 the Crown requisitioned, and became the owner of, land in a rural area which was then converted into an airfield. From 1955 until 1959 two hangars built on the airfield during wartime were used to store civil defence vehicles while the rest of the airfield was returned to agricultural use. In 1959 the former owner of the land received planning permission to use the hangars to store agricultural products subject to the removal of the hangars by 31st December 1970, and subsequently in 1961 he and his family trustees purchased the freehold of the hangar site from the Crown. They then leased it back to the Crown for a term of 40 years at a nominal rent. In 1962 a rubber company received planning permission to use the hangars as warehouses subject to their removal by 31st December 1972, and subsequently purchased the 40-year lease from the Crown at auction. The particulars of sale referred to the county council's policy, stated in the county development plan, of securing the removal of wartime buildings built in open countryside. The company used the hangars to store synthetic rubber and in 1970 applied for a 30-year extension of their planning permission. The local district council refused the application on the grounds that the hangars were an undesirable intrusion into a rural landscape. The company continued to use the hangars after 1972 and in 1973 the council served enforcement notices on them. The company appealed to the Secretary of State who, after a local inquiry, decided that the condition requiring the removal of the hangars was invalid and that as the company had started using them before 1963 they had an indefeasible right under s 87 of the Town and Country Planning Act 1971 to continue using them. In so deciding the Secretary of State applied a policy that it was in all cases

unreasonable to impose a condition requiring the removal of a building on the expiry of
permission for a temporary change of use of an existing building. The local planning *a*
authority appealed to the Divisional Court which dismissed their appeal. The authority
further appealed, contending that under s 29(1)*a* of the 1971 Act they were required when
granting planning permission to 'have regard to the provisions of the development plan'
and could grant permission 'subject to such conditions as they [thought] fit'. On the
hearing of the appeal the rubber company contended that as the hangars had previously
been used as a 'repository' by the Crown and as they themselves were continuing to use *b*
them for that purpose or purposes of the same class the use came within class X*b* of the
schedule to the Town and Country Planning (Use Classes) Order 1972 and therefore
planning permission was not necessary to continue that use.

Held – The appeal would be allowed for the following reasons—
(i) A local planning authority's discretion, under s 29(1) of the 1971 Act, to impose such *c*
conditions as they thought fit on the grant of planning permission was to be exercised
reasonably, and whether a condition requiring the removal of a building at the end of a
temporary change of use of an existing building was reasonable depended on the
circumstances. The county development plan stated that the local planning authority
would seek to secure the removal of wartime buildings such as the hangars, that statement
had been referred to in the particulars of sale, the rubber company's application for *d*
planning permission had been in the nature of an application for temporary use only, and
they had bought at auction knowing that they would be required to remove the hangars
at the end of the temporary use. In those circumstances the condition imposed by the local
planning authority requiring the removal of the hangars was not unreasonable (see p 249
a and *c* to *e*, p 251 *a* to *c* and *e f*, p 252 *a* to *d* and *g h*, p 253 *f* to *h*, and p 254 *a*, post); dictum
of Lord Denning in *Pyx Granite Co Ltd v Minister of Housing and Local Government* [1958] 1 *e*
All ER at 633 explained.
(ii) The hangars had not been used as a 'repository', whether within the ordinary
meaning of that term or in the sense of a place where goods were stored away to be kept
for the purposes of keeping them safe as part of a storage business, either when used by the
Crown to store civil defence vehicles or (per Lord Denning MR and Lawton LJ) when used
by the rubber company to store synthetic rubber. They did not therefore come within *f*
class X of the 1950 order and permission had been required to change the use (see p 249 *g*
to p 250 *a*, p 251 *a*, p 252 *e* to *h* and p 254 *f g*, post); dictum of Lord Denning MR in *G Percy
Trentham v Gloucestershire County Council* [1966] 1 All ER at 703 applied.
Per Lord Denning MR. The maxim qui sentit commodum sentire debet et onus applies
to planning cases so that a person who applies for and accepts planning permission cannot
later deny that that permission was required if the grant of permission has opened up a *g*
new chapter in the planning history of the site (see p 250 *c d*, post).

Notes
For conditions attaching planning permission, see 37 Halsbury's Laws (3rd Edn) 304, para
414, and for cases on the subject, see 45 Digest (Repl) 340–343, 56–64.
For the Town and Country Planning Act 1971, s 29, see Halsbury's Statutes (3rd Edn) *h*
1619.
For the Town and Country Planning (Use Classes) Order 1972, Sch, class X, see 21
Halsbury's Statutory Instruments (3rd Reissue) 141.

Cases referred to in judgments
Brayhead (Ascot) Ltd v Berkshire County Council [1964] 1 All ER 149, [1964] 2 QB 303, [1964] *j*
2 WLR 507, 128 JP 167, 62 LGR 162, 15 P & CR 423, DC, 45 Digest (Repl) 348, 81.

a Section 29(1), so far as material, is set out at p 253 *b*, post
b Class X, so far as material, specifies: 'Use as a . . . repository for any purpose.'

Chertsey Urban District Council v Mixnam's Properties Ltd [1964] 2 All ER 627, [1965] AC 735, [1964] 2 WLR 1210, 128 JP 405, 62 LGR 528, 15 P & CR 331, sub nom *Mixnam's Properties Ltd v Chertsey Urban District Council* [1964] RVR 632, HL, 45 Digest (Repl) 359, 126.

Crabb v Arun District Council [1975] 3 All ER 865, [1976] Ch 179, [1975] 3 WLR 847, CA, Digest (Cont Vol D) 312, 1250a.

East Barnet Urban District Council v British Transport Commission [1961] 3 All ER 878, [1962] 2 QB 484, [1962] 2 WLR 134, 126 JP 1, 60 LGR 41, 13 P & CR 127, DC, 45 Digest (Repl) 329, 17.

Fawcett Properties Ltd v Buckingham County Council [1960] 3 All ER 503, [1961] AC 636, [1960] 3 WLR 831, 125 JP 8, 50 LGR 69, 12 P & CR 1, HL, 45 Digest (Repl) 342, 60.

Gray v Minister of Housing and Local Government (1969) 68 LGR 15, CA, Digest (Cont Vol C) 963, 30n.

Hall & Co Ltd v Shoreham-by-Sea Urban District Council [1964] 1 All ER 1, [1964] 1 WLR 240, 128 JP 120, 62 LGR 206, 15 P & CR 119, CA, 45 Digest (Repl) 342, 61.

Halsall v Brizell [1957] 1 All ER 371, [1957] Ch 169, [1957] 2 WLR 123, Digest (Cont Vol B) 641, 2719a.

Ives (ER) Investments Ltd v High [1967] 1 All ER 504, [1967] 2 QB 379, [1967] 2 WLR 789, CA, Digest (Cont Vol C) 828, 925c.

Kingston-upon-Thames Royal London Borough Council v Secretary of State for the Environment [1974] 1 All ER 193, [1973] 1 WLR 1549, 138 JP 131, 72 LGR 206, 26 P & CR 480, DC, Digest (Cont Vol D) 923, 61c.

Mounsdon v Weymouth and Melcombe Regis Corpn [1960] 1 All ER 538, [1960] 1 QB 645, [1960] 2 WLR 484, 124 JP 231, 58 LGR 144, 11 P & CR 103, 45 Digest (Repl) 326, 8.

Petticoat Lane Rentals Ltd v Secretary of State for the Environment [1971] 2 All ER 793, [1971] 1 WLR 1112, 135 JP 410, 69 LGR 504, 22 P & CR 703, DC, Digest (Cont Vol D) 932, 119a.

Prossor v Minister of Housing and Local Government (1968) 67 LGR 109, DC, Digest (Cont Vol C) 971, 61b.

Pyx Granite Co Ltd v Minister of Housing and Local Government [1959] 3 All ER 1, [1960] AC 260, [1959] 3 WLR 346, 123 JP 429, 58 LGR 1, 10 P & CR 319, HL; *rvsg* [1958] 1 All ER 625, [1958] 1 QB 554, [1958] 2 WLR 371, 56 LGR 171, 9 P & CR 204, CA, 45 Digest (Repl) 336, 37.

Trentham (G Percy) Ltd v Gloucestershire County Council [1966] 1 All ER 701, [1966] 1 WLR 506, 130 JP 179, 64 LGR 134, CA, Digest (Cont Vol B) 689, 30d.

Appeal

The Newbury District Council ('the local planning authority') appealed against the decision of the Divisional Court of the Queen's Bench Division dated 18th February 1977 dismissing their appeal against an order of the Secretary of State for the Environment dated 24th July 1975 allowing the appeal of the International Synthetic Rubber Co Ltd ('the rubber company') against two enforcement notices served on them by the local planning authority in respect of their alleged failure to comply with a condition attached to planning permission granted to them for the use of two hangars at Membury Airfield, Lambourn Woodlands, Berkshire, namely that the buildings be removed at the expiration of the period ending 31st December 1972. The facts are set out in the judgment of Lord Denning MR.

Peter Boydell QC and *R M K Gray* for the local planning authority.
Christopher Symons for the Secretary of State.
David Widdicombe QC and *Anthony J Anderson* for the rubber company.

Cur adv vult

13th July. The following judgments were read.

LORD DENNING MR. Before the 1939–45 war the stretch of land was delightfully rural. It was in open country next to an old earthwork of the stone age called Membury Fort in the downlands of north Wiltshire. But during the war the Crown requisitioned it and became the owners of it. It was turned into an airfield, with long concrete runways and huge hangars, used by the armed services for their military operations. After the war the air force gave up the airfield and gradually the area was restored to agricultural use. The concrete runways were broken up and turned into fields again. But not the hangars. They remained huge black structures of corrugated iron despoiling the landscape. They were used for storage. At first the Ministry of Agriculture used them to cope with the food shortage. They stored supplies in the hangars and distributed them as rations to the towns and cities. That went on for six years until 1953. A year or two later the Home Office made use of the hangars for civil defence. They stored vehicles in them for issue in the event of a national emergency. There were 152 Bedford self-propelled fire-pumps ('Green Goddesses') and 10 Morris equipment vehicles. They were stored away like clothes in moth-balls. That went on until 1959 when the Home Office gave it up.

It then became known that the Crown was thinking of selling the site of the airfield and the hangars. This was of interest to the pre-war owner of the land, Mr J G Gilbey, and his family trustees. He came to a provisional agreement with the Crown and applied for planning permission for the hangars. He said that he wanted them for agricultural purposes so as to store fertilisers and corn. The local council on 2nd December 1959 granted him planning permission for this purpose:

> 'Change of use of hangars at Membury Airfield ... to allow for storage of agricultural products. [Subject to these conditions:] 1. The buildings shall be removed at the expiration of the period ending 31st December, 1970. 2. No fertiliser shall be stored in the buildings which give rise to offence by reason of smell. [For this reason:] To safeguard the amenities of the area.'

After obtaining this permission the Gilbey trustees negotiated with the Air Ministry. On 30th November 1961 they bought the freehold of the site from the Crown for £9,000 and granted a lease back to the Crown for 40 years at £2 a year.

Soon afterwards a rubber company became interested in the hangars. They thought them very suitable for the storage of synthetic rubber. The company was called the International Synthetic Rubber Co Ltd. It was wholly owned by the big rubber companies of the world.

On 7th May 1962 this rubber company applied for planning permission. They stated in their application that the hangars were used for the 'storage of synthetic rubber' and they asked for permission for their use 'as warehouses for the storage of synthetic rubber'. They said in a covering letter: 'As we are prospective buyers from the Air Ministry, it would be appreciated if the planning authorities could see their way to giving their permission to cover as long a period forward as is possible.'

On 31st May 1962 (before they bought the hangars) they were given planning permission for:

> 'Use of two hangars on Membury Airfield as warehouses. [Subject to these conditions:] 1. The buildings shall be removed at the expiration of the period ending December 31st, 1972. 2. The use shall be confined to storage and no materials shall be stored which give rise to offence by reason of smell. [For this reason:] 1. To accord with the local planning authority's policy regarding industrial development in rural areas. 2. To safeguard the amenities of the area.'

Having got that permission, which covered them for the next ten years, up to 31st December 1972, the rubber company proceeded to purchase the hangars. There was a sale by the Crown by auction on 26th July 1962 at Newbury of the 40-year lease at a ground rent of £2 a year. The particulars of sale contained an important quotation from the development plan about the future. It said:

> 'The consent of the Berkshire County Council has been obtained for the use of these hangars for storage purposes until December 31st, 1970 . . . [The revised county map has been amended so as to conform with the county council policy for such sites. The written statement says that:] Problems have arisen from time to time regarding the use of buildings on sites relinquished by government departments. These are often suitable in design for industrial or storage use, although frequently their location in open countryside renders them unsuitable in location as permanent centres of employment and detrimental to landscape amenities. The local planning authority will normally only permit permanent changes of use in localities appropriate in the light of their general policy objectives for the distribution of employment; *otherwise they will seek to secure removal of the buildings. Temporary periods of changed use may be permitted in particular circumstances.*'

The auction was held on 26th July 1962. The 40-year lease was knocked down to the rubber company for £22,000. No doubt they made their bid, knowing that their permission only carried them for ten years. They knew they had to remove the hangars by 31st December 1972. Yet they now seek to say that they are not so bound. To this I will return.

The rubber company continued thenceforward for several years to use the hangars for storing their synthetic rubber. In November 1970, realising that their permission was coming to an end in December 1972, they applied for an extension for 30 years. On 4th January 1971 the Hungerford District Council refused it. They gave as their reason that the proposal conflicted with the county development plan, that it was within an area of outstanding beauty, and—

> 'The development is very conspicuous from the adjoining highway and represents undesirable alien intrusion into the rural landscape to the detriment of the amenities of the area'.

The rubber company appealed to the minister against that refusal.

On 31st December 1972 the rubber company ought to have ceased using the hangars and removed them. They did not do so. They continued to use them in defiance of the conditions. The council gave them a good deal of grace, but in November 1973 served enforcement notices. The rubber company appealed to the minister. They contended that the condition was void, or that they were authorised to use them as warehouses.

In 1973 there was a local inquiry. The inspector was clearly of opinion that, on planning merits, the hangars ought to be removed. '. . . there can be no doubt,' he said, 'they are large, prominent, and ugly in what must have been and could be a pleasant rural scene . . .' But he thought that on legal grounds they could not be removed, nor could the rubber company be stopped from using them. He thought that the condition requiring their removal was void, because it was 'a condition extraneous to the proposed use'.

The minister gave his decision in a letter of July 1975. He held that the condition was invalid, and that the planning permission itself was void, as in *Hall & Co Ltd v Shoreham-by-Sea Urban District Council*[1]. Nevertheless the rubber company could not be stopped from using them. The hangars were very unsightly and ought on the planning merits to be removed, but the rubber company had an indefeasible right to go on using them because they had started using them before 1963: see s 87 of the Town and Country Planning Act 1971.

---

1   [1964] 1 All ER 1, [1964] 1 WLR 240

The local planning authority appealed to the Divisional Court. They dismissed the appeal. The local planning authority appeal to this court. The rubber company resist the appeal. So does the minister.

The present view of the ministry

The present view of the ministry is contained in a circular which was issued in 1968 and is numbered 5/68. It is to the effect that, when an applicant applies for permission to *change the use of an existing building*, the local planning authority, when granting permission, can impose a condition limiting the period of time during which the building may be so used: but cannot impose a condition requiring the building to be *removed* at the end of that time. The crucial sentence in the circular is this: 'A condition requiring the removal of an existing building, whether on the application site or not, will only be reasonable if the need for that removal springs directly from the fact that a new building is to be erected.'

This view of the ministry (as appears from the circular itself) is based on some words of mine in *Pyx Granite Co Ltd v Minister of Housing and Local Government*[1]:

'Although the planning authorities are given very wide powers to impose "such conditions as they think fit", nevertheless the law says that those conditions, to be valid, must fairly and reasonably relate to the permitted development.'

Those words have been approved by the House of Lords in *Fawcett Properties Ltd v Buckingham County Council*[2] by Lord Keith of Avonholm and by Lord Jenkins, and in *Chertsey Urban District Council v Mixnam's Properties Ltd*[3] by Lord Reid and by Lord Guest.

Now apply those words to an application to change the use of an existing building, say, from a retail warehouse into a furniture repository. The Ministry think that a condition, to be valid, must fairly and reasonably relate to *that change of use*, by putting limitations on its use as a furniture respository, but that it cannot validly require the removal of the building itself. A condition could, therefore, limit the period of use to ten years, but it could not require the pulling down of the building at the end of the ten years.

In order to support this view, reference is made to the wording of s 30(1)(b) of the 1971 Act. That makes it clear that where permission is granted authorising 'any building works' (e g by erecting a new building) it is legitimate to enforce a condition 'for requiring the removal' of it. But that provision does not extend to cases where the permission is only for a change of use.

The consequences of the ministry's view

If the view of the Ministry is correct, it leads to remarkable results, as this present case shows. The only way in which the local planning authority could have got these hideous hangars removed would be by acting under s 51 or s 52 of the 1971 Act.

Under s 51 the local planning authority could give a notice requiring the removal, but they would have to pay all the costs of the removal and also compensation to the rubber company under s 170 of the 1971 Act; which would be, we are told, a very large sum for the local people to bear.

Under s 52 the local planning authority might in 1962 have come to an agreement with the rubber company, by which the rubber company (on being granted planning permission) could have agreed to remove the hangars at the end of the ten years. But the trouble about any such agreement was that, at that time, a positive covenant did not run with the land. So it could not bind the successors of the rubber company. It is possible now under s 126 of the Housing Act 1974. (It was suggested that the Berkshire County Council might have been able to do it under their local Act, but I was not satisfied about this.)

---

1   [1958] 1 All ER 625 at 633, [1958] 1 QB 554 at 572
2   [1960] 3 All ER 503 at 515, 522, [1961] AC 636 at 674, 685
3   [1964] 2 All ER 627 at 631–632, 637, [1965] AC 735 at 751, 761

The ministry's view is wrong

It seems to me that the ministry's view is wrong. They put too narrow a construction on the words which I used in the *Pyx Granite* case[1]. They did not have sufficient regard to the provisions of the development plan or the generality of s 29(1).

The development plan dealt specifically with 'the use of buildings on sites relinquished by government departments'. It said that the local planning authority 'will seek to secure removal of the buildings. Temporary permission of changed use may be permitted in particular circumstances'.

Expanded a little, it is plain that the development plan contemplated that wartime buildings, like these hangars, should be removed in due course, but that, pending removal, permission could be given for them to be retained temporarily and used for some changed use, such as storage.

The development plan was referred to in the particulars of the auction sale. No doubt the rubber company knew all about it when they applied for planning permission. In the circumstances their application should, I think, be interpreted as an application for 'temporary use'. So that in answer to the question: 'Give a brief description of the proposed development', the rubber company's answer should have been: 'Temporary use of the two hangars at present on Membury Airfield as warehouses for the storage of synthetic rubber.' And the permission should have been likewise in the same words, 'temporary use'. So interpreted, it is plain that a condition which specified a period of 'temporary use', and a condition which required 'removal' at the end of that period, both related fairly and reasonably to the permitted development, ie to the temporary use.

If you now turn back to the conditions imposed by the local planning authority and the reasons given for them, you will see that they are perfectly good. They require the removal of the hangars at the end of ten years and gave as the reason the local planning authority's policy as set out in the development plan. To my mind they related fairly and reasonably to the permitted development and are valid.

Use classes order

The rubber company now fall back on their second line of defence. They say that in 1962 they did not need to ask for planning permission because there was an existing use as a 'repository': and they could change to another use in the same class. They rely on the Town and Country Planning (Use Classes) Order 1972[2], class X, which says that development does not include use for a purpose of this class: 'Use as a wholesale warehouse or repository for any purpose.'

The rubber company say that their use of the hangars for storing synthetic rubber was use as a 'repository'. The word 'repository' is very vague. It must in this class be narrower than 'warehouse'. The typical use of 'repository' is in describing a furniture repository or a repository for keeping archives. Having these in mind, I ventured in *G Percy Trenthan v Gloucestershire County Council*[3] to say that: 'A repository means a place where goods are stored away, to be kept for the sake of keeping them safe, as part of a storage business.'

Counsel for the rubber company suggested that those last words 'as part of a storage business' were erroneous, and that I should have said 'as an end in itself'. He suggested that when the Home Office had the fire-pumps in one of the hangars, it was a 'repository', and when the rubber company had all its synthetic rubber there, it was a 'repository'. Alternatively, he referred to the wide meaning given to the word 'business' in other contexts.

The one answer I can give to this argument is that it is a matter of impression, depending on the meaning one gives to the word 'repository' in one's own vocabulary. My opinion

---

1   [1958] 1 All ER 625 at 633, [1958] 1 QB 554 at 572
2   SI 1972 No 1385
3   [1966] 1 All ER 701 at 703, [1966] 1 WLR 506 at 512

is that no one conversant with the English language would dream of calling these hangars a 'repository' when filled with fire-pumps or synthetic rubber.

I would, therefore, reject this claim under the use classes order.

Blowing hot and cold

In case I am wrong about 'repository', I must turn to the final point, which is this. Seeing that the rubber company accepted the grant of planning permission in 1962 (subject to the condition of removal), can they now turn round and say that they did not need planning permission at all, being entitled, as they say, to use the hangars for storing rubber without any permission at all?

Counsel for the rubber company submitted that they could. He referred to *Mounsdon v Weymouth and Melcombe Regis Corpn*[1] and *East Barnet Urban District Council v British Transport Commission*[2]. But counsel for the planning authority referred to *Brayhead (Ascot) Ltd v Berkshire County Council*[3], *Prossor v Ministry of Housing*[4], *Gray v Minister of Housing and Local Government*[5], *Petticoat Lane Rentals Ltd v Secretary of State for the Environment*[6] and *Kingston-upon-Thames Royal London Borough Council v Secretary of State for the Environment*[7].

To my mind the maxim of law and equity applies here: qui sentit commodum sentire debet et onus. He who takes the benefit must accept it with the burdens that go with it. It has been applied recently in *Halsall v Brizell*[8] and *E R Ives Investments Ltd v High*[9]. It is an instance of the general principle of equity considered in *Crabb v Arun District Council*[10] and it is, in my view, particularly applicable in planning cases. At any rate in those cases where the grant of planning permission opens a new chapter in the planning history of the site. Take this very case. In 1962 the rubber company must have thought it necessary to get planning permission before they bought these hangars. They knew that, without planning permission, they could do nothing with the hangars. They had no thought of going back and finding out the past history, so as to see if there was any existing use of which they could avail themselves. They were only too pleased when they were granted planning permission for ten years on the condition that they pulled the hangars down at the end of it. They bought the land on that basis. They did not dream of appealing against the condition because they realised that it was perfectly fair and reasonable. It is quite contrary to equity and justice that they should be allowed to say, now that the ten years have come to an end, 'We never needed planning permission at all', and for that purpose to rake up past history of use 15 or 20 years before, when witnesses have died, memories become blurred, and documents lost or destroyed. The truth is that, back in 1962, they had two inconsistent courses open to them. One was to apply for a grant of planning permission; the other was to rely on any existing use rights that might be attached to the site. Once they opted for planning permission, and accepted it without objection, they had made their bed and must lie on it. No doubt they did not know of the past history, but that was only because they did not choose to rely on it. They should not be allowed to bring it up again now.

Conclusion

In conclusion I will just remind you of these facts. In 1962 this rubber company were given planning permission to use these two hangars for the next ten years on condition that they removed them at the end on 31st December 1972. They did not honour that obligation. They have raised issues and fought them with much tenacity and at great

1   [1960] 1 All ER 538, [1960] 1 QB 645
2   [1961] 3 All ER 878, [1962] 2 QB 484
3   [1964] 1 All ER 149, [1964] 2 QB 303
4   (1968) 67 LGR 109
5   (1969) 68 LGR 15
6   [1971] 2 All ER 793, [1971] 1 WLR 1112
7   [1974] 1 All ER 193, [1973] 1 WLR 1549
8   [1957] 1 All ER 371, [1957] Ch 169
9   [1967] 1 All ER 504 at 507, [1967] 2 QB 379 at 394
10 [1975] 3 All ER 865 at 871–872, [1976] Ch 179 at 187–188

expense ever since. So much so that the delays have gone beyond all bounds. Now six years later the hangars are still there. It is high time that they were removed, and obliterated from the landscape. I would allow the appeal accordingly.

LAWTON LJ. The main question for decision is this: was the Secretary of State wrong in thinking, as he clearly did, that when a local planning authority grants permission for a change of use of any building, it can never impose a condition requiring the removal of this building after the end of a specific number of years.

The relevant statutory provision, s 29(1) of the Town and Country Planning Act 1971, says that a local planning authority, subject to specific statutory restrictions which do not apply in this case, 'may grant planning permission either unconditionally or subject to such conditions as they think fit'. This discretion must be used reasonably: see *Pyx Granite Co Ltd v Ministry of Housing and Local Government*[1] and *Fawcett Properties Ltd v Buckingham County Council*[2]. Any other restrictions must be found in the words of the statute itself: see *Chertsey Urban District Council v Mixnam's Properties Ltd*[3] per Viscount Radcliffe.

In this context what does 'using a discretion reasonably' mean? The words are not statutory: they reflect the judicial concept that those who are given statutory powers should use them in a fair and reasonable way and for the purposes for which they were given. In the *Pyx Granite* case[4], Lord Denning expressed this concept in relation to the application of conditions to planning permission as follows:

'... nevertheless the law says that those conditions, to be valid, must fairly and reasonably relate to the permitted development. The planning authority are not at liberty to use their powers for an ulterior object, however desirable that object may seem to be in the public interest.'

In *Fawcett's* case[5] Lord Morton, Lord Keith and Lord Jenkins cited these words with obvious approval and founded part of their reasoning on them. Lord Denning himself[6] made it clear that what he had said in the *Pyx Granite* case[4], and what has been referred to so often since, was but a way of putting that a planning authority should act reasonably. This is what the Secretary of State should concern himself with when reviewing a local planning authority's exercise of discretion under s 29 of the 1971 Act. He will be helped, of course, by applying what Lord Denning said in the *Pyx Granite* case[4]; but what Lord Denning said must not be construed as if they were statutory words.

I turn now to consider whether any other restrictions besides reasonableness are placed on the exercise of a local planning authority's discretion under s 29(1). If there are any they must be found in the 1971 Act itself. The authority must 'have regard to the provisions of the development plan, so far as material to the application and to any other material consideration ...' Having regard to the opening words of s 30(1), viz 'without prejudice to the generality of section 29(1)', I can see no reason for thinking that the remainder of the section puts any further restrictions on the discretion given by s 29(1).

The county development plan was put in evidence before the inspector. The 'written statement of the first review county map' stated that local planning authorities would normally only permit permanent changes of use in the light of their general policy objective for the distribution of employment; otherwise they would seek to secure the removal of wartime buildings. It went on to provide that *temporary* periods of changed use

---

1   [1958] 1 All ER 625, [1958] 1 QB 554
2   [1960] 3 All ER 503, [1961] AC 636
3   [1964] 2 All ER 627 at 634, [1965] AC 735 at 755
4   [1958] 1 All ER 625 at 633, [1958] 1 QB 554 at 572
5   [1960] 3 All ER 503 at 509, 515, 522, [1961] AC 636 at 665, 674, 685
6   *Fawcett Properties Ltd v Buckingham County Council* [1960] 3 All ER 503 at 518, [1961] AC 636 at 678–679

might be permitted in particular circumstances. The planning permission granted to the rubber company was for a temporary change of use. It was a step in furtherance of the local planning authority's policy objectives for the return to agricultural use of the land on which the hangars stood. It did, in my judgment, relate fairly and reasonably to the permitted development, which was the temporary use of the hangars, pending the attainment of the policy objective. Anyway, having regard to the provisions of the county development plan, it was reasonable for the local planning authority to grant permission for a change of use for a limited period on the condition that at the end of that period the company should remove the hangars. There was nothing oppressive about this condition. The company knew what the planning objectives were. They bought at auction knowing what the condition was. The price at which the lease of the hangars was knocked down to them would have reflected the burden of complying with the condition at the end of the period of temporary use. There was no evidence that the local planning authority when imposing the condition had had any motive other than the attainment of their policy objectives. It was never suggested that they imposed the condition in order to avoid having to act under s 51, a course which would have led to their having to pay compensation. In my judgment the Secretary of State has tied his hands with restrictions which did not exist. In many cases a condition requiring the removal of buildings might be unreasonable, but not in this one. The condition imposed by the local planning authority in my judgment was a valid one. The Secretary of State should have upheld the enforcement notice.

I turn now to counsel's submission for the rubber company that even if the condition was valid it was put on a planning permission which had no effect in law because the company had no need for it. When using the hangars as they did, they were reverting to a lawful existing use, viz that of a repository under class X of the Town and Country Planning (Use Classes) Order 1972. This class refers to 'use as a wholesale warehouse or repository for any purpose'. The word 'repository' has to be construed in its context in this class. When it is so construed the concept of a commercial undertaking comes to mind. This, no doubt, led Lord Denning MR to define 'repository' in the terms he did in *G Percy Trentham v Gloucestershire County Council*[1]. I agree with that definition. There is, however, a simple way of dealing with this point. As a matter of the ordinary modern usage of the English language, I am sure that no literate person would say that the use to which the Home Office had put the hangars in the 1950s was or that the company are now, using them as a repository. It follows that there was no prior lawful existing use of which the company could take advantage. They did require planning permission for the use they intended.

Attracted though I am by Lord Denning MR's comments on the application of the maxim qui sentit commodum sentire debet et onus to the facts of this case I do not find it necessary to decide the appeal on that ground.

I too would allow the appeal.

BROWNE LJ. I agree that this appeal should be allowed.

1 The validity of the condition
I agree with Lord Denning MR and Lawton LJ that, for the reasons they have given, this condition is valid.

The Secretary of State in his decision letter on 24th July 1975 said:

'It is considered however in the circumstances of this case where planning permission was sought merely for a change of use of existing substantial buildings, hat a condition requiring the removal of those buildings after the expiration of a specific number of years was not sufficiently related to the change of use in respect of which the planning permission was granted and was unreasonable. It is therefore concluded that the condition was invalid.'

---

1 [1966] 1 All ER 701 at 703, [1966] 1 WLR 506 at 512

Counsel for the Secretary of State submitted that this was a finding of fact. I do not agree. In my view, it is a holding of law that such a condition can never be valid, a conclusion no doubt based on the statement in circular 5/68 which Lord Denning MR has quoted.

Section 29(1) of the Town and Country Planning Act 1971 is in very wide terms:

> '. . . where an application is made to a local planning authority for planning permission, that authority, in dealing with the application, shall have regard to the provisions of the development plan, so far as material to the application, and to any other material considerations, and—(a) . . . may grant planning permission, either unconditionally or subject to such conditions as they may think fit; or (b) may refuse planning permission.'

I agree with Lawton LJ that s 30(1) cannot have been intended to narrow the powers of the local planning authority under s 29(1), having regard to its opening words: 'Without prejudice to the generality of section 29(1) . . .'

But it is now well established that *some* limitation must be put on the power of a local planning authority to impose conditions under s 29(1)(a). The statement by Lord Denning in *Pyx Granite*[1], which Lord Denning MR and Lawton LJ have already quoted, has since been consistently applied. Counsel for the Secretary of State and for the rubber company submit that this limitation should be applied strictly. They emphasise the references to 'the application' in s 29(1), and to 'the purposes of or in connection with the development authorised by the permission' in s 30(1)(a), which they say lay down the same test of what conditions can be validly imposed. They say that the 'application' and the permission in this case were for 'development' by a change of use, and that although the planning authority could validly have imposed a condition requiring a cessation of that use at the end of a specified period the condition requiring the removal of the hangars did not 'fairly and reasonably relate to the permitted development'.

I agree with Lord Denning MR and Lawton LJ that in the circumstances of this case this is to put too narrow an interpretation on Lord Denning's test. ' "Development" . . . means the carrying out of . . . operations in, on, over or under land, or the making of any material change in the use of any dwellings or other land' (s 22(1)). All 'development', whether by 'operations' or by change of use, must relate to some particular land or building (by s 290(1) 'land' includes a building). The 'land' to which the rubber company's application related was the hangars and the permission was for 'development' of the hangars. The rubber company's application of 3rd May 1962, though not clearly expressed, was an application for the development of these two hangars by a change of use. I agree with Lord Denning MR and Lawton LJ that it should be construed as an application for *temporary* use. The particulars of the auction sale of the hangars contained the extract from the development plan, which Lord Denning MR has quoted, which made it clear that the existing permission for the use of the hangars was only until 31st December 1970, that the local planning authority was only prepared to grant temporary permission for their use and that their policy was to secure their removal. It is clear from the rubber company's letter of 7th May 1962 to the planning authority, sending their application, that they realised that only a temporary permission would be granted, though they hoped to get (and did get) an extension beyond 31st December 1970. In imposing this condition the planning authority clearly did 'have regard to the provisions of the development plan', as s 29(1) required them to do. I think it was a 'material consideration' that, as counsel for the planning authority satisfied me, there was no method in 1962 of securing that (in accordance with their policy) the hangars would be removed in 1972 except by this condition. The Secretary of State accepted in his decision letter that the planning authority would not have granted a permanent permission, but the effect of his decision is that the rubber company have got a permanent immunity from enforcement because their change of use took place before 31st December 1963 (see s 87(1)).

---

1   [1958] 1 All ER 625 at 633, [1958] 1 QB 554 at 572

I agree with Lord Denning MR and Lawton LJ that in the circumstances of this case this condition did 'fairly and reasonably' relate to the 'permitted development' of the land in question, ie, the temporary use of the hangars.

So far as the authorities go, I think they are against the respondents' narrow construction of the statute and of Lord Denning's test in *Pyx Granite*[1]. *Fawcett Properties Ltd v Buckingham County Council*[2] was the converse of this case. The House of Lords held that a condition relating to the use of the land could validly be attached to a permission for building operations. Counsel for the rubber company submitted that the power of a planning authority to impose conditions on a grant of permission for operations is wider than the power to impose conditions on a permission for change of use. I cannot see why; both are permissions for the development of land. He referred us to s 33(2) of the 1971 Act, but so far as I can see the House of Lords in the *Fawcett Properties Ltd* case[2] did not rely on the corresponding s 18(3) of the Town and Country Planning Act 1947, though it was referred to in argument. In *Hall & Co Ltd v Shoreham-on-Sea Urban District Council*[3] this court held that the condition there in question (which I think on the respondents' test would have been invalid) did fairly and reasonably relate to the permitted development (see Willmer LJ and Harman LJ) although on the very special facts of that case they held that it was unreasonable. The case[4] referred to by Lord Denning in *Pyx Granite*[5] seems to me different and distinguishable (see also *Kingston-upon-Thames Royal London Borough Council v Secretary of State for the Environment*[6]); here the condition relates to the land to the development of which the application related, but there it related to different land and had no connection with that development, though it was directed to carrying out the *general* policy of the planning authority.

2 The Town and Country Planning (Use Classes) Order 1972

I understood counsel's argument for the rubber company rather differently from Lord Denning MR and Lawton LJ. I understood his submission to be that the use by the Home Office was 'as a repository', and that the use by the rubber company was 'as a wholesale warehouse', so that by virtue of Town and Country Planning (Use Classes) Order 1972 this change of use was deemed not to involve development of the land. But, whichever way it is put, the vital question is the same: was the use by the Home Office 'use as a repository'? The order does not include a class of 'use for storage'; the uses covered by class X must therefore, I think, be intended to have some special characteristics other than merely storage. I agree with Lord Denning MR and Lawton LJ that whether one applies the ordinary meaning of the word or the definition given by Lord Denning MR in *G Percy Trentham Ltd v Gloucestershire County Council*[7] the use by the Home Office was not 'use as a repository'.

3 Blowing hot and cold

In view of our decision on the second question, this point does not arise. I think it raises a difficult question, and to answer it would involve an examination of the authorities to which Lord Denning MR has referred and others, including the decisions of the House of Lords in *Pyx Granite Co Ltd v Minister of Housing and Local Government*[8] and in *Fawcett*

---

1   [1958] 1 All ER 625 at 633, [1958] 1 QB 554 at 572
2   [1960] 3 All ER 503, [1961] AC 636
3   [1964] 1 All ER 1 at 7, 13, [1964] 1 WLR 240 at 248, 255
4   Bulletin of selected Appeal Decisions (VII/12)
5   [1958] 1 All ER 625 at 633, [1958] 1 QB 554 at 573
6   [1974] 1 All ER 193 at 198–199, [1973] 1 WLR 1549 at 1555–1557
7   [1966] 1 All ER 701 at 703, [1966] 1 WLR 506 at 512
8   [1959] 3 All ER 1, [1960] AC 260

Properties Ltd v Buckingham County Council[1]. In my view it would be undesirable to embark on a series of obiter dicta about it. I will only say that as at present advised I am afraid that I do not agree with Lord Denning MR on this point, except where the circumstances are as in *Prossor v Minister of Housing and Local Government*[2] and the cases which have followed and applied that decision, viz where a new planning unit, and indeed in those cases a new physical unit, has been created.

Appeal allowed. Leave to appeal to the House of Lords refused.

Solicitors: *Sharpe, Pritchard & Co*, agents for *W J Turner*, Newbury (for the planning authority); *Treasury Solicitor*; *Herbert Smith & Co* (for the rubber company).

Gavin Gore-Andrew Esq   Barrister.

---

1   [1960] 3 All ER 503, [1961] AC 636
2   (1968) 67 LGR 109

Malone v Commissioner of Police of the Metropolis

COURT OF APPEAL, CIVIL DIVISION

STEPHENSON AND ROSKILL LJJ

19th, 22nd, 23rd, 26th MAY 1978

Police – Power to retain property relevant to criminal proceedings – Police searching plaintiff's house and seizing stolen property and large amounts of English and foreign currency – Plaintiff charged with handling and conspiracy to handle stolen property – No charge made in respect of currency – Currency not made an exhibit – Whether police entitled to retain currency as material evidence in respect of charges against plaintiff – Whether police entitled to retain currency in anticipation of restitution, compensation or forfeiture order being made against plaintiff if convicted – Theft Act 1968, s 28(1)(c) – Powers of Criminal Courts Act 1973, ss 35, 43.

The plaintiff was suspected by the police of receiving and handling stolen goods. The police acting under a search warrant searched the plaintiff's house and found a large number of goods alleged to have been stolen. They also found in a concealed cupboard a clock movement alleged to been stolen, English banknotes to the value of over £7,000 and United States and Italian banknotes to the value of about £3,000. The plaintiff was charged with handling stolen goods and conspiracy to do so dishonestly. No charges were made in respect of the banknotes but they were however seized and retained by the police despite demands for their return. The plaintiff commenced an action in detinue claiming delivery up of the banknotes. The plaintiff claimed that he required the money to pay the legal fees of his trial. The police conceded that the banknotes were not the subject of charges against the plaintiff and had not been made an exhibit at the plaintiff's committal proceedings but contended (i) that they had reason to believe that the banknotes were to be used for the purchase of stolen property and were thus material evidence in connection with the offences for which the plaintiff had been charged, and as such they were entitled to retain them until the trial, and (ii) that the banknotes might be the subject of a compensation or a forfeiture order under s 35ᵃ or s 43ᵇ of the Powers of Criminal Courts Act 1973 or a restitution order under s 28(1)(c)ᶜ of the Theft Act 1968. On a summons by the plaintiff for judgment under RSC Ord 14 the judge held that the banknotes themselves were not the best evidence of the money seized, since their production at the trial would prove nothing that the witness who discovered it could not prove without producing it, and that there was no justification for the police keeping the money for the speculative purpose of an application for a compensation or forfeiture order. The judge accordingly ordered the banknotes to be returned to the plaintiff. The police appealed.

Held – (i) The police had no power to retain property lawfully seized from an accused person if it was not stolen or the subject of any charges unless the retention was justified on ascertainable grounds. However, where the property was a reasonably necessary and valuable part of the evidence material to the charges against the accused it was in the public interest, having regard to the unpredictability of the course of a criminal trial and the risk to the administration of justice if the property were not available as evidence, for the police to retain the property until the trial, and that public interest prevailed over the right of the individual not to be deprived of his property. Because the banknotes were part of the evidence material to the charges against the plaintiff and because it could not be predicted with sufficient certainty that there would be no circumstances under which it would be necessary to adduce the banknotes in evidence at the plaintiff's trial, the police were

---

a   Section 35, so far as material, is set out at p 265 *b c*, post

b   Section 43, so far as material, is set out at p 265 *e f*, post

c   Section 28(1), so far as material, is set out at p 268 *g*, post

entitled to retain them until the trial. The appeal would therefore be allowed (see p 262 *e f*, p 263 *d e*, p 266 *f*, p 270 *j* to p 271 *d* and p 272 *d*, post); *R v Barnett* (1829) 3 C & P 600, *R v O'Donnell* (1835) 7 C & P 138, *R v Rooney* (1836) 7 C & P 515, and *Ghani v Jones* [1969] 3 All ER 1700 distinguished.

(ii) The police had no power under either s 35 or s 43 of the 1973 Act or s 28 of the 1968 Act to retain money or property seized from an accused person solely in anticipation of the possibility of a compensation, forfeiture or restitution order being made against the accused if he was convicted, and the court would not develop the common law to embrace such a power (see p 263 *g h*, p 264 *f* to *h*, p 265 *a b*, p 266 *b* to *d* and *f*, post); dictum of Scrutton LJ in *Jagger v Jagger* [1926] All ER Rep at 618 applied.

Per Curiam. Where it appears that a person was in possession of foreign currency contrary to the provisions of the Exchange Control Act 1947 it would not be right to order the return of that currency to the person even if he were entitled to recover it on other grounds, and if the court is of the opinion that the possession was unlawful, whether under the 1947 Act or otherwise, it is the court's duty to take the point of its own motion irrespective of whether it has been raised by the Crown (see p 266 *f g*, p 271 *e f* and p 272 *b* and *d*, post).

Notes

For the seizure of property by police on effecting a search, see 11 Halsbury's Laws (4th Edn) para 126, and for cases on the subject of search and search warrants, see 14(1) Digest (Reissue) 215, 216, 1566–1578.

For the Theft Act 1968, s 28(1), as substituted by the Criminal Justice Act 1972, s 64(1) and Sch 5, see 42 Halsbury's Statutes (3rd Edn) 153.

For the Powers of Criminal Courts Act 1973, ss 35, 43, see 43 ibid 331, 337.

Cases referred to in judgments

American Cyanamid Co v Ethicon Ltd [1975] 1 All ER 504, [1975] AC 396, [1975] 2 WLR 316, [1975] RPC 513, HL, Digest (Cont Vol D) 536, 152a.

Dillon v O'Brien and Davis (1887) 16 Cox CC 245, 14(1) Digest (Reissue) 193, *915.

Ghani v Jones [1969] 3 All ER 1700, [1970] 1 QB 693, [1969] 3 WLR 1158, 134 JP 166, CA; *affg* [1969] 3 All ER 720, [1970] 1 QB 693, Digest (Cont Vol C) 158, 607b.

Gordon v Chief Comr of Metropolitan Police [1910] 2 KB 1080, [1908–10] All ER Rep 192, 79 LJKB 957, 103 LT 338, 74 JP 437, CA, 14(1) Digest (Reissue) 216, 1574.

Jagger v Jagger [1926] P 93, [1926] All ER Rep 613, 95 LJP 83, 135 LT 1, CA, 27(2) Digest (Reissue) 849, 6774.

Mareva Compania Naviera SA v International Bulkcarriers Ltd [1975] 2 Lloyd's 509, CA.

R v Barnett (1829) 3 C & P 600, 172 ER 563, 14(1) Digest (Reissue) 192, 1371.

R v Bunce (1978) 66 Cr App R 109.

R v Hinde [1977] RTR 328, 64 Cr App R 213, CA.

R v Lushington, ex parte Otto [1894] 1 QB 420, 70 LT 412, 58 JP 282, 42 WR 411, 17 Cox CC 754, 10 R 418, sub nom *Re Ebstein, ex parte Otto* 10 TLR 57, DC, 22 Digest (Reissue) 469, 4698.

R v O'Donnell (1835) 7 C & P 138, 3 Nev & MMC 397, 173 ER 61, 14(1) Digest (Reissue) 192, 1373.

R v Rooney (1836) 7 C & P 515, 173 ER 228, 14(1) Digest (Reissue) 192, 1377.

R v Thompson (1978) 66 Cr App R 130, CA.

Siskina (Cargo Owners) v Distos Compania Naviera SA, The Siskina [1977] 3 All ER 803, [1977] 3 WLR 818, HL.

Truman (Frank) Export Ltd v Metropolitan Police Comr [1977] 3 All ER 431, [1977] QB 952, [1977] 3 WLR 257, 64 Cr App R 248.

Interlocutory appeal

This was an appeal by the defendant, the Commissioner of Police of the Metropolis, against a decision of Wien J dated 2nd May 1978 made in chambers on appeal from Master Elton, granting the plaintiff, James Malone, a mandatory injunction ordering the commissioner to return to the plaintiff Bank of England notes, United States dollars and Italian lira seized by the police on 22nd March 1977 from the plaintiff's house at 15 Aldebert Terrace, London SW8. The facts are set out in the judgment of Stephenson LJ.

John Hazan QC and *Leonard Gerber* for the commissioner.
Daniel Serota and *Charles Gordon* for the plaintiff.

Cur adv vult

26th May. The following judgments were read.

STEPHENSON LJ. This case concerns a large amount of money in English and foreign currency seized and retained by the police on behalf of the appellant commissioner (the defendant) but claimed as his property by the respondent (the plaintiff).

In March 1978, by specially indorsed writ, the plaintiff claimed delivery up of 514 Bank of England notes to the value of over £6,000 and United States dollar notes and Italian lira notes to the value, at present exchange rates, of about £3,000. He alleged that they had been wrongfully in the commissioner's possession for a year (since 22nd March 1977) and the commissioner had refused to deliver them up on demand. He also claimed damages for their detention. The circumstances in which the police had taken the notes and by which the commissioner claimed to be authorised by law to take and detain them are set out in para 3 of his defence served on 10th April 1978:

'(a) From the beginning of 1977 Police Officers commenced an observation on the activities of the Plaintiff and various of his associates. [I will not read out paras (b) to (e).]

'(f) Immediately thereafter the search warrant was executed and Police Officers took possession of a large number of items from the said house which were subsequently identified by witnesses to be goods stolen from them by means of burglary.

'(g) On the 22nd March 1977 after the arrest of the Plaintiff Detective Sergeant Ware in possession of a search warrant in respect of 15 Aldebert Terrace went to the said address with other officers and together with the wife of the Plaintiff who had been arrested on a charge of dishonestly handling stolen goods knowing or believing the same to be stolen.

'(h) The search warrant was then executed and amongst property seized by Detective Sergeant Branchflower were the various bank notes the subject of the proceedings herein which together with a grandfather clock movement were found in a concealed wall cupboard in the basement kitchen of the aforesaid premises.

'(i) The grandfather clock movement has been identified as stolen by means of a burglary, and other property seized has been identified subsequently by witnesses to be goods stolen from them by means of burglary.

'(j) On the 26 September 1977 the Plaintiff and eight other persons were committed for trial from the Horseferry Road Magistrates Court to the Inner London Crown Court.

'(k) The indictment against the Plaintiff and his co-accused charges the Plaintiff with conspiracy to dishonestly handle stolen goods between the 1st January 1976 and the 23rd March 1977 and also with four substantive counts of handling stolen goods.'

On 29th March 1978 the plaintiff's advisers took the remarkable step of issuing a summons for judgment under RSC Ord 14. That summons was supported by an affidavit from an articled clerk in the firm of the plaintiff's solicitors swearing that he verily believed that there was no defence to the action.

At the hearing of the summons Master Elton had before him four further affidavits. The plaintiff himself swore that, in addition to the sum of money claimed, police officers had seized the sum of £1,419 in Bank of England notes which had been returned to him through his solicitors on 29th March 1977. The senior partner in the firm of his solicitors set out two requests in 1977 for the return of the sum of about £11,000 and swore:

'(2) Detective Sergeant Ware refused to release the said money giving the reason on each occasion that if the Plaintiff were to be found guilty at his trial he, Detective Sergeant Ware, might be criticised by the trial judge in the event that a compensation order or an order for costs were made against the Plaintiff and it transpired that such orders could not be satisfied without the aid of the sum of about £11,000.'

It was not disputed before us that the £1,419 was found on the plaintiff's person when arrested and was returned to him a week later, and that Det Sgt Ware had said substantially what he was alleged to have said in the paragraph I have just read.

In opposition to that summons the commissioner filed affidavits by Det Sgt Branchflower and Det Sgt Ware. The former corrected the number found on two denominations of English bank notes, which increased the total value of those to over £7,000, and swore to their discovery as subsequently particularised in the defence. The latter, who was the officer in charge of the case against the plaintiff, deposed to the plaintiff's committal, produced schedules of stolen property including that found at the plaintiff's two addresses, and concluded with these paragraphs:

'(6) With regard to the various bank notes seized by Detective Sergeant Branchflower on the 22nd March 1977 from the concealed wall cupboard at 15 Aldebert Terrace consisting of notes of English, American and Italian denominations I have reason to believe on the available evidence that this was money used by the Plaintiff to pay burglars, thieves and other dishonest handlers for stolen property he was purchasing and accordingly the bank notes will be valuable and the best evidence in the Plaintiff's forthcoming trial.

'(7) Accordingly I am advised and verily believe that there is a proper Defence to the Plaintiff's claim and ask this Honourable Court to dismiss the application for leave to sign judgment and grant the [commissioner] unconditional leave to defend.'

It is not disputed, notwithstanding this affidavit and the return of the £1,419, that the plaintiff has been granted legal aid to defend himself on these charges. Instead of dismissing the application and ordering the plaintiff to pay the costs forthwith under RSC Ord 14, r 7(1), the master gave the commissioner unconditional leave to defend, and the commissioner served the defence from which I have already read. That led the plaintiff's legal advisers to take two further steps in the action: to appeal against the master's order and to amend the statement of claim on 27th April 1978 by adding a claim for an injunction (in terms unspecified).

On 2nd May the plaintiff's appeal and his application for a mandatory injunction ordering the defendant forthwith to deliver up to the plaintiff the bank notes referred to in the statement of claim came together before Wien J. In the approved note which we have of his judgment the judge stated that 'the matter can be disposed of by my deciding the application for an injunction'. He read the affidavits I have already mentioned and a further affidavit from another member of the firm of the plaintiff's solicitors in these terms. I read from Mr Klahn's affidavit:

'(1) I have perused the committal documents in my possession regarding the Plaintiff's trial at the Inner London Crown Court on the 6th June 1978 and the banknotes referred to in the Plaintiff's Statement of Claim are not exhibits in the trial. I produce list of exhibits . . .

'(2) I have been informed by the Plaintiff and verily believe that although he has substantial assets in his two properties in London and Dorking, he has at present very limited liquid assets and requires the money he is claiming in his action in order to pay his Solicitors fees at his trial on the 6th June 1978.'

No argument was addressed to him on the application of *American Cyanamid v Ethicon Ltd*[1], but the argument was confined to two points, to which I must come in due course. At

---

1   [1975] 1 All ER 504, [1975] AC 396

the end of the argument the judge made no order on the appeal except that the costs of the appeal were to be costs in the cause; but he granted the injunction, ordered the costs of the application for it to be the plaintiff's in any event and stayed execution for seven days pending an appeal.

I at first found this a surprising result of the hearing of the appeal and application. If the judge thought, as he clearly did, that the commissioner's detention of the notes was unlawful, why did he not allow the appeal, for there was nothing left of his action except a possible but unreal claim for nominal damages? Yet he left the master's unconditional leave to defend and ordered costs to be costs in a cause which his injunction had brought to an end. If, on the other hand, he thought that there was an arguable defence and an issue to be tried, why did he grant the injunction?

The answer appears to be that both parties agreed to his disposing of the whole action in this way, as was done by Talbot J in *Ghani v Jones*[1]; so that the judge cannot be criticised for making two apparently inconsistent orders. It was important that the fate of the bank notes should be decided before the criminal trial came on. Accordingly no point was raised in the commissioner's notice of appeal that an injunction was not an appropriate remedy on the ground that there is a serious issue to be tried, damages would be an adequate remedy and the balance of convenience tips against the injunction granted. And though at one time counsel was disposed to argue the point on behalf of the commissioner, he agrees with counsel for the plaintiff that we should dispose of the action by deciding the issues between them on the grounds raised in the notice of appeal. I feel bound to express my opinion that, had we been asked to consider that other ground, counsel for the plaintiff would have had the greatest difficulty in persuading me that this injunction should have been granted, whether the commissioner's claim to these notes is or is not well founded. I doubt whether we ought not to allow the appeal on that ground. But I yield to the wish of both parties to have this appeal decided on the important points which have been argued here and below.

It is not disputed in these proceedings that the police officers acted lawfully in seizing the English bank notes and foreign currency, although counsel for the plaintiff reserved the right to argue the contrary elsewhere. The only question is whether it is necessary for the commissioner to detain them until the trial of the plaintiff is concluded. If it is necessary, the judge was wrong to grant the injunction ordering their release and the appeal should be allowed. If it is not necessary, he was right and the appeal should be dismissed.

The commissioner rested his case before the judge that retention of these notes was necessary on two grounds: (1) that the notes were material evidence in connection with the offences for which the plaintiff had been committed for trial; (2) that they might be the subject of a forfeiture order under s 43 of the Powers of Criminal Courts Act 1973.

On the first point the judge held that the production of the money proved nothing that the witness who discovered it in the cupboard could not prove without producing it. He said:

'The applicant's contentions are that there is no question of the notes being produced to prove any material fact. The police rely on the fact that a large amount of money in notes was found at the [plaintiff's] premises at the time the search warrant was executed. The relevant evidence can be given by the police officer who conducted the search. I have no doubt that this evidence will not be disputed. The evidence of the police officer is the best evidence of the money seized, not the money itself. The production of the money is of no benefit to anyone; so the first ground on which the police claim the right to retain the money fails.'

On the second point he thought that it would be difficult to prove the conditions necessary to satisfy s 43. He said:

'The [plaintiff] contends that the police should not retain the money for an event that may never occur and which is highly improbable. In *Ghani v Jones*[2] Lord

---

1 [1969] 3 All ER 720 at 723, [1970] 1 QB 693 at 698
2 [1969] 3 All ER 1700 at 1705, [1970] 1 QB 693 at 708–709

Denning MR sets out certain requisites where a person has not been arrested or charged, which is not the case here. These requirements are not intended to be all-embracing, but it seems to me beyond any doubt that police must not keep money, not alleged to be stolen, longer than necessary for the purpose of evidence. I see no justification at all for the police to retain the money for no other purpose than to invite the court which may or may not make an order under s 43. On the evidence before me it is not the duty of the police to retain property purely for that speculative purpose.'

His conclusion on both points he stated thus:

'While the police were initially entitled to seize the money, counsel for the [plaintiff] is, in my opinion, correct in submitting that they are no longer entitled to retain it. What is the best evidence is the fact that it was seized and there is no justification for the police keeping it for the speculative purpose of an application under s 43. I do not see how or on what grounds the Crown Court could ever be satisfied that the money was intended to be used to pay thieves or receivers.'

The first point is not, to my mind, easy to decide. The notes are not alleged to be stolen nor to be the proceeds of selling stolen property, but to be for use in paying for the purchase of stolen property. They were not made an exhibit, so may not have been literally 'produced in court' by a witness so as to make it right and necessary for the court or the police to preserve and retain them until the trial is concluded: *R v Lushington, ex parte Otto*[1], per Wright J. But I suspect that it was for reasons of administrative convenience that they were not made an exhibit, certainly not, as counsel for the plaintiff suggested, because the Crown does not intend to produce them at the trial; and they were referred to in detail, including some of them being wrapped in Midland Bank plastic bags, by Det Sgt Branchflower in his statement produced to the committing magistrates' court under s 2 of the Criminal Justice Act 1967. I can see no material difference between the two procedures for the purpose of deciding whether it was necessary for the police to detain them, except that, if they had been produced and exhibited and it were necessary to detain them, they could not be safely returned to the plaintiff without leave of the Crown Court. So the question is whether they were required, in addition to the officers' evidence about them, to prove the offences charged in the indictment against the plaintiff.

Counsel for the plaintiff is instructed that the evidence as to them, their number and denominations, their hiding place and their discovery, is accepted by the plaintiff as given in Det Sgt Branchflower's statement and will not be disputed at the trial. Nor will that evidence be objected to as inadmissible. In other words, it is not disputed that the officer's evidence is material, and reasonably believed to be so, as tending to prove the charges on which the plaintiff is being prosecuted, within the law as declared by Lord Denning MR in *Ghani v Jones*[2]. There Lord Denning MR said:

'I take it to be settled law, without citing cases, that the officers are entitled to take any goods which they find in his possession or in his house which they reasonably believe to be material evidence in relation to the crime for which he is arrested or for which they enter. If in the course of their search they come on any other goods which show him to be implicated in some other crime, they may take them provided they act reasonably and detain them no longer than is necessary.'

Compare what he went on to say[3], and the judgment of Swanwick J in *Frank Truman Export Ltd v Metropolitan Police Comr*[4]. I accept the second part of the statement of the law

1   [1894] 1 QB 420 at 423
2   [1969] 3 All ER 1700 at 1703, [1970] 1 QB 693 at 706
3   [1969] 3 All ER 1700 at 1705, [1970] 1 QB 693 at 709
4   [1977] 3 All ER 431, [1977] QB 952

as to seizure of property in Halsbury's Laws of England[1]. The paragraph is very much cut down from what it must have originally contained. It simply reads in this way:

'A constable effecting a search should not take property which is in no way connected with the offence alleged to have been committed by the person arrested; but if, in the course of the search, he comes upon other property which shows a person to be implicated in some other offence, he may take that property also, provided he acts reasonably and retains it no longer than is necessary. The police are entitled to retain property relevant to the offence charged for the purpose of its production in court but may not retain it for longer than the period required for the trial or any appeal.'

The first sentence would be relevant if the plaintiff were being prosecuted for an offence against the Exchange Control Act 1947, but it is only the second sentence which is directly relevant to this appeal, and it compels us to allow it unless counsel for the plaintiff is right in his submission to us, as to the judge, that the production at the trial of the actual notes is not necessary in this case. He relies on *Gordon v Chief Comr of Metropolitan Police*[2], per Fletcher Moulton LJ, and the observation of Lord Denning MR in *Ghani v Jones*[3]: 'If a copy [of an article such as a passport or letter] will suffice, it should be made and the original returned.' I find it impossible to assume that the plaintiff will continue to admit the police officers' evidence about the notes or to be sure that the actual notes will not help the prosecution to prove to the jury the offences charged in the indictment. Juries may be irrational, but I do not regard it as unreasonable to believe that circumstances difficult to predict may arise at the trial in which the police witnesses may be discredited or handicapped in their evidence by being unable to produce the actual notes to the court and jury. It is not necessary to suppose that the plaintiff may, at the trial, go back on the admission made on his instructions to counsel appearing for him before us, although nothing could stop him from doing so, and accuse the police officers of 'planting' the notes on him. It is only necessary to remind oneself how unpredictable is the course of a criminal trial and how important it is for the Crown to prove every link in the chain of evidence leading to proof of the offences charged. These notes seem to me to differ from the money found on the plaintiff in much more than their value. They are also wholly different from the passport, notebook and letters released in *Ghani v Jones*[4]. There there was no charge preferred against the owners or possessors of the documents and I am by no means sure that if they had been charged Lord Denning MR would have considered that copies of those documents would have sufficed and the originals could be released. Had these notes been made exhibits, their release before the conclusion of the plaintiff's trial would have been more difficult, as counsel for the plaintiff concedes. If I had then been asked to release them to the plaintiff, I would have refused to do so, and I would refuse to do so, although they are not exhibits because they will, in my opinion, 'form material evidence in his prosecution' for the offences of conspiracy and receiving on which he has been committed for trial: see *Dillon v O'Brien and Davis*[5], per Palles CB.

Counsel for the plaintiff has called our attention to three old decisions at nisi prius in which (before the days of legal aid) judges ordered sums of money found on prisoners to be restored to them in order to enable them to make their defence, where the money was in no way material to the charges on which they were to be tried: see *R v Barnett*[6], *R v O'Donnell*[7] and *R v Rooney*[8]. If I could say that these notes were in no way material to the

---

1   11 Halsbury's Laws (4th Edn) para 126
2   [1910] 2 KB 1080 at 1094, [1908–10] All ER Rep 192 at 198
3   [1969] 3 All ER 1700 at 1705, [1970] 1 QB 693 at 709
4   [1969] 3 All ER 1700, [1970] 1 QB 693
5   (1887) 16 Cox CC 245 at 249
6   (1829) 3 C & P 600
7   (1835) 7 C & P 138
8   (1836) 7 C & P 515

charges against the plaintiff, I would follow those decisions and let the injunction stand. But I cannot say that, knowing the circumstances disclosed in the evidence of the police officers and set out in the defence, including the discovery of the notes hidden with stolen clock parts in a concealed wall cupboard, but not knowing what the plaintiff's evidence about these notes and his dealings in antiques may be.

If the officers can give their evidence about them, that evidence is material to the charges and the only question is the narrow one: are the actual notes a reasonably necessary, and valuable, part of that evidence? I am not sure that that is the same question as the question: what is the best evidence? The judge called the fact that the notes were seized the best evidence but I doubt if the officers' evidence of seizure is 'better' than the evidence of the notes themselves. If the two questions differ, I would ask the first and give it an affirmative answer.

I was unfavourably impressed, as I think was the judge, by the reliance of the police officers on reasons other than the importance of these notes as evidence for the Crown.

But police officers are naturally concerned with criticisms which the court may make; the value of the notes as evidence is stressed in Det Sgt Ware's affidavit, though not so prominently as in the defence; and it is for the court to give proper weight to the views of the police but to make up its own mind and decide for itself whether justice requires that the original notes should be available as evidence.

I hesitate to give effect to what may appear speculative in balancing the public interest in the conviction of the guilty against the right of the individual, presumed innocent, not to be deprived of his own property, even for a time, unless public policy requires the deprivation and makes it lawful. Where a man is charged with conspiracy and the scope of relevant evidence is thereby enlarged, the court must be even more careful not to confiscate his property without justification. In all the circumstances of this case, however, I conclude that the balance tips on the side of the public interest and I differ, with hesitation, from the judge's opinion that the notes are not the best evidence and, therefore, of benefit to no one, judge, jury or prosecution, in tending to prove the offences charged. I would accordingly allow the appeal on this ground.

The second point has had a chequered career in this court and undergone more than one metamorphosis. Counsel for the commissioner first asked us to consider the power of the court of trial to make a restitution order under s 28(1)(c) of the Theft Act 1968, as substituted by the Criminal Justice Act 1972, in place of its power to make a forfeiture order under s 43 of the Powers of Criminal Courts Act 1973. Counsel for the plaintiff did not object to the substitution although the earlier section was not pleaded in the defence, or argued before the judge, or raised in the notice of appeal. Then counsel for the commissioner asked us to consider the powers given by both sections and a third, again relied on for the first time in this court, the power to make a compensation order given by s 35 of the Powers of Criminal Courts Act 1973. Counsel for the plaintiff continued to be accommodating and we have considered all three powers. But at an early stage of our consideration counsel for the commissioner abandoned s 28(1)(c) as inapplicable to this case and I say no more about that enactment except that in its substituted form, set out in Sch 5 to the Criminal Justice Act 1972, it is clearly confined to cases in which stolen goods are no longer in the possession of the person convicted but can be specified and valued, whereas in this case the commissioner concedes that all the stolen goods referred to in the indictment were either in the possession of the plaintiff and therefore recoverable themselves or unspecified and therefore incapable of valuation.

We were therefore left to consider whether the commissioner was justified in retaining these notes until the trial was concluded because their retention would enable the court of trial to consider making an order on conviction under s 35 or s 43 of the 1973 Act. But once more the point for our consideration took on a new shape, this time at the request of counsel for the plaintiff and without objection from counsel for the commissioner. Whereas the point, as stated and decided by the judge, was whether the possibility of the court of trial making an order was too speculative to make the retention of the notes lawful, counsel for the plaintiff challenged the court's power to make any order under either section if the evidence was not material and the judge was right on his first ground. He assured us that he had taken this point, fundamental to his case and of general importance, before the judge, but there is no trace of it in the note of his judgment, and it took counsel for the commissioner and the court by surprise. It is nevertheless an important point on which we have heard full argument because both parties wish us to decide it, and I think we should decide it, raising, as it does, an issue of interest alike to the police and to persons subjected to arrest and search by the police.

Counsel submits on behalf of the plaintiff that the commissioner has no right to detain any property for any purpose, including compensation, restitution or forfeiture, unless it is reasonably required as material evidence or it is goods alleged to be stolen or the fruits of goods alleged to be stolen. If these sums of money are not so required, contrary to what I have decided, admittedly not being goods, or the fruits of goods, alleged to be stolen, they must be returned. Counsel submits, on behalf of the commissioner, that on the contrary the commissioner has a right to detain for those particular purposes any property reasonably suspected of being connected with the crimes charged or, I think he must logically and did ultimately submit, with any crime. Even if these sums of money are not so required, they may be detained for those purposes.

It is the plaintiff's case that the authorities establish a right at common law to seize and detain as long as reasonably necessary money like other property; but no one, not even a police officer, has a right at common law or under any statute to detain money or other property belonging to a person being prosecuted or sued simply to provide security or compensation or punishment or satisfaction of a judgment. In *Jagger v Jagger*[1] Scrutton LJ said:

'I am not aware of any statutory or other power in the court to restrain a person from dealing with his property at a time when no order against him has been made.'

Matrimonial legislation has made inroads on that since then. The courts have qualified it recently by granting *Mareva*[2] injunctions. But the courts will not permit any general encroachment on a defendant's right to do what he likes with his own property by freezing his assets in the hands of the police or anybody else: see the comments of Lord Hailsham of St Marylebone in *The Siskina*[3], with which Lord Simon of Glaisdale and Lord Russell of Killowen agreed[4].

The common law can develop in many ways, but I would accept it as clear law that, generally speaking, the right or power to deprive a defendant of his property even for a time, whether in criminal or in civil proceedings, for the purpose of punishing him by forfeiture or compensating the victim of his wrongdoing by any form of restitution can only be conferred by express and unambiguous statutory provisions. There is admittedly no such provision in the three enactments on which the plaintiff here relies, even if they are not construed as strictly as a criminal statute should be: see eg *R v Hinde*[5].

Counsel for the commissioner answers this point not by challenging that statement of what the common law right to detain property *was* but by asking us to develop or expand the common law by asserting that there *is* now a power to detain it for the exercise of the new powers conferred on criminal courts by those three enactments. His submission in its final form was that two of these powers, those conferred by s 28 of the 1968 Act and s 35 of the 1973 Act, give speedy relief to losers of property or other victims of crime by restitution or compensation, an object which would be to a considerable extent defeated without the extended power he asks us to assert; and one of those powers, the power of forfeiture conferred by s 43 of the 1973 Act, is conferred in language which envisages or assumes or implies that extended power. And that extended power is necessary, and

1 [1926] P 93 at 102, [1926] All ER Rep 613 at 618
2 See *Mareva Compania Naviera SA v International Bulkcarriers Ltd* [1975] 2 Lloyd's Rep 509
3 [1977] 3 All ER 803 at 828–829, [1977] 3 WLR 818 at 829–830
4 [1977] 3 All ER 803 at 830, [1977] 3 WLR 818 at 831
5 (1977) 66 Cr App R 213 at 216

clearly regarded by Parliament as necessary, to defeat the sophisticated crime which threatens society in this country today.

I find no warrant for that expansion or assumption in these enactments, their object or the language in which that object has been expressed.

I need not read s 28. It certainly gives the court wide powers to order restitution, but it certainly cannot apply to these notes, and counsel for the commissioner admits that it does not by itself support the extension of police powers for which he contends. Section 35 provides:

'(1) Subject to the provisions of this Part of this Act, a court by or before which a person is convicted of an offence, in addition to dealing with him in any other way, may, on application or otherwise, make an order (in this Act referred to as "a compensation order") requiring him to pay compensation for any personal injury, loss or damage resulting from that offence or any other offence which is taken into consideration by the court in determining sentence . . .

'(4) In determining whether to make a compensation order against any person, and in determining the amount to be paid by any person under such an order, the court shall have regard to his means so far as they appear or are known to the court.'

As counsel for the plaintiff points out, nowhere in the section is there any reference to the source from which compensation is to be paid for loss or damage resulting from an offence. The section itself confers no power to seize or retain anything, and again counsel for the commissioner can find in it, by itself, no support for this contention of his. But he does claim support for it in the remaining enactment, to which I now turn. Section 43 provides:

'(1) Where a person is convicted of an offence punishable on indictment with imprisonment for a term of two years or more and the court by or before which he is convicted is satisfied that any property which was in his possession or under his control at the time of his apprehension—(a) has been used for the purpose of committing, or facilitating the commission of, any offence; or (b) was intended by him to be used for that purpose; the court may make an order under this section in respect of that property . . .

'(3) An order under this section shall operate to deprive the offender of his rights, if any, in the property to which it relates, and the property shall (if not already in their possession) be taken into the possession of the police.

'(4) The Police (Property) Act 1897 shall apply, with the following modifications, to property which is in the possession of the police by virtue of this section . . .'

and then the subsection goes on to state the modifications.

This section, too, confers no power to seize or retain anything. Counsel for the plaintiff conceded that it applies to money (compare the definition of 'property' in s 4(1) of the 1968 Act); and it covers property which was in a convicted person's possession at the time of his apprehension but is, at the date of conviction, already in the possession of the police. It also covers property which is not then in their possession.

Now it may be that the powers conferred by these three sections could be more extensively used if the police had their powers of detaining property extended as counsel for the commissioner submits that they have been or should be. But it cannot be said that there is not considerable scope for the exercise of the court's powers under all three sections without any extension of the powers of the police. There is nothing to prevent a court taking into account money seized and returned to a convicted thief or receiver before conviction as part of his means and requiring him to pay compensation accordingly. There is nothing to prevent a court from depriving him of property used, or intended for use, for purposes of crime, whether that property is money or the more usual motor car and whether it is in the possession of the convicted thief or receiver or of the police or some other person. Indeed, counsel for the commissioner conceded that he got no help from s 35, or from the Theft Act 1968, but he argued that the language of s 43 did presuppose that the police had the power to take into possession and keep in their possession property used, or intended for use, for the purposes of committing any offence. He relied particularly on the words in parenthesis in s 43(3), contending that they postulated that property so used, or intended to be so used, could lawfully be in the possession of the police before an order was made under the section. But the words in parenthesis could, in my judgment, apply to property used, for example, for the purpose of committing the particular offence with which the convicted person had been charged, and they do not begin to suggest, let alone require, the existence or addition of an extended police power to detain his property.

If such a power or powers as counsel for the commissioner wants the police to have, or the courts to assert that they have, are now required for the protection of the public against the increase of crime, it is for Parliament, not for the courts, to grant them. Until I listened to this argument, I had never heard that the statute book was a source of the common law. The argument has nothing to commend it but its audacity. Even counsel for the commissioner could not make it viable. I reject it.

I therefore conclude that the commissioner has no right to detain these notes for the purpose of enabling the court of trial to consider making an order under s 43 or any other statutory provision which we have been asked to consider. I would uphold the plaintiff's objection in the form which it has now taken and would not allow the appeal on this ground.

It is therefore unnecessary to consider the plaintiff's objection in its first form to the commissioner's argument on this point and to decide whether the judge was right in holding that the court of trial was so unlikely to exercise its statutory power over these notes that their detention for that purpose could not be justified.

There remains the fourth ground in the notice of appeal:

> '(4) It would be against public policy for the [commissioner] to be ordered to return the large amount of foreign currency in American dollars and Italian lire to the Plaintiff even though no criminal charges have been brought against the Plaintiff in respect of his possession of the said currency.'

This would appear to allege in support of the appeal what has not yet been pleaded in the defence or alleged in any prosecution, that the plaintiff, in possessing the foreign currency seized, was committing an offence against s 2 of the Exchange Control Act 1947.

On this topic, as on other points in the case, I agree with all that will be said by Roskill LJ in the judgment which I have had the benefit of reading in draft. I would allow the appeal and discharge the injunction on the ground that the production of all the notes retained by the commissioner may be relevant and necessary to the case for the prosecution at the plaintiff's trial the week after next.

ROSKILL LJ. This appeal raises an important point of principle in relation to police powers. It is the duty of the courts to protect the freedom and property of the individual against arbitrary action by the executive, whatever the form which the particular action may take. But the courts, when performing that duty, must always have in mind that the administration of justice must not be hampered and that from time to time the rights of individuals have to yield to a wider public interest which requires the abridgment of individual rights. The Commissioner of Police of the Metropolis claims that the present is a case in which that wider interest must prevail over the private interest of the plaintiff, which is immediately to receive back a substantial sum which by concession is his but of the possession of which he was lawfully deprived at the time of his arrest in March 1977. The plaintiff, on the other hand, asserts the paramountcy of his personal right of property. The judge, Wien J, decided this matter in favour of the plaintiff. Hence this appeal by the commissioner.

The facts admit of no dispute and have been fully stated by Stephenson LJ. Both the sterling and the foreign currency, possession of which the plaintiff seeks to recover from the commissioner, are admitted to be the plaintiff's property. For brevity I shall call these 'the money', and I shall ignore, in this part of the judgment, the question raised by the court itself (it was not raised before Wien J) and indicated in the notice of appeal of the commissioner, whether, all else apart, the provisions of the Exchange Control Act 1947 in any event operate to bar the plaintiff's claim to recover possession of the foreign currency, the plaintiff having no Treasury permission to hold that foreign currency or to refrain from disposing of it otherwise than in accordance with the 1947 Act.

It was not disputed before us that the search which led to the discovery of this money was lawful and that the seizure of the money following the search was also lawful. Counsel for the plaintiff, did, however, reserve the right to argue the contrary elsewhere, if necessary. The sole question for decision is whether the continued retention of the money by the commissioner is lawful. As already stated, the judge held that it was not. Before dealing with the substantial issues in this appeal I would say something of the procedure which has been adopted in this case, no doubt with the best of intentions, to secure a speedy decision but with what I would regard as somewhat irregular results. In the first instance, the plaintiff, after issuing his writ, sought judgment against the defendant under RSC Ord. 14. I am afraid I do not begin to follow how it could seriously have been thought that the commissioner did not have at least an arguable defence to this claim. Yet an articled clerk in the employment of the plaintiff's solicitors permitted himself to swear he believed that there was no defence to the action. Not surprisingly, in those circumstances, Master Elton gave unconditional leave to the commissioner to defend. For my part I regard it as quite wrong that RSC Ord 14 proceedings should have been started. The plaintiff then appealed to the judge in chambers still somewhat surprisingly seeking judgment under RSC Ord 14. But he also, by a fresh summons, added a claim against the commissioner for a mandatory injunction for the delivery up of the money. The master, of course, had had no power to grant such a mandatory injunction had it initially been sought, but the judge in chambers had such power. Conveniently the appeal in the RSC Ord 14 proceedings and the summons for the mandatory injunction were heard by Wien J together. The judge dealt with the matter, seemingly without objection from either party, by making no order on the appeal in the RSC Ord 14 proceedings, but, considering that the plaintiff's contentions were correct by granting a mandatory injunction against the commissioner. Since such a mandatory injunction must dispose of the action if this money were handed over to the plaintiff, in my view it ought only to have been granted if there were, in all the circumstances, clearly no defence to this action, as was the position in *Ghani v Jones*[1]. Yet if there were no defence to the action judgment should have been entered under RSC Ord 14 for the plaintiff. It seems to me, with all respect to the judge, that his two orders were mutually inconsistent, though this appears to have been almost by consent.

Before us the appeal has been argued on a far wider basis than it was before the judge. Indeed, by the time the argument was concluded the case might well have been unrecognisable by him or by anyone present before him. Both sides sought our decision irrespective of the matters which had been pleaded or argued before the judge, and we were pressed to deal with this appeal in effect as if it were an appeal from a decision on the trial of an action determined on an agreed statement of facts or on a preliminary point of law. In order to help the parties on a matter which we were told required urgent decision before the plaintiff's trial begins early next month we agreed to proceed on this basis, but in my view our consent so to do must not be taken as approval by this court of the course which was adopted below, which strikes me as not only irregular and not complying with the principles on which mandatory injunctions are granted, but as resulting in two mutually inconsistent orders. The factual position in *Ghani v Jones*[1], where a mandatory injunction was granted notwithstanding that it is in effect disposed of the action, was very different. See the final passage of the judgment of Talbot J[2]; a decision subsequently approved in this court. But in that case there were no RSC Ord 14 proceedings.

---

1   [1969] 3 All ER 1700, [1970] 1 QB 693
2   [1969] 3 All ER 720 at 723, [1970] 1 QB 693 at 698

The commissioner sought to defend his continued retention of the money on two main grounds. Whilst he accepted that it could not be justified on the ground that the money itself was the subject of a criminal charge, he claimed that it was material evidence in relation to both the conspiracy and the substantive charges which the plaintiff had to face at his forthcoming trial, or at the least was, in the circumstances in which the money had been found in close physical proximity to certain stolen parts of a grandfather clock, sufficiently closely connected with the subject-matter of those charges as to be liable to be lawfully retained by him until the conclusion of the relevant criminal proceedings.

Alternatively he argued that he was entitled to retain the money until the conclusion of these criminal proceedings in order that the money might then be available in the event of the plaintiff's conviction so that the court of trial might, if it thought fit, thereupon avail itself of the money for the purpose of making a restitution order under s 28 of the Theft Act 1968 (as amended), or one or more compensation orders under s 35 of the Powers of Criminal Courts Act 1973, or a forfeiture order under s 43 of that last-mentioned Act. Of those three relevant statutory provisions only s 43 had been pleaded in the commissioner's defence, but no objection was raised before us on behalf of the plaintiff to the commissioner's reliance on those two other statutory provisions. These last-mentioned contentions are, we are told, of general importance to police forces throughout the country.

It seems apparent from an affidavit of one of the police officers involved in the case that that officer feared that if the money were not retained so as to facilitate the making of one or more of these orders in the event of the plaintiff's conviction there might be sharp judicial criticism of the police for releasing the money to the plaintiff so that it was no longer available for this purpose, a point of view of an experienced police officer which I can readily understand.

In the further alternative, counsel for the commissioner argued that if, as the plaintiff contended, none of these statutory provisions justified the continued retention of the money, this court ought, and I quote counsel for the commissioner's words, 'to develop the common law to assert that power' which the commissioner claimed to exist in order to justify that retention which ex hypothesi those three recent statutory provisions did not of themselves justify, a proposition which counsel for the plaintiff at once roundly condemned as offending against all the ordinary canons of statutory construction.

Though the various questions were argued before us in the order in which I have just indicated, I propose to deal with the three statutory provisions first, for, as will shortly emerge, I find myself unable to find in any of them any justification for the continued retention of the money. I will deal first with s 28 of the Theft Act 1968 (as amended). Reliance was placed, on behalf of the commissioner, on the provisions of s 28(1)(c) which, as substituted, reads:

> '... the court may order that a sum not exceeding the value of the first-mentioned goods shall be paid, out of any money of the person convicted which was taken out of his possession on his apprehension, to any person who, if those goods were in the possession of the person convicted, would be entitled to recover them from him.'

It was argued at first that it was enough to justify the making of an order under s 28(1)(c) if the money so taken could be shown to have some connection with reference to theft. It seems to me that the argument for the commissioner overlooks the importance of the opening words of para (c). There is there a reference back to 'the first-mentioned goods'. That, in the context, must mean the goods referred to in the opening of sub-s (1), namely goods which have been stolen. That is the first prerequisite for making an order. The second is that someone, in this case the plaintiff, has been convicted of some offence with reference to the theft; it does not matter whether or not stealing is the gist of that offence. Then the court may, under para (a), order anyone, not necessarily the convicted person, having possession or control of those stolen goods to restore them to anyone entitled to recover them from him, or, under para (b), where those goods have, as it were, been converted in whole or in part into other goods, order those other goods to be similarly delivered up, or, under para (c), in a case where, if those stolen goods were still in the possession of the convicted person, the person claiming the money could have recovered possession of those goods from him, order a sum not exceeding the value of those goods to be paid out of any money of the convicted person which was taken out of his possession on his apprehension. When faced with this difficulty, that is, the absence of any relevant stolen goods, I did not understand counsel for the commissioner seriously further to press his argument under this section.

I turn next to s 35 of the 1973 Act. I would observe that whereas both s 28 of the 1968 Act and s 43 of the 1973 Act refer to money in the former case and to property in the latter case as the possible source of subject-matter of any order which the court may make under those sections, s 35 makes no similar reference. It simply empowers the making of a compensation order. The section is wholly silent as to the source of funds whence any order made by the court is to be satisfied. Other statutory provisions constitute an elaborate code whereby compensation orders may be enforced by the court, by imprisonment in appropriate cases: see the discussion of these powers in *R v Bunce*[1]. Further, the court is required, as has frequently been emphasised in the Criminal Division of this court, to have regard to the means of the offender against whom such an order is sought following conviction. Counsel for the plaintiff drew our attention to the principle stated in *Jagger v Jagger*[2], that in the absence of any statutory power to the contrary a person is not to be restrained by the court from dealing with his own property as he wishes at a time when no order of a court of competent jurisdiction has been made against him: see especially the judgment of Scrutton LJ[3]. He also drew our attention to the statement of the law by Lord Hailsham of St Marylebone in *The Siskina*[4], that generally speaking an unsecured creditor cannot convert himself into a partially secured creditor merely by bringing an action against an alleged debtor and then seeking to freeze his assets by injunction, a principle now admittedly somewhat eroded, at least in the case of foreign based defendants with assets in this country, by the so-called *Mareva*[5] injunction. But if the commissioner is entitled legitimately to claim to retain moneys found in an accused person's possession, admittedly his own and not the subject of any charge, against the contingency of a court, on that accused person's conviction (if any) at some future and maybe distant date, making one or more compensation orders against him, the defendant is almost constituting himself and other police authorities similarly placed a stakeholder or perhaps a trustee for a class of possible future beneficiaries who would or might thereby become almost partially secured creditors at the expense of others perhaps less fortunate. I cannot think that Parliament intended this result, nor can I read s 35 as authorising the police to retain money, not the subject of a charge and not required as evidence, found in the possession of an accused person and that person's property, against any such contingency. In truth s 35 was designed to afford a cheap and convenient form of relief to persons dishonestly deprived of the property or otherwise injured or afflicted. It was not concerned with anything else.

Finally as to s 43, although from the terms of the note which we have of the judge's judgment this matter appears to have been argued before him on the basis that, though s 43 did give the requisite power, the present was not a suitable case for the exercise of that power. Counsel for the plaintiff, before us, contended that the section gave no such power, saying that he had advanced this argument before the judge. Section 43 differs from s 35 in that sub-s (3) does contemplate that property will or may have remained in police possession from arrest until the conclusion of the trial. But the section is contained in a criminal statute and it must be strictly construed: see *R v Hinde*[6] and, more recently, *R v*

1   (1978) 66 Cr App R 109
2   [1926] P 93, [1926] All ER Rep 613
3   [1926] P 93 at 102, [1926] All ER Rep 613 at 618
4   [1977] 3 All ER 803 at 828, [1977] 3 WLR 818 at 829
5   [1975] 2 Lloyd's Rep 509
6   (1977) 64 Cr App R 213

Thompson[1]. The original purpose of this section is well known. It may be that the language of the section is wide enough to justify the making of orders for the forfeiture of money as being 'property' within this section provided that the other prerequisites set out in the section for the making of the order are satisfied. But I can find nothing in the section to justify the police retaining moneys of his own which have been found on an accused person at the time of his arrest merely against the possible contingency that an order may thereafter be made under s 43.

Ultimately counsel for the commissioner found himself constrained to admit that in none of the three statutory provisions could he point to any specific power conferred on the police to retain money admittedly lawfully seized in the first instance solely in anticipation of the possibility of orders being made under one or more of those sections in the event of conviction. But he argued that the common law should now be developed and extended by the court to justify such retention which the language of the relevant statutory provisions does not justify. With respect, this is an impossible argument. Compensation orders, restitution orders and forfeiture orders are, in their modern form, the creation of recent statutes. Before those creations the common law could not and did not justify the retention of such moneys for use for purposes which did not then exist. When the power to make the orders was given, the statutes were silent on this crucial question. To extend the common law to justify what Parliament has not empowered is to write into the statutes that which has not been included in them. I know of no warrant for such construction. If the police require such powers for this purpose, and one can appreciate that in this day and age it might be convenient for them to have them, the police must seek the requisite powers from Parliament, if they can obtain them. This further argument therefore fails.

If, therefore, this appeal is to succeed it must be on other grounds. I agree with counsel for the plaintiff when he says that if the commissioner is to succeed he must show that there is a common law power which justifies that which he claims to be entitled to do. Counsel for the plaintiff relied on the five propositions stated by Lord Denning MR in his judgment in *Ghani v Jones*[2]. As already stated, counsel for the plaintiff did not seek to challenge the legality of the seizure of this money. But he argued that this money was not required as material evidence against the plaintiff, either on the conspiracy charge or on the substantive charges of dishonestly handling stolen property, and that therefore the police had no right to retain it further. He accepted that if this money could be shown to be material evidence either on the conspiracy charge or on the substantive charges, there would be a right to retain it as such evidence until the conclusion of the trial. Counsel for the plaintiff relied on the statement of the police officer who made the search and found the money, which was put in evidence at the magistrates' court at the time of the committal proceedings against the plaintiff and his co-accused. This statement related how and where the money was found. The money itself was not made an exhibit at the magistrates' court. Counsel for the plaintiff said that the plaintiff would be willing at the trial to admit the whole of the contents of that officer's statement without his being called. The material fact was, he contended, and Wien J accepted this, that the money had been found in the circumstances related in the statement, but proof of that fact did not require the production of the money itself in evidence and this was, he argued, why the money itself had not been exhibited in the magistrates' court.

For my part I do not attach great importance to the failure formally to exhibit the money though, had it been so exhibited, counsel for the plaintiff's argument might, as he frankly accepted, have been more difficult for him to advance. There may well have been administrative reasons for not exhibiting it.

It seems to me that the line of authorities to which counsel for the plaintiff referred, and to which I do not find it necessary to refer in detail, show that there is no general power in the police, when they have lawfully seized property which is thereafter not the subject of any charge and is clearly shown not to have been stolen, to retain that property as against

---

1   (1978) 66 Cr App R 130
2   [1969] 3 All ER 1700 at 1705, [1970] 1 QB 693 at 708–709

the person entitled to possession of it against some uncertain future contingency. The police must be able to justify the retention of such property in such circumstances on some clearly ascertainable ground. To my mind the only question in this case is whether it can be predicted with sufficient certainty that under no circumstances, irrespective of the fact that that money was not exhibited in the committal proceedings, will it become necessary to adduce that money in evidence at the trial which starts next month, so that it can now, without risk to the administration of justice, be safely returned to the plaintiff. If it became necessary for the prosecution to adduce that money in evidence, it would obviously gravely hamper the administration of justice if that money had been handed back and spent, so that it was no longer available to be put in evidence whenever required. Whatever counsel for the plaintiff's present instructions are (and, of course, I unreservedly accept that he has received those instructions I have mentioned) as to the course which the plaintiff at present intends to take at the trial, this will be a long trial and it seems to me quite impossible to predict, at this juncture, every turn which that long trial may ultimately take. It is not difficult to envisage circumstances in which it might become highly material for that money to be produced, either on behalf of the Crown or of the defence, even though the Crown do not seek to say that the money itself was stolen and have not so far exhibited it as part of the police officer's evidence. I think, therefore, on this narrow ground the commissioner is entitled to retain this money until the conclusion of the criminal proceedings against the plaintiff, and in this respect I venture to disagree with the judge. On this ground I would allow the appeal and discharge the injunction.

So far I have said nothing about the position under the Exchange Control Act 1947. This Act, of course, does not touch the sterling which was found in the plaintiff's possession. But I am quite unable to see how it can be said that the plaintiff's possession of the dollars and the lire in question was otherwise than unlawful, having regard to the clear statutory obligation on him under s 2 of the 1947 Act to sell that foreign currency to the Treasury or to an authorised dealer unless, of course, he could obtain authority to retain that foreign currency in his own possession. There was no suggestion in evidence that he had any such authority. Although no point was taken before the judge under the 1947 Act, the point is now taken, albeit without specific reference to the Act, in the notice of appeal. If the court were of the opinion that the plaintiff's possession of any part of the money was unlawful, whether under the Act or otherwise, it would be the court's duty to take the point of its own motion irrespective of whether it had been raised by the defendant, and this the court has done. Ultimately I did not understand counsel for the plaintiff to contend that the plaintiff's original possession of the foreign currency had been lawful. But he strenuously argued that he, the plaintiff, had not been prosecuted for any offence under the 1947 Act, though the police had known of his possession and apparent breach of the statute for a long time. As to this point, I do not think it impossible that he may still be prosecuted for such an offence.

Principally, however, counsel for the plaintiff relied on the decision of this court in *Gordon v Chief Comr of Metropolitan Police*[1], where a predecessor of the commissioner sought to justify his refusal to return moneys to the plaintiff which were the proceeds of street bookmaking on the ground of their supposed unlawful origin. Particular reliance was placed on passages[2] in the judgments of Vaughan-Williams, Fletcher Moulton, and Buckley LJJ. But the facts of *Gordon's* case[1] are clearly distinguishable from those in the present case. There was nothing unlawful about the plaintiff's possession of the proceeds of street bookmaking. He was entitled to retain those whatever their origin, even though he might not have been able to sue to recover for the bets from those who owed them. But his right to immediate possession of that money was undoubted. In the present case the plaintiff's initial possession was unlawful, for he ought to have sold the foreign currency to the Treasury or to an authorised dealer. Here the seizure of the foreign currency by the police was perfectly lawful. Ought the court, then, to lend its aid to grant an equitable remedy to a plaintiff who, in relation to the foreign currency, had no lawful right to immediate possession, to enable him to regain immediate possession from the defendant whose taking of the foreign currency from the plaintiff under the search warrant was lawful? In my view, whether or not the maxim ex turpi causa non oritur actio strictly applies, it would not be right, in those circumstances, to grant a mandatory injunction for the return of the foreign currency, even if, contrary to my view, the plaintiff were entitled to recover on other grounds. And if it were wrong for those reasons to grant equitable relief in relation to the foreign currency, I would not think it right, in those circumstances, for the court in its discretion to grant the like relief in relation to the sterling.

I do not wish to rest my decision, in a case which raises wider issues, on this last-mentioned ground, but even had I come to the opposite conclusion in the plaintiff's favour on the matters on which I have decided in favour of the commissioner I would have thought that this last-mentioned ground operated as a complete bar to the grant of a mandatory injunction for the recovery of the dollars and the lire, and that the court, in its discretion, should, in those circumstances, refuse the like relief in relation to the sterling.

Since writing this judgment I have had the advantage of reading in draft the judgment just delivered by Stephenson LJ. I find myself in complete agreement with him on all points.

In the result I would allow the appeal and discharge the injunction.

Appeal allowed; injunction discharged; leave to appeal to the House of Lords refused.

Solicitors: *Solicitor, Metropolitan Police*; *Davis Hanson* (for the plaintiff).

L I Zysman Esq Barrister.

a

Pearson and others v Inland Revenue Commissioners

CHANCERY DIVISION
FOX J
b 26th, 27th, 28th, 31st JULY 1978

Capital transfer tax – Settlement – Interest in possession – Beneficiary entitled under settlement to income of property subject to trustees' power to accumulate – Whether beneficiary's interest a present interest or an interest in reversion or remainder – Whether beneficiary's interest an interest in possession – Finance Act 1975, Sch 5, para 6(2).

c

Under a settlement made in 1964 the settlor settled a trust fund on such one or more of his children and their issue as the trustees should appoint during a specified period ('the trust period'). The settlement further provided that until and subject to such appointment the d trustees were to accumulate so much (if any) of the income of the trust fund as they thought fit, during a period of 21 years from the date of the settlement. Subject to that, the trustees were to hold the capital and income of the trust fund in equal shares absolutely for such of the children of the settlor as attained the age of 21 or married under that age. The settlor had three daughters, including F, and by the end of February 1974 all three had attained the age of 21 years. In exercise of their overriding power of appointment, the e trustees, by a deed of appointment dated 20th March 1976, irrevocably appointed that the sum of £16,000 was to be held on trust to pay the income to F during her life or the trust period, whichever was the shorter. The Crown claimed that by reason of the existence of the trustees' power of accumulation F had no interest in possession in any part of the trust fund prior to the appointment, and accordingly, when F became entitled to an interest in possession in the £16,000 on the execution of the deed of appointment, the trustees f became liable to capital transfer tax under para 6(2)[a] of Sch 5 to the Finance Act 1975. The trustees contended that since all three daughters had attained the age of 21 prior to 26th March 1974 (the date on which, by virtue of s 20(5) of the 1975 Act, dispositions could become chargeable transfers) they had by then already become entitled to interests in possession in the trust fund and accordingly the appointment of the £16,000 to F on 20th March 1976 did not involve a capital distribution attracting liability to capital transfer tax.

g

Held – An interest in possession existed where the interest conferred the right to present enjoyment of the subject-matter of the interest. A person entitled to the income of property subject to a power of accumulation was entitled to a present interest giving a present right to whatever income was not accumulated. It followed therefore that, at the time of the appointment, F was already entitled to an interest in possession in the trust h fund and accordingly the appointment did not involve a capital distribution out of the trust fund that was liable to capital transfer tax (see p 277 j, p 278 d, p 284 h, p 285 f g and p 286 a, post).

Attorney-General v Power [1906] 2 IR 272 and *Gartside v Inland Revenue Comrs* [1968] 1 All ER 121 distinguished.

j
_____

a   Paragraph 6(2) provides: 'Where a person becomes entitled to an interest in possession in the whole or any part of the property comprised in a settlement at a time when no such interest subsists in the property or that part, a capital distribution shall be treated as being made out of the property or that part of the property; and the amount of the distribution shall be taken to be equal to the value at that time of the property or, if the interest is in part only of that property, of that part.'

Notes

For the meaning of interest in possession, see 19 Halsbury's Laws (4th Edn) para 636.
   For the Finance Act 1975, Sch 5, para 6, see 45 Halsbury's Statutes (3rd Edn) 1889.

Cases referred to in judgment

Allen-Meyrick's Will Trusts, Re, Mangnall v Allen-Meyrick [1966] 1 All ER 740, [1966] 1 WLR
   499, Digest (Cont Vol B) 733, *3435*.
Attorney-General v Power [1906] 2 IR 272, 21 Digest (Repl) 33, **40*.
Buttle's Will Trusts, Re, Buttle v Inland Revenue Comrs [1977] 3 All ER 1039, [1977] 1 WLR
   1200, [1977] STC 459, CA.
Gartside v Inland Revenue Comrs [1968] 1 All ER 121, [1968] AC 553, [1968] 2 WLR 277,
   [1967] TR 309, 46 ATC 323, HL, Digest (Cont Vol C) 326, *74b*.
Jones, Re (1884) 26 Ch D 736, 53 LJ Ch 807, 50 LT 466, CA, 40 Digest (Repl) 797, *2776*.
Locker's Settlement Trusts, Re, Meachem v Sachs [1978] 1 All ER 216, [1977] 1 WLR 1323.
Morgan, Re (1883) 24 Ch D 114, 53 LJ Ch 85, 48 LT 964, 40 Digest (Repl) 797, *2775*.

Cases also cited

Aylwin's Trusts, Re (1878) LR 16 Eq 585.
Beit's Will Trusts, Re, Beit v Inland Revenue Comrs [1951] 2 All ER 1002, [1952] Ch 53, CA.
Gourju's Will Trusts, Re, Starling v Custodian of Enemy Property [1942] 2 All ER 605, [1943]
   Ch 24.
Gulbenkian's Settlement Trusts, Re, Whishaw v Stephens [1968] 3 All ER 785, [1970] AC 521,
   HL.
Gulbenkian's Settlement Trusts, Re (No 2), Stephens v Maun [1969] 2 All ER 1173, [1970]
   Ch 408.
McPhail v Doulton [1970] 2 All ER 228, [1971] AC 424, HL.
Master's Settlement, Re, Master v Master [1911] 1 Ch 321.
Sainsbury v Inland Revenue Comrs [1969] 3 All ER 919, [1970] Ch 24.
Weir's Settlement, Re, McPherson v Inland Revenue Comrs [1970] 1 All ER 297, [1971] Ch 145,
   CA.

Adjourned summons

By originating summons issued on 12th July 1977 the plaintiffs, Clifford Pearson, Arthur
Cope Pilkington and John Murray McKenzie ('the trustees'), sought a declaration, inter alia,
that for the purposes of Sch 5 to the Finance Act 1975 a settlement made on 30th
November 1964 by the settlor, Sir Richard Pilkington, was such as to confer on the
principal beneficiaries, namely the daughters of the settlor, Fiona Pilkington ('Fiona'),
Victoria Serena Pilkington ('Serena') and Diana Penelope Julia Pilkington ('Julia'), interests
which on 27th March 1974 were beneficial interests in possession in equal shares in the
trust fund. The facts are set out in the judgment.

D J Nicholls QC and *C H McCall* for the trustees.
Martin Nourse QC and *M C Hart* for the Crown.

Cur adv vult

31st July. **FOX J** read the following judgment: This case concerns a claim for capital
transfer tax under the Finance Act 1975. The issue is the meaning of the expression
'interest in possession' in Part III of and Sch 5 to that Act.

   By a settlement of 30th November 1964 Sir Richard Pilkington ('the settlor') settled a
trust fund on the following trusts: (i) (By cl 2 of the settlement) On trust as to both capital
and income for such one or more of a class consisting of the children of the settlor
(whenever born) and their issue, and the wives, husbands, widows or widowers of such
children and issue as the trustees of the settlement should by deed appoint during a period
(which has not yet determined) referred to in the settlement as the trust period. (ii) (By cl

3 of the settlement) In default of and until and subject to any such appointment on trust: (a) during (in effect) a period of 21 years from the date of the settlement on trust that—

> '... the Trustees shall accumulate so much (if any) of the income of the Trust Fund as they shall think fit by investing the same and the resulting income thereof in any manner hereinafter authorised as an accretion to the capital of the Trust Fund and as one fund with such capital for all purposes',

(b) subject thereto and to the powers by the settlement or by law conferred on the trustees, on trust as to both capital and income of the trust fund for such of the children of the settlor (whenever born) as should attain the age of 21 years or marry under that age, and if more than one in equal shares absolutely with trusts over.

The only other provision of the settlement to which I need refer is cl 21, which is in the following terms:

> 'The Trustees may at any time or times apply any income of the Trust Fund in or towards the payment or discharge of any duties taxes costs charges fees or other outgoings which but for the provisions of this clause would be payable out of or charged upon the capital of the Trust Fund or any part thereof.'

The settlor has had three children. They are Fiona (born in 1947), Serena (born in 1949) and Julia (born in February 1953). The position thus far, therefore, is that subject to the trustees' overriding power of appointment and to the trustees' power to accumulate income during the 21-year period, and to the possibility of partial defeasance on the birth of further children to the settlor, the trust fund was to be held on trust for such of the three daughters as attained 21 years of age or married, and in equal shares absolutely. By the end of February 1974 all three daughters had attained 21 years.

In exercise of the overriding power of appointment, the trustees made the following appointments: (i) By an appointment of 8th August 1974 the trustees revocably appointed that the freehold property 10 Norland Place, London, be held on trust that Serena be entitled to occupy it without payment of rent and without impeachment of waste, she paying the rates and other outgoings and keeping the property in good repair and fully insured. (ii) By an appointment of 6th September 1974 the trustees revocably appointed that the freehold property 9 Selwood Place, London, be held on trust that Fiona be entitled to occupy it without payment of rent and on similar terms to Serena's in respect of 10 Norland Place. (iii) By an appointment of 20th March 1976 the trustees irrevocably appointed that the sum of £16,000 be held on trust to pay the income to Fiona during her life or the trust period referred to in the settlement, whichever should be the shorter. (iv) By an appointment of 8th April 1977 the trustees revocably appointed (a) that the freehold property 43 Cresswell Place, London, be held on trust that Julia be entitled to occupy it during her life without payment of rent and on similar terms to Serena's in respect of 10 Norland Place, (b) that the sum of £16,000 be held on trust for Julia during her life.

The Finance Act 1975 abolished estate duty and introduced capital transfer tax. It received the Royal Assent on 13th March 1975. By s 19 the tax is to be charged on the value transferred by a chargeable transfer. By s 20(2) a transfer of value is any disposition made by a person as a result of which the value of his estate immediately after the disposition is less than it would have been but for the disposition; and the amount by which it is less is the amount transferred by the transfer. By s 20(5) a chargeable transfer is any transfer of value made by an individual after 26th March 1974. By s 22 it is provided that on the death of any person tax should be charged as if immediately before his death he had made a transfer of value and the value transferred by it had been equal to the value of his estate immediately before his death.

Settlements are (by s 21 of the Act) dealt with by Sch 5. The material provisions of that schedule are as follows. By para 3(1) a person entitled to an interest in possession in settled property is treated as beneficially entitled to the property in which the interest subsists. Paragraph 4 provides:

'(1) Where a person beneficially entitled to an interest in possession ... disposes of his interest the disposal—(a) is not a transfer of value; but (b) shall be treated for the purposes of this Schedule as the coming to an end of his interest ...

'(2) Where at any time during the life of a person beneficially entitled to an interest in possession in any property comprised in a settlement his interest comes to an end, tax shall be charged ... as if at that time he had made a transfer of value and the value transferred had been equal to the value of the property in which his interest subsisted.'

Paragraph 6 provides:

'(1) Where a distribution payment is made out of property comprised in a settlement and at the time the payment is made no interest in possession subsists in the property ... out of which the payment is made, the payment is in this Schedule referred to as a capital distribution. [I should interpose here that a 'distribution payment' is by virtue of the definition in para 11(7), in effect, any payment or transfer not of an income nature.]

'(2) Where a person becomes entitled to an interest in possession in the whole or any part of the property comprised in a settlement at a time when no such interest subsists in the property or that part, a capital distribution shall be treated as being made out of the property or that part of the property; and the amount of the distribution shall be taken to be equal to the value at that time of the property or, if the interest is in part only of that property, of that part.'

By para 6(4) tax is charged on any capital distribution as on the value transferred by a chargeable transfer where the value transferred less the tax payable on it is equal to the amount of the capital distribution.

The result of these provisions is that the statute makes a distinction, of fundamental importance to the operation of capital transfer tax in relation to settlements, between settlements where an interest in possession subsists in the settled property and those where it does not. That distinction corresponds (putting the matter very loosely) to the difference between discretionary trusts and fixed interest trusts. Discretionary trusts had a destructive effect on estate duty as a tax, and under the Finance Act 1975 they (or, to be accurate, trusts where there is no interest in possession) are subjected to a regime of greater severity than where an interest in possession exists. They become subject to a charge for tax every ten years; and tax is chargeable when capital is distributed or interests in possession arise in settled property. Credit is given for the previous payment of tax under the periodic charge.

Although the distinction between trusts where there is an interest in possession and those where there is not is fundamental to the operation of the provisions of the Act relating to settlements, the Act contains no useful definition of 'interest in possession' so far as England is concerned. Paragraph 10(10) merely declares that 'interest in possession' means an interest in possession to which an individual is beneficially entitled or, if certain conditions are satisfied, an interest in possession to which a company is beneficially entitled. As regards Scotland, para 1(9) of Sch 5 provides:

'In the application of this Schedule to Scotland, any reference to an interest in possession in settled property is a reference to an interest of any kind under a settlement actually being enjoyed by the person in right of that interest ...'

The matter arises in the present case in the following way. The Crown assert that under the appointment of 20th March 1976 Fiona became entitled to an interest in possession in the £16,000 at a time when no such interest subsisted in that part of the trust fund. They contend that by reason of the existence of the power of accumulation, no such interest in possession existed until the execution of the appointment under which, admittedly, Fiona was entitled to an interest in possession in the £16,000. The Crown claim, therefore, that capital transfer tax became payable by reason of the appointment under para 6(2) of Sch 5. The trustees contend that since, prior to 26th March 1974, all the three daughters had attained 21, there were subsisting interests in possession since they were absolutely entitled in equal shares to all unaccumulated income.

By the originating summons now before me, the trustees ask for a declaration that for the purposes of Sch 5 to the Finance Act 1975 the settlement conferred on the three daughters' interests which on 27th March 1974 were beneficial interests in possession in equal shares of the trust fund. The summons also raises a subsidiary question whether, if the appointment of 20th March 1976 gave rise to a charge to capital transfer tax, in calculating the tax any account falls to be taken of any property comprised in the appointments of 8th August 1974 and 6th September 1974.

I come to the more detailed submissions of the parties on the question of the meaning of 'interest in possession' for the purposes of the present case. The Crown's contentions are as follows: (A) For the purposes of Part III of the Act, there is an interest in possession in settled property if the holder of the interest is entitled to the net income (if any) of the property as it arises but not if the income is subject to a discretion or power in whatever form which can be exercised so as to withhold it from him after it has arisen. (B) On 26th March 1974 there was no interest in possession in the trust fund because: (i) the trustees' duty from time to time was to consider whether income as it arose should (a) be paid to the three daughters in equal shares or (b) be accumulated or (c) be dealt with partly in the one way and partly in the other; (ii) accordingly, the provisions of the settlement were in substance the same as provisions which (a) conferred power on the trustees for a period of 21 years to pay so much (if any) of the income of the trust fund as they should think fit to the three daughters in equal shares, (b) imposed a trust during the like period to accumulate any income not so paid and, subject as aforesaid, (c) gave the capital to the settlor's children in equal shares absolutely; (iii) in the circumstances, since fiscal legislation is concerned with substance and not with form, the present case is on all fours with *Attorney-General v Power*[1] and *Gartside v Inland Revenue Comrs*[2].

The trustees contend (a) that the expression 'interest in possession' is the same as that used in the estate duty legislation; (b) that in the estate duty legislation, and in the law generally, the term has a well recognised meaning; it distinguishes an interest in possession from one in reversion. Under that meaning the existence of a prior power which trustees can exercise or not to deal with income (whether by way of appointment or by way of payment or application to or for the benefit of others or by way of accumulation or by way of use for capital purposes or otherwise) does not of itself convert an interest which would otherwise be an interest in possession into an interest not in possession; (c) that in the Finance Act 1975 the expression has the same meaning as in the estate duty legislation.

In the course of the argument certain matters emerged as being common ground. These are as follows: (i) in the Finance Act 1975 the expression 'interest in possession' has the same meaning as in the estate duty legislation; (ii) that, at the material times, each of the daughters had an 'interest' in the trust fund within the meaning of the expression 'interest in possession'. The only question therefore is whether the interest was 'in possession'; (iii) it makes no difference to the present issue whether the power of accumulation has been exercised or not.

As I mention later it is not suggested by the Crown that the overriding power of appointment in cl 2 of the settlement prevents the interests of the daughters from being interests in possession. For the purpose of determining the question of principle the case can be equated with a trust to pay the income of property to A during his life but subject to a power to the trustees to accumulate income and add it to capital.

In its general use in English law, the expression 'interest in possession' has traditionally been used to connote present enjoyment. It distinguishes the estate or interest from one in remainder or reversion. Thus, in Fearne on Contingent Remainders[3] it is said:

---

1   [1906] 2 IR 272
2   [1968] 1 All ER 121, [1968] AC 553
3   10th Edn (1844), p 2

'An estate is vested, when there is an immediate fixed right of present or future enjoyment An estate is vested in possession, when there exists a right of present enjoyment. An estate is vested in interest, when there is a present fixed right of future enjoyment.'

These definitions indicate that an interest is not in possession if there is merely a present right of future enjoyment. There must be a present right of present enjoyment.

The same approach is to be found in Re Morgan[1]. That was a case on the Settled Land Act 1882. North J says this:

'In my opinion this case does come under sect. 58, sub-sect. 2. That section first of all contains a provision that "each person shall, when the estate or interest of each of them is in possession, have the powers of a tenant for life under this Act as if each of them were a tenant for life". I think "possession" there clearly means possession properly so called as distinguished from remainder or reversion, and does not draw any distinction as regards a person in possession personally or by his guardian if an infant. I think it means possession as distinguished from reversion.'

The observations in Re Jones[2] of Baggallay and Lindley LJJ are to the same effect.

For the purposes of that traditional distinction, it seems to me that the interest of a person who is entitled to the income of property subject only to a power in the trustees to accumulate is an interest in possession and not in reversion or remainder. The latter interests are future interests, which the former is not; it is a present interest, giving a present right to whatever income is not accumulated. I observe, in passing, that that appears to be consistent with the Settled Land Act 1925, s 20(1)(viii) (which in substance re-enacted similar provisions in the Settled Land Act 1882). That provides as follows:

'Each of the following persons being of full age shall, when his estate or interest is in possession, have the powers of a tenant for life under this Act, (namely) . . . (viii) A person entitled to the income of land under a trust or direction for payment thereof to him during his own or any other life, whether or not subject to expenses of management or to a trust for accumulation of income for any purpose, or until sale of the land, or until forfeiture, cesser or determination by any means of his interest therein . . .'

This evidently contemplates that an interest can be in possession although it is subject to some provision for accumulation. It is no doubt necessary for the purpose of this provision to distinguish between a future interest which is to arise only when a trust for accumulation has determined and a present interest which is subject to a provision for accumulation. But if the case is properly characterised as the latter, the section contemplates that the interest can be an interest in possession notwithstanding the accumulation provision.

In the law of estate duty the expression 'interest in possession' was of importance. Until 1969 its main importance was in relation to s 5(3) of the Finance Act 1894 (which gave an exemption where an interest under a settlement failed or determined by reason of death before it became an interest in possession) and s 43 of the Finance Act 1940 (under which, put generally, duty was chargeable if an interest limited to cease on a death determined 'after becoming an interest in possession' and the life tenant died thereafter within the statutory period).

There is no authority as to the position in the law of estate duty of a person entitled to income subject to a power of accumulation. But if, prior to 1969, a fund was held on trust for A for life and then to B for life but subject to a power of accumulation which was subsisting at A's death, it seems to me that on A's death the fund would have passed for estate duty purposes under s 2(1)(b) of the Finance Act 1894 because A had an interest ceasing on his death. So far as my own experience goes, I agree with counsel for the trustees that it would not then have been generally supposed in the profession that the

1　(1883) 24 Ch D 114 at 116
2　(1884) 26 Ch D 736 at 741, 744

claim for estate duty (or the claim under s 43 of the Finance Act 1940, if the life interest was surrendered in A's lifetime) could be met by the contention that, because of the power of accumulation, the interest failed before it became an interest in possession. I should observe here that it is the Crown's case that the mere existence of a power of accumulation would prevent the interest from being an interest in possession.

The well-known judgment of Palles CB in *Attorney-General v Power*[1], to which I will refer later, proceeds on the basis that in s 5(3) of the Finance Act 1894 the expression 'interest in possession' is used in its traditional sense. Palles CB[2] said it meant possession properly so called as distinct from remainder or reversion. It seems to me probable that that is the sense in which it was used throughout the estate duty legislation prior to 1969.

I come to the Finance Act 1969. Section 2(1)(b) of the Finance Act 1894 imposed a charge for duty in respect of property in which the deceased or any other person had an interest ceasing on the death of the deceased. That section was repealed by s 36(2) of the Finance Act 1969. It was replaced by what was called 'the substituted section 2(1)(b)', which imposed a charge to duty on property in respect of which—

> '(i) at any time during the period of seven years ending with the date of the deceased's death the property was comprised in a settlement and the deceased was entitled to a beneficial interest in possession in that property as . . . a beneficiary under the settlement; or (ii) the property being or having been comprised as aforesaid and the deceased having at a time before the period of seven years aforesaid been entitled to such an interest in that property as is mentioned in sub-paragraph (i) of this paragraph which determined . . . at a date before the beginning of that period, the deceased was not at all times during that period entirely excluded from possession and enjoyment of the property . . . ; or (iii) the property being, or having at a time after 15th April 1969 been, comprised in settled property subject to a trust conferring a discretion on the trustees or some other person as to the application of all or part of any of the combined income of all the property from time to time subject to that trust which is for the time being available for distribution . . . (aa) the deceased having immediately before the date of his death been eligible to benefit as a result of the discretion aforesaid and the property in question having at that date been subject to the trust, the deceased has so benefited at any time during the material period (that is to say, so much of the period of seven years ending with that date as falls after 15th April 1963) at which the property was subject to the trust . . .'

The Crown contend that where property is, for example, held on trust for A for life subject to a power of accumulation the case falls within sub-para (iii)(aa) above of the substituted s 2(1)(b). The trustees contend that it falls within sub-para (i). It does not seem to me that such an interest falls at all naturally within the language of cl (aa). To come within the provision the deceased must have been 'eligible to benefit as a result of the discretion'. That is perfectly apt language to cover the case of a trust to apply the income for such one or more of a class as the trustees think fit. Each member of the class is eligible to benefit from the exercise of the discretion. The Shorter Oxford Dictionary defines 'eligible' as 'fit or proper to be chosen'. The word, it seems to me, implies an element of selection. It is true that if the trustees decide not to accumulate then A, in the example which I have given, will benefit (as will the capital reversioners if the trustees decide to accumulate), but one would not normally describe A or the reversioners as 'eligible' to benefit from this discretion. They are simply persons who automatically benefit or suffer because of their interests in the trust property. The discretion is not concerned with the eligibility of beneficiaries, but simply with whether to accumulate or not.

Looking at s 36 by itself, therefore, I should have felt some doubt whether the case of a life interest subject to a power of accumulation comes within cl (aa). If it does not, one must look for the charging provision elsewhere. That brings me to s 37(1)(a), which is in the following terms:

1 [1906] 2 IR 272
2 [1906] 2 IR 272 at 279

'Where on any death estate duty falls to be charged on any property by virtue of
sub-paragraph (i) or (ii) of the substituted section 2(1)(b) by reason of an interest in that
property—(a) if that interest did not confer a right to receive the whole of any income
of that property during the whole of the relevant period, that is to say, any period
during which the deceased was entitled to that interest which falls within the period
of seven years ending with the relevant date, namely—(i) if the interest determined
or was disposed of at a date before the death, that date, or (ii) in any other case, the date
of the death, but conferred a right to receive a part of that income which varied in
accordance with, or as the result of, the exercise of any power in that behalf, there shall
be treated as passing on the death by virtue of the said sub-paragraph (i) or (ii) part
only of that property, being a part bearing to the whole of that property the same
proportion as the aggregate amount received by the deceased during the relevant
period out of that income by virtue of that interest bears to the aggregate amount of
that income during that period.'

Now that is dealing only with cases falling within sub-paras (i) or (ii) of the substituted
s 2(1)(b). No interest falls within those sub-paragraphs unless it is an interest in
possession. Section 37(1)(a), however, appears plainly to contemplate that a right to receive
income of an amount which varies as a result of the exercise of a power can still be within
sub-para (i) or (ii) and, therefore, will be an interest in possession. The interest of a life
tenant subject to a power of accumulation is, it seems to me, just such an interest as is dealt
with by s 37(1)(a). That subsection is, of course, dealing only with the case where, during
the relevant period, the interest gave to the deceased a right to receive only part of the
income. There was no need to deal with the case where he actually received the whole
income, since s 37(1)(a) is a relieving provision and, where the whole income was received
in right of an interest in possession, there was no need to give relief. Relief was necessary
only where the deceased, though he had an interest in possession in the whole income, in
fact received only part.

Re Buttle's Will Trusts[1] is consistent with the view that, under the 1969 Act, a person
entitled to income subject to a power in the trustees to apply the income for other purposes
was entitled to an interest in possession. The point was not argued, but nobody seems to
have doubted that the next-of-kin, who were entitled subject to the trustees' power to apply
income and capital for the benefit of any of the descendants of the testator's parents who
were 'in real need', were entitled to interests in possession. Stamp LJ said[2]:

'[Counsel] concedes that at the relevant time the residuary estate was within the
meaning of s 2(1)(b)(i) of the substituted section, comprised in a settlement. He also,
I think, concedes, as indeed must follow, that Mr Buttle [one of the next-of-kin] was
entitled to a beneficial interest in possession in that property within the meaning of
the charging provision.'

It seems to me, therefore, that in the Finance Act 1969 an entitlement to income subject
to a power of accumulation is dealt with by the substituted s 2(1)(b)(i) and is thus regarded
as an interest in possession. Whether there was any alternative claim under the substituted
s 2(1)(b)(iii)(aa) I need not consider further; for the reasons which I have given I feel doubt
whether there was. But, be that as it may, the 1969 Act does seem to me to assume that
such an interest is in possession. I should emphasise that it is not 'deemed' to be an interest
in possession; if it is within the substituted s 2(1)(b)(i), it must actually be an interest in
possession.

It is the Crown's contention that the present case is no different in substance from
Attorney-General v Power[3] and *Gartside v Inland Revenue Comrs*[4]. In *Attorney-General v Power*[3],
property was limited to trustees in trust for the future-born children of a marriage as

1   [1977] 3 All ER 1039, [1977] 1 WLR 1200
2   [1977] 3 All ER 1039 at 1045, [1977] 1 WLR 1200 at 1210
3   [1906] 2 IR 272
4   [1968] 1 All ER 121, [1968] AC 553

tenants in common with remainders over of the share of a child dying under 21. This was subject to a proviso that if anyone who, but for the proviso, would be entitled to the possession of the premises or to an undivided share should being male be under 21 the trustees should enter into the possession or receipt of the rents and profits, and should during the minority apply such annual sums as they thought proper for his benefit and accumulate the balance on trust for the child if he attained 21 but if he should not then for the person who ultimately became entitled to the corpus. One of the children was Hubert. He died an infant; and there were two other children who attained 21. The issue was whether Hubert died before becoming entitled to an interest in possession so that the exemption in s 5(3) of the Finance Act 1894 was available. It was held that the interest was not in possession.

Palles CB said[1]: 'Was Hubert's interest an interest "in possession", which I agree with the Attorney-General, means possession properly so called as distinct from remainder or reversion.' And in a later passage he said[2]:

> 'Had Hubert here been entitled to the entire surplus of the rents and profits of his share, I should have held his estate was one in possession; but being, as I hold him to be, entitled to part only of that surplus, and that fluctuating, uncertain and incapable of being defined or ascertained irrespective of its application, I must hold his estate is not in possession and that such sums as he might receive for maintenance were payable to him, not by reason of his vested estate which must be taken to be subject to the estate or interest of the trustees, but as maintenance *eo nomine*, out of the express trust for its payment to him of the interim income of an estate, the present income of which was not his but the trustees.'

The essence of that decision, I think, is this. Hubert was not entitled to an interest in possession by virtue of his fee simple estate. The fee simple estate did not carry the interim income at all. That income was wholly captured by the trusts for maintenance and accumulation. And under the latter trusts Hubert had no present right to income at all; he was merely the object of a discretionary trust with a contingent interest in accumulations. There was no circumstance in which, during his minority, he was entitled to any income as of right.

In *Gartside v Inland Revenue Comrs*[3], a one-fourth share of a fund was held on trust during the lifetime of John to pay or apply the whole or any part of the income for the maintenance or benefit of John or during his life for his wife or children or any one or more of them to the exclusion of the other or others of them in such manner as the trustees should think fit. John died in 1963. In 1962, the trustees had advanced certain sums of capital to his children. The question was whether those advances attracted duty on John's death under s 43 of the Finance Act 1940 by reason of the determination therein during the statutory period of an interest in possession limited to cease on death. It was held by the House of Lords that they did not. None of the objects of the discretionary trusts had, individually, any interest in the trust property since the trustees had an absolute discretion whether to distribute income or to withhold distribution in any year; and if they did distribute it was entirely a matter for their discretion whether they gave all or none of it to any beneficiary. As regards the discretionary objects as a group, they had no interest either since any undistributed income was subject to a trust for accumulation, and although the trustees had power to treat any accumulations as income of the current year they could not be compelled to do so. Again, it is a case where the beneficiary was not entitled to any income as of right in any circumstances.

I do not think it is correct to say that the present case is in substance on all fours with those two authorities. The position as to the trustees' power of accumulation, as I understand it, is this. The power is purely permissive. The trustees are not bound to

---

1   [1906] 2 IR 272 at 279
2   [1906] 2 IR 272 at 280
3   [1968] 1 All ER 121, [1968] AC 553

exercise it. If they do exercise it, they must do so within a reasonable period after the income has arisen: see *Re Allen-Meyrick's Will Trusts*[1] and *Re Locker's Settlement Trusts*[2].

The result, it seems to me, is that the daughters would be entitled as of right to income of their shares in each of the following circumstances: (a) if the trustees decide not to accumulate that income; (b) if the trustees fail to agree as to whether they should accumulate or not; (c) if the trustees, having allowed a reasonable period to elapse after receipt of income, have reached no decision whether to accumulate or not. In each of those cases the daughter will be entitled to the income as of right. She will be entitled to it, not because the trustees have decided to give it to her (as would be the case of Hubert in *Attorney-General v Power*[3] or the discretionary objects in *Gartside v Inland Revenue Comrs*[4]) but because she is entitled to it in right of what is, beyond doubt, her interest in the trust fund. She is entitled to it by reason of her vested interest (which was the circumstance that Palles CB remarked was lacking in *Attorney-General v Power*[3]). In *Attorney-General v Power*[3] and *Gartside v Inland Revenue Comrs*[4] the beneficiaries got nothing unless the trustees decided to give it to them. In the present case the daughters are absolutely entitled to income unless the trustees decide to accumulate that income.

There are thus substantial differences between this case, on the one hand, and *Attorney-General v Power*[3] and *Gartside v Inland Revenue Comrs*[4], on the other. A consequence of the fact that what the daughters take they take in right of their interests is that, as between the daughters, the trustees have no discretion at all. If the trustees decide not to accumulate, they cannot divert income away from one daughter and give it to another. The income is captured by the vested interests. The Crown contend that the position is the same as that of a trust under which, during a period of 21 years, the trustees have power to pay so much if any of the income as they think fit to the three daughters in equal shares and subject thereto the income is to be held on trust to accumulate it. That, I think, shows to some extent the artificiality of the attempt to assimilate the two cases. A power over income which can be exercised only by distributing income equally among the objects would, if such a power has ever been created at all, be most unusual; it is difficult to see any point in such a provision.

There are other differences also between the present case and cases such as *Attorney-General v Power*[3] and *Gartside v Inland Revenue Comrs*[4] (which are cases of discretionary objects pure and simple). In the present case the daughters have interests which can be the subject of voluntary assignments; the objects of a discretionary trust or of a power have not. And the position as to apportionment of accruing income is different in the case of somebody who becomes entitled in right of an interest from that of a person who merely receives income as a discretionary object. If a person entitled to an interest, say, for life dies in mid-quarter there will be apportionment. A discretionary object reserves only what is appointed to him.

The result, in my view, is that while there are similarities in that both in *Attorney-General v Power*[3] and *Gartside v Inland Revenue Comrs*[4] and in the present case the trustees could prevent income reaching the beneficiaries, the differences between this case, on the one hand, and *Attorney-General v Power*[3] and *Gartside v Inland Revenue Comrs*[4], on the other, are substantial and not matters of mere form.

There remains the Crown's wider submission that for the purposes of the Finance Act 1975 there is an interest in possession in settled property if the holder of the interest is entitled to the net income (if any) of the property as it arises but not if the income is subject to a discretion or power which can be exercised so as to withhold it from him after it arises. It is the Crown's case, in effect, that from that proposition two things follow: (i) The existence of a power of revocation or of an overriding power of appointment (such as that contained in cl 2 of the settlement in the present case) will not have the consequence

1 [1966] 1 All ER 740, [1966] 1 WLR 499
2 [1978] 1 All ER 216 at 219, [1977] 1 WLR 1323 at 1326
3 [1906] 2 IR 272
4 [1968] 1 All ER 121, [1968] AC 553

that a present entitlement to income which is subject to such power is not an interest in possession since the beneficiary will be entitled to any income already received by the trustees when the power of revocation or power of appointment is exercised. It is accepted, therefore, that an interest can be an interest in possession even though it is subject to a power of revocation or an overriding power of appointment. (ii) The essential distinction between an overriding power and a power of revocation, on the one hand, and a power to accumulate, on the other, is that in the latter case the discretion of the trustees operates over income which has already been received by them. The beneficiary cannot insist on receiving the income because the trustees must have a reasonable time in which to decide whether to accumulate or not; and if they decide to accumulate the beneficiary will not get the income at all.

The Crown's proposition, it seems to me, gives rise to a number of difficulties. First, it has been common form for many years now for settlements to confer on trustees wide powers of applying income for all sorts of purposes, for example, in payment of the costs of improvements to land and in payment of capital taxes. Clause 21 of the present settlement contains such powers: it authorises payment out of income of any duties, taxes, charges, fees or other outgoings which but for the provisions of the clause would be payable out of capital. That is a convenient provision. But if the Crown are correct, it seems to me that if a fund is held on trust for A for life and the settlement includes such a power, then the life interest is not in possession during periods when the practical situation is such that the power could be exercised to absorb the income (or would not be in possession as to the whole when the power could be exercised to absorb part). Such a power would plainly be exercisable over income after it had arisen, and could prevent its receipt by the life tenant. So far as the beneficiaries' right to receive income is concerned, the position is no different from that where a power of accumulation exists. Counsel for the Crown accepts, I think, that on the Crown's view a power such as that in cl 21 could have the effect of determining whether there was an interest in possession or not. That would be a curious consequence of powers which are really intended as aids to administration of the trust. One would get the same problem if there is simply a power to use income to pay the cost of improvements to land.

Secondly, if a power such as that contained in cl 21 has the effect of determining whether an interest is in possession or not, the result in terms of liability to capital transfer tax may be startling. Suppose a power to pay capital taxes out of income; and suppose a period when no liability to the capital tax exists. A liability of large amount is then incurred (say to capital gains tax). Consistently with the Crown's view, what was previously a life interest in possession is determined (with a resulting charge to capital transfer tax). The capital gains tax having been paid, the life interest in possession would then arise again, with a further charge to capital transfer tax, and so on. Similarly, if there is a power to effect improvements to land out of income, if a fund consisting of equities is sold and converted into land, the transposition of investments might result in a charge to capital transfer tax.

Another example of the operation of the principle as formulated by the Crown is the case where property is held on trust for A for life but the trustees have power to apply income for the benefit of his children. The birth of a child would determine A's life interest in possession with a resulting claim to capital transfer tax. The death of the child would restore it to possession with a similar claim.

Thirdly, the Crown's proposition is that there is a life interest in possession in settled property if the holder of the interest is entitled to the net income (if any) of the property as it arises. But what is meant by 'net income'? The outgoings which are properly payable out of income must depend on the provisions of the settlement. The income receivable by a life tenant may be reduced or extinguished by any one or more of a number of powers, for example, a power of accumulation, a power to apply income in payment of capital improvements to land or premiums on a policy on the life tenant's life. If trustees are authorised to pay the cost of capital improvements to land out of income, there is no satisfactory distinction (so far as determining the 'net income' available for distribution is concerned) between the position arising under such a power and that arising under powers relating to payments which are more of an income nature; it is simply an incident of the life interest. It may be well after the end of the year before the trustees are in a position to decide whether to pay for improvements out of income or not. If they decide to do so, the cost may swallow up the whole or a large part of the income. Does such a power negative the existence of an interest in possession? If the answer is, No, what realistic difference is there between such a power and a power to accumulate? In both cases income is in effect being applied in augmentation of capital. If the answer is, Yes, one is faced with the problems, which I have mentioned, of intermittent powers which may cause interests in possession to arise and disappear again.

All these considerations lead me to doubt whether the test based on the distinction between cases where the beneficiary is entitled to income as it arises and cases where the trustees have power to withhold income after it has arisen is satisfactory. The fact is that an income beneficiary's right to income is always a right to receive what remains after the trustees have exercised the powers which by the general law or by the settlement are conferred on them in respect of that income. The trustees are always entitled to a reasonable time in which to exercise the powers. They can thus retain income as it arises and, depending on the mode of exercise of the powers, divert it from the beneficiary altogether. Even in the simple case of charges of an income nature (for example, repairs), a period may well have to elapse after the end of the year before the trustees are able to decide whether to repair or not. The beneficiary's right to receive income is deferred and interfered with accordingly.

I was referred by counsel for the Crown to the observations of Lord Reid in *Gartside v Inland Revenue Comrs*[1], where Lord Reid said:

> 'To have an interest in possession does not merely mean that you possess the interest. You also possess an interest in expectancy for you may be able to assign it and you can rely on it to prevent the trustees from dissipating the trust fund. "In possession" must mean that your interest enables you to claim now whatever may be the subject of the interest. For instance, if it is the current income from a certain fund your claim may yield nothing if there is no income, but your claim is a valid claim, and if there is any income you are entitled to get it; but a right to require trustees to consider whether they will pay you something does not enable you to claim anything. If the trustees do decide to pay you something, you do not get it by reason of having the right to have your case considered: you get it only because the trustees have decided to give it to you.'

I do not read that passage as meaning that Lord Reid was dissenting from the ordinary contrast between possession and expectancy. The word 'now' is used to distinguish a present from a future right. And if one asks, 'What is the subject-matter of the daughters' interests?', the answer, I think, is that it is the whole income of the trust fund but as diminished by any exercise of the trustees' powers thereover. The fundamental difference between this case and *Gartside v Inland Revenue Comrs*[2] is emphasised by the concluding part of Lord Reid's observations. The daughters, if they receive income, do not get it because the trustees have decided to give it to them: they get it directly from their interest in the trust fund; and not the less so because it is only available for distribution because of the mode in which the trustees have exercised their powers. Their interest is a present and not a future interest.

It seems to me that the essential question is not whether a beneficiary can say of any income as it arises, 'That is mine'. In all but the simplest cases he will very often not be able to say that because the income will be subject to various administrative powers of the trustees. Nor, it seems to me, is the quantum of income which ultimately reaches the beneficiary a material matter. The fundamental question, I think, is whether his

---

1 [1968] 1 All ER 121 at 128, [1968] AC 553 at 607
2 1 All ER 121, [1968] AC 553

entitlement, whatever, if anything, it may turn out to be in terms of quantum, is a present entitlement in right of an interest in the trust property subject only to the proper exercise of the trustees' powers. And, an entitlement is a present entitlement notwithstanding that the trustees have, as they must have, a reasonable time in which to consider what course to adopt as to exercise of powers. It is not necessary for me to consider any question of the possibility of the existence of interests which are neither in possession nor in reversion since it seems to me that the daughters' interests, conferring as they did present rights of enjoyment, were in possession.

Looking at the whole matter in practical terms, it does not seem to me that either answer to the problem is satisfactory in all circumstances. Suppose that the power of accumulation is used to the full so that the life tenant gets nothing, and the power is still subsisting at his death. If the interest of the life tenant is an interest in possession, there will be a charge to tax on his death which might be regarded as unsatisfactory. But now suppose that the interest is not to be regarded as an interest in possession and that the power of accumulation is never used at all. On the determination of the power while the life tenant is living (and being a power of accumulation it is necessarily subject to the statutory limits) there would be a claim for tax on the determination, since a life interest in possession would then commence. There seems to me no sensible reason for such a claim to tax, which might cause much hardship to the life tenant.

I should add that there is no question in the present case of the trustees seeking to utilise a tax avoidance device or seeking to take advantage of a loophole in the statute. Capital transfer tax will, if the trustees are right and the interests are in possession, inevitably be payable when the daughters die or if their interests in possession are determined by an exercise of the overriding power by, for example, appointments to their children. But transfers of capital to them personally, to the extent of their one-third shares, will not attract tax which they would if the interests are not in possession.

In summary, the position seems to me to be this: (i) It is common ground that each of the daughters had, at all material times, an 'interest' in the trust fund in the strict conveyancing sense. The only question is whether that interest was in possession. (ii) It is common ground that the existence of the overriding power of appointment in cl 2 of the settlement does not prevent the interests from being in possession. It is the Crown's case that the reason for that is that the power cannot affect income already in the trustees' hands. (iii) In English trust law the expression 'interest in possession' is used to distinguish the interest from one in expectancy. By that test it seems to me that the interests are in possession, since they confer a present right to receive whatever income is the subject-matter of the interests for the time being. They are not interests in expectancy, which are future interests. These are present interests, with rights to present enjoyment. (iv) It is common ground that the expression 'interest in possession' has the same meaning in the Finance Act 1975 as in the estate duty legislation. Section 37 of the Finance Act 1969 seems to me to recognise that a present entitlement to income subject to a power which may diminish it is an interest in possession. I see no reason to suppose that that diverges from the meaning of the expression prior to 1969 in the estate duty law. (v) *Attorney-General v Power*[1] and *Gartside v Inland Revenue Comrs*[2] are in substance quite different cases from the present. (vi) The distinction between cases where the trustees have power to withhold income and those where they have no such power is not a satisfactory basis for determining the existence of an interest in possession. It produces in practice unreal distinctions and, in addition, unsatisfactory results by giving rise to intermittent interests in possession.

The result, it seems to me, is that both in trust law and in the law of estate duty the expression was used in the same sense. Further, it is used in the same sense in the Finance Act 1975. That sense is the traditional distinction between interests in possession and in reversion. In the terms of that distinction the interests in the present case are, it seems to me, interests in possession.

---

1 [1906] 2 IR 272
2 [1968] 1 All ER 121, [1968] AC 553

Accordingly, I think that the trustees succeed and are entitled to the declaration which they seek in para 1 of the originating summons. The subsidiary question does not arise.

Declaration granted.

Solicitors: *Alsop, Stevens, Batesons & Co* (for the trustees); *Solicitor of Inland Revenue.*

Rengan Krishnan Esq   Barrister.

Jones v Wrotham Park Settled Estates and another

HOUSE OF LORDS

LORD DIPLOCK, LORD SALMON, LORD EDMUND-DAVIES, LORD FRASER OF TULLYBELTON AND LORD RUSSELL OF KILLOWEN

30th, 31st OCTOBER, 2nd, 6th NOVEMBER, 13th DECEMBER 1978

Landlord and tenant – Leasehold enfranchisement – Agreement purporting to exclude or modify right to acquire freehold – Freeholder granting concurrent lease of house to third party before service of tenant's notice to acquire freehold – Concurrent lease having effect of increasing price payable by tenant for freehold – Whether concurrent lease modifying tenant's right to acquire freehold – Whether concurrent lease providing for imposition of penalty or disability on tenant seeking to acquire freehold – Leasehold Reform Act 1967, s 23(1).

In 1962 the tenant and her husband were granted a lease of a house for a term of 87 years expiring on 25th December 2048 at a yearly rent of £15. By a notice dated 5th October 1973 and served on 8th October they gave notice, under the Leasehold Reform Act 1967, to the freeholder that they desired to acquire the freehold. On 6th October, between the date of the notice and service of it, the freeholder, as a device to increase the value of the freehold, granted a lease of the house ('the concurrent lease') to a company ('the reversioner') for a term of 300 years from 25th December 1970 subject to and with the benefit of the 1962 lease. The rent payable under the concurrent lease was a peppercorn until the expiry of the 1962 lease and a rack rent thereafter. The concurrent lease provided, in para (5) of Sch 4, that if a sublease of the house was granted by the reversioner then the rent payable under the concurrent lease, for the period of the sublease, would be the rack rent obtainable at the commencement of the term of the sublease. The parties failing to reach agreement on the price payable by the tenant for acquisition of the freehold, the tenant referred the matter to the Lands Tribunal. Before the tribunal there were three alternative agreed valuations: the first, on the assumption that the valuers should ignore the concurrent lease, produced an agreed figure of £300 payable to the freeholder, being £50 payable to the freeholder and £250 payable to the reversioner in respect of the concurrent lease; the second, on the assumption that the provisions of the concurrent lease except for para (5) of Sch 4 were to be taken into account, produced the same agreed figure of £300; the third, on the assumption that all the provisions of the concurrent lease including para (5) of Sch 4 were to be taken into account, produced an agreed figure of £4,000 payable to the freeholder and nothing payable to the reversioner. The freeholder contended that, because of s 9(1)[a] of the 1967 Act, the third assumption was correct. The tenant conceded that the concurrent lease was a valid lease and not a sham and that s 9 required the valuation to be made on the footing that the reversioner was to be deemed to have granted a sublease, within para (5) of Sch 4, but contended that the agreement contained in para (5) of Sch 4 was rendered void by s 23(1)[b] of the 1967 Act because it was an 'agreement relating to' the tenant's tenancy which '[purported] to . . . modify' her right to acquire the freehold and

a Section 9(1), as far as material, is set out at p 291 *e f*, post
b Section 23(1) is set out at p 293 *h j*, post

furthermore imposed a 'penalty or disability on the tenant' in the event of her acquiring or claiming the right to acquire the freehold. The tribunal held that the agreement was not an agreement relating to the tenancy since the tenant was not a party to it, and furthermore it did not purport to modify the tenant's right to acquire the freehold since, although it dramatically reduced the value of that right, the right itself remained absolute and unqualified. Accordingly, the tribunal determined that £4,000 was the price payable by the tenant. The tenant appealed to the Court of Appeal which allowed her appeal^c, holding that the concurrent lease was capable of being an agreement 'relating to' her tenancy, within s 23(1), and therefore void notwithstanding that she was not a party to it and was in fact void because coupled with the tenant's concession that the reversioner was to be deemed to have granted a sublease within the meaning of para (5) of Sch 4 it increased the price of the freehold on enfranchisement from £300 to £4,000 and thereby purported to modify the tenant's right to acquire the freehold. The court substituted as the price payable for the freehold a sum of £300. On appeal by the freeholder to the House of Lords the tenant sought to withdraw the concession that the valuation was to be made on the footing that the reversioner was to be deemed to have granted a sublease within the meaning of para (5) of Sch 4 and sought leave to amend the case stated to include that point. A question arose whether the House of Lords had power to amend a case stated.

Held – (i) The House of Lords had power in proper case to amend a case stated and leave would be given to the tenant to do so in order to argue that the valuation was to be made on the footing that the reversioner was not to be deemed to have granted a sublease within the meaning of para (5) of Sch 4 to the concurrent lease. However, the tenant had in the event been right to make the concession because under s 9(1)(a) of the 1967 Act the same result was arrived at whether the tenant claiming the freehold had or had not previously obtained an extension of the term under that Act (see p 288 f, p 289 h, p 290 e f, and p 293 c to e, post).

(ii) The concurrent lease had not modified the tenant's right to acquire the freehold because although the effect of para (5) of Sch 4 to the concurrent lease may have been to modify the terms on which the tenant could acquire the freehold it had not modified the right itself. The statutory right to acquire the freehold was a right to acquire all the reversionary interests at a total of the market price appropriate to those various interests in whatever circumstances might affect those interests at the time of the notice of enfranchisement, including e g the circumstances which would exist if the tenant first gave notice requiring an extension of the lease, when the reversioner would have to pay a vacant possession rack rent to the freeholder until the year 2098 while only receiving the ground rent. Nor did para (5) have the effect of imposing a penalty or disability on the tenant in the event of the tenant acquiring or claiming a right to enfranchisement. Accordingly, para (5) was not invalidated by s 23(1) of the 1967 Act. It followed therefore that, taking para (5) into account, the price for the freehold under s 9 of the 1967 Act was to be fixed on the basis of the rent to which the freeholder was entitled under the concurrent lease, i e £4,000. The appeal would therefore be allowed (see p 288 f, p 289 h, p 290 e f, p 293 g, p 294 g to 295 g and j, post).

Decision of the Court of Appeal [1978] 3 All ER 527 reversed.

Notes

For agreements excluding or modifying a right to acquire the freehold which are void, see Supplement to 23 Halsbury's Laws (3rd Edn) para 1774.

For the Leasehold Reform Act 1967, s 23, see 18 Halsbury's Statutes (3rd Edn) 678.

Cases referred to in opinions

Brandling v Barrington (1827) 6 B & C 467, 9 Dow & Ry KB 609, 5 LJOSKB 181, 108 ER 523, 44 Digest (Repl) 272, 992.

---

c [1978] 3 All ER 527

Gladstone v Bower [1960] 3 All ER 353, [1960] 2 QB 384, [1960] 3 WLR 575, 58 LGR 313,
CA, 2 Digest (Reissue) 15, 46.
Greenhalgh v Arderne Cinemas Ltd [1946] 1 All ER 512, CA, 9 Digest (Reissue) 234, 1424.
Johnson v Moreton [1978] 3 All ER 37, [1978] 3 WLR 538, HL.
Joseph v Joseph [1966] 3 All ER 486, [1967] Ch 78, [1966] 3 WLR 631, CA, 31(2) Digest
(Reissue) 940, 7707.
Kammins Ballrooms Co Ltd v Zenith Investments (Torquay) Ltd [1970] 2 All ER 871, [1971] AC
850, [1970] 3 WLR 287, 22 P & CR 74, HL, 31(2) Digest (Reissue) 953, 7757.
White v Bristol Aeroplane Co Ltd [1953] 1 All ER 40, [1953] Ch 68, [1953] 2 WLR 144, CA,
9 Digest (Reissue) 235, 1425.

Appeal

This was an appeal by the freeholder, Wentworth Securities Co Ltd ('Wentworth') against
a decision of the Court of Appeal[1] (Stephenson, Orr and Goff LJJ) dated 26th January 1978
allowing an appeal by the respondent, Mrs Lena Jones ('the tenant'), on a case stated from
a decision of the Land Tribunal (chairman V G Wellings Esq QC) dated 15th October 1976
determining that the price payable by the tenant under s 9 of the Leasehold Reform Act
1967 for the acquisition of the freehold of a house at 45 Wellesley Crescent, Potters Bar,
Hertfordshire, of which she was the occupying tenant, was £4,000 to the freeholder,
Wentworth, and nil to the reversioner, Wrotham Park Settled Estates ('Wrotham'). The
facts are set out in the opinion of Lord Russell of Killowen.

E G Nugee QC and *S J Sher* for Wentworth.
Nigel Hague for the tenant.
Wrotham was not represented.

Their Lordships took time for consideration.

13th December. The following opinions were delivered.

LORD DIPLOCK. My Lords, I have read in advance the speech of my noble and learned
friend, Lord Russell of Killowen, and for the reasons which he gives, which I too find
compelling, I would allow this appeal.

One must start with the assumption that the intermediate lease between Wentworth
Securities Ltd ('Wentworth') as landlord and Wrotham Park Settled Estates ('Wrotham') as
tenant is not a sham; that is to say, that however disadvantageous it may appear to be
financially to Wrotham (an unlimited company), if at any time a tenant occupying the
demised premises as his residence exercises his right under the Leasehold Reform Act 1967
to acquire the freehold or an extended lease, Wentworth will nevertheless enforce and
Wrotham will comply with the covenants of the lease relating to the rent that will become
payable by Wrotham to Wentworth in that event. The effect of those covenants, as my
noble and learned friend points out, is to increase the price at which the freehold can be
acquired by the resident tenant under the relevant provisions of the Act to a figure
substantially greater than that at which it could have been acquired by him if the
intermediate lease had not been made; though they make no difference to the terms on
which the resident tenant could acquire an extended lease. The existence of the covenants,
if they are to be treated as valid and effective for the purpose of assessing the price payable
by the resident tenant for acquiring the freehold under the Act, will act as a financial
deterrent to him from acquiring the freehold instead of exercising his alternative right
under the Act to acquire an extended lease. It is not for your Lordships to speculate what
fiscal or other advantages Wentworth and Wrotham hope to derive from the course they
have chosen to adopt. It is evident from the care and ingenuity with which the scheme has
been devised that the two companies entered into it with their eyes open to what its
financial consequences to them will be if it is held to be valid.

---

1   [1978] 3 All ER 527, [1978] 3 WLR 585

My Lords, it would seem most unlikely that either the draftsman of the Leasehold Reform Act 1967, or those members of either House of Parliament by whose votes it was passed, had envisaged the possibility that any ground landlord would enter into an intermediate lease in the precise terms adopted by Wentworth and Wrotham or in any other terms which would have the same economic consequences as between ground landlord and intermediate tenant. If it has been envisaged it seems likely that the draftsman would have done something about it to prevent its having the effect of enhancing the price payable by the resident tenant for the freehold; but how he would set about achieving this and what words he would have used to do so is a matter of pure speculation.

My Lords, I am not reluctant to adopt a purposive construction where to apply the literal meaning of the legislative language used would lead to results which would clearly defeat the purposes of the Act. But in doing so the task on which a court of justice is engaged remains one of construction, even where this involves reading into the Act words which are not expressly included in it. *Kammins Ballrooms Co Ltd v Zenith Investments (Torquay) Ltd*[1] provides an instance of this; but in that case the three conditions that must be fulfilled in order to justify this course were satisfied. First, it was possible to determine from a consideration of the provisions of the Act read as a whole precisely what the mischief was that it was the purpose of the Act to remedy; secondly, it was apparent that the draftsman and Parliament had by inadvertence overlooked, and so omitted to deal with, an eventuality that required to be dealt with if the purpose of the Act was to be achieved; and thirdly, it was possible to state with certainty what were the additional words that would have been inserted by the draftsman and approved by Parliament had their attention been drawn to the omission before the Bill passed into law. Unless this third condition is fulfilled any attempt by a court of justice to repair the omission in the Act cannot be justified as an exercise of its jurisdiction to determine what is the meaning of a written law which Parliament has passed. Such an attempt crosses the boundary between construction and legislation. It becomes a usurpation of a function which under the constitution of this country is vested in the legislature to the exclusion of the courts.

My Lords, in the instant case I do not find it possible to state with any certainty what words would have been inserted in the Act to fill the gap that has now been revealed by the intermediate lease granted by Wentworth to Wrotham. Any suggestion that the parliamentary intention was that, notwithstanding the existence and terms of any intermediate lease, the price to be paid by the resident tenant for the freehold was to be the investment value of the reversion subject only to his own lease (as extended) must be discarded for the reasons given by my noble and learned friend. The notion that Parliament would have inserted in the Act a clause limited to requiring that covenants in an intermediate lease in the precise terms of those in the lease by Wentworth to Wrotham should alone be ignored in assessing the price of the freehold is fanciful; and might indeed • have converted the Bill into a hybrid Bill for which a special procedure must be followed in Parliament. But what Parliament would have done somewhere between those two extremes is, as I have said, a matter of pure speculation.

LORD SALMON. My Lords, with some reluctance I agree that, for the cogent reasons stated by my noble and learned friend, Lord Russell of Killowen, this appeal must be allowed, and I add only a few observations of my own.

On 6th October 1973 Wentworth Securities Ltd was, amongst other things, the freeholder of an estate at Potters Bar, Hertfordshire, on which stood about 100 houses, all of which had been let to its tenant occupiers from 1961 for 87 years at a yearly rental of £15, the tenant occupiers having paid for the building of their homes. On 6th October 1973 Wentworth granted concurrent leases to a company called Wrotham Park Settled Estates (with which it had connections) of all the houses on the Potters Bar estate (including the tenant's house) for 300 years, subject to the existing leases and at a peppercorn rent until the expiry of the tenants' leases, and at a rack rent thereafter.

---

1   [1970] 2 All ER 871, [1971] AC 850

This somewhat odd, possibly unique and certainly ingenious transaction was not a sham: it was a reality. It was, however, admittedly a device to discourage tenants from acquiring the freehold of their homes by exercising their rights under the Leasehold Reform Act 1967.

A few days after the transaction to which I have referred was entered into, the tenant served the statutory notice calling for the freehold of her home. But for the transaction into which the companies had entered, the tenant could have acquired the freehold of her home for £300. As it was, the transaction, which was completed two days before the tenant's notice was served, sent the market price for the freehold of the tenant's home up from £300 to £4,000.

In my opinion, it was clearly the policy of the legislature under the 1967 Act that a tenant should obtain the freehold of his home at the ordinary market price and not at a price which had been inflated by a transaction such as the present. I have no doubt that if it had ever occurred to the legislature that a transaction such as the present might have been devised and put into operation clear words would have been introduced into the Act which would preclude such a transaction from affecting the market price which the tenant would have to pay for the freehold of his home. As it is, no such words appear in the Act; and accordingly it contains a gap. It is well settled, however, that the courts have no power to fill in any gap in an Act, even if satisfied that, had the legislature been aware of the gap, it would have filled it in: *Johnson v Moreton*[1], *Gladstone v Bower*[2] and *Brandling v Barrington*[3] per Lord Tenterden CJ. Accordingly, there is nothing to be done by this House, sitting in its judicial capacity, other than to allow the appeal. It may, however, perhaps be worth consideration in other quarters whether the Act should be amended.

LORD EDMUND-DAVIES. My Lords, for the reasons developed in the speech of my noble and learned friend, Lord Russell of Killowen, with which I am in complete agreement, I concur in holding that this appeal should be allowed and in the order proposed by him.

LORD FRASER OF TULLYBELTON. My Lords, I have had the advantage of reading in advance the speech prepared by my noble and learned friend, Lord Russell of Killowen. I entirely agree with his reasoning and his conclusion, and I cannot usefully add anything.

I would allow the appeal and make an order in the terms proposed by my noble and learned friend.

LORD RUSSELL OF KILLOWEN. My Lords, the respondent, Mrs Jones (together with her late husband), became in 1962 lessees from the freeholder (now the appellant Wentworth Securities Ltd) ('Wentworth') of a semi-detached house, 45 Wellesley Crescent, Potters Bar, for a term of years expiring in December 2048 at a yearly rent of £15. They at the same time paid to the builder some £3,700 for building the house. They and subsequently she remained in the house as a residence. In 1967 the Leasehold Reform Act 1967 became law. Thereunder a resident tenant suitably qualified was enabled on giving a suitable notice or notices before the expiration of the original term to those entitled to reversionary interests in the land to demand an extension of his term by 50 years, or a conveyance to him of the freehold, or (in that order, of course) both. The qualifications need not be exactly rehearsed: the term had to be sufficiently long, the rent sufficiently low and the rateable value sufficiently low, and the tenant had to fulfil a time qualification of residence in the premises as his only or main residence. It suffices to say that Mrs Jones was a qualified tenant when on 8th October 1973 she served notice calling for the freehold.

Had the facts been as thus far stated it is clear from the agreement between the valuers that the price payable for the freehold to Wentworth under the statutory provisions for its

---

1   [1978] 3 All ER 37, [1978] 3 WLR 538
2   [1960] 3 All ER 353, [1960] 2 QB 384
3   (1827) 6 B & C 467 at 475

calculation would have been about £300. However shortly before service of the tenant's notice Wentworth granted a lease to Wrotham Park Settled Estates ('Wrotham'), an unlimited company with extensive property and property management interests, which Wentworth contends results in the tenant having to pay to Wentworth a sum of £4,000, a figure agreed by the valuers on the assumptions for which Wentworth contends, unless the tenant resiles, as she is entitled by the Act to do, from her wish to acquire the freehold.

Before looking at the terms of the Wrotham lease, which to say the least are as between Wentworth and Wrotham unusual, one or two facts must be noticed. The house now in question is one of about 100 similar houses on this laid-out estate; the lease of each is of the same length at the same rent, and no doubt in most if not all cases there is a tenant qualified to serve a notice under the Act; so that this case is of wide import. An estate of this size benefits from well qualified management. Wentworth is trustee of a family trust, and I can have no doubt that the same family is beneficially interested in some degree in Wrotham, though I do not of course suggest identity of beneficial interests. Finally, any suggestion that the Wrotham lease was in any part a sham was absolutely disclaimed on behalf of the tenant, and vigorously denied on behalf of Wentworth, for whom it was (correctly) pointed out that legitimate avoidance of fiscal burdens is sometimes apt to lead to odd-looking transactions between taxpayers.

But first I must advert to the statutory provisions for payment by the tenant in the event of his serving a relevant notice. If he requires a 50 year extension (which in the instant case would extend the lease to December 2098) the provisions are simple: starting in 2048 he pays during the rest of the lease what was described as a 'modern ground rent', with a provision for re-assessment thereof half way through the extension. In the case of service of a notice calling for the freehold the price is to be ascertained according to s 9(1)(a):

> '. . . the price payable . . . on a conveyance . . . shall be the amount which at the relevant time the house and premises, if sold in the open market by a willing seller, might be expected to realise on the following assumptions:— (a) on the assumption that the vendor was selling for an estate in fee simple, subject to the tenancy but on the assumption that this Part of this Act conferred no right to acquire the freehold; and if the tenancy has not been extended under this Part of this Act, on the assumption that . . . it was to be so extended.'

(I quote in its original form; it has been amended but not in a respect now relevant.)

I remark at this point that the second of those assumptions is designed in favour of the reversioner, while the third of those assumptions is designed in favour of the tenant (by postponing the reversion by 50 years) so as to put a tenant who had not previously claimed an extension on a par with one who had. All this is simple if there is but one reversioner to the tenancy, the free holder. But problems arise when, as here, there is more than one person interested in the reversion to the tenancy. It might have been thought a reasonable system to adopt in such case to ascertain the price appropriate to the simple case that I have mentioned, and divide among the reversionary interests in appropriate proportions. But Parliament decided on something different. In such a case Sch 1, para 7(1)(b), requires that—

> 'a separate price shall be payable in accordance with section 9 for each of the interests superior to the tenancy in possession, and . . . section 9 shall apply to the computation of that price with such modifications as are appropriate to relate it to a sale of the interest in question subject to any tenancies intermediate between that interest and the tenancy in possession . . .'

I turn to the Wrotham lease, saying at the outset that the critical aspect of it is that if and when Wrotham grants a tenancy of the house, which is involved in the third assumption in s 9(1)(a), Wentworth becomes entitled to a vacant possession rack rent from Wrotham, which it is claimed has the effect on the valuers' agreed figures of throwing up a price of £4,000 for the freehold.

The Wrotham lease was dated 6th October 1973 (after the date of the preparation of the tenant's notice but before its service). It demised no 45 for a term of 300 years from 25th December 1970 subject to and with the benefit of the tenant's lease. Wrotham thus became the owner of the immediate reversion to the tenant's lease, and entitled to receive the £15 per annum. The provisions for rent payable by Wrotham, set out in Sch 4 to the lease, may be summarised as follows: (1) until 25th December 2048, the term date of the tenant's lease, a peppercorn; (2) from 25th December 2048 to 25th December 2098, the 'extended' term date of the tenant's lease, a rack rent as at 25th December 2048 to be determined as there provided; (3) from 25th December 2098 for the rest of the term a rack rent as at that date; (4) rack rent in paras (2) and (3) was defined as the best yearly rent for which the premises could be let in the open market for a term equal to the unexpired residue of the term of the lease at the date of ascertainment. Paragraph (5), the crucial paragraph, is in these terms:

'If and so often as a sub-lease (not being a tenancy from year to year or any lesser interest) is granted by [Wrotham] of the whole of the Premises the annual rent payable hereunder shall for the period beginning with the commencement of the term granted by the sub-lease and ending with the termination thereof (however the same determines and if the term is extended by virtue of any enactment then ending with the termination of the term so extended) be (in lieu of the foregoing rents) an amount equal to the best yearly rent for which the Premises could be let in the open market at the commencement of such term with vacant possession free from all incumbrances (including the existing lease) for a term equal to the term granted by the sub-lease such amount to be ascertained (in default of agreement) by arbitration as aforesaid.'

Paragraph (6) was in these terms:

'PROVIDED ALWAYS that if (whether by virtue of the provisions of Paragraph (5) of this Schedule or otherwise) the yearly rent which would (apart from this Paragraph (6)) be for the time being payable hereunder shall be more than the yearly rent reserved by any sub-lease granted by [Wrotham] (whether in pursuance of the provisions of the Leasehold Reform Act 1967 or any amendment or re-enactment thereof or otherwise howsoever) then the yearly rent payable hereunder under paragraphs (2) and (3) of this Schedule shall be reduced to a peppercorn during a period (hereafter called "a rent free period") from the actual termination of the term of such sub-lease (howsoever the same shall determine and if the term shall be extended by Statute then from the termination of the term as so extended) on the 25th December 2048 or the expiration of any rent free period referably to any earlier sub-lease (whichever shall be the later date) until the expiration of a period equal to twice the actual duration of such sub-lease or the expiration of the term hereby granted (whichever shall last occur).'

It will thus be seen that, if the price ascertained under s 9 for the freehold is to be based on an assumption of an extended lease, that assumption triggers off the operation of para (5) of the Wrotham schedule, and Wentworth can say that its freehold is entitled to the rent exigible under that paragraph and to a value inflated accordingly. And this was indeed the design.

One other point is to be mentioned on the Wrotham lease. In the given circumstances under para (5) of Sch 4 whereunder Wrotham on an extension of the tenant's term has to pay a vacant possession rack rent while receiving only the £15 per annum until 2048 and a modern ground rent until 2098, Wrotham would be entitled under Sch 1, para 11, to the Act to surrender the Wrotham lease and Wentworth could not rely on that para (5). But cl 6 of the Wrotham lease stopped that gap. It reads:

'IT IS HEREBY AGREED AND DECLARED that the provisions for the reduction of rent contained in Paragraph (6) of the Fourth Schedule hereto are in substitution for and not in addition to the right of surrender conferred on [Wrotham] by paragraph 11 of the First Schedule of the Leasehold Reform Act 1967 and [Wrotham] hereby covenants with [Wentworth] that in consideration of the premises it will not exercise the right of surrender conferred by the said paragraph 11 on any occasion when the same might otherwise become exercisable.'

Before the Lands Tribunal and the Court of Appeal counsel for the tenant accepted that this would be so, and relied only on the provisions of s 23, to which I will come. In the Court of Appeal it was suggested that in fact it was well arguable that the s 9 assumption did not have that effect. But counsel for the tenant did not accept that suggestion. The judgments of the Court of Appeal returned to that suggestion with some favour, and very understandably counsel sought leave to raise and argue it, notwithstanding that he had not accepted it below. Had leave been refused the tenants' association (backing the tenant) might well have felt that they might have been let down by counsel in the light of the comments by the Court of Appeal. To raise the point, amendment of the case stated as to the questions posed was necessary. A question was raised whether this House had power to amend a case stated. I am of opinion that in a proper case it has. A further suggestion was made that if this point were now taken it would impinge on an area where evidence might have been called at the Lands Tribunal, but the only suggestion of such an area was that the tenant's lease might have become forfeit. This appears to me quite artificial: it is really inconceivable that evidence could have been led to suggest even the possibility of a lease of that length at that rent ever being effectually forfeited. Accordingly leave was given and the case stated amended to include the point.

However, in my opinion counsel for the tenant was right to think that the point was not sound. He argued valiantly to the contrary, on the lines that the assumption need not and should not be followed through to trigger off para (5) in the Wrotham lease schedule. But I take it to be clear that the intention in s 9(1)(a) was to arrive at the same result whether the tenant claiming the freehold had or had not previously obtained the extension. In this case if the tenant had obtained the extension before seeking to acquire the freehold there would be no question on that later attempt of making any assumption: para (5) would necessarily have been already triggered off with Wentworth entitled to the vacant possession rack rent from Wrotham from the time of the extension notice.

Counsel for the tenant sought to put a rather different point on s 9, on the lines that it was designed or should be construed as designed to fix the price only at the investment value of the reversion subject to the tenant's lease (extended). But this suggestion appears to me to involve that it should be apportioned between reversionary interests, and this, as I have remarked, is not permitted by Sch 1, para 7, to the Act.

Before turning then to s 23 I observe that if the tenant is unwilling in the end to accept the freehold but later contents herself with an extension, Wrotham will be at once saddled with vacant possession rack rent for this house until 2098 while receiving only the ground rent. And this may be multiplied 100 times. It would seem an unhappy situation for Wrotham, but for all I know it may suit both Wentworth and Wrotham.

Section 23(1) is in the following terms:

'Except as provided by this section, any agreement relating to a tenancy (whether contained in the instrument creating the tenancy or not and whether made before the creation of the tenancy or not) shall be void in so far as it purports to exclude or modify any right to acquire the freehold or an extended lease or right to compensation under this Part of this Act, or provides for the termination or surrender of the tenancy in the event of a tenant acquiring or claiming any such right or for the imposition of any penalty or disability on the tenant in that event.'

Four questions on these provisions were raised in argument. (1) Was the Wrotham lease an agreement relating to the tenant's tenancy? (2) If so, did it modify the tenant's right to acquire the freehold by virtue of the operation of para (5) of Sch 4 and cl 6? (3) In any event did it 'purport' so to do? (4) Alternatively did those provisions of the Wrotham lease provide for the imposition of any penalty or disability on the tenant in the event of her claiming the right to acquire the freehold? For Wentworth it was contended that each of those questions should be answered in the negative.

My Lords, I propose in the first instance to address myself to questions (2) and (4), for if Wentworth be right on those questions the other two do not call for an answer.

The Lands Tribunal member on question (2) considered that there was no modification of the tenant's right to acquire the freehold. He said: '... paragraph 5 of the 4th Schedule ... does not ... modify the tenant's right to acquire the freehold. That remains absolute and unqualified.'

In the Court of Appeal the contrary view was taken on question (2). The valuers, on the basis that para (5) of Sch 4 to and cl 6 of the Wrotham lease were to be ignored in assessing the price to be paid for the two reversionary interests, valued that of Wrotham at £250 and the freehold at £50, a total of prices to be paid of £300. And as I have indicated, had the Wrotham lease not been executed, the price for the freehold would have been approximately £300. But with the benefit of Wrotham's onerous liability for vacant possession rack rent the price to be paid for the freehold was agreed at £4,000, Wrotham's lease having for Wrotham a substantial negative value. Wrotham took no part in the Court of Appeal or before your Lordship's House. Orr LJ[1] criticised the Lands Tribunal on this point as ignoring the fact—

'that until the act of enfranchisement £300 remained the proper price for the freehold, calculated in accordance with the Act and apart from para 5 of Sch 4 the exercise of the right of enfranchisement could not increase the price, but para 5 ... makes it do so, and in that respect ... modifies the right.'

Goff LJ[2] approached this question in a similar way, stressing that immediately before the Wrotham lease the price for the freehold calculated in accordance with the Act was £300. He said that immediately after the execution of the Wrotham lease, right down at least until the tenant had actually exercised the right of enfranchisement, that was still the proper price, because Wentworth could not get more than a nominal rent from any concurrent lessee during the subsistence of the tenancy. Apart from para (5) the exercise of the right of enfranchisement could not increase that price. Therefore the operation of para (5), throwing up a price of £4,000, did modify that right.

Stephenson LJ[3] agreed that notwithstanding the Wrotham lease the price payable in accordance with s 9 was £300, 'at least until the tenant exercised her right of enfranchisement'. He took a broad line against an 'ingenious device' to reduce the apparent value of the tenant's right, which he could not believe the legislature intended to permit.

Counsel for Wentworth criticised these approaches of the Court of Appeal as unsound. He said that it was fallacious to say that there was a right to acquire the freehold of £300 which was modified by the operation of para (5) of the Wrotham lease. The statutory right to acquire the freehold was a right to acquire all the reversionary interests at a total of the market prices appropriate to the various reversionary interests in whatever circumstances might affect those reversionary interests at the time of notice of enfranchisement. Suppose the Wrotham lease to antedate by a considerable time any action by the tenant; suppose the tenant to give first notice requiring an extension of the lease; assume (as one must) the Wrotham lease to be a genuine transaction between Wentworth and Wrotham. There could be no doubt that after the extension Wentworth would be entitled to the vacant possession rack rent from the time of notice of extension. Could para (5) then be said, on the occasion of a later notice of enfranchisement, to modify the right to enfranchise? Suppose alternatively that the Wrotham lease had been created before the passing of the 1967 Act, though with the terms of the Bill in mind? It must be borne in mind that there may be many legitimate justifications for an otherwise puzzling form of concurrent lease, such as a lease at a reverse premium, which may affect the calculation of prices under

1   [1978] 3 All ER 527 at 535, [1978] 3 WLR 585 at 596
2   [1978] 3 All ER 527 at 537, [1978] 3 WLR 585 at 598
3   [1978] 3 All ER 527 at 539, [1978] 3 WLR 585 at 601

s 9(1)(*a*) of the Act, and these should not be held to be void modifications of the right of enfranchisement. In truth the effect of para (5) of Sch 4 to the Wrotham lease may modify the *terms* on which the tenant may acquire the freehold, but it does not modify the right itself. Further, to describe what was done as an ingenious device is irrelevantly pejorative: a man is entitled to avoid a claim against his prima facie legal rights by adoption of a genuine disposition of those rights. For Wentworth it was additionally argued that the Act is expropriatory of Wentworth (which it is) and this should affect the construction to be attributed to the statutory language. I attribute minimal if any force to this point, and regard only the statutory provisions. It was accordingly contended for Wentworth that the price for the freehold under s 9 must be properly fixed on the basis of the rent to which Wentworth was entitled under the Wrotham lease, viz £4,000; that is how the machinery of the Act operates on the circumstances as they exist. By analogy with company cases such as *Greenhalgh v Arderne Cinemas Ltd*[1] and *White v Bristol Aeroplane Co Ltd*[2] the Wrotham lease did not affect or modify the right to enfranchise but only the terms on which that right might be exercised or enjoyed.

Counsel for the tenant sought to support the decision of the Court of Appeal on this question not only on their grounds but also on a further ground. It was argued that in any valuation to ascertain the price or prices under s 9 there are two determining factors. One is the formula laid down by s 9 in combination with Sch 1, para 7, to the Act. The other consists in the data to which that formula is to be applied. If (it was argued) a provision altered either formula or data it would (if adverse to the tenant) modify the right to enfranchisement. In particular it was said that this would be so if the alteration of data was 'artificial' and one to take place on the very event of an enfranchisement notice.

My Lords, I am unable to accept on this question the views of the Court of Appeal or the contentions in support of them by counsel in this House. I find the contentions for Wentworth to the contrary compelling. Granted that the rights of Wentworth under the Wrotham lease are genuine I cannot accept that they can be disregarded in assessing the price of the freehold under s 9. Nor do I accept that a genuine modification of the situation to which the statutory system of calculation of the price applies is a modification of the right of enfranchisement, which remains untouched save as to the cost of enforcement of the right. There is ample scope for the operation of s 23(1) without embracing this case; I need only give the example of a provision postponing the right of enfranchisement until near the end of the tenancy term.

I turn next to the question whether the operation of the Wrotham lease was such that it, by para (5) of Sch 4 and cl 6, provides for the imposition of any penalty or disability on the tenant in the event of the tenant acquiring or claiming a right to enfranchisement. The Lands Tribunal and all members of the Court of Appeal were of opinion that this could not be said, and I, my Lords, am content to agree with them.

In those circumstances, if I am right on questions (2) and (4) it is not necessary to decide questions (1) and (3) and I prefer to leave them to a case in which they are essential. I would only comment on question (1) that counsel for Wentworth was not minded to adopt the narrow view of the Lands Tribunal that an agreement 'relating to the tenancy' must be one to which the tenant must be a party: he would go somewhat wider. He also contended on question (3) that 'purports' is confined to an express provision, relying on the Oxford English Dictionary and challenging the view of the Court of Appeal in *Joseph v Joseph*[3]. I refer to these contentions without further comment.

Accordingly I would allow this appeal, which will reinstate the opinion of the Lands Tribunal that the price to be paid by the tenant if she wishes to pursue her claim to enfranchisement will be £4,000 to Wentworth and nil to Wrotham. As a technical matter question (2) in the amended case stated should be answered in the affirmative. As a result of the terms on which the Court of Appeal gave leave to appeal to this House, and on which

1   [1946] 1 All ER 512
2   [1953] 1 All ER 40, [1953] Ch 65
3   [1966] 3 All ER 486, [1967] Ch 78

your Lordships gave leave to raise the point under s 9, the orders for costs below should remain undisturbed and there should be no order for costs in this House.

I cannot, my Lords, leave this case without referring once more to the curious situation that if all the 100 odd tenants seek 50 year extensions, Wrotham will be (apparently) in a very unhappy position. Whether this offers an opportunity for some adjustment on enfranchisements I know not.

Appeal allowed.

Solicitors: *Boodle Hatfield & Co* (for Wentworth); *Sherwood & Co*, agents for *Andrew Rowntree*, Potters Bar (for the tenant).

Mary Rose Plummer   Barrister.

Re Barlow's Will Trusts

CHANCERY DIVISION
BROWNE-WILKINSON J
3rd, 6th, 13th, 26th, 27th, 28th JULY 1978

Will – Residue – Division – Trust for sale of residue subject to 'any members of my family and any friends of mine who may wish to do so' being allowed to purchase testatrix's paintings at less than current market value – Whether 'friends' too vague to be given legal effect – Whether 'family' confined to next-of-kin or extending to all blood relatives.

The testatrix died in 1975 leaving a valuable collection of paintings. She was unmarried and her most immediate survivors were eight nephews and nieces, 24 great nephews and nieces and 14 great great nephews and nieces. By her will the testatrix made a bequest to a great niece described as such, and made specific bequests of some of the paintings. She directed her executor to sell the remainder of the collection subject to the provision that 'any members of my family and any friends of mine who may wish to do so' be allowed to purchase any of the paintings at the price shown in a catalogue compiled in 1970 or at probate value, whichever was the lower. Both prices were considerably lower than current market values. By a summons the executor sought the determination of the court of the questions, inter alia, (i) whether the direction was void for uncertainty because the provision was too vague to be given legal effect and (ii) who were to be treated as being members of the testatrix's 'family', which, in the absence of descendants, could mean either her next-of-kin only or everyone related by blood to her.

Held – (i) The direction to allow 'friends' of the testatrix to purchase her paintings did not require all members of a class of donee to be established before it took effect because any uncertainty as to some of the persons who may have been intended to take did not in any way affect the quantum of the gift to those who undoubtedly qualified, and the direction would therefore be valid merely if it was possible to say that one or more claimants qualified, irrespective of how difficult it might be to decide whether others qualified. As the testatrix would have had acquaintances so close that, on any reasonable basis, anyone would consider them her friends, the direction was not void for uncertainty. Whether a particular claimant qualified depended, inter alia, on whether his relationship with the testatrix was of long standing, whether it was a social as opposed to a business or professional relationship and whether when circumstances permitted they met frequently (see p 299 d to g and p 300 b and d e, post); *Re Allen, Faith v Allen* [1953] 2 All ER 898 applied; *Re Gulbenkian's Settlement Trust, Whishaw v Stephens* [1968] 3 All ER 785 and *McPhail v Doulton* [1970] 2 All ER 228 distinguished.

(ii) In the absence of any issue of the testatrix or of any intention expressed in the will to benefit a narrower class, the expression 'family' meant those related by blood to the testatrix, and because the gift was not such that all members of the class described as the testatrix's family had to be established before the gift took effect the rule of construction limiting gifts to relations to the statutory next-of-kin did not apply. Moreover the bequest to a great niece who was described as such indicated that the testatrix regarded her as a member of her family even though she was not one of her next-of-kin. It followed that anyone who proved a blood relationship with the testatrix was entitled to purchase the paintings (see p 301 b to f, post).

Notes

For identification of donees under a will, see 39 Halsbury's Laws (3rd Edn) 1054, 1062, paras 1579, 1586.

For certainty of objects under a trust, see 38 ibid 835, para 1399.

Cases referred to in judgment

Allen, Re, Faith v Allen [1953] 2 All ER 898, [1953] Ch 810, [1953] 3 WLR 637, CA; subsequent proceedings [1954] 1 All ER 526, [1954] Ch 295, [1954] 2 WLR 333, 19 Digest (Repl) 241, 8.

Brown v Gould [1971] 2 All ER 1505, [1972] Ch 53, [1971] 3 WLR 334, 22 P & CR 871, 31(1) Digest (Reissue) 285, 2351.

Gansloser's Will Trusts, Re, Chartered Bank of India, Australia and China v Chillingworth [1951] 2 All ER 936, [1952] Ch 30, CA, 49 Digest (Repl) 797, 7492.

Gibbard, Re, Public Trustee v Davis [1966] 1 All ER 273, [1967] 1 WLR 42, Digest (Cont Vol B) 602, 1330a.

Gulbenkian's Settlement Trusts, Re, Whishaw v Stephens [1968] 3 All ER 785, [1970] AC 508, [1968] 3 WLR 1127, HL, Digest (Cont Vol C) 806, 1330b.

Lloyd's Trust Investments, Re (24th June 1970) unreported.

McPhail v Doulton [1970] 2 All ER 228, [1971] AC 424, [1970] 2 WLR 1110, HL; rvsg sub nom *Re Baden's Deed Trusts, Baden v Smith* [1969] 1 All ER 1016, [1969] 2 Ch 388, [1969] 3 WLR 12, CA, Digest (Cont Vol C) 805, 1324a.

Tuck's Settlements Trusts, Re, Public Trustee v Tuck [1978] 1 All ER 1047, [1978] Ch 49, [1978] 2 WLR 411, CA.

Summons

On 22nd November 1977 the plaintiff, the Royal Exchange Assurance, the executors of the will of Helen Alice Dorothy Barlow deceased ('the testatrix'), issued a summons asking the court to make a declaration whether, on its true construction cl 5(a) of the will, which provided, inter alia, that the executors were 'to allow any members of [the testatrix's] family and any friends of [the testatrix's] who may wish to do so to purchase' certain pictures, (i) entitled only the next-of-kin to purchase, or (ii) entitled next-of-kin or friends to purchase, or (iii) entitled next-of-kin and friends to purchase, or (iv) entitled family, whether next-of-kin or not, and friends to purchase, or (v) was void and of no effect, or (vi) took effect in some other way and if so in what way. The defendants were (1) the National Council of Social Service, (2) Sir Thomas Erasmus Barlow Bt, (3) Dr Rosalind Penelope Kennedy and (4) the Rev Frank Coventry, all of whom claimed to be beneficially interested under the will. The facts are set out in the judgment.

J A Moncaster for the plaintiff.
George Hesketh for the first defendant.
V R Chapman for the second defendant.
D J T Parry for the third defendant.
Miles Shillingford for the fourth defendant.

Cur adv vult

28th July. **BROWNE-WILKINSON J** read the following judgment: This summons raises a number of questions on the will of Helen Alice Dorothy Barlow, who died on 16th September 1975. She had a valuable collection of paintings.

By cl 4 of her will, dated 8th September 1970, she made specific bequests of a number of them. Then by cl 5(a) she provided as follows:

> 'I GIVE AND BEQUEATH all my pictures not hereby specifically disposed of unto the Corporation [I interpose to say that that is the executor] upon trust to distribute any which may be specified in written instructions placed with this my Will among the persons or bodies named in such instructions subject thereto upon trust for sale but I DIRECT the Corporation to allow any members of my family and any friends of mine who may wish to do so to purchase any of such pictures at the prices shown in Mr. Fry's catalogue or at the values placed upon them by valuation for Probate purposes at the date of my death, whichever shall be the lower. The Corporation shall hold the net proceeds of sale of such pictures as are sold by them as part of my residuary estate.'

The written instructions referred to in the first part of cl 5(a) were not admitted to probate. Therefore, apart from the pictures specifically bequeathed, the rest of the testatrix's pictures are directed by cl 5(a) to be sold subject to the rights of the testatrix's family and friends to purchase them at valuation.

The pictures passing under cl 5(a) are of considerable quality, though not of outstanding importance. Mr Fry's catalogue referred to in the clause was made in 1970. Mr Fry also made the valuation for probate purposes, when he put a total value of £28,130 on the pictures in question. The values for probate purposes of most of the pictures are substantially greater than the values appearing in the 1970 catalogue. The present day value of the pictures must certainly be greater still. Therefore, the right to purchase conferred by cl 5(a) on the testatrix's family and friends is a beneficial right of some value.

The main questions which arise for my decision are (a) whether the direction to allow members of the family and friends to purchase the pictures is void for uncertainty since the meaning of the word 'friends' is too vague to be given legal effect and (b) what persons are to be treated as being members of the testatrix's family. I will deal first with the question of uncertainty.

Those arguing against the validity of the gift in favour of the friends contend that, in the absence of any guidance from the testatrix, the question 'Who were her friends?' is incapable of being answered. The word is said to be 'conceptually uncertain' since there are so many different degrees of friendship and it is impossible to say which degree the testatrix had in mind. In support of this argument they rely on Lord Upjohn's remarks in *Re Gulbenkian's Settlement Trusts, Whishaw v Stephens*[1] and the decision of the House of Lords in *McPhail v Doulton*[2] (on appeal from *Re Baden's Deed Trusts*[3]) to the effect that it must be possible to say who is within and who without the class of friends. They say that since the testatrix intended all her friends to have the opportunity to acquire a picture it is necessary to be able to ascertain with certainty all the members of that class.

Counsel for the fourth defendant, who argued in favour of the validity of the gift, contended that the tests laid down in the *Gulbenkian* case[4] and *McPhail v Doulton*[2] were not applicable to this case. The test, he says, is that laid down by the Court of Appeal in *Re Allen*[5] as appropriate in cases where the validity of a condition precedent or description is in issue, namely that the gift is valid if it is possible to say of one or more persons that he or they

---

1 [1968] 3 All ER 785 at 792–793, [1970] AC 508 at 523–524
2 [1970] 2 All ER 228, [1971] AC 424
3 [1969] 1 All ER 1016, [1969] 2 Ch 388
4 [1968] 3 All ER 785, [1970] AC 508
5 [1953] 2 All ER 898, [1953] Ch 810

undoubtedly qualify even though it may be difficult to say of others whether or not they qualify.

The distinction between the *Gulbenkian*[1] test and the *Re Allen*[2] test is, in my judgment, well exemplified by the word 'friends'. The word has a great range of meanings; indeed, its exact meaning probably varies slightly from person to person. Some would include only those with whom they had been on intimate terms over a long period; others would include acquaintances whom they liked. Some would include people with whom their relationship was primarily one of business; others would not. Indeed, many people, if asked to draw up a complete list of their friends, would probably have some difficulty in deciding whether certain of the people they knew were really 'friends' as opposed to 'acquaintances'. Therefore, if the nature of the gift was such that it was legally necessary to draw up a complete list of 'friends' of the testatrix, or to be able to say of any person that 'he is not a friend', the whole gift would probably fail even as to those who, by any conceivable test, were friends. But in the case of a gift of a kind which does not require one to establish all the members of the class (eg 'a gift of £10 to each of my friends'), it may be possible to say of some people that, on any test, they qualify. Thus in *Re Allen*[3] Evershed MR took the example of a gift to X 'if he is a tall man'; a man 6 feet 6 inches tall could be said on any reasonable basis to satisfy the test, although it might be impossible to say whether a man, say, 5 feet 10 inches high satisfied the requirement.

So in this case, in my judgment, there are acquaintances of a kind so close that, on any reasonable basis, anyone would treat them as being 'friends'. Therefore, by allowing the disposition to take effect in their favour, one would certainly be giving effect to part of the testatrix's intention even though as to others it is impossible to say whether or not they satisfy the test.

In my judgment, it is clear that Lord Upjohn in *Re Gulbenkian*[4] was considering only cases where it was necessary to establish all the members of the class. He made it clear that the reason for the rule is that in a gift which requires one to establish all the members of the class (eg 'a gift to my friends in equal shares') you cannot hold the gift good in part, since the quantum of each friend's share depends on how many friends there are. So all persons intended to benefit by the donor must be ascertained if any effect is to be given to the gift. In my judgment, the adoption of Lord Upjohn's test by the House of Lords in *McPhail v Doulton*[5] is based on the same reasoning, even though in that case the House of Lords held that it was only necessary to be able to survey the class of objects of a power of appointment and not to establish who all the members were. But such reasoning has no application to a case where there is a condition or description attached to one or more individual gifts; in such cases, uncertainty as to some other persons who may have been intended to take does not in any way affect the quantum of the gift to persons who undoubtedly possess the qualification. Hence, in my judgment, the different test laid down in *Re Allen*[2]. The recent decision of the Court of Appeal in *Re Tuck's Settlement Trust*[6] establishes that the test in *Re Allen*[2] is still the appropriate test in considering such gifts, notwithstanding the *Gulbenkian*[1] and *McPhail v Doulton*[5] decisions: see per Lord Russell of Killowen[7].

Accordingly, in my judgment, the proper result in this case depends on whether the disposition in cl 5(a) is properly to be regarded as a series of individual gifts to persons answering the description 'friend' (in which case it will be valid), or a gift which requires the whole class of friends to be established (in which case it will probably fail).

---

1   [1968] 3 All ER 785, [1970] AC 508
2   [1953] 2 All ER 898, [1953] Ch 810
3   2 All ER 898 at 901, [1953] Ch 810 at 817
4   [1968] 3 All ER 785 at 792, [1970] AC 508 at 524
5   [1970] 2 All ER 228, [1971] AC 424
6   [1978] 1 All ER 1047, [1978] Ch 49
7   1 All ER 1047 at 1056, [1978] Ch 49 at 65

The effect of cl 5(a) is to confer on friends of the testatrix a series of options to purchase. Although it is obviously desirable as a practical matter that steps should be taken to inform those entitled to the options of their rights, it is common ground that there is no legal necessity to do so. Therefore, each person coming forward to exercise the option has to prove that he is a friend; it is not legally necessary, in my judgment, to discover who all the friends are. In order to decide whether an individual is entitled to purchase, all that is required is that the executors should be able to say of that individual whether he has proved that he is a friend. The word 'friend', therefore, is a description or qualification of the option holder.

It was suggested that by allowing undoubted friends to take I would be altering the testatrix's intentions. It is said that she intended all her friends to have a chance to buy any given picture, and since some people she might have regarded as friends will not be able to apply, the number of competitors for that picture will be reduced. This may be so, but I cannot regard this factor as making it legally necessary to establish the whole class of friends. The testatrix's intention was that a friend should acquire a picture. My decision gives effect to that intention.

I therefore hold that the disposition does not fail for uncertainty, but that anyone who can prove that by any reasonable test he or she must have been a friend of the testatrix is entitled to exercise the option. Without seeking to lay down any exhaustive definition of such test, it may be helpful if I indicate certain minimum requirements: (a) the relationship must have been a long-standing one; (b) the relationship must have been a social relationship as opposed to a business or professional relationship; (c) although there may have been long periods when circumstances prevented the testatrix and the applicant from meeting, when circumstances did permit they must have met frequently. If in any case the executors entertain any real doubt whether an applicant qualifies, they can apply to the court to decide the issue.

Finally on this aspect of the case I should notice two further cases to which I was referred. The first is *Re Gibbard*[1], in which Plowman J upheld the validity of a power to appoint to 'any of my old friends'. It is not necessary for me to decide whether that decision is still good law, in that it applied the *Re Allen*[2] test to powers of appointment. But it does show that, if the *Re Allen*[2] test is the correct test, the word 'friends' is not too uncertain to be given effect. Secondly, in *Re Lloyd's Trust Instruments*[3] (unreported but extracts from which are to be found in *Brown v Gould*[4], Megarry J stated:

'If there is a trust for "my old friends", all concerned are faced with uncertainty as to the concept or idea enshrined in those words. It may not be difficult to resolve that "old" means not "aged" but "of long standing"; but then there is the question of how long is "long". Friendship, too, is a concept with almost infinite shades of meaning. Where the concept is uncertain, the gift is void. Where the concept is certain, then mere difficulty in tracing and discovering those who are entitled normally does not invalidate the gift.'

The extract that I have read itself shows that the judge was considering a trust for 'my old friends' (which required the whole class to be ascertained) and not such a case as I have to deal with. In my judgment, that dictum was not intended to apply to such a case as I have before me.

I turn now to the question, who are to be treated as 'members of my family'? It is not suggested that this class is too uncertain. The contest is between those who say that only the next-of-kin of the testatrix are entitled and those who say that everyone related by blood to the testatrix is included.

---

1   [1966] 1 All ER 273, [1961] 1 WLR 42
2   [1953] 2 All ER 898, [1953] Ch 810
3   (24th June 1970) unreported
4   [1971] 2 All ER 1505 at 1507, [1972] Ch 53 at 57

The testatrix was unmarried; therefore the word 'family' cannot refer to her descendants. She had two brothers, Sir James and Sir Thomas Barlow, who survived to adulthood, a brother who died without issue during the 1914–18 war, and a sister who died in infancy. She was survived by eight nephews and nieces, 24 great nephews and nieces, and 14 great great nephews and nieces. A number of these were infants. Her will includes a gift to a great niece (so described) who would not be one of her next-of-kin. No doubt there are very many more remote relations.

In the absence of issue, the prima facie meaning of 'family' means 'relations', that is to say those related by blood. The context of the will may show that the testatrix had a special class in mind, but I can find no sufficient context in this will to find that the testatrix meant any narrower class to take. However, there is a rule of construction that limits gifts to relations to the statutory next-of-kin of the testator. The authorities clearly establish that the reason for this rule is that, unless such a limitation is introduced, the gift would fail for uncertainty, it being impossible to establish all the persons who are related by blood, however remotely: see Jarman on Wills[1]. That this is the reason for the rule is made abundantly clear by Jenkins LJ in *Re Gansloser's Will Trusts*[2] where he describes this need for limiting the class to next-of-kin as 'justification for imputing a wholly conventional and artificial intention to the testator'.

In the case of a gift to 'my relations in equal shares', such an artificial construction is necessary to save the gift from failing for uncertainty. But for the same reasons as I have sought to give in dealing with the word 'friends', in this particular case the option to the members of the family would not in any event fail for uncertainty even if it included all the testatrix's blood relations; anyone seeking to exercise the option would have to prove simply that he had a blood relationship.

There being, therefore, no reason to give the words in this will an artificially limited meaning, I decline to do so. The fact that in the will the testatrix described a beneficiary as her great niece strongly suggests that she regarded that beneficiary as a member of her family. Yet that great niece is not one of her next-of-kin. Accordingly, the artificially limited construction would defeat the testatrix's intention. There being no need so to construe the clause in order to validate it, I hold that the word has its ordinary meaning and includes all persons related by blood to the testatrix.

Declaration accordingly.

Solicitors: *Robertson, Thomas & Stevens*, Amersham (for the plaintiff and the third defendant); *Palmer, Paletz & Mark* (for the first defendant); *Wood, Nash & Winter's* (for the second defendant); *Farrer & Co* (for the fourth defendant).

Hazel Hartman   Barrister.

---

1   8th Edn (1951), p 1621
2   [1951] 2 All ER 936 at 946, [1952] Ch 30 at 46–47

Re Mesco Properties Ltd

CHANCERY DIVISION
BRIGHTMAN J
17th, 18th, 19th OCTOBER, 7th NOVEMBER 1978

Company – Compulsory winding-up – Corporation tax on chargeable gains – Priority of liquidator's fees over tax – Company compulsorily wound up – Assets sold following winding-up order – Resulting liability to corporation tax on chargeable gains – Liquidator's balance less than amount liable to corporation tax – Whether corporation tax an expense incurred in realising assets – Whether corporation tax a necessary disbursement by the liquidator – Whether corporation tax a charge or expense incurred in the winding-up – Whether corporation tax ranking in priority to costs of petition and liquidator's fees – Whether court having discretion to order payment of liquidator's fees before payment of tax – Companies Act 1948, s 267 – Companies (Winding-up) Rules 1949 (SI 1949 No 330), r 195(1).

A company was compulsorily wound up and its properties subsequently sold. After discharging encumbrances and paying costs and other liabilities the liquidator held a balance of some £520,000. As a result of the sale of the properties the company was assessed to corporation tax of £634,440 on chargeable gains. The liquidator sought the determination of the court whether the company's liability to account to the Crown in respect of the corporation tax (i) was part of 'the fees or expenses properly incurred in preserving, realising or getting in the assets' of the company, within r 195(1)[a] of the Companies (Winding-up) Rules 1949 (in which case the tax ranked in front of the costs of the winding-up petition and the liquidator's fees) or part of the 'necessary disbursements of [the] liquidator', within r 195(1) (in which case the tax ranked after the costs of the petition but ahead of the liquidator's fees); or (ii) was part of 'the costs, charges and expenses incurred in the winding up', within s 267[b] of the Companies Act 1948 (in which case the court had power to order that the tax rank after the costs of the petition and the liquidator's fees).

Held – (i) On the true construction of r 195(1) of the 1949 rules corporation tax arising on a capital gain made by a liquidator when he sold an asset was not an expense incurred in realising that asset since it did not assist the sale and was not a necessary result of it but was merely a possible consequence of the sale (see p 306 *d* to *f* and *h*, post); dictum of Maugham J in *Re Beni-Felkai Mining Co Ltd* [1933] All ER Rep at 696–697 applied.

(ii) Since the tax was not an expense incurred in realising assets it was therefore a necessary disbursement of the liquidator, within r 195(1). However it was also a charge or expense incurred in the winding-up, within s 267 of the 1948 Act, and the court therefore had power to vary the priority in which the tax was paid in relation to other charges or expenses incurred in the winding-up. In the circumstances the court would order that the liquidator's fees rank ahead of the liability for corporation tax (see p 305 *a* and p 306 *f* to *h*, post); *Re Beni-Felkai Mining Co Ltd* [1933] All ER Rep 693 applied.

---

a   Rule 195(1), so far as material, provides: 'The assets of a Company in a winding-up by the Court remaining after payment of the fees and expenses properly incurred in preserving, realising or getting in the assets . . . shall . . . be liable to . . . payments, which shall be made in the following order . . . *First.*—The taxed costs of the petition . . . *Next.*—The remuneration of the special manager (if any). *Next.*—The costs and expenses of any person who makes or concurs in making, the Company's statement of affairs. *Next.*—The taxed charges of any shorthand writer . . . *Next.*—The necessary disbursements of any Liquidator . . . other than expenses properly incurred in preserving, realising or getting in the assets . . . *Next.*—The costs of any person properly employed by such Liquidator. *Next.*—The remuneration of any such Liquidator . . .'

b   Section 267 provides: 'The court may, in the event of the assets being insufficient to satisfy the liabilities, make an order as to the payment out of the assets of the costs, charges and expenses incurred in the winding up in such order of priority as the court thinks just.'

Notes

For priority for payment of tax in a winding-up, see 7 Halsbury's Laws (4th Edn) paras 1285, 1316, for the application of assets in a winding-up, see ibid paras 1310, 1497, and for cases on the subject, see 10 Digest (Reissue) 1075–1076, 1148, 6596–6600, 7146–7149.

For the Companies Act 1948, s 267, see 5 Halsbury's Statutes (3rd Edn) 319.

For the Companies (Winding-up) Rules 1949, r 195, see 4 Halsbury's Statutory Instruments (Third Reissue) 186.

Cases referred to in judgment

Beni-Felkai Mining Co Ltd, Re [1934] Ch 406, [1933] All ER Rep 693, 18 Tax Cas 632, 103 LJ Ch 187, 150 LT 370, [1934] B & CR 14, 10 Digest (Reissue) 1152, 7170.

General Rolling Stock Co, Re, Chapman's Case (1866) LR 1 Eq 346, 35 Beav 207, 12 Jun NS 44, 55 ER 874, 9 Digest (Reissue) 579, 3455.

Cases also cited

McMeekin (a bankrupt), Re [1974] STC 429, 48 Tax Cas 725.

Webb v Whiffin (1872) LR 5 HL 711.

Whitney v Inland Revenue Comrs [1926] AC 37, 10 Tax Cas 88, HL.

Adjourned summons

By summons dated 28th April 1978, Gerhard Adolf Weiss, the liquidator of Mesco Properties Ltd ('the company'), sought the determination of the following questions and the following relief: (1) whether the liability of the company to account to the Commissioners of Inland Revenue in respect of chargeable gains on disposals by (i) the Co-operative Bank Ltd ('the bank') in exercise of its powers as mortgagee, (ii) the receiver appointed by the bank in exercise of its powers as mortgagee, and (iii) the liquidator of the company during winding-up by the court of assets vested in the company arose (a) as a fee or expense properly incurred in preserving, realising or getting in the company's assets within the meaning of r 195(1) of the Companies (Winding-up) Rules 1949[1], or (b) as a necessary disbursement of the liquidator within the meaning of r 195(1), or (c) as a debt or some other liability ranking pari passu with the claims of the ordinary unsecured creditors of the company, or (d) as some other liability; and (2) whether in any event the liability was a cost, charge or expense of the winding-up within the meaning of s 267 of the Companies Act 1948; and (3) in the event that the liability ranked in order of priority ahead of the remuneration of the liquidator within r 195(1) an order under s 267 of the 1948 Act that the remuneration of the liquidator down to his release be allowed in full in priority to the liability. The Commissioners of Inland Revenue were respondents to the summons.

Allan Heyman QC and *James Munby* for the liquidator.
Peter Gibson for the commissioners.

Cur adv vult

7th November. **BRIGHTMAN J** read the following judgment: This summons relates to a company known as Mesco Properties Ltd. This was one of a number of companies which defrauded banks of large sums of money by means of forged documents and bogus valuations. A compulsory winding-up order was made on 21st December 1970. The present application is by the liquidator to determine certain questions of priority. The Commissioners of Inland Revenue are the respondents.

Before the commencement of the winding-up, namely in September 1970, the Co-operative Bank Ltd appointed a receiver of certain of the company's properties which had been charged in its favour. Between 1971 and 1973 nine of these properties were sold by the receiver at prices substantially in excess of the cost of acquisition. In 1971 a further property charged in favour of the bank, of which a receiver had not been appointed, was

---

1   SI 1949 No 330

sold by the bank as mortgagee at a substantial profit over the company's acquisition price. Between 1971 and 1976 11 more properties were sold by the liquidator, some of which were subject to charges and some of which were unencumbered. In these cases also the properties were mostly realised at prices in excess of cost.

In the result, chargeable gains have accrued under the capital gains tax legislation initiated by the Finance Act 1965. Under s 22(7) of that Act a sale by a mortgagee or receiver is treated as if it had been effected by the mortgagee or receiver as nominee for the mortgagor, so that the mortgagor is the person assessable to tax on any chargeable gains so realised. Under s 22(8) an asset subject to a charge at the date of disposition is treated as being disposed of free of such charge so that the gross proceeds of sale are taken into account for the purposes of computing any chargeable gain.

As a result of these realisations there accrued to the liquidator a net balance of £736,197 after discharging encumbrances and costs. Chargeable gains accruing to a company are liable to corporation tax under s 238 of the Income and Corporation Taxes Act 1970. Under section 243(2) of the 1970 Act a company is chargeable to corporation tax on profits arising in the winding-up thereof. Under s 238(4) of the 1970 Act such profits include chargeable gains. The total liability to corporation tax on these chargeable gains has been calculated at £634,440. This is only about £100,000 less than the balance of the proceeds of sale which came into the hands of the liquidator. Indeed, the corporation tax liability could well have exceeded the net balance, in which case it would have paid the liquidator to abandon the properties if by so doing he could have avoided liability to tax. The liquidator has a balance in hand of about £520,000, which is less than the corporation tax due.

At this stage I am concerned only with the first two paragraphs of the summons. The first question asked can be stated as follows: (A) whether the corporation tax is part of 'the fees and expenses properly incurred in preserving, realising or getting in the assets' within the meaning of the opening words of r 195(1) of the Companies (Winding-up) Rules 1949. If so, the tax is one of the first payments to be made by the liquidator out of the assets. The tax would rank in front of the costs of the winding-up petition, the liquidator's remuneration and the other matters mentioned in the paragraphs of r 195(1); (B) if not, whether the tax is part of the 'necessary disbursements of any Liquidator appointed in the winding-up by the Court other than expenses properly incurred in preserving, realising or getting in the assets heretofore provided for.' This is the fifth paragraph of r 195(1). The tax would then rank after the taxed costs of the petition and certain other matters, but in front of the liquidator's fees; (C) if not, whether the tax is a debt or liability ranking pari passu with the claims of the ordinary unsecured creditors. This alternative was abandoned before me, because it is accepted that only liabilities which are subsisting at the date of the winding-up order are capable of proof: see *Re General Rolling Stock Co*[1]; (D) alternatively, whether the tax is postponed to the debts of the unsecured creditors. In this case, the fees of the liquidator could be paid in full.

The second question is whether the tax comes within the expression 'the costs, charges and expenses incurred in the winding up' in s 267 of the Companies Act 1948. If so, the court would have power to make an order for the payment thereof out of the assets in such order of priority as the court considered just, and could therefore postpone the tax to the costs of the petition and the fees of the liquidator.

The summons raises these questions separately in respect of tax on chargeable gains on disposals respectively by the bank, the receiver and the liquidator, but in fact there is no distinction to be drawn, since in each case the gain accrues to the company and the liquidator is the proper person to discharge the tax so occasioned.

It is conceded by the Crown that the tax in question is not preferential under s 319 of the 1948 Act.

As I have already said, s 243(2) of the Income and Corporation Taxes Act 1970 expressly enacts that a company is chargeable to corporation tax on a capital gain arising in the winding-up. It follows that the tax is a charge which the liquidator is bound to discharge

1   (1866) LR 1 Eq 346

by payment, to the extent that assets are available. It is, therefore, to my mind, beyond argument that the payment of the tax is a 'necessary disbursement' of the liquidator and must come within the fifth paragraph of r 195(1) of the 1949 rules unless it is an expense 'properly incurred in preserving, realising or getting in the assets', in which case it is excepted from the fifth paragraph because it falls within the opening words of sub-r (1).

One can start, therefore, by ruling out construction (D) as well as construction (C). The tax cannot rank with or after the debts of unsecured creditors. It is either an expense incurred in realising or getting in the assets or a necessary disbursement of the liquidator which is not properly described as an expense so incurred.

There is no reported authority which directly solves this question. However, there are certain obiter dicta in *Re Beni-Felkai Mining Co Ltd*[1] to which I will come later. In that case the company was in voluntary liquidation under the Companies (Consolidation) Act 1908. Section 171 of the 1908 Act, corresponding to s 267 of the Companies Act 1948, provided that:

> 'The court may, in the event of the assets being insufficient to satisfy the liabilities, make an order as to the payment out of the assets of the costs, charges, and expenses incurred in the winding up in such order of priority as the court thinks just.'

Under s 193 of the 1908 Act that power was exercisable in a voluntary winding-up. Section 196 of the 1908 Act, corresponding to s 309 of the 1948 Act, provided that:

> 'All costs, charges and expenses properly incurred in the voluntary winding-up of a company, including the remuneration of the liquidator, shall be payable out of the assets of the company in priority to all other claims.'

The liquidator carried on the company's business at a profit for the purpose of realisation and thereby incurred a liability for income tax under Sch D. The Crown claimed that the tax was an expense incurred in the winding-up of the company within the meaning of s 196 and was therefore not postponed to the liquidator's remuneration, as it would have been if outside the ambit of this section. Maugham J, considering ss 171 and 196 together, said[2]:

> 'I have a difficulty in seeing how a liquidator who, in the course of his liquidation carries on the business of the company at a profit, the consequence being the assessment of the company to income tax, can avoid the conclusion that this is one of the expenses in the winding-up. It is curious that in the authorities to which I have been referred the phrase does not seem to have been used by the Court. In my opinion rates and taxes—and for this purpose I can group them together, although there is for some purposes a distinction between them—falling due subsequently to the winding up are part of the expenses of the winding up.'

Maugham J therefore concluded that it was open to him under s 171 to determine the order of priority as between the charge to income tax and the remuneration of the liquidator.

That decision does not answer the question before me, namely whether construction (A) or construction (B) is correct. The words I have to consider are 'expenses properly incurred in realising or getting in the assets', not 'expenses incurred in the winding up'. The former expression is much narrower. However, in reaching his decision Maugham J did consider r 187 (1) of the Companies (Winding-up) Rules 1909, which was the same as the present r 195(1) except for minor differences in wording. Priority was given by r 187(1) of the 1909 rules to 'the payment of the fees and actual expenses incurred in realising or getting in the assets'. The wording is very similar to the opening words of the present r 195(1). The fifth paragraph of r 187(1) refers to 'the Liquidator's necessary disbursements, other than actual expenses of realisation heretofore provided for'.

---

1   [1934] Ch 406, [1933] All ER Rep 693, 18 Tax Cas 632
2   Ch 406 at 418, [1933] All ER Rep 693 at 697, 18 Tax Cas 632 at 635–636

Maugham J said[1]:

'That rule, of course, does not apply to the present case, which, as I have said, is a case of voluntary liquidation. It may, however, be useful by way of analogy, as showing what the framers of the rules considered to be the fair way of dealing with the case where the assets available were not sufficient to pay the whole of those various costs and expenses in full and to leave anything over for the creditors of the company in the ordinary way. Accordingly, as the rule is not strictly applicable and is not binding on me, I am at liberty to disregard it if I think it just, and in any case the rule is expressed to be subject to any Order of the Court, but I think I ought to express the opinion which I have formed that income tax incurred under Schedule D by a liquidator in carrying on the business of a company after the date of liquidation is not strictly within the words "fees and actual expenses incurred in realising or getting in the assets." It would be going too far, I think, to hold that the rule gives income tax priority over the taxed costs of a petition and a number of other costs which are intended to come early in the scale of priorities. I am more doubtful whether an income tax liability so incurred may not be within the words "the liquidator's necessary disbursements." That, however, is a matter on which I think I had better not express a final opinion at the present time.'

I respectfully agree with his conclusion, given obiter, that in the case of a compulsory liquidation income tax incurred by the liquidator under Sch D in carrying on the business of the company after the date of the order is not an expense incurred in realising or getting in the assets notwithstanding he is carrying on the business in the course of the performance of his duty to realise and get in the assets; nor do I think that corporation tax on a capital gain made by the liquidator when he sells an asset is 'an expense incurred in realising' that asset. It is not like the fees payable to a solicitor or to an estate agent in connection with a sale, or the advertising costs of a sale, which are clearly part of the expenses of the sale. The tax does not assist the liquidator to sell. Nor is it a necessary result of the sale. It is merely a possible consequence of a sale at a profit. Even when a sale has been made at a profit the liquidator may not know whether ultimately any tax will be payable. This will depend on what, if any, profits, including both income and chargeable gains, or losses, arise in that financial year and whether any losses can be carried forward from a previous year. The tax is merely a possible consequence of the realisation of an asset at a profit. It is not an expense which the liquidator incurs for the purposes of, or as a direct result of, realising that asset, and therefore it is not, in my view, an expense incurred in realising it. However, it seems to me equally clear, as I have already indicated, that the tax is a necessary disbursement of the liquidator and therefore falls within the fifth paragraph of r 195(1) of the 1949 rules.

I turn now to the second question. *Re Beni-Felkai Mining Co Ltd*[2] is a direct authority that Sch D income tax is a charge or expense 'incurred in the winding up' within the meaning of what is now s 267 of the 1948 Act. It seems to me equally clear that corporation tax is also such a charge or expense. This follows from the decision which I have already made that the tax is a necessary disbursement of the liquidator.

I therefore decide against what I have called construction (A) and in favour of construction (B). I will also declare that the tax is a cost, charge or expense incurred in the winding-up within the meaning of s 267 of the 1948 Act.

[His Lordship, after hearing further submissions by counsel, then ordered that the remuneration of the liquidator down to his release be allowed in full in priority to the company's liability to corporation tax.]

Order in same terms as questions (1)(b), (2) and (3) of the summons.

Solicitors: *Herbert Smith & Co* (for the liquidator); *Solicitor of Inland Revenue.*

Evelyn Budd   Barrister.

---

1 [1934] Ch 406 at 417, [1933] All ER Rep 693 at 696–697, 18 Tax Cas 632 at 634–635
2 Ch 406, [1933] All ER Rep 693, 18 Tax Cas 632

Federal Commerce and Navigation Ltd v Molena Alpha Inc and others
The Nanfri, The Benfri, The Lorfri

HOUSE OF LORDS

LORD WILBERFORCE, VISCOUNT DILHORNE, LORD FRASER OF TULLYBELTON, LORD RUSSELL OF KILLOWEN AND LORD SCARMAN

3rd, 4th, 5th, 9th, 10th, 11th OCTOBER, 23rd NOVEMBER 1978

Contract – Repudiation – Anticipatory breach – Charterparty – Shipowners threatening to instruct master to withdraw from charterers right to sign bills of lading 'freight pre-paid' – Charterers treating owners' conduct as repudiation of charterparty – Whether owners' conduct anticipatory breach of charterparty – Whether breach amounting to repudiation of charterparty – Whether charterers entitled to terminate charterparty.

By three time charterparties, dated 1st November 1974, in identical form, the respective owners of three vessels let them to charterers for a period of six years. They were to be used for the carriage of grain and steel on c i f terms. The shippers would therefore pay the freight for the carriage in advance and receive bills of lading marked 'freight pre-paid'. The charterparties provided: (i) by cl 9*[a]* that the master was to be under the orders of the charterers as regards employment, agency or other arrangements and that the charterers were to indemnify the owners against all consequences or liability arising from the master signing the bills of lading; (ii) by cl 11 that the charterers were entitled to make deductions from the hire in the event of specified occurrences, one of which was time being lost or expenses incurred by slow steaming; and (iii) by cl 18*[b]* that the owners were to have a lien on all cargoes and sub-freight belonging to the time charterers and on any bill of lading for all claims under the charterparties. By virtue of cl 9 the charterers, on behalf of the master, issued and signed bills of lading and the freight was paid to them or their agents. In 1977 a dispute arose between the parties regarding various deductions which the charterers had made from the hire paid and regarding the general right of the charterers to make deductions from the hire. On 19th September the charterers informed the owners that they intended to deduct, under cl 11, $47,122·43 from the hire due on one of the vessels on 1st October on account of slow steaming during a voyage in 1975 following engine repairs. On 20th September the owners refused to authorise the deduction and demanded payment of the full hire instalment but the charterers nevertheless proceeded to deduct the $47,122·43. On 4th October the owners informed the charterers by telex that they were instructing the masters of the three vessels (i) to withdraw all authority to the charterers or their agents to sign bills of lading, (ii) to refuse to sign any bill of lading endorsed 'freight pre-paid' and (iii) to insist that all bills of lading should bear an endorsement stating that all the terms, conditions and exceptions of the charterparties were incorporated 'including the lien under clause 18 on bill of lading freight as well as sub-freight belonging to the [charterers]'. At the same time the owners issued instructions to the masters in those terms knowing that their action would place the charterers in serious difficulties because the charterers had sub-chartered the vessels to shippers to whom these terms would be unacceptable and who would blacklist the vessels and the charterers from the grain and steel trades, unless bills of lading were issued promptly freight pre-paid and not claused by reference to a time charterparty. On 5th October the charterers demanded the withdrawal of the owners' instructions to the masters. The owners refused to withdraw unless all the

---

a   Clause 9, so far as material, is set out at p 316 *e*, post

b   Clause 18 provided: 'The Owners to have a lien upon all cargoes and sub-freights belonging to the Time-Charterers and any Bill of Lading freight for all claims under this Charter, and the Charterers to have a lien on the Vessel for all moneys paid in advance and not earned.'

disputed deductions from hire were paid. The charterers thereupon telexed on the same
day the owners that their conduct was a repudiation of the charterparties which the   *a*
charterers accepted without prejudice to their rights and that they considered the
charterparties to be terminated forthwith. Termination would have had a serious effect on
the shipowners because shipping hire rates were then much lower than the rates obtaining
in 1974. The parties entered into a 'without prejudice' agreement as a result of which the
three vessels remained in service, the charterers paid the disputed deductions and agreed
to make no more deductions without the owners' consent, and bills of lading marked   *b*
'freight pre-paid' were issued without endorsement. The question whether the
charterparties had been terminated by repudiation and acceptance was referred to
arbitration. The umpire found in favour of the charterers but stated his award in the form
of a special case, the questions for the decision of the court being whether the charterers
had validly terminated the charterparties on 5th October and whether the charterers were
entitled to deduct from hire without the consent of the owners claims which arose either   *c*
under cl 11 of the charterparty or which constituted an equitable set-off. The judge held
that the charterers had not validly terminated the charterparties because the owners' action
on 4th October had merely created a temporary impasse which had been speedily resolved
by the 'without prejudice' agreement. He further held that the charterers were entitled to
make deductions without the owners' consent both under cl 11 and by way of equitable set-
off. On appeal, the Court of Appeal[c] held that the owners' action on 4th October amounted   *d*
to an anticipatory breach of the charterparties and the charterers were therefore entitled to
treat them as terminated. The court further held that the charterers were entitled to
deduct without the owners' consent valid claims arising under cl 11 or by way of equitable
set-off notwithstanding the rule of law that freight payable under a voyage charterparty
was payable in full without deduction. The owners appealed to the House of Lords,
contending, inter alia, that cl 18 entitled them to instruct the masters to refuse to sign bills   *e*
of lading freight pre-paid and to clause them by a reference to the time charters. The
deduction issue was not argued before the House.

Held – The appeal would be dismissed for the following reasons—
  (i) On the construction of cll 9 and 18 of the charterparties according to their ordinary
meaning, the owners' lien under cl 18 only gave the owners a lien if and when cargoes   *f*
belonging to the charterers were carried or sub-freights became due to them and did not
entitle the owners to interfere with the charterers' primary right under cl 9 to use the
vessels as they thought fit and to direct the masters as to their use. Furthermore, in the
circumstances of the trades for which the vessels were chartered the only sensible
construction of the charterparties was that cl 18 had not given the owners the right to
require the charterers to procure that shippers' cargoes were carried on terms giving the   *g*
owners a lien over them. It was within the charterers' powers under cl 9 to require the
masters to sign freight pre-paid bills of lading and the owners' attempt to prevent the
masters from doing so was an anticipatory, or (per Viscount Dilhorne and Lord Russell of
Killowen) actual, breach of cl 9 of the charterparties (see p 312 j to p 313 d and g h, p 316
a b and g to j, p 317 c, p 318 g to j, p 319 a b and p 320 g, post).
  (ii) Furthermore, although cl 9 was not a condition of the contract so that any breach of   *h*
it automatically amounted to a repudiation, the actual breach which had occurred, by
threatening to deprive the charterers of substantially the whole benefit of the contract, had
gone to the root of the contract since the charterparties would then have become useless for
the purpose for which they were entered into, and the breach was therefore such as to
entitle the charterers to terminate them (see p 313 j to p 314 a and g to j, p 315 b c and h,
p 316 a c, p 317 d, p 318 a to e, p 319 c e and p 320 b c and f g, post); dicta of Diplock LJ in   *j*
Hong Kong Fir Shipping Co Ltd v Kawasaki Kisen Kaisha Ltd [1962] 1 All ER at 489 and of
Buckley LJ in *Decro-Wall International SA v Practitioners in Marketing Ltd* [1971] 2 All ER at
232 applied.

c   [1978] 3 All ER 1066

Per Lord Wilberforce. A threat to commit a breach, having radical consequences, is nonetheless serious because it is disproportionate to the intended effect. Furthermore, if a party's conduct is such as to amount to a threatened repudiatory breach, his subjective desire to maintain the contract cannot prevent the other party from drawing the consequences of his actions (see p 315 *f g*, post).

Decision of the Court of Appeal [1978] 3 All ER 1066 affirmed in part.

Notes

For a ship's master's authority to sign bills of lading, see 35 Halsbury's Laws (3rd Edn) 285, 339–341, paras 425, 485–488, and for cases on the subject, see 41 Digest (Repl) 242, 276–278, 626–636, 934–955.

For anticipatory breach and repudiation of contract generally, see 9 Halsbury's Laws (4th Edn) paras 546–550, and for cases on the subject, see 12 Digest (Reissue) 411–416, 3032–3049.

Cases referred to in opinions

Aries Tanker Corpn v Total Transport Ltd [1977] 1 All ER 398, [1977] 1 WLR 185, [1977] 1 Lloyd's Rep 334, HL.

Decro-Wall International SA v Practitioners in Marketing Ltd [1971] 2 All ER 216, [1971] 1 WLR 361, CA, 12 Digest (Reissue) 415, 3049.

Freeth v Burr (1874) LR 9 CP 208, [1874–80] All ER Rep 750, 43 LJCP 91, 29 LT 773, 12 Digest (Reissue) 413, 3042.

Hong Kong Fir Shipping Co Ltd v Kawasaki Kisen Kaisha Ltd [1962] 1 All ER 474, [1962] 2 QB 26, [1962] 2 WLR 474, [1961] 2 Lloyd's Rep 478, CA, 41 Digest (Repl) 363, 1553.

Shaffer (James) Ltd v Findlay Durham & Brodie [1953] 1 WLR 106, CA, 12 Digest (Reissue) 414, 3046.

Shillito, The (1897) 3 Com Cas 44, 41 Digest (Repl) 540, 3179.

Smyth (Ross T) & Co Ltd v T D Bailey, Son & Co [1940] 3 All ER 60, 164 LT 102, 45 Com Cas 292, HL, 39 Digest (Repl) 611, 1239.

Sweet & Maxwell Ltd v Universal News Services Ltd [1964] 3 All ER 30, [1964] 2 QB 699, [1964] 3 WLR 356, CA, 12 Digest (Reissue) 415, 3048.

Turner v Haji Goolam Mahomed Azam [1904] AC 826, 74 LJPC 17, 91 LT 216, 9 Asp MLC 588, PC, 41 Digest (Repl) 277, 947.

Appeals

On 12th December 1974 retroactive to 1st November 1973 Molena Trust Inc as bareboat chartered owners concluded three identical time charterparties on Baltime 1939 forms (with additions and amendments) with Federal Commerce and Navigation (1974) Ltd of Montreal, Quebec, Canada, a subsidiary of Federal Commerce and Navigation Ltd ('the charterers'), for the hire by the charterers of three vessels, the Nanfri, the Benfri and the Lorfri, for a period of six years. Subsequently Molena Alpha Inc, Molena Beta Inc and Molena Gamma Inc ('the owners') each acquired title to one of the vessels and each was substituted for Molena Trust Inc as the owners in the respective charterparties. The charterparties contained arbitration clauses providing that any dispute arising thereunder was to be referred to arbitration in London. During the course of 1977 disputes arose between the parties as to the validity of various deductions which the charterers had made from hire and as to the general right of the charterers to make deductions from hire. Those issues were submitted to arbitration. In September 1977 the charterers informed the owners that they intended to deduct the sum of $47,122·43 from hire due on the Nanfri on 1st October. The charterers made the deduction despite the owners' objection. On 4th October the owners informed the charterers that they would refuse to allow freight pre-paid bills of lading to be issued and would insist that all bills of lading be claused to incorporate the time charterparties, and in particular cl 18 thereof under which the owners were to have a lien on all cargoes and sub-freights belonging to the time charterers and any bill of lading freight for all claims under the charterparties. On the same day the owners instructed their masters to this effect. Despite the charterers' protest, and their reiterated offer to secure the owners by placing the amount of all disputed deductions from hire in escrow, they affirmed that they intended to enforce their stated intention unless they were paid all disputed deductions. On 5th October the charterers gave notice terminating the charterparties. The parties then went to arbitration on the issue, inter alia, whether the charterers were justified in terminating the charterparties. The arbitrators disagreed and the umpire (Clifford A L Clark Esq) stated his award in each case in the form of a special case. The questions of law for the opinion of the court in each case were: (1) whether on the true construction of the charterparty the charterers were entitled to deduct from hire without the consent of the owners valid claims which (a) arose under cl 11 of the charterparty or (b) constituted an equitable set-off; and (2) whether the charterers had validly terminated the charterparty on 5th October 1977. Subject to the opinion of the court the umpire answered all questions in the affirmative. By order dated 23rd February 1978 Kerr J answered question 1(a) and (b) in the affirmative and question (2) in the negative and remitted the case to the umpire. The charterers appealed and the owners cross-appealed to the Court of Appeal[1] (Lord Denning MR, Goff and Cumming-Bruce LJJ) which on 18th April 1978 restored the findings of the umpire. The owners appealed to the House of Lords. The facts are summarised in the opinion of Lord Wilberforce. They are set out fully in the judgment of Lord Denning MR in the Court of Appeal[2].

Robert Alexander QC, Nicholas Phillips QC and *Adrian M Ginsberg* for the owners.
Gordon Pollock and *Peter Gross* for the charterers.

Their Lordships took time for consideration.

23rd November. The following opinions were delivered.

LORD WILBERFORCE. My Lords, this litigation arises from three charterparties in identical form dated 1st November 1974, and amended by addenda dated 12th June 1975, by which the appellants ('the owners') chartered three vessels called the Nanfri, the Benfri and the Lorfri to the respondents ('the charterers') for six years. Because of the world recession in shipping the charters were, at the time when the relevant events occurred, advantageous to the owners and disadvantageous to the charterers. It is therefore in the charterers' interest to contend that the charters are at an end. Their contention is that the owners have committed a repudiatory breach of contract so that they were entitled, as they did in October 1977, to determine the charters. Separate litigation has arisen regarding each of the three ships, but this has been consolidated, and I shall deal with the dispute as a single identical issue which equally affects each contract.

The relevant facts are fully given in the award in the form of a special case made by the umpire (the matter having gone to arbitration) and these, with the relevant clauses in the charterparties, appear in the judgments of Kerr J[3] and of the Court of Appeal[1]. No doubt they will be restated in the report of this appeal. I shall not set them out at length. The relevant points which, as it appears to me are necessary for the decision of these appeals, are the following.

1. The charters, being time charters on Baltime 1939 form, provided for the payment of hire in advance on the 1st and 16th of each month. There was a clause (cl 11) allowing deductions to be made from hire in specified events, one of which was the event of time being lost, or expense incurred, through slow steaming. It appears that in the initial years of the charters certain deductions from hire were made by the charterers under cl 11, some of which were agreed with the owners in advance; others were the subject of discussion and subsequent agreement. In 1975 the charterers put forward a claim in respect of slow steaming of the Nanfri. The owners did not agree with this claim and suggested that it be

taken to arbitration, but this suggestion was not taken up by the charterers, and the claim remained dormant until September 1977. In July and September 1977 the charterers made deductions in respect of each of the three vessels which the owners did not agree: they contended that the charterers had over-deducted some $46,000. On 19th September 1977 the charterers resurrected the 1975 slow steaming claim and said that in respect of it they intended to deduct some $47,000 from the Nanfri hire due on 1st October. The owners rejected this claim. On 21st September they gave notice of arbitration in respect of the validity of the deductions of $46,000 and also on the question of principle whether the charterers had any right unilaterally to deduct sums not agreed as valid. The charterers proceeded to make the threatened deductions from 1st October hire.

2. Early in October, the owners, having consulted lawyers in London and in New York, gave instructions to their masters to refuse to sign bills of lading marked 'freight pre-paid' and to insist that all bills of lading should be 'claused' so as to incorporate the terms of the charters. On 4th October the owners, by telex of their managers, informed the charterers of this action. The charterers protested against these instructions and insisted that they be withdrawn. The owners replied that they would withdraw the instructions if all unilateral deductions were immediately paid. On 5th October the charterers telexed that they treated the owners' conduct as repudiation of the charters and that they terminated the charters.

3. A 'without prejudice' agreement was immediately entered into by which the three vessels remained in service, all disputed deductions were paid, the charterers agreed to make no more deductions without the owners' approval, and freight pre-paid bills of lading were issued without any reference therein to the charterparties.

4. Findings made by the umpire include the following. (a) The owners and their managers knew at all material times that the charterers wished to use the vessels for Great Lakes trade, involving outward carriage of grain and inward carriage of steel. They also knew that each of these types of shipment was usually made on c i f terms in which it would be usual for freight pre-paid bills of lading to be issued clean of any reference to a time charter. (b) The owners and their managers knew that refusal to issue freight pre-paid bills was likely to cause the charterers severe commercial embarrassment and possibly substantial liability to third parties. (c) The owners intended that the effect of their action (as communicated in the October telexes) would be that the charterers would pay the disputed deductions under protest and that all issues would shortly be resolved by arbitration. (d) The consequences for the charterers of the orders issued by the owners on 4th October were extremely serious since, unless the charterers could ensure the issue of freight pre-paid bills of lading not claused by reference to a time charterparty, the vessels would be largely debarred from the grain and steel trade, the charterers would be unable to comply with existing obligations to sub-charterers, and the charterers were likely to be blacklisted by Continental Grain (their sub-charterers and one of the world's largest shippers of grain) and likely to incur substantial liabilities to that company if cargoes currently being loaded or about to be loaded did not have promptly issued freight pre-paid bills of lading.

My Lords, before attacking the real question in these appeals, which is whether the owner's actions were repudiatory, it is necessary to clarify the situation as regards the right of the charterers to make deductions. There are two separate questions. The first concerns the scope of the contractual right to make deductions, under cl 11 of the charterparties; the second the right, apart from cl 11, to make deductions by way of equitable set-off. The nature of the latter was discussed to some extent, in relation to voyage charters, in *Aries Tanker Corpn v Total Transport Ltd, The Aries*[1], and in earlier cases there referred to, but there is room for argument, at least in this House, how far what was there laid down applies to time charters.

As regards the contractual claims, the umpire made only provisional findings. These were that part of the slow steaming deduction made from the Nanfri hire in October was

---

1   [1977] 1 All ER 398, [1977] 1 WLR 185

probably justified but not all, that the owners believed all the July and September deductions to be invalid and that the owners knew that part of the deductions (presumably of that made in respect of the slow steaming claim) was valid. In these circumstances the issue between the parties would be whether, in order to entitle the charterers under cl 11 to make a deduction, their claim must be (a) previously established as valid or (b) bona fide believed to be valid and calculated on a reasonable basis, or whether (c) a deduction may be made of any sum claimed whether ultimately found to be valid or not.

Kerr J and the Court of Appeal were able to deal with the main issue of repudiation independently of whatever answer should be given to the questions regarding deductions. Kerr J held that the owners' conduct did not amount to repudiation of the contract, but, formally, also held that the charterers were entitled to deduct under cl 11 and also by way of equitable set-off claims believed to be valid and calculated on a reasonable basis. In other words, he held the owners' conduct not to be repudiatory although they were substantially wrong on the deduction issue.

The Court of Appeal unanimously held the owners' conduct to be repudiatory but they differed on the deduction questions. All three members held in favour of the charterers that all the deductions in dispute could be made under cl 11 as held by Kerr J. As regards equitable set-off, Lord Denning MR and Goff LJ held that such a right existed in relation to time charters (so distinguishing *The Aries*[1]), and Cumming Bruce LJ to the contrary thought that it did not. From this analysis it appears clear that the answer to the main issue as regards repudiation does not depend on the answer to be given on the deduction issues. Counsel at the bar agreed that this was so, and in view of this, and there being no definite findings of fact on the deduction issues themselves, did not address arguments on them. While therefore I recognise the interest which the commercial community may have in decision of them whether as they arise under a contractual right to deduct, or under a general doctrine of equitable set-off, I must reluctantly agree to decline this task on the present occasion.

I come then to the issue of repudiation. It is first necessary to see whether the owners' conduct on 4th October 1977 was a breach of contract at all. Counsel for the owners contended that it was not. His argument was that the owners, while giving the charterers very wide powers under cl 9 of the charterparties ('the Master to be under the orders of the Charterers as regards employment, agency, or other arrangements') which would include in general the power to require the master to issue bills of lading, nevertheless always retained the right to insist that any action required to be taken by the master, or taken by the charterers themselves, should be in accordance with the terms and provisions of the charterparty as a whole. This, it was said, would lead to two results. First, the owners would be within their rights in insisting that bills of lading should be 'claused' by a reference to the time charters; secondly, that the owners would be entitled to object to (and to instruct their masters to refuse) bills of lading which derogated from their right of lien on cargoes, sub-freights and bill of lading freight, as expressly conferred by cl 18.

There can be no exception taken to a general proposition that a charterparty, as any other contract, must be taken as a whole: the obligations and rights created by one clause must be read in the light of the fact that it forms part of a complex of contractual provisions. Some charters in fact contain in clauses corresponding to cl 9 such words as 'without prejudice to the charter' which no doubt emphasise this point. But it may well be that a particular clause is so clearly worded, and its purpose so clear, as to resist any suggestion that it should be limited, or written down, on account of some supposed inconsistency with the general purpose of the contract or by some other clause in the contract.

It is important in this connection to have in mind that the present charters are time charters, the nature and purpose of which is to enable the charterers to use the vessels during the period of the charters for trading in whatever manner they think fit. The issue of bills of lading in a particular form may be vital for the charterers' trade, and indeed in relation to this trade, which involves c if or c & f contracts, the issue of freight pre-paid bills

---

1   [1977] 1 All ER 398, [1977] 1 WLR 185

of lading is essential if the trade is to be maintained. Furthermore, cl 9, as is usual in time charters, contains an indemnity clause against all consequences or liabilities arising from the master signing bills of lading. This underlines the power of the charterers, in the course of exploiting the vessel, to decide what bills of lading are appropriate for their trade and to instruct the masters to issue such bills, the owners being protected by the indemnity clause.

Then what limitations are there on this power? It must be clear that the owners cannot require bills of lading to be claused so as to incorporate the terms of the time charter: such a requirement would be contrary to the whole commercial purpose of the charterers. But the owners contend that at any rate the charterers have no right to require the master to issue bills of lading which would defeat the owners' right of lien, which under cl 18 extends to 'all cargoes and sub-freights belonging to the Time-Charterers and any Bill of Lading freight'. A freight pre-paid bill of lading might prejudice this lien, since, if the freight had been paid before the lien was sought to be exercised, there would be nothing on which it could operate.

In my opinion this argument attributes too much force to the lien clause. This clause, just as much as cl 9, must be read in the context of the whole contract, and must be related to the commercial situation which exists under time charters. The lien clause must be read as giving the owners a lien on such freights or sub-freights as, in the event, come to be payable, and which in fact are payable, under any sub-charter or bill of lading, but it cannot be read as interfering with the time charterers' primary right to use the ship and to direct the master as to its use. Such authority as there is in relation to time charters supports this view. In *The Shillito*[1], an action between the master and the owners, the judgment of Barnes J contains this passage:

> 'The charterer [in fact a time charterer] has a right to present any bills he chooses, and although there is a lien clause, it is inoperative, because the bills of lading contain no reference to the charterparty, and there is no freight on which a lien can be exercised.'

The master was held not to be negligent in signing bills showing freight paid in advance, and the inference is that he was bound to do so. In *Turner v Haji Goolam Mahomed Azam*[2], the time charter contained the words 'without prejudice to this charter'. In the judgment of the Privy Council it is said[3]:

> 'These words introduce a difficulty. It is said that they limit the authority of the captain to sign bills of lading which do not preserve to the owners . . . their lien on all goods under condition 22. This construction is a possible construction, but it has long ago been rejected both by commercial men and by judicial decision.'

It is true that these decisions bear on the authority of the master to sign bills of lading rather than directly on the powers of the time charterers, but I think it must follow from their reasoning that to require the master to sign freight pre-paid bills of lading is not to require him to act inconsistently with the charter, that to do so is within the powers of the time charterers and that for the owners to prevent their masters from acting on any such requirement is a breach of the time charter, specifically a breach of cl 9. If the masters had in the present case acted on the owners' instructions, an actual breach would, in my view, have been committed; they did not in fact do so because the without prejudice agreement was immediately made. But the owners' instructions (communicated to the charterers) clearly constituted a threat of a breach or an anticipatory breach of the contract.

Was this then such a threatened or anticipatory breach as to entitle the charterers to put an end to the charters? It was argued for the charterers that cl 9 of the charters amounted to a condition of the contract, so that any breach of it automatically gave the charterers the

---

1   (1897) 3 Com Cas 44 at 49
2   [1904] AC 826
3   AC 826 at 836–837

right to put an end to it. I do not agree with this. The clause is not drafted as a condition, and on its face it admits of being breached in a number of ways some of which might be far from serious and would certainly not go to the root of the contract. I regard the clause as one breaches of which must be examined on their individual demerits. Was this breach, or threatened breach, repudiatory or not? I shall not set out at any length the numerous authorities on anticipatory breach: this is one of the more perspicuous branches of the law of contract and the modern position is clear. The form of the critical question may differ slightly as it is put in relation to varying situations: per Lord Coleridge CJ in *Freeth v Burr*[1], as—

> '. . . an intimation of an intention to abandon and altogether to refuse performance of the contract [or to] evince an intention no longer to be bound by the contract.'

Or, per Lord Wright in *Ross T Smyth & Co Ltd v T D Bailey, Son & Co*[2]:

> 'I do not say that it is necessary to show that the party alleged to have repudiated should have an actual intention not to fulfil the contract. He may intend in fact to fulfil it, but may be determined to do so only in a manner substantially inconsistent with his obligations, and not in any other way.'

Or, per Diplock LJ in *Hong Kong Fir Shipping Co Ltd v Kawasaki Kisen Kaisha Ltd*[3], such as to deprive—

> 'the charterers of substantially the whole benefit which it was the intention of the parties . . . that the charterers should obtain from the further performance of their own contractual undertakings.'

Or, per Buckley LJ in *Decro-Wall International SA v Practitioners in Marketing Ltd*[4]:

> 'To constitute repudiation, the threatened breach must be such as to deprive the injured party of a substantial part of the benefit to which he is entitled under the contract . . . will the consequences of the breach be such that it would be unfair to the injured party to hold him to the contract and leave him to the remedy in damages . . .?'

The difference in expression between these two last formulations does not, in my opinion, reflect a divergence of principle, but arises from and is related to the particular contract under consideration. They represent, in other words, applications to different contracts of the common principle that to amount to repudiation a breach must go to the root of the contract.

My Lords, I do not think there can be any doubt that the owners' breach or threatened breach in the present case, consisting in their announcement that their masters would refuse to issue bills of lading freight pre-paid and not 'claused' so as to refer to the charters, prima facie went to the root of the contract as depriving the charterers of substantially the whole benefit of the contract. This is clear from the findings of the umpire to which I have already referred. It was in fact the owners' intention to put irresistible pressure on the charterers ('to compel the Charterers to pay over all sums deducted from hire by the Charterers which the Owners disputed, irrespective of whether such deductions should ultimately be determined to be valid or invalid': see the award, para 27), through the action they threatened to take. If the charterers had not given way, the charters would have become useless for the purpose for which they were granted. I do not think that this was disputed by the owners; in any event it was not disputable. What was said was that the action of the owners, in the circumstances in which it was taken, should not be taken to be repudiatory. They had, on 21st September 1977, referred the whole question of deductions to arbitration; in a short time the whole issue would be cleared up one way or another, after

1   (1874) LR 9 CP 208 at 213
2   [1940] 3 All ER 60 at 72
3   [1962] 1 All ER 474 at 489, [1962] 2 QB 26 at 72
4   [1971] 2 All ER 216 at 232, [1971] 1 WLR 361 at 380

which the charters would continue to be operated in accordance with the arbitrators' decision. The owners' action was of an interim character designed to have effect only until the position as to deductions could be clarified. The owners' interest was strongly in the direction of maintaining the charters; their move was simply a tactical one designed to resolve a doubtful situation. The sums which they were forcing the charterers to pay were inconsiderable. The charterers had already offered to pay them in 'escrow'.

My Lords, with genuine respect for the judgment of Kerr J who in substance agreed with this argument, I find myself obliged to reject it. Even if I were prepared to accept the assumption that arbitration proceedings set in motion on 21st September 1977 would be rapidly concluded through an early and speedy hearing, without a case being stated and without appeals in the courts (all of which must in fact be speculative), even so the owners' action must be regarded as going to the root of the contract. The issue of freight pre-paid bills of lading in respect of each of the three vessels was an urgent, indeed an immediate, requirement. The Nanfri completed loading a cargo, shipped by Continental Grain for Europe, on 5th October 1977; the Benfri, on passage to Chicago, was to load a cargo in Duluth for Europe; the Lorfri had loaded one parcel of grain for Continental Grain on 3rd October in respect of which a separate bill of lading was to be issued, and thereafter she was scheduled to load the balance of her capacity from Continental Grain at other Great Lakes ports.

These were pending transactions, and 'The Charterers were likely to incur very substantial liabilities to Continental Grain if the cargoes which were being loaded or which were about to be loaded on 5th October were not completed and if freight pre-paid unclaused bills of lading were not issued promptly' (see the award, para 28). Blacklisting by Continental Grain was likely to follow (ibid). Thus the resolution of the deductions issue by arbitration, however soon this might be achieved, would still have left the charterers in a position where they might have lost the whole benefit of the time charters. That a 'without prejudice' agreement was in fact entered into which averted these consequences is of course irrelevant though the fact that it was made does underline the extent of the pressure on the charterers. It is also irrelevant that the steps the charterers were being compelled, under threat of a breach of contract, to take were not very serious for them. A threat to commit a breach, having radical consequences, is nonetheless serious because it is disproportionate to the intended effect. It is thirdly irrelevant that it was in the owners' real interest to continue the charters rather than put an end to them. If a party's conduct is such as to amount to a threatened repudiatory breach, his subjective desire to maintain the contract cannot prevent the other party from drawing the consequences of his actions. The two cases relied on by the owners (*James Shaffer Ltd v Findlay Durham & Brodie*[1] and *Sweet & Maxwell Ltd v Universal News Services Ltd*[2]) do not support a contrary proposition, and would only be relevant here if the owners' action had been confined to asserting their own view, possibly erroneous, as to the effect of the contract. They went, in fact, far beyond this when they threatened a breach of the contract with serious consequences.

For these reasons I agree with the decision of the Court of Appeal that the charterers were entitled to determine the contracts. The appeals must accordingly be dismissed with costs.

VISCOUNT DILHORNE. My Lords, now that I have had the advantage of reading the speech of my noble and learned friend, Lord Wilberforce, I do not think any useful purpose would be served by my delivering the speech I had prepared.

It is indeed unfortunate that determination of the question whether deductions can lawfully be made by way of equitable set-off from the hire payable under a time charter and the question whether, if deductions can be made either by way of equitable set-off or by virtue of provisions in the charterparty, the charterers are entitled to deduct (a) only amounts which they have established their right to deduct or which they have agreed with

1   [1953] 1 WLR 106
2   [1964] 3 All ER 30, [1964] 2 QB 699

the owners or (b) sums to which they bona fide believe they are entitled calculated on a reasonable basis or (c) any sum they claim to be due to them whether or not it is must be left to another occasion.

Save in one minor respect I entirely agree with the reasoning and the conclusions reached by my noble and learned friend.

The point on which I differ from his is that I think the giving by the owners of instructions to the masters to refuse to sign bills of lading marked 'freight pre-paid' and to insist that all bills of lading should be 'claused' was an actual and not anticipatory breach of contract as it amounted to a breach of cl 9 of the charterparty whereby it was agreed that the masters should be under the orders of the charterers.

However it makes no difference whether the conduct of the owners amounted to an actual breach or an anticipatory breach for, as my noble and learned friend has so clearly demonstrated, their conduct was repudiatory.

I agree that the appeals should be dismissed.

LORD FRASER OF TULLYBELTON. My Lords, the only question now remaining in this appeal is whether the charterers (respondents) validly terminated the charterparty on 5th October 1977. It raises two issues: (1) whether the owners (appellants), by asserting a right to control the form of bill of lading, had acted or threatened to act in breach of the charterparty, a time charter on the Baltime form, and (2) if so, whether their breach amounted to repudiation of the contract, entitling the charterers to terminate it.

On the former of these issues the umpire and all the judges who have considered it have been against the owners. As I agree with that view, I shall summarise my reasons briefly. Clause 9 of the charterparty provides in the second and third sentences as follows:

'The Master to be under the orders of the Charterers as regards employment, agency, or other arrangements. The Charterers to indemnify the Owners against all consequences or liabilities arising from the Master, Officers or Agents signing Bills of Lading or other documents or otherwise complying with such orders . . .'

The latter sentence shows beyond possibility of doubt that the signing of bills of lading was included among the respects in which the master was to be under the charterers' orders. Accordingly when the owners on 4th October 1977 instructed the master to refuse to sign any bill of lading endorsed 'freight pre-paid' and which did not bear an endorsement referring to the conditions of the charterparty, they were in breach of their obligation under cl 9 unless that obligation is to be read as qualified by some other provision of the charterparty. The argument was that it was qualified by cl 18. But in my opinion there is no conflict or inconsistency between cll 9 and 18 and no need to regard the former as being qualified by the latter. Clause 18 does not give to the owners any right to require that the charterers shall procure that cargoes (not belonging to the charterers) shall be carried on terms that give the owners a lien over them or that there shall be in existence sub-freights over which the owners can exercise their lien. The effect of cl 18 was simply that, if and when there were cargoes belonging to the charterers or sub-freights due to them, the owners were to have a lien over them, whatever the exact meaning of a 'lien' on sub-freights may be.

That is the effect of reading the clauses according to their ordinary meaning. It is powerfully reinforced by the consideration that, if the instructions issued by the owners to masters on 4th October had been carried out, the consequences for the charterers would, as found by the umpire in para 28 of his award, have been 'extremely serious', and they would have been largely debarred from using the ships for the trade for which they had hired them under these time charters. It is therefore difficult to suppose, as a matter of commercial sense, that the contract can have entitled the owners to give such instructions; if it did, the owners could at any time have held a pistol to the charterers' head and demanded that the charterparty be amended in any way that seemed good to them.

Further, the main reason why the owners contended that they were entitled to instruct the master to refuse to sign clean bills of lading was that, if he did sign, they would lose their co-called 'lien' on any sub-freights that might be due from the shippers to the charterers. I doubt very much whether the contention is well-founded. The bills of lading are a contract between the shipper and the shipowner (see *Turner v Haji Goolam Mahomed Azam*[1]) and they would not affect the rights and obligations of the shipowners and charterers inter se including such rights as the owners have under cl 18. No doubt the shipper or his consignee, holding clean bills of lading, would be entitled to have the cargo unloaded free from lien, but if in fact the shipper had not paid the freight due to the charterers I do not think he could rely on the clean bill of lading in defence to a claim for payment. The only question for him would be to whom the payment was due.

We heard some argument as to whether, if the result of carrying out the owner's instructions would have been a breach of their contract, a breach had been actually committed or merely threatened. In the circumstances of this case it would not make any difference, but my view is that the breach was only threatened. True, the instructions were actually given to the masters and the charterers were so informed, but the issue of instructions was merely a preparatory step, useful in making the threat realistic and necessary to enable it to be carried out quickly. The instructions given by the owners to their own servants could be cancelled at any time and the umpire found that the charterers knew that if they paid the disputed deductions the instructions to the masters would be withdrawn. That is what happened; the threat to the charterers was enough and it did not have to be put into action.

The second issue is whether the threat, if it had been carried out, would have been repudiatory. It was argued that the second sentence in cl 9 under which the master was to be under the orders of the charterer contained a 'condition', the breach of which entitled the charterers at once to terminate the contract. I do not agree. It is clearly not expressed as a condition. Nor in my opinion is it converted into a condition, or strengthened in any way, by the third sentence of cl 43 of the charterparty which was relied on by the charterers. That sentence provides:

> 'Owner hereby expressly undertakes and agrees that it will at no time use or employ the Vessel in any manner inconsistent with the terms of this Charter or with the Owner's obligations hereunder, or with the legitimate orders for the employment of the Vessel given from time to time by the Charterer . . .'

The owner's instructions as to the form of bills of lading to be signed by the master cannot be regarded as 'employing' the vessel in a manner inconsistent with the charter and the sentence appears to me to have no bearing on the construction of cl 9.

It is easy to imagine minor breaches of the charterers' orders that would be of no consequence in the performance of the contract as a whole. The argument for the charterers was that the second sentence in cl 9 contained hidden within itself two obligations: first, an obligation on the owners to place the master under the orders to the charterers and, second, an obligation on the master to obey those orders. Only the first of these was said to be a condition, on the ground that it went to the root of the contract. So failure by the master to carry out an order from the charterers in any respect, however trivial, would be a breach of a condition (and therefore repudiatory) if caused by the owner's failure to place him under the charterers' orders, but would only be a breach of contract (giving rise to a claim for perhaps minimal damages) if caused by the master's personal fault. Everything would depend on the cause of disobedience. That seems to me to be unacceptable.

Treating the second sentence of cl 9 then as an innominate or intermediate term, I proceed to consider whether the threatened breach of it here was so fundamental as to amount to repudiation of the contract. The test of repudiation has been formulated in various ways by different judges. I shall adopt the formulation by Buckley LJ in *Decro-Wall International SA v Practitioners in Marketing Ltd*[2] as follows:

---

1   [1904] AC 826
2   [1971] 2 All ER 216 at 232, [1971] 1 WLR 361 at 380

> '. . . will the consequences of the breach be such that it would be unfair to the injured party to hold him to the contract and leave him to his remedy in damages as and when a breach or breaches may occur? If this would be so, then a repudiation has taken place.'

Judged by that test I have no doubt that the breach here was repudiatory. The whole purpose of the contract from the charterers' point of view was that they should have the use of the ship for carrying on their trade from the Great Lakes, but if the owner's threat had been carried out it would have been ruinous to that trade. I need not repeat the umpire's findings as to the consequences in full but I attach particular importance to his finding in para 28(iii):

> 'The Charterers were likely to be blacklisted as grain carriers by Continental Grain, which is one of the world's largest shippers of grain. In consequence the Charterers' reputation would be very seriously damaged and they would probably have been unable to obtain business for the vessels from other major shippers of grain.'

Such damage to their reputation might well have been lasting and not limited to the duration of actual interruption of the trade. In face of that finding, I am, with all respect to Kerr J, unable to agree with his view that the owners were only creating a 'temporary impasse'. It was said that the breach was not repudiatory because the owners were merely reacting against the charterers' unilateral deductions from the hire, and particularly against their revival of a stale claim for deductions. This is really a plea in mitigation but it does not affect the result. If the owners' reaction involved committing a breach that went to the root of the contract, they cannot in my opinion escape the legal consequences by pleading that they had been provoked. I would therefore hold that the breach was repudiatory.

For these reasons I would dismiss the appeals.

LORD RUSSELL OF KILLOWEN. My Lords, as these three cases have progressed there fall for decision in each of them only two questions, the same in each case. The first question is whether the owner committed a breach of contract in instructing the master to refuse to sign bills of lading marked 'freight pre-paid' and threatening to adhere to those instructions.

It is quite clear that cl 9 prima facie confers on the time charterers the right to require bills of lading to be so marked. The contention of the owners is that (at least when hire is allegedly in arrear by unjustified deductions) the instructions to the masters were justified because that marking of bills of lading detracted from the owners' lien rights (so labelled) under cl 18. This, and this only, was the justification advanced by the owners for their actions. But this attempted justification involves a fallacy. That marking of bills of lading could not possibly detract from the cl 18 'lien' rights.

The fact that cl 18 refers expressly to bill of lading freights appears to me to add nothing to the lien conferred by that clause on sub-freights belonging to the charterers, and serves only to distract the mind from the true scope of the lien. The lien operates as an equitable charge on what is due from the shippers to the charterers, and in order to be effective requires an ability to intercept the sub-freight (by notice of claim) before it is paid by shipper to charterer. The simple question is whether the marking of bills of lading freight pre-paid interferes with that ability to intercept. It cannot. If freight is in fact pre-paid before issue of the bill of lading, cadit quaestio. If not, how does the marking freight pre-paid interfere with such ability to intercept as may be available to the other? For these reasons I say that the justification suggested by the owners for their actions is fallacious.

For the owners the only answer put forward was that it would be strange that, if the master for the owner signed a bill of lading freight pre-paid, the owner should demand of the shipper that freight *not* paid should be paid to the owner. I see nothing impossible in this. The shipper would if necessary interplead. He could not, not having paid the freight, assert that he *had* paid; nor could he assert an estoppel against the owner: he would be simply faced with rival claims, not caring which was right, and knowing only that he owed someone the sub-freight.

For those reasons I have no doubt that the owners were in their actions guilty of a breach of contract.

I would have been prepared also to arrive at the same conclusion on a different ground, that is, that in the particular circumstances of the trade for which these vessels were time chartered it was preponderantly essential, as concerned with c i f or c & f contracts, that bills of lading should be marked freight pre-paid. In such circumstances I cannot conclude that the actions and proposed actions of the owners were a sensibly justifiable intervention with the charter's cl 9 requirements as to the marking of bills of lading; in other words in the circumstances of the charter cl 18 must relevantly yield to cl 9 to make sense.

Having reached that conclusion on the first question, the second question is whether the breach of contract by the owners was such as entitled the charterers to treat it as repudiation of the charter contracts by the owners.

For the charterers it was contended that cl 9 involved either expressly or by implication a strict *condition* that the charterers' rights thereunder would not be breached by the owners, so that any breach by the owners would entitle the charterers to assert repudiation. I do not favour that approach. In recent cases it has not found favour. It was argued that if the masters disobeyed an order by the charterers it would (or could) be a mere breach of warranty: it might be a minor matter. But if the owners countermanded an order by the charterers under cl 9 it must be a breach of a condition. I am not content with this division, attractive as it was at first submission. I would be unwilling to hold that every contradiction by the owner of an order by the charterer to the master was necessarily repudiatory of the charter contract.

But the question remains whether this particular contradiction could properly be regarded as repudiatory, as it was considered by the umpire and all members of the Court of Appeal, though not by Kerr J.

The question is whether, objectively regarded and in all the circumstances of the case, the conduct of the owners can properly be said to strike at the root or essence of this contract. In my opinion it can. As I have said the ability to have bills of lading issued marked freight pre-paid was essential to the time charterers' exploitation of the vessels in trading therewith; and this was of course known to the owners. Counsel for the owners frankly admitted in argument that the instructions to the masters would have been fatal to the charterers' trade. Indeed, on the crucial date of 5th October bills of lading in respect of two of the three vessels were due to be called for that very day. The special case made the following findings in para 28:

> 'The consequences for the Charterers of the Orders issued by the Owners on 4th October 1977 were extremely serious, in that (i) Unless the Charterers could ensure the issue of freight prepaid bills of lading which were not claused with any reference to a time charterparty the vessels were largely debarred from use by the Charterers in the grain and steel trades, since nearly all of the shippers of grain and steel would not agree to accept bills of lading if they were either non-freight prepaid or claused with a reference to a time charter. (ii) The Charterers would be unable to comply with their existing obligations to sub-charterers. (iii) The Charterers were likely to be blacklisted as grain carriers by Continental Grain, which is one of the world's largest shippers of grain. In consequence the Charterers' reputation would be very seriously damaged and they would probably have been unable to obtain business for the vessels from other major shippers of grain. (iv) The Charterers were likely to incur very substantial liabilities to Continental Grain if the cargoes which were being loaded or which were about to be loaded on 5th October were not completed and if freight prepaid unclaused bills of lading were not issued promptly.'

And in para 26 it was found that the owners knew that the charterers were likely to suffer those consequences.

It was contended for the owners that their breach should not be regarded as striking at the root or essence of the contract because they had already set on foot arbitration proceedings designed to decide the disputed questions of deductions from hire, that such arbitration could produce a decision within a reasonably short time, that the question whether the owner's instructions to the masters were or were not breaches of contract could be raised and solved in that arbitration, and that thereafter a considerable period of the time charters would remain to the charterers. Accordingly, it was contended, in those circumstances it could not be said that in the action of the owners (if persisted in) would deprive the charterers of more than some part of the benefit of their contract, and so should not be regarded as striking at the root or essence of the contract. I do not accept that contention. Having regard to the findings in the special case I cannot regard the conduct of the owners as something which, if persisted in, would lead merely to a temporary suspension of the charterers benefits under the charter.

It was further contended for the owners that, in so far as they made it plain that the instructions to the masters would be withdrawn if the charterers paid at once to the owners the total of the unpaid hire the deduction of which was disputed, the breach of threatened breach, however grave, being in a sense conditional, could not be regarded as repudiation. And, it was added, since the charterers were anyway prepared to place the disputed amount 'in escrow' it was reasonable to insist on that condition, inasmuch as if in arbitration it proved that the deductions were justifiable there would be plenty of scope under the charter thereafter for the charterers to recoup themselves by deduction from future hire obligations.

I am not able to accept this contention that a breach or threatened breach of the character now in question escapes the quality of being repudiatory because it is indicated that it will not be pursued if the other party to the contract gives way in a field of dispute thereunder; and I do not think that it matters whether the indication is phrased thus, or whether it is indicated that the breach will be pursued unless the other party gives way.

A further contention for the owners was that their action or threat could not seriously and objectively be regarded as repudiation, because the hire rates under this time charter were greater than the current going rates, and termination of the charters could only harm the owners. That the owners would be so harmed is true, but that does not appear to me to detract from the essential gravity of the breach and threatened breach so as to reduce it to the level of a mere tactical exercise of 'muscle', or even bluff.

I am accordingly of opinion that there was here repudiation by the owners accepted by the charterers, and would dismiss these appeals.

LORD SCARMAN. My Lords, I have had the advantage of reading in draft the speech delivered by my noble and learned friend, Lord Wilberforce. I agree with it, and for the reasons which he gives I would dismiss the appeals with costs.

Appeals dismissed.

Solicitors: *Richards, Butler & Co* (for the owners); *Ince & Co* (for the charterers).

Mary Rose Plummer   Barrister.

Tyrer v Smart (Inspector of Taxes)

HOUSE OF LORDS

LORD DIPLOCK, LORD SALMON, LORD EDMUND-DAVIES, LORD FRASER OF TULLYBELTON AND LORD RUSSELL OF KILLOWEN

6th, 7th NOVEMBER, 13th DECEMBER 1978

Income tax – Emoluments from office or employment – Preferential right to apply for shares – Company offering shares for sale to public – Ten per cent of shares reserved at preferential price for employees – Whether employee's profit on purchase of shares at preferential price an emolument deriving from his employment – Finance Act 1956, Sch 2, para 1(1).

In 1969 the parent company of a group of companies decided to become a public company and to offer for sale 5,600,000 ordinary shares. The sale was by tender through a bank at a uniform price ('the striking price') which was to be the highest price at which sufficient applications for all shares offered were received. Ten per cent of the shares on offer were reserved at a price of 20s per share for those employees of the group who had been employed for five years or more and who wished to accept the offer. No limit was put on the number of shares for which an employee could subscribe. On 9th March 1969 the taxpayer, who was an eligible employee, applied for 5,000 shares and enclosed his cheque for £5,000. The offer for sale closed on 12th March. On 13th March a striking price of 25s per share was announced. On 17th March the taxpayer's application was accepted. Dealings started on the Stock Exchange on 18th March and at the close of business on that day the shares had risen to 27s 6d. The taxpayer was assessed to income tax under Sch E on the advantage which had accrued to him by the purchase of the shares on the ground that it was an 'emolument' from his employment, within para 1(1)[a] of Sch 2 to the Finance Act 1956. He appealed to the Special Commissioners who found that the purpose of the offer of shares to employees at the preferential price was to encourage them to identify with the company and to induce them to be loyal employees with an understanding of and sense of involvement in the affairs and fortunes of the group. The commissioners further found that the taxpayer had had no particular confidence when he made his application that the shares would increase in price, and that the value of the shares on 17th March when the taxpayer's legal right to them arose was 24s. On those findings the commissioners held that the advantage which had accrued from the shares had been given to the taxpayer by the company in return for his being an employee of the group and that his employment had been the source of that advantage. Accordingly they held that he was assessable to tax in respect of the difference between the value of the shares on 17th March and the price at which he had purchased them, a total of £1,000. On the taxpayer's appeal the judge[b] reversed that decision on the ground that, although the taxpayer would not have had the opportunity to purchase the shares if he had not been an employee of the group, the benefit which had accrued to him from the shares had resulted from his decision as a private individual, and not as an employee, to take the commercial risk of investing in the shares. Accordingly, the judge held that the taxpayer was not liable to tax on the increase in the value of the shares. The Court of Appeal[c] affirmed that decision. The Crown appealed to the House of Lords.

Held – The appeal would be allowed because, although a different tribunal might well have reached the opposite conclusion, there was sufficient evidence before the commissioners for them to hold that the benefit or perquisite of being able to obtain the

---

a   Paragraph 1(1), so far as material, provides: 'Tax under Case I, II or III shall . . . be chargeable on the full amount of the emoluments falling under that Case . . . and the expression "emoluments" shall include all salaries, fees, wages, perquisites and profits whatsoever.'

b   [1976] 3 All ER 537, [1976] STC 521

c   [1978] 1 All ER 1089, [1978] STC 141

shares at an advantageous price was an inducement to the taxpayer to become and continue to be a loyal employee and was accordingly an emolument from his employment. The commissioners' decision was not one which no reasonable commissioners properly instructed as to the relevant law could have arrived at and there were therefore no grounds for reversing their decision (see p 325 *e* to p 326 *b*, p 328 *a* to *e*, p 330 *d* to *h* and p 331 *d* to *g*, post).

Dictum of Lord Radcliffe in *Edwards (Inspector of Taxes) v Bairstow* [1955] 3 All ER at 57 applied.

Decision of the Court of Appeal [1978] 1 All ER 1089 reversed.

Notes

For taxation of emoluments, see 23 Halsbury's Laws (4th Edn) para 641, and for a case on the subject, see 28(1) Digest (Reissue) 332, *1194*.

For the Finance Act 1956, Sch 2, para 1, see 36 Halsbury's Statutes (2nd Edn) 448.

For 1970–71 and subsequent years of assessment, para 1 of Sch 2 to the 1956 Act has been replaced by the Income and Corporation Taxes Act 1970, s 183.

Cases referred to in opinions

Abbott v Philbin (Inspector of Taxes) [1960] 2 All ER 763, [1961] AC 352, [1960] 3 WLR 255, 39 Tax Cas 82, [1960] TR 171, 39 ATC 221, 53 R & IT 487, HL, 28(1) Digest (Reissue) 345, *1249*.

Bentley (Inspector of Taxes) v Evans (1959) 39 Tax Cas 132, [1959] TR 117, 38 ATC 108, 52 R & IT 277, 28(1) Digest (Reissue) 346, *1250*.

Ede (Inspector of Taxes) v Wilson and Cornwall [1945] 1 All ER 367, 26 Tax Cas 381, 28(1) Digest (Reissue) 327, *1170*.

Edwards (Inspector of Taxes) v Bairstow [1955] 3 All ER 48, [1956] AC 14, [1955] 3 WLR 410, 36 Tax Cas 207, [1955] TR 209, 34 ATC 198, 48 R & IT 534, HL, 28(1) Digest (Reissue) 566, *2089*.

Hochstrasser (Inspector of Taxes) v Mayes [1959] 3 All ER 817, [1960] AC 376, [1960] 2 WLR 63, 38 Tax Cas 673, [1959] TR 355, 38 ATC 360, 53 R & IT 12, HL, 28(1) Digest (Reissue) 326, *1164*.

Laidler v Perry (Inspector of Taxes) [1965] 2 All ER 121, [1966] AC 16, [1965] 2 WLR 1171, 42 Tax Cas 351, [1965] TR 123, 44 ATC 114, HL, 28(1) Digest (Reissue) 338, *1226*.

Salmon v Weight (Inspector of Taxes) [1935] All ER Rep 904, 19 Tax Cas 174, 153 LT 55, HL, 28(1) Digest (Reissue) 329, *1179*.

Appeal

This was an appeal by the Crown against the decision of the Court of Appeal[1] (Buckley, Eveleigh LJJ and Sir John Pennycuick) dated 1st December 1977 affirming the judgment of Brightman J[2] dated 23rd July 1976 whereby he allowed the appeal of the taxpayer, Arthur Adrian Andersen Tyrer, against an assessment to income tax under Sch E for the years 1968–69 in respect of a benefit which had accrued to him from a preferential right as an employee to apply for shares in a company. The facts are set out in the opinion of Lord Diplock.

Patrick Medd QC and *Michael Hart* for the Crown.
Michael Nolan QC and *James Holroyd Pearce* for the taxpayer.

Their Lordships took time for consideration.

13th December. The following opinions were delivered.

---

1 [1978] 1 All ER 1089, [1978] 1 WLR 415, [1978] STC 141
2 [1976] 3 All ER 537, [1977] 1 WLR 1, [1976] STC 521

LORD DIPLOCK. My Lords, this adds another to the long series of cases which raise the question whether a particular benefit capable of being turned into money and granted to an employee by his employer or a parent company of his employer forms part of the employee's emoluments from his employment so as to be taxable under Sch E. 'Emoluments' in this context include, in addition to all salaries, fees and wages, all 'perquisites and profits whatsoever'. The test to be applied is well established. It is whether the benefit represents a reward or return for the employee's services, whether past, current or future, or whether it was bestowed on him for some other reason. The borderline may be a fine one, as is illustrated by two cases in this House: *Hochstrasser (Inspector of Taxes) v Mayes*[1], in which the benefit was held not to be part of the employee's emoluments, and *Laidler v Perry (Inspector of Taxes)*[2], in which a benefit granted by the parent company of the employer was held to be part of the employee's emoluments.

Where the benefit is granted by and at the expense of the employer or its parent company, as distinct from benefits derived from third parties, such as a huntsman's field money or a taxi driver's tips, the purpose of the employer in granting the benefit to the employee is an important factor in determining whether it is properly to be regarded as a reward or return for the employee's services. The employer's motives in conferring the benefit may be mixed and the determination of what constitutes his dominant purpose is a question of fact for the commissioners to determine. Their finding on this matter is therefore one with which a court whose jurisdiction on appeal is limited to correcting errors of law by the commissioners should be slow to interfere.

In the instant case, the taxpayer was a senior employee of a company called Rentokil Ltd, which was one of a number of subsidiary companies in a group, the parent of which was called Rentokil Group Ltd ('the parent company') a private company in which the major shareholder was a Danish company. Early in 1969 it was decided for good commercial reasons that the parent company should go public. The scheme put up for this was that the Danish company should sell to the Westminster Bank part of its holding of shares in the parent company and that a further block of shares should be issued by that company to the bank. Nine-tenths of those shares were to be offered by the bank to the public by tender at a price not less than 20s per share; the remaining tenth was to be offered at the fixed price of 20s per share to employees of the parent company and its subsidiaries who had been employed for five years or more. The shares to be offered to the public by tender were underwritten at 20s per share and an arrangement had been reached with two executive directors of the parent company that they would take up any balance of the shares offered to employees which were not applied for.

For the shares made available by the Danish company and the newly issued shares the price to be paid by the bank was to be for those that were sold by the bank by tender, 3d less than the tender price struck; for those sold to employees it was to be 3d less than the price of 20s at which they were made available to employees.

Applications by employees for shares at the price of 20s had to be made by 12th March 1969, before the tender price was struck. They had to be accompanied by a cheque for the full price and, once made, were irrevocable. The tender price was in fact struck on 13th March at 25s per share.

The taxpayer, Mr Tyrer, who had duly applied on 9th March for 5,000 shares, received a fully-paid renouncable letter of acceptance for them on 17th March, the day before the market on the Stock Exchange opened. It was held by the commissioners that the value of the shares on 17th March 1969, when the taxpayer's legal right to them arose, was 24s. When dealings started on the Stock Exchange on the following day there was a stag market; the price at the close of dealings had risen to 27s 6d.

The benefit of which the taxpayer availed himself was the right to subscribe at what it was expected would prove to be a preferential price. The expectation was realised and, on the finding of the commissioners, the value of the benefit obtained by the taxpayer was 4s

---

1   [1959] 3 All ER 817, [1960] AC 376, 38 Tax Cas 673
2   [1965] 2 All ER 121, [1966] AC 16, 42 Tax Cas 351

on each share allotted to him, making a total of £1,000, on which they held him to be assessable to tax. The value was considerably higher once the market had opened.

The crucial finding of fact by the commissioners as to the company's purpose in making the shares available to employees is that it was to encourage established employees of the company and of companies within the group to become shareholders in the parent company. The aim, said the commissioners, was 'to achieve a better relationship with the employees so that they would become and continue to be loyal employees, having an understanding of and a sense of involvement in the affairs and fortunes of the Rentokil group'. This the commissioners held was an advantage afforded to the taxpayer in return for acting as or being an employee, within the meaning of that expression as used by Viscount Radcliffe in *Hochstrasser (Inspector of Taxes) v Mayes*[1].

The commissioners stated a case for the opinion of the High Court on two questions of law: '(a) whether we made an error of law in holding that an emolument arose to the appellant from his office or employment when he acquired 5,000 shares in the Company for £5,000; and (b) whether in law the value of that emolument should be taken to be some figure other than the £1,000 which we estimated it to be on the basis of the evidence submitted to us.'

Brightman J[2] answered the first question in favour of the taxpayer; so, the second did not arise. His judgment was upheld by the Court of Appeal[3] (Buckley, Eveleigh LJJ and Sir John Pennycuick). From their decision this appeal is brought by the Crown to your Lordships' House.

It was contended by the Crown in the light of the commissioners' finding as to the purpose of the parent company in making the offer to its subsidiaries' employees that there was no relevant distinction between the instant case and two other cases which were decided by this House, in which employees of companies availed themselves of an offer to acquire shares in the company at a preferential price. The first is *Weight (Inspector of Taxes) v Salmon*[4], in which the taxpayer was granted a right to subscribe at par for shares in a well-known public company whose market value at the time the right was granted was higher than their par value. In that case it was expressly stated in the resolutions by the board of directors to grant the taxpayer this right that the right was granted 'having regard to the eminent and special services rendered' by the taxpayer in the preceding year. In the instant case the absence of a similar explicit statement in the resolution of the board of the parent company is made good by the finding of fact by the commissioners as to what the purpose of the parent company was in granting to employees the right to acquire shares on preferential terms. The second case is *Abbott v Philbin (Inspector of Taxes)*[5] where the taxpayer, who was a senior employee of a company, was granted in October 1954 the right to acquire, at the price of £20, an option to subscribe for up to 2,000 shares of the company at the price of 68s 6d per share. He paid his £20 in 1954 but did not exercise the option until a few years later when the market price of the shares was 82s per share. The question in the appeal to this House in that case was whether he was assessable in the year in which he exercised the option for the difference between the market price at which the shares then stood and the 68s 6d at which he acquired them or was assessable on the value of the option in the year 1954 when he acquired, less, in either case, £20 which was the cost to him of acquiring it. It was taken for granted in this House that the option given to the taxpayer was a perquisite or profit from his employment and it was held that it fell to be assessed at the value at the date at which he acquired it for the price of £20. A corresponding basis, the value of the shares, when the respondent taxpayer acquired them, was adopted by the commissioners in the instant case.

Brightman J considered that these two cases and others like them (*Ede (Inspector of Taxes)*

1 [1959] 3 All ER 817, [1960] AC 376
2 [1976] 3 All ER 537, [1977] 1 WLR 1, [1976] STC 521
3 [1978] 1 All ER 1089, [1978] 1 WLR 415, [1978] STC 141
4 (1935) 19 Tax Cas 174, [1935] All ER Rep 904
5 [1960] 2 All ER 763, [1961] AC 352, 39 Tax Cas 82

v Wilson and Cornwall[1] and *Bentley (Inspector of Taxes) v Evans*[2]) had nothing in common with the instant case because when the taxpayer availed himself of the proffered opportunity to subscribe for shares at 20s it was by no means certain that the tender price would be struck at a figure higher than 20s or that the shares would command a higher price than that in the market when it opened. To avail himself of the benefit, the taxpayer had to be prepared to take a certain view of the market and to back his judgment with his own money of which he also had to have some available for investment. It was possible, as Brightman J pointed out, for him to have incurred a loss by taking up the shares.

My Lords, whenever marketable securities are offered to favoured individuals on terms more advantageous than those on which they are offered to the public (in the instant case, at a price which could not be more and was likely to be less than that at which the public was able to acquire them) the individual accepting the special offer runs some risk, however small the risk may be, that he will lose by accepting it. In *Weight (Inspector of Taxes) v Salmon*[3] the risk that the taxpayer might lose by accepting the offer to subscribe was minimal. In the report of *Abbott (Inspector of Taxes) v Philbin*[4] in this House there is no material on which to assess the risk that the taxpayer's £20 which he paid for the option to buy shares might have proved to be a bad investment. The very fact that he accepts the offer is a strong indication that the risk is one which the taxpayer thinks is worth taking. In the instant case, looked at with the benefit of hindsight, there can be no question that the preferential terms offered to the taxpayer did, in the result, secure for him a substantial financial benefit; and a reading of the prospectus which accompanied the offer of the shares and the fact that four days after his application the tender price was struck at 25s suggests that it would be quite unrealistic to suppose that when he applied for 5,000 shares there was not a strong probability that the market in them would open, as in the result it did, at a figure substantially higher than the price of 20s at which they were offered to the employees of the company.

My Lords, it does not seem to me that the fact that there was some element of risk when the taxpayer applied for his shares and that, as found by the commissioners, he himself had at that time 'no particular confidence that the shares would have a value in excess of the minimum price' can affect the finding of fact of the commissioners that the purpose of the offer of shares to employees at a preferential price was so that the offerees 'would become and continue to be loyal employees, having an understanding of and a sense of involvement in the affairs and fortunes of the Rentokil group'.

That seems to me a clear finding that the offer was made as a reward for past (since he had to have served five years to qualify for the offer) and more particularly for future services and accordingly was made to him in return for acting as or being an employee.

In my view it is not possible to bring the commissioners' finding to this effect within the well-known principle stated by Lord Radcliffe in *Edwards (Inspector of Taxes) v Bairstow*[5] that the court has power to interfere with a determination of commissioners if the facts found 'are such that no person acting judicially and properly instructed as to the relevant law could have come to the determination under appeal'. It is only in these circumstances that the court 'has no option but to assume that there has been some misconception of the law and that this has been responsible for the determination'.

It may be that different conclusions of fact as to the purpose of the company's offer might have been reached on the evidence by different deciders of the fact. The borderline between a profit which is an emolument from an employment and one which is not may, in some cases, be a narrow one. Even if it were the case that any of your Lordships might not necessarily have reached the same conclusion on the evidence before them as the commissioners did in the instant case if this were a field in which it lay within the

1   [1945] 1 All ER 367, 26 Tax Cas 381
2   (1959) 39 Tax Cas 132
3   (1935) 19 Tax Cas 174, [1935] All ER Rep 904
4   [1960] 2 All ER 763, [1961] AC 352
5   [1955] 3 All ER 48 at 57, [1956] AC 14 at 36, 36 Tax Cas 207 at 229

jurisdiction of the courts of justice to decide questions of fact, I can see no ground for saying that there was any error of law involved in the commissioner's determination. I would accordingly allow this appeal.

On the question of the value of the emolument, as the commissioners heard evidence as to the value of the shares on the day that they were issued, which was the day before the market opened and was agreed to be the date on which the value of the emolument was to be assessed, their finding was clearly one of fact and I can see no grounds at all for interfering.

LORD SALMON. My Lords, all the relevant facts in this appeal have been fully and lucidly set out by my noble and learned friend, Lord Diplock. I shall only briefly draw attention to what I regard as some of the most cardinal facts.

In 1969 it was agreed that Rentokil Group Ltd, then a private company, should go public with a capital of 5,600,000 ordinary shares of 2s each. Permission was obtained from the Stock Exchange to reserve and offer 10 per cent of these shares for sale at 20s a share to all employees of the company and of its subsidiaries in the United Kingdom of five years' standing, and to employees abroad of managerial status. An offer for sale by tender of the balance of 90 per cent of the shares at a minimum price of 20s per share (which was the price at which the shares had been underwritten) was made to the public on 12th March 1969 and closed on that date. The 'striking price' of 25s a share was announced on 13th March 1969. At that figure the shares were three times oversubscribed. In the meantime special application forms had been issued to all the employees to whom I have referred, one of whom was the taxpayer. He filled in his form applying for 5,000 shares and returned it with his cheque for £5,000 to the company's secretary on 9th March 1969. The acceptance of his application reached him on 17th March 1969; and on that day he became the legal owner of the 5,000 shares. Dealings in the company shares on the Stock Exchange did not open until the following day.

It is now undisputed that the value of the shares on 17th March was 24s a share. Accordingly, the 5,000 shares which the taxpayer had acquired on that day for £5,000 were then worth £1,000 more than the price he had paid for them. The question is whether the taxpayer is assessable to income tax on that £1,000. This depends on whether that sum was an emolument from his employment. Income tax under Sch E is assessable on all emoluments derived from employment: see the Finance Act 1956, s 10(1). Schedule 2 to that Act provides by para 1(1) that 'the expression "emoluments" shall include all . . . perquisites and profits whatsoever'. A perquisite is, in my view, any advantage which has a money value and which the employee receives from his employer for services he has rendered or is expected to render in the course of his employment.

It is clearly impossible to foretell the future price of any shares with certainty. Accordingly, no one can ever have been certain, when the employees were given the opportunity of making an application to buy the shares at 20s each, that these shares would be worth more than that figure on the day of their acquisition. Nevertheless, it is not surprising that 20s a share was regarded as an advantageous price and that the shares would fetch a substantially higher price when the market opened. The accountants' report in the prospectus showed that the company had a remarkably successful growth record. Its pre-tax profits had risen steadily from £273,000 for the year ending 31st December 1959 to £1,525,000 for the year ending 31st December 1968.

As I have already pointed out, the 'striking price' was 25s a share on 13th March and the special commissioners found that the 5,000 shares acquired by the taxpayer on 17th March were then worth £6,000. Incidentally, their closing price on the Stock Exchange on 18th March was 27s 6d per share.

Accordingly, I am certainly not surprised that the special commissioners, Brightman J and the Court of Appeal all apparently accepted that the advantage of being enabled to acquire 5,000 shares at 20s a share was a benefit conferred on the taxpayer by the company. The special commissioners, however, found that this benefit was a perquisite which arose from the taxpayer's employment, whilst Brightman J and the Court of Appeal held that it was not.

The special commissioners' finding was a finding of fact. No appellate tribunal may reverse such a finding merely on the ground that they might probably have arrived at a different conclusion. The commissioners' finding can be reversed on appeal only if the appellate tribunal is convinced that, on the evidence recorded in the case stated, no reasonable commissioners could have arrived at such a finding.

In *Edwards (Inspector of Taxes) v Bairstow*[1] Viscount Simonds said:

> '... it is universally conceded that, though it is a pure finding of fact, it may be set aside on grounds which have been stated in various ways but are, I think, fairly summarised by saying that the court should take that course if it appears that the commissioners have acted without any evidence, or on a view of the facts which could not reasonably be entertained.'

And Lord Radcliffe said[2]:

> '... it may be that the facts found are such that no person acting judicially and properly instructed as to the relevant law could have come to the determination under appeal. In those circumstances, too, the court must intervene. It has no option but to assume that there has been some misconception of the law, and that this has been responsible for the determination. So there, too, there has been error in point of law. I do not think that it much matters whether this state of affairs is described as one in which there is no evidence to support the determination, or as one in which the evidence is inconsistent with, and contradictory of, the determination, or as one in which the true and only reasonable conclusion contradicts the determination.'

In the present case, the commissioners said in their case stated:

> 'We accept that the purpose of the Company ... in arranging for shares to be offered on favourable terms to established employees ... was to encourage such employees to become shareholders of, or to increase their shareholdings in the parent company. ... If employees became members of the parent company, they would identify with the group. The aim, we were told, was to achieve a better relationship with the employees so that they would become and continue to be loyal employees, having an understanding of and a sense of involvement in the affairs and fortunes of [the company].'

The facts in *Laidler v Perry (Inspector of Taxes)*[3] (in which your Lordship's house found in favour of the Crown) were different from those in the present case. In that case, each employee from the lowest to those holding high executive positions was given £10 every Christmas. An observation of Lord Donovan in that case seems to me to be very much the point in the present one. Lord Dovovan said[4]:

> 'The admitted facts are that the company disbursed these sums to "help to maintain a feeling of happiness among the staff and to foster a spirit of personal relationship between management and staff". *In less roundabout language that simply means in order to maintain the quality of service given by the staff. Looked at in this way, the payments were an inducement to each recipient to go on working well ...*' (The emphasis is mine.)

It is only necessary to substitute for the words 'the payments', the words 'the benefit or perquisite of being able to obtain the shares at an advantageous price' to make Lord Donovan's comment as applicable to the passage from the case stated, which I have recited above, as it was to the case stated in *Laidler v Perry (Inspector of Taxes)*[3]. Speaking for

---

1   [1955] 3 All ER 48 at 53, [1956] AC 14 at 29, 36 Tax Cas 207 at 224
2   [1955] 3 All ER 48 at 57, [1956] AC 14 at 36, 36 Tax Cas 207 at 229
3   [1965] 2 All ER 121, [1966] AC 16, 42 Tax Cas 351
4   [1965] 2 All ER 121 at 128, [1966] AC 16 at 35–36, 42 Tax Cas 351 at 366

myself, I think that I would have been likely to have come to the same conclusion as did the commissioners. I certainly have no doubt that it is impossible to say that no reasonable commissioners could have come to that conclusion. Even discounting the exceptional experience and distinction of these commissioners, I find it equally impossible to agree that their findings of fact could support the argument that they must have misdirected themselves on the law. I have no doubt that the perquisite afforded to each employee was an inducement to go on working well. The company could have received 25s a share for each of the 560,000 shares allotted to the staff. Accordingly, the company deprived itself of upwards of £100,000 and distributed that sum amongst the staff 'to achieve a better relationship with the employees so that they would become and continue to be loyal employees, having an understanding of and a sense of involvement in the affairs and fortunes of [the company]'.

I have therefore come to the conclusion, with some reluctance, that no grounds exist on which the decision of the commissioners could properly be reversed. I say with reluctance because, in my view, the company's scheme was excellent. If generally adopted, it might well be of great advantage to industry and to the country's economy in general. It seems a pity to discourage employees from participating in such schemes by assessing them to income tax on the comparatively small profit they would gain on acquiring their shares, particularly as such a tax would produce only a derisively small sum of money in comparison with the substantial benefits which the public economy might well derive from such schemes. This policy consideration, however, can, of course, carry no weight with this House sitting in its judicial capacity. It might, however, perhaps deserve examination in other quarters.

My Lords, I would allow this appeal.

LORD EDMUND-DAVIES. My Lords, there is less to this appeal than meets the eye. And, with respect to those who have thought differently, my conclusion is that it poses a simple question of law calling for nothing more than a short answer. That does not, however, mean that the appeal can properly be disposed of in a sentence. The relevant facts have been related in the speech of my noble and learned friend, Lord Diplock. In considering them, it is important to have in mind throughout that this is an appeal from a decision of the Special Commissioners confirming an assessment to tax under Sch E 'in respect of any office or employment on emoluments therefrom' (Finance Act 1956, s 10(1)), Sch 2 providing by para 1(1) that 'the expression "emoluments" shall include all salaries, fees, wages, perquisites and profits whatsoever'.

Taxability in such cases as the present accordingly depends on the answers to two questions: (1) has the employee received an 'emolument'? and (2) if he has, was it an emolument *from* his office or employment? Unless both questions demand an affirmative answer, it is common ground that the finding of Brightman J and of the Court of Appeal in favour of the taxpayer must be upheld and the appeal dismissed.

As to the first question, it was contended for the taxpayer before the Special Commissioners that the most which the company could be said to have provided for him or for any other employees to whom application forms were sent was an opportunity to apply for shares at a price which might or might not prove favourable. As to the second question, the contention then raised was that any profit accruing to the taxpayer (ie the excess in value of his 5,000 shares over 20s a share) was derived from the normal operation of the market and not from his office or employment.

Before Brightman J and the Court of Appeal discussion was, understandably enough, concentrated largely, if not entirely, on the second question. In this, as in many other cases, they cannot be separately considered, and, indeed, they were coalesced in the first question of law raised by the Special Commissioners in their stated case. In my judgment the taxpayer here (in common with all other employees who had served for the minimum period of five years) was the recipient of an advantage (or 'emolument') which was not enjoyed by the public at large, viz the right to subscribe for shares at what was expected

would prove a preferential price, the employers undertaking to issue sufficient shares at 20s
a to meet employees' applications regardless of how the market behaved.

Accordingly, as I think, the second question is the only one which may reasonably have
presented the Special Commissioners with any difficulty. Was the advantage conferred on
employees of five years' service and on nobody else attributable to their employment? The
obvious fact that the taxpayer would not have enjoyed this benefit had he not been such an
employee is not decisive (*Hochstrasser (Inspector of Taxes) v Mayes*[1], per Lord Radcliffe) and,
b for myself, I respectfully accept as correct Brightman J's summary of the 'guidelines' laid
down by decided cases in dealing with this second question. He said[2]:

> 'It may be asked whether the benefit was a remuneration or reward or return for
> the services of the taxpayer. If so, the reward is an emolument from the employment:
> see, for example, *Hochstrasser (Inspector of Taxes) v Mayes*[3] and *Laidler v Perry (Inspector
> of Taxes)*[4]. It may also be asked whether the employment was the causa causans or
c > merely the causa sine qua non of the reward. If the former, the reward is an
> emolument: see other passages in *Hochstrasser v Mayes*[5] and *Laidler v Perry*[6].'

Applying those tests to the facts of the instant case, the taxpayer contends that the proper
conclusion is that the opportunity afforded certain employees to apply for an allotment of
shares on preferential terms was to encourage them to identify themselves with the
d employer rather than to remunerate or reward them for services and depended solely on
how much of their own money they were prepared to invest; and, indeed, that only about
one-half of the eligible employees in fact applied, leaving 151,018 out of the 560,000 shares
reserved for employees to be taken up by directors.

Such contentions prevailed before Brightman J and in the Court of Appeal. Dealing
with the taxpayer's application for 5,000 shares, Buckley LJ said[7]:

e
> 'He would not have had the opportunity to make it if he had not been an employee
> of that company, but the considerations which affected his mind in making the
> decision must have been personal to him as a private individual: how much money
> he could afford to invest in shares of the parent company; would the investment be
> a wise one from his point of view; would the shares in the short term or the long term
> be likely to be worth what he was going to pay for them; what income would they be
f > likely to yield, and so on? On the findings of the commissioners there was no
> certainty about these matters when the taxpayer made his decision; they were matters
> on which he had to make judgments. I think the decision involved a real commercial
> risk. They were matters quite unrelated to his relation with the subsidiary company,
> as an employee of that company, or his remoter relationship with the parent company,
> as an employee of one of its subsidiaries ... In my judgment the right to the shares
g > arose, not from the opportunity afforded by the company's scheme, but from the
> taxpayer's decision to take advantage of it.'

I have to say, with respect, that I see much force in these words and in the similarly
expressed views of Eveleigh LJ and Sir John Pennycuick. And it has to be borne in mind
that the conclusion of the Court of Appeal was arrived at after express adversion to the
h finding of the Special Commissioners that—

---

1   [1959] 3 All ER 817 at 823, [1960] AC 376 at 391, 38 Tax Cas 673 at 707
2   [1976] 3 All ER 537 at 546, [1977] 1 WLR 1 at 4, [1976] STC 521 at 530
3   [1959] 3 All ER 817 at 822, 826–827, [1960] AC 376 at 389–390, 396–397, 38 Tax Cas 673 at 706,
     711, per Viscount Simonds and Lord Denning
j 4   [1964] 3 All ER 329 at 331, 332, [1965] Ch 192 at 199, 200, 42 Tax Cas 351 at 360, 361, per Lord
     Denning MR and Danckwerts LJ
5   [1959] 3 All ER 817 at 821, 825, [1960] AC 376 at 387–389, 394–395, 38 Tax Cas 673 at 705, 709,
     per Viscount Simonds and Lord Cohen
6   [1965] 2 All ER 121 at 126, [1966] AC 16 at 33, 42 Tax Cas 351 at 365, per Lord Reid
7   [1978] 1 All ER 1089 at 1094–1095, [1978] 1 WLR 415 at 421, [1978] STC 141 at 146–147

'... the purpose of the Company ... in arranging for shares to be offered on favourable terms to established employees ... on the occasion of the parent Company of the group becoming a public company, was to encourage such employees to become shareholders of, or to increase their shareholdings in the parent company. ... If employees became members of the parent company, they would identify with the group. The aim, we were told, was to achieve a better relationship with the employees so that they would become and continue to be loyal employees, having an understanding of and a sense of involvement in the affairs and fortunes of the Rentokil group.'

On this basis, did the advantage conferred on eligible employees constitute a reward or return for their services, bearing in mind that, in the words of Sir John Pennycuick[1], 'A reward or return for services may, of course, be a reward or return for services in the present, the future or, I think, the past'?

The Special Commissioners concluded that—

'... the advantage which accrued to the [taxpayer] ... was an advantage afforded to him in return for acting as or being an employee within the meaning of that expression as used by Lord Radcliffe in *Hochstrasser (Inspector of Taxes) v Mayes*[2].'

My Lords, not everyone would have so concluded. Indeed, I have been and remain dubious that I myself would have done so. But such is not the proper approach. On the contrary, your Lordships have no entitlement to differ from the Special Commissioners' finding of fact regarding attributability unless, in the words of Lord Radcliffe in *Edwards (Inspector of Taxes) v Bairstow*[3], '... the facts found are such that no person acting judicially and properly instructed as to the relevant law could have come to the determination under appeal'. Only then may an appellate court hold that 'It has no option but to assume that there had been some misconception of the law and that this has been responsible for the determination'. There can be no room for thinking that the highly distinguished Special Commissioners who stated this case were under any misconception regarding the relevant law, nor, indeed, has it been suggested that they were. And so, after considerable expenditure of space and the use of many words, we come to that 'simple question of law calling for nothing more than a short answer' to which I adverted in my opening remarks. *Can* it be said that the conclusion of fact arrived at by the Special Commissioners regarding the attributability of the advantage conferred on the taxpayer in the present case was one which no person acting judicially could have come to? Put more specifically, did the only reasonable conclusion contradict their determination that the advantage the taxpayer enjoyed was extended as a reward for past services and as an inducement for the future? I have to say that I think these questions demand a negative answer and that I am accordingly obliged to hold that this appeal should be allowed.

LORD FRASER OF TULLYBELTON. My Lords, at the end of the hearing of this appeal I was inclined to dismiss it on the ground that the conclusion of the Special Commissioners was unreasonable in the sense explained by Lord Radcliffe in *Edwards (Inspector of Taxes) v Bairstow*[3]. But further reflection, and consideration of the speech prepared by my noble and learned friend, Lord Diplock, which I have seen in draft, has convinced me that, even though the Special Commissioners' conclusion is one that many judges might disagree with, it cannot properly be described as unreasonable. It is therefore not one that I am entitled to interfere with.

The facts of this case differ in several respects from those in *Weight (Inspector of Taxes) v Salmon*[4] and these differences, taken together, would certainly have justified the Special

---

1   [1978] 1 All ER 1089 at 1096, [1978] 1 WLR 415 at 423, [1978] STC 141 at 148
2   [1959] 3 All ER 817 at 823–824, [1960] AC 376 at 391–392, 38 Tax Cas 673 at 707–708
3   [1955] 3 All ER 48 at 57, [1956] AC 14 at 36, 36 Tax Cas 207 at 229
4   (1935) 19 Tax Cas 174, [1935] All ER Rep 904

Commissioners if they had found that the cases were distinguishable and that the advantage
which the taxpayer obtained by acquiring 5,000 shares in the company at 20s each did not
arise from his employment. The advantage accrued only when shares were allotted to him
at a price lower than the striking price for allotment to members of the public. Before
allotment he had no right to any shares and no other legal right of any relevant kind: see
Weight (Inspector of Taxes) v Salmon[1], per Lord Atkin. But shares could not have been
allotted to him unless he had applied for them, and his application required an investment
decision on his part. There is therefore, in my opinion, clearly room for the view that the
advantage is attributable to, or caused by, the taxpayers' own decision to apply for 5,000
shares. He had to take a view of the company's prospects and of his own willingness to risk
his money and he might quite well have decided not to apply for any shares, as many of the
other employees who were entitled to apply did in fact decide. The decision was unlike
that in *Salmon's case*[2] where, in a practical sense, there can have been little doubt that the
taxpayer would take up the limited number of shares for which he was entitled to apply.
The number of shares to be applied for in this case was a matter for the individual
judgment of the taxpayer. These were the considerations that weighed with the learned
judge, and also in the Court of Appeal with Buckley LJ who said[3]: 'In my judgment the
right to the shares arose, not from the opportunity afforded by the company's scheme, but
from the taxpayer's decision to take advantage of it.'

While I sympathise with that view, I have reached the opinion that it depends on
weighing the relative importance to be attached to the various primary facts, and that it
cannot be said to raise a question of law. Even in *Salmon's case*[2] the decision to apply for the
shares must have involved some element of risk and some personal decision by the
taxpayer, and so must have the decision to take up the option in *Abbott v Philbin (Inspector
of Taxes)*[4]. The most that can be said is that the decisions in those cases were much easier
than the decision in this case. But that is a difference only of degree.

For these reasons I also would allow this appeal and restore the order of the Special
Commissioners on both questions.

LORD RUSSELL OF KILLOWEN. My Lords, ordinarily, since your Lordships are
differing from the conclusion reached by Brightman J and the three members of the Court
of Appeal, I would feel it incumbent on me to express my conclusions in my own words.
But I have had the advantage of studying in draft the speech prepared by my noble and
learned friend, Lord Diplock, and I trust that it will not be thought disrespectful to the
views expressed below if I content myself with saying that I am in entire agreement with
it and do not attempt to paint the lily.

Appeal allowed.

Solicitors: *Solicitor of Inland Revenue ; Denton, Hall & Burgin* (for the taxpayer).

Mary Rose Plummer　　Barrister.

1　(1935) 19 Tax Cas 174 at 193, [1935] All ER Rep 904 at 910
2　19 Tax Cas 174, [1935] All ER Rep 904
3　[1978] 1 All ER 1089 at 1095, [1977] 1 WLR 415 at 421, [1978] STC 141 at 147
4　[1960] 2 All ER 763, [1961] AC 352, 39 Tax Cas 82 at 115

Lim Poh Choo v Camden and Islington Area Health Authority

QUEEN'S BENCH DIVISION
BRISTOW J
22nd, 23rd, 24th, 25th NOVEMBER, 7th DECEMBER 1977

COURT OF APPEAL, CIVIL DIVISION
LORD DENNING MR, LAWTON AND BROWNE LJJ
6th, 7th, 8th, 9th, 12th JUNE, 7th JULY 1978

Damages – Personal injury – Loss of future earnings – Doctor – Doctor with good prospects of becoming consultant suffering irreparable brain damage following operation – Injury due to negligence of hospital – Doctor requiring total care for rest of her life – Expectation of life 37 years – Doctor only intermittently sentient – No dependants – Whether award should include sum for loss of future earnings – Whether allowance should be made for inflation.

On 28th February 1973 the plaintiff, a senior pyschiatric registrar, was admitted to a hospital controlled by the defendant health authority for a minor gynaecological operation. She was 36 years old and a reasonably healthy woman. On 1st March, immediately after the operation, she suffered a cardiac arrest and irreparable brain damage due to the negligence of one of the defendants' staff. She had no dependants. She had however an elderly mother in Penang and a married sister in England. She was flown home to Penang where she was looked after by her mother and one full-time servant and two part-time servants. Through her mother she brought an action for damages for personal injuries against the defendants. At the trial of the action in 1977 the only issue was the quantum of damages. There was evidence that her expectation of life was 37 years, that if she had not suffered the cardiac arrest and brain damage she would almost certainly have become a consultant psychiatrist by 1978, that since her operation she had been a helpless invalid and only intermittently sentient and that her condition was such that she would require total care for the rest of her life either at home or in an institution. The judge found, inter alia, that she had little appreciation of what had happened to her, that her mother would probably only be able to look after her for seven years and that, as there was no suitable institution in Penang where she could be satisfactorily cared for thereafter, she would probably have to return to England then and be placed in an institution near her sister. He assessed the damages in the conventional way under the following heads: (i) *special damages to the date of trial*—£25,809 plus interest; (ii) *cost of future care*: (a) at home in Penang for seven years ('disregarding any purely domestic element [to] avoid any overlap with the loss of future earnings') at £2,600 per annum—£18,200, which he discounted to £17,500 to take account of the fact that part of the award would earn interest before it was expended; (b) thereafter at an institution in England at £8,000 per annum, to which multiplicand he applied a multiplier of 11 (making some reduction to allow for the purely domestic element and some increase for prospective inflation)—£88,000; total cost of future care—£105,500; (iii) *pain, suffering and loss of amenities*—£25,930; (iv) (a) *loss of future earnings* as a national health service consultant with some private practice in England at £6,000 per annum, to which multiplicand he applied a multiplier of 14 (to include a small increase to build in some anti-inflation protection)—£84,000; (b) *loss of pension rights*—£8,000 (giving a total under (a) and (b) of £92,000). He then considered the total sum of £249,239 to see (i) whether it did justice between the parties and (ii) how it compared with other awards. He concluded that it was high but not disproportionately so for someone who was only 41 and in the plaintiff's condition. The defendants appealed against the quantum of the award, contending, inter alia, (i) that where the injuries were as grave as the plaintiff's and where there were no dependants compensation awarded should not include an item for loss of future earnings, (ii) that even if loss of future earnings, had to be included, the judge had not made enough allowance for the overlap between that head of damage and the cost of future care, (iii) that he should not have made any allowance for future inflation and (iv) that the sum awarded for pain, suffering and loss of amenities was too high and should be a conventional figure analogous to that given for loss of expectation of life in fatal accident cases.

Held (Lord Denning MR dissenting) – The appeal would be dismissed for the following reasons—

(i) The court was bound by precedent to take into account the plaintiff's loss of her earning capacity and pension rights and to treat them as a separate item of damages. They were benefits of which she had been deprived by the negligence of a member of the defendants' staff and she was not debarred from recovering for the loss of them by reason of the fact that she was also entitled to recover the expenses of the different standard of living imposed on her by the defendants (see p 345 *c d*, p 348 *e*, p 353 *c d*, p 354 *c* to *e* and p 357 *c*, post); dicta of Lord Pearce in *H West & Son Ltd v Shephard* [1963] 2 All ER at 645–646 and of Orr LJ in *Taylor v Bristol Omnibus Co Ltd* [1975] 2 All ER at 1114 approved; *Phillips v London and South Western Railway Co* [1874–80] All ER Rep 1176 applied; *Fletcher v Autocar & Transporters Ltd* [1968] 1 All ER 726 explained.

(ii) The judge had made allowance for overlap between the cost of future care and the loss of future earnings (see p 346 *e f*, p 347 *j* and p 356 *f* to *h*, post).

(iii) The case came within the limited exception to the rule against making an allowance for inflation because the evidence showed that the assumed annuity which the sum awarded for future loss would purchase was large enough to attract a high rate of tax (see p 347 *b* to *d*, p 348 *a* and p 356 *a b*, post); dictum of Lord Fraser of Tullybelton in *Cookson v Knowles* [1978] 2 All ER at 616 applied.

(iv) There were no grounds for awarding only a modest sum for the plaintiff's pain, suffering and loss of amenities. She was not wholly insentient and the sum awarded might even be on the low side. It was certainly not exceptional in comparison with awards in other cases (see p 347 *h j*, p 350 *e* and p 357 *b*, post).

(v) Looked at as a whole, the total sum awarded was fair and reasonable in the circumstances (see p 348 *b* to *d* and p 357 *a* and *d e*, post).

Notes
For the measure of damages in personal injuries cases, see 12 Halsbury's Laws (4th Edn) paras 1145–1158, and for cases on the subject, see 17 Digest (Reissue) 116, 221, *190, 932,* and 36(1) ibid 313–318, 337, 362–363, *1263–1282, 1345, 1468–1473.*

Cases referred to in judgments
Armsworth v South Eastern Railway Co (1847) 11 Jur 758, 36(1) Digest (Reissue) 362, *1468.*
Benham v Gambling [1941] 1 All ER 7, [1941] AC 157, 110 LJKB 49, 164 LT 290, HL, 36(1) Digest 383, *1544.*
Bolton v Essex Area Health Authority [1977] The Times, 8th November.
Cavanagh v Ulster Weaving Co Ltd [1959] 2 All ER 745, [1960] AC 145, [1959] 3 WLR 262, [1959] 2 Lloyd's Rep 165, HL, 34 Digest (Repl) 262, *1864.*
Cookson v Knowles [1977] 2 All ER 820, [1977] QB 913, [1977] 3 WLR 279, [1977] 2 Lloyd's Rep 412, CA; *affd* [1978] 2 All ER 604, [1978] 2 WLR 978, HL.
Derby v McCarty and Leeds Health Authority (29th July 1977, Sheffield Crown Court), unreported.
Fletcher v Autocar & Transporters Ltd [1968] 1 All ER 726, [1968] 2 QB 322, [1968] 2 WLR 743, [1968] 1 Lloyd's Rep 317, CA, 36(1) Digest (Reissue) 314, *1271.*
Mitchell (by his next friend Mitchell) v Mulholland (No 2) [1971] 2 All ER 1205, [1972] 1 QB 65, [1971] 2 WLR 1271, [1971] 1 Lloyd's Rep 462, CA, 36(1) Digest (Reissue) 315, *1273.*

Oliver v Ashman [1960] 3 All ER 677, [1961] 1 QB 337, [1960] 3 WLR 924; *affd* on different grounds [1961] 3 All ER 323, [1962] 2 QB 210, [1961] 3 WLR 669, CA, 36(1) Digest (Reissue) 313, 1267.

Phillips v London and South Western Railway Co (1879) 4 QBD 406, 48 LJQB 693, 40 LT 813; *affd* 5 QBD 78, 41 LT 121, 43 JP 749, CA; *subsequent proceedings* 5 CPD 280, [1874–80] All ER Rep 1176, 49 LJQB 233, 42 LT 6, 44 JP 217, CA, 17 Digest (Reissue) 221, 932.

Roach v Yates [1937] 3 All ER 442, [1938] 1 KB 256, 107 LJKB 170, CA, 36(1) Digest (Reissue) 317, 1277.

Rowley v London and North Western Railway Co (1873) LR 8 Exch 221, [1861–73] All ER Rep 823, 42 LJ Ex 153, 29 LT 180, Ex Ch, 36(1) Digest (Reissue) 362, 1469.

Shearman v Folland [1950] 1 All ER 976, [1950] 2 KB 43, CA, 36(1) Digest (Reissue) 337, 1345.

Sinclair v O'Byrne (8th April 1976, Leeds Crown Court), unreported.

Skelton v Collins (1966) 115 CLR 94, [1966] ALR 449, 30 Digest (Reissue) 267, *380.

Smith v Central Asbestos Co Ltd [1971] 3 All ER 204, [1972] 1 QB 244, [1971] 3 WLR 206, [1971] 2 Lloyd's Rep 151, CA; *affd sub nom Central Asbestos Co Ltd v Dodd* [1972] 2 All ER 1135, [1973] AC 518, [1972] 3 WLR 333, [1972] 2 Lloyd's Rep 413, HL, 17 Digest (Reissue) 116, 190.

Taylor v Bristol Omnibus Co Ltd [1975] 2 All ER 1107, [1975] 1 WLR 1054, CA, Digest (Cont Vol D) 272, 191a.

Taylor v O'Connor [1970] 1 All ER 365, [1971] AC 115, [1970] 2 WLR 472, 49 ATC 37, [1970] TR 37, HL, 36(1) Digest (Reissue) 362, 1472.

West (H) & Son Ltd v Shephard [1963] 2 All ER 625, [1964] AC 326, [1963] 2 WLR 1359, HL, 36(1) Digest (Reissue) 314, 1269.

Wise v Kaye [1962] 1 All ER 257, [1962] 1 QB 638, [1962] 2 WLR 96, CA, 36(1) Digest (Reissue) 313, 1268.

Young v Percival [1974] 3 All ER 677, [1975] 1 WLR 17, [1975] 1 Lloyd's Rep 130, CA, 36(1) Digest (Reissue) 363, 1473.

Cases also cited

Davis v Johnson [1978] 1 All ER 1132, [1978] 2 WLR 553, HL.
Farrell v Alexander [1976] 2 All ER 721, [1977] AC 59, HL.
Jefford v Gee [1970] 1 All ER 1202, [1970] 2 QB 130, CA.
Malyon v Plummer [1963] 2 All ER 344, [1964] 1 QB 330.
Rose v Ford [1937] 3 All ER 359, [1937] AC 826, HL.

Action

This was an action by the plaintiff, Dr Lim Poh Choo (suing by her mother and next friend, Lim Gim Hoe), against the defendants, Camden and Islington Area Health Authority, for damages for personal injury, loss, damage and expense sustained by reason of the negligence of the defendants, their servants or agents, on or about 1st March 1973 in the course of the provision of medical treatment. The defendants admitted liability and at the trial of the action the only issue was the quantum of damages. The facts are set out in the judgment.

Christopher French QC and *George Newman* for the plaintiff.
John Davies QC and *Peter Scott* for the defendants.

Cur adv vult

7th December. **BRISTOW J** read the following judgment: On 28th February 1973 Dr Lim Poh Choo, a 36 year old senior psychiatric registrar working for the New Southgate Group of Hospitals and the Royal Free Hospital, was admitted to the Elizabeth Garrett Anderson Hospital for minor gynaecological surgery. Following on the operation which took place next morning she suffered a cardiac arrest as the result of the failure by someone,

for whom the Camden and Islington Area Health Authority is vicariously responsible, to
a take reasonable care for her safety.

The consequences have been disastrous. Before 1st March 1973 she was in mid-career
practising in her chosen field of medicine. She had qualified in Singapore in 1963 at the
age of 26. In the next few years she served in junior house appointments in Singapore and
worked for a short time as a general practitioner in Hong Kong. Then her lawyer father
fell ill and she returned to Malaya and in 1967 started training in psychiatric medicine at
b University Hospital, Kuala Lumpur. In 1971 she came to England. She worked first as a
full time clinical assistant at the Halliwick Hospital and gained her Diploma in Psychiatric
Medicine. In 1972 she was appointed Senior Registrar at the hospital complex for which
she was working at the time of the accident. Although she failed the exam for membership
of the Royal College of Psychiatrists, a necessary qualification for consultant status in
England, in autumn 1972, her performance and quality were such that she was confidently
c expected to pass, probably at the April 1973 sitting. The career structure in the national
_health service is such that barring accidents or a decision to move into another field she
would have become a consultant psychiatrist by 1978, if not earlier.

As a result of what happened on 1st March 1973 she was in coma for two weeks, and on
regaining consciousness she did not talk, had two epileptic fits, and could not walk. In the
Wolfson Rehabilitation Unit she recovered the ability to walk a little with help and to
d speak a few words. On 25th September 1973, six months after the disaster, she was
assessed by the consultant neurologist at the Royal Free Hospital as suffering from diffuse
brain damage producing a lack of co-ordination in all four limbs, and to be depressed and
withdrawn with difficulty in speaking. Tests at the Maudsley Hospital showed that her
disabilities were purely organic in origin, due to the extensive brain damage caused by the
cardiac arrest.

e Dr Lim's mother, a retired teacher, now a widow living in Penang, decided that the right
place for her to be cared for was at home, so she was flown home on 2nd February 1974.
She spent from 28th February to 7th June 1975 in the Department of Rehabilitation
Medicine, Tan Tock Sing Hospital, Singapore under the care of Dr Don and Dr Loong. She
was found to be depressed, occasionally aggressive, and totally dependent on others in all
self care activities including feeding, toileting and grooming, and her speech was
f impaired. This condition was the result of gross neurological deficit arising from the brain
damage. She could not walk without help or propel her wheel chair. Their conclusion was
that she would require maximum personal assistance for the rest of her life and would not
be able to function as a doctor.

The picture which emerges from the agreed medical reports is that of a helpless invalid
who will require nursing for the rest of her life, and is only intermittently sentient. When
g she is sentient it looks as if it is at a comparatively low level and though she sometimes
remembers that she was a doctor in England Dr Lim is so intellectually impaired that she
does not appreciate what has happened to her. This picture was borne out by the evidence
of Dr McQuaide of St Andrews Hospital, Northampton, who examined Dr Lim at her
mother's home in Penang in July 1976. He found her emotional state to be blank and she
was completely lacking in volition and spontaneity. Her powers of reasoning were
h impossible to test.

Dr McQuaide's conclusion was that she showed evidence of dementia and gross physical
disability due to severe cerebral damage. She would always need total care at home or in
an institution and would never get better. If she continues to be cared for as she is by her
mother at present, her expectation of continued existence, for you cannot call it life, will
not be shortened. Otherwise it will almost certainly be less than average.

j That a doctor who had so much to offer to the mentally ill should be subjected by want
of care in hospital to the appalling disability from which Dr Lim is condemned to suffer for
the rest of her existence is a very great tragedy. Her mother, who has been in court
throughout the trial, in which counsel on both sides have given me the greatest possible
help, will realise that the law cannot pretend to compensate her daughter for the
destruction of her life. The court can only award a sum of money, and in justice to the

defendants as well as to Dr Lim that sum must be in proportion to awards in other cases of those who have suffered injuries of comparable severity.

I have been helpfully referred by counsel to the relevant authorities, and especially *Fletcher v Autocars & Transporters Ltd*[1] and *Taylor v O'Connor*[2]. I bear in mind the warnings against awarding damages which might overlap from one into another of the categories into which the authorities require me to divide the problem in order to reach a fair result.

I also bear in mind what is said in the authorities about the question of protecting plaintiffs against the consequences of future inflation, because damages have to be awarded once for all here and now. In *Taylor v O'Connor*[2] the accident which caused the death of the plaintiff's husband took place in June 1965. The award of damages by Lyell J at first instance was on 8th May 1968. The House of Lords gave judgment on 21st January 1970. Lord Pearson dealt[3] with this aspect of the matter where he commented on the fact that Lyell J had increased the multiplier to a modest extent to shield the plaintiff to some extent against the effects of inflation. Lord Pearson said:

'Certainly it is right to have regard to the prospect of continuing inflation as an important factor in the situation, but I do not think that a mere increase in the multiplier is a suitable method of protecting against inflation, although it achieves something. I think that protection against inflation is to be sought by investment policy, and that the lump sum of damages should be assessed on the basis that it will be invested with the aim of obtaining some capital appreciation to offset the probable rise in the cost of living.'

In 1970 the rise in oil prices and the acceleration in wage demands to figures with which we are now familiar, were still in the future, and relatively stable money was the context in which these words of Lord Pearson were uttered. But since 1970 our world has dramatically changed. We have experienced inflation at rates approaching 30% in a single year. We see government doing its best to reduce inflation to single figures, with success said to be dependent on trade unions being content with wage settlements of the order of 10%. We have passed through three years in which investment advisers could hardly do more than say, 'If you take our advice you might, if all goes well, reduce the impact on you of the certain rise in the cost of living.'

In these circumstances I take the view that the court must do what it reasonably can to protect a plaintiff against inflation, and that what the House of Lords thought it wrong for Lyell J to do in the conditions of 1968 it is right to do in 1977 when we can see more clearly where the world is going.

I will now consider the assessment of the appropriate damages under the various heads:

1 *Future care of Dr Lim*

This is clearly the first priority. For her there is nothing the law can do other than to try to provide enough for her to be reasonably looked after for the rest of her days. It is clear on the evidence that her mother, now aged 71, will look after Dr Lim at home in Penang for as long as she is able. But the time will come when she can do so no longer. What then?

Dr Lim has a sister, Mrs Plowright, herself a Ph D (London), married to a member of the BBC staff, living in Hampstead with her husband and two small children. She has a brother who is an architect, married to a German girl, living and working in Kuala Lumpur with three boys, twins aged 12 and a six year old. The brother's wife finds living in Malaya difficult, and Mr Lim has contemplated emigration and work somewhere else in the world for that reason.

1 [1968] 1 All ER 726, [1968] 2 QB 322
2 [1970] 1 All ER 365, [1971] AC 115
3 [1970] 1 All ER 365 at 378–379, [1971] AC 115 at 142–143

I have to put myself in the position of the officious bystander at the family conference which in my judgment is going to take place, probably in seven years time, about what is to be done with Dr Lim when her mother can no longer look after her. In my judgment the probable situation then will be, Mr and Mrs Plowright in London, Mr and Mrs Lim, if still based in Kuala Lumpur, anxious to emigrate. Neither branch of the family would contemplate leaving Dr Lim alone in Malaya, where the evidence is that there are no institutions which could cope satisfactorily with her as a long term patient. In my judgment the joint family answer will be that Dr Lim should go to England and be cared for in an institution within range of Mrs Plowright. Neither family as it seems to me, can reasonably be expected to care for her at home.

The cost of caring for Dr Lim at home in Penang, disregarding any purely domestic element and so avoiding any overlap with the loss of future earnings problem, I find to be approximately £2,600 per year. The straight £2,600 × 7 = £18,200 must be discounted to some extent because part of the award will earn interest before it is expended. In my judgment £17,500 is the appropriate figure for 7 years of future care of Dr Lim in Penang.

On this basis, when Dr Lim is expected to be brought to London she will be 47 years old. What is the proper multiplier for the remaining care element? Her expectation of life according to the tables will be in the order of a further 30 years. In this case I must make a substantial discount because of the accelerated payment, some reduction for the contingency that she will not reach the average age, some reduction to allow for the purely domestic element, and some increase for prospective inflation. Balancing these elements as best I can I find the appropriate multiplier for the period of future care in England to be 11.

On the evidence the present cost of looking after Dr Lim in an appropriate institution in England is in the order of £8,000 per year. So £88,000 is the appropriate figure to allow for future care in London, making a total for the cost of future care, the top priority, of £105,500.

2 Cost of care of Dr Lim to date

On the evidence the cost of care of Dr Lim at home in Penang to date is the cost of one full time and two part-time servants, plus a physiotherapist five times a week and visits from the family doctor and medicines, amounting to $850 a month. It is agreed that the rate of exchange should be taken at $4·25 to the £, making a monthly figure of £200. Dr Lim has been looked after on this basis for approximately 40 months, so the total under this head is £8,000.

3 'Out of pockets' to date

These are agreed to a large extent. The accepted items amount to £3,296. I find the approximate figure for the disputed item as follows: telephone £300. So the total here is £3,596.

4 Loss of earnings to date

Dr Lim received her salary for some time after the accident. Taking that into account, her net loss of earnings to date is £14,213, an average of £3,158 per annum.

5 Loss of future earnings

I have no evidence other than her history of Dr Lim's plans for a career as a consultant. There are more opportunities in England though the rewards in Malaya are greater. Her sister is fixed in England. Her brother is not fixed in Malaya. On the probabilities I conclude that she would have practised as a consultant in England.

Assuming the present national health service salary rates, and allowing for a small amount of earnings from private practice, in my judgment the fair multiplicand to take is £6,000. Including a small increase to build in some anti-inflation protection, 14 looks like an appropriate multiplier. On this basis the figure for loss of future earnings is £84,000.

6 Loss of pension rights

Had Dr Lim reached pensionable age and lived her life-table span of 12 years thereafter, she would have received £49,866 pension. Discounting that amount by the appropriate percentage if she received it now, the figure is £18,500. But I must make a further discount for the contingency that Dr Lim would never have reached pensionable age at all, or if she did would not have survived the 12 tabular years, although she might have survived far longer. There are even more imponderables under this head, and I think the appropriate award would be £8,000.

7 General damages for pain and suffering and loss of the amenities of life

Under this head we pass from the wholly or partly calculable into the field of convention. Dr Lim's loss of the amenities of her good and useful life is total. On the evidence, her appreciation of that loss, and so the agony which knowing what you have lost must cause, is nil, or very small. In the light of the authorities in my judgment the right conventional award would be £20,000.

When we add up the total of the individual sums reached by the above approach the total is £243,309. It is then necessary to look at the total and ask ourselves whether it does justice to both parties. Dr Lim's situation is terrible. £243,309 is a very large sum for a hospital authority to have to pay by way of damages. The most that can be done for Dr Lim herself is to look after her. She has no dependants so that when she dies it is likely, though I have no evidence about it, that her estate will pass to her brother and sister and enure for the benefit of her nephews and nieces.

As a rough cross check of the appropriateness of such an award it is interesting to see what net income Dr Lim would receive by buying an annuity with an amount equal to those elements which relate only to the future and to the pain and suffering element, that is £217,500. A payment of £200,000 would produce a net income of £12,896 per annum with no inflation hedge. With the cost of care in England in what seems an appropriate but in no way luxurious or extravagant institution presently £8,000 per year, and the present inflationary trends, does £217,500 to look after the future and compensate for being condemned to a living death look too much?

If we were to approach the problem on the basis considered by Diplock LJ in *Fletcher v Autocars & Transporters Ltd*[1] but not held to be right by the court, we would have to take into account only the cost of care to date and the cost of future care, being those elements which go to Dr Lim's 'happiness', with a 'pain and suffering' figure, in her case nominal, plus 'out of pockets'. Loss of earnings and pension rights as Dr Lim is now make no difference whatever to her. That loss simply affects the benefits that would pass on to others on her death. The total award on that basis would be say £117,500. Using the same rough cross check, £100,000 would produce an annuity of £7,540 net, not enough to cover the present annual cost of care in England. £150,000 would produce an annuity of £10,131.

In my judgment the authorities require me to take into account the loss of earnings amounts and to award a pain and suffering and loss of amenity sum proportionate to other awards in cases of injury of the maximum severity. Going by this road the total award is high, but not in my judgment, disproportionately high when I remember that Dr Lim is only 41, there is no reason to suppose that her expectation of existence has been reduced, and she will need total care for the rest of her days.

There will be judgement for the sum of £243,309 plus interest of the appropriate amount on the appropriate elements, liberty to apply if the amount of interest cannot be agreed.

The award of £20,000 for the general damages for pain and suffering and loss of the amenities of life is assessed on the pre-*Cookson v Knowles*[2] basis, so as to be comparable with other awards and assuming that it carries interest. Since it is the *Cookson v Knowles*[2] basis

---

1   [1968] 1 All ER 726, [1968] 2 QB 322
2   [1977] 2 All ER 820, [1977] QB 913

that should be applied now that must be increased by the amount of interest it would have carried, and so the total damages must be increased by the amount which, before that decision, would have been awarded by way of interest.

There will be a stay of execution as to £100,000.

Judgment for the plaintiff for £243,309 plus interest; defendants to pay £111,590 within 14 days; stay of execution as to balance pending appeal.

K Mydeen Esq   Barrister.

Appeal

The defendants appealed against the judgment of Bristow J. By a respondent's notice under RSC Ord 59, r 6(1)(2), the plaintiff gave notice that at the hearing of the appeal she would contend that the judgment of Bristow J should be varied, or, alternatively, affirmed on grounds additional to those relied on before the judge, namely (i) that while the award of £20,000 damages for pain, suffering and loss of amenities would have been a proper sum in 1974, it was an insufficient sum to be awarded in 1977, and/or (ii) that she was entitled to interest pursuant to s 3 of the Law Reform (Miscellaneous Provisions) Act 1934, as amended by s 22 of the Administration of Justice Act 1969, on a proper award in 1977.

John Davies QC and *Peter Scott* QC for the defendants.
Christopher French QC and *George Newman* for the plaintiff.

Cur adv vult

7th July. The following judgments were read.

LORD DENNING MR. It happened on 1st March 1973. A lady doctor, Dr Lim Poh Choo, had gone into hospital for a minor gynaecological operation. It was for dilatation and curettage. She was quite a healthy woman. She was put under a general anaesthetic. The operation was performed. She was moved from the operating theatre to the recovery room. Whilst she was still unconscious she began to go blue. The doctors call it cyanosis. This was a sign of trouble. It showed that her breathing had been affected. The recovery sister sent for help. They gave her oxygen, but nevertheless the cyanosis increased. Five minutes later her breathing stopped. This affected her heart. The blood stopped flowing to her brain. She suffered what the doctors call 'cardiac arrest'. The heart was massaged. After 25 minutes her breathing was restored to normal. She was brought back to life. The more's the pity of it! For it was a living death. Her brain was severely damaged beyond repair. She was in a deep coma for two weeks. At length she recovered consciousness but could not talk. She had two epileptic fits. After four months she could speak a few words and could walk a little with help. Now five years later she is still helpless. Her mind is gone. She can speak a few words, but without meaning or sense. She cannot dress, bath herself or attend to her toilet. In the words of the specialist, she 'shows evidence of dementia and gross physical disability due to severe cerebral damage . . . She will always need total care either at home or in an institution.'

Now by her mother (who is her next friend) she has brought an action for damages against the health authority. At first they denied liability; as indeed they well might. Accidents such as this do happen in operations through sheer misadventure, some allergy or sensitivity in the patient to a particular drug, without negligence at all. But, after consideration the health authority accepted liability; and the only issue is the amount of damages. The judge has awarded nearly £250,000. It is a staggering figure. It is the highest sum ever yet awarded in these courts. The health authority appeal to this court on this amount.

In considering damages in personal injury cases, it is often said: 'The defendants are wrongdoers. So make them pay up in full. They do not deserve any consideration.' That is a tendentious way of putting the case. The accident, like this one, may have been due to a pardonable error such as may befall any one of us. I stress this so as to remove the misapprehension, so often repeated, that the plaintiff is entitled to be *fully* compensated for all the loss and detriment she has suffered. That is not the law. She is only entitled to what is, in the circumstances, a *fair* compensation, fair both to her and to the defendants. The defendants are not wrongdoers. They are simply the people who have to foot the bill. They are, as the lawyers say, only vicariously liable. In this case it is in the long run the taxpayers who have to pay. It is worth recording the wise words of Parke B over a century ago:

> 'Scarcely any sum could compensate a labouring man for the loss of a limb, yet you do not in such a case give him enough to maintain him for life . . . You are not to consider the value of existence as if you were bargaining with an annuity office . . . I advise you to take a reasonable view of the case and give what you consider fair compensation'

(see *Armsworth v South Eastern Railway Co*[1], quoted with approval by Brett J in *Rowley v London and North Western Railway Co*[2] and approved in the leading case of *Phillips v London and South Western Railway Co*[3]).

The lady here was born on 18th October 1936. So at the operation in 1973 she was 36. She is now 41. She was educated in Malaya. In 1963 at the age of 26 she qualified as a doctor and specialised in psychiatry. She was for eight years working in hospitals out there. She came to England in 1971, when she was 34. She passed her Diploma in Psychiatry and was appointed a Senior Registrar at the Friern Hospital. She was due in April 1973 to take her examination for membership of the Royal College of Psychiatrists. Two distinguished doctors described Dr Lim as 'a remarkably good doctor, intelligent, conscientious, reliable, able to make good contact with patients, supportive to and popular with the nursing staff'. Each doctor regarded it as almost certain that she would have passed her membership examination and obtained a post as a consultant psychiatrist within four or five years.'

The disaster happened on 1st March 1973. She lay stricken in hospitals in England for several months. Then, on 2nd February 1974, she was flown back to Malaya. She was then taken to her mother's home in Penang where she has been ever since, save for a month or two in a nursing home in Singapore. Her mother looks after her, together with the help of one full-time servant and two part-time servants. It is doubtful, however, how long her mother will be able to look after her. It has been suggested that the best thing would be for her to be moved back to England and put in an institution here where she could be cared for; especially as she has a married sister living here in London.

If this lady had died under the operation, as in former times she would probably have done, then, even though it was due to the fault of the hospital, the damages would have been minimal. She had no relatives dependent on her. So there would be no payment under the Fatal Accidents Acts. The only sum to be awarded to her estate would be the conventional sum of £750 for loss of expectation of life.

But now, by reason of the advances of medical science, she was snatched back from death under the operation and has been brought back to a life which is not worth living. The body has been kept alive, but the mind is gone. The doctors and nurses, with the aids available today, say that they can keep the body going for the normal expectation of life. In her case 37 years. But every moment of it distressing to her and those about her. Sadness and happiness are all alike to her. Many might say: ''Twere better she had died.'

Such cases, we are told, are not uncommon, and we are faced with the problem: on what principles should compensation be awarded to her? As I said in *Taylor v Bristol Omnibus Co Ltd*[4] the subject needs radical reappraisal. This case gives the opportunity for it.

1 (1847) 11 Jur 758 at 760
2 (1873) LR 8 Exch 221 at 230, [1861–73] All ER Rep 823 at 830
3 (1879) 5 QBD 78 at 79
4 [1975] 2 All ER 1107 at 1113, [1975] 1 WLR 1054 at 1060

On principle

One thing is beyond doubt; fair compensation must mean that she is to be kept in as much comfort and tended with as much care as compassion for her so rightfully demands; and that she should not want for anything that money can buy. But I see no justification in law or in morals awarding to her large sums of money in addition to those needed to keep her in comfort. Such extra sums will avail her nothing. She herself can make no use of them. All that will happen to them is that they will be accumulated during her lifetime at high interest rates of which 80% or more will go to the Revenue. Invested well the capital will be worth more and more. She will be unable to dispose of any of it by will, since she has not the mental capacity to make a will. On her death, all will go to her nearest relatives, or if she has none then, I suppose to the Crown as bona vacantia; and the Crown will not know what to do with the money. If she should not last the 37 years, but die within five years, as a layman may think very probable, this huge sum will do no one any good. It was for reasons such as these that Lord Pearson's Commission recommended that non-pecuniary damages should no longer be recoverable for permanent unconsciousness[1]. Similar reasoning seems to me to apply to permanent insensibility.

One cannot forget, also, that in these days after such an accident as this, the relatives, and the doctors, are faced with an agonising decision: is she to be kept alive? Or is she to be allowed to die? Is the thread of life to be maintained to the utmost reach of science? Or should it be let fall and nature takes its inevitable course? Such a decision should not be influenced in the least by a law which whispers in the ear: 'If she is kept alive, there will be large sums of compensation payable—for the benefit of the relatives; whereas, if she dies there will be nothing.' Rather those about her should say: 'For mercy's sake, let the end come now.'

To be fair to her relatives in this case, to be fair to her mother, her sister and her brother, they do not ask for anything more than fair compensation on the grounds that I have stated. They want nothing for themselves. They seek to uphold this large award of £250,000 solely so as to ensure that the expenses of nursing and attendance shall be met, whatever the future may bring in the way of inflation. Their fears on this score can, I believe, be met in other ways, as I will show.

It is a modern problem, the impact of modern science, in prolonging life in a body destitute of mind. To my mind on principle fair compensation requires that there should be ample provision in terms of money for comfort and care during the lifetime of the sufferer such as to safeguard her in all foreseeable contingencies, including the effect of inflation; that, if he or she has any dependants, they should be compensated for any pecuniary loss which they suffer by reason of his or her incapacity and inability to earn, just as if he or she had died and compensation was being awarded under the Fatal Accident Acts. Beyond that there can be conventional sums for pain and suffering and loss of amenities, but these should not be too large, seeing that they will do her no good, and can only accumulate during her lifetime to benefit others who survive after her death. This is reinforced by the views of Lord Pearson's Commission[2]. Half of them thought there should be a statutory maximum of £20,000. The other half thought that there should not be a statutory maximum but that the Court of Appeal should exercise a restraining hand.

I may add, too, that if these sums get too large, we are in danger of injuring the body politic; just as medical malpractice cases have done in the United States of America. As large sums are awarded, premiums for insurance rise higher and higher, and these are passed to the public in the shape of higher and higher fees for medical attention. By contrast, we have here a national health service. But the health authorities cannot stand huge sums without impeding their service to the community. The funds available come out of the pockets of the taxpayers. They have to be carefully husbanded and spent on essential services, They should not be dissipated in paying more than fair compensation.

---

1   Report of the Royal Commission on Civil Liability and Compensation for Personal Injury (Cmnd 7054–I), paras 393, 398

2   Cmnd 7054–I, paras 391 392

In many of these cases the national health service willingly provides full care, nursing and attention without charging anything for it. Surely this, too, should go to reduce the amount awarded against them. The damages should not be inflated so as to cover the cost of being kept in the most expensive nursing home. It has been known, I am not saying in this case, that when such damages have been awarded, the relatives have afterwards arranged to take advantage of the facilities afforded by the national health service (see Lord Pearson's report[1]), and thus save money for themselves.

The authorities

Such being the position in principle, I turn to see whether there is any authority which prevents it. The practice is now established and cannot be gainsaid that, in personal injury cases, the award of damages is assessed under four main heads: first, special damages in the shape of money actually expended; second, cost of future nursing and attendance and medical expenses; third, pain and suffering and loss of amenities; fourth, loss of future earnings.

I need not comment on the first two items except to say that the sum is to include compensation for the services of wife or husband, mother or father, given voluntarily and gratuitously. So far as the third item is concerned, we have the authority of the House of Lords for giving an award of a substantial sum for pain and suffering and loss of amenities: see *H West & Son Ltd v Shephard*[2]; but we have the suggestion of Lord Pearson's Commission[3] that it should be a modest sum, with a maximum, some suggest, of £20,000. So far as inflation is concerned, we have it established by the House of Lords that it is not to be taken into account in the ordinary run of cases, but there are exceptional cases (where the sum awarded attracts high tax) where allowance may be made for future inflation: see *Young v Percival*[4] as qualified in *Cookson v Knowles*[5].

The real problem is the fourth item, the loss of future earnings. It is often assumed that these are to be calculated on an annuity basis and given as an additional award over and above the other items. The courts take an appropriate sum for his annual earnings and an appropriate multiplier, and add the result on to the other items. That method may be good enough when the injured man was a married man with a family, who was in work at the time of the accident, and would have continued to work until his retirement but for the accident, and lives at home after the accident with little extra expense. His loss of earnings, calculated in that way, is a fair compensation for the dependency of his family on him, as in the asbestosis cases; see *Smith v Central Asbestos Co Ltd*[6]. But in cases like the present, that method gives more than fair compensation. Much more. Whilst unconscious or insensible, he gets his full salary without doing any work for it and no expenses out of it; and at the same time he gets his full board and keep at a very expensive nursing home. In *Fletcher v Autocars & Transporters Ltd*[7] I tried to modify it by invoking a doctrine of 'overlapping'. In *Taylor v Bristol Omnibus Co Ltd*[8] I sought to reduce the sum for loss of future earnings, but my brethren persuaded me otherwise. And I know of several good judges of first instance who have expressed their unease at the high figures which in these cases of severe brain damage, notably Kilner Brown J in *Sinclair v O'Byrne*[9] and Jupp J in *Derby v McCarty and Leeds Health Authority*[10].

---

1 Cmnd 7054–I, para 341
2 [1963] 2 All ER 625, [1964] AC 326
3 Cmnd 7054–I, paras 377–392
4 [1974] 3 All ER 677 at 685–688, [1975] 1 WLR 17 at 26–29
5 [1978] 2 All ER 604, [1978] 2 WLR 978
6 [1971] 3 All ER 204 at 208–214, [1972] 1 QB 244 at 255–263
7 [1968] 1 All ER 726, [1968] 2 QB 322
8 [1975] 2 All ER 1107, [1975] 1 WLR 1054
9 (8th April 1976) unreported
10 (29th July 1977) unreported

As this case will, I hope, go to the House of Lords, I take my stand on principle. In my opinion when a plaintiff is rendered unconscious or insensible, fair compensation should not include an item for loss of earnings as such, but instead it should include an item for pecuniary loss suffered by the dependants of the injured man by reason of his accident. After all, if that is the compensation regarded as fair by the legislature in case of his natural death, it may justly be regarded as fair in case of his living death, provided also that full compensation is also given for every expense that may be incurred on his behalf and every service that may be rendered to him by relatives and friends. The cost of keeping the plaintiff for the rest of his days will exceed by far the salary or wages that he would have earned if he never had been injured. It is not fair to the defendants to make them pay both.

Similarly, if *Oliver v Ashman*[1] is overruled by the House of Lords and a man is given compensation for his loss of earnings during his 'lost years', there again these should be calculated, not for loss of earnings as such, but for the pecuniary loss suffered by his dependants during those lost years. In *Skelton v Collins*[2] the High Court of Australia only awarded £2,000, which was far less than any actuarial calculation.

Application to this case

The first item is the cost of nursing and keep of the plaintiff for the rest of her days.

This lady was unmarried with no one dependent on her, nor likely to be. Beyond doubt the damages must provide for the cost of nursing and attendance and keep for the rest of her days. If she is looked after by her mother and the servants at their home in Penang, the sum must include not only the outgoings on doctors, nurses, medicines, and the like; but also a sum for food and nourishment; and to recompense the mother and staff; and a proportion of the outgoings on the house; and so forth. If she is moved over to England, the sum must include the cost of any nursing home or institution, and any other expenses that may have to be incurred.

The difficulty in this item is to know how long she is likely to stay in Penang; and whether she is likely to come over to England, or not. This is most uncertain. The judge thought that she would probably stay in Penang for another seven years at an expense of £2,600 a year, and then come to England for a further 30 years at £8,000 a year—at present day costs. But additional evidence was tendered before us to show that her mother was frail and could not look after her in Penang very much longer; and in that case Dr Lim might be brought to England very soon.

Apart from these uncertainties, there are these other matters to be taken into account, the fact that the payment will be a lump sum which will be paid immediately and can be invested to produce income, which will be subject to tax; the possibility that she may not live the expected span of 37 years; and that the costs in Penang or in England will go up with inflation; and the possibility (as has happened in other cases) that after expenses have been awarded on the basis of an expensive nursing home, it is afterwards saved by taking advantage of the facilities of the national health service; (see Lord Pearson's report[3]).

So many are the uncertainties and contingencies that I do not think it can be solved by actuarial evidence. Nor do I think it desirable. There should be a simpler method which is available to all the many people who have to consider the amount. Sometimes in negotiations for a settlement. Sometimes by decision in a court. Experience shows that, in order to ascertain nursing expenses (over the rest of expected life) or loss of earnings or dependency (over the rest of working life) the best way is to take an appropriate multiplicand and multiply it by an appropriate multiplier. The practitioners in this field have become very expert in it, once the courts have shown the way.

---

1   [1960] 3 All ER 677, [1961] 1 QB 337; *affd* on different grounds [1961] 3 All ER 323, [1962] 2 QB 210, CA
2   (1965) 115 CLR 94
3   Cmnd 7054–I, paras 340–341

In the result, I assess the damages in this case as follows:

Cost of nursing and care to date of trial (as found by the judge)		£8,000·00
Out-of-pocket expenses to date (as found by the judge)		£3,596·00
Cost of future nursing, care and keep (allowing for possibility of early return to England)	£7,000 a year	
Number of years purchase (increased for inflation)	15	
Total (same as found by the judge)		£105,000·00
Pain and suffering and loss of amenities		£20,000·00
		£136,596·00

The fears of the relatives

The relatives fear that a sum of this magnitude may not be sufficient. They need not fear. If the usual course is adopted, the sum will be put under the control of the Court of Protection. If the lady should die in a few years' time, as may well be the case, the greater part of it will still be intact and will go to the relatives themselves.

She may, however, live a very long time. I cannot think that she will live so long as to outlive this large sum of money. The Court of Protection, with its expert advice, will be able to see that it will suffice. But, in the remote contingency that she should live to a great age, there is nowadays machinery in the Rules of the Supreme Court by which this sum of £136,596 can be regarded as an interim award[1]. It needs some ingenuity to adapt the rules, but I think it could be done. If it is regarded as an interim award, it will be open to her, by her next friend, in that remote contingency, to come back for an additional award to last out the rest of her days. Alternatively, and more simply, without adapting the rules, the health service can be asked to give an undertaking to pay whatever extra is necessary or to look after her in comfort in that very remote contingency. I have no doubt they would give such an undertaking. Such a solution would be much more fair than awarding an immense sum now; and it would offer a satisfactory middle course between the rival views on periodic payments expressed in the report of Lord Pearson's Commission[2].

I would add that the Master of the Court of Protection has provided for us a most interesting analysis of 46 cases where large sums have been awarded in cases of severe brain damage. They show how well these sums are administered by the court. But they also show that, in no case, even in the more recent times, has the figure exceeded £130,000. If it be right to have some regard to the scale of awards in these cases, the present award is far, far above the current scale. It is just about double.

I would, therefore, allow this appeal and reduce the award to £136,596·00, with the appropriate interest.

Lawton LJ cannot be here, but Browne LJ will read his judgment.

LAWTON LJ (read by Browne LJ). The award in this case of just over a quarter of a million pounds is startling. Counsel on behalf of the defendants described it as absurd. In a full and careful judgment Bristow J set out how he had reached this sum: £105,000 for future care; £8,000 for care to date; £3,596 for out-of-pocket expenses to date; £84,000 for loss of future earnings; £8,000 for loss of pension rights; £20,000 for pain and suffering and the loss of the amenities of life; and a sum for interest calculated in accordance with the guidelines set out by this court in *Cookson v Knowles*[3].

---

1 Cf RSC Ord 29, Part II
2 Cmnd 7054–I, paras 555–630
3 [1977] 2 All ER 820, [1977] QB 913

The conventional method of assessing damages

Nearly all who are concerned with personal injury claims, whether as judges, barristers, solicitors or insurance company claims managers would have made their own assessments of damages in the same kind of way; and the experienced amongst them would have taken care, as Bristow J said he did, to ensure first that there was no overlapping between the heads of damage, as they are called, and secondly that the sum to be awarded, when looked at in the round, was fair and reasonable. All my professional lifetime claims have been settled and awards fixed in this sort of way; and it is pertinent to remember that the great majority of claims are settled without the issue of a writ. In *H West & Sons Ltd v Shephard*[1], all the members of the House of Lords seem to have approached the assessment of damages in the conventional way to which I have referred although two, Lords Reid and Devlin, differed from their brethren as to the sum to be assessed for the physical injury and loss of the amenities of life sustained by the plaintiff.

Departure from the conventional method

Lord Denning MR in his judgment has said that in cases in which the injuries are as grave as in this case and there are no dependants, compensation should not include an item for loss of earnings. As is usual with him what he has said has a compelling attraction; but in this case I have had to remind myself that, like the centurion at Capharnaum, I am a man under authority, that of the decided cases binding on this court. There may be, as Lord Denning MR has said, sound reasons for thinking that awards of this size, which have been assessed in the conventional way, will injure the body politic. Parliament may decide to take action against such danger as there may be. I cannot see how we can do so without departing from the principles enunciated by this court nearly a hundred years ago in the much litigated case of *Phillips v London and South Western Railway Co*[2] and followed ever since.

The authorities

The plaintiff in *Phillips v London and South Western Railway Co*[2], before the accident out of which his claim arose, had practised as a physician and as such had earned a substantial income. The reports do not say what his injuries were; but Cockburn CJ[3] said this about them:

> 'The plaintiff was a man of middle age and of robust health. His health had been irreparably injured to such a degree as to render life a burden and source of the utmost misery. He has undergone a great amount of pain and suffering. The probability is that he will never recover. His condition is at once helpless and hopeless . . . Medical attendance still is and is likely to be for a long time necessary.'

At first instance the trial judge, Field J, directed the jury as to the heads of damage in respect of which the plaintiff was entitled to compensation (the details of his direction are set out in the report of the Court of Appeal proceedings[4]). He told the jury to consider what sum should be given for the plaintiff's loss of future earnings and directed them to take account of the contingencies of life. The jury awarded a sum which showed that they could not have made any, or any proper, provision for loss of future earnings. The plaintiff asked for a new trial. The Divisional Court ordered one[5]. The defendants appealed. This court[6] (James, Brett and Cotton LJJ) confirmed the order for a new trial and did not accept a submission that Field J had misdirected the jury as to the assessment of damages.

1   [1963] 2 All ER 625 at 630, 632, 645, [1964] AC 326 at 344, 347–348, 369, per Lord Tucker, Lord Morris of Borth-y-Gest and Lord Pearce
2   (1879) 4 QBD 406; *affd* 5 QBD 78, CA; *subsequent proceedings* 5 CPD 280, [1874–80] All ER Rep 1176, CA
3   4 QBD 406 at 408
4   5 QBD 78 at 78–82
5   4 QBD 406
6   5 QBD 78

There was a new trial before Lord Coleridge CJ. By this time it seems likely that the prognosis was better than when the case was before Field J. The jury awarded the plaintiff £16,000, a figure which at the present value of the pound sterling would be the equivalent of well over £100,000 and might be about £200,000. Lord Coleridge CJ had directed them to take into account loss of future earnings. This time the defendants applied to the Divisional Court for a new trial[1]. They were unsuccessful. They then appealed to this court. One of the arguments put by the defendants' counsel, the redoubtable Serjeant Ballantine, was that the plaintiff's loss of professional income was too remote and ought not to have been taken into account. This court[2] (Bramwell, Brett and Cotton LJJ) would have none of this. Each member of this court thought that loss of future earnings had to be taken into account when assessing damages.

At no time during this protracted litigation was the precise method of calculating prospective pecuniary loss in issue; but during argument on the occasion of the first appeal to this court, James LJ said[3]:

'The proper direction to the jury, as it seems to me, would have been to tell them to calculate the value of the income as a life annuity, and then make allowance for its being subject to the contingencies of the plaintiff retiring, failing in his practice, and so forth.'

This direction was adopted by this court in *Roach v Yates*[4], a case not unlike the present one: see per Greer and Slesser LJJ.

The calculation of loss of earnings

Since then, and probably for decades before, the loss of future earnings in cases where on the evidence the plaintiff was likely to be unable to earn anything for the rest of his life has been calculated on what Lord Fraser in *Cookson v Knowles*[5] referred to as the assumed annuity basis. As far as I know *Phillips v London and South Western Railway Co*[2] has never been questioned by the House of Lords. In *H West & Son Ltd v Shephard*[6] it was cited with obvious approval by Lord Morris of Borth-y-Gest, by Lord Devlin and by Lord Pearce. I consider myself bound to follow and apply *Phillips v London and South Western Railway Co*[2]. This means that when reviewing Bristow J's award I must take into account the plaintiff's pecuniary loss arising from her loss of future earnings and pension rights. Perhaps it would be more accurate, as counsel for the defendants submitted, to describe this loss as that of her earning capacity. However it is described, what Bristow J had to do was to consider all the factors, save one, mentioned by Lord Tucker in *Cavanagh v Ulster Weaving Co Ltd*[7]. In that case, Lord Tucker said in respect of a labourer, aged 20, who had lost a leg:

'... the jury had, *of course*, [my emphasis] to consider what he might reasonably have been expected to earn during a working life of perhaps forty-five or fifty years, taking account of the fall in the value of money, the tendency for wages to rise and the possibility of his improving his status in the labour market contrasted with his present position and future prospects in the event of an increase in the number of unemployed.'

The reference to the factor of inflation must now be understood and applied in the

1   (1879) 5 CPD 280 at 281–285
2   5 CPD 280, [1874–80] All ER Rep 1176
3   5 QBD 78 at 84
4   [1937] 3 All ER 442 at 446, 448, [1938] 1 KB 256 at 266, 269
5   [1978] 2 All ER 604 at 616, [1978] 2 WLR 978 at 991
6   [1963] 2 All ER 625 at 631, 637, 643, [1964] AC 326 at 346, 356, 365
7   [1959] 2 All ER 745 at 749–750, [1960] AC 145 at 163–164

limited way explained by Lord Diplock and Lord Fraser in *Cookson v Knowles*[1]. Bristow J heard evidence about the plaintiff's expectation of life, which was only slightly less than the normal for a woman of her age, about what her chances of becoming a consultant psychiatrist would have been and what she would have been likely to earn as such in the national health service with some private practice after the deduction of tax. In addition he had expert evidence as to what the incidence of taxation would be if he calculated her loss under this head on an assumed annuity basis, as in my judgment he was entitled to do. On the figures produced there would have been a substantial tax element. This would bring into operation the exception to the general rule against making allowance for inflation to which Lord Fraser referred in his speech in *Cookson v Knowles*[2]. He made an allowance for inflation by increasing the multiplier. This is what Lord Fraser said could be done when there is a high tax element in the calculation. In my judgment the calculation he made was right. The sums which he awarded for loss of future earnings (£84,000) and pension rights (£8,000) must be added to the other heads of damage. As I agree with Lord Denning MR what the sums for those other heads should be, it follows that I would confirm the trial judge's award.

Outstanding points

For the sake of completeness, however, I shall deal shortly with three of counsel for the defendants' submissions; first, that Bristow J should not have found on the evidence that there was a probability that the plaintiff would be brought to England when her mother died or became too frail to look after her in Penang; secondly, that the sum awarded for pain and suffering and the loss of the amenities of life was too high and should have been a conventional one of the *Benham v Gambling*[3] kind, albeit much greater, and thirdly, that no allowance of any kind should have been made for future inflation.

England or Penang

The evidence about what was likely to happen to the plaintiff when her mother could no longer look after her was vague; and some of it was tainted with hearsay: see the sentence in Dr MacQuaide's report about there being no suitable institutions in Malaysia for patients such as the plaintiff. In my judgment the trial judge was entitled to find on such evidence as there was that the plaintiff one day would have to be cared for in England. The defendants as a subordinate body of the Department of Health and Social Security retained Dr MacQuaide to find out what were the plaintiff's circumstances in Penang. If they had any reason to think that he was wrong about there being no suitable institutions in Malaysia, with the resources of the state behind them, they could easily have shown that he was wrong.

The loss of the amenities of life

I do not accept that the plaintiff was in such an insensitive condition that it can be assumed that she does not appreciate what her condition is. Her mother told Dr MacQuaide that sometimes she laughs and cries. The plaintiff has not been reduced to the condition of a zombie. She retains some memory of what she learned whilst in training for her profession as a doctor. The fact that she cannot express what she feels does not mean she does not feel at all. Far from £20,000 being too high a sum for this head of damage, it may be too low. But as the trial judge may not have allowed enough for overlap between future loss of earnings and the cost of future care I would not alter his final figure.

---

1   [1978] 2 All ER 604, [1978] 2 WLR 978
2   [1978] 2 All ER 604 at 616, [1978] 2 WLR 978 at 991
3   [1941] 1 All ER 7, [1941] AC 157

The factor of inflation

As to inflation I have read the speech of Lord Fraser[1], with which Viscount Dilhorne, Lord Salmon and Lord Scarman agreed, in the same sense as Lord Denning MR has done and as meaning that in exceptional cases where there is a high tax factor, inflation can be taken into account when calculating the heads of damage for which the assumed annuity method is appropriate.

Conclusions

I end as I began. This is a startling award; but it is not an absurd one. A number of factors have gone to make it as high as it is. There is the long expectation of life, some 30 years, during most of which, but for this appalling accident, the plaintiff would probably have been earning a substantial income. Above all there is the fact of inflation in recent years. As I have already pointed out the present day equivalent in purchasing power of the £16,000 which Mr Phillips[2] was awarded in 1879 would probably be nearly £200,000; and as counsel for the plaintiff pointed out the present day equivalent of the £51,447 awarded by this court in *Fletcher v Autocars & Transporters Ltd*[3], a quantity surveyor, who was 56 at the time of the accident and had an expectation of life of 16 years, would be about £150,000 when account is taken of the inflation factors set out in Kemp and Kemp[4]. Lord Denning MR has commented that any sum over that necessary for the plaintiff's care will avail her nothing and will accumulate at high interest rates for the benefit of her relatives who have told us through counsel for the plaintiff that they want none of it. This may be so; but with respect, it is optimistic speculation. My concern for the plaintiff is that the award may not be enough for her care during her lifetime. If inflation goes on during the next decade like it has done in the past one, those having charge of the plaintiff may have difficulty in paying her maintenance costs. Anyway on the authorities the courts should not concern themselves with what happens to any damages awarded: see *H West & Son Ltd v Shephard*[5] per Lord Reid, Lord Morris of Borth-y-Gest, Lord Devlin and Lord Pearce.

I would dismiss the appeal.

BROWNE LJ. I agree with Lawton LJ that this appeal should be dismissed. On 28th February 1973 the plaintiff, at the age of 36, could look forward to a successful life in her chosen branch of her chosen profession, a life which would no doubt have given satisfaction to herself and been of great value to her patients. She is said to have been 'a remarkably good doctor, intelligent, conscientious, reliable, able to make good contact with patients, supportive to and popular with the nursing staff, and a loyal member of [the] team' and to have shown 'great promise' (as confirmed by Professor Russell of the Royal Free Hospital). She had come to England in 1971, and was already Senior Registrar at Friern Hospital, working between the New Southgate Group of Hospitals and the Royal Free Hospital. In all probability she would have reached the status of consultant psychiatrist within four or five years.

On 1st March 1973, as a result of negligence for which the defendants admitted liability (though, counsel for the plaintiff told us, only on the day before the trial), she lost everything, except her life. I cannot do better than adopt what the judge said[6]:

'That a doctor who had so much to offer to the mentally ill should be subjected by want of care in hospital to the appalling disability from which Dr Lim is condemned to suffer for the rest of her existence is a very great tragedy. Her mother, who has been in court throughout the trial, in which counsel on both sides have given me the

---

1 *Cookson v Knowles* [1978] 2 All ER 604 at 616, [1978] 2 WLR 978 at 991
2 *Phillips v London and South Western Railway Co* (1879) 5 CPD 280, [1874–80] All ER Rep 1176
3 [1968] 1 All ER 726, [1968] 2 QB 322
4 The Quantum of Damages (4th Edn, 1975), vol 2, p 601
5 [1963] 2 All ER 625 at 629, 633, 641, 642, [1964] AC 326 at 341–342, 349, 363, 364
6 See pp 335–336, ante

greatest possible help, will realise that the law cannot pretend to compensate her daughter for the destruction of her life. The court can only award a sum of money, and in justice to the defendants as well as to Dr Lim that sum must be in proportion to awards in other cases of those who have suffered injuries of comparable severity.'

As I understand it, the defendants at the trial did not put forward any constructive suggestions for dealing with the disastrous situation which had been created by the negligence for which they are responsible, although I suppose that as an area health authority they ought to be in a good position to make such suggestions. Now on this appeal they challenge all the major items in the total damages and interest of £254,765 awarded by the judge. It is convenient to divide these damages, as counsel for the defendants did, into two main heads: physical damage (or non-economic loss) and economic loss, though of course, in the end, one must look at the total.

Physical damage or non-economic loss
Under this head the judge awarded £25,930. In form, he split this item into £20,000 damages and £5,930 interest. As I understand it, the reason why he did it in this form was this. In *Cookson v Knowles*[1] this court said (obiter) that damages under this head should be assessed as at the date of the trial and that therefore no interest should be awarded. When the present case was before Bristow J, *Cookson v Knowles*[2] had been decided by this court and was under appeal to the House of Lords but the House had not given its decision. Bristow J assessed the damages on the 'pre-*Cookson v Knowles*[2] basis' so as to be comparable with other awards. He increased that amount to the '*Cookson v Knowles*[2] basis' by adding the amount which would have been awarded as interest before that decision. The House of Lords left this point open (see Lord Diplock's[3] speech), and I think we must follow what was said by this court. I treat the judge's award as an award of £26,000 as at the date of the trial.

Counsel for the defendants would have wished to argue that in a case like this, where there was (he said) no appreciation by the plaintiff of her loss and she had been reduced to 'living death', the damages ought to be a conventional figure analogous to the conventional figures which are given for loss of expectation of life when the victim has been killed (see *Benham v Gambling*[4]). But he rightly recognised and accepted that this argument was not open to him in face of the decisions of this court in *Wise v Kaye*[5] and of the House of Lords in *H West & Son Ltd v Shephard*[6]. He submitted, however, that this head of damages in cases like this should be limited to a 'conventional' figure of £10,000–£15,000.

Counsel for the plaintiff disputed counsel for the defendants' suggestion that the plaintiff had no appreciation of her loss. He referred us to the medical evidence, and submitted that this is by no means what is sometimes called a 'cabbage' case; he described it as a 'twilight case, with the twilight sometimes getting lighter and sometimes darker'.

I think counsel for the plaintiff is right about this. I do not think I need refer in detail to the agreed medical reports. Their effect is that the plaintiff's moods vary widely. On good days she has some memory of the past (including it seems some memory of having been a doctor) can understand a little, can read a little, can speak a little. At other times 'she would lapse into a depressed, withdrawn, non-responsive, non-communicative and even non-co-operative behaviour not unlike a child of a few years old'. At times, she appears to be deeply miserable. One doctor says that 'her intellectual functions were probably better than what could be drawn out of her'. As to her physical condition, the medical reports fully support the judge's findings that—

1   [1977] 2 All ER 820 at 823, [1977] QB 913 at 921
2   [1977] 2 All ER 820, [1977] QB 913
3   [1978] 2 All ER 604 at 612, [1978] 2 WLR 978 at 987
4   [1941] 1 All ER 7, [1941] AC 157
5   [1962] 1 All ER 257, [1962] 1 QB 638
6   [1963] 2 All ER 625, [1964] AC 326

'the picture which emerges from the agreed medical reports is that of a helpless invalid who will require nursing for the rest of her life, and is only intermittently sentient'.

The report of Dr MacQuaide, who went out to Penang in July 1976 to examine the plaintiff on behalf of the defendants, was that:

'She will always need total care either at home or in an institution. I do not consider that significant improvement is likely to occur in the future and certainly not to a degree that would enable her to look after herself.'

He reported that if the plaintiff continues to get the personal attention she has had since she went home to Penang he could see no reason why her life expectancy should be shortened, though if the standard of care should deteriorate significantly her life expectancy would almost certainly be less than average. Her normal expectation of life at the date of the trial would have been about 37 years. The judge said:

'Dr Lim's loss of the amenities of her good and useful life is total. On the evidence, her appreciation of that loss, and so the agony which knowing what you have lost must cause, is nil, or very small.'

As I understand the medical reports, I think the judge rather underrated the plaintiff's appreciation.

Any award of damages under this head can only be 'conventional' in the sense that there can be no money equivalent for losses of this kind. But I can see no justification for counsel for the defendants suggestion of a 'conventional' figure of £10,000 or £15,000 in this type of case; each case must depend on its own facts, as is illustrated by the comparable cases to which we were referred. In my view, the judge's award is amply supported by the damages awarded in those cases.

In *Wise v Kaye*[1], where the accident was in 1958 and the trial in 1961, the damages under this head were £15,000. In that case the plaintiff had been unconscious ever since the accident and there was no prospect that she would ever recover consciousness; she was aged 20 at the time of the accident; 'No doctor could say how long the plaintiff will live, but it was accepted that she cannot be expected to endure for anything approaching a normal span of life.'[2] The majority of this court (Sellers and Upjohn LJJ, Diplock LJ dissenting) held: (i) that *Benham v Gambling*[3] had no application; (ii) that it was irrelevant that the plaintiff herself could not use or enjoy the damages, and that in the end they would probably pass to her next-of-kin; (iii) that the plaintiff was entitled to damages for the physical injury and loss of amenities which she had sustained (though not for pain and suffering) even though she had no realisation of what had happened to her.

In *H West & Son Ltd v Shephard*[4] the plaintiff was aged 41 at the time of the accident in 1959; she probably had some realisation of what had happened to her (certainly more than the plaintiff in *Wise v Kaye*[1]); her expectation of life had been reduced to five years from about the date of the trial. The judge in 1962 awarded £17,500 for physical injuries and loss of amenities, holding that because she had some appreciation of her condition she was in a worse position than the plaintiff in *Wise v Kaye*[1], but that the damages were limited by the limitation of her expectation of life to five years. He gave nothing for pain and suffering. This award was upheld by this court and by the majority of the House of Lords[4]. The plaintiff in that case was about the same age as the plaintiff in this case; she had perhaps rather more appreciation of her condition (though I am not sure of this); on the

---

1   [1962] 1 All ER 257, [1962] 1 QB 638
2   [1962] 1 All ER 257 at 260, [1962] 1 QB 638 at 646
3   [1941] 1 All ER 7, [1941] AC 157
4   [1963] 2 All ER 625, [1964] AC 326

other hand, she had only an expectation of life of five years, as against something like 30 years in this case. All the members of the House, except Lord Devlin but including Lord Reid, who dissented as to the result, held[1] that *Benham v Gambling*[2] did not apply; that the way in which a plaintiff spends the damages is irrelevant and that therefore the fact that a plaintiff can get no personal benefit for them is irrelevant; and that the expected period of life was relevant. The majority[3] (Lord Morris of Borth-y-Gest, with whom Lord Tucker agreed, and Lord Pearce) in dismissing the appeal approved the decision of the majority of this court in *Wise v Kaye*[4], and, as I understand it, the judge's view that Mrs Shephard was entitled to rather more damages than Miss Wise because she had some realisation of her condition.

In *Fletcher v Autocar & Transporters Ltd*[5] the plaintiff was aged 56 at the time of the accident in 1964; his expectation of life was about 16 years; he had little if any appreciation of what had happened to him but suffered some pain; his physical injuries were less than those in *Wise v Kaye*[4] and *H West & Son Ltd v Shephard*[6]. The judge in 1967 awarded £10,000 for pain, suffering and loss of amenities. Diplock LJ[7] thought that if there had been no overlap with loss of earnings a figure of £15,000 would not have been wrong and Salmon LJ[8] would have awarded £17,000.

In *Taylor v Bristol Omnibus Co Ltd*[9] the accident was in 1968 and the trial in 1974. The plaintiff was in 1968 aged 3½. He was completely helpless but was aware of his condition; his expectation of life was not reduced to any great extent. This court upheld £27,500 damages for pain, suffering and loss of amenities.

Counsel for the plaintiff put before us an advance copy of a table which is to appear in the new edition of Kemp and Kemp, The Quantum of Damages[10], showing the value of the pound at various dates. Without going into detailed figures, it is clear that if the awards in the four cases to which I have referred are translated into their 1977 equivalents they would be far more than the £20,000 or £26,000 awarded by the judge in the present case, something like £40,000 or £50,000 or even more.

Finally, in *Bolton v Essex Area Health Authority*[11], decided a month before Bristow J's decision in the present case (we were provided with a copy of the judgment), Thompson J awarded £40,000 under this head. The accident was in 1975. The plaintiff was aged 53. His expectation of life was about 10 years. He was paralysed and unable to speak, but his intellect appeared to have escaped damage, and he could understand and communicate, although not properly or easily. By comparison with the present case, his faculties were less completed affected, and I should suppose that he therefore had more realisation of the loss he had suffered, but his expectation of life was much less.

In my judgment, Bristow J made no mistake in principle on this head of damages and his award was not excessive in comparison with the other cases to which I have referred. It is enough at this stage to say that £20,000 or £26,000 was in my view not excessive, but by her respondent's notice the plaintiff alleges that it was insufficient.

Economic loss

Leaving interest out of account, the sums awarded by the judge under this general head were:

1 [1963] 2 All ER 625 at 629, 630, 632, 645–646, [1964] AC 326 at 343, 344, 348, 369, per Lord Reid, Lord Tucker, Lord Morris of Borth-y-Gest and Lord Pearce, respectively
2 [1941] 1 All ER 7, [1941] AC 157
3 [1963] 2 All ER 625 at 630, 634–636, 646, [1964] AC 326 at 344, 351–353, 370
4 [1962] 1 All ER 257, [1962] 1 QB 638
5 [1968] 1 All ER 726, [1968] 2 QB 322
6 [1963] 2 All ER 625, [1964] AC 326
7 [1968] 1 All ER 726 at 744, [1968] 2 QB 322 at 353
8 [1968] 1 All ER 726 at 752, [1968] 2 QB 322 at 366
9 [1975] 2 All ER 1107, [1975] 1 WLR 1054
10 Cf 4th Edn (1975), vol 2, p 601
11 [1977] The Times, 8th November

Special damages

Cost of care to date of trial	£8,000
Out of pocket expenses to date of trial	£3,596
Loss of earnings to date of trial	£14,213
	£25,809

Loss of future earnings

£6,000 a year multiplied by 14	£84,000
Loss of pension rights	£8,000
	£92,000

Cost of future care

7 years in Malaysia at £2,600 a year	
£18,200 discounted to £17,500	£17,500
Thereafter in England at £8,000 a year	
multiplied by 11	£88,000
	£105,500

Counsel for the defendants attacked these awards on two matters of principle, and also made various detailed criticisms. The matters of principle were: (i) duplication between future loss of earnings and cost of care; (ii) the way in which the judge dealt with inflation.

As to (i), counsel for the defendants' submission in its primary form was, as I understand it, that nothing should be awarded for loss of future earnings in the circumstances of this case. He said that what he called the 'basic fallacy' was to regard loss of future earnings as an item of damages 'in its own right'. He said, and I quote from his written submissions which he helpfully put before us, that 'the plaintiff's loss is not a loss of earnings, but the material loss he suffers by not being able to live and to keep his family (if he has one) in the life-style which his rate of earning, and his earning prospects, enable him to do'. This may well be right, but it seems to me only a matter of words. I agree of course that the earnings to be considered are the net earnings, after deducting the expenses of earning them (eg fares going to work), but I am afraid that I simply cannot understand the rest of the argument set out in para 7.2 of his written submissions[1]. The effect seems to be that if the labourer is worthy of his hire, and the value of his work is equal to what he is paid for it, he gets nothing for loss of earnings. However, counsel for the defendants' concluding submission was:

'The true question is, what is the cost of keeping the plaintiff in reasonable comfort

---

1   Paragraph 7.2 read: '"Loss of Earnings" are not and cannot be an item of legal damage in personal injury cases, because there is no legal way of evaluating the worth to the plaintiff of his job if he is not working. The fact that the accident prevents him from working is not to the point, because it still leaves the value of the essential factor in the equation unresolved. If the plaintiff earns £X for work, and is prevented from working, and, therefore, earning, his loss in law is not £X, but £X − £Y (Y being the value of the work necessary to earn X). In principle, the position is exactly the same as that of a ship owner, whose ship is damaged and prevented from earning £X freight. His loss is not £X, but £X − £Y (the cost of running the ship). The crucial difference is, that in the case of the shipowner, his net loss can be priced; in the case of a worker it cannot; a fortiori because earnings are the price of labour.'

for the rest of her life, and of keeping the plaintiff's dependants (if any) in a style and comfort commensurate with the plaintiff's earnings, past and prospective, for the estimated duration of her working life?'

In another paragraph of the submissions it is said:

'Her loss, therefore, is not a loss of earnings, but consists of the inability to use her earnings for the purposes for which she would have used them, but for the accident. The enjoyment she would have got from that alternative use is already compensated in the figure for loss of amenities. What then has she lost? Since (i) there was, and there could be, no evidence that she would have saved anything from her earnings, and (ii) her maintenance is wholly covered by an additional award of £6,000, she cannot be said to have suffered a greater loss than the sum required for her care.'

In my judgment, counsel for the defendants' submissions are wrong, both on principle and authority. At least since *Phillips v London and South Western Railway Co*[1], to which Lawton LJ has referred in detail, loss of future earnings has been treated as a separate item of damages 'in its own right' in personal injury cases. In several of the cases to which I have referred under the heading of physical injury or non-economic loss damages were awarded under the separate heads of future loss of earnings and future care. The exceptions were *Wise v Kaye*[2] where the plaintiff was being cared for free of charge by the national health service, but an award was made for future loss of earnings, and *H West & Son Ltd v Shephard*[3], where I understand the position was the same. In my judgment this court cannot and should not depart from this well-settled practice. I am confirmed in this view by what Lord Pearce said in *H West & Son Ltd v Shephard*[4] and what Orr LJ (with whom Stamp LJ agreed) said in *Taylor v Bristol Omnibus Co Ltd*[5]. In that case, the majority of this court, with whom Lord Denning MR rather reluctantly agreed, rejected what seems to have been the same argument as that put forward by counsel for the defendants, and Lord Denning MR said[6]: 'This suggestion is, however, contrary to present practice'.

The only authority which gives any support to counsel for the defendants' argument is *Fletcher v Autocar & Transporters Ltd*[7], in which Lord Denning MR and Diplock LJ held that the damages in respect of future loss of earnings and future care should be reduced; Salmon LJ dissented. Neither of the majority held that *nothing* should be given for future loss of earnings. Lord Denning MR[8] thought that the plaintiff should only—

'be compensated for his loss of future earnings to the extent that he would have used them for supporting his wife in comfort for the rest of her life, including any savings that he would have made out of his earnings, if uninjured.'

He also pointed out the danger of overlapping between sums awarded for loss of future earnings and those awarded for loss of amenities and for future care. Diplock LJ reduced the sums awarded by the judge for loss of future earnings and for future care. He too pointed out the danger of overlapping between damages for loss of future earnings and for loss of amenities. But as I understand it, the actual ground of his decision that the damages under these heads should be reduced was that, as a result of a detailed criticism of the judge's figures for loss of future earnings (which he reduced from £32,000 to £22,000) and

1 (1879) 5 CPD 280, [1874–80] All ER Rep 1176
2 [1962] 1 All ER 257, [1962] 1 QB 638
3 [1963] 2 All ER 625, [1964] AC 326
4 [1963] 2 All ER 625 at 645–646 [1964] AC 326 at 369
5 [1975] 2 All ER 1107, [1975] 1 WLR 1054
6 [1975] 2 All ER 1107 at 1113, [1975] 1 WLR 1054 at 1059
7 [1968] 1 All ER 726 at 733–734, 737–739 [1968] 2 QB 322 at 336–337, 341–345
8 [1968] 1 All ER 726 at 734, [1968] 2 QB 322 at 337

the cost of future care, he thought the figures were too high, and not because of overlapping. He did think there was some overlapping between loss of future earnings *a* and general damages for loss of amenity. It is true that he referred to a method of assessing damages on the lines of counsel for the defendants' submission in the present case, but he introduced this part of his judgment by saying[1]:

> 'Although ... it is not a conventional way of assessing damages, it is, I think possible, to check very roughly whether a total award of £51,000 accords with what, *b* in agreement with LORD DENNING, M.R., I think that social justice requires in [this] case ...'

Salmon LJ would have dismissed the appeal. In my judgment *Fletcher v Autocars & Transporters Ltd*[2] does not, as a matter of decision, support counsel for the defendants' primary submission, and we are bound by *Taylor v Bristol Omnibus Co Ltd*[3] to reject it; in that case Lord Denning MR referred to *Fletcher*[2] and cannot have thought it was *c* inconsistent with the decision in *Taylor*[3], with which he agreed.

I think that counsel for the defendants' argument is also wrong in principle. Whether you call this head of damages loss of future earnings or whether you call it loss of the standard of living which those earnings would have enabled the plaintiff to enjoy, she has been deprived of it by negligence for which the defendants are responsible. I can see no reason why she should be debarred from recovering this loss because she is also entitled to *d* recover the expenses of a different standard of living imposed on her by the defendants; the two are not connected. Further, it seems to me that it would be quite impossible for a court to investigate how a plaintiff would have spent or saved his or her earnings if he or she had not been injured. I think that the most which can and should be done is to see that as far as possible there is no overlapping between the sums awarded for loss of future earnings and the cost of future care in respect of the 'domestic element' (food, rent, *e* electricity etc), as was done in *Shearman v Folland*[4] and *Mitchell v Mulholland (No 2)*[5] per Sir Gordon Willmer. Bristow J did this.

Counsel for the defendants also made some subsidiary criticisms of the judge's award under this head: (i) the way in which the judge dealt with inflation: I will come to this later; (ii) overlapping; I will deal with this under costs of future care; (iii) expenses to be *f* deducted from earnings.

Counsel for the plaintiff rightly accepts that the plaintiff's expenses of earning her salary must be deducted in calculating her future loss of earnings. Counsel for the defendants submits that the judge did not make any or any sufficient deduction. Mr Eccleshall, the accountant who gave evidence on behalf of the plaintiff, calculated the plaintiff's future earnings on the alternative assumptions that she would have gone on working in the United Kingdom or that she would have gone back to Malaysia and worked there. His *g* estimate of her average future earnings (after deduction of tax and national insurance contributions) if she had stayed in the United Kingdom was £6,700 a year. If she had gone back to Malaysia, her net earnings would have been substantially higher, I gather mainly because of lower taxation. Bristow J found that on the probabilities she would have practised in England, and found that a fair multiplicand would be £6,000. Counsel for the defendants accepts the judge's figure of £6,000, but submits that £3,000 should be *h* deducted for expenses. I understood this submission to be based on two answers given by Mr Eccleshall in cross-examination:

---

1 [1968] 1 All ER 726 at 743, [1968] 2 QB 322 at 352
2 [1968] 1 All ER 726, [1968] 2 QB 322
3 [1975] 2 All ER 1107, [1975] 1 WLR 1054
4 [1950] 1 All ER 976, [1950] 2 KB 43
5 [1971] 2 All ER 1205 at 1222, [1972] 1 QB 65 at 88

Q. As an accountant who deals with people's affairs do you think you can help us on this. Would I be very far out if I were to suggest to you that it would cost a professional person like a consultant about £3,000 a year to live in this country today. *A.* I should think that would be a pretty low figure. I only have my own expenses to go by and I know they are more than that.

'*Q.* Of course when we are dealing with a consultant, a consultant would have to have rooms to practise from if he or she were carrying on private practice. *A.* Yes.'

The first question and answer seem to relate to the whole cost of living, not to the plaintiff's expenses of earning her salary and fees. As to the consulting room, the assumption was that the plaintiff would have worked as a consultant in the national health service, for which she would not have had to provide a consulting room. Mr Eccleshall's figures do include some fees for private practice, but they are comparatively small and seem unlikely to involve much expense. The judge reduced Mr Eccleshall's estimate of £6,700 a year to £6,000, which I think is ample. In my view there is nothing in this point.

Inflation

Bristow J referred to *Taylor v O'Connor*[1] and the changes in circumstances since then and said[2]:

'In these circumstances I take the view that the court must do what it reasonably can to protect a plaintiff against inflation, and that what the House of Lords thought it wrong for Lyell J to do in the conditions of 1968 it is right to do in 1977 when we can see more clearly where the world is going.'

He took future inflation into account at two points. In the multiplier for cost of future care he made 'some increase for prospective inflation', and in the multiplier for loss of future earnings he included 'a small increase to build in some anti-inflation protection'. Counsel for the defendants submits that he should not have taken it into account at all.

In *Taylor v O'Connor*[3] Lord Reid said that 'it would, I think, be quite unrealistic to refuse to take [future inflation] into account at all', though he thought that it would not make much difference in that case because of high rates of interest and capital appreciation. He also held that taxation must be taken into account[4]. It is even more unrealistic to refuse today to take future inflation into account. But until the decision of the House of Lords in *Cookson v Knowles*[5] there were decisions binding on this court that future inflation must not be taken into account: see *Young v Percival*[6] and *Cookson v Knowles*[7]. In my judgment, however, the House of Lords has held in *Cookson v Knowles*[5] (a) that future inflation 'is taken care of in a rough and ready way' by the fact that damages are normally awarded on the basis of the conventional multipliers which assume a rate of interest of 4% or 5%, whereas the actual rates of interest today are very much higher (per Lord Diplock[8], and per Lord Fraser of Tullybelton[9] with whom Viscount Dilhorne, Lord Salmon and Lord Scarman agreed), but (b) that in—

'exceptional cases, where the annuity is large enough to attract income tax at a high rate ... it might be appropriate to increase the multiplier, or to allow for future inflation in some other way [according to the evidence in the case],'

1   [1970] 1 All ER 365, [1971] AC 115
2   See p 336, ante
3   [1970] 1 All ER 365 at 368–369, [1971] AC 115 at 130
4   [1970] 1 All ER 365 at 367–368, [1971] AC 115 at 128–129
5   [1978] 2 All ER 604, [1978] 2 WLR 978
6   [1974] 3 All ER 677, [1975] 1 WLR 17
7   [1977] 2 All ER 820, [1977] QB 913
8   [1978] 2 All ER 604 at 610–611, [1978] 2 WLR 978 at 984–986
9   [1978] 2 All ER 604 at 615–616, [1978] 2 WLR 978 at 990–991

(per Lord Fraser of Tullybelton[1]; and see per Lord Diplock[2]) inflation can be largely offset by investment policy 'at any rate if the rate of tax on the dependant's gross income is low'. The present case seems to me to be one of the exceptional cases referred to by Lord Fraser; the high incidence of tax on the assumed annuity in this case is shown on Mr Eccleshall's exhibit. In my view, the judge (who seems to have had premonition of what the House of Lords was going to say in *Cookson v Knowles*[3]) made no mistake in principle on this point and I am not satisfied that he made any excessive allowance.

Cost of future care

Counsel for the defendants challenged the judge's finding that the probability was that the plaintiff would have to come to England about seven years after the trial to be looked after here. He also submitted that the judge had not made enough allowance for overlap between loss of future earnings (if his primary submission on that point was rejected) and cost of future care.

As to the first point, I agree with Lawton LJ that the evidence was vague, but in my view the judge was entitled to find as he did. The additional evidence which was put before us supports the view that she may have to come here sooner than the judge thought.

The information that there were no satisfactory institutions in Malaysia which could cope satisfactorily with the plaintiff came from Dr MacQuaide's report of 4th August 1976. At that stage he was advising the defendants. At the trial he was called as a witness for the plaintiff. The defendants had ample time and opportunity to find out whether this information was correct, but no questions were put to Dr MacQuaide in cross-examination to suggest that it was not. The plaintiff's mother is over 70 and is not in good health. Dr MacQuaide said in evidence that at the time of the trial (November 1977) she was not as well as when he had seen her a year before; she suffered from osteo-arthritis of the knees and was very much more crippled than she had been. No one suggested any possibility except that the plaintiff should be looked after either in her mother's house in Penang or in an institution in England. I have no hesitation in drawing the inference that fairly soon (probably sooner than the judge's finding of seven years) the plaintiff will have to come to England to be looked after here.

As to overlap, the judge had this problem in mind. In his figure for care in her mother's house at Penang he allowed nothing for the 'domestic element', in order to avoid overlap. He allowed nothing for the value of the mother's services, which he could have done. On this part of the award I think he made an ample allowance for overlap. On the figure for care in England, he allowed for the 'domestic element' by a reduction in the multiplier. It is not clear how much he allowed, and this seems to be an unorthodox way of dealing with this problem. But, without going into details of the figures, I agree with counsel for the plaintiff that the judge pared the figures of the cost of care in England to the bone and beyond, and so made a further provision for overlap. Mr Eccleshall's figure (at 1977 prices) was £8,500 a year on a modest basis, and the judge reduced this to £8,000. There was no question of her being kept in the most expensive nursing home. Dr MacQuaide's figure for care at St Andrew's Hospital, Northampton, was about £13,000 a year initially, though it would be less if she was later put in a long-term ward. In my view, the judge made ample allowance for overlapping.

Conclusion.

The paramount consideration in this case must be that the plaintiff should be looked after for the rest of her life. I entirely accept that this is the only consideration of her family. If the figure of £8,000 a year as the cost in 1977 of her care in England is right, I think there

1   [1978] 2 All ER 604 at 616, [1978] 2 WLR 978 at 991
2   [1978] 2 All ER 604 at 610, [1978] 2 WLR 978 at 985
3   [1978] 2 All ER 604, [1978] 2 WLR 978

is a real risk that the damages awarded may not enable this sum to be provided if she survives for anything like her expectation of life (see Mr Eccleshall's evidence)). At least, I am not satisfied that they are excessive for this purpose. We are not entitled to tinker with the judge's award, and I have no wish to do so. If (which I do not accept) the judge made insufficient allowance in favour of the defendants under some heads, I think that the award under the head of non-economic loss might well have been higher, and he might well have held that the probabilities were that the plaintiff might have to come to this country sooner than in seven years time.

I have had the advantage of reading the judgments which Lord Denning MR and Lawton LJ have delivered. I agree with Lord Denning MR that the principles on which damages are awarded in personal injury cases need re-appraisal, not only in cases like this but in all cases. High inflation and high taxation have completely distorted the traditional methods of assessment. Mr Eccleshall's evidence illustrates that in a case where heavy damages are awarded a large part of the damages which a defendant has to pay is paid for the benefit of the Revenue and not of the plaintiff; it is a matter of chance that in this particular case it is merely a transfer from one pocket of the state to another. But I agree with Lawton LJ that we are bound by the authorities to which he refers to hold that we cannot do what Lord Denning MR would do; see also per Stamp and Orr LJJ in *Taylor v Bristol Omnibus Co Ltd*[1]. Nor am I satisfied that his figure of £136,596 would produce a just result in this case. According to Mr Eccleshall's evidence a capital sum of £100,000 would produce a spendable income of £7,540 a year and of £150,000 a spendable income of £10,131. The figure of £8,000 a year for future care in England was based on 1977 prices, and I cannot believe that an income of this sort would be enough to provide for the plaintiff's needs if she lives for the expected 30 years, or even if she only lives for 10 or 15 or 20 years. I know of no authority which would enable this court at this stage (or a trial judge) to make an interim award as suggested by Lord Denning MR; RSC Ord 29, rr 9 to 16, would not authorise such an order.

As I have said, I would dismiss this appeal.

Appeal dismissed. Leave to appeal to the House of Lords on condition that the defendants not seek to disturb the order in the Court of Appeal as to costs.

Solicitors: *J Tickle & Co* (for the defendants); *Coward Chance* (for the plaintiff).

Sumra Green   Barrister.

---

1   [1975] 2 All ER 1107 at 1114, [1975] 1 WLR 1054 at 1060, 1061

Re Slocock's Will Trusts

CHANCERY DIVISION
GRAHAM J
22nd JUNE, 6th JULY 1978

Deed – Rectification – Deed of release – Deed not effecting parties' common intention – Deed giving tax advantage if rectified – Whether court should order rectification – Whether tax advantage if rectification ordered a bar to relief.

By his will the testator devised one-third of his residuary estate to his daughter, the first plaintiff, on trust to pay her the income of it for life and after her death to hold the capital and income on trust for her issue as she should appoint. In December 1969 the first plaintiff appointed that after her death her share of residue was to be held on trust for her two children, the second and third plaintiffs. At the same time the first plaintiff also executed a deed releasing to the second and third plaintiffs her life interest in that part of her share of residue represented by the securities specified in the deed of release. In 1972 lands owned by the testator's family were sold to a development company in consideration for the allocation of shares in the company and a specified sum of money. The first plaintiff as a residuary legatee under the testator's will was beneficially entitled to a share of the proceeds of the sale. To facilitate the transaction with the development company and provide for an orderly realisation and distribution between the various beneficiaries of the proceeds of the sale, a management company was formed to receive and distribute the proceeds. The various beneficiaries were allotted 1p shares in the management company in the proportions of their holdings. The management company was purely administrative and held the moneys and securities received by it in a fiduciary capacity and not beneficially. In 1973 the three plaintiffs consulted a solicitor as to the first plaintiff's share in the proceeds of the sale, and it was decided that the first plaintiff should by deed surrender her life interest in the proceeds to the second and third plaintiffs. The deed was designed to reduce or avoid the payment of tax on the death of the first plaintiff. The deed failed to carry out the plaintiffs' intention because, due to the solicitor's erroneous belief that the first plaintiff's shares in the management company carried with them her beneficial interest in the proceeds of sale, the deed released to the second and third plaintiffs the first plaintiff's shares in the management company only and not her beneficial interest in the proceeds of the sale. The plaintiffs issued a summons against the trustees of the first plaintiff's settled share of residue seeking rectification of the deed of release to give effect to the plaintiffs' common intention. Rectification if granted would also result in the avoidance of the necessity to pay capital transfer tax. On the question whether the court should exercise its discretion to order rectification where the effect of the rectification was to give a tax advantage,

Held – In its equitable jurisdiction the court had a discretion to rectify a document where it was satisfied that the document did not carry out the common intention of the parties. Since parties were entitled to enter into any transaction which was legal and, in particular, were entitled to arrange their affairs to avoid payment of tax if they legitimately could, there was no reason why a mistake made in a document legitimately designed to avoid the payment of tax should not be corrected. The Crown was not in a privileged position with respect to such a document and it would not be a correct exercise of the court's discretion in such circumstances to refuse rectification merely because the Crown would thereby be deprived of tax. It followed that the court would order rectification of the deed of release to give effect to the common intention of the plaintiffs (see p 363 c to e and g, post).

Re Colebrook's Conveyances [1973] 1 All ER 132 applied.

Whiteside v Whiteside [1949] 2 All ER 913 and dictum of Graham J in *Re Colebrook's Conveyance* [1973] 1 All ER at 134 explained.

Notes

For rectification, see 26 Halsbury's Laws (3rd Edn) 914–921, paras 1698–1710, and for cases on the subject, see 35 Digest (Repl) 135–145, 291–362.

Cases referred to in judgment

Butlin's Settlement Trust, Butlin v Butlin [1976] 2 All ER 483, [1976] Ch 251, [1976] 2 WLR 425.

Colebrook's Conveyances, Re, Taylor v Taylor [1973] 1 All ER 132, [1972] 1 WLR 1397, 24 P & CR 249, Digest (Cont Vol D) 811, 3085c.

Van der Linde v Van der Linde [1947] Ch 306, [1947] LJR 592, 170 LT 297, 35 Digest (Repl) 140, 321.

Whiteside v Whiteside [1949] 2 All ER 913, [1950] Ch 65, CA; *affg* [1949] 1 All ER 755, [1949] Ch 448, 27(2) Digest (Reissue) 846, 6736.

Case also cited

Weir v Van Tromp (1900) 16 TLR 531.

Summons

By a summons dated 1st July 1977 the plaintiffs, Margery Martin Scott, Jane Alderson Nadin and Elizabeth Grace Alderson Purkis, the sole beneficiaries under a settled share of residue and a settled legacy under the trusts of the will of Walter Charles Slocock deceased ('the testator'), sought rectification by the court of a deed of release dated 12th July 1973 between the first plaintiff of the one part and the second and third plaintiffs of the other part whereby it was intended that the first plaintiff should surrender her life interest in the proceeds of sale of her settled share of the residue in favour of the second and third plaintiffs. The first plaintiff died on 31st August 1977 and on 17th March 1978 Master Chamberlain ordered that the proceedings in the action be carried on by the second and third plaintiffs. The defendants were Richard Mark Goodrich and Michael Anthony Croft Baker, the present trustees of the first plaintiff's settled share of residue and settled legacy under the trusts of the will of the testator. After 17th March 1978 the second defendant was also sued in his additional capacity as the personal representative of the first plaintiff. The facts are set out in the judgment.

Nigel Hague for the plaintiffs.
Nicholas Patten for the trustees.

Cur adv vult

6th July. **GRAHAM J** read the following judgment: By this summons the plaintiffs ask the court to rectify a deed of release. The effect of such rectification if granted will be to avoid the necessity to pay to the Crown the full rate of capital transfer tax. Fifteen per cent was allowed under the Finance Act 1969 if the settlor survived for four out of the seven years which were necessary to escape estate duty altogether. The Finance Act 1975, s 22, adopts the same figure in respect of capital transfer tax, and, if the facts are such that a reduction of estate duty could have been claimed under Sch 17 to the 1969 Act, the same reduction of capital transfer tax, which has superseded estate duty, is still granted.

The relevant facts are as follows. Walter Charles Slocock ('the testator') made his will in August 1920. He died in 1926 and probate of his will was granted in 1927. He had two sons and a daughter. The first plaintiff, Mrs Scott, who is now dead, was his daughter, and the second and third plaintiffs are, in turn, her daughters. From the affidavit of the second plaintiff it is seen that the testator devised and bequeathed his residuary estate to pay the net income to his wife, while alive, and after her death equally between his two sons and Mrs Scott. It was also directed that Mrs Scott's share of the residue should be held on trust to pay the income thereof to her for life, and, after her death, as to the capital and income, on trust to her issue as she should by deed or will appoint.

The testator's will was duly proved in February 1927 in the Principal Probate Registry. The Public Trustee is, and was at all material times, sole trustee of the will. As a result of deeds of appointment in 1973 and 1975 the defendants were eventually appointed trustees of Mrs Scott's settled one-third share of the residue and the settled legacy. On 26th December 1969 Mrs Scott, in exercise of the power conferred on her by the will, appointed that the trust funds from time to time representing the settled share of residue and her settled legacy, from and immediately after her decease, be held on trust for the second and third plaintiffs. By the first deed of release dated 27th December 1969 Mrs Scott released her life interest in the parts of her settled share of residue and settled legacy represented by the stocks, funds and securities specified in the schedule therein.

Prior to 1973 the Public Trustee, as trustee of the will of the testator, owned certain lands at Woking, Surrey. Other neighbouring lands were owned by other members of the testator's family and by a family company, and in 1971–72 negotiations took place for the sale of all these lands to Trafalgar House Investments Ltd ('Trafalgar') for development purposes. These negotiations culminated in the master agreement relating to the whole development which was called the 'Goldsworth development'. The consideration for the sale to Trafalgar consisted of two elements: an element consisting of securities in Trafalgar credited as fully paid to be made by instalments, and an additional consideration of some £70,765 payable on completion. The master agreement, after certain variations, was completed on 2nd March 1973. To facilitate the implementation of the master agreement and to provide for the orderly sale of the securities in Trafalgar, and for the proceeds of such sale to be allocated under the master agreement, it was agreed by a family agreement dated 2nd March 1973 that a company called 'Slocock Goldsworthy Development Management Co' ('the management company') should be responsible for receiving the various profits and distributing them to the various beneficiaries. For this purpose the various beneficiaries received an allotment of 1p shares in the management company in the proportions of their various holdings. The management company was at all times only a management company with purely administrative functions. Moneys and securities received were to be held in a fiduciary capacity only and at no time did it own beneficial assets of any substance. This is confirmed by the audited accounts of July 1972 to March 1976 prepared by Messrs Thomson McLintock & Co.

In 1973 the three plaintiffs consulted a Mr Parkes, a solicitor, of Friar Street, Reading, about the master agreement and Mrs Scott's settled share of residue, and it was decided that Mrs Scott should surrender her life interest in the proceeds of sale of her settled share of residue in favour of the second and third plaintiffs. A deed of release dated 12th July 1973, the subject of these proceedings, was entered into with the intention of carrying such surrender into effect. It is clear that such deed did not do so, and the object of these proceedings is to obtain its rectification in the way indicated in the summons. Examination of this deed of release will show that it only released 210 ordinary shares in the management company to each of the second and third plaintiffs, and did not release any beneficial share comprised in the settled share of residue of the securities, moneys and other assets from time to time representing the proceeds of sale of Mrs Scott's interest under the will. It seems clear that Mr Parkes erroneously thought that the various land holdings and shareholdings which were the subject of the management company had been transferred to the management company in exchange for shares in that company. He apparently at all times assumed that such shares in the management company carried with them the proceeds of sale of the management company under the master agreement, and that the release of Mrs Scott's life interest in these shares would effectively release her life interest in the proceeds of sale. It was not until 22nd February 1974 when the management company's accountants, Messrs Thomson McLintock & Co, advised that the stamp duty on the deed of release was nominal only, as was confirmed by the adjudication of 'nil' on 22nd February 1974, that Mr Parkes realised that he had been mistaken.

Mrs Scott died on 31st August 1977, after the proceedings had started, and an order to carry on was granted to the second and third plaintiffs on 17th March 1978.

I am satisfied that the facts are as set out above and that it was the intention of Mrs Scott by the 1973 deed of release to release her life interest in the whole of the proceeds of sale of the management company comprised in her settled share, as is set out in the second plaintiff's affidavit. It is on this basis quite clear that the deed of release in question does not give effect to the true intention of the parties, and the question for decision is whether it should be rectified.

The plaintiffs' solicitor gave notice of these proceedings on 29th July 1977 to the Capital Taxes Office, and to the Inspector of Taxes, Woking 1 District, and they have replied to the effect that the Crown does not wish to take part in the proceedings and will regard themselves as bound by the decision of this court in the matter of the relief sought. In their letter of 30th September 1977, in so saying, the Commissioners of Inland Revenue required that the attention of the court should be properly drawn to *Whiteside v Whiteside*[1]; they added also, for what they are worth, the words 'provided that the order does not appear wrong for any reason'. I am not clear as to the intention of this addition, which, if the commissioners do not appear, can have no effect. But I should say that the *Whiteside* case[1] has been fully and properly drawn to my attention by counsel for the plaintiffs, and will be discussed hereafter.

The general principle in regard to rectification is clearly stated in Snell's Principles of Equity in the following words[2]:

> 'If by mistake a written instrument does not accord with the true agreement between the parties, equity has power to reform, or rectify, that instrument so as to make it accord with the true agreement. What is rectified is not a mistake in the transaction itself but a mistake in the way in which that transaction has been expressed in writing. "Courts of Equity do not rectify contracts; they may and do rectify instruments purporting to have been made in pursuance of the terms of contracts"[3].'

It also seems clear that rectification may be made in the case of a provision in favour of a volunteer. Nor is there anything to prevent a volunteer claiming such rectification, at any rate after the settlor's death: see Snell[4] and *Butlin v Butlin*[5] where Brightman J held that the court had power to rectify a settlement notwithstanding that it was a voluntary one and not the result of a bargain. In his judgment he made it clear that the principle was that the court would rectify the document so that it expressed the true intentions of the parties.

In *Whiteside v Whiteside*[1] in the Court of Appeal the facts were that the plaintiff executed a deed in favour of his former wife after the dissolution of marriage, to provide her with maintenance. As executed the deed obliged the plaintiff to pay her 'the sum of £1,000 per annum free of . . . income tax up to but not exceeding 7s. 6d. in the £'. These last words were substituted by the plaintiff's solicitor for the words 'such a sum after deduction of income-tax at the rate of not more than 7s.6d. in the £ as shall represent £1,000 per annum', originally inserted in the draft as prepared by the wife's solicitor. It was clearly, one would suppose, the plaintiff's intention that his wife should receive £1,000 after tax up to the stated rate had been deducted. The Crown at first allowed the deduction from the plaintiff's surtax on the footing that he was liable to pay on that basis, but later refused

1   [1949] 2 All ER 913, [1950] Ch 65
2   27th Edn (1973), p 610
3   *Mackenzie v Coulson* (1869) LR 8 Eq 368 at 375, per James V-C
4   27th Edn (1973), p 616
5   [1976] 2 All ER 483, [1976] Ch 251

to allow the deduction, and the plaintiff then asked for rectification of the deed by substituting the words 'such an annual sum as after deduction of British income-tax at the rate of 7s.6d. in the £, will leave £1,000', While the action was pending, the plaintiff executed a supplementary deed which included the proposed rectification so as to make him legally bound to pay the full amount of £1,000 as from the date of execution of the supplementary deed, as in fact he had previously done. The headnote[1] states that the court would not rectify, because (1) the plaintiff was seeking to obtain a rectification which would restore the deed to the state in which it would have been but for the error of the plaintiff by his solicitor, and (2) that the question of tax was never present in the mind of the plaintiff's former wife, so that rectification was being asked for, when, owing to the execution of the supplementary deed, there was no issue between the parties.

I do not find the decision very easy to follow, but it seems clear, contrary to the facts in the present case, that the court in *Whiteside v Whiteside*[2] was not satisfied that it was the intention of both parties at the date of the original deed that the wife should receive the £1,000 free tax, so as to enable the husband to claim a benefit from the point of view of surtax. Cohen LJ, for example, states[3]: '. . . there is no evidence that it was the common intention of the parties to secure him that benefit.' Furthermore, the plaintiff, through the hand of his solicitor, quite deliberately altered the words originally suggested in the draft prepared by the wife's solicitor which would in fact have given him the tax advantage which he was seeking by the application to rectify. It was strongly arguable, therefore, that it hardly lay in his mouth to say that the deed did not represent his intention at the time of signing it. There are some words of Evershed MR[4], quoting his own words in *Van der Linde v Van der Linde*[5], which might be thought to question whether the court should exercise its discretion to rectify where the object of the party seeking rectification is solely to obtain a tax advantage. Evershed MR, however, goes on to make it clear that his words in question were merely a statement of the argument and were unnecessary for his decision in *Van der Linde v Van der Linde*[6].

It may possibly be that the Crown asked that *Whiteside v Whiteside*[2] should be brought to the notice of the court because it was thought the court might take the view, perhaps basing itself on the words of Evershed MR, that it ought not to rectify where the only effect of such rectification is to give a tax advantage. I do not think that such a proposition stated in such general terms can be correct. Nor do I think that there is anything in *Whiteside v Whiteside*[2] which says that it is.

I was reminded by counsel for the plaintiffs that in *Re Colebrook's Conveyances*[7] I had myself considered *Whiteside v Whiteside*[2] on a previous occasion and had distinguished *Re Colebrook's Conveyance*[7] from it. In *Re Colebrook's Conveyances*[7] I found that the document in question did not carry out the intention of the parties, and decided that it should be rectified to enable it to do so. I went on to hold that, if such rectification had the incidental result of giving a tax advantage to one of the parties, that was no reason for refusal of the application. In commenting on *Whiteside v Whiteside*[2], I said[8]:

'. . . it may well be an authority for saying that if the only result of the rectification of an error *which was due to the plaintiff himself*, will be to give the plaintiff a tax advantage, then that may well be a good reason for refusing to exercise the equitable jurisdiction.'

---

1   [1950] Ch 65
2   [1949] 2 All ER 913, [1950] Ch 65
3   [1949] 2 All ER 913 at 918, [1950] Ch 65 at 77
4   [1949] 2 All ER 913 at 915, [1950] Ch 65 at 72
5   [1947] Ch 306 at 311
6   [1974] Ch 306
7   [1973] 1 All ER 132, [1972] 1 WLR 1397
8   [1973] 1 All ER 132 at 134, [1972] 1 WLR 1397 at 1399

As I have already said, in *Whiteside v Whiteside*[1] the court based itself on two facts: firstly, that there was no evidence of intention on the wife's part to avoid payment of tax and, secondly, that the mistake came about by a deliberate alteration on the plaintiff's own part of words originally put into the draft prepared by the wife's solicitor, which, if not altered, would have given him the tax advantage which he was seeking by rectification. I would not like my words in *Re Colebrook's Conveyances*[2] about *Whiteside v Whiteside*[1] to be thought to be more general than they are when read strictly, and, in particular, that they should be thought to be suggesting that *Whiteside v Whiteside*[1] can be taken to be an authority for refusal of rectification where the main, or indeed only, object of the original transaction is legitimate avoidance of tax.

The true principles governing these matters I conceive to be as follows. (1) The court has a discretion to rectify where it is satisfied that the document does not carry out the intention of the parties. This is the basic principle. (2) Parties are entitled to enter into any transaction which is legal, and, in particular, are entitled to arrange their affairs to avoid payment of tax if they legitimately can. The Finance Acts 1969 and 1975 tell them explicitly how they can do so in the case of estate duty and capital transfer tax. (3) If a mistake is made in a document legitimately designed to avoid the payment of tax, there is no reason why it should not be corrected. The Crown is in no privileged position qua such a document. It would not be a correct exercise of the discretion in such circumstances to refuse rectification merely because the Crown would thereby be deprived of an accidental and unexpected windfall. (4) As counsel for the trustees submitted, neither *Whiteside v Whiteside*[1] nor any other case contains anything which compels the court to the conclusion that rectification of a document should be refused where the sole purpose of seeking it is to enable the parties to obtain a legitimate fiscal advantage which it was their common intention to obtain at the time of the execution of the document.

I should perhaps add that in *Whiteside v Whiteside*[1] it was said that, as the parties had voluntarily executed a supplemental deed incorporating the proposed rectification, there was nothing between the parties which was outstanding and needed rectification. It was suggested that it might be argued here that the death of Mrs Scott meant that the capital assets in question had now passed anyway to the second and third plaintiffs, so that rectification is unnecessary so far as capital is concerned. This may be true, but it does not deal with the case of past income which they could not get unless the release was rectified so as to back-date the effect on income. The facts in this case are thus different from those in *Whiteside v Whiteside*[1] in that respect.

For the reasons given above, therefore, I consider that the court should rectify the release in question in the manner asked for in the summons, and I make an order accordingly.

Order accordingly.

Solicitors: *Theodore Goddard & Co* (for the plaintiffs and the trustees).

Evelyn Budd   Barrister.

---

1   [1949] 2 All ER 913, [1950] Ch 65
2   [1973] 1 All ER 132 at 134, [1972] 1 WLR 1397 at 1399

Practice Direction

CHANCERY DIVISION

Practice – Trial – Order for early trial – Summons for directions adjourned from judge to master – Documents to be lodged with master's summons clerk.

1. When a judge, on hearing a motion, directs a speedy trial of the action it is now usual **b** for the judge to treat the summons for directions in the action as before him (subject to the issue of a pro-forma summons) and to give preliminary directions, adjourning the rest of the summons to the master on a fixed date in order that the master may consider the progress of the action and give such further directions as may be necessary to enable the action to be set down for hearing without delay.

2. Solicitors are reminded that the master needs to be supplied with copies of the **c** relevant papers before the date fixed by the judge. The solicitors to the party at whose instance the order for speedy trial was made and who have issued the pro-forma summons (normally the plaintiff's solicitors) must accordingly, not less than two days before the date of the adjourned hearing, lodge with the master's summons clerk (a) copies of the writ and all subsequent pleadings and notices, (b) a copy of the summons for directions issued pro-forma, (c) a certified or office copy of the judge's order or, if it has not yet been perfected, **d** a copy of the draft order or, if it has not been drafted, counsel's brief endorsed with the judge's directions and (d) the duplicate appearance and a copy of any civil aid certificate.

3. If the master has not been supplied with these papers in due time before the adjourned hearing and accordingly has to order a further adjournment it is likely to be at the expense of the party in default.

By the direction of the Vice-Chancellor.

R E BALL
Chief Master.

31st January 1979

Pearlman v Keepers and Governors of Harrow School

COURT OF APPEAL, CIVIL DIVISION
LORD DENNING MR, GEOFFREY LANE AND EVELEIGH LJJ
24th, 25th, 26th MAY, 14th JULY 1978

Certiorari – Jurisdiction – Certiorari to quash county court decision – Error on face of record – Misconstruction by judge of words in statute conferring jurisdiction – Statute providing that decision of county court to be 'final and conclusive' – Whether error of law going to court's jurisdiction – Whether certiorari lies to quash decision – County Courts Act 1959, s 107 – Housing Act 1974, Sch 8, para 2(2).

Landlord and tenant – Leasehold enfranchisement – Improvement of house by execution of works amounting to structural alteration, extension or addition – Central heating system – Whether installation of central heating system a 'structural alteration . . . or addition' – Housing Act 1974, Sch 8, para 1(2).

The tenant resided in a three-storied house in London which he held on a long lease at a low rent. He removed the old coal-fired central heating system and installed a modern gas-fired one which supplied hot water and heat for the 20 radiators which he installed and connected to the walls. The boiler for the system, which was in the kitchen on the ground floor, was connected to a tank in the roof by pipes which ran from the ground floor, through holes in the walls, floors and ceilings, to the roof. The boiler was also connected to the electrical system which powered it, and to the flue and the chimney which for the purpose of the system was lined with asbestos. Once installed the pipes could not be removed. The improvement effected by the installation of the new central heating system increased the rateable value of the house to £1,597, which took it outside the limit of rateable value of £1,500 prescribed by the Leasehold Reform Act 1967 for the application of the enfranchisement provisions in that Act to houses in Greater London. The tenant wished to claim the benefit of those provisions. He therefore applied to the landlords, under the 1967 Act and Sch 8[a] to the Housing Act 1974, seeking their agreement to a reduction in the rateable value to £1,487, on the ground that the central heating system was an 'improvement made by the execution of works amounting to structural alteration, extension or addition', within para 1(2) of Sch 8 to the 1974 Act. The landlords did not agree and the tenant applied to the county court, under para 2(2) of Sch 8, for a declaration

---

a Schedule 8, so far as material, provides:
  '1. (1) Where the tenant . . . has made or contributed to the cost of an improvement on the premises comprised in the tenancy and the improvement is one to which this Schedule applies, then, if the tenant serves on the landlord a notice in the prescribed form requiring him to agree to a reduction under this Schedule, their rateable value . . . shall be reduced by such amount, if any, as may be agreed or determined in accordance with the following provisions of this Schedule.
  '(2) This Schedule applies to any improvement made by the execution of works amounting to structural alteration, extension or addition.
  '2. (1) The amount of any such reduction may at any time be agreed in writing between the landlord and the tenant.
  '(2) Where, at the expiration of a period of six weeks from the service of a notice under paragraph 1 of this Schedule any of the following matters has not been agreed in writing between the landlord and the tenant, that is to say,—(a) whether the improvement specified in the notice is an improvement to which this Schedule applies; (b) what works were involved in it; (c) whether the tenant . . . made it or contributed to its cost; and (d) what proportion his contribution, if any, bears to the whole cost; the county court may on the application of the tenant determine that matter, and any such determination shall be final and conclusive.'

that the system was an improvement, within para 1(2), and that the rateable value should be reduced. The county court judge determined, under para 2(2)(a), that the heating system was not an improvement amounting to works of structural alteration and refused the declaration. In reaching that decision the judge rejected the meaning of 'structural alteration' adopted by another county court judge in a similar case. Paragraph 2(2) of Sch 8 provided that the judge's determination was to be 'final and conclusive'. The tenant applied to the Divisional Court for an order of certiorari to quash the judge's decision on the ground of error of law on the face of the record, namely his conclusion that the system did not amount to structural alteration. The Divisional Court refused leave to apply for certiorari. The tenant appealed to the Court of Appeal. On the appeal the landlords conceded that s 107[b] of the County Courts Act 1959 did not affect the power to issue certiorari to quash a county court decision for absence of jurisdiction but contended that it did exclude certiorari for error of law on the face of the record.

Held – (i) 'Structural alteration . . . or addition', within para 1(2) of Sch 8 to the 1974 Act, meant an alteration or addition which involved the structure or fabric of a house, as opposed to the mere provision of equipment. The central heating system, by affecting and being connected to the fabric of the house, amounted to a 'structural alteration . . . or addition' to the house, within para 1(2). It followed that the judge had misconstrued the meaning of the words 'structural alteration' and that his decision was wrong (see p 369 j to p 370 a and d, p 372 h, p 373 j to p 374 b, p 378 g and p 379 c, post).

(ii) (Geoffrey Lane LJ dissenting) The judge's misconstruction of the words in para 1(2) of Sch 8 was an error of law which went to his jurisdiction under para 2(2) to determine the tenant's application, because (per Lord Denning MR) no court had jurisdiction to make an error of law on which the decision of the case depended, and by misconstruing the words 'structural alteration' the judge had made such an error of law and thereby deprived himself of the jurisdiction to go on and determine the matters set out in sub-paras (b), (c) and (d) of para 2(2), or (per Eveleigh LJ) the judge had gone outside his jurisdiction under para 2(2) by asking himself the wrong question when he asked whether the central heating system amounted to a 'structural alteration' on the wrong meaning of those words. It followed that, even though the judge's determination was final and conclusive under the 1974 Act, certiorari would issue to quash the determination for want of jurisdiction. Accordingly the appeal would be allowed (see p 371 h j, p 372 c to e and j, p 377 b and h, p 378 b and p 379 b and f, post); dictum of Coleridge J in Bunbury v Fuller (1853) 9 Exch at 140 and Anisminic Ltd v Foreign Compensation Commission [1969] 1 All ER 208 applied.

Per Curiam. The 1959 Act does not exclude certiorari where the county court judge has acted in excess of his jurisdiction (see p 371 g and p 379 e, post).

Per Lord Denning MR. Section 107 of the 1959 Act applies only to proceedings under that Act and has no application to a decision by a county court judge under Sch 8 to the 1974 Act. In such a case certiorari lies when the judge goes outside his jurisdiction or there is an error of law on the face of the record (see p 371 c and f and p 372 g, post).

Notes

For the exclusion of certiorari by statute generally, see 1 Halsbury's Laws (4th Edn) paras 155–158.

For the exclusion of certiorari to quash a judgment or order of the county court, see 10 ibid para 653.

For the County Courts Act 1959, s 107, see 7 Halsbury's Statutes (3rd Edn) 370.

For the Housing Act 1974, s 118 and Sch 8, see 44 ibid 594, 609.

Cases referred to in judgments

Anisminic Ltd v Foreign Compensation Commission [1969] 1 All ER 208, [1969] 2 AC 147,

---

b   Section 107, so far as material, is set out at p 371 a b, post

[1969] 2 WLR 163, HL; *rvsg* [1967] 2 All ER 986, [1968] QB 862, [1967] 3 WLR 382, CA, Digest (Cont Vol C) 281, *2557b*.

Armah v Government of Ghana [1966] 3 All ER 177, [1968] AC 192, [1966] 3 WLR 828, HL, Digest (Cont Vol B) 296, *157a*.

Blagrave's Settled Estates, Re [1903] 1 Ch 560, [1900–3] All ER Rep 319, 72 LJ Ch 317, CA, 20 Digest (Repl) 208, *28*.

Bradlaugh, Ex parte (1878) 3 QBD 509, 47 LJMC 105, 38 LT 680, 42 JP 583, DC, 16 Digest (Repl) 495, *3183*.

British Launderers' Research Association v Hendon Borough Rating Authority [1949] 1 All ER 21, [1949] 1 KB 462, [1949] LJR 646, 113 JP 72, 47 LGR 113, CA, 38 Digest (Repl) 583, *627*.

Brutus v Cozens [1972] 2 All ER 1297, [1973] AC 854, [1972] 3 WLR 521, 136 JP 636, sub nom *Cozens v Brutus* 56 Cr App R 799, HL, Digest (Cont Vol D) 211, *7271a*.

Bunbury v Fuller (1853) 9 Exch 111, 23 LJ Ex 29, 23 LTOS 131, 17 JP 790, 1 CLR 893, 156 ER 47, Exch, 11 Digest (Repl) 78, *994*.

Cardiff Rating Authority and Cardiff Assessment Committee v Guest Keen Baldwin's Iron and Steel Co Ltd [1949] 1 All ER 27, [1949] 1 KB 385, [1949] LJR 713, 113 JP 78, 47 LGR 159, CA, 38 Digest (Repl) 630, *955*.

Challis v Watson [1913] 1 KB 547, [1911–13] All ER Rep 661, 82 LJKB 529, 108 LT 505, DC, 13 Digest (Reissue) 534, *4482*.

Clarke's Settlement, Re [1902] 2 Ch 327, 71 LJ Ch 593, 86 LT 653, 20 Digest (Repl) 208, *27*.

Dyson Holdings Ltd v Fox [1975] 3 All ER 1030, [1976] QB 503, [1975] 3 WLR 744, CA, Digest (Cont Vol D) 592, *7646a*.

Gaskell's Settled Estates, Re [1894] 1 Ch 485, 63 LJ Ch 243, 70 LT 554, 8 R 67, 30 Digest (Reissue) 377, *144*.

Gilmore's Application, Re [1957] 1 All ER 796, sub nom *R v Medical Appeal Tribunal, ex parte Gilmore* [1957] 1 QB 574, [1957] 2 WLR 498, CA, 34 Digest (Repl) 665, *4584*.

Hall v Arnold [1950] 1 All ER 993, [1950] 2 KB 543, 114 JP 293, 48 LGR 443, DC, 25 Digest (Repl) 356, *382*.

Lee v Hay's Wharf Ltd's Proprietors [1940] 3 All ER 282, [1940] 2 KB 306, 109 LJKB 797, 163 LT 117, CA, 13 Digest (Reissue) 535, *4494*.

Pickering v Phillimore (10th May 1976) unreported, West London County Court.

Pyx Granite Co Ltd v Ministry of Housing and Local Government [1959] 3 All ER 1, [1960] AC 260, [1959] 3 WLR 346, 123 JP 429, 58 LGR 1, 10 P & CR 319, HL, 45 Digest (Repl) 336, *37*.

R v His Honour Judge Donald Hurst, ex parte Smith [1960] 2 All ER 385, [1960] 2 QB 133, [1960] 2 WLR 961, 58 LGR 348, DC, 20 Digest (Repl) 43, *270*.

Tehrani v Rostron [1971] 3 All ER 790, [1972] 1 QB 182, [1971] 3 All ER 612, 136 JP 40, CA, Digest (Cont Vol D) 637, *1822a*.

Westminster Corpn v Gordon Hotels Ltd [1908] AC 142, 77 LJKB 520, 98 LT 681, 72 JP 201, 6 LGR 520, HL; *affg* [1907] 1 KB 910, CA, 38 Digest (Repl) 209, *318*.

Woodhouse v Peter Brotherhood Ltd [1972] 3 All ER 91, [1972] 2 QB 520, [1972] 3 WLR 215, [1972] ICR 186, CA, Digest (Cont Vol D) 671, *816Afcb*.

Appeal

By an application under Sch 8, para 2(2), to the Housing Act 1974, dated 22nd June 1976, Sidney Pearlman ('the tenant') applied to the county court for declarations (1) that as a consequence of improvements carried out by him to premises at 1 Vale Close, Maida Vale, London W9, the rateable value of the premises for the purposes of the Leasehold Reform Act 1967 should be reduced from £1,597·00 to £1,487·00, and (2) that the improvements were the execution of works amounting to the structural alteration or extension of the premises or a structural addition thereto, and the proportion of the cost of the works borne by the tenant was £2,404·54. The respondents to the application were the Keepers and Governors of Harrow School ('the landlords'). By a judgment given on 26th November 1976 his Honour Judge Curtis-Raleigh sitting in the Bloomsbury and Marylebone County

Court found that the improvements, namely the installation of a central heating system, were not works of structural alteration, and refused the declaration. The tenant applied to the Divisional Court of the Queen's Bench Division for an order of certiorari to remove the judge's decision into that court for the purpose of quashing it on the ground that the decision disclosed an error of law on the face of the record, namely the conclusion that the improvements were not works amounting to structural alteration, extension or addition to the premises. On 5th April 1977 the Divisional Court refused the tenant leave to apply for an order of certiorari. The tenant appealed pursuant to leave of the Court of Appeal. The grounds of the appeal were (1) that the order of the county court judge disclosed an error of law on the face of the record, (2) that the Divisional Court were wrong in law, or wrongly exercised their discretion, in holding that the case was not an appropriate one for the issue of an order of certiorari, (3) that the tenant had no other means of redress to correct the error of law made by the county court judge except by applying for an order of certiorari and (4) that it was a matter of public disquiet that different county courts could come to a different conclusion on the same facts, and that that situation could only be put right by the intervention of the Court of Appeal. The facts are set out in the judgments of Lord Denning MR.

Lionel Read QC and *Matthew Horton* for the tenant.
Alistair Dawson QC and *Joseph Harper* for the landlords.

Cur adv vult

14th July. The following judgments were read.

LORD DENNING MR. The Leasehold Reform Act 1967 conferred a great benefit on some tenants. They were tenants who resided in houses which they held on long leases at a low rent. It gave them a right to acquire the freehold on very favourable terms. But it did not apply to large houses. In the London area it only applied to houses of a rateable value of not more than £400. Later on the valuation lists were reviewed, and all rateable values were much increased. By an amendment the Act was extended so as to apply in the London area to houses of a rateable value of not more than £1,500: see s 118 of the Housing Act 1974.

Now there are many houses in the London area where the tenants have done improvements to the property at their own cost; and the rateable value has been increased on that account. The house might be assessed at over £1,500 just because of the tenant's improvements. Parliament realised that it was very unfair on a tenant that he should be deprived of the benefit of the 1967 Act simply by reason of improvements which he himself had made. So in the 1974 Act Parliament inserted provisions enabling the tenant in such a case to get the rateable value reduced for the purpose of the 1967 Act. These provisions are s 118(3) of and Sch 8 to the 1974 Act.

The procedure is for the tenant to serve a notice on the landlord saying that he made the improvements at his own cost and wants the rateable value reduced. The landlord may agree. But if he disagrees the matter is referred to the county court judge. He has to determine whether the tenant has a legitimate case for a reduction: but he does not determine the quantum of it. That is to be referred to the valuation officer for him to certify the amount of the reduction.

The house and the improvements

The house is 1 Vale Close, Maida Vale, London W9. It is a good-sized house with three floors. It is owned by the Governors of Harrow School. They let it in 1933 on a long lease for 88 years, so that it is due to expire in 2021 AD. The leaseholder is Mr Sidney Pearlman, who has occupied it as his residence for over 30 years. When he went there it had an old-fashioned heating system. There was a coal-fired boiler in the kitchen. It supplied hot water for the sinks and baths, and two radiators, one in the hall and the other on the first floor landing. The rooms in the house were heated by ordinary coal fires.

In 1960 Mr Pearlman scrapped that system. He installed a modern full central heating system. It supplied 18 radiators and towel-rails all over the house. It supplied hot water to baths, sinks, and so forth. It was fired with gas. The boiler was in the kitchen. It was connected with the flue and the chimney. There was asbestos lining inserted right up the chimney. Pipes were laid from the boiler on the ground floor up to the top floor, passing under floors and through ceilings and walls, some of them load bearing, from room to room right up to a metal tank in the roof space. Holes had to be made in the ceilings and walls and made good afterwards. Each radiator was connected to the walls with brackets. In 1971 Mr Pearlman had two more radiators installed.

That work undoubtedly was a great improvement to the house and went to increase its rateable value. In the latest revaluation the rateable value of the house was £1,597. This was over £1,500 and, as things stood, Mr Pearlman was unable to claim the benefit of the Leasehold Reform Act 1967: because that was limited to houses in London of less than £1,500 rateable value. In the circumstances, Mr Pearlman applied to his landlords asking them to agree to a reduction in the rateable value. He proposed that the rateable value should be reduced to £1,487. He said that, by installing the full central heating system, he had himself made improvements, increasing the rateable value, and that that increase should not count against him for the purposes of the Leashold Reform Act 1967.

The landlords did not agree. So Mr Pearlman applied to the county court judge. On 26th November 1976 the judge refused Mr Pearlman's request. Mr Pearlman says that the determination of the judge was wrong in law.

The law

In order to qualify for a reduction, the improvement must be an 'improvement made by the execution of works amounting to structural alteration, extension or addition'. Those are the words of Sch 8, para 1(2), to the 1974 Act. They are simple English words, but they have been interpreted by different judges differently. At any rate, when the judges have had to apply them to the installation of a full central heating system. In each house the primary facts have been exactly the same, or near enough the same, but one judge has found one way. Another the other way. One judge has held that the installation is a 'structural alteration'. Another has found that it is not. It is said, nevertheless, that, being simple English words, we should not interfere. Neither decision can be said to be unreasonable. So let each decision stand. Reliance is placed for this purpose on the speech of Lord Reid in *Brutus v Cozens*[1].

I am afraid that I cannot accept this argument. As I pointed out in *Dyson Holdings Ltd v Fox*[2], when an ordinary word comes to be applied to similar facts, in one case after another, it would be intolerable if half of the judges gave one answer and the other half another. No one would know where he stood. No lawyer could advise his client what to do. In such circumstances, it is the duty of a court of appeal to give a definite ruling one way or the other. However simple the words, their interpretation is a matter of law. They have to be applied, in case after case, by lawyers; and it is necessary, in the interests of certainty, that they should always be given the same interpretation, and always applied in the same way: see our two rating cases: *British Launderers' Research Association v Hendon Borough Rating Authority*[3] and *Cardiff Rating Authority v Guest Keen Baldwin's Iron and Steel Co Ltd*[4]; and *Woodhouse v Peter Brotherhood*[5].

Applying the words of Sch 8 to the house here, I am of opinion that the installation of full central heating to this house was 'an improvement made by the execution of works

---

1   [1972] 2 All ER 1297, [1973] AC 854
2   [1975] 3 All ER 1030 at 1034, [1976] QB 503 at 510
3   [1949] 1 All ER 21 at 25–26, [1949] 1 KB 462 at 471–472
4   [1949] 1 All ER 27 at 30, [1949] 1 KB 385 at 396
5   [1972] 3 All ER 91 at 95, [1972] 2 QB 520 536–537

amounting to structural alteration . . . or addition'. It involved a good deal of tampering with the structure by making holes in walls and partitions, by lining the chimney with asbestos, and so forth. Much more than is involved in installing fitted cupboards instead of wardrobes, or a modern fireplace instead of old fire-dogs.

This is confirmed by the practice of rating authorities. They have always held that, when full central heating is installed, the rateable value of the house is increased. So much so that they have a formula for calculating the increase according to the number of rooms that are centrally heated: and the increase dates from the time when the central heating was installed, on the ground that it was a 'structural alteration' within ss 68 (4)(b) and 79(2)(b) of the General Rate Act 1967. Stronger still is the fact that when the installation was made after 1st April 1974, Parliament has expressly said that no increase is to be made in the rateable value by reason of the 'structural alterations' involved in installing a central heating system: see s 21(1)(a) of the Local Government Act 1974.

The contrary view was supported by some cases under the Settled Land Acts 1882 and 1890. The point there arose about the early form of heating houses by hot water through pipes. It was held that the tenant for life had to install it himself out of his income, and that he could not require his trustees to pay it out of capital (see Re Gaskell's Settled Estate[1]) because it was not a structural alteration (see Re Clarke's Settlement[2] affirmed in this court in Re Blagrave's Settled Estates[3]). I find no help in those cases, concerned as they were with a different statute, worded differently, in a different context altogether.

My conclusion is, therefore, that in the previous case[4] his Honour Judge White was right, and that in the present case his Honour Judge Curtis-Raleigh was wrong. The installation of a full central heating system is a 'structural alteration . . . or addition' within Sch 8 to the 1974 Act. But is it possible for this court to correct the decision of Judge Curtis-Raleigh? That brings me to the point of jurisdiction.

Jurisdiction

There is an express provision in the 1974 Act which makes the decision of the judge in the county court 'final and conclusive'. It is Sch 8, para 2(2). It applies, among other matters, to the question whether the improvement is one to which the schedule applies. If such a question is not agreed, then '. . . the county court may, on the application of the tenant, determine that matter, and any such determination shall be final and conclusive'.

Those words 'final and conclusive' have been considered by the courts a hundred times. It has been uniformly held that they preclude any appeal to a higher court in the sense of an appeal proper where the higher court reviews the decision of the lower tribunal and substitutes its own decision for that of the lower tribunal: see Westminster Corpn v Golden Hotels[5] and Hall v Arnold[6]. But those words do not preclude the High Court from correcting the errors of the lower tribunal by means of certiorari, now called judicial review. Notwithstanding that a decision is by a statute made 'final and conclusive', certiorari can still issue for excess of jurisdiction, or for error of law on the face of the record: see Re Gilmore's Application[7]; or a declaration can be made by the High Court to determine the rights of the parties. It can declare the law by which they are bound, irrespective of what the lower tribunal has done: see Pyx Granite Co Ltd v Ministry of Housing and Local Government[8]. It can even consider the point of law by means of a case stated: see Tehrani v Rostron[9].

1   [1894] 1 Ch 485
2   [1902] 2 Ch 327 at 331
3   [1903] 1 Ch 560 at 562, 563, [1900–3] All ER Rep 319 at 321
4   *Pickering v Phillimore* (10th May 1976) unreported
5   [1907] 1 KB 910; [1908] AC 142
6   [1950] 1 All ER 993, [1950] 2 KB 543
7   [1957] 1 All ER 796 at 801, [1957] 1 QB 574 at 583
8   [1959] 3 All ER 1, [1960] AC 260
9   [1971] 3 All ER 790, [1972] 1 QB 182

The 'no certiorari clause', s 107

But it is said here that those decisions apply only to lower tribunals, and that they do not apply to county courts. It is said that Parliament has taken away certiorari to county courts. This argument is based on s 107 of the County Courts Act 1959 which says:

'Subject to the provisions of any other Act relating to county courts, no judgment or order of any judge of county courts, nor any proceedings brought before him or pending in his court, shall be removed by appeal, motion, certiorari or otherwise into any other court whatever, except in the manner and according to the provisions in this Act mentioned.'

To my mind that provision has no application to the present case. It applies only to proceedings under the 1959 Act, just as if the words 'under this Act' were written into it. Certiorari is taken away in proceedings in which the 1959 Act gives jurisdiction to county courts, such as s 39 (actions of contract and tort), s 48 (recovery of land), s 52 (equity jurisdiction) and s 56 (Admiralty jurisdiction). In all such matters certiorari does not lie: but instead the statute gives a right of appeal on points of law: see s 108. In so interpreting s 107, I am following the lead of Cockburn CJ in *Ex parte Bradlaugh*[1], where there was a 'no certiorari clause'. He said: 'I entertain very serious doubts whether that provision does not apply only to matters in respect if which jurisdiction is given by that statute, and not to matters in which jurisdiction is given by subsequent statutes.'

I am confirmed in this view by reference to s 108 of the 1959 Act, which gives an appeal to the Court of Appeal on points of law. It seems to me to be dealing with matters in respect of which the 1959 Act gives jurisdiction to the county court: and not to matters in respect of which jurisdiction is given by subsequent Acts.

Moreover, in subsequent Acts giving fresh jurisdiction to the county court (additional to that in the 1959 Act), Parliament has expressly said whether there is to be an appeal (as in the Building Societies Act 1962, s 72(5)), or no appeal (as in the Industrial and Provident Societies Act 1965, s 42(3)(*b*)). In both those cases it uses the words 'final and conclusive' leaving the remedy by certiorari or declaration unimpaired.

So I would hold that certiorari lies in the case of a decision by the judge in the county court under Sch 8 to the 1974 Act when he goes outside his jurisdiction or there is an error of law on the face of the record.

Jurisdictional error

But even if s 107 does apply to this case, it only excludes certiorari for error of law on the face of the record. It does not exclude the power of the High Court to issue certiorari for absence of jurisdiction. It has been held that certiorari will issue to a county court judge if he acts without jurisdiction in the matter: see *R v His Honour Judge Donald Hurst, ex parte Smith*[2]. If he makes a wrong finding on a matter on which his jurisdiction depends, he makes a jurisdictional error, and certiorari will lie to quash his decision: see *Anisminic Ltd v Foreign Compensation Commission*[3] by Lord Wilberforce. But the distinction between an error which entails absence of jurisdiction and an error made within the jurisdiction is very fine. So fine indeed that it is rapidly being eroded. Take this very case. When the judge held that the installation of a full central heating system was not a 'structural alteration or addition' we all think, all three of us, that he went wrong in point of law. He misconstrued those words. That error can be described on the one hand as an error which went to his jurisdiction. In this way: if he had held that it was a 'structural alteration . . . or addition' he would have had jurisdiction to go on and determine the various matters set out in sub-paras (*b*), (*c*) and (*d*) of para 2(2) of Sch 8. By holding that it was not a 'structural alteration . . . or addition' he deprived himself of jurisdiction to determine those matters. On the other hand, his error can equally well be described as an error made by him within his

1   (1878) 3 QBD 509 at 512
2   [1960] 2 All ER 385, [1960] 2 QB 133
3   [1969] 1 All ER 208 at 244, [1969] 2 AC 147 at 208

jurisdiction. It can plausibly be said that he had jurisdiction to enquire into the meaning of the words 'structural alteration . . . or addition'; and that his wrong interpretation of *a* them was only an error within his jurisdiction, and not an error taking him outside it.

That illustration could be repeated in nearly all these cases. So fine is the distinction that in truth the High Court has a choice before it whether to interfere with an inferior court on a point of law. If it chooses to interfere, it can formulate its decision in the words: 'The court below had no jurisdiction to decide this point wrongly as it did.' If it does not choose to interfere, it can say: 'The court had jurisdiction to decide it wrongly, and did so.' Softly *b* be it stated, but that is the reason for the difference between the decision of the Court of Appeal in *Anisminic*[1] and the House of Lords[2].

I would suggest that this distinction should now be discarded. The High Court has, and should have, jurisdiction to control the proceedings of inferior courts and tribunals by way of judicial review. When they go wrong in law, the High Court should have power to put them right. Not only in the instant case to do justice to the complainant, but also so as to *c* secure that all courts and tribunals, when faced with the same point of law, should decide it in the same way. It is intolerable that a citizen's rights in point of law should depend on which judge tries his case, or in what court it is heard. The way to get things right is to hold thus: no court or tribunal has any jurisdiction to make an error of law on which the decision of the case depends. If it makes such an error, it goes outside its jurisdiction and certiorari will lie to correct it. In this case the finding, that the installation of a central *d* heating system was not a 'structural alteration', was an error on which the jurisdiction of the county court depended: and, because of that error, the county court judge was quite wrong to dismiss the application outright. He ought to have found that the installation was an 'improvement' within Sch 8, para 2(2)(*a*), and gone on to determine the other matters referred to in Sch 8, para 2(2)(*b*), (*c*) and (*d*).

On these grounds I am of opinion that certiorari lies to quash the determination of the *e* county court judge, even though it was made by statute 'final and conclusive'.

Appeal

In case certiorari does not lie, the tenant submitted that he had a remedy by way of appeal, and he asked to be given leave out of time. He submitted that the words 'final and conclusive' meant that the determination of the county court judge was final and conclusive *f* on the facts, but not on the law: see *Tehrani v Rostron*[3]. Accordingly, he submitted that he could appeal under s 108 of the County Courts Act 1959.

I must say that, if I had been of opinion that certiorari did not lie, I would have held that the tenant could have appealed under s 108: because I would never accept a situation where different judges on the same set of facts could come to different conclusions on points of law. I would have held that 'final and conclusive' excluded appeal on the facts but not on *g* the law. But, as I have already said, I think that s 108, like s 107, is confined to the jurisdiction conferred in county court judges by the 1959 Act itself. Neither section applies to new jurisdiction created under new statutes, such as the Housing Act 1974, Sch 8. And it is because neither section applies that I am of opinion that certiorari does lie.

Conclusion   *h*

In my opinion the county court judge made an error of law when he determined that the installation of a full central heating system was not a 'structural alteration . . . or addition' to the house. His decision was made by the statute 'final and conclusive'. Those words do not exclude remedy by certiorari, that is, by judicial review. I would, therefore, allow the appeal and make an order quashing his decision and declaring that the improvement made by Mr Pearlman fell within Sch 8, para 2(1) of the 1974 Act, and *j* remitting the matter to the county court to determine the remaining matters.

---

1   [1967] 2 All ER 986, [1968] QB 862
2   [1969] 1 All ER 208, [1969] 2 AC 147
3   [1971] 3 All ER 790 at 793, [1972] 1 QB 182 at 187

GEOFFREY LANE LJ. The tenant, Mr Pearlman, holds from the landlords 1 Vale Close, Maida Vale, London W9, under an 88 year lease due to expire in the year 2021. He is anxious to take advantage of the provisions of the Leasehold Reform Act 1967 to acquire the freehold of the house on advantageous terms. The landlords are equally anxious that he should not. By virtue of s 118 of the Housing Act 1974 where the rateable value of houses in the London area is more than £1,500 the 1967 Act has no application. The rateable value of this house is £1,597. Therefore at first sight it seems that the landlords are safe. However, Sch 8 to the 1974 Act provides machinery whereby the rateable value of a house may for the purposes of the 1967 Act be notionally reduced in circumstances where a tenant has made improvements to the premises 'by the execution of works amounting to structural alteration, extension or addition'.

It is not disputed that the tenant carried out extensive works in the house between 1960 and 1971. They consisted of removing the old central heating system which had been fired by a solid fuel boiler serving the hot water system and a couple of radiators and replacing it with a modern small-bore gas-burning system to heat the domestic water and no less than 20 radiators. He proposed to the landlords that these improvements had resulted in an increase in the rateable value and that without them the value would be reduced to £1,487. The landlords did not agree that this was a relevant improvement, and the matter accordingly went to the county court for decision under the terms of Sch 8, para 2(2):

> 'Where . . . any of the following matters has not been agreed in writing between the landlord and the tenant, that is to say,—(a) whether the improvement . . . is an improvement to which this Schedule applies . . . the county court may on the application of the tenant determine that matter, and any such determination shall be final and conclusive.'

The county court judge determined that the improvements were not 'by the execution of works amounting to structural alteration, extension or addition', and Mr Pearlman now seeks an order from this court that the judge was wrong. He is particularly aggrieved because it seems that in other county courts on basically similar facts the decision has gone in favour of the tenant. There is a lot to be said for the view that the outcome of litigation should not depend on which particular judge is sitting in the county court on the day of trial, but that cannot be an overriding consideration.

There are two issues. First, what is the meaning of the words 'works amounting to structural alteration, extension or addition'? Secondly, to what extent do the words of Sch 8, para 2(2)(a), 'such determination shall be final and conclusive', inhibit the tenant from obtaining redress from this court?

'Structural alteration'

The new central heating system entailed the usual work being carried out. The gas-fired boiler is a substantial affair. It is connected not only to the various radiators and towel-rails, but also, of course, to the cold water supply. It must also be connected to the electrical system (to provide power for the circulating pump and the programming mechanism) and the gas supply. It is also connected to the flue and chimney. The chimney has been lined to prevent damage through condensation. The pipes from the boiler have been run under the ground floor coming up at starting levels to most of the rooms. They pass through holes which have been made specially in the walls, load-bearing and otherwise, and in the floors and ceilings. The piping eventually rises to the roof space where it is connected to the metal header-tank and overflow pipe. It would be impossible to remove the piping. It would be possible to remove the boiler, but only by dismantling it.

'Structural' in this context means, I believe, something which involves the fabric of the house as opposed to the provision merely of a piece of equipment. It matters not whether the fabric in question is load-bearing or otherwise, if there is any substantial alteration, extension or addition to the fabric of the house the words of the schedule are satisfied. I have no doubt that the works done here 'amount to' such alteration or addition. The system is connected in permanent fashion to the gas, water and electrical installations which are part of the fabric of the house. The walls, floors and ceilings have been drilled with holes to accommodate the piping. The flue is connected in permanent fashion to the chimney (part of the fabric) which has itself been altered by lining. This is not merely the provision of equipment: it amounts to alteration and addition to the structure.

I do not derive assistance from decisions such as *Re Gaskell's Settled Estates*[1] which was made on different facts and on the words of the Settled Land Acts 1882 and 1890 which were not the same as the words under consideration here. The judge in the present case was, I think, wrong in the conclusion which he reached on this aspect of the case.

Has this court any power to intervene?

By s 107 of the County Courts Act 1959:

'. . . no judgment or order of any judge of county courts, nor any proceedings brought before him or pending in his court, shall be removed by appeal, motion, certiorari or otherwise into any other court whatever, except . . . according to the provisions in this Act mentioned.'

These words are designed to deal with two separate situations. First, a judgment or order which has already been given or made by the court, and secondly any proceedings which have not yet reached the stage of judgment or order. The section removes the remedy of certiorari in either case. Section 115(1) of the 1959 Act provides:

'The High Court . . . may order the removal into the High Court, by order of certiorari or otherwise, of any proceedings commenced in a county court, if the High Court . . . thinks it desirable that the proceedings should be heard and determined in the High Court.'

It is clear from the words themselves that that section applies only to the second type of situation, namely where the proceedings have not yet reached judgment or order. Otherwise the matter would already have been 'determined' by the county court. This conclusion is confirmed by s 117(1): 'The grant by the High Court . . . of leave to make an application for an order of certiorari . . . to a county court shall, if the High Court . . . so directs, operate as a stay of proceedings in question . . .' If completed proceedings were contemplated this section would be meaningless.

Thus what the 1959 Act has done is to abolish certiorari for error of law on the face of the record as a method of attacking a judgment or order of the county court. It has retained certiorari as a method of removing a pending or uncompleted action from the county court to the High Court: see *Challis v Watson*[2] by Lush J (a decision on s 126 of the County Courts Act 1888 which was in similar terms to s 115) and *Lee v Hay's Wharf Ltd's Proprietors*[3] (a decision under s 111 of the County Courts Act 1934). The action in the present case is not uncompleted. The judgment has been delivered. Therefore neither of those two forms of certiorari are available to the tenant.

Counsel on behalf of the landlords has conceded however that the 1959 Act has not affected the power of the High Court in a proper case to remove and quash a decision of the county court which was made in excess of that court's jurisdiction. It must follow that the only basis for an order of certiorari would be if the judge had acted in excess of his jurisdiction.

Is there an appeal on a point of law?

Section 108 of the 1959 Act gives a general right of appeal to the Court of Appeal on a point of law to any party who is dissatisfied with the judge's determination. Section 109

1 [1894] 1 Ch 485
2 [1913] 1 KB 547, [1911–13] All ER Rep 661
3 [1940] 3 All ER 282, [1940] 2 KB 306

specifies the circumstances in which there may be an appeal on a question of fact. None of them is applicable here.

What then is the effect of the words of Sch 8, para 2, to the Housing Act 1974, 'such determination shall be final and conclusive'? Since there is in any event no appeal on fact, the words of the schedule can only apply to questions of law and one must therefore conclude that they are effective to bar an appeal on a point of law. There is nothing else to which they can apply.

It follows from that reasoning that the only circumstances in which this court can correct what is to my mind the error of the county court judge is if he was acting in excess of his jurisdiction as opposed to merely making an error of law in his judgment by misinterpreting the meaning of 'structural alteration . . . or addition'.

In order to determine the ambit of the words 'excess of jurisdiction' one must turn to the decision of the House of Lords in *Anisminic Ltd v Foreign Compensation Commission*[1]. The effect of the majority speeches in that case may perhaps be expressed as follows. Where words in a statute purport to oust the jurisdiction of the High Court to review the decision of an inferior tribunal they must be construed strictly. That is to say, if there is more than one way in which they can reasonably be construed the construction which impairs the power of the High Court the least should be selected. A provision to the effect that the determination of a tribunal 'shall not be called in question in any court of law' does not exclude the power of the High Court to quash a decision which has been reached by the tribunal acting in excess of its jurisdiction. Jurisdiction in this sense has a wide meaning. It includes any case where the apparent determination of the tribunal turns out on examination to be a nullity, because it cannot properly be called a determination at all. Lord Reid said this[2]:

> 'But there are many cases where, although the tribunal had jurisdiction to enter on the enquiry, it has done or failed to do something in the course of the enquiry which is of such a nature that its decision is a nullity. It may have given its decision in bad faith. It may have made a decision which it had no power to make. It may have failed in the course of the enquiry to comply with the requirements of natural justice. It may in perfect good faith have misconstrued the provisions giving it power to act so that it failed to deal with the question remitted to it and decided some question which was not remitted to it. It may have refused to take into account something which it was required to take into account. Or it may have based its decision on some matter which, under the provisions setting it up, it had no right to take into account. I do not intend this list to be exhaustive. But if it decides a question remitted to it for decision without committing any of these errors it is as much entitled to decide that question wrongly as it is to decide it rightly.'

In that case the Foreign Compensation Commission in adjudicating on the appellants' claim to compensation considered that they were bound by the relevant order to determine whether the appellants had a 'successor in title' and if so whether that successor was a British national. Having decided that there was such a successor and that he was not a British national they considered themselves obliged to reject the claim. In fact the order did not require them to make any determination at all about 'successors in title' or their nationality and the commission was basing its decision 'on some matter which, under the provisions setting it up, it had no right to take into account'. Therefore the apparent or purported determination was a nullity and no determination at all and was not protected by the words of ouster. Lord Wilberforce, expressing similar views in somewhat different terms, said this[3]:

---

1   [1969] 1 All ER 208, [1969] 2 AC 147
2   [1969] 1 All ER 208 at 213–214, [1969] 2 AC 147 at 171
3   [1969] 1 All ER 208 at 246, [1969] 2 AC 147 at 210

'. . . the cases in which a tribunal has been held to have passed outside its proper limits are not limited to those in which it had no power to enter on its enquiry or its jurisdiction, or has not satisfied a condition precedent. Certainly such cases exist (for example *Ex p. Bradlaugh*[1]) but they do not exhaust the principle. A tribunal may quite properly validly enter on its task and in the course of carrying it out may make a decision which is invalid—not merely erroneous. This may be described as "asking the wrong question" or "applying the wrong test"—expressions not wholly satisfactory since they do not, in themselves, distinguish between doing something which is not in the tribunal's area and doing something wrong within that area—a crucial distinction which the court has to make.'

It is plain that this decision makes the ambit of excess of jurisdiction very wide, but does it embrace what the judge did in the present case?

For my part I am unable to see what the judge did which went outside the proper area of his enquiry. He seems to have taken the view that the word 'structural' qualifies the following words, 'alteration, extension or addition' and does not qualify the part of the house to which the alterations etc are made. That is to say the words do not mean 'non-structural alterations or additions to a structure'. Assuming he was wrong in that method of interpreting the words of Sch 8 to the 1974 Act, it does not seem to me to be going outside his terms of reference in any way at all, nor does it contravene any of the precepts suggested by their Lordships which I have already cited. The question is not whether he made a wrong decision, but whether he enquired into and decided a matter which he had no right to consider: see per Lord Reid[2].

The judge summarised matters in the final passage of his judgment as follows: 'I think in the final analysis it is a matter of first impression tested by argument, analogy and illustration and finally it is a question of fact. There can be little doubt. I do not intend to give any definition at all.' In short what he is saying is that in his view the works executed by the tenant did not amount to structural alteration or addition, within the ordinary meaning of those words. I am, I fear, unable to see how that determination, assuming it to be an erroneous determination, can properly be said to be a determination which he was not entitled to make. The judge is considering the words in the schedule which he ought to consider. He is not embarking on some unauthorised or extraneous or irrelevant exercise. All he has done is to come to what appears to this court to be a wrong conclusion on a difficult question. It seems to me that, if this judge is acting outside his jurisdiction, so then is every judge who comes to a wrong decision on a point of law. Accordingly, I take the view that no form of certiorari is available to the tenant. I am fortified in this view of the matter by the fact that counsel for the tenant accepted that the judge was acting within his jurisdiction, and added that 'the nature of the judge's error was within his jurisdiction and was in relation to his interpretation and construction of the schedule'. Consequently counsel for the landlords did not feel himself obliged to address us on the *Anisminic*[3] line of argument. Indeed for that reason alone I would have been reluctant to allow the appeal.

I would accordingly dismiss this appeal.

EVELEIGH LJ. By Sch 8, para 2(2), to the Housing Act 1974 the judge in the county court is given a trenchant power. His determination on certain matters is made final and conclusive. That finality will affect not only the immediate parties but also their successors. His determination will be virtually decisive in many cases of the wider question, namely whether or not the tenant has the right to buy the freehold and, should that question come before the High Court in an action by the tenant claiming that right, the determination of the county court judge affecting as it does the vital factor of rateable value will be binding on that court. Apart from para 2(2) of Sch 8 the judge would have

---

1   (1878) 3 QBD 509
2   [1969] 1 All ER 208 at 216, [1969] 2 AC 147 at 174
3   [1969] 1 All ER 208, [1969] 2 AC 147

no say in the matter at all. The simple determination could not come within the exercise of his general jurisdiction as a judge of the county court. By Sch 8 he is given arbitral power. Parliament would look on it in another light also. It has imposed on him a duty. That duty is to answer certain questions which the law is asking. In so far as he answers them his determination is binding. If he answers some other question he is wasting everybody's time. He is not performing his duty. He is not exercising any power granted to him by Parliament. His decision is ultra vires. It is a nullity. Because his jurisdiction extends to answering a different question only, the determination which he has made will be outside his jurisdiction.

I believe that this is the approach to the question indicated by *Anisminic Ltd v Foreign Compensation Commission*[1]. I do not regard that decision as being in any way revolutionary. It has been said that the power of the court by certiorari to control errors of law has lain dormant for over a hundred years. This assertion is more pertinent in relation to an error on the face of the record made within the jurisdiction or intra vires. It is not true of certiorari used to ensure that the tribunal does not exceed its jurisdictional power.

In Wade on Administrative Law[2] we read:

'. . . the rule that a determination which is ultra vires may always be challenged in the High Court. This is no more than the corollary of the main principle of jurisdictional control, which ordains that no tribunal can give itself jurisdiction which it does not possess.'

In other words a tribunal cannot give itself power to decide a question that Parliament has not empowered it to answer. The absurdity of allowing the tribunal so to do is all the more apparent when Parliament has made the answer of the tribunal binding on other courts. That the answer to a question which has not been asked should be binding on a court as the answer to a totally different question which Parliament requires to be asked is utterly absurd.

In *Bunbury v Fuller*[3] Coleridge J said:

'Now it is a general rule, that no Court of limited jurisdiction can give itself jurisdiction by a wrong decision on a point collateral to the merits of the case upon which the limit to its jurisdiction depends; and however its decision may be final on all particulars, making up together that subject-matter which, if true, is within its jurisdiction, and, however necessary in many cases it may be for it to make a preliminary inquiry, whether some collateral matter be or be not within the limits, yet, upon this preliminary question, its decision must always be open to inquiry in the superior Court.'

In the present case, before the tribunal could embark on its enquiry, it was necessary for it to decide the meaning of the question it was required to answer. This was a collateral matter. It had nothing to do with the merits of the case. It was indeed 'a point collateral to the merits of the case upon which the limit to its jurisdiction depend'.

It is not for the county court judge to decide, ie to lay down, what 'structural alteration, extension or addition' means, although of course he has to comprehend what it means before he can answer the question he is empowered to decide under Sch 8, para 2(2). Parliament determines what structural alteration means. If the county court judge proceeds to answer the question having wrongly comprehended its meaning his decision is a nullity.

Fundamentally it is necessary to ask if the '. . . tribunal has jurisdiction to enter on the enquiry and to decide a particular issue . . .': see Lord Reid in *Armah v Government of Ghana*[4]. The fundamental question which the court is entitled to and must decide is

---

1 [1969] 2 AC 147 at 234, per Browne J
2 4th Edn (1977), p 232
3 (1853) 9 Exch 111 at 140
4 [1966] 3 All ER 177 at 187, [1968] AC 192 at 234

whether the judge was entitled to enter on the enquiry he in fact made. He had to ask whether the work was 'works amounting to structural alteration, extension or addition'. If in his mind those words meant X and by using those words Parliament meant Y the judge was answering a question he was not asked.

It is clear to my mind that the reason why two judges on identical facts gave different answers to the question was because one understood it to mean one thing and the other understood it to mean another. The facts of the cases permit of no other explanation. In the case before this court we can discover how the judge understood the question. He has delivered a judgment in which he explains his approach to the words 'works amounting to structural alteration, extension or addition'. In my opinion he wrongly understood the meaning of those words. He therefore did not answer the question he was asked. In *Anisminic*[1] Lord Pearce said:

'It would lead to an absurd situation if a tribunal, having been given a circumscribed area of enquiry, carved out from the general jurisdiction of the courts, were entitled of its own motion to extend that area by misconstruing the limits of its mandate to enquire and decide as set out in the Act of Parliament. If, for instance, Parliament were to carve out an area of enquiry within which an inferior domestic tribunal could give certain relief to wives against their husbands, it would not lie within the power of that tribunal to extend the area of enquiry and decision, i.e., jurisdiction, thus committed to it by construing "wives" as including all women who, without marriage, cohabited with a man for a substantial period . . .'

By the use of certiorari the courts ensure that the right question is answered and that the answer to the wrong question is not accepted. The courts thus ensure that a decision is arrived at in accordance with Parliament's intention. Lord Pearce said[2]:

'It is simply an enforcement of Parliament's mandate to the tribunal. If the tribunal is intended, on a true construction of the Act, to enquire into and finally decide questions within a certain area, the courts' supervisory duty is to see that it makes the authorised enquiry according to natural justice and arrives at a decision whether right or wrong. They will intervene if the tribunal asks itself the wrong questions (i.e., questions other than those which Parliament directed it to ask itself).'

There are several passages in the speeches of their Lordships to the same effect, namely that if the tribunal answers the wrong question its determination is a nullity.

One must therefore seek to determine what the question was which the county court judge was required to ask. The judge had to ask himself whether the improvement specified in the notice was 'an improvement . . . to which this Schedule applies'. He could only answer that question if he knew what it was to which the schedule applied. Schedule 8, para 1(2), reads: 'This Schedule applies to any improvement made by the execution of works amounting to structural alteration, extension or addition.' In my opinion 'structural' means appertaining to the fabric of a building so as to be a part of the complex whole. In *Pickering v Phillimore*[3] his Honour Judge White said:

'A house is a "complex unity", particularly a modern house. "Structural" implies concern with the "constituent or material" parts of that unity. What are the "constituent" or "material" parts? In my judgment in any ordinary sense they involve more than simply the load bearing elements, for example the four walls, the roof and the foundations. The constituent parts are more complex than that.' [He then suggested a definition of "structural" as being] Appertaining to the basic fabric and parts of the house as distinguished from its decorations and fittings.'

The judge said that it would be wrong to describe the central heating system as mainly

---

1   [1969] 1 All ER 208 at 233, [1969] 2 AC 147 at 194
2   [1969] 1 All ER 208 at 233–234, [1969] 2 AC 147 at 195
3   (10th May 1976) unreported

a fittings for throughout the house the system became built into it and became part of it in a layman's sense.

In my opinion Judge White has the right conception of what Parliament meant by structural. In the case before this court the county court judge perhaps wisely did not attempt a definition. There is much to be said for that approach. Alternative definitions often take the matter no further. However when a word has more than one meaning the court has to make up its mind which meaning it will adopt and it is helpful if it says so not *b* as an alternative definition but as an explanation of what Parliament meant by the words in question. However the judge did reject the meaning adopted by Judge White. From this it follows that he was proceeding on some other meaning of the word and consequently asked himself the wrong question.

I agree with the judgments just delivered that the central heating in this case comes within the wording of the schedule. In the course of argument there was some conjecture *c* as to why the expression used was 'works amounting to . . .' In my opinion it is because we have to look at the final result. That which is achieved must amount to a structural alteration, extension or addition. Work that simply involves structural alteration will not necessarily come within the definition. I have had some difficulty in persuading myself that there is no appeal on a point of law from the decision of the judge in the county court. I have been inclined to treat his determination as final and conclusive only on questions of *d* fact. Paragraph 2(2) of Sch 8 lists matters for the judge's determination which is made final and conclusive but I regard them all as questions of fact. It may well be, however, that as the decision was a nullity the court must say that there is nothing to appeal against. Therefore, I regard the remedy of certiorari as more appropriate to the present situation. I agree with the judgments just delivered that the County Court Act 1959 does not exclude certiorari in the kind of case which goes to jurisdiction. I would also add that for myself *e* I did not understand counsel for the tenant to say that the judge was acting within his jurisdiction in the sense with which the *Anisminic* case[1] deals. He seemed to be taking the view that, because this was a judge and not a tribunal, different considerations applied. He was wrong in that, and I think he realised this when he came to reply when he developed the argument more fully. In any event, certiorari is a matter for the court to decide where necessary, and I therefore agree with Lord Denning MR that certiorari should go in this *f* case.

Appeal allowed. Leave to appeal to the House of Lords granted.

Solicitors: *Enever, Freeman & Co*, Ruislip (for the tenant); *Fladgate & Co* (for the landlords).

g   Gavin Gore-Andrews Esq   Barrister.

---

1   [1969] 1 All ER 208, [1969] 2 AC 147

George Veflings Rederi A/S v President of India
and other appeals
The Bellami, The Pearl Merchant, The Doric Chariot

COURT OF APPEAL, CIVIL DIVISION
LORD DENNING MR, GEOFFREY LANE AND EVELEIGH LJJ
10th MAY 1978

Money – Currency – Date at which rate of exchange calculated – Charterparty providing for demurrage to be calculated in dollars – No provision for payment in sterling – Freight payable in sterling in London at rate of exchange on bill of lading date – Charterers paying demurrage in sterling at rate of exchange on bill of lading date – Fall in value of sterling between bill of lading date and date of payment – Whether demurrage required to be paid at rate of exchange on bill of lading date or date of payment.

In two separate charterparties demurrage was to be paid at a rate calculated in US dollars while freight was to be paid in British external sterling at the 'exchange rate ruling on Bill of Lading date'. In the first case the bill of lading date was February 1975 and the charterers incurred demurrage in May amounting to $US 66,219. In December 1975 and May 1976 they paid in sterling the equivalent of the demurrage due in US dollars at the rate of exchange on the bill of lading date. Because of the fall in sterling against the dollar between February 1975 and the dates of payment, the sterling paid yielded substantially less dollars when the payments were made than it would have yielded in February 1975. The owners of the vessel claimed the shortfall, contending that the rate of exchange applicable to demurrage was that ruling at the date of payment. The charterers contended that the same rate of exchange applied to payment of both demurrage and freight, namely that ruling on the bill of lading date. Alternatively, they contended that the applicable rate of exchange for payment of demurrage was that ruling when the demurrage was incurred, ie May 1975, which also produced a shortfall although less than that produced by exchange at the rate ruling at the dates of payment.

In the second case the charterers similarly paid in sterling the equivalent of the demurrage due at the rate of exchange ruling on the bill of lading date. On the owners claiming the difference between the sum paid and the sterling required to be paid to yield the same amount of US dollars at the rate of exchange on the date of payment, the charterers contended that the relevant rate of exchange was that ruling when laytime accounts were settled and the demurrage calculated. Furthermore, they contended that the money of payment of the demurrage, as well as the money of account, was sterling because the charterparty provided that freight was payable in London in sterling, and the charterparty was governed by English law.

Held – Where a charterparty provided that demurrage was to be calculated in US dollars, and did not provide for it to be paid in sterling, the reasonable inference was that the money of payment, as well as the money of account, was US dollars, even though the charterparty provided for freight to be payable in sterling, and for the contract to be governed by English law. Since the money of payment and account of demurrage was US dollars, the rate of exchange was that prevailing at the date of payment of the demurrage and, accordingly, in each case the owners were entitled to the difference between the sum actually paid and the sum required to be paid at the rate of exchange ruling at the date of payment to yield the amount due in US dollars and to have that balance awarded in US dollars (see p 383 *j* to p 384 *a* and *c* to *f*, post).

Miliangos v George Frank (Textiles) Ltd [1975] 3 All ER 801 applied.

Decision of Donaldson J [1978] 3 All ER 838 affirmed.

Notes

For the conversion of money payable in foreign currency into sterling, see 27 Halsbury's Laws (3rd Edn) 6, para 5, and for cases on the subject, see 35 Digest (Repl) 194–196, 51–59.

Cases referred to in judgments

Miliangos v George Frank (Textiles) Ltd [1975] 3 All ER 801, [1976] AC 443, [1975] 3 WLR 758, [1976] 1 Lloyd's Rep 201, HL, Digest (Cont Vol D) 571, 6786.

Woodhouse AC Israel Cocoa Ltd SA v Nigerian Produce Marketing Co Ltd [1971] 1 All ER 665, [1971] 2 QB 23, [1971] 2 WLR 272, [1971] Lloyd's Rep 25, CA; *affd* [1972] 2 All ER 271, [1972] AC 741, [1972] 2 WLR 1090, [1972] 1 Lloyd's Rep 439, HL, Digest (Cont Vol D) 43, 1154d.

Appeals

George Veflings Rederi A/S v President of India, The Bellami

By a charterparty in the Ferticon form dated 28th February 1975 the claimants, George Veflings Rederi A/S ('the owners') chartered the vessel Bellami to the respondent, the President of India ('the charterers') for a voyage from Europe to India. Disputes were to be settled in London by arbitration. The charterparty provided that demurrage should be paid at the rate of $US 2,500 per day or pro rata, that the cargo should be delivered on freight being paid in British sterling and that freight should be paid in London by the charterers in British external sterling, 90% within seven days of submission of the necessary documents and the balance after completion of discharge and settlement of demurrage, at the rate expressed in US dollars. In the event the owners became entitled to demurrage and, on 7th November 1975, agreed to accept the charterers' calculation of the demurrage at $US 153,348·95. On 3rd December the charterers paid to the owners' account in London £63,334·62 which at the rate of exchange prevailing at the date of the bills of lading was the equivalent in US dollars of the demurrage incurred but, at the rate of exchange prevailing at the date of the payment was equivalent to only $US 127,840·93, leaving a net shortfall of $US 24,870·32. In an arbitration the owners claimed the amount of the shortfall contending that the demurrage was payable in US dollars or in such amount of sterling as would at the date of the payment of the demurrage enable the owners to buy the same amount of dollars. The charterers contended that the appropriate rate of exchange was that prevailing at the date of the bills of lading, and, therefore, their liability for demurrage was discharged, or alternatively, that the appropriate rate of exchange was that prevailing when the parties reached agreement as to the quantum of the demurrage, ie on 7th November 1975, and that accordingly the payment of the £63,334·62 had partially discharged the liability for demurrage and there remained outstanding only the sum of $US 21,813·65. The arbitrators awarded, in favour of the owners, that $US 24,870·32 was due and owing from the charterers, and stated their award in the form of a special case requesting the opinion of the court as to whether there was any sum due from the charterers to the owners and if so the amount. On 30th January 1978 Donaldson J[1] held that the rate of exchange ruling at the date of payment was the proper rate of exchange and accordingly upheld the arbitrators' award. The charterers appealed. The facts are set out in the judgment of Lord Denning MR.

Monrovia Tramp Shipping Co v President of India, The Pearl Merchant

By a voyage charterparty in the Ferticon form dated 5th February 1975 the claimants, Monrovia Tramp Shipping Co ('the owners'), chartered the vessel Pearl Merchant to the

---

1   [1978] 3 All ER 838, [1978] 1 WLR 982

respondent, the President of India ('the charterers'), for a voyage from Europe to India. Disputes were to be settled in London by arbitrators. The charterparty provided that *a* freight was payable in sterling at rates expressed in US dollars and was to be paid by the charterers to the owners in accordance with cl 30 of the charterparty in London in British external sterling, at the exchange rate ruling on the bill of lading date, and that demurrage was to be paid at the rate of $US 2,800 per running day or pro rata. Demurrage accrued at Bombay between 21st April and 15th May 1975 which at the charterparty rate amounted to $US 66,219·56 net after deduction of commission. On 23rd December 1975 and 3rd *b* May 1976 the charterers paid to the owners a total sum of £27,689·75 in settlement of the demurrage on the basis that the rate of exchange ruling on the bill of lading date, which was applicable to the payment of freight under cl 30 of the charterparty, was also applicable in discharging the liability for demurrage. In an arbitration the owners contended that the rate of exchange applicable to determine the amount of sterling payable to satisfy the claim for demurrage was the rate ruling on the date of payment of the demurrage. The charterers *c* contended that the rate of exchange applicable was that ruling on the bill of lading date or, alternatively, that the applicable rate was that ruling on the 25 days during which the demurrage accrued at Bombay. The arbitrators awarded that the rate of exchange ruling on the dates when the demurrage was actually paid was the applicable rate and, applying that rate, the total payment of £27,689·75 made on those dates produced only $US 54,924·04, and accordingly the charterers had failed to discharge their liability for the *d* net demurrage in the sum of $US 11,295·52, ie $US 66,219·56 less the sum of $US 54,924·04. The arbitrators stated their award in the form of a special case requesting the decision of the court as to whether on the facts found and the true construction of the charterparty the charterers had discharged their liability for demurrage and, if not, to what extent it was discharged by the payment of the £27,689·75. On 20th February 1978 Donaldson J upheld the arbitrators' award. The charterers appealed. The facts are set out *e* in the judgment of Lord Denning MR.

Marperfecta Compania Naviera S/A v President of India, The Doric Chariot

By a voyage charterparty on the Ferticon form dated 12th April 1975 the claimants, Marperfecta Compania Naviera SA ('the owners'), chartered the vessel Doric Chariot to the respondent, the President of India ('the charterers'), for a voyage from the US Gulf to India. Disputes were to be settled by arbitration in London. The charterparty contained terms for the payment of freight and demurrage similar to the terms of the charterparty relating to the Pearl Merchant. The vessel completed discharge on 16th December 1975. Demurrage in the net amount of $US 114,084·01 was incurred by the charterers. On 12th February 1976 the charterers paid the owners the sum of £49,042·16 in sterling which at *g* the exchange rate ruling on the bill of lading date yielded the net amount of dollars due for demurrage, but on the rate of exchange ruling on the date of payment yielded only $US 99,359·42. In an arbitration the owners contended that the rate of exchange applicable to determine the amount of sterling payable to satisfy the claim for demurrage was that ruling on the date of payment of the demurrage. The charterers contended that the rate of exchange applicable was that ruling on the bill of lading date or, alternatively, that *h* ruling on the date discharge was completed or, in the further alternative, that ruling on the 44 days during which demurrage accrued under the terms of the charterparty. The arbitrators awarded that the rate of exchange applicable to the payment of the demurrage was that ruling on 16th December, and on that basis the charterers' payment fell short of the net amount of demurrage by the sum of $US 13,351·41, and to that extent the owners' claim succeeded. The award was stated in the form of a special case requesting the decision of the court as to whether on the true construction of the charterparty and the facts found the charterers had discharged their liability in respect of demurrage in the amount of $US 114,084·01, and if not, to what extent such liability was discharged by the payment on 12th February 1976 of the £49,042·16. On 5th April 1978 Lloyd J held that the rate of exchange applicable to demurrage was that ruling on the date when the charterers had in fact paid the owners and accordingly that the charterers had discharged their liability to the owners in the amount of $US 99,359·42 only and remained liable to the owners in the sum of $US 14,724·59. The charterers appealed.

A R Barrowclough QC and *Vasant Kothari* for the charterers.
Bernard Rix for the owners in the first appeal.
R J Thomas for the owners in the second and third appeals.

LORD DENNING MR. These three cases raise a point about the currency in which demurrage is payable. Typical is the case of the Pearl Merchant. In February 1975 the vessel was chartered to carry a cargo of fertiliser from Europe to India. She completed discharging at Bombay on 15th May 1975. At Bombay demurrage accrued between 21st April and 15th May 1975 over a total period of 24 days. By cl 9 of the charterparty: 'If the vessel is detained longer than the time allowed for loading and/or discharging demurrage shall be paid at $[US] 2,800 per running day.'

The vessel carried the goods through to India. On arriving in India, she was discharged at Bombay. She finished discharging on 15th May 1975. Demurrage accrued while she was at Bombay over 24 days. The total came to $US 66,219·56.

At the bill of lading date in February 1975 the rate of exchange was $US 2·3915 to the pound sterling. At the date in April or May 1975 (on which the demurrage was incurred under the charterparty) the pound had weakened. The rate of exchange was then $US 2·3370 to the pound sterling. The demurrage was eventually paid a good deal later, on 23rd December 1975. By that time the rate of exchange had fallen to $US 2·0225 to the pound sterling.

The question is how is the demurrage to be paid? The total is $US 66,219·56. Which is the rate of exchange? Is it to be taken at the bill of lading rate of $US 2·3915 to the pound sterling? Or at the rate when demurrage was incurred which was $US 2·3370 to the pound sterling? Or at the rate on the date when it was paid which was $US 2·0225 to the pound sterling?

In the first place, the charterers claim that the rate of exchange should be taken as at the date of the bill of lading in February 1975. They rely on cl 30 of the charterparty which was in these terms:

'The freight shall be paid in London to N.G. Livanos Maritime Co. Ltd., current account at Williams and Glyn's Bank Ltd., 22 St. Mary Axe, London EC3 by Charterers in British external sterling, 90 percent within 7 days of submission of documents to the Indian High Commission, London but while claiming the 90 percent freight Owners to submit their debit note, in triplicate, together with supporting documents such as the Bill of Lading and Charter Party. Balance freight will be paid after completion of discharge and settlement of demurrage/despatch on production of paid voucher from the Charterers' broker to whom commission is due under the terms of the Charter Party. Freight payable on nett Bill of Lading weight at exchange rate ruling on Bill of Lading date. Entire freight to be on vessel's Owners risk up to 7 days from signing Bills of Lading.'

The charterers rely on one sentence in that clause: 'Freight payable on nett Bill of Lading weight at exchange rate ruling on Bill of Lading date', together with the sentence which refers to the ten per cent balance freight: 'Balance freight will be paid after completion of discharge and settlement of demurrage.'

It seems to me that, although the freight was payable at the February rate, it is different with demurrage. I see no reason whatever for making the demurrage payable at the February rate. The bill of lading date does not apply to demurrage. That is the first point. In the second place, the charterers claim that demurrage should be payable at the rate of exchange prevailing in May 1975 when it was incurred. That would have been the rate before *Miliangos v George Frank (Textiles) Ltd*[1]. But since the *Miliangos* case[1] the law on this subject has been revolutionised. It seems to me clear that the rate of exchange should be the rate prevailing at the date of payment. That is the second point.

The Bellami raises a third point. In the case of the Bellami demurrage was payable at the rate of $US 2,500 per day. The goods were loaded in Europe in March 1975 and discharging was completed in Calcutta on 1st August 1975. Demurrage was earned for 61 days coming to $US 153,348. The charterers claimed that the rate of exchange should be taken at the date when the calculations were completed, which was 7th November 1975 when the rate was US $2·8680 to the pound sterling. The remaining date would be the day of payment, 3rd December 1975, when the rate was $US 2·0185 to the pound sterling.

On this point we have had much discussion as to the 'money of account' and 'the money of payment'. The difference was explained in *Woodhouse AC Israel Cocoa Ltd SA v Nigerian Produce Marketing Co Ltd*[2]. It seems to me that in all three cases, so far as demurrage was concerned, the money of account was US dollars. What about the money of payment? The charterers sought to say that the money of payment was sterling. They rely on the fact that the freight was payable in London in British external sterling and because the contract was governed by English law. But demurrage is different from freight. I see no reason to think that demurrage was payable in sterling. So far as demurrage was concerned, the money of account was US dollars and the money of payment was also US dollars. The rate of exchange should be taken at the date of payment, not at the date of calculation. This is the clear result of the *Miliangos* case[1].

When you find, as here, that the demurrage is to be calculated in US dollars and that there is no provision for it to be paid in sterling, then it is a reasonable inference that the money is payable in US dollars. In each case the owners are entitled to have the balance awarded in US dollars.

I think the arbitrators in each of these cases were correct, and I would dismiss the appeals accordingly.

GEOFFREY LANE LJ. I agree.

EVELEIGH LJ. I also agree.

Appeals dismissed. Leave to appeal to the House of Lords refused.

Solicitors: *Stocken & Co* (for the charterers); *Sinclair, Roche & Temperley* (for the owners in the first appeal); *Holman, Fenwick & Willan* (for the owners in the second and third appeals).

Gavin Gore-Andrews Esq   Barrister.

---

1   [1975] 3 All ER 801, [1976] AC 443
2   [1971] 1 All ER 665, [1971] 2 QB 23

Clark v Inland Revenue Commissioners

CHANCERY DIVISION
FOX J
29th, 30th JUNE, 31st JULY 1978

Income tax – Tax advantage – Transaction in securities – Bona fide commercial reasons – Commercial reasons – Taxpayer and his brother selling all the issued share capital in H Ltd to a family company to perpetuate family control of another company – Taxpayer selling his shares in H Ltd for the purpose of raising money to purchase neighbouring farm to improve his farming business – Sale of shares resulting in tax advantage – Whether sale of shares carried out for 'bona fide commercial reasons' – Income and Corporation Taxes Act 1970, s 460(1).

The taxpayer was a farmer who owned a 400 acre farm. He also owned 50 per cent of the shares in H Ltd which was a private investment company. The other 50 per cent of the shares was owned by the taxpayer's brother. The assets of H Ltd consisted mainly of quoted shares in a public company, C Ltd, of which the taxpayer's father was chairman and managing director. The taxpayer also owned shares in E Ltd which was a private investment company. The other shares of E Ltd were held by members of the taxpayer's family or by family trusts. Late in 1969 the taxpayer learnt that an adjoining farm was shortly to be sold by auction and he decided to purchase it. He considered that he would require about £50,000 to complete the purchase and decided to sell his shares in H Ltd to raise that sum. His brother decided that if the taxpayer was going to sell he also would sell his shares in H Ltd, and, to meet their father's wish that control of C Ltd be kept within the family, the taxpayer and his brother sold the total shareholding in H Ltd to E Ltd for £102,000. The taxpayer used his half of the proceeds to purchase the adjoining farm. The Crown considered that the taxpayer had obtained a tax advantage in consequence of a transaction in securities (ie the sale of the shares in H Ltd) within s 460(1)[a] of the Income and Corporation Taxes Act 1970 and accordingly issued a notice under s 460(3) specifying adjustments necessary to counteract the tax advantage obtained. The taxpayer appealed against the notice to the Special Commissioners. He conceded that he had obtained a tax advantage from the transaction but contended that the transaction was carried out 'for bona fide commercial reasons' and did not have 'as [its] main object, or one of [its] main objects, to enable tax advantages to be obtained' and therefore came within the exception referred to in s 460(1). The commissioners accepted that the taxpayer's principal reason for carrying out the transaction had been to obtain the sum required to purchase the adjoining farm, that there had been commercial reasons for him doing so, and that the transaction had not had the obtaining of a tax advantage as its main object. They held however that for the transaction to have been carried out for bona fide commercial reasons, within s 460(1), it was necessary for it to have been connected with the taxpayer's interest in the companies concerned which the taxpayer's farming venture had not been. They therefore upheld the notices. The taxpayer appealed.

Held – On the true construction of s 460(1) of the 1970 Act the commercial reason for carrying out a transaction did not have to be connected with the taxpayer's interests in the companies concerned before the taxpayer could claim to be exempted from s 460. It was sufficient if, having regard to the context of all the circumstances which gave rise to the transaction, it was carried out for a commercial reason, which need not be intrinsic to the transaction. On the facts, the predominant reason for the taxpayer carrying out the transaction was the wholly commercial reason of acquiring the adjoining farm and he was therefore entitled to exception from s 460. The appeal would therefore be allowed (see p 394 j to p 395 a and c d and j to p 396 b and e to g and p 397 a b, post).

Dictum of Lord Pearce in *Inland Revenue Comrs v Brebner* [1967] 1 All ER at 781 applied.

---

a   Section 460, so far as material, is set out at p 393 c d, post.

Notes

For cancellation of tax advantages from certain transactions in securities, see 23 Halsbury's Laws (4th Edn) para 1462, and for cases on the subject, see 28(1) Digest (Reissue) 489–492, 1753–1759.

For the Income and Corporation Taxes Act 1970, s 460, 33 Halsbury's Statutes (3rd Edn) 591.

Cases referred to in judgment

Cleary v Inland Revenue Comrs [1967] 2 All ER 48, [1968] AC 766, [1967] 2 WLR 1271, 44 Tax Cas 399, 46 ATC 51, [1967] TR 57, HL, 28(1) Digest (Reissue) 489, 1753.

Inland Revenue Comrs v Brebner [1967] 1 All ER 779, [1967] 2 AC 18, [1967] 2 WLR 1001, 43 Tax Cas 705, 46 ATC 17, [1967] TR 21, 1967 SC(HL) 31, HL, 28(1) Digest (Reissue) 490, 1755.

Inland Revenue Comrs v Brown [1971] 3 All ER 502, [1971] 1 WLR 1495, 47 Tax Cas 217, 50 ATC 211, [1971] TR 185, CA, Digest (Cont Vol D) 495, 1759a.

Case also cited

Inland Revenue Comrs v Goodwin [1976] 1 All ER 481, [1976] 1 WLR 191, [1976] STC 28, HL.

Case stated

1. At a meeting of the Commissioners for the Special Purposes of the Income Tax Acts held on 2nd and 3rd May 1977, Robin Clark ('Robin') appealed against a notice dated 13th May 1976 given by the Commissioners of Inland Revenue under the provisions of s 460(3) of the Income and Corporation Taxes Act 1970 and against the following assessments to tax made in accordance therewith: 1970–71, income tax Sch D, Case VI, £51,000; 1970–71, surtax (further assessment), £51,000.

[Paragraphs 2 and 3 listed the witnesses who gave evidence and the documents proved or admitted before the commissioners.]

4. As a result of the evidence both oral and documentary adduced before them, the commissioners found the following facts proved or admitted.

Equity. (1) Equity was incorporated in 1938 as a private company with the name of Langholm Investment Trust Ltd; its name was changed to The Equity Trust Ltd in 1962. Among the objects stated in its memorandum of association were:

'To carry on the business of an investment trust company, and in particular to invest in land, tenements and hereditaments, and to purchase, subscribe for or otherwise acquire, and to hold and dispose of shares, stocks, debentures, debenture stocks, bonds, obligations and securities.'

(2) Only one class of shares (£1 ordinary shares) in Equity was ever authorised or issued. The original allotment of 7,300 £1 ordinary shares was made for cash to:

James Walkinshaw Wishart	1
George William Alexander Gray	1
Robert (Robin's father)	4,648
Mrs Mary Black Clark ('Mary')	
Robert's wife	2,650
	7,300

Equity made subsequent allotments at various times of its shares, some for cash and some by way of capitalising sums standing to the credit of its capital reserve account and applying them in paying up bonus allotments of shares to the existing shareholders. By 1960 the total issued share capital was 100,000 and subsequent bonus issues of 400,000 and 500,000 brought the total to 500,000 and 1,000,000 in 1963 and 1971 respectively. Since at least 1950 all the shares had at all times been held by Robert, Mary, Colin (Robin's brother), Robin, Robin's wife Patricia and trustees of trusts of which Robin, Colin and their respective wives and issue were the principal beneficiaries under discretionary trusts. On 6th April 1970 the shares were held as follows:

Robert	12,600
Mary	12,600
Colin	187,000
Robin	187,000
James Harold MacDonald, Sir John Johnson Campbell and Colin as trustees for Robin, his issue and any wife of his	50,400
James Harold MacDonald, Sir John Johnson Campbell and Robin as trustees for Colin, his issue and any wife of his	50,400
	500,000

(3) At all material times Equity operated as an investment company; its investments were principally in securities issued by other companies. On 5th April 1970 Equity held more than ten per cent of the issued equity share capital of 11 other companies, and in nine of these 11 companies Equity held more than 30 per cent of the issued equity share capital (including Caledonian Associated Cinemas Ltd ('Caledonian') and W Lang (Timber) Ltd). At all material times Equity was a private company and none of its shares or other securities was authorised to be dealt in on a stock exchange in the United Kingdom. (4) At the material times Robert was the governing director of Equity and each of Robin and Colin was a director. Under art 93 of the articles of association of Equity no resolution of the directors 'shall be valid and effective without the consent of the Governing Director'.

Highland. (5) Highland was incorporated in 1958 as a private company. Among the objects stated in its memorandum of association were: 'To carry on the business of an Investment Company and to acquire and hold stocks, shares, debentures . . . ' (6) Only one class of shares (£1 Ordinary shares) in Highland was ever authorised and at all material times its issued share capital was 2,000 shares. Of these, Colin became entitled to 1,000 shares in 1965 from a trust and Robin became entitled to 1,000 shares in 1968 from another trust. On 6th April 1970 Colin and Robin each held 1,000 shares. (7) At all material times Highland operated as an investment company. By 6th April 1970 its principal fixed asset was 80,001 5 shilling ordinary shares in Caledonian representing 20 per cent of the issued ordinary share capital of Caledonian.

Caledonian. (8) Caledonian was incorporated in 1935. At the material time it was a public company whose shares were dealt in on the Glasgow Stock Exchange and subsequently on the London Stock Exchange. At 6th April 1970 the issued share capital of Caledonian was £243,181 divided into 400,000 5 shilling ordinary shares and 143,181 £1 seven per cent cumulative preference shares. Among the holders of 5 shilling ordinary shares at that date were:

Robert	2,667
Equity	130,361
Highland	80,001
W Lang (Timber) Ltd	2,000
Others	184,971
	400,000

(9) At the material time Caledonian carried on business principally as cinema and bingo hall proprietors. It had several subsidiaries engaged in, among other activities, finance, *a* property development and dealing in photographic equipment.

Sale by Colin and Robin to Equity of their shares in Highland. (10) On 6th April 1970 each of Colin and Robin sold his entire holding of shares in Highland to Equity for £51,000. Payment was to be made in cash on the same day. £102,000 represented the net asset value of Highland, taking its shares in Caledonian at the mid-market price at which they were *b* quoted in the Stock Exchange official list. (11) On 22nd March 1971 Highland sold its 80,001 5 shilling ordinary shares in Caledonian to Equity for £100,001, representing the mid-market price at which those shares were quoted in the Stock Exchange official list. The £100,001 was left outstanding on loan from Highland to Equity, and remained on loan when a resolution for the members' voluntary liquidation of Highland was passed on 27th September 1972. (12) (a) Apart from his interest in family companies Robin had *c* qualified as a chartered accountant (although he had never been in practice as such). He was, as he still is, a farmer and owned a 400 acre farm in Wiltshire. Robert disapproved of this farming venture. Late in 1969 Robin learned that Lower Penn Farm, a 273 acre farm which adjoined his own, was to be sold by auction in the spring of 1970. He thought (and events proved him right) that it would be profitable to buy it and to run the two farms as one. He regarded this chance to buy the adjoining farm as the opportunity of a lifetime *d* as the resultant entity could be farmed more efficiently. In the expectation that the price of Lower Penn Farm would be about £70,000 (he eventually bought it by private treaty for about £65,000) he reviewed his resources. He had about £20,000 in cash and decided that his shares in Highland (whose assets were entirely quoted shares) were the easiest to value and sell and that they would fetch much about the extra cash he needed. He had no personal investments quoted on the Stock Exchange. (b) As Robin did not have a majority *e* shareholding in Highland he thought that it would be easier to sell his shares if Colin who owned the other 50 per cent of them was to join him in the sale. Accordingly he suggested to Colin that they should together sell all the issued capital in Highland. (c) Robin discussed his plans with Robert. The latter was strenuously opposed to the Highland shares being sold at all, and certainly to their being sold outside the family with the consequent loss of the family control of Caledonian. Robert was chairman and managing director of *f* Caledonian and was determined, if possible, to retain those offices. He had recently lost his offices as deputy chairman and chief executive of a large public company which had been taken over. This had caused him much distress and he feared that the same thing might happen if the Clark family lost control of Caledonian. He was also anxious about the welfare of other long serving employees of Caledonian if that company was to be taken over. Robert suggested to Robin that instead of selling his Highland shares he should *g* borrow from the bank. Robin, however, did not wish to borrow: he wanted to stand on his own feet and believed that he could best do so by selling the shares to raise the cash that he needed. (d) Robert then persuaded Robin that the best course was to sell the Highland shares to Equity instead of to outsiders, thus achieving a situation which fitted in with the general intention of a scheme which had been recommended by Peat Marwick Mitchell & Co ('Peat') in 1965 for the simplification of the structure of a number of companies in *h* which the Clark family had interests. It was one of the features of Peat's recommendations that Equity should as an investment holding company act as parent company to the whole family group. Peat's scheme did not, however, involve large sums of cash being extracted from the family companies for the benefit of shareholders. In the first year following Peat's recommendations some progress had been made in their implementation but thereafter no progress had been made as the family could not agree about one of the major *j* features of the scheme, a matter not otherwise relevant to the present proceedings. The sale of the Highland shares to Equity, although it was a limited step in the direction of Peat's recommendations, did not (being a sale for cash) conform to them in detail and it did not accompany a comprehensive implementation of those parts of the scheme that had not at that time been put into effect. (e) Colin had no immediate need of cash and would not have thought of selling his Highland shares if Robin had not been selling his; but he did not want to be left with a 50 per cent holding if his brother had disposed of the remaining 50 per cent. He took the view that this would reduce the value of his holding and that the prudent course would be to join Robin in the sale so that each of them would get a better price than if he were selling separately. Subsidiary reasons for Colin's joining in the sale were that he wanted to oblige his brother Robin and his father Robert. Colin, like his brother Robin, had qualified as a chartered accountant but had never been in practice as such. He is an art historian. (f) Following his discussion with Robert, Robin drew up a memorandum on 7th January 1970 and sent it to Peat for comment. The memorandum included the following:

> 'The Shareholders (ie Robin Clark 50% and Colin Clark 50%) wish to realise their investment in "Highland". There are two methods by which this could be done: (1) By selling the shares of "Highland". The sale would have to be to another "connected company" as the family wish to retain control of "CAC". This would involve a proper valuation of the shares in "Highland" to insure the sale is for full value. (2) By liquidating the company and (a) distributing the "CAC" shares in "specie" or (b) by selling the "CAC" shares and distributing the cash sale proceeds.'

This memorandum was among a variety of matters discussed on 21st January between Robert, Robin and Mr Parsons, a partner in Peat, when it was agreed that Peat should prepare a memorandum for discussion with counsel. At the same meeting it was agreed that Robert should prepare a detailed memorandum setting out all the points that he would like to discuss in connection with a proposed general reorganisation of his family group of companies. Subsequently Peat produced a memorandum for counsel but counsel's advice was not taken then or at any time about the proposed sale of shares in Highland. Peat also produced a draft memorandum dated 9th April 1970 about the proposed general reorganisation. In essence the recommendations were an updating of the 1965 scheme; the intention being that in due course shares in Equity should be issued to the public with a view to the shares being quoted. The main body of the scheme had not been implemented at the time of the proceedings before the commissioners. (g) It never occurred to either Robin or Colin that the sale of shares in Highland involved his withdrawing cash in tax free form from Equity or that it might be vulnerable to s 460 or that it was anything other than the sale of an asset for a capital money consideration. Mr Parsons was fully aware of the tax implications of the transaction. He did not, however, mention s 460 to his clients because he assumed that the escape clause would apply.

5. It was contended on behalf of Robin that: (i) the sale of shares in Highland was carried out for bona fide commercial reasons, namely (a) the improvement of Robin's livelihood as a farmer, (b) the protection of Robert's post as chairman and chief executive of Caledonian, and (c) for the re-organisation in accordance with Peat's recommendation of the family company structure; (ii) the sale was carried out in the ordinary course of making or managing investments; Equity in making the investment acquiring control thereby of Caledonian and Robin and Colin in making the sale managing investments; (iii) the tax advantage obtained by Robin was incidental to the sale and not a main object of it; and (iv) the notice under s 460(3) should be cancelled and the assessments made in accordance therewith should be quashed.

6. It was contended on behalf of the Crown that: (i) for a scheme of transactions to have been carried out for bona fide commercial reasons within the meaning of the first limb of the escape clause in s 460(3) it was not necessary that the only reasons for the transactions were bona fide commercial reasons, but the predominant or paramount reasons had to be bona fide commercial reasons; (ii) none of the reasons for which either Robin or Colin carried out the sale of his Highland shares was bona fide commercial; (iii) the sale was not carried out in the ordinary course of making or managing investments; (iv) the inference from the evidence was that the main object or one of the main objects of the sale was to enable a tax advantage to be obtained; and (v) the notice under s 460(3) and the assessments made in accordance therewith should be upheld.

[Paragraph 7 set out the cases[1] cited before the commissioners]

8. The commissioners who heard the appeal gave their decision in writing on 14th June 1977 as follows:

'1. It is common ground that prima facie section 460 Income and Corporation Taxes Act 1970 applies to each of the [taxpayers] in respect of the transaction whereby he sold to Equity his 50 per cent shareholding in Highland. The only question therefore for our decision is whether either or both of them can successfully invoke the escape clause in section 460(1).

'2. Having considered the evidence, both documentary and oral, adduced before us, we find:

'As regards *Robin*—(a) The principal reason for his carrying out the transaction was to get money to buy a farm adjoining one that he already owned. (b) There were good commercial reasons for him to enlarge his farm as he did. (c) A subsidiary reason for the transaction was that it fitted in with a scheme which had been recommended by accountants acting for the family group of companies for simplifying the group's structure; but this had only a minor influence on his decision. (d) The transaction took the form it did (ie, a sale within the group instead of a sale in the open market) to meet his father's strongly expressed desire to keep the family control of Caledonian (shares in which were Highland's only asset), so ensuring that his father could retain his office of chairman and managing director of Caledonian. This was not a reason why Robin sold his shares but it was a substantial reason why he sold them to whom he did. (e) Scanty evidence only was adduced before us as to what commercial benefit Robin (as distinct from his father) expected to accrue to the family companies from the simplification scheme or from securing his father's tenure as an officer of Caledonian and we make no findings on the point. (f) Although he was a qualified Chartered Accountant, he had never been in private practice and it never occurred to him that the transaction involved his withdrawing cash in tax free form from a family company in which he himself was a substantial shareholder or that it might be vulnerable to section 460, or that it was anything other than the sale of an asset for a capital money consideration. (g) His accountant Mr Parsons, partner in Messrs Peat Marwick Mitchell & Co, was fully aware of the tax implications of the transaction. He therefore knew that it would result in a "tax advantage" as defined in section 460. He did not, however, mention section 460 to his clients because he assumed the escape clause would apply. We infer that, so far as Mr Parsons' motives may be relevant, it was not his object to enable the "tax advantage" to be obtained. (h) The assets of Equity, in which Robin had a 37 per cent interest, had a value of several million pounds sterling.

'As regards *Colin*—(i) His principal reason for carrying out the transaction was to protect his own interests. Although Robin's 50 per cent holding in Highland was to be sold to a family company, Colin took the view that his own 50 per cent holding would then be worth less than when he and his brother together owned all the shares. If Robin had not been selling his shares Colin would not have sold his. He had no immediate need of cash and he invested the proceeds of sale in gilt-edged securities and equity shares quoted on the Stock Exchange. (j) His subsidiary reasons were: (i) Robin had asked him to join in the transaction and he wanted to oblige his brother and help him get a better price from the purchaser, who would then acquire a 100 per cent interest in Highland. (ii) He wished, in the same way as Robin, to meet his father's wishes. These subsidiary reasons had, however, only a minor influence on Colin's decision. (k) Our findings in sub-paragraphs (f) (g) and (h) above apply to Colin just as they apply to Robin.

1   *Cleary v Inland Revenue Comrs* [1967] 2 All ER 48, [1968] AC 766, 44 Tax Cas 399, HL; *Inland Revenue Comrs v Brebner* [1967] 1 All ER 779, [1967] 2 AC 18, 43 Tax Cas 705, HL; *Inland Revenue Comrs v Brown* [1971] 3 All ER 502, [1971] 1 WLR 1495, 47 Tax Cas 217, CA; *Inland Revenue Comrs v Goodwin* [1976] 1 All ER 481, [1976] 1 WLR 191, [1976] STC 28, HL

'3. We now consider the escape clause in section 460(1) in the light of the above findings:

'As regards *Robin*—(a) In our view, and we so hold, his transaction did not have as its main object, or one of its main objects, to enable tax advantages to be obtained. (b) Although he sold his shares to raise money to be used for commercial purposes, we do not think that this, standing alone, justifies our concluding that his transaction was carried out for bona fide commercial reasons. We think that, in circumstances such as obtain here, to satisfy this limb of the escape clause the commercial reason must be connected with the vendor's interests in companies concerned in or affected by the transaction. Robin's farming venture, although commercial in nature, was something quite separate from his interests in companies in the family group. We hold, therefore, that the principal reason for which Robin carried out the transaction was not a "commercial reason" within the intent of the escape clause. (c) While we would hold that a substantial bona fide commercial reason for carrying out a transaction is sufficient to satisfy the relevant limb of the escape clause even though the principal reasons were not commercial, we do not think that either the reason at paragraph 2(c) above or (so far as it amounted to anything more than a desire to please his father) the reason at sub-paragraph 2(d), even assuming it to be commercial (as to which we have expressed no opinion), is of sufficient substance to be taken into account for the purposes of the escape clause. (d) We think that the transaction, taking the form that it did (sale to a family company) for the reasons that it did (to retain family control of Caledonian), cannot be said, without unduly straining the use of words, to have been carried out in the "ordinary course of making and managing investments". We hold, therefore, that it is not protected by that limb of the escape clause.

'As regards *Colin*—(e) In our view, and we so hold, his transaction did not have as its main object, or one of its main objects, to enable tax advantages to be obtained. (f) We do not think that any commercial reasons for carrying out the transactions entered into his thinking. We hold that his transaction was not carried out for commercial reasons. (g) His transaction was clearly not carried out in the course of "making" investments. But we find more difficult the question whether it might be said to have been carried out in the ordinary course of "managing" investments. The transaction was to a great extent thrust upon him by his brother. He conceived the value of his investment in Highland to be threatened and protected his interests by sale of that investment in the most favourable way open to him, ie, to the buyer of his brother's shares, and re-investing the proceeds. And, put in those simple terms, that is what any prudent investor would do in the ordinary course of managing his investments. It is true that the threat to Colin arose in a very special way and was met in a very special way but that does not alter the fact that in principle he reacted to a situation that was none of his seeking in the same way that any other prudent investor would react. We think that Colin's action took place "in the ordinary course of . . . managing investments".

'4. We hold therefore that the escape clause in section 460(1) applies to Colin but not to Robin. Colin's appeal succeeds. Robin's fails. We cancel the section 460(3) notice to Colin and quash the income tax and surtax assessments made in accordance with it. We uphold the notice to Robin and confirm the income tax and surtax assessments made in accordance with it.'

9. Robin immediately after the determination of the appeal declared his dissatisfaction with the determination as being erroneous in point of law and required the commissioners to state a case for the opinion of the High Court pursuant to s 56 of the Taxes Management Act 1970.

10. The questions of law for the opinion of the court were whether there was evidence on which the commissioners could reach their decision and whether such decision was correct in law.

David Shirley for the taxpayer.
C H McCall for the Crown.

31st July. **FOX J** read the following judgment: This is an appeal by the taxpayer, Mr   *a*
Robin Clark (to whom I shall refer as 'Robin'), from a decision of the Special Commissioners
whereby they dismissed his appeal against a notice dated 13th May 1976 given by the
Commissioners of Inland Revenue under s 460 of the Income and Corporation Taxes Act
1970. Robin is a farmer. He is the son of Mr Robert Clark (to whom I shall refer as
'Robert'), and he has a brother named Colin.

There are three companies concerned in the case. These are as follows: (1) The Equity   *b*
Trust Ltd ('Equity'). Equity is a private company. It was incorporated in 1938, and
operates as an investment trust company. On 6th April 1970, the issued share capital of
500,000 shares was held as follows: Robert, 12,600; Mary (Robert's wife), 12,600; Colin,
187,000; Robin, 187,000; Trustees for Robin and his family, 50,400; Trustees for Colin
and his family, 50,400; a total of 500,000.

(2) Highland and Caledonian Finance Ltd ('Highland'). Highland is a private company   *c*
and was incorporated in 1958. At all material times it operated as an investment company,
and its issued share capital was 2,000 shares. On 6th April 1970 those shares were held as
to half by Robin and as to the other half by Colin. The principal asset of Highland on 6th
April 1970 was a holding of 80,001 ordinary shares in a company called Caledonian
Associated Cinemas Ltd ('Caledonian').

(3) Caledonian. Caledonian was incorporated in 1935. It carried on business as cinema   *d*
and bingo hall proprietors. At all material times it was a public company whose shares
were quoted on the Glasgow (and latterly on the London) Stock Exchange. On 6th April
1970 the issued share capital of Caledonian was 400,000 5 shilling ordinary shares and
143,181 £1 seven per cent cumulative preference shares. The holders of the 5 shilling
ordinary shares were: Robert (Robin's father), 2,667; Equity, 130,361; Highland, 80,001;
others, 186,971; a total of 400,000.   *e*

Robin, as I have said, is a farmer. Prior to 1970 he was already engaged in farming and
had a 400 acre farm in Wiltshire. Late in 1969 Robin learned that Lower Penn Farm,
which was a 273 acre farm adjoining his own, was to be sold by auction in the spring of
1970. It was Robin's opinion (and the Special Commissioners found that events proved
him right) that it would be profitable to buy Lower Penn and run the two farms as one.
The case stated records: 'He regarded this chance to buy the adjoining farm as the   *f*
opportunity of a lifetime as the resultant entity could be farmed more efficiently.'

Robin expected the price of the Lower Penn to be about £70,000. He had £20,000
available in cash, and he decided that his shares in Highland (the assets of which were
quoted shares) were the easiest to value and sell and that they would produce roughly the
amount of extra cash which he needed. Robin had no quoted investments of his own. As
Robin did not have a majority interest in Highland, he thought that it would be easier for   *g*
him to sell if Colin sold his holding as well, so that the purchaser could be offered the entire
share capital.

The opposition to this proposal came from Robert. He did not want the Highland shares
to be sold at all; and certainly he did not want them to be sold to a stranger, since that
would mean that the family would or might lose control of Caledonian, of which Robert
was chairman and managing director. Robert did not want to lose those offices; he had   *h*
recently lost his offices as deputy chairman and chief executive of a public company, and
he feared that the same might happen if the Clark family lost control of Caledonian.
Robert suggested that Robin should borrow the amount which he required. Robin
rejected that. He said that he wanted to stand on his own feet and could best do so by
selling his shares.

The upshot was that Robert persuaded Robin that the best course was to sell the   *j*
Highland shares to Equity instead of to outsiders. The control of Caledonian would thus
remain in the family. The proposal also fitted in with the general intention of a scheme
recommended by accountants, Messrs Peat Marwick Mitchell & Co, in 1965 for the
simplification of the structure of a number of companies in which the Clark family were
interested. That scheme, however, did not involve large sums of money being extracted

from the companies for the benefit of shareholders. Virtually no progress had been made as regards the Peat Marwick scheme by 1970.

Colin's attitude to the sale of the Highland shares was this. Left to himself, he would not have sold at all at that stage; he had no need for cash. But he did not want to be left with a 50 per cent holding if Robin sold. He took the view that this would reduce the value of his holding, and that the prudent course would be to join in the sale with Robin. Accordingly, on 6th April 1970 Colin and Robin each sold to Equity his holding in Highland for the sum of £51,000; £102,000 in all. That sum represented the net asset value of Highland taking its shares in Caledonian at mid-market prices. Robin in fact purchased Lower Penn Farm for slightly less than he had anticipated: he paid about £65,000.

Section 460(1) of the Income and Corporation Taxes Act 1970 is in the following terms:

> 'Where—(a) in any such circumstances as are mentioned in section 461 below, and
> (b) in consequence of a transaction in securities or of the combined effect of two or more such transactions, a person is in a position to obtain, or has obtained, a tax advantage, then unless he shows that the transaction or transactions were carried out either for bona fide commercial reasons or in the ordinary course of making or managing investments, and that none of them had as their main object, or one of their main objects, to enable tax advantages to be obtained, this section shall apply to him in respect of that transaction or those transactions...'

Section 460(3) provides that where the section applies to any person in respect of any transaction or transactions the tax advantage shall be counteracted by certain adjustments to be specified by notice in writing.

The notice of 13th May 1976 to which I have referred stated that the Board of Inland Revenue, being of opinion that s 460 applied to Robin by reason of a transaction consisting of the sale of the Highland shares, gave notice of certain adjustments to counteract the tax advantage. A similar notice was given to Colin. In consequence of the adjustments, Robin and Colin were assessed to income tax and surtax in the sums of £51,000 each for 1970–71. They both appealed to the Special Commissioners.

It is not in dispute that by reason of the sale of the Highland shares Robin and Colin obtained a tax advantage and that accordingly s 460 applies unless the exempting provisions of s 460(1) are satisfied. That is the consequence of the decision in *Cleary v Inland Revenue Comrs*[1]. The essential issues before the Special Commissioners, therefore, were whether Robin and Colin had established two things: first, that it was not the main object or one of the main objects of the transaction to enable tax advantages to be obtained; secondly, that the transaction was carried out either for bona fide commercial reasons or in the ordinary course of making or managing investments.

The Special Commissioners found as regards Robin: (a) the principal reason for his carrying out the transaction was to get money to buy a farm adjoining the one that he already owned; (b) there were good commercial reasons for him to enlarge his farm as he did; (c) a subsidiary reason for the transaction was that it fitted in with Messrs Peat Marwick's scheme for simplifying the structure of the family group of companies, but that this had only a minor influence on his decision; (d) the transaction took the form it did (that is to say, a sale within the group instead of a sale on the open market) to meet his father's strongly expressed desire to keep the family control of Caledonian. This was not a reason why Robin sold his shares, but it was a substantial reason why he sold them to whom he did; (e) there was only scanty evidence as to what commercial benefit Robin (as distinct from his father) expected to accrue from the simplification scheme or from securing his father's tenure as an officer of Caledonian; (f) it never occurred to either Robin or Colin that the sale of the Highland shares involved withdrawing cash in tax-free form from Equity, or that it was anything more than the sale of an asset for a capital money

---

1   [1967] 2 All ER 48, [1968] AC 766, 44 Tax Cas 399

consideration. The commissioners held that the transaction did not have as its main object or one of its main objects to enable tax advantages to be obtained.

The commissioners made certain findings as regards Colin. I need not recount these except to mention that the commissioners found (a) that his transaction did not have as its main object or one of its main objects to enable tax advantages to be obtained, (b) that his principal reason for carrying out the transaction was to protect his own interests, since he took the view that his own 50 per cent holding in Highland would, if Robin alone sold his holding, be worth less than when he and Robin together owned all the shares, and (c) a subsidiary reason for Colin's transaction was that he wished in the same way as Robin to meet his father's wishes.

The consequence of those findings was that both Robin and Colin had established that it was not the main object or one of the main objects of the transactions to enable tax advantages to be obtained. The only question, therefore, was whether the transaction was carried out either for bona fide commercial reasons or in the ordinary course of making or managing investments.

The commissioners' conclusions on these matters, as regards Robin, were as follows. They stated that although Robin—

'sold his shares to raise money to be used for commercial purposes, we do not think that this, standing alone, justifies our concluding that his transaction was carried out for bona fide commercial reasons. We think that, in circumstances such as obtain here, to satisfy this limb of the escape clause the commercial reason must be connected with the vendor's interests in companies concerned in or affected by the transaction. Robin's farming venture, although commercial in nature, was something quite separate from his interests in companies in the family group.'

The commissioners, therefore, went on to hold 'that the principal reason for which Robin carried out the transaction was not a "commercial reason" within the intent of the escape clause' in s 460.

The commissioners also decided that neither the fact that the transaction fitted in with Peat Marwick's scheme for the family companies nor the fact that the sale took the form it did (that is to say, a sale to Equity and not on the open market) to meet Robert's wishes as to family control of Caledonian was of sufficient substance to be taken into account for the purposes of the escape clause. Accordingly, the commissioners rejected Robin's contention that the transaction was carried out for bona fide commercial reasons. The commissioners also rejected Robin's contention that the transaction was carried out in the ordinary course of making or managing investments. They took the view that it would unduly strain the use of the words so to describe the transaction.

As regards Colin, the commissioners held that no commercial reasons for entering into the transaction entered into Colin's thinking, and that accordingly he did not carry out the transaction for commercial reasons. They held, however, that he did carry out the transaction in the ordinary course of managing investments, since he believed that the value of his investment in Highland would be threatened if Robin sold and he did not.

The result was that, before the commissioners, Robin's appeal failed but Colin's succeeded. Robin now appeals to this court. The Crown also appealed against the decision in Colin's favour, but that appeal has been abandoned.

I come, then, to the first question on Robin's appeal: was the transaction carried out for bona fide commercial reasons? The Special Commissioners found that it was not. That is a matter of fact and, if the commissioners properly directed themselves on the relevant matters of law, I cannot go behind their decision.

It seems to me, however, that the commissioners, in reaching their conclusion, did misdirect themselves as to the law. They state (in para 3(b) of their decision) that to satisfy the escape clause in s 460 'the commercial reason must be connected with the vendor's interests in companies concerned in or affected by the transaction'. That seems to me to be altogether too narrow an approach. Section 460, in my view, contains no such qualification. The section merely requires that the transaction must be 'carried out for bona fide commercial reasons'. That language is entirely at large. If the taxpayer can prove that the transaction was carried out for bona fide commercial reasons, he satisfies the requirement of the section. And 'carried out', I think, means carried out by the taxpayer, in this case Robin.

It is said by the Crown that, while the commissioners' language which I have quoted may, taken by itself, be unsatisfactory, it is saved by the fact that the commissioners qualify it by the words 'in circumstances such as obtain here'. I do not think that those rather imprecise words do have a saving effect. The fact remains, it seems to me, that the language of the section is unqualified. The sole question is the nature of the reason for which the transaction was carried out. There is no requirement in the section of a nexus with particular parties affected by or in some way concerned in the transaction. It does not seem to me that the commissioners approached the matter on that basis. In the circumstances, I take the view that the Special Commissioners misdirected themselves in law and that accordingly the matter is at large before me.

Now it is not in dispute that the transaction was, in every respect, bona fide. The only issue is whether it was carried out for commercial reasons. In deciding that, one must, I think, look at the transaction in the context of all the circumstances which gave rise to it. Looked at by itself, the reason for the sale of the Highland shares, from Robin's point of view, was simply to obtain money. But one cannot, I think, just look at the sale in isolation. It must be considered against the background of the facts which gave rise to it and, in particular, of the circumstance which set the whole matter in motion, which was Robin's intended purchase of Lower Penn Farm.

In *Inland Revenue Comrs v Brebner*[1] the taxpayer was a director of a company carrying on business as coal merchants. In 1959 a take-over bid was made which, if successful, was likely to put an end to the company's activities. Most of the directors, including the taxpayer, had interests in fishing companies which received favourable terms from the company and which would be in difficulties with their coal-burning ships if the company ceased to operate. Accordingly, the taxpayer and five others made a successful counter-offer for the company's shares. They financed that purchase by borrowing from a bank. It had been understood from the beginning by the members of the group that their repayment to the bank would be effected as far as possible by taking assets out of the company. Nearly two years after the purchase, moneys were quite lawfully extracted from the company by a series of resolutions in circumstances from which a tax advantage was obtained. The Special Commissioners found that the transactions in question had been entered into for bona fide commercial reasons. They also found that, although admittedly a tax advantage had been obtained, this advantage was an ancillary result of the main object and that the transactions did not have as their main object or one of their main objects to enable tax advantages to be obtained. The Crown contended that that was not a conclusion to which, on the evidence, the commissioners could reasonably have come. The commissioners should, it was contended, have isolated the later part of the transaction from the earlier, and that the actual resolutions which finally obtained the tax advantage must have had as their main object the tax advantage since it was to that alone that the resolutions were referable. That was rejected by the House of Lords. Lord Pearce said[2]:

> 'The subsection would be robbed of all practical meaning if one had to isolate one part of the carrying out of the arrangement, namely, the actual resolutions which resulted in the tax advantage, and divorce it from the object of the whole arrangement. The method of carrying it out was intended as one part of a whole which was dominated by other considerations.'

In the present case, it seems to me, the sale of the shares was merely part of a whole

1   [1967] 1 All ER 779, [1967] 2 AC 18, 43 Tax Cas 705
2   [1967] 1 All ER 779 at 781, [1967] 2 AC 18 at 27, 43 Tax Cas 705 at 715

which was dominated by Robin's wish to acquire Lower Penn. The sale of the shares had no purpose other than to finance that purchase, any more than the extraction of the money from the company in *Inland Revenue Comrs v Brebner*[1] had any purpose but to pay (by discharging the debt to the bank) the purchase price of the shares in that case. If one asks, 'For what reason did Robin carry out the sale of the shares?', the answer must be, 'In order to buy Lower Penn'. He had no other reason for selling at all. The commissioners found as a fact that there were good commercial reasons for acquiring Lower Penn. The result, it seems to me, is that the transaction (the sale of the shares) was carried out for bona fide commercial reasons.

Now it is true that the reason why Robin sold to Equity (as opposed to selling on the open market) was because of pressure by his father. But the essence of the transaction was that it was simply a bona fide sale by Robin. The identity of the purchaser was acceptable to his father and unobjectionable to him; it is not suggested that he got other than a fair price. In these circumstances, I cannot see that the identity of the purchaser alters the fact that he carried out the sale for commercial reasons.

Further, one must not altogether lose sight of Colin's attitude. In order to achieve a sale of the entirety of the shareholding in Highland, Robin had to carry Colin with him. Colin, the commissioners found, wished, in the same way as Robin, to comply with his father's wishes. In general, it seems to me that, looked at from Robin's point of view, the predominant reason for doing everything that he did was the wholly commercial one of acquiring Lower Penn. His purpose was to acquire Lower Penn. For that reason he had to sell the shares. The identity of the purchaser was immaterial to him provided he got full value.

It is contended by the Crown that to be within the escape clause the 'commercial reasons' must be, as it is said, 'intrinsic' to the transaction. *Inland Revenue Comrs v Brebner*[1] is cited as an example of the sort of circumstances that the section requires. The acquisition was for commercial reasons, mainly the preservation of the value of the interests of the members of the group in the fishing companies. In the present case, the sale of the shares, it is said, was simply to raise cash.

That approach seems to me to produce very unreal distinctions. In both cases the taxpayer was concerned to acquire property. In both cases he was concerned to acquire it for good commercial reasons. In both cases those reasons were largely based on the impact of the property to be acquired on property already owned, in *Inland Revenue Comrs v Brebner*[1] the fishing companies and in the present case Robin's existing farm. And in both cases the question was how to raise the purchase money. In *Inland Revenue Comrs v Brebner*[1] it was raised by borrowing from the bank and then extracting the amount from the company. In the present case it was raised simply by the sale of the Highland shares. Looking at the overall position in both cases, what was done was done for good commercial reasons.

I was referred by counsel for the Crown to *Inland Revenue Comrs v Brown*[2], and in particular to the observations of Russell LJ, where he says:

> 'It seems to me that one does not show that a transaction of sale of securities for full consideration to a company already owned by oneself is a transaction entered into for bona fide commercial reasons, merely by saying that it is such a sale transaction, and that one wanted the money.'

That, with respect, is plainly correct. The matter has to be considered in the context of all the relevant facts and not merely part of them. In *Inland Revenue Comrs v Brown*[3] the issue was whether the tribunal could properly conclude that the transactions were not carried out for bona fide commercial reasons. That depended on all the evidence. There was, for example, evidence that the taxpayer had over the years, in managing the affairs of the

---

1   [1967] 1 All ER 779, [1967] 2 AC 18, 43 Tax Cas 705
2   [1971] 3 All ER 502 at 512, [1971] 1 WLR 1495 at 1502, 47 Tax Cas 217 at 239
3   [1971] 3 All ER 502, [1971] 1 WLR 1495, 47 Tax Cas 217

companies, taken every possible opportunity, by cessations and the like, of minimising tax. That was not conclusive against the taxpayer, but it was a factor that the tribunal was entitled to consider.

The present case was a perfectly honest transaction entered into, as the commissioners found, without the object of obtaining tax advantages. So far as Robin was concerned, the predominant reason for it and everything that he did was wholly commercial. In the circumstances I think that the case comes within the first limb of the escape clause and that the appeal succeeds. It is not, in the event, necessary for me to consider the question whether the second limb is applicable.

Appeal allowed.

Solicitors: *A V C Astley* (for the taxpayer); *Solicitor of Inland Revenue.*

Rengan Krishnan Esq   Barrister.

The Rena K

QUEEN'S BENCH DIVISION (ADMIRALTY COURT)
BRANDON J
12th, 13th, 14th, 16th DECEMBER 1977, 12th JANUARY, 17th FEBRUARY 1978

Shipping – Bill of lading – Incorporation of terms of charterparty – Arbitration clause – General clause incorporating terms and conditions of charterparty and specifically incorporating arbitration clause – Arbitration clause providing that any dispute arising under charterparty to be referred to arbitration – Dispute arising under bills of lading – Whether dispute one which parties had agreed to refer to arbitration.

Arbitration – Stay of court proceedings – Exception where arbitration agreement incapable of being performed – Party alleged to be unable to satisfy award if award made against him – Whether arbitration agreement 'incapable of being performed' – Arbitration Act 1975, s 1(1).

Admiralty – Jurisdiction – Action in rem – Arrest of ship – Stay of proceedings – Arbitration agreement – Court bound to grant stay – Whether court bound to order release of ship from arrest – Arbitration Act 1975, s 1(1).

Injunction – Interlocutory – Danger that defendant may transfer assets out of jurisdiction – Arbitration agreement – Stay of court proceedings – Whether plaintiff entitled to injunction to provide him with security for payment of any award he may obtain in the arbitration – Arbitration Act 1950, s 12(6)(f)(h).

The Rena K was owned by a Panamanian company ('the shipowners'), a one-ship company managed and controlled from Greece. A Mauritian company ('the charterers') chartered the ship in 1977 under a voyage charterparty to carry from Mauritius to Liverpool a cargo of sugar sold on cif terms by the charterers to an English company ('the cargo owners'). The charterparty contained a London arbitration clause and the bills of lading issued in respect of the shipment provided that 'All terms, clauses, conditions and exceptions including the Arbitration Clause [in the charterparty were] hereby incorporated'. The bills of lading were endorsed to the cargo owners. During the voyage almost a quarter of the sugar was ruined and had to be jettisoned. While the voyage was still in progress the cargo owners brought an action in rem against the Rena K and in personam against the shipowners claiming, under the bills of lading, damages of £549,000, with interest, for breach of contract in relation to the carriage of the cargo. The Rena K was entered in the books of a protection and indemnity association ('the P & I club') which agreed to indemnify the shipowners in respect of liability for loss of, or damage to, cargo carried in her. Rule 6 of the P & I club's rules provided, however, that the club was not obliged to indemnify a member in respect of liability unless and until the member had himself first discharged the liability out of moneys belonging to him absolutely and not by way of loan or otherwise. Rule 8(k) further provided that the club might reduce the amount of a member's claim if he had not taken such steps to protect his interests as he would have done if the ship had not been entered for protection and indemnity. The Rena K arrived in Liverpool in July 1977 and the cargo owners applied ex parte for a Mareva^a injunction restraining the shipowners from dealing with moneys payable to their bankers in London in respect of freight due under the charterparty. An interim injunction was granted. On 27th July the Rena K was arrested. On 28th July the shipowners entered an appearance in the action and issued a notice of motion seeking (i) a stay of the action, under s 1^b of the Arbitration Act 1975, on the ground that the dispute to which the action related was one which the parties had agreed should be referred to arbitration, and (ii) the release of the Rena K from arrest. Pending the determination of the questions raised by the notice of motion an agreement was reached between the cargo owners on the one hand and the shipowners and the P & I club on the other whereby it was arranged that, without prejudice to any rights which the cargo owners might have, the Rena K would be released from arrest and the club would put up security for the claim on behalf of the shipowners in the form of a letter of undertaking in the sum of £390,000 (being the current value of the ship). The letter was to be cancelled and returned to the club if the court subsequently decided (i) that the shipowners were entitled to a stay, (ii) that as a result of the stay the Rena K should be unconditionally released and (iii) that the cargo owners were not entitled, by way of alternative security for their claim, to a Mareva injunction. On 8th December the shipowners and the P & I club applied by summons for the determination of the question whether by virtue of the agreement the club was entitled to the cancellation and return to it of the letter of undertaking given pursuant to it. By consent the summons and the application for a stay of the original action were heard together. At the hearing the cargo owners contended, inter alia, (i) that since the dispute between them and the shipowners arose under the bills of lading, and the arbitration clause in the charterparty related only to disputes arising under it, there was no agreement to refer the matter to arbitration, (ii) that, in any event, the court should refuse to order a stay of the action because the arbitration was 'incapable of being performed', within the meaning of s 1(1) of the 1975 Act, as the shipowners' financial resources were such that, if an award was made against them, they would not be able to pay the full amount of it, (iii) that, even if the shipowners were entitled to a stay, they were not automatically entitled to an order for the unconditional release of the ship from arrest and (iv) that, even if the shipowners were entitled to such an order, the cargo owners were entitled, by way of alternative security for their claim, to a Mareva injunction in respect of the ship notwithstanding that the arbitration had not been commenced.

Held – (1) The fact that the arbitration clause in the charterparty was expressly incorporated into the bills of lading showed that the parties to the bills of lading had intended the provisions of that clause to apply to disputes arising under the bills of lading. It followed that the dispute was one which the parties had agreed to refer to arbitration (see p 404 d and p 405 c to e, post).

(2) The shipowners were entitled, as at 28th July, to a stay of the cargo owners' action because—

(i) on the true construction of s 1(1) of the 1975 Act the words 'incapable of being performed' referred only to the question whether an arbitration agreement was capable of being performed up to the stage when it resulted in an award and did not extend to the question whether, once an award was made, the party against whom it was made would be

---

a See *Mareva Compania Naviera SA v International Bulkcarriers Ltd* [1975] 2 Lloyd's 509 and *Nippon Yusen Kaisha v Karageorgis* [1975] 3 All ER 282, CA

b Section 1, so far as material, is set out at p 405 g to p 406 a, post

capable of satisfying it. Accordingly, for the purposes of s 1(1), it was irrelevant whether the shipowners would be capable of satisfying any award made against them (see p 407 *b* to *e*, post);

(ii) in any event, the cargo owners had failed to show that if they were to succeed in the arbitration and obtain an award in respect of the full amount of their claim the shipowners would be incapable of satisfying it, for although it had been established that the shipowners would not be able to satisfy more than half of it out of their own resources, the possibility that the P & I club would in fact satisfy the award direct on its member's behalf had not been eliminated (see p 408 *g* to *j*, post).

(3) There was nothing in s 1(1) of the 1975 Act which obliged the court, whenever it granted a stay of an action in rem in which security had been obtained, to make an order for the unconditional release of that security. Under RSC Ord 75, r 13(4)*c*, the court had a discretion as to what order it would make with regard to such security. In a case where the stay would in all probability be final, and there would in consequence be no judgment in the action to be satisfied, the court should exercise its discretion by ordering the release of the security, but in a case where the stay might not be final and there might therefore be a judgment in the action to be satisfied, the court should exercise its discretion either by refusing to release the security or by releasing it subject to a condition that the defendant provide alternative security for payment of any award in the arbitration. In the instant case, if an award was made against the shipowners and they were unable to satisfy it, the cargo owners would be entitled to have the stay of the action removed and to proceed to a judgment in rem in it because a cause of action in rem did not become merged in an arbitration award. It followed (i) that the shipowners were not entitled, as at 28th July, along with and consequent on the stay of the action, to the unconditional release of the ship from arrest and (ii) that the P & I club was not entitled to the return and cancellation of its letter of undertaking (see p 415 *e* to *j*, p 417 *a* to *d* and p 420 *d e*, post); *The Cap Bon* [1967] 1 Lloyd's Rep 543 and *The Golden Trader* [1974] 2 All ER 686 considered.

Per Curiam. Under s 12(6)(*f*) and (*h*)*d* of the Arbitration Act 1950 the court has power to grant a Mareva injunction for the purpose of, and in relation to, an arbitration which has not yet been commenced, and to do so subject to a term providing for the arbitration to be commenced within a specified time, together with such other terms, if any, as the court thinks fit (see p 418 *f* to *h*, post).

Notes

For arrest of ship in actions in rem, see 1 Halsbury's Laws (4th Edn) para 305, for conditions determining release from arrest, see ibid para 385, and for cases on arrest of ships, see 1 Digest (Repl) 191–193, 762–782.

For stay of proceedings in Admiralty actions in rem, see 1 Halsbury's Laws (4th Edn) para 440.

For stay of court proceedings in arbitration cases, see 2 ibid paras 555–567, and for cases on the subject, see 2 Digest (Repl) 477–481, 346–369.

For injunction restraining arbitration proceedings, see 2 Halsbury's Laws (4th Edn) para 518, and for cases on the subject, see 2 Digest (Repl) 489–500, 465–481.

For the Arbitration Act 1950, s 12, see 2 Halsbury's Statutes (3rd Edn) 444.

For the Arbitration Act 1975, s 1, see 45 ibid 33.

Cases referred to in judgment

Annefield The [1971] 1 All ER 394, [1971] P 160, [1971] 2 WLR 320, [1971] 1 Lloyd's Rep 1, CA, Digest (Cont Vol D) 37, 156*e*.

Athenée, The (1922) 11 Ll L Rep 6, CA.

Atlantic Star, The [1973] 2 All ER 175, [1974] AC 436, [1973] 2 WLR 795, [1973] 2 Lloyd's Rep 197, HL, 11 Digest (Reissue) 645, 1777.

---

c   Rule 13(4), so far as material, is set out at p 415 *d*, post
d   Section 12(6), so far as material, is set out at p 418 *b*, post

Bengal, The (1859) Sw 468, 166 ER 1220, 21 Digest (Repl) 277, 506.

Bremer Oeltransport GmbH v Drewry [1933] 1 KB 753, [1933] All ER Rep 851, 102 LJKB 360, 148 LT 540, 45 Ll L Rep 133, CA, 2 Digest (Repl) 700, 2128.

Cap Bon, The [1967] 1 Lloyd's Rep 543.

Cella, The (1888) 13 PD 82, 57 LJP 55, 59 LT 125, 6 Asp MLC 293, CA, 1 Digest (Repl) 191, 767.

Eleftheria, The [1969] 2 All ER 641, [1970] P 94, [1969] 2 WLR 1073, [1969] 1 Lloyd's Rep 237, 11 Digest (Reissue) 633, 1691.

Fehmarn, The [1958] 1 All ER 333, [1958] 1 WLR 159, [1957] 2 Lloyd's Rep 551, CA; *affg* [1957] 2 All ER 707, [1957] 1 WLR 815, [1957] 1 Lloyd's Rep 511, 1 Digest (Repl) 175, 606.

Foresta Romana SA v Georges Mabro (Owners) (1940) 66 Ll L Rep 139.

Gascoyne v Edwards (1826) 1 Y & J 19, 148 ER 569, 2 Digest (Repl) 672, 1884.

Golden Trader, The [1974] 2 All ER 686, [1975] QB 348, [1974] 3 WLR 16, [1974] 1 Lloyd's Rep 378, Digest (Cont Vol D) 39, 369d.

Hamilton & Co v Mackie & Sons (1889) 5 TLR 677, CA, 2 Digest (Repl) 442, 152.

John and Mary, The (1859) Sw 471, 3 LT 123, 166 ER 1221, 21 Digest (Repl) 280, 523.

Makefjell, The [1975] 1 Lloyd's Rep 520; *affd* [1976] 2 Lloyd's Rep 29, CA.

Merak, The [1965] 1 All ER 230, [1965] P 223, [1965] 2 WLR 250, [1964] 2 Lloyd's Rep 527, Digest (Cont Vol B) 25, 156a.

Njegos, The [1936] P 90, [1935] All ER Rep 863, 105 LJP 49, 155 LT 109, 18 Asp MLC 609, 2 Digest (Repl) 443, 156.

Phonizien, The [1966] 1 Lloyd's Rep 150.

Rasu Maritima S A v Perusahaan Pertambangan Minyak Dan Gas Bumi Nagara (Pertamina) and Government of Indonesia (as interveners) [1977] 3 All ER 324, [1978] QB 644, [1977] 3 WLR 518, [1977] 2 Lloyd's Rep 397, CA.

Siskina (Cargo Owners) v Distos Compania Naviera SA, The Siskina [1977] 3 All ER 803, [1977] 3 WLR 818, [1978] 1 Lloyd's Rep 1, HL.

Sylph, The (1867) LR 2 A & E 24, 37 LJ Adm 14, 17 LT 519, 3 Mar LC 37, 1 Digest (Repl) 168, 549.

Thomas (TW) & Co Ltd v Portsea Steamship Co Ltd [1912] AC 1, 12 Asp MLC 23, HL; *affg* sub nom *The Portsmouth* [1911] P 54, CA, 2 Digest (Repl) 442, 155.

Yeo v Tatem, The Orient (1871) LR 3 PC 696, 8 Moo PCC 74, 40 LJ Adm 29, 24 LT 918, 20 WR 6, 1 Asp MLC 108, 17 ER 241, PC, 42 Digest (Repl) 1087, 9000.

Cases also cited

Carl-Zeiss-Stiftung v Rayner and Keeler Ltd (No 2) [1966] 2 All ER 536, [1967] 1 AC 853, HL.

King v Hoare (1844) 13 M & W 494, 153 ER 206.

MacCabe v Joynt [1901] 2 Ir R 115, DC.

Nelson v Couch (1863) 15 CBNS 99, 143 ER 721.

Purser & Co (Hillingdon) Ltd v Jackson [1976] 3 All ER 641, [1977] QB 166.

Speak v Taylor (1893) 10 TLR 224.

Motion and originating summons

By a writ issued on 24th June 1977 the plaintiffs, Mauritius Sugar Syndicate, Tate & Lyle Sugar Refineries Ltd ('the cargo owners'), Emcar Ltd and Adam & Co Ltd, brought an action in rem against the Rena K and in personam against the owners of the Rena K, Black Lion Shipping Co SA ('the shipowners'), claiming damages for breach of contract and duty in and about the carriage of cargo. On 27th July the Rena K was arrested. On 28th July the shipowners entered an appearance in the action and applied, by notice of motion, for an order (i) that all further proceedings in the action be stayed pursuant to s 1(1) of the Arbitration Act 1975, (ii) that the Rena K be released from arrest. On the same day an agreement was made between the plaintiffs on the one hand and by the shipowners and London Steamship Owners' Mutual Insurance Association Ltd ('the P & I club') pursuant to which the Rena K was to be released from arrest and the P & I club was to put up security for the claim on behalf of the shipowners in the form of a letter of undertaking in the sum of £390,000. The letter was to be cancelled and returned to the P & I club if the court subsequently decided (1) that the shipowners were entitled to a stay, (ii) that as a consequence of the stay the Rena K was to be unconditionally released and (iii) the cargo owners were not entitled by way of alternative security for their claim to a Mareva injunction. By an originating summons, dated 8th December, the shipowners and the P & I club sought the determination of the court whether on the true construction of the agreement of 28th July the club was entitled to the cancellation and return to them of the letter of undertaking in the sum of £390,000 given by them pursuant to it. By consent the application for the stay of the original action and the originating summons were heard together.

M N Howard for the shipowners and the P & I club.
David Grace for the plaintiffs.

Cur adv vult

17th February. **BRANDON J** read the following judgment: These proceedings arise out of the carriage of a cargo of about 11,150 metric tons of sugar from Port Louis, Mauritius, to Liverpool in the Greek ship Rena K during May, June and July 1977.

The sugar concerned was sold by the Mauritius Sugar Syndicate to Tate & Lyle Refineries Ltd on cif terms. The Rena K was chartered for the carriage by the Mauritius Sugar Syndicate from her owners, Black Lion Shipping Co SA, under a voyage charterparty dated London 13th April 1977. The latter is a Panamanian company managed and controlled from Greece.

The cargo was shipped for the Mauritius Sugar Syndicate by two agents of theirs, Emcar Ltd and Adam & Co Ltd, and two bills of lading were issued in respect of such shipment. One bill of lading was on Emcar Ltd's form and the other on Adam & Co Ltd's form. In either case the agent was named as shipper in the bill of lading although acting as agent only.

The Rena K left Port Louis on 17th May 1977. On 20th May there was an entry of sea water into her no 4 hold. As a result of this a quantity of about 2,440 metric tons of sugar in that space was ruined. Later, after the Rena K had proceeded to Durban for examination and temporary repairs, the whole of the ruined sugar was jettisoned.

On 24th June, while the voyage was still in progress, the Mauritius Sugar Syndicate, Tate & Lyle Refineries Ltd Emcar Ltd, and Adam & Co Ltd, began an action in this court both in rem against the Rena K and in personam against Black Lion Shipping Co SA. The claim endorsed on the writ was for damages for breach of contract and duty in and about the carriage of the cargo. The amount claimed is said by the plaintiffs to be £549,000 with interest and costs, that figure being calculated on the basis of a total loss of 2,440 metric tons of sugar with a sound arrived value of £225 per metric ton.

On 11th July the Rena K arrived at Liverpool, and on 24th or 25th July discharge of the rest of her cargo began. On 25th July the plaintiffs applied ex parte for a Mareva injunction restraining the defendants from dealing with money payable to their bankers in London in respect of freight due under the charterparty. An interim injunction effective for 28 days or until further order was granted, with liberty to the defendants to apply on short notice to vary or discharge the order.

On 27th July the writ, in so far as it was in rem, was served on the Rena K and she was arrested in the action. At the same time solicitors acting for the defendants accepted service of the writ in so far as it was in personam. On 28th July the defendants entered an appearance in the action, and on the same day they issued a notice of motion asking, first, for a stay of the action on the ground that the dispute to which it related was one which the parties had agreed to refer to arbitration, and, secondly, along with and consequent on such stay, for the release of the Rena K from arrest.

It was then the last day but one of the Trinity sittings, and there was insufficient time for the questions raised by the notice of motion to be adequately argued and decided. In these circumstances an agreement was reached between the plaintiffs on the one hand and the defendants and their protection and indemnity association, London Steamship Owners' Mutual Insurance Association Ltd ('the P & I club') on the other hand, which would allow the Rena K to be released while preserving for the plaintiffs all such rights as they might at that stage have had to retain security for their claim by keeping the Rena K under arrest, or, if such arrest was not maintainable, by obtaining comparable security in the form of a Mareva injunction relating to the ship which they would in that event have applied for in the alternative.

The principal terms of the agreement to which I have referred are contained in a telex from the solicitors for the plaintiffs to the solicitors for the defendants, dated 27th July 1977, and can be summarised as follows: (a) that the P & I club should put up security for the claim on behalf of the defendants in the form of a letter of undertaking in the sum of £390,000; (b) that this letter of undertaking should be cancelled and returned by the plaintiffs to the P & I club if the court should subsequently decide that as at 28th July 1977: (1) the defendants were entitled to a stay of the action on the ground that there was an agreement to refer the dispute to which it related to arbitration, (2) as a consequence of such stay the defendants were further entitled to the unconditional release of the Rena K from arrest and (3) the plaintiffs were not entitled, by way of alternative security for their claim, to a Mareva injunction restraining the defendants from removing the Rena K from the jurisdiction; and (c) that the Rena K should meanwhile be released from arrest.

The sum of £390,000 referred to in term (a) above was based on the estimated value of the Rena K in the condition in which she was at that time.

In accordance with that agreement the P & I club put up security in the form of a letter of undertaking in the sum of £390,000 and the Rena K was released from arrest. A consent order was further made adjourning the hearing of the defendants' application for a stay to 12th December 1977.

On 8th December a further proceeding was begun by originating summons in which Black Lion Shipping Co SA and the P & I club were named as plaintiffs and the Mauritius Sugar Syndicate, Tate & Lyle Refineries Ltd, Emcar Ltd and Adam & Co Ltd as defendants. In that originating summons, as subsequently amended, the plaintiffs ask the court to determine in effect whether, by virtue of the agreement which I summarised above, the P & I club is entitled to the cancellation and return to them of the letter of undertaking in the sum of £390,000 given by them pursuant to it.

On 9th December the four defendants to the originating summons entered an appearance to it, and it was agreed by all the parties concerned that the originating summons should be heard at the same time as the adjourned application for a stay in the original action.

As I have indicated above, four persons, the Mauritius Sugar Syndicate, Tate & Lyle Refineries Ltd, Emcar Ltd and Adam & Co Ltd, were named as plaintiffs in the original action and again as defendants in the further proceedings begun by originating summons. It is, however, common ground that the title to sue for substantial damages in respect of the cargo which was lost is vested in Tate & Lyle Refineries Ltd, and in them alone, as endorsees of the two bills of lading to which I referred earlier, and that the existence of the other three plaintiffs can, therefore, for all practical purposes be disregarded. It is further common ground that, in these circumstances, the relevant terms of carriage for the purposes of the claim are those contained in those bills of lading.

In the rest of this judgment I shall refer to the effective plaintiffs, Tate & Lyle Refineries Ltd, as the cargo owners, to Black Lion Shipping Co SA as the shipowners, to London Steamship Owners' Mutual Insurance Association Ltd as the P & I club or, simply, the club and to the Rena K as the ship.

Before I state and examine the various questions which arise in this matter, I think it is right to say something about the nature and strength of the prima facie case which the cargo owners have shown in respect of their claim.

There was put in evidence a report of T R Little & Co dated 13th June of a survey made by them of the ship at Durban on 1st June and following days. According to that report the ingress of sea water into no 4 hold resulted from defects in the hull of the ship of such a character that they must have been in existence at the commencement of the voyage and have made her unseaworthy at that time. Since the carriage of the cargo was on Hague Rule terms, it would be for the shipowners, in order to resist the cargo owners' claim successfully, to show that, although the ship was unseaworthy, they had exercised due diligence to make her seaworthy. While the possibility of the shipowners' discharging the burden of proof which would be on them in this respect cannot be excluded, the inference which I draw from the survey report is, to put the matter no higher, that they would be likely to have considerable difficulty in doing so.

In these circumstances I am of opinion that the cargo owners have shown a very strong prima facie case on the merits in support of their claim.

Four main questions were argued before me as follows. (1) Is the dispute to which the cargo owners' action relates one which the parties have agreed should be referred to arbitration? (2) If so, were the shipowners entitled, as at 28th July 1977, to a stay of the action? (3) If so, were the shipowners also entitled, as at 28th July 1977, along with and consequent on such stay, to the unconditional release of the ship from arrest? (4) If so, were the cargo owners entitled, as at 28th July 1977, by way of alternative security for their claim, to a Mareva injunction in respect of the ship?

I shall examine each of these four questions in turn.

1 Is the dispute to which the cargo owners' action relates one which the parties
have agreed should be referred to arbitration?

The charterparty between the Mauritius Sugar Syndicate and the shipowners dated 13th April 1977, to which I referred earlier, contains the following provision:

> 'Any dispute which may arise under this Charter to be settled in arbitration in London, each party appointing an arbitrator, and should they be unable to agree, the decision of an umpire selected by them to be final. The arbitrators and umpire all to be commercial men. This submission may be made a rule of the High Court of Justice in England by either party.'

The bill of lading on Emcar Ltd's form, which has terms printed or typed on both its face and its reverse side, contains several references to the charterparty. On the main part of the face of the bill of lading there are words acknowledging the shipment of the goods at the port of loading and providing for their delivery at the port of discharge to order. Then there follow, mainly in print but partly in type, these two sentences:

> 'Freight for the said goods to be paid as laid down in Charter Party. All conditions of the Charter Party dated 13th April, 1977 including exception clause, are incorporated in the Bill of Lading.'

On the left hand side of the face of the bill of lading these words appear again in type: 'Freight payable as laid down in Charter Party.'

On the reverse side of the bill of lading there are a number of standard printed clauses, some of which, as appear from their terms, are designed for inclusion in a charterparty rather than in a bill of lading. Right at the end, following this series of standard clauses, comes the following further printed clause:

> 'All other terms, conditions, clauses and exceptions including the Arbitration Clause as well as the Negligence Clause and Cesser Clause as per Charter Party. In case of conflict between the terms of the Charter Party and those of the Bill of Lading, the former shall prevail.'

The bill of lading on Adam & Co Ltd's form, which has terms printed or typed on its face only, also contains several similar references to the charterparty. There are two references to freight being paid or payable 'as laid down in Charter Party dated London 13 April

1977'. In addition there is a clause on the left hand side of the bill of lading towards the top which reads: 'All terms, clauses, conditions and exceptions including the Arbitration Clause, the Negligence Clause and the Cesser Clause of the Charter Party dated London 13 April 1977 are hereby incorporated.' This clause is all in print except for the date of the charterparty which is typed.

Those being the relevant terms of the charterparty and the two bills of lading, the problem of construction which arises is this. Both bills of lading contain clauses incorporating all the terms, clauses, conditions and exceptions of the charterparty, including, by express description, the arbitration clause contained in the latter contract. That clause itself, however, by its own terms relates only to disputes arising under the charterparty. What then is the effect, if any, of its incorporation?

For the cargo owners it was contended that the incorporation had no effect at all because, when the arbitration clause was read into the bills of lading, it did not by its terms apply to disputes arising under them, but only to disputes arising under the charterparty. Nor, it was further argued, was there any justification for manipulating or adapting the wording of the clause, when read into the bills of lading, so as to make it apply to disputes arising under the bills of lading instead of disputes arising under the charterparty.

For the shipowners, on the other hand, it was contended that the fact that the arbitration clause was expressly incorporated by description showed clearly that the parties to the bills of lading intended the provisions of that clause to apply in principle to disputes arising under the bills of lading. It followed, so the argument went on, that some manipulation or adaptation of the wording of the clause, when read into the bills of lading, was justified in order to give effect to that clearly shown intention.

A long series of authorities has established that, where a charterparty contains an arbitration clause providing for arbitration of disputes arising under it, general words in a bill of lading incorporating into it all the terms and conditions, or all the terms, conditions and clauses, of such charterparty, are not sufficient to bring such arbitration clause into the bill of lading so as to make its provisions applicable to disputes arising under that document: see *Hamilton v Mackie & Sons Ltd*[1], *T W Thomas & Co Ltd v Portsea Steamship Co Ltd*[2], *The Njegos*[3], *The Phonizien*[4] and *The Annefield*[5].

By contrast it has been held that, where an arbitration clause in a charterparty provides for arbitration of disputes arising not only under the charterparty itself but also under any bill of lading issued pursuant to it general words of incorporation in such a bill of lading of the kind referred to above are sufficient to bring in the arbitration clause so as to make it applicable to disputes arising under that bill of lading: see *The Merak*[6].

In the authorities mentioned above a distinction has been drawn between clauses in the relevant charterparty which are directly germane to the shipment, carriage and delivery of the goods covered by the bill of lading and other clauses which are not directly germane to such matters.

Referring to this distinction Lord Denning MR said in *The Annefield*[7]:

'I would say that a clause which is directly germane to the subject-matter of the bill of lading (ie to the shipment, carriage and delivery of goods) can and should be incorporated into the bill of lading contract, even though it may involve a degree of manipulation of the words in order to fit exactly the bill of lading. But, if the clause is one which is not thus directly germane, it should not be incorporated into the bill of lading contract unless it is done explicitly in clear words either in the bill of lading or in the charterparty.'

1   (1889) 5 TLR 677
2   [1912] AC 1
3   [1936] P 90, [1935] All ER Rep 863
4   [1966] 1 Lloyd's Rep 150
5   [1971] 1 All ER 394, [1971] P 160
6   [1965] 1 All ER 230, [1965] P 223
7   [1971] 1 All ER 394 at 406, [1971] P 160 at 184

Counsel for the cargo owners argued, on the basis of these authorities, that an arbitration clause in a charterparty, being a clause which was not directly germane to the shipment, carriage and delivery of the goods, could never be brought into a bill of lading and made applicable to disputes arising under that document if it was necessary to manipulate the wording of the clause in order to achieve that end. He contended that it made no difference, for this purpose, whether the words of incorporation contained in the bill of lading were general words without any specific reference to the arbitration clause in the charterparty, as in all the authorities relied on, or general words to which a specific reference to such clause was added, as in the present case.

I cannot accept this last contention. It was an essential element in the facts of the cases referred to that the words of incorporation in the bill of lading were general words without specific reference to the arbitration clause in the charterparty; the conclusions reached on the questions of construction involved depended entirely on that circumstance; and the judgments of the judges who decided the cases must be read and understood in the light of it.

The present case is, in my view, clearly distinguishable, in that there were added to the usual general words of incorporation in the two bills of lading the further specific words 'including the arbitration clause'. The addition of these words must, as it seems to me, mean that the parties to the bills of lading intended the provisions of the arbitration clause in the charterparty to apply in principle to disputes arising under the bills of lading; and, if it is necessary, as it obviously is, to manipulate or adapt part of the wording of that clause in order to give effect to that intention, then I am clearly of opinion that this should be done.

For the reasons which I have given I prefer the argument for the shipowners so that for the cargo owners on this part of the case. I hold that, on the true construction of the bills of lading, the provisions for arbitration contained in the arbitration clause of the charterparty were brought into the bills of lading and made applicable to disputes arising under them.

The cargo owners' claim in the action is brought under the bills of lading, so that the dispute to which the action relates is a dispute arising under those documents. It follows, on the view which I have expressed above, that the dispute is one which the parties have, by the terms of the bills of lading, agreed to refer to arbitration.

2 *If the dispute to which the action relates is one which the parties have*
   agreed to refer to arbitration, were the shipowners entitled, as at 28th July 1977,
   to a stay of the action?

Section 1 of the Arbitration Act 1975, which came into operation on 23rd December 1975, provides, so far as material:

> '(1) If any party to an arbitration agreement to which this section applies . . . commences any legal proceedings in any court against any other party to the agreement . . . in respect of any matter agreed to be referred, any party to the proceedings may at any time after appearance, and before delivering any pleading or taking any other steps in the proceedings, apply to the court to stay the proceedings; and the court, unless satisfied that the arbitration agreement is null and void, inoperative or incapable of being performed or that there is not in fact any dispute between the parties with regard to the matter agreed to be referred, shall make an order staying the proceedings.

> '(2) This section applies to any arbitration agreement which is not a domestic arbitration agreement; and neither section 4(1) of the Arbitration Act 1950 nor section 4 of the Arbitration Act (Northern Ireland) 1937 shall apply to an arbitration agreement to which this section applies . . .

> '(4) In this section "domestic arbitration agreement" means an arbitration agreement which does not provide, expressly or by implication, for arbitration in a State other than the United Kingdom and to which neither—(a) an individual who is a national of, or habitually resident in, any State other than the United Kingdom; nor (b) a body

corporate which is incorporated in, or whose central management and control is exercised in, any State other than the United Kingdom; is a party at the time the proceedings are commenced.'

On the basis of the court's answer to question 1, it was conceded for the cargo owners that, since the shipowners were a body corporate incorporated in Panama, and since also their central management and control were exercised in Greece, the arbitration agreement concerned was not a domestic arbitration agreement with s 3(1) above, and that s 1(1) was accordingly applicable to the case.

At the commencement of the hearing before me it was further conceded for the cargo owners that, since s 1(1) applied to the case, the court was bound to make an order staying their action. Subsequently, however, this further concession was, with the leave of the court, withdrawn, and it was contended instead for the cargo owners that an order staying the action should be refused on the ground that the shipowners did not have the financial resources with which to satisfy an award against them if made, and that the arbitration agreement was therefore 'incapable of being performed' within the meaning of that expression as used in s 1(1). This contention was, not surprisingly, strongly disputed on behalf of the shipowners.

This contention for the cargo owners raises two questions. The first question is one of law. It is whether an arbitration agreement is 'incapable of being performed' within the meaning of s 1(1) of the 1975 Act if the financial position of one of the parties to it is such that, in the event of an award being made against him in an arbitration held pursuant to the agreement, he would not be able to pay the amount of the award. The second question is one of fact. It is whether the financial position of the shipowners in this case is such that, if the cargo owners were to succeed in an arbitration against them and obtain an award in respect of their claim, the shipowners would be unable to satisfy such award.

So far as the first question, that of law, is concerned the argument for the cargo owners was as follows. Any person who enters into an arbitration agreement impliedly undertakes that he will pay any award made against him in an arbitration held pursuant to such agreement: see *Bremer Oeltransport GmbH v Drewry*[1]. Performance of an arbitration agreement involves, therefore, not only the appointment of an arbitral tribunal in accordance with such agreement, the conduct before that tribunal of such proceedings as may be appropriate, and, following such proceedings, an adjudication by the tribunal on the matters referred to it and the issue of an award. Performance of an arbitration agreement involves also, as an essential element in the whole process, the payment of the amount of the award by the party against whom it is made. That being so, where a claim by A against B is the subject-matter of an arbitration agreement, and it is shown that, in the event of A succeeding in an arbitration held pursuant to such agreement and obtaining an award in respect of his claim against B, B will not be able, by reason of his impecuniosity, to pay the amount of the award, then the arbitration agreement concerned is, in that essential respect, incapable of being performed, and should be so treated for the purposes of s 1(1) of the 1975 Act.

In considering whether this argument is sound or not it is necessary to have regard to the background and purpose of the 1975 Act. The Act was passed to give effect to the New York Convention on the Recognition and Enforcement of Foreign Arbitral Awards[2] concluded on 10th June 1958. It is an essential preliminary to the recognition and enforcement of arbitral awards that the arbitration agreements capable of resulting in such awards being made should themselves first be recognised and enforced. Section 1 of the 1975 Act, giving effect to para 3 of art II of the convention, compels the recognition and enforcement of convention (ie non-domestic) arbitration agreements by requiring a court,

---

1　[1933] 1 KB 753, [1933] All ER Rep 851
2　TS 20 (1976); Cmnd 6419; previously published as Cmnd 1515

except in certain specified cases, to stay any legal proceedings brought in respect of a matter referred to arbitration under such an agreement. Sections 2, 3 and 4 of the 1975 Act, giving effect to arts III, IV and V of the convention, go on to deal with the recognition and enforcement of the awards themselves after they have been made.

The exceptional cases in which the court is not bound to recognise and enforce a convention arbitration agreement by granting a stay of legal proceedings are defined in s 1(1) of the 1975 Act as those in which the court is satisfied that the arbitration agreement concerned is 'null and void, inoperative or incapable of being performed', or that 'there is not in fact any dispute between the parties with regard to the matter agreed to be referred'. The whole of the expression 'null and void, inoperative or incapable of being performed', as so used, is taken directly from para 3 of art II of the convention.

It follows from what is said above that the context in which the words 'incapable of being performed' are used is the context of the recognition and enforcement of arbitration agreements which, if valid and effective, will result in awards being made, and not the context of the recognition and enforcements of such awards themselves after they have been made. Having regard to that context it appears to me that the words 'incapable of being performed' should be construed as referring only to the question whether an arbitration agreement is capable of being performed up to the stage when it results in an award and should not be construed as extending to the question whether, once an award has been made, the party against whom it is made will be capable of satisfying it.

There is the further point that, even if the words 'incapable of being performed' were given the extended meaning discussed above, the fact that, if an award were made against one party, he would be incapable of satisfying it would not necessarily mean that the arbitration agreement was incapable of being performed. This is because the arbitration might also result in the award being made against the other party, in which case the incapacity concerned would be irrelevant.

For the reasons which I have given I decide this first point of law against the cargo owners. I hold that the fact that one of the parties to an arbitration agreement would be incapable of satisfying an award if it should be made against him does not make such agreement 'incapable of being performed' within the meaning of s 1(1) of the 1975 Act.

Since I may be wrong on the point of construction, however, I shall go on to consider whether it is in this case shown that, if an award were to be made against the shipowners, they would be incapable of satisfying it. This involves consideration of the financial position of the shipowners, including their rights as members of the P & I club, a subject which will in any case be highly material in relation to questions 3 and 4 later.

I shall consider first the financial position of the shipowners apart from such rights as they may have as members of the club. They are, as I indicated earlier, a company incorporated in Panama whose central management and control are exercised in Greece. Their only asset, apart from the charterparty freight in respect of which a Mareva injunction was granted earlier, and possibly also some further money payable to them by way of demurrage under the same charterparty, is the ship herself. That, at any rate, is the inference which I feel bound to draw in the absence of any evidence from the shipowners themselves to the contrary.

I understand that separate security representing the freight, and possibly also the demurrage, has been provided unconditionally by the club, and that the amount of such security is about £5,000. There was, however, no clear evidence about these matters before me, and the actual figure may be a little different.

The ship, according to affidavit evidence from the managers of the P & I club, A Bilbrough & Co Ltd, is at present laid up in Greece. There is no evidence about her present value, but, since she has been laid up for a considerable period of time without permanent repairs being done to her, I infer that it is substantially less than the £390,000 at which she was valued in July 1977.

If the cargo owners were to succeed fully in an arbitration in respect of their claim, the amount of the award, including interest and costs, would be likely to be about £700,000.

It is clear that, even after allowing for part of such award being met out of the separate security representing the freight and possibly also the demurrage, realisation by the shipowners of their only other asset in the form of the ship would provide a fund quite insufficient to satisfy the balance of the award.

The conclusion to which I feel bound to come, therefore, is that, if the cargo owners were to succeed in an arbitration and obtain an award in respect of the full amount of their claim, the shipowners would be incapable, out of their own resources alone, of satisfying more than a part, probably less than half, of the amount of the award. This proportion would, moreover, be much decreased if the shipowners, between now and the time when the award became payable, sold the ship and disposed of the proceeds in one way or another.

The question then arises whether the award would be satisfied by the P & I club on the shipowners' behalf. The ship was entered in the P & I club at the material time and the shipowners' calls had been paid up to date. They were therefore entitled, subject to the relevant rules of the P & I club, to be indemnified by the club in respect of liability for loss of or damage to cargo carried in the ship.

The relevant rules, however, which come under the heading 'Class 5. The Protecting and Indemnity Rules', include rr 6 and 8(k). Rule 6 provides that, unless the committee otherwise decides, the club is not obliged to indemnify a member in respect of a liability unless and until the member has himself first discharged the liability out of money belonging to him absolutely and not by way of loan or otherwise. Rule 8(k) provides that the club may, whenever it thinks fit, reduce the amount of a member's claim on the ground that he has not taken such steps to protect his interests as he would have done if the ship had not been entered for protection and indemnity.

The affidavit from the P & I club's managers, to which I referred earlier, contained evidence also about the way in which rr 6 and 8(k) mentioned above are applied in practice. As regards r 6 the evidence amounts to this: that, in the case of large claims like that involved in the present case, the committee often agrees to a member's request that the club should pay the claimant direct without insisting on the members discharging the claim out of his own resources first. No indication is however given by the deponent as to the criteria by which the committee makes its decisions on these matters. As regards r 8(k) the evidence is that the committee very seldom exercises its powers under this rule, even though there may be circumstances which would justify it in doing so.

The result of the above is that the question whether, if the shipowners could not pay the award or a large part of it themselves from their own resources, the P & I club would pay it directly on their behalf is left entirely open. The shipowners have no legal right to insist on the club doing so, and the club has an unfettered discretion, exercised on no principles revealed in evidence, to decline to do so. On the other hand the club often does agree to make such payments, and it is at least possible that it would do so in this case.

The burden of proof on the question whether, if the cargo owners were to succeed in an arbitration and obtain an award in respect of the whole of their claim, the shipowners would be incapable of satisfying the award lies, in my view, on the cargo owners. So far as satisfaction of the award, except in part, out of the shipowners' own resources is concerned, I consider that the cargo owners have discharged that burden of proof. So far as satisfaction of the award in full by the P & I club on the shipowners' behalf is concerned, however, I consider that the cargo owners have not discharged the burden, because the evidence shows a clear possibility that the P & I club would satisfy the award direct on its member's behalf and the cargo owners are unable to eliminate that possibility.

The result of the conclusions to which I have come on the matters discussed above is that the contention for the cargo owners, that the court should in this case refuse a stay under s 1(1) of the 1975 Act on the ground that the arbitration agreement is incapable of being performed, fails both on the law and the facts.

It follows that I answer question 2 by holding that the shipowners were, as at 28th July 1977, entitled under s 1(1) to a stay of the cargo owners' action.

3 *If the shipowners were entitled to, as at 28th July 1977, a stay of the cargo owners'*
action, were they also entitled, along with and consequent on such stay, to the
unconditional release of the ship from arrest?

It was contended for the shipowners that, whenever an action in rem in which a ship is
under arrest is stayed under s 1(1) of the 1975 Act, an order for the unconditional release
of the ship from arrest must also be made, and that the court has no discretion, whatever
the circumstances of any particular case, to refuse such order. In support of this contention
counsel for the shipowners relied on two comparatively recent cases decided by me in this
court which he said were together conclusive of the matter. These were *The Cap Bon*[1] and
The Golden Trader[2].

In *The Cap Bon*[1] there was a claim by charterers against shipowners for damage to cargo
carried under a charterparty containing a London arbitration clause. The charterers began
two proceedings against the shipowners in respect of the claim: first, an action in rem in
the Liverpool District Registry, in which they arrested the ship concerned, and in which
the shipowners, having appeared, gave bail in order to obtain her release; and, secondly,
arbitration proceedings under the arbitration clause in the charterparty. The charterers
did not proceed with the action but were ready and willing to proceed with the arbitration,
their plan being that, if and when they obtained an award in their favour in the arbitration,
they would be able to enforce it against the bail in the action. The shipowners applied by
summons to the district registrar for an order that the action either be proceeded with by
the charterers or else be dismissed and the bail given in it released. The district registrar
refused the order sought, but on appeal I took a different view and made an order that,
unless the charterers proceeded with the action by serving a statement of claim within 21
days, the action should stand dismissed and the bail bond should be cancelled.

My decision was based on two propositions of law, one positive and one negative, which
I considered flowed from the nature and form of the provisions in the Administration of
Justice Act 1956, by which jurisdiction in rem is conferred on the Admiralty Court. The
first and positive proposition is that the purpose of arresting a ship in an action in rem is
to provide the plaintiff with security for the payment of any judgment which he may
obtain in such action, or of any sum which may become payable to him under a settlement
of such action. The second and negative proposition is that it is not the purpose of arresting
a ship in an action in rem to provide the plaintiff with security for payment of an award
which he may obtain in an arbitration of the same claim as that raised in the action, and the
court therefore has no jurisdiction to arrest a ship, or keep her under arrest, for such other
purpose.

On the basis of these propositions I held that the charterers' plan was misconceived, in
that they could never enforce any award which they might obtain in the arbitration against
the bail given in the action. That being so, I thought that the charterers should be
compelled to choose between the two courses available to them, either pursuing their
claim in the action with the advantage of the security obtained by them in it or pursuing
their claim in the arbitration without that advantage.

It is to be observed that this was not a case where a defendant to an action was seeking
to have it stayed, either because he preferred to arbitrate or because he wished to have the
security which he had been compelled to give released. It was rather a case in which one
party, who was asserting a claim against another party, had set on foot at the same time two
separate proceedings in respect of such claim, one an action in rem and the other an
arbitration. He wished, however, to have the claim decided in the arbitration, and was
only using the action as a means of obtaining security for the award which he hoped to
obtain in the former proceeding. The other party contended that he was not entitled, as
a matter of law, to do that, and I upheld that contention.

In *The Golden Trader*[2] the facts were in many respects similar to those in the present

1   [1967] 1 Lloyd's Rep 543
2   [1974] 2 All ER 686, [1975] QB 348

case. A ship had been chartered by Dutch charterers from shipowners residing and carrying on business in Eire. The charterers had a claim against the shipowners for alleged breaches of the charterparty. The charterers began an action in rem against the ship in this court in respect of their claim and arrested her in that action. The shipowners then applied, first, for a stay of the action on the ground that the dispute to which it related was covered by the arbitration clause in the charterparty, and, secondly, along with and consequent on such stay, for the release of the ship from arrest.

The 1975 Act had not yet been passed at that time, and the application for a stay had to be decided under s 4 of the Arbitration Act 1950, which dealt separately in two subsections with non-protocol cases on the one hand and protocol cases on the other. So far as non-protocol cases are concerned, s 4(1) gave the court, subject to certain specified conditions, a discretionary power to stay an action relating to a matter agreed to be referred to arbitration. So far as protocol cases are concerned, s 4(2) imposed on the court, again subject to certain specified conditions, a mandatory duty to stay an action relating to a matter agreed to be so referred.   Section 28 of the 1950 Act further drew a distinction, so far as attaching terms to orders for a stay is concerned, between discretionary orders in non-protocol cases made under s 4(1) and mandatory orders in protocol cases made under s 4(2). The effect of the distinction was that the court had power to attach terms as to costs or other matters to orders made under s 4(1), but had no power to do so in the case of orders made under s 4(2).

I pointed out in my judgment in *The Golden Trader*[1] that, although the question for decision in that case arose on a stay granted under s 4(2) of the 1950 Act, it was part of a larger problem which arose whenever an action in rem, in which the property proceeded against had been arrested, or bail or other security had been given to prevent or obtain release from arrest, was subsequently stayed on the ground that the dispute ought properly to be decided by another tribunal. The same problem arose in three other kinds of cases, which I described shortly for convenience as 'non-protocol arbitration cases', 'foreign jurisdiction clause cases' and 'vexation cases' respectively: it was what to do with the security when the action was stayed.

I went on to say that there were, in principle, three ways in which this problem, which arose in these three other kinds of case, also, could be dealt with. The first method was for the court to retain the security to satisfy any judgment or award of the other tribunal. I called this 'the retention method', and pointed out that it was the method contemplated by the International Convention relating to the Arrest of Sea-going Ships 1952[2] ('the Brussels Arrest Convention') to which the United Kingdom was a party. The second method was for the court to release the security, but only subject to a term that the defendants provided other equivalent security outside the court to satisfy the judgment or award of the other tribunal. I called this 'the alternative security method', and gave examples of its use in foreign jurisdiction clause cases (*The Eleftheria*[3]) and in vexation cases (*The Atlantic Star*[4]). It appeared to me then that the alternative security method could also be used in non-protocol arbitration cases (ie cases under s 4(1) of the 1950 Act), where the grant of a stay, as in foreign jurisdiction clause cases and vexation cases, was discretionary and not mandatory. I still think that to be so, although the cases concerned should now, as a result of the 1975 Act, be renamed 'domestic arbitration cases'.

It was common ground in *The Golden Trader*[1] that the case was a protocol case to which s 4(2) rather than s 4(1) of the 1950 Act applied. If the decision in *The Cap Bon*[5] was correct, the court had no jurisdiction to use the retention method of dealing with the security; and, since it was a protocol case under s 4(2), s 28 meant that the alternative security method, in the form of attaching a term to the order for a stay, was not available either.

1   [1974] 2 All ER 686, [1975] QB 348
2   Misc 13 (1952), Cmd 8954, art 7, paras 1–4
3   [1969] 2 All ER 641, [1970] P 94
4   [1973] 2 All ER 175, [1974] AC 436
5   [1967] 1 Lloyd's Rep 543

In this situation it would have been open to counsel for the cargo owners to invite me to treat my earlier decision in *The Cap Bon*[1], that the court had no jurisdiction to use the retention method, as wrong and to depart from it. He did not, however, do this, but accepted that *The Cap Bon*[1] had been correctly decided and sought to resist the shipowners' application for the release of the ship on other grounds. His contention was that, although the court was bound to make an unconditional order for a stay, it was not also bound to make at the same time an order for the release of the ship. His main ground for this contention was that the stay was not final, and that the security therefore could and should be retained by the court to cater for the possibility of the stay later being removed and the action then proceeding to judgment. This argument did not conflict with the decision in *The Cap Bon*[1], for what was being suggested was not retention of the security for the inadmissible purpose of satisfying an award in the arbitration, but retention of the security for the proper purpose of satisfying a judgment in the action which might still, in certain hypothetical events, be obtained by the cargo owners.

Counsel for the cargo owners relied on a second and alternative ground for the court not releasing the ship. This was that, once the cargo owners had begun an arbitration, they would be entitled to apply to the court under s 12(6)(*f*) of the 1950 Act for an order securing the amount in dispute, and the court would have power, on such application, to order the arrest of the ship in order to provide such security. In these circumstances the existing arrest should be maintained at least until the cargo owners had had an opportunity of making such application and the court had adjudicated one way or the other on it.

A further possibility was canvassed in argument, at my suggestion if I remember correctly. This was that, if the court would be justified, on the first ground relied on by counsel for the cargo owners, in refusing an order for the release of the ship, it might also be justified in making such order for release but attaching to it a term with regard to the provision of alternative security. That would involve using, in effect, the alternative security method of dealing with the problem, but employing slightly different procedural means, which did not conflict with s 28 of the 1950 Act, for the purpose.

The conclusion with regard to these matters which I reached were as follows. (1) That the court had no jurisdiction to keep the ship under arrest in order to provide the cargo owners with security for an award in the arbitration. It only had jurisdiction to keep her under arrest in order to provide security for a judgment or settlement in the action. This conclusion accorded with my earlier decision in *The Cap Bon*[1], which was not, as I have said, challenged by counsel for the cargo owners, and which appeared to me in any event to derive support from the approach adopted in three earlier cases which I examined: *The Athenée*[2], *Foresta Romana SA v Georges Mabro (Owners)*[3] and *The Fehmarn*[4]. (2) That a stay of the action, not being final, could later be removed for good cause, in which case the action could still proceed to judgment or settlement. (3) That good cause for removal of the stay might arise if the arbitration subsequently (in the words of s 4(2) of the 1950 Act) became inoperative or could not proceed. There was, however, no evidence of there being more than a remote possibility of events of that kind supervening in that case. The court would not, therefore, be justified in keeping the ship under arrest in order to cater for the possibility of the stay being removed and the action proceeding by reason of such supervening events. (4) That failure by the shipowners to satisfy any award which the cargo owners might later obtain in the arbitration would not necessarily be good cause for the removal of the stay. In the event of such failure the cargo owners would be entitled either to enforce the award as a judgment under s 26 of the 1950 Act or to sue for breach of the

1   [1967] 1 Lloyd's Rep 543
2   (1922) 11 Ll L Rep 6
3   (1940) 66 Ll L Rep 139
4   [1957] 2 All ER 707, [1957] 1 WLR 815; *affd* [1958] 1 All ER 333, [1958] 1 WLR 159

arbitration agreement (see *Bremer Oeltransport GmbH v Drewry*[1] to which I referred earlier). There was no evidence before the court to suggest that the shipowners, if an award were to be made against them, would not pay under it. The court would not, therefore, be justified in keeping the ship under arrest in order to cater for the possibility of the stay being removed and the action proceeding by reason of the shipowners not paying under an award. (5) That s 12(6)(*f*) of the 1950 Act did not give the court power to arrest a ship, or to keep her under arrest, in order to provide security for the claim of a claimant in an arbitration. The argument for the cargo owners based on that provision accordingly failed. (6) That since, in all probability at least, the stay would be final and there would be no judgment or settlement in the action to be satisfied, the court should make an unconditional order for the release of the ship, and should not qualify such order by attaching to it a term with regard to the provision of alternative security.

In *The Golden Trader*[2] the question of stay was, as I explained, governed by s 4(2) of the 1950 Act. That subsection was repealed by the 1975 Act and replaced by the provisions of s 1 of the latter Act which I set out earlier. The 1975 Act further repealed the proviso to s 28 of the 1950 Act, which had prohibited the attachment of any terms as to costs or other matters to orders made under s 4(2).

It might perhaps have been contended in the present case that, since the 1975 Act contained no express prohibition against attaching terms as to costs or other matters to orders for a stay under s 1(1) of that Act, the court had a discretion to do so. Counsel for the cargo owners, however, did not argue that this was so, but accepted that orders for a stay made under s 1(1) of the 1975 Act, like orders for a stay made under s 4(2) of the 1950 Act, had to be unconditional, that is to say without any terms of any kind attached to them.

I think that this concession was rightly made for, where a statute requires the court, in a specified situation, to make an order of a particular kind, the court can, in general, only attach terms to such order if the statute gives it express power to do so. The situation under the 1950 Act was that s 28 expressly gave the court power to attach terms to various kinds of orders, including orders made under s 4(1), while providing that the court should not have the same power in relation to orders made under s 4(2). The situation under the 1975 Act is that no power to attach terms to orders for a stay is expressly given, and I do not think that any such power can be implied.

Counsel for the shipowners contended, as I indicated earlier, that the question whether, on a stay being granted, the ship should be unconditionally released, was concluded in the shipowners' favour by the previous decisions of this court in *The Cap Bon*[3] and *The Golden Trader*[2]. Counsel for the cargo owners did not accept that this was so, because the present case was, he said, distinguishable from *The Golden Trader*[2]. If he was wrong about that, however, he fell back on the submission that the two cases were wrongly decided and ought not to be followed.

In considering these matters it is, I think, necessary to distinguish between two aspects of the problem. The first aspect is whether the view which I expressed in *The Cap Bon*[3] and followed in *The Golden Trader*[2], that the court has no jurisdiction to arrest a ship, or keep her under arrest, in order to provide a plaintiff with security for payment of an arbitration award, as distinct from payment of a judgment or settlement in the action in rem concerned, is correct or not. The second aspect is whether, assuming that view to be correct, the court nevertheless has a discretion, when it grants a mandatory stay under the 1975 Act of an action in rem in which a ship has been arrested, to refuse to release the ship from arrest unless alternative security for payment of an award in the arbitration is provided; or, to put the same thing in a different way, to attach to any order made for the release of the ship, as distinct from the order for the stay of the action, a term relating to the provision of such alternative security.

1   [1933] 1 KB 753, [1933] All ER Rep 851
2   [1974] 2 All ER 686, [1975] QB 348
3   [1967] 1 Lloyd's Rep 543

I shall refer to these two aspects of the problem as the jurisdiction point and the discretion point respectively.

The jurisdiction point

The conclusion on the jurisdiction point which I reached in *The Cap Bon*[1] and followed in *The Golden Trader*[2] was, from the point of view of what I believe that the law on the matter ought to be, as distinct from what I felt obliged to hold that it was, an unsatisfactory conclusion.

I say this for two reasons. The first reason is that I think that, quite apart from any international convention relating to the matter to which the United Kingdom is a party, the court should have power, when it grants a stay, on the ground that the dispute should be decided by another tribunal, of an action in rem in which security has been obtained, to retain such security to satisfy any judgment or award of the other tribunal. When the grant of a stay is discretionary, as in domestic arbitration cases, foreign jurisdiction clauses cases and vexation cases, the court can get round the lack of such power, and has in practice got round it, by using the alternative security method. It would, however, be more satisfactory, in my view, even in those cases, to use the retention method, which is both more simple and direct, and which is, I believe, commonly used in other jurisdictions.

The second reason is that art 7 of the Brussels Arrest Convention[3], to which the United Kingdom is a party, contemplates that a court, which stays an action on the ground that the dispute should be decided by another tribunal, will have power to retain any security obtained in the action for the purposes mentioned above. I drew attention to this fact, as I said earlier, in the course of my judgment in *The Golden Trader*[2]. I further thought it right to point out at the end of my judgment in that case that, if the view on the jurisdiction point which I had formed was correct, this court did not have the power which the convention contemplated that it would have, and this was a situation which could not be regarded as satisfactory and which it would be desirable for Parliament to remedy.

I have said that counsel for the cargo owners submitted, by way of alternative argument in support of his case, that the opinion on the jurisdiction point which I formed in *The Cap Bon*[1] and followed in *The Golden Trader*[2] was wrong. In view of that submission I have reconsidered carefully the reasons which led me to form that opinion, and it will be apparent, from the observations which I have made above, that I should be in no way reluctant to change it if I were persuaded that it would be right to do so. Having re-examined the whole question, however, I remain of the same opinion that, without some statutory authority, which does not unfortunately at present exist (although it could, of course, easily be given), the court has no jurisdiction to use the retention method, that is to say to retain security not for the purpose of satisfying a judgment or settlement in the action in which the security has been given, but to satisfy the judgment or award of another tribunal.

The discretion point

There was a controversy before me as to what *The Golden Trader*[2] actually decided. For the shipowners it was said that it decided that, in every case where the court grants a mandatory stay of an action in rem in which the ship proceeded against has been arrested, it is bound also to make an unconditional order for the release of the ship. If the case decided that, and decided it correctly, then it follows that the shipowners in this case were entitled, as at 28th July 1977, along with a stay of the cargo owners' action, to an unconditional order for the release of the ship.

1   [1967] 1 Lloyd's Rep 543
2   [1974] 2 All ER 686, [1975] QB 348
3   Misc 13 (1952), Cmd 8594

For the cargo owners it was said that the decision in *The Golden Trader*[1], that the shipowners were entitled to an unconditional order for the release of the ship, was related *a* to the finding made by the court in that case, that in all probability the stay would be final and that there would therefore be no judgment in the action to be satisfied. In these circumstances, the decision left open the question whether, in other cases where it was shown that the stay might well not be final and there might well therefore still be a judgment in the action to be satisfied, the court might not be justified in keeping the ship under arrest or only releasing her subject to a term for the provision of alternative *b* security. Alternatively, if the case laid down the general rule which the shipowners said it did, it was to this extent at least wrong.

The relevant passage in my judgment in *The Golden Trader*[2] reads as follows:

> 'In theory I do not see why, if it is appropriate to use the alternative security method in non-protocol arbitration cases, foreign jurisdiction clause cases and vexation cases, *c* where the grant of a stay is discretionary, it should not also be appropriate to use it in protocol arbitration cases, where the grant of a stay is mandatory, even if the procedure employed for the purpose has to be slightly different. On further examination of the point, however, I think that protocol arbitration cases must, in this respect, be treated differently. Counsel for the defendants argued that to attach a term for the provision of alternative security to the order for release, while not offending against the letter *d* of s 28 of the 1950 Act, would offend against its spirit. While this may be the right way to put the matter, I should prefer to put it differently as follows. The starting point, if *The Cap Bon*[3] is right, is that the court can only retain the security to satisfy a judgment or compromise in the action itself. It follows that, if the courts stays the action, *so that there will, in all probability at least, be no judgment or compromise in the action to be satisfied*, it must then release the security. Putting it shortly, if there is a stay, *e* there must, as a necessary consequence, be a release. In cases where the grant of a stay is discretionary, the court can refuse a stay unless alternative security is provided. The defendant then has to choose between having a stay subject to a term for the provision of such security and not having a stay at all. If he chooses the former, then, subject to his complying with the term, he gets both a stay and a release; if he chooses the latter, he gets neither. By contrast, in protocol arbitration cases, where the grant of a stay is *f* mandatory, the court cannot refuse a stay unless alternative security is granted. It is bound to grant a stay in any event, and, since release is a necessary consequence of a · stay, it is bound also to grant a release.' [The emphasis is mine.]

I can well understand this passage being read as meaning that, in all cases where the stay of an action in rem is mandatory, the security obtained in it must be unconditionally *g* released. It was, however, not necessary for me to go so far as that in order to decide the case before me, and the words italicised show that my views were being expressed in relation to a case in which in all probability the stay of the action would be final and there would therefore be no judgment in the action to be satisfied. In these circumstances I think that counsel for the cargo owners was right in saying either that the case left open the question as to what order should be made in other cases in which it was shown that the stay *h* might well not be final, and that there might well therefore still be a judgment in the action to be satisfied, or alternatively that, if the case did not leave that question open, it ought to have done so and was to that extent wrong.

On the footing that the question is an open one, it was suggested for the shipowners that a party to an arbitration agreement should be treated as having, by entering into such an *j*

1   [1974] 2 All ER 686, [1975] QB 348
2   [1974] 2 All ER 686 at 696, [1975] QB 348 at 359–360
3   [1967] 1 Lloyd's Rep 543

agreement, abandoned the rights which he would otherwise have had to security for any claim covered by the agreement.

I do not accept this proposition at all. The choice of forum for the determination of the merits of a dispute is one thing. The right to security in respect of maritime claims under the Admiralty law of this country is another. This distinction has been recognised and given effect to by the way in which the court has exercised its discretion in foreign jurisdiction clause cases and vexation cases, in which it has either treated the plaintiff's right to security as a material factor in refusing a stay (The Athenée[1] and The Fehmarn[2]) or else has only granted a stay subject to a term for the provision of alternative security (The Eleftheria[3] and The Atlantic Star[4], and more recently The Makefjell[5]).

If this distinction between choice of forum on the one hand and right to security on the other is recognised and given effect to in foreign jurisdiction clause cases and vexation cases, I cannot see any good reason why it should not equally be recognised and given effect to in arbitration cases, whether the grant of a stay is discretionary under s 4(1) of the 1950 Act, or, as in the present case, mandatory under s 1(1) of the 1975 Act.

I would stress again in this connection also that the distinction in question is clearly recognised and given effect to by the Brussels Arrest Convention[6].

The process by which property, which has been lawfully arrested in an action in rem, can be released at the instance of the party interested in it, is the making by the court of an order for the issue of a release under RSC Ord 75, r 13(4). That rule provides, so far as material: 'A release may be issued at the instance of a party interested in the property under arrest if the court so orders . . .' That rule, as I understand it, gives the court a discretion, when an application for an order for the issue of a release is made, whether to make such order or not. The discretion so given is, so far as the terms of the rule go, unfettered, but it must, like any other discretion, be exercised judicially.

There is nothing in s 1(1) of the 1975 Act which obliges the court, whenever it grants a stay of an action in rem in which security has been obtained, to make an order for the unconditional release of such security. Nor did s 4(2) of the 1950 Act, now repealed, impose any such obligation. That being so, I think that it is a matter for the discretion of the court, acting under the rule referred to above, what order it should make with regard to such security, and that the way in which it exercises that discretion must depend on the circumstances of each particular case.

If, on the one hand, the case is one where in all probability the stay will be final and there will therefore never be any judgment in the action to be satisfied, the court should exercise its discretion by releasing the security unconditionally, as was done in The Golden Trader[7]. If, on the other hand, the case is one where the stay may well not be final and there may well therefore still be a judgment in the action to be satisfied, the court should exercise its discretion either by refusing to release the security at all or by only releasing it subject to a term that the defendants shall provide alternative security for payment of any award in the arbitration.

On this view of the law it is necessary to consider, in relation to the facts of this particular case, whether in all probability the stay will be final and there will therefore never be any judgment in the action to be satisfied or whether the stay may well not be final and there may well therefore still be a judgment in the action to be satisfied.

It is in this respect that counsel for the cargo owners contended that the present case was clearly distinguishable from The Golden Trader[7]. There was, he said, ample evidence to

---

1   (1922) 11 Ll L Rep 6
2   [1958] 1 All ER 333, [1958] 1 WLR 159
3   [1969] 2 All ER 641, [1970] P 94
4   [1973] 2 All ER 175, [1974] AC 436
5   [1975] 1 Lloyd's Rep 528; [1976] 2 Lloyd's Rep 29
6   Misc 13 (1952), Cmd 8954
7   [1974] 2 All ER 686, [1975] QB 348

show that, if the cargo owners obtained an award in respect of the full amount of their claim, the shipowners might well be unable to satisfy it, even if all available steps to enforce the award were taken. In that event the cargo owners would be entitled to have the stay of the action removed and to obtain a judgment in rem against the shipowners in it. That judgment would, however, be worthless unless there were security still available against which it could be satisfied. Justice to the cargo owners therefore demanded that the court should either, as at 28th July 1977, have kept the ship under arrest to serve as such security or alternatively should only have released her subject to a term that the shipowners provided alternative security to satisfy an award in the arbitration.

Counsel for the shipowners contended that it was wrong to suggest that, if an award should be made against the shipowners and they should be unable to satisfy it, the cargo owners would then be in a position to have the stay of the action removed and to obtain a judgment in rem in it. It was wrong, he said, because, once an award was made, the cargo owners' cause of action would become merged in the award and would therefore no longer be available to them for prosecution in the action. In these circumstances the whole argument for the cargo owners broke down, and the whole basis for keeping the ship under arrest, or only releasing her subject to a term for the provision of alternative security, disappeared.

This contention involves a consideration of the law of merger in relation, first, to arbitral awards, and, secondly, to causes of action in rem. I am prepared to assume, without finally deciding, that, just as a cause of action in personam which is adjudicated on by an English court merges in the judgment of that court, so also a similar cause of action which is adjudicated on by an English arbitral tribunal merges in the award of that tribunal. That is the view which is expressed in Spencer-Bower and Turner on The Doctrine of Res Judicata[1], and it appears to be supposed at least by *Gascoyne v Edwards*[2], and possibly also by certain other cases to which I was referred.

It has, however, been held that a cause of action in rem, being of a different character from a cause of action in personam, does not merge in a judgment in personam, but remains available to the person who has it so long as, and to the extent that, such judgment remains unsatisfied: *The Bengal*[3], *The John and Mary*[4] and; *The Cella*[5]; see also *The Sylph*[6] (although this may have turned partly on an express reservation made in the submission to arbitration concerned) and *Yeo v Tatem, The Orient*[7]. The situation must, in my view, be the same in the case of an arbitral award, which is likewise based on a cause of action in personam.

It was argued for the shipowners that this exception to the general rule of merger applied only when the cause of action in rem was founded on a maritime lien, which the cargo owners' claim in the present case is not. The first two cases referred to above, *The Bengal*[3] and *The John and Mary*[4], were certainly maritime lien cases, the claim in the former being for wages and in the latter for damage by collision. But the observations of Hannen P in the third case, *The Cella*[8], related to a claim for repairs and necessaries made under s 4 of the Admiralty Court Act 1861 in respect of which the plaintiff had no maritime lien, but only, like the cargo owners in the present case, a statutory right of action in rem. I cannot see any good reason in principle for distinguishing in this respect between a cause of action founded on a maritime lien and one founded on a statutory right in rem. It appears to me,

1   2nd Edn (1969), p 362, para 433
2   (1826) 1 Y & J 19, 148 ER 569
3   (1859) Sw 468, 166 ER 1220
4   (1859) Sw 471, 166 ER 1221
5   (1888) 13 PD 82
6   (1867) LR 2 A & E 24
7   (1871) LR 3 PC 696
8   13 PD 82 at 85

therefore, both on principle and on authority, that the distinction suggested is not a valid one.

The result is that I accept the argument of counsel for the cargo owners that, if an award should be made against the shipowners and they should be unable to satisfy it, the cargo owners would be entitled to have the stay of the action removed and to proceed to a judgment in rem in it.

I examined earlier, in relation to question 2, the financial situation of the shipowners and the position of the club in the matter. As a result of that examination I have no hesitation in concluding that this is a case in which, if the cargo owners should obtain an award in respect of the full amount of their claim, the shipowners might well be unable to satisfy it, either themselves or through the medium of the club. It follows, on my view, that a cause of action in rem does not, as a matter of law, become merged in an arbitral award, that this is a case where the stay might well not be final and that there might well therefore still be a judgment in the action to be satisfied.

In these circumstances, applying the principles for the exercise of the court's discretion which I concluded earlier were the right principles to apply, I consider that the court ought in this case to have exercised its discretion, as at 28th July 1977, by either keeping the ship under arrest or by only releasing her subject to a term for the provision of alternative security.

It follows that I answer question 3 by saying that the shipowners were not entitled, as at 28th July 1977, along with and consequent on the stay of the action, to the unconditional release of the ship from arrest.

4 *If, as at 28th July 1977, the shipowners were entitled to the unconditional release*
of the ship from arrest, were the cargo owners then entitled, by way of alternative
security for their claim, to a Mareva injunction in respect of the ship?

This further question only arises if I am wrong on question 3.

The power of the High Court to grant Mareva injunctions under s 45 of the Supreme Court of Judicature (Consolidation) Act 1925 has been established by a series of recent decisions of the Court of Appeal culminating in *Rasu Maritima SA v Perusahaan Pertambangan Minyak Dan Gas Bumi Nagara (Pertamina)*[1]. Further, the House of Lords, while reserving the question of the correctness of those decisions, was prepared to assume the existence of the power, in principle, for the purpose of its decision in *The Siskina*[2].

A Mareva injunction is granted in a case where a plaintiff has brought an action here against a foreign defendant, and the latter has money or chattels within the jurisdiction which, if he were not prevented from doing so, he would be free to remove out of the jurisdiction before the plaintiff could bring the action to trial, and, if successful, obtain and enforce a judgment against him.

The injunction takes the form of an order restraining the defendant, by himself, his servants or agents, from selling, disposing of or otherwise dealing with such money or chattels or from removing them out of the jurisdiction, usually until further order. Its purpose is to ensure that, if the plaintiff succeeds in the action, there will be property of the defendant available here out of which the judgment which the plaintiff obtains in it can be satisfied.

On the footing that the procedure is available to provide a plaintiff, in a case where no question of arbitration arises, with security for any judgment which he may obtain in an action, I see no good reason in principle why it should not also be available to provide a plaintiff, whose action is being stayed on the application of a defendant in order that the claim may be decided by arbitration in accordance with an arbitration agreement between them, with security for the payment of any award which the plaintiff may obtain in the arbitration. I have further been informed by counsel that the Commercial Court has granted injunctions on this extended basis in a number of unreported cases.

---

1   [1977] 3 All ER 324, [1978] QB 644
2   [1977] 3 All ER 803, [1977] 3 WLR 818

I doubt whether specific statutory authority, beyond the general authority conferred on the court by s 45 of the Supreme Court of Judicature (Consolidation) Act 1925 is required to justify this extension of the Mareva injunction procedure. If such specific authority is required, however, I think that it is to be found in s 12(6) of the 1950 Act, which provides so far as material:

> 'The High Court shall have, for the purpose of and in relation to a reference, the same power of making orders in respect of . . . (*f*) securing the amount in dispute in the reference . . . and (*h*) interim injunctions . . . as it has for the purpose of and in relation to an action . . .'

As I mentioned earlier, it was argued for the charterers in *The Golden Trader*[1] that s 12(6)(*f*) above gave the court power to arrest a ship in order to secure the amount in dispute in an arbitration once such arbitration had been commenced. Counsel for the cargo owners in the present case went a stage further and argued that the provision gave the court power to do this not only once the arbitration concerned had been commenced, but also in anticipation of its commencement.

I was unable to accept the basic argument with regard to s 12(6)(*f*) put forward for the charterers in *The Golden Trader*[1], because it appeared to me that, on the true construction of that provision, it did not cover the arresting of a ship, or the keeping of a ship under arrest, in the exercise of the court's jurisdiction in rem at all. The provision refers to the power of 'making orders in respect of . . . securing the amount in dispute'. This did not seem to me to be appropriate language to describe the process of arrest in an action in rem, because such arrest does not result from the making of any order by the court, but from the party concerned himself causing a warrant of arrest to be issued under RSC Ord 75, r 5, subject to the requirements of that rule. The matters to which I thought the provision did relate were the court's powers of securing amounts in dispute in various other ways, for instance by making orders under RSC Ord 29, rr 2(3) and 6.

I still think that s 12(6)(*f*) does not cover the arresting of a ship, or the keeping of a ship under arrest, in the exercise of the court's jurisdiction in rem. It follows that I am equally unable to accept the extended argument as to the effect of that provision put forward for the cargo owners in the present case. The point involved in the extension itself, however, is a separate one, and I shall return to it shortly.

Although I cannot, for the reasons which I have given, accept that s 12(6)(*f*) covers the arresting of a ship, or the keeping of a ship under arrest, it appears to me that both s 12(6)(*f*) and s 12(6)(*h*) cover the granting of a Mareva injunction, and so give the court the same power to grant such an injunction for the purpose of and in relation to an arbitration as it has for the purpose of and in relation to an action or matter in the court.

As to the question whether the court can exercise such power not only once the arbitration concerned has been commenced but also in anticipation of its commencement, it is to be observed that RSC Ord 29, r 1(3), gives the court power to grant interim injunctions, for the purpose of and in relation to an action or matter in the court, before the writ or originating summons by which the cause or matter is to be begun has been issued, and, in such cases, to impose terms providing for the issue of the writ or originating summons, together with such other terms as it thinks fit.

It follows, in my view, that the court has power under s 12(6)(*f*) and (*h*) to grant a Mareva injunction for the purpose of and in relation to an arbitration which has not yet been commenced, and to do so subject to a term providing for the arbitration to be commenced within a specified time, together with such other terms, if any, as it thinks fit.

Various arguments were advanced for the shipowners against the application of the procedure of Mareva injunctions to ships. Firstly, it was said that, because the Administration of Justice Act 1956 provided for the arrest of ships in Admiralty actions in rem, it impliedly excluded ships from the categories of chattels in respect of which a

---

1   [1974] 2 All ER 686, [1975] QB 348

Mareva injunction could be granted under s 45 of the Supreme Court of Judicature (Consolidation) Act 1925. If that were not so, it was said, a plaintiff with a maritime claim might obtain a Mareva injunction in respect of two or more ships, or proceed in rem against one ship and obtain a Mareva injunction in respect of one or more other ships, and by these means obtain security for a larger amount than he could by proceeding in rem against a single ship (which was all he was allowed to do) under the 1956 Act. Secondly, it was said that, if a plaintiff was in the difficulty that he was not entitled, in a case like the present one, to ensure security for his claim by having a ship kept under arrest in the exercise of the court's jurisdiction in rem, he should not be allowed to get round that difficulty, and achieve substantially the same result, by obtaining a Mareva injunction relating to the same ship. Thirdly, it was said that the grant of a Mareva injunction in respect of a ship gave rise, or might well give rise, to a number of inconveniences. The ship would not be in the custody of the Admiralty Marshal, so that the control and effective enforcement of her detention provided by such custody would not be available. The detention of the ship might further create an obstruction in a port or elsewhere to the prejudice of a port authority or other third parties.

I do not find these arguments at all convincing. As regards the first and second arguments, it is to be observed that the shipowners entered an unconditional appearance to the cargo owners' action, so that it is not only an action in rem against the ship but also an action in personam against them. The rights given to the plaintiffs by the Supreme Court of Judicature (Consolidation) Act 1925 and the Administration of Justice Act 1956 are cumulative, not alternative: see particularly s 43 of the 1925 Act. That being so, I cannot see why the circumstance that the cargo owners cannot (if it be the case) maintain security for their claim by having the ship kept under arrest by the court in the exercise of its jurisdiction in rem should be a reason why they should not be entitled to obtain alternative security for their claim by means of a Mareva injunction relating to the ship granted by the court in the exercise of its jurisdiction in personam. On the contrary, the fact that they are unable, in their efforts to ensure security for their claim, to use one of the two methods potentially available for the purpose, seems to me to afford a very good reason why they should be permitted to use the other.

The questions of a plaintiff obtaining a Mareva injunction in respect of several ships, or of combining an arrest of one ship in proceedings in rem with the obtaining of a Mareva injunction in respect of one or more other ships in proceedings in personam, do not arise for consideration in this case. I would, however, just say that the prospect of a plaintiff being able to obtain several kinds of security cumulatively in respect of the same claim, if the size of such claim justifies it, is not one which fills me with any consternation or dismay.

As regards the third argument, I do not think that the fact that the ship will not be in the custody of the Admiralty Marshal is of any particular significance. The court grants injunctions in the expectation that they will be obeyed, not disobeyed, and a Mareva injunction relating to a ship does not differ in principle, so far as enforcement is concerned, from a similar injunction in respect of any other moveable chattel. As to third parties, if they should be adversely affected by the injunction, I think that they would be entitled to intervene in the proceedings in order to protect their interests.

The result is that I approach this matter on the basis that the court had power, as at 28th July 1977, to grant a Mareva injunction in this case, and that the only question is whether, in the words of s 45 of the Supreme Court of Judicature (Consolidation) Act 1925, it would have appeared to the court just and convenient to do so. That would have been a matter for the discretion of the court, having regard to the particular circumstances of the case.

Considering the matter as at 28th July 1977, there were two strong points in favour of granting a Mareva injunction. The first point was that the cargo owners had a very strong prima facie case in support of their claim. The second point was that, if an injunction were not granted, the cargo owners, assuming that they obtained an award, might well be unable to recover more than a comparatively small part of it. I have explained earlier why each of these matters should be so and do not need to do so again here.

There was one apparently strong point against granting an injunction. It was that the ship was a trading asset, and that, if the shipowners were compelled by an injunction to keep her here, they would lose the benefit of trading her. The strength of the point is, however, apparent only, for we now know that, since the ship was released, the shipowners have not used her for trading but have laid her up in Greece without carrying out permanent repairs to her. It may be said that this circumstance could not have been known in advance as at 28th July 1977. The intentions of the shipowners at that time would, however, have had to be investigated, and it would have been for them to prove that they intended to continue trading the ship. They adduced no evidence to show that, whatever it is now known in fact happened, it was then their intention to do so.

In any case there is a certain artificiality about the concept that, if a Mareva injunction had been granted, the ship would have remained here, for it is obvious from what in fact happened that the club would have given a letter of undertaking rather than have allowed their members' ship to be detained here indefinitely.

Having considered all the relevant circumstances of the case, including particularly the main points discussed above, I should on 28th July 1977, if it had been necessary for me to decide whether to grant a Mareva injunction or not, have exercised my discretion by granting such injunction, subject, I think, to a term providing for the arbitration to be commenced within a specified time.

It follows that I answer question 4 in the affirmative.

I have now examined and answered each of the four main questions which were argued before me. The result of my answers to questions 1 and 2 is that, on the shipowners' adjourned application in the cargo owners' action, there must be an order for a stay of the action. The result of my answer to question 3, or, if that is wrong, of my answer to question 4, is that, on the originating summons issued by the shipowners and the club, there must be a declaration that the club is not entitled to the return and cancellation of its letter of undertaking.

Order accordingly

Solicitors: *Ince & Co* (for the plaintiffs); *Hill Dickinson & Co* (for the defendants).

N P Metcalfe Esq   Barrister.

Owners of the mv Eleftherotria v Owners of the mv Despina R

The Despina R

Services Europe Atlantique Sud (SEAS) v Stockholms Rederiaktiebolag SVEA

The Folias

HOUSE OF LORDS
LORD WILBERFORCE, LORD DIPLOCK, LORD SALMON, LORD RUSSELL OF KILLOWEN AND LORD KEITH OF KINKEL
17th, 18th, 19th, 20th JULY, 19th OCTOBER 1978

Judgment – Foreign currency – Jurisdiction to order payment of sum expressed in foreign currency – Damages for tort – Currency in which judgment to be given – Loss and expenditure incurred in several foreign currencies in consequence of tort – Whether court having jurisdiction to give judgment for sum expressed in currency other than sterling – Whether damages to be awarded in plaintiff's own currency or currencies in which expenditure or loss directly and immediately incurred.

Arbitration – Award – Foreign currency – Damages – Breach of contract – Currency in which damages to be awarded – Charterparty governed by English law – Currency of contract US dollars – Cargo arriving at Brazilian port of discharge in damaged condition due to unseaworthiness of ship – French charterers purchasing Brazilian cruzeiros with French francs to settle claims by cargo receivers – Whether charterers' loss incurred in French francs or Brazilian cruzeiros – Whether damages to be awarded in currency in which loss incurred or currency which reflected charterers' actual loss.

The Despina R

In 1974 the Eleftherotria, a Greek ship owned by the plaintiffs and managed for them by a company having its principal place of business in New York, was damaged in a collision off Shanghai with another Greek ship, the Despina R, owned by the defendants. Temporary repairs were done to the Eleftherotria in Shangai. They were paid for by the plaintiffs in Chinese currency, renmimbi yuan ('RMB'). A survey, also carried out in Shanghai, was paid for in US dollars. The ship proceeded to Yokohama, where the plaintiffs incurred further expenditure which was paid for in Japanese yen. The ship sailed to Los Angeles where permanent repairs were carried out and paid for in US dollars. The plaintiff also incurred expenses in London in respect of the damaged ship which were paid for in sterling. The plaintiffs purchased the RMB, yen and sterling used to pay for the repairs and expenses with US dollars and used a US dollar account in New York for all the payments. The plaintiffs brought an action in England against the defendants alleging negligence and claiming damages for the collision. Negotiations followed and the parties agreed, inter alia, that the defendants were 85% to blame for the collision and would pay as damages 85% of the loss and damage occasioned to the plaintiffs by reason of the collision. In accordance with the terms of the settlement the plaintiffs applied for the separate trial of the question whether, where the plaintiffs had suffered loss or damage in a currency other than sterling, the court could give judgment for a sum expressed in that foreign currency. Brandon J[a] answered the question in the affirmative and held that the plaintiffs

---

were entitled to be awarded damages in the currencies in which the expenditure or loss had been directly and immediately incurred, ie in RMB, yen, sterling and US dollars. He indicated that he would have liked to have held that the plaintiffs were entitled to be awarded damages in US dollars, the currency in which the plaintiffs operated, but that he was precluded by authority from doing so. The defendants appealed, contending that damages for a tort could only be awarded in sterling and that the foreign currency had to be converted into sterling at the date when the loss or damage was sustained. The plaintiffs cross-appealed, contending that they were entitled to be awarded damages in US dollars. The Court of Appeal[b] dismissed the appeal and allowed the cross-appeal. The defendants appealed to the House of Lords.

Held – Where a plaintiff had suffered damage or sustained loss in a foreign currency as the result of a tort committed against him and had used his own currency, whether sterling or otherwise, to obtain the amount of foreign currency required to make good the damage or loss or if his loss could only be appropriately measured in his own currency, then, applying the principle of restitutio in integrum and having regard to the fact that English courts and arbitrators were able to award damages in currency other than sterling, the plaintiff's loss or damage was to be measured in his own currency, and not in the foreign currency or necessarily in sterling, provided his own currency was the currency in which his loss was felt and was the currency which it was reasonably foreseeable he would have had to spend, by virtue of being the currency in which he generally operated or with which he had the closest connection. If the plaintiff was not able to show that the currency he had expended to obtain the foreign currency was the currency in which he normally conducted his operations, his loss or damage was to be measured in the currency in which it immediately arose. Since the currency in which the plaintiffs generally operated and with which they had the closest connection was US dollars and since that was the currency in which they had effectively had to bear the loss, they were entitled to be awarded damages in US dollars. The appeal would therefore be dismissed (see p 426 *f g*, p 427 *c d*, p 428 *a* to *c* and *f*, p 431 *g h*, p 432 *e* to *g* and p 433 *c*, post).

Miliangos v George Frank (Textiles) Ltd [1975] 3 All ER 801 applied.

Owners of Steamship Celia v Owners of Steamship Volturno, The Volturno [1921] All ER Rep 110 distinguished.

Decision of the Court of Appeal [1977] 3 All ER 874 affirmed.

The Folias

A French company ('the charterers') chartered a ship from its Swedish owners to carry a cargo from Spain to Brazil. The charterparty contained a London arbitration clause and the proper law of the contract was English law. During the voyage the ship's refrigerating machinery failed and the cargo arrived in Brazil in a damaged condition. The Brazilian receivers of the cargo claimed against the charterers as issuers of the bills of lading for the damage to the cargo. On 11th August 1972 the charterers, whose place of business was Paris and who conducted their business in French francs, settled the cargo receivers' claim in Brazilian cruzeiros which they had purchased with French francs. The charterers then claimed from the Swedish owners the amount of French francs expended on the ground that the owners had been in breach of the warranty of seaworthiness in the charter. In the course of the ensuing arbitration proceedings, the owners accepted liability and admitted that the measure of damage was the amount the charterers had had to pay to the cargo receivers, but disputed the currency in which they should pay damages to the charterers. Between August 1972 and the time of the arbitration the cruzeiro had devalued markedly against the French franc to a little over half its value. The owners contended that the award should be expressed in cruzeiros. On 24th July 1975 the arbitrators, rejecting that contention, made an award for payment of the amount of French francs claimed by the charterers. The arbitrators, however, stated a special case for the opinion of the High Court as to whether the charterers were entitled to an award in French francs. The judge[c] held

---

b   [1977] 3 All ER 874 at 892

c   [1977] 3 All ER 945

a that the award should be in cruzeiros in the absence of a contrary intention in the contract, the damages having to be calculated in the currency in which the loss had been incurred. The charterers appealed to the Court of Appeal^d which allowed the appeal and restored the arbitrators' award. The owners appealed to the House of Lords.

Held – Where the proper law of a contract was English law and the contract specified a particular currency as the currency of account and payment in respect of all transactions *b* arising under the contract, then any damages awarded under the contract were to be awarded in the currency of the contract, since that was the currency with which the contract had the closest and most real connection. However, where it was not apparent from the terms of the contract that damages for breach were to be awarded in a currency specified for the satisfaction of obligations under the contract, then damages were to be awarded in the currency which most truly expressed the plaintiff's loss. In ascertaining *c* that currency the questions to be asked were what the currency was which would as nearly as possible compensate the plaintiff in accordance with the principle of restitutio in integrum and whether the parties were to be taken to have had that currency in contemplation. Since it was not apparent from the charterparty in what currency damages for breach should be awarded and since the charterers' actual loss was the amount of the French francs expended by them in acquiring the cruzeiros necessary to settle the cargo *d* receivers' claim, the arbitrators had been right to express the award in French francs. The appeal would therefore be dismissed (see p 429 *d* to p 430 *a*, p 431 *b c* and p 433 *b c*, post).

Miliangos v George Frank (Textiles) Ltd [1975] 3 All ER 801 and *Jugoslavenska Oceanska Plovidba v Castle Investment Co Inc* [1973] 3 All ER 498 applied.

Jean Kraut AG v Albany Fabrics Ltd [1977] 2 All ER 116 and *Federal Commerce and Navigation Co Ltd v Tradax Export SA* [1977] 2 All ER 41 approved.

e *Di Ferdinando v Simon, Smits & Co Ltd* [1920] All ER Rep 347 and *The Canadian Transport* (1932) 43 Ll L Rep 409 distinguished.

Decision of the Court of Appeal [1978] 2 All ER 764 affirmed.

Notes

f For damages for breach of contract, the currency of which is foreign currency, see 8 Halsbury's Laws (4th Edn) para 613.

For damages in tort, see 37 Halsbury's Laws (3rd Edn) 141, para 251.

For foreign currency liabilities converted into sterling for enforcement, see 27 ibid 6, para 5.

For judgments for a sum of money payable in foreign currency, see 12 Halsbury's Laws (4th Edn) para 1201, and for cases on the subject, see 17 Digest (Reissue) 203–205, 749–758.

g

Cases referred to in opinions

Canadian Transport, The (1932) 43 Ll L Rep 409, CA.

Celia (Steamship) (Owners) v Owners of Steamship Volturno [1921] 2 AC 544, [1921] All ER Rep 110, 90 LJP 385, 126 LT 1, 15 ASP MLC 374, 27 Com Cas 46, HL, 17 Digest *h* (Reissue) 204, *753*.

Di Ferdinando v Simon, Smits & Co Ltd [1920] 3 KB 409, [1920] All ER Rep 347, 89 LJKB 1039, 124 LT 117, 25 Com Cas 37, CA, 17 Digest (Reissue) 204, *754*.

Federal Commerce and Navigation Co Ltd v Tradax Export SA, The Maratha Envoy [1977] 2 All ER 41, [1977] QB 324, [1977] 2 WLR 122, [1977] 1 Lloyd's Rep 217, CA; rvsd [1977] 2 All ER 849, [1978] AC 1, [1977] 3 WLR 126, [1977] 2 Lloyd's Rep 301, HL.

j *Kraut (Jean) AG v Albany Fabrics Ltd* [1977] 2 All ER 116, [1977] QB 182, [1976] 3 WLR 872, [1976] 2 Lloyd's Rep 350.

Jugoslavenska Oceanska Plovidba v Castle Investment Inc [1977] 3 All ER 498, [1974] QB 292, [1973] 3 WLR 847, [1973] 2 Lloyd's Rep 1, CA, Digest (Cont Vol D) 46, *2136a*.

d [1978] 2 All ER 764

Miliangos v George Frank (Textiles) Ltd [1975] 3 All ER 801, [1976] AC 443, [1975] 3 WLR
758, [1976] 1 Lloyd's Rep 201, HL, Digest (Cont Vol D) 691, 64c.

United Railways of the Havana and Regla Warehouses Ltd, Re [1960] 2 All ER 332, [1961] AC
1007, [1960] 2 WLR 969, HL, 11 Digest (Reissue) 489, 919.

Appeals

The Despina R

On 21st April 1974 a collision took place off Shanghai between two Greek ships, the
Eleftherotria, owned by the plaintiffs, and the Despina R, owned by the defendants. Both
ships were damaged. On 18th July 1974 the plaintiffs brought an action against the
defendants claiming damages for the collision on the ground that it was caused by the
negligence of the defendants, their servants or agents. The defendants raised a counterclaim
in respect of damage done to the Despina R. On 7th July 1976, following negotiations, it
was agreed between the parties, inter alia, that the defendants were 85% to blame for the
collision, that the defendants' counterclaim be dismissed, that the defendants should pay
to the plaintiffs as damages 85% of the loss and damage occasioned to the plaintiffs by
reason of the collision and that, subject to liberty, given to either party, to apply to the
Admiralty judge to determine in what currency the damages would be payable, such
damages should, failing agreement, be referred to the Admiralty registrar for assessment.
The agreement was filed in the Admiralty Registry and on 9th July the plaintiffs filed their
claim for damages. On 12th July, on an application for directions made by the plaintiffs
pursuant to the liberty reserved in the agreement of settlement, Brandon J ordered that the
following questions arising in the action should be tried separately: (a) whether, where the
plaintiffs had suffered damage or sustained loss in a currency other than sterling, they were
entitled to recover damages in respect of such damage or loss expressed in such other
currency; (b) if, in such a case, the plaintiffs were only entitled to recover damages
expressed in sterling at what date the conversion into sterling was to be made. On 28th
January 1977 Brandon J[1] held that the plaintiffs were entitled to recover damages in the
various foreign currencies in which the expenditure or loss had been immediately
incurred. The defendants appealed and the plaintiffs cross-appealed. On 17th June the
Court of Appeal[1] (Stephenson, Orr and Cumming-Bruce LJJ) dismissed the defendants'
appeal and allowed the plaintiffs' cross-appeal, holding that the damages should be awarded
in US dollars. The defendants appealed to the House of Lords. The facts are set out in the
opinion of Lord Wilberforce.

The Folias

By a time charterparty in New York Produce Exchange form dated 5th July 1971 the
respondents, Services Europe Atlantique Sud (SEAS) of Paris ('the charterers'), chartered the
motor vessel Folias from the appellants, Stockholms Rederiaktiebolag SVEA of Stockholm
('the owners'), for the carriage of onions from Valencia, Spain, to ports in Brazil. The
onions arrived in a damaged condition for which the owners admitted liability. A dispute
between the parties as to the currency in which damages should be assessed was referred to
arbitration. The arbitrators (Robert Reed Esq and Donald Davies Esq) awarded the
charterers the damages in French francs but stated their award in the form of a special case
requesting the opinion of the court on the following questions: (1) whether on the facts
found and on the true construction of the charterparty the charterers were entitled to an
award in French francs; (2) if the answer to (1) was no, then (a) what currency was to be
used for the award, Brazilian cruzeiros, US dollars, or pounds sterling, and (b) what was the
appropriate date for rate of exchange purposes. Robert Goff J[2] answered question (1) 'No'
and question (2)(a) 'Brazilian cruzeiros'. The charterers appealed to the Court of Appeal[3]
(Lord Denning MR, Ormrod and Geoffrey Lane LJJ) which allowed their appeal and

---

1   [1977] 3 All ER 874, [1977] 3 WLR 597
2   [1977] 3 All ER 945, [1977] 3 WLR 176
3   [1978] 2 All ER 764, [1978] 2 WLR 887

restored the arbitrators' award. The owners appealed to the House of Lords. The facts are set out in the opinion of Lord Wilberforce.

Nicholas Phillips QC and *John Reeder* for the owners of the Despina R.
C Staughton QC, M N Howard and *Sarah Miller* for the owners of the Eleftherotria.
N Merriman and *Timothy Young* for the owners of the Folias.
Gordon Pollock for the charterers of the Folias.

Their Lordships took time for consideration.

19th October. The following opinions were delivered.

LORD WILBERFORCE. My Lords, in *Miliangos v George Frank (Textiles) Ltd*[1], this House decided that a plaintiff suing for a debt payable in Swiss francs under a contract governed by Swiss law could claim and recover judgment in this country in Swiss francs. Whether the same, or a similar, rule could be applied to cases where (i) a plaintiff sues for damages in tort, or (ii) a plaintiff sues for damages for breach of contract were questions expressly left open for later decision. These questions were regulated before *Miliangos*[1] as to tort by *Owners of Steamship Celia v Owners of Steamship Volturno, The Volturno*[2] and as to contract by *Di Ferdinando v Simon, Smits & Co Ltd*[3], which decided that judgment in an English court could only be given in sterling converted from any foreign currency as at the date of the wrong. Now these questions are directly raised in the present appeals in each of which your Lordships have the advantage of judgments of the Court of Appeal and of judgments of high quality at first instance. These enable the House, as it could not have done in *Miliangos*[1], to consider some of the problems which may exist in the varied cases of torts and breaches of contract.

1.   *The Despina R*

The Eleftherotria and the Despina R are two Greek vessels which collided in April 1974 off Shanghai. On 7th July 1976 a settlement was arrived at under which it was agreed that the defendants should pay to the plaintiffs 85% of the loss and damage caused to the defendants by the collision. This is therefore a tort case based on negligence.

After the collision the Eleftherotria was taken to Shanghai where temporary repairs were carried out. She then went to Yokohama for permanent repairs, but it turned out that these could not be carried out for some time. She was therefore ordered to Los Angeles, California, USA, for permanent repairs. Expenses were incurred under various headings (particularised in the judgment of Brandon J) in foreign currencies, namely, renmimbi yuan ('RMB'), Japanese yen, US dollars, and as to a small amount in sterling. The owners of the ship are a Liberian company with head office in Piraeus (Greece). She was managed by managing agents with their principal place of business in the State of New York, USA. The bank account used for all payments in and out on behalf of the plaintiffs in respect of the ship was a US dollar account in New York, so all the expenses incurred in the foreign currencies other than US dollars were met by transferring US dollars from this account. The expenses incurred in US dollars were met directly by payment in that currency from New York.

The judge ordered that the following questions be tried separately, namely: (a) whether, where the plaintiffs have suffered damage or sustained loss in a currency other than sterling, they are entitled to recover damages in respect of such damage or loss expressed in such other currency; (b) if, in such a case, the plaintiffs are only entitled to recover damages expressed in sterling, at what date the conversion into sterling should be made. Under question (a) there are two alternatives. The first is to take the currency in which the

---

1   [1975] 3 All ER 801, [1976] AC 443
2   [1921] 2 AC 544, [1921] All ER Rep 110
3   [1920] 3 KB 409, [1920] All ER Rep 347

expense or loss was immediately sustained. This I shall call 'the expenditure currency'. The second is to take the currency in which the loss was effectively felt or borne by the plaintiff, having regard to the currency in which he generally operates or with which he has the closest connection. This I shall call 'the plaintiff's currency'. These two solutions have to be considered side by side with the third possible solution, namely, the sterling solution, taken at the date when the loss occurred (applying *The Volturno*[1]) or at some other date.

I consider first *The Volturno*[1]. Although, as in this case, there had been expenses for repairs incurred in foreign currency, these were not in issue on the appeal. That was only concerned with a claim for damages in respect of detention which was assessed in Italian lire. It was thought to be clear at that time that an English court could only give judgment for a sum in sterling, and it is this which formed the basis of the decision arrived at, namely that conversion must be made at the date of the breach and not at the date of judgment. This most clearly appears in the speech of Lord Sumner. He states[2] the argument in favour of conversion at the date of judgment: the creditor in that event would get the exact sum to which he was entitled. This would inevitably, he says, introduce a speculative element into all transactions: waiting to convert the currency until the date of judgment only adds the uncertainty of exchange to the uncertainty of the law's delays. There is no answer to this, he continues, except that the claimant's right is exclusively a right to lire and would result in a judgment for lire, if only an English court was, so to speak, competent to express itself in Italian. Earlier he had described the agreed numbers of lire as only part of the foreign language in which the court is informed of the damage sustained, which, like the rest of the foreign evidence, must be translated into English as at the date when the damage accrues.

The whole of this process of argument flows from the accepted inability of the court to receive a claim in lire and to give judgment in lire. The same point underlies just as clearly the opinion of Lord Parmoor[3]:

'The necessity for transferring into English money damages ascertained in a foreign currency arises in the fact that the Courts of this country have no jurisdiction to order payment of money except in English currency.'

The contrary view, based firmly on the principle of restitutio in integrum, is clearly stated by Lord Carson[4].

My Lords, I do not think that there can now be any doubt that, given the ability of an English court (and of arbitrators sitting in this country) to give judgment or to make an award in a foreign currency, to give a judgment in the currency in which the loss was sustained produces a juster result than one which fixes the plaintiff with a sum in sterling taken at the date of the breach or of the loss. I need not expand on this because the point has been clearly made both in *Miliangos*[5], and in cases which have followed it, as well as in commentators who, prior to *Miliangos*[5], advocated abandonment of the sterling breach-date rule. To fix such a plaintiff with sterling commits him to the risk of changes in the value of a currency with which he has no connection; to award him a sum in the currency of the expenditure or loss, or that in which he bears the expenditure or loss, gives him exactly what he has lost and commits him only to the risk of changes in the value of that currency, or those currencies, which are either his currency or those which he chosen to use.

I shall consider the objections against the use of that currency or those currencies, but first it is necessary to decide between the expenditure currency and the plaintiff's currency, a matter which gave the judges below some difficulty. Brandon J would have preferred

1   [1921] 2 AC 544, [1921] All ER Rep 110
2   [1921] 2 AC 544 at 558, [1921] All ER Rep 110 at 116–117
3   [1921] 2 AC 544 at 560, [1921] All ER Rep 110 at 118
4   [1921] 2 AC 544 at 566–567, [1921] All ER Rep 110 at 120–121
5   [1975] 3 All ER 801, [1976] AC 443

adoption of the plaintiff's currency but he considered himself prevented from doing so by *The Canadian Transport*[1], a collision case decided by a strong Court of Appeal. There the loss was originally suffered in Argentinian pesos but a claim was made which involved converting pesos into sterling, sterling into francs at one rate and francs into sterling at another rate, thus producing an exchange profit for the cargo owners. The decision of the Court of Appeal, against the cargo owners, was based in part on their rejection of the treble exchange manoeuvre and in part on their acceptance of the necessity of giving judgment in sterling. They could not have given judgment in either pesos or francs. In my opinion, and I agree with the Court of Appeal in the present case on this, this case, like *The Volturno*[2], does not preclude a decision in favour of the plaintiff's currency or the currency of the loss (there it would have been francs or pesos) once the possibility of giving judgment in a foreign currency exists.

I return to consider the alternatives.

My Lords, in my opinion, this question can be solved by applying the normal principles which govern the assessment of damages in cases of tort (I shall deal with contract cases in the second appeal). These are the principles of restitutio in integrum and that of the reasonable foreseeability of the damage sustained. It appears to me that a plaintiff, who normally conducts his business through a particular currency, and who, when other currencies are immediately involved, uses his own currency to obtain those currencies, can reasonably say that the loss he sustains is to be measured not by the immediate currencies in which the loss first emerges but by the amount of his own currency, which in the normal course of operation, he uses to obtain those currencies. This is the currency in which his loss is felt, and is the currency which it is reasonably foreseeable he will have to spend.

There are some objections to this, but I think they can be answered. First, it is said that to use the method of finding the loss in the plaintiff's currency would involve the court or arbitrators in complicated enquiries. I am not convinced of this. The plaintiff has to prove his loss: if he wishes to present his claim in his own currency, the burden is on him to show to the satisfaction of the tribunal that his operations are conducted in that currency and that in fact it was his currency that was used, in a normal manner, to meet the expenditure for which he claims or that his loss can only be appropriately measured in that currency (this would apply in the case of a total loss of a vessel which cannot be dealt with by the 'expenditure' method). The same answer can be given to the objection that some companies, particularly large multi-national companies, maintain accounts and operate in several currencies. Here again it is for the plaintiff to satisfy the court or arbitrators that the use of the particular currency was in the course of normal operations of that company and was reasonably foreseeable. Then it is said that this method produces inequality between plaintiffs. Two claimants who suffer a similar loss may come out with different sums according to the currency in which they trade. But if the losses of both plaintiffs are suffered at the same time, the amounts awarded to each of them should be equivalent even if awarded in different currencies; if at different times, this might justify difference in treatment. If it happened that the currencies of the two plaintiffs relatively changed in value before the date of judgment, that would be a risk which each plaintiff would have to accept. Each would still receive, for himself, compensation for *his* loss.

Finally it is said (and this argument would apply equally if the expenditure currency were taken) that uncertainty will take the place of certainty under the present rule. Undoubtedly the present (sterling-breach-date) rule produces certainty, but it is often simpler to produce an unjust rule than a just one. The question is whether, in order to produce a just, or juster, rule, too high a price has to be paid in terms of certainty.

I do not think so. I do not see any reason why legal advisers, or insurers, should not be able, from their knowledge of the circumstances, to assess the extent of probable liability. The most difficult step is to assess the quantum of each head of damage. Once this is done,

1   (1932) 43 Ll L Rep 409
2   [1921] 2 AC 544, [1921] All ER Rep 110

it should not be difficult, on the basis of information which the plaintiff must provide, to agree or disagree with his claim for the relevant currency. I wish to make it clear that I would not approve of a hard and fast rule that in all cases where a plaintiff suffers a loss or damage in a foreign currency the right currency to take for the purpose of his claim is 'the plaintiff's currency'. I should refer to the definition I have used of this expression and emphasise that it does not suggest the use of a personal currency attached, like nationality, to a plaintiff, but a currency which he is able to show is that in which he normally conducts trading operations. Use of this currency for assessment of damage may and probably will be appropriate in cases of international commerce. But even in that field, and still more outside it, cases may arise in which a plaintiff will not be able to show that in the normal course of events he would use, and be expected to use, the currency, or one of several currencies, in which he normally conducts his operations (the burden being on him to show this) and consequently the conclusion will be that the loss is felt in the currency in which it immediately arose. To say that this produces a measure of uncertainty may be true, but this is an uncertainty which arises in the nature of things from the variety of human experience. To resolve it is part of the normal process of adjudication. To attempt to confine this within a rigid formula would be likely to produce injustices which the courts and arbitrators would have to put themselves to much trouble to avoid.

Apart from these general considerations there are certain special problems which may arise in Admiralty cases to which attention was rightly drawn by Brandon J. I do not think it necessary, or wise, to comment on them in detail for I am satisfied that they do not in themselves create insuperable, or great, difficulties in the way of adopting the plaintiff's currency, where to do so is appropriate. Brandon J expressed on them provisional views which must clearly command respect and which demonstrate that the problems are soluble. I think it best to leave such cases to be decided as they arise in the light of full argument. Lastly there are some difficulties foreseen by the Court of Appeal[1]. I appreciate these but I think that the answer to them lies in the necessity for a plaintiff, claiming a judgment in the plaintiff's currency, to prove his case, that his loss was naturally and foreseeably borne in that currency. There should be no automatic and invariable rule to this effect; if, in the circumstances, he fails to satisfy the court or arbitrators, they may give judgment or award in whatever other currency represents his loss.

In my opinion the Court of Appeal reached a right conclusion on this case and I would dismiss the appeal.

2. The Folias

This case arises out of a charterparty under which the owners chartered the Folias to charterers for a round voyage from the Mediterranean to the East Coast, South America. The hire was expressed to be payable in US dollars, but there was a provision that in any general average adjustment disbursements in foreign currencies were to be exchanged in a European convertible currency or in sterling or in US dollars. The owners are a Swedish firm of shipowners and the charterers are a French company which operates shipping services. The proper law of the contract was English law.

In July 1971 the charterers shipped a cargo of onions at Valencia in Spain for carriage to Brazilian ports. They issued bills of lading in their own name. There was a failure of the vessel's refrigeration as a result of which the cargo was found to be damaged on discharge. The cargo receivers claimed against the charterers and, with the concurrence of the owners as to quantum, this claim was settled in August 1972 by a payment in Brazilian currency of 456,250 cruzeiros. In addition, the charterers incurred legal and other expenses.

The charterers discharged the cargo receivers' claim by purchasing the necessary amount of cruzieros with French francs. The arbitrators found that French francs were the currency in which the charterers accounted and that it was reasonable to contemplate that,

---

1   [1977] 3 All ER 874 at 901–902, [1977] 3 WLR 597 at 628

a being a French corporation and having their place of business in Paris, they would have to use French francs to purchase other currencies to meet cargo claims.

The charterers then claimed against the owners for the French francs which they had expended and for the amount of their expenses. In the alternative they claimed the equivalent in US dollars, that being said to be the currency of the contract (viz the charterparty). The basis of their claim was for damages for breach of the contract of affreightment.

b The claim was referred to arbitration in London, and the arbitrators held that they had jurisdiction to make an award in a foreign currency; in this they followed the decision of the Court of Appeal in *Jugoslavenska Oceanska Plovidba v Castle Investment Co Inc*[1]. They recorded that, along with other City of London arbitrators, they had frequently since that case made awards in a currency which was not the currency of the contract. They awarded the sum claimed in French francs for the reason that this seemed to them to be the most *c* appropriate and just result. On the hearing of the special case, Robert Goff J set aside the arbitrators' award and held that damages should have been awarded in Brazilian cruzeiros. This judgment was in turn reversed by the Court of Appeal which restored the award of the arbitrators.

My Lords, the effect of the decision of this House in *Miliangos*[2] is that, in contractual as in other cases, a judgment (in which for convenience I include an award) can be given in *d* a currency other than sterling. Whether it should be, and, in a case where there is more than one eligible currency, in which currency, must depend on general principles of the law of contract and on rules of conflict of laws. The former require application, as nearly as possible of the principle of restitutio in integrum, regard being had to what was in the reasonable contemplation of the parties. The latter involve ascertainment of the proper law of the contract, and application of that law. If the proper law is English, the first step *e* must be to see whether, expressly or by implication, the contract provides an answer to the currency question. This may lead to selection of the 'currency of the contract'. If from the terms of the contract it appears that the parties have accepted a currency as the currency of account and payment in respect of all transactions arising under the contract, then it would be proper to give a judgment for damages in that currency. This is, I think, the case which Lord Denning MR had in mind when he said:

f '[Arbitrators] should make their award in that currency because it is the proper currency of the contract. By that I mean that it is the currency with which the payments under the contract have the closest and most real connection'

(see *Jugoslavenska Oceanska Plovidba v Castle Investment Co Inc*[3]).

But there may be cases in which, although obligations under the contract are to be met *g* in a specified currency, or currencies, the right conclusion may be that there is no intention shown that damages for breach of the contract should be given in that currency or currencies. I do not think that Lord Denning MR was intending to exclude such cases. Indeed in the present case he said[4], in words which I would adopt, 'the plaintiff should be compensated for the expense or loss in the currency which most truly expresses his loss'. In the present case the fact that US dollars have been named as the currency in which *h* payments in respect of hire and other contractual payments are to be made provides no necessary or indeed plausible reason why damages for breach of the contract should be paid in that currency. The terms of other contracts may lead to a similar conclusion.

If then the contract fails to provide a decisive interpretation, the damage should be calculated in the currency in which the loss was felt by the plaintiff or 'which most truly expresses his loss'. This is not limited to that in which it first and immediately arose. In *j* ascertaining which this currency is, the court must ask what is the currency, payment in

1   [1973] 3 All ER 498, [1974] QB 292
2   [1975] 3 All ER 801, [1976] AC 443
3   [1973] 3 All ER 498 at 501, [1974] QB 292 at 298
4   [1978] 2 All ER 764 at 769, [1978] 2 WLR 887 at 892

which will as nearly as possible compensate the plaintiff in accordance with the principle of restitution, and whether the parties must be taken reasonably to have had this in contemplation. It would be impossible to devise a simple rule, other than the general principles I have mentioned, to cover cases on the sale of goods, on contracts of employment, on international carriage by sea or air: in any of these types of contracts the terms of the individual agreement will be important.

My Lords, it is obvious that this analysis, involving as it does a reversion to the ordinary law governing damages for breach of contract, necessitates a departure from older cases decided on the sterling-breach-date rule. I should comment on some of the latter.

Di Ferdinando v Simon, Smits & Co Ltd[1] was clearly decided on the sterling-breach-date principle so that the foundations of it have been impaired. It is possible, as suggested by Lord Denning MR[2], that the same results could have been reached if judgment had been given so as truly to express the plaintiff's loss, but the case itself can no longer be regarded as authoritative. The decision of Eveleigh J in *Jean Kraut A G v Albany Fabrics Ltd*[3] is in line with the principles I have endeavoured to state. The learned judge in effect applied to a claim in damages the same rule as *Miliangos*[4] applied to debt, thus applying, in reverse, the principles which led Viscount Simonds in *Re United Railways of Havana and Regla Warehouses Ltd*[5] to apply the same rule to debt as he held to apply to damages. *Federal Commerce and Navigation Co Ltd v Tradax Export SA, The Maratha Envoy*[6] I would regard as a decision on the 'currency of the contract' and correct on that basis. *The Canadian Transport*[7] I have already mentioned when dealing with the appeal in *The Despina R.* I regard the decision as depending on the sterling-breach-date rule which was thought to prevent a choice between the currency of expenditure and the currency of the plaintiff. Finally I would regard the original last paragraph of r 172 of Dicey and Morris on The Conflict of Laws[8], based as it is on existing authorities, as requiring revision, or reinterpretation, so as, at least, to reflect the principle that, subject to the terms of the contract, damages should be recoverable in the currency which most truly expresses the plaintiff's loss.

The present case is concerned with a charterparty for carriage by sea, the parties to which are Swedish and French. It was in the contemplation of the parties that delivery of the goods carried might be made in any of a number of countries with a currency different from that of either of the parties. Loss might be suffered, through non-delivery or incomplete delivery, or delivery of damaged or unsuitable goods, in any of those countries, and if any such loss were to fall on the charterer he in turn might have a claim against the shipowners. Although the proper law of the contract was accepted to be English by virtue of a London arbitration clause, neither of the parties to the contract, nor the contract itself, nor the claim which arose against the charterers, nor that by his charterers against the owners, had any connection with sterling, so that prima facie this would be a case for giving judgment in a foreign currency. This is not disputed in the present appeal, and the only question is which is the appropriate currency in which to measure the loss.

Prima facie, there is much to be said in favour of measuring the loss in cruzeiros; the argument for this was powerfully stated by Robert Goff J. The initial liability of the charterers was measured in that currency by the difference between the value of sound goods arrived at the port of discharge and the damaged value at that port. To require or admit a further conversion can be said to introduce an unnecessary complication brought about by an act of the charterers' choice. I am unable in the end to accept this argument.

1 [1920] 3 KB 409, [1920] All ER Rep 347
2 [1978] 2 All ER 764 at 771, [1978] 2 WLR 887 at 894
3 [1977] 2 All ER 116, [1977] QB 182
4 [1975] 3 All 801, [1976] AC 443
5 [1960] 2 All ER 332, [1961] AC 1007
6 [1977] 2 All ER 41, [1977] QB 324, CA (not appealed on this point)
7 (1932) 43 Ll L Rep 409
8 9th Edn (1973), p 894

The essential question is what was the loss suffered by the charterers. I do not find this to be identical with that suffered by the cargo receivers: the charterers' claim against the owners is not one for indemnity in respect of expenditure sustained but is one for damages for breach of contract. Robert Goff J makes this plain in his judgment[1]: '... the charterers' claim [as formulated] was a claim for damages, on the basis that [they] incurred a personal liability to the receivers under the bills of lading which they were compelled to discharge.' I think it must follow from this that their loss, which they claim as damages, was the discharge of the receivers' claim, together with the legal and other expenses they incurred. They discharged all these by providing francs, until they provided the francs to meet the receivers' claim they suffered no loss. Then secondly was this loss the kind of loss which, under the contract, they were entitled to recover against the owners? The answer to this is provided by the arbitrators' finding that it was reasonable to contemplate that the charterers, being a French corporation and having their place of business in Paris, would have to use French francs to purchase other currencies to settle cargo claims arising under the bills of lading. So in my opinion the charterers' recoverable loss was, according to normal principle, the sum of French francs which they paid.

My Lords, there may be many variants of situations (*The Canadian Transport*[2] is one), in which a loss arises immediately in the form of expenditure or indebtedness in one currency, but is ultimately felt in another, which other may be the normal trading currency of the plaintiff. In my opinion a decision in what currency the loss was borne or felt can be expressed as equivalent to finding which currency sum appropriately or justly reflects the recoverable loss. This is essentially a matter for arbitrators to determine. A rule that arbitrators may make their award in the currency best suited to achieve an appropriate and just result should be a flexible rule in which account must be taken of the circumstances in which the loss arose, in which the loss was converted into a money sum, and in which it was felt by the plaintiff. In some cases the 'immediate loss' currency may be appropriate, in others the currency in which it was borne by the plaintiff. There will be still others in which the appropriate currency is the currency of the contract. Awards of arbitrators based on their appreciation of the circumstances in which the foreign currency came to be provided should not be set aside for, as such, they involve no error of law.

The arbitrators' decision in the present case was both within the permissible area of decision, and further was in my opinion right.

I agree with the Court of Appeal that the award ought not to have been set aside and with the judgments in that court. I would dismiss the appeal.

LORD DIPLOCK. My Lords, in each of these appeals I have had the advantage of reading in advance the speech of my noble and learned friend, Lord Wilberforce. I agree with what he says and, for the reasons that he gives, would dismiss both these appeals.

LORD SALMON. My Lords, I agree with my noble and learned friend, Lord Wilberforce, that, for the reasons stated in his written speech, both these appeals should be dismissed.

LORD RUSSELL OF KILLOWEN.

1. *The Despina R*

My Lords, this appeal, heard immediately before that in *The Folias*, concerned a collision in the China seas between The Despina R (the defendants) and the Eleftherotria (the plaintiffs), the negligent responsibility of the defendants being agreed at 85%. As a result of the damage the plaintiffs incurred repair and other costs in various currencies. The first

1   [1977] 3 All ER 945 at 949, [1977] 3 WLR 176 at 179
2   (1932) 43 Ll L Rep 409

question is whether having regard to the decision in this House in the *Miliangos* case[1] the approach in *The Volturno*[2] should still be adhered to. In *The Volturno* decision[2] there were two salient features which together led to the one conclusion that judgment should be given in the amount of sterling resulting from conversion of the foreign currency expended at the breach date, a factor which might well result in hardship to a claimant in this country from a decline in the exchange rate of sterling. One salient feature was the theory that a claim could only be made here in sterling; the other was that damages had to be assessed at the breach date.

The first question is whether it flows, or should flow, from the *Miliangos* case[1] that in a case such as the present of damages for tort a claim may be made and judgment given here in a foreign currency. The *Miliangos* case[1] was one of debt in a foreign currency, and it may rightly be said that the parties were in agreement that the payment should be made in that currency, whereas in the case of damages for tort it is at least highly unlikely that there should be such agreement, and it was not so here. But the rule that a claim here must be made only in sterling and judgment given only in sterling is basically a rule of procedure, and in my opinion it is undesirable that the rule of procedure should be retained for a claim for damages (whether in tort or for breach of contract) while departed from in a case of debt. I observe in this connection that Viscount Simonds in particular in the *Havana* case[3] considered that damages and debt should follow the same procedural rule.

If this be right the second feature of *The Volturno*[2] is no longer of relevance, since there would be no question of conversion of the relevant foreign currency into sterling at the breach date, with the concomitant hardship to a plaintiff of a weakening of the exchange rate of sterling in what might be a long delay between damage done and judgment.

There remains in this appeal the question in what foreign currency the plaintiffs are to be entitled to claim: is it to be a mixed bag of Chinese RMB, yen and US dollars, or is it to be US dollars? (I doubt if it makes a great deal of difference in this case because the bulk of the direct expenditure and loss to the plaintiffs was in US dollars.) In this case the plaintiffs' business was conducted in US dollars, it being managed in New York. The other foreign currency was necessarily acquired in exchange for US dollars. The true loss of the plaintiffs was a loss of US dollars, and in pursuit of the remedy of restitutio in integrum, or full and proper compensation, I conclude that the claim and judgment should be for the US dollars lost. It may be said that there is in any given case support in simplicity for a system by which you take as the relevant foreign currency the currency of direct disbursement; but that simplicity may lead away from a true and fair assessment of the damage sustained by the claimant.

I have not overlooked the arguments advanced based on complications involved in departure from *The Volturno*[2] in fields such as set-off, counterclaim, limitation of liability, insolvency. They do not arise in this case, and should not be incapable of just solutions when they do arise. I do not propose to advance hypothetical solutions.

I would dismiss this appeal.

2.   *The Folias*

This appeal raises the question of a claim for damages by the charterers for breach by the owners of a warranty of seaworthiness. The refrigeration plant in The Folias which the charterers had chartered to carry onions from Spain to Brazil was defective; the onions were damaged; the charterers having issued the bills of lading were liable to the receivers in Brazil and paid them a substantial sum in cruzeiros.

It was common ground between the parties that this claim for breach of contract was properly advanced in arbitration here in terms of a currency other than sterling; and that, as I have indicated in my speech in *The Despina R* appeal, is correct.

---

1   [1975] 3 All ER 801, [1976] AC 443
2   [1921] 2 AC 544, [1921] All ER Rep 110
3   [1960] 2 All ER 332, [1961] AC 1007

The charterers are a French company which conducts its business basically in French **a** francs. In order to pay the receivers of the onions in cruzeiros the charterers had to dip into their assets to produce the francs required to acquire those cruzeiros. In what foreign currency were the charterers entitled to make their claim here? Should it be in cruzeiros, as the owners claim? Or should it be in French francs, as the charterers claimed and the arbitrators awarded?

My Lords, in this case also the goal of restitutio in integrum is the aim. In cases such as **b** this for damages for breach of contract, subject of course to questions of remoteness, the question is what is truly the claimant's loss resulting from the breach of contract? True, the direct disbursement was in cruzeiros; but in order to make that disbursement the charterers had perforce to expend francs, against which by the time of the award cruzeiros had steeply (and indeed predictably) declined. The arbitrators found that 'It was reasonable to contemplate that the charterers, being a French corporation and having their place of **c** business in Paris, would have to use French francs to purchase other currencies to settle cargo claims arising under the bills of lading'.

In my opinion the award was properly made in French francs, and I would dismiss this appeal.

LORD KEITH OF KINKEL. My Lords, I agree that each of these appeals should be **d** dismissed for the reasons stated by my noble and learned friend, Lord Wilberforce.

Appeals dismissed.

Solicitors: *Holman Fenwick & Willan* (for the owners of the Despina R and the charterers of the Folias); *Hill Dickinson & Co* (for the owners of the Eleftherotria); *William A Crump & Son* **e** (for the owners of the Folias).

Mary Rose Plummer   Barrister.

Re a debtor (No 2283 of 1976), ex parte the debtor v Hill Samuel & Co Ltd

COURT OF APPEAL, CIVIL DIVISION

BUCKLEY, BRIDGE LJJ AND SIR DAVID CAIRNS

10th, 11th, 12th, 13th APRIL 1978

Bankruptcy – Practice – Evidence – Debtor abroad – Cross-examination on debtor's affidavits – Debtor applying to be cross-examined abroad – Petitioning creditor seeking exclusion of affidavits if debtor not attending court for cross-examination – Whether application for cross-examination abroad should be dismissed – Whether question of admissibility of affidavits if debtor failed to attend court for cross-examination should be postponed until trial of petition – RSC Ord 38, r 2(3).

In November 1976 a petitioning creditor presented a petition in bankruptcy against the debtor alleging as the act of bankruptcy that he had remained out of England and intended to remain abroad for the purpose of defeating or delaying his creditors. The debtor gave notice that he would oppose the making of a receiving order on the ground that the bankruptcy court had no jurisdiction to make an order against him because he was not ordinarily resident or carrying on business in England at the date of the alleged act of bankruptcy. The debtor filed affidavits in support of his contention deposing that he had legitimately left England to make his home abroad (in Spain) and to commence business there, and had acquired a domicile of choice in Spain. In September 1977 he applied for an order that cross-examination on his affidavits should be conducted in Spain. A registrar dismissed that application. On 14th December the petitioning creditor applied to a second registrar for an order that the debtor's affidavits should not be admitted in evidence unless he attended court in England for cross-examination on them. On 19th December the second registrar declined to make the order sought because of the debtor's pending appeal against the dismissal of his application, and because the question of excluding the affidavits was a matter to be determined when the petition came on for hearing, and not before. If the debtor came to England he was at risk of being imprisoned under warrants for his arrest issued by a magistrate in connection with summonses against him charging corrupt practices. The debtor contended that the summonses disclosed no offence, and had obtained leave to move for mandamus against the magistrate but the Divisional Court had not yet determined that matter. The debtor appealed against the dismissal of his application to be cross-examined in Spain. The petitioning creditor appealed against the refusal to make the order sought excluding the affidavits.

Held – Both appeals would be dismissed for the following reasons—

(i) In exercising its discretion whether to order cross-examination abroad, the court had to have regard to all the relevant circumstances and to decide which course was preferable in justice. Having regard to the subjective nature of the questions in issue on the petition, ie the debtor's intention at the material date in regard to his residence, domicile etc, it would be unjust to the petitioning creditor if the debtor were not cross-examined before the court in England. Although, therefore, the possibility of the debtor's arrest was a matter for the court to take into consideration in exercising its discretion, it was not one which, in the circumstances, should be given very great weight, and should not prejudice the desirability in the interests of justice that he should be cross-examined in England. Moreover, the debtor's return to England would not prejudice his objection to the court's jurisdiction, and to order cross-examination abroad would result in delay and additional expense. It followed that the registrar had properly exercised his discretion in refusing the debtor's application (see p 438 f, p 439 a to d and f to h, p 440 b and h and p 441 d, post).

(ii) Since RSC Ord 38, r 2(3)ᵃ, contemplated that the trial court might give leave to read an affidavit notwithstanding that the deponent had failed to comply with an order to attend for cross-examination, it would be wrong, in ordinary circumstances, to anticipate exercise of that discretion for it ought to be exercised in the light of all the circumstances known to the court at the time when it was sought to read the affidavit. Accordingly, in deciding that the admissibility of the debtor's affidavits ought to be determined at the hearing of the petition, and not before, and in declining on that ground to make any order on the petitioning creditor's application, the registrar had properly exercised his discretion (see p 440 e to h and p 441 d, post).

Per Curiam. There is no statutory provision in bankruptcy legislation and no bankruptcy rule or practice which requires the exclusion of an affidavit if a deponent ordered to attend for cross-examination or to whom notice to attend has been given fails to do so. However, if the debtor does not attend for cross-examination he is at risk that his evidence will not be admitted (see p 437 j to p 438 a and e, p 440 h, and p 441 d, post).

Notes

For cross-examination on affidavits filed in bankruptcy proceedings, see 3 Halsbury's Laws (4th Edn) paras 982–983, and for cases on the subject, see 4 Digest (Reissue) 554–557, 4838–4879.

Cases referred to in judgments

Bottomley, Re, ex parte Brougham (1915) 84 LKJB 1020, [1915] HBR 75, 4 Digest (Reissue) 556, 4866.
Brauch (a debtor), ex parte Britannic Securities & Investments Ltd, Re [1978] 1 All ER 1004, [1977] 3 WLR 354, CA.
Debtor (No 12 of 1970), Re a, ex parte Official Receiver v the Debtor [1971] 2 All ER 1494, [1971] 1 WLR 1212, CA; *affg* [1971] 1 All ER 504, [1971] 1 WLR 261, 4 Digest (Reissue) 1643.
Evans v Bartlam [1937] 2 All ER 646, [1937] AC 473, 106 LJKB 568, HL, 50 Digest (Repl) 169, 1458.
Maxwell v Keun [1928] 1 KB 645, [1927] All ER Rep 335, 97 LJKB 305, 138 LT 310, CA, 30 Digest (Reissue) 169, 32.
New v Burns (1894) 64 LJQB 104, 71 LT 681, 14 R 339, CA, 22 Digest (Reissue) 631, 6668.
Ottaway, Re, ex parte Child (1882) 20 Ch D 126, 51 LJ Ch 494, 46 LT 118, CA, 4 Digest (Reissue) 556, 4864.
Ross v Woodford [1894] 1 Ch 38, 63 LJ Ch 191, 70 LT 22, 8 R 20, 22 Digest (Reissue) 631, 6669.

Cases also cited

Bird, Re, ex parte the Debtor v Inland Revenue Comrs [1962] 2 All ER 406, [1962] 1 WLR 686, CA.
Bottomley v Bell (1915) 31 TLR 591, CA
Boyse, Re, Crofton v Crofton (1880) 15 Ch D 591.
Cohen, Re, ex parte Trustee [1924] 2 Ch 515, CA.
Dilworth v Comr of Stamps [1899] AC 99, PC.
Lucas, Re, Bennett v Lucas [1952] 1 All ER 102.

Appeals

On 8th November 1976 the petitioning creditor, Hill Samuel & Co Ltd, presented a petition in bankruptcy for a receiving order to be made against the debtor, Malcolm Robert

---

a   Rule 2(3) is set out at p 438 b c, post

Ross. On 16th September 1977 the debtor, who was residing in Spain, applied for an order that his cross-examination on affidavits sworn by him opposing the making of a receiving *a* order should be conducted in Spain. On 6th October Mr Registrar Wheaton dismissed the application. The debtor appealed. On 14th December the petitioning creditor applied for an order that the debtor's affidavits should not be admitted in evidence unless he attended for cross-examination on them. On 19th December Mr Registrar Parbury declined to make the order sought and made no order on the petitioning creditor's application. The petitioning creditor appealed on the grounds (1) that the order sought was in accordance *b* with the usual bankruptcy practice that the affidavit of a deponent who did not attend for cross-examination notwithstanding notice or an order requiring his attendance could not be read, (2) that the registrar was wrong in deciding that he should not determine the petitioning creditor's application before the debtor's appeal against Mr Registrar Wheaton's order was determined, (3) that he was wrong in deciding that it was premature for him to make any order concerning the admission in evidence of the debtor's affidavits, (4) that he *c* attached no or insufficient weight to the convenience of making the order sought prior to the hearing of the debtor's appeal and (5) that the registrar erred as a matter of principle and/or in the exercise of his discretion in refusing to make the order sought. The facts are set out in the judgment of Buckley LJ.

Muir Hunter QC and *Christopher Brougham* for the debtor. *d*
John Vallat for the petitioning creditor.

BUCKLEY LJ. There are here two appeals before the court; one is an appeal by the *e* debtor against the refusal by Mr Registrar Wheaton to direct that he, the debtor, should be cross-examined on his affidavits in Spain and the other is an appeal by the petitioning creditor against the refusal by Mr Registrar Parbury to order that the debtor's affidavits filed in this matter, of which there are two in number, be not admitted in evidence unless he attends for cross-examination.

The history of the matter is this. On 27th July 1976 the petitioning creditor obtained *f* a judgment against the debtor on a guarantee in a sum of £272,722·83, that action having been commenced in May of that year. On 8th November 1976 the petitioning creditor presented the petition, and the act of bankruptcy relied on is set out in para 4 of the petition in the following terms:

'That the [debtor] within three months before the date of the presentation of this Petition has committed the following act of bankruptcy, namely, that with intent to *g* defeat or delay his creditors the [debtor], being out of England, remained out of England or otherwise absented himself on or about 1st September 1976 and with like intent has continued to remain out of England or otherwise absent himself down to the date hereof.'

The debtor in his evidence asserts that he left England in August 1975 with the intention *h* of thereafter residing abroad and that he has continued to reside abroad and now is engaged in the business of property development or exploitation in Spain.

The first hearing of the petition took place on 28th March, when directions were given. At that stage no application was made for cross-examination of the debtor abroad. On 25th March the debtor had given notice of his intention to oppose the making of a receiving order and said that he intended to contend that the bankruptcy court had no jurisdiction to make such an order. In support of that contention he had filed an affidavit, sworn on 25th March 1977, in which he had deposed to the fact that on or about 21st August 1975 he had left England with the intention of making his home on the continent and starting business there, and that he had, at or about that time, resigned his directorships of all companies of which he was a director; and he went on to say that from the time he

left England until May 1976 he was travelling round Europe, but that finally in that
a month he decided to concentrate his business activities in Spain and to reside there
permanently. He said: 'When I left England in August 1975 my intention was to reside on
the Continent of Europe and not to return to England to live or to carry on business there
and that is still my firm intention.' In para 6 of the affidavit he said that he had not
remained out of England or absented himself from England with the intent of defeating
or delaying his creditors, but that he had remained out of England because he left England
b with the intention of taking up residence abroad, and he put forward a claim to have
acquired a domicile of choice in Spain.

A date for the substantive hearing of the petition had been fixed for some time in the
month of May 1977, but by agreement that date was vacated and a new date was fixed at
13th October 1977 for the determination of the dispute raised by the debtor's notice. The
petitioning creditor was then given 21 days within which to file evidence and the debtor
c was directed to file evidence within 21 days thereafter. In fact, the petitioning creditor did
not file evidence until early in September 1977 and the debtor filed his second affidavit in
answer to that further evidence by the petitioning creditor on 1st October 1977. In that
affidavit he dealt with various transactions in respect of property in this country and
property abroad, and said in para 2(b) that it was correct that until August 1975 to a
substantial extent he had carried on his business through a number of limited companies
d which he either controlled or in which he had a shareholding. That form of words seems
to me to suggest that the debtor is conceding or recognising that, to some extent at any rate,
he did carry on business down to August 1975 on his own account otherwise than through
limited companies. I do not think it is necessary for me to refer in any detail to the
evidence contained in that affidavit.

On 16th September 1977, and not until that date, the debtor applied by motion for an
e order that his cross-examination on his affidavits should be conducted in Spain. That
application came before Mr Registrar Wheaton on 6th October 1977, only one week before
the date fixed for the hearing of the petition with a view to determining the dispute raised
by the debtor as to the jurisdiction of the bankruptcy court. The registrar then dismissed
the application and it is from that dismissal that the debtor appeals.

On 13th October, that being the date that was fixed earlier, as I have mentioned, the
f petition came before Mr Registrar Parbury, when he adjourned it generally with liberty to
apply to restore, on account of the fact that an appeal from Mr Registrar Wheaton's
decision of 6th October was then pending. On 14th December the petitioning creditor
applied for a direction that the debtor's two affidavits be not admitted in evidence unless
the debtor attended for cross-examination thereon; that application came on for hearing
before Mr Registrar Parbury on 19th December, when the registrar declined to make the
g order sought by the petitioning creditor and continued the adjournment of the petition
generally. That is the decision from which the petitioning creditor now appeals.

The objection to the jurisdiction raised by the debtor is founded on ss 1(2)(b) and 4(1)(d)
of the Bankruptcy Act 1914. Under s 1(2) the question arises whether, at the date of the act
of bankruptcy relied on, the debtor was ordinarily resident, or had a place of residence, in
England, and whether at that date he was carrying on business in England personally or by
h means of an agent or manager. The petition contains no allegation about carrying on
business, or the absence of carrying on business, by the debtor at any relevant date, but
counsel for the petitioning creditor submits that that would not exclude the point from
consideration. Under s 4(1)(d) the question arises whether the debtor is domiciled in
England or whether within a year before the date of the presentation of the petition he was
ordinarily resident in England or had a dwelling-house or place of business in England, or
j carried on business in England personally or by means of an agent or manager. These are
questions the investigation of which must involve consideration of the debtor's state of
mind at the relevant time; they are matters which give rise to subjective questions on the
debtor's state of mind.

There is no statutory provision in the bankruptcy legislation and no bankruptcy rule or
practice direction which positively requires the exclusion of an affidavit if a deponent who

has been ordered to attend for cross-examination, or to whom notice to attend for cross-examination has been given, fails to do so. But in *Re Bottomley, ex parte Brougham*[1], Horridge J, referring to *Re Ottaway, ex parte Child*[2] and r 33 of the Bankruptcy Rules then in operation, said that an affidavit could not be read in such circumstances as I have mentioned and that the practice in the bankruptcy court was the same as that of the High Court.

The High Court practice is regulated now by RSC Ord 38, r 2(3), which provides that:

'In any cause or matter begun by originating summons, originating motion or petition, and on any application made by summons or motion, evidence may be given by affidavit unless in the case of any such cause, matter or application any provision of these rules otherwise provides or the Court otherwise directs, [and now come the relevant words] but the Court may, on the application of any party, order the attendance for cross-examination of the person making any such affidavit, and where, after such an order has been made, the person in question does not attend, his affidavit shall not be used as evidence without the leave of the Court.'

It is true that the Bankruptcy Rules 1952[3] provide by r 390 that 'Save as provided by these Rules, the Rules of the Supreme Court shall not apply to any proceedings in bankruptcy'; but counsel for the petitioning creditor is I think inclined to concede that probably, in the absence of any positive rule in the Bankruptcy Rules regulating matters of this kind, the court might be disposed to apply the Rules of the Supreme Court by way of analogy though not directly applicable.

However that may be, if the debtor does not attend for cross-examination he is at least at risk that his evidence will not be admitted. It is common ground between the parties that the question whether or not an order for cross-examination out of the jurisdiction should be made is a matter for the discretion of the court who is asked so to direct.

We have been referred to certain cases which indicate that in an action commenced by writ the court may look more benevolently on an application by a defendant that his evidence should be taken before an examiner, or on commission, abroad, than it would look on an application by a plaintiff for a like order in relation to his own evidence. The cases to which our attention has been drawn are *Ross v Woodford*[4] and *New v Burns*[5]. But as in all cases of any exercise of judicial discretion the court must, in my opinion, pay regard to all the relevant circumstances and decide which of the available courses is preferable in the interests of justice.

It is important to mention that in June 1977 certain summonses were issued out of the Birmingham Magistrates' Court charging the debtor with corrupt practices, and two warrants for his arrest have been issued in association with those summonses, which are not backed for bail. The debtor sought to obtain an order from the magistrate quashing the summonses on the ground that they disclosed no offence recognisable by English law, but the magistrate declined to entertain that submission. The debtor applied in the Divisional Court for leave to move for an order of mandamus; he has obtained leave to move but the matter has not yet been determined by the Divisional Court and stands in that position. So as things are at the present time, if the debtor comes to this country he is at risk of being detained.

Counsel for the debtor contends that if the debtor is compelled to return to this country not only will he be at the risk I have just mentioned but he might also be liable to be served with other bankruptcy proceedings than those in which this appeal is before the court, to which no objection to the jurisdiction of the court might be available; or he might be

---

1   (1915) 84 LJKB 1020
2   (1882) 20 Ch D 126
3   SI 1952 No 2113
4   [1894] 1 Ch 38
5   (1894) 64 LJQB 104

exposed to service with other forms of process which he would not be exposed to while he is out of the country; and counsel contends that to force the debtor to return would be to force him to concede that his intent in remaining abroad has been to delay or defeat the claim of his creditors.

I confess that I am not myself able to follow that contention. There seems to me to be nothing in it, for returning to this country to make good his objection to the jurisdiction could not, as it seems to me, give rise to any inference that he in any way concedes that his absence abroad is due to an intention to delay or defeat the claims of his creditors. His return to this country will not, as it seems to me, prejudice his objection to the jurisdiction in any way if it is a valid objection, and could not affect any questions arising in relation to what his present domicile is or where his ordinary residence is or has been at any time, or any question about his carrying on business in this country at any particular time.

But counsel for the debtor places great reliance on the outstanding warrants for the debtor's arrest; he contends that this is a conclusive factor in the matter. It is, I have no doubt, something which must be taken into consideration by the court, amongst the other relevant circumstances, in deciding whether or not to make the order for examination out of the country which is sought; but for my part I do not think that it should be given any very great weight in deciding whether or not to make the order. I think there is great force in counsel's submission for the petitioning creditor that the possibility of the debtor's arrest if he comes to this country ought not to prejudice the claims of the petitioning creditor that cross-examination of the debtor before the court in this country is very highly desirable in this case having regard to the nature of the issues which have to be decided.

Junior counsel for the debtor in the course of his reply has referred us to *Maxwell v Keun*[1] and to the case in the House of Lords of *Evans v Bartlam*[2] in support of the proposition that, if a particular exercise of judicial discretion is such as to work an injustice to one of the parties, an appellate court will interfere with the exercise of that discretion and put the matter right.

In the present case, if the debtor is right in his contention that the summonses which have been issued against him do not disclose any offence known to English law, or if in fact he is innocent of any such offence, he has, as Bridge LJ pointed out in the course of the argument, nothing to fear, although it may be that his being temporarily taken into custody pending the determination of those questions might prejudice his business activities abroad and otherwise interfere with his life in a way that would be disadvantageous to him. But we have also to consider the interests of the petitioning creditor and, as I have emphasised earlier in this judgment, the questions which have to be decided are questions subjective to the debtor, questions of his frame of mind, his intention at various dates in relation to his residence, domicile and so forth, and those are matters in respect of which it seems to me that the physical presence of the debtor here to be cross-examined before the registrar before whom the petition comes to be heard is of very high importance; and in this case it would, in my judgment, work an injustice to the petitioning creditor if the debtor were not to attend for cross-examination in this country.

There is not only that consideration to consider but also the circumstances of delay which must result from ordering examination of the debtor abroad, and the additional expense which would be involved in that connection. The debtor's application for examination abroad did also extend to the evidence of other witnesses resident in Spain, but that matter has not been ventilated in this court and I do not think I need say anything about it.

Mr Registrar Wheaton, when he gave his decision, did not give any reasons for it. In *Re a debtor*[3] Stamp J expressed the view that if a judge does not give reasons for a decision an appellate court may infer that he has gone wrong in exercising his discretion; but in the present case we have the advantage of a note of the submissions which were made to the

---

1   [1928] 1 KB 645, [1927] All ER Rep 335
2   [1937] 2 All ER 646, [1937] AC 473
3   [1971] 1 All ER 504 at 508, [1971] 1 WLR 261 at 266

registrar, and that note shows that the relevant points were raised. It may have been that they were not discussed at any great length, but I think they are shown to have been raised. I think we must assume that the registrar took those matters into consideration, and consequently it seems to me that we should not interfere with his discretion unless those matters were such that he could not properly have exercised his discretion in the way in which he did, from which one would infer that he must in some way or other have misdirected himself either about the law or about the weight to be given to the various circumstances before him in evidence and otherwise. I cannot find any grounds for saying that he did exercise his discretion in accordance with any wrong principle or without paying attention to all the matters to which he ought to have paid attention, and accordingly I think that in this case we should not interfere with the way in which he decided the question then before him, from which it follows that in my judgment the debtor's appeal fails.

With regard to the petitioning creditor's appeal, the question of whether or not an order should be made at the stage when the application was made to Mr Registrar Parbury excluding the debtor's affidavits from consideration unless he attends for cross-examination was undoubtedly one of discretion. As I understand it, the registrar took the view that the application was premature, that the matter was one which ought to be determined at the time when the petition came on for hearing and not earlier.

Counsel, in support of the petitioning creditor's appeal, has relied on arguments of convenience, saying that if the question is left to be determined at the hearing and the affidavit is then excluded, there may be an appeal from that point, which will involve further delay.

I have referred to RSC Ord 38, r 2(3), which contemplates that in High Court proceedings the court may give leave to read an affidavit notwithstanding that the deponent who has been ordered to attend for cross-examination fails to do so, and in that context the court referred to must, I think, be the trial court, for it will not be until the trial that it can be known, at any rate in normal circumstances, whether the defendant will or will not attend for cross-examination. It seems to me that in ordinary circumstances it would be wrong to anticipate the exercise of this discretion by the trial judge, for the discretion should be exercised, I think, in the light of all the circumstances known to the court at the relevant time, that is to say when the affidavit is sought to be read, and that will include what has emerged from the evidence of witnesses adduced before the question of admitting or excluding the deponent's affidavit arises at the trial.

In this case also there seems to me to be no indication that the registrar exercised his discretion on any wrong principle, or that he failed to take into account all the matters which he ought to have taken into account or that he took into account any matters which he ought not to have taken into account.

In these circumstances once again I do not think that we should interfere with the registrar's decision in the matter and I would dismiss the petitioning creditor's appeal also.

BRIDGE LJ. I agree that both appeals before the court should be dismissed for all the reasons given in the judgment of Buckley LJ.

I only wish to make brief reference to two points which were canvassed in argument before us at some length, and I do so out of an abundance of caution, only to make clear, as I understand it, that the court is not purporting to decide either of those points, a decision not being necessary for the purpose of determining either of the appeals before us.

The first issue that was raised was an issue as to the proper construction of s 1(2) of the Bankruptcy Act 1914. Counsel for the debtor contended that in order that he should be held to be a debtor within the meaning of s 1(2) it would have to be shown that he fell within one of the four categories, (a), (b), (c) or (d), set out in s 1(2). The contrary argument for the petitioning creditor, addressed to us by counsel for the petitioning creditor, is that a person who is a British subject is a debtor within the meaning of that subsection whether or not he falls within one of the four lettered categories.

As I say, for the purpose of deciding the present appeals, it is unnecessary to express any opinion on that issue, though of course it will be an issue before the registrar before whom the petition comes to be heard.

It is common ground that in any event, in order to establish jurisdiction, the petitioning creditor will have to show that the debtor falls within one or other of the classes enumerated in s 4(1)(d) of the 1914 Act. But here again there is an issue, and the issue here is whether the petitioning creditor is confined, in relation to that issue, to allegations set out in his petition, or whether he can go outside the terms of his petition and show other grounds on which the debtor can be brought within s 4(1)(d), and here counsel for the petitioning creditor, in support of the view that he is not limited to what is alleged in the petition, relies on a decision at first instance of Mr Registrar Hunt in *Re Brauch*[1], which subsequently came on appeal to this court but in this court the point presently at issue was not canvassed and was therefore not decided. Here again, it is quite unnecessary for present purposes to express any view, and I have said what I have said only to make clear that when the matter does come for hearing before a bankruptcy registrar, when it is to be anticipated that those two points will undoubtedly be raised, the registrar will have to decide them without the assistance, or encumbrance, as the case may be, of any decision of this court.

SIR DAVID CAIRNS. I agree with both the judgments delivered, and have nothing of my own to add.

Appeals dismissed. Leave to appeal to House of Lords refused.

Solicitors: *David Lee & Co* (for the debtor); *Coward Chance* (for the petitioning creditors).

J H Fazan Esq   Barrister.

Lord Lilford v Glynn

COURT OF APPEAL, CIVIL DIVISION
STAMP, ORR AND GEOFFREY LANE LJJ
10th, 11th APRIL, 12th MAY 1978

Divorce – Financial provision – Child – Settlement – Jurisdiction – Exercise of jurisdiction – Millionaire father – Whether settlement required to restrict provision of income after child attains 18 – Whether if marriage had continued a wealthy father to be regarded as obliged to make settlement in favour of child – Matrimonial Causes Act 1973, ss 24(1)(b), 25(2), 29.

In 1969 the marriage between the husband and wife was dissolved and the husband, who was a millionaire, made pursuant to agreement between the parties approved by the court substantial financial provision for the wife, and provided a trust fund of £30,000 to meet the cost of educating the two children of the marriage, daughters aged 15 and 13, who were to remain in the wife's care. The fund proved insufficient to pay the school fees and provide for the children's maintenance at home. The wife therefore applied to the court

---

1   [1978] 1 All ER 1004, [1977] 3 WLR 354

for periodical payments for the benefit of the children. By agreement between the parties the court, in June 1973, ordered the husband to pay each child until she attained 18 periodical payments of £1,320 a year less tax, and ordered those payments to be increased from July 1976 by a defined percentage to meet inflation. In June 1976 the wife sought a variation of the order for periodical payments, security for such payments and lump sum payments for the benefit of the children, on the ground that the current periodical payments did not make reasonable provision for the children in the light of the expenditure required to maintain them at the standard they would have enjoyed if the marriage had continued. Subsequently the application was amended to include an order for a settlement on each child. The trustees of the fund deposed that the income of the fund was insufficient to pay all the school fees. In December 1977 a judge made an order on the amended application requiring the husband to make periodical payments of £1,812 a year less tax to each child until she attained 18 and to secure such payments, to pay the children's school fees, and to settle on each child the sum of £25,000. The husband appealed against that part of the order requiring him to pay the school fees and provide a settlement for each child.

Held – The appeal would be allowed for the following reasons—

(i) Since the husband had created the trust fund of £30,000 to provide for the cost of educating the children, it would be unjust to him, and would defeat the object of the trust, to place on him the primary liability for the school fees and to leave the trustees to accumulate the income of the fund for the prospective benefit of the children after their education was completed. Accordingly, the order to pay the school fees would be revoked and in lieu thereof the court would accept an undertaking by the husband to pay, term by term, the balance of the fees unpaid by the trustees (see p 445 g to j and p 448 b c, post).

(ii) Although the court was empowered under s 24(1)(b)[a] of the Matrimonial Causes Act 1973 to order the settlements ordered to be made on the children, the settlements, if made, would be a continuing provision and would not be subject to the restrictions imposed by s 29[b] of the 1973 Act on the making of orders in favour of children beyond the age of 18. Having regard, therefore, to those restrictions, the court should not exercise that power so as to order settlements making provision for the payment of income to the children during the whole of their life. Furthermore, although under s 25(2)[c] of the 1973 Act the court was required to exercise the power to order a settlement so as to place the children in the financial position they would have been in if the marriage had continued and each party had discharged his or her financial obligations and responsibilities towards the children, even the richest father was not to be regarded as under a financial obligation or responsibility to provide the settlements envisaged by the judge on children who were under no disability and whose maintenance and education were secure. It followed that the judge had been wrong to order the settlements (see p 446 j to p 447 e and h j and p 448 b c, post); dicta of Bagnall J in *Harnett v Harnett* [1973] 2 All ER at 598 and of Scarman LJ in *Chamberlain v Chamberlain* [1974] 1 All ER at 38 applied.

Notes

For financial provision and property adjustment orders after a decree of divorce, see 13 Halsbury's Laws (4th Edn) para 1052.

For the matters to which the court must have regard in exercising its power to make orders for financial provision, see ibid para 1060.

For the Matrimonial Causes Act 1973, ss 24, 25 and 29, see 43 Halsbury's Statutes (3rd Edn) 566, 567, 574.

---

a   Section 24(1), so far as material, is set out at p 446 a to c, post
b   Section 29, so far as material, is set out at p 446 c to f, post
c   Section 25(2), so far as material, is set out at p 447 c d, post

Cases referred to in judgment

Chamberlain v Chamberlain [1974] 1 All ER 33, [1973] 1 WLR 1557, CA, Digest (Cont Vol D) 426, 6962Abb.

Harnett v Harnett [1973] 2 All ER 593, [1973] Fam 156, [1973] 3 WLR 1; *affd* [1974] 1 All ER 764, [1974] 1 WLR 219, CA, Digest (Cont Vol D) 429, 6962Aj.

Appeal

The former husband, George Vernon Powys, Baron Lilford, appealed against an order of Payne J made on 13th December 1977 whereby, on the application of the former wife, Muriel Norma Glynn (formerly Muriel Norma Powys, Lady Lilford), it was ordered, inter alia, that the husband should pay the school fees of the two children of the marriage, and should settle on each child a sum of £25,000 for her life and thereafter for her children if any, and failing issue, for the surviving child and her issue. The facts are set out in the judgment of the court.

Joseph Jackson QC and *John Stannard* for the husband.
E Somerset Jones and *Marilyn Mornington-Abrathat* for the wife.

Cur adv vult

12th May. **ORR LJ** read the following judgment of the court: This is an appeal by the former husband of the respondent (but for convenience we shall refer to the parties as 'the husband' and 'the wife') against those parts of an order made by Payne J on 13th December 1977 whereby it was ordered that the husband should pay all the school fees of each of the two children of the marriage, both girls, Clara, then aged 15, and Emma, then aged 13, and should also settle a sum of £25,000 on trust for each of these children for life, and, after her death, for her child or children, if any, and, failing children, for the other surviving daughter and her issue. On the same hearing Payne J further ordered that the husband should pay, by way of periodical payments, £1,812 a year, less tax, to each of the two daughters until they respectively attained the age of 18, or further order, and that these payments, as well as the payment of the school fees, should be secured by the husband, but the husband does not appeal against those parts of the order.

The marriage of the parties took place on 23rd December 1961, being the husband's fourth and the wife's second marriage, and both have remarried since the divorce. The husband, who is aged 47, was born in South Africa, but came to school in England, and in 1949, following the death of a distant relative, succeeded to the title of Lord Lilford and an interest in substantial property, of which he acquired the capital on a variation of trusts in 1968. After attending school and university here he returned to South Africa, where he married his first and second wives, both marriages ending in divorce. In 1958 he returned to England with his third wife, also South African, but that marriage also ended in divorce and, by reason of the form of the obligation which he undertook to maintain her, he was, at the time of the hearing before Payne J, paying her a sum of £14,000 per year. There were no children of these three marriages. Following the break-up of his subsequent marriage to the respondent, the husband returned to South Africa in 1975, where he is now living with his fifth wife, whom he married in 1969 and by whom he has a son and two daughters, and he has decided not to return to England. He is undoubtedly a millionaire, and has said informally that he may well be worth £3 million. His attitude has been that it would take longer to make a detailed investigation of his resources than it would to try his fourth wife's claims, and that he has sufficient means to meet any supplemental provision for the children which could be sensibly expended.

This history of his marriage to the wife can be briefly summarised. She brought no financial assets into the marriage. He made some financial provision for her former husband and also for her two children, both girls, and one of them married. The parties lived at Heskin Hall, in Lancashire, which he left in September 1967. She later took wardship proceedings as a result of which the children of the marriage were made wards of court in March 1968. On 9th May of that year the husband petitioned for divorce alleging cruelty and adultery, but the suit was compromised on agreed terms, which were approved by his Honour Judge Bailey on 14th February 1969, and subsequently embodied in a formal agreement, including the following provisions:

'(1) That the wife would not oppose a decreee on the ground of her cruelty and the husband would not proceed on his allegations of adultery.

'(2) That he would pay her a sum of £20,000 and a further sum of £15,000, to be secured, and would convey to her Heskin Hall and its contents, with certain exceptions.

'(3) That he would pay £30,000 to his and his wife's solicitors out of which they were to pay such capital sum as might be required to provide basic school fees for the children, and the balance, and also certain silver, was to be settled on trusts for the children's benefit.'

The payments to the wife, for which this agreement provided, were in addition to substantial gifts of money, shares (half of which the wife has presented to her present husband) and jewellery made by the husband to the wife, and his transfer to her of a house in Halsey Street, and it is not in dispute that, as a result, she has now money and assets worth at least £200,000, and possibly considerably more.

Following the approval of the agreement the husband obtained a decree nisi in May 1969, which was made absolute in August of the same year, and thereafter both parties remarried, the children remaining, by agreement, in the care of the wife.

On 19th August 1971 the wife gave notice of an application for periodic payments for the benefit of the children, and later deposed in an affidavit that the trustees of the children's settlement, who had previously paid her £125 a quarter for the maintenance of the children, had notified her that they could not continue these payments. The trustees, in an affidavit, stated that so long as the children remained at their present school it was their intention to pay the fees and the cost of uniforms out of the income of the trust fund, if necessary resorting to capital, but that there would be no income available for home maintenance. In these circumstances the parties signed a schedule of agreed terms which recited the desire of both of them that the school bills should be rendered by the school to the trustees and paid by them direct to the school, and they assumed that the trustees would so administer the trust as to give effect to those wishes. On this basis an order was made on 11th June 1973 by Hollings J which provided, inter alia:

'(1) that the husband should pay to each of the children periodical payments for the year beginning on 1 June 1972 of £1,200, less tax, and as from 1 July 1973, £1,320 a year, less tax, until the children should respectively attain the age of 18; and

'(2) that by consent, and to provide for inflation, the payments of £1,320 per year should be increased in the year beginning 1 July 1976, and subsequent years, by a defined percentage . . .'

it being also stated by leading counsel for the wife that the parties were agreed that neither of them intended to make any application for the variation of these benefits until after 31st May 1976.

On 30th June 1976 the wife gave notice of the application which was in due course to come before Payne J and in which she originally sought variation of the order of Hollings J for periodical payments, an order for security for such payments and lump sum payments for the benefit of each of the children, but the application was amended at the hearing to include an order for a settlement for the benefit of each child.

In her affidavit in support of this application the wife claimed that the periodical payments currently being made, even if adjusted to take account of inflation, did not make reasonable provision for the maintenance of the children, and also alleged that the husband intended to transfer his property out of the jurisdiction, if he had not already done so; and in a subsequent affidavit she claimed that in order to maintain a home and standard of living commensurate with what the children would have enjoyed if the marriage had continued she had to incur approximate annual expenditure of some £19,800.

In an affidavit in answer the husband alleged that he had had to pay a balance of the school fees after the trustees had made their contribution, and had twice had to pay the entire fees; but he admitted that he had decided not to return to England and, in order to minimise taxation, had transferred assets abroad, including his family trust assets. There was also an affidavit by a South African lawyer to the effect that South African law provides for reciprocal enforcement of maintenance orders as between the United Kingdom and South Africa, and that the relevant South African provisions are effective in practice for that purpose.

An affidavit was also sworn by the trustees of the children's settlement deposing that they had applied £5,000 from the capital of the trust fund in the purchase of educational annuities for the children which would have been sufficient at their former school, but that the children had been sent to a different school where the fees were very much higher, and that in these circumstances, having paid out the whole of the trust income of £1,300 towards payment of the fees, they had applied to the husband to pay the balance, which he had done. They further deposed that the book value of the capital of the trust fund is some £42,000, including the silver.

On the material which we have summarised Payne J, on 13th December 1977, made the order under appeal, and since the husband does not challenge those parts of the order which require him to make periodic payments of £1,812 per annum, less tax, for each of the children until they attain 18 years of age, and also to secure such payments and the payment of the school fees, the only questions arising on the appeal are whether the judge was right in ordering, first, that the husband should pay the school fees of the children, and, secondly, that he should settle a sum of £25,000 on each of them.

The first of these issues does not admit of long discussion. The reason given by the judge for this part of the order was that, rather than to have the complications of extracting income from the trustees towards the payment of the fees, it was not unreasonable to impose on the husband the obligation of paying the fees and to leave the trustees free to use the trust income in other ways for the benefit of the children, or, if the trustees thought fit, to accumulate it with the capital so as to benefit the children when they are older. If the matter involved only the mechanics of payment of the school fees we can see some force in this argument, but the circumstances of the present case were that the husband had clearly created the trust with the main object of meeting the cost of the girls' education and had provided for that purpose a sum of £30,000, the income of which (with the expenditure of a modest part of the capital in the purchase of educational annuities) may well have appeared likely to be sufficient for that purpose and probably would have been but for subsequent inflation. In these circumstances it would, in our judgment, be unjust to the husband to place on him a primary liability to pay the fees, leaving the trustees free, if they should think fit, to accumulate the income of the trust for the prospective benefit of the children after their education has been completed.

To do so would, in our judgment, be to defeat the object for which the trust was created, and we would, for these reasons, allow the appeal on this issue and, in lieu of the order made by the judge, would accept an undertaking from the husband that he will pay, term by term, any balance of the school fees which the trustees do not pay, and will provide, as he is willing to do, security for the payments so undertaken to be made, as well as security for the periodical payments of £1,812 per annum, less tax, for each child.

The other ground of appeal concerns the settlement of £25,000 which the judge ordered in respect of each child, and raises two questions: the first, whether the judge had power to order such settlements; and the second, whether in all the circumstances of this case he was right to do so.

Section 24 of the Matrimonial Causes Act 1973 provides, so far as material, as follows:

'(1) On granting a decree of divorce, a decree of nullity of marriage or a decree of judicial separation or at any time thereafter (whether, in the case of a decree of divorce or of nullity of marriage, before or after the decree is made absolute), the court may make any one or more of the following orders, that is to say—(a) an order that a party to the marriage shall transfer to the other party, to any child of the family or to such person as may be specified in the order for the benefit of such a child such property as may be so specified, being property to which the first-mentioned party is entitled, either in possession or reversion; (b) an order that a settlement of such property as may be so specified, being property to which a party to the marriage is so entitled, be made to the satisfaction of the court for the benefit of the other party to the marriage and of the children of the family or either or any of them . . . subject, however, in the case of an order under paragraph (a) above, to the restrictions imposed by section 29(1) and (3) below on the making of orders for a transfer of property in favour of children who have attained the age of eighteen . . .'

Section 29, so far as material, provides:

'(1) Subject to subsection (3) below, no financial provision order and no order for a transfer of property under section 24(1)(a) above shall be made in favour of a child who has attained the age of 18.

'(2) The term to be specified in a periodical payments or secured periodical payments order in favour of a child may begin with the date of the making of an application for the order in question or any later date but—(a) shall not in the first instance extend beyond the date of the birthday of the child next following his attaining the upper limit of the compulsory school age (that is to say, the age that is for the time being that limit by virtue of section 35 of the Education Act 1944 together with any Order in Council made under that section) unless the court thinks it right in the circumstances of the case to specify a later date; and (b) shall not in any event, subject to subsection (3) below, extend beyond the date of the child's eighteenth birthday.

'(3) Subsection (1) above, and paragraph (b) of subsection (2) shall not apply in the case of a child, if it appears to the court that—(a) the child is, or will be, or if an order were made without complying with either or both of those provisions would be, receiving instruction at an educational establishment or undergoing training for a trade, profession or vocation, whether or not he is also, or will also be, in gainful employment; or (b) there are special circumstances which justify the making of an order without complying with either or both of those provisions.'

Section 23, so far as material, provides:

'(1) On granting a decree of divorce, a decree of nullity of marriage or a decree of judicial separation or at any time thereafter (whether, in the case of a decree of divorce or of nullity of marriage, before or after the decree is made absolute), the court may make any one or more of the following orders, that is to say . . . (d) an order that a party to the marriage shall make to such person as may be specified in the order for the benefit of a child of the family, or to such a child, such periodical payments, for such term, as may be so specified; (e) an order that a party to the marriage shall secure to such person as may be so specified for the benefit of such a child, or to such a child, to the satisfaction of the court, such periodical payments, for such terms, as may be so specified; (f) an order that a party to the marriage shall pay to such person as may be so specified for the benefit of such a child, or to such a child, such lump sum as may be so specified; subject, however, in the case of an order under paragraph (d), (e) or (f) above, to the restrictions imposed by section 29(1) and (3) below on the making of financial provision orders in favour of children who have attained the age of eighteen . . .'

It is clear from the terms of s 23(1)(d) of the 1973 Act, and the concluding words of that subsection, that periodical payments for a child may only be ordered up to the age of 18, but it is difficult to see how similar restrictions to those already cited could have been imposed on the power to order a settlement under s 24(1)(b) of the 1973 Act, since a settlement is a continuing provision and it would have been an absurdity to provide that the beneficial trusts in a settlement for the benefit of a child should be subject to a restriction corresponding to those included in s 29 and not be exercisable in favour of a child who has attained the age of 18 years.

In these circumstances there was, in our judgment, power under the 1973 Act to order a settlement in the present case, but it does not follow that on divorce a father whose means permit it ought to be ordered to make a settlement in favour of a child of his marriage. There being expressed restrictions on the powers of making financial provision in the shape of periodical payments, lump sum payments or transfers of property in favour of children who have already attained 18, it could not be right, in our judgment, for the court to exercise the power to order a father to settle funds so as to make provision for the payment of income to the child during the whole life of the child. Furthermore, one finds in s 25(2) of the 1973 Act, which lays down the duty of the court in deciding whether to exercise its powers under (inter alia) s 24(1)(b), that the court is so to exercise the power to order a settlement, like the other powers there referred to, as to place the child '... in the financial position in which the child would have been if the marriage had not broken down and each of the parties to the marriage had properly discharged his or her financial obligations and responsibilities towards him'. Whatever the precise meaning of that phrase a father, even the richest father, ought not to be regarded as under 'financial obligations or responsibilities' to provide funds for the purposes of such settlement as are envisaged in this case on children who are under no disability and whose maintenance and education are secure. We find support for this view in the following passages from the judgments of Scarman LJ in *Chamberlain v Chamberlain*[1] and of Bagnall J in *Harnett v Harnett*[2]. In the first of these cases Scarman LJ said[3]:

> 'Equally, I think the learned judge erred in this case in settling the house so that the beneficial interest at the end of the day became that of the children in equal shares. The order that the registrar made provided for the care and upbringing of the children in this house until they should finish full-time education. I think that that was an appropriate order. There are no circumstances in this case to suggest that any of these children had special circumstances that required them to make demands on their parents after the conclusion of their full-time education. The capital asset, the house, was acquired by the work and by the resources of their parents, and, provided their parents meet their responsibilities to their children as long as their children are dependent, this seems to me an asset that should revert then to the parents. Accordingly, I think that the learned judge was wrong to order a settlement and I think the learned registrar was right to divide this house in the way in which he did, beneficially between husband and wife, and to provide that at the end of the education of the children the house could be sold and the proceeds divided between the parents.'

In the second case Bagnall J said[4] that—

> '... in the vast majority of cases the financial position of a child of a subsisting marriage is simply to be afforded shelter, food and education, according to the means of his parents.'

For these reasons we think that Payne J was wrong in his approach to this issue but in any event, in our judgment, the order which he made was not justified in the circumstances of this case. There is not in this context, one rule for millionaires and another for less wealthy fathers, and in our judgment there was no means of judging whether the father, if the

1   [1974] 1 All ER 33, [1973] 1 WLR 1557
2   [1973] 2 All ER 593, [1973] Fam 156
3   [1974] 1 All ER 33 at 38, [1973] 1 WLR 1557 at 1564–1565
4   [1973] 2 All ER 593 at 598, [1973] Fam 156 at 161

marriage had continued, would or would not have made a settlement in favour of the daughters. He might or he might not, and there was no reason to suppose that the first course was more likely than the other in view of the fact that he had already made a substantial settlement for the daughters in the form of the trust deed.

We would add that the fact that the daughters have lost, by reason of the husband settling in South Africa, their rights under the Inheritance (Provision for Family and Dependants) Act 1975 is, in our view, irrelevant for the present purposes even if they have no corresponding rights under South African law.

For these reasons we would allow the appeal and reverse the judge's orders for the execution of a settlement and for the payment by the husband of the school fees, and in lieu of the latter order would accept an undertaking by the husband in the terms we have indicated.

Appeal allowed. Leave to appeal to the House of Lords refused.

Solicitors: *Alsop, Stevens, Batesons & Co* (for the husband); *Rutherfords*, Liverpool (for the wife).

Avtar S Virdi Esq   Barrister.

Jackson v Hall and another

COURT OF APPEAL, CIVIL DIVISION

LORD DENNING MR, LAWTON AND BRANDON LJJ

4th, 5th, 21st DECEMBER 1978

Agricultural holding – Tenancy – Death of tenant – Eligibility of survivor of tenant for grant of new tenancy – Date at which eligibility to be determined – Tenant of agricultural holding dying – Whether a survivor of tenant required to be eligible at date of tenant's death – Whether a survivor who later acquires eligibility entitled to apply for new tenancy – Agriculture (Miscellaneous Provisions) Act 1976, s 18(2).

A father and his two sons farmed in partnership two adjacent farms, a freehold property and a leasehold property. The freehold farm, which was a commercial unit within the meaning of Part II of the Agriculture Act 1967, was owned by the father but leased to the partnership. When the father died the sons continued to farm both farms as partners, but the lessors of the leasehold farm gave the executors of the deceased notice to quit. Very shortly after, one of the sons assigned to his brother all his estate and interest in the freehold farm and then applied to an agricultural land tribunal under s 20[a] of the Agriculture (Miscellaneous Provisions) Act 1976 claiming to be eligible for the grant of a new tenancy by virtue, inter alia, of being a 'survivor of the deceased [tenant]' and 'not [being] the occupier of a commercial unit of agricultural land', for the purposes of s 18(2)[b] of that Act. The lessors contended that the preconditions of eligibility laid down by s 18(2) had to be fulfilled by an applicant at the date of the deceased tenant's death and that at the date of his father's death the applicant was, together with his brother, the occupier of a commercial unit and therefore not eligible for the grant of a new tenancy. The tribunal decided that the appropriate date for determining the preconditions of eligibility was the date of the father's death and dismissed the application. On a case stated to the High Court the judge upheld the tribunal's decision. The son appealed.

Held (Brandon LJ dissenting) – A person who was a survivor of a deceased tenant and who, within the time limited for making an application, became eligible for the grant of a new tenancy was not precluded by s 18(2) of the 1976 Act from applying for the grant of a new tenancy, since 'survivor' could refer to a continuing state of surviving the deceased during which time eligibility could be acquired, and s 18(2) had not specified in terms that a survivor had to be eligible at the moment of the deceased tenant's death. Furthermore, s 20 merely required the tribunal to be satisfied that an applicant 'is' an eligible person, i e that he was eligible at the date of the application and of the hearing of the application, and that indicated that eligibility could be acquired after the death of the previous tenant. Since the son was both a survivor of the previous tenant and, as required by s 20(1), was at the date of his application eligible to apply for a new tenancy by virtue of his not being the occupier of a commercial unit at that date, he was entitled to have his application considered on its merits by the tribunal. The appeal would therefore be allowed (see p 452 *d* to *h*, p 453 *e* to *h* and p 454 *b*, post).

Notes

For succession on death of a tenant of an agricultural holding, see Supplement to 1 Halsbury's Laws (4th Edn) para 1011A.1–3.

For the Agriculture (Miscellaneous Provisions) Act 1976, ss 18, 20, see 46 Halsbury's Statutes (3rd Edn) 31, 36.

---

a   Section 20, so far as material, is set out at p 452 *c*, post.
b   Section 18(2) is set out at p 453 *b c*, post.

Cases referred to in judgments

Benninga (Mitcham) Ltd v Bijstra [1945] 2 All ER 433, [1946] KB 58, 115 LJKB 28, 173 LT
298, CA, 31 (2) Digest (Reissue) 1089, 8493.

Betty's Cafés Ltd v Phillips Furnishing Stores Ltd [1958] 1 All ER 607, [1959] 1 AC 20, [1958]
2 WLR 513, HL, 31(2) Digest (Reissue) 961, 7779.

Harrison-Broadley v Smith [1964] 1 All ER 867, [1964] 1 WLR 456, CA, Digest (Cont Vol B)
15, 15b

Inland Revenue Comrs v Duke of Westminster [1936] AC 1, [1935] All ER Rep 259, 104 LJKB
383, 153 LT 223, 19 Tax Cas 490, HL, 28(1) Digest (Reissue) 507, 1845.

Kimpson v Markham [1921] 2 KB 157, 90 LJKB 393, 124 LT 790, 19 LGR 346, DC, 31(2)
Digest (Reissue) 1110, 8615.

Zbytniewski v Broughton [1956] 3 All ER 348, [1956] 2 QB 673, [1956] 3 WLR 630, CA, 31(2)
Digest (Reissue) 1086, 8471.

Cases also cited

Hulme v Earl of Aylesford and Trustees of Earl of Aylesford's Settlement (1965) (1978) 245
Estates Gazette 851.

Jones v Burgoyne (1963) 188 Estates Gazette 497.

Morris (BT) v Master, Wardens and Commonalty of Merchant Venturers of the City of Bristol
(26th May 1978) (East Midlands Agricultural Land Tribunal), unreported.

Nevile v Hardy [1921] 1 Ch 404.

Pocock v Carter [1912] 1 Ch 663.

Public Trustee v McKay (Minister of Health) [1969] NZLR 995.

Westminster Bank Ltd v Zang [1966] 1 All ER 114, [1966] AC 182, HL.

Wykes' Will Trusts, Re, Riddington v Spencer [1961] 1 All ER 470, [1961] Ch 229.

Appeal

The applicant, Graham Christopher Jackson, appealed against a judgment of Sir Douglas
Frank QC, sitting as a deputy judge of the High Court on 5th July 1978, in respect of an
award in the form of a special case stated by the agricultural land tribunal for the
Yorkshire/Lancashire area (chairman Mr F Stephenson) on the application dated 23rd June
1977 by the applicant seeking a direction that he was entitled to a tenancy of the holding
known as Grange Farm, Keyingham, owned by the respondents, William Horner Hall and
Geoffrey Alan Marr, trustees of the estate of Geoffrey Edwards Marr, deceased. The
question of law for the determination of the court was whether the tribunal came to a
correct conclusion in law in holding that the applicant did not qualify as an 'eligible
person', within the meaning of s 18(2) of the Agriculture (Miscellaneous Provisions) Act
1976, and thereby refusing a direction under that Act entitling the applicant to a tenancy
of the holding. The judge decided that the tribunal's conclusion was correct in law and
upheld its decision. The facts are set out in the judgment of Lord Denning MR.

E C Evans-Lombe QC and *Clifford Joseph* for the applicant.
Alan Sebestyen for the respondents.

Cur adv vult

21st December. The following judgments were read.

LORD DENNING MR. Under the Agricultural Holdings Act 1948 the tenant of a farm
was given security of tenure during his life: but it ceased on his death. When he died, the
landlord could turn out his widow and family. He could give them notice to quit so long
as he did it within three months after the tenant's death: see s 24(2)(g) of the 1948 Act. In
1976 Parliament extended this protection so as to give security to a member of his family
after his death. Take for instance a son. If he had been working on his father's farm for the
last five years, and had no other farm of his own, he could apply for a new tenancy to
himself. But he had to show that he was an 'eligible person'. The question in this case is

whether he has to be an 'eligible person' at the date of his father's death, or whether it is sufficient if he is eligible at the date of his application to the tribunal. The point has given rise to differences of opinion between the various agricultural land tribunals. So we have to settle it.

Such being the question, I will state the facts which give rise to it. The farmer here was James Jackson of Keyingham, north of the Humber. He died on 22nd March 1977, leaving two sons, Graham and Martin Jackson. The father had farmed two holdings, which I must describe. One was Grange Farm of 519 acres. It was owned by the Marr trustees. The father was the legal tenant. But he and his two sons were partners in the farming business; and they carried on Grange Farm as partners. The other was White House Farm of 400 acres. It was next door to Grange Farm. It was owned by the father himself, but he had let it on a legal tenancy to the partnership of himself and his two sons; and they carried on White House Farm as partners. White House Farm was a 'commercial unit' within s 40 of the Agriculture Act 1967, because it was large enough to give full-time employment for an occupier and one man.

No doubt the partners carried on the two farms together as one unit of agriculture. That was obviously the most efficient and economical way of running the business.

The father died, as I have said, on 22nd March 1977. The two sons were, of course, secure in White House Farm because of their succession to their father, who was the owner. But they were not secure in Grange Farm because that was owned by the Marr trustees. These trustees, on the father's death, gave them notice to quit. As a result, the sons would have had to quit Grange Farm unless they could take advantage of the Agriculture (Miscellaneous Provisions) Act 1976 so as to claim a family succession. To do this the two sons, or one of them, had to be an 'eligible person'.

'Eligible person' is defined in s 18(2) of the 1976 Act. It has three requisites, paras (a), (b) and (c). Each of the two sons satisfied para (a), the family relationship of being a 'child', and para (b), the length of service, not less than five years on the farm. But there was this third requisite:

'(c) he is not the occupier of a commercial unit of agricultural land within the meaning of Part II of the Agriculture Act 1967, or, if he is, occupies it as a licensee only.'

Now, *at the date of the father's death*, neither of the sons could satisfy that requirement: because at that date they were the occupiers of White House Farm, which was a 'commercial unit' and they occupied it as tenants and not as licensees only.

But, *soon after the father's death*, the two sons took legal advice; and in consequence they took steps to get Graham out of White House Farm. On 22nd June 1977 Graham assigned to his brother Martin all his interest in White House Farm. So thereafter Martin was the sole owner of White House Farm. If Graham should visit it afterwards, he would do so as a licensee only: see *Harrison-Broadley v Smith*[1].

Having taken those legal steps, on the very next day, 23rd June 1977, just within the permitted three months from 23rd March 1977, Graham applied to the tribunal for a tenancy of Grange Farm. He said that *at the date* (the date of his application) he was an 'eligible person'. He satisfied all the requirements, paras (a), (b) and (c). In particular he satisfied para (c) because he was no longer the occupier of a commercial unit at White House Farm, or, if he was, he occupied it as a licensee only.

The tribunal seems to have regarded the assignment by Graham to Martin as a 'contrivance'. The judge regarded it as a 'subterfuge'. So regarding it, they made short work of it. They said that the material date was the date of the death; and not the date of the application to the tribunal.

I do not so regard the conduct of the two sons. This was a legitimate transaction done so as to keep the two farms together. To keep them in the family and to farm them as one efficient and economic unit. If they had to give up Grange Farm and be confined to White

---

1 [1964] 1 All ER 867, [1964] 1 WLR 456

House Farm only, it might be disastrous for their business. The transaction may or may not have achieved the desired result, that I will soon consider, but I would not subscribe to the view that there was anything discreditable in it, any more than there was anything discreditable in the Duke of Westminster paying his gardener his wages by way of a deed of annuity: see *Inland Revenue Comrs v Duke of Westminster*[1]. It was a legitimate way of avoiding a stern law.

So I turn to the question of law in the case stated. In order to qualify as an 'eligible person', what is the material date? Is it the date of the death of the deceased? Or is it the date of the application?

To my mind this question is solved by reference to the actual words of s 20(1) and (2). These read:

> '(1) Any eligible person may within the relevant period apply to the Tribunal for a direction entitling him to a tenancy of the holding.
>
> '(2) Where only one application is made under this section the Tribunal, if satisfied that the applicant is an eligible person, shall determine whether he is in their opinion a suitable person to become the tenant of the holding.'

Note the present tense. Under sub-s (1) the words refer to the date of the application. Under sub-s (2) they refer to the date of the hearing by the tribunal. Taking the two subsections together, it seems to me that the applicant must, in the ordinary way, satisfy the requirement of being an 'eligible person' both at the date of the application and at the date of the hearing. But not at the date of death. This solution is similar to that reached by the court in cases under the Rent Restriction Acts: see *Kimpson v Markham*[2], *Benninga (Mitcham) Ltd v Bijstra*[3], *Zbytniewski v Broughton*[4]; and under the Landlord and Tenant Act 1954: see *Betty's Cafés Ltd v Phillips Furnishing Stores Ltd*[5].

On the other side emphasis was placed on the words 'survivor of the deceased' in the definition of 'eligible person' in s 18(2). But that seems to me to be neutral. At the date of the application the son is a 'survivor of the deceased'. Likewise, at the date of the hearing he is a 'survivor of the deceased'. In order to insist on the date of death, you would have to insert the words 'at the date of the death of the deceased' after the words 'in whose case' and before the words 'the following conditions are satisfied—(*a*) . . . (*b*) . . . and (*c*) . . .' I see no reason to insert those words.

Other matters were raised which were said to point in favour of one or other construction. But these all seem to me to be neutral. One thing, however, which does influence me is that, before the date of the death, the family could make an arrangement so as to ensure the succession of one son. So why should they not do it after his death? The clever far-sighted families will consult their lawyers before the death. The nice good-natured ones will wait till after the old man has died. I would not let them lose on that account. I would hold that a family can, by appropriate arrangements, ensure that a son shall be an 'eligible person' so long as the transaction is carried out before the date of the application.

I would allow the appeal and hold that eligibility is to be determined, not at the date of death, but at the date of the application and the hearing.

LAWTON LJ. By the Agriculture (Miscellaneous Provisions) Act 1976, Parliament gave four classes of persons, who were 'eligible' as defined in that Act, the right to apply to an agricultural land tribunal for a tenancy of an agricultural holding of a deceased tenant. These tribunals have a legally qualified chairman and two members who are not lawyers. It was such a tribunal, sitting in the Yorkshire and Lancashire area, which had to construe

1   [1936] AC 1, [1935] All ER Rep 259
2   [1921] 2 KB 157
3   [1945] 2 All ER 433, [1946] KB 58
4   [1956] 3 All ER 348, [1956] 2 QB 673
5   [1958] 1 All ER 607 at 612–613, [1959] 1 AC 20 at 34–35

a definition section (s 18(2)) which has thrown up for the consideration of this court niceties of grammar and of the meaning of one word. Counsel for the respondents argued for grammatical purity and a restricted meaning, counsel for the applicant for a wider meaning.

The grammatical purity for which counsel for the respondents contended is said by him to come from the correct parsing of the words—

> '"eligible person" means . . . a survivor of the deceased in whose case the following conditions are satisfied—(*a*) he falls within paragraphs (*a*) to (*d*) of subsection (1) above; (*b*) in the seven years ending with the date of death his only or principal source of livelihood throughout a continuous period of not less than five years, or two or more discontinous periods together amounting to not less than five years, derived from his agricultural work on the holding or on an agricultural unit of which the holding forms part; and (*c*) he is not the occupier of a commercial unit of agricultural land . . . or, if he is, occupies it as a licensee only.'

If a survivor of the deceased means, and can only mean, a person who is to be identified as going on living at the moment of the tenant's death, that person to be eligible must then have all the qualifications set out in paras (*a*), (*b*) and (*c*); and for the purpose of specifying those qualifications at that moment the use of the present tense in para (*c*) is both appropriate and correct.

Counsel for the respondents went on to submit that this construction of a statutory definition slots easily into sections of the Act in which it has to be applied, the most important being s 20. Eligibility is fixed by reference to the past and must continue up to the dates of application and determination (see s 20(1) and (2)).

There is much force in the suggested construction of counsel for the respondents. It is a possible one. But is it the only one? If there is another construction, which should be preferred?

The alternative construction is derived from the concept that a survivor of a deceased lives on. His state as such continues until he himself dies. In the ordinary usage of the English language this is a common meaning as is shown by such phrases as 'he is a survivor of the First World War'. If being a survivor is a continuing state, then the qualification set out in para (*c*) is one which an otherwise eligible person can acquire within any relevant period and it need not be one acquired on the tenant's death. The use of the present tense in para (*c*) ensures that the person applying under s 20(1) then has the necessary qualification and continues to have it when the tribunal considers his application. This construction finds some support in the use of the passive tense in s 18(1) in the words 'the sole . . . tenant of an agricultural holding dies and *is survived* by any of the following persons . . .'

In my judgment the alternative construction is the one which would the more easily be given by literate persons, especially as para (*c*) omits any reference to the time of death which might well have been there in the interests of clarity. This seems to have been the construction put on para (*c*) of s 18(2) by the draftsman of the statutory form which has to be used when an application is made to a tribunal under s 20: see the Agricultural Land Tribunals (Succession to Agricultural Tenancies) Order 1976[1], r 2, and the appendix to the order. Paragraph 11 of Form 1 (succession), is as follows:

> '(*a*) I occupy as owner-occupier/tenant/licensee the following agricultural land [*give particulars of the land occupied, including area*]:—
> '(*b*) I do not occupy any other agricultural land.

The form does not require the applicant to state what agricultural land he occupied when the tenant died, as it would have done had the draftsman thought that s 18(2) should be construed as counsel for the respondents submitted it should be. The form cannot, of course, be a guide to the construction of s 18(2). Such value as it has lies only in showing

---

1   SI 1976 No 2183

what a draftsman, used to looking closely at words, thought the ones used in s 18(2) meant.

I can see nothing in the policy of the 1976 Act which should lead me to prefer the construction of counsel for the respondents to that of counsel for the applicant. The broad policy of the 1976 Act is clear: anyone taking over a deceased tenant's holding must not be an occupier of another 'commercial unit' when he applies for a direction entitling him to do so. Anyone having another 'commercial unit' may divest himself of it in expectation of the tenant's death, and probably will do so if he takes legal advice. Such a divesting would not be contrary to the policy of the 1976 Act. In my opinion a divesting between death and an application under s 20 would be no more contrary to the policy of the 1976 Act than one before death. If applicants enter into colourable transactions which are mere sham divestings, the tribunals can disregard them.

I would allow the appeal.

BRANDON LJ. Part II of the Agriculture (Miscellaneous Provisions) Act 1976 ('the Act') provides for the succession to tenancies of agricultural holdings by survivors of deceased tenants after their deaths. Applications for such succession are made to and decided by the agricultural land tribunal for the area concerned.

Under s 20(1) of the Act the right of a survivor of a deceased tenant to apply to the tribunal for a direction entitling him to become the tenant of the relevant holding depends on his being an 'eligible person'. Further, under s 20(2) the tribunal to which the application is made must first of all, before deciding whether the applicant is suitable to become the tenant, be satisfied that he is an 'eligible person'.

Under s 18(2) an 'eligible person' means a survivor who possesses three specified qualifications. Qualification (a) is that he should have been either the spouse or a sibling or a child (actual or by treatment) of the deceased. Qualification (b) is that his only or principal income should, during a specified period or periods before the death, have derived from his agricultural work on the holding or on an agricultural unit of which the holding forms part. Qualification (c) is that 'he is not the occupier of a commercial unit of agricultural land within the meaning of Part II of the Agriculture Act 1967 or, if he is, occupies it as licensee only'.

The question for decision in this appeal is at what time or times an applicant has to possess qualification (c) above in order to have the right, as an 'eligible person', to apply under s 20(1), and in order to enable the tribunal to be satisfied that he is such a person under s 20(2). The Agricultural Land Tribunal (Yorkshire/Lancashire Area), and the High Court (Sir Douglas Frank QC sitting as a deputy judge) on a case stated by that tribunal, have both decided that the relevant time is the deceased's death. The applicant, who does not, if that view is correct, possess qualification (c) in this case, appeals against the latter decision, contending that there are two relevant times and that these are, firstly, the time of the application to the tribunal, and, secondly, the time of the hearing before it.

In support of the applicant's contention reliance has been placed on the use of the present tense, firstly, in the phrases 'he is not the occupier' and 'or, if he is, occupies it as a licensee only' in para (c) of the definition of eligible person in s 18(2), and, secondly, in the phrase 'that the applicant is an eligible person' in s 20(2). The applicant's interpretation of the Act was further said to be supported by *Kimpson v Markham*[1], a decision on the Rent Acts.

In my judgment the contention for the applicant is wrong, and the decisions of the tribunal and Sir Douglas Frank QC are right, for the following reasons.

Firstly, 'eligible person' is defined in s 18(2) as 'a survivor of the deceased in whose case the following conditions are satisfied', the conditions concerned being those set out in paras (a), (b) and (c) following. It seems to me that this subsection, by making the test of eligibility whether certain conditions are satisfied in the case of a survivor, that is to say (to use the related language of s 18(1)) a person by whom the deceased is survived, must by necessary implication be providing that the test should be applied at the time of survivorship, that is to say the time of the deceased's death.

---

1   [1921] 2 KB 157

Secondly, the questions whether conditions (a) and (b) are satisfied in the case of a survivor clearly fall to be decided by reference to the time of the deceased's death. It is, therefore, a natural interpretation of the definition of 'eligible person' as a whole that the question whether condition (c) is satisfied should also be decided by reference to the same time.

Thirdly, the use of the present tense in the phrases 'he is not the occupier' and 'or, if he is, occupies it as a licensee only' in para (c) of the definition of 'eligible person' in s 18(2) is no more significant than the use of the same tense in the phrase 'he falls within paragraphs (a) to (d)' in para (a), or in the phrase 'agricultural unit of which the holding forms part' in para (b). The latter phrase, despite the use of the present tense, must surely relate to the time of death.

Fourthly, s 20(1) provides that an 'eligible person' may apply to the tribunal within 'the relevant period', which is defined in s 18(2) as being (subject to certain exceptions which are not material) the period of three months beginning with the day after the date of the deceased's death. It seems to me that, if an 'eligible person' can apply at any time from one day after the deceased's death to 91 days or thereabouts after it, the test of his eligibility must be a test as applicable on the first day as on any subsequent day up to the last. This will only be so if the question whether condition (c) is satisfied in his case is decided by reference to the time of the deceased's death.

Fifthly, the use of the present tense in the phrase 'that the applicant is an eligible person' in s 20(2) is not significant. 'Eligible' means the same as 'qualified'. The question whether a person is presently qualified in one respect or another will, more often than not, depend on whether certain conditions were satisfied in his case in the past. For instance a barrister is presently qualified if he was called to the Bar in the past, and a doctor is presently qualified if he acquired the necessary medical qualifications in the past. That being so, there is no difficulty in interpreting the phrase 'that the applicant is an eligible person' in s 20(2) as meaning 'is eligible because he possessed the necessary qualifications, including qualification (c), at the time of the deceased's death'.

Sixthly, the contention for the applicant that there are two relevant times for the satisfying of condition (c), namely the time of the application and the time of the hearing before the tribunal, itself necessarily involves interpreting the phrase 'that the applicant is an eligible person' in s 20(2) as referring, so far as the earlier of those two times is concerned, to the past. If there were any problem, therefore, about the use of the present tense in that phrase (which I do not think, for my fifth reason set out above, that there is) the applicant's interpretation would not eliminate such problem.

Seventhly, it seems to me more consistent with any policy of the Act which can reasonably be attributed to the legislature that the test of eligibility for succession contained in para (c) of the definition of 'eligible person' in s 18(2) should be applied by reference to the situation of a survivor as it exists at the time of the deceased's death rather than by reference to some different situation of his which has come into existence between the time of the deceased's death and the time of such survivor's application to the tribunal anything up to three months later.

So far as *Kimpson v Markham*[1], the authority on the Rent Acts relied on by the applicant, is concerned, I would only say that, since it is a decision on a different statute, I do not think it affords any real assistance in the interpretation of the statute here concerned. In any case it cannot be in any way decisive of such interpretation.

My conclusion on this matter differs from that of the other two members of the court and I express it therefore with diffidence. For the reasons which I have given, however, I would dismiss the appeal.

Appeal allowed. Leave to appeal to the House of Lords granted.

---

1   [1921] 2 KB 157

Solicitors: *Warren, Murton & Co*, agents for *Stamp, Jackson & Procter*, Hull (for the applicant); *Collyer-Bristow & Co*, agents for *Chambers Thomas & Williamson*, Hull (for the respondents).

Sumra Green Barrister

Shields v E Coomes (Holdings) Ltd

COURT OF APPEAL, CIVIL DIVISION
LORD DENNING MR, ORR AND BRIDGE LJJ
7th, 8th, 10th, 13th MARCH, 27th APRIL 1978

Employment – Equality of treatment between men and women – Like work – Difference between employees' work not of practical importance in relation to terms and conditions of employment – Male and female counterhands employed in betting shop – Man employed to deal with trouble in shop – Trouble not having in fact arisen – Whether difference in contractual obligations a difference of practical importance – Whether variation in pay due to a material difference other than sex – Equal Pay Act 1970 (as amended by the Sex Discrimination Act 1975), s 1(3)(4).

The employers owned 90 betting shops. In 81 shops the two counterhands employed were both women. In respect of the remaining nine shops the employers adopted the policy of employing one male and one female counterhand, the male counterhand being employed because they considered those shops to be located in areas where there might be trouble from awkward customers or criminal intruders. Under their contracts of employment the male counterhands were required to work longer hours, to open the shop, and to carry cash between the shop and other shops or the employers' head office. The men were paid £1·06 per hour and the women £0·92 per hour. The applicant was a woman counterhand employed at one of the nine shops having a male counterhand, at which however there had never been any trouble. The applicant complained to an industrial tribunal claiming to be entitled to the same rate of pay as her male counterpart in the shop. The tribunal decided that the claim arose under the Equal Pay Act 1970 and dismissed it on the grounds that although the work of male and female counterhands was of 'a broadly similar nature', within s 1(4)[a] of the 1970 Act, the security and cash-carrying duties of the male counterhands amounted to a difference 'of practical importance in relation to terms and conditions of employment'. The applicant appealed to the Employment Appeal Tribunal which allowed her appeal on the ground, inter alia, that it had not been shown by the employers that any variation between the contracts of male and female counterhands was due to a material difference other than sex and therefore under s 1(1) and (3) of the 1970 Act the applicant's contract was to be deemed to include an equality clause. The employers appealed.

---

a Section 1, so far as material, provides:
  '(1) If the terms of a contract under which a woman is employed at an establishment in Great Britain do not include (directly or by reference to a collective agreement or otherwise) an equality clause they shall be deemed to include one . . .
  '(3) An equality clause shall not operate in relation to a variation between the woman's contract and the man's contract if the employer proves that the variation is genuinely due to a material difference (other than the difference of sex) between her case and his.
  '(4) A woman is to be regarded as employed on like work with men if, but only if, her work and theirs is of the same or a broadly similar nature, and the differences (if any) between the things she does and the things they do are not of practical importance in relation to terms and conditions of employment; and accordingly in comparing her work with theirs regard shall be had to the frequency or otherwise with which any such differences occur in practice as well as to the nature and extent of the differences . . .'

Held – The appeal would be dismissed for the following reasons—

(i) When the work of male and female employees was of 'a broadly similar nature', then in deciding whether differences between their respective duties were 'not of practical importance in relation to terms and conditions of employment', within s 1(4) of the 1970 Act, the comparison to be made was that between the work actually done by the male and female employees having regard to the nature, extent and frequency of any differences in that work, and not between their respective contractual obligations. The male counterhand's cash-carrying duties did not make his job significantly different from the applicant's and he had in fact never been called on to exercise his security function. There was therefore no difference of practical importance between the applicant's job and that of her male counterpart (see p 463 g h, p 465 a to c, p 467 h to p 468 c, p 471 j to p 472 a h and j and p 473 a to c, post).

(ii) The variation in pay between the applicant and her male counterpart was not 'genuinely due to a material difference (other than the difference of sex)', within s 1(3) of the 1970 Act, since the employers' policy in employing male counterhands simply because they were male and not, for example, because they had been trained as security guards was discriminatory. The applicant was therefore entitled to be regarded as employed on like work with a male counterhand (see p 465 d to g, p 468 c d, p 471 c d and p 473 f, post).

Per Curiam. The Sex Discrimination Act 1975 and the Equal Pay Act 1970 form a single code (see p 463 b, p 467 b to d and p 470 f, post).

Notes

For equal treatment of men and women as regards terms and conditions of employment, see 16 Halsbury's Laws (4th Edn) para 767.

For the Equal Pay Act 1970, s 1, as amended by the Sex Discrimination Act 1975, see 45 Halsbury's Statutes (3rd Edn) 290.

Cases referred to in judgment

Amies v Inner London Education Authority [1977] 2 All ER 100, [1977] ICR 308, EAT.

Brennan v Prince William Hospital Corpn (1974) 503 F 2d 282.

British Leyland Ltd v Powell [1978] IRLR 57, EAT.

Capper Pass Ltd v Lawton [1977] 2 All ER 11, [1977] QB 852, [1977] 2 WLR 26, [1977] ICR 83, EAT.

Costa v Ente Nazionale per l'Energia Elettrica (ENEL) [1964] ECR 585, [1964] CMLR 425, CJEC.

Defrenne (Gabrielle) v Société Anonyme Belge de Navigation Aérienne (SABENA) [1976] ECR 455, [1976] ICR 547, CJEC.

Dugdale v Kraft Foods Ltd [1977] 1 All ER 454, [1977] ICR 48, EAT.

Eaton Ltd v Nuttall [1977] 3 All ER 1131, [1977] 1 WLR 549, [1977] ICR 272, EAT.

Electrolux Ltd v Hutchinson [1977] ICR 252, EAT.

NV Algemene Transport-en Expeditie Onderneming van Gend & Loos v Nederlandse administratie der belastingen [1963] ECR 1, [1963] CMLR 105, CJEC.

National Vulcan Engineering Insurance Group Ltd v Wade [1978] 3 All ER 121, [1978] 3 WLR 214, [1978] ICR 800, CA.

Navy, Army and Air Force Institutes v Varley [1977] 1 All ER 840, [1977] 1 WLR 149, [1977] ICR 11, EAT.

Reyners v Belgian State [1974] ECR 631, CJEC.

Shultz v American Can Co-Dixie Products (1970) 424 F 2d 356.

Shultz v Wheaton Glass Co (1970) 421 F 2d 259.

Snoxell v Vauxhall Motors Ltd [1977] 3 All ER 770, [1978] QB 11, [1977] 3 WLR 189, [1977] ICR 700, EAT.

Van Duyn v Home Office (No 2) [1975] 3 All ER 190, [1975] Ch 358, [1975] 2 WLR 760, [1974] ECR 1337, [1975] 1 CMLR 1, CJEC, Digest (Cont Vol D) 317, 4.

Waddington v Leicester Council for Voluntary Services [1977] 2 All ER 633, [1977] 1 WLR 544, [1977] ICR 266, EAT.

Cases also cited

ARW Transformers Ltd v Cupples [1977] IRLR 228, EAT.
Askew v Victoria Sporting Club Ltd [1976] ICR 302, EAT.
Director of Public Prosecutions v Hester [1972] 3 All ER 1056, [1973] AC 296, HL.
Early (Charles) & Marriott (Witney) Ltd v Smith [1977] 3 All ER 770, [1978] QB 11, EAT.
Edmonds v Computer Services (South-West) Ltd [1977] IRLR 359, EAT.
Hodgson v Brookhaven General Hospital (1970) 436 F 2d 719.
Macarthys Ltd v Smith [1978] 2 All ER 746, [1978] 1 WLR 849, EAT.
National Coal Board v Sherwin [1978] ICR 700, EAT.
Nothman v London Borough of Barnet [1978] 1 All ER 1243, [1978] 1 WLR 220, CA.
Peake v Automotive Products Ltd [1978] 1 All ER 106, [1978] QB 233, CA.
Redland Roof Tiles Ltd v Harper [1977] ICR 349, EAT.
Salomon v Comrs of Customs and Excise [1966] 3 All ER 871, [1967] 2 QB 116, CA.
Waddington v Miah [1974] 2 All ER 377, [1974] 1 WLR 683, HL.

Appeal

The employers, E Coomes (Holdings) Ltd ('the company'), appealed against a decision of the Employment Appeal Tribunal (Bristow J, Mr B L Mackie and Miss P Smith) dated 16th February 1977 to allow an appeal by an employee of the company, Sandra Shields ('the applicant'), from a majority decision of an industrial tribunal (chairman Mr Clifford G White) sitting in London on 27th July 1976 dismissing the applicant's complaint that she was entitled to the same rate of pay as a male counterhand and employed with the applicant in the employers' betting shop in Sussex Street, Pimlico, London. The facts are set out in the judgment of Lord Denning MR.

Mark Potter for the company.
Eldred Tabachnik for the applicant.
Anthony Lester QC for the Equal Opportunities Commission.

Cur adv vult

27th April. The following judgments were read.

LORD DENNING MR. E Coomes (Holdings) Ltd are bookmakers, alias turf accountants. They have 90 betting shops, 60 of them in south-east London, and the remaining 30 in south coast towns, such as Ramsgate, where they have five. In 81 of the shops they have two counterhands, who are both women. But in nine of the shops one of the counterhands is a man, and the other is a woman. The reason why they have a man in those nine is because they are situated in areas where the company anticipate there may be trouble from customers and others: and a man is needed to cope with it, if it arises.

One of these nine shops is in Sussex Street, Pimlico. The industrial tribunal describes it thus:

'The company has a policy of employing some male counterhands at each of those nine shops, not only as a possible deterrent to attack or possible entry or other trouble, but also to ensure that, if trouble arises, physical help shall be available on the spot to repel it until such time as the police are given an opportunity of arriving.'

The company took over this shop in 1973. They were told that trouble had been experienced there before they took over, but the company have not themselves had any trouble in their three years of ownership. The company say that 'this period of calm [has been] ensured by employing suitable male personnel, particularly on the counter where he is readily visible'. The man is especially important when the shop is opened in the mornings 'as a cover or precaution against illegal entry when the opening of the shop makes it most vulnerable to attack'. The man is needed, too, 'from time to time to transport cash to and from [their] shop' and other shops or head office.

Those findings make it clear that, at those nine shops in troublesome areas, the man fills a protective role. He does the same work at the counter as the woman counterhand. He takes the bets and receives and pays out the money. But, in his protective role, he works longer hours. He has to be at the shop when it is opened and most vulnerable, whereas the woman comes half-an-hour later. He is required to work a basic week of $37\frac{1}{2}$ hours a week as compared with a woman counterhand who does $32\frac{1}{2}$ hours.

Now here is the point: at 81 shops in trouble-free areas, the counterhands are all women and receive £0·92 per hour. But at the nine shops in troublesome areas the man counterhand is paid £1·06 per hour, and the women £0·92 per hour.

Now the woman counterhand at the Sussex Street shop claims that she does like work with the man and should receive £1·06 per hour, the same as he. The industrial tribunal, by a majority of two to one, rejected her claim.

The majority view of the evidence was that:

'. . . although the Sussex Street shop had enjoyed its three-year period of peace, it was genuinely and reasonably a requirement of [the company] that it should employ at least one male counterhand in present circumstances to perform those duties of detection and deterrence and (where required) of security. The employment of a male employee, being able to give assistance of this nature as and when required (albeit at extra cost) can be likened to the payment of an insurance premium to insure against trouble . . . that was a reasonable requirement and stipulation . . . an obligation within the terms and conditions of employment . . . and . . . having regard thereto and his longer basic week, all represented differences (real and existing and of practical importance) between ["his work and hers"]'

The minority view was 'that the alleged differences could not be regarded as real or that, if they existed, they were not of any practical importance'.

The woman appealed to the Employment Appeal Tribunal. They allowed her appeal. But I am afraid they were under a misapprehension. They thought that the company employed male counterhands not only at the nine shops in the troublesome areas, but also at the 81 trouble-free shops as well and that at all the 90 shops the male counterhands were paid more money than the women. They said: 'All the male counterhands, whether exercising [the protective] functions or not, got the same money, and this was 14p more than . . . the girls.' Before us this was acknowledged to be a mistake. There were no male counterhands employed except at the nine shops where trouble was feared. So the decision of the Employment Appeal Tribunal can be put on one side.

The company appeal to this court. They say that a large sum of money is involved. This is true. If the woman counterhand gets an increase of £0·14 per hour, so will the women in the other eight shops in the troublesome areas. And so will the women in all the 81 shops in the trouble-free areas: because each of those women counterhands will be able to say that she does like work, not only with the woman counterhand in Sussex Street, but also with the man counterhand there. The company's wage bill will go up at least £45,000 a year, and probably more.

The discussion before us ranged far and wide, in which we had the assistance of counsel on behalf of the Equal Opportunities Commission. He introduced us to the law of the European Communities on the subject of 'equal pay and sex discrimination'. He showed us that much of it is directly applicable in this country. So much so that I propose to set out the major provisions of Community law, and later see how they apply to the problem in hand.

Community law

Parliament has decreed that all the rights and obligations arising under the EEC Treaty are to be given legal effect: see s 2(1) of the European Communities Act 1972. Amongst these rights and obligations are those contained in art 119 of the EEC Treaty. It lays down firmly the principle of 'equal pay for equal work'. It says:

'Each Member State shall during the first stage ensure and subsequently maintain
the application of the principle that men and women should receive equal pay for
equal work. For the purpose of this Article, "pay" means the ordinary basic or
minimum wage or salary and any other consideration, whether in cash or in kind,
which the worker receives directly or indirectly, in respect of his employment from
his employer. Equal pay without discrimination based on sex means: (a) that pay for
the *same* work at piece rates shall be calculated on the basis of the *same* unit of
measurement; (b) that pay for work at *time* rates shall be the same for the *same* job.'
(emphasis mine)

The principle was easy to apply when men and women did the *same* work: such as when
they were both schoolteachers, or both bank clerks, or both waiting at table, doing exactly
the *same* work. But it ran into trouble when the work was not quite the same or the job a
little different. Employers were able to make a 'wage differential' between the sexes by
making differences in 'job content' between the man's work and the woman's work; or by
giving the work of the men a different 'job description' or a different 'job classification'
from that of women.

To meet such intrusions on the 'principle of equal pay', the European Community
extended it to the 'principle of equal value'. It was extended so as to apply not only when
it was the *same* work but also when it was work of *equal value*. This 'principle of equal
value' was introduced into Community law by a Council directive of 10th February 1975[1],
which said:

'The principle of equal pay for men and women outlined in Article 119 of the
Treaty, hereinafter called "principle of equal pay", means, for the same work or for
work *to which equal value is attributed*, the elimination of all discrimination on ground
of sex with regard to all aspects and conditions of remuneration. In particular, when
a job classification system is used for determining pay, it must be based on the same
criteria for both men and women, and so drawn up as to exclude any discrimination
on grounds of sex.' (emphasis mine)

So much for discrimination in the field of pay. But there remained other ways in which
there was discrimination against women: such as employing only men for jobs which
could be done equally well by women, for instance, in the professions or in business. To
exclude this, the slogan 'equal pay for equal work' became the apothegm 'no discrimination
on ground of sex'. The European Community announced its adherence to this principle
in 1976. By a directive of 9th February 1976[2], the Council declared that its purpose was—

'to put into effect in the Member States the principle of equal treatment for men
and women as regards access to employment, including promotion, and to vocational
training and as regards working conditions,'

and made enacting clauses, accordingly.

Applying the EEC Treaty provisions in England

If you were to read art 119 with the eyes of an English lawyer, you would think that that
article, and the directives following on it, imposed on the *member states* an obligation to pass
legislation so as to ensure equal pay for equal work, but that it had no direct application of
its own force in England. You would think that the English courts could wait and do
nothing until they saw an Act on the statute book to give effect to 'the principle of equal
pay', or 'the principle of equal value', or 'the principle of equal treatment'. But, if you
should think that, you would be wrong.

Long before the United Kingdom joined the European Community, the European
Court had laid down two principles of great importance to all member states and their

---

1   EEC Council Directive 75/117, art 1
2   EEC Council Directive 76/207, art 1

citizens. When we joined the Community, our Parliament enacted that we should abide
a by those principles laid down by the European Court: see s 3(1) of the European
Communities Act 1972. These two principles are the twin pillars on which Community
law rests. They uphold the standing of Community law as an independent legal order. It
is a law which is common to all member states and must be applied in all of them.

The first is the principle of 'direct applicability'. It arises whenever the EEC Treaty
imposes an obligation on member states to pass legislation on this subject or that. For
b instance, art 119 says: 'Each member state shall ... ensure ... that men and women shall
receive equal pay for equal work.' It is obvious that, if any member state failed to pass
legislation to implement that article, it might become a dead letter within that state. In
order to overcome any such evasion of the treaty, the European Court has declared that
many of the articles of the treaty are 'directly applicable' in any member state. This means
that any citizen in a member state can bring proceedings in his own national courts to
enforce the rights and obligations contained in this or that article of the treaty. He need
c not wait for his own Parliament to legislate. He can require his own courts to enforce his
Treaty rights. It is not every article which permits of 'direct applicability'. It is only those
articles which are sufficiently clear, precise and unconditional as not to require any further
measure of implementation. This principle was enunciated by the European Court in
1963 in *NV Algemene Transport-en Expeditie Onderneming van Gend & Loos v Nederlandse
administratie der belastingen*[1]. It was applied to art 119 in the case of the Belgian air hostess,
d Gabrielle Defrenne. She claimed equal pay with the cabin steward. Although Belgium
had not legislated to give effect to art 119, the European Court held that she was entitled
to sue in the national courts of Belgium to enforce her right to equal pay: see *Defrenne
(Gabrielle) v Société Anonyme Belge de Navigation Aérienne (SABENA)*[2]. The principle has also
been applied to art 48 concerning the freedom of movement of workers (see *Van Duyn v
Home Office (No 2)*[3]); and to art 52 concerning the right to take up activities as an advocate
e (see *Reyners v Belgian State*[4]); and to other articles.

The second is the principle of 'the supremacy of Community law'. It arises whenever
there is a conflict or inconsistency between the law contained in an article of the EEC
Treaty and the law contained in the internal law of one of the member states, whether
passed before or after joining the Community. It says that in any such event the law of the
f European Community shall prevail over that of the internal law of the member state. This
principle was enunciated by the European Court in 1964 in *Costa v Ente Nazionale per
l'Energia Elettrica (ENEL)*[5], and has been frequently affirmed since, especially in a recent
case from Italy[6]. The principle is obviously necessary in the economic field where
Community law requires levies to be made on goods to go into Community funds, and
refunds to be made. It would be intolerable if one country interpreted the regulations
g differently from another. This principle applies to art 119 also. Suppose that the
Parliament of the United Kingdom were to pass a statute inconsistent with art 119: as, for
instance, if the Equal Pay Act 1970 gave the right to equal pay only to unmarried women.
I should have thought that a married woman could bring an action in the High Court to
enforce the right to equal pay given to her by art 119. I may add that I should have
thought that she could bring a claim before the industrial tribunals, also. It seems to me
h that when the Parliament of the United Kingdom sets up a tribunal to carry out its treaty
obligations, the tribunal has jurisdiction to apply Community law, and should apply it, in
the confident expectation that that is what Parliament intended. If such a tribunal should
find any ambiguity in the statutes or any inconsistency with Community law, then it
should resolve it by giving the primacy to Community law. In this respect I would go

j 1   [1963] ECR 1 at 12
2   [1976] ECR 455
3   [1975] 3 All ER 190, [1975] Ch 358
4   [1974] ECR 631
5   [1964] ECR 585 at 594
6   *Amministrazione delle Finanze dello Stato v Simmenthal SpA* [1978] ECR 629

further than Bristow J in *Amies v Inner London Education Authority*[1]; and than Phillips J in *Snoxell v Vauxhall Motors Ltd*[2] (where the 'red circle' cases were considered). I think that Community law applies not only in the High Court, but also in the industrial tribunals and the Employment Appeal Tribunal. An appeal lies in all these cases to the Court of Appeal. So they should all apply the same law.

Thus far I have spoken only of the articles of the treaty. The same also applies to regulations. Article 189 says expressly that a regulation 'shall be binding in its entirety and directly applicable in all Member States'. That assumes, of course, that it is sufficiently clear, precise and unconditional to be applied without more ado.

Directives stand on a somewhat different footing. Article 189 says that 'A directive shall be binding, as to the result to be achieved ... but shall leave to the national authorities the choice of form and methods'. You might think from that article that a directive could never have direct effect; and that it would always be for the national authorities to implement it. But the European Court has laid emphasis on the word 'binding'. The European Court has held that the national courts can, in some cases, give direct effect to a directive: such as in *Van Duyn v Home Office (No 2)*[3], where the court held that the directive there in question 'confers on individual rights which are enforceable by them in the courts of a member state, and which the national courts must protect'. I do not pause here to say whether or not the directives issued under art 119 have direct effect. If need be, I would refer that question to the European Court. But the principles should be regarded as 'binding as to the result to be achieved'.

All this shows that the flowing tide of Community law is coming in fast. It has not stopped at high-water mark. It has broken the dykes and the banks. It has submerged the surrounding land. So much so that we have to learn to become amphibious if we wish to keep our heads above water.

The United States legislation

Whereas Community law on this subject is directly applicable in England, the United States legislation is not. But it is apparent from internal evidence that the English legislation is based a good deal on the United States experience. So it is instructive to glance at their law for a moment. It is contained in an Act of Congress passed in 1963 called the 'Equal Pay Act of 1963'[4].

The underlying principle is the 'principle of equal value'; that is, that when men and women are doing jobs of *equal value*, they are to receive equal pay. Employers are required to pay women wages at the same rate as men 'for equal work on jobs the performance of which requires equal skill, effort and responsibility, and which are performed under similar working conditions'[5].

But there is an exception in the case of 'individual merit' where a particular man or woman may get more money for the job if he or she specially deserves it. This exception is stated to apply where payment is made 'pursuant to (i) a seniority system; (ii) a merit system; (iii) a system which measures earnings by quantity or quality of production; or (iv) a differential based on any other factor other than sex'[5]. We were referred to cases in the United States Court of Appeal which considered that enactment. They look at any particular job, and ask: what is the rate for the job based on an hourly rate? Some jobs demand more of the workers in respect of skill, effort or responsibility than other jobs. So much so that the worker is entitled to higher pay on that account. This is called a 'wage differential'. Each person doing the same job is entitled to be paid the 'rate for the job' irrespective of his sex. In contrast the American cases allow an exception by way of a 'merit

---

1   [1977] 2 All ER 100 at 104–105
2   [1977] 3 All ER 770 at 783, [1978] QB 11 at 34
3   [1975] 3 All ER 190 at 206, [1975] Ch 358 at 377
4   77 Stat 56 (1963)
5   77 Stat 56 (1963) §3

system' in which unequal pay for equal work may be justified by the merits of an individual worker, provided that it is not based on a difference of sex.

The English statutes

The English statutes are plainly designed so as to implement the EEC Treaty and the directives issued by the Council. They are the Sex Discrimination Act 1975, to which is scheduled the Equal Pay Act 1970, as amended. All came into force on 29th December 1975. They must all be taken together. But the task of construing them is like fitting together a jig-saw puzzle. The pieces are all jumbled up together, in two boxes. One is labelled the Sex Discrimination Act 1975; the other, the Equal Pay Act 1970. You pick up a piece from one box and try to fit it in. It does not. So you try a piece from the other box. That does not fit either. In despair you take a look at the picture by the makers. It is the guide[1] issued by the Home Office. Counsel on behalf of the Equal Opportunities Commission recommended especially para 3.18, which he says will show the distinction between the two Acts. Even that will not make you jump with joy. You will not find the missing pieces unless you are very discriminating.

The only thing that is clear to me is that, when men and women are engaged on like work in the same establishment, the women are to be paid the same 'rate for the job' as the men. That is usually an hourly rate. But an exception can be made where a man deserves more than the woman because he has special personal claims to a higher rate because of his superior skill or responsibility or merit, so long as it is not based on the difference in sex. I turn to the sections which bear this out.

Section 1(4)—'like work'

When a woman claims equal pay with a man in the same employment, she has first to show that she is employed on 'like work' with him. This is defined in s 1(4), which proceeds in this fashion:

First, her work and that of the men must be 'of the same or a broadly similar nature'. Instances of the 'same nature' are men and women bank cashiers at the same counter; or men and women serving meals in the same restaurant. Instances of a 'broadly similar nature' are men and women shop assistants in different sections of the same department store; or a woman cook who prepares lunches for the directors and the men chefs who cook breakfast, lunch and teas for the employees in the canteen: see *Capper Pass Ltd v Lawton*[2].

Second, there must be an enquiry into (i) the 'differences . . . between the things [that the woman] does and the things [that the men do]', and (ii) a comparison of them so as to see 'the nature and extent of the differences' and 'the frequency or otherwise with which such differences occur in practice' and (iii) a decision as to whether these differences are or are not 'of practical importance in regard to terms and conditions of employment'.

This involves a comparison of the two jobs, the woman's job and the man's job, and making an evaluation of each job as a job irrespective of the sex of the worker and of any special personal skill or merit that he or she may have. This evaluation should be made in terms of the 'rate for the job', usually a payment of so much per hour. The rate should represent the value of each job in terms of the demand made on a worker under such headings as effort, skill, responsibility and decision. If the value of the man's job is worth more than the value of the woman's job, it is legitimate that the man should receive a higher 'rate for the job' than the woman. For instance, a man who is dealing with production schedules may deal with far more important items than the woman, entailing far more serious consequences from a wrong decision. So his job should be rated higher than hers: see *Eaton Ltd v Nuttall*[3]. But, if the value of the woman's job is equal to the man's job, each should receive the same rate for the job. This principle of 'equal value' is so important that you should ignore differences between the two jobs which are 'not of

---

1   Sex Discrimination, A guide to the Sex Discrimination Act 1975
2   [1977] 2 All ER 11, [1977] QB 852
3   [1977] 3 All ER 1131, [1977] 1 WLR 549

practical importance'. The employer should not be able to avoid the principle by introducing comparatively small differences in 'job content' between men and women; nor by giving the work a different 'job description'. Thus where a woman driver in a catering department drives vans within the factory premises to and from the kitchens, and a man driver in a transport section drives vans on the public highway, it could properly be held that the differences were 'not of practical importance' and she should receive the same 'rate for the job' an hour rate as he: see *British Leyland Ltd v Powell*[1]. Again in a hospital, the attendance on patients may be done by women called 'nurses' and men called 'orderlies': and there may be differences in 'job content' in that, while both do many similar things, the men 'orderlies' deal with the special needs of men patients, but these differences are not such as to warrant a 'wage differential' between the nurses and the orderlies: see *Brennan v Prince William Hospital Corpn*[2].

Nor should the employer be able to avoid the principle of 'equal value' by having the work (at the same job) done by night or for longer hours. The only legitimate way of dealing with night work or for longer hours is by paying a night shift premium or overtime rate assessed at a reasonable figure. Article 119 of the EEC Treaty says specifically that the 'pay for work at time rates shall be the same for the same job'. The decided cases are to the same effect: see *Shultz v American Can Co-Dixie Products*[3], *Dugdale v Kraft Foods Ltd*[4] and *Electrolux Ltd v Hutchinson*[5].

If it is found that the differences are 'not of practical importance' then the woman is employed on 'like work' with the men; and her contract is deemed to include an equality clause giving her the same 'rate for the job' as the men: see s 1(1) (2).

Section 1(3)—personal differences

Section 1(3) says that a variation in pay is justifiable 'if the employer proves that the variation is genuinely due to a material difference (other than the difference of sex) between her case and his'.

This subsection deals with cases where the woman and the man are doing 'like work' but the personal equation of the man is such that he deserves to be paid at a higher rate than the woman. Even the two jobs, viewed as jobs, are evaluated equally, nevertheless there may, quite genuinely, be 'material differences' between the two people who are doing them, which merit a variation in pay, irrespective of whether it is a man or woman doing the job. One instance is length of service. In many occupations, a worker, be he man or woman, gets an increment from time to time, according to his seniority or length of service. Another instance is special personal skill or qualifications. In many occupations a degree or diploma is a qualification for higher pay, irrespective of sex. So is a higher grading for skill or capacity within the firm itself: see *National Vulcan Engineering Insurance Group Ltd v Wade*[6]. Likewise, a bigger ouput or productivity may warrant a 'wage differential' so long as it is not based on sex. So may the place of work: see *Navy, Army and Air Force Institutes v Varley*[7]. In all these cases the two jobs are evaluated equally as jobs, but, nevertheless, there are material differences (other than sex) which warrant a 'wage differential' between the two persons doing them.

But the escape route offered by s 1(3) is so open to abuse that the section requires that the variation should be 'genuinely due' to the difference and that the employer should 'prove' it, not by an excessively high standard of proof but by the ordinary standard of the balance of probabilities: see *National Vulcan Engineering Insurance Group Ltd v Wade*[6].

---

1   [1978] IRLR 57
2   (1974) 503 F 2d 282 at 283
3   (1970) 424 F 2d 356 at 358
4   [1977] 1 All ER 454 at 458
5   [1977] ICR 252
6   [1978] 3 All ER 121, [1978] 3 WLR 214
7   [1977] 1 All ER 840, [1977] 1 WLR 149

Application to this case

In this case the woman and the man were employed on work of a broadly similar nature. They were both counterhands. There were several differences between the things she did and the things which he did. For instance, he started at opening time and worked longer hours; but this did not, by itself, warrant a difference in the 'rate for the job'. He carried cash from shop to shop or to head office. But this difference was, by itself, 'not of practical importance'. The one difference of any significance between them was that the man filled a protective role. He was a watchdog ready to bark and scare off intruders. This difference, when taken with the others, amounted to differences which the majority of the industrial tribunal found were 'real and existing and of practical importance'. Accepting this finding, I do not think these differences could or did affect the 'rate for the job'. Both the woman and the man worked alongside one another hour after hour, doing precisely the same work. She should, therefore, receive the same hourly rate as he. It is rather like the difference between a barman and a barmaid. They do the same work as one another in serving drinks. Each has his or her own way of dealing with awkward customers. Each is subject to the same risk of abuse or unpleasantness. But, whichever way each adopts in dealing with awkward customers, the job of each, as a job, is of equivalent rating. Each should, therefore, receive the same 'rate for the job'. It comes within s 1(4) as 'like work'.

It would be otherwise if the difference was based on any special personal qualification that he had; as, for instance, if he was a fierce and formidable figure, trained to tackle intruders, then there might be a variation such as to warrant a 'wage differential' under s 1(3). But no such special personal qualification is suggested. The only difference between the two jobs is on the ground of sex. He may have been a small nervous man, who could not say boo to a goose. She may have been as fierce and formidable as a battle-axe. Such differences, whatever they were, did not have any relation to the terms and conditions of employment. They did not affect the 'rate for the job'.

I confess, however, that I have felt great difficulty in overcoming the finding of the industrial tribunal that the differences, especially the protective role of the man, were 'real and existing and of practical importance'. I thought for some time that this protective role should be rewarded by some additional bonus or premium. But my difficulties on this score have been resolved by giving supremacy to Community law. Under that law it is imperative that 'pay for work at time rates shall be the same for the same job'; and that 'all discrimination on the ground of sex shall be eliminated with regard to all aspects and conditions of remuneration'. The differences found by the majority of the industrial tribunal are all based on sex. They are because he is a man. He only gets the higher hourly rate because he is a man. In order to eliminate all discrimination, there should be an equality clause written into the woman's contract.

I would, therefore dismiss the appeal.

ORR LJ. In this case the industrial tribunal, correctly in my judgment, for reasons to which I shall later refer, directed themselves in the first paragraph of their decision that, although the originating application referred to a question to be decided under the Sex Discrimination Act 1975, it was clear that the claim was one arising under ss 1 and 2 of the Equal Pay Act 1970. But having so directed themselves, and considering the case, as they clearly did, with great care, they appear to have ignored s 1(3) of the 1970 Act, as substituted by s 8(1) of the 1975 Act, and the references in the second paragraph of their decision to the terms of sub-s (2) of s 1 of the 1970 Act suggests that they may, at least at that stage, have been looking at the original and not at the substituted sub-s (2).

The tribunal decided by a majority of two to one that there were differences between the things done by the applicant and those done by Mr Rolls, and that such differences were all of regular frequency in practice and of practical importance in relation to the terms and conditions of employment. It has been common ground on this appeal that one of the differences found by them, namely that Mr Rolls's basic week was 37½ hours and the applicant's was 32½ hours, is not a relevant difference for the present purposes. The other differences accepted by the majority of the tribunal were that Mr Rolls was required to be available (i) during the opening hours of the shop for the purposes of deterring, and if necessary repelling, violence within the shop and also unlawful intruders, (ii) at the time of opening of the shop by the manager since the shop was considered to be specially vulnerable at that time, (iii) to transport cash between the shop and other shops of the company, or to and from the company's head office. Finally, (iv) the majority accepted as relevant to the requirement of frequency that for the above purposes the company were entitled to take the view, which they applied as a matter of policy, that a male clerk should be continuously employed in each of the nine shops which they considered to lie in a potential trouble area.

The minority of the tribunal, on the other hand, took the view that the alleged differences could not be regarded as real, or if they were real, as not of any practical importance, and they attached some weight in this context to the fact that the applicant had on occasions been present, in the absence of Mr Rolls, when the shop was opened, and had once herself opened it in the absence of the manager, and had also volunteered on one occasion to collect money from another of the company's shops.

From this decision of the industrial tribunal, the applicant appealed to the Employment Appeal Tribunal which, in a judgment delivered by Bristow J, allowed the appeal and in default of agreement gave the applicant leave to amend her application so as to include a claim for arrears of pay or damages.

In his judgment Bristow J referred to the fact that there had been no evidence that male counter clerks in the nine shops which were considered to fall within the potential trouble area were paid any more than male counter clerks in the other 81 of the company's shops in which the additional protective and deterrent functions were considered unnecessary. The £0·14 differential as between the male and female counter clerks in the nine shops within the trouble area having been the only differential of which evidence had been given by Mr Jeffery, a director and the general manager of the company, and who had also conducted their case before the industrial tribunal.

On this basis the Employment Appeal Tribunal, while accepting that there were differences between the things done by the applicant and those done by Mr Rolls, held that such differences were not of practical importance in relation to terms and conditions of employment, and that this was clearly indicated by the fact that the protective and deterrent part of Mr Rolls's job was not regarded as worth any more than was paid to the male counter clerks outside the trouble area, and they concluded that in this respect the majority of the industrial tribunal must have misdirected themselves and gone wrong in law.

This was the first reason given by the Employment Appeal Tribunal for allowing the appeal but it has in this court been alleged on behalf of the company, and not disputed on behalf of the applicant, whose advisers have had an opportunity of verifying the facts, that the appeal tribunal were under a misapprehension in assuming, in the absence of evidence to the contrary, that male counter clerks are employed in the other 81 shops and also in assuming that they are paid at the same rate of £0·14 per hour in excess of the wages paid to women. It will be necessary therefore to consider whether the conclusion reached by the appeal tribunal in this case was justified on grounds other than their wrong assumption as respects other shops. Moreover, the matter does not rest there because the appeal tribunal, after referring to the supposed employment of males in the other shops at a wage of £0·14 per hour more than was paid to the women, observed that it was for this reason impossible to escape the conclusion that the money differential rested on sex. They went on, however, to say that, quite apart from the consideration as to rate of pay, Mr Rolls was required to perform his function as protector and deterrent simply because he was a man and not because he was in any way trained in security guard duties or unarmed combat, and that in their view selected and trained women could have done that part of his job as well as he, and for this reason also they allowed the appeal on a second ground that, within the meaning of s 1(3) of the Equal Pay Act 1970 (as substituted by s 8(1) of the Sex

Discrimination Act 1975) the variation in the rate of pay was not in their judgment genuinely due to a material difference other than sex.

On this appeal counsel for the company (the appellants) has challenged both these grounds on which the Employment Appeal Tribunal reversed the industrial tribunal, his attack on the first ground being based on the wrong assumption made by the appeal tribunal as to the employment of men in the other 81 shops, and also on the conclusion reached by the majority of the industrial tribunal, and his attack on the second ground being that the applicant had never sought or wished to be employed in the security duties assigned to Mr Rolls, and that ss 6 and 7 of the Sex Discrimination Act 1975, contained in Part II of that Act entitled 'Discrimination in the Employment Field', are of no relevance to the present case.

In my judgment, however, it is clear beyond doubt that the Equal Pay Act 1970, enacted on 29th May of that year but with a provision contained in s 9 that it should come into force on 29th December 1975, and the Sex Discrimination Act 1975, which was brought into force (with exceptions irrelevant for the present purposes) on the same date, form in effect two parts of a single code directed against sex discrimination both in the field of employment and in other fields, and designed to fulfil the obligations in those respects of the United Kingdom under art 119 of the EEC Treaty. That they constitute a single code is in my judgment clear from their expressed objects and their being brought into force on the same day, and from the circumstances that s 8 of the Sex Discrimination Act substituted new sub-ss (1), (2) and (3) in the place of those originally enacted in s 1 of the Equal Pay Act, and most important of all, from the care which has been taken in the Sex Discrimination Act to specify in relation to 'Discrimination in the Employment Field', under which of the two Acts proceedings are in given circumstances to be taken. Examples are ss 6(5) and 8(3) of the Sex Discrimination Act and the effect of the provisions clearly is that proceedings lie under the Equal Pay Act where there is a contractual relation and under the Sex Discrimination Act where there is not. In the present case there was a contract of employment between the applicant and the company and, by virtue of s 6(5) of the Sex Discrimination Act, s 6(1)(*b*) of the same Act (which provides that it is unlawful for a person, 'in relation to employment by him . . . to discriminate against a woman . . . in the terms on which he offers her that employment') does not apply, and the appropriate remedy is under ss 1 and 3 of the Equal Pay Act. By contrast, had the applicant in the present case refused the offer of employment made to her, with the result that no contract came into being, her remedy would have been under s 6(1)(*b*) of the Sex Discrimination Act. These and other sample cases put to us by counsel for the Equal Opportunities Commission clearly indicate, in my judgment, that the two Acts are to be regarded as complementary parts of a single code, and underline the necessity of so construing each part of the code as to produce a harmonious result.

The first question arising in the appeal is whether the industrial tribunal, having rightly found that, for the purposes of s 1(4) of the Equal Pay Act, the applicant's work and Mr Rolls's work was of a broadly similar nature were justified on the evidence in further finding (by a majority) that the differences (if any) between the things she did and the things he did were of practical importance in relation to terms and conditions of employment. The subsection by its terms requires that in comparing her work with his regard should be had to the frequency with which any such differences occur in practice as well as the nature and extent of the differences, and it is abundantly clear, in my judgment, that the comparison which the subsection requires to be made is not between the respective contractual obligations but between the things done and the frequency with which they are done. But it is equally clear from the terms of the decision of the industrial tribunal that the majority of the members misdirected themselves in this respect by paying too great attention to the contractual obligations and too little to the acts in fact done and their frequency, and in particular to the fact that Mr Rolls had never in fact, on the evidence, had to deal with any disturbance or attempted violence. It is true that the arrangement made by the company for dealing with such incidents was, apart from the Equal Pay Act and Sex Discrimination Act, a sensible one, and the fact that no trouble in fact arose does not establish that they were being over cautious in making that arrangement at the nine shops, but the fact that Mr Rolls did not in fact ever have to deal with any trouble is by the terms of s 1(4) very material for the present purposes and in my judgment much too little regard was paid to it by the tribunal. The same consideration applies to the duty of Mr Rolls to be present at the opening of the shop by the manager, plainly a sensible precaution, but here again there has been no untoward incident and this was a matter which the tribunal were required to take into account. Considering the totality of the evidence, and with great respect to the tribunal, I find the conclusion inescapable that they must have either misdirected themselves as to the law or adopted a view of the facts which was not justified by the evidence, and for the same reasons I am satisfied that the appeal tribunal, putting aside their wrong assumption as to the employment of men in the other shops, came to a right conclusion on this issue.

The second question in the appeal involves s 1(3) of the Equal Pay Act (as substituted by the Sex Discrimination Act, s 58(1)) which provides an alternative ground of relief to an employer who fails under s 1(4) but by its terms imposes a burden of proof on the employer. In my judgment it cannot in the present case assist the employers in view of their acknowledged policy of sex discrimination in the selection of employees for the nine shops, and in my judgment, putting aside the wrong assumption as to the employment of males in the other shops, the appeal tribunal were entirely right in their conclusion that the money differential rested on sex alone.

I would add that in the course of the argument on this appeal we were addressed at some length and very helpfully as to the possible relevance, for the purpose of construction of the Equal Pay and Sex Discrimination Acts, of art 119 of the EEC Treaty and the subsequent directives dated 10th February 1975[1] and 9th February 1976[2] of the Council of the European Communities, but for the reasons I have given I do not think that the applicant needs the assistance which it was claimed could be derived from those sources. I accept, on the authority of the European Court in *Defrenne (Gabrielle) v Société Anonyme Belge de Navigation Aérienne (SABENA)*[3], that the principle of equal pay embodied in art 119 of the EEC Treaty is enforceable as part of the law of the United Kingdom, but I would reserve for a case in which it arises for decision the question whether the same principle extends to the two directives, to which I have earlier referred, of the Council of the European Communities. In my view the judgment of the European Court in *Van Duyn v Home Office (No 2)*[4], which was concerned with a different article of the EEC Treaty, and in which it was accepted that directives of the Council of the European Communities, unlike regulations, do not necessarily have direct effect in each member state, is not decisive one way or the other in the present context.

I would also add that we were referred in argument to a large number of reported cases, most of them decided by the Employment Appeal Tribunal, but the present case must in my judgment depend on its own facts, and for this reason, while the authorities were properly and helpfully cited, I found them of limited assistance.

For the reasons I have given I would dismiss this appeal.

BRIDGE LJ. The company, the appellants, operate a chain of 90 betting shops. At most of these the counterhands employed are female. But nine shops ('the trouble shops') are situated in areas where it is anticipated that there may be trouble from awkward customers or criminal intruders. At the trouble shops the company, as the industrial tribunal found, operate—

'a policy of employing some male counterhands ... not only as a possible deterrent to attack or forcible entry or other trouble but also to ensure that, if trouble arises,

---

1 EEC Council Directive 75/117
2 EEC Council Directive 76/207
3 [1976] ECR 455
4 [1975] 3 All ER 190, [1975] Ch 358

a   then physical help shall be available on the spot to repel it until such time as the police are given an opportunity of arriving.'

The company's shop at Sussex Street, London, SWI, is one of the trouble shops, though since the company took it over in 1973 there has been no trouble there in fact. The applicant was one of two counterhands employed at the Sussex Street shop. The other was a Mr Rolls. She was paid £0·92 per hour. He was paid £1·06 per hour. She claimed to be

b   entitled to the same rate of pay as his by virtue of an equality clause under s 1(2)(a) of the Equal Pay Act 1970 on the ground that they were employed on like work. The industrial tribunal by a majority rejected the applicant's claim. Purporting to apply s 1(4) they found that his work and hers were of a broadly similar nature, but that there were differences between the things she did and the things he did of practical importance in relation to terms and conditions of employment, so that the applicant's claim to be employed on like

c   work with a man failed. The Employment Appeal Tribunal reversed this decision primarily on the ground that the supposed differences could not be the real reason for the difference in pay since male counterhands employed elsewhere than at the trouble shops were also paid the higher rate. This conclusion was based on an erroneous inference of fact which the Employment Appeal Tribunal drew from the evidence. No male counterhands have been employed by the company at any material time except at the trouble shops. An

d   alternative ground relied on by the Employment Appeal Tribunal and expressed very shortly in their judgment treated the case as depending on s 1(3). In my judgment the crucial provision on which the case depends is that in s 1(4). Accordingly the proper approach for this court must be to examine de novo the decision of the industrial tribunal to see whether it exhibits any error of law and if so whether the facts are sufficiently clear to enable us to arrive at a firm result or whether the case should go back for rehearing.

e   At the end of the day I am satisfied that the issue arising for decision can be resolved within a narrow compass and that the application of the provisions of s 1 of the Equal Pay Act to the facts of the case leads to a perfectly clear conclusion. We have, however, had the advantage of hearing penetrating arguments ranging over the whole scheme of the legislation comprised in the Sex Discrimination Act and the Equal Pay Act, which is embodied in its amended form in Sch 1 to the Sex Discrimination Act. Since this is the

f   first opportunity this court has had to consider this subject-matter in a reserved judgment, it may not be out of place to take note of the background to the legislation and of the salient features of the policy which underlies it.

Article 119 of the EEC Treaty already enshrines the principle 'that men and women should receive equal pay for equal work'. In *Defrenne (Gabrielle) v Société Anonyme Belge de Navigation Aérienne (SABENA)*[1] the European Court held that this principle of equal pay was

g   of direct effect, that is to say it was a principle of law enforceable between individuals as part of the municipal law of member states. The principle must accordingly be applied as part of our law under the provisions of s 2 of the European Communities Act 1972. It follows that if the employment provisions of the Equal Pay Act had not been enacted the courts in this country themselves would have had the duty of giving effect to the broad general principle derived from the treaty.

h   However it is important to note the limitations set by the European Court on the direct applicability of art 119. They said in *Defrenne's case*[2]:

'(18) For the purposes of the implementation of these provisions a distinction must be drawn within the whole area of application of Article 119 between, first, direct and overt discrimination which may be identified solely with the aid of the criteria based on equal work and equal pay referred to by the article in question and, secondly,

j   indirect and disguised discrimination which can only be identified by reference to more explicit implementing provisions of a Community or national character. (19) It is impossible not to recognise that the complete implementation of the aim pursued

---

1   [1976] ECR 455, [1976] ICR 547
2   [1976] ECR 455 at 473, [1976] ICR 547 at 566

by Article 119 by means of the elimination of all discrimination, direct or indirect, between men and women workers, not only as regards individual undertakings but also entire branches of industry and even of the economic system as a whole, may in certain cases involve the elaboration of criteria whose implementation necessitates the taking of appropriate measures at Community and national level.'

The further measures taken at Community level are Directives 75/117/EEC and 76/207/EEC of the Council of the European Communities. There is no decision of the European Court that any of the provisions of these two directives are of direct effect.

The directives are clearly intended to be implemented at national level by national legislation. In this country they have been so implemented by the Sex Discrimination Act and the Equal Pay Act.

It may be that the directives could be prayed in aid to assist in resolving some ambiguity in the English statutes. As no such ambiguity arises in the instant case, there is, in my judgment, no occasion to resort to the directives.

In the United States a code closely analogous to the employment provisions of the Sex Discrimination Act and the Equal Pay Act is found in the United States Equal Pay Act of 1963[1] of which it has been said[2]:

'The Act was intended as a broad charter of women's rights in the economic field. It sought to overcome the age-old belief in women's inferiority and to eliminate the depressing effects on living standards of reduced wages for female workers and the economic and social consequences which flow from it.'

The same could be said of the English Acts. The underlying philosophy is well expressed in a passage from the White Paper which foreshadowed the legislation, 'Equality for Women'[3]:

'Beyond the basic physiological difference between men and women lies a whole range of differences between individual men and individual women in all aspects of human ability. The differences within each sex far outweigh the differences between the sexes. But there is insufficient recognition that the variations of character and ability within each sex are greater and more significant than the differences between the sexes.'

In the sphere of employment the provisions of the Sex Discrimination Act and the Equal Pay Act aimed at eliminating discrimination on grounds of sex are closely interlocking and provided in effect a single comprehensive code. The particular provisions designed to prevent overlapping between the two Acts are complex, and it may often be difficult to determine whether a particular matter of complaint falls to be redressed under one Act or the other. But what is abundantly clear is that both Acts should be construed and applied as a harmonious whole and in such a way that the broad principles which underlie the whole scheme of legislation are not frustrated by a narrow interpretation or restrictive application of particular provisions.

What those broad principles are is nowhere more clearly shown than in the provisions of ss 6 and 7 of the Sex Discrimination Act designed to eliminate discrimination on grounds of sex in the provision of employment opportunities and in the selection criteria which may properly be applied in determining suitability for employment. The general rule is that any presumption of an inherent superiority of one sex over the other in the qualifications required for any employment is to be outlawed. Exceptions to this general rule are permitted only to the extent that they are specifically spelled out in the defined categories where being a man (or woman) is to be admitted as 'a genuine occupational qualification for a job'. It is significant that the demands a job may make on the employee's physical strength or stamina are specifically excluded from consideration under the

1 77 Stat 56 (1963)
2 *Shultz v Wheaton Glass Co* (1970) 421 F 2d 259 at 265
3 Cmnd 5724, para 16

excepted categories. In relation to the kind of work which police or security officers may
be called on to perform it is again significant that there is no exception to the general rule
which would permit any presumption that men are inherently better qualified for the
work than women on the ground either of any supposed superior courage, resourcefulness
and ability to deal with trouble or that they can properly be exposed to danger from which
women should be protected. This principle is emphasised by s 17 of the Sex Discrimination Act from which it is clear that the employment provisions of both the Sex Discrimination Act and the Equal Pay Act are applicable to employment in police forces and that
in relation to such employment men and women may be treated differently only in certain
strictly limited respects which are for present purposes immaterial.

If one bears these aspects of the general scheme of the legislation in mind, the result
arrived at by the majority of the industrial tribunal is, to say the least, a surprising one.
True, the case was concerned not with job selection but with remuneration. Nevertheless
the company's employment policy was clearly in conflict with the principles which the
legislation embodies. The company were perfectly frank about it. Their case in a nutshell
was that men were employed as counterhands in the trouble shops because they were men;
that if trouble arose the men rather than the women would have to dealt with it, and that
this justified paying them a higher hourly rate than the women.

The matter falls for decision, as already stated, under s 1 of the Equal Pay Act. In
comparing the applicant's position with that of her fellow counterhand, Mr Rolls, three
possible questions fell to be answered, as they would in any case where a woman claims an
equality clause by virtue of employment on like work with a man under s 1(2)(a). First,
was their work of the same or a broadly similar nature? Secondly, if so, were any
differences between the things she did and the things he did (regard being had to the
frequency, nature and extent of such differences) of practical importance in relation to
terms and conditions of employment? These first two questions arise under s 1(4) which
defines like work. The legal burden of proving that she is employed on like work with a
man rests on the woman claimant. But if the first question is answered in her favour, an
evidential burden of showing differences of practical importance rests on the employers.
The third question under s 1(3) arises only if the woman has established that she is
employed on like work with a man. Can the employer then prove that any variation
between the woman's contract and the man's is genuinely due to a material difference
(other than the difference of sex) between her case and his? If so, her claim to an equality
clause is defeated.

We have referred to a number of reported decisions of the Employment Appeal Tribunal
in which the proper approach to these questions has been considered. The first question,
whether the work of the man and woman to be compared is of the same or of a broadly
similar nature, does not appear to have given rise to difficulties. In relation to the second
question, whether differences between the things done by the employees being compared
are of practical importance in relation to terms and conditions of employment, I would
respectfully adopt as correct the general approach expressed by Phillips J giving the
judgment of the Employment Appeal Tribunal in *Capper Pass Ltd v Lawton*[1] where he said:

> 'In answering that question the industrial tribunal will be guided by the concluding
> words of the subsection. But again, it seems to us, trivial differences, or differences
> not likely in the real world to be reflected in the terms and conditions of employment,
> ought to be disregarded. In other words, once it is determined that work is of a
> broadly similar nature it should be regarded as being like work unless the differences
> are plainly of a kind which the industrial tribunal in its experience would expect to
> find reflected in the terms and conditions of employment.'

In considering this second question, it has been emphasised in a number of cases that a
difference between duties which the man and woman whose work is being compared are

---

1   [1977] 2 All ER 11 at 14, [1977] QB 852 at 857

under a contractual obligation to perform is not a relevant difference unless it results in an
actual difference in what is done in practice. It is by comparing their observed activities
not their notional paper obligations that the relevant differences are to be ascertained. This
is an important principle. Where the differences between the employees to be compared
are not reflected in differences in things done, they fall for consideration only when the
third question is asked, viz: is the variation between the woman's contract and the man's
(a difference in rate of pay or other contractual benefits) genuinely due to a material
difference (other than the difference of sex) between her case and his? The kind of
differences which can be considered at this stage are manifold and it would be undesirable
to attempt to categorise or limit them. A difference in mere seniority, whether measured
by age or length of service, would be an obvious example. It may nevertheless be difficult
to draw a clear line of demarcation between differences proper for consideration under
s 1(4) and those which can only be considered under s 1(3). The Employment Appeal
Tribunal has held that differences in the degree of responsibility borne by two employees
may properly lead to the conclusion that there are differences between the things they do
for the purposes of sub-s (4), even though it may be difficult to pinpoint and identify the
precise differentiation of activity: see *Waddington v Leicester Council for Voluntary Services*[1]
and *Eaton Ltd v Nuttall*[2]. No doubt this principle is correct, though how far it can be
applied to the facts of particular cases may be debatable and must in the end be a matter of
degree. The important thing is that the words of sub-s (4), 'differences . . . between the
things she does and the things they do', should in no way be strained beyond their natural
and ordinary meaning. If the differences relied on to justify the more favourable treatment
of a man than a woman cannot fairly be brought within these words, the employer still has
the full protection of the fall-back provision in sub-s (3) provided always that he can
discharge the onus of making good his case of justification in accordance with the terms of
that subsection.

    The decision of the industrial tribunal in this case, having found the work of Mr Rolls
and the applicant to be of a broadly similar nature, introduces the five differences relied on
by the company and accepted by the majority of the tribunal as 'differences of practical
importance between the things done by the applicant and the things which Mr Rolls is
required by his terms and conditions of employment to do'. Here and elsewhere it is
apparent that the majority misdirected themselves as to the statutory test under s 1(4) by
comparing contractual obligations rather than things done. The first difference was said
to be that 'it is important that there should be a male employee to counter the application
of force within the shop or to reject unlawful intruders'. It will be convenient to call this
the difference in security function. Two of the remaining four differences (the necessity
for a male counterhand to be present at the morning opening of the shop, when it was said
to be vulnerable, and the fact that Mr Rolls was one of a team of male counterhands
employed at the trouble shops) were no more than aspects of the difference in security
function and added nothing of substance to it. The remaining differences were said to be
a difference in cash carrying duties and a difference in working hours. It has been
conceded throughout by counsel for the company that the difference in working hours was
an irrelevant factor. A careful analysis of the evidence leads to the conclusion that, apart
from a notional difference in contractual obligations, there was no significant differences
between the things done by the applicant and the things done by Mr Rolls in relation to
cash carrying duties which could provide material to support the decision of the
majority. The ultimate question, therefore, and that to which the main argument has
been directed is whether the decision of the majority can be supported by reference to the
difference in security function. Counsel for the company has strenuously contended that
this alone reveals a difference of practical importance in relation to terms and conditions of
employment between the things done by the respondent and the things done by Mr Rolls
and that the majority of the industrial tribunal must be taken to have so found. He

1   [1977] 2 All ER 633, [1977] 1 WLR 544
2   [1977] 3 All ER 1131, [1977] 1 WLR 549

analyses Mr Rolls's security responsibility as involving three different aspects: first, it was his duty by his mere male presence to deter trouble; secondly, he had to be constantly on the alert for trouble; thirdly, if trouble had ever arisen, it would have been his responsibility not the applicant's to deal with it. With respect, it seems to me that it would be a complete misuse of language to say that any of these factors represented a difference between the things the respondent did and the things that Mr Rolls did in the course of their employment as counterhands, let alone a difference of practical importance. The fact that the first and third factors never in the event called for any action on Mr Rolls's part is obvious. The second factor might, in other circumstances, involve the practical activity of keeping watch, as in the case of a store detective, but to suppose that such watchkeeping was called for in a small betting shop employing two counterhands is quite unrealistic and there is no hint of it in the evidence. I have no hesitation in concluding that the majority of the industrial tribunal erred in rejecting the applicant's claim that she was employed on like work with Mr Rolls.

Counsel for the company has sought to support the majority's decision in favour of the company on the alternative ground under s 1(3) that Mr Rolls's higher rate of pay was genuinely due to a material difference (other than the difference of sex) between the applicant's case and the case of Mr Rolls, contending in substance that the higher rate of pay simply reflected the additional security responsibilities borne by Mr Rolls. There is no finding to that effect and I gravely doubt whether there was any evidence which could support such a finding. But this contention on behalf of the company fails for a more fundamental reason. It falls foul of the principle correctly enunciated by Phillips J, giving the judgment of the Employment Appeal Tribunal, in *Snoxell v Vauxhall Motors Ltd*[1], that—

> 'an employer can never establish in the terms of s 1(3) that the variation between the woman's contract and the man's contract is genuinely due to a material difference (other than the difference of sex) between her case and his when it can be seen that past sex discrimination has contributed to the variation.'

The difference in pay between the appellant and Mr Rolls sprang from the undisguised policy of sex discrimination which the company operated in selecting employees for the trouble shops. It could not, therefore, possibly be justified under s 1(3). If the company had employed persons specially trained as security guards who were recruited from either sex, entirely different considerations would arise, but that is certainly not the case.

I would dismiss the appeal.

Appeal dismissed.

Solicitors: *Prothero & Prothero* (for the company); *Pattinson & Brewer* (for the applicant); *Angharad Savage* (for the Equal Opportunities Commission).

Sumra Green   Barrister.

---

1 [1977] 3 All ER 770 at 779, [1978] QB 11 at 28

Clay Cross (Quarry Service) Ltd v Fletcher

COURT OF APPEAL, CIVIL DIVISION
LORD DENNING MR, LAWTON AND BROWNE LJJ
27th, 28th, 29th JUNE, 11th JULY 1978

Employment – Equality of treatment between men and women – Variation between woman's and man's contract due to a material difference other than sex – Circumstances to be considered in determining whether variation due to a difference other than sex – Employers forced to recruit male employee at higher wage than existing female employees – Whether circumstances in which male employed relevant in deciding whether difference in pay due to material difference other than sex – Equal Pay Act 1970, s 1(3).

The applicant was employed by the employers as one of three clerks at the rate of £35 per week. When one of the other clerks left the only suitable replacement was a man receiving £43 per week from his existing employers. Since he would not change jobs for less, he was employed by the employers at that rate. Following a wage increase of £6 per week to all the clerks and a job evaluation study which increased the applicant's wages, the applicant was paid £43·46 per week while the male clerk was paid £49 per week. The applicant applied to an industrial tribunal claiming that she was entitled under the Equal Pay Act 1970 to equal pay with the male clerk because both were doing the same job. The tribunal upheld the applicant's claim. The employers appealed to the Employment Appeal Tribunal which upheld their appeal on the ground that the difference in pay arose because the male clerk had been paid more in his previous job, and was therefore 'genuinely due to a material difference (other than the difference of sex)', within s 1(3)[a] of the 1970 Act. The applicant appealed.

Held – Whether a variation in wages paid to a male and female employee employed on like work was due to a 'material difference' other than sex, within s 1(3) of the 1970 Act, depended on a comparison of the personal equation of each employee, ie that which appertained to each employee in his or her job by way of qualifications, experience, length of service, special skills etc. The circumstances in which the respective employees came to be employed and the economic reasons or market pressures which caused one to be employed at a higher wage than the other were irrelevant in making that comparison. Since the employers had not therefore shown that the variation between the applicant's and the male clerk's wage was due to a material difference other than sex, the appeal would be allowed and the applicant awarded the same pay as the male clerk (see p 477 a to f, p 478 g to p 479 a, p 480 g to p 481 a g, p 482 g and p 483 a to c, post).

Dictum of Lord Denning MR in *Shields v E Coomes (Holdings) Ltd* at p 464, ante, applied.

Notes

For equal treatment of men and women regarding terms and conditions of employment, see 16 Halsbury's Laws (4th Edn) para 767.

For the Equal Pay Act 1970, s 1, as amended by the Sex Discrimination Act 1975, see 45 Halsbury's Statutes (3rd Edn) 290.

Cases referred to in judgments

Brennan v City Stores Inc (1973) 479 F 2d 235.
Corning Glass Works v Brennan (1974) 417 US 188.
Griggs v Duke Power Co (1971) 401 US 424.
Hodgson v Brookhaven General Hospital (1970) 436 F 2d 719.
Hodgson v J M Fields Inc (1971) 335 F Supp 731.

---

a   Section 1(3) is set out at p 476 *d e*, post

National Coal Board v Sherwin [1978] ICR 700, [1978] IRLR 122, EAT.
Shields v E Coomes (Holdings) Ltd p 456, ante, [1978] 1 WLR 1408, CA.
Shultz v Wheaton Glass Co (1970) 421 F 2d 259.

Cases also cited
Brennan v Prince William Hospital Corpn (1974) 563 F 2d 282.
Brennan v Victoria Bank and Trust Co (1974) 493 F 2d 896.
Defrenne (Gabrielle) v Société Anonyme Belge de Navigation Aérienne (SABENA) [1976] ECR 455, [1976] ICR 547, CJEC.
National Vulcan Engineering Insurance Group Ltd v Wade [1977] 3 All ER 634, [1977] ICR 455, EAT.
Snoxell v Vauxhall Motors Ltd [1977] 3 All ER 770, [1978] QB 11, EAT.
Sotgiu v Deutsche Bundespost [1974] ECR 153, CJEC.
Thieffry v Conseil de l'Ordre des Avocats à la Cour de Paris [1978] QB 315, CJEC.

Appeal
The employee, Karen Fletcher, appealed from the decision of the Employment Appeal Tribunal[1] (Kilner-Brown J, Mrs D Ewing and Mr W L Kendall) dated 22nd April 1977 to allow an appeal by the employer, Clay Cross (Quarry Services) Ltd ('Clay Cross'), from the majority decision of an industrial tribunal (chairman Mr A L Gordon) sitting at Shrewsbury on 18th August 1976 upholding the employee's complaint that she was entitled to the same rate of pay as a male clerk employed by the employers. The facts are set out in the judgment of Lord Denning MR.

Anthony Lester QC and *Eldred Tabachnik* for Mrs Fletcher.
Charles Gibson for Clay Cross.

Cur adv vult

11th July. The following judgments were read.

LORD DENNING MR. The Clay Cross company employs three clerks in their sales office. One of them, a Mrs Fletcher, is a young woman of 22 years of age. She started with them in May 1972. She was the senior of the three. In June 1975 one of the others left and the company advertised the vacancy. They had only three applications for the job. Only one of the applicants was worthy of consideration. He was a man, Mr Tunnicliffe. They interviewed him, but not the others. He was a young man aged 24. He said he wanted £43 a week. That was what he was getting from his then employers, and he would not come for less. So the company employed him at that wage. That was much more than the other two clerks in the office were getting. They were both women, and were receiving only £35 a week. Mrs Fletcher spent quite a long time helping to train Mr Tunnicliffe. But she did not ask for equal pay at that time. The Equal Pay Act 1970 had not then come into force. It only came into force six months later on 29th December 1975.

In February 1976 the company increased the wages of all the clerks by £6 a week. So Mrs Fletcher and the other woman went up to £41 a week, and Mr Tunnicliffe to £49 a week.

About this time the company employed a firm of consultants to carry out a job evaluation scheme. These consultants recommended that the appropriate wage for the work of a sales clerk was £43·46 a week. That showed that Mrs Fletcher was being underpaid and Mr Tunnicliffe was being overpaid. So the company increased Mrs Fletcher's pay from £41 to £43·46 (the rate for the job) and back-dated it to 29th December 1975. They did not reduce Mr Tunnicliffe's wage. They felt they could not reduce it. So it remained at £49.

1 [1977] ICR 868

In June 1976 Mrs Fletcher applied to the industrial tribunal, and filled in her own application:

> 'I wish to make a claim under the Equal Pay Act, 1970, for the following reason: I work alongside a man doing the same job. My weekly wage is £43·46. The man concerned's wage is £49·00. I would also like to point out that I have been with the company for four years, and the man concerned [has] only been employed for approx. 9 months.'

The company resisted the claim. The case was heard in August 1976. Mrs Fletcher conducted her own case. The company were represented by a solicitor. By a majority of two to one the industrial tribunal decided in favour of Mrs Fletcher. They awarded her the same pay as Mr Tunnicliffe, £49 a week. The company appealed to the Employment Appeal Tribunal. They held in favour of the company and rejected the woman's claim. Mrs Fletcher appeals to this court.

Mrs Fletcher's case

There is no doubt that Mrs Fletcher made out a prima facie case. She proved that she was employed on like work with a man in the same employment and that her wages were less than his. So her contract is deemed to include an equality clause by which her wages are to be brought up so as to equal his: see s 1(2)(a) of the Equal Pay Act 1970.

In order to avoid payment, the Clay Cross company rely on the exception contained in s 1(3) of the Equal Pay Act 1970, which reads:

> 'An equality clause shall not operate in relation to a variation between the woman's contract and the man's contract if the employer proves that the variation is genuinely due to a material difference (other than the difference of sex) between her case and his.'

There was undoubtedly a variation here between her pay and his. The question is: what was the variation due to? Was it due to a material difference (other than sex) between her case and his?

The reasoning of the Employment Appeal Tribunal

As I read the decision of the Employment Appeal Tribunal, they thought that the issue depended on the employer's state of mind, on the reason why he paid the man more than the woman. If the reason had nothing to do with sex, they could pay him more. They relied on the evidence of the managing director, who said: 'We did not specify in the advertisement whether we were seeking a man or a woman. Sex was of no importance. If Tunnicliffe had been a woman asking £43, we would have employed her at that rate.'

I am sorry that the managing director was not cross-examined. But Mrs Fletcher was in person and could not be expected to do so. Any experienced advocate would have asked him: 'If you took on a new woman at £43, what would the other two women have said? Would you have kept those two on at £35 whilst paying the new woman £43 for the like work?' The managing director, if he told the truth, would have had to answer: 'I could not possibly have done that. I would have had to increase those two to £43; or, alternatively, kept them at £35 and not taken on the new woman.' Nevertheless the managing director was not cross-examined and the Employment Appeal Tribunal felt that his reasons were decisive. They said[1]:

> 'The industrial tribunal accepted that it was a matter of indifference to the employers whether they engaged a male or a female clerk. The only reason why they had to pay Mr. Tunnicliffe more was because he had previously been paid more in another job. It was not because he was a man . . . the reason here was nothing to do with Mr. Tunnicliffe's sex . . . the only basis on which they could get him was to pay him more money . . .'

---

1   [1977] ICR 868 at 871

In so deciding the case, the Employment Appeal Tribunal fell, I think, into error. The issue does not depend on the employer's state of mind. It does not depend on his reasons for paying the man more. The employer may not intend to discriminate against the woman by paying her less; but, if the result of his actions is that she is discriminated against, then his conduct is unlawful, whether he intended it or not.

Material difference
The issue depends on whether there is a material difference (other than sex) between her case and his. Take heed to those words, 'between her case and his'. They show that the tribunal is to have regard to *her* and to *him*, to the personal equation of the woman as compared to that of the man, irrespective of any extrinsic forces which led to the variation in pay. As I said in *Shields v E Coomes (Holdings) Ltd*[1], the subsection applies when 'the personal equation of the man is such that he deserves to be paid at a higher rate than the woman'. Thus the personal equation of the man may warrant a wage differential if he has much longer length of service; or has superior skill or qualifications; or gives bigger output or productivity; or has been placed, owing to down-grading, in a protected pay category, vividly described as 'red circled'; or to other circumstances personal to him in doing his job.

But the tribunal is not to have regard to any extrinsic forces which have led to the man being paid more. An employer cannot avoid his obligations under the 1970 Act by saying: 'I paid him more because he asked for more', or 'I paid her less because she was willing to come for less'. If any such excuse were permitted, the Act would be a dead letter. Those are the very reasons why there was unequal pay before the statute. They were the very circumstances in which the statute was intended to operate.

Nor can the employer avoid his obligations by giving the reasons why he submitted to the extrinsic forces. As for instance by saying: 'He asked for that sum because it was what he was getting in his previous job', or 'He was the only applicant for the job, so I had no option'. In such cases the employer may beat his breast, and say: 'I did not pay him more because he was a man. I paid it because he was the only suitable person who applied for the job. Man or woman made no difference to me.' Those are reasons personal to the employer. If any such reasons were permitted as an excuse, the door would be wide open. Every employer who wished to avoid the statute would walk straight through it.

In saying this, I find support from the words of Phillips J in *National Coal Board v Sherwin*[2]:

> 'The general principle [is] that it is no justification for a refusal to pay the same wages to women doing the same work as a man to say that the man could not have been recruited for less,'

and he applied it to the man in that case, saying[3]:

> '. . . what was being paid was the rate necessary to secure his services. For ourselves, we do not see why this is a material difference between his case and that of the complainants.'

Other cases
During the argument in this case, counsel for Mrs Fletcher drew our attention to the European Community law and to United States law. I found them helpful.

(i) *Community law*
In *Shields v E Coomes (Holdings) Ltd*[4] I pointed out that art 119 of the EEC Treaty is part of our law. It provides equal pay for equal work. It contains no exception, such as is in

---

1   See p 464, ante
2   [1978] ICR 700 at 710
3   [1978] ICR 700 at 711
4   Page 456, ante

s 1(3) of the Equal Pay Act 1970. But I have no doubt that the European court, with its liberal approach, would introduce an exception on the same lines. I do not suggest that we should refer the matter to them. Suffice it that I feel confident that it would have regard to the personal equation of the man and the woman, and not to any extrinsic forces.

(ii) *United States law*

The Equal Pay Act of 1963[1] expressly permitted a difference in the pay of men and women if it was made pursuant to 'a differential based on any other factor other than sex'. That was a 'general catch-all provision': see *Corning Glass Works v Brennan*[2]. But, even so, it was much limited by the courts: for, if it were widely interpreted, there was a danger that the exception would swallow up the rule. In an oft-quoted passage, the United States Court of Appeals said in *Shultz v Wheaton Glass Co*[3]:

'The Act was intended as a broad charter of women's rights in the economic field. It sought to overcome the age-old belief in women's inferiority and to eliminate the depressing effects on living standards of reduced wages for female workers and the social consequences which flow from it.'

In interpreting the provision, the courts in the United States held that the 1963 Act was violated even though the employer had no intention to discriminate. If he so conducted his affairs that women were paid less than men for like work, that was an infringement of the Act, whether he intended it or not: see *Hodgson v J M Fields Inc*[4]. So also the Act was violated even though 'market forces' brought about the difference in pay. Thus where women were very willing to work for less than men on work which was broadly similar, such as men selling men's clothes in the men's department, and women selling women's clothes in the women's department, the Act was violated: see *Hodgson v Brookhaven General Hospital*[5], *Brennan v City Stores*[6]. Nor was it any excuse that the discrimination was not open and direct, but covert and indirect. Thus, when there was a law which prohibited women from working at night, so that only men could be employed on night work, that was no reason for paying the men a higher rate for the job. The women were entitled to the same rate for the job, but the men were entitled to a reasonable, but not excessive, allowance as a night-shift premium: see *Corning Glass Works v Brennan*[2]. Nor could the effect of the Act be avoided by imposing unnecessary qualifications for the job, so that many more men could qualify than women. Thus, in a racial discrimination case, where a job did not require any special educational attainments, it was unlawful to require all applicants to have a high-school education, thus excluding a disproportionately large number of negroes: see *Griggs v Duke Power Co*[7].

Those cases show that the United States courts, with all their wide experience of the problem, have come to the same results as we come to here.

Conclusion

In my opinion, on the evidence in this case, the lower pay of Mrs Fletcher below that of Mr Tunnicliffe was not due to a 'material difference' between her case and his. It was due to extrinsic circumstances, namely that he could not be recruited for the work except by paying him more. That was the decision of the majority of the industrial tribunal, and I agree with them. As there was no material difference, she was entitled to the same rate of pay as he was getting, that is £49 per week. If there had been a 'material difference

---

1   77 Stat 56 (1963)
2   (1974) 417 US 188
3   (1970) 421 F 2d 259 at 265
4   (1971) 335 F Supp 731
5   (1970) 436 F 2d 719
6   (1973) 479 F 2d 235
7   (1971) 401 US 424

between her case and his', I should have thought it necessary to remit the case for a fresh hearing to enquire whether it was not due to the difference in sex.

I would, therefore, allow the appeal, and restore the decision of the industrial tribunal.

LAWTON LJ. On 29th December 1975 the day on which the Equal Pay Act 1970, as amended by the Sex Discrimination Act 1975, came into operation, Mrs Fletcher was working for Clay Cross (Quarry Services) Ltd alongside a Mr Tunnicliffe and a Mrs Holland. All three were doing the same job as sales clerks. Mrs Fletcher had been doing the job since May 1972. Her wages were £35·71 per week. Mr Tunnicliffe, who was about the same age as Mrs Fletcher, had joined the company in June 1975 but he was being paid £43 per week. He had replaced another clerk who had left. Mrs Holland was paid slightly less than Mrs Fletcher because she was less experienced. In the first half of 1976 the company carried out a job evaluation scheme. As a result Mrs Fletcher was paid £43·46 per week back-dated to 29th December 1975; but Mr Tunnicliffe was paid £49 per week back-dated to the same date. Understandably Mrs Fletcher did not like this difference. She thought it was wrong because of the Equal Pay Act 1970 as amended. She applied to an industrial tribunal to look into her case. She prepared her own application and put her case in it fully and accurately as follows: 'I work alongside a man doing the same job. My weekly wage is £43·46. The man concerned's wage is £49·00.'

At the hearing she proved what she had alleged in her application. She established a strong prima facie case under the combined operation of the Sex Discrimination Act 1975 and the Equal Pay Act 1970. In order to rebut it the company had to prove that the variation between Mrs Fletcher's wage and Mr Tunnicliffe's was 'genuinely due to a material difference (other than the difference of sex) between her case and his': see s 1(3) of the Equal Pay Act 1970. They tried to do so through their managing director, a Mr Lund. The tribunal adjudged him to have been an honest witness. He said that the company's concern was to get a replacement for the clerk who had left. The sex of anyone taking the job was irrelevant. They would have employed any suitable person who applied. Mr Tunnicliffe was the only suitable applicant who did apply. He wanted a wage of £43 per week because that was what he was getting in the job he then had. The company took him on at the wage for which he had asked.

Consideration of the effect in law of these few facts has occupied this court for two and a half days. We have had to consider two decisions of this court, two of the Employment Appeals Tribunal, six of the United States federal courts, two of the United States Supreme Court, two of the European Court, art 119 of the EEC Treaty and a Community Council direction. In addition counsel for Clay Cross submitted that for the proper determination of this case further evidence should have been put before the industrial tribunal for the purpose of finding out whether the wage which Mr Tunnicliffe received from his former employers reflected a sex differential. On the basis of the United States decisions there was a good reason for this submission. He shrank from suggesting that Mrs Fletcher should have called this evidence. The absurdity of expecting a sales clerk in her mid twenties who was presenting her own case to do so was obvious to him. He suggested that the chairman of the tribunal should have asked questions of the witnesses who were called to find out why Mr Tunnicliffe had been paid his former wage. I found all these complications disturbing. Parliament intended that industrial tribunals should provide a quick and cheap remedy for what it had decided were injustices in the employment sphere. The procedure was to be such that both employers and employees could present their cases without having to go to lawyers for help. Within a few years legalism has started to take over. It must be driven back if possible. If the wording of the relevant statutes has opened the door to legal subtleties, there is nothing the courts can do to stop what I regard as an unfortunate development. The remedy lies with Parliament. If, however, there are uncertainties in the statutes, when construing them the courts should, I think, lean in favour of a simplicity in meaning which will safeguard informality in procedure. In the presentation of this appeal, counsel on both sides have not been prolix, nor have they shown symptoms of suffering from the prevalent modern forensic ailment of the excessive citation of cases. Their excellent displays of legal learning have been necessary for the construction of a subsection of the Equal Pay Act 1970 which occupies four lines in the Queen's Printer's copy of it.

Counsel for Clay Cross submitted that a scarcity of applicants had caused the company to pay the wages asked. As there was no evidence to show that this scarcity arose out of any differences between the rates of wages paid to men and women for this kind of work (as had been established in a number of the United States cases to which we were referred) and the company had not intended to discriminate against women, the reason why there was a variation in wage rates was an economic one which had nothing to do with the mischief which Parliament had tried to curb. This economic factor had operated in Mr Tunnicliffe's case. This made his case different from hers in a real and relevant sense with the result that the company could take advantage of the defence provided by s 1(3). The Employment Appeal Tribunal accepted this argument.

Counsel on behalf of Mrs Fletcher submitted that a reason such as that put forward by the company in this case ('we had to pay what was asked by the only person we could find to do the job') is in law incapable of being 'a material difference (other than the difference of sex) between her case and his': s 1(3) of the 1970 Act. Further, if economic factors of the kind relied on by Clay Cross could constitute a material difference there could be a conflict between the Equal Pay Act 1970 and art 119 of the EEC Treaty, as applied in the United Kingdom by the European Communities Act 1972. This article says that 'men and women should receive equal pay for equal work'. There is no let out for the employer who pays a man more than a woman because the labour market is such that in order to get a worker, whether male or female, he has to pay a male applicant more than he is paying his women workers. The position under the EEC Treaty is different from that under the United States Equal Pay Act of 1963, which provides exceptions to the general principle of equal pay for equal work. They are where 'payment is made pursuant to (i) a seniority system; (ii) a merit system; (iii) a system which measures earnings by quantity or quality of production; or (iv) a differential based on any other factor than sex'. Counsel for Mrs Fletcher pointed out that, although the United States statute does make provision for differentials based on economic factors unconnected with sex and historically it has been considered in the drafting of the equivalent United Kingdom statute, the wording of the exception provision in the Equal Pay Act 1970 is different.

What does s 1(3) in its context in both the Equal Pay Act 1973 and the Sex Discrimination Act 1975 mean? The context is important. The overall object of both Acts is to ensure that women are treated no less favourably than men. If a woman is treated less favourably than a man there is a presumption of discrimination which can only be rebutted in the sphere of employment if the employer brings himself within s 1(3). He cannot do so merely by proving that he did not intend to discriminate. There are more ways of discriminating against women than by deliberately setting out to do so: see s 1(1)(b) of the Sex Discrimination Act 1975. If lack of intention had provided a lawful excuse for variation, s 1(3) would surely have been worded differently. The variation must have been genuinely due to (that is, caused by) a material difference (that is, one which was relevant and real) between (and now come the important words) her case and his. What is her case? And what is his? In my judgment her case embraces what appertains to her *in* her job, such as the qualifications she brought to it, the length of time she has been in it, the skill she has acquired, the responsibilities she has undertaken and where and under what conditions she has to do it. It is on this kind of basis that her case is to be compared with that of the man. What does not appertain to her job or to his are the circumstances in which they came to be employed. These are collateral to the jobs as such. This was the approach of Lord Denning MR in *Shields v E Coomes (Holdings) Ltd*[1]. In the course of his judgment in that case, referring to s 1(3) of the Equal Pay Act 1970, he said[2]: 'This subsection deals with

---

1   Page 456, ante
2   See p 464, ante

cases where the woman and the man are doing "like work" but the personal equation of the man is such that he deserves to be paid at a higher rate than the woman.'

For example, a woman chemist with a recently acquired doctorate who is given a job in a forensic science laboratory is not entitled under the Equal Pay Act 1970 to be paid the same salary as the man working alongside her who has the same degree from the same university but who has 25 years' experience behind him. Nor could she reasonably expect to be so paid. Their personal equations would be different. The position would be otherwise if a few months after her appointment a man with the same qualifications as hers and straight from the university were paid a higher salary merely because he asked for it and at the time there were no other applicants for the job. That is this case. When Mr Tunnicliffe was appointed his personal equation was the same as Mrs Fletcher's so far as the company knew or cared when employing him. After he had started work the company appreciated that he had better educational qualifications than Mrs Fletcher and a potential for doing another kind of job and for which they were willing to train him. Had Mrs Fletcher been a candidate for this new job her personal equation would not have been the same as his.

The construction which I have put on s 1(3) should be easy to apply by industrial tribunals. There will be no need for evidence to be called as to why a man, who is the subject for comparison with a woman applicant, was paid a higher wage in another job than she is getting so as to prove, or disprove, that there was an element of sexual discrimination in the differing rates of pay. There will be no need, thankfully, for the kind of statistical evidence covering a period of 28 months, supported by four complicated graphs, which was used in the United States case of *Hodgson v J M Fields Inc*[1]. Further, this construction will make evasion more difficult. If the payment of higher wages or salaries to men merely because they asked for them, and would not accept work if they did not get what they asked for, was a valid reason for not paying women at the same rates, the Equal Pay Act 1970 could not work as Parliament intended it to do.

Another advantage of the construction which I put on s 1(3) is that it brings our law into line with Community law. As I have already commented, art 119 of the EEC Treaty provides for no exceptions at all. When construing art 119 the European Court may have to evolve some exceptions such as arise from personal equations. It is most unlikely to evolve an exception based on such a vague conception as economic factors or market pressures. To do so would strike at the object of the article. In the labour market women have always been in a worse position than men. Under both art 119 and the Equal Pay Act 1970 that was no longer to be so.

I would allow the appeal.

BROWNE LJ. I agree that this appeal must be allowed.

Mr Tunnicliffe was engaged by Clay Cross before the Equal Pay Act 1970 came into force. The industrial tribunal found that it was a matter of indifference to the employers whether they engaged a male or a female clerk. Mr Lund (their managing director) said that if Mr Tunnicliffe had been a woman on £43 they would have engaged her at that rate. Mr Tunnicliffe would not come to Clay Cross for less than he was already receiving. There is no evidence why he was being paid more by his previous employers than Mrs Fletcher was paid by Clay Cross. He may not have been overpaid. There may have been some special reason why he was paid more. Nor was there any evidence (as there was in the United States cases to which we were referred) that the general market rate for women was less than the general market rate for men. I do not think that the United States cases help with our present problem.

After the job evaluation, Mrs Fletcher was paid what was assessed to be the rate for her job and Mr Tunnicliffe was overpaid. The result of the decision of the industrial tribunal is that she too will be over-paid; and this will continue indefinitely.

1   (1971) 335 F Supp 731

On those facts I have a good deal of sympathy for the reasoning of the Employment Appeal Tribunal, and at first I thought it was conclusive. They said[1]:

'Upon the given and proved facts in this case we are entirely of the opinion that [counsel for Clay Cross] is right, when one asks oneself what would have been the position if a female had been in the same situation as Mr. Tunnicliffe—of equal ability, going to do the same work, but, because she was previously paid a higher wage, would only come if she was given the higher wage. This is why that particular finding of fact to which reference has been made becomes of vital importance. The industrial tribunal accepted that it was a matter of indifference to the employers whether they engaged a male or a female clerk. The only reason why they had to pay Mr. Tunnicliffe more was because he had previously been paid more in another job. It was not because he was a man. Secondly, it was inevitably, as they found, a genuine reason. It was inevitably, as we think, a material reason because it was in fact the only reason. Once one applies oneself to the facts of this case in that way it seems to us inevitable that any tribunal would be driven to say that in the particular circumstances the employers shouldered that heavy burden, shouldered it successfully and plainly demonstrated that the reason here was nothing to do with Mr. Tunnicliffe's sex; it was a perfectly genuine and a most important and material matter, that the only basis on which they could get him was to pay him more money than the applicant doing the same work already employed.'

The long title of the Equal Pay Act 1970 is: 'An Act to prevent discrimination, as regards terms and conditions of employment, between men and women', and it is common ground that the 1970 Act should be construed as one with the Sex Discrimination Act 1975. One might therefore suppose that the 1970 Act had no application where, as here, there was no intention on the part of the employer to discriminate against Mrs Fletcher by reason of her sex, and the reason for the difference between her pay and Mr Tunnicliffe's had nothing to do with her sex. But the *effect* of what happened was that although Mrs Fletcher and Mr Tunnicliffe were doing 'like work' she was being paid less than he was.

If s 1(3) had provided that an equality clause shall not operate if the employer proves that the variation is genuinely not due to a difference of sex, Clay Cross would clearly be entitled to succeed. But this is not what it provides. It provides that:

'An equality clause shall not operate in relation to a variation between the woman's contract and the man's contract if the employer proves that the variation is genuinely due to a material difference (other than the difference of sex) between her case and his.'

The subsection clearly requires a comparison between her 'case' and his. The sort of 'differences' referred to by Lord Denning MR in *Shields v E Coomes (Holdings) Ltd*[2] are obviously 'material' and capable of justifying a 'variation', length of service, special skill and qualifications and so on, what was called in the argument the 'personal equation'. So perhaps might the fact that the man was being paid more for benevolent reasons, eg because he had a sick wife and a large family, or (at any rate in some cases) that he was a 'red circle' case. But the only difference in the present case was that Mr Tunnicliffe was not willing to come to Clay Cross for less than he was being paid in his previous job, and that Clay Cross were willing to agree because they could not get anyone else. The fact that Clay Cross could not get anyone else is not a difference between his case and hers; it is a general bargaining factor common to any applicant. (Although the point was not raised in argument, it is not clear that this really was a difference; if at the time when Mr Tunnicliffe was engaged Mrs Fletcher had asked for an increase and threatened to leave if she did not get it, Clay Cross would presumably have had to agree.)

I do not think it is necessary or desirable to try to lay down in this case any general rule

---

1   (1977) ICR 868 at 871
2   Page 456, ante

about what is or is not capable of being a 'material difference'. This will have to be worked out in particular cases as they arise. It is enough to say that counsel for Mrs Fletcher convinced me that it would frustrate the purpose of the 1970 Act if the mere facts that a man asks for more than a woman is being paid for like work and that the employer agrees because of some bargaining factor (other than some personal characteristic or qualification to the advantage of the man) are enough to satisfy s 1(3). If this was enough, it would apply not only to a prospective new employee but to an existing employee who asked for an increase and threatened to leave if he did not get it. Or to a case where all the men in a factory asked for an increase and threatened to strike if they did not get it. In the end, I have come to the conclusion that this is the position in this case, that Clay Cross have not discharged the burden imposed by s 1(3) and that the appeal must therefore be allowed and the decision of the industrial tribunal restored.

I would only add that it seems to me unnecessarily complicated to approach the problem in two stages, as the Employment Appeal Tribunal suggested in *National Coal Board v Sherwin*[1], (i) is there a material difference? and (ii) is it a difference other than sex? I think it is all one question: is the variation 'genuinely due to a material difference (other than the difference of sex)...'? Once the 'material difference' has been identified, it will be obvious whether or not it is one of sex.

Appeal allowed.

Solicitors: *Pattinson & Brewer* (for Mrs Fletcher); *Knight & Sons,* Newcastle under Lyme (for Clay Cross).

Gavin Gore-Andrews Esq   Barrister.

Maynard v Osmond (No 2)

COURT OF APPEAL, CIVIL DIVISION
LORD DENNING MR, ORR AND BRANDON LJJ
3rd, 4th OCTOBER 1978

Legal aid – Unassisted person's costs out of legal aid fund – Just and equitable – Unsuccessful appeal to Court of Appeal by assisted party – Appeal on a point of constitutional importance – Unassisted party a police authority funded out of central funds – Whether just and equitable that police authority's costs be paid out of legal aid fund – Legal Aid Act 1974, s 13(2).

A police constable who was charged with a breach of discipline and subsequently denied legal representation at the hearing of the charge, brought an action against his chief constable claiming that as a police constable he was entitled to legal representation in disciplinary proceedings. The judge dismissed the action and the Court of Appeal[a] upheld that decision. The police constable had been legally aided throughout and at the conclusion of the Court of Appeal hearing the court ordered him to pay costs, but as he was legally aided the order was not to be enforced except on further application to the court. The chief constable, acting on behalf of his police authority, applied as an unassisted party for payment of his costs (amounting to £3,000) out of the legal aid fund, under s 13(2)[b] of the Legal Aid Act 1974, contending that it was 'just and equitable in all the circumstances that provision for those costs should be made out of public funds'. The Law Society, as the custodian of the legal aid fund, objected, contending that as the police authority was a public authority which received money from central funds just as the legal aid fund did the authority should bear its own costs.

1 [1978] ICR 700 at 705–706
a [1977] 1 All ER 64, [1977] QB 240
b Section 13(2) is set out at p 486 *b c,* post

Held – For the purposes of s 13(2) of the 1974 Act it was just and equitable that the legal aid fund should bear the police authority's costs since, by taking up the case on behalf of the police constable, the fund had been responsible for the litigation, and also since the case had raised a point of some constitutional importance affecting all police authorities and many other people. In those circumstances it would not be right for the costs to fall on the authority alone (see p 486 *h* to p 487 *c* and p 488 *b c*, post).

Per Curiam. When an unassisted party succeeds against an assisted party in the Court of Appeal and the unassisted party wishes to recover his costs from the legal aid fund the court, having determined the amount to be paid by the assisted person and the legal aid fund respectively, should then state its intention whether the legal aid fund should bear all or 'part of the unassisted party's costs, and ten weeks' notice of that intention should be given to the Legal Aid Committee to enable them to appear and object to the proposed order (see p 487 *d* to *j* and p 488 *b c*, post).

Notes

For the award of costs to an unassisted party out of the legal aid fund, see Supplement to 30 Halsbury's Laws (3rd Edn) para 933A.

For the Legal Aid Act 1974, s 13, see 44 Halsbury's Statutes (3rd Edn) 1053.

Case referred to in judgment

Saunders (Executrix of estate of Rose Maud Gallie (deceased)) v Anglia Building Society) (formerly Northampton Town and County Building Society) (No 2) [1971] 1 All ER 243, [1971] AC 1039, [1971] 2 WLR 349, HL, Digest (Cont Vol D) 706, 4463a.

Cases also cited

Bahamas International Trust Co Ltd v Threadgold [1974] 3 All ER 881, [1974] 1 WLR at 1523, HL.

Baron v Phillips [1978] Court of Appeal Transcript 282.

Davies v Taylor (No 2) [1973] 1 All ER 959, [1974] AC 225, HL.

General Accident, Fire & Life Assurance Corpn Ltd v Foster [1972] 3 All ER 877, [1973] QB 50, CA.

Lewis v Averay (No 2) [1973] 2 All ER 229, [1973] 1 WLR 510, CA.

Maynard v Osmond [1977] 1 All ER 64, [1977] QB 240, CA.

McDonnell v McDonnell [1977] 1 All ER 766, [1977] 1 WLR 34, CA.

O'Brien v Robinson (No 2) [1973] 1 All ER 969, [1973] 1 WLR 515, HL.

S v S (unassisted party's costs) [1978] 1 All ER 934, [1978] 1 WLR 11, CA.

Shiloh Spinners Ltd v Harding [1973] 1 All ER 90, [1973] AC 691, HL.

Wozniak v Wozniak [1953] 1 All ER 1192, [1953] P 179, CA.

Application

By a writ dated 15th April 1976 the plaintiff, Jeremy George Maynard, a police constable in the Hampshire Police Force, brought an action against the defendant, Sir Douglas Osmond, the Chief Constable of Hampshire, claiming, inter alia, declarations (i) that the plaintiff was entitled to be represented by a solicitor or counsel of his choice at disciplinary proceedings brought against him, (ii) that under reg 8(6) of the Police (Discipline) Regulations 1965[1] the defendant had a discretion whether or not to permit the plaintiff to be represented by a solicitor or counsel of his choice at the disciplinary proceedings, and (iii) that if reg 8(6) prohibited the defendant from exercising such a discretion the regulation was ultra vires and invalid. The plaintiff was legally aided. On 24th May 1976 Griffiths J[2] refused the declarations and ordered that the plaintiff pay the defendant's costs, the order not to be enforced without the leave of the court. On 13th July 1976 the Court

---

1   SI 1965 No 543
2   [1977] 1 All ER 64 at 66

of Appeal[1] (Lord Denning MR, Orr and Waller LJJ) dismissed the plaintiff's appeal. The court then considered the matter of costs. The defendant applied for the order of Griffiths J to be varied so that the plaintiff should be ordered to pay the costs below limited to the amount of his contribution to legal aid and applied for the costs of the appeal to be paid out of the legal aid fund. The Court of Appeal refused the defendant's application and ordered that the costs of the successful defendant and unassisted party be paid out of the legal aid fund, subject to the Law Society being allowed within 21 days to make any representations they wished. On 11th March 1977 application was made by the Law Society to stay the order on the ground that no proper consideration had been given to its making and that the court should consider making an order against the plaintiff. The facts are set out in the judgment of Lord Denning MR.

Duncan Matheson for the Law Society.
Michael Brooke for the defendant.

LORD DENNING MR. The question before us is one of costs arising out of a case which was heard some years ago. The facts of the case are these. One night in November 1975, at Alton in Hampshire, three young men were making a great deal of noise. At twenty past two that morning all the people in the neighbourhood were awakened by the noise, and the police were called. The three men were eventually escorted to the police station and put in the cells. There happened to be a young police constable called Jeremy Maynard in the police station that night. He belonged to the same club as the three young men who had been making the noise. Later he accused the police sergeant of assaulting one of the men. I will not go into all the details of what is said to have happened. It has been the subject of civil proceedings. The upshot of it all was that this young police constable, who reported the alleged assault, was charged with a disciplinary offence under the police regulations for, in effect, making an accusation against the police sergeant which was unfounded. Faced with that charge, Pc Maynard went to lawyers. They advised him that he ought to have counsel to represent him before the disciplinary tribunal.

The police regulations do not make any provision for a constable to be represented by lawyers on a disciplinary charge. He can be represented by another police officer; and arrangements are available whereby he can get a very good police officer, perhaps from another area, to defend him. That was not acceptable to Pc Maynard's lawyers. So they, on his behalf, obtained legal aid to test the position in the courts. An action was brought before Griffiths J seeking a declaration that Pc Maynard was entitled to legal representation before the police tribunal. Griffiths J held that Pc Maynard was not entitled to be represented by lawyers; and, as he was legally aided, the judge made an order that the costs should not be enforced except with the leave of the court. The matter then came before this court on appeal from Griffiths J's judgment. It is reported in *Maynard v Osmond*[1].

Again Pc Maynard was represented by lawyers. He was legally aided. Queen's counsel and junior counsel were instructed on his behalf. The case was argued for some five days before us. We reserved judgment, and upheld the judge on the matter. We held that Pc Maynard was not entitled to be represented by lawyers at the disciplinary tribunal. The right course was for him to have another police officer as a friend to represent him. So the decision of the court was against Pc Maynard and in favour of Sir Douglas Osmond, who was the Chief Constable of Hampshire.

As I said, Pc Maynard had been legally aided throughout as he could not pay the costs himself. On the other hand, Sir Douglas Osmond, representing the Hampshire police authority, had been put to a great deal of costs in order to defend this unsuccessful claim by Pc Maynard. We are told that those costs amounted to some £3,000.

The question then arose as to whether the Hampshire police authority could recover their costs from the legal aid fund, the legal aid fund having supported Pc Maynard all the

---

1   [1977] 1 All ER 64, [1977] QB 240

way through. That is the matter which has been debated before us today. It has raised points on the circumstances in which unassisted persons, that is, the Hampshire police authority in this case, can recover their costs against the legal aid fund when the person it has supported loses his case. That matter is the subject of legislation. The Legal Aid Act 1974, s 13, says that an unassisted party can in special circumstances get an order for payment out of the legal aid fund of the whole or any part of the costs incurred by him. The material subsection is sub-s (2), which says:

'An order may be made under this section in respect of any costs if (and only if) the court is satisfied that it is just and equitable in all the circumstances that provision for those costs should be made out of public funds; and before making such an order the court shall in every case (whether or not application is made in that behalf) consider what orders should be made for costs against the party receiving legal aid and for determining his liability in respect of such costs.'

I will start with the end first, '. . . the court shall in every case . . . consider what orders should be made for costs against the party receiving legal aid and for determining his liability in respect of such costs.' That means in this case that it is our duty to consider what order would be made against Pc Maynard himself. (We are told that he has since retired from the force so he is Mr Maynard now.) We have to consider what order is to be made against him and to determine his liability.

In this particular case the order which was made against him by this court was that he should pay the costs but, as he was legally aided, the order should not be enforced except on further application to this court. That is a very common form of order made by this court in legally aided cases. I am not sure how far it conforms with the statutory requirements, but it is a very common order and it seems to me that it sufficiently complies with the statute. It means that the legally aided person is not to pay any costs at all unless there is a further application to the court, as, for instance, if he comes into a great deal of money or something of that kind. That is the first matter to be considered. In this particular case it has been considered, namely an order was made against Mr Maynard which was not to be enforced except on further application to the court.

That leads to the earlier part of the section: 'An order may be made [against the Legal Aid Fund] . . . if (and only if) the court is satisfied that it is just and equitable in all the circumstances that provision for those costs should be made out of public funds . . .' This is the 'just and equitable' point. The question is whether in this particular case it is just and equitable that the legal aid fund should pay the costs of the Hampshire police authority out of their funds. The fact that an unassisted party has a good deal of money does not mean that it is not just and equitable to make an order against the legal aid fund. Orders have been made in favour of building societies, insurance companies and the like. In the Court of Appeal it is often just and equitable that their costs should be paid if they have been put to expense by an unsuccessful assisted person coming to this court.

It is suggested to us that a public authority, like the Hampshire police authority, is in a different position from an insurance company or a building society because the legal aid fund receives its money from central funds (from the government) and the Hampshire police authority also received its money directly or indirectly from public funds. About a quarter comes from the ratepayers of Hampshire and about three-quarters from central funds (that is, from the taxpayer). It is said that, on that account, a public authority or a local authority is in a different position from an insurance company or a building society.

I am afraid that I cannot go with that agrument at all. It seems to me that if the legal aid fund takes up a case on behalf of an assisted person and put an authority to a great deal of expense in fighting it, it is often just and equitable that the authority should have its costs from the legal aid fund. It is that fund, after all, which has been responsible for the litigation and has led to all the legal costs being incurred.

Take this particular case. It raised a point of some constitutional importance, namely whether police constables were entitled to legal representation on a disciplinary charge. No doubt it was right and proper for it to be decided as a point of law. But not at the expense of the Hampshire police authority only. It affected all police authorities and many other people. When a point of law has to be elucidated like this between litigants, and it goes up to the Court of Appeal or to the House of Lords, it is not right that costs should fall on an individual or a concern. They should fall on the legal aid fund. The fund is particularly appropriate to deal with matters of this kind. That was the position in *Saunders v Anglia Building Society (No 2)*[1]. It was a case about the principle of non est factum. Lord Reid said[2]:

'In this case it enabled the whole vexed matter of non est factum to be re-examined. This seems to me a typical case where the costs of . . . the successful respondent should come out of public funds.'

The same applies here to the costs of the Hampshire police authority. It is just and equitable in this case that the costs should come out of the legal aid fund.

But I would not confine it to cases which involve important points of law. I think the principle should be extended so as to be of general application. It seems that whenever the legal aid fund takes up cases for assisted persons and brings another party before the courts, then, if the case fails, it is often just and equitable that the legal aid fund should pay the costs of the unassisted party.

We have had some discussion here today as to the right procedure in these matters. It has been pointed out very helpfully by counsel for the Law Society that so far as this court is concerned (I am not dealing with the courts of first instance at the moment because there is a question of financial hardship coming in there; I am only dealing with the costs so far as this court is concerned) it is quite plain on the 1974 Act that if at the end of the appeal the assisted party loses and the other party desires to recover its costs from the legal aid fund the court has to consider what order should be made for costs against the party receiving legal aid and for determining his liability. It is often not practical to have a formal enquiry as to means and so forth or further hearings. Such an enquiry would cost more than it is worth. The simpler and better course is for the court, then and there, informally to enquire of counsel what are the means of the assisted party, what was his legal aid contribution, what were the circumstances in which legal aid was granted, and so forth. From this informal enquiry, the court should glean such information as it can, and consider what order should be made. For instance, it might then and there make an order for the assisted person to pay £100 or £200, or whatever it may be. The court may make an order that the assisted party himself should pay so much of the costs. As to the balance, the court can then go on and decide whether or not the legal aid fund should be asked to pay it.

Then as to the legal aid fund. It seems that the right and convenient course is that this court at the end of the hearing should consider and state, if it thinks fit, that its present intention is that the costs incurred by the unassisted party, or so much of them as may be directed, should be paid out of the legal aid fund. Although that is its present intention, nevertheless the order is not to be drawn up and further steps are not to be taken until notice has been served on the area secretary of the Legal Aid Committee. The Legal Aid Committee have suggested that a period of ten weeks' notice should be given to the Legal Aid Committee to come in and object if they wish to do so. That is fair enough. If, within ten weeks, the area secretary decides to come in and object to the order being made against the legal aid fund, then they can come in and make their objections. If they do not object in that time, the order will be made in accordance with the declared intention. If they do object, they will be heard before any order is made against the legal aid fund.

In this particular case we do not order any specific sum against Mr Maynard. The order is to be simply in the form, which is used so often, for him to pay the costs, not to be enforced except on further application to the court. So far as the legal aid fund itself is concerned, having heard what has been said about what is just and equitable and the like,

1   [1971] 1 All ER 243, [1971] AC 1039
2   [1971] 1 All ER 243 at 247, [1971] AC 1039 at 1048

it seems to me that this is a case where the costs in this court of the unassisted party, the Hampshire police authority, should be paid by the legal aid fund. That is the costs in this court. We are not dealing with the costs at first instance. There are special provisions in the 1974 Act about them. There is the question of financial hardship to be considered. We will not deal with those today. We could deal with it if an application were made in regard to it, and we would have to do what the court of first instance should have done. But that does not arise today, and I say no more about it.

As I say, the order in this case is that the legal aid fund should pay the costs of the unassisted party.

ORR LJ. I agree.

BRANDON LJ. I agree with the order proposed. I would just like to say one thing about the question of costs against the assisted party. I do not for a moment suggest that the order which has been made in this case, namely an order that he should pay the costs not to be enforced without the leave of the court, should be different. For my part, however, I think it is for consideration for the future whether it is not the duty of this court under s 13(2) of the Legal Aid Act 1974 to go further than that and determine the liability of the assisted person, so that in a case like the present, where the intention of the court is that he shall have no liability, the court should say so by determining his liability as nil. For myself I think that would be a more convenient way of doing it and one more in accord with the wording of the 1974 Act.

Application dismissed. Costs incurred by the defendant in the plaintiff's appeal to the Court of Appeal to be paid out of the legal aid fund.

Solicitors: *Law Society*; *R A Leyland*, Winchester (for the defendant).

Sumra Green   Barrister.

Trapp v Mackie

HOUSE OF LORDS
LORD DIPLOCK, LORD SALMON, LORD EDMUND-DAVIES, LORD FRASER OF TULLYBELTON AND LORD
RUSSELL OF KILLOWEN
8th, 9th NOVEMBER, 13th DECEMBER 1978

Action – Immunity from civil action – Witness – Tribunal – Privilege of witness – Inquiry set up by Minister to report on whether dismissal of teacher reasonably justifiable – Tribunal holding inquiry and reporting to Minister – Minister making final determination – Tribunal's report leading directly to, or being major influence on, Minister's determination – Whether evidence of witness at inquiry absolutely privileged – Education (Scotland) Act 1946, ss 63, 81(3).

The appellant, the headmaster of a school in Scotland, was dismissed from his post by the local education authority. The respondent was the chairman of the education authority. Pursuant to s 81(3)[a] of the Education (Scotland) Act 1946, the appellant petitioned the Secretary of State for Scotland to set up an inquiry into the reasons for his dismissal. Under the power conferred on him by s 63 of that Act the Minister ordered a local inquiry to be held into whether the appellant's dismissal was reasonably justifiable and appointed a Queen's Counsel as the commissioner to hold the inquiry. The commissioner's function was to report to the Minister. The issue before him, ie whether or not the dismissal was reasonably justifiable, was an issue between adverse parties (the appellant and the education authority) similar to issues commonly decided by courts of law. The inquiry was held in public and the procedure adopted by the commissioner was similar to that in a court of law. The respondent gave evidence at the inquiry. The commissioner reported to the Minister that the appellant's dismissal was reasonably justifiable. The commissioner's opinion was not, under the 1946 Act, binding on the Minister, but the Minister's power under s 81(3) to take further action, namely to require the education authority to reconsider its resolution, or to uphold the dismissal, was dependent on receipt of the commissioner's report and the opinion he formed as a result of it. Moreover, in practice the Minister was unlikely to overrule the commissioner's opinion. The opinion reached by the Minister finally determined the issue between the parties. The Minister accepted the commissioner's report and upheld the dismissal. The appellant brought an action against the respondent alleging that the evidence he had given at the inquiry was maliciously false and had caused the commissioner to report to the Minister adversely to the appellant, and claimed damages for the loss, injury and damage which he alleged he had suffered as a result of the evidence. The respondent pleaded that the action was irrelevant and should be dismissed because absolute privilege attached to the evidence given at the inquiry. The Lord Ordinary and, on appeal, the Second Division of the Court of Session, upheld the respondent's plea and dismissed the appellant's action. He appealed to the House of Lords.

Held – Provided that a tribunal was one recognised by law, there was no single element which would be conclusive to show that it had attributes sufficiently similar to those of a court of law to create absolute privilege for the testimony of witnesses before it. It was not, however, essential that the tribunal itself should have power finally to determine the issue before it, and absolute privilege might apply if the inquiry by the tribunal was a step leading directly to, or was a major influence on, the final determination of that issue by the authority who had appointed the tribunal. Since the inquiry had been set up under statutory authority to decide an issue in dispute between adverse parties under a procedure which was similar to that in a court of law, and since the commissioner's report was an essential step towards an effective decision on the issue by the Minister, who also had power to award costs, the inquiry was one at which witnesses were protected by absolute

---

a   Section 81(3) is set out at p 492 *f g*, post

privilege. It followed that the appeal would be dismissed (see p 492 *a* to *c*, p 494 *e f*, p 495 *a* to p 496 *a*, p 499 *c* to *f* and p 500 *c* to *g*, post).

Dawkins v Lord Rokeby (1873) LR 8 QB 255 and dictum of Lord Atkin in *O'Connor v Waldron* [1934] All ER Rep at 283 applied.

O'Connor v Waldron [1934] All ER Rep 281 distinguished.

Dictum of Lord Sankey LC in *Shell Co of Australia Ltd v Federal Comr of Taxation* [1930] All ER Rep at 679 explained.

Per Lord Diplock. In deciding whether a particular tribunal is of such a kind as to attract absolute privilege for witnesses the court is engaged in the task of balancing against one another public interests which conflict, namely the general interest that the law should provide a remedy to the citizen whose good name and reputation is traduced by malicious falsehoods and the particular interest that witnesses before tribunals recognised by law should give their testimony free from any fear of being harassed by an action alleging that they acted from malice (see p 492 *a b* and p 494 *j* to p 495 *a*, post).

Notes

For absolute privilege and tribunals to which the doctrine extends, see 24 Halsbury's Laws (3rd Edn) 49–50, paras 89–90, and for cases on the subject, see 32 Digest (Repl) 118–120, 1393–1416.

Cases referred to in opinions

Barratt v Kearns [1905] 1 KB 504, 74 LJKB 318, 92 LT 255, CA, 32 Digest (Repl) 120, *1411*.

Collins v Henry Whiteway & Co Ltd [1927] 2 KB 378, 96 LJKB 790, 137 LT 297, 32 Digest (Repl) 120, *1413*.

Dawkins v Lord Rokeby (1873) LR 8 QB 255, 42 LJQB 63, 28 LT 134, Ex Ch; *affd* (1875) LR 7 HL 744, [1874–80] All ER Rep 994, 45 LJQB 8, 33 LT 196, 40 JP 20, HL, 32 Digest (Repl) 119, *1404*.

Lincoln v Daniels [1961] 3 All ER 740, [1962] 1 QB 237, [1961] 3 WLR 866, CA, 3 Digest (Reissue) 747, *4459*.

O'Connor v Waldron [1935] AC 76, [1934] All ER Rep 281, 104 LJPC 21, 152 LT 289, PC, 32 Digest (Repl) 126, **485*.

Roy v Prior [1970] 2 All ER 729, [1971] AC 470, [1970] 3 WLR 202, 134 JP 615, HL, Digest (Cont Vol C) 1, *218a*.

Royal Aquarium and Summer and Winter Garden Society Ltd v Parkinson [1892] 1 QB 431, [1891–4] All ER Rep 429, 61 LJQB 409, 66 LT 513, 56 JP 404, CA, 32 Digest (Repl) 148, *1671*.

Shell Co of Australia Ltd v Federal Comr of Taxation [1931] AC 275, [1930] All ER Rep 671, 100 LJPC 55, 144 LT 421, 16 Digest (Repl) 115, *20*.

Slack v Barr (1918) 82 JP 91, 1918 1 SLT 133, 32 Digest (Repl) 121, **451*.

Watson v M'Ewan, Watson v Jones [1905] AC 480, [1904–7] All ER Rep 1, 74 LJPC 151, 93 LT 489, 1905 7 F (HL) 109, HL, 32 Digest (Repl) 126, *1476*.

Williamson v Umphray and Robertson (1890) 17 R (Ct of Sess) 905.

Appeal

This was an appeal by the pursuer, Dr George Trapp ('the appellant'), against an interlocutor pronounced by the Second Division of the Court of Session in Scotland (the Lord Justice Clerk (Lord Wheatley), Lord Thomson and Lord Stott) dated 28th March 1978 affirming an interlocutor of the Lord Ordinary (Lord Ross) dated 24th June 1977 whereby the Lord Ordinary dismissed the appellant's action against the defender, Maitland Mackie ('the respondent'), for damages for loss, injury and damage which he claimed to have suffered as a result of 'maliciously false evidence' which he alleged had been given by the respondent at a local inquiry held pursuant to the Education (Scotland) Act 1946. The facts are set out in the opinion of Lord Diplock.

The appellant appeared in person.

J P H Mackay QC (Dean of Faculty) and *A C Hamilton* (also of the Scottish Bar) for the respondent.

Their Lordships took time for consideration.

13th December. The following opinions were delivered.

LORD DIPLOCK. My Lords, this is an appeal by the pursuer, Dr Trapp ('the appellant'), against an interlocutor pronounced by the Second Division of the Court of Session dismissing the appellant's action against the defender, Mr Mackie ('the respondent'), for damages for loss, injury and damage which he claims to have suffered as a result of 'maliciously false evidence' alleged to have been given by the respondent at a local inquiry held pursuant to the Education (Scotland) Act 1946 in the summer of 1960.

In 1959 the appellant was rector (headmaster) of the Gordon Schools at Huntly. On 30th November 1959 he was dismissed from his post by the Aberdeenshire Education Committee of which the respondent was then the chairman. The appellant petitioned the Secretary of State for an inquiry into the reasons for his dismissal. The Secretary of State appointed Mr Manuel Kissen QC (as he then was) to hold a local inquiry into the matter. It was in the course of that inquiry that the respondent gave the evidence on which the appellant seeks to found this action.

When the record had been closed, the Lord Ordinary (Lord Ross) dismissed the action on the ground that the occasion on which the words complained of were spoken was one on which the respondent was entitled to absolute privilege. The appellant's motion for review of the Lord Ordinary's interlocutor was dismissed by the Second Division of the Court of Session. Their unanimous decision was delivered on 28th March 1978 by the Lord Justice Clerk (Lord Wheatley).

My Lords, on the immunity from suit of witnesses in respect of evidence they have given before courts of justice and tribunals acting in a manner similar to courts of justice, there is no difference between the law of Scotland and the law of England. That absolute privilege attaches to words spoken or written in the course of giving evidence in proceedings in a court of justice is a rule of law, based on public policy, that has been established since earliest times. That the like privilege extends to evidence given before tribunals which, although not courts of justice, nevertheless act in a manner similar to that in which courts of justice act was established more than a hundred years ago by the decision of this House in *Dawkins v Lord Rokeby*[1], where the unanimous answer of the judges to the question asked them by the House was adopted and the ratio decidendi of the judgment of the Court of Exchequer Chamber[2] was approved.

The kind of tribunal in which the evidence of witnesses is entitled to absolute privilege was described by Lord Atkin in *O'Connor v Waldron*[3] as a tribunal which 'has similar attributes to a court of justice or acts in a manner similar to that in which such courts act'. That the 'or' in this phrase is not intended to be disjunctive is apparent from the fact that Lord Atkin was confirming the accuracy of the law as it had been stated by Lord Esher MR in *Royal Aquarium and Summer and Winter Garden Society Ltd v Parkinson*[4]. Lord Esher MR, having spoken of 'an authorised inquiry which, though not before a Court of justice, is before a tribunal which has similar attributes', went on to explain that what he meant by similar attributes was 'acting . . . in a manner as nearly as possible similar to that in which a Court of justice acts in respect of an inquiry before it'.

In the course of the hearing which, as in both courts below, has been conducted by the appellant in person with skill and erudition, your Lordships' attention has been drawn to what must be nearly every reported case on this topic in Scotland, and in England where

---

1   (1875) LR 7 HL 744, [1874–80] All ER Rep 994
2   (1873) LR 8 QB 255
3   [1935] AC 76 at 81, [1934] All ER Rep 281 at 283
4   [1892] 1 QB 431 at 442, [1891–4] All ER Rep 429 at 432

most of the authorities are to be found. I do not find it necessary to refer to them. They provide examples of inquiries and tribunals which have been held to fall on one or other *a* side of a line which as Lord Atkin said in *O'Connor v Waldron*[1] 'is not capable of very precise limitation'.

No single touchstone emerges from the cases; but this is not surprising, for the rule of law is one which involves the balancing of conflicting public policies, one general: that the law should provide a remedy to the citizen whose good name and reputation is traduced by malicious falsehoods uttered by another; the other particular: that witnesses before *b* tribunals recognised by law should, in the words of the answer of the judges in *Dawkins v Lord Rokeby*[2], 'give their testimony free from any fear of being harassed by an action of an allegation, *whether true or false*, that they acted from malice'.

So, to decide whether a tribunal acts in a manner similar to courts of justice and thus is of such a kind as will attract absolute, as distinct from qualified, privilege for witnesses when they give testimony before it, one must consider first, under what authority the *c* tribunal acts, secondly, the nature of the question into which it is its duty to inquire, thirdly, the procedure adopted by it in carrying out the inquiry and, fourthly, the legal consequences of the conclusion reached by the tribunal as a result of the inquiry.

To attract absolute privilege for the testimony of witnesses the tribunal, by whatever name it is described, must be 'recognised by law', a phrase first used by the Court of Exchequer Chamber in *Dawkins v Lord Rokeby*[3]. This is a sine qua non; the absolute *d* privilege does not attach to purely domestic tribunals. Although the description 'recognised by law' is not necessarily confined to tribunals constituted or recognised by Act of Parliament (see *Lincoln v Daniels*[4]) it embraces all that are, and so includes the local inquiry in the instant case at which the respondent's evidence was given. This was held by the commissioner, Mr Kissen QC, appointed for the purpose by the Secretary of State under ss 63 and 81(3) of the Education (Scotland) Act 1946. *e*

The nature of the question into which it was the commissioner's duty to inquire is stated in s 81. Subsections (1) and (2) deal with the dismissal of a certificated teacher by resolution of an education authority. They require that the teacher should be given notice of the resolution but contain no provision for him to be heard by the committee before the resolution is passed. Subsection (3) is as follows:

'If at any time within six weeks after the adoption of a resolution for the dismissal *f* of a certificated teacher a petition shall be presented to the Secretary of State by the said teacher, praying for an inquiry into the reasons for the dismissal, the Secretary of State shall make such inquiry as he sees fit, and if as the result of such inquiry he is of opinion that the dismissal is not reasonably justifiable he shall communicate such opinion to the education authority with a view to reconsideration of the resolution, and in the event of the education authority not departing from the resolution within *g* six weeks thereafter may attach to the resolution the condition that the education authority shall pay to the teacher such sum not exceeding one year's salary as the Secretary of State may determine; and any sum so determined may be recovered by the teacher as a debt from the education authority.'

The inquiry is thus initiated by a petition by the aggrieved teacher to the Secretary of *h* State. The question into which it thereupon becomes the duty of the Secretary of State to inquire is whether the dismissal of the teacher was reasonably justifiable. Such a question partakes of the nature of a lis inter partes, an issue raised between the dismissed teacher and the education authority no different from the kind of issues between pursuer and defender that daily form the subject-matter of civil suits in courts of justice.

Section 81(3) gives to the Secretary of State a discretion as to the means that he will adopt *j*

---

1   [1935] AC 76 at 81, [1934] All ER Rep 281 at 283
2   (1875) LR 7 HL 744 at 753, [1874–80] All ER Rep 994 at 995
3   (1873) LR 8 QB 255 at 263
4   [1961] 3 All ER 740, [1962] 1 QB 237

in making the inquiry called for by the subsection; but the nature of the question that is the subject of the inquiry will make it appropriate in most cases arising under the subsection to adopt a procedure which will enable the parties to the dispute, the teacher and the education authority, to address oral argument and to adduce evidence in support of their respective contentions. The procedure which the Act provides by which this can be done is a local inquiry. Section 63 empowers the Secretary of State to cause a local inquiry to be held for the purpose of the exercise of any of his functions under the Act. If he exercises this power, as he did in the instant case, the provisions of Sch 1 have effect with regard to the inquiry.

Under Sch 1, a local inquiry is held by a commissioner appointed by the Secretary of State. The commissioner's function is to hold the inquiry and to report thereon to the Secretary of State. The schedule gives the commissioner a wide discretion as to the procedure to be adopted at a local inquiry. It leaves it to him to adopt the procedure appropriate to the kind of question into which he is appointed to inquire. This is necessary since questions of very different kinds from those arising under s 81(3) may also be the subject of local inquiries, such as, for example, schemes prepared by education authorities for the exercise of their powers and duties under the Act for which the approval of the Secretary of State is needed. For such inquiries the procedure followed in a court of justice may be quite unsuitable, but the schedule equips the commissioner with the necessary powers to enable him to conduct the inquiry before him in a manner similar to that in which contested civil actions are conducted in the regular courts of justice, where the question into which he is appointed to inquire renders appropriate this manner of proceeding.

Thus, the commissioner, by para 3, is armed with powers to compel the attendance of witnesses and the production of documents. These powers are backed by penal sanctions under para 6; but, by para 3, proviso (ii), they are made subject to the same privilege to refuse to answer or to produce a document as 'if the inquiry were a proceeding in a court of law'. By para 4 the commissioner may require evidence before him to be given on oath; by para 5 the inquiry is to be held in public unless the Secretary of State otherwise directs.

That the Secretary of State considered that the question into which he was required by the appellant to make inquiry in the instant case was one which called for the adoption at the local inquiry of a procedure similar to that adopted by a court of justice may, perhaps, be inferred from his appointment of a distinguished senior member of the Scots Bar to act as commissioner. Mr Kissen QC, in his formal letter to the parties, the appellant and the Aberdeenshire Education Authority, announced the procedure which he proposed to adopt at the inquiry, apparently with the agreement of the parties. The relevant paragraphs are as follows:

'As has already been agreed at the meeting at my Chambers on 25th March, 1960, I shall expect the County Council to lead evidence first. [The appellant] will then lead his evidence and the County Council will have the right to lead further evidence if necessary. The question of onus of proof is reserved. In conformity with the normal legal practice, I propose to allow examination, cross-examination and re-examination of any witnesses who give evidence at the inquiry and at the close of the evidence to afford the representatives of both sides opportunity to address me on the evidence which has been led. I propose to take any oral evidence on oath. In the circumstances it will be for the legal advisers of both parties to decide what evidence they desire to tender at the inquiry. It is not my intention to cite witnesses unless requested to do so by either party. If either party has difficulty in securing attendance of any necessary witness I shall be prepared, on being satisfied by said party that such witness is a necessary witness, to exercise the powers I have under Paragraph 3 of the First Schedule to the Act of 1946. I shall expect to receive a list of the names and addresses of witnesses by 7th June, 1960. Inventories of productions and any copies should also be lodged by that date.'

The procedure there described was followed at the inquiry. It is indistinguishable from
that followed in a court of justice in trying a contested issue in a civil case.   *a*

There remain to be considered the legal consequences of the conclusion reached by the
tribunal as a result of the inquiry. The commissioner's function is to report to the Secretary
of State on the question into which he was appointed to inquire, viz whether or not the
dismissal of the appellant was reasonably justifiable. It was his opinion on that matter and
the material on which his opinion was based that was to form the subject-matter of his
report. It is true that an opinion expressed by the commissioner as to whether or not the   *b*
dismissal was reasonably justifiable is not binding in law on the Secretary of State, although
in practice on an issue such as this where there are adverse parties equally entitled to have
justice done to them it would take a bold Secretary of State to overrule a legally qualified
commissioner whom he himself had selected for appointment. Where he has chosen to
cause a local inquiry to be held, his power to take further action under s 81(3) is dependent
on his receiving the report and forming an opinion as the result of it. The legal   *c*
consequence of the report is that, if the opinion that it causes the Secretary of State to reach
is that the dismissal was not reasonably justifiable, he must so inform the education
authority with the consequences in that event for which s 81(3) provides; while if the
report causes him to reach the opinion that the dismissal was reasonably justifiable he has
no power of further action, and the matter ends there. In either event the issue between
the teacher and the education authority is finally determined. The Secretary of State has   *d*
also power, in the exercise of which he would no doubt be influenced by the commissioner's
report, to order one of the parties to the inquiry to pay the expenses of the other party and
his order is enforceable in the same way as a decree arbitral (Sch 1, paras 7 and 8).

My Lords, these consequences of the conclusion reached by the commissioner at the
close of the inquiry differ from the consequences of decisions of a court of justice in that
the latter are binding and authoritative in their own right (whether subject to appeal or   *e*
not), whereas the conclusion reached by the commissioner as to whether or not the
dismissal was reasonably justifiable has in strict law no binding effect unless and until it is
adopted by the Secretary of State. It is not authoritative in its own right however
improbable it may be in practice that the Secretary of State will not adopt it. But this
distinction between the report of the commissioner and decisions of courts of justice, while
it may be relevant in constitutional questions as to what constitutes an exercise of judicial   *f*
power, has never been regarded as sufficient to exclude tribunals which report to a higher
authority, with whom the ultimate decision rests, their opinion on some question into
which they are authorised by law to inquire, for the assistance of that higher authority in
reaching its decision. In *Dawkins v Lord Rokeby*[1] the military court of inquiry with which
that case was concerned was a tribunal of this kind. It reported its opinion to the
commander-in-chief in whom the decision-making power was vested. *Barratt v Kearns*[2]   *g*
provides another example. The tribunal there consisted of commissioners appointed by a
bishop, under powers conferred by statute, to report to him whether the duties of a
benefice had been adequately performed. A report of the opinion of a majority of the
commissioners that the duties had *not* been adequately performed was a condition
precedent to the bishop's power to take any further action against the incumbent, but it did
not put him under any obligation to do so; the decision whether to or not was, in strict law,   *h*
his alone. It may not be out of place to mention that when your Lordships are sitting as an
appellate committee of this House or as the Judicial Committee of the Privy Council, the
result of your deliberations is a report of your collective opinion in the one case to this
House and in the other to Her Majesty in Council. In strict law the opinion so reported
does not become binding and authoritative until agreed to by this House or by Her Majesty
in Council, as the case may be.   *j*

In deciding whether a particular tribunal is of such a kind as to attract absolute privilege

1   (1875) LR 7 HL 744, [1874–80] All ER Rep 994
2   [1905] 1 KB 504

for witnesses when they give testimony before it, your Lordships are engaged in the task of balancing against one another public interests which conflict. In such a task legal technicalities have at most a minor part to play. Where the report of a tribunal though not necessarily decisive as a matter of legal theory nevertheless in practice has a major influence on the final decision that in law is binding and authoritative, the same considerations apply to such a tribunal as those that weigh the balance down in favour of absolute privilege for evidence given before a tribunal whose decisions are in strict law binding and authoritative in their own right.

The result of this examination of the nature of the tribunal before which the respondent gave the evidence on which the appellant seeks to raise his action in the instant case is that it shared with courts of justice the following characteristics. (1) It was authorised by law; it was constituted pursuant to an Act of Parliament. (2) It was inquiring into an issue in dispute between adverse parties of a kind similar to issues that commonly fall to be decided by courts of justice. (3) The inquiry was held in public. (4) Decisions as to what oral evidence should be led and what documents should be tendered or their production called for by the adverse party were left to the contending parties. (5) Witnesses whom either of the adverse parties wished to call were compellable, under penal sanctions, to give oral evidence or to produce documents as havers; and were entitled to the same privilege to refuse to answer a question or to produce a document as would apply if the inquiry were a proceeding in a court of law. (6) The oral evidence was given on oath; if it were false to the knowledge of the witness he would incur criminal liability for the offence of perjury. (7) Witnesses who gave oral testimony were subject to examination-in-chief and re-examination by the party calling them and to cross-examination by the adverse party, in accordance with the normal procedure of courts of law. (8) The adverse parties were entitled to be, and were in fact, represented by legally qualified advocates or solicitors and these were given the opportunity of addressing the tribunal on the evidence that had been led. (9) The opinion of the tribunal as reported to the Secretary of State, even though not of itself decisive of the issue in dispute between the adverse parties, would have a major influence on his decision either to require the education committee to reconsider its resolution to dismiss the appellant or to let the matter rest. (10) As a result of the report either of the parties to the inquiry might be ordered by the Secretary of State to pay the whole or part of the expenses of appearing at the inquiry incurred by the adverse party; and such expenses would be recoverable in the same manner as expenses incurred in a civil action in a court of law.

My Lords, I am far from suggesting either that the presence of any one of these characteristics taken in isolation would suffice to attract absolute privilege for witnesses in respect of testimony given by them before a tribunal or that the absence of any one of these characteristics would be fatal to the existence of such absolute privilege. An appeal which has been argued on one side by a litigant in person, however skilfully, does not, in my view, afford an appropriate occasion for stating propositions of law in any wider terms than are necessary to dispose of that particular appeal. I would therefore content myself by saying that the cumulative effect of the ten characteristics that I have listed are more than enough to justify the contention of the respondent that the tribunal before which he gave the evidence on which the appellant seeks to raise his action was 'acting . . . in a manner as nearly as possible similar to that in which a Court of justice acts in respect of an inquiry before it'[1]. The words complained of were therefore published on an occasion when the respondent was entitled to absolute privilege. No action may be raised against him in respect of them. For that reason I would dismiss this appeal.

LORD SALMON. My Lords, for the reason stated in the speeches of my noble and learned friends, Lord Diplock and Lord Fraser of Tullybelton, with which I agree, I would dismiss this appeal.

---

1   *Royal Aquarium and Summer and Winter Garden Society Ltd v Parkinson* [1892] 1 QB 431 at 442, [1891–4] All ER Rep 429 at 432, per Lord Esher MR

LORD EDMUND-DAVIES. My Lords, for the reasons set out in the speeches of my noble and learned friends, Lord Diplock and Lord Fraser of Tullybelton, with which I am in respectful agreement, I concur in holding that this appeal should be dismissed.

LORD FRASER OF TULLYBELTON. My Lords, this appeal raises an important question as to the circumstances in which a witness, giving evidence before a tribunal which is not a court of law, is protected by absolute privilege. The appellant formerly held the office of rector of the Gordon Schools at Huntly in Aberdeenshire. He was dismissed from that office by a resolution of the Aberdeenshire Education Committee passed on 30th November 1959, just 19 years ago. Thereafter he petitioned the Secretary of State, as he was entitled to do by s 81(3) of the Education (Scotland) Act 1946, asking for an inquiry into the reasons for his dismissal. The Secretary of State ordered an inquiry and appointed Mr Manuel Kissen QC as commissioner to hold it. At the inquiry evidence was given by the respondent who was chairman of the Education Committee of Aberdeen County Council and had taken a prominent part in the events leading up to the appellant's dismissal. The appellant's case is that the evidence given by the respondent was false, and was known by him to be false, that the respondent bore malice towards the appellant (for reasons that are averred), that the false evidence caused the commissioner to report adversely to the appellant with the result that the Secretary of State, who accepted the report, upheld the appellant's dismissal. He says that he suffered loss in consequence. His case is conveniently summed up in his first plea-in-law thus: 'The pursuer having suffered loss, injury and damage by the said maliciously false evidence of the defender is entitled to reparation from him therefor.'

The action is apparently not based on defamation but on some other form of verbal injury, either convicium or malicious falsehood. There may be room for doubt about the exact meaning of these words[1] and about whether either of them would apply to this action. But in view of the opinion that I have formed on the question of privilege, it is unnecessary for me to investigate what might have been interesting questions as to the legal basis of the action, and the sufficiency of the averments.

The respondent denies the material averments of fact and, among other pleas, he has a general plea that the whole action is irrelevant. The general plea was supported by an argument that he was entitled to absolute privilege for his evidence and it thus raises the question whether the inquiry held by Mr Kissen QC was one to which such privilege attached. Both the Lord Ordinary and the Second Division decided that question adversely to the appellant.

It will be convenient first to consider the legal principles to be applied. It is, and has long been, well settled that no action will lie against a witness for words spoken in giving evidence in a court even if the evidence is falsely and maliciously given. In *Watson v M'Ewan*[2], Lord Halsbury LC said that was 'settled law and cannot be doubted'. He went on thus:

> 'The remedy against a witness who has given evidence which is false and injurious to another is to indict him for perjury; but for very obvious reasons, the conduct of legal procedure by Courts of justice, *with the necessity of compelling witnesses to attend,* involves as one of the necessities of the administration of justice the immunity of witnesses from action being brought against them in respect of evidence they have given.' (My italics.)

That case decided that the same immunity attached to statements made on precognition with a view to giving evidence. The rule was reaffirmed recently in *Roy v Prior*[3] and its justification was explained by Lord Wilberforce thus[4]:

---

1   See the report of the Committee on Defamation (1975) Cmnd 5909, paras 595–598
2   [1905] AC 480 at 486, cf [1904–7] All ER Rep 1 at 3
3   [1970] 2 All ER 729, [1971] AC 470
4   [1970] 2 All ER 729 at 736, [1971] AC 470 at 480

'The reasons why immunity is traditionally (and for this purpose I accept the tradition) conferred on witnesses in respect of evidence given in court, are in order that they may give their evidence fearlessly and to avoid a multiplicity of actions in which the value or truth of their evidence would be tried over again. Moreover, the trial process contains in itself, in the subjection to cross-examination and confrontation with other evidence, some safeguard against careless, malicious or untruthful evidence.'

The rule has been extended beyond courts of justice and has been held to apply to authorised inquiries before tribunals which, though not courts of justice, have similar attributes: see *Royal Aquarium and Summer and Winter Garden Society Ltd v Parkinson*[1], per Lord Esher MR. In *O'Connor v Waldron*[2] Lord Atkin giving the advice of the Judicial Committee said this:

'In their Lordships' opinion the law on the subject was accurately stated by Lord Esher in *Royal Aquarium, etc., Ltd* v. *Parkinson*[1], where he says that the privilege "applies wherever there is an authorized inquiry which, though not before a Court of justice, is before a tribunal which has similar attributes ... This doctrine has never been extended further than to courts of justice and tribunals acting in a manner similar to that in which such Courts act." The question therefore in every case is whether the tribunal in question has similar attributes to a court of justice or acts in a manner similar to that in which such courts act? This is of necessity a differentia which is not capable of very precise limitation.'

The question mentioned by Lord Atkin is exactly the question which arises in the present case and it it necessary to see what attributes have been treated as significant for this purpose. In *Dawkins v Lord Rokeby*[3] it was held that absolute privilege applied to evidence given to a court of inquiry set up by the commander-in-chief in the case of a witness who, being a military man, could have been compelled under Queen's Regulations to attend and give evidence. In the Court of Exchequer Chamber Kelly CB said[4]:

'Under these regulations officers in the army, if required by competent military authority to attend, are compellable to attend and give evidence ... There is, therefore, no sound reason or principle upon which such a witness, called upon to give evidence in such a court, should not be entitled to the same protection and immunity as any other witness in any of the courts of law or equity in Westminster Hall. He is equally compellable to appear and give evidence, and punishable in case of refusal. And it would be unreasonable and unjust to hold him liable to a heavy punishment if he refuse to answer the question put to him, and liable to an action at law for damages if he answers them and his answers happen to reflect upon the character of another.'

Clearly compellability was the decisive factor there and the decision was reached notwithstanding certain factors which might have been considered as detracting from the status of the court of inquiry, videlicit (1) Queen's Regulations expressly provided: 'A court of inquiry is not to be considered in any light as a judicial body.' (2) The court had no power to administer an oath. (3) It sat in private. (4) It could not itself come to a final decision or adjudication on any issue. Its function was to report to the commander-in-chief and to[5]—

'give, after due investigation, their opinion as to the validity of the charges in the sense in which [the plaintiff] presses them against his superior officers, and also [to]

1   [1892] 1 QB 431 at 442, [1891–4] All ER Rep 429 at 432
2   [1935] AC 76 at 81, [1934] All ER Rep 281 at 283
3   (1873) LR 8 QB 255; *affd* (1875) LR 7 HL 744, [1874–80] All ER Rep 994
4   LR 8 QB 255 at 267
5   LR 8 QB 255 at 258

give their opinion upon [the plaintiff's] conduct generally, as evinced by the correspondence submitted, and state how far they consider the service will be benefited, or the contrary, by placing [the plaintiff] in command of a battalion of Guards when the occasion presents itself.'

Any decision would be made by the commander-in-chief.

The principle of the decision in *Dawkins v Lord Rokeby*[1] was accepted as applicable in Scotland (subject to one exception which is not material for the present purpose and which may I think be more apparent than real) by Lord President Inglis in *Williamson v Umphray and Robertson*[2].

Absolute privilege has also been held to apply to evidence given at an inquiry by a commission set up by a bishop under the Pluralities Act 1838 to report to the bishop whether the duties of an incumbent were being properly performed: *Barratt v Kearns*[3]. Here again the final decision was to be taken not by the commission but by the bishop.

In *Slack v Barr*[4] Lord Anderson in the Outer House held that absolute privilege attached to evidence given before an arbitration tribunal under the Munitions of War Act 1915. His decision was given on the assumption (though without deciding) that the tribunal did not have power to compel witnesses to attend. Further authority showing that absolute privilege may apply to proceedings before a tribunal which does not have power to compel the attendance of witnesses is to be found in the opinion of Sellers LJ in *Lincoln v Daniels*[5], referring to a disciplinary tribunal of benchers of one of the Inns of Court.

There have on the other hand been decisions negativing absolute privilege. It was held not to attach to proceedings before a meeting of the London County Council for granting licences for music and dancing because its function of granting licences was regarded as administrative and not judicial, and also because its constitution and procedure were not analogous to that of a law court: *Royal Aquarium and Summer and Winter Garden Society Ltd v Parkinson*[6]. Fry LJ contrasted its procedure with that of a court, and described the latter in words that are illuminating for the present case. He said[7]:

'Courts are, for the most part, controlled and presided over by some person selected as specially qualified for the purpose; and they have generally a fixed and dignified course of procedure, which tends to minimise the risks that might flow from this absolute immunity.'

In *Collins v Henry Whiteway & Co Ltd*[8] communications to a court of referees under the Unemployment Insurance Act 1920 were held not entitled to absolute privilege because that was not a body deciding between parties, nor did its decision affect criminally or otherwise the status of an individual.

The case on which the appellant mainly relied was *O'Connor v Waldron*[9], where the Judicial Committee held that an inquiry under the (Canadian) Combines Investigation Act 1927 was not an absolutely privileged occasion, so as to render the commissioner who conducted it immune from liability for defamatory words spoken in the course of its proceedings. In that case the tribunal had power to administer oaths and to summon witnesses, but it was also entitled to use methods of investigation entirely unlike those used by a judge. Moreover the inquiry could not lead to a decision of any issue either by the commissioner who held it or by the Minister to whom his report was to be transmitted.

---

1   (1875) LR 7 HL 744, [1874–80] All ER Rep 994
2   (1890) 17 R (Ct of Sess) 905
3   [1905] 1 KB 504
4   1918 1 SLT 133
5   [1961] 3 All ER 740 at 745, [1962] 1 QB 237 at 250
6   [1892] 1 QB 431, [1891–4] All ER Rep 429
7   [1892] 1 QB 431 at 447, [1891–4] All ER Rep 429 at 434
8   [1927] 2 KB 378
9   [1935] AC 76, [1934] All ER Rep 281

The most that could happen was that, if as a result of the report the Minister considered that an offence under the Act had been committed, he could remit the report with any evidence taken to the appropriate authority for prosecution. The whole inquiry was therefore merely a preliminary investigation. Lord Atkin, after the passage quoted above from his speech, went on to say this[1]:

'It is only necessary to remember that the commissioner by the Act is empowered to enter premises and examine the books, papers and records of suspected persons to see how far his functions differ from those of a judge. His conclusion is expressed in a report; it determines no rights, nor the guilt or innocence of anyone. It does not even initiate any proceedings, which have to be left to the ordinary criminal procedure . . . the fact that a tribunal may be exercising merely administrative functions though in so doing it must act "judicially" is well established, and appears clearly from the *Royal Aquarium* case[2] above cited. If it is exercising such functions it seems to be immaterial whether it is armed with the powers of a court of justice in summoning witnesses, administering oaths and punishing disobedience to its orders made for the purpose of effectuating its inquiries . . .'

Consideration of the cases shows that, provided the tribunal is one recognised by law, there is no single element the presence or absence of which will be conclusive in showing whether it has attributes sufficiently similar to those of a court of law to create absolute privilege. It is not essential that the tribunal itself should have power to determine the issue before it, and a statement by Lord Sankey LC in *Shell Co of Australia Ltd v Federal Comr of Taxation*[3], which at first sight appears to indicate the contrary, is not truly in pari materia. It was directed to the different question of the meaning of 'judicial power' in s 71 of the Australian Constitution. Cases such as *Dawkins v Lord Rokeby*[4] and *Barratt v Kearns*[5] show that absolute privilege may apply if the inquiry is a step leading directly toward determination of an issue by the authority who appointed it. In each case the object of the tribunal, its constitution and its manner of proceeding must all be considered before the question can be answered.

I must therefore refer to the statutory provisions that applied to the inquiry in the present case. The inquiry was set up by the Secretary of State under the Education (Scotland) Act 1946. By s 78(1) of the Act teachers in local authority schools are appointed during the pleasure of the local authority. But s 81(1) provides that no resolution of an education authority for dismissal of a teacher shall be valid unless due notice has been given to the teacher and unless certain procedural rules are observed. Thereafter sub-s (3) may come into play. It is as follows:

'If at any time within six weeks after the adoption of a resolution for the dismissal of a certificated teacher a petition shall be presented to the Secretary of State by the said teacher, praying for an inquiry into the reasons for the dismissal, the Secretary of State shall make such inquiry as he sees fit, and if *as the result of such inquiry* he is of opinion that the dismissal is not reasonably justifiable he shall communicate such opinion to the education authority with a view to reconsideration of the resolution, and in the event of the education authority not departing from the resolution within six weeks thereafter may attach to the resolution the condition that the education authority shall pay to the teacher such sum not exceeding one year's salary as the Secretary of State may determine . . .' (My italics.)

---

1 [1935] AC 76 at 82, [1934] All ER Rep 281 at 283
2 [1892] 1 QB 431, [1891–4] All ER Rep 429
3 [1931] AC 275 at 295, [1930] All ER Rep 671 at 679
4 (1875) LR 7 HL 744, [1874–80] All ER Rep 994
5 [1905] 1 KB 504

One of the forms of inquiry which the Secretary of State may see fit to set up is a local inquiry under s 63 of the Act which empowers him to cause a local inquiry to be held 'for the purpose of the exercise of any of his functions under this Act'. The rules for the conduct of a local inquiry are set out in Sch 1 to the Act. It is too long to quote in full but certain of its provisions show that the inquiry was intended to follow broadly the type of procedure that would be followed in a court of law. Paragraph 3 provides that the commissioner may 'require' any person to attend to give evidence but adds the significant proviso:

'(ii) Nothing in this paragraph shall empower the commissioner to require any person to produce any book or document or to answer any question which he would be entitled, on the ground of privilege or confidentiality, to refuse to produce or to answer if the inquiry were a proceeding in a court of law.'

Later paragraphs provide that the commissioner may administer oaths, that the inquiry is to be held in public unless the Secretary of State otherwise directs, and that the Secretary of State may make orders as to the expenses incurred by the parties appearing at the inquiry.

Against that background I have reached the opinion that the inquiry in the present case is one at which witnesses are protected by absolute privilege. I rely particularly on the following factors. 1. The inquiry was set up under statutory authority. 2. The object of the inquiry was to enable the Secretary of State to decide a definite issue which was in dispute between the appellant and the education authority, namely whether his dismissal was reasonably justifiable, and it was an essential step towards an effective decision: see the words italicised above in s 81(3). It was quite different from the preliminary investigation in *O'Connor v Waldron*[1]. It therefore possessed the element which in my opinion was the most important for the present purpose. 3. The commissioner was a Queen's Counsel. He was to sit in public. His power to compel witnesses and havers to attend (and the proviso for privilege and confidentiality) and his power to administer the oath all point to a 'fixed and dignified course of procedure'. 4. The commissioner's letter dated 3rd May 1960, giving notice of the inquiry, and informing parties that he proposed 'in conformity with the normal legal practice' to allow examination, cross-examination and re-examination of witnesses, points in the same direction. 5. So does the power of a Secretary of State to award expenses.

I would dismiss the appeal and find the appellant liable to the respondent for the expenses of the appeal.

LORD RUSSELL OF KILLOWEN. My Lords, I have had the advantage of reading in advance the speeches prepared by my noble and learned friends, Lord Diplock and Lord Fraser of Tullybelton. I agree with them and with their conclusion that this appeal should be dismissed.

Appeal dismissed.

Solicitors: *Martin & Co,* agents for *Shepherd & Wedderburn WS,* Edinburgh (for the respondent).

Mary Rose Plummer Barrister.

---

1 [1935] AC 76, [1934] All ER Rep 281

a
Customs and Excise Commissioners v Mechanical Services (Trailer Engineers) Ltd

COURT OF APPEAL, CIVIL DIVISION
MEGAW, BROWNE AND WALLER LJJ
22nd, 23rd NOVEMBER, 13th DECEMBER 1978

b

Value added tax – Higher rate – Boats and aircraft – Goods suitable for use as part of boats or boat accessories – Suitable for – Items capable of being used as parts of boats or boat accessories – Items equally capable of being used for other purposes – Items not designed or adapted for use as parts of boats or boat accessories – Trailer couplings and winches – Whether couplings and winches 'goods of a kind suitable for use as parts of' trailers for carrying boats – Whether subject to tax at higher
c *rate – Finance (No 2) Act 1975, Sch 7, Group 3, item 6.*

The taxpayer company supplied lightweight trailer equipment used for the on and off loading and carrying of boats. Included amongst the equipment were trailer couplings and winches. The coupling was a standard fitting capable of being used to link any trailer of any nature to a towing vehicle. It consisted of a fitting on the trailer which fitted over
d a boss or bar attached to the towing vehicle and which provided a pivotal connection. There was nothing intrinsic in its design or construction which particularly fitted it for the purpose of a boat trailer. The winch was a small article consisting of a ratchet mechanism and drum around which passed a cable which was capable through reduction gearing of dragging an object in a horizontal direction. One of the many uses to which it could be put was the loading of a boat onto a trailer. In February 1976 the taxpayer company sold two
e couplings to one of its customers and two winches to another and charged value added tax at the then higher rate of 25%. The taxpayer company enquired of the commissioners whether it was right in so doing and the commissioners confirmed that the items supplied fell within item 6 of Group 3[a] of Sch 7 to the Finance (No 2) Act 1975 and were thus liable to the higher rate of value added tax. The value added tax tribunal allowed an appeal by the taxpayer company, holding that since the winches and couplings were goods of a kind
f used for a multiplicity of purposes they were not goods 'designed' or 'adapted', and therefore were not 'suitable', for use as parts of a trailer for carrying boats, within item 6 of Group 3. The Crown appealed to the Divisional Court of the Queen's Bench Division[b] which allowed its appeal holding that the word 'suitable' in item 6 was to be given its ordinary meaning, ie 'suited' or 'well fitted', and was not to be restricted to meaning 'designed' or 'adapted for' and accordingly the couplings and winches were 'goods of a kind
g suitable for use as parts of' trailers for carrying boats, within item 6. The taxpayer company appealed to the Court of Appeal.

Held – The phrase 'goods of a kind suitable for use as parts of' trailers for carrying boats in item 6 meant a kind or genus of goods specifically designed or intended for purposes ancillary to boats, even though it could be used for other purposes. Although the trailer
h couplings and winches were suitable for use as parts of trailers for carrying boats, since they were not made exclusively or primarily for such use they were not goods of a kind suitable for use as parts of trailers for carrying boats within item 6. Accordingly the taxpayer company was not liable to pay value added tax at the higher rate on couplings and winches which were not used on pleasure boat trailers. The appeal would accordingly be allowed, (see p 508 *a* to *c* and *f h*, p 509 *d* and *g h*, p 510 *c* to *d*, p 511 *b* to *j* and p 512 *b c*, post).
j   Decision of the Divisional Court of the Queen's Bench Division [1978] 1 All ER 204 reversed.

---

a   Group 3, so far as material, is set out at p 503 *f g*, post
b   [1978] 1 All ER 204, [1977] STC 485

Notes
For the rates of value added tax, see 12 Halsbury's Laws (4th Edn) para 865.

For the Finance (No 2) Act 1975, Sch 7, Group 3, see 45 Halsbury's Statutes (3rd Edn) 213.

Case referred to in judgments
Luke v Inland Revenue Comrs [1963] 1 All ER 655, [1963] AC 557, [1963] 2 WLR 559, 40 Tax Cas 630, 1963 SC (HL) 65, 42 ATC 21, [1963] TR 21, [1963] SLT 129, HL, 28(1) Digest (Reissue) 332, 1200.

Cases also cited
Canadian Eagle Oil Co Ltd v R [1945] 2 All ER 499, [1946] AC 119, 27 Tax Cas 205, CA.
Roberts v Granada TV Rental Ltd [1970] 2 All ER 764, [1970] 1 WLR 889, 46 Tax Cas 295.

Appeal
This was an appeal by Mechanical Services (Trailer Engineers) Ltd ('the taxpayer company') against the decision of the Divisional Court of the Queen's Bench Division[1] (Lord Widgery CJ and Watkins J, O'Connor J dissenting) given on 25th July 1977 allowing an appeal by the Crown from a decision of a value added tax tribunal sitting at Manchester dated 25th May 1976 whereby the tribunal by a majority allowed an appeal by the taxpayer company against a decision of the Commissioners of Customs and Excise that the supply of two articles, namely trailer couplings and winches sold by the taxpayer company, was chargeable to value added tax at the higher rate. The facts are set out in the judgment of Browne LJ.

Andrew Park QC for the taxpayer company.
Philip Vallance for the Crown.

Cur adv vult

13th December. The following judgments were read.

BROWNE LJ (delivering the first judgment at the invitation of Megaw LJ). This is an appeal by Mechanical Services (Trailer Engineers) Ltd ('the taxpayer company') from a decision of the Divisional Court[1] given on 25th July 1977. The Divisional Court by a majority (Lord Widgery CJ and Watkins J, O'Connor J dissenting) allowed an appeal by the Crown from a decision of the value added tax tribunal dated 25th May 1976, but gave leave to appeal to this court. The tribunal had by a majority of two to one allowed an appeal by the taxpayer company from a decision of the Commissioners of Customs and Excise that certain couplings and winches supplied by the taxpayer company were subject to value added tax at the higher rate (then 25% and now 12½%) as opposed to the standard rate (then 10% and now 8%).

Value added tax was originally imposed by the Finance Act 1972. It is a tax on the supply of goods and services and also on the importation of goods. The present case is concerned with the supply of goods. There is no need to go into the details of the incidence of the tax as laid down in the 1972 Act. There is no dispute that value added tax is payable on the supply of the goods here in question, and the only question is about the rate. It is only necessary to refer to s 9(1) and (3) of the 1972 Act. Section 9 provides:

'(1) Subject to the following provisions of this section, tax shall be charged at the rate of ten per cent., and shall be charged—(a) on the supply of goods or services, by reference to the value of the supply as determined under this Part of this Act; and (b) [deals with the charge on the importation of goods] . . .

---

1   [1978] 1 All ER 204, [1978] 1 WLR 56, [1977] STC 485

'(3) The Treasury may by order increase or decrease the rate for the time being in force by such percentage thereof, not exceeding 20 per cent., as may be specified in the order, but any such order shall cease to be in force at the expiration of a period of one year from the date on which it takes effect, unless continued in force by a further order under this subsection . . .'

The Finance Act 1972 was amended by the Finance (No 2) Act 1975. Section 17 of that Act provides:

'(1) Subsection (1) of section 9 of the Finance Act 1972 shall have effect as if in its application to—(a) a supply which is of a description for the time being specified in Schedule 7 to this Act or is a supply of goods or services of a description for the time being so specified . . . the rate of 25 per cent. ("the higher rate") were substituted for the rate specified in it ("the standard rate"); and any order made under subsection (3) of that section may apply to both the standard rate and the higher rate or to only one of them . . .

'(2) The Treasury may by order vary Schedule 7 to this Act by adding to or deleting from it any description or by varying any description for the time being specified in it . . .

'(4) Schedule 7 to this Act shall be interpreted in accordance with the notes contained in it; and accordingly the power conferred by subsection (2) above includes power to add to, delete or vary those notes.

'(5) The descriptions of Groups in Schedule 7 to this Act are for ease of reference only and shall not affect the interpretation of the descriptions of items in those Groups . . .'

Schedule 7 to the 1975 Act contains eight 'Groups'. The group which is directly relevant to this case is Group 3, but in the course of the argument we were referred to a number of the provisions in other groups. Group 3 is headed 'Boats and Aircraft', and as originally enacted it contained the following provisions relevant to this case:

'Item No.
'1. Boats—(a) of a gross tonnage of less than 15 tons; or (b) designed for use for recreation or pleasure; except boats which are of a kind used solely as liferafts and comply with the requirements of [certain rules under the Merchant Shipping Act 1894].
'2. Boats adapted for use for recreation or pleasure . . .
'5. The following accessories to goods within item 1 or item 2, namely . . . (f) trailers and trolleys.
'6. Goods of a kind suitable for use as parts of goods within item 1 or item 5, except goods within the exceptions from item 5 of Group 1 . . .'

Item 5 of Group 1, incorporated by the provision in item 6 of Group 3 which I have just read, is as follows:

'Goods of a kind suitable for use as parts of goods comprised in items 1 to 4, except—(a) nuts, bolts, screws, screw caps, nails, washers, eyelets, rivets . . .'

Then paras (b), (c), (d), (e) and (f) deal with other, what may be called general purpose, components.

It seems clear that the general intention of Group 3 was to subject pleasure-boats and their accessories to the higher rate of tax.

The facts found by the tribunal are these:

'The coupling is, we find, a standard fitting which is capable of being used to link any trailer of any nature, or any article of equipment fitted with wheels, to a towing vehicle. It consists of a fitting on the trailer which fits over a boss or bar attached to the towing vehicle, and which provides a pivotal connection, and it has a ratchet mechanism for quick release: there is nothing intrinsically in its design or construction which indicates, or particularly fits it for, the purposes of a boat trailer: it is an all-purpose component. The winch is a small article consisting of a ratchet mechanism and a drum around which passes a cable which is capable through reduction gearing of dragging any object in a horizontal direction. It can be used, and is used without adaptation, for the purposes of loading a boat on to a trailer: equally there are a diversity of other uses to which it may be put in connection with a trailer as, for example, moving a broken down vehicle on to a low loading platform. It also has a variety of uses unconnected with trailers.'

The tribunal also adopted as a finding of fact an important part of the evidence of Mr Badland, the managing director of the taxpayer company. I quote from the decision:

'Mr. Badland did not seek to argue that such use [that is, use on boat trailers] was minimal; very fairly he admitted that it was measurable but, he said, the predominant use was for purposes other than in connection with boat trailers and the tribunal is prepared to adopt this statement as a finding of fact.'

The decisions of the majority and the minority of the tribunal are:

'The view of the minority is that the words of Group 3 of Schedule 7 must be given their strict meaning and that the test to be applied is to ask oneself the question posed by those words, namely: Are these components or either of them suitable for use as parts of boat trailers? Having regard to the evidence that they are so used, the minority considers that this question admits only of an affirmative answer.'

There is then a reference to a decision of the London tribunal, and the decision in the present case goes on:

'But the principle underlying that decision, which the minority would follow, is that once a suitability in connection with boats has been established other suitabilities are irrelevant. Furthermore in relation to the [taxpayer company's] argument based on the presumed intentions of Parliament it seems to the minority that, so far as any intention is to be collected from the wording of Group 3, such intention is contrary to that contended for by the [taxpayer company]: where exceptions are intended they are clearly specified in item 6 by reference to item 5 of Group 1. Accordingly the minority would dismiss this appeal. The majority of the tribunal, on the other hand, has approached the matter from the point of view that the two items in question are predominantly of a general industrial nature and suitability and that their use in connection with boat trailers is a comparatively recent superimposition upon such general industrial use and suitability: their use and suitability in connection with boat trailers is accordingly, in the judgment of the majority, subordinate to such general use and the words "suitable for use as parts of goods" where they appear in item 6 should be construed accordingly. In reaching this conclusion the majority does not consider that such suitability and use in boat trailers is de minimis: that would be contrary to the evidence. But upon the tribunal's unanimous findings of fact such suitability and use are subordinate to the general industrial use and the word "suitable" in item 6 should be given a restricted construction as meaning "designed" or "adapted": if a wide construction were to be accorded to the word "suitable" in the context of item 6 the effect would not only be to bring many articles of general industrial application within the higher rate of tax but also to lead to articles formerly subject to the standard rate coming overnight into the higher rate by reason of the discovery that they were capable of being used as parts of higher rated goods.'

As I have said, there was a difference of opinion in the Divisional Court. Watkins J said[1]:

---

1   [1978] 1 All ER 204 at 207, [1978] 1 WLR 56 at 60, [1977] STC 485 at 488

'So the sole point in issue is whether the word "suitable" as used in the 1975 Act bears its commonly understood meaning, that is "suited for" or "well fitted for", or has it to be construed more strictly as meaning "designed" or "adapted" .'

He then set out the facts found, the relevant statutory provisions, the decision of the tribunal, and the contentions of the parties. He quoted from the speech of Lord Reid in *Luke v Inland Revenue Comrs*[1], as to the circumstances in which it is legitimate to 'do some violence' to the words of a statute. O'Connor J also quoted this passage, and drew the opposite conclusion from it as applied to this case. Watkins J stated his conclusion thus[2]:

'I have come, though bereft of enthusiasm for it, to the conclusion that the decision of the tribunal was wrong. I am not sure that the intention of Parliament was other than to bring about the result which the ordinary meaning of the word "suitable" produces. So I am not prepared to do a violence to it by giving this ordinary, well-understood English word a meaning which I do not believe it either has or should have. To do so would, in my opinion, blur the distinction which undoubtedly exists between the word "suitable" and the equally well-understood and different words "adapted" and "designed". If, as I believe, Parliament has produced, either intentionally or unwittingly through bad drafting of parts of Sch 7, an absurd and unjust application of the higher rate of value added tax it should by order, as it is entitled to do, right the wrong. And the sooner the better. I observe that the facts in *Luke's* case are vastly different from those which confront this court. And I add, with respect, that the doing of violence to well-understood English words used in a statute should I think be sparingly done and only done when the intention of Parliament is obvious and would be thwarted were it not for the draftsman's failure to use a word which precisely and aptly produces the intended effect of the legislation under consideration. I do not believe the instant case demands such intervention from this court. I would allow the appeal.'

Lord Widgery CJ agreed that the appeal should be allowed. He said[3]:

'I accept that for an article to be an accessory to goods within item 1 or item 2 of Group 3, that article must be designed or adapted to such use. No other guidance is supplied by the Finance (No 2) Act 1975, and I think that this is the plain meaning of "accessory". When one comes to deal with parts of goods under item 6 of Group 3, the only requirement is that they be "suitable" for such use as parts. On my reasoning, so far, a trolley does not come within Group 3 unless designed or adapted for use as an accessory to a boat. Hence a coupling does not come within Group 3 unless it is suitable for use as part of a trolley so designed or adapted. I do not think that the coupling (or part) must, in addition, be designed or adapted for use in a trolley which is in turn designed or adapted as an accessory to a boat.'

O'Connor J, in his dissenting judgment, said[4]:

'The commissioners contend that the words "suitable for use as parts" must be given their ordinary meaning so that anything which is normally a component of a higher rated article inevitably is suitable for use as a part of it. In support of this contention, the commissioners point to the nuts and bolts exception and say that but for the exception all these everyday articles would be caught by the "suitable for use as parts" provision and themselves have to bear the higher rate of value added tax

---

1 [1963] 1 All ER 655 at 664, [1963] AC 557 at 577, 40 Tax Cas 630 at 646
2 [1978] 1 All ER 204 at 209–210, [1978] 1 WLR 56 at 63, [1977] STC 485 at 490–491
3 [1978] 1 All ER 204 at 210, [1978] 1 WLR 56 at 63, [1977] STC 485 at 491
4 [1978] 1 All ER 204 at 206, [1978] 1 WLR 56 at 59, [1977] STC 485 at 487

regardless of the use to which they were to be put. This is a powerful argument but, like the majority of the tribunal, I find that I cannot accept it. If an unrestricted meaning is given to the word "suitable", then the chargeability of the higher rate of tax becomes capricious and uncertain. That a restricted meaning must be given to many of the provisions of the 1975 Act is I think clear; the instant case provides an example. It is only trailers that are accessories to boats that are chargeable with the higher rate of tax. What makes a trailer an accessory to a boat? It cannot be the mere capacity of having a boat loaded on it for that would catch every trailer in the land. To my mind the only workable construction is to say that it is only trailers which are designed or adapted for the carriage of boats that can be accessories of boats. Let me give another example. Group 1, item 1(c) expressly exempts electric water heaters ordinarily installed as fixtures. Many yacht marinas and caravan sites provide electric power points for their customers. If an electric water heater is installed in a boat or caravan, I have no doubt that it becomes a part of it, and if "suitable" is given an unrestricted meaning we have the absurd result of one section of the schedule expressly exempting electric water heaters and by a sidewind two other groups of the same schedule imposing the tax on that article. See Group 3, item 6 and Group 4, items 1, 2 and 3 and the notes to items 1 and 2.'

O'Connor J then quoted the same passage from the speech of Lord Reid in *Luke v Inland Revenue Comrs*[1] which Watkins J quoted, and went on[2]:

'If I am right in the view that I have formed that the trailers themselves must be designed or adapted for the carriage of boats, then it seems to me permissible to hold that "Goods suitable for use as parts" of such trailers only become suitable if they are themselves designed or adapted for such use. The nuts and bolts exception will bite on parts which are so designed or adapted and a rational interpretation of Sch 7 is achieved. For these reasons I would dismiss this appeal.'

Counsel for the taxpayer company submits that the results of the construction put forward by the Crown and accepted by the majority of the Divisional Court are so absurd and unjust that Parliament cannot have intended them. These results also affect Groups 1, 2, 4 and 5, which all contain exactly the same provision as Group 3, item 6. In particular he relies on: (1) the fact that the couplings and winches with which this appeal is concerned are predominantly used for purposes which have nothing to do with boats; if the majority of the Divisional Court is right, all of them will pay tax at the higher rate. (2) He suggests that any raw materials, such as wood, steel, or glass, which could be used as components in pleasure boats or their accessories, would pay tax at the higher rate. I do not think that raw materials which have to have something more done to them before they are 'suitable for use as parts' would be caught by the higher rate, even on the Crown's interpretation, but there must be many 'goods' (for example planks of wood or steel sections of particular dimensions) which are suitable for use in boats or boat trailers (or caravans: Group 4) without anything more being done to them. (3) The example given by O'Connor J of the electric water heater. I can see no convincing explanation of or answer to this anomaly.

Counsel for the Crown accepted that there may inevitably be anomalies in this legislation, but he submitted that they could be mitigated to an acceptable level or removed (a) by the power of the Treasury under s 17(2) and (4) of the 1975 Act to amend Sch 7, and (b) by the exercise by the commissioners of their administrative discretion in administering the tax.

As to (a), the existence of this power is, I think, a relevant factor in considering what was the intention of Parliament, but I doubt whether we are entitled to look at subsequent amendments actually made in deciding what that intention was; I think we can only look

---

1 [1963] 1 All ER 655 at 664, [1963] AC 557 at 577, 40 Tax Cas 630 at 646
2 [1978] 1 All ER 204 at 207, [1978] 1 WLR 56 at 60, [1977] STC 485 at 488

at the Act as enacted. Amendments have been made by a number of orders in 1975[1], 1976[2] and 1977[3].

We were helpfully supplied by counsel with an agreed document setting out the various amendments and the dates when they came into effect. Only the first of these orders[4] had come into force before what the parties agree was the relevant date in this case, the date when the goods in question were supplied on 11th February 1976. Its effect on Group 3 was to introduce an exception into item 5(d) and to exclude item 3 from item 10. It seems to me that none of the amendments which have subsequently been made, even if we are entitled to take them into account, affect the problem we have to decide. I think the most which can be said is that Parliament thought it right to give the Treasury power to amend the schedule, apparently in any way they thought fit, either by including or excluding items; it appears from counsel's agreed document that some of the amendments add to the exceptions from charge and others add new items to be charged. I find it impossible to say that this is a satisfactory answer to counsel for the taxpayer company's arguments on anomalies.

As to (b), I understand counsel for the Crown to be saying that the commissioners could and would deal with anomalies by not enforcing the law when they thought this inexpedient. This argument seems to raise echoes of the 17th century, when one of the great issues between King and Parliament was the general dispensing power, and I have no hesitation in rejecting it as an answer to counsel for the taxpayer company.

What the Crown is seeking in this case to charge at the higher rate are parts of accessories to pleasure boats. As O'Connor J pointed out, articles cannot be accessories to boats unless they are designed or adapted for use (or perhaps predominantly used) for purposes ancillary to boats, and it seems strange that parts not specifically designed or intended for use in connection with boats and predominantly used for other purposes should all be caught by the higher rate. Counsel for the taxpayer company submits that Group 3, item 6, only applies to goods which are specifically designed or intended by their manufacturer to be used as parts of pleasure boats or their accessories, or which are in fact predominantly used for that purpose.

The argument in favour of the Crown's interpretation can be simply stated. 1. 'Suitable' in its ordinary meaning means 'suited for' or 'well-fitted for', as Watkins J said in the Divisional Court[5]. 2. It is clear that the couplings and winches here in question are in this sense suitable for use as parts of trailers or trolleys which are accessories to pleasure boats, since they are in fact used to a measurable extent for that purpose. 3. Parliament has shown by the exceptions to Group 1, item 5 (incorporated by reference in Group 3, item 6) that it had in mind the problem of goods suitable for a number of different uses; those of such goods which are specified in these exceptions are excluded from the higher charge and any which are not so specified are subject to the higher charge. 4. When this schedule means 'designed' or 'adapted' it says so: see Group 3, item 1(b) and Group 4, item 2 ('designed') and Group 2, note (1), Group 3, item 2, and Group 5, note (1) ('adapted'). 5. Where in this schedule Parliament means goods suitable or used 'mainly' or 'solely' for some purpose, it says so: see Group 1, item 1, exception (j) ('goods suitable for domestic use as, and only as . . .') and Group 1, item 5(e) ('goods of a kind used mainly . . .').

This argument seemed to me for some time to be conclusive in favour of the Crown, but in the end I have come to the conclusion that it fails to take into account all the words of Group 3, item 6. If the item had read 'Goods suitable for use as parts . . .', it would be very

---

1 Value Added Tax (Higher Rate) Order 1975 (SI 1975 No 1297), Value Added Tax (Higher Rate) (No 2) Order 1975 (SI 1975 No 2010)

2 Value Added Tax (Consolidation) Order 1976 (SI 1976 No 128), art 5, Sch 3, Value Added Tax (Higher Rate) Order 1976 (SI 1976 No 2027)

3 Value Added Tax (Higher Rate) Order 1977 (SI 1977 No 1786), Value Added Tax (Consolidation) Order 1977 (SI 1977 No 2092)

4 SI 1975 No 1297

5 [1978] 1 All ER 204 at 207, [1978] 1 WLR 56 at 60, [1977] STC 485 at 488

difficult, if not impossible, to reject the Crown's interpretation in spite of the anomalies which I think it would produce. But this item reads 'Goods *of a kind* suitable for use in boats'. The words 'of a kind' must be intended to add something to the meaning of 'goods suitable'; in item 1, exception (*j*) and Group 4, item 1, 'suitable' is used without this addition. They must be intended either to widen or to limit 'Goods . . . suitable for use'. It might be argued that they are intended to widen the description; it might be said that all raw materials such as steel, wood or glass are 'of a *kind* suitable for use as parts of' boats, because some goods of that kind are suitable. This result is so absurd that it cannot have been intended. The only alternative is that they were intended to narrow the effect of the description. It seems to me that 'Goods of a kind' must refer to some class or category or genus of goods which has characteristics in common, and that it is necessary to identify the 'kind' to which the goods in question in any particular case belong. The question is then not whether the particular goods in question are 'suitable', but whether the 'kind' to which they belong is suitable. I cannot identify any 'kind' to which the couplings and winches here in question belong which is narrower than *all* couplings and winches. Many couplings and winches are not suitable for use as parts of pleasure boats or their accessories, and I am therefore of the opinion that the couplings and winches with which we are concerned are not 'Goods of a kind suitable for use as parts' within Group 3, item 6. There are no doubt goods (for example possibly some winches) which are solely or primarily designed or intended by their manufacturer, or in fact predominantly used, as parts of pleasure boats or their accessories. In such a case, it would be possible to identify such goods as a separate 'kind' (a sub-species so to speak of the 'kind' of winches generally) and (for example) winches of this sub-species would be 'goods of a kind suitable for use as parts'. This construction of 'Goods of a kind' seems to me to be consistent with the use of this phrase elsewhere in the schedule. In particular, I think it is supported by the exception in Group 3, item 1(*b*) of 'boats which are of a kind used solely as liferafts'. It seems to me likely that Parliament intended to except only boats specifically designed or intended for use as liferafts, and not all boats which simply happen to be so used. This construction would remove the anomalies pointed out by counsel for the taxpayer company. It would still leave ample scope for the operation of the exceptions in Group 1, item 5; when goods are identified as being 'of a kind suitable for use as parts' as I construe that phrase, components within the exceptions would still be exempted from the higher rate.

I would therefore allow the appeal, set aside the decision of the Divisional Court, declare that the supplies of the couplings and winches here in question are not liable to value added tax at the higher rate, and restore the decision of the tribunal.

This decision will not prevent the commissioners from recovering tax at the higher rate on all couplings and winches which are in fact used on pleasure boat trailers. The trailer as a whole will be charged at the higher rate, including these parts. What it will prevent is what I think the grossly unjust result that the commissioners are authorised to levy the higher rate on the great majority of these goods which are used for purposes which have nothing whatever to do with boats or boat trailers. In such cases the person who pays would be the ultimate user, unless he happens to be registered for value added tax.

WALLER LJ (read by Browne LJ). I agree with the judgment of Browne LJ and with that of Megaw LJ, which I have had the advantage of reading in draft. I will, however, express my own view shortly in my own words.

The question which arises for consideration in this case is whether trailer couplings and winches fall within the definition of item 6 of Group 3. Trailer couplings and winches are sold by the taxpayer company for a number of purposes but also for use in connection with boats. The tribunal found as a fact that the use for boats was measurable but that the predominant use was for purposes other than in connection with boat trailers. The effect of being higher rated would involve a higher rating for all trailer couplings and winches whether or not they were being used in connection with boats.

The phrase 'of a kind suitable for use as parts of goods' can have two possible meanings: (1) it may mean of a kind suitable for use in a boat even though it was designed for something quite different. This might be described as accidentally suitable for use in connection with boats; or (2) alternatively it may mean of a kind designedly suitable for use in a boat even though it can be used for other purposes. In other words, if it was designed for other purposes it would not come within this definition.

The first meaning is that contended for by the Crown and the second meaning is that contended for by the taxpayer company. If the former meaning is correct, it would mean that all the other users would have to pay the higher rate of value added tax and although some of them would be able to recover it back if they were registered for value added tax, there would be others who, having nothing to do with boats and aircraft, would be paying the higher rate with no chance of recovering it. In so far as the couplings or winches were being used for boats the Crown would suffer no loss of revenue on the alternative view, because when incorporated in a trailer or boat the higher rate would be paid on the whole article, including the coupling or winch.

It is said by the Crown that any anomalies resulting from this interpretation can be cured by regulation and that some have been cured since the passage of the 1975 Act. It is further said that the fact of making exceptions, for example Group 1, item 5, nuts and bolts etc, indicates that unless an article is specifically excepted it will be included in the definition. The reply is made to that that the exception of nuts and bolts etc is really put in out of an abundance of caution because such articles are of general use, not designed for any particular market, and to except them makes the position absolutely clear but does not affect the precise definition of 'suitable'.

In my opinion, the more limited meaning is that which should be adopted.

(1) The group, part of which it is claimed by the Crown produces this wide-reaching effect, is headed 'Boats and Aircraft', and under that heading are set out those goods which attract the higher rate of value added tax. I would expect to find anything designed to be suitable for boats or aircraft to be included under this heading. It would be surprising, to say the least, if, for example, a winch, which for years had been used largely for agriculture, was suddenly included because some winches were used for boat trailers. If the words compel such meaning I would accept it, but in my view they do not. As I have indicated above, the tribunal found that the predominant use was for purposes other than those in connection with boats, and this indicates that these trailer couplings and winches were designed for use other than in boats. It is anomalous to tax them at a higher rate because they happen to be useful in boats also.

(2) If the phrase 'suitable for use as parts of goods' is taken literally, it would cover a very wide range of goods; if taken literally it would apply to pieces of wood which were cut to particular lengths for manufacturing or repairing a trailer. It would apply to sheets of glass which were being cut to the size of a window for a boat or caravan, or to steel sections to fit a trailer. Taking the broad meaning each of these could be covered by the definition. But in my view the statute cannot have intended to cover all raw material of a kind I have mentioned. It would be very difficult for the supplier of wood to decide whether it was going to be used as parts of goods within item 5. The phrase, however, contains the words 'of a kind suitable for use as'. The words 'of a kind' must be given some meaning. The very wide meaning of 'suitable' could hardly be wider. Why, then, have the words 'of a kind' been added? 'Kind' suggests a limitation. It may mean description or genus. Therefore the description must be related to boats; it must be either of a description suitable for use or of a genus suitable for use in boats. The limitation is that it applies only to goods of a kind which are related to boats or aircraft.

(3) I also find the example quoted, and the reasoning adopted, by O'Connor J convincing. The argument by which it was sought to answer his reasoning was that electric water heaters do not become parts of goods within item 1 or item 5. However, when one looks at note (1) to Group 4, where the phrase 'removable contents of a kind not ordinarily installed as fixtures' is used, it would seem that electric water heaters might well be of a kind ordinarily installed as fixtures and therefore they would be part of the boat. Thus the anomaly would be that that which was taken out by Group 1, item 1(c) would be put back by the construction suggested by the Crown of Group 3, item 6.

Both the taxpayer company and the Crown have submitted that the alternative view produced anomalies; and there is no doubt that either interpretation does produce some anomalies. There was cited to us the dictum of Lord Reid in *Luke v Inland Revenue Comrs*[1], where he accepts that it is sometimes necessary to do some violence to the words of the statute. In my judgment it is not necessary to do violence to the words of the statute in this case. The ordinary meaning of 'suitable' of course, would have no restriction at all; but to make the kind of restriction which the taxpayer company argue would, in my view, remove many anomalies. It would make sense of the title to the group by restricting its application to articles which come within that group; it would avoid the fortuitous injustice of imposing a higher rate on winches and couplings which have nothing whatever to do with boats, and the argument of the Crown that it would be difficult to operate because of determining the design intended is, in my view, of very little substance. The difficulties, if they exist, would be comparatively small and the interpretation proposed by Megaw and Browne LJJ would avoid injustice.

MEGAW LJ. The relevant statutory provisions and facts have been set out in the judgment delivered by Browne LJ. I agree with his reasoning and conclusions.

It would in my opinion be odd, indeed, if Parliament intended by the formula used in item 6 of Group 3 in Sch 7 to render an article ('goods') subject to the higher rate of value added tax merely because it is incidentally suitable to be used as a part of a pleasure boat or a pleasure boat carrying trailer, despite the fact that the article, at and from the time of its manufacture, is likely to be used ('likely' representing odds of, say, 9 to 1 on, or possibly even greater odds) for one or other of a large variety of uses, all of which are unconnected with boats or boat carrying trailers. If it were not for the incidental suitability, the article would be subject only to the normal rate of value added tax. But, if the submission of the Crown is right as to the construction of the words used in item 6 of Group 3, the result would be that such an article would be subjected to the higher rate of tax.

If this is what Parliament intended, so be it. Yet, if the suggested interpretation were right, it would, in my view, lead to remarkable and substantial, not merely theoretical, anomalies, or even absurdities, such as were instanced by O'Connor J in his dissenting judgment in the Divisional Court. Thus, an electric water heater suitable for domestic use would be expressly excepted from the higher rate of duty by the provisions of Group 1, but would be subjected to the higher rate by the provisions of Group 3. That would produce what I think would be a novel problem for the courts to solve: where Parliament in one and the same Act says that the answer to the selfsame question is both 'Yes' and 'No'. For reasons which I shall give later, however, it seems to me that, fortunately, that insoluble problem does not arise, on the true interpretation of the words used.

Another very strange result, if the suggested interpretation were right, would, as was submitted in the argument of counsel for the taxpayer company, be this: that such ordinary articles of general use as pieces of timber, sheets of glass and steel sections would always be subject to the higher rate of tax. That would come about because a piece of timber could obviously be suitable for use as a part of a pleasure boat, for example, for deck planking; glass could be used for a boat window; a steel section for the making of a trailer for carrying a boat. Nobody, I think, would be disposed to deny that, if Parliament wished to make such articles as these subject to the higher rate of value added tax, irrespective of their particular use, the achieving of that result by way of Group 3, item 6, would be a remarkably indirect and tortuous way to reach the result.

During much of the argument, however, I thought that it was very difficult to escape from the conclusion that the words meant what was suggested by the Crown. This was particularly so because of the exception from item 6 of 'goods within the exceptions from item 5 of Group 1'. I found it hard to see any sensible purpose for providing those exceptions unless the opening words of item 6 had the meaning which was suggested for the Crown.

---

1 [1963] 1 All ER 655 at 664, [1963] AC 557 at 577, 40 Tax Cas 630 at 646

If the words used in item 6 had been 'Goods suitable for use as parts', the argument on behalf of the Crown, however unattractive its consequences, would have been, at least, very difficult to rebut. The coupling and the winch which are here the relevant articles (the 'goods') are in themselves and by themselves suitable, in any ordinary meaning of that word, for use as parts of the boats covered by item 1 or of the trailers covered, as accessories, by item 5(f).

But the words used in item 6 are not 'Goods suitable for use'. They are 'Goods *of a kind* suitable for use'. Presumably the three words 'of a kind' have not been introduced merely for elegance of prosody or to provide meaningless padding. They have been introduced in order to affect the meaning. They do affect the meaning. It is not 'the goods' (the particular articles, here the coupling and the winch) which have to be suitable for use as parts. It is the kind of goods to which those particular articles belong, their genus, which has to be thus suitable. The addition of 'of a kind' would be meaningless if goods which are themselves suitable are necessarily also goods of a kind which is suitable. So the question is not whether the particular articles are suitable. The question is, first, what is the relevant 'kind of goods' of which they are members; and, secondly, is that kind of goods, generically, suitable for use as parts of the goods comprised in items 1 and 5 of Group 3.

How then do you ascertain what is the relevant kind, what is the relevant genus, to which the specific articles belong? To identify the 'kind' to which a particular article belongs, you must ascertain first what is the common characteristic which turns a collection of individual articles into a 'kind'. In the context of item 6 (and the other provisions of the schedule where the words 'goods of a kind' are used), the characteristic must relate to suitability for use for some purpose. Next, as the example given by O'Connor J demonstrates, a particular article cannot, for the purpose of these statutory provisions, be treated as belonging to more than one kind. If it could, the electric water heater which is suitable for domestic use and which can also be used as part of a boat would be both excluded from and included in the higher rate. The only way in which the relevant kind can be ascertained is by ascertaining what is the exclusive or primary purpose for which the specific article is made, or, perhaps, if this should be different, for which it is used. (We do not have to consider that alternative in this case; nor do we have to consider the case of an article which is made equally for two different purposes).

If the article (in the present case the coupling or the winch) is made exclusively or primarily for use as a part of the relevant boats or trailers, then that characteristic establishes and identifies its kind for the purpose of the schedule, including item 6. This article, and any other coupling or winch which, though not identical, is made exclusively or primarily for that use is 'goods of a kind' which falls within item 6 of Group 3 and which is thus subject to the higher rate. If it is made exclusively for some other use, no question can arise. If it is made primarily for some other use, then, even though it may incidentally be used suitably as a part of a relevant boat or trailer, it is not of a kind which falls within item 6. It is of a different kind for that purpose, and it cannot be of both kinds. If the article has no exclusive or primary use, but can suitably be used for any one of a number of different uses, none of them being its primary use, then its kind, the only 'kind' to which it can belong for the purpose of item 6, is a kind which includes all such multi-use articles. But it is no more a kind suitable for use as a part of relevant boats and trailers than it is a kind suitable for use as a part of a domestic hot water boiler or a farm tractor or whatever all and any of the other uses may be. It cannot be of more than one kind for the purpose of item 6. Therefore the article is not within item 6, at any rate if multi-purpose couplings or winches include among their number, as must be the case, couplings or winches which would not be suitable as use for parts of the relevant boats or trailers.

This meaning of item 6, as it seems to me, is not impossible, nor even difficult, to reconcile with the provisions of item 5 of Group 1, the exceptions wherein are expressly made exceptions to item 6 of Group 3. If it were not for the express exclusion of, for example, nuts, bolts, screws and nails from the higher rate of tax, those articles might well come (each and every one of them, whatever its intended or actual use) within that higher rate of tax, merely by reason of the fact that any nut, bolt, screw or nail whatever its shape, size or other qualities, could, quite possibly, be suitable for use as a part of some boat or trailer within Group 3, item 1 or item 5. So, even on my interpretation of 'goods of a kind' in item 6 of Group 3, all nuts, bolts etc, unless they were expressly excepted, could at least be in danger of coming, in their totality and in whatever actual use, within the higher rate of tax, as being 'goods of a kind suitable . . .' That, I assume, Parliament regarded as being at least undesirable, if not absurd. Hence these express exceptions in item 5 of Group 1. But if I am right about the intended, and the true, effect of the words 'of a kind' in item 6 (and elsewhere, where they occur, in the schedule) it was not necessary expressly to except the coupling and the winch with which we are here concerned, or other articles which similarly have a secondary or adventitious suitability for use as part of boats or trailers. It was not necessary because the kind of goods to which they are properly to be regarded as belonging is not a kind which is suitable; and the fact that the individual, specific, articles are incidentally suitable does not bring them within item 6.

I would therefore allow the appeal.

Appeal allowed. Decision of Divisional Court set aside. Declaration that the supplies of couplings and winches in question are not liable to value added tax at the higher rate. Decision of tribunal restored. Leave to appeal on terms as to costs.

Solicitors: *Porter, Hope & Porter*, Bolton (for the taxpayer company); *Solicitor for the Customs and Excise.*

Mary Rose Plummer Barrister.

Re Earl of Strafford (deceased)
Royal Bank of Scotland Ltd v Byng and others

COURT OF APPEAL, CIVIL DIVISION
BUCKLEY, LAWTON AND GOFF LJJ
14th, 17th, 18th, 20th JULY 1978

Trust and trustee – Power of trustee – Compromise – Exercise of power – Consideration for compromise – Consideration including surrender by adverse claimant of life interest under trust – Continuing interests under trust thereby accelerated – Whether compromise within power of trustee – Whether surrender effecting variation of trust – Trustee Act 1925, s 15(f).

By his will the testator settled lands and bequeathed all his chattels on trusts under which, inter alia, successive life interests were given to his daughters (the third and fourth defendants), then to a grandson (the first defendant), and then to other grandsons (the fifth and sixth defendants). The third and fourth defendants were also entitled absolutely to the estate of their mother, the testator's wife. The testator and his wife owned many works of art and other valuable chattels; some belonged to the testator and some to his wife. After their deaths in 1951, the third and fourth defendants allocated certain chattels to the wife's estate and the remainder to the testator's estate. Subsequently it appeared that the chattels allocated to the wife's estate might have belonged to the testator, and a dispute arose as to whether those chattels formed part of the testator's estate. In 1968 under a scheme of arrangement all the property passing under the testator's will became the property of an estate company (the second defendant). Because of doubts whether disputed chattels found to belong to the testator's estate fell within the scheme and passed to the second defendant or should be held on the original will trusts, the third to sixth defendants put forward to the trustee of the testator's will proposed terms of compromise regarding the disputed chattels. Under those terms the trustee was to abandon its claim to approximately half the disputed chattels, and the other half was to be held on the testator's will trusts with the qualification that the third and fourth defendants, the adverse claimants, and also the fifth and sixth defendants, were to surrender their life interests in the share of the chattels taken by the trustee. The first and second defendants opposed the compromise. The trustee sought the decision of the court whether the compromise should be accepted, and surrendered to the court its discretion to compromise under s 15[a] of the Trustee Act 1925. Megarry V-C[b] held, without going into the merits of the compromise, that he had jurisdiction to approve it on the ground that it was one which lay within the trustee's power under s 15. The first and second defendants appealed, contending (i) that without the surrender of the life interests the compromise would not reflect the strength of the trustee's claim to all the disputed chattels and (ii) that s 15 only conferred administrative powers on a trustee and did not empower him to compromise a claim to trust property in consideration of the surrender by the adverse claimants of their life interests under the trust, without the consent of all the beneficiaries, because that would constitute a variation of the trust which was outside the scope of the trustee's power under s 15.

Held – The surrender of a limited interest under a settlement did not of itself have the effect of varying the trusts of the settlement but merely eliminated a pre-existing interest while leaving the trusts intact. Since s 15 of the 1925 Act conferred on a trustee wide and flexible powers of compromising and settling disputes, subject to exercising those powers with due regard to the interest of the beneficiaries, a trustee was entitled, in determining

---

a   Section 15, so far as material, is set out at p 517 *d e,* post
b   [1978] 3 All ER 18

whether a compromise of a dispute over assets was justifiable under s 15, to weigh the extent by which the value of the recovered assets under the compromise fell short of the true measure of the trustee's prospect of success on the claim against the advantages obtained for the continuing beneficiaries from the acceleration of their interests by the surrender under the compromise of prior life interests under the trust. The fact that the value of the surrendered interests could not be reflected in the capital account of the fund was not a ground for excluding them from consideration in determining whether the compromise was beneficial to the continuing beneficiaries. It followed that neither s 15 nor any general principle of law restricted the trustee's exercise of its discretion under s 15, and accordingly the court had jurisdiction to direct the trustee to implement the compromise. The appeal would therefore be dismissed (see p 520 g to p 521 a and f to j, p 522 d to f, p 523 c to f and p 524 c, post).

Chapman v Chapman [1954] 1 All ER 798 distinguished.

Decision of Megarry V-C [1978] 3 All ER 18 affirmed.

Notes

For a trustee's power to compromise a claim, see 38 Halsbury's Laws (3rd Edn) 1021, para 1760, and for cases on the subject, see 47 Digest (Repl) 426, 3086–3087.

For the Trustee Act 1925, s 15, see 38 Halsbury's Statutes (3rd Edn) 118.

Cases referred to in judgments

Chapman v Chapman [1954] 1 All ER 798, [1954] AC 429, [1954] 2 WLR 723, 33 ATC 84, 47 R & IT 310, HL; *affg sub nom Re Chapman's Settlement Trusts, Chapman v Chapman* [1953] 1 All ER 103, [1953] Ch 218, [1953] 2 WLR 94, CA, 47 Digest (Repl) 329, 2973.

Craven's Estate, Re, Lloyds Bank Ltd v Cockburn (No 2) [1937] 3 All ER 33, [1937] Ch 431, 106 LJ Ch 311, 47 Digest (Repl) 372, 3332.

Walker, Re, Walker v Duncombe [1901] 1 Ch 871, 70 LJ Ch 417, 84 LT 193, 28(2) Digest (Reissue) 753, 866.

Cases also cited

National Provincial Bank Ltd v Hyam [1942] 2 All ER 224, *sub nom Re Ezekiel's Settlement Trusts, National Provincial Bank v Hyam* [1942] Ch 230, CA.

Owens, Re, Jones v Owens (1882) 47 LT 61, CA.

Appeal

This was an appeal by Julian Michael Edmund Byng ('the first defendant') and Wrotham Park Settled Estates ('the second defendant') against the judgment of Megarry V-C[1] given on 10th May 1978 declaring that the court had jurisdiction under s 15 of the Trustee Act 1925, notwithstanding the opposition of the first and second defendants, to direct the plaintiff, the Royal Bank of Scotland Ltd ('the trustee'), the sole trustee of the will trust of the sixth Earl of Strafford, deceased ('the testator'), to compromise a claim to the ownership of disputed chattels put forward by the Honourable Florence Elizabeth Alice Byng ('the third defendant') and the Honourable Mary Millicent Rachel Naylor ('the fourth defendant'), the adverse claimants to the chattels, and their children, the fifth and sixth defendants. The seventh and eighth defendants were entitled under the will to successive life interests on the conclusion of the interest of the sixth defendant, and the ninth defendant to an entailed estate on the conclusion of the interest of the eighth defendant. The grounds of the appeal were, inter alia, that s 15 conferred administrative powers only and did not authorise a trustee, or the court where the trustee had surrendered his discretion to the court, to enter into a compromise of a dispute the terms of which effected a variation of the beneficial interest subsisting under the trust, that the terms of the compromise did effect a variation of the will trusts, and that Megarry V-C had erred in law in holding that he had jurisdiction to direct the trustee to compromise the claim. The facts are set out in the judgment of Buckley LJ.

1 [1978] 3 All ER 18

Edward Nugee QC and *David Lowe* for the first and second defendants.
Peter Horsfield QC for the trustee.
Robert Walker for the third to sixth defendants.
The seventh to ninth defendants did not appear.

BUCKLEY LJ. The sixth Earl of Strafford ('the testator') died on 24th December 1951, some two months after his wife ('the countess'), who died on 2nd October 1951. The third and fourth defendants in these proceedings, Lady Elizabeth Byng and Lady Mary Naylor, are his two daughters. They are the legal personal representatives of their mother, the countess, and under her will they are absolutely entitled to her estate in equal shares. The plaintiff, the Royal Bank of Scotland Ltd ('the trustee'), is the sole executor and trustee of the will of the testator. By that will, by cl 3, he devised his mansion house, Wrotham Park in the County of Middlesex, and his house in St James's Square, on trusts under which the countess, if she had survived him, would have taken a life interest, with remainder on trust to secure a jointure for each of his daughters, and subject thereto on trusts under which the third defendant took a first life interest, and subject thereto the fourth defendant took a life interest, subject to which the first defendant, Mr Julian Byng, who is the son of the third defendant, took a life interest; after which Mr Christopher Naylor, a son of the fourth defendant, took a life interest; after which Mr Edmund Naylor, her other son took a life interest; after which, in the events which have happened, the present earl took a life interest (he is a collateral relation of the other parties, being a descendant, I think, of the fifth earl); after which his son, Viscount Enfield took a life interest (they are the seventh and eighth defendants); after which Lord Enfield's son, the ninth defendant, took an entailed estate.

By cl 5 of the will the testator bequeathed all his chattels, subject to certain exceptions which I need not refer to, on trust that they should devolve with the settled land. There were a considerable number of works of art and other valuable chattels in and about the houses of the testator and countess, some of which were considered to belong to him and some to her, and after both the testator and the countess had died the third and fourth defendants arrived at decisions as to which of these chattels belonged to the estate of their mother, the countess, and which belonged to the estate of their father, the testator, and the allocations which they then made of these chattels to the two estates were acted on, they taking under their mother's will those chattels which were allocated to her estate as their own absolute property.

Since that time it appears that evidence has been found which at any rate suggests that some of the chattels so allocated to the countess's estate were in fact the property of the testator; it is said that some of these chattels, notwithstanding that they came from sources connected with the countess's family, had nevertheless been bought by the testator, either from her late father or on the market, so that those chattels were in truth his property and not the property of the countess; and so a dispute has arisen whether a considerable number of articles of value form part of one estate or part of the other. We are told that the value of the disputed chattels is upwards of £170,000 in the aggregate.

In 1968 an order was made under the Variation of Trusts Act 1958, varying the trusts of the will of the testator. Under that scheme of arrangement all the property which passed under the will of the testator has become the property of the second defendant, Wrotham Park Settled Estates, which is an incorporated company; but there is a doubt whether that scheme of arrangement extends to, and has any effect on, the disputed chattels so far as they belonged to the estate of the testator.

In these circumstances the trustee took out an originating summons in March 1976, asking for directions whether it should institute proceedings against the third and fourth defendants and any other and what persons, to recover the disputed chattels. In those proceedings all the persons having interests under the original will trusts affecting the settled estate were made defendants, including the third and fourth defendants. When that summons came before the judge the third and fourth defendants, although parties to the proceedings, were excluded from any contentious discussion of the matter and Megarry V-C, before whom the matter came, indicated at that stage that he considered that a sufficient case had been shown to justify the bringing of proceedings against the third and fourth defendants.

At the time of that hearing the advisers of the third and fourth defendants had been permitted to see the uncontroversial evidence filed in support of the summons, but not the bulk of the evidence, which dealt with the position in relation to the dispute. Counsel for the third and fourth defendants asked to be allowed to see that evidence on the ground that this was a family dispute and should be dealt with in that way. The trustee supported that application but the judge, having seen and studied the evidence, decided that he would not accede to that application and he then indicated that he thought that proceedings should be instituted, but he granted an adjournment to allow counsel for the third and fourth defendants to obtain instructions, particularly in relation to the question whether those proceedings should be taken by way of originating summons or whether the matter should be litigated in an action commenced by writ with the full panoply of pleadings.

The matter came back before Megarry V-C on 7th and 14th November, when counsel for the third and fourth defendants, who was also appearing for the fifth and sixth defendants, indicated that his clients would not consent to the proceedings being by way of originating summons and urged that the proceedings should be by way of a full-scale action commenced by writ. Megarry V-C then varied his directions with regard to access to the evidence which had been filed on the summons, and directed that counsel for the third, fourth, fifth and sixth defendants should be allowed to see the controversial evidence in the case and he directed that the proceedings to be taken by the trustee against the third and fourth defendants should be by way of originating summons on which an enquiry might be directed as to which of the disputed chattels constituted part of the estate of the testator. No appeal was taken from that decision of Megarry V-C, and accordingly that is the way in which the matter would have proceeded; but that course of proceeding was overtaken by events, because on 27th February 1978 the solicitors for the third, fourth, fifth and sixth defendants wrote a letter to the trustee putting forward proposed terms of compromise of the dispute relating to the ownership of the chattels. The nature of the proposal was stated by Megarry V-C in the course of his judgment as follows[1]:

'Broadly the terms are, first, that the [trustee] should abandon the claim as regards those chattels which the third and fourth defendants have either sold or given away. Second, that subject to the third defendant retaining her life interest in certain items, and subject to enough of the other chattels being sold to pay the costs of these proceedings, the remaining chattels should be divided as to one-fifth to the third and fourth defendants absolutely, and as to the remaining four-fifths to the [trustee] to hold on the trusts of the testator's will, with the important qualification that neither the third nor fourth defendants (nor the fourth defendant's sons) would claim any interest under those trusts. There would thus in effect be a surrender by the third and fourth defendants of their respective life interests in the remaining four-fifths, with the consequent acceleration of the first defendant's life interest in them from third place to first.'

The letter in question gave what were described as rough estimates of the values of the various categories into which the chattels were to be divided for the purposes of the proposed compromise, the result of which is that under the compromise the trustee would abandon its claim to approximately half the disputed chattels and that the other half should be held on the trusts applicable to the estate of the testator, the third defendant retaining a life interest in certain specific items which she desired to enjoy for the remainder of her life.

Perhaps it is convenient to say at this point that neither the first defendant nor the second defendant the estate company, would resist the suggestion that the third defendant should be allowed to enjoy the use of those chattels during the remainder of her life.

That compromise having been proposed, the matter was restored to Megarry V-C, and

---

1   [1978] 3 All ER 18 at 19–20, [1978] 3 WLR 224 at 225

the trustee surrendered to him its discretion under s 15 of the Trustee Act 1925, asking for directions whether it should enter into the compromise or not.

The matter was heard for five days in chambers; it was adjourned into court for Megarry V-C to give judgment[1] confined to the question whether in the circumstances the court had jurisdiction to approve the compromise, or direct the trustee to enter into the compromise, under s 15 of the 1925 Act. Megarry V-C came to the conclusion that the court had such jurisdiction, and on 10th May 1978 he made an order declaring that the court had jurisdiction under s 15 of the 1925 Act, notwithstanding the opposition of the first and second defendants, to direct the trustee to compromise the claim referred to in the originating summons, that is to say, the claim as to ownership of the disputed chattels, on terms substantially similar to those set out in the letter to which I have referred. It is from that order that this appeal is brought. It will be appreciated that the only question which is raised is the question of jurisdiction, that is to say, the question of the scope of the discretion of a trustee under s 15 of the 1925 Act. The merits of the proposed compromise were not adjudicated on by Megarry V-C in his judgment and we are not at this stage concerned with them.

Section 15 of the 1925 Act so far as relevant to the present case is in the following terms:

> 'A personal representative, or two or more trustees acting together, or, subject to the restrictions imposed in regard to receipts by a sole trustee not being a trust corporation, a sole acting trustee where by the instrument, if any, creating the trust, or by statute, a sole trustee is authorised to execute the trusts and powers reposed in him, may, if and as he or they think fit ... (d) accept any composition or any security, real or personal, for any debt or for any property, real or personal, claimed; or ... (f) compromise, compound, abandon, submit to arbitration, or otherwise settle any debt, account, claim, or thing whatever relating to the testator's or intestate's estate or to the trust; and for any of those purposes may enter into, give, execute, and do such agreements, instruments of composition or arrangement, releases, and other things as to him or them seem expedient, without being responsible for any loss occasioned by any act or thing so done by him or them in good faith.'

No assessment has been made, or at any rate, no such assessment has been formulated before us, of the measure of the plaintiff's prospect of success in its claim to the disputed chattels. Before Megarry V-C it seems that the argument proceeded on the basis that the measure could not be better than an 85% chance; indeed, the identity of the disputed chattels has not yet been defined, for there has not yet been any enquiry which would result in identifying the chattels which the trustee ought to claim as being property of the testator.

Counsel for the first two defendants, the appellants in this court, submits that without the surrender of the life interest of the third, fourth, fifth and sixth defendants in the chattels which are to be taken by the trustee under the compromise, the compromise would not reflect the strength of the trustee's claim against the adverse claimants. This may have been the basis of the discussion before Megarry V-C, but I do not think we can regard this as certain.

Counsel for the first two defendants further submits that s 15 of the 1925 Act confers only administrative powers on a trustee and he says that consequently a trustee cannot in the exercise of his discretion under that section accept as part of the consideration for a compromise a surrender of an interest under the trust of which he is a trustee without the consent of all the other beneficiaries. In support of this he says that property recovered as the result of the prosecution or the compromise of a claim must be brought into the trust accounts as an asset of the trust, which could not be done in relation to a surrendered

---

1   [1978] 3 All ER 18, [1978] 3 WLR 224

beneficial interest where such surrender forms part of the consideration for the compromise of a claim. Counsel for the first two defendants says that, although trustees have an undoubted power to compound claims against other parties where this is for the benefit of the trust estate, and he has referred us to some of such cases, they have no power, either under the general law of equity, or by statute, to abandon any part of a claim to property as an asset of their trust in consideration of a beneficiary giving up a beneficial interest under the trust. He referred us to the statutory predecessors of s 15 of the 1925 Act; that is to say to s 30 of Lord Cranworth's Act[1], the Conveyancing and Law of Property Act 1881, s 37 and the Trustee Act 1893, s 21; and he cited *Re Craven's Estate, Lloyds Bank Ltd v Cockburn (No 2)*[2], where Farwell J said of s 57 of the 1925 Act that the word 'expedient' in that section means expedient for the trust as a whole. In this connection counsel criticised what Megarry V-C said in his judgment where he said[3]:

> 'The only question on jurisdiction is whether what is done falls fairly within the words of the section, such as the term "compromise . . . any . . . claim". Second, in exercising the power, the only criterion is whether the compromise is fair as regards all the beneficiaries.'

Counsel suggested that that put on the word 'expedient' in s 15 a different interpretation from the interpretation placed by Farwell J on the same word in s 57 in *Re Craven's Estate*[4]. I cannot myself see any grounds for distinction. 'Expedient for the trust as a whole' must mean, it seems to me, the same as 'expedient in the interests of all the beneficiaries under the trust', provided that it be kept in mind that, in considering the interests of the beneficiaries collectively, trustees must take into account the effect of what is proposed on the several individual interests of the beneficiaries and hold the scale fairly between them.

Counsel for the first two defendants further contended that the only purpose and effect of the statutory provisions which I have mentioned was to simplify conveyancing practice by conferring a statutory power on trustees which skilful draftsmen before 1860 were accustomed to provide for in express terms in trust instruments; and he said that the various statutory provisions displayed no intention to confer on trustees power to give up a claim to trust property in consideration of a surrender of a beneficiary's interest under the trusts. He went on to contend that the court itself has limited powers to authorise trustees to depart from the strict letter of their trust, and that it should not be supposed that the statutes were intended to confer wider powers on trustees than the court itself possessed.

In this connection he referred us to *Chapman v Chapman*[5], both in this court, and in the House of Lords. The effect of the decision in that case is perhaps most concisely stated by Lord Simonds LC where he said this[6]:

> 'The major proposition I state in the words of one of the great masters of equity, FARWELL, J., in *Re Walker*[7]: "I decline to accept any suggestion that the court has an inherent jurisdiction to alter a man's will because it thinks it beneficial. It seems to me that is quite impossible." It should then be asked what are the exceptions to this rule. They seem to me to be reasonably clearly defined. There is no doubt that the Chancellor (whether by virtue of the paternal power or in the execution of a trust, it matters not) had, and exercised, the jurisdiction to change the nature of an infant's property from real to personal estate and vice versa, though this jurisdiction was generally so exercised as to preserve rights of testamentary disposition and of succession. Equally, there is no doubt that, from an early date, the court assumed the power, sometimes for that purpose ignoring the direction of a settlor, to provide

---

1   23 & 24 Vict c 145 (Powers of Trustees, Mortgagees etc) (1860)
2   [1937] 3 All ER 33 at 42, [1937] Ch 431 at 436
3   [1978] 3 All ER 18 at 22, [1978] 3 WLR 224 at 229
4   [1937] 3 All ER 18, [1937] Ch 431
5   [1953] 1 All ER 103, [1953] Ch 218; [1954] 1 All ER 798, [1954] AC 429
6   [1954] 1 All ER 798 at 802, [1954] AC 429 at 445
7   [1901] 1 Ch 871 at 885

maintenance for an infant, and, rarely, for an adult, beneficiary. So, too, the court had power in the administration of trust property to direct that by way of salvage some transaction unauthorised by the trust instrument should be carried out. Nothing is more significant than the repeated assertions by the court that mere expediency was not enough to found the jurisdiction. Lastly, and I can find no other than these four categories, the court had power to sanction a compromise by an infant in a suit to which that infant was a party by next friend or guardian ad litem. This jurisdiction, it may be noted, is exercisable alike in the Queen's Bench Division and the Chancery Division and whether or not the court is in course of executing a trust.'

That statement of the law was elaborated at greater length by Lord Morton in his speech[1], with which Lord Simonds LC expressly agreed[2].

The decision was to the effect that a judge of the Chancery Division—

'. . . has no inherent jurisdiction, in the execution of the trusts of a settlement, to sanction, on behalf of infant beneficiaries and unborn persons, a rearrangement of the trusts of that settlement for no other purpose than to secure an adventitious benefit (e.g., that estate duty payable in a certain event will, in consequence of the rearrangement, not be payable in respect of the trust funds) [and that] The power of the court to sanction a compromise by an infant in a suit to which he is a party cannot be extended to cover cases in which there is no real dispute as to rights but in which it is sought by way of bargain between the beneficiaries to rearrange the beneficial interests under the trust instrument and to bind infants and unborn persons.'[3]

Those propositions are of course now indisputable; the question is how far they are applicable in the present case.

There is a doubt, at present unresolved and one which has not been judicially investigated, whether such of the disputed chattels as belonged to the testator's estate are held on the will trusts in their original form or are caught by the scheme of arrangement, in which event they belong to the second defendant absolutely. The proposed compromise does not touch this. The question is expressly left open by the letter of 27th February 1978. In the first alternative there is no doubt about what the will trusts are. In the latter alternative there is no doubt that the second defendant is in equity entitled absolutely to such of the disputed chattels as belong to the testator's estate. The unresolved doubt does not, however, depend only on the construction of the scheme of arrangement, but also, apparently, on whether the scheme itself may be liable to rectification.

The dispute which is sought to be compromised at the present stage is not a dispute between beneficiaries or those claiming to be beneficiaries under the trusts, but a dispute between the trustee and claimants whose claims are adverse to the trusts. It so happens that the adverse claimants are also beneficiaries under the will trusts in their original form, but this does not affect the fact that the claim sought to be compromised is not one between beneficiaries but one against the trust estate. Had the proposed compromise been merely that the trustee should abandon its claim to, say, one half in value of the disputed chattels and that the adverse claimants, that is, the third and fourth defendants, should abandon their claims to the other half, there could be no doubt that the trustee could effect such a compromise or composition under s 15 provided that it considered in good faith that such a compromise was beneficial to the trust estate, that is to say, to all the beneficiaries in accordance with their several interests in the trust estate. Can the inclusion in the proposed compromise of a term that the adverse claimants and the fourth and fifth defendants shall surrender their life interests in that part of the chattels to be taken by the trustee exclude the compromise from the scope of the trustee's discretion under the section? The first two

---

1   [1954] 1 All ER 798 at 810, [1954] AC 429 at 456
2   [1954] 1 All ER 798 at 800, [1954] AC 429 at 442
3   [1954] AC 429 at 430

defendants so contend. The argument is based on a contention that if the surrender of the life interests is a necessary part of the consideration for the compromise, without which the consideration would be insufficient, it must follow that the share of the chattels to be taken by the trustee does not, by itself, reflect the value of the trustee's prospect of success in its claim to the disputed chattels. Consequently the trustee would be giving up part of its claim to the disputed assets in return for the surrenders which, it is contended, would involve an impermissible variation by the trustee of the beneficial interest under the trust, without the consent of the beneficiaries affected.

The argument is illustrated by counsel for the first and second defendants by means of a fictitious example: suppose a residuary estate be settled on A for life with remainder to B absolutely, and suppose that the testator has a claim against A for the sum of £10,000, in respect of which the claim is a strong claim but not certain of success in litigation; and that the value of the claim should therefore be discounted by 15%, making its value £8,500. Various solutions might emerge. The trustees could undoubtedly accept £8,500 in settlement of the claim, and the trustees having become entitled to £8,500 in cash from A, A and B between them could agree to partition that sum, A taking £4,500 and B taking £4,000. Such a partition would be one arrived at by a free agreement between A and B and would not be imposed by the trustees on them. Or A, B and the trustees could, by a tripartite arrangement, achieve the same result, A paying £4,000 to the trustees to be held immediately on trust for B absolutely. Or A might be unwilling to pay the trustees more than, say, £4,000 but be willing to surrender his life interest in that sum. In such circumstances can the trustee bind B to the compromise by accepting the £4,000 from A in conjunction with a surrender of his life interest? Counsel for the first two defendants submits that this clearly could not be the case if the £4,000 was not the most that could be recovered from A, and that by agreeing to such a compromise the trustee would be effecting a variation of the trusts of the settlement, B getting something different from what the testator gave him.

Just so, it is contended in the present case that the trustee cannot without the consent of all the beneficiaries bind any of them under s 15 by a compromise under which what will be recovered as part of the capital of the trust fund is less in value than the measure of the trustee's prospect of success in its claim against the third and fourth defendants to recover all the disputed chattels, for if the value of what is recovered is less than the measure of the trustee's prospect of success the trustee will, it is said, be imposing on non-consenting beneficiaries a partition between the third and fourth defendants as adversely claiming life tenants on the one hand and non-consenting remaindermen on the other of the value of the trustee's claim against the third and fourth defendants.

In my judgment this argument, ingenious as it is, proceeds on too narrow an interpretation of s 15 and a misapplication of the principles enunciated in *Chapman v Chapman*[1]. The language of s 15 is, it appears to me, very wide. It would, I think, be undesirable to seek to restrict its operation in any way unless legal principles require this, for it seems to me to be advantageous that trustees should enjoy wide and flexible powers of compromising and settling disputes, always bearing in mind that such a power, however wide, must be exercised with due regard for the interests of those whose interests it is the duty of the trustees to protect. I see nothing in the language of the section to restrict the scope of the power. Accordingly, any restriction must be found if anywhere, in the general law.

So I ask myself whether the proposed compromise conflicts in any way with any principle enunciated in *Chapman v Chapman*[1], or otherwise established. In my judgment the surrender of a limited interest under a settlement does not of itself have the effect of varying the trusts of that settlement. It eliminates a pre-existing interest under the

---

1   [1954] 1 All ER 798, [1954] AC 429

settlement, but leaves the trusts intact. A trustee cannot control or prohibit dealings by competent beneficiaries with their interests under the settlement. His obligation is to protect the interests which from time to time subsist under the trusts of the settlement. If the owner of a limited interest proposed to put an end to it by surrendering it, the trustees cannot prevent him from doing so and are only concerned to see that the rights which arise or are advanced in consequence of the surrender are given proper effect.

If the assets of a trust include a claim against some person, be he a stranger to the trust or a beneficiary under the trust, that claim is an asset of the trust. The trustees may enforce the claim, sell it, compromise it or compound it, or (if it be worthless) abandon it. In any case but the last the fruit of enforcing, selling or compromising the claim will replace the claim as an asset of the trust. None of these transactions involves any variation of the trusts or of the beneficial interests under them; there is merely a change in the composition of the trust fund. If the trustees compromise the claim at an unduly low level, they may be liable for breach of trust, but no variation of the trusts is involved. The trust fund will thenceforth comprise, in addition to other assets, the fruit of the compromise plus a claim against the culpable trustees. Maybe it would be possible in certain circumstances to get the compromise set aside, but otherwise the beneficiary's only remedy would be against the trustees personally.

Let me assume that in the present case the value of the share of the disputed chattels which the trustee will in consequence of the compromise hold on the trusts applicable to the testator's estate is sufficient to reflect the measure of the trustee's prospect of success in prosecuting its claim to all the disputed chattels. In this case the surrender of the life interests need not be relied on to justify the compromise. They constitute in effect a gratuitous addition to the consideration for the compromise. Moreover, the compromise must be justifiable whether the second defendant is absolutely entitled under the scheme of arrangement to the share of the chattels recovered by the trustee, or whether those chattels will be held on the original will trusts.

Now let me assume that the value of the share of the disputed chattels which will be held on the trusts applicable to the testator's estate is insufficient to reflect the measure of the trustee's prospect of success. In this case can the surrender of the life interest legitimately be taken into account in determining whether the compromise is a justifiable one for the trustee to enter into? I have already indicated my reasons for thinking that no inadmissible variation of the trusts of the testator's estate are involved. If the trustee were embarking on the enquiry with a view to exercising its own discretion under s 15, it would in my judgment be incumbent on the trustee to consider carefully all the consequences which would flow from the implementation of the compromise, including for instance its fiscal incidence and possibly the expenses which might attend the enjoyment of their interests by the successive beneficiaries. The trustee would then have to weigh against the extent by which the value of the recovered chattels fell short of the true measure of the prospect of the trustee's success on the claim, that is to say, the extent to which the capital of the trust property has been disappointed by the compromise, to the consequent disadvantage of the successive beneficiaries in relation to their several successive interests, against the advantages obtained by those beneficiaries respectively by reason of the acceleration of their interests. I do not regard the fact that the value of a surrendered limited interest cannot be reflected in the capital account of the trust fund as a ground for excluding it from consideration in determining whether a compromise is beneficial to those beneficiaries who have continuing interests under the trust. The surrendering life tenants are in effect assigning their interests to the trustee to the intent that they shall be applied to accelerating all succeeding interests. Each surrender is, or may be, a valuable benefit conferred on all those who have continuing interests under the trusts. It seems to me perfectly proper to take such a benefit into account in judging the propriety of the compromise. The trustee having in the present case surrendered its discretion to the court, the court should take these matters into consideration, just as the trustee should if there had been no surrender of discretion.

But it must, it seems to me, be borne in mind that, on the assumption that under the scheme of arrangement all the recovered chattels will belong to the second defendant absolutely, the purported surrender of the life interests will be valueless because on this assumption there will be no such interests to surrender. The assumption is, however, not yet established as valid. We are not in a position to judge how likely it is to be valid. It is suggested that it would be vigorously contested and with at least some, and possibly substantial, hope of success. It is said, therefore, that the second defendant might obtain some benefit from the purported surrender of the life interests, because this would eliminate four potential vigorous opponents to the second defendant's claim under the scheme of arrangement and leave only the first and ninth defendants.

I should have mentioned earlier that the interests under the will trusts of the seventh and eighth defendants have now all merged in the ultimate entailed interest of the ninth defendant as the result of dealings between those three defendants.

The elimination of the life interests would leave only the first and ninth defendants to dispute the second defendant's claim under the scheme of arrangement, and both of those defendants are known to be likely to favour a negotiated settlement of this question. These also would, I think, be considerations which it would be legitimate for the court to take into account in deciding how to act under s 15, giving them such weight as may be thought to be appropriate. Although the question is not one which the compromise seeks to dispose of, its existence is, it seems to me, relevant to the exercise of the discretion under s 15 in the manner I have indicated, but not to the scope of the power available to the trustee or the court under the section.

For these reasons I do not find any principle of law which should restrict the exercise by the trustee of the discretion conferred by s 15 in the present case. Accordingly, I am of the opinion that Megarry V-C was right in his conclusion that the court has jurisdiction under s 15 to direct the trustee to implement the proposed compromise. In so saying, I do not express any opinion as to how the judge should exercise his discretion, which must depend on his assessment, in the light of all the relevant circumstances, of the merits of the proposal. I would consequently dismiss this appeal.

LAWTON LJ. I agree with the judgment delivered by Buckley LJ, and have only one short comment to make. I make it knowing that, unlike my brethren, I bring to the elucidation of the issues in this appeal little more than a knowledge of the English language and some experience in the application of the canons of construction to statutes. That limited experience is, however, enough to enable me to form a judgment in this dispute.

I say that because as I see the problem, it turns on the construction of s 15 of the Trustee Act 1925. That section gives trustees a discretion to do six types of act; they are set out in the lettered paragraphs of the section. The opening words indicate that the trustees are to have a wide discretion in doing the specified acts. Not only are they to have a wide discretion to do them, but the concluding words of the section give them wide powers to carry out what they have decided to do.

The relevant power comes in para (f), and the relevant part is this: the trustees may, as they think fit, compromise a claim relating to the trust. The word 'compromise', according to the Concise Oxford Dictionary, means to settle disputes by mutual concessions. It follows, therefore, that if the trustee in this case is compromising the claim which it is making against the third, fourth, fifth and sixth defendants, there must be some making of mutual concessions. As the claim relates to chattels, it follows as a matter of construction, so it seems to me, that there must be the making of mutual concessions relating to the chattels.

What the proposed compromise comes to is this, that the trustee must give up approximately half of its claim; that is the concession which it is making.

The third, fourth, fifth and sixth defendants have also got to make a concession if there is to be a compromise. The concession which they are making is, as I understand it, that they are giving up their interest under the will in relation to the chattels which the trustee is to have. So, on the face of it, there is a compromise; and it is a compromise relating to the trust because it involves chattels which the trustee claims are part of the trust. Seemingly the proposed compromise is within the terms of s 15.

However, the trustee, though having a wide discretion must act fairly and reasonably,
and if it uses the power to compromise for purposes other than to procure a compromise,
it will be misusing the powers given by s 15.

The essence of counsel's case for the first and second defendants has been that what is
proposed is outside the terms of s 15 because it amounts to a variation of the trust. It is
conceded by the trustee and by counsel for the third, fourth, fifth and sixth defendants,
that the trustee cannot vary the terms of the trust under guise of compromising the
claim. It follows, therefore, that the central issue in this appeal is whether the compromise
constitutes a variation of the trust.

Every time trustees claim that certain property belongs to a trust, if they succeed, that
property will accrue to the trust, and if it accrues to the trust the beneficiaries under the
trust will get something more than they had before. But that result is not a variation of the
trust; and if, for the purposes of compromise, the trustees do not get as much as they hoped
to get and have to make concessions, the beneficiaries will not get as much as they might
have hoped to get; but that again does not, in my judgment, amount to a variation of the
trust. If the other parties to the dispute make a concession which adds something to the
corpus of the trust, then that again in my judgment does not vary the trust.

What is proposed should come about in this case is that the third and fourth defendants
and those claiming under them should surrender their interests in some of the disputed
chattels. That will make more property available for the other beneficiaries; but, as I have
already said, in my judgment it will not amount to a variation of the trust.

It is for those reasons, in addition to those advanced by Buckley LJ, that I would dismiss
this appeal.

GOFF LJ. I also agree.

I share the view expressed by Buckley LJ that the very wide words of s 15 of the Trustee
Act 1925 should be given a wide construction. They are indeed wide words, because there
is a provision in para (d) authorising the trustees to 'accept any composition or any security,
real or personal, for any debt or for any property, real or personal, claimed'; and then there
is a further power in para (f), in these terms: '. . . compromise, compound, abandon,
submit to arbitration, or otherwise settle any debt, account, claim, or thing whatever
relating to the testator's or intestate's estate or to the trust.' For my part, I do not see
anything in the proposed compromise which is outside the powers conferred by s 15.

Chapman v Chapman[1], on which counsel for the first and second defendants relied, is
distinguishable because there was in that case no dispute as to the rights of the parties at
all. The surrender of the life interests of the adverse claimants in this case is something
which they are entitled to do without the consent of anyone, and the argument on which
counsel's case for the first and second defendants rests is that in the circumstances it
involves a variation of the interests of the beneficiaries, because the compromise is, in
analysis, two things rolled into one: first, a compromise of the estate's claim against the
adverse claimants; and, secondly, a partition between the beneficiaries of the chattels
which, as the result of the first transaction, are left in the estate and subject to the trusts on
which it is held.

But I do not agree that that is a correct analysis. I do not think that the trustee, or the
beneficiaries, are partitioning either the estate's claim or the chattels themselves. All that
the trustee is doing is one thing, namely to compromise the estate's claim in respect of the
chattels.

Of course if, when the matter is further investigated, it appears that more is being given
up by the trustee than is justified by the prospects of success in litigation, and having regard
to the costs which will be involved and considerations of that nature, it will be for Megarry
V-C to consider whether or not in his view this is sufficiently offset by the surrender of the

_____

1   [1954] 1 All ER 798, [1954] AC 429

life interests, and whether the compromise as a whole is for the benefit of all the beneficiaries, but that, in my judgment, is a matter of merits, not jurisdiction.

The position is, of course, complicated by the doubt as to what trusts do indeed affect whatever chattels are, as the result of litigation or compromise, found to be part of the testator's estate, and if the estate company be the true beneficiary it can derive no direct benefit from the surrender of the life interests, for there are none to be surrendered. But it may nevertheless benefit from the fact that a compromise is achieved, and there is the indirect benefit suggested by counsel for the trustee, to which Megarry V-C will give such weight as he may think fit. It will be for him to consider whether, in his view, the compromise as a whole is for the benefit of all the beneficiaries, taking into account, of course, the fact that if the estate company be the beneficiary, there are, as I have observed, no life interests to be surrendered. But it is not for this court to fetter him in any way in the exercise of his discretion and, like Buckley LJ, I do not attempt to do so.

In my judgment, for the reasons Buckley and Lawton LJJ have given and for the reasons which I have briefly added, the proposed compromise, and any similar compromise is something which the trustee has the power to enter into under s 15, and of which the court may approve in the exercise of the discretion surrendered to it by the trustee.

I therefore agree that this appeal fails.

Appeal dismissed. Leave to appeal to the House of Lords refused.

Solicitors: *Farrer & Co* (for the trustee); *Boodle, Hatfield & Co* (for the first and second defendants); *Charles Russell & Co* and *Frere, Cholmeley & Co* (for the third to sixth defendants).

J H Fazan Esq Barrister.

R v Harbax Singh

COURT OF APPEAL, CRIMINAL DIVISION
ROSKILL LJ, ACKNER AND STOCKER JJ
10th AUGUST 1978

Criminal law – Bail – Absconding from bail – Crown Court's jurisdiction to deal with absconder – Whether Crown Court having jurisdiction to commit absconder summarily for criminal contempt of court – Bail Act 1976, s 6(5).

Section 6 of the Bail Act 1976 has created a new offence of absconding from bail which, under s 6(5)[a], may be punished either as a summary offence triable only in a magistrates' court, with additional power to commit for sentence to the Crown Court, or as if it were a criminal contempt of court, in which case the Crown Court may direct that summary proceedings be begun in a magistrates' court, or if it thinks fit, may commit the offender summarily without the necessity of proceedings in the Divisional Court, notwithstanding that there has been no contempt in the face of the court (see p 527 *a b* and *e* to *j*, post).

Notes

For contempt of court, see 9 Halsbury's Laws (4th Edn) para 87, and for cases on the subject, see 16 Digest (Repl) 17–18, 102–120.

For the jurisdiction of the Divisional Court to commit for contempt in criminal proceedings, see 9 Halsbury's Laws (4th Edn) para 89.

For the Bail Act 1976, s 6, see 46 Halsbury's Statutes (3rd Edn) 298.

Case referred to in judgment

Balogh v Crown Court at St Albans [1974] 3 All ER 283, sub nom *Balogh v St Albans Crown Court* [1975] QB 73, [1974] 3 WLR 314, 138 JP 703, CA, Digest (Cont Vol D) 253, 92a.

---

a   Section 6(5) is set out at p 525 *f*, post

Appeal

On 20th July 1978 at the Central Criminal Court before his Honour Judge Edward Clarke QC the appellant, Harbax Singh, admitted to failing to answer to his bail during his trial with others on charges of blackmail, robbery and assault. He was sentenced to three months' immediate imprisonment. He applied for leave to appeal against sentence on the grounds, inter alia, (i) that the judge had erred in treating the appellant's conduct as a criminal contempt of court in that the judge had no power under s 6 of the Bail Act 1976 summarily to commit an absconder to prison if there was no contempt in the face of the court, and (ii) that there was no immediate urgency justifying the judge in dealing summarily with the matter. The facts are set out in the judgment of the court.

Andrew Collins for the appellant.
J H Robbins for the Crown.

ROSKILL LJ delivered the following judgment of the court: This is an application by Harbax Singh for leave to appeal against a sentence of three months' imprisonment passed on him by his Honour Judge Edward Clarke QC at the Central Criminal Court on 20th July for the newly created offence of 'absconding', to use the word which appears in the side-note to s 6 of the Bail Act 1976. It is notorious that that statute has created problems for magistrates' courts and the Crown Court, but the present is the first case, so far as we are aware, in which this court has had to consider this offence.

Section 3(1) of the 1976 Act reads thus: 'A person granted bail in criminal proceedings shall be under a duty to surrender to custody, and that duty is enforceable in accordance with section 6 of this Act.' One therefore turns to s 6. The side note to s 6, which I have mentioned, reads 'Offence of absconding by person released on bail'. Curiously enough, that phrase is not mentioned in the substantive provision of the statute, and strictly the side-note is irrelevant for the purpose of construing the statute. Section 6 provides:

'(1) If a person who has been released on bail in criminal proceedings fails without reasonable cause to surrender to custody he shall be guilty of an offence . . .
'(3) It shall be for the accused to prove that he had reasonable cause for his failure to surrender to custody . . .'

Section 6(5), which is the important subsection for the purpose of the present appeal, reads thus:

'An offence under subsection (1) or (2) [I have not read sub-s (2) which is irrelevant] above shall be punishable either on summary conviction or as if it were a criminal contempt of court.'

Section 6(6) gives certain powers to magistrates' courts when dealing with the matter, and provides:

'Where a magistrates' court convicts a person of an offence under subsection (1) or (2) above the court may, if it thinks—(a) that the circumstances of the offence are such that greater punishment should be inflicted for that offence than the court has power to inflict, or (b) in a case where it commits that person for trial to the Crown Court for another offence, that it would be appropriate for him to be dealt with for the offence under subsection (1) or (2) above by the court before which he is tried for the other offence, commit him in custody or on bail to the Crown Court for sentence.'

Section 6(7) provides:

'A person who is convicted summarily of an offence under subsection (1) or (2) above and is not committed to the Crown Court for sentence shall be liable to imprisonment for a term not exceeding 3 months or to a fine not exceeding £400 or to both and a person who is so committed for sentence or is dealt with as for such a contempt shall be liable to imprisonment for a term not exceeding 12 months or to a fine or to both.'

The facts of this case fall within a narrow compass. According to the prosecution this man and others were involved on 31st January 1977 in offences of blackmail, robbery and assault. They were arrested and committed for trial to the Central Criminal Court; they were released on bail in their own recognisances and with sureties of £1,000 each. That trial was listed to come on at the Central Criminal Court on Thursday, 6th July 1978. But, no doubt through pressure of work, it did not start on that day. It began on Friday, 7th July 1978 before Judge Clarke and a jury. The applicant surrendered properly into the custody of that court on that day. The judge, equally properly, made a fresh order for bail under the 1976 Act and the applicant was on bail over the ensuing weekend. But unfortunately, and this is all the cause of the trouble, on the Sunday night, this is common ground, he went out and got not merely drunk but so drunk that his hangover on the Monday morning was such that he was incapable of appearing at the Central Criminal Court at 10.30 am when he was due to surrender. As a result his trial and that of his co-accused could not proceed. The judge was annoyed, and rightly so, that there should be such a waste of public time because of conduct of this character. Ultimately he was brought to the Central Criminal Court and the trial was resumed at 2 o'clock that Monday afternoon, 10th July. The judge thereupon most properly revoked the order for bail and remanded him in custody until the end of the trial.

On Wednesday, 19th July, the jury disagreed and, we are told, the judge discharged the jury finally at or about 6 o'clock that evening. The applicant was again remanded in custody. On the next day, Thursday, 20th July, he was brought before Judge Clarke. He was represented by counsel. He admitted the offence of failing to surrender to his bail, the offence created by s 6(1) of the 1976 Act. The judge dealt with the matter summarily, if I may use that word, as if it were a criminal contempt of court and sentenced him to three months' imprisonment.

This case, we are told, raises for the first time in this court the question of what are the powers of a Crown Court judge in these circumstances. That, in our view, must depend on the true construction of s 6(5) of the 1976 Act. But before I deal with that, it may be useful to say how this matter comes before the Criminal Division of this court and not the Civil Division.

The Administration of Justice Act 1960 for the first time gave a right of appeal to the Civil Division of the Court of Appeal in cases of committal for contempt of court. Section 13(6) provides:

'This section does not apply to a conviction or sentence in respect of which an appeal lies under Part I of the Criminal Appeal Act 1968, or to a decision of the criminal division of the Court of Appeal under that Part of that Act; and for the purposes of the said Part I and of this subsection an order for the punishment of any person for contempt of court in proceedings in which he has a right of appeal against his sentence shall be treated as part of that sentence.'

As a result of the passing of the 1976 Act, the Rules of the Supreme Court were altered by the Rules of the Supreme Court (Amendment) (Bail) 1978[1]. I need only refer to r 2, which provides:

'Order 59, rule 20, shall be amended as follow: . . . (7) The jurisdiction of the Court of Appeal under section 13 of the Administration of Justice Act 1960 to hear and determine any appeal from an order or decision of the Crown Court dealing with an offence under section 6 of the Bail Act 1976 as if it were a contempt of court shall be exercised by the criminal division of the Court of Appeal.'

I mention this provision to show how this present application comes to this division and not the Civil Division of this court.

It is argued, if I may say so, with conspicuous ability by counsel for the appellant that the judge had neither right nor power to send this man to prison in the circumstances in which

---

1   SI 1978 No 251

he did so. It is said that this was not a contempt in the face of the court, and there was no
immediate urgency which justified the judge dealing with him summarily in the way he
did. It is necessary, in order to consider this part of counsel for the appellant's argument,
to look at s 6(5). It seems to us plain that s 6 has created a wholly new offence and sub-s
(5) is providing how that wholly new offence, when proved, may be punished. It becomes
punishable either on summary conviction, which of course means on commission for a
summary offence triable in a magistrates' court (then one finds the ensuing provisions in
sub-s (6), which are designed to permit a greater sentence than that permissible in a
magistrates' court in circumstances where a greater sentence is thought desirable), or, and
this is the all important provision, as if the offence were a criminal contempt of court.

Counsel for the appellant drew our attention to two earlier statutory provisions: the first
is s 3(1) of the Criminal Procedure (Attendance of Witnesses) Act 1965, which provides:

> 'Any person who without just excuse disobeys a witness order or witness summons
> requiring him to attend before any court shall be guilty of contempt of that court and
> may be punished summarily by that court as if his contempt had been committed in
> the face of the court.'

The second is s 20(2) of the Juries Act 1974, which creates certain offences, in the case of
defaulting jurors. Subsection (2) provides: 'An offence under subsection (1) above [for
failure to attend when duly summoned] shall be punishable either on summary conviction
or as if it were criminal contempt of court committed in the face of the court.' Thus,
argues counsel for the appellant, in two antecedent statutory references to committal for
contempt the punishment is to be as if these were criminal contempt in the face of the
court. But those last words are not to be found in s 6(5) of the 1976 Act, and therefore there
is no power under that subsection to punish as if there were contempt committed in the
face of the court.

One must look at the structure and purpose of s 6. It seems clear that it has, as I said a
moment ago, created a wholly new offence punishable in one of two ways. It can be
punished as if it were a summary offence, triable in and only in a magistrates' court, with
additional power to commit for sentence to the Crown Court, or as if it were a criminal
contempt of the court.

This court finds itself unable to agree with the underlying premise of counsel's argument
for the appellant that the omission of words such as 'contempt committed in the face of the
court' limits the powers accorded by s 6(5). On the contrary we think the omission is
deliberate and is designed to give a court other than a magistrates' court, that is the Crown
Court, power to deal with an offender as if he had committed a criminal contempt of court,
leaving the Crown Court to deal with him in whatever way as the Crown Court could do
if he were guilty of criminal contempt of court. In some cases it may not be appropriate
to deal with the offender summarily in this way. We are not deciding this question finally
since it does not arise, but one can imagine circumstances in which there might be a
dispute whether or not particular facts amounted to absconding; the judge might then
think that that was not a suitable matter for determination by him summarily under the
latter part of sub-s (5). In such a case he might think it right to direct that summary
proceedings should be begun before a magistrates' court, or he might think he could deal
with the matter adequately himself.

But the purpose of the provision seems to us to be to create swift and simple alternative
remedies, either by way of proceedings for a summary offence or by way of committal for
what is to be treated as a criminal contempt of court, without the necessity for more
elaborate proceedings of a kind which sometimes are necessary when questions of criminal
contempt of court arise. We cannot think Parliament contemplated in this subsection that
in such cases there should be proceedings in the Divisional Court[1] or, as counsel for the
appellant suggested, by way of a revival of the somewhat archaic practice of indicting for
criminal contempt, if indeed that latter course is still open in view of the language of s 6.

---

1   See, e g, RSC Ord 52, r 1(2)(a)(ii)

For those reasons, we think Judge Clarke did have full and sufficient powers to deal with the matter in the way he did. Here was a man who had deliberately made it impossible for himself to answer to the bail that had been granted over the weekend by his own act of getting blind drunk on that Sunday night. We see no reason in the circumstances why the judge, in the public interest, should not have taken a serious view of this matter, because the applicant by his conduct wasted the court's time, the jury's time, and the time of the police and of scores of other persons for half a day. We think it was perfectly proper to act as he did.

The only other question is whether or not in all the circumstances three months was excessive. It will be observed that that is the maximum custodial sentence on summary conviction. We think in all the circumstances the gravity of the offence will be sufficiently marked, particularly as the applicant is going to be remanded in custody, if we reduce the three months to one month. To that extent only, granting leave to appeal and treating this as the hearing of the appeal with the consent of counsel for the appellant, the appeal succeeds.

I should have mentioned that reliance was placed by counsel for the appellant on the decision of the Court of Appeal (Civil Division) in *Balogh v Crown Court at St Albans*[1]. We do not find it necessary to consider that decision in detail. It was of course given in different circumstances and before the passing of the 1976 Act. We do not think that the decision assists in the solution of the problem with which we are here concerned.

For those reasons the appeal will be allowed to the extent only of reducing the three months to one month. The judge was absolutely right to pass an immediate custodial sentence in order to mark the fact that those who behave in this way must expect additional punishment.

Appeal allowed in part.   Sentence varied.

Solicitors: *Hatten, Wyatt & Co*, Gravesend (for the appellant); *Solicitor, Metropolitan Police*.

N P Metcalfe Esq   Barrister.

---

1   [1974] 3 All ER 283, [1975] QB 73

Re Sarflax Ltd

CHANCERY DIVISION
OLIVER J
12th, 13th, 14th, 25th APRIL 1978

Company – Winding-up – Fraudulent trading – Company disposing of assets and paying other debts without taking into account pending claim against it – Whether company 'carrying on business' – Whether company's conduct showed 'intention to defraud creditor' – Companies Act 1948, s 332(1).

In 1966 S Ltd contracted to sell goods to Italian buyers. The goods supplied were not satisfactory and the buyers rescinded the contract. In 1970 they brought an action in the English courts against S Ltd claiming damages but later allowed the action to lapse. On 13th January 1971 S Ltd passed a resolution to cease trading as from the close of business on 30th April 1971. It sold its fixed assets, stock-in-trade and work in progress to its parent company at a price equal to their book value. The price was set off pro tanto against a debt due to the parent company. Over the next two years S Ltd's remaining assets were got in and were employed in discharging S Ltd's debts but no account was taken of a pending claim against S Ltd by the Italian buyers in an action commenced in the Italian courts in October 1971. On 23rd September 1973 S Ltd went into voluntary liquidation and a liquidator was appointed. In November 1973 the buyers obtained judgment against S Ltd in the Italian courts. The liquidator admitted proof of the judgment debt in the liquidation. He applied for a declaration, under s 332(1)[a] of the Companies Act 1948, (i) that, from 13th January 1971 until 7th September 1973, the business of S Ltd was carried on with intent to defraud creditors (and in particular, one creditor, the Italian buyers) in that its directors and the parent company ('the respondents'), knowing that S Ltd was unable to pay its debts in full, had caused S Ltd's assets to be distributed amongst its creditors (other than the buyers) to the intent that such creditors (and, in particular, the parent company) should be preferred to the buyers, and (ii) that the respondents were jointly and severally liable to pay him a sum equal to the amount of the loss found to have been caused to the buyers (ie the amount to which the buyers would have been entitled if all S Ltd's assets had been retained and distributed pari passu amongst all its creditors including the buyers). The respondents applied for the summons to be struck out as disclosing no cause of action on the grounds (i) that the mere collection and distribution of assets did not constitute 'carrying on business', within s 332(1) of the 1948 Act, and (ii), that there was no intention to defraud.

Held – (i) The phrase 'carrying on business' in s 332(1) of the 1948 Act was not synonymous with actively carrying on trade. The collection of assets acquired in the course of business and the distribution of the proceeds of those assets in the discharge of business liabilities could constitute 'carrying on business' and in the present case did so because there was a continuous course of active conduct and not merely a passive suffering of undischarged liabilities (see p 534 h j and p 535 b, post); *Theophile v Solicitor-General* [1950] 1 All ER 405 and *Re Bird, ex parte the Debtor v Inland Revenue Comrs* [1962] 2 All ER 406 applied.

(ii) Where, however, a debtor knew or had good grounds to suspect that he would not have sufficient assets to pay all his creditors in full, the mere preference of one creditor over another did not amount to an 'intention to defraud', within s 332(1). It followed that, since the liquidator had merely alleged that the respondents intended to prefer all S Ltd's other creditors to the buyers, his summons disclosed no reasonable cause of action and would accordingly be dismissed (see p 535 f g and p 545 g h, post); *Tomkins v Saffery* (1877) 3 App Cas 213 applied.

---

a Section 332(1), so far as material, is set out at p 534 c d, post

Notes

For fraudulent trading, see 18 Halsbury's Laws (4th Edn) paras 1384–1389, and for cases on the subject, see 24 Digest (Repl) 1131–1133, 138–146.

For the Companies Act 1948, s 332, see 5 Halsbury's Statutes (3rd Edn) 361.

Cases referred to in judgment

Alton v Harrison, Poyser v Harrison (1869) LR 4 Ch App 622, 38 LJ Ch 669, 21 LT 282, LJ; 25 Digest (Repl) 207, *254.*

Bird, Re, ex parte the Debtor v Inland Revenue Comrs [1962] 2 All ER 406, [1962] 1 WLR 686, [1962] TR 173, 41 ATC 137, CA, 4 Digest (Reissue) 25, *208.*

Cooper (Gerald) Chemicals Ltd, Re [1978] 2 All ER 49, [1978] Ch 262, [1978] 2 WLR 866.

Darvill v Terry (1861) 6 H & N 807, 30 LJ Ex 355, 158 ER 333, 25 Digest (Repl) 222, *393.*

Drummond-Jackson v British Medical Association [1970] 1 All ER 1094, [1970] 1 WLR 688, CA, Digest (Cont Vol C) 1075, *510a.*

Fasey, Re, ex parte Trustees [1923] 2 Ch 1, 92 LJ Ch 400, 129 LT 132, [1923] B & CR 8, CA, 25 Digest (Repl) 176, *44.*

Glegg v Bromley [1912] 3 KB 474, [1911–13] All ER Rep 1138, 81 LJKB 1081, 106 LT 825, CA, 25 Digest (Repl) 189, *134.*

Holbird v Anderson (1793) 5 Term Rep 235, 101 ER 132, 25 Digest (Repl) 226, *422.*

Hubbuck & Sons Ltd v Wilkinson Heywood & Clark Ltd [1899] 1 QB 86, [1895–9] All ER Rep 244, 68 LJQB 34, 79 LT 429, CA, 50 Digest (Repl) 49, *381.*

Lloyd's Furniture Palace Ltd, Re, Evans v Lloyd's Furniture Palace Ltd [1925] Ch 853, [1925] All ER Rep 439, 25 LJ Ch 140, 134 LT 241, [1926] B & CR 29, 25 Digest (Repl) 227, *434.*

Middleton v Pollock, ex parte Elliott (1876) 2 Ch D 104, 45 LJ Ch 293, 25 Digest (Repl) 221, *380.*

Murray-Watson Ltd, Re, Re Lincomb Hall (Hartlebury) Ltd (6th April 1977) unreported.

Nagle v Feilden [1966] 1 All ER 689, [1966] 2 QB 633, [1966] 2 WLR 1027, CA, Digest (Cont Vol B) 323, *585a.*

Patrick and Lyon Ltd, Re [1933] Ch 786, [1933] All ER Rep 590, 102 LJ Ch 300, 149 LT 231, [1933] B & CR 151, 10 Digest (Reissue) 1031, *6321.*

Rondel v Worsley [1967] 3 All ER 993, [1969] AC 191, [1967] 3 WLR 1666, HL, Digest (Cont Vol C) 42, *284a.*

Roy v Prior [1969] 3 All ER 1153, [1970] 1 QB 283, [1969] 3 WLR 635, CA; *rvsd* [1970] 2 All ER 729, [1971] AC 470, [1970] 3 WLR 202, 134 JP 615, HL, Digest (Cont Vol C) 1, *218a.*

Schmidt v Secretary of State for Home Affairs [1969] 1 All ER 904, [1969] 2 Ch 149, [1969] 2 WLR 337, 133 JP 274, CA, 2 Digest (Reissue) 203, *1160.*

Theophile v Solicitor-General [1950] 1 All ER 405, [1950] AC 186, 43 R & IT 180, HL, 4 Digest (Reissue) 25, *207.*

Tomkins v Saffery (1877) 3 App Cas 213, 47 LJ Bcy 11, 37 LT 758, HL; *affg* sub nom *Ex parte Saffery, Re Cooke* 4 Ch D 555, CA, 4 Digest (Reissue) 59, *495.*

Wiseman v Borneman [1969] 3 All ER 275, [1971] AC 297, [1969] 3 WLR 706, 45 Tax Cas 540, [1969] TR 279, 48 ATC 278, HL, 28(1) Digest (Reissue) 493, *1760.*

Wood v Dixie (1845) 7 QB 892, 5 LTOS 286, 9 Jur 798, 115 ER 724, 25 Digest (Repl) 221, *384.*

Cases also cited

Art Reproduction Co Ltd, Re [1951] 2 All ER 984, [1952] Ch 89.

Charterbridge Corpn v Lloyds Bank Ltd [1969] 2 All ER 1185, [1970] Ch 62.

Daniels v Daniels [1978] 2 All ER 89, [1978] Ch 406.

Eichholz (deceased), Re [1959] 1 All ER 166, [1959] Ch 708.

Freeman v Pope (1870) LR 5 Ch App 538.

Lee, Behrens & Co Ltd, Re [1932] 2 Ch 46, [1932] All ER Rep 889.

Leitch (William C) Brothers Ltd, Re [1932] 2 Ch 71, [1932] All ER Rep 892.

Lloyds Bank Ltd v Marcan [1973] 3 All ER 754, [1973] 1 WLR 339, CA.

Morgan v Odham's Press Ltd [1971] 2 All ER 1156, [1971] 1 WLR 1239, HL.
Parke v Daily News [1962] 2 All ER 929, [1962] Ch 927.
Rawlplug Co Ltd v Kamvale Properties Ltd (1968) 20 P & CR 32.
Roith (W & M) Ltd, Re [1967] 1 All ER 427, [1967] 1 WLR 432.
Wenlock v Moloney [1965] 2 All ER 871, [1965] 1 WLR 1238, CA.

Adjourned summons

On 12th November 1975 the liquidator of Sarflax Ltd ('the company') applied, under s 332 of the Companies Act 1948, for (i) a declaration that from 13th January 1971 until 7th September 1973 (the date of the commencement of the winding-up of the company) the business of the company was carried on with intent to defraud creditors (and, in particular, Serrature Auto Ferroviare Edili spa ('SAFE'), a creditor of the company) or for other fraudulent purposes in that the respondents, John Savell Freeman, Annie Marie Freeman and Tom Geoffrey Allison, as directors of the company and Fine Blanking (Shoreham) Ltd ('the parent company') as the holding company of the company well knowing that the company was unable to pay its debts in full caused the assets of the company to be distributed amongst its creditors (other than SAFE) to the intent that such creditors (and, in particular, the parent company) should be preferred to SAFE; (ii) a declaration that the respondents were knowingly parties to the carrying on of the business of the company in that manner; (iii) an inquiry into what loss had been caused to SAFE by the carrying on of the business of the company in that manner; (iv) a declaration that the respondents were jointly and severally liable to pay to the liquidator on behalf of SAFE a sum equal to the amount of the loss found to have been caused to SAFE; (v) an order that the respondents pay to the liquidator the sum in respect of which they were declared to be liable. Points of claim were delivered pursuant to an order of Mr Registrar Dearbergh dated 18th November 1975. The third respondent ceased to be a party to the proceedings. Points of defence were served on 20th January 1976. By a summons, dated 22nd September 1977, the three remaining respondents applied for an order that the proceedings against them be struck out on the ground that the allegations set out in the points of claim disclosed no reasonable cause of action against them or otherwise constituted an abuse of the process of the court. The facts are set out in the judgment.

Leolin Price QC and *Robin Potts* for the respondents.
J M Chadwick for the liquidator.

Cur adv vult

25th April. **OLIVER J** read the following judgment: This is an application by the respondents to a summons under s 332 of the Companies Act 1948 to strike out the summons and the points of claim served thereunder pursuant to the registrar's directions for pleading on the grounds that (a) the points of claim disclose no reasonable cause of action against the respondents and (b) that the summons is an abuse of the process of the court. Some evidence has been filed in support of the second ground directed to showing that the only creditor alleged to have been defrauded was not, at any material time, a creditor at all because its claim was statute-barred. I can, however, dispose of that ground straight away without any detailed consideration of the contention because it emerged that, although no evidence in answer has been filed by the liquidator (because it was considered inappropriate to do so on an application of this sort) some, at least, of the relevant facts are in dispute and an application of this type is, as counsel concedes on behalf of the respondents, not an appropriate proceeding for trying disputed questions of fact. If, therefore, he fails on his first ground, those questions must be left to be disposed of at the trial and, in that event, he seeks leave to amend his points of defence to raise them.

I turn therefore to the only live issue now raised by the respondents' summons: do the liquidator's points of claim, assuming all the allegations of fact made in them to be proved, give rise to a claim against the respondents which has any reasonable prospect of success? Before I turn to the points of claim themselves, it is convenient to give a brief summary of the background against which the proceedings are brought. The applicant is the liquidator appointed in the voluntary winding-up of Sarflax Ltd (formerly called Fine Blanking Ltd) to which I will refer to as 'the company'. The first two respondents are individuals who were formerly directors both of the company and of Fine Blanking (Shoreham) Ltd, now the third respondent, to which I will refer as 'the parent company', of which the company was a wholly owned subsidiary; and they owned, if not the whole, at least the major part of the issued capital of the parent company. There was a third individual respondent who was, or was alleged to be, in the same position as the other two, but he ceased to be a party to the proceedings in circumstances which are not entirely clear to me but which do not matter for present purposes.

It seems that, at the material time, the company, which appears to have carried on a business of manufacturing machine-tools, was substantially indebted to the parent company and there is no suggestion that that indebtedness was otherwise than genuine or bona fide incurred in the course of the company's trading. In September 1966 it entered into a contract to supply a particular type of press to an Italian lock-making company, Serrature Auto Ferroviare Edili spa (known as 'SAFE' for short) which was incorporated and resident in Italy and the proper law of the contract appears to have been the law of the Republic of Italy. It contained, indeed, an express term that disputes were to be determined by the court in Turin. The press was supplied but it did not work satisfactorily and a dispute arose about the responsibility for this. This dispute resulted in SAFE rescinding or purporting to rescind the contract under Italian law and advancing a claim against the company for damages.

In November 1970 it commenced proceedings in the Queen's Bench Division claiming something over £80,000 plus interest, but after the company had entered an appearance under protest, that action was not proceeded with and was allowed to lapse without the point of jurisdiction being determined. In October 1971 a new action was commenced by SAFE in the Italian courts in Turin and that seems to have proceeded with varying degrees of celerity over the next two years. The company appeared and was originally represented but at some stage its Italian advisers withdrew from the case and in November 1973, the company taking no part in the proceedings, a judgment was entered against it in the Second Civil Division of the Civil and Penal Tribunal of Turin in a sum of 120,465,690 lire (about £86,000).

In the meantime, pursuant to a resolution passed in January 1971, the company had ceased to trade as from the close of business on 30th April 1971 and its fixed assets, stock-in-trade and work in progress had been sold to the parent company at a price equal to their book value, such price being set off pro tanto against the debt due to the parent company. There is no suggestion that this sale was otherwise than at a proper price. Over the next two years the remaining assets of the company were got in and were applied in discharging the company's established debts but without any account being taken of the pending claim by SAFE. On 23rd September 1973 a resolution was passed for the voluntary winding-up of the company and the applicant was appointed to be its liquidator. After receipt of the judgment of the Turin court he admitted SAFE's proof in the liquidation, and he now brings proceedings in which he claims that the collection of the company's assets and their distribution in defraying the debts of the company without making pari passu provision for SAFE's claim constituted the carrying on of the company's business with intent to defraud a creditor (namely SAFE) and claims against the respondents personally an order under s 332 limited to making good the loss to SAFE so occasioned, that is to say, the payment of the sum to which SAFE would be entitled if all the company's assets had been retained and distributed pari passu among all the company's creditors including SAFE. That is the claim which counsel for the respondents seeks to have struck out and I must first see how it is put in the points of claim.

The points of claim begin with some definitions which I do not think I need read in full. It refers to the individual respondents by their names; it refers to the parent company as 'the Parent Company' and it defines 'the S.A.F.E.' Claim' as meaning the claim for damages by SAFE. In para 2 it sets out that the company was a subsidiary at all material times of the parent company and the individual respondents were directors of the company and the parent company and held the majority of the shares in the parent company beneficially.

Then in para 3 it sets out the contract between SAFE and the company, to which I have referred, and the breach of the obligations under the contract by the company and concludes:

> 'On or before 13th May 1969, S.A.F.E. (as it was entitled to do) elected to treat that contract as discharged, and to claim damages for breach. On 6th November 1970, upon the delivery of the said Statement of Claim [that is the statement of claim in the English action] if not before, the S.A.F.E. Claim was quantified at £80,509 or thereabouts, with interest thereon.'

Then in para 4 it goes on to allege that at all material times prior to 30th April 1971 the facts mentioned in the previous paragraph were well known to the respondents or to the parent company and Mr Freeman, one of the respondents, and at all times the respondents were well aware that there was no substantial defence to the SAFE claim. That arises from advice which they had received. In the alternative, it is alleged that at no material time prior to 30th April did the respondents have any reasonable grounds for a belief that there was a substantial defence to the SAFE claim.

Then it sets out in para 5 a meeting of the board of directors held on 13th January 1971 at which the individual respondents were present at which it was resolved that the company should cease to trade on 30th April 1971, and it was further resolved that, at the close of business on that day, the fixed assets of the company be sold to the parent company at open market value, and the stock-in-trade and work in progress be sold to the parent company at net realisable value.

Paragraph 6 sets out the financial position of the company at the close of business on 30th April 1971, showing fixed assets, stock-in-trade and work in progress of £44,210, trade debtors of £38,062, and cash at bank at £6,241. That amounted in all to £88,513. That was against liabilities consisting of debts due to the parent company of £47,863, and debts due to other trade creditors (excluding the SAFE claim), £38,569, making a total of £86,432. The end result of that is a surplus of assets over liabilities before providing for the SAFE claim of £2,081. It is then alleged that accordingly on 30th April 1971 the respondents, or (in the alternative) the parent company and Mr Freeman, were well aware that, after making any reasonable provision for the SAFE claim, the company was insolvent and unable to pay its debts in full.

It then sets out in para 7 that at the close of business on 30th April 1971 the company sold to the parent company (in pursuance of the resolution to which I have referred) its fixed assets at the price of £28,557 and its stock-in-trade and work in progress at the price of £15,653, and that the said sums were set off against the debt due by the company to the parent company. In the circumstances that the company was unable to pay its debts in full, the parent company was thereby preferred to the other creditors of the company and (in particular) to SAFE. The sums which I have mentioned as the price of the fixed assets and stock-in-trade added together amount to the figure shown in para 6 as the value of fixed assets, stock-in-trade and work in progress, that is £44,210, which was some £3,000 less than the amount due to the parent company.

In para 8 it is said that during the period from 30th April 1971 until July 1973, the company received from its trade debtors the sum of £38,050 or thereabouts, and applied the same (together with the cash at bank) (a) in satisfying the balance of the debt due to the parent company, (b) in satisfying the debts of the other trade creditors (excluding the SAFE claim), and (c) in paying administration expenses and legal fees. In the circumstances that the company was unable to pay its debts in full, the parent company and the trade creditors (other than SAFE) were thereby preferred to SAFE.

In para 9 it sets out the resolution to wind up and alleges a statement of affairs in which it was disclosed that the company had no assets.

In para 10 it sets out the judgment of the Turin court. The substantial allegation arising out of all this is in para 11. It is here that one finds the nub of the case which is made by the applicant. Paragraph 11 reads:

'In the circumstances during the period from 13th January 1971 until 7th September 1973, the business of the Company was carried on with intent to defraud creditors (and, in particular, S.A.F.E.) or for other fraudulent purposes, in that the Respondents, (or, in the alternative, the Parent Company and Mr Freeman) well knowing that the Company was unable to pay its debts in full caused the assets of the company to be distributed amongst its creditors (other than S.A.F.E.) to the intent that such creditors (and, in particular, the Parent Company) should be preferred to S.A.F.E.'

It then proceeds with a claim for relief claiming a declaration that from 13th January 1971 until 7th September 1973 the business of the company was carried on with intent to defraud creditors or for other fraudulent purposes, and that the respondents were knowingly parties to that and consequential relief.

Section 332 of the 1948 Act is in the following terms. Subsection (1) is the only one I need to read for present purposes:

'If in the course of the winding up of a company it appears that any business of the company has been carried on with intent to defraud creditors of the company or creditors of any other person or for any fraudulent purpose, the court, on the application of the official receiver, or the liquidator or any creditor or contributory of the company, may, if it thinks proper so to do, declare that any persons who were knowingly parties to the carrying on of the business in manner aforesaid shall be personally responsible, without any limitation of liability, for all or any of the debts or other liabilities of the company as the court may direct . . .'

Counsel's first point for the respondents is that, whatever else may be said, the points of claim disclose nothing but the closing down of the company's business and the collection and distribution of its assets. That is, he suggests, (a) the very negation of carrying on business, and (b) constitutes simply a single transaction carried out at the cessation of trading which cannot possibly fall within the ambit of the section. He relies on certain observations of mine in *Re Murray-Watson Ltd, Re Lincomb Hall (Hartlebury) Ltd*[1] in which, in relation to some particularly complicated pleadings relating to a scheme of inter-company transfers, I sought to analyse the impact of the section on an isolated transaction with a view to testing whether it could be said that an individual respondent in that case had been party to the carrying on of a business. It may be that some of the observations there made require some qualification in the light of the subsequent decision of Templeman J in *Re Gerald Cooper Chemicals Ltd*[2]; but, whether this is so or not, I do not think that they help counsel for the respondents in the present context, where what is involved is a continuous course of conduct in collecting in what was due to the company from its trading operations and in discharging the obligations incurred in those trading operations.

The question of whether a course of conduct of this description can constitute the carrying on of a business is not one which fell to be considered either in *Re Murray-Watson Ltd*[1] or in *Re Gerald Cooper Chemicals Ltd*[3] but I feel quite unable to say that the expression 'carrying on any business' in the section is necessarily synonymous with actively carrying on trade or that the collection of assets acquired in the course of business and the distribution of the proceeds of those assets in the discharge of business liabilities cannot constitute the carrying on of 'any business' for the purposes of the section. The decision of

---

1   (6th April 1977) unreported
2   [1978] 2 All ER 49, [1978] 2 WLR 866
3   [1978] 2 All ER 49, [1978] Ch 262

the House of Lords in *Theophile v Solicitor-General*[1], and *Re Bird*[2] appear to me to point very strongly in the opposite direction. Admittedly those cases were decided on s 4(1) of the Bankruptcy Act 1914 where the expression used is 'carried on business in England, personally or by means of an agent or manager', but they establish that, at least for the purpose of that section, a bankrupt carries on business until he has performed all the obligations that the fact of trade imposes on him. The instant case is really a fortiori because there was here not merely a passive suffering of undischarged liabilities but a continuous course of active conduct in the collection and distribution of the business assets.

Counsel's next submission for the respondents is, however, a much more formidable one. Granted, he says, that the collection of assets and payment of debts can constitute the carrying on of a business, nevertheless what the court is concerned with here is a composite expression 'has carried on any business with intent to defraud creditors'. Now when one looks at the points of claim (and disregarding the opening words of para 11 which are not an allegation of fact but merely the expression of a conclusion that the facts alleged fall within the statutory words) what is alleged here as the carrying on of a business with intent to defraud creditors? And the answer is that all that is alleged is (a) the collection and realisation of assets, which cannot possibly, without more, constitute fraud, and (b) the application of the proceeds of collection and realisation in paying creditors, as to the validity of whose debts no contest is raised, in preference to the claim of SAFE.

The only intention which is alleged, and the only intention which *can* be alleged, is an intention to prefer and that, counsel submits, cannot be an intention to defraud, for to say that a man intends to prefer one creditor over another is to say no more than that he intends to do that which the law permits him to do subject only to the risk that such preference may be nullified if he subsequently becomes bankrupt. The critical allegations express or implicit in the pleading are: (a) that SAFE was a known creditor of the company (although the *precise* extent of the liability was not yet crystallised); (b) that the total amount of the company's liabilities (including that to SAFE) exceeded the company's assets; (c) that the respondents knew this and knew (because the company had ceased trading) that there would be no further assets from which debts could be discharged; and (d) that having this knowledge the respondents caused the assets of the company to be applied in discharging the company's liabilities (other than that to SAFE) and thereby intentionally preferred the other creditors of the company to SAFE.

Now that is all that is alleged and the question at issue may be expressed thus: where a debtor, knowing or having good grounds to suspect that he had not and will not have, sufficient assets to pay all his creditors in full, pays some but not others (or, I think, it must follow, pays unequal proportions of those creditor's debts) with the consequence that some creditor either is not paid at all or is paid a lesser proportion of his debt than that which is paid to the other creditors, is that per se fraudulent conduct on the part of the debtor in the sense in which the word 'fraudulent' is used in s 332 of the 1948 Act?

Counsel for the liquidator submits that I do not have to decide the question. This is a striking out application which is not suitable for the determination of difficult points of law which ought to be left to the trial and all that he had to do, he submits, is to satisfy me that the point is an arguable one. Now it is perfectly true that in *Hubbuck & Sons Ltd v Wilkinson Heywood & Clark Ltd*[3] Lindley MR expressed the view that, where the point of law was one requiring argument and careful consideration, the more appropriate method of deciding the case was to set the point down as a preliminary point under what is now RSC Ord 33, r 3, the jurisdiction to strike out summarily being reserved for 'cases which are plain and obvious, so that any master or judge can say at once that the statement of claim . . . is insufficient, even if proved, to entitle the plaintiff to what he asks'. In fact, however, the matter has been extensively argued before me for three days and it seems to

1   [1950] 1 All ER 405, [1950] AC 186
2   [1962] 2 All ER 406, [1962] 1 WLR 686
3   [1899] 1 QB 86 at 91, [1895–9] All ER Rep 244 at 247

me wholly inappropriate, if on the arguments I am able to form a clear conclusion, that I should decline to decide it on this summons and leave it to the parties to bring the matter before the court again under a different procedure in which there will be adduced (either before me or before some other judge) the same arguments and authorities as those which have been adduced before me.

If I am now satisfied that the points of claim disclose no reasonable cause of action it seems to me to be wrong that I should refrain from striking it out simply because there exists some more appropriate procedure for bringing the same question before the court.

I have been referred to *Drummond-Jackson v British Medical Association*[1] where Lord Pearson says this:

> 'Over a long period of years it has been firmly established by many authorities that the power to strike out a statement of claim as disclosing no reasonable cause of action is a summary power which should be exercised only in plain and obvious cases. The authorities are collected in The Supreme Court Practice 1970[2] under the heading "Exercise of powers under this Rule" in the notes under Ord 18, r 19. One which might be added is *Nagle v Feilden*[3]. Reference has been made to four recent cases: *Rondel v Worsley*[4], *Wiseman v Borneman*[5], *Roy v Prior*[6] and *Schmidt v Secretary of State for Home Affairs*[7]. In each of these cases there was an important question of principle involved, and the hearing of the application under RSC Ord 18, r 19, was much longer and more elaborate than is usual, but the final decision was that the alleged cause of action was clearly unsustainable, and so the statement of claim disclosed no reasonable cause of action and was ordered to be struck out. There was no departure from the principle that the order for striking out should only be made if it becomes plain and obvious that the claim or defence cannot succeed, but the procedural method was unusual in that there was a relatively long and elaborate instead of a short and summary hearing. It must be within the discretion of the courts to adopt this unusual procedural method in special cases where it seemed to be advantageous. But I do not think that there has been or should be any general change in the practice with regard to applications under the rule.'

On the face of it counsel's proposition for the liquidator appears both novel and bold. It involves this: that a debtor who reasonably suspects that the value of the assets likely to be available to him is exceeded by the amount of his liabilities must, in effect, suspend payment to all his creditors until the full amount of his liabilities is ascertained or risk a charge of fraud. None of the authorities to which I have been referred gives any support for such a proposition and, indeed, the very words of s 44 of the Bankruptcy Act 1914 appear to be to militate against it. That section provides:

> '(1) Every conveyance or transfer of property, or charge thereon made, every payment made, every obligation incurred, and every judicial proceeding taken or suffered by any person unable to pay his debts as they become due from his own money in favour of any creditor, or of any person in trust for any creditor, with a view of giving such creditor, or any surety or guarantor for the debt due to such creditor, a preference over the other creditors, shall, if the person making, taking, paying or suffering the same is adjudged bankrupt on a bankruptcy petition presented within three months after the date of making, taking, paying or suffering the same, be deemed fraudulent and void as against the trustee in bankruptcy . . .'

---

1 [1970] 1 All ER 1094 at 1101, [1970] 1 WLR 688 at 695–696
2 Vol I, p 284, para 18/19/3
3 [1966] 1 All ER 689 at 695, 697, [1966] 2 QB 633 at 648, 651
4 [1967] 3 All ER 993, [1969] AC 191
5 [1969] 3 All ER 275, [1967] AC 297
6 [1969] 3 All ER 1153, [1970] 1 QB 283
7 [1969] 1 All ER 904, [1969] 2 Ch 149

Where A is deemed to be B the hypothesis is that, apart from the deeming provision, A is not in fact B; and the very fact that the legislature thought it necessary to deem a payment made with a view to preferring to be fraudulent and void suggests that, apart from this provision, it would not be so. Counsel for the liquidator seeks to escape from this by suggesting that there are two types of preference, those which are innocent because the debtor does not necessarily know that the effect will be to defeat other creditors, and those which are fraudulent where the debtor is aware that the necessary effect of paying one creditor is going to be that another goes short. The latter, he says, might well be open to attack in any event under s 172 of the Law of Property Act 1925 (or formerly under the statute of Elizabeth I[1] which that section replaced) but s 44 of the 1914 Act has the dual effect of excluding, where it applies, any defence of lack of notice in the payee which otherwise might be available and of including innocent preferences within its ambit.

I do not think that I can accept that. A preference, by definition, seems to me to be the payment of one creditor to the exclusion, in whole or in part, of another and it postulates, in its very nature, a deficiency of assets to pay all creditors. A payment 'with intent to prefer' or with a view to preferring necessarily, therefore, presupposes a knowledge on the part of the payer that his assets are insufficient to pay all, so that the actual fraudulent intent which counsel for the liquidator ascribes to *some* of the preferential payments to which the section refers must apply in fact, by definition, to *all* such payments. And if it is in *fact* fraud intentionally to pay A to the detriment of B, why was it thought necessary to 'deem' such payments to be fraudulent?

But the matter does not rest purely on deductive argument from the intention of the legislature as it emerges from the 1914 Act. If counsel for the liquidator is right and the mere intentional preference of one creditor over another is fraud, the tolerance of equity of the personal representative's right of preference, which existed up to 1972[2], is, as counsel for the respondents points out, inexplicable and wholly illogical. How could the law protect and uphold in a personal representative, charged with the payment of the debts of a deceased, that which, if done by the deceased himself, would be categorised as fraudulent?

There is, in fact, a long line of authority in relation to fraudulent conveyances from which there can be deduced, and, in my judgment, unequivocally deduced, the proposition that, apart from the provisions of the 1914 Act, a man may discharge his liabilities in any order he pleases. Now of course s 172 of the Law of Property Act 1925 and the statute of Elizabeth I which preceded it were directed at something quite different from that at which the Bankruptcy Acts were directed. The former were aimed at transfers intended to defeat, hinder, delay or defraud creditors, the latter at distributing the debtor's property pari passu. Nevertheless, if the mere preference of one creditor over another constituted fraud in the eye of the law, one would expect to find that treated as a relevant intent for the purposes of determining whether or not a transfer was fraudulent and void. The authorities however are all the other way. Counsel for the liquidator points out that all the cases were decided under the statute of Elizabeth I which began by declaring that all conveyances made 'to the End Purpose and Intent to delay hinder or defraud Creditors' should be deemed and taken 'to be clearly and utterly void' and then went on, in a proviso, to except those made for good consideration and bona fide without notice in the transferee of the fraudulent purpose. The cases, he suggests, were concerned not with the fraudulent intent but with the somewhat narrow meaning of the expression 'bona fide' which was construed as meaning merely that the document genuinely did what it was purporting to do and was not a mere sham or cloak for preserving an interest to the grantor.

Now certainly this is true of some of the earlier cases. *Holbird v Anderson*[3] and *Alton v Harrison*[4] are cases in point. But over and over again we find the courts expressing the view

---

1   13 Eliz I c 5 (1571) (Fraudulent Conveyances)
2   The Administration of Estates Act 1971
3   (1793) 5 Term Rep 235, 101 ER 132
4   (1869) LR 4 Ch App 622

that there is nothing in the statute which prohibits a debtor from preferring one creditor over another, and while it is true that in a number, perhaps the majority of the cases, the courts were considering the validity of a defence raised under the proviso that the conveyance was 'bona fide' I would find counsel's argument for the liquidator more persuasive if it were not for the fact that, in a number of these cases, it was quite evident that the transferee was aware of the transferor's intention to prefer him. If, therefore, that intention per se were, as a matter of law, a fraudulent intention, the defence under the proviso which was held to be available to the transferee in those cases could not have been so held. Indeed, in *Holbird v Anderson*[1] itself we find Lord Kenyon CJ, saying this:

'There was no fraud in this case. The plaintiff was preferred by his debtor, Charter, not with a view of any benefit to the latter, but merely to secure the payment of a just debt to the former, in which I see no illegality or injustice.'

Ashurst J said in a very short judgment[1]:

'The reason why executors are confined in their preference to those of equal degree, is, because otherwise it would amount to a devastavit. But inter vivos all are of the same degree; and anyone may be preferred in this manner.'

In *Wood v Dixie*[2] (a case of the provision of security to a creditor to defeat an execution) Coltman J directed the jury that 'if the intention of the transaction was to defeat the execution creditor, the conveyance was void as against him'. The Court of Queen's Bench held that direction to be wrong and in *Darvill v Terry*[3] Martin B observed: 'I am not aware of any case in which the law so laid down has since been disputed.' That was a case of a bill of sale executed as security for a debt (as both parties knew) to defeat a pending execution. The direction to the jury was that if they were of opinion that the parties really intended to pass the property to the plaintiff 'it was no objection to the bill of sale that the parties had come to that arrangement with a view of defeating the defendant's execution'[4]. Pollock CB remarked[5]: '... such assignment is valid, though made for the express purpose of defeating a particular creditor.'

Middleton v Pollock[6] was a case where a deceased debtor had, shortly prior to his death, declared himself a trustee of certain property as security for a particular debt. It was held that even if he had knowledge of his insolvency, the transaction was not avoided by the statute.

The argument of Mr Fry, who appeared for the creditor in that case, was as follows[7]:

'We admit that the doctrine of fraudulent preference has no application, there being no bankruptcy ... But under the statute of *Elizabeth* ... a gift, to be good as against creditors, must not only be made on good consideration, as this gift was, but also *bonâ fide*, which this gift was not ... A gift is not *bonâ fide* within the statute that has for its object the preferring of a few favoured creditors in the event of the debtor's insolvency; for good faith requires that he shall do no such thing.'

So this is a case which was directly related, as counsel for the liquidator has pointed out, to the proviso to the statute relating to the meaning of the words 'bona fide'.

We find Jessel MR saying that the argument was confined to the question of bona fides. He continued[8]:

---

1   (1793) 5 Term Rep 235 at 238, 101 ER 132 at 134
2   (1845) 7 QB 892 at 893, 115 ER 724
3   (1861) 6 H & N 807 at 812, 158 ER 333 at 335
4   6 H & N 807 at 808, 158 ER 333 at 334
5   6 H & N 807 at 811, 158 ER 333 at 334, 335
6   (1876) 2 Ch D 104
7   2 Ch D 104 at 106
8   2 Ch D 104 at 108

'The first argument was that Mr. *Pollock* intended to give a preference to his selected body of clients, that is, to give them a valid security against his property, but to give that valid security as a preferential payment or security. As between these preferred clients and the rest of his clients, whatever may be the morality of the case, as far as I know, there is no law which prevents a man in insolvent circumstances from preferring one of his creditors to another, except the bankruptcy law. Under the bankruptcy law, no doubt a man in insolvent circumstances is not entitled, without pressure, at all events, to pay one creditor and to leave the other creditors unpaid. But Mr. *Pollock* was not a bankrupt, and the bankruptcy law has no application to him. It has been decided, if decision were wanted, that a payment is *bonâ fide* within the meaning of the statute of *Elizabeth*, although the man who made the payment was insolvent at the time to his own knowledge, and even although the creditors who accepted the money knew it. Therefore, the mere fact of the deliberate intention of Mr. *Pollock*, if he entertained that deliberate intention, of preferring, in case of insolvency, this selected list of clients to the others, would not be sufficient to avoid this claim.'

At the end of his judgment, he says[1]: 'Consequently, I think it was intended by him that these securities should have the exact operation which the law would give them, and in that sense, therefore, they were *bonâ fide*.'

So here, although the ground for the decision was the restricted meaning of 'bona fide', as appears from the words last quoted, nevertheless there is the clear statement that the mere preference plus knowledge does not bring the statute into play.

This is echoed again in *Glegg v Bromley*[2]. Vaughan Williams LJ said:

'Finally, I may say that I had taken it for granted throughout my judgment that mere preference of one creditor over another does not bring the case within the statute 13 Eliz. c.5, even though the parties may have been minded to defeat a particular creditor.'

Fletcher Moulton LJ said this[3]:

'In my opinion the sole object of the deed was to transfer to Mr. Glegg by way of charge the future accounts therein referred to, and this was also its sole effect. It may fairly be regarded as a deliberate attempt to prefer Mr. Glegg to any creditors that might thereafter arise. I am not sure whether there were any creditors at the date at which the deed was actually made, but if so, it operated to give him a like preference over them. Now it is well settled law that apart from the rules of bankruptcy a person may pay his debts in any order he pleases, and may charge his property as he will as security for paying those debts. The covenous assignments referred to in the 13 Elizabeth are mock assignments whereby in some form or other the assignor reserves some benefit to himself, but an out and out assignment by way of charge to secure an actual existing creditor is not within the class of assignments which are affected by that statute . . .'

But the clearest expression is that of Parker J. I think that it is worth reading the whole of this passage. He said[4]:

'The only remaining point is I think, that which was argued under the statute of 13 Eliz. c.5. Now the scheme of that statute is this: By it all conveyances and assignments made with intent to hinder and delay creditors are rendered void against all creditors hindered or delayed by their operation. There is, however, a proviso for the protection

---

1   (1876) 2 Ch D 104 at 109
2   [1912] 3 KB 474 at 484, [1911–13] All ER Rep 1138 at 1143
3   [1912] 3 KB 474 at 485, [1911–13] All ER Rep 1138 at 1144
4   [1912] 3 KB 474 at 492, [1911–13] All ER Rep 1138 at 1147

of a purchaser for good consideration without notice of the illegal intention. In the authorities which deal with the statute it is not always clear whether the judges are dealing with the operative part of the Act or with the proviso. The illegal intent under the operative part is a question of fact for the jury or the judge sitting as a jury. On the one hand the want of consideration for the conveyance or assignment is a material fact in considering whether there was any illegal intent, but it is not conclusive that there existed any such intent. In the same way consideration was by no means conclusive that there was no illegal intent. When, however, one comes to deal with the proviso, it is quite clear that any person relying on the proviso must prove both good consideration and the fact that he had no notice of the illegal intent. Now in the present case it is really quite unnecessary to consider the proviso, for every one is agreed, and I think it is quite clear on the evidence, that if there was any fraudulent intention, the mortgagee had notice of it. The question therefore is really a question which reduces itself to this: Does a debtor who gives his creditor security with the intention of preferring him to other creditors or another creditor, and consequently defeating or delaying such other creditors or creditor, have an illegal intention within the meaning of the statute? In my opinion it is well decided that he has not, and as far as I can gather no distinction has ever been drawn in the cases between a preference given for fresh security and a preference given without any fresh security.'

This unanimous decision of the Court of Appeal is really inexplicable if the giving of the preference by the wife to her husband had itself constituted a fraudulent intent because the defence under the proviso could not, in that event, possibly have been available to him.

A case in which there was both fraudulent intent and an unsuccessful attempt to rely on the proviso was *Re Fasey*[1]. The argument is worth looking at. Mr Clayton, who appeared for a creditor to whom property had been transferred by a bankrupt, submitted[2]:

'1. An intention to prefer a particular creditor and thus to exclude and defeat the other creditors does not bring the case within the statute of 13 Eliz. c.5 . . . 2. The fact that the assignor was insolvent at the time he made the assignment and that the assignee knew it does not bring the case within the statute. 3. The fact that the assignor is dealing with substantially the whole of his property, although very material in cases of bankruptcy, does not bring the case within the statute . . .'

Lord Sterndale MR said[3]:

'Mr. Clayton for the appellant company very properly pointed out to us, and substantiated his point by several authorities, that the considerations that apply to a question under the statute of Elizabeth are very different from those that apply to the question of fraudulent preference in bankruptcy, because a fraudulent preference constitutes an act of bankruptcy. There is no doubt that the considerations are quite different, although the same circumstances may have to be taken into consideration in each case. I do not think the proposition that a conveyance or transfer for the purpose of giving a fraudulent preference to one creditor is not a defrauding of the creditors generally and would not come within the statute of Elizabeth, can be inverted so as to enable the debtor to say: "I did intend to defraud my creditors, I did intend to hinder them, I did intend to delay them, but incidentally to that intention I did give one of them some benefit, therefore what I did cannot come within the statute of Elizabeth in law." That proposition so inverted cannot be maintained as a general principle.'

1   [1923] 2 Ch 1
2   [1923] 2 Ch 1 at 10
3   [1923] 2 Ch 1 at 11–12

There implicitly Lord Sterndale MR is recognising the validity of the proposition which he says cannot be inverted. He concludes his judgment by saying[1]:

'That being so I think the transaction comes clearly within the statute of 13 Eliz. c.5. Its real object was to defeat and delay the creditors, and the fact that one creditor, the solicitor, incidentally got a benefit does not seem to me to prevent the transaction from being void. It was not a transaction for the purpose of giving the solicitor a preference over other creditors; no doubt it did so incidentally, or might have done so, but that was not its object. The object of it was to keep substantially the assets of the business and the goodwill of the business for the bankrupt himself and to exclude his creditors from payment of their debts.'

There again, one finds implicit in that the recognition that if the real object had been to give the creditor a preference it would not have been fraudulent within the statute. Warrington LJ said[2]:

'I quite agree it is well settled that the fact that a transaction is and is intended to be a preference of a particular creditor does not of itself bring the transaction within the statute of Elizabeth.'

Finally, perhaps the most striking case is *Re Lloyd's Furniture Palace Ltd*[3]. Here a company agreed to issue debentures to cover past and future loans, but by arrangement with the debenture holder (a director) deferred actually issuing them in order not to damage its credit with other creditors. So this was a case where there was a clear intent to prefer and clear knowledge of that intent in the creditor preferred. When the company got into financial difficulties, the debentures were issued. Some six months later the company was wound up. The liquidator, being unable to avail himself of the provisions of the predecessor of s 320 of the Companies Act 1948 as a result of the lapse of time, sought to have the debentures declared void under the statute of Elizabeth I. Romer J said this[4]:

'Now it was not disputed by Mr. Luxmoore [for the trustee in bankruptcy] that if the debentures in the present case were (to quote the words of the statute) "devised and contrived of malice fraud covin collusion or guile to the end purpose and intent to delay hinder or defraud creditors" of the company they are avoided by the statute as against the liquidator. Whether they were or were not so devised or contrived is the question I have to determine. The statute of Elizabeth has, as is well known, been the subject of judicial consideration in a great number of reported cases, to many of which my attention was called in argument. Those cases seem to establish the principle that a conveyance is not avoided by the statute merely because it is made with the intention of preferring, and does in the result prefer, one creditor of the grantor over the others. In *Alton v. Harrison*[5], Giffard L.J., in reference to a deed executed by a debtor at a time when he knew that a writ of sequestration would be issued against him said: "If the deed is bona fide—that is, if it is not a mere cloak for retaining a benefit to the grantor—it is a good deed under the statute of Elizabeth." In *Middleton v. Pollock*[6] Jessel M.R. said: "The meaning of the statute is that the debtor must not retain a benefit for himself. It has no regard whatever to the question of preference or priority amongst the creditors of the debtor".'

He then refers to *Glegg v Bromley*[7] and the passage of the judgment of Fletcher Moulton LJ to which I have referred and to the judgment of Parker J. He continued[8]:

1   [1923] 2 Ch 1 at 14
2   [1923] 2 Ch 1 at 16
3   [1925] Ch 853, [1925] All ER Rep 439
4   [1925] Ch 853 at 860, [1925] All ER Rep 439 at 442–443
5   (1869) LR 4 Ch App 622 at 626
6   (1876) 2 Ch D 104 at 108–109
7   [1912] 3 KB 474 at 485, [1911–13] All ER Rep 1138 at 1144
8   [1925] Ch 853 at 861–862, [1925] All ER Rep 439 at 443–444

'. . . in the present case there can be no doubt that Evans committed a fraud upon the company's other creditors, that the company was a party to this fraud, and that, by reason of the fraud, a benefit was secured to the company. But the real fraud on the creditors consisted, not in taking the debentures, but in deliberately postponing their issue until June, 1922, so that the company should be enabled to obtain credit in the meantime. In the same way, it was not the issue of the debentures [and of course it was the issue of the debentures which constituted the preference in this case] but the postponement of that issue, that benefited the company. I cannot find in the circumstances of the case anything more than a fraudulent intention throughout to prefer Evans to the other creditors, carried into effect when the debentures were issued. But if, as appears to be established by the authorities, a present fraudulent intention to prefer one creditor over the others is not sufficient under the statute to avoid a conveyance to that creditor, unless the debtor is himself in some way benefited by the conveyance, I am unable to see how the conveyance is avoided merely because the debtor always had the intention to prefer the creditor at some time or another. I should have been glad if I had been able to avoid these debentures issued to Evans. But, in view of the authorities, I cannot, after giving the matter my best consideration, see how I can do so under the statute of Elizabeth: Mr. Topham [for the liquidator] has not suggested any other ground upon which I can do so at the instance of the liquidator.'

Counsel for the liquidator derives some comfort from the use by Romer J of the words 'fraudulent intention to prefer'[1] which, he suggests, shows that the judge considered that the intention to prefer was per se fraudulent. But that, on analysis seems to me to be an impossible contention. I think that Romer J was using, and can only have been using, the word in the rather artificial sense in which it is used in relation to s 44 of the Bankruptcy Act 1914. If he had really been of opinion that the mere intention to prefer involved actual fraud, he could not have come to the conclusion that the debentures were good, because in the state of knowledge of the debenture holder, there could not have been any defence available to him under the proviso.

Counsel for the liquidator argues nevertheless that, whatever may be the position under the statute of Elizabeth I, to pay one creditor in the knowledge that the result will be that another will go unpaid is to use the words of Maugham J in *Re Patrick and Lyon Ltd*[2] words which 'connote actual dishonesty involving, according to current notions of fair trading among commercial men, real moral blame' and therefore fraudulent within s 332. This would carry greater force if it were not for the following passage from the same judgment. Maugham J said this[3]:

'In my opinion it is not used [and he is talking here about the word "fraud"] in the same sense as that in which the word "fraud" is used in [s 265 of the Companies Act 1929]. There, following the example set by s. 44 of the Bankruptcy Act, 1914, and by s. 92 of the Bankruptcy Act, 1869, both of which deal with the avoidance of fraudulent preferences, the Legislature has thought fit to state that certain acts are to be deemed a fraudulent preference and to be invalid accordingly. A fraudulent preference within the meaning of the Companies Act, 1929, or the Bankruptcy Act, 1914, whether in the case of a company or an individual, possibly may not involve moral blame at all. For example, there may be a discrimination between creditors, irrespective of pressure, on grounds with which most people would sympathize. Again, there is nothing in the language of s. 266 of the Companies Act, 1929 (which enables a floating charge created within six months of a winding up to be attacked in certain circumstances), to indicate that the Legislature took the view that the creation

1   [1925] Ch 853 at 862, [1925] All ER Rep 439 at 443
2   [1933] Ch 786 at 790, [1933] All ER 590 at 593
3   [1933] Ch 786 at 790–791, [1933] All ER Rep 590 at 593

of such a charge when the company is insolvent is fraudulent, however blameworthy it may be. That appears from the fact that the right to attack such a floating charge is limited to cases where the company goes into liquidation within six months of the creation of it. Coming to the present case, I think that in exercising jurisdiction under s. 275 the Court, however little it may approve of the conduct of the director who is being attacked, is bound to consider whether he has been guilty of a dishonest fraud, and it is hardly necessary for me to point out that the onus is upon the person who seeks to make good the charge, whether he be the official receiver, or the liquidator, or a creditor, or a contributory.'

Counsel for the liquidator further argues that whatever may be the position as regards other creditors the preference of the debt due to the parent company is on a different footing. But there is no suggestion in the points of claim that that indebtedness was not genuine and bona fide nor is there any allegation that the realisation of assets was improper. The only thing relied on as constituting fraudulent trading is the preference; and the preference of the parent company in this case is no different from the preference which occurred in *Re Lloyd's Furniture Palace Ltd* [1] where the preferred creditor was himself a director and shareholder and indeed the promoter of the company.

To uphold counsel's contentions for the liquidator would, quite apart from flying in the face of a long line of authorities (among which *Glegg v Bromley* [2] appears to me to be a direct decision of the Court of Appeal which is binding on me), involve a departure from some very strong expressions of opinion in the House of Lords in *Tomkins v Saffrey* [3] where certain rules of the Stock Exchange fell to be considered. In substance they provided for the collection by official assignees appointed by the Stock Exchange of a defaulter's Stock Exchange assets for distribution in payment exclusively of claims arising from Stock Exchange transactions. Under these rules, a defaulter had handed over to the official assignees a sum for distribution only among his Stock Exchange creditors. This was clearly a preference, but their Lordships expressed themselves quite unable to ascribe any moral blame to it. The Court of Appeal had had some hard words to say about the debtor's conduct and the rules: see *Ex parte Saffery, Re Cooke* [4] where James LJ, delivering the judgment of the court, said:

> 'It was suggested that this was done merely in obedience to the rules and regulations of the *Stock Exchange*. My answer to that is that the *Stock Exchange* is not an *Alsatia*. The Queen's laws are paramount there and the Queen's writ runs even into the sacred precincts of *Capel Court*.'

A little later on, he said:

> 'It was suggested that in this particular transaction the man was not minded to make a preference to anybody, but he was only induced to do it and was only doing it for his own emolument and benefit, with a view to being reinstated again on the *Stock Exchange*. Putting the thing in plain language, it was this: An insolvent on the eve of the bankruptcy takes some of his creditors' money to provide himself a comfortable resting-place after his bankruptcy, and a special body of creditors say to him this: "Cheat your other creditors for our benefit, and we will re-admit you as a proper and worthy member of our fraternity." If anything were wanting, this supplies it. It shews how improper and utterly illegal the whole transaction was.'

In the House of Lords, however, this view of the matter, that the preference of the Stock Exchange creditors was fraudulent and improper in the sense of actual impropriety or

---

1 [1925] 1 Ch 853, [1925] All ER Rep 439
2 [1912] 3 KB 474, [1911–13] All ER Rep 1138
3 (1877) 3 App Cas 213
4 (1876) 4 Ch D 555 at 561

fraud, was expressly rejected by at least three of their Lordships, although they were unanimous in upholding the Court of Appeal decision that what had been done constituted a fraudulent preference under the bankruptcy laws and that the assignees had at least constructive, if not actual, knowledge of it. Lord Cairns LC said[1]: '. . . I can see nothing whatever in those rules which is deserving of any anidmadversion whatever. They seem to me to be judicious and business-like rules.' Later he said[2]:

> '. . . they are in this position as to that—they knew the amount of the bankrupt's assets, they knew the amount of their own debts, they knew therefore that if there was another creditor undoubtedly they must be receiving a preference over that other creditor.'

A little later on, he went on to say[3]:

> 'I desire, however, to impute to these gentlemen no departure from principles of rectitude or morality, and I regret that by what I think was a misapprehension of some expressions which fell from the Court below some feeling of dissatisfaction had arisen on the part of the Appellants, as if something had been said in the Court below which was intended to impute, to those who were represented by the Appellants, a departure from correct and honourable action. My Lords, I read the statements which were made, and the expressions which were used by the learned Lord Justice who delivered the judgment of the Court below, as referring not to the facts of the case, but rather to certain arguments which perhaps with too great confidence had been placed before him as to the law applicable to the case. I repeat, I see nothing whatever in what was done here, upon the *Stock Exchange*, which was not perfectly consistent with honourable feeling and honourable conduct, but I repeat also, that there was, underlying the whole of what was done, the one infirmity, namely, the question of whether there was an outside creditor who would not be bound by what was done.'

Lord O'Hagan said[4]:

> '. . . I am of the same opinion, and I too feel bound to say that I see nothing in the case which impeaches the integrity, in purpose or in action, of the *Stock Exchange*. This appeal appears to me to have been prosecuted very much under the influence of irritated feeling; but the words that produced that feeling may be accounted for in the way suggested by my noble and learned friend, without any imputation of impropriety either as to the rules of the body or the proceedings of its members. I think there is no ground whatever for such an imputation;'

Later he said[5]:

> 'The bankrupt was in an insolvent condition. He was indebted to two classes of persons—the members of the *Stock Exchange* and his general creditors . . . in these circumstances he entered into an arrangement, which, however it may be regarded, was clearly made in the terms of the statute "with a view to giving preference" as against one class of creditors in favour of others. The facts of the case could scarcely be represented in more precise and fitting words. A preference was given as soon as, according to the rules of the *Stock Exchange*, the declaration of insolvency authorized the official assignees, for the exclusive benefit of creditors who were members of it, to seize upon the greater portion of the assets by impounding the balance at the *Bank of England*. The practical effect of the notice is thus described by the bankrupt [and he

---

1   (1877) 3 App Cas 213 at 220
2   3 App Cas 213 at 227
3   3 App Cas 213 at 227–228
4   3 App Cas 213 at 228
5   3 App Cas 213 at 231

read the passage and then he said:] But however that may have been, the paragraph plainly shews the understanding and intention of the parties to have been that the *Stock Exchange* creditors should be primarily and exclusively secured.'

That again is echoed in the speech of Lord Blackburn, who said[1]:

'Consequently those assets which, according to this honorary agreement, the defaulter was bound to hand over to the official assignees are to be distributed solely and exclusively to those creditors whose claims arise out of *Stock Exchange* transactions. It is impossible, as it seems to me, not to see that if that be done, these assets, to whatever extent they go, whether they be the whole of the assets or a portion of the assets, are to be so distributed as to give preference to creditors arising out of *Stock Exchange* transactions, over creditors arising out of other than *Stock Exchange* transactions. I do not know that any words can make it clearer than the rule itself does; it says they are to distribute the assets, and they are to recognise no claim except one that arises out of a *Stock Exchange* transaction. That would clearly be a preference.'

Later he said[2]:

'It seems to me to be clear as a matter of fact that he paid this money to the official assignees, because when he became a member of the *Stock Exchange* he had entered into an honorary engagement that he would, in the event of his becoming a defaulter, pay the money to them which they were to distribute to his *Stock Exchange* creditors, who were to be preferred to the others. I do not think there is anything morally dishonest in that, nor anything which in the great majority of cases would produce hardship. Nevertheless, the fact that it is voluntarily paid with the view to give certain creditors, namely, the *Stock Exchange* creditors, an undue preference, is one which I cannot bring myself to doubt.'

He then goes on to say that quite clearly the official assignees had, if not actual, constructive notice of the preference. Lord Gordon said again[3]:

'My Lords, I entirely agree with the rest of your Lordships with reference to the disposal of this case. The observations of the Lord Justice in the Court of Appeal were probably made more in consequence of the line of argument which was submitted to him than with a view to suggest the idea that the members of the *Stock Exchange* intended to get rid of the binding effect of the equitable laws of bankruptcy, which must continue to be binding upon them.'

In the light of the authorities to which I have referred I think that I am bound to accept counsel's submissions on behalf of the respondents.

It is unnecessary for me to decide, and I do not decide, that there may not be circumstances of a very peculiar nature involving preferential payments from which the intention required by s 332 could be inferred. What is alleged here, and it is all that the liquidator relies on, is the bare fact of preference and in the light of the authorities to which I have referred the proposition that that, per se, constitutes fraud within the meaning of the section is not one which is, in my judgment, arguable with any prospect of success. I therefore am of the view that the points of claim, assuming every allegation of fact contained in them to be true and proved, do not, without more, disclose any reasonable cause of action and I must order them to be struck out.

Order accordingly.

Solicitors: *Courts & Co* (for the respondents); *Pritchard Englefield & Tobin* (for the liquidator).

Evelyn Budd Barrister.

---

1   (1877) 3 App Cas 213 at 233–234
2   3 App Cas 213 at 235–236
3   3 App Cas 213 at 238

Re Christie (deceased)
Christie v Keeble

CHANCERY DIVISION

VIVIAN PRICE QC SITTING AS A DEPUTY JUDGE OF THE HIGH COURT

20th, 21st JULY 1978

Family provision – Reasonable provision for maintenance – Provision for applicant other than husband or wife of deceased – Son – Mother's will devising one house to son and another house to daughter – Mother selling house devised to son and replacing it with smaller house – Devise of house to son ineffective and his entitlement under will restricted to half share of residue – Whether will making reasonable financial provision for son's 'maintenance' – Whether applicant required to prove financial difficulty to qualify for provision – Inheritance (Provision for Family and Dependants) Act 1975, ss 1(2)(b), 3(1).

By her will made in 1963 the mother devised her interest in a house in London to her daughter, her interest in a house in Essex to her son, and her residuary estate to the son and daughter in equal shares. On her husband's death in 1971 the mother inherited a half share in the London house and the whole of the Essex house where she was then living. In that year she executed a deed of gift to the daughter of her half share in the London house thereby satisfying the gift to the daughter in the will. In 1976 the mother sold the Essex house for £12,800 and replaced it with a smaller house in Essex which she bought for £9,000. The balance remained in her bank account. Later that year she died. Her residuary estate amounted to some £13,000. Since the house in Essex devised to the son had been sold at the date of the mother's death, the gift to him in the will was ineffective, and he was only entitled to a half share of the residuary estate under the will. The son was in his middle thirties, married and with two young children to support and educate. He owned a house worth about £14,000 which was subject to a mortgage of £6,000. He applied under s 1(1) of the Inheritance (Provision for Family and Dependants) Act 1975 for reasonable financial provision from his mother's estate, contending that she had intended that he should have the house in Essex which was devised to him or its replacement, and that 'reasonable financial provision' for him, within s 1(2)(b)[a] of the 1975 Act, meant that the replacement house should be transferred to him and what remained of the estate should constitute the residue. There was uncontradicted evidence that the mother had expressed the intention of altering her will to devise the replacement house to the son. The daughter opposed the application on the ground that as the son was not in need of maintenance and the will had provided him with a half share in the residuary estate he did not qualify for reasonable financial provision within s 1(2)(b).

Held – Although in the case of an application, other than by the husband or wife of the deceased, for reasonable financial provision under s 1(2)(b) of the 1975 Act, 'reasonable financial provision' meant provision for the applicant's maintenance, that did not imply that the applicant had to prove that he was destitute or in financial difficulty in order to qualify for provision. Having regard to the considerations specified in s 3(1)[b] of the 1975 Act, 'maintenance', in s 1(2)(b), referred to the maintenance of the way of life, well-being, health and financial security of the applicant and his immediate family. Accordingly, to qualify under the 1975 Act the applicant had to prove that the disposition of the deceased's estate did not make financial provision for such maintenance as it would be reasonable for him to receive in all the circumstances. On that test, and considering in particular the mother's intention that the daughter should have her interest in one of the properties and

---

a   Section 1(2) is set out at p 549 *d e*, post

b   Section 3(1), so far as material, is set out at p 549 *f* to *h*, post

the son her interest in the other, the mother's will had not made reasonable financial provision for the son's maintenance. The application would therefore be allowed and an order made transferring the replacement house to the son and dividing the residue of the estate between him and the daughter (see p 550 *e* to *h* and p 551 *g* to 552 *a*, post).

Notes

For matters to which the court is to have regard on an application for financial provision from a deceased's estate, see 17 Halsbury's Laws (4th Edn) para 1337.

For the Inheritance (Provision for Family and Dependants) Act 1975, ss 1, 3, see 45 Halsbury's Statutes (3rd Edn) 496, 501.

Originating summons

By an originating summons dated 25th August 1977 the plaintiff, Graham John Christie ('the son'), applied for an order for reasonable financial provision to be made for him out of the net estate of his mother, Grace Annie Victoria Christie ('the deceased'), under s 1 of the Inheritance (Provision for Family and Dependants) Act 1975. The defendant to the application was Ethel Violet Keeble, the plaintiff's sister ('the daughter'). The facts are set out in the judgment.

David Gerrey for the son.
John Trenhaile for the daughter.

VIVIAN PRICE QC. Grace Annie Victoria Christie ('the deceased') of 9 Edison Road, Holland-on-Sea, Essex, formerly of 76 Median Road, Clapton, London E5, died on 19th December 1976. Her will dated 23rd September 1963 was proved on 21st March 1977 in the Ipswich District Probate Registry by her two children, Graham John Christie ('the son') and Ethel Violet Keeble ('the daughter'), who were granted letters of administration of the deceased's estate and who had been appointed in her will as executors and trustees of the will.

At the time when she made her will in 1963 the deceased was living with the daughter and her family at 76 Median Road together with her husband, Mr Charlie Christie. That house at that time was owned jointly by Mr Charlie Christie and the daughter's husband and, indeed, from that time until 1968 or 1969 the deceased and her husband continued to live with the daughter and her family at the house in Median Road, Clapton. The son also lived in the same house at Median Road up until his marriage in 1966.

After 1968 or 1969 the deceased had moved with her husband to 26 Ingarfield Road, Holland-on-Sea, Essex, which had been left to her husband in 1963 by two friends of the family, Mrs Florence Bell and Miss Edith Heath.

On the death of her husband in 1971 the deceased inherited 26 Ingarfield Road and her husband's half share of 76 Median Road, Clapton. The year 1971 is of significance since in that same year in which she inherited her husband's half share in 76 Median Road, Clapton, the deceased executed a deed of gift of that half share to her daughter. The significance can be seen from a consideration of her will of 23rd September 1963. Under cl 3 of her will she had given all her estate and effects whatsoever and wheresoever to her husband, Charlie Christie, absolutely, but since he had died in 1971, then by cl 4 of the will, cll 5, 6 and 7 took effect. Under cl 6(b) the deceased devised and bequeathed all her estate and interest at the time of her death in the freehold dwelling-house, with the outbuildings and land belonging to or held with the same and known as 76 Median Road, Clapton, London E5 to her daughter absolutely. Thus in 1971 by her deed of gift the deceased had carried into effect that part of her intention, as expressed in her will, that related to the transfer of her interest in 76 Median Road to her daughter.

The other portions of the will that came into effect in 1971 on Mr Charlie Christie's death, were: first of all, cl 5 whereby, she states, 'I APPOINT my son, GRAHAM CHRISTIE (if and when he shall attain the age of twenty one years) and my daughter ETHEL KEEBLE (hereinafter called "my Trustees") to be the EXECUTORS and TRUSTEES of this my Will'.

Clause 6 provides:

'I DEVISE and bequeath:—a). All my estate and interest at the time of my death in the freehold dwellinghouse with the outbuildings and land belonging to or held with the same and known as 26, Ingarfield Road Holland-on-Sea in the County of Essex to my said son Graham Christie absolutely [(b) I have already read] c). I direct that all duties leviable at my death in respect of the foregoing devises or in respect of the property comprised therein shall be paid as part of my testamentary expenses out of my general personal estate.'

Clause 7 provides:

'SUBJECT to the devises hereinbefore given I GIVE my residuary estate to such of my said son Graham Christie and my said daughter Ethel Keeble as shall survive me and if both shall so survive me in equal shares absolutely.'

Thus after 1971 the position was that the daughter had already received the property interest that was to be left to her under the deceased's will while the son's future property interest under that will remained in the possession of the deceased. The deceased, indeed, continued to live at 26 Ingarfield Road, Holland-on-Sea, during her widowhood.

By the summer of 1976, however, she had decided to move from 26 Ingarfield Road because she was finding the house and garden there too large for her and too expensive to maintain. She therefore planned to move into a smaller property. By November 1976 she carried this plan into effect, had sold 26 Ingarfield Road, for £12,800, and had bought 9 Edison Road, Holland-on-Sea, into which she moved on 22nd November.

Less than one month later, on 19th December, the deceased died and, her husband having predeceased her, then, as I have said, the son and daughter were appointed under cl 5 of her will to be her executors and trustees. Clause 6(a) could have no effect since at the time of her death she had neither estate nor interest in 26 Ingarfield Road. Similarly, cl 6(b) could have no effect since at the time of her death she had neither estate nor interest in 76 Median Road, Clapton. Clause 7 effectively became the only operative clause of her will pursuant to which the son and the daughter share equally in the residuary estate which amounted to the sum of £13,613.

The son, however, complains that this division was not his mother's intention which was, so he asserts, that at her death he should have 26 Ingarfield Road, or its replacement, 9 Edison Road, while his sister, Mrs Keeble, should have his mother's interest in 76 Median Road. Only after these dispositions had been made, so the son asserts, should the residuary estate be divided between himself and his sister. It was in those circumstances that the son had issued the present summons under the Inheritance (Provision for Family and Dependants) Act 1975, asking for an order that such reasonable financial provision as the court thinks just be made to him out of his mother's estate. At the hearing of the summons before me, it was submitted on the son's behalf that 'reasonable financial provision' for him under the Act would be an order for the transfer to him of 9 Edison Road with the residue being then divided equally between himself and his sister.

The first question that I have to decide is whether the son's application under the 1975 Act is well founded in law since its whole basis is challenged by the daughter. She asserts that her brother is not in need of maintenance and assistance, and the provision made for him in their mother's will, being something over £6,500, is reasonable when viewed objectively. She, therefore, says that his application under the 1975 Act is misconceived in law and should be dismissed.

Under s 1 of the 1975 Act, application for financial provision from a deceased's estate may be made by any of the persons specified in paras (a) to (e) of sub-s (1), on the ground that the disposition of the deceased's estate effected by his will or the law relating to intestacy, or the combination of his will and that law, is not such as to make reasonable financial provision for the applicant.

As one would expect from the short title of the Act, the Inheritance (Provision for Family and Dependants) Act 1975, the persons specified in paras (a) to (e) of sub-s (1) are respectively either persons having a family connection with the deceased or a dependant of the deceased. Thus, (a) is the wife or husband of the deceased; (b) is a former wife or husband of the deceased who has not remarried; (c) is a child of the deceased; (d) is any person (not being a child of the deceased) who, in the case of any marriage to which the deceased was at any time a party, was treated by the deceased as a child of the family in relation to that marriage. All these deal with people having some family relationship with the deceased. Then (e) is any person (not being a person included in the foregoing paragraphs of the subsection) who immediately before the death of the deceased was being maintained, either wholly or partly, by the deceased.

The son qualifies, of course, under para (c) as a child of the deceased, and the question is whether the disposition of his mother's estate effected by her will is not such as to make 'reasonable financial provision' for him.

'Reasonable financial provision' is defined in s 1(2) which draws a sharp distinction between financial provision for the husband or wife of the deceased and financial provision for any of the other classes of persons qualifying under paras (a) to (e) of sub-s (1). Thus, sub-s (2) is in the following terms:

'In this Act "reasonable financial provision"—(a) in the case of an application made by virtue of subsection (1)(a) above by the husband or wife of the deceased (except where the marriage with the deceased was the subject of a decree of judicial separation and at the date of death the decree was in force and the separation was continuing), means such financial provision as it would be reasonable in all the circumstances of the case for a husband or wife to receive, whether or not that provision is required for his or her maintenance; (b) in the case of any other application [which, of course, includes the present one] made by virtue of subsection (1) above, means such financial provision as it would be reasonable in all the circumstances of the case for the applicant to receive for his maintenance.'

In considering that question, I am directed to consider the various matters specified in s 3 of the 1975 Act. Section 3(1) makes it clear that in considering both the question whether reasonable financial provision has in fact been made and the question whether, and in what manner, the court shall exercise its powers to make an order under s 2, the court shall have regard to the following matters:

'(a) the financial resources and financial needs which the applicant has or is likely to have in the foreseeable future; (b) the financial resources and financial needs which any other applicant for an order under section 2 of this Act has or is likely to have in the foreseeable future; (c) the financial resources and financial needs which any beneficiary of the estate of the deceased has or is likely to have in the foreseeable future; (d) any obligations and responsibilities which the deceased had towards any applicant for an order under the said section 2 or towards any beneficiary of the estate of the deceased; (e) the size and nature of the net estate of the deceased; (f) any physical or mental disability of any applicant for an order under the said section 2 or any beneficiary of the estate of the deceased; (g) any other matter, including the conduct of the applicant or any other person, which in the circumstances of the case the court may consider relevant.'

Of those matters, under those paragraphs, the following are relevant for consideration. Under para (a) I must thus have regard to the financial resources and financial needs which the son has or is likely to have in the foreseeable future; under para (c) the financial resources and financial needs which the daughter has or is likely to have in the foreseeable future; under para (d) possibly any obligations and responsibilities which the deceased had towards the son or the daughter; under para (e) the size and nature of the deceased's estate; under para (g) any other matter, including the conduct of the son or the deceased or the daughter which the court, in the circumstances of the case, may consider relevant.

In addition, I must refer to some of the other subsections of s 3. Subsection (2) has no relevance. The first part of sub-s (3), however, I must read:

'Without prejudice to the generality of paragraph (*g*) of subsection (1) above, where an application for an order under section 2 of this Act is made by virtue of section 1(1)(*c*) [that is the son's application] or 1(1)(*d*) of this Act, the court shall, in addition to the matters specifically mentioned in paragraphs (*a*) to (*f*) of that subsection, have regard to the manner in which the applicant was being or in which he might expect to be educated or trained . . .'

I read it only to observe that there is no evidence before me that the son is embarking or proposing to embark on any scheme of further education at any time in the future. Then sub-s (4) has no relevance. Subsection (5) directs that:

'In considering the matters to which the court is required to have regard under this section, the court shall take into account the facts as known to the court at the date of the hearing.'

Finally, under sub-s (6):

'In considering the financial resources of any person for the purposes of this section the court shall take into account his earning capacity and in considering the financial needs of any person for the purposes of this section the court shall take into account his financial obligations and responsibilities.'

It is in the light of all these considerations that I have to decide the question arising under s 1 of the 1975 Act, namely whether in general terms the disposition of the deceased's estate effected by his will or the law relating to intestacy, or a combination of his will and that law, is not such as to make in the case of an application other than by a husband or wife of the deceased such financial provision as it would be reasonable for the applicant to receive for his maintenance.

In my judgment, the financial provision that is thus contemplated is not necessarily financial provision that would be 'required' for the applicant's maintenance. The contrast between paras (*a*) and (*b*) of s 1(2), in my judgment, makes this clear. Nor in my judgment does the use of the word 'maintenance' carry with it any implication that the applicant, in order to qualify, must be in any way in a state of destitution or financial difficulty. Nor in my judgment is it useful to refer to the test as being an objective test, whatever that word may mean, in the context of this Act which directs the court to consider the particular and personal matters set out in s 3.

In my judgment, the word 'maintenance' refers to no more and no less than the applicant's way of life and well-being, his health, financial security and allied matters such as the well-being, health and financial security of his immediate family for whom he is responsible. Thus the question that the court has to consider under the 1975 Act on an application by a person other than the husband and wife of the deceased is, in my judgment, whether the disposition of the deceased's estate effected by his will or the law relating to intestacy or the combination of his will and that law is not such as would make reasonable financial provision for the applicant in the sense of such financial provision as it would be reasonable in all the circumstances of the case for the applicant to receive for the maintenance of his way of life and well-being, his health and financial security and the well-being, health and financial security of his immediate family for whom he is responsible.

Under s 2, before the court considers whether it should make an order, it has to be satisfied that the disposition of the deceased's estate did not make reasonable financial provision for the applicant and it is clear that the burden of so satisfying the court must rest on the applicant.

On that basis I now turn to examine, as a matter of fact, the question of whether the disposition of the deceased's estate effected by her will was not such as to make such financial provision for the son as it would be reasonable in all the circumstances of the case for the son to receive for his maintenance in the sense that I have indicated before.

The evidence before me comprised three affidavits by the son, one affidavit by his wife,

Mrs Georgina Ann Christie, and one affidavit by Mr Kenneth Levy Brown, all in support of the application, while the daughter swore two affidavits in opposition.

At the hearing of the summons the son and Mr Brown were cross-examined by counsel for the daughter, while the daughter in turn was cross-examined on the son's behalf. The son's wife was not cross-examined. All the witnesses seemed to me to give their evidence in a careful and frank manner. The daughter, in particular, did not allow her natural anxiety that the disposition of her mother's estate effected by her mother's will should not be disturbed in any way to affect her evidence.

I have carefully taken into account the financial circumstances of both the son and the daughter. I do not think that it is necessary for me to rehearse them in detail, but only draw the conclusion that for both of them any money that they respectively were to receive from their mother's estate would clearly be of great use to them. The son has a house worth approximately £14,000 with a £6,000 mortgage, and has two young children to support and educate. The daughter's two sons are grown up and able to contribute to the household expenses and the daughter, with her husband, owns the house in which they live. On the other hand, the son is in his middle thirties while the daughter is 20 years older and no doubt reasonably to be expected to be considering provision for her old age. At one time, for a period of five years, the deceased lived with her daughter, but after she left, no doubt, the daughter did not see quite so much of her mother. In the evidence before me there was some attention paid to such matters as how frequently the son, on the one hand, visited the deceased as compared with his sister, and also whether he did more maintenance and other odd jobs about the house for his mother than did the daughter or her family. I am bound to say that I attach no importance to such matters since, it seems to me, that visiting and helping a widowed mother is no more and no less than an expression of natural affection as between a son and his mother, on the one hand, and a daughter and her mother, on the other hand. I do not think that it is useful or desirable for a court, when considering an application such as the present one, to attempt to strike a balance sheet between the expressions of natural affection of one child of the deceased as against another. Nor do I think that in the circumstances of this case any significance or assistance is to be gained by considering whether the deceased had any special obligations towards the son as opposed to his sister. There is no evidence that she treated the one in any way differently from the other. The size and nature of the estate of the deceased is, however, of significance since it shows that the £12,800 received by the deceased for 26 Ingarfield Road was applied as to £9,000, or thereabouts, for the purchase of 9 Edison Road while the remainder was left in her bank accounts.

It is, in my judgment, quite clear on the evidence that the deceased had the intention at all times right up to her death that her daughter would have her interest in the one property while her son should have her interest in the other. The 1963 will explicitly states this intention. In 1971 the deceased put part of her intention into effect by making a deed of gift of her half share of 76 Median Road to her daughter. In July 1976 the house at 26 Ingarfield Road was still intended by the deceased to go to her son. In my judgment, when she sold that house it remained her intention that her son should have the replacement. The son in his evidence stated that his mother expressed the intention of altering her will so as to devise the replacement property to him. His evidence was not shaken in cross-examination nor was the evidence of the like effect of Mr Brown. The son's wife in her affidavit stated that when she and the son visited the deceased in July 1976, the deceased said that the house and garden at Ingarfield Road was becoming too large for her and that she was planning to move to a smaller property. According to the son's wife, the deceased stated that not only would she find the property easier to manage, but 'also that [the son] and I would, when she died, and such property became ours'. The son's wife was not cross-examined and I accept her evidence.

In all these circumstances, I am satisfied that the disposition of the deceased's estate effected by her 1963 will did not make such financial provision for the son as was reasonable in all the circumstances of the case for him to receive for his maintenance. In her very fair evidence the daughter straightforwardly agreed that it was probable that she

had benefited more than her brother.   In my judgment, it is fair and just that this
application should be allowed to redress the balance, and, accordingly, I order that the *a*
house and garden at Edison Road be transferred to the son and that the residue of the estate
be divided into equal shares between him and his sister.

Order accordingly.

Solicitors: *Prestons & Kerlys* (for the son); *Corsellis & Berney* (for the daughter).

b

Tokunbo Williams Barrister.

Universal Corporation v Five Ways Properties Ltd

c

COURT OF APPEAL, CIVIL DIVISION
BUCKLEY AND EVELEIGH LJJ
30th, 31st OCTOBER 1978

Sale of land – Deposit – Forfeiture – Purchaser's failure to complete – Purchaser unable to complete
because purchaser's bank not arranging transfer of funds in time – Vendor rescinding contract and *d*
forfeiting deposit – Purchaser able to complete 14 days after rescission – Purchaser claiming return
of deposit – Whether contract frustrated by failure of purchaser's bank to transfer funds in time –
Whether court having jurisdiction to order return of deposit if it thought fit – Whether if court
having jurisdiction it should exercise discretion to order return of deposit – Law of Property Act
1925, s 49(2).

e

By a contract dated 21st December 1977 the purchasers agreed to buy a property in London
from the vendors for £885,000.   The purchasers paid a deposit of £88,500 and completion
was to be on 24th January 1978.   The purchasers intended financing the purchase from
money deposited in a bank in Nigeria and instructed the bank to transfer the balance of the
purchase price to their London solicitors.   Because of a change in the exchange control
regulations in force in Nigeria there was a delay in the transmission of the money to *f*
London and the purchasers were unable to complete on 24th January.   On that date the
vendors served a 28 day completion notice on the purchasers in accordance with the terms
of the contract.   The notice expired on 22nd February and, the purchasers having failed to
complete, the vendors rescinded the contract on that date and purported to forfeit the
deposit.   The purchasers' money arrived in London from Nigeria on 6th March but the
vendors declined to proceed with the contract.   The purchasers brought an action against *g*
the vendors seeking to recover the deposit on the grounds that the contract had been
frustrated or alternatively that the court should, if it thought fit, order repayment of the
deposit under s 49(2)[a] of the Law of Property Act 1925.   On an application by the vendors,
Walton J[b] ordered that the writ and statement be struck out, holding, inter alia, that the
court had no jurisdiction under s 49(2) to order the return of a deposit if the vendors would
have been granted specific performance had they applied for such relief, and that in any *h*
event it would not be just and equitable to deprive the vendors of a deposit to which in law
they were entitled.   The purchasers appealed.

Held – (i) Although the purchasers were unable to complete by the completion date, the
contract was not incapable of performance and nothing had happened to make performance
of the contract significantly different from that which was contracted for.   The fact that the *j*
purchasers did not have the money to complete the contract on the due date did not
therefore amount to a frustration of the contract (see p 544, *d* to *f* and p 556 *d*, post); dictum

---

a   Section 49(2) is set out at p 554 *g*, post
b   [1978] 3 All ER 1131

of Lord Radcliffe in *Davis Contractors Ltd v Fareham Urban District Council* [1956] 2 All ER at 160 applied.

(ii) On the true construction of s 49(2) of the 1925 Act, which was designed simply to do justice between vendor and purchaser, the court had an unqualified discretion to order repayment of a deposit where the justice of the case so required it as being the fairest course between the parties, subject only to the discretion being exercised judicially and with regard to all relevant considerations, including the terms of the contract. It followed that there was an issue between the parties whether the vendor should be permitted to retain the deposit or alternatively ordered to return it under s 49(2) and be left to seek damages, and that issue should be left to the trial judge or tried as a separate issue. The appeal would therefore be allowed (see p 555 *a b* and *e* to *g* and p 556 *a* to *c*, post); *Schindler v Pigault* (1975) 30 P & CR 328 approved.

Decision of Walton J [1978] 3 All ER 1131 reversed.

Notes

For the right to recovery of deposit by the purchaser, see 34 Halsbury's Laws (3rd Edn) 328–330, paras 557–558, and for cases on the subject, see 40 Digest (Repl) 246–261, 2067–2200.

For the Law of Property Act 1925, s 49 see 27 Halsbury's Statutes (3rd Edn) 424.

Cases referred to in judgments

Davis Contractors Ltd v Fareham Urban District Council [1956] 2 All ER 145, [1956] AC 696, [1956] 3 WLR 37, 54 LGR 289, HL, 12 Digest (Reissue) 507, 3518.
Schindler v Pigault (1975) 30 P & CR 328.

Cases also cited

British Movietonews Ltd v London and District Cinemas Ltd [1951] 2 All ER 617, [1952] AC 166, HL.
Evans v Bartlam [1937] 2 All ER 646, [1937] AC 473, HL.
Hunt (Charles) Ltd v Palmer [1931] 2 Ch 287, [1931] All ER Rep 815.
Macara (James) Ltd v Barclay [1944] 2 All ER 589, [1945] 1 KB 148, CA.

Appeal

By writ of summons issued on 13th March 1978, the plaintiffs, Universal Corpn, brought an action against the defendants, Five Ways Properties Ltd, claiming repayment of the deposit of £88,500, together with interest, paid by the plaintiffs to the defendants in respect of the purchase by the plaintiffs of the freehold property known as Dorset House, Upper Gloucester Place, London, which, by contract dated 21st December 1977, the defendants had agreed to sell to them. The defendants, by notice of motion dated 29th March 1978, sought an order under RSC Ord 18, r 19, and/or the inherent jurisdiction of the court that the statement of claim to be struck out and the action dismissed on the ground that the statement of claim disclosed no reasonable cause of action and/or was frivolous or vexatious and/or was an abuse of the process of the court and/or was bound to fail. On 28th April 1978 Walton J[1] struck out the writ and statement of claim as disclosing no cause of action. The plaintiffs appealed to the Court of Appeal. The facts are summarised in the judgment of Buckley LJ. They are fully set out in the judgment of Walton J in the Chancery Division[2].

T L G Cullen QC and *Anthony Thompson* for the plaintiffs.
Gerald Godfrey QC and *Joseph Harper* for the defendants.

BUCKLEY LJ. This is an appeal from an order of Walton J,[1] whereby he struck out the writ and statement of claim in this action under RSC Ord 18, r 19, or under the inherent jurisdiction of the court, on the ground that the plaintiff was bound to fail, that the action was one which could not possibly succeed.

---

1   [1978] 3 All ER 1131
2   [1978] 3 All ER 1131 at 1133–1135

The case arises on a contract for the sale of a piece of property in London to the plaintiff at the price of £885,000, a deposit of £88,500 being paid on exchange of contracts. The facts, and statement of claim which has been served, are set out carefully by the judge in his judgment in the court below[1] and I do not propose to recapitulate that material.

The plaintiff's case for the repayment of the deposit is founded on two contentions: first, that the contract was frustrated and, secondly, a claim under the Law of Property Act 1925, s 49(2). The plaintiff is a Liberian company. It proposed to finance the purchase out of funds in Nigeria. It has no place of business in this country and apparently it has no funds at its disposal in this country.

Unhappily for the plaintiff, owing to complications arising out of a change in the Nigerian exchange control law, the plaintiff was unable to have the necessary moneys at its disposal in London by the date fixed for completion after time had been made of the essence of the contract. Consequently the defendant gave notice under condition 22 of the National Conditions of Sale, 19th Edn, which were incorporated in the contract, rescinding the contract and forfeiting the deposit; that was on 22nd February last.

The money became available to the plaintiff company in London on 6th March 1978, 12 days after the notice of rescission. On 12th March the plaintiff issued its writ, and on 29th March the defendant moved to strike out the writ and statement of claim. On 28th April the judge made the order appealed from.

The judge dealt with the topic of frustration quite shortly. He said[2]:

'But quite emphatically the doctrine of frustration cannot be brought into play merely because the purchaser finds, for whatever reason, he has not got the money to complete the contract.'

That seems to me to be an accurate and proper statement. Certainly the plaintiff was unable, by reason of matters beyond its control, to complete the contract when it should have done so, but this is something quite different from the contract having become incapable of performance; nor, in my view, can it be suggested that anything had happened to make the performance of the contract, in the circumstances existing at the date for completion, significantly different from what was contracted for: see *Davis Contractors Ltd v Fareham Urban District Council*[3]. On the material before the court, in my judgment, no frustration is shown to have occurred.

The alternative claim is put forward under s 49(2) of the Law of Property Act 1925, which is in these terms:

'Where the court refuses to grant specific performance of a contract, or in any action for the return of a deposit, the court may, if it thinks fit, order the repayment of any deposit.'

The judge thought that it would be surprising if Parliament had, by that provision, conferred on the courts an absolute unfettered jurisdiction to interfere in a bargain between vendor and purchaser whenever it thought fit to do so, without the remotest hint of any guidelines as to how what he described as 'that quite extraordinary jurisdiction' should be exercised.

He reached a preferred view on the construction of s 49(2) that the jurisdiction only exists where the vendor could, but has not, sued for specific performance, on which basis the judge said that the subsection was simply not applicable to a case of the present nature, which is one in which the vendor, had he issued the writ for specific performance in time, must have been granted such a decree beyond all question. With deference to Walton J, this seems to me to confuse the question in what circumstances the jurisdiction exists with the question in what circumstances the court will exercise it in favour of the purchaser.

The judge, however, went on to say that, if he were wrong in his preferred view as being too narrow, it was obvious that there must be severe limits on the operation of the

1 [1978] 3 All ER 1131 at 1133–1135
2 [1978] 3 All ER 1131 at 1135
3 [1956] 2 All ER 145 at 160, [1956] AC 696 at 729, per Lord Radcliffe

subsection. It is not, he said, designed simply to do justice between vendor and purchaser. Looking at s 49(2) in its terms, having regard to the language used in it and without regard to extraneous considerations, this seems to be precisely what the section in fact is.

By way of supporting, or establishing, his view, the judge asked[1]: '. . . when can it be just and equitable to deprive the vendor of the whole of the moneys to which he is at law entitled?' It seems to me that this is, or may be, precisely the problem which the section presents to the court, for it confers on the judge a discretion, which is unqualified by any language of the subsection, to order or refuse repayment of the deposit, a discretion which must, of course, be exercised judicially and with regard to all relevant considerations, including the very important consideration of the terms of the contract into which the parties have chosen to enter.

With respect to the judge, it does not seem to me to follow, as he thought, that a purchaser can only succeed in a claim to repayment of the deposit if the vendor's conduct has been open to criticism in some way which Walton J described as having some mark of equitable disfavour attached to it.

In the course of argument, we have been referred to the principle of construction which is stated in Maxwell on Statutes[2] where it is said that 'it is a canon of interpretation that all words, if they be general and not precise, are to be restricted to the fitness of the matter, that is, to be construed as particular if the intention be particular'. That, as I understand it, is a reference to the well-known doctrine of having regard to the mischief which the enactment is intended to deal with; but that doctrine, as I understand it, does not entitle the court to disregard the plain and natural meaning of wide general terms in a statute. If the language is equivocal and requires construction, then the doctrine is a proper one to refer to; but if the language is quite plain then the duty of the court is to give effect to what Parliament has said, and it seems to me that in the present case Parliament has conferred a wide and general discretion.

I prefer to the judge's approach to the construction of this subsection the approach of Megarry V-C, who has expressed the view that the jurisdiction is one to be exercised where the justice of the case requires: see what he said in *Schindler v Pigault*[3]. In this connection I take the word 'justice' to be used in a wide sense, indicating that repayment must be ordered in any circumstances which make this the fairest course between the two parties. It is, I think, relevant in the present case that condition 22 of the National Conditions does not confer on the vendor an unqualified right to forfeit a deposit. The words in para 3 of the condition are: '. . . the purchaser's deposit may be forfeited (unless the court otherwise directs).' This formula may well have been adopted with the terms of s 49(2) in mind. However that may be, in my view the language makes clear that the vendor has not an absolute right to retain a deposit paid by a purchaser who is in default under the condition.

Walton J properly drew attention to the fact that the statement of claim contains no suggestion that the defendant knew that the plaintiff was going to obtain its finance for the purchase from Nigeria. That position has changed since the matter was before the judge, for counsel for the plaintiff has now stated that he is instructed that the plaintiff is in a position to allege that the defendant was at all relevant times aware that the plaintiff needed to bring funds from abroad in order to complete the purchase, and he has sought leave to amend the statement of claim accordingly. It is not for us, on this appeal, to attempt to prejudge the issues in the action, but we must remember that the statement of claim should only be struck out if it is clear that the claim cannot succeed, or that it is in some other way an abuse of the process of the court. It is not clear to me that, when the circumstances are investigated at the trial, the trial judge might not justifiably reach the conclusion that, having regard to all the relevant circumstances, including those in which the notice of rescission and forfeiture were given, it would not be more just to order

1   [1978] 3 All ER 1131 at 1137
2   12th Edn (1969), p 86
3   (1975) 30 P & CR 328

repayment of the deposit, leaving the defendant such remedy in damages as may be available to it, than to allow it to retain the very substantial deposit which was paid in this case.

I would allow this appeal.

EVELEIGH LJ. I am not wholly confident of the extent of the jurisdiction of the judge under s 49(2) of the Law of Property Act 1925. But I am confident that the limit contended for by the defendant is not plain and obvious. That being so, in my judgment the procedure adopted was wrong.

If there is an arguable point of law, which there clearly is in this case, then the matter should more appropriately be set down under RSC Ord 33, r 3.

This case raises not only the question of construction of s 49, but also the effect of condition 22 of the National Conditions of Sale, with the important words in that paragraph: '. . . the purchaser's deposit may be forfeited (unless the court otherwise directs).' The precise effect of those words, either standing alone in a contract, or perhaps read in conjunction with s 49(2), will give rise, I have little doubt, to a great deal of argument on either side.

It has been submitted in this case that s 49(2), although it has general words, has a specific intent, and consequently those words should be read in a narrow sense. That submission, as I see it, begs the whole question of what the intent of s 49(2) is.

For those reasons, therefore, I would allow this appeal.

In so far as the question of frustration is concerned, I agree with all that has been said on that matter by Buckley LJ.

Appeal allowed.

Solicitors: *Heald & Nickinson* (for the plaintiffs); *Linklaters & Paines* (for the defendants).

J H Fazan Esq Barrister.

C v C (divorce: exceptional hardship)

COURT OF APPEAL, CIVIL DIVISION

ORMROD, WALLER AND BRANDON LJJ

31st OCTOBER, 7th, 8th, 23rd NOVEMBER 1978

Divorce – Petition – Petition within three years of marriage – Discretion to allow – Exceptional hardship or exceptional depravity – Homosexual husband – Wife discovering husband homosexual after marriage – Husband becoming impotent and losing interest in wife a few weeks after marriage and leaving her shortly afterwards – Whether effect of husband's conduct on wife amounting to exceptional hardship – Matrimonial Causes Act 1973, s 3(2).

The parties married on 15th October 1977 having had a successful and normal sexual relationship for some three years prior to the marriage. A few weeks after the marriage took place the husband became impotent and by 19th December 1977 he ceased to attempt intercourse with the wife and on 5th February 1978 he left the matrimonial home. The wife discovered that the husband was homosexual, that he had had homosexual relations before the marriage and that he was incapable of having normal sexual relationship with her. On 30th June 1978 she applied for leave to a petition for divorce within three years from the date of the marriage alleging both exceptional hardship to her and exceptional depravity by the husband under s 3(2)[a] of the Matrimonial Causes Act 1973. The judge

---

a Section 3(2) provides: 'A judge of the court may, on an application made to him, allow the presentation of a petition for divorce within the specified period on the ground that the case is one of exceptional hardship suffered by the petitioner or of exceptional depravity on the part of the respondent; but in determining the application the judge shall have regard to the interests of any child of the family and to the question whether there is reasonable probability of a reconciliation between the parties during the specified period.'

held that she had not made out a case on either ground and refused the application. The wife appealed against the judge's finding that the case was not one of exceptional hardship suffered by her but not against his finding that the husband's homosexual behaviour did not amount to exceptional depravity.

Held – Having regard to the fact that for the purposes of s 3(2) of the 1973 Act 'exceptional hardship' included hardship arising from the conduct of the other spouse, the husband's conduct in leading the wife to expect a normal sexual relationship in marriage which he was then unable to sustain had caused her exceptional hardship. The wife would therefore be granted leave under s 3(2) on the ground of exceptional hardship to present a petition for divorce within three years of marriage. The appeal would accordingly be allowed (see p 560 e f, post).

Per Curiam. Since it is now accepted that in dealing with an application for leave to petition for divorce within three years from the date of marriage the judge may properly take into account hardship arising from the conduct of the other spouse, present hardship and hardship arising from having to wait until the specified period has elapsed, it seems to be unneccessary in the great majority of cases to rely on exceptional depravity with all its unpleasant overtones and difficulties. In practice, when it is alleged, the proposed petitioner often relies for proof of the element of exceptional depravity on the effect of the conduct on him or her (see p 560 a b, post).

Notes

For principles on which leave to present a petition within three years of marriage is granted, see 13 Halsbury's Laws (4th Edn) para 559, and for cases on the subject, see 27(1) Digest (Reissue) 355–357, 2614–2628.

For the Matrimonial Causes Act 1973, s 3, see 43 Halsbury's Statutes (3rd Edn) 546.

Cases referred to in judgment

Blackwell v Blackwell (1973) 117 Sol Jo 939, CA.
Bowman v Bowman [1949] 2 All ER 127, [1949] P 353, [1949] LJR 1416, CA, 27(1) Digest (Reissue) 355, 2618.
Brewer v Brewer [1964] 1 All ER 539, [1964] 1 WLR 403, CA, 27(1) Digest (Reissue) 356, 2621.
Fisher v Fisher [1948] P 263, CA, 27(1) Digest (Reissue) 355, 2617.
Hillier v Hillier and Latham [1958] 2 All ER 261, [1958] P 186, [1958] 2 WLR 937, CA, 27(1) Digest (Reissue) 356, 2622.
Winter v Winter [1944] P 72, 113 LJP 49, 171 LT 111, CA, 27(1) Digest (Reissue) 355, 2614.

Cases also cited

C v C [1967] 1 All ER 928, [1967] P 298.
Sanders v Sanders (1967) 111 Sol Jo 481, CA.
V v V [1966] 3 All ER 493, [1966] 1 WLR 1589, CA.
W v W [1966] 2 All ER 889, [1967] P 291.

Appeal

The wife appealed against an order of his Honour Judge Sleeman made at the Birmingham County Court on 3rd August 1978 refusing her application, dated 30th June 1978, for an order giving her leave under s 3(2) of the Matrimonial Causes Act 1973 to file a petition for the dissolution of her marriage to the husband before the expiration of three years from the date of the marriage. The facts are set out in the judgment of the court.

Margaret Booth QC and *Patricia Deeley* for the wife.
Nicholas Wilson for the Queen's Proctor as amicus curiae.
The husband did not appear.

Cur adv vult

23rd November. **ORMROD LJ** read the following judgment of the court: This is an appeal from an order made by his Honour Judge Sleeman on 3rd August 1978, sitting at

Birmingham, dismissing an application by the wife under the Matrimonial Causes Act 1973, s 3(2), for leave to present a petition for dissolution within the 'specified period', that is, three years from the date of the marriage. The application was based on both exceptional hardship and exceptional depravity. The judge held that the wife had not made out her case on either ground and therefore dismissed the application.

The material before the judge consisted of a short affidavit by the wife, exhibiting and verifying the contents of the proposed petition, and an affidavit by a man who need not be referred to by name. The substance of the wife's case was that the marriage, which took place on 15th October 1977, had proved to be a disastrous failure within a few weeks because soon after the honeymoon to all intents and purposes the husband became impotent. At the same time he showed less and less interest in the wife and spent much of his time with a young male cousin of whom he seemed to be very fond. By 19th December the husband had ceased to attempt intercourse and on 5th January 1978 he left the matrimonial home. From then on the marriage was dead. During this period the husband from time to time made distressing remarks to the wife such as that he did not like women's bodies and was frightened of women. He refused to consult a marriage guidance counsellor. The wife became increasingly suspicious that the husband was 'queer', but he denied it. However, soon after the parting the wife spoke to a mutual friend, the deponent to the supporting affidavit, and from him learnt that on two occasions shortly before the marriage the husband had made overt homosexual advances to him.

There was very little other evidence of hardship except that the wife said that she had lost a stone in weight. This was not confirmed by medical or other evidence.

It is not very surprising that on this evidence the judge declined to find either exceptional hardship or exceptional depravity.

The wife appealed. When the appeal first came on for the hearing she was represented by junior counsel who said that she intended to argue that the judge was wrong on both findings. The husband, though then represented by counsel, indicated, through counsel, that he did not intend to take an active part in the appeal. In these circumstances, it seemed that the appeal was likely to raise issues of general importance. Moreover, apart from one case, *Blackwell v Blackwell*[1], this section does not appear to have been considered by the Court of Appeal since the new code of divorce law came into force in 1970. We, therefore, thought it right to ask for the assistance of the Queen's Proctor and adjourned the matter, giving leave to the wife to adduce further evidence, if so advised.

On the resumed hearing, the wife was represented by Queen's Counsel, and junior counsel, and the Queen's Proctor appeared by counsel. We are greatly indebted to all counsel and the Queen's Proctor in this case for their able arguments and for reviewing this branch of the law so fully and helpfully. We admitted two further affidavits, by the wife and her supporting witness, which contained a considerable amount of new and relevant material. In the result we decided to allow the appeal and gave the wife leave to present a petition on the ground of exceptional hardship, but not on the alternative ground of exceptional depravity, and reserved our reasons which we now give.

Section 3 of the 1973 Act, and its predecessors, have troubled judges who have to apply their provisions ever since these were first introduced by s 1 of the Matrimonial Causes Act 1937. The principal difficulty lies in knowing what standards to use in assessing exceptional hardship and what is meant by the phrase 'exceptional depravity'. Both involve value judgments of an unusually subjective character, so much so that in the earlier cases in this court these appeals were treated as appeals from the exercise of a purely discretionary jurisdiction (*Winter v Winter*[2] and *Fisher v Fisher*[3]). Later in *Brewer v Brewer*[4], it was held that exceptional hardship or exceptional depravity involved provisional findings of fact. The difficulty arises, partly, because all decisions at first instance are made in

---

1   (1973) 117 Sol Jo 939.
2   [1944] P 72
3   [1948] P 263
4   [1964] 1 All ER 539, [1964] 1 WLR 403

chambers and therefore cannot be reported, and, partly, because the reported cases in this
court do not give much, if any, guidance on the standards to be applied. Moreover,
standards in society in these matters are not stable and are subject to considerable changes
over comparatively short periods of time.

Hardship is a concept with which judges are familiar in various contexts though it is
often difficult to decide whether it can properly be called exceptional. A considerable
degree of hardship is inevitable when a marriage breaks down in the first three years.

Exceptional depravity, on the other hand, is much more difficult. The word 'depravity'
has fallen out of general use (it is not included in Fowler's Modern English Usage) so that
it now conveys only a vague idea of very unpleasant conduct. In 1937 it may have carried
to contemporary minds a much more specific meaning, but norms of behaviour,
particularly in the sexual sense, have changed greatly in the last 40 years. It is unlikely that
the meaning of 'depravity' and 'exceptional depravity' suggested by Denning LJ in *Bowman
v Bowman*[1] would find much support today.

In contrast, the change in the basis of divorce from the matrimonial offence to
irretrievable breakdown with the expectation of relatively easy divorce may have increased
the hardship involved in waiting for the specified period to elapse.

The legislative history of s 1 of the 1937 Act is interesting and illuminating and we are
indebted to counsel for the Queen's Proctor for his research on this aspect of the case. From
1857 to 1937 there was no statutory restriction in point of time on the presentation of
petitions for divorce, though the ground was, of course, confined to adultery, except in the
case of a wife who could rely on rape, sodomy etc. When the Marriage Bill, as it was
originally called, was presented to Parliament in 1937, it provided for a considerable
extension of the grounds for divorce and for nullity, but imposed an absolute ban on the
presentation of petitions for a period of five years from the date of marriage. There was no
'escape clause' of any kind. In this form, the Bill passed the House of Commons and it
seems probable that this clause was an important factor in securing its passage. But when
the Bill reached the House of Lords cl 1 ran into very heavy opposition. Lord Atkin
described it as a 'terrible clause', and was strongly supported by the legal peers, most of
whom objected to any kind of time limit. Eventually the period of five years was amended
to three years and Lord Maugham successfully moved a further amendment to introduce
a proviso in the same terms as those which now appear in the first part of s 3(2) of the 1973
Act. When the Bill returned to the Commons Mr A P Herbert moved a further
amendment which is now the second part of s 3(2).

Bucknill LJ was therefore plainly right when he said in *Fisher v Fisher*[2] that this provision
was 'enacted not only to deter people from rushing into ill-advised marriages, but also to
prevent them from rushing out of marriage so soon as they discovered that their marriage
was not what they expected'. It is equally clear that the proviso was intended to provide for
cases where the three year bar would operate unduly harshly and cause injustice. It seems
therefore unlikely that Parliament intended to create two separate ways of avoiding the
bar, although the proviso is expressed unequivocally in a disjunctive form. It is difficult
to imagine a case where exceptional depravity does not cause exceptional hardship but it
is possible that the draftsman was thinking primarily of hardship arising from the enforced
delay in starting divorce proceedings.

These queries are reflected in the judgments in some of the reported cases in this court.
In *Bowman v Bowman*[3] Bucknill and Denning LJJ both accepted that hardship arising from
the conduct of the other spouse could be taken into account under the first limb of the
proviso, whereas Romer LJ in *Hillier v Hillier and Latham*[4] thought that exceptional hardship
meant primarily hardship arising from the enforced delay. Willmer and Pearson LJJ in

1   [1949] 2 All ER 127 at 128–129, [1949] P 353 at 356–357
2   [1948] P 263 at 264
3   [1949] 2 All ER 127 at 128, [1949] P 353 at 355, 356
4   [1958] 2 All ER 261 at 263, [1958] P 185 at 191

Brewer v Brewer[1] took the other view, relying on the use of the word 'suffered' in the past tense.

Be that as it may, it is now accepted that in dealing with these applications the judge may properly take into account hardship arising from the conduct of the other spouse, present hardship, and hardship arising from having to wait until the specified period has elapsed. In these circumstances it seems to be unnecessary in the great majority of these cases to rely on exceptional depravity with all its unpleasant overtones and difficulties. In practice, when it is alleged, the proposed petitioner often relies for proof of the element of exceptional depravity on the effect of the conduct on him or her.

This is precisely what occurred in this case. Counsel for the wife said at the outset of her argument that she did not intend to argue that the homosexual behaviour alleged against the husband could properly be said to amount to exceptional depravity. She did argue, however, that there were sufficient aggravating factors in the case to justify such a finding. All of these, in fact, impinged directly on the wife and we think provide much more convincing evidence of hardship than of depravity.

Most of these factors emerged from the further evidence filed in this court which showed that for about three years or more before marriage the parties in this case had been having a normal and successful heterosexual relationship, albeit somewhat intermittently. At one stage their relationship was broken off and the wife formed an attachment to another man which seems to have aroused the husband's jealousy so that he quickly came back on the scene and disrupted this new relationship and resumed the affair with the wife. It is now clear, however, assuming the evidence to be true, that the husband was also having occasional homosexual relations with at least one man. Whether deliberately or otherwise, he certainly led the wife to think that he was a normally heterosexual man and that their marriage would be a sexually normal one. No doubt he hoped it would be and he may have been hoping to suppress his homosexuality by marrying an attractive girl. The result was very different, for he seems quickly to have become incapable of sustaining such a relationship sexually or otherwise. To the wife the experience must have been bewildering and deeply hurtful and, as the truth dawned on her, extremely distressing.

In these circumstances we think that the wife has made out a case of exceptional hardship but not of exceptional depravity. We accordingly allowed the appeal and gave leave to present a petition of divorce under s 3(2) of the 1973 Act.

May I just repeat that this case ought to be reported only by initials.

Appeal allowed.

Solicitors: *Cartwright & Lewis*, Birmingham (for the wife); *Queen's Proctor*.

Avtar S Virdi Esq   Barrister.

---

1   [1964] 1 All ER 539, [1964] 1 WLR 403

Diamond v Bank of London & Montreal Ltd

COURT OF APPEAL, CIVIL DIVISION
LORD DENNING MR, STEPHENSON AND SHAW LJJ
6th, 7th NOVEMBER 1978

Practice – Service out of the jurisdiction – Action founded on tort committed within jurisdiction – Fraudulent or negligent misrepresentation made by telephone and telex from Bahamas to England – Misrepresentation received and acted on by plaintiff in England – Whether tort committed in England – RSC Ord 11, r 1(1)(h).

In 1974 the plaintiff, a London commodity broker, wished to purchase a consignment of one million tonnes of sugar of undisclosed origin from a US broker acting for undisclosed sellers. In accordance with the normal practice in commodity broking neither broker was willing to disclose the identity of his client or the respective source or destination of the sugar. Instead each nominated a bank to give the necessary assurances, the US broker nominating the defendants, a bank in Nassau in the Bahamas, to give an assurance that the consignment was available and the sellers were genuine, and the plaintiff nominating a London bank to confirm the creditworthiness of the buyer. The plaintiff alleged that between 4th and 8th January 1974 the defendants' manager confirmed by telex and telephone that the sugar was available and that the US brokers were respectably constituted and had done deals of considerable magnitude through the defendants and were well able to undertake the sale. On 8th January the plaintiff's bank received a telex from the defendants confirming the availability of the sugar. When asked to authenticate this telex the defendants' manager sent a telex on 11th January that 'Without responsibility on the part of the bank we confirm on behalf of a client availability' of the sugar. In fact the sugar did not exist and the transaction was never completed. The plaintiff issued a writ against the defendants claiming damages for negligent misrepresentations made by the defendants' manager and alleging that he had had a buyer arranged for the sugar and had refused an offer of sugar from the alternative source, thus losing £2,000,000 in commission. Parker J refused to allow the writ to be served out of the jurisdiction because, inter alia, the action was not 'founded on a tort committed within the jurisdiction' for the purposes of RSC Ord 11, r 1(1)(h)[a], since the negligence had been committed in Nassau. The plaintiff issued a second writ against the defendants claiming damages for fraudulent misrepresentation but Donaldson J refused to allow service out of the jurisdiction for the same reason as Parker J. The plaintiff appealed. At the hearing the defendants contended, inter alia, that they were protected by the disclaimer of responsibility in the telex of 11th January and by s 6[b] of the Statute of Frauds Amendment Act 1828 which prevented an action being brought in respect of a 'representation or assurance made or concerning or relating to the character, conduct, credit, ability, trade, or dealings of any other person . . . unless such representation or assurance be made in writing, signed by the party to be charged, therewith'.

Held – (i) The tort of fraudulent or negligent misrepresentation when made by telephone or telex were committed at the place where the message was received and acted on, and not the place from which it was sent. Since the representation by the defendants' manager had been received and acted on by the plaintiff in London, the tort had been committed within the jurisdiction for the purposes of RSC Ord 11, r 1(1)(h), and the court therefore had discretion to give leave for the writ to be served out of the jurisdiction (see p 564 *b c* and *f g*,

---

a   Rule 1(1), so far as material, provides: '. . . service of a writ, or notice of a writ, out of the jurisdiction is permissible with the leave of the Court in the following cases, that is to say . . . (h) if the action begun by the writ is founded on a tort committed within the jurisdiction . . .'

b   Section 6 is set out at p 564 *h* to p 565 *a*, post

p 566 *b* and *f* to *h*, p 567 *b c* and *h* and p 568 *a b* and *d* post); *Original Blouse Co Ltd v Bruck Mills Ltd* (1963) 42 DLR (2d) 174 and *Bata v Bata* [1948] WN 366 applied; *Cordova Land Co v Victor Brothers Inc* [1966] 1 WLR 793 and dicta of Goddard LJ and of du Parcq LJ in *George Monro Ltd v American Cuanamid and Chemical Corpn* [1944] 1 All ER at 389–390 distinguished.

(ii) The court was not precluded by s 6 of the 1828 Act from giving leave since the Act only extended to representations relating to the creditworthiness of a person. The Act might therefore protect the defendants in respect of any representations that the seller was genuine but not that the sugar was available (see p 565 *b* to *d* and p 568 *a b*, post).

(iii) However, the court would not in the circumstances exercise its discretion because it was doubtful whether the bank was liable in view of the disclaimer of responsibility in the confirming telex of 11th January, although (per Shaw LJ) the plaintiff was entitled to rely on the contents of the telex of 8th January despite the fact that it was not authenticated. In any event there was insufficient evidence that the plaintiff had suffered damage since there were no particulars of the alternative offer of sugar which the plaintiff had turned down or of the terms of the offer and the commission the plaintiff would have received on it. The plaintiff had therefore not made out a good arguable case justifying leave to serve the writ out of the jurisdiction and accordingly the appeal would be dismissed (see p 565 *f* to *h*, p 567 *h* and p 568 *a* and *c* post).

Notes

For service out of the jurisdiction, see 30 Halsbury's Laws (3rd Edn) 323, para 588, and for cases on service out of the jurisdiction found on tort committed within the jurisdiction, see 50 Digest (Reissue) 352–353, 766–771.

Cases referred to in judgments

Anderson (WB) & Sons Ltd v Rhodes (Liverpool) Ltd [1967] 2 All ER 850, 36(1) Digest (Reissue) 26, 88.

Banbury v Bank of Montreal [1918] AC 626, [1918–19] All ER Rep 1, 87 LJKB 1158, 119 LT 446, HL, 51 Digest (Repl) 831, *3855*.

Bata v Bata [1948] WN 366, CA, 50 Digest (Repl) 353, *770*.

Briess v Woolley [1954] 1 All ER 909, [1954] AC 333, HL, 9 Digest (Reissue) 492, *2941*.

Cordova Land Co v Victor Brothers Inc [1966] 1 WLR 793, 50 Digest (Repl) 351, *757*.

Director of Public Prosecutions v Stonehouse [1977] 2 All ER 909, [1978] AC 55, [1977] 3 WLR 143, HL.

Distillers Co (Biochemicals) Ltd v Thompson [1971] 1 All ER 694, [1971] AC 458, [1971] 2 WLR 441, PC.

Entores Ltd v Miles Far East Corpn [1955] 2 All ER 493, [1955] 2 QB 327, [1955] 3 WLR 48, [1955] 1 Lloyd's Rep 511, CA, 50 Digest (Repl) 341, *688*.

Hirst v West Riding Union Banking Co Ltd [1901] 2 KB 560, [1900–3] All ER Rep 782, 70 LJKB 828, 85 LT 3, CA, 1 Digest (Reissue) 90.

Monro (George) Ltd v American Cuanamid and Chemical Corpn [1944] 1 All ER 386, [1944] KB 432, 113 LJKB 235, 170 LT 281, CA, 50 Digest (Repl) 374, *917*.

Original Blouse Co Ltd v Bruck Mills Ltd (1963) 42 DLR (2d) 174.

R v Baxter [1971] 2 All ER 359, [1972] 1 QB 1, [1971] 2 WLR 1138, 135 JP 345, 55 Cr App R 214, CA, 14(1) Digest (Reissue) 169, *1195*.

R v Ellis [1899] 1 QB 230, 68 LJQB 103, 79 LT 532, 62 JP 838, 19 Cox CC 210, CCR, 14(1) Digest (Reissue) 155, *1089*.

Secretary of State for Trade v Markus [1975] 1 All ER 958, [1976] AC 35, [1975] 2 WLR 708, 139 JP 301, 61 Cr App R 58, HL, 14(1) Digest (Reissue) 156, *1092*.

Swift v Jewsbury (P O) and Goddard (1874) LR 9 QB 301, 43 LJQB 56, 30 LT 31, Ex Ch, 1 Digest (Repl) 321, *89*.

Case also cited

Treacy v Director of Public Prosecutions [1971] 1 All ER 110, [1971] AC 537, HL.

Appeal

The plaintiff, Hyman Richard Diamond, appealed against the judgment of Donaldson J given on 4th May 1978 dismissing his appeal against the decision of Master Bickford-Smith on 2nd December 1977 setting aside service on the defendants, the Bank of London & Montreal Ltd, at Nassau in the Bahamas, of a writ issued on 29th July 1977 by the plaintiff against the defendants claiming damages arising out of fraudulent misrepresentations alleged to have been made by a servant or agent of the defendants whereby he lost £2,000,000 in commission. The facts are set out in the judgment of Lord Denning MR.

Christopher Cocharane for the plaintiff.
James Leckie for the defendant.

LORD DENNING MR. At the beginning of 1974 the market in sugar was extremely volatile. Brokers were anxious to get hold of sugar and sell it on behalf of clients. This case concerns a supposed deal for a huge quantity of sugar; about one million tonnes of it. I say a 'supposed deal' because we now know there was no sugar available at all. But two commodity brokers at that time thought there was this huge consignment of a million tonnes of sugar available somewhere. One of the commodity brokers was Mr Hyman Richard Diamond in London, and the other was an American company called Niram Corpn Inc ('Niram') of Nashua, New Hampshire. They did not want to disclose the names of their clients on either side; nor did they want to disclose the origin of the sugar. It might have been from Brazil or from one of the West Indian islands. Some suspicious person might think it was coming from Cuba and was being diverted to Europe instead of Russia. At all events, the brokers did not disclose their clients on either side for their own good reasons. Nevertheless the brokers wanted an assurance that the sugar was available and that there were sound people behind the deal, so that, if it went through, all would be well. For that purpose the practice of these brokers on either side was to get a prime bank to confirm the availability of the sugar and the genuineness of the supplier and of the buyer. In this case the selling broker named the Bank of London & Montreal Ltd as the prime bank to confirm the sellers. It is based in Nassau in the Bahamas. It is wholly owned by Lloyds Bank International Ltd, which in turn is a subsidiary of Lloyds Bank Ltd. It is, of course, a very reputable bank.

Mr Diamond, the London broker, got in touch with the trustee manager of the bank in Nassau, Mr Bease. Mr Diamond says that, by telex and telephone messages from Nassau to London, Mr Bease in Nassau confirmed that there was a million tonnes of sugar available, that the brokers for the sellers were respectable, that they had done deals of considerable magnitude, that he had seen the documents and all was genuine. Mr Diamond in London says that he relied on those assurances and he made arrangements to sell half a million tonnes to a company called Aztecs in Liechtenstein. He put forward, as prime bank for the buyers, the Australia and New Zealand Bank. Mr Diamond further says that he had an offer of sugar from an alternative source of supply which he turned down in consequence of the assurances which were given to him by Mr Bease in Nassau.

Mr Diamond now alleges that the assurances given him by Mr Bease were false. He says they were fraudulent because there was never any sugar available, and that the selling brokers were not respectable. He says that Mr Bease knew this, but gave the assurances in the hope of getting a private commission for himself out of the deal. So Mr Diamond alleges that it was plain fraud on the part of Mr Bease in Nassau for which his employers the Bank of London & Montreal Ltd are answerable. In these circumstances, Mr Diamond has brought an action against the Bank of London & Montreal Ltd. As they are based in Nassau, he seeks leave to serve out of the jurisdiction.

I may say in passing that previously Mr Diamond had issued a writ against the bank for negligent misrepresentation. Parker J refused leave to serve it out of the jurisdiction. Now Mr Diamond has issued a second writ. In it he alleges fraudulent misrepresentation against the Bank of London & Montreal Ltd, and seeks leave to serve it out of the jurisdiction on this account.

A preliminary point arises on it. It is whether the case comes within RSC Ord 11, r 1(h). That rule only permits service out of the jurisdiction if the action begun by the writ is 'founded on a tort committed within the jurisdiction'. Donaldson J held that this tort of fraudulent misrepresentation was not committed within the jurisdiction. It was committed in Nassau where Mr Bease sent off the telex and from where he spoke on the telephone. Donaldson J was influenced by some observations made by Winn J in *Cordova Land Co Ltd v Victor Brothers Inc*[1].

I do not think this preliminary objection should be upheld. It seems to me that in the case of fraudulent misrepresentation, when it is made by telephone or by telex, as it was here, the tort is committed at the place where the message is received, wherever it is heard on the telephone by the receiver or tapped out by the telex machine in the receiver's office. It was so held in Canada in *Original Blouse Co Ltd v Bruck Mills Ltd*[2]. The judge said that, when a communication is made by telephone or by telex, it is to be regarded in the same way as a letter sent by hand or a message sent by word of mouth by a messenger to the recipient. In such a case there could be no doubt that the fraudulent misrepresentation was made at the point where it was received and where it was acted on. It is rather similar to what we have held in regard to contracts: see *Entores Ltd v Miles Far East Corpn*[3].

The *Cordova* case[1] is quite distinguishable. A fraudulent misrepresentation was made in Boston, USA, by the master of a ship who signed bills of lading and handed them to the shipper in Boston. Later on the bills of lading were indorsed to buyers in England. It seems to me clear that the tort was committed in Boston where the bills of lading were handed over, and not in England. There were some observations made by Winn J but they were obiter dicta and not by any means intended to be of general application.

We were also referred to *George Monro Ltd v American Cuanamid and Chemical Corpn*[4], where Goddard LJ made some observations obiter about the tort of negligence, but nothing to affect the tort of fraudulent misrepresentation. Much nearer to the present case are cases of the publication of a libel. When a letter or paper is sent from one country to another, the tort is committed in the place where the publication takes place. That is shown in *Bata v Bata*[5].

The truth is that each tort has to be considered on its own to see where it is committed. In many torts the place may be where the damage is done, such as in *Distillers Co (Biochemicals) Ltd v Thompson*[6]. Distillers sent the thalidamide drug out from England to Australia. A woman took it in Australia with the result that her baby was born deformed. It was held that the tort was committed in New South Wales. Every tort must be considered separately. In the case of fraudulent misrepresentation it seems to me that the tort is committed at the place where the representation is received and acted on, and not the place from which it was sent. Logically, it seems to me, the same applies to a negligent misrepresentation by telephone or by telex. It is committed where it is received and acted on.

In my opinion, therefore, the court has jurisdiction to give leave to serve this writ out of the jurisdiction. It remains to be seen whether the court in its discretion should give leave.

To get leave Mr Diamond must show that he has a good arguable case. Counsel for the bank submitted that Mr Diamond had no case. He drew our attention to Lord Tenterden's Act[7]. Section 6 says:

> 'No action shall be brought whereby to charge any person upon or by reason of any representation or assurance made or given concerning or relating to the character,

1   [1966] 1 WLR 793
2   (1963) 42 DLR (2d) 174
3   [1955] 2 All ER 493, [1955] 2 QB 327
4   [1944] 1 All ER 386 at 389, [1944] KB 432 at 439–440
5   [1948] WN 366
6   [1971] 1 All ER 694, [1971] AC 458
7   9 Geo 4 c 14, the Statute of Frauds Amendment Act 1828

conduct, credit, ability, trade, or dealings of any other person, to the intent or purpose that such other person may obtain credit, money, or goods upon [sic], unless such representation or assurance be made in writing signed by the party to be charged therewith.'

We have been shown some very interesting cases on that section. They are *Swift v Jewsbury* (*P O*) *and Goddard*[1], *Hirst v West Riding Union Banking Co Ltd*[2], *Banbury v Bank of Montreal*[3], and finally *W B Anderson & Sons Ltd v Rhodes* (*Liverpool*) *Ltd*[4]. Those cases show that Lord Tenterden's Act does not apply to negligent representations, but it does apply to fraudulent representations. Even then, it only extends to fraudulent representations which relate in some way to the credit or creditworthiness of a person.

In this particular case it seems to me that the Act may protect the bank in respect of the allegations in para 8, when it is said that Mr Bease confirmed that Niram were respectably constituted and had done deals of considerable magnitude through the defendants and were well able to undertake the contract for a million tonnes of sugar. On the other hand, I think it is doubtful whether it applies so as to protect the bank with regard to the other allegation that they confirmed the availability of one million tonnes of white crystalline sugar. So, although Lord Tenterden's Act might well afford a good defence to a number of these allegations, I doubt whether for present purposes it could be safely said to afford a defence to the others.

So I turn to the next point. Counsel for the bank submitted that Mr Diamond in any case did not rely on these representations. A number of telexes were sent from Mr Bease in Nassau in which he said: 'We confirm availability of one million tons'; but these were not authenticated as between the banks. Eventually on 11th January the confirmation came through with an important qualification. It said: 'Without responsibility on the part of the bank we confirm on behalf of a client availability of one million M/T white crystalline sugar.' The bank say that, by that telex, they made it clear that they were not taking any responsibility in the matter. There seems to me to be quite a good deal in this point. I doubt very much whether the bank can be made liable when they expressly said 'Without responsibility'.

But there is one final point which seems to me to be strong. Did Mr Diamond suffer any damage as a result of the supposed fraudulent representations? In his statement of claim he said this: 'In further reliance on the Defendants aforesaid fraudulent misrepresentation the Plaintiff turned down the offer of an alternative supply of sugar from which he could have satisfied Aztecs' order for 500,000 metric tons of sugar.' He gives not a single particular saying what that offer was or where the alternative supply of sugar was to come from. It appears from the affidavits that there were a lot of bogus people going around offering sugar at this time. People were saying they had sugar when they had not. In the first action for negligent misrepresentation Parker J was much impressed by the absence of proof of damage. He said: 'There is no evidence that the plaintiff would have been able to obtain other supplies and, if obtained, would have got commission or like commission.'

That point seems to me to be decisive. But I need not take each point individually. Taking these three points which the defendants raised, I find it impossible to say that Mr Diamond has a good arguable case for damages so as to justify leave to serve out of the jurisdiction. All the cases show that we should be careful before granting leave to serve out of the jurisdiction. This is not a proper case for leave to serve out. I would dismiss the appeal.

STEPHENSON LJ. The plaintiff's claim in this second action is for damages arising out of the fraudulent misrepresentation of one Robert McLean Bease, the manager of the

1   (1874) LR 9 QB 301
2   [1901] KB 560, [1900–3] All ER Rep 782
3   [1918] AC 626, [1918–19] All ER Rep 1
4   [1967] 2 All ER 850

defendants' bank in Nassau in the Bahamas, by telephone and telex between 4th January 1974 and 7th March 1974 whereby the plaintiff was induced to act to his disadvantage and suffered loss and damage. The misrepresentations are alleged to have been telephoned and telexed by Mr Bease in Nassau in the Bahamas to the plaintiff in London. Is his action 'founded on a tort committed within the jurisdiction'? Only if so have our courts jurisdiction to give him leave to serve his writ on the defendants outside the jurisdiction under RSC Ord 11, r 1(1)(h).

Donaldson J felt bound by the decision of Winn J in *Cordova Land Co v Victor Brothers Inc*[1], to which Lord Denning MR has referred, to hold that the substance of the tort of fraudulent misrepresentation on which the plaintiff's action was founded was committed in Nassau outside the jurisdiction and not within the jurisdiction. I agree with Lord Denning MR that it was committed within the jurisdiction.

The question we have to answer is broadly the same as that which Winn J found difficult and answered with some doubt in favour of the defendant representor. It is also related to the wider question left open by Scott LJ in *George Monro v American Cuanamid and Chemical Corpn*[2] and by Lord Pearson giving the judgment of the Judicial Committee in *Distillers Co (Biochemicals) Ltd v Thompson*[3]. The case closest to this on its facts is, however, *Original Blouse Co Ltd v Bruck Mills Ltd*[4], to which Lord Denning MR has referred, which was decided by Aikens J in the Supreme Court of British Columbia in favour of the plaintiff representee.

The choice between the plaintiff and the defendants in this case depends on the nature of the tort of deceit or fraudulent misrepresentation and the correct analysis of the different stages by which the tort is complete and the cause of action is founded on it. It begins with the statement issuing from the defendant by word of mouth or through recording by telex or in writing. That statement is then received, believed and acted on by the plaintiff to his resulting damage and loss. All these different stages may be divided from each other in time and space. If A speaks his representation to B in the same room, there is no appreciable change of time or space until B comes, perhaps later, to act on the representation. If A writes his representation to B on the other side of the world, the appreciable changes begin at the beginning, and what begins on one date and in one place takes effect at a later date and in another place. But it is settled law that A's misrepresentation, however fraudulent and morally wrong, does not become tortious until B not merely receives it but acts on it: see *Briess v Woolley*[5] per Lord Tucker; and the passage which was cited by Aikens J in the *Original Blouse* case[6] from the 13th edition of Salmond on the Law of Torts[7] and which I think is exactly reproduced in the current edition[8]. The damage may be suffered when and where B acts or begins to act on the representation, but it may be suffered at a later time and at a different place. Although A's part of the tort is committed where and when he speaks or telexes or writes the misrepresentation, B's part is needed to complete the tort by acting on the representation, and the tort is committed, in my judgment, where and when he does so act. This is so whether the true analysis be that the misrepresentation is not made by the defendant until it is communicated or received (as Aikens J held), or it is made but it is not a tort until it is received and acted on, which is the point of time when its falsity has to be proved, or it is made in the Bahamas but it is continued here or is repeated to the plaintiff here.

A false statement or representation made fraudulently (and also, I agree with Lord Denning MR, if made negligently) resembles defamation, which needs publication before

---

1 [1966] 1 WLR 793
2 [1944] 1 All ER 386 at 387, [1944] KB 432 at 437
3 [1971] 1 All ER 694 at 700–701, [1971] AC 458 at 469
4 (1963) 42 DLR (2d) 174
5 [1954] 1 All ER 909 at 918, [1954] AC 333 at 353
6 (1963) 42 DLR (2d) 174 at 181
7 (1961), p 665
8 17th Edn (1977), p 387

it becomes the tort of libel or slander, more closely than it resembles other negligent acts or omissions, which only become tortious when they cause damage. The decision in *Bata v Bata*[1b] is accordingly more relevant to our decision of the preliminary question where this tort was committed than the obiter opinions of Goddard and du Parcq LJJ in the *George Monro* case[2]. In other cases of negligence the plaintiff has to suffer damage from the negligent act or omission for it to be actionable. In deceit, as in slander, the false representation or (in most cases) the defamatory publication has to cause damage to be actionable, but no damage to the plaintiff is necessary for the tort to be committed. The defamatory matter must, however, be published and the false representation must be effective or there is no tort. It is this requirement of the tort in question in this appeal, that the defendant's misrepresentation must be effective and operate on the plaintiff's mind, which distinguishes this tort from others, and, in my judgment, determines the preliminary point of jurisdiction in the plaintiff's favour.

This allegation of this tort within the civil jurisdiction of the High Court accords with what has been decided in such cases as *Director of Public Prosecutions v Stonehouse*[3] and in *R v Ellis*[4], *R v Baxter*[5] and *Secretary of State for Trade v Markus*[6] which were there cited. The similar offences of obtaining money or property by false pretences or deception come within the criminal jurisdiction of our courts where the false pretence or deception is initiated outside this country but operates on persons and property in this country, or would so operate if successfully attempted.

I agree that there may be different considerations in founding civil jurisdiction under RSC Ord 11, r 1, and criminal jurisdiction. The defendants' servant or agent would not be liable to prosecution here unless he came or could be brought from Nassau to this country. The similar criminal offence is what has been called a 'result crime' and so is justiciable where the property is obtained and not where the party induced to part with it happens to be at the time of inducement. It would, however, be anomalous and regrettable if the same lies with the same effect, for which he could be prosecuted if he were here, could not render him liable to be sued here, whether or not this court would wish to exercise the discretion given by the rule against him and allow him to be sued here.

To decide that the tort alleged against the defendants was committed within the jurisdiction does not, in my opinion, overrule Winn J's decision in the *Cordova* case[7]. There the representation by clean bills of lading that the goods sold were not defective was a representation made in Boston to whatever persons the bills of lading might come to before ever they came to the buyers in this country. It is therefore unnecessary to suppose that by an 'act, which was wrongful at the moment when it was committed,'[8] the judge meant, as counsel for the defendants has argued, representations that were morally wrong but not tortious, or tortious ex post facto. While uncertain how far what the judge said about jurisdiction can be considered as obiter dictum, I suspect that the judge might well have taken the opposite view and held that the representation fell within the paragraph if he had not decided to exercise his discretion against the defendant or if he had had the *Original Blouse* case[9] cited to him.

For these reasons I agree that the substance of the tort which is alleged to have been committed by the defendants' servant or agent was committed within the jurisdiction, and I agree accordingly that the appeal on the preliminary point will have to be allowed. But I also agree with Lord Denning MR that we should not exercise our discretion in the plaintiff's favour because he has not made out a good arguable case for the reasons which

1   [1948] WN 366
2   [1944] 1 All ER 386 at 389–390, [1944] KB 432 at 440–441
3   [1977] 2 All ER 909, [1978] AC 55
4   [1899] 1 QB 230
5   [1971] 2 All ER 359, [1972] 1 QB 1
6   [1975] 1 All ER 958, [1976] AC 35
7   [1966] 1 WLR 793
8a   [1966] 1 WLR 793 at 799
9   (1963) 42 DLR (2d) 174

Lord Denning MR has given. I am impressed by the impression which this case made on
Parker J without any reference to a possible defence under Lord Tenterden's Act. I would
therefore dismiss the appeal on the same grounds as Lord Denning MR.

SHAW LJ. I agree with both judgments. I would add only two observations of my
own. The first is that it appears to me to be quite clear that the scope of Lord Tenterden's
Act does not cover the matters relied on by the plaintiff in this action. That statute, despite
its comprehensive language, applies only to representations as to creditworthiness.

The other matter is that, although the telex on which the plaintiff relied was not
authenticated, that does not seem to me to preclude that it was intended to communicate
something and that its contents were in fact communicated. Accordingly the plaintiff was
entitled to rely on the contents of that telex as he said he did.

Where I think the plaintiff fails in setting up a good arguable case is that it was the very
substance of his claim that he had an alternative source of supply from which he could have
provided the sugar to sell to the intended buyer. There is only the most tenuous basis for
the assertion that such a source of supply existed. There may be enough to give rise to a
prima facie case, but not enough to suggest a good arguable case. While counsel's
submissions for the plaintiff on that matter were made with equal succinctness and ability,
I am not satisfied that there is sufficient to justify this court in exercising its discretion in
the way he seeks.

I would therefore allow the appeal on the preliminary point and dismiss the appeal on
the question of discretion.

Appeal dismissed.

Solicitors: *Tatton, Gaskell & Tatton* (for the plaintiff); *Bischoff & Co* (for the defendant).

Frances Rustin Barrister.

Quennell v Maltby and another

COURT OF APPEAL, CIVIL DIVISION
LORD DENNING MR, BRIDGE AND TEMPLEMAN LJJ
14th, 15th NOVEMBER 1978

*Mortgage – Action by mortgagee for possession – House subject to statutory tenancy under Rent
Acts – Unauthorised tenancy of mortgaged property – Tenancy not binding on mortgagee –
Mortgagor wishing to obtain vacant possession in order to sell property – Mortgagee bringing
action for possession against tenant on mortgagor's behalf – Whether mortgagee acting bona fide to
protect security – Whether mortgagee entitled to possession against tenant.*

The landlord owned a house worth between £30,000 and £40,000 which he mortgaged to
his bank to secure an overdraft of £2,500. The mortgage contained a covenant that the
landlord would not let or lease the house without the bank's consent. In breach of this
covenant the landlord let the house to a tenant who became a statutory tenant protected by
the Rent Acts. The landlord, wishing to gain vacant possession of the property in order to
sell it, approached the bank to bring an action against the tenant for possession, since the
tenancy, being made in breach of the covenant, was not binding on the bank. The bank
declined as their position as mortgagee was not in jeopardy. The landlord's wife then paid
off the amount owing to the bank, the mortgage was transferred into her name, and she
brought an action for possession against the tenant contending that she stood in the bank's
shoes and, like the bank, was not bound by the tenancy. The judge upheld her claim. On
appeal,

Held – The court was entitled to, and would, look behind the formal legal relationship of the parties, since a mortgagee would not be granted possession unless it was sought bona fide and reasonably for the purpose of enforcing the security. The landlord's wife had brought the action not to enforce payment of the amount due under the mortgage nor to protect her security but with the ulterior motive of assisting her husband in obtaining vacant possession and thereby defeating the protection afforded to the tenant by the Rent Acts. In those circumstances she was to be treated as the landlord's agent and the action as being brought by the landlord. The appeal would therefore be allowed and possession refused (see p 571 *e* to p 572 *b* and *h* to p 573 *a*, post).

Dudley and District Benefit Building Society v Emerson [1949] 2 All ER 252 distinguished.

Notes
For the effect of tenancies granted by a mortgagor or chargee after the charge is created, see 27 Halsbury's Laws (3rd Edn) 255, para 464 and 4 Halsbury's Laws (4th Edn) para 1683.

Case referred to in judgments
Dudley and District Benefit Building Society v Emerson [1949] 2 All ER 252, [1949] Ch 707, [1949] LJR 1441, CA, 31(2) Digest (Reissue) 978, 7865.

Cases also cited
Barclays Bank Ltd v Stasek [1956] 3 All ER 439, [1957] Ch 28.
Bolton Building Society v Cobb [1965] 3 All ER 814, [1966] 1 WLR 1.
Bungalows (Maidenhead) Ltd v Mason [1954] 1 All ER 1002, [1954] 1 WLR 769, CA.
Chatsworth Properties Ltd v Effiom [1971] 1 All ER 604, [1971] 1 WLR 144.
Collins v Claughton [1959] 1 All ER 95, [1959] 1 WLR 145, CA.
Evans v Elliot (1838) 9 Ad & El 342, 112 ER 1242.
Feyereisel v Parry [1952] 1 All ER 728, sub nom *Feyereisel v Turnidge* [1952] 2 QB 29, CA.
Jessamine Investment Co v Schwartz [1976] 3 All ER 521, [1978] QB 264, CA.
Lloyd v Sadler [1978] 2 All ER 529, [1978] QB 774, CA.
London and County (A & D) Ltd v Wilfred Sportsman Ltd [1970] 2 All ER 600, [1971] Ch 764, CA.
Murray, Bull & Co Ltd v Murray [1952] 2 All ER 1079, [1953] 1 QB 211.
Parker v Braithwaite [1952] 2 All ER 837, [1952] 2 TLR 731.
Property Holding Co Ltd v Clark [1948] 1 All ER 165, [1948] 1 KB 630, CA.
Stroud Building Society v Delamont [1960] 1 All ER 749, [1960] 1 WLR 431.

Appeal
The defendant, Peter Jeffrey Maltby appealed against the judgment of his Honour Judge Granville Wingate QC at Lewes County Court on 14th June 1978 granting the plaintiff, Joan Marilyn Gillespie Quennell, possession of the house at 6 Wallands Crescent, Lewes, Sussex, as mortagee. The house was owned by the plaintiff's husband, Peter Courtney Quennell, who was also the mortgagor of the property. The facts are set out in the judgment of Lord Denning MR.

David Lamming for Mr Maltby.
Paul de la Piquerie for Mrs Quennell.

LORD DENNING MR. If the judgment of the judge below is right, it will open a gap in the protection which is afforded to tenants by the Rent Acts. I will first give the facts.

Mr Quennell is a gentleman who lives in Cheyne Row in London. But he is the owner of a large house in Lewes. It is No 6 Wallands Crescent, Lewes, with about nine bedrooms. He has an agent in Lewes who looks after it for him. The house is very suitable for students. In 1973 the agent let it to some students of the University of Sussex. Two of them became the tenants. They were Mr Maltby and Mr Jack. They were let into possession for a term of one year at a rent of £90 a month, expiring on 31st December 1974. They had other students there with them, about nine students in the house.

Whilst Mr Maltby and Mr Jack were tenants, Mr Quennell borrowed money from Barclays Bank and mortgaged this house to secure the loan. It was only for the sum of £2,500. He executed a legal charge on 13th August 1974 in favour of Barclays Bank to cover any moneys which might from time to time be owing to the bank. In that legal charge there was this clause, cl 4, which is in common form:

> 'During the continuance of this security no statutory or other power of granting or agreeing to grant or of accepting or agreeing to accept surrenders of leases or tenancies of the Mortgaged Property or any part thereof shall be capable of being exercised by the Mortgagor without the previous consent in writing of the Bank . . .'

That meant thereafter from 13th August 1974 so long as this legal charge subsisted to the bank, Mr Quennell could not let the premises or accept surrenders without the consent in writing of the bank.

The tenancy of Mr Maltby and Mr Jack came to an end at the end of December 1974. The house was then relet to two other students, a Mr Quilter and Mr Lyth, again for a year. It was not relet to Mr Maltby because it was thought he was going to the United States. As it happened Mr Maltby did not go to the United States. In fact he stayed on living in the house. So did several other students.

At all events, the important thing to note is that the bank did not give its consent to this letting to Mr Quilter and Mr Lyth. No one asked the bank for its consent. No one realised it was necessary. No one interfered and nothing happened. That year 1975 passed. Then at the end of that year there was a fresh letting. This was between Mr Quennell as landlord and Mr Maltby and a Mr Lupton as tenants. That tenancy lasted until December 1976. Again no one asked the bank for consent. No one realised it was necessary. And from January 1977 onwards the tenants remained as statutory tenants, paying the rent to the agents.

The position then arose that Mr Quennell wanted to get possession of the house. If he could get vacant possession, he could sell it at a high price. It might be worth £30,000 to £40,000 with vacant possession. Mr Quennell started proceedings for nuisance and annoyance, but he dropped them. Then he went to lawyers for advice. After consulting them, in October 1977 Mr Quennell went to the bank and told them about the tenants in the house. The bank had not heard before about the various changes in the tenancies. Even when they were told the bank made it clear that they had no intention of taking any proceedings to enter the property or to turn the tenants out or anything of that kind. The bank were not concerned to get possession.

Then Mr Quennell's lawyers in London advised him that there was a good way in which possession could be achieved. This is what it was: Mr Quennell's wife, Mrs Quennell, paid off the bank. She paid the £2,500 which was owing to the bank and took a transfer of the charge. The bank transferred it to her by a transfer dated 17th January 1978.

Then Mrs Quennell brought proceedings against the tenants Mr Maltby and Mr Lupton seeking possession. She said that she stood in the shoes of the bank; and, seeing that the tenancy was granted without the consent of the bank, it was void. So she could recover possession.

The judge accepted this submission. He held that the wife, Mrs Quennell, was entitled to possession of the premises and could turn Mr Maltby and all the other students out of the house.

Now it has been held that, when the bank holds a charge and there is a clause in it whereby there are to be no tenancies granted or surrendered except with the consent of the bank in writing, then in those circumstances, if the mortgagor does thereafter grant tenancies without the consent of the bank, then those tenancies are not binding on the bank, and the tenants are not entitled to the protection of the Rent Acts. That was decided

in *Dudley and District Benefit Building Society v Emerson*[1]. Mrs Quennell relies on that case.
She says that, as transferee of the legal charge, she stands in the shoes of the bank and can
obtain possession.

The judge accepted that submission. His decision, if right, opens the way to widespread
evasion of the Rent Acts. If the owner of a house wishes to obtain vacant possession, all he
has to do is charge it to the bank for a small sum; then grant a new tenancy without telling
the bank; then get his wife to pay off the bank and take a transfer; then get the wife to sue
for possession.

That indeed was what happened here. In October 1977, when Mr Quennell went to the
bank, he told them about the tenancies. They said that they did not intend to take
proceedings. So he got Mrs Quennell to do it. In evidence, she said:

> 'I paid £2,500. This was for my husband. I took the charge to make the debt to his
> Bank less onerous. I was aware he wanted to obtain possession of the house to sell it.
> I merely paid off the charge. These proceedings have been brought to get possession
> to sell.'

So the objective is plain. It was not to enforce the security or to obtain repayment or
anything of that kind. It was in order to get possession of the house and to overcome the
protection of the Rent Acts.

Is that permissible? It seems to me that this is one of those cases where equity steps in
to mitigate the rigour of the law. Long years ago it did the same when it invented the
equity of redemption. As is said in Snell's Principles of Equity[2]:

> 'The courts of equity left the legal effect of the transaction unaltered but declared
> it to be unreasonable and against conscience that the mortgagee should retain as
> owner for his own benefit what was intended as a mere security.'

So here in modern times equity can step in so as to prevent a mortgagee, or a transferee
from him, from getting possession of a house contrary to the justice of the case. A
mortgagee will be restrained from getting possession except when it is sought bona fide
and reasonably for the purpose of enforcing the security and then only subject to such
conditions as the court thinks fit to impose. When the bank itself or a building society
lends the money, then it may well be right to allow the mortgagee to obtain possession
when the borrower is in default. But so long as the interest is paid and there is nothing
outstanding, equity has ample power to restrain any unjust use of the right to possession.

It is plain that in this transaction Mr and Mrs Quennell had an ulterior motive. It was
not done to enforce the security or due payment of the principal or interest. It was done
for the purpose of getting possession of the house in order to resell it at a profit. It was done
so as to avoid the protection which the Rent Acts afford to tenants in their occupation. If
Mr Quennell himself had sought to evict the tenants, he would not be allowed to do so. He
could not say the tenancies were void. He would be estopped from saying so. They
certainly would be protected against him. Are they protected against his wife now that she
is the transferee of the charge? In my opinion they are protected, for this simple reason:
she is not seeking possession for the purpose of enforcing the loan or the interest of
anything of that kind. She is doing it simply for an ulterior purpose of getting possession
of the house, contrary to the intention of Parliament as expressed in the Rent Acts.

On that simple ground it seems to me that this action fails and it should be dismissed.
The legal right to possession is not to be enforced when it is sought for an ulterior motive.
I would on this account allow the appeal and dismiss the action for possession.

BRIDGE LJ. I entirely agree. The situation arising in this case is one, it seems to me, in
which the court is not only entitled but bound to look behind the formal legal relationship
between the parties to see what is the true ɾ ɩbstance of the matter. Once one does that, on

---

[1] [1949] 2 All ER 252, [1949] Ch 707
[2] 27th Edn (1973), p 376

the facts of this case it is as plain as a pikestaff that the purpose of the bringing of these
proceedings via Mrs Quennell is not for her own benefit to protect or enforce the security　*a*
which she holds as the transferee of the legal charge but for the benefit of her husband as
mortgagor to enable him to sell the property with the benefit of vacant possession. In
substance she is suing as his agent. That being so, it seems to me inevitably to follow that
she can be in no better position in these proceedings than her husband would be if they had
been brought in his name. If they had been brought in his name, it is clear that the
defendants would have had an unanswerable defence under the Rent Acts.　*b*

I agree that the appeal should be allowed.

TEMPLEMAN LJ. I agree that the appeal should be allowed. The landlord, Mr　*c*
Quennell, finding that he was incumbered by a statutory tenant and not able to reap the
benefit of a sale with vacant possession, devised, under advice, a scheme whereby he might
obtain vacant possession. It so happened that the landlord had mortgaged the property to
his bank to secure his overdraft and other borrowings, and the mortgage contained a
common form prohibition on any lettings without the consent of the mortgagee bank.　*d*
The lease to the statutory tenant was made by the landlord after the date of the mortgage
without the consent of the bank and was therefore in breach of the landlord's covenant
contained in the mortgage. That lease was binding on the landlord but void against the
bank. On expiry of the lease the tenant became a statutory tenant as against the landlord
but not as against the bank.

The landlord being unable to get possession from his own statutory tenant approached　*e*
the bank and asked the bank to bring an action against the tenant for possession. This
would then enable the landlord to sell the property with vacant possession. The bank very
properly declined to take any such action which was not required to protect their position
as mortgagee. The amount of the debt owed by the landlord to the bank was £2,500, the
rent payable by the tenants exceeded £1,000 a year, and the property was worth in the
region of £30,000 to £40,000. The bank in these circumstances rightly refused to do for　*f*
the landlord that which the landlord could not do for himself.

The landlord, again under advice and undaunted, conceived an alternative method of
obtaining vacant possession. His wife paid off the debt of £2,500 owed to the bank by her
husband, the landlord; and the bank, as they were bound to do, accepted that payment and
transferred the mortgage to the wife. The landlord's wife (then the mortgagee) was owed
£2,500 by her husband; and she, at the request of her husband, brought an action against　*g*
the tenant for possession claiming that the lease made by her husband is not binding on her
as mortgagee and that she can therefore obtain possession and then sell to the benefit of
herself and her husband.

As I say, the authorities establish that as a matter of law a lease made in breach of
covenant by a mortgagor is void against the mortgagee and, I assume for present purposes
(but without deciding), is also void against the transferee unless the lease is adopted by the　*h*
mortgagee. Neither the bank nor the wife adopted the tenancy.

The estate, rights and powers of a mortgagee, however, are only vested in a mortgagee
to protect his position as a mortgagee and to enable him to obtain repayment. Subject to
this, the property belongs in equity to the mortgagor. In the present case it is clear from
the facts and the evidence that the mortgagee Mrs Quennell is not bona fide exercising her
rights and powers for her own purposes as mortgagee but for the purpose of enabling the　*j*
landlord mortgagor (her own husband) to repudiate his contractual obligations and defeat
the statutory tenancy of the tenant which is binding on the landlord. Mrs Quennell does
not even pretend to be acting in her own interests as mortgagee. She brings this action to
oblige her husband. In my judgment the court must therefore treat this action, although
in form brought by a mortgagee, as an action brought for and on behalf of the landlord

mortgagor. The court should deal with it as though the mortgagor landlord were the
a plaintiff, and on that basis possession will not be ordered.

Appeal allowed.

Solicitors: *Donne, Mileham & Haddock*, Brighton (for Mr Maltby); *Anscomb, Hollingworth* (for
Mrs Quennell).

b

Sumra Green   Barrister

Old Grovebury Manor Farm Ltd v W Seymour
c # Plant Sales & Hire Ltd and another

CHANCERY DIVISION
BRIGHTMAN J
22ND, 24TH MAY 1978

d *Landlord and tenant – Action for possession – Claim for mesne profits – Interim payments order
– Application by landlord for interim payments order pending determination of action –
Counterclaim by defendant for damages for harassment – Counterclaim exceeding amount of claim
for mesne profits – Defendant liable for rent or mesne profits whether he won or lost counterclaim
– Whether court having power to make order for interim payments – RSC Ord 29, r 18.*

e In January 1975 the plaintiff leased a garage and petrol filling station to a tenant for three
years. The lease contained a covenant against assignment without the plaintiff's consent.
In September 1976 the tenant, without the plaintiff's consent, purported to assign the lease
to the defendant, who occupied the premises from that date. The plaintiff brought an
action against the defendant claiming possession and rent or mesne profits until delivery
up of possession. The defendant alleged that he was entitled to occupy the premises. The
f amount due for the defendant's use and occupation of the premises was about £11,000.
The defendant counterclaimed for damages exceeding £20,000 for harassment arising out
of alleged obstruction and intimidation by the plaintiff which had reduced petrol sales.
The counterclaim was made in good faith and was not without merit as was shown by the
fact that the defendant had obtained an undertaking from the plaintiff not to molest or
assault the defendant's employees and the plaintiff had been fined £250 for breach of that
g undertaking. The plaintiff applied under RSC Ord 29, r 18[a], for an order against the
defendant for interim payments for use and occupation of the premises. The defendant
would be liable for rent or mesne profits whether he won or lost on the counterclaim. On
the question whether the court should make the order sought by the plaintiff,

Held – The court's discretion under RSC Ord 29, r 18, to award interim payments in
h respect of mesne profits against the defendant in an action for possession of land was not
exercisable where the defendant had a bona fide counterclaim against the plaintiff which
exceeded the amount of the claim for mesne profits, for r 18 was not intended to give the
plaintiff money which he would not be entitled to receive at the conclusion of the action
if the counterclaim succeeded. Accordingly, the plaintiff was not entitled to the order
sought (see p 576 *d* to *f*, post).

j

Cases referred to in judgment
Hart v Rogers [1916] 1 KB 646, 85 LJKB 273, 114 LT 329, 31(1) Digest (Reissue) 500, 4126.
Moore v Assignment Courier Ltd [1977] 2 All ER 842, [1977] 1 WLR 638, CA.

a   Rule 18 is set out at p 575 *c* to *f*, post.

Case also cited

Rookes v Barnard [1964] 1 All ER 367, [1964] AC 1129, HL.

Summons

By a writ and statement of claim served on 7th January 1977 the plaintiff, Old Grovebury Manor Farm Ltd, the landlord of property demised to James Brian Armstrong ('the second defendant') for a term of three years, claimed, inter alia, possession of the property against W Seymour Plant Sales and Hire Ltd ('the first defendant') and the second defendant, and rent or alternatively mesne profits at the rate of £7,000 a year from the date of service of the writ until delivery up of possession. By a summons dated 26th January 1978 the plaintiff applied for an order under RSC Ord 29, r 18 against the first defendant for an interim payment for use and occupation of the property, and for periodical payments thereafter for use and occupation while the action was pending. The facts are set out in the judgment.

Cyril W F Newman for the plaintiff.
M K I Kennedy for the first defendant.

BRIGHTMAN J. This is an application by a landlord for relief under RSC Ord 29, r 18. That order relates to interlocutory injunctions, interim preservation of property and interim payments.

Before the coming into force of the Rules of the Supreme Court (Amendment No 3) 1977[1], an order for an interim payment pending trial was confined to a payment on account of damages in respect of personal injury[2]. Shortly stated, such an order can be made if the defendant has admitted liability, or if the plaintiff has obtained a judgment for damages to be assessed, or if the court is satisfied that the plaintiff will succeed at the trial and obtained judgment for damages. In such a case the rules provide that the court may, if it thinks fit, order an interim payment of such amount as it thinks just, not exceeding a reasonable proportion of the damages which, in the opinion of the court, are likely to be recovered by the plaintiff. It follows that an order for an interim payment of this sort may involve a preliminary determination by the court of the merits of the case. No other orders for interim payments could previously be made under RSC Ord 29.

On 20th January 1977 the Court of Appeal gave judgment in *Moore v Assignment Courier Ltd*[3]. The question in issue was this: where a landlord purports to forfeit a lease but the tenant remains in occupation, is the landlord entitled to be paid, pending a determination of the landlord's forfeiture action, a periodic sum representing either rent or mesne profits? Clearly, in such a case, assuming no cross-claim, the landlord must at the end of the day be entitled to some payment in respect of the tenant's occupation, either as rent, if the occupation turns out to be lawful, or as mesne profits if the occupation turns out to be unlawful. The question before the Court of Appeal was whether it had jurisdiction to order an interim payment corresponding to the minimum amount which, one way or the other, the landlord would ultimately receive for the use of his land. The court decided that it had no such jurisdiction.

The injustice highlighted by that case led on 21st November 1977 to the addition of r 18 to RSC Ord 29. This rule came into force on 11th January 1978 and is now invoked by the plaintiff.

The facts of the case can be told very shortly. On 3rd January 1975 the plaintiff, a company which carries on a farming business, leased a piece of land to Mr J B Armstrong ('the second defendant') for three years for use as a garage and petrol filling station. On 23rd September 1976 the second defendant purported to assign the lease to the first defendant, W Seymour Plant Sales and Hire Ltd, without the consent of the plaintiff as

---

1   SI 1977 No 1955
2   See RSC Ord 29, rr 9–17
3   [1977] 2 All ER 842, [1977] 1 WLR 638

required by a covenant in the lease. The plaintiff alleged that this was a breach of
covenant. On 27th September 1976 it issued a writ for forfeiture of the lease. The lease
was due to end on 1st January 1978. The first defendant claims that there has been an
effective exercise of an option to renew for a further three years under a provision in the
lease; alternatively, the first defendant claims that the term continues to exist under the
Landlord and Tenant Act 1954 as a business tenancy. The second defendant, the original
tenant, is bankrupt. It is common ground that he has no interest in the action.

The first defendant has been in occupation of the garage premises since September
1976. It has not paid one penny for such occupation, although at one stage payments of
rent were offered. These were refused because the plaintiff feared that acceptance might
compromise its claim for forfeiture. This is precisely the situation which the new r 18 is
designed to meet. On the facts so far narrated the plaintiff is bound to receive either rent
or mesne profits. Rule 18 reads as follows:

'(1) Where in an action in which there is a claim for possession of land it appears to
the Court that, in the event of a final judgment or order being given or made in
favour of the plaintiff, the defendant would be held liable to pay to the plaintiff a sum
of money in respect of the defendant's use and occupation of the land during the
pendency of the action, the Court may, on the application of the plaintiff, and without
prejudice to any contentions of the parties as to the nature or character of the sum to
be paid by the defendant, order the defendant to make a payment (in this rule referred
to as an "interim payment") on account of that sum.

'(2) No such order for an interim payment shall be made unless it appears to the
Court that, even if a final judgment or order were given or made in favour of the
defendant, he would still be under an obligation to pay the plaintiff for his use and
occupation of the land, whether by way of rent, mesne profits or otherwise.

'(3) An order under this rule may be for the payment of—(a) a sum not exceeding
the amount which, if a final judgment or order were given or made in favour of the
defendant, would be payable by him in respect of his use and occupation of the land
up to the date of the order, or (b) periodical payments during the pendency of the
action, or (c) a combination of both.

'(4) Subject to Order 80, rule 12, the amount of any interim payment ordered to be
made shall be paid to the plaintiff unless the order provides for it to be paid into court;
and when the amount is paid into court, the Court may, on the ex parte application
of the plaintiff, order the whole or any part of it to be paid out to him at such time as
the Court thinks fit.'

The conditions, therefore, which must be satisfied to justify an order for an interim
payment are: (i) that if the landlord won the action, the defendant would be liable to pay
the landlord a sum of money in respect of his use and occupation of the land during the
pendency of the action; and, (ii) that if the defendant won the action, the defendant would
still be under an obligation to pay the landlord for his use and occupation of the land.

Prima facie the plaintiff is clearly entitled to an order for an interim payment under
r 18. Admittedly, r 18 is discretionary and not mandatory, but on any ordinary exercise
of the court's discretion it is hardly to be doubted that an order for an interim payment
would be made in the present case, in the absence of other relevant factors.

The problem which arises here flows from the fact that the first defendant has made a
cross-claim against the plaintiff. The first defendant alleges that ever since it went into
occupation as assignee or purported assignee it has been the victim of a course of harassment
by the plaintiff. The first defendant claims that it has suffered damage in excess of £20,000
as a result of the wrongful activities of the plaintiff or its officers or servants. These large
damages are based on an alleged reduction of petrol sales due to obstruction and
intimidation on the part of the plaintiff. The first defendant has raised a counterclaim
against the plaintiff accordingly.

The counterclaim is not devoid of merit, and is not advanced in bad faith or
vexatiously. In May 1977 the plaintiff, on a motion for an injunction, gave an undertaking

until judgment or further order not to molest or assault the officers or servants of the first
defendant and not to interfere with its quiet and peaceful enjoyment of the premises. On *a*
24th June 1977 the first defendant moved to commit for contempt of court arising out of
breach of that undertaking. On 8th March 1978 the plaintiff was fined £250 for
contempt. So clearly the counterclaim has substance.

The amount now due to the plaintiff for rent or for use and occupation is at its highest
(on the agreed figures) of the order of £11,400. The first defendant's counterclaim is of the
order of £20,000. The plaintiff, nevertheless, submits that I ought to make an order for *b*
interim payments in respect of the first defendant's use and occupation of the land. It is
unjust, it is said, that the plaintiff should see its land occupied by the defendant without
any payment being made. The plaintiff relies on the proposition, usually accepted as
correct, that a tenant cannot set off damages for breach of covenant against a claim for rent:
see *Hart v Rogers*[1]. It also submits that the only conditions imposed by r 18 are: (i) that if
a final judgment or order is made in favour of the plaintiff the defendant will be held liable *c*
to pay for the use and occupation, and (ii) that if a final judgment or order is made in favour
of the defendant, the defendant will still be liable to pay for use and occupation. Those
conditions are satisfied, it is submitted, because the first defendant, win or lose, must be
liable either for rent or for mesne profits. Furthermore, the plaintiff says it is assessed to
tax on rent which it does not receive at present. I express no view on the rightness of that
assessment since the plaintiff does not claim to be entitled to rent and does not yet have any *d*
judgment or order in its favour for mesne profits, and is not in occupation.

In my view, the plaintiff's approach to r 18 is not correct. I think that r 18 is directed
only to the simple case of a claim for possession of land without the complication of a bona
fide cross-claim which may absorb the whole amount of the landlord's claim. Rule 18 is
not intended to give a landlord money which at the end of the day he may never be entitled
to receive owing to the success of defendant's cross-claim. If the first defendant were an *e*
undisputed tenant and the plaintiff were suing for rent, so that the plaintiff was entitled to
summary judgment under RSC Ord 14 for the amount of the rent, the existence of a bona
fide cross-claim on the part of the tenant would almost certainly entitle the tenant to a stay
of execution under RSC Ord 14, r 3(2), at any rate if the cross-claim exceeded the claim for
rent. I do not see why it should be proper for the court under Ord 29 to order an interim
payment in the face of a bona fide cross-claim of greater amount just because the plaintiff's *f*
claim is for mesne profits as an alternative to rent and is therefore within the wording of
Ord 29 instead of Ord 14.

In these circumstances, I make no order in favour of the plaintiff.

No order on summons.

g

Solicitors: *Wilkins & Son*, Aylesbury (for the plaintiff); *Neve, Son & Co*, Luton (for the first
defendant).

Evelyn Budd—Barrister.

---

1   [1916] 1 KB 646

R v Thomas
R v Ferguson

COURT OF APPEAL, CRIMINAL DIVISION
LORD WIDGERY CJ, BRIDGE LJ AND WIEN J
7th NOVEMBER 1978

Criminal law – Obstructing course of justice – Common law offence – Interference by dishonest, corrupt or threatening means – Applicants giving registered numbers of unmarked police cars to suspected person to assist him in avoiding arrest – Whether applicants guilty of attempting to pervert the course of justice – Whether dishonest, corrupt or threatening interference essential element of offence.

The applicants discovered that they were being kept under observation by police officers in unmarked cars. An associate of theirs suspected of committing a number of bank robberies was also being kept under observation by the police and the applicants passed on to him the registration numbers of the unmarked cars in order to assist him in avoiding arrest. The applicants were arrested and charged with the common law offence of attempting to pervert the course of justice. They were found guilty and sentenced to three years' imprisonment. They appealed against their conviction contending that there had to be interference by dishonest, corrupt or threatening means before the common law offence was committed.

Held – Any act calculated to assist a person known to be suspected by the police in avoiding arrest was an interference with the police in their function of seeking to arrest suspected persons, and therefore interference such as the giving of some information or warning to a suspect which was intended to assist and did assist the subject to avoid arrest amounted to perverting or attempting to pervert the administration of justice, notwithstanding that the interference did not involve dishonest, corrupt or threatening conduct. The applicants had therefore been rightly convicted and their appeals would be dismissed (see p 580 *d* to *h* and p 581 *e* to *g*, post).

Dictum of Lord MacDermott CJ in *R v Bailey* [1965] NI at 26 applied.

Notes

For perversion of the course of justice, see 11 Halsbury's Laws (4th Edn) para 955, and for cases on the subject, see 15 Digest (Reissue) 975–977, 8423–8446.

For the Criminal Law Act 1967, s 4, see 8 Halsbury's Statutes (3rd Edn) 555.

Cases referred to in judgment

R v Bailey [1956] NI 15, CCA, 15 Digest (Reissue) 1090, *6994.
R v Britton [1973] RTR 502, CA, Digest (Cont Vol D) 878, 322fd.
R v Panayiotou [1973] 3 All ER 112, [1973] 1 WLR 1032, 137 JP 699, 57 Cr App R 762, CA, 15 Digest (Reissue) 977, 8446.
R v Vreones [1891] 1 QB 360, 60 LJMC 62, 64 LT 309, 55 JP 536, 17 Cox CC 267, CCR, 15 Digest (Reissue) 974, 8412.

Cases also cited

R v Kellett [1975] 3 All ER 468, [1976] QB 372, CA.
R v Sharpe, R v Stringer [1938] 1 All ER 48, CCA.

Appeal

Derek Thomas and William John Ferguson applied for leave to appeal against their conviction at the Central Criminal Court on 28th April 1978 before his Honour Judge Argyle QC and a jury on a charge of attempting to pervert the course of justice. The applicants were sentenced to three years' imprisonment. The hearing of the application was treated as the hearing of the appeal. The facts appear in the judgment of the court.

M Birnbaum for the applicant Thomas.
G Bathurst Norman for the applicant Ferguson.
R Amlot for the Crown.

BRIDGE LJ delivered the following judgment of the court: On 28th April 1978 at the Central Criminal Court the two applicants were convicted of attempting to pervert the course of justice and sentenced to three years' imprisonment. The indictment against them contained two counts. The first alleged an attempt to pervert the course of justice by supplying John Charles Short with the registration numbers of certain vehicles to assist the said John Charles Short to avoid arrest and prosecution for robbery. The second count was laid under s 4 (1) of the Criminal Law Act 1967, and the particulars were that on or about 9th December 1976, after John Charles Short had committed an arrestable offence, namely robbery, knowing or believing the said John Charles Short to be guilty of that offence or of some other arrestable offence without lawful authority or reasonable excuse, supplied the said John Charles Short with the registration numbers of certain police vehicles with intent to impede the apprehension or prosecution of the said John Charles Short.

At the close of the case for the prosecution a submission was made to the trial judge that on that second count there was no case for either applicant to answer on the footing that there was no evidence that either of them knew or believed that Short was guilty of the arrestable offence mentioned or any other arrestable offence. The judge upheld that submission and directed an acquittal of the s 4 offence.

The applicants now seek leave to appeal against their conviction for the common law offence of attempting to pervert the course of justice.

The point raised in the appeal is a short but important one, and the factual basis giving rise to it can, I hope, be quite shortly summarised. At the material time when the acts relied on as constituting criminal conduct on the part of these applicants were committed, the man named in both counts in the indictment, John Charles Short, was, it is common ground, a man whom the police were keeping under observation and whom in due course they intended to arrest as a person whom they suspected to have been guilty of committing one or more bank robberies. According to the facts which must be taken to have been proved, what the applicants had done was, finding themselves under observation by police officers who were travelling in unmarked police vehicles, to give the numbers of those police vehicles to Short with a view to assisting him in avoiding arrest as a suspect.

The directions which the judge gave to the jury with regard to the elements which they must find proved in relation to the common law offence were in the following terms. He said:

> 'In this particular case the Crown has brought this charge involving perverting the course of public justice. What is alleged here is that this man Short, being wanted for a very serious crime, was being protected in various ways by various people. What is said here is that Ferguson and Thomas were playing their part in that perverting the course of public justice by supplying Short with the numbers of police cars which were watching him or pursuing him. Put in its starkest form, and getting away from this case for a moment, perverting the course of public justice when it is known a man is wanted for an offence is obviously, or can be, a very serious matter.'

Then he said: 'Looking again at the charge, first of all the Crown has got to prove the attempt.' He later gave the jury a further direction as to what was involved in an attempt, which has not been the subject of any criticism. He continued:

> 'Secondly it has got to prove by supplying Short with the registration numbers of certain police vehicles these accused, and you must consider their cases separately,

intended to assist Short to avoid arrest and prosecution for robbery. Finally, you have to be satisfied, if that is proved, this was done in order to try to pervert the course of public justice.'

The submission made on behalf of both applicants is to this effect, that, in the light of the judge's withdrawal of the case from the jury under s 4 of the Criminal Law Act 1967, it must be assumed that neither of these accused had any knowledge or belief in the guilt of Short of any of the robberies of which he was suspected. Then, so runs the argument, since they could not be convicted of an offence under s 4 of the 1967 Act, which is the statutory replacement of the old offence of being an accessory after the fact, neither could they be convicted, lacking knowledge of the guilt of Short of any offence of which he was suspected, of the offence of attempting to pervert the course of justice.

Counsel for the Crown has concisely summarised the four propositions on which he relies in support of the contention that the jury could properly convict of this offence and that the evidence disclosed an offence. First, he says that it is well established that it is a common law offence to do any act which has a tendency and is intended to pervert the administration of public justice.

I pause there to observe that that proposition is well supported by the authority of R v Vreones[1]. Indeed the proposition comes in terms from the judgment of Pollock B[2] in that case, and the proposition is in no way controverted by counsel for the applicants.

The second of counsel's propositions is in these terms. Doing an act calculated to assist another to avoid arrest, knowing he is wanted by police as a suspect, falls into the category of offences of perverting the administration of public justice. It will be necessary to come back to that second proposition later on in this judgment, for it is on the validity and scope of that proposition that in the end the propriety of these convictions depends.

The third proposition, which again is not controverted by counsel for the applicants, is to the effect that the course of public justice may be perverted before any proceedings in court are commenced.

The fourth proposition is to the effect, which is in a measure in controversy, that it matters not that the applicants were not and could not be prosecuted and convicted under s 4 of the 1967 Act.

It is convenient to dispose of the issue as regards that fourth proposition before returning to the second proposition, which is at the heart and kernel of the matter. It seems to us that counsel's fourth proposition is conclusively established by the authority of this court in R v Panayiotou[3]. This was a case of conspiracy to pervert or obstruct the course of justice, the conspiracy alleged being an attempt to persuade by threats a lady who had made a complaint of rape to withdraw her complaint and not to give evidence in accordance with the statement she had made to the police.

In giving the judgment of the court, Scarman LJ said[4], as regards the relationship between the common law offence with which we are here concerned and the statutory offences created by ss 4 and 5 of the 1967 Act:

'The Criminal Law Act 1967 has created certain statutory offences of acting to impede the apprehension or prosecution of an offender (s 4) and of concealing offences or giving false information (s 5): but, though it has abolished the crime of compounding an offence (other than treason), it is silent as to the common law offence of perverting or obstructing the course of justice. We do not read ss 4 and 5 as codifying the law in this field: it is not therefore to be inferred from this silence that the offence no longer exists.'

1   [1891] 1 QB 360
2   [1891] 1 QB 360 at 369
3   [1973] 3 All ER 112, [1973] 1 WLR 1032
4   [1973] 3 All ER 112 at 115, [1973] 1 WLR 1032 at 1035

The authority on which essentially counsel for the Crown relies for his second proposition, to revert to that, is a decision of the Court of Criminal Appeal in Northern Ireland in *R v Bailey*[1]. That was a case of a man who had made a false confession to the police implicating two other men and himself in a murder. He was convicted on an indictment which described his offence as effecting a public mischief. It was said by Lord MacDermott CJ, in giving judgment, that it could more appropriately have been prosecuted as the offence of perverting the course of public justice.

The particular passage in which Lord MacDermott CJ considered the scope of the offence of perverting the course of justice is where he said[2]:

'But the administration of public justice, particularly in the criminal sphere, cannot well be confined to the processes of adjudication. In point of principle we think it comprehends functions that nowadays belong, in practice almost exlusively, to the police, such as the investigation of offences and the arrest of suspected persons; and we see no good reason for regarding these preliminaries as beyond the scope of the category we are now considering.'

In the face of that important statement of principle, counsel for the applicants does not, sensibly and rightly in our view, feel able to mount a root and branch attack on the soundness of counsel's second proposition for the Crown. What he does by way of an alternative to that is to say that, whilst the proposition is sound as far as it goes, it is a proposition which can only be invoked in a limited class of cases.

How he puts the submission on behalf of the applicant Thomas is to say that indeed there can be an interference with the course of justice at the stage when police officers are concerned to arrest someone suspected of a criminal offence, but such an interference amounting to the common law offence of perverting public justice can only be constituted where the interference itself is sought to be effected by some dishonest, corrupt or threatening means. Counsel accepts that, if a person dishonestly deflected a police officer from arresting a suspect by giving him deliberately false information, or if a person corruptly deflected a police officer from arresting the suspect by bribing him, or if a person threateningly deflected a police officer from arresting a suspect by an offer of violence, in each of those cases he would be guilty of the common law offence of which these applicants were convicted. But, so the argument runs, if the act which has frustrated the police officer's attempt to arrest the suspect was no more than the giving of some information or warning to the suspect, as here, which was intended to assist, and did assist, the suspect to avoid arrest, then that is not sufficient to constitute the offence of attempting to pervert or perverting the course of public justice.

We have considered that submission with care. We appreciate that the established cases do not in terms show any instance of a conviction of this common law offence on facts which are on all fours with the facts before the court today. But we are unable in principle to accept the logic or validity of the distinction which counsel seeks to draw between an interference with the police in their activity, which is certainly part of the administration of justice, of seeking to arrest suspected persons, which is done in a dishonest, corrupt or threatening way and an interference which consists of such acts as were here involved.

We gain support for that conclusion in principle from the last authority which was brought to our attention in the course of argument, which was *R v Britton*[3]. That was a case of a motorist who, having been stopped after committing a moving traffic offence and required to take a breathalyser test, went into his own house, and before the breathalyser could be administered to him took a drink from a bottle of some alcoholic liquor, thereby, on well established authority, putting himself beyond the reach of the procedure leading to a conviction for driving with excess alcohol in the blood. He had been convicted of attempting to defeat the course of justice. It was argued in that case that he had fairly

---

1   [1956] NI 15

2   [1956] NI 15 at 26

3   [1973] RTR 502

escaped prosecution under the statute through a statutory loophole which it was for Parliament alone to stop.

That argument was rejected, and the important passage in the judgment of the court, given by Lord Widgery CJ, is that in which the court recited with approval and acceptance the argument which was adduced in support of the conviction by counsel then appearing for the Crown[1]:

'[Counsel for the Crown], supporting the conviction, invites us to say that the offence is proved if there is some course upon which justice has embarked and the accused deliberately tampers with that course or interferes with it. I have not perhaps exactly recorded [counsel's] words, and he will forgive me if I do not do entire justice to the way he put it, but that was the substance of it. The emphasis of his argument, of course, is that there must be some course upon which justice has embarked before there can be any proper case of interference with that course. He submits that in the present case the course of justice is mapped out by the Road Safety Act 1967, the precise steps to be taken are there laid down, and once a police officer has reached the stage of setting that course of action in motion by requiring the provision of a specimen of breath for a breath test from a motorist, then, says [counsel] anything which the accused does thereafter which interferes with and upsets the due working out of the statutory course of action is within the scope of the offence which was charged here.'

It is to be observed on the facts of that case that it could not possibly have been said that the act of taking additional alcoholic drink after his driving had ceased involved a dishonest, corrupt or threating course of conduct on the part of the appellant. There, as here, there had been some course on which justice had embarked: there, the statutory procedure initiated by the request for a specimen of breath made by the police officer; here, the common law procedure of investigating a crime leading in due course, if not frustrated, to the arrest of a suspect.

For those reasons we have come to the conclusion that the facts here did disclose an offence, and that the principal directions, to which reference has already been made, which the judge gave to the jury were beyond criticism.

Certain other complaints about aspects of the summing-up have been addressed to the court by counsel for the applicant Ferguson, but we can find no substance in those matters. It seems to us that they are complaints about particular references to the facts which it was perfectly within the judge's province to comment on in the way he did, and we can find no ground on which it could properly be concluded, having rejected the main argument in respect of these applications, that there was any misdirection to the jury which would justify interfering with either of these convictions.

Accordingly, the applications for leave to appeal against conviction are refused.

Applications refused.

8th December. The Court of Appeal (Lord Widgery CJ, Cumming-Bruce LJ and Drake J) refused leave to appeal to the House of Lords but certified under s 33 (2) of the Criminal Appeal Act 1968 that the following point of law of general public importance was involved in the decision: whether a person commits the offence of attempting to pervert the course of public justice if he does an act intended to assist another to evade lawful arrest with knowledge that the other is wanted by the police as a suspect.

1st February 1979. The Appeal Committee (Lord Wilberforce, Lord Fraser of Tullybelton and Lord Scarman) dismissed the petition for leave to appeal.

Solicitors: *Sears Blok* (for the applicant Thomas); *Registrar of Criminal Appeals* (for the applicant Ferguson); *Director of Public Prosecutions.*

N P Metcalfe Esq   Barrister.

---

1   [1973] RTR 502 at 506–507

Re Southard & Co Ltd

CHANCERY DIVISION
BRIGHTMAN J
22nd, 23rd NOVEMBER 1978

Company – Compulsory winding-up – Winding-up order – Court's discretion to make winding-up order – Voluntary liquidation in progress – Petitioning and supporting creditor members of same group of companies as company in liquidation and having majority in value of debts – Opposing creditors independent of group and greater in number but having minority in value of debts – Whether nature of petitioning and supporting creditors' debts relevant in depriving petitioning creditor of prima facie right to winding-up order – Whether number of opposing creditors to be taken into account – Companies Act 1948, s 346(2).

In September 1978 the parent company ('the petitioning creditor') of a group of companies placed a wholly owned subsidiary in voluntary liquidation and subsequently appointed a liquidator. On 11th October the petitioning creditor presented a winding-up petition for the compulsory liquidation of the company. The petition was founded on an alleged unsecured debt of the company of £40,504, and the ground of the petition was that the company's assets would be realised more expeditiously and economically if there was a compulsory winding-up. The petition was supported by another company in the same group which claimed to be an unsecured creditor for £49,000. The petition was opposed by seven creditors not connected with the group who were creditors of the company for a total of about £12,000 and who wished to continue with the voluntary liquidation. There was no evidence that a compulsory liquidation would be quicker or more economical than the voluntary liquidation. The petitioning creditor contended that a winding-up order should be made because domestic debts, ie debts owing to the parent or subsidiary companies, were not to be discounted if the domestic creditors supported rather than opposed the petition, and if the domestic debts were not discounted the opposing creditors were in the minority in the value of their debts.

Held – Although generally the court ought not to deprive a petitioning creditor of his prima facie right to a winding-up order unless the opposing creditors were the majority in the value of their debts, where the petitioning and supporting creditors belonged to the same group of companies as the company in liquidation the court should have regard to the nature of their debts, i e that they were domestic debts owed from a member company, and, even though they were the majority in value, the value of their debts ought not to carry decisive weight since, in the absence of contrary evidence, the court had to assume that where the petitioning creditor was the parent company it had had power to control the activities of the company in liquidation. Furthermore, s 346[a] of the Companies Act 1948 did not debar the court from having regard to the number of the opposing creditors. In the circumstances that the petition was opposed by seven independent creditors, that the petitioning and supporting creditors belonged to the same group of companies as the company in liquidation, and in the absence of evidence that a compulsory liquidation would be more effective, the court would prefer the view of the opposing creditors even though they were the minority in the value of their debts. Accordingly, the court would exercise its discretion to dismiss the petition and allow the voluntary liquidation to proceed (see p 585 g h, p 586 b c, p 587 b to j and p 588 a b, post).

---

a   Section 346, so far as material, provides:
      '(1) The court may, as to all matters relating to the winding up of a company, have regard to the wishes of the creditors . . .
      '(2) In the case of creditors, regard shall be had to the value of each creditor's debt. . .'

Notes

For creditors' wishes and the value of their debts in relation to a winding-up, see 7 Halsbury's Laws (4th Edn) para 1033, and for cases on the subject, see 10 Digest (Reissue) 945–948, 5531–5553.

For the Companies Act 1948, s 346, see 5 Halsbury's Statutes (3rd Edn) 369.

Cases referred to in judgment

ABC Coupler & Engineering Co Ltd, Re [1961] 1 All ER 354, [1961] 1 WLR 243, 10 Digest (Reissue) 946, 5541.

Home Remedies Ltd, Re [1942] 2 All ER 552, [1943] Ch 1, 112 LJ Ch 36, 167 LT 362, 10 Digest (Reissue) 1201, 7477.

Karsberg (B) Ltd, Re [1955] 3 All ER 854, [1956] 1 WLR 57, CA, 10 Digest (Reissue) 1201, 7478.

Macrae (P & J) Ltd, Re [1961] 1 All ER 302, [1961] 1 WLR 229, CA, 10 Digest (Reissue) 1121, 6932.

Millward (James) & Co Ltd, Re [1940] 1 All ER 347, [1940] Ch 333, 109 LJ Ch 161, 162 LT 257, [1940–41] B & CR 7, 10 Digest (Reissue) 1199, 7468.

Swain (J D) Ltd, Re [1965] 2 All ER 761, [1965] 1 WLR 909, CA, 10 Digest (Reissue) 946, 5542.

Vuma Ltd, Re [1960] 3 All ER 629, [1960] 1 WLR 1283, CA, 10 Digest (Reissue) 948, 5553.

Winding-up petition

By a petition presented on 11th October 1978 by Seton Trust Ltd ('the petitioning creditor') to wind up Southard & Co Ltd ('the company'), it was alleged that the company was indebted to the petitioning creditor in the sum of £40,504, that on 18th September 1978 at an extraordinary general meeting of the company a special resolution for the voluntary winding-up of the company was passed, that at a creditors' meeting on 11th October 1978 joint liquidators were appointed, that the company was insolvent and unable to pay its debts, that the petitioning creditor believed that the assets of the company would be realised more expeditiously and more economically by the Official Receiver than by the joint liquidators and that in the circumstances it was just and equitable that the company should be wound up by the court. The petition was opposed by seven creditors ('the opposing creditors'). The facts are set out in the judgment.

Jeremiah Harman QC and *Oliver Albery* for the petitioning creditor.
John Lindsay for the opposing creditors.

BRIGHTMAN J. This is a creditors' petition to wind up a company. The petition is presented by the parent company ('the petitioning creditor') and is supported by an associated company. The petitioning creditor has already placed the company in voluntary liquidation. The petitioning creditor and its associated company now desire a compulsory order; the minority of creditors wish the voluntary liquidation to continue. Reasons are given on each side. The question of law is on what principles this court should exercise its undoubted discretion to make or refuse a winding-up order.

The company was incorporated in March 1960. It carried on business as wine merchants. It is a wholly owned subsidiary of the petitioning creditor. The paid-up capital of the company is £113,450. According to the evidence of the petitioning creditor, at some time before the end of May this year the company was indebted to the National Westminster Bank Ltd in about £101,000 on loan account and about £53,000 on overdraft account. On 24th May the company gave Barclays Bank Ltd a debenture to secure future indebtedness, charging all its assets and undertaking. Thirteen days later, on 6th June, Barclays Bank Ltd paid £153,968 to National Westminster Bank Ltd and took over the debt. This was done at the request of the company and was supported by the guarantee of the petitioning creditor.

On 18th September 1978 the petitioning creditor placed the company in creditors' voluntary liquidation. At that date the company is said to have owed the petitioning creditor £47,140. Mr Stevens was appointed liquidator by the petitioning creditor or its nominees. According to a statement of affairs signed by Mr Stevens the company was hopelessly insolvent. Bank overdraft and loan accounted for £174,000, trade creditors were £73,000, loans from the petitioning creditor and its associated company amounted to £84,000. The estimated deficiency was about £188,000. On 26th September the petitioning creditor assigned to 24 persons £14,400 of its debt, leaving it as a creditor for £32,740. There were 24 assignments, each of £600. The purpose of this transaction is not explained. The apparent consequence was to increase the number of individual creditors able to vote on relevant occasions.

On 10th October the company held a meeting of its creditors. Mr George Auger and Mr Leonard Curtis were appointed liquidators by the creditors in place of Mr Stevens. They are chartered accountants specialising in insolvencies. On the next day the petitioning creditor presented a winding-up petition founded on an alleged debt of £40,504, described as 'money lent'. On 13th October the petitioning creditor paid Barclays Bank £175,348 for an assignment of its then debt and of the debenture. The petitioning creditor was, as I have said, the guarantor of that debt. At some time thereafter the petitioning creditor appointed Mr Stevens as receiver and manager, so that he is back in the saddle, in a manner of speaking. On 20th October the petitioning creditor obtained a re-assignment of the £14,400. The petitioning creditor has valued its security at £150,000, so that it claims to be an unsecured creditor for about £25,000 plus £47,000.

The petition is supported by Scandic Credit & Commerce Ltd ('Scandic'). It is registered in the Bahamas and was formerly called the National Union Bank Ltd. Scandic claims to be a creditor for £49,000.

I will say a word about the relationship of the petitioning and supporting creditors and the company. They are all members of the same group. At the head is Seton Securities Ltd. The petitioning creditor is a subsidiary of Seton Securities Ltd. The company in liquidation is a subsidiary of the petitioning creditor. Scandic is a subsidiary of Seton Securities Ltd, via another stirps. So, in the result, one finds that the petitioning and supporting creditors, and the bankrupt company, are all of the same family, controlled by Seton Securities Ltd. The petitioning creditor, which was originally content in its capacity as shareholder that its wholly-owned subsidiary should be placed in voluntary liquidation, now in its capacity as creditor desires that its subsidiary should be wound up by the court.

The petition is opposed by Gilbey Vintners Ltd, which is a creditor for £409, and by seven other creditors. I disregard one of such creditors whose debt is almost certainly preferred. The debts of the seven relevant creditors amount to about £12,000 compared with an unsecured indebtedness of the petitioning and supporting creditors amounting to many times that figure.

During the course of the hearing counsel for the opposing creditors received instructions to appear for three further creditors claiming total debts of £7,000. They are ex-employees. A small amount of this indebtedness may be preferred. The amounts of the individual debts were not known when the application was made. On the whole, I think it would be more fair to the petitioning creditor on this occasion to refuse leave to add these three creditors to the list out of time.

I turn initially to the law. The question really amounts to this: how decisive are the wishes of the majority in value of the creditors where they seek a winding-up by the court, and the minority seek a continuation of a voluntary liquidation? This point does not appear to be directly covered by reported authority. All the recent relevant cases, with the exception of *ABC Coupler & Engineering Co Ltd*[1], were reviewed by the Court of Appeal in

---

1	[1961] 1 All ER 354, [1961] 1 WLR 243

Re J D Swain Ltd[1]. None falls quite into the pattern of the instant case. In *Re James Millward & Co Ltd*[2] the choice, as in the present case, was compulsory liquidation or continued voluntary liquidation. There was no opposition to a compulsory winding-up order except from the company itself. Not surprisingly, I would think, the petitioner was held entitled to the order ex debito justitiae. That was a decision of the Court of Appeal reversing Bennett J. In *Re Home Remedies Ltd*[3] the choice was the same, compulsory order or continued voluntary liquidation. But in this case a majority of creditors opposed an order. So the wishes of the majority prevailed in the absence of any sufficient evidence to show why their wishes should be disregarded. That was a decision of Simonds J. In *Re B Karsberg Ltd*[4] the choice was the same, the pattern was the same and the result was the same. That was a decision of the Court of Appeal reversing Vaisey J. In *Re Vuma Ltd*[5] the choice was compulsory liquidation or no liquidation. The petition was opposed by a majority but no reasons were given. The petitioning creditor was held entitled to his order ex debito justitiae. That was a decision of the Court of Appeal reversing Buckley J. In *Re P & J Macrae Ltd*[6] the choice was the same, the pattern was the same and the result was the same. That was a decision of the Court of Appeal upholding the decision of a county court judge. In *Re ABC Coupler & Engineering Co Ltd*[7], which I mentioned earlier, the choice was the same and the pattern was the same, but with this distinction, that there was evidence filed on behalf of the majority opposition which contained reasoned grounds for refusing a winding-up order. No order was made by Pennycuick J. Lastly, in *Re J D Swain Ltd*[1] the choice was between compulsory liquidation or continued voluntary liquidation. The majority of creditors opposed the petition which was dismissed at first instance by Pennycuick J and also on appeal. The decision is accurately recorded in the holding as follows[8]:

> '(1) that whether or not it was proper to make an order for the compulsory winding up of an insolvent company was a matter entirely within the discretion of the judge, whose decision could not be interfered with on appeal unless he had erred in law . . . (2) That where there was no voluntary liquidation in progress and the majority of creditors opposed an order for compulsory winding up, the court would ordinarily require them to buttress their opposition with valid reasons, but that where the majority of creditors wished to continue an existing voluntary liquidation, the court would ordinarily require the petitioning creditor to show some special reason or circumstance for having a compulsory liquidation; that in the present case since the majority of creditors wished to continue an existing liquidation and since the petitioning creditor had not shown any special reason or circumstance for having a compulsory liquidation, the petition would be dismissed.'

I have made this brief summary of previous cases as they have a consistent thread running through them. As has often been said, the decision in a case such as the present is a matter for the discretion of the judge. However, it is clear that the court ought not to deprive a petitioning creditor of his prima facie right to a winding-up order unless there is an opposing majority, and, if there is no voluntary liquidation in existence or in contemplation, unless there are good reasons for such opposition. I have been told that there is no reported case where the court has denied a creditor his prima facie right to a winding-up order ex debito justitiae at the instance of a minority of opposing creditors.

---

1 [1965] 2 All ER 761, [1965] 1 WLR 909
2 [1940] 1 All ER 347, [1940] Ch 333
3 [1942] 2 All ER 552, [1943] Ch 1
4 [1955] 3 All ER 854, [1956] 1 WLR 57
5 [1960] 3 All ER 629, [1960] 1 WLR 1283
6 [1961] 1 All ER 302, [1961] 1 WLR 229
7 [1961] 1 All ER 354, [1961] 1 WLR 243
8 [1965] 1 WLR 909

While conceding that the petitioning creditor's right to a winding-up order is only a prima facie right, counsel for the petitioning and supporting creditors submitted that if the opposition is in a minority, so that the majority are on the side of the creditor seeking to exercise his prima facie right, the court will not deny a winding-up order save in the most exceptional circumstances. Debts owing to subsidiary companies, and other like debts of an inside or 'domestic' nature, are commonly discounted by the court in evaluating the weight of the opposition to a winding-up order: see, for example, the *ABC Coupler* case[1]. Counsel submitted that domestic debts should not be discounted where the domestic creditors in question are supporting and not opposing the petition.

It would, I think, be wrong for me to seek to lay down any rules as to how the court should exercise its discretion. My proper course is to have regard to the value of the debts of the creditors supporting and opposing a winding-up order, and the nature of those debts, to the reasons given by the minority for desiring the court to override the wishes of the majority, and, since the majority have given reasons, to examine those reasons.

Mr Logan, who is a director of the petitioning creditor and a chartered accountant, deposes that the petitioning creditor believes that the assets of the company in liquidation will be realised more quickly and at less cost by the Official Receiver than by the existing voluntary liquidators. No other reasons are advanced by the petitioning creditor for now preferring a compulsory liquidation to a voluntary liquidation. I asked counsel for the petitioning and supporting creditors whether he wished to apply for leave to put in evidence challenging the appointment of the voluntary liquidators on any personal grounds. He said that he did not. So the efficiency and integrity of the voluntary liquidators are not in issue.

I have before me an affidavit of Mr Curtis who is a partner in Messrs Leonard Curtis & Co, who are chartered accountants specialising in insolvencies. He deposes that Mr Auger is a member of Messrs Stoy Hayward & Co, who are also chartered accountants specialising in insolvencies. Mr Curtis would not normally consider it appropriate to take sides in a dispute as to whether there should be a compulsory or a voluntary liquidation. He says that he swears this affidavit at the request of Gilbey Vintners Ltd, which were originally the only opposing creditors on the list, in order, he says, to deal with matters outside the knowledge of that company. Mr Curtis deposes that it is at this stage impossible for him to assess the true indebtedness of the company to the petitioning creditor and Scandic. In relation to an investigation into the affairs of the company Mr Curtis says this:

> '6. I regard it as important in the winding up, by whoever conducted, that there be an investigation by a disinterested person into the circumstances surrounding the grant of the Debenture of the 24th May 1978, to which Mr Logan's Affidavit refers. It is plain that by September 1978 the Company was hopelessly insolvent; it may or may not have been insolvent to the knowledge of its officers earlier than that. I would not wish to say more because at this stage my views could only be speculation, but it is obvious that the validity of the Debenture and the manner in which the Company traded-on down to September 1978 are topics which could very materially affect the position of the Company's unsecured trade creditors.

> '7. Mr Auger and I intend to conduct such an investigation as Joint Liquidators in the voluntary winding up. How much work will be involved I cannot say; it may be that at an early stage the Debenture will emerge as valid and the latter days of trading as entirely proper. Equally, it may be that early research will lead to doubts which might increase as work progresses. Mr Auger and I appreciate and accept that this may well be work for which we are not remunerated adequately, or, as is not unlikely, at all. But, like men in most professions, we accept that there is an element of 'swings and roundabouts' in our professional remuneration. Some matters which occasionally lead to good receipts comparatively easily earned lead to a moral obligation to do work for little or nothing where a strong case exists that the work should be done. This is

---

1   [1961] 1 All ER 354, [1961] 1 WLR 243

such a case; an independent investigation of the kind I have mentioned ought to be carried out and, if Mr Auger and I remain Joint Liquidators in the voluntary winding up, it will be.'

The debenture could conceivably be invalid under s 322 of the Companies Act 1948, as a floating charge created within 12 months of the winding-up. There might conceivably be a liability on certain persons under s 332 for permitting the company to trade when insolvent. The petitioning creditor, for its part, deposes that it is quite prepared to have the affairs of the company and the validity of the debenture investigated. I have to exercise a discretion in reaching my decision. I bear very much in mind that in terms of value, the creditors seeking a winding-up order vastly exceed the opposing creditors. This is not decisive but it is important. I also bear in mind that an unpaid creditor has a prima facie right to a winding-up order, even if a voluntary liquidation is on foot.

On the other hand, I bear in mind the following factors against a compulsory liquidation.

(1) The petitioning and supporting creditors object to a voluntary liquidation on two grounds only: (a) that the assets of the company will be realised more expeditiously; (b) that the assets of the company will be realised more economically, if there is a compulsory liquidation. As regards speed, there is no evidence whatever before me to support the proposition that the Official Receiver will be quicker than Mr Curtis and Mr Auger. I am not impressed by the suggestion that the Official Receiver will be cheaper. There is no absolute standard of cheapness which can in my opinion sensibly be used. If the Official Receiver, as will sometimes be the case, is limited in his activities by the funds which come into his hands and are thus available to finance investigations, and perhaps litigation, while the voluntary liquidators are willing, as they say, to take a broader view on the question of costs, it is possible that a compulsory liquidation will be cheaper but less fruitful, and a voluntary liquidation more expensive, but more fruitful. In para 6 (c) of Mr Logan's first affidavit he says that at a meeting of creditors on 10th October he heard Mr Curtis, in reply to a suggestion that his services were more expensive than the Official Receiver's, impliedly admit that he and his fellow professional liquidator would be more expensive than the Official Receiver. Mr Curtis denies any such conversation. There has been no cross-examination and I think it correct to disregard that paragraph.

(2) The petition is presented and supported only by creditors who belong to the same group of companies as the company in liquidation. Their wishes do not carry with me a weight commensurate with the size of the alleged indebtedness. The company is a subsidiary of the petitioning creditor. The petitioning creditor is prima facie morally responsible for the insolvency and large indebtedness of the company, unless and until the contrary is shown. The supporting creditor is a member of the same group. The insolvency of the company and its considerable indebtedness could be the result of mismanagement or lack of control by its parent company, which is the petitioning creditor. Certainly, in the absence of evidence to the contrary I must assume that the petitioning creditor had it in its power to control the activities of the company which is now bankrupt. I therefore take the view that the size of the indebtedness of the company to the petitioning creditor and the supporting creditor, all of which have operated under the same aegis, ought not to carry decisive weight.

(3) Section 346 of the 1948 Act authorises me, and in practical terms virtually requires me, to have regard to the value of the debts owed to the respective creditors. But it does not debar me from also having regard to the number of creditors ranged against the petition, even though their debts are relatively small. So I bear in mind that there are in this case seven totally independent creditors who opt for a continued voluntary liquidation, compared with the two 'domestic' creditors who opt, on slender grounds in my view, for a compulsory liquidation.

(4) If a compulsory liquidation is so much more advantageous than a voluntary liquidation, I ask myself: how did it come about that the petitioning creditor, who owned all the shares in the bankrupt company, originally put it into voluntary liquidation instead of seeking a compulsory order? That question is not answered by the evidence.

As I have said, the question before me is a matter of discretion. In all the circumstances I have formed a clear conviction that I ought to exercise my discretion by leaving the voluntary liquidation to proceed undisturbed. The opposing creditors have made out a case which, on the evidence and the arguments submitted to me, convince me that I ought to prefer the views of the minority to the wishes of the majority. I therefore dismiss the petition.

Order accordingly.

Solicitors: *Janners* (for the petitioning creditor); *Evan Davies & Co* (for the opposing creditors).

Evelyn Budd   Barrister.

Inland Revenue Commissioners v McMullen and others

COURT OF APPEAL, CIVIL DIVISION
STAMP, ORR AND BRIDGE LJJ
5th, 6th, 7th, 10th JULY, 18th OCTOBER 1978

Charity – Benefit to community – Education – Recreational charity – Sport – Promotion and encouragement of sport – Trust to promote, encourage and provide facilities for pupils of schools and universities to play association football and other games – Whether an educational charity – Whether a trust for purposes beneficial to community – Whether facilities provided in interests of social welfare – Recreational Charities Act 1958, s 1(1).

The objects of a trust, set out in the trust deed, were to organise, provide or assist in the organisation and provision of facilities to enable and encourage pupils of schools and universities to 'Play Association football or other games or sports and thereby to assist in ensuring that due attention is given to [their] physical education and development'. The Charity Commissioners registered the trust as a charity. The Crown appealed against the registration on the ground that the objects of the trust were not exclusively charitable. The trustees of the deed contended that the objects of the trust were exclusively charitable because (i) the trust was established for the advancement of education, (ii) it was established for a purpose beneficial to the community and (iii) it was deemed to be established for exclusively charitable purposes by virtue of s 1(1)[a] of the Recreational Charities Act 1958. The trustees conceded, however, that under the trust the games and sports for which facilities could be provided need not be enjoyed as part of the curriculum of a school or university. Walton J[b] held (i) that the trust could not be classified as an educational charity because its object was the mere encouragement of games and sports and that object was not made subservient to the advancement of education, (ii) nor could it be classified as a trust for a purpose beneficial to the community because the trust fund could be applied for non-charitable purposes and (iii) the trust could not be deemed to be charitable under s 1(1) of the 1958 Act because the provision of facilities under the deed was not 'in the interests of social welfare', within s 1(1). The trustees appealed.

Held (Bridge LJ dissenting) – The appeal would be dismissed for the following reasons—
      (i) On the true construction of the deed the trust had the single object of promoting the physical education and development of pupils at school and university by the playing of

---

a   Section 1, so far as material, is set out at p 593 *d* to *f*, post
b   [1978] 1 All ER 230

association football and other games and sports. Nevertheless a trust to promote the physical education and development of pupils was not a trust for the promotion of education either in the ordinary sense of that word or in its legal sense, because it was a trust merely for the encouragement of games and sports which were not required to be enjoyed as part of the curriculum of a school or university. A non-charitable gift could not be converted into a charitable gift for the promotion of education simply by limiting the objects of the trust to pupils at school or university (see p 591 *j* to p 592 *d*, p 594 *d f* and p 595 *a b*, post); *Re Nottage, Jones v Palmer* [1895–9] All ER Rep 1203 applied; *Re Mariette, Mariette v Governing Body of Aldenham School* [1914–15] All ER Rep 794 and *London Hospital Medical College v Inland Revenue Comrs* [1976] 2 All ER 113 distinguished.

(ii) Furthermore, although by promoting exercise and physical recreation the trust qualified as a trust beneficial to the community, and was therefore prima facie charitable, it failed to qualify as a charitable trust for a purpose beneficial to the community because, on the true construction of the deed, the trust fund could be applied for non-charitable purposes, for the word 'play' embraced engaging in sports as well as games and, accordingly, the fund could be applied, consistently with the deed, in promoting sports such as fishing, shooting, fox hunting and yachting, the promotion of which was not a charitable purpose (see p 592 *h* to p 593 *c*, p 594 *d* and p 595 *b c*, post); *Re Nottage, Jones v Palmer* [1895–9] All ER Rep 1203, *Dunne v Byrne* [1911–13] All ER Rep 1105 and *Incorporated Council of Law Reporting for England and Wales v Attorney-General* [1971] 3 All ER 1029 applied.

(iii) Nor could the trust be deemed to be charitable under s 1(1) of the 1958 Act for, although the trust fund could be used to provide facilities which were 'in the interests of social welfare', within s 1(1), it could also, consistently with the deed, be used to provide facilities for forms of sports the promotion of which was not in the interests of social welfare. It did not follow that, because the facilities under the trust were primarily intended for pupils at school or university, they were provided with the object of improving the pupils' 'conditions of life', within s 1(2) of the 1958 Act; on the true construction of the deed the facilities were to be provided simply for those pupils who played a game or sport irrespective of their conditions of life (see p 593 *g* to p 594 *b* and *d* and p 595 *d*, post).

Per Stamp LJ. The 1958 Act does not validate trust deeds but merely provides that the provision of facilities which might not otherwise be regarded as charitable shall be so regarded (see p 594 *b c*, post).

Decision of Walton J [1978] 1 All ER 230 affirmed.

Notes

For the meaning of charitable purposes, see 5 Halsbury's Laws (4th Edn) paras 502, 504–507. For charities for educational purposes, see ibid paras 522–527, and for cases on the subject, see 8(1) Digest (Reissue) 256–266, *112–157*.

For recreational charities, see 5 Halsbury's Laws (4th Edn) paras 544–547.

For the Recreational Charities Act 1958, s 1, see 3 Halsbury's Statutes (3rd Edn) 584.

Cases referred to in judgments

Brisbane City Council v Attorney-General for Queensland [1978] 3 All ER 30, [1978] 3 WLR 299, PC.

Dunne v Byrne [1912] AC 407, [1911–13] All ER Rep 1105, 81 LJPC 202, 106 LT 394, PC, 8(1) Digest (Reissue) 318, *575*.

Income Tax Special Purposes Comrs v Pemsel [1891] AC 531, [1891–4] All ER Rep 28, 61 LJQB 265, 65 LT 621, 55 JP 805, 3 Tax Cas 53, HL, 8(1) Digest (Reissue) 236, *1*.

Incorporated Council of Law Reporting for England and Wales v Attorney-General [1971] 3 All ER 1029, [1972] Ch 73, [1971] 3 WLR 853, 47 Tax Cas 321, CA, 8(1) Digest (Reissue) 260, *137*.

London Hospital Medical College v Inland Revenue Comrs [1976] 2 All ER 113, [1976] 1 WLR 613.

Mariette, Re, Mariette v Governing Body of Aldenham School [1915] 2 Ch 284, [1914–15] All ER Rep 794, 84 LJ Ch 825, 113 LT 920, 8(1) Digest (Reissue) 257, *119*.

McDougall (Arthur) Fund, Re the Trusts of the, Thompson v Fitzgerald [1956] 3 All ER 867,
　[1957] 1 WLR 81, 8(1) Digest (Reissue) 313, *533*.
Nottage, Re, Jones v Palmer [1895] 2 Ch 649, [1895–9] All ER Rep 1203, 64 LJ Ch 695, 73
　LT 269, 12 R 571, CA, 8(1) Digest (Reissue) 300, *418*.
Strakosch, Re, Temperley v Attorney-General [1949] 2 All ER 6, [1949] Ch 529, [1949] LJR
　1477, 8(1) Digest (Reissue) 312, *522*.
Wedgwood, Re, Allen v Wedgwood [1915] 1 Ch 113, 84 LJ Ch 107, 112 LT 66, CA, 8(1) Digest
　(Reissue) 287, *331*.
Williams' (Sir Howell Jones) Trustees v Inland Revenue Comrs [1947] 1 All ER 513, [1947] AC
　447, [1948] LJR 644, 176 LT 462, 27 Tax Cas 409, HL, 28(1) Digest (Reissue) 17, *54*.

Appeal

The first three defendants, Anthony Derek McMullen, Professor Sir Harold Thompson and
Leonard Thomas Shipman, the trustees of the Football Association Youth Trust ('the trust'),
appealed against a judgment of Walton J[1] given on 13th July 1971 whereby he allowed an
appeal by the Crown from a decision of the Charity Commissioners for England and Wales,
reversed the commissioners' determination that the trust was a charity and should be
entered in the register of charities under s 4 of the Charities Act 1960, and declared that the
trust was not entitled to be registered as a charity because its objects were not charitable or
exclusively charitable. The fourth defendant, pursuant to RSC Ord 108, r 5(2), was the
Attorney-General. The facts are summarised out in the judgment of Stamp LJ. They are
fully set out in the judgment of Walton J in the Chancery -Division[2].

Andrew Morritt QC and *Spencer G Maurice* for the trustees.
Donald Rattee QC for the Crown.
John Mummery for the Attorney-General.

　　　　　　　　　　　　　　　　　　　　　　　　　　　　　　　　Cur adv vult

18th October. The following judgments were read.

STAMP LJ (read by Orr LJ). This is an appeal from an order of Walton J[1] made on 13th
July 1977 whereby he allowed an appeal by the Commissioners of Inland Revenue against
a decision of the Charity Commissioners to register a trust known as the Football
Association Youth Trust as a charity pursuant to s 4 of the Charities Act 1960.
　The case in the court below is fully reported[1] and I need not set out the facts. The
relevant parts of the trust deed, for I do not think in the end that anything turns on the
construction of the recitals, are contained in cl 3 of the deed which is in the following
terms:

　　'The objects of the Trust are—(a) to organise or provide or assist in the organisation
　and provision of facilities which will enable and encourage pupils of Schools and
　Universities in any part of the United Kingdom to play Association Football or other
　games or sports and thereby to assist in ensuring that due attention is given to the
　physical education and development of such pupils as well as the development and
　occupation of their minds and with a view to furthering this object (i) to provide or
　assist in the provision of Association Football or games or sports equipment of every
　kind for the use of such pupils as aforesaid (ii) to provide or assist in the provision of
　courses lectures demonstrations and coaching for pupils of Schools and Universities in
　any part of the United Kingdom and for teachers who organise or supervise playing
　and coaching of Association Football or other games or sports at such Schools and
　Universities as aforesaid (iii) to promote provide or assist in the promotion and
　provision of training colleges for the purpose of training teachers in the coaching of
　Association Football or other games or sports at such Schools and Universities as
　aforesaid (iv) to lay out manage equip and maintain or assist in the laying out

---

1　[1978] 1 All ER 230, [1978] 1 WLR 664
2　[1978] 1 All ER 230 at 233–236, [1978] 1 WLR 664 at 666–669

management equipment and maintenance of playing fields or appropriate indoor facilities or accommodation (whether vested in the Trustees or not) to be used for the teaching and playing of Association Football or other sports or games by such pupils as aforesaid (b) to organise or provide or assist in the organisation or provision of facilities for physical recreation in the interests of social welfare in any part of the United Kingdom (with the object of improving the conditions of life for the boys and girls for whom the same are provided) for boys and girls who are under the age of twenty-one years and who by reason of their youth or social and economic circumstances have need of such facilities.'

I confess I have found great difficulty in attaching any precise or clear meaning to the phrase 'physical education and development of such pupils . . .' where those words appear in cl 3(a) of the trust deed. Walton J[1] took the view that the settlor or draftsman wrongly assumed that the 'organisation and provision of facilities which will enable and encourage pupils . . . to play Association Football . . .' would automatically assist in ensuring that due attention is given to physical education and development. In my view, however, the proper approach to the construction of para (a) is to construe 'physical education and development', which I find an elusive phrase, as connoting something which the playing of association football will assist in ensuring.

Counsel for the trustees of the deed, arguing that the trust fell to be regarded as an educational trust, was indeed, I think, disposed to accept this latter view. He submitted that the trustees in deciding what facilities to provide were bound to consider whether a contemplated facility would or would not assist in ensuring that due attention was given to the physical education and development of the pupils, and that the trust had a single object consisting of the physical education and development of the pupils. Paragraph (a) must be read as a whole and clearly I think it is not *any* games and sports for which facilities may be provided consistently with the terms of the trust deed but only those of a physical character. But in relation to association football the settlor has made it clear that, for the purpose of the trust, facilities which do enable and encourage pupils to play that game are to be regarded as 'thereby' assisting in ensuring that due attention is given to their physical education and development.

A game of association football is a game of association football, as well (or as ill) calculated to assist in ensuring that due attention is given to the physical education and development of the 22 pupil players whether it is played at Wembley before an audience numbering many thousands, at a school as a house match, or on one of many pitches in one of the parks. So far as regards the effect on the players, one game of association football is so like another that it is quite impossible for the trustees to say in relation to association football that some facilities do and some do not assist in ensuring that due attention is given to the physical education and development of the pupils. In relation to other games and sports, however, the trustees are in my judgment constrained to have regard to the phrase 'the physical education and development' so that facilities for the playing of a sedentary game indoors would not be authorised. Thus the words 'physical education and development' cannot be rejected as mere surplusage or as showing a failure to appreciate that association football does not assist in ensuring that result, but must be construed as indicating something which a young man acquires when playing such games as association football. And whatever that something may mean it has in my judgment nothing whatever to do with education in the sense in which that word is used in relation to the law of charities.

Sub-clauses (ii) to (iv) inclusive of sub-para (a) of cl 3 fortify me in my conclusion that the object of the trust is the 'physical education and development of pupils of schools and universities' in the sense that the playing of association football has that result and so promotes that object. Each of the facilities described in those sub-paragraphs appears to be calculated to promote skill in the playing of association football and other games or sports,

---

1   [1978] 1 All ER 230 at 239, [1978] 1 WLR 664 at 673

thus, so it is assumed, furthering the physical education and development of those who play them.

I would summarise my judgment on this part of the case by saying that as a matter of construction the expression 'physical education and development' where it appears in para (a) connotes something which a young man or boy must expect to obtain by playing the game of association football and that a trust to promote the physical education and development when the words are construed in that sense is not a trust for the promotion of 'education' in any ordinary sense of that term, or in the sense that that word is used in the law of charity.

I must emphasise that counsel for the trustees did not contend that on the true construction of the deed the games and sports for which facilities are to be provided are to be enjoyed as part of the curriculum of a school or university. It follows that the reasoning by which Eve J concluded in *Re Mariette, Mariette v Governing Body of Aldenham School*[1] that the gift there, which was to an institution which was a school, and so itself clearly an educational charity, for a purpose of the school, was itself a charitable gift, is not applicable although the particular purpose for which the gift was made was the erection of fives courts. *London Hospital Medical College v Inland Revenue Comrs*[2] is similarly distinguishable. You do not however convert what would not otherwise qualify as a charitable gift into a charitable gift by limiting the object of the trust to those persons who are pupils of, or, if you will, are being educated at, a school or university.

I turn to consider the submission that the trust is charitable as falling within the fourth class of charitable purposes defined in *Income Tax Special Purposes Comrs v Pemsel*[3] as a trust beneficial to the community within the spirit and intendment of the preamble to 43 Eliz I c 4[4].

As Lord Wilberforce remarked in the Privy Council in the recent case of *Brisbane City Council v Attorney-General*[5] the lack of precision of the latter words has to be made good by reference to decided authorities which, as has been said, are legion and not easy to reconcile: see *Sir Howell Jones Williams' Trustees v Inland Revenue Comrs*[6]. In the latter case, however, the House of Lords[7] laid it down very clearly that in order to come within the fourth class the gift must be not only for the benefit of the community but beneficial in a way which the law regards as charitable and within the spirit and intendment of the statute (see also *Re Strakosch*[8]).

It can hardly be doubted that exercise and physical recreation are today objects which are of benefit to the community and a trust to provide facilities for exercise and physical recreation accordingly would qualify as a trust for objects beneficial to the community. And so the trust in the instant case ought in my opinion and judgment to be so regarded. And since it was the decision of the majority of this court in *Incorporated Council of Law Reporting for England and Wales v Attorney-General*[9] that objects of general utility or for purposes beneficial to the community are 'prima facie' charitable, this would lead to the conclusion that the trust sought to be set up by the trust deed is indeed 'charitable' within the fourth class. I must, if I can, reconcile this decision with *Sir Howell Jones Williams' Trustees v Inland Revenue Comrs*[6] or if I cannot I must, as I understand it, follow the more recent decision in this court. For this purpose I take refuge in the words 'prima facie' in the *Council of Law Reporting* case[9], for I find that although the trust here qualifies as a trust for objects beneficial to the community and so is prima facie charitable, when one comes to

---

1 [1915] 2 Ch 284, [1914–15] All ER Rep 794
2 [1976] 2 All ER 113, [1976] 1 WLR 613
3 [1891] AC 531 at 583, [1891–4] All ER Rep 28 at 55
4 Charitable Uses Act 1601
5 [1978] 3 All ER 30, [1978] 3 WLR 299
6 [1947] 1 All ER 513, [1947] AC 447
7 [1947] 1 All ER 513 at 518, [1947] AC 447 at 455
8 [1949] 2 All ER 6, [1949] Ch 529
9 [1971] 3 All ER 1029, [1972] Ch 73

consider in what manner the trust money might be applied one finds that it might be applied for purposes which are not charitable.

Here the trustees could in my judgment, consistently with the terms of the trust deed, apply the whole of the trust fund in providing facilities which would enable and encourage pupils of schools and universities to engage in such sports as fishing, shooting, fox hunting and yachting. None of those sports is in my judgment less well adapted than association football to 'ensure that due attention is given to the physical education and development' of those people who engage therein. There is clear authority of this court that a trust for such purposes is not charitable (see Re Nottage[1]), and it is also clear that if on the true construction of a trust instrument the trust property may consistently therewith be applied for purposes which are not charitable, the trust fails (see Lord Macnaghten in Dunne v Byrne[2]).

I have not forgotten that the word 'play' is the word used in para (a) and of course that is not an appropriate word to describe engaging in fishing, shooting, fox hunting or yachting. Nevertheless in the context in which one finds the word 'play', to 'play association football or other games or sports', the word 'play' must extend to embrace engaging in a sport.

I turn to consider the submission that the trust is one falling within s 1 of the Recreational Charities Act 1958. That section provides as follows:

'(1) Subject to the provisions of this Act, it shall be and be deemed always to have been charitable to provide, or assist in the provision of, facilities for recreation or other leisure-time occupation, if the facilities are provided in the interests of social welfare: Provided that nothing in this section shall be taken to derogate from the principle that a trust or institution to be charitable must be for the public benefit.

'(2) The requirement of the foregoing subsection that the facilities are provided in the interests of social welfare shall not be treated as satisfied unless—(a) the facilities are provided with the object of improving the conditions of life for the persons for whom the facilities are primarily intended; and (b) either—(i) those persons have need of such facilities as aforesaid by reason of their youth, age, infirmity or disablement, poverty or social and economic circumstances; or (ii) the facilities are to be available to the members or female members of the public at large ...'

I will assume, as I think did the judge in the court below, that the trust declared by cl 3(a) of the trust deed is a trust to provide facilities for recreation and that there is in it the necessary element of public benefit spoken of in s 1(1) of the 1958 Act. The question then turns on whether the facilities to be provided satisfy the requirement that they are to be provided 'in the interests of social welfare'.

Even if the phrase 'in the interests of social welfare' fell to be construed without the limitation imposed by s 1(2) I would take the view, reading the provisions of the trust deed as a whole, that it could not be said of it that the facilities provided, or to be provided, pursuant to cl 3(a) are provided in the interests of 'social welfare'. No doubt the funds could, consistently with the terms of the trust, be applied in such a way that they did, and were intended to, promote the interests of social welfare. The purchase of a playing field in part of a great town where there were no facilities for fresh air or recreation to be used by the public at large for the playing of games might well qualify. But an application of the funds in encouraging the pupils of what I may call a 'rugger' school to play 'soccer' would on the one hand be authorised by cl 3(a) and on the other hand could hardly satisfy the social welfare requirement of s 1(1) of the 1958 Act. Similarly, to provide facilities for one or other of the sports which I have mentioned would hardly be an application of the trust fund for the promotion of social welfare. When one comes to the limitation of the meaning of the phrase 'the facilities are provided in the interests of social welfare' found in s 1(2), and finds that to satisfy that requirement the facilities must be provided 'with the object of improving the conditions of life for the persons for whom the facilities are primarily intended', the difficulty of fitting the instant trust into the Act is underlined. One has to ask the question: who are the persons for whom the facilities are primarily intended? If the answer be that the facilities are primarily intended for pupils of schools and universities in any part of the United Kingdom, and I can think of no other answer, it cannot in my judgment with any show of reason be argued that the facilities are provided with the object of improving the conditions of life for the pupils of such schools and universities. Of course they are not. The facilities are to be provided for those of them who are persuaded to, or do, play football or some other game or sport quite irrespective of their conditions of life.

I must add this. The Act does not validate trust deeds but merely provides that the provision of facilities which might not otherwise be regarded as charitable shall be so regarded. It does not validate trusts which embrace other objects which are not charitable or which authorise the application of the trust fund for non-charitable purposes. Accordingly if it be correct that on the true construction of the deed in the instant case the trustees could, consistently with the terms of the trust deed, utilise the trust fund in providing facilities for fox hunting, for example, which if there be such a thing as 'physical education and development' would be a fine sport to promote it, then the trust could only be saved by the Act if the fox hunting had to be provided 'in the interests of social welfare'.

In my judgment Walton J in the court below came to the correct conclusion and I would dismiss this appeal.

ORR LJ. I agree that this appeal should be dismissed for the reasons given by Stamp LJ and I only add a brief judgment of my own because of the different conclusions reached in the judgment to be delivered by Bridge LJ.

As to the construction of cl 3(a) of the trust deed, two points arise of which the first concerns the effect of the words 'and thereby to assist in ensuring that attention is paid to the physical education and development of such pupils . . . as well as the development and occupation of their minds'. Walton J[1] took the view that these words expressed no more than an erroneous view of the draftsman as to the effect of the earlier part of cl 3(a) of the deed and could not control the operation of that part. I agree, but I agree with Stamp LJ that the proper approach to the words in question is to construe 'physical education and development' as denoting something which the playing of association football will assist in ensuring, with the result that the trust has the single object of physical education and development of the pupils.

The second question of construction is whether the use of the word 'play' in the passage 'to play Association Football or other games or sports' in cl 3(a) is restrictive of the kinds of sports therein referred to. But the verb 'play' is inappropriate to any sport which is not a game, and clearly in my judgment it denotes 'participate in'.

As to the law applying to the cases, we were referred in argument to a very large number of cases, but those which seem to me to be most helpful for the present purposes are *Re Nottage*[2] in which it was held by this court that a gift for the encouragement of a sport, though it might be beneficial to the public, could not be upheld as charitable: *Re Mariette*[3] (subsequently followed in *London Hospital Medical College v Inland Revenue Comrs*[4]) where it was held that such a gift to a school which was itself a charity was a valid charitable bequest; and as to general principles the speech of Lord Simonds in *Sir Howell Jones Williams' Trustees v Inland Revenue Comrs*[5], in which he pointed out that it remains the law that a trust is not charitable unless it is within the spirit and intendment of the preamble to the statute 43 Eliz I c 4 and that not every object of general utility must necessarily be a charity. To these

---

1   [1978] 1 All ER 230 at 239, [1978] 1 WLR 664 at 673
2   [1895] 2 Ch 649, [1895–9] All ER Rep 1203
3   [1915] 2 Ch 284, [1914–15] All ER Rep 794
4   [1976] 2 All ER 113, [1976] 1 WLR 613
5   [1947] 1 All ER 513 at 518, [1947] AC 447 at 455

authorities I would add the statement of Lord Macnaghten in *Dunne v Byrne*[1] that if trust property on the true construction of the trust instrument and consistently therewith may be applied for purposes which are not charitable, the trust fails.

On the first issue in the appeal, whether the trust in question is charitable within the first class of charitable purposes defined by Lord Macnaghten in *Income Tax Special Purposes Commissioners v Pemsel*[2], I agree with Stamp LJ that the trust here in question, however beneficial it may be, is not a trust for the promotion of education either in the ordinary sense of that word or in the sense in which it is used in the law of charity, and I also agree that on the facts of the present case it cannot be distinguished from the principle laid down in *Re Nottage*[3] on the basis of the reasoning applied in *Re Mariette*[4] and the *London Hospital* case[5].

On the next issue, whether the trust is charitable within Lord Macnaghten's fourth class as being for purposes beneficial to the community I accept that the trust is prima facie charitable, but agree with Stamp LJ that on the authority of *Dunne v Byrne*[6] the trust must fail on the ground that the trustees could, consistently with the trust deed, apply the fund towards sports of which, on the authority of *Re Nottage*[3], the promotion is not a charitable purpose.

The remaining issue is whether the facilities to be provided under the trust are provided .'in the interests of social welfare' for the purpose of s 1 of the Recreational Charities Act 1958 and on this issue I agree with Stamp LJ that, while the trust funds could under the terms of the trust be applied in such a manner as to comply with this requirement, they could also, consistently with the trust provisions, be applied to forms of sport of which the promotion could not possibly be said to be in the interests of social welfare.

For these reasons, agreeing with Stamp LJ, I would dismiss this appeal.

BRIDGE LJ. I am very conscious that, in contrast with Stamp and Orr LJJ, I have no experience in the field of charity law, and it is with diffidence and regret that I express a different conclusion.

The first question which arises in this appeal is whether the object of the Football Association Youth Trust which is defined in cl 3(a) of the trust deed of 30th October 1972 is charitable as being for the advancement of education. The arguments of counsel took us helpfully through all the authorities having any relevance in this field, but in the end I believe this question is a short one which turns on the construction of the language of the clause. For convenience of reference I set out the words of the clause which define the object divided into two parts: the first part is '. . . to organise or provide or assist in the organisation and provision of facilities which will enable and encourage pupils of Schools and Universities in any part of the United Kingdom to play Association Football or other games or sports'. The second part is: '. . . and thereby to assist in ensuring that due attention is given to the physical education and development of such pupils as well as to the development and occupation of their minds . . .'

The ensuing words 'and with a view to furthering this object' must refer back to both the first and second parts envisaged as defining a composite object to which all that follows in sub-clauses (i) to (iv) is subordinate. The judge, apparently confining his attention to the first part, declared[7] that this was 'on its face simply a trust to promote the playing of games'. He later explained[8] his disregard of the second part as based on acceptance of the submission that it only expresses 'the draftsman's erroneous view of the effect of the [first

1   [1912] AC 407 at 411, [1911–13] All ER Rep 1105 at 1108
2   [1891] AC 531 at 583, [1891–4] All ER Rep 28 at 55
3   [1895] 2 Ch 649, [1895–9] All ER Rep 1203
4   [1915] 2 Ch 284, [1914–15] All ER Rep 794
5   [1976] 2 All ER 113, [1976] 1 WLR 613
6   [1912] AC 407, [1911–13] All ER Rep 1105
7   [1978] 1 All ER 230 at 236, [1978] 1 WLR 664 at 670
8   [1978] 1 All ER 230 at 239, [1978] 1 WLR 664 at 673

part], and cannot control the operation of that part'. With all respect to the judge, I am quite unable to accept this approach. I know of no canon of construction whereby one part of a document, being in no way repugnant, can be thus dismissed as expressing a mistaken interpretation by the draftsman himself of what he intended by some other part. All parts of a document must be read as conveying the totality of the draftsman's intention and so far as possible harmonised on the premise that each part was included as having some positive role to play in expressing that intention. Applying these principles I can see no difficulty in harmonising the two parts of cl 3(a) or in assigning to both a significant effect in denoting the object which this clause empowers the trustees to promote. The first part of the clause places no limitation on the kind of games or sports which are to be facilitated and encouraged and if it stood alone, would include purely sedentary games. But the second part makes clear that it is only such games or sports as are capable of promoting physical education or development as are intended. This is an obvious and simple demonstration of the necessity for giving some effect to the second part of the clause in controlling the operation of the first part. I see no reason, however, why it should not be construed as indicating to the trustees not only the nature of the games or sports which they are to encourage but also the wider considerations they must keep in mind in deciding whether or not in any particular circumstances it is appropriate that particular sporting facilities should be provided at the expense of the trust. If this is a fair reading of cl 3(a), it is by no means simply a trust to promote the playing of games. The three elements which determine the essential character of the trust are: (i) the facilities to be provided are to be for games or sports (including but not limited to football) having a potential value for physical education and development; (ii) the beneficiaries qualifying to enjoy the facilities are to be all persons engaged in any formal educational process; (iii) the overriding objective to be served by the provision of the facilities is to ensure that the physical side of the beneficiaries' education is not neglected.

On the face of it this construction of cl 3(a) seems to me to create a valid charitable trust for an exclusively educational purpose. It is not disputed that the class of beneficiaries represents a sufficiently important section of the community to provide the necessary public element. The importance of the part which organised sporting activities can and should play in the overall educational development of the young citizen at every stage of the educational process can hardly be over-emphasised.

As against this view, however, a number of objections have been advanced. First, it has been argued by counsel for the Crown that if once the second part of cl 3(a) is allowed to affect the construction of the clause, the result is that the clause becomes so vague that the purposes of the trust could not be carried into execution by the court, and hence no valid charitable trust is created. It is certainly possible to envisage situations in which it might be difficult to give a confident answer to the question whether the facilities proposed to be provided would or would not serve the purpose of ensuring due attention to physical education and development. Given a class of beneficiaries as wide as pupils of schools and universities, as defined in the trust deed, it may perhaps be difficult to postulate a situation where facilities to be provided for members of the class for any sport with potential value for physical education could be said to fall clearly outside the terms of the trust on the ground that they were not necessary to ensure due attention to physical education and development. Conversely, however, there could be not the slightest difficulty for the court or for trustees to identify situations where a clear need for enhanced opportunities for physical education and development was established and to direct the resources of the trust to the provision of facilities to meet that need. In my judgment neither the considerable width of the object defined by cl 3(a), nor the difficulty of drawing with precision its outer boundary are considerations effective to defeat its charitable status. As Kennedy LJ observed in *Re Wedgwood*[1]:

'There are, I suppose, very few, if any, charities of a wide character, such as, to take

---

1   [1915] 1 Ch 113 at 121

an imaginary case, a charity for the relief of poor mechanics, in regard to which it would not be easy for ingenuity to suggest difficulties of discrimination.'

A second objection, closely related perhaps to the first, is summarised in the following passage from the judge's judgment[1]:

'This is not a case where the sports and games are made part of, and hence subservient to, the concept of education as a whole, as is the case where the facilities are under the control of the educational establishment itself. There is in this trust deed no requirement for the trustees to carry out the duties thereby laid on them in conjunction with any particular institution; their activities will be entirely extra-curricular.'

I do not myself see the force of this point. Assisting existing educational establishments to provide enhanced sporting facilities may be one way, and perhaps the best way, of ensuring that the declared educational objective of cl 3(a) is achieved. But I cannot see why it need necessarily be the only way. The process of education is not confined to school or university hours, terms or premises and the fact that organised sporting facilities may be provided away from school or university on an extra-curricular basis does not mean that they can have no educational value. On the contrary, the importance of such facilities is expressly recognised by s 53 of the Education Act 1944.

The judge saw a third and fatal objection to the charitable status claimed for cl 3(a) in the ability of the trustees to apply their funds in 'the provision of sports equipment and in laying out and equipping both playing fields and indoor facilities and accommodation' at schools conducted for profit. Counsel for the Crown advanced no argument in support of this view and I need say no more than that counsel for the Trustees satisfied me that any such application of trust funds would involve a breach of trust, since the property in question would pass out of control of the trustees and could be diverted by the new owners to purposes not within the trust.

A fourth objection, which the judge considered[2] without expressing any concluded view about it, suggests that cl 9 of the trust deed, whereunder the chairman for the time being of the Football Association is to be ex officio chairman of the trustees and the executive committee of the Football Association is to have the power of appointing new trustees, may be considered as throwing light on the objects set out in cl 3 and may lead to the conclusion that the real object of the trust is to promote the game of football as such by, for example, the early discovery and encouragement of potential professional footballers. It is not, of course, suggested that the trust deed is in any way a sham or that the trustees will commit any breach of trust. In these circumstances it is not legitimate, as it seems to me, to look at the identity of the trustees or at the supposed motives of the founders of the trust as throwing light on the objects defined in cl 3: see *Re the Trusts of the Arthur McDougall Fund*[3] per Upjohn J and *Incorporated Council of Law Reporting for England and Wales v Attorney-General*[4] per Buckley LJ.

Accordingly I reach a conclusion favourable to the trustees on the ground that the trust created by cl 3(a) falls within the second category of Lord Macnaghten's classification of charities in *Income Tax Special Purposes Comrs v Pemsel*[5] as being for the advancement of education. Having reached that conclusion, I do not feel that I can usefully express any opinion on the question whether, if it were not within the second category, it would fall within the fourth category as being for other purposes beneficial to the community.

I turn therefore to consider whether the object defined by cl 3(a) is charitable under the express terms of s 1 of the Recreational Charities Act 1958. Are the facilities for recreation

1   [1978] 1 All ER 230 at 238–239, [1978] 1 WLR 664 at 672
2   [1978] 1 All ER 230 at 234, [1978] 1 WLR 664 at 668
3   [1956] 3 All ER 867 at 874, [1957] 1 WLR 81 at 91
4   [1971] 3 All ER 1029 at 1043, [1972] Ch 73 at 99
5   [1891] AC 531 at 583, [1891–4] All ER Rep 28 at 55

contemplated in this clause to be 'provided in the interests of social welfare' under s 1(1)? If this phrase stood without further statutory elaboration, I should not hesitate to decide that sporting facilities for persons undergoing any formal process of education are provided in the interests of social welfare. Save in the sense that the interests of social welfare can only be served by the meeting of some social need, I cannot accept the judge's view[1] that the interests of social welfare can only be served in relation to some 'deprived' class. The judge found this view reinforced by the requirement of s 1(2)(a) that the facilities must be provided 'with the object of improving the conditions of life for the persons for whom the facilities are primarily intended'. Here again I can see no reason to conclude that only the deprived can have their conditions of life improved. Hyde Park improves the conditions of life for residents in Mayfair and Belgravia as much as for those in Pimlico or the Portobello Road, and the village hall may improve the conditions of life for the squire and his family as well as for the cottagers. The persons for whom the facilities here are primarily intended are pupils of schools and universities, as defined in the trust deed, and these facilities are in my judgment unquestionably to be provided with the object of improving their conditions of life. Accordingly the ultimate question on which the application of the statute to this trust depends, is whether the requirements of s 1(2)(b)(i) are satisfied on the ground that such pupils as a class have need of facilities for games or sports which will promote their physical education and development by reason either of their youth or of their social and economic circumstances, or both. The overwhelming majority of pupils within the definition are young persons and the tiny minority of mature students can be ignored as de minimis. There cannot surely be any doubt that young persons as part of their education do need facilities for organised games and sports both by reason of their youth and by reason of their social and economic circumstances. They cannot provide such facilities for themselves but are dependent on what is provided for them. There is overwhelming evidence that for the class as a whole the facilities available to meet the need are wholly inadequate: see the Report of the Wolfenden Committee on Sport[2]; the Second Report of the House of Lords Select Committee on Sport and Leisure[3]; and the White Paper on Sport and Recreation[4].

Accordingly I have reached the clear conclusion that all the requirements of the statute are here satisfied and I would allow the appeal on that ground also.

Appeal dismissed. Leave to appeal to the House of Lords granted.

Solicitors: *Chethams* (for the trustees); *Solicitor of Inland Revenue*; *Treasury Solicitor*.

Avtar S Virdi Esq   Barrister.

---

1   [1978] 1 All ER 230 at 241, [1978] 1 WLR 664 at 675
2   Sport and the Community (Central Council for Physical Recreation (1960))
3   (1960) Cmnd 193–I
4   (1975) Cmnd 6200

Re Emmadart Ltd

CHANCERY DIVISION
BRIGHTMAN J
21st NOVEMBER, 5th DECEMBER 1978

Company – Compulsory winding-up – Petition by receiver under debenture – Petition in company's name – Winding-up approved by board of directors but not by company in general meeting – Debenture conferring power to take possession of company's assets and do other acts incidental or conducive to that power – Petition presented to secure company's exemption from rates on unoccupied property – Whether board having power to present petition without approval of shareholders – Whether receiver having same power – Whether receiver having power under debenture to present petition – Companies Act 1948, Sch 1, Table A, Part 1, art 80.

A debenture executed by a company over all its undertakings and assets provided that a receiver appointed under the debenture should be the company's agent and should have power to take possession of the property charged, and to do all other acts and things 'incidental or conducive' to any power conferred by the debenture. The company's articles of association incorporated art 80^a of Table A of the Companies Act 1948 which provided that the business of the company should be 'managed' by the directors. The company became insolvent with an estimated deficiency of £40,000 and a receiver was duly appointed under the debenture. The company owned the lease of a shop which had been unoccupied for 2½ years and in respect of which the local rating authority demanded rates of £3,000 from the company. The company was liable for the rates unless it was able to claim exemption under reg 2^b of the Rating (Exemption of Unoccupied Property) Regulations 1967 on the ground, inter alia, that it was subject to a winding-up order. With the object of gaining that exemption the receiver, in the name of the company and as its agent, presented a petition for the compulsory winding-up of the company on the ground that it was just and equitable for the company to be wound up. The directors of the company knew of the petition and did not oppose it but a winding-up had not been approved by the company in general meeting. It was contended for the company (i) that the receiver had authority to present the petition because, having regard to the company's insolvency, it was competent for the board of directors to present a winding-up petition without the authorisation of the company in general meeting, and the receiver, as receiver of the company's entire undertaking, was invested with the powers of the board of directors, or, alternatively, (ii) that the receiver had authority to present the petition under the terms of the debenture.

Held – (i) The receiver had no power to present the petition as the company's agent because, unless the articles of association conferred on the board of directors power to present a winding-up petition, the board had no power to present a petition without a resolution of the company in general meeting. Therefore, even if the receiver had the same power to present a winding-up petition as the board of directors had, the receiver had no power on that ground to present the petition, for the power conferred on the board by art 80 of Table A of the 1948 Act to manage the company did not include power to wind it up (see p 604 g to j and p 605 c d, post); *Smith v Duke of Manchester* (1883) 24 Ch D 611 and *Re Galway and Salthill Tramway Co* [1918] 1 IR 62 applied.

---

a Article 80, so far as material, provides: 'The business of the company shall be managed by the directors, who . . . may exercise all such powers of the company as are not, by the Act or by these regulations, required to be exercised by the company in general meeting . . .'

b Regulation 2, so far as material, provides: 'No rates shall be payable . . . in respect of a hereditament for, or for any part of the three months beginning with the day following the end of, any period during which . . . (d) the owner is a company which is subject to a winding-up order made under the Companies Act 1948 . . .'

(ii) However, the receiver did have power under the debenture to present the petition in the name of the company, because presentation of the petition was 'incidental or conducive' to the power to take possession of the company's assets conferred by the debenture, for the effect of a winding-up order would be to protect the company's assets from depletion by a levy of rates, and, protection of the assets, though not expressly mentioned in s 109 of the Law of Property Act 1925 or in the debenture, was incidental to the power to take possession. In all the circumstances the court would exercise its discretion by making a winding-up order (see p 605 e to h, post); dictum of Shaw LJ in *Newhart Developments Ltd v Co-operative Commercial Bank Ltd* [1978] 2 All ER at 900 explained.

Per Curiam. The practice under which the board of directors of an insolvent company presents in the name of the company but without reference to the shareholders a petition for its winding up where it seems to the board to be the sensible course is wrong and ought no longer to be pursued unless the articles confer the requisite authority (see p 605 b c, post).

Notes

For presenting a petition, see 7 Halsbury's Laws (4th Edn) para 1002, and for cases on the subject, see 10 Digest (Reissue) 930–943, 5415–5525.

For the Companies Act 1948, Sch 1, Table A, art 80, see 5 Halsbury's Statutes (3rd Edn) 449.

For the Rating (Exemption of Unoccupied Property) Regulations 1967, reg 2, see 18 Halsbury's Statutory Instruments (Third Reissue) 177.

Cases referred to in judgment

Birmacley Products Pty Ltd, Re [1942] ALR 276, 10 Digest (Reissue) 930, *2643.

Galway & Salthill Tramways Co, Re [1918] 1 IR 62, 52 ILT 41, 10 Digest (Reissue) 930, *2644.

Lawson (Inspector of Taxes) v Hosemaster Machine Co Ltd [1965] 3 All ER 401, [1965] 1 WLR 1399, 43 Tax Cas 337; *rvsd* [1966] 2 All ER 944, [1966] 1 WLR 1300, 43 Tax Cas 337, CA, 10 Digest (Reissue) 878, 5080.

Newhart Developments Ltd v Co-operative Commercial Bank Ltd [1978] 2 All ER 896, [1978] QB 814, [1978] 2 WLR 636, CA.

Smith v Duke of Manchester (1883) 24 Ch D 611, 53 LJ Ch 96, 49 LT 96, 9 Digest (Reissue) 750, 4463.

Standard Bank of Australia Ltd, Re (1898) 24 VLR 304, 10 Digest (Reissue) 930, *2642.

Cases also cited

Gough's Garages Ltd v Pugsley [1930] 1 KB 615, CA.

Johnson (B) & Co (Builders) Ltd, Re [1955] 2 All ER 775, [1955] Ch 634, CA.

Sowman v David Samuel Trust Ltd [1978] 1 All ER 616, [1978] 1 WLR 22.

Winding-up petition

An amended petition to wind up Emmadart Ltd ('the company') was presented by the company itself through the agency of its receiver and manager, Maurice Ernest Bulley, appointed under a debenture issued by the company in favour of Barclays Bank Ltd ('the bank'). The petition stated that the company was insolvent and unable to pay its debts and that in the circumstances it was just and equitable that it should be wound up. The petition was not opposed, and the only question for the determination of the court was whether the receiver had authority to present the petition in the name of the company. The facts are set out in the judgment.

Michael Crystal for the company.

Cur adv vult

5th December. **BRIGHTMAN J** read the following judgment: This is a petition to wind up Emmadart Ltd ('the company'), presented by the company itself through the agency of its receiver and manager, Mr Bulley.

On 28th June 1973 the company executed a debenture in favour of Barclays Bank Ltd ('the bank') in order to secure its banking account. The debenture contained a first floating charge over all the undertaking and assets of the company. It provided that, at any time after a demand for payment, the bank might appoint a receiver or manager of all or any of the property thereby charged. Clause 6(c) provided that the receiver should be the agent of the company and should have all powers conferred by the Law of Property Act 1925 on a receiver appointed thereunder and should in particular have certain specified powers of which the only material ones are:

> '(i) To take possession of collect and get in all or any part of the property hereby charged and for that purpose to take any proceedings in the name of the Company or otherwise as he shall think fit . . . (viii) to do all such other acts and things as may be considered to be incidental or conducive to any of the matters or powers aforesaid and which he lawfully may or can do.'

On 26th April 1976 the bank appointed Mr Bulley to be receiver and manager of all the property of the company, to enter on and take possession of the same; the receiver was to have all powers conferred on him by the debenture and by law.

The petition was presented on 19th September 1978 as the petition of the receiver himself but was later amended so as to be the petition of the company by the agency of the receiver.

The unamended petition was duly served at the registered office of the company, which was unoccupied. It was separately served on Mrs Ellis, the secretary of the company, at 26 High Street, Stamford, who was made a respondent, although not so required by the Companies (Winding-up) Rules 1949[1]. When it became the petition of the company itself, it did not require to be served: see r 29. However, in the amended petition Mr Ellis, the only known director of the company, was added as a respondent. He is the husband or former husband of Mrs Ellis. Determined but unsuccessful attempts were made to serve him. The only relevance of the service of Mrs Ellis and attempted service of Mr Ellis is that there is, to my mind, no possibility that this petition has escaped the notice of the officers of the company and it is clear that they do not oppose a winding-up order. The only opposition has come from the Bench and in the circumstances of this case that is a reluctant opposition.

The company is hopelessly insolvent. It owes £28,000 to the bank and has an estimated deficiency of £40,000. The company has a shop in King's Lynn on a 25-year lease at an annual rent of £4,000. The shop has been unoccupied over the last 2½ years. The receiver has tried without success to realise it. The rating authority is the West Norfolk District Council. The council has demanded rates from the company of some £3,000, to which the council is entitled unless the shop is exempt under r 2 of the Rating (Exemption of Unoccupied Property) Regulations 1967[2]. The only relevant exemptions are under paras (d) and (e), which apply if the owner of the premises is a company subject to a winding-up order or in voluntary liquidation.

The object of presenting the petition is to get a winding-up order and thus gain exemption from rates in respect of the vacant premises. The bank, as a creditor, is entitled to present a petition but is reluctant, for business reasons into which I need not go, to present its own petition. It is willing and indeed anxious that the receiver should do so in the name of the company, if that course is available as a matter of procedure.

Section 222 of the Companies Act 1948 defines the circumstances in which a company may be wound up by the court. Section 224 defines the persons by whom a petition may be presented. Section 222 provides that a company may be wound up by the court if

---

1   SI 1949 No 330
2   SI 1967 No 954

(among other things) it has by special resolution so resolved, or is unable to pay its debts, or if it is just and equitable that it should be wound up. Section 224 provides that a petition may be presented by the company or by a creditor or by a shareholder; there are certain qualifications which I need not mention. It is clear that a person who holds shares in a solvent company may present a petition if (1) a special resolution to wind up has been passed or (2) it is just and equitable that the company should be wound up. It is equally clear that the company itself may present a petition if (1) such a resolution has been passed or (2) the company cannot pay its debts or (3) it is just and equitable that the company should be wound up.

No special resolution has been passed in the present case. The receiver, relying on his authority as agent, has presented the petition.

There is no doubt that the company is unable to pay its debts and that therefore circumstances exist in which the court has jurisdiction to wind up the company. It is equally clear that the company has the right to present a petition founded on such insolvency. The only question is whether the receiver has the authority which he professes to present such a petition in the name of the company. This is nothing more nor less than a question of agency.

Counsel who appears, or (to avoid prejudging the issue) I should perhaps say purports to appear, for the company makes two submissions. First he submits that the board of directors of a company can present a petition in the name of the company if the company is insolvent, and that a receiver and manager of the entire undertaking of a company has, in general, vested in him all the powers of the board. Therefore, he submits, the receiver can, in the name of the company, present this petition. Secondly, he submits that, quite apart from the authority of the board, the receiver has authority to present a petition in the instant case under the terms of the receivership in order to protect the property of the company.

As regards the first submission, the appointment of a receiver for debenture holders suspends the powers of the directors over the assets of which the receiver has been appointed, so far as requisite to enable the receiver to discharge his functions: see *Lawson (Inspector of Taxes) v Hosemaster Machine Co Ltd*[1] and *Newhart Developments Ltd v Co-operative Commercial Bank Ltd*[2]. It is therefore at least arguable that if a receiver is appointed of the whole undertaking of the company and the company is insolvent, the receiver would have the like power to present a petition for a compulsory liquidation as the directors themselves would have possessed had the receiver not been appointed. I do not think that such an argument is necessarily correct (see *Newhart Developments Ltd v Co-operative Commercial Bank Ltd*[3]) but I am prepared to assume it for present purposes without so deciding; for counsel concedes that it is fundamental to his submission that it should be competent for the board of directors to present a petition to wind up the company on their own motion, having regard to the admitted insolvency of the company. It is to that point alone that I shall direct my attention in this part of my judgment.

Counsel has carried out some extensive researches into the law, which is not as clear and decisive in his favour as the textbooks seem to suggest. As regards the principal textbooks: (1) the following note appears in Buckley on the Companies Acts[4], edited by the late Mr J B Lindon QC:

'It has been held in Ireland that directors are not entitled to present a winding up petition in the company's name without the authority of a general meeting, though a general meeting can ratify their action in having done so. But in England this decision has not been followed and orders have been made on the petition of a company presented by the agency of its directors without the authority of a general meeting.'

1   [1965] 3 All ER 401 at 410, [1965] 1 WLR 1399 at 1410
2   [1978] 2 All ER 896, [1978] QB 814
3   [1978] 2 All ER 896 at 900, [1978] QB 814 at 819
4   13th Edn (1957), pp 462–463

The first sentence of this statement has appeared in all editions of Buckley since 1924. The second sentence, however, is a gloss which is not to be found in Buckley until 1957. (2) Palmer's Company Law says this[1]:

'It has been held in Ireland that the directors cannot present a petition in the name of the company without the sanction of a general meeting, but there seems to be no justification for this ruling in the words of the Act, and it has not been followed in English cases.'

In *Smith v Duke of Manchester*[2], decided by Bacon V-C in 1883, the directors of a company pursuant to a board resolution presented a petition for winding-up, without reference to the shareholders. The petition was dismissed and the directors proposed to appeal. The plaintiff shareholder, in a representative action, moved the court for an interlocutory injunction to restrain the defendants, who were four of the directors and their solicitors, from using the company's money to pay the costs of the petition and of the proposed appeal. The Companies Act 1862 was similar to the current Act as regards the presentation of winding-up petitions. Bacon V-C said this[3]:

'The statute enables a company to take its own proceedings for winding-up, but then there must be a meeting of the shareholders, and the shareholders would have a right to vote upon the very important question of whether this company should be destroyed or not.'

This case was followed in Australia in *Re Standard Bank of Australia Ltd*[4]. This was a decision of the Supreme Court of Victoria. The powers conferred on the directors by art 128 of the articles of association were similar to the powers set out in art 80 of the current Table A. The judge said this[5]:

'The ordinary powers of directors are powers given to them to carry on the business of the company. The whole idea of the persons who bring the company into existence is as a rule for the continuance of that company, and for the carrying on of its business, and to make profits. It is said by the directors, however, that whatever may have been their power generally, they have power to present this petition to the Court under art. 128. [The judge read the article.] It is said those words give power to the directors to do everything that the company can do, unless there is something in the Act which restricts them or requires the company itself to do it. In my opinion those words cannot be rendered in that unlimited way. The article says the "business of the company shall be managed," and in construing the article those words must be kept in mind. The "business of the company shall be managed"—that is, for the purpose of conducting the business of the company all these powers are given, not for the purpose of destroying the company.'

Reference was made to the decision in *Smith v Duke of Manchester*[2]. The petition was dismissed.

In *Re Galway and Salthill Tramways Co*[6], which is the case alluded to in Buckley on the Companies Acts[7] and Palmer's Company Law[1], a petition was presented in the name of the company pursuant to a decision of the directors and without reference to the shareholders. The company had been incorporated by a special Act of Parliament[8] which

---

1 22nd Edn (1976), vol 1, p 891, para 81–12
2 (1883) 24 Ch D 611
3 24 Ch D 611 at 615
4 (1898) 24 VLR 304
5 24 VLR 304 at 306–307
6 [1918] 1 IR 62
7 13th Edn (1957), pp 462–463
8 The Galway and Salthill Tramways Act 1877 (40 & 41 Vict c ccxxxvii)

included the Companies Clauses Consolidation Act 1845, but I think nothing turns on this. O'Connor MR said[1]:

'The point is, had the directors, without the authority of the company conferred by general meeting of the share-holders, the right to present a petition for winding up? Counsel in support of the petition maintain that they have, and they say that the authority is conferred by s. 90 of the Companies Clauses Act, 1845. That section enacts that the directors shall have the management and superintendence of the affairs of the company, and they may lawfully exercise all the powers of the company, except as to all such matters as are directed by that or the special Act to be transacted by a general meeting of the company. Counsel contend that all the powers of the company are thereby vested in the directors, except such as are specially excepted, and that the power of presenting a petition for winding up is not within the exceptions. But in my opinion that part of the section which gives the directors all the powers of the company subject to the exception must be read along with the opening words giving powers of management, and is merely in aid of the proper and effective exercise of such powers. If I am right in this, the powers of the directors are only powers of managing, and, if the argument relied on is sound, a winding up of the company must come within the scope of its management. But the object of management is the working of the company's undertaking, while the object of a winding-up is its stoppage. On this ground alone I would hold that the directors had no power to present the petition in the present case . . .'

He added later in his judgment[2]:

'. . . it was quite within the powers of the company to authorize the filing of a petition on its own behalf for a winding-up. That being so, it has now power to ratify the petition already filed without authority.'

Smith v Duke of Manchester[3] was referred to in the course of argument.

There is one further Australian case, *Re Birmacley Products Pty Ltd*[4]. This was also a decision of the Supreme Court of Victoria. The winding-up petition was presented in the name of the company pursuant to a resolution of the board of directors and without reference to the shareholders. The powers of the board were again regulated by an article in much the same form as art 80 of the current Table A in this country. Counsel for the company and the majority shareholder, who opposed the petition, relied on the three cases to which I have already referred. The petition was dismissed.

None of these cases is, I think, strictly binding on me. In particular the decision in *Smith v Duke of Manchester*[3] was on motion and not at the trial of the action. However, they appear to me to be of persuasive authority and based on sound principles. I propose to follow them. The position, in my view, is this. It would be theoretically possible for the articles of association of a company to be drawn in terms which confer power on the board of directors to present a winding-up petition. But an article on the lines of art 80 of Table A is not so drawn. The board of directors can resolve to present a petition in the name of the company but such action by the board must be authorised or ratified by the company in general meeting. Clearly the board can cause a petition to be presented in the name of the company if a special resolution has already been passed resolving that the company be wound up by the court, because that is expressly covered by s 222(a) of the 1948 Act. The board can also properly act on an ordinary resolution of the shareholders conferring the requisite authority on the board provided that his does not contravene any provision in the articles.

---

1 [1918] 1 IR 62 at 65
2 [1918] 1 IR 62 at 66
3 (1883) 24 Ch D 611
4 [1942] ALR 276

I have been told that over the years a winding-up order has often been made on a petition presented by an insolvent company pursuant to a resolution of the board of directors and without reference to the shareholders. That would seem to be so. It is certainly so stated in the passage that I have read from Buckley on the Companies Acts[1]. Despite the defect in the petition, any order so made will be fully valid and effective unless and until it is recalled. I express no view as to whether it would be competent for the court to recall an order so made. The practice which seems to have grown up, under which a board of directors of an insolvent company presents a petition in the name of the company where this seems to the board to be the sensible course, but without reference to the shareholders, is in my opinion wrong and ought no longer to be pursued, unless the articles confer the requisite authority, which art 80 of Table A does not. What is stated in Buckley[1] to be the law according to Irish authority is in my view equally the law in this country. I express this view with greater confidence on finding that it coincides with the conclusion expressed by Lord Cohen and Raymond Walton, when contributing the title Companies to the third edition of Halsbury's Laws of England[2], and by Walton J when contributing this title to the fourth edition[3].

In the instant case the articles of association of the company incorporate art 80 of Table A. There is no other article on which reliance can be placed. Accordingly counsel's first submission fails.

The authority of a receiver is not, however, coterminous with the authority of the board of directors. The powers of the receiver stem from (i) the powers contained in the memorandum and articles of association of the company to create mortgages and charges, coupled with (ii) the particular powers which have been conferred on a duly appointed receiver pursuant to the due exercise of the company's borrowing powers. In the instant case the debenture has been regularly created, the receiver has been duly appointed and the powers which I have already read have been properly conferred on the receiver. The only question, therefore, is whether the presentation of the petition by the receiver in the name of the company is incidental or conducive to any of the matters or powers mentioned in cl 6(c) of the debenture. In my judgment the protection and preservation of the assets of the company in respect of which the receiver has been appointed, though not expressly mentioned in s 109 of the Law of Property Act 1925 or in cl 6(c) of the debenture, are incidental to his possession of such assets. As the company is unable to pay its debts, and a winding-up order will have the effect of protecting the assets under the control of the receiver from depletion by a levy of rates in respect of vacant property, I am of the opinion that the receiver has the requisite authority by virtue of his appointment to present a petition in the name of the company, and the court has jurisdiction to make a winding-up order on that petition. The order is, of course, discretionary and the receiver, unlike a creditor, cannot claim the right to a winding-up order ex debito justitiae. The discretion of the court is all important. The petition has been brought to the attention of those who might be concerned to oppose it and the secretary of the company has been made a respondent and served. In the special circumstances I think it is right that I should exercise my discretion and make a winding-up order. This decision is in no way inconsistent with the observations of Shaw LJ in *Newhart Developments Ltd v Co-operative Commercial Bank Ltd*[4], when he said: 'One has got to see what the function of the receiver is. It is not, of course, to wind up the company.' Those words were spoken in a wholly different context.

Winding-up order made.

Solicitors: *Lee, Bolton & Lee*, agent for *Roythorne & Co*, Spalding (for the company).

Evelyn Budd   Barrister.

---

1   13th Edn (1957), pp 462–463
2   6 Halsbury's Laws (3rd Edn) 536, para 1036
3   7 Halsbury's Laws (4th Edn) para 1002
4   [1978] 2 All ER 896 at 900, [1978] QB 814 at 819

Methuen-Campbell v Walters

COURT OF APPEAL, CIVIL DIVISION
BUCKLEY, ROSKILL AND GOFF LJJ
15th, 16th, 19th, 21st JUNE 1978

Landlord and tenant – Leasehold enfranchisement – Premises – House and other premises – Appurtenance let with house – Paddock demised and occupied with house on land to be enfranchised – Whether paddock an 'appurtenance' to house – Whether 'appurtenance' restricted to incorporeal right where principal subject-matter land – Whether 'appurtenance' limited to land within curtilage of house – Whether paddock within curtilage of house – Leasehold Reform Act 1967, s 2(3).

A lease made in 1894 demised for a term of 99 years, at a low rent, a parcel of land with the dwelling-house, stables and offices erected thereon. The house lay at the northern part of the land. South of it, at a lower level, was a garden and further south, again at a lower level, was an area of rough pasture known as the paddock. On the plan to the lease there was an unbroken line across the whole of the property denoting the boundary between the garden and the paddock. Moreover at all material times a post and wire fence had divided the garden from the paddock, and although there had once been a gate in the fence giving access from the garden to the paddock it had fallen into disrepair and the opening had been boarded up. The tenant became lessee of the demised property in 1929. When her children were young the family quite often used the paddock for recreational purposes but subsequently that user had greatly diminished and from 1950 a licensee of the tenant had used the paddock to graze his pony. In January 1973 the tenant served notice on the landlord of the demised property, under the Leasehold Reform Act 1967, that she desired to acquire the freehold of the property. The landlord applied for a declaration that the house and premises which, under s 1(1)[a] of the 1967 Act, the tenant was entitled to have conveyed to her did not include the paddock because it was not a 'garden' or an 'appurtenance' to the house within the definition of premises in s 2(3)[b] of the 1967 Act. The judge held that although the paddock was not a 'garden' it was an 'appurtenance' to the house, within s 2(3). Accordingly he dismissed the landlord's application and made the counter-declaration sought by the tenant that the paddock was included in the house and premises to be enfranchised. The landlord appealed contending that only an incorporeal hereditament could be appurtenant to land, but if the paddock was capable of being appurtenant to the house it did not satisfy the proper test of an appurtenance. The tenant contended that an 'appurtenance' included anything used and occupied with or for the benefit of the principal land. She also contended that the paddock was a 'garden', within s 2(3).

Held – The appeal would be allowed for the following reasons—

(i) The original and strict meaning of 'appurtenance', preventing land from being appurtenant to other land, yielded to a wider meaning if the context in which the word appeared made it apparent that it should do so, and in the context of s 2(3) of the 1967 Act 'appurtenance' included land which was appurtenant to the house to be enfranchised, but even so, it did not extend to land which was not within the curtilage of the house (see p 613 e, p 614 f g, p 615 a d e, p 618 c f g, p 619 b to e and g, p 620 a d f g and p 622 c d and h, post); *Hill v Grange* (1556) 1 Plowd 164 and *Trim v Sturminster Rural District Council* [1938] 2 All ER 168 applied.

(ii) Whether land fell within the curtilage of other land was a question of fact and although the house and paddock were demised and occupied together, and the paddock provided a valuable amenity or convenience for the occupant of the house, since at all material times the paddock had been physically separated from the house, it was not within the curtilage of the house. It followed that the paddock was not an appurtenance

---

a   Section 1 (1), so far as material, is set out at p 608 g, post
b   Section 2(3) is set out at p 608 h, post

to the house, within s 2(3) (see p 615 *c*, p 617 *a b*, p 619 *f g*, p 620 *a*, p 621 *a b* and *h*, and p 622 *e* to *j*, post); *Leach v Leach* [1878] WN 79 disapproved.

(iii) Furthermore, where there was a cultivated garden which was separated from an adjoining piece of rough pasture, the rough pasture could not be regarded as part of the garden. Accordingly the paddock was not a garden, within s 2(3) (see p 616 *g h*, p 619 *a b* and p 620 *a*, post).

Per Curiam. In dealing with an Act such as the 1967 Act which is an expropriatory Act since it gives a right to a tenant in the nature of compulsory purchase, the court should not give too liberal a construction to the words defining that which the tenant is given the right to purchase; it is for the tenant to show that on the facts found he can properly bring his claim within the language of the Act (see p 610 *a b*, p 615 *e*, p 619 *h* and p 620 *a e*, post).

Per Buckley and Goff LJJ. The strict meaning of appurtenant has so far yielded to context as to be dead and to be replaced by another meaning, which is that all that passes on a demise as appurtenant is that which would pass without express mention (see p 613 *h* to p 614 *a* and p 620 *g h*, post).

Per Buckley LJ. For one corporeal hereditament to fall within the curtilage of another, the former must be so intimately associated with the latter as to lead to the conclusion that the former forms part and parcel of the latter (see p 621 *f g*, post).

Notes

For the meaning of house and premises, see Supplement to 22 Halsbury's Laws (3rd Edn) para 1777, and for cases on the subject, see 31(1) Digest (Reissue) 176–177, 1491–1492.

For the Leasehold Reform Act 1967, s 2, see 18 Halsbury's Statutes (3rd Edn) 636.

Cases referred to in judgments

Barnes v Southsea Railway Co (1884) 27 Ch D 536, 51 LT 762, 11 Digest (Reissue) 215, *651*.

Bettisworth's Case, Hayward v Bettisworth (1580) 2 Co Rep 31b, 76 ER 482, sub nom *Hayward v Bettesworth* Moore KB 250, 17 Digest (Reissue) 430, *1916*.

Bryan v Wetherhead (1625) Cro Car 17, 79 ER 620, 17 Digest (Reissue) 430, *1918*.

Buck d Whalley v Nurton (1797) 1 Bos & P 53, 126 ER 774, 48 Digest (Repl) 443, *3949*.

Busgard v Capel (1828) 8 B & C 141, 2 Man & Ry KB 197, 6 LJOSKB 267, 108 ER 996; affd sub nom *Capel v Busgard* (1829) 6 Bing 150, Ex Ch, 31(1) Digest (Reissue) 463, *3797*.

Clymo (Valuation Officer) v Shell-Mex and BP Ltd (1963) 10 RRC 85, [1963] RVR 471, [1963] RA 191, CA.

Cuthbert v Robinson (1882) 51 LJ Ch 238, 46 LT 57, 17 Digest (Reissue) 430, *1914*.

Evans v Angell (1858) 26 Beav 202, 5 Jur NS 134, 32 LTOS 382, 53 ER 874, 48 Digest (Reissue) 543, *5093*.

Hearn v Allen (1627) Cro Car 57, Hut 85, 79 ER 652, 48 Digest (Repl) 561, *5271*.

Hill v Grange (1556) 1 Plowd 164, 2 Dyer 130 b, 75 ER 253, 17 Digest (Reissue) 293, *593*.

Leach v Leach [1878] WN 79.

Lister v Pickford (1865) 34 Beav 576, [1861–73] All ER Rep 374, 6 New Rep 243, 34 LJ Ch 582, 12 LT 587, 11 Jur NS 649, 55 ER 757, 17 Digest (Reissue) 430, *1913*.

Pulling v London, Chatham & Dover Railway Co (1864) 3 De GJ & Sm 661, 4 New Rep 386, 33 LJ Ch 505, 10 LT 741, 28 JP 499, 10 Jur NS 665, 46 ER 793, 11 Digest (Reissue) 213, *628*.

St Thomas's Hospital (Governors) v Charing Cross Railway Co (1861) 1 John & H 400, 30 LJ Ch 395, 4 LT 13, 25 JP 771, 7 Jur NS 256, 70 ER 802, 11 Digest (Reissue) 195, *471*.

Trim v Sturminster Rural District Council [1938] 2 All ER 168, [1938] 2 KB 508, 107 LJKB 687, 159 LT 7, 102 JP 249, 36 LGR 319, CA, 26 Digest (Repl) 687, *46*.

Cases also cited

Marson v London, Chatham & Dover Railway Co (1868) LR 6 Eq 101.

Sovmots Investments Ltd v Secretary of State for the Environment [1977] 2 All ER 385, [1977] QB 411, HL.

Appeal

By an originating application dated 3rd August 1976 Christopher Paul Mansel Methuen-

Campbell ('the landlord') applied for (i) a declaration that the house and premises known as The Gables, Reynoldston, Gower, which the respondent, Kate Evelyn Walters ('the tenant'), was entitled to have conveyed to her by the landlord under a notice dated 2nd January 1973 of her desire to enfranchise the property under Part I of the Leasehold Reform Act 1967, did not include a paddock situated on the south western side of the property, (ii) in the alternative, a declaration that the house and premises did not include that part of the paddock coloured blue on the plan drawn on a lease made on 27th August 1894 and (iii) an order that the tenant forthwith quit and deliver up possession of the said land coloured blue on the plan. On 11th July 1977 Mr Michael Evans QC sitting as a deputy circuit judge at Swansea County Court gave judgment for the tenant and declared that she was entitled to a declaration that the whole of the paddock was included in the house and premises known as The Gables for the purpose of the 1967 Act. The landlord appealed. By a respondent's notice the tenant gave notice that she would seek to affirm the judge's decision on the additional or alternative ground that if the paddock was not an appurtenance it was comprehended within the word 'garden' in s 2(3) of the 1967 Act. The facts are set out in the judgment of Goff LJ.

Jules Sher for the landlord.
Ian Edwards-Jones QC and *Trefor Hughes* for the tenant.

GOFF LJ delivered the first judgment at the invitation of Buckley LJ. This is an appeal from a judgment, or order, dated 19th August 1977 of Michael Evans QC, sitting as a deputy circuit judge in the Swansea County Court, in a matter arising under the Leasehold Reform Act 1967. Proceedings were commenced by an originating application dated 3rd August 1976, and the dispute between the parties is how much of the demised premises should be included in an enfranchisement under the 1967 Act. The applicant ('the landlord'), who is also the appellant, is tenant for life under a settlement created by the will of Emily Charlotte Talbot, who died in 1918 and whose will and codicils were proved in the Principal Probate Registry on 10th January 1919. As such, he is the estate owner of the demised premises and his title is admitted.

The relevant lease is dated 27th August 1894 and was made between the same Emily Charlotte Talbot of the one part and Horatio Edward Rawling of the other part. It was assigned to the tenant, the respondent to the originating application and this appeal, by an assignment dated 31st October 1929. Her title is also admitted.

I must draw attention to a number of sections of the 1967 Act and read certain extracts therefrom. I start with s 1(1) which says:

'This Part of this Act shall have effect to confer on a tenant of a leasehold house, occupying the house as his residence, a right to acquire on fair terms the freehold or an extended lease of the house and premises where . . . [and then follow certain conditions].'

Then I pass to s 2(3), which is as follows:

'Subject to the following provisions of this section, where in relation to a house let to and occupied by a tenant reference is made in this Part of this Act to the house and premises, the reference to premises is to be taken as referring to any garage, outhouse, garden, yard and appurtenances which at the relevant time are let to him with the house and are occupied with and used for the purposes of the house or any part of it by him or by another occupant.'

I pass on to s 8 which gives the right to enfranchisement:

'(1) Where a tenant of a house has under this Part of this Act a right to acquire the freehold, and gives to the landlord written notice of his desire to have the freehold, then except as provided by this Part of this Act the landlord shall be bound to make to the tenant, and the tenant to accept, (at the price and on the conditions so provided)' a grant of the house and premises for an estate in fee simple absolute, subject to the tenancy and to tenant's incumbrances, but otherwise free from incumbrances.'

Section 9 is the section which determines the price. I need not read the whole of it but s 9(1), so far as material, and as amended retrospectively by s 82 of the Housing Act 1969, is as follows:

'Subject to subsection (2) below, the price payable for a house and premises on a conveyance under section 8 above shall be the amount which at the relevant time the house and premises, if sold in the open market by a willing seller, (with the tenant and members of his family who reside in the house not buying or seeking to buy) might be expected to realise on the following assumptions:—(a) on the assumption that the vendor was selling for an estate in fee simple, subject to the tenancy but on the assumption that this Part of this Act conferred no right to acquire the freehold, and if the tenancy has not been extended under this Part of this Act, on the assumption that (subject to the landlord's rights under section 17 below) it was to be so extended.'

Section 14 deals with the alternative option, the right of the tenant to take an extension of the lease instead of to acquire the freehold, and s 15 describes the terms of any extended lease. Subsection (1) of that section provides that it shall be a tenancy on the same terms as the existing tenancy but with such modifications as may be required or appropriate, and s 15(2) deals with the rent:

'The new tenancy shall provide that as from the original term date the rent payable for the house and premises shall be a rent ascertained or to be ascertained as follows:— (a) the rent shall be a ground rent in the sense that it shall represent the letting value of the site (without including anything for value of buildings on the site) for the uses to which the house and premises have been put since the commencement of the existing tenancy, other than uses which by the terms of the new tenancy are not permitted or are permitted only with the landlord's consent.'

Those two sections, ss 14 and 15, further provide that the new tenancy shall be a 50-year tenancy, with one rent review.

So it will be seen that where the tenant exercises an option to take a new tenancy, the ground rent is fixed at the date of the expiration of the old tenancy. The landlord can, as I have said, have one rent review; and it is also provided that the tenant is to pay the costs varying from time to time of the landlord's liability for services or repairs. Further by s 15(7) the terms are subject to any agreement to the contrary between the parties.

The only other section of importance which I should read is s 10 which deals with the rights to be included on a conveyance of the freehold. Section 10(1) is as follows:

'Except for the purpose of preserving or recognising any existing interest of the landlord in tenant's incumbrances or any existing right or interest of any other person, a conveyance executed to give effect to section 8 above shall not be framed so as to exclude or restrict the general words implied in conveyances under section 62 of the Law of Property Act 1925, or the all-estate clause implied under section 63, unless the tenant consents to the exclusion or restriction; but the landlord shall not be bound to convey to the tenant any better title than that which he has or could require to be vested in him ...'

The expression 'relevant time' in the 1967 Act is defined by s 37(1)(d) as meaning: '... in relation to a person's claim to acquire the freehold or an extended lease under this Part of this Act, the time when he gives notice in accordance with this Act of his desire to have it.'

It will be seen that the assumption required to be made under s 9(1)(a) gives the tenant electing to call for a sale of the freehold the benefit of his right to a new lease, and although under such a lease the landlord would get a modern, and therefore increased, ground rent with one, but only one, rent review, still obviously the price will be less, and I think substantially less, than it would be if the value of the freehold were assessed as if it were subject only to the original lease, at all events where the enfranchisement is near the end of the long term.

Counsel for the tenant says, and says rightly, that this is not a penal provision, and he says that Parliament itself has declared that the prescribed terms are fair and, therefore, there should be no leaning on construction one way or the other. Counsel for the landlord, however, says that the 1967 Act is expropriatory and is giving a right of compulsory purchase, and that we ought therefore to construe it strictly. I think there is force in the latter submission. Too much weight should not be attached to it, but on the other hand we should not be too ready to give too liberal a construction to the words defining what the tenant is given a right to purchase.

I turn now to describe the property. It consists of a house and land now known as The Gables, Reynoldston, Gower, in West Glamorganshire. Whether that is the original house which existed at the time of the demise, and whether, if so, it has been altered or to what extent, I do not know, for the lease contained a covenant by the tenant forthwith at his own expense to erect, alter and rebuild and (if specially required) according to plans and elevations to be first approved of by the lessor; but nothing turns on that.

The house lies at the northern part of the demised premises. South of the house, and at a lower level, there is a garden, and still further south and also again at a lower level, an area of rough pasture which has been referred to as the paddock. There was at all material times a post and wire fence dividing the garden from the paddock, but originally it included a gateway, it was a wicket gate, giving access from the garden to the paddock, with concrete steps leading down from the one to the other. There are also a considerable number of trees along this fence on the cultivated garden side. On the plan to the lease the garden and part of the paddock were alike coloured pink. The southern part of the paddock was coloured blue, but there is no significance in that for present purposes. It represents an area over which the lease reserves to the landlord a right to re-enter, the rent being thereupon reduced by an amount calculated at the rate of £8 per acre. The plan to the lease, however, does show an unbroken line drawn across the whole of the property, which appears to denote the boundary between the garden and the paddock.

In course of time the gate to the paddock became broken down; it was not replaced with a new gate but was roughly closed off. The landlord's surveyor described it as an opening boarded up with planks. Mr Walters, the tenant's son, called it an old gateway now obstructed by a broken wooden gate. The judge did not think the differing descriptions mattered, and he said that the photograph which we have seen spoke for itself. He said: 'The gateway or opening was and is an access to the paddock from the house area' and so in a sense it was; but it was not an open access from the time when it was boarded up. It was no longer a gate which one could open. The evidence shows that this gate was broken down and the opening roughly closed up before, and remained so at the relevant time, that is, 2nd January 1973. The evidence of the tenant's son was that it was blocked up in this way because sheep, and occasionally ponies, strayed from the paddock into the garden.

At the south-west corner of the paddock there was another gate leading into a public highway, but the landlord's agent gave evidence that it was not in use and that one had to climb that gate to get into the paddock that way.

I shall read the parcels from the lease itself. They are:

> 'ALL THAT piece or parcel of land with the dwellinghouse stables and offices erected thereon situate in the village and parish of Reynoldstone in the County of Glamorgan on the southern side of the highway road leading from Fairy Hill to Penrice and now in the occupation of the lessee ALL which said premises are delineated in the plan in the margin hereof and therein coloured pink and blue and contain in all by admeasurement two acres one rood and three perches or thereabouts with power to the Lessee his executors administrators or assigns to alter or rebuild the said dwellinghouse in conformity with the covenant hereinafter contained.'

The area of the house and garden is 0·5 of an acre and of the paddock 1·6 of an acre. The lease was for a term of 99 years from 25th March 1893 at a yearly rent of £16. It is

common ground that it is a long lease at a low rent to which the 1967 Act applies, the
rateable value falling within the prescribed limit.

a   The issue is whether the tenant is entitled to a conveyance of the whole of the demised
premises, or whether the landlord is entitled to exclude the paddock as not falling within
the words 'house and premises'. The tenant in fact served a notice desiring to have the
freehold as long ago as 1st January 1968, and in the schedule thereto the premises were
described as: 'Dwellinghouse and land comprised in lease dated 27-8-1894 between Miss
Emily Talbot and Dr. Horatio Rawling.' There were some negotiations about price after
b this and ultimately the notice lapsed, and the tenant served another notice, that being the
one with which we are concerned. That is dated 2nd January 1973. In the schedule to that
notice the property is described as 'House garden and land, known as The Gables,
Reynoldston'.

    In his notice in reply the landlord took the point that the tenant was currently barred
c under s 9(3) of the 1967 Act because of her failure to proceed to completion under the 1968
notice, which was not then five years old. This was a misapprehension, because no price
had ever been agreed, and, therefore, that section had no application and the objection was
withdrawn by letter dated 22nd January 1974.

    In her answer to the originating application the tenant relied on this letter as an estoppel
precluding the landlord from objecting to the inclusion of the paddock, but the deputy
d county court judge ruled against this and there is no appeal on that point.

    So that all that is before us is the question whether the paddock falls within the words
'house and premises'.

    At the trial it was thought that the question turned solely on the definition of 'premises'
in s 2(3), of which it was considered that the only relevant words were 'garden' and
'appurtenances'. The judge held that the paddock was not garden, but that it was an
e appurtenance. He found as follows: '. . . the uses to which the paddock has been put
continuously over the years down to the present day have been for the purposes of the
house by [the tenant] and other occupants.' He therefore dismissed the landlord's
originating application for a declaration—

f   '. . . that the house and premises which the [tenant] is entitled to have conveyed to
her by the [landlord] pursuant to a notice of desire to enfranchise the above-mentioned
property dated the Second day of January 1973 given by the [tenant] to the [landlord]
under and by virtue of Part I of the Leasehold Reform Act 1967 do not include the
paddock.'

And he made the counter-declaration sought by the tenant—

g   '. . . that the whole of the said paddock is included in the said house and premises
for the purposes of the said Act and that the [tenant] is entitled to have the same
conveyed to her pursuant to the said Notice of desire to enfranchise.'

    The landlord contends that the judge was wrong, first because the paddock could not as
a matter of law be appurtenant to the house since only an incorporeal hereditament can be
appurtenant to land, secondly because, even if it could be, it did not satisfy the proper test
h for determining what is appurtenant, and ought not to be so held, and thirdly because the
conditions as to user in s 2(3) were not satisfied at the relevant time. The tenant, of course,
disputes all these contentions, but in addition, by a respondent's notice she claims that the
paddock was 'garden' within the meaning of that expression in s 2(3), and by an
amendment which we have allowed she contends further—

j   '. . . that the judgment of the Learned Judge should be upheld on the ground that
the relevant paddock is in the circumstances of this case, and in the alternative to
being "appurtenant", or part of the "garden", itself within the scope of the term "a
house" as used in Part I of the Leasehold Reform Act 1967.'

Appeal lies only on a point of law, but the landlord submits that there was no evidence
to support the judge's finding of fact which I have read.

The tenant and her family came to the house in 1929. There was then the mother and
father and three children, a son, Mr Walters, who gave the evidence, and two daughters,   *a*
one two years older and the other two years younger than the son. The whole family left
the property at the outbreak of war and it was sublet. The tenant and her husband
returned in 1944 but the children, who had grown up and married, did not live there
again, save only the younger sister who lost her husband in 1968 and then returned to live
with her mother.

The father died in 1949 and thereafter the son, Mr Walters, visited the property quite   *b*
frequently, that is to say, for three weeks every annual holiday and for eight to ten
weekends a year, until his sister returned home, and thereafter his visits were less frequent,
principally I think because he was no longer concerned about his mother being alone, but
they did not cease altogether and they continued until after the relevant time, so that he
was able to give some evidence about the state of affairs at that time, although the younger
sister was not called as a witness.   *c*

In recent years a doctor, who had been in partnership with the younger sister's husband,
also came to live at the house. The son, Mr Walters, said that he had a home there for three
years, so it would seem that he must have come some time in 1972. The doctor, the
mother and the younger sister all left the house finally in 1975.

The evidence showed that the paddock was used quite often for recreational purposes by
the family in the early years when the children were young. After the war, however, the   *d*
use was greatly diminished, but it was still used by the grandchildren when they were
visiting, and by other persons with the permission of the tenant. From about 1950 a local
builder used it for grazing his pony under an informal agreement with the tenant. This
was for their mutual benefit, she having the grass kept down and he obtaining feed for his
animal and a safe place in which to keep it. He also did odd jobs about the house. He was
clearly not a visitor, but this intermittent use did not in any way detract from the tenant's   *e*
occupation; indeed, it was user by her licensee.

Counsel for the landlord placed much reliance on the way in which, as the family grew
up, user of the paddock diminished, and on the fact that, as I have observed, the evidence
showed that the gateway leading to the paddock was broken down and the opening
blocked up by the relevant time, 2nd January 1973, although I think, looking at the
photograph, that any reasonably agile person would not have had great difficulty in getting   *f*
through, or over, the fence from the garden into the paddock.

In my judgment, however, if the paddock could on the true construction of the words
used in s 2(3), that is to say, 'any garage, outhouse, garden, yard, and appurtenances which
at the relevant time are let to him with the house and are occupied with and used for the
purposes of the house as part of the premises', and on the evidence as to user in the early
days, fall within those words then it was still so at the relevant time. There was no   *g*
sufficient change to exclude it. I need not consider the evidence as to user further at this
stage, for one must first consider whether on construction the words of s 2(3) are wide
enough to include the paddock. It may be that it will be necessary to go on to consider
further whether there was any evidence on which the judge could find as he did, that the
user at the relevant time was for the purposes of the house within the meaning of s 2(3),
whatever those words may mean.   *h*

There is only one other point I need mention. In 1961 the landlord's agent caused an
application for outline planning permission to be made in the tenant's name, and it was
granted on 15th January 1961 for not more than five houses. It is clear, however, that this
was not because of any intention on the part of the tenant or her family to build on it, but
simply because she wanted to buy the freehold, and there were negotiations to that end.
The landlord's agent requested that this application be made to assist him in arriving at a
valuation by testing whether the land had any development potential, and in my judgment
this incident has no relevance to anything that we have to decide.

Now I have to consider, on those facts, the problem which arises under s 2(3) of the 1967
Act in determining whether the paddock falls within the house and premises which the
tenant is entitled to enfranchise. The original strict meaning of 'appurtenances' required

that the thing appurtenant should be of the same character as the principal subject-matter. Therefore, land could not be appurtenant to land and any attempt to make it so was void. This is clearly stated in Coke on Littleton[1]:

'Concerning things appendant and appurtenant two things are implied. First, that prescription (which regularly is the mother thereof) doth not make any thing appendant or appurtenant, unless the thing appendant or appurtenant agree in quality and nature to the thing whereunto it is appendant or appurtenant; as a thing corporeall cannot properly be appendant to a thing corporeall, nor a thing incorporeall to a thing incorporeall.'

The same was very clearly held in *Busgard v Capel*[2], where Lord Tenterden CJ said:

'It is difficult to understand what is really meant by that part of the finding of the jury, "that the exclusive use of the land of the river Thames opposite to and in front of the said wharf ground between high and low water mark, as well when covered with water as dry, for the accommodation of the tenants of the wharf, was demised as appurtenant to the said wharf ground and premises; but that the land itself between high and low water mark was not demised." [After adverting to the difficulty of understanding how the exclusive use could be demised and the land not, he continued:] If the meaning of this finding be that the land itself was demised as appurtenant to the wharf, that would be a finding that one piece of land was appurtenant to another, which, in point of law, cannot be. If, on the other hand, the meaning be that the use and enjoyment of this land passed as appurtenant, that would be mere privilege or easement, and the rent would not issue out of that . . .'

This strict meaning would yield to a context, however, not only in a will but also in a deed, as was shown in *Hill v Grange*[3], where the following occurs:

'And all the four justices agreed unanimously that the averment or pleading that the land has been always appurtenant to the messuage is not good here, and also they agreed that land might not be appurtenant to a messuage in the true and proper definition of an appurtenance. But yet all of them (except Brown, Justice, who did not speak to this point) agreed that the word (*appertaining* to the messuage) shall be here taken in the sense of *usually occupied* with the messuage, or *lying* to the messuage, for when *appertaining* is placed with the said other words [that of course is a reference to context], it cannot have its proper signification, as it is said before, and therefore it shall have such signification as was intended between the parties, or else it shall be void, which it must not be by any means, for it is commonly used in the sense of *occupied with*, or *lying to, ut supra*, and being placed with the said other words it cannot be taken in any other sense, nor can it have any other meaning than is agreeable with law, and forasmuch as it is commonly used in that sense, it is the office of Judges to take and expound the words, which common people use to express their meaning, according to their meaning, and therefore it shall be here taken not according to the true definition of it, because that does not stand with the matter, but in such sense as the party intended it.'

There, however, for what it is worth, it is to be observed that the word was 'appertaining' and not 'appurtenant'. Indeed, I think the strict meaning has so far yielded to context as to be really dead and to be replaced by another, which is that all that passes on a demise as

1   Co Litt (16th Edn, 1809), p 121b, s 184
2   (1828) 8 B & C 141 at 150, 108 ER 996 at 999
3   (1556) 1 Plowd 164 at 170, 75 ER 253 at 263

appurtenant is that which would pass without express mention: see *Evans v Angell*[1], where
Romilly MR said: 'Therefore if these pieces of land pass at all they must do so under the
word "appurtenances"', and he did not say, 'which they cannot do because they are land   *a*
and not an incorporeal hereditament'. But he went on later to say[2]:

> 'The word "appurtenances" has a distinct and definite meaning, and though it may
> be enlarged by the context, yet the burden of proof lies on those who so contend.
> *Prima facie*, it imports nothing more than what is strictly appertaining to the subject
> matter of the devise or grant, and which would, in truth, pass without being specially   *b*
> mentioned.'

That the strict meaning had acquired the signification I have mentioned must, I think,
be the explanation of the fact that in *Buck d Whalley v Nurton*[3], Eyre CJ and Heath J applied
the strict rule and excluded all other lands; they held that an orchard was included in the
grant.
    The present position seems to me to be clearly stated by Slesser LJ in *Trim v Sturminster*   *c*
Rural District Council[4], in which he said:

> 'The question for the decision of this court is whether, in coming to that conclusion,
> [the judge] was correct in law. In my opinion [he] was wrong in law in coming to any
> such conclusion. In the definition to which I have referred, certain specific matters
> are mentioned—that is to say, any yard, garden and outhouses—and then follows the   *d*
> word "appurtenances". The word "appurtenances" has had applied to it, through a
> long series of cases mostly dealing with the meaning of the word in demises, a certain
> limited meaning, and it is now beyond question that, broadly speaking, nothing will
> pass, in the case of a demise, by the word "appurtenances" which would not equally
> pass under a conveyance of the principal subject-matter without the addition of that
> word "appurtenances". That is to say, as pointed out in the early case of *Bryan v.*   *e*
> *Wetherhead*[5], in 1625, the word "appurtenances" will pass with the house, the orchard,
> yard, curtilage and gardens, but not the land and that view, as far as I understand the
> authorities, has never been departed from, except that in certain cases it has been held,
> on the material in those cases, that the word "appurtenances" may be competent to
> pass incorporeal hereditaments but no case has been cited to us in which the word
> "appurtenances" has ever been extended to include land which does not fall within the   *f*
> curtilage of the yard of the house itself—that is, within the parcel of the demise of the
> house.'

That confines 'appurtenances' to the curtilage of the house.
    Counsel for the tenant argued that the present legal meaning is wide, and is indeed the
same as the popular meaning foreshadowed as long ago as the third year of the reign of
Philip and Mary in *Hill v Grange*[6]. He submits that the legal meaning of the word today   *g*
comprehends anything used and occupied with, or to the benefit of, the house, either as a
matter of convenience or as an amenity, but in the face of *Trim v Sturminster Rural District
Council*[7] I do not think it possible so to hold.
    But if that be not the legal meaning (and in my view it is not) then counsel for the tenant
says that there is here a context which will give it that wider meaning. He relies on the fact   *h*
that the word 'appurtenances' in s 2(3) follows the words 'garage, outhouse, garden and
yard'; secondly, that the definition includes the words '. . . let to him with the house and
occupied with and used for the purposes of the house', and he rightly points out that

1   (1858) 26 Beav 202 at 205, 53 ER 874 at 875
2   26 Beav 202 at 205, 53 ER 874 at 876
3   (1797) 1 Bos & P 53, 126 ER 774
4   [1938] 2 All ER 168 at 170, [1938] 2 KB 508 at 515–516
5   (1625) Cro Car 17, 79 ER 620
6   (1556) 1 Plowd 164, 75 ER 253
7   [1938] 2 All ER 168, [1938] 2 KB 508

j

although one might use a right of light, one certainly could not occupy it; and, thirdly, that the subject of incorporeal hereditaments is so comprehensively dealt with by s 10. If indeed context be needed to enable the word 'appurtenances' to include corporeal, as distinct from incorporeal, hereditaments, I would agree, but I see nothing in that context to enlarge the meaning of the word 'appurtenance' beyond the curtilage of the house.

Alternatively he says, on the facts of this case, the paddock is in any event within the curtilage. He relied on the fact that the house, garden and paddock were all let as one entire unit, but I think that in itself is not relevant, certainly not of much weight. But he relied also on the evidence of the tenant's son, Mr Walters, that the land is vital to the enjoyment of the house, that the house and field are one unit and that there is a clear view to the south. He also relied strongly on the evidence of a surveyor who said: 'In my view the paddock is an essential element in the use of this type of house; any purchaser would expect some land with it.' This evidence, however, and the rest of the evidence as to user, which I need not review in detail, goes, I think, no further than to show that the paddock is a valuable amenity. It does not make it an appurtenance and it does not show it to be within the curtilage of the house. Counsel for the tenant submits that the paddock is all part of the residential unit and that we ought to take a broad, common sense, view of the word 'appurtenance' itself, or of the definition of 'house and premises' as a whole, and, if necessary, to treat the paddock as part of the house itself, or as being within the word 'garden'. But the 1967 Act is not one dealing with residential units. It is one giving people whose houses are held on long leases at a low rent security of tenure in their homes, and it specifies what is meant by 'house and premises'.

Without in effect not following *Trim v Sturminster Rural District Council*[1] which I am not prepared to do, even though it may be distinguishable, I cannot go along with these submissions of counsel for the tenant, or adopt the wide construction which he would seek to put on s 2(3), and I bear in mind also what I have already adverted to, but not, I hope, giving it too much weight, that this is a section which gives the tenant a compulsory right of purchase, and is thus expropriatory.

Counsel for the tenant relied very much on a number of cases under s 92 of the Lands Clauses Consolidation Act 1845, but there the problem was different. Here, as I have said, we are dealing with an expropriatory act, whereas there the court was considering the converse, a section protecting the landlord from undue expropriation. I do not think these cases help very much, but perhaps I should refer to two of them.

The first is *Barnes v Southsea Railway Co*[2]. There there was a house which fronted onto a highway; there was land in front of the house, between the house and the road with a way to the front of the premises; behind it there was a yard and over against the boundary walls some buildings described as kennels, and behind it a laid out garden. The whole of that area and property was enclosed within one boundary, and in the corner there were double gates giving access to a paddock outside that boundary. There ran from the double gates to another highway a path, or road, giving access from that highway to the rear of the premises. The railway company wished to acquire a part of that back way in and a part of the paddock and the owner claimed, under s 92, that they could not do that but were bound to take the house as a whole. He succeeded in that contention.

Counsel for the tenant says that that is a decision that the paddock was considered to be part of the house. It may be that that can be spelt out of the relief claimed, because the notice of motion sought to restrain the company from taking further proceedings to assess the amount of the compensation and from entering on or taking any other proceedings for the purpose of obtaining possession of the land comprised in the notice, save on the condition that they should acquire the whole house. Reading the judgment however, I think that the ratio decidendi and all that the court was dealing with was the road which ran across the paddock and not the rest of the paddock itself. But even if it be otherwise,

---

1 [1938] 2 All ER 168, [1938] 2 KB 508
2 (1884) 27 Ch D 536

this was a special case in that it afforded the rear access to the premises so that there was a direct nexus between the paddock and the rest of the property, enclosed in the boundary to which I have referred.   *a*

Bacon V-C in his judgment said[1]:

'To his house so constructed the entrance for visitors is on one side, and the entrance and the exit for the use and enjoyment of the house is on the other side; and for that purpose he, the owner of the house, has made a part of his piece of land into a roadway   *b* by which he carries away from his house all the refuse or all that needs to be carried away, and by which he gets from the railway station coals, goods and other necessaries; and that forms the entrance to the backyard of his house.'

In my view this case is really against him because, unless one stops at the curtilage of the house, when one seeks to give a secondary meaning to 'appurtenance' beyond the strict legal meaning, there is nowhere to stop, short of the whole of the demised premises, apart   *c* from the qualification in s 1(3) of the 1967 Act, which says:

'This Part of this Act shall not confer on the tenant of a house any right by reference to his occupation of it as his residence (but shall apply as if he were not so occupying it) at any time when—(a) it is let to and occupied by him with other land or premises to which it is ancillary.'   *d*

Once one departs from the curtilage, I think that one might produce some extravagant results. This objection is supported by what Bacon V-C said in *Barnes v Southsea Railway Co*[2], quoting from *Pulling v London, Chatham & Dover Railway Co*[3]. The relevant quotation is as follows:

'Then the Lord Justice says further, "If, indeed, it is to be held that these fields are   *e* part of the appellant's house, I do not see why every part of a large park would not be entitled to be considered as part of the mansion standing in the park, and to pass by a conveyance of the mansion."'

The other s 92 case which I would mention is that of *St Thomas's Hospital (Governors) v Charing Cross Railway Co*[4]. But there the court was dealing actually with the building,   *f* albeit it was a detached new wing, and with part of the garden. So that case, in my judgment, affords no support for counsel's argument for the tenant.

In my view it is impossible to treat this paddock as part of the house simpliciter, so I reject that. Likewise, for reasons which I will give in a moment, in my view it cannot be regarded as part of the garden. However, the garden is not itself part of the house and it would, I think, be extraordinary if, that being so, this paddock, separated from the house   *g* by the garden, could be regarded as part of the house.

So far as the garden is concerned, counsel for the tenant says that you can have a formal cultivated garden and a wild garden, and no doubt it is true that some people do have such a corner, or part, in their pleasure garden. But when you have, as here, a cultivated garden and a piece of rough pasture ground separated from one another, and apparently marked as separate in the lease plan, I do not think it is possible to regard that rough pasture (the   *h* paddock) as being garden.

So in the end, in my judgment, the crux of the problem becomes: is this within the curtilage?

The word 'curtilage' is defined in the Oxford English Dictionary as 'a small court, yard, or piece of ground attached to a dwellinghouse and forming one enclosure with it'.   *j*

---

1   (1884) 27 Ch D 536 at 542
2   27 Ch D 536 at 544
3   (1864) 3 De GJ & Sm 661 at 670, 46 ER 793 at 797
4   (1861) 1 John & H 400, 70 ER 802

Stroud's Judicial Dictionary[1] suggests that it may be wider than that. We have looked at some of the cases cited in Stroud, but I do not think they afford us any assistance. What is within the curtilage is a question of fact in each case, and for myself I cannot feel that this comparatively extensive piece of pasture ought to be so regarded, particularly where, as here, it was clearly divided off physically from the house and garden right from the start and certainly at all material times.

Counsel for the tenant has threatened that the consequences of this construction of the section would be that one would find all over the country large numbers of small pieces of land which could not be enfranchised and which would be left in the hands of the respective landlords as property of no real use or value to them, although the various tenants, if they could have enfranchisement, would have obtained value and benefit out of those small pieces of land. But I do not think that in practice that would be so, although the 1967 Act does not, of course, necessarily give the tenant the right in every case to everything contained in his demise.

In that connection I would conclude my reasoning by citing the concluding words of Upjohn LJ's judgment in *Clymo (Valuation Officer) v Shell-Mex and BP Ltd*[2], a case in which he quoted with approval the passage which I have read from Slesser LJ's judgment in *Trim v Sturminster Rural District Council*[3]. Upjohn LJ's words were:

'This appeal was said to raise some important question of principle on which guidance was required, but we cannot see that it raises any question of principle at all. The whole problem is a question of mixed fact and law but depends very largely on the facts. Provided a piece of land satisfied the concept of being an appurtenance, it is a question of fact and of circumstance whether it is an appurtenance.'

In my judgment, for the reasons which I have given, this piece of land does not satisfy the concept of being an appurtenance but what the position will be in other cases will depend first on the question of law whether the piece of land in question does satisfy that concept, and secondly whether on the facts of the particular case it ought to be regarded as an appurtenance.

For these reasons I would allow the appeal, discharge the declaration that has been made and substitute the counter-declaration which I have read.

ROSKILL LJ. I have reached the conclusion, like Goff LJ, that this appeal succeeds. As we are differing from the learned deputy county court judge who gave a most careful judgment, and in deference to the arguments to which we have listened over a period of some four days, which have included the citation of authority as far back as the reign of Queen Mary Tudor as well as of more recent date, I will endeavour to give my own reasons.

In the ultimate analysis it seems to me that the determination of this appeal depends on the true construction of a very few words in s 2(3) of the Leasehold Reform Act 1967. We have been referred to a number of decisions on other statutes in which the word 'appurtenance' occurs, notably s 92 of the Lands Clauses Consolidation Act 1845. We have also been referred to other decisions on the Housing Act 1936 and the Housing Act 1957, where the same word has appeared. We have also, as Goff LJ said at the end of his judgment, been referred to the decision of this court in *Clymo (Valuation Officer) v Shell-Mex and BP Ltd*[4], where the same word appears in a different context in the Rating and Valuation Act 1925.

This word makes its appearance throughout the reports in a number of different contexts. Sometimes it has arisen for consideration as a matter of the construction of a will or a deed, and on other occasions as the matter of the construction of a statute. The meaning that is to be given must depend on the context in which it appears.

---

1   4th Edn (1971), vol 1, p 663, curtilage (7)
2   (1963) 10 RRC 85 at 98–99
3   [1938] 2 All ER 168 at 170, [1938] 2 KB 508 at 515–516
4   10 RRC 85

If one looks at the history of the use of the word 'appurtenant' there seems to be no doubt that originally conveyancers did give it an exceedingly restricted meaning. Goff LJ referred to *Hill v Grange*[1]; I quote a passage which appears just before the passage which Goff LJ quoted[2]:

'And afterwards all the four justices argued, all whose argument I heard, except the beginning of Staunford's argument [Staunford was apparently a Justice of the Common Bench], and what I here affirm touching the beginning thereof, I report upon the credible information of others. And they all argued to the same intent, and agreed unanimously that land could not be appurtenant to a messuage in the true sense of the word *appertaining*. For a messuage consists of two things, viz. the land and the edifice, and before it was built upon it was but land, and then land cannot be appurtenant to land.'

One therefore starts from that basic meaning, which was repeated by Romilly MR in *Evans v Angell*[3], but it is also clear that that being a restricted meaning, that construction will yield without great difficulty to the context in which the word appeared; and indeed later the passage to which Goff LJ referred in *Hill v Grange*[1], and much relied on by counsel for the tenant, shows that even as far back as 1556 the courts were ready to give a wider interpretation to the word 'appurtenant' than that which the strict doctrine of the conveyancers of the day required. Whether it is right to say that today the strict meaning is dead or whether it would be better to say that a context in which this word should be given a strict meaning would now be extremely rare is perhaps more a matter of language than anything else.

For my own part, I confess that I was attracted by counsel for the landlord's first though not his main point that in the context in which this word is used in s 2(3) it might be possible, even today, to give the word its strict meaning. My reason for so thinking is that, when one looks at the context of the subsection, immediately before the word 'appurtenances' one finds 'garage, outhouse, garden and yard', all corporeal hereditaments. It occurred to me that it was at least a possible view that, in that context and following four specific corporeal hereditaments, the intention was to use the word 'appurtenances' in its strict meaning. But the more I have listened to the arguments and considered these other cases, the more I am led to the conclusion that in this context it is impossible to give this narrow meaning to this word, and I think counsel for the tenant is right when he said that to give it this narrow meaning makes nonsense of the rest of the language, because it cannot be said that a party can occupy or use an incorporeal hereditament such as an easement of light.

So I start from the view, as does Goff LJ, that the word 'appurtenances' has here to be given its wider meaning. But that is not to say that it should be treated as synonymous with what counsel for the tenant has called 'a residential unit as a whole'. One has to consider s 2(3) in the context of the 1967 Act as a whole, and I ask myself, to what is the tenant entitled under this section? He is entitled to demand the enfranchisement of the house and the premises, provided that he is, as a first condition, the tenant of a leasehold house. But the 1967 Act does not go on to say that he shall be entitled to the enfranchisement of the house and premises, the premises being the whole of that which he occupies by reason of the demise from which his right arises. It would have been very easy to have defined the scope of the tenant's entitlement under s 2(3) as the whole of the property which the tenant occupies under the demise, and to have said that he should be entitled to enfranchise the whole of what counsel for the tenant would call 'the residential unit'. That would not have been difficult to enact, but the 1967 Act does not so state. The

1   (1556) 1 Plowd 164 at 170, 75 ER 253 at 263
2   1 Plowd 164 at 170, 75 ER 253 at 262
3   (1958) 26 Beav 202 at 205, 53 ER 874 at 876

Act states that that which he is entitled to enfranchise is the house (which is given what I might call an inclusive definition) and the premises, which are given an exhaustive definition; that exhaustive definition, to which Goff LJ has already referred, is that 'the premises' must be taken to refer to any garage, outhouse, garden, yard and appurtenance.

In my judgment, therefore, the question is whether or not (leaving on one side the further argument that this paddock forms part of the house or of the garden; and for the reasons Goff LJ has given I think it is impossible to say that it is either) this paddock can fairly be said to be an appurtenance of the house, giving 'appurtenance' a reasonably wide meaning, though not treating it as synonymous with all the land instantly occupied by the tenant seeking enfranchisement.

It is at this point that one does get some assistance from the cases. It seems to be clear that the cases show that the courts have never yet, even when treating 'appurtenance' as apt to cover a corporeal hereditament, gone as far as construing the word as including land which does not itself fall within the curtilage of the house in question; and, like Goff LJ, I think it would be almost impossible to decide this case in favour of the tenant without ignoring the decision of this court in *Trim v Sturminster Rural District Council*[1]. Goff LJ has read the relevant passage from the judgment of Slesser LJ[2] and I shall not repeat it; but I would draw attention to the fact that that passage was expressly approved by Upjohn LJ giving the judgment of the court in the *Clymo* case[3], to which reference has already been made. Both decisions are binding on this court. They can only be departed from or distinguished if in the particular context the word 'appurtenances' can be given an even wider meaning than that which those cases show may be given to it. It seems to me that in the context of s 2(3) of the 1967 Act it is impossible to give any wider meaning to the word than to treat it, as Slesser LJ did, as in effect synonymous with the curtilage of the house.

It was suggested by counsel for the tenant that even so this paddock could be said to be within the curtilage of this house. This is, as Goff LJ has said, a mixed question of law and fact. There is no finding by the deputy judge that this paddock was within the curtilage, and if he had found that it was, I confess that I would have wondered whether, on the evidence, that view was correct as a matter of law.

Goff LJ has described the geographical layout of the paddock. It is well apart from the house physically, though contiguous with the garden, and I do not think that, giving the word 'curtilage' its ordinary meaning by any possible legitimate construction can it be extended so as to include the paddock which the tenant is seeking to enfranchise.

So, for those reasons, in addition to the reasons which Goff LJ has given, I have reached the conclusion that, with all respect to the deputy judge's contrary view, the paddock cannot be said to be part of the curtilage of the house, and unless it can it is not an appurtenance within the subsection, and since it is not I do not think it is possible for the tenant to succeed.

I would only add this. I do not think it right to describe the 1967 Act as confiscatory legislation; it is a statute which obliges a landlord to enfranchise the tenant at a price fixed by the statute. Rather, it is in the nature of a compulsory purchase. But where someone is seeking to exercise such a right given by statute it seems to me that it is for the person seeking to exercise that right to show that on the facts found he can properly bring his claim within the language of the statute which confers that right on him; in my judgment the tenant cannot do so.

I would allow the appeal, set aside the declaration granted by the deputy judge and, subject to hearing counsel, substitute the alternative declaration to which Goff LJ referred at the end of his judgment.

---

1   [1938] 2 All ER 168, [1938] 2 KB 508
2   [1938] 2 All ER 168 at 170, [1938] 2 KB 508 at 515–516
3   (1963) 10 RRC 85 at 98–99

BUCKLEY LJ. I agree; I also would only add something of my own out of respect for the deputy judge and for the arguments which have been presented to us.

The word 'appurtenance' in English law is a term of art which, according to its original and strict meaning, where the principal subject-matter is land, does not include land but is restricted to incorporeal rights: see Coke on Littleton[1], the passage which Goff LJ has read; *Hill v Grange*[2]; *Buszard v Capel*[3]; *Evans v Angell*[4]; *Lister v Pickford*[5]; *Cuthbert v Robinson*[6].

It would seem that the verb 'appertain' may not perhaps have quite so technical a meaning. I note that in *Evans v Angell*[7] Romilly MR said:

'In the first place, it is to be observed that the word here is simply "appurtenances", not "lands appertaining to", or any equivalent words. It must, therefore, be distinguished from that class of cases which rest on such words. This distinction is taken in *Hearn* v. *Allen*[8].'

Later he said[9]:

'There is a still further class of cases which must be distinguished from those to which I have already referred, where the words are not simply "appurtenances" but "lands appurtenant" or "lands appertaining thereto," and the like. They rest on a totally different footing . . .'

But the technical meaning of the word 'appurtenance' will yield to a context and perhaps, with the passage of years, it has become easier for it to do so. Thus in a will the word may carry land if the context and circumstances indicate that the testator so intended: *Buck d Whalley v Nurton*[10]; *Cuthbert v Robinson*[6].

In a statute, if the legislature uses a technical term, it should in my opinion be taken to use it in its technical sense unless it is plain that something else was intended. I agree with the view expressed by Goff LJ that in an Act such as the Leasehold Reform Act 1967, which, although it is not a confiscatory Act is certainly a disproprietory Act, if there is any doubt as to the way in which language should be construed, it should be construed in favour of the party who is to be dispropriated rather than otherwise.

In *Clymo (Valuation Officer) v Shell-Mex and BP Ltd*[11], it was held (see per Upjohn LJ) that the word 'appurtenances' as used in the Rating and Valuation Act 1925, s 22, in the context in which it is there to be found, extends to land described as appurtenant to houses or buildings. It was I think clear from the context afforded by s 22(1) and (4) of that Act that the word there was used as applying to land. In such a case the question of what corporeal property is included as appurtenant in any particular case must depend in part on the construction of the instrument and in part on the circumstances of the case; in other words, the question is one of mixed law and fact.

In the absence of some contrary indication the word 'appurtenances', in a context which shows that it is used in a sense capable of extending to corporeal hereditaments, will not be understood to extend to any land which would not pass under a conveyance of the principal subject-matter without being specifically mentioned, that is to say, to extend only to land or buildings within the curtilage of the principal subject-matter.

---

1   Co Litt (16th Edn, 1809), p 121b, s 184

2   (1556) 1 Plowd 164, 75 ER 253

3   (1828) 8 B & C 141, 108 ER 996

4   (1858) 26 Beav 202, 53 ER 874

5   (1865) 34 Beav 576, [1861–73] All ER Rep 374

6   (1882) 51 LJ Ch 238

7   26 Beav 202 at 205, 53 ER 874 at 876

8   (1627) Cro Car 57, 79 ER 534

9   26 Beav 202 at 206, 53 ER 874 at 876

10 (1797) 1 Bos & P 53, 126 ER 774

11 (1963) 10 RRC 85 at 98–99

Perhaps I may refer to one other ancient authority in this connection. It is *Bettisworth's Case*[1], where I find this stated: 'For, when a man makes a feoffment of a messuage *cum pertinentiis*, he departs with nothing thereby but what is parcel of the house, *scil.* the buildings, curtilage, and garden.' See also *Trim v Sturminster Rural District Council*[2], and in particular the passage which has already been read by Goff LJ, and what was said in the *Clymo* case[3] by Upjohn LJ. What lies within the curtilage is a question of fact, depending on the physical features and circumstances of the principal subject-matter.

For the purposes of this appeal I will assume in the tenant's favour the word 'appurtenances' in s 2(3) of the Act is apt to include land. It may be that the reference in that section to 'occupation' and 'use' is sufficient to admit such an interpretation. It then becomes a question whether the paddock can be aptly described as an appurtenance of The Gables, for the 1967 Act only applies to the house and premises. The relevant house in this case is The Gables and the word 'premises' must be interpreted in relation to the house in accordance with the definition contained in s 2(3).

The tenant has submitted that in this case the paddock would pass under a conveyance of The Gables without any specific mention of the paddock. The paddock is said to be a parcel of the house, having been both let and occupied with it. The judge so held, but I do not find myself able to agree with that view. We have been referred to no cases going that length, except perhaps *Leach v Leach*[4]. Unless it can be said that in that case the description of the property devised as the testator's mansion house afforded a context justifying an extended construction of the word 'appurtenances', which I very much doubt, I do not think that the very liberal construction adopted by Malins V-C should be regarded as good law.

What then is meant by the curtilage of a property? In my judgment it is not sufficient to constitute two pieces of land parts of one and the same curtilage that they should have been conveyed or demised together, for a single conveyance or lease can comprise more than one parcel of land, neither of which need be in any sense an appurtenance of the other or within the curtilage of the other. Nor is it sufficient that they have been occupied together. Nor is the test whether the enjoyment of one is advantageous or convenient or necessary for the full enjoyment of the other. A piece of land may fall clearly within the curtilage of a parcel conveyed without its contributing in any significant way to the convenience or value of the rest of the parcel. On the other hand, it may be very advantageous or convenient to the owner of one parcel of land also to own an adjoining parcel, although it may be clear from the facts that the two parcels are entirely distinct pieces of property. In my judgment, for one corporeal hereditament to fall within the curtilage of another, the former must be so intimately associated with the latter as to lead to the conclusion that the former in truth forms part and parcel of the latter. There can be very few houses indeed that do not have associated with them at least some few square yards of land, constituting a yard or a basement area or passageway or something of the kind, owned and enjoyed with the house, which on a reasonable view could only be regarded as part of the messuage and such small pieces of land would be held to fall within the curtilage of the messuage. This may extend to ancillary buildings, structures or areas such as outhouses, a garage, a driveway, a garden and so forth. How far it is appropriate to regard this identity as parts of one messuage or parcel of land as extending must depend on the character and the circumstances of the items under consideration. To the extent that it is reasonable to regard them as constituting one messuage or parcel of land, they will be properly regarded as all falling within one curtilage; they constitute an integral whole. The conveyance of that messuage or parcel by general description without reference to metes or bounds, or to the several component parts of it, will pass all those component parts sub silentio. Thus a conveyance of The Gables without more, will pass everything within

1   (1580) 2 Co Rep 31b at 32a, 76 ER 482 at 483
2   [1938] 2 All ER 168 at 170, [1938] 2 KB 508 at 515–516
3   (1963) 10 RRC 85 at 98–99
4   [1878] WN 79

the curtilage to which that description applies, because every component part falls within the description. The converse proposition, that because an item of property will pass sub silentio under such a conveyance of The Gables it is therefore within the curtilage of The Gables, cannot in my opinion be maintained, for that confuses cause with effect.

If a conveyance of The Gables simpliciter will pass all the component parts of what lies within the curtilage, to add the words 'and the appurtenances thereof' adds nothing to the effect of the conveyance so far as those component parts are concerned. This was recognised by Romilly MR in *Evans v Angell*[1], to which I have already referred, and by Slesser LJ in *Trim v Sturminster Rural District Council*[2]. So construed, the word serves no purpose save as a conveyancing precaution of the kind which was effected before 1881 by the addition of numerous and often inappropriate general words to parcels described in a conveyance.

Under the 1967 Act we are concerned with the enfranchisement of a leasehold house occupied as a dwelling-house, in the instant case The Gables. The tenant is entitled to enfranchisement of that house and the premises, and the term 'premises' is defined in s 2(3). In the present case the words 'garage, outhouse, garden and yard' are not applicable. So the question is whether the paddock can be properly recognised as an appurtenance of the dwelling-house. 'Appurtenance' for this purpose is in my judgment confined to what is within the curtilage of The Gables.

So the question comes to this: whether the paddock is within the curtilage of the house. In other words, would the paddock pass under a conveyance of 'all that house known as The Gables'?

The tenant has submitted that the house and the paddock all constitute one residential unit but, as Goff LJ has stressed in the judgment which he has delivered, there is nothing in the 1967 Act about residential units; we have to consider what are the premises, as defined, which go with the house. I am quite ready to accept that the common ownership of the house and the paddock is advantageous to the occupant of the house and that the availability of the paddock to the occupant of the house may be something which adds to the value of the right to occupy the house. It does so, however, in my view because the common ownership of the house and the paddock provides an amenity, or a convenience, for the occupants of the house which enhances the value of the house; but the paddock can serve that purpose perfectly well without being part and parcel of the house.

The evidence established that the garden has at all material times been surrounded by a fence, fencing it in with the house and separating it from the paddock, a fence in which there was a gate until the date which has been mentioned in Goff LJ's judgment. But the presence of the gate does not in my judgment detract from the fact that the garden was separated physically from the paddock by a fence. The garden no doubt serves the intimate domestic purposes of the house, and the enjoyment of those uses of the garden is an integral part of the enjoyment of the house as a residence. The enjoyment of the paddock serves, as I say, to provide what may be a valuable amenity and convenience but is not, I think, a use of a kind such as to negative the fact that the paddock was at all material times separated from that plot of land, namely the garden, within which the house is situate.

For these reasons, which are substantially those which have already been expressed by Roskill and Goff LJJ, I am unable to agree with the conclusion at which the deputy judge arrived. I reach the conclusion that the paddock is not within the curtilage of the house and so, within the true construction of the 1967 Act, cannot be regarded as an appurtenance of the house. Consequently in my judgment this appeal succeeds.

ROSKILL LJ. May I just add that I respectfully agree with what has fallen from Buckley LJ with regard to the decision of Malins V-C in *Leach v Leach*[3]; it is a decision which may

---

1   (1858) 26 Beav 202 at 205
2   [1938] 2 All ER 168 at 170, [1938] 2 KB 508 at 515–516
3   [1878] WN 79

have been dictated, unless something else supported it other than what appears in the very brief report, more by sympathy with the widow than with regard to the accuracy of the language used.

Appeal allowed. Leave to appeal to the House of Lords refused.

Solicitors: *Dawson & Co* (for the landlord); *L C Thomas & Son*, Neath (for the tenant).

J H Fazan Esq Barrister.

Re Bucks Constabulary Widows' and Orphans' Fund Friendly Society
Thompson v Holdsworth and others (No 2)

CHANCERY DIVISION
WALTON J
30th JUNE, 11th, 21st JULY 1978

Friendly society – Dissolution – Surplus assets – Distribution – Whether surplus assets should pass to members or to Crown as bona vacantia – Friendly Societies Act 1896, s 49(1).

Friendly society – Dissolution – Surplus assets – Distribution – Method of distribution – No provision in rules as to method of division – Whether surplus assets should be divided among members in equal shares or in proportion to amount contributed by each member.

The Bucks Constabulary Widows' and Orphans' Fund Friendly Society ('the society') was established primarily to provide, by voluntary contributions from its members, for the relief of widows and orphans of deceased members of the Bucks Constabulary. The society was registered under the Friendly Societies Act 1896. By s 49(1)[a] the property of such a society vested in its trustees for the use and benefit of the society, its members and persons claiming through them. The society's rules made no provision for the distribution of its assets in the event of the society being wound up. In April 1968 the Bucks Constabulary was amalgamated with other constabularies to form the Thames Valley Constabulary. In October 1968 the society resolved that it should be wound up, that annuities should be purchased for the beneficiaries of the society and that the assets of the society should be transferred to the benevolent fund of the Thames Valley Constabulary ('the Thames Valley fund') to purchase for beneficiaries of the society the right of entry into the Thames Valley fund. Accordingly an instrument of dissolution was sent to the members of the society which provided, by para 5, that after payment of debts and the expenses of the dissolution the funds and property of the society were to be applied (i) in the purchase of annuities for the beneficiaries, (ii) in the grant of £40,000 to the Thames Valley fund, and (iii) in transferring the balance of the society's assets to a fund for the benefit of serving members of the former Bucks Constabulary ('the Bucks fund'). The instrument of dissolution was signed by the majority of members of the society and the society was dissolved. The court subsequently held[b] that the society's trustee was not authorised by s 79(4) of the 1896 Act or by para 5(2) and (3) of the instrument of dissolution to transfer the surplus assets to the Thames Valley fund and the Bucks fund. The trustee then applied to the court to determine (i) whether the surplus assets should be distributed among the persons who were members of the society at the date of its dissolution or whether, as the Crown claimed, they should

---

a   Section 49(1) is set out at p 628 c, post
b   [1978] 2 All ER 571

pass to the Crown as bona vacantia, and (ii) if the assets were to be distributed among the members, whether they should be distributed in equal shares or in proportion to the subscriptions respectively paid by the persons who were members of the society at the date of its dissolution.

Held – (i) As there were members of the society in existence at the time of its dissolution, the surplus assets were held on trust for such members to the total exclusion of any claim on behalf of the Crown (see p 628 *f* to *j* and p 636 *e f*, post); *Tierney v Tough* [1914] 1 IR 142 applied; *Cunnack v Edwards* [1896] 2 Ch 679, *Braithwaite v Attorney-General* [1909] 1 Ch 510 and *Re West Sussex Constabulary's Widows, Children and Benevolent (1930) Fund Trusts* [1970] 1 All ER 544 distinguished.

(ii) Claims of members of a friendly society inter se on surplus funds held on trust for their benefit were governed exclusively by the contract between them, and where the contract provided no other method of distribution such funds were prima facie distributable in equal shares. Since there were no grounds for holding that the surplus assets should be distributed on any other basis, they were to be distributed in equal shares among the persons who were members at the date of the society's dissolution and the estates of those who had died since that date (see p 636 *h* to p 637 *c h* and *j* and p 639 *g*, post); *Tierney v Tough* [1914] 1 IR 142 considered.

Notes

For the dissolution of a friendly society, see 19 Halsbury's Laws (4th Edn) paras 303–313, and for cases on distribution of funds, see 25 Digest (Repl) 363–365, 447–456.

For the Friendly Societies Act 1896, ss 49, 79, see 14 Halsbury's Statutes (3rd Edn) 286, 306.

The Friendly Societies Act 1896, except s 22, and ss 62 and 64 to 67 in certain respects, was repealed by the Friendly Societies Act 1974, a consolidating measure. Sections 49 and 79 of the 1896 Act were replaced respectively by ss 54 and 94 of the 1974 Act.

Cases referred to in judgments

Braithwaite v Attorney-General [1909] 1 Ch 510, 78 LJ Ch 314, 100 LT 599, 73 JP 209, 8(1) Digest (Reissue) 296, 392.

Bucks Constabulary Widows' and Orphans' Fund Friendly Society, Re, Thompson v Holdsworth [1978] 2 All ER 571, [1978] 1 WLR 641.

Cunnack v Edwards [1895] 1 Ch 489; *rvsd* [1896] 2 Ch 679, 65 LJ Ch 801, 75 LT 122, 61 JP 36, CA, 8(1) Digest (Reissue) 296, 391.

Customs and Excise Officers' Mutual Guarantee Fund, Re, Robson v Attorney-General [1917] 2 Ch 18, 86 LJ Ch 457, 117 LT 86, 8(1) Digest (Reissue) 297, 397.

Gillingham Bus Disaster Fund, Re, Bowman v Official Solicitor [1958] 1 All ER 37, [1958] Ch 300, [1957] 3 WLR 1069; *affd* [1958] 2 All ER 749, [1959] Ch 62, [1958] 3 WLR 325, CA, 8(1) Digest (Reissue) 319, 579.

Hobourn Aero Components Ltd's Air-Raid Distress Fund, Re, Ryan v Forrest [1945] 2 All ER 711, [1946] Ch 86, 115 LJ Ch 50, 174 LT 91; *affd* [1946] 1 All ER 501, [1946] Ch 194, 115 LJ Ch 158, 174 LT 428, CA, 8(1) Digest (Reissue) 250, 72.

Lead Co's Workmen's Fund Society, Re, Lowes v Governor and Co for Smelting Down Lead with Pit and Sea Coal [1904] 2 Ch 196, [1904–7] All ER Rep 933, 73 LJ Ch 628, 91 LT 433, 25 Digest (Repl) 363, 444.

Printers and Transferrers Amalgamated Trades Protection Society, Re [1899] 2 Ch 184, 45 Digest (Repl) 555, 1334.

Recher's Will Trusts, Re, National Westminster Bank Ltd v National Anti-Vivisection Society Ltd [1971] 3 All ER 401, [1972] Ch 526, [1971] 3 WLR 321, 8(1) Digest (Reissue) 297, 398.

St Andrew's Allotment Association's Trusts, Re, Sargeant v Probert [1969] 1 All ER 147, [1969] 1 WLR 229, 20 P & CR 404, Digest (Cont Vol C) 896, 20a.

St James' Club, Re (1852) 2 De GM & G 383, 19 LTOS 307, 16 Jur 1075, 42 ER 920, 8(2) Digest (Reissue) 612, 1.

Sick and Funeral Society of St John's Sunday School, Golcar, Re, Dyson v Davies [1972] 2 All ER

a   439, [1973] Ch 51, [1972] 2 WLR 962, 8(2) Digest (Reissue) 618, 32.
Tierney v Tough [1914] 1 IR 142, 25 Digest (Repl) 364, *179.
*West Sussex Constabulary's Widows, Children and Benevolent (1930) Fund Trusts, Re, Barnett v
    Ketteringham* [1970] 1 All ER 544, [1971] Ch 1, [1970] 2 WLR 848, Digest (Cont Vol C)
    1041, 937a.
William Denby & Sons Ltd Sick and Benevolent Fund, Re, Rowling v Wilks [1971] 2 All ER 1196,
b   [1971] 1 WLR 973, Digest (Cont Vol D) 356, 457.

Cases also cited
Blackburn Philanthropic Assurance Co Ltd, Re [1914] 2 Ch 430.
Sawyer v Sawyer (1885) 28 Ch D 595.

c **Adjourned summons**

The Bucks Constabulary Widows' and Orphans' Fund Friendly Society ('the society') was
established to provide by voluntary contributions of the members for the relief of widows
and orphans of deceased members of the Bucks Constabulary, insurance of moneys to be
paid on the death of a member of that constabulary and the relief of members of the
constabulary during sickness or infirmity. The society was registered under the Friendly
d Societies Act 1896. In April 1968 the Bucks Constabulary was amalgamated with other
constabularies to form the Thames Valley Constabulary. In October 1968 the society
resolved that it should be wound up, that annuities should be purchased for the
beneficiaries of the society and that assets of the society should be transferred to the
benevolent fund of the Thames Valley Constabulary ('the Thames Valley fund') to purchase
for beneficiaries of the society the right of entry into the Thames Valley fund. Accordingly
e in December 1968 an instrument of dissolution was sent to members of the society which
provided, by para 5, that after payment of debts and the expenses of dissolution, the funds
and property of the society were to be applied in (1) the purchase of the annuities, (2) the
grant of £40,000 to the Thames Valley fund, and (3) the donation of the balance of the
society's assets to the Bucks fund, a fund for the benefit of serving members of the former
Bucks Constabulary. The instrument of dissolution was signed by a sufficient majority of
f the members of the society and the society was dissolved on 14th October 1969. The
annuities were purchased and £40,000 was paid to the Thames Valley fund. The balance
of the society's funds, amounting to some £30,000, remained in the hands of the plaintiff,
George William Thompson, the sole trustee of the society. On 14th June 1973 he took out
a summons for the court's determination of certain questions. Question 1 was whether, by
virtue of the execution by the members of the society of the instruments of dissolution and
g by virtue of the Friendly Societies Act 1896, the plaintiff as trustee of the society was
effectively authorised to dispose of the funds and property of the society in accordance with
para 5 of the instruments of dissolution. On 27th April 1977 Megarry V-C[1] held that the
plaintiff was not authorised to dispose of the funds in accordance with para 5(2) and (3).
The plaintiff then sought the court's determination of questions 3 and 4 of the summons.
Question 3 was whether the funds and property of the society, which were or should
h become vested in or under the legal control of the plaintiff as trustee of the society, ought
to be held by him (a) on trust for the Bucks Benevolent Trustees, or (b) on trust to distribute
them among the persons now living and the estates of the persons now dead who were
members of the society at the date of its dissolution, or (c) on trust for the Crown as bona
vacantia, or (d) on some other and what trusts. Question 4 was, if question 3 was answered
in the sense of para (b), whether the funds and property ought to be distributed among
j such persons and estates (a) in equal shares, or (b) in proportion to the subscriptions
respectively paid by the persons who were members of the society at the date of its
dissolution, or (c) in some other and what shares. The defendants were (1) David
Holdsworth, the trustee of the Thames Valley Constabulary Benevolent Fund, (2) George

---

1   [1978] 2 All ER 571, [1978] 1 WLR 641

Whitton Wilkinson, a trustee of the Bucks Constabulary Benevolent Fund, (3) Hywel Wyn
Edwards, who claimed to be one of the persons beneficially interested in the funds and
property of the society, who had not signed the instrument of dissolution, (4) the Treasury
Solicitor, (5) Alexander Leonard, who claimed to be another of the persons beneficially
interested in the funds and property of the society, who had signed the instrument of
dissolution. An order was made staying proceedings against the first and second
defendants.

Robert Reid for the plaintiff.
Richard McCombe for the third defendant.
John Knox for the Treasury Solicitor.
Judith Jackson for the fifth defendant.

Cur adv vult

11th July. **WALTON J** read the following judgment with respect to question 3: The
relevant facts are all set out in the judgment of Megarry V-C[1] on the first question raised
by the originating summons herein, and I need not repeat them. Megarry V-C decided
that the instrument of dissolution made on the dissolution of the Bucks Constabulary
Widows' and Orphans' Fund Friendly Society ('the society') was ineffective for its
purpose. The next question which arises, and which was argued before me on 30th June
1978, is as to the destination of the assets of the friendly society which were thus
purportedly, but invalidly, disposed of. There are basically two claimants to the fund, the
Solicitor for the Affairs of Her Majesty's Treasury, who claims the assets as ownerless
property, bona vacantia, and the members of the friendly society at the date of its
dissolution on 14th October 1969.

Before considering the relevant legislation, the Friendly Societies Act 1896, since largely
replaced by the Friendly Societies Act 1974, and the decided cases, it is I think desirable to
view the question of the property of unincorporated associations in the round. If a number
of persons associate together, for whatever purpose, if that purpose is one which involves
the acquisition of cash or property of any magnitude, then, for practical purposes, some
one or more persons have to act in the capacity of treasurers or holders of the property. In
any sophisticated association there will accordingly be one or more trustees in whom the
property which is acquired by the association will be vested. These trustees will of course
not hold such property on their own behalf. Usually there will be a committee of some
description which will run the affairs of the association; though of course in a small
association the committee may well comprise all the members; and the normal course of
events will be that the trustee, if there is a formal trustee, will declare that he holds the
property of the association in his hands on trust to deal with it as directed by the
committee. If the trust deed is a shade more sophisticated it may add that the trustee holds
the assets on trust for the members in accordance with the rules of the association. Now
in all such cases it appears to me quite clear that, unless under the rules governing the
association the property thereof has been wholly devoted to charity, or unless and to the
extent to which the other trusts have validly been declared of such property, the persons,
and the only persons, interested therein are the members. Save by way of a valid declaration
of trust in their favour, there is no scope for any other person acquiring any rights in the
property of the association, although of course it may well be that third parties may obtain
contractual or proprietary rights, such as a mortgage, over those assets as the result of a
valid contract with the trustees or members of the committee as representing the
association.

I can see no reason for thinking that this analysis is any different whether the purpose for
which the members of the association associate are a social club, a sporting club, to establish
a widows' and orphans' fund, to obtain a separate Parliament for Cornwall, or to further the
advance of alchemy. It matters not. All the assets of the association are held in trust for its
members (of course subject to the contractual claims of anybody having a valid contract

[1] [1978] 2 All ER 571, [1978] 1 WLR 641

with the association) save and except to the extent to which valid trusts have otherwise

a   been declared of its property. I would adopt the analysis made by Brightman J in *Re Recher's Will Trusts*[1]:

'A trust for non-charitable purposes, as distinct from a trust for individuals, is clearly void because there is no beneficiary. It does not, however, follow that persons cannot band themselves together as an association or society, pay subscriptions and validly devote their funds in pursuit of some lawful non-charitable purpose. An

b   obvious example is a members' social club. But it is not essential that the members should only intend to secure direct personal advantages to themselves. The association may be one in which personal advantages to the members are combined with the pursuit of some outside purpose. Or the association may be one which offers no personal benefit at all to the members, the funds of the association being applied exclusively to the pursuit of some outside purpose. Such an association of persons is

c   bound, I would think, to have some sort of constitution, ie the rights and liabilities of the members of the association will inevitably depend on some form of contract inter se, usually evidenced by a set of rules. In the present case it appears to me clear that life members, the ordinary members and the associate members of the London and Provincial Society were bound together by a contract inter se. Any such member was entitled to the rights and subject to the liabilities defined by the rules. If the

d   committee acted contrary to the rules, an individual member would be entitled to take proceedings in the courts to compel observance of the rules or to recover damages for any loss he had suffered as a result of the breach of contract. As and when a member paid his subscription to the association, he would be subjecting his money to the disposition and expenditure thereof laid down by the rules. That is to say, the member would be bound to permit, and entitled to require, the honorary trustees and

e   other members of the society to deal with that subscription in accordance with the lawful directions of the committee. Those directions would include the expenditure of that subscription, as part of the general funds of the association, in furthering the objects of the association. The resultant situation, on analysis, is that the London and Provincial Society represented an organisation of individuals bound together by a contract under which their subscriptions became, as it were, mandated towards a

f   certain type of expenditure as adumbrated in r 1. Just as the two parties to a bipartite bargain can vary or terminate their contract by mutual assent, so it must follow that the life members, ordinary members and associate members of the London and Provincial Society could, at any moment of time, by unanimous agreement (òr by majority vote, if the rules so prescribe), vary or terminate their multi-partite contract. There would be no limit to the type of variation or termination to which all

g   might agree. There is no private trust or trust for charitable purposes or other trust to hinder the process. It follows that if all members agreed, they could decide to wind up the London and Provincial Society and divide the net assets among themselves beneficially. No one would have any locus standi to stop them so doing. The contract is the same as any other contract and concerns only those who are parties to it, that is to say, the members of the society. The funds of such an association may, of course,

h   be derived not only from the subscriptions of the contracting parties but also from donations from non-contracting parties and legacies from persons who have died. In the case of a donation which is not accompanied by any words which purport to impose a trust, it seems to me that the gift takes effect in favour of the existing members of the association as an accretion to the funds which are the subject-matter of the contract which such members have made inter se, and falls to be dealt with in

j   precisely the same way as the funds which the members themselves have subscribed. So, in the case of a legacy. In the absence of words which purport to impose a trust, the legacy is a gift to the members beneficially, not as joint tenants or as tenants in common so as to entitle each member to an immediate distributive share, but as an

---

1   [1971] 3 All ER 401 at 407–408, [1972] Ch 526 at 538–539

accretion to the funds which are the subject-matter of the contract which the members have made inter se.'   *a*

All this doubtless seems quite elementary, but it appears to me to have been lost sight of to some extent in some of the decisions which I shall hereafter have to consider in detail in relation to the destination on dissolution of the funds of unincorporated associations.

Now in the present case I am dealing with a society which was registered under the Friendly Societies Act 1896. This does not have any effect at all on the unincorporated nature of the society, or (as I have in substance already indicated) on the way in which its *b* property is held. But the latter point is in fact made very explicit by the provisions of s 49(1) of the 1896 Act which reads as follows:

> 'All property belonging to a registered society, whether acquired before or after the society is registered, shall vest in the trustees for the time being of the society, for the use and benefit of the society and the members thereof, and of all persons claiming *c* through the members according to the rules of the society.'

There can be no doubt, therefore, that in the present case the whole of the property of the society is vested in the trustees for the use and benefit of the society and the members thereof and of all persons claiming through the members according to the rules of the society. I do not think I need go through the rules in detail. They are precisely what one would expect in the case of an association whose main purpose in life was to enable *d* members to make provision for widows and orphans. Members paid a contribution in exchange for which in the event of their deaths their widows and children would receive various benefits. There is a minimal benefit for which provision is made in the case of a member suffering very severe illness indeed, but, as counsel for the Treasury Solicitor was able to demonstrate from an analysis of the accounts, virtually the entire expenditure of the association was, as indeed one would expect, on the provision of widows' and orphans' *e* benefits. But, of course, there is no trust whatsoever declared in their favour. I am not called on, I think, to decide whether they are, within the meaning of s 49(1), persons claiming through the members according to the rules of the society, or whether they are simply the beneficiaries of stipulations by the members for the benefit of third parties. All parties are agreed that accrued rights of such persons must be given full effect. There is indeed no rule which says what is to happen to surplus assets of the society on a *f* dissolution. But in view of s 49(1) there is no need. The assets must continue to be held, the society having been dissolved, and the widows and orphans being out of the way, simply for the use and benefit of the members of the society, albeit they will all now be former members.

This indeed appears so obvious that in a work of great authority on all matters connected with friendly societies, Baden Fuller[1], the learned author says this: *g*

> 'If the rules provide for the termination of the society they usually also provide for the distribution of the funds in that event, but if on the termination of a society no provision has been made by the rules for the distribution of its funds, such funds are divisible among the existing members at the time of the termination or dissolution in proportion to the amount contributed by each member for entrance fees and subscriptions, but irrespective of fines or payments made to members in accordance *h* with the rules.'

In my judgment this accurately represents the law, at any rate so far as the beneficiaries of the trust on dissolution are concerned, although not necessarily so far as the quantum of their respective interests is concerned; a matter which still remains to be argued. The effective point is that the claims of the Treasury Solicitor to the funds as bona vacantia are unsustainable in the present case. I say 'in the present case' because there are undoubtedly *j* cases where the assets of an unincorporated association do become bona vacantia. To quote Baden Fuller again[2]:

---

1   The Law of Friendly Societies (4th Edn, 1926), p 186
2   Ibid, pp 186–187

a

'A society may sometimes become defunct or moribund by its members either all dying or becoming so reduced in numbers that it is impossible either to continue the society or to dissolve it by instrument; in such cases the surplus funds, after all existing claims (if any) under the rules have been satisfied or provided for, are not divisible among the surviving members ... or the last survivor ... or the representative of the last survivor ... nor is there any resulting trust in favour of the personal representatives of the members of the society ... not even in favour of

b

honorary members in respect of donations by them ... but a society which, though moribund, had at a testator's death one member and three annuitant beneficiaries, was held to be existing so as to prevent the lapse of a legacy bequeathed to it by the testator ... In these circumstances two cases seem to occur: if the purposes of the society are charitable, the surplus will be applicable *cy-près* ... but if the society is not a charity, the surplus belongs to the Crown as *bona vacantia*.'

c

Before I turn to a consideration of the authorities, it is I think pertinent to observe that all unincorporated societies rest in contract to this extent, that there is an implied contract between all of the members inter se governed by the rules of the society. In default of any rule to the contrary, and it will seldom if ever be that there is such a rule, when a member ceases to be a member of the association he ipso facto ceases to have any interest in its

d

funds. Once again, so far as friendly societies are concerned, this is made very clear by s 49(1), that it is the members, the present members, who, alone, have any right in the assets. As membership always ceases on death, past members or the estates of deceased members therefore have no interest in the assets. Further, unless expressly so provided by the rules, unincorporated societies are not really tontine societies, intended to provide benefits for the longest liver of the members. Therefore, although it is difficult to say in

e

any given case precisely when a society becomes moribund, it is quite clear that if a society is reduced to a single member neither he, still less his personal representatives on his behalf, can say he is or was the society and therefore entitled solely to its fund. It may be that it will be sufficient for the society's continued existence if there are two members, but if there is only one the society as such must cease to exist. There is no association, since one can hardly associate with oneself or enjoy one's own society. And so indeed the assets have

f

become ownerless.

I now turn to the authorities. The first case is that of *Cunnack v Edwards*[1]. It is I think necessary to deal with the facts and arguments put forward in that case with some little care. The association there in question was established in 1810 to raise a fund by the subscriptions, fines and forfeitures of its members, to provide annuities for the widows of its deceased members. It was later registered under the Friendly Societies Act 1829. This

g

Act was repealed later, but its material provisions remained in force with regard to societies registered thereunder. There was no provision in that Act corresponding to s 49(1) of the 1896 Act. Sections 3, 8 and 26 are material but I cannot improve on the summary thereof given by Rigby LJ in the Court of Appeal[2]:

'Sect. 3 makes it obligatory on every society established under the Act, before confirmation of the rules by justices as afterwards directed, to declare, by one or more

h

of the rules to be confirmed, all and every the intents and purposes for which the society is intended to be established, and by such rules to direct all and every the uses and purposes to which the money which shall from time to time be subscribed, paid or given to or for the use or benefit of such society, or which shall arise therefrom, or in any wise shall belong to the society, shall be appropriated and applied, and in what circumstances any member of the society or other person shall become entitled to any

j

part thereof. Sect. 8 provides for the rules, when confirmed, becoming binding on the members and officers of the society and the several contributories thereto. Sect. 26 provides for the dissolution of the society, and, among other things, that it shall not

1   [1895] 1 Ch 489; *on appeal* [1896] 2 Ch 679
2   [1896] 2 Ch 679 at 687–689

be lawful for the society, by any rule made on the dissolution or determination, to direct the division or distribution of any part of the stock or fund to or amongst the members, other than for carrying into effect the general intents and purposes of the society declared by them and confirmed by the justices. Sect. 39 provides that the Act is to extend to all friendly societies thereafter to be established, and also to societies already established as soon as they should think fit to conform to it.'

The scheme of the 1829 Act thus was that the rules must specify all the circumstances under which any member of the society might become entitled to any part of its assets, and that on a dissolution the distribution of the assets had to conform to the general intents and purposes of the society. It is at once apparent why in that case an alteration of the rules was essential before any member could take any part of the assets, as, on their face, the rules were exclusively concerned with the provision of the relief of the widows of deceased members. There was no provision whatsoever relating to any members. In the course of time the society was reduced to two members, one an honorary member who was in fact the ultimate survivor, but who had disclaimed any interest in the society's assets, the other an ordinary member who died and whose personal representative claimed the surplus of the assets of the society after provision had been made for the payment of the last annuity to the last widow. There was a claim that the society was a charity, but with that claim we are not concerned. Now the argument for the personal representatives was first of all that the successive members of the society were entitled to its surplus assets and that the last survivor of the ordinary members was therefore entitled to them by survivorship. I have already noted that this argument is untenable because there is no idea in any such societies that they are simply tontines. The next argument was that he could have held a meeting and voted the funds to himself. It was of course necessary to put the argument in this way because of the provisions of the 1829 Act which I have read. It would not have been necessary in the case of an association which had not registered under the Act, but of course in any event the result would have been the same having regard to the tontine point. And finally as a last throw the argument was put forward that there was a resulting trust on the basis that every subscription made and fine paid by the deceased member was paid to create a trust in favour of the widows, and to the extent to which this created a fund in excess of what was required the moneys resulted back to the members. In the court of first instance Chitty J[1] disposed of the first argument by taking the tontine point, of the second by saying that even if the last member could have held a meeting he never did, but he acceded to the third submission. He held that the members had in substance settled their subscriptions by way of trust. In my judgment the short answer to the contention put in this way ought to have been, as is pointed out in a later case, that the money was not paid to establish a trust but by way of contract so that no resulting trust came into the picture at all. In the Court of Appeal[2] the only point argued apart from the question of charity was the third, the resulting trust point, and in my view Lord Halsbury LC did indeed decide against this point on the contractual basis, for what he said was this[3]:

'Chitty J. has held that there is a resulting trust in favour of the personal representatives of those who contributed to the fund. I think we are all of opinion that that view cannot be maintained. The entire beneficial interest has been exhausted in respect of each contributor. It was, as I shall have to repeat in another view of the case, a perfectly businesslike arrangement: each man contributed a certain sum of money to a common fund upon the bargain that his widow was to receive, upon terms definitely settled, a certain annuity proportionate to the time during which the husband had contributed to the common fund. There never was and there never could be any interest remaining in the contributor other than the right that his wife, if she survived him, should become entitled to a widow's portion thus provided. This

---

1   [1895] 1 Ch 489
2   [1896] 2 Ch 679
3   [1896] 2 Ch 679 at 681

was the final and exhaustive destination of all the sums contributed to the common fund. Under these circumstances, I am at a loss to see what room there is for the contention that there is any resulting trust.'

A L Smith LJ took the same position. He said[1]:

'Each subscriber to this common fund (I am not now dealing with honorary members) did so upon the terms that if he left a widow the trustees of the society should out of that fund provide for her in the prescribed manner during her widowhood. If a member died leaving no widow, there was no resulting trust in favour of his personal representative upon his death; his subscriptions were not to be returned to them, but were to remain with the society and form part of its common fund. If a member left a widow she was to be provided for during her widowhood, and although the amount of subscriptions the member had paid might possibly not have been exhausted by making the contemplated provision for his widow, nevertheless the surplus was not to be returned to his personal representatives when the widow died, but the whole beneficial interest in what was left also formed part of the common fund of the society. In neither case was there any resulting trust in favour of the representatives of the deceased member.'

So I think it is fair to say he also really took the contractual position and his last remark is of course completely justified having regard to the combination of the expressed objects of the society and s 26 of the Act. Rigby LJ, after, as I have already noticed, calling specific attention to the relevant provisions of the 1829 Act, concluded as follows[2]:

'The members were not cestuis que trust of the funds or of any part thereof, but persons who, under contracts or quasi-contracts with the society, secured for valuable consideration certain contingent benefits for their widows which could be enforced by the widows in manner provided by the Acts. Any surplus would, according to the scheme of the rules, be properly used up (under appropriate amendments of the rules) either in payment of larger annuities or in reduction of contributions. It is true that no such alterations were made, and it is now too late so to distribute funds; but I do not think that such omission can give to the contracting parties any benefit which they did not bargain for. The rules, which, according to the Act, are to state all the uses of the stock, contain no provision in favour of members. It is difficult to see why the personal representatives of deceased members should be entitled to any money produced by voluntary contributions, fines and forfeitures, but no doctrine of resulting trust would entitle them.'

So a careful examination of that case reveals that the really crucial fact was that the rules were required to state all the uses applicable to the assets of the society and they stated none in favour of members. On dissolution s 26 governed, and following on the absence of any provision in favour of members in the rules the members were not entitled to any interest in the assets. Hence the inescapable conclusion that the surplus assets had no owner and must go to the Crown. At the risk of repetition, the combined effect of the rules and the 1829 Act made it quite impossible for any argument to the effect that on dissolution the assets vested in the then members in some shares and proportions, which is the normal argument to be put forward in such a case. The case therefore did not decide that this was not the usual position in the case of an unincorporated association not then registered under the Friendly Societies Act.

The next case to which I was referred was *Re Printers and Transferrers Amalgamated Trades Protection Society*[3]. I am afraid that I get little assistance from that case. There, there was no claim by the Crown to the assets as bona vacantia, obviously correctly, but the

---

1   [1896] 2 Ch 679 at 683
2   [1896] 2 Ch 679 at 689
3   [1899] 2 Ch 184

distribution which was ordered was on the basis of a resulting trust apparently influenced
by Chitty J's decision at first instance in the case just cited[1]. With all respect to the judge   *a*
who decided that case, I do not think that the method of distribution employed could, in
the light of the judgment in the Court of Appeal in *Cunnack v Edwards*[2], ever have been
correct.

The next case was *Braithwaite v Attorney-General*[3]. Although it is undeniably correct that
no mention was made at any point in the case of the fact in express terms, the society there
in question having been established as a friendly society in the year 1808 and actually   *b*
registered under the 1793 Act, was, like the society in *Cunnack v Edwards*[2], governed by the
provisions of the 1829 Act. It is therefore hardly surprising that, after deciding the new
point, namely that the contributions of honorary members were absolute gifts to the
society and could not be recovered, it was held that the benefited members, of whom there
were just two surviving both drawing annuities, did not take the fund. This was a straight
following of *Cunnack v Edwards*[2] on identical legislation. The rules made no further   *c*
provision for benefited members and hence it is not to be wondered at that Swinfen Eady J
summed the matter up in three pithy paragraphs of the report as follows[4]:

> 'In the present case the two surviving benefited members are entitled to the
> annuities for which their contract of membership provides, but not to any other
> interest in the funds. The entire beneficial interest has been exhausted in respect of   *d*
> each deceased benefited member, and when the annuities to the two surviving
> members cease to be payable upon their respective deaths, they too will have
> exhausted all their beneficial interest in the funds. All possible claimants to the fund
> having now been disposed of, I decide that the surplus of the benefited members' fund
> and the children's fund belongs to the Crown as bona vacantia.'

The next case is one from Ireland, *Tierney v Tough*[5]. O'Connor MR, though concurring   *e*
in the decision, criticised the reasoning in the *Printers* case[6] along the lines which appeal to
me and which I have already noted. It is true that he did not in any way allude to the
statutory provisions which appear to me to have played so large a part in *Cunnack v
Edwards*[2], but the basis on which he rested his decision is short, simple and wholly
convincing. It must be borne in mind that this was simply the case of an unincorporated   *f*
association. No question of the statutory provisions arose. He put it thus[7]:

> 'The conclusion which I have arrived at in the present case is, that the fund belongs
> to the existing members, and I think that the true reason is to be found in the fact that
> the accumulated fund is the property of the society, which is composed of individual
> members. The society is only the aggregation of those individuals, and the property
> of the former is the property of the latter. This is not a case in which all the members   *g*
> have disappeared and their claims have been satisfied, or never arose, as in *Cunnack v
> Edwards*[2]. There are here existing members with unsatisfied claims against the
> fund. As I said before, and I think this cannot be controverted, if the existing
> members, with the assent of their committee and their trustee, agree to divide the
> fund among themselves, there is no person qualified to call them to account for so
> doing. The fund is a private one. On the authorities it is clear that there is no   *h*
> charitable trust attaching to it, and I think I have shown that the fund cannot be
> regarded as bona vacantia. The Attorney-General then has no claim.' .

1   *Cunnack v Edwards* [1895] 1 Ch 489
2   [1896] 2 Ch 679
3   [1909] 1 Ch 510
4   [1909] 1 Ch 510 at 520
5   [1914] 1 IR 142
6   [1899] 2 Ch 184
7   [1914] 1 IR 142 at 155–156

The next case was *Re Customs and Excise Officers' Mutual Guarantee Fund, Robson v Attorney-General*[1]. I do not consider that this case adds anything by way of theory to the matter. The fund there in question became wholly unnecessary as a result of changes in Excise practice on 31st December 1914, when there were still members of the fund in existence, and it was held to be distributable amongst the members then living accordingly. Although the decision in *Re St Andrew's Allotment Association's Trusts*[2] is fully in line with the analysis which I have made, I do not think it in fact adds anything thereto. In *Re William Denby & Sons Ltd Sick and Benevolent Fund*[3] the main finding was that, as the substratum of the association had not gone, it continued, but Brightman J said this[4]:

'One matter is common ground. It is accepted by all counsel that a fund of this sort is founded in contract and not in trust. That is to say, the right of a member of the fund to receive benefits is a contractual right and the member ceases to have any interest in the fund if and when he has received the totality of the benefits to which he was contractually entitled. In other words, there is no possible claim by any member founded on a resulting trust. I turn to the question whether the fund has already been dissolved or terminated so that its assets have already become distributable. If it has been dissolved or terminated, the members entitled to participate would prima facie be those persons who were members at the date of dissolution or termination'

and he refers to the *Printers and Transferrers* case[5], *Re Lead Co's Workmen's Fund Society*[6] and *Re St Andrew's Allotment Association's Trusts*[2]. Once again, this is fully in line with the principle of the cases as I see them.

Finally, although there is at any rate one later case, for the purpose of this review there comes a case which gives me great concern, *Re West Sussex Constabulary's Widows, Children and Benevolent (1930) Fund Trusts*[7]. The case is indeed easily distinguishable from the present case in that what was there under consideration was a simple unincorporated association and not a friendly society, so that the provisions of s 49(1) of the 1896 Act do not apply. Otherwise the facts in that case present remarkable parallels to the facts in the present case. Goff J decided that the surplus funds had become bona vacantia. The headnote of that case, so far as material, reads as follows[8]:

'Members of the West Sussex Constabulary subscribed to a fund for the purpose of granting allowances to widows and dependants of deceased members. Revenue was also derived from other sources including the proceeds of: (a) entertainments, raffles and sweepstakes; (b) collecting-boxes; (c) donations, including legacies. On January 1, 1968, the constabulary was amalgamated with other police forces. On June 7, 1968, a meeting of members resolved to amend the fund's rules enabling them to wind up the fund and distribute its assets under a scheme prescribed in the resolution. On a summons by the trustees for the court's approval of the proposed method of dealing with the fund the court ruled that the meeting of June 7, 1968, was abortive for there were no members after December 31, 1967, capable of holding a meeting, amending the rules, or winding up the fund. On the question what in those circumstances was the destination of the fund:—Held, (1) that the fund could not, on the analogy of the members' club cases, belong to the members themselves since, as

---

1   [1917] 2 Ch 18
2   [1969] 1 All ER 147, [1969] 1 WLR 229
3   [1971] 2 All ER 1196, [1971] 1 WLR 973
4   [1971] 2 All ER 1196 at 1201, [1971] 1 WLR 973 at 978
5   [1899] 2 Ch 184
6   [1904] 2 Ch 196, [1904–7] All ER Rep 933
7   [1970] 1 All ER 544, [1971] Ch 1
8   [1971] Ch 1 at 1–2

the rules stood, only third parties could benefit; that there could not be a resulting trust for members since their money had been put up on a contractual, and not a trust basis; that accordingly, their contributions, apart from any claim members might have in contract arising from frustration or total failure of consideration, were bona vacantia. *Cunnack v. Edwards*[1] applied . . .'

And the material parts of that judgment read as follows[2]:

'First it was submitted that it belongs exclusively and in equal shares to all those persons now living who were members on 31st December 1967 and the personal representatives of all the then members since deceased, to all of whom I will refer collectively as 'the surviving members'. That argument is based on the analogy of the members' club cases, and the decisions in *Re Printers and Transferrers Amalgamated Trades Protection Society*[3], *Re Lead Co's Workmen's Fund Society, Lowes v Governor and Co for Smelting Down Lead with Pit and Sea Coal*[4] and the Irish case, *Tierney v Tough*[5]. The ratio decidendi of the first two of those cases was that there was a resulting trust, but that would not give the whole fund to the surviving members unless r 10 could somehow be made to carry to them the contributions of the former members despite the failure of the purposes of the fund, as was pointed out by Sir Charles O'Connor MR in *Tierney's* case[6], and unless, indeed, the moneys raised from outside sources also could somehow be made to accrue to the surviving members. I agree with Ungoed-Thomas J that the ratio decidendi of *Tierney's* case[5] is to be preferred: see *Re St Andrew's Allotment Association's Trusts, Sargeant v Probert*[7]. This brings one back to the principle of the members' clubs, and I cannot accept that as applicable, for these reasons. First, it simply does not look like it. This was nothing but a pensions or dependent relatives fund not at all akin to a club. Secondly, in all the cases where the surviving members have taken, with the sole exception of *Tierney's* case[5], the club, society or organisation existed for the benefit of the members for the time being exclusively, whereas in the present case as in *Cunnack v Edwards*[8], only third parties could benefit. Moreover, in *Tierney's* case[5] the exception was minimal and discretionary and can, I think, fairly be disregarded. Finally, this very argument was advanced and rejected by Chitty J in the *Cunnack* case[9] at first instance, and was abandoned on the hearing of the appeal[8]. That judgment also disposes of the further argument that the surviving members had power to amend the rules under r 14 and could, therefore, have reduced the fund into possession and so ought to be treated as the owners of it or the persons for whose benefit it existed at the crucial moment. They had the power but they did not exercise it, and it is now too late. Then it was argued that there is a resulting trust, with several possible consequences. If this be the right view there must be a primary division into three parts, one representing contributions from former members, another contributions from the surviving members, and the third moneys raised from outside sources. The surviving members then take the second, and possibly by virtue of r 10 the first also. Rule 10 is as follows: "Any member who voluntarily terminates his membership shall forfeit all claim against the Fund except in the case of a member transferring to a similar Fund of

---

1   [1895] 1 Ch 489, [1896] 2 Ch 679
2   [1970] 1 All ER 544 at 546–548, [1971] Ch 1 at 8–10
3   [1899] 2 Ch 184
4   [1904] 2 Ch 196, [1904–7] All ER Rep 933
5   [1914] 1 IR 142
6   [1914] 1 IR 142 at 155
7   [1969] 1 All ER 147 at 152–153, [1969] 1 WLR 229 at 238
8   [1896] 2 Ch 679
9   [1895] 1 Ch 489

another force in which instance the contributions paid by the member to the West Sussex Constabulary's Widows, Children and Benevolent (1930) Fund may be paid into the Fund of the force to which the member transfers." Alternatively, the first may belong to the past members on the footing that r 10 is operative so long only as the fund is a going concern, or may be bona vacantia. The third is distributable in whole or in part between those who provided the money, or again is bona vacantia. In my judgment the doctrine of resulting trust is clearly inapplicable to the contributions of both classes. Those persons who remained members until their deaths are in any event excluded because they have had all they contracted for, either because their widows and dependants have received or are in receipt of the prescribed benefits, or because they did not have a widow or dependants. In my view that is inherent in all the speeches in the Court of Appeal in *Cunnack v Edwards*[1]. Further, whatever the effect of r 10 may be on the contribution of those members who left prematurely, they and the surviving members alike are also unable to claim under a resulting trust, because they put up their money on a contractual basis and not one of trust: see per Harman J, in *Re Gillingham Bus Disaster Fund, Bowman v Official Solicitor*[2]. The only case which has given me difficulty on this aspect of the matter is *Re Hobourn Aero Components Ltd's Air-Raid Distress Fund, Ryan v Forrest*[3], where in somewhat similar circumstances it was held there was a resulting trust. The argument postulated, I think, the distinction between contract and trust but in another connection, namely whether the fund was charitable. There was in that case a resolution to wind up but that was not, at all events as expressed, the ratio decidendi (see per Cohen J[4]) but as his Lordship observed there was no argument for bona vacantia. Moreover no rules or regulations were ever made and although in fact £1 per month was paid or saved for each member serving with the forces, there were no prescribed contractual benefits. In my judgment that case is therefore distinguishable. Accordingly, in my judgment all the contributions of both classes are bona vacantia, but I must make a reservation with respect to possible contractual rights. In *Cunnack v Edwards*[1] and *Braithwaite v A-G*[5], all the members had received or provision had been made for all the contractual benefits. Here the matter has been cut short. Those persons who died whilst still in membership cannot, I conceive, have any rights, because in their case the contract has been fully worked out, and on a contractual basis I would think that members who retired would be precluded from making any claim by r 10, although that is perhaps more arguable. The surviving members, on the other hand, may well have a right in contract on the ground of frustration or total failure of consideration, and that right may embrace contributions made by past members, though I do not see how it could apply to moneys raised from outside sources. I have not, however, heard any argument based on contract and therefore the declarations I propose to make will be subject to the reservation which I will later formulate. This will not prevent those parts of the fund which are bona vacantia from being paid over to the Crown as it has offered to give a full indemnity to the trustees.'

and the judge then turned to consider the destination of moneys from outside sources, with which of course I am not here concerned.

It will be observed that the first reason given by the judge for his decision is that he could not accept the principle of the members' clubs as applicable. This is a very interesting reason, because it is flatly contrary to the successful argument of Mr Ingle Joyce who

1   [1896] 2 Ch 679
2   [1958] 1 All ER 37 at 43, [1958] Ch 300 at 314
3   [1945] 2 All ER 711, [1946] Ch 86
4   [1945] 2 All ER 711 at 718, [1946] Ch 86 at 97
5   [1909] 1 Ch 510

appeared for the Attorney-General in the case Goff J purported to follow, *Cunnack v Edwards*[1]. His argument was as follows[2]:

'This society was nothing more than a club, in which the members had no transmissible interest: *In re St. James' Club*[3]. Whatever the members, or even the surviving member, might have done while alive, when they died their interest in the assets of the club died with them.'

and in the Court of Appeal[4] he used the arguments he had used below. If all that Goff J meant was that the purposes of the fund before him were totally different from those of a members' club then of course one must agree, but if he meant to imply that there was some totally different principle of law applicable one must ask why that should be. His second reason is that in all the cases where the surviving members had taken, the organisation existed for the benefit of the members for the time being exclusively. This may be so, so far as actual decisions go, but what is the principle? Why are the members not in control, complete control, save as to any existing contractual rights, of the assets belonging to their organisation? One could understand the position being different if valid trusts had been declared of the assets in favour of third parties, for example charities, but that this was emphatically not the case was demonstrated by the fact that Goff J recognised that the members could have altered the rules prior to dissolution and put the assets into their own pockets. If there was no obstacle to their doing this, it shows in my judgment quite clearly that the money was theirs all the time. Finally he purports to follow *Cunnack v Edwards*[4] and it will be seen from the analysis which I have already made of that case that it was extremely special in its facts, resting on a curious provision of the 1829 Act which is no longer applicable. As I have already indicated, in the light of s 49(1) of the 1896 Act the case before Goff J[5] is readily distinguishable, but I regret that, quite apart from that, I am wholly unable to square it with the relevant principles of law applicable.

The conclusion therefore is that, as on dissolution there were members of the society here in question in existence, its assets are held on trust for such members to the total exclusion of any claim on behalf of the Crown. The remaining question under this head which falls now to be argued is, of course, whether they are simply held per capita, or, as suggested in some of the cases, in proportion to the contributions made by each.

Question 3 answered in sense 3(b)

On 21st July the court heard argument on question 4 and then delivered the following judgment.

WALTON J. The relevant facts, of course, are all set out in the judgment of Megarry V-C in this matter when it came before the court of first instance[6], and I do not propose to repeat them. But the question has now arisen, consequent on my previous decision that in fact the surplus funds of this friendly society belong to its members, first of all as to whether those surplus funds ought to be distributed basically between such members in equal shares, or, alternatively, in proportion to the subscriptions respectively paid by the persons who were the members of the friendly society at the date of the dissolution thereof.

I think that there is no doubt that, as a result of modern cases springing basically from the decision of O'Connor MR in *Tierney v Tough*[7], judicial opinion has been hardening and

1　[1895] 1 Ch 489
2　[1895] 1 Ch 489 at 494
3　(1852) 2 De GM & G 383 at 387
4　[1896] 2 Ch 679
5　[1970] 1 All ER 544, [1971] Ch 1
6　[1978] 2 All ER 571, [1978] 1 WLR 641
7　[1914] 1 IR 142

is now firmly set along the lines that the interests and rights of persons who are members of any type of unincorporated association are governed exclusively by contract, that is to say the rights between themselves and their rights to any surplus assets. I say that to make it perfectly clear that I have not overlooked the fact that the assets of the society are usually vested in trustees on trust for the members. But that is quite a separate and distinct trust bearing no relation to the claims of the members inter se on the surplus funds so held on trust for their benefit.

That being the case, prima facie there can be no doubt at all but that the distribution is on the basis of equality, because, as between a number of people contractually interested in a fund, there is no other method of distribution if no other method is provided by the terms of the contract, and it is not for one moment suggested here that there is any other method of distribution provided by the contract. We are, of course, dealing here with a friendly society, but that really makes no difference to the principle. The Friendly Societies Acts do not incorporate the friendly society in any way and the only effect that it has is, as I pointed out in my previous judgment in this case, that there is a section which makes it crystal clear in the Friendly Societies Act 1896 that the assets are indeed held on trust for the members.

Now the fact that the prima facie rule is a matter of equality has been recently laid down, not of course for the first time, in two cases to which I need do no more than refer, *Re St Andrew's Allotment Association's Trusts*[1], a decision of the late Ungoed-Thomas J, and *Re Sick and Funeral Society of St John's Sunday School, Golcar*, a decision of Megarry J[2]. Neither of those cases was, however, the case of a friendly society, and there are a number of previous decisions in connection with friendly societies, and, indeed *Tierney v Tough*[3] itself is such a case, where the basis of distribution according to the subscriptions paid by the persons among whom the fund is to be distributed has been applied, and it has been suggested that perhaps those decisions are to be explained along the lines that a friendly society, or similar society, is thinking more of benefits to members, and that, thinking naturally of benefits to members, you think, on the other side of the coin, of subscriptions paid by members. But in my judgment that is not a satisfactory distinction of any description, because one is now dealing with what happens at the end of the life of the association; there are surplus funds, funds which have not been required to carry out the purposes of the association, and it does not seem to me it is a suitable method of distribution to say that one then looks to see what the purposes of the society were while the society was a going concern.

An ingenious argument has been put up by counsel for the third and fifth defendants, who are ad idem on this particular point, which runs very simply as follows: the members of the society are entitled in equity to the surplus funds which are distributable among them, therefore they are to be distributed among them according to equitable principles and those principles should, like all equitable principles, be moulded to fit the circumstances of the case, and in one case it would therefore be equitable to distribute in equal shares, in another case it might be equitable to distribute in proportion to the subscriptions that they have paid, and I suppose that in another case it might be equitable to distribute according to the length of their respective feet, following a very well known equitable precedent. Well, I completely deny the basic premise. The members are not entitled in equity to the fund: they are entitled at law. It is a matter, so far as the members are concerned, of pure contract, and, being a matter of pure contract, it is, in my judgment, as far as distribution is concerned, completely divorced from all questions of equitable doctrines. It is a matter of simple entitlement, and that entitlement, in my judgment, at this time of day must be, and can only be, in equal shares.

However, that is not the end of the matter, because we now have to consider the situation which has in fact happened, whereby the surplus assets of the society have first of

---

1   [1969] 1 All ER 147, [1969] 1 WLR 229
2   [1972] 2 All ER 439, [1973] Ch 51
3   [1914] 1 IR 142

all been perfectly properly applied in the purchase of annuities for continuing beneficiaries, not members, under the rules. And then, secondly, in the grant to the Thames Valley Constabulary Benevolent Fund of the sum of £40,000, which has unfortunately been paid over, but which should not have been paid over; and also the balance remaining which was intended to be paid over to the Bucks Constabulary Benevolent Fund but has in fact not been paid over to them. The £40,000 in fact we now know, as a result of the evidence which has been put in on behalf of the fifth defendant, Alexander Leonard (which does no more than make an accurate analysis of the documents in front of the court), was really paid to secure the membership in the Thames Valley Benevolent Fund of beneficiaries of the Bucks Constabulary Widows' and Orphans' Fund Friendly Society, and not for the serving police officers themselves, who were entitled to, and largely did, under the existing rules of the Thames Valley Police Benevolent Fund, join that fund on their own behalf.

Counsel for the third defendant, whom it would suit to put this argument forward, has said that all those members who signed the instrument of dissolution, in which provision was made for this payment must be treated as having given a direction in respect of their own beneficial interest, and, therefore, they are to be debited in the pro rata distribution which I have already indicated would otherwise take place, with a corresponding slice of the £40,000, corresponding to the number of people who agreed to this distribution. Counsel for the fifth defendant, on the other hand, invites me to have a look at the document that such people as did sign it did in fact sign, and the accompanying letter. That letter reads, as far as material, as follows:

'Further to the informative letter . . . the Annual General Meeting of the Fund was held at Aylesbury, on 31st October, 1968 and the suggestion put forward by your management committee, that the Fund be dissolved, etc., was well and truly discussed. The outcome of the Meeting was the passing of the following resolutions.—1. That the fund be wound up. [And then I pass over resolutions 2. to 5.] 6. That assets be realised to purchase annuities for all present beneficiaries and others to be transferred to the Thames Valley Benevolent Fund to purchase the right of entry into that Fund for all present and future beneficiaries. The foregoing resolutions are necessary to commence winding-up proceedings and to safeguard the payments to beneficiaries during the process, but they themselves are not sufficient to close the Fund; this is your right as a member of the Fund and you must signify your assent by voting in duplicate, on the attached copies of the Instrument of Dissolution. The Fund cannot wind up until sufficient members, with a minimum of five-sixths of the voting power, have agreed in writing to this being done. [The letter then sets out the voting formula and goes on:] If you agree to the Fund being wound up, sign your name on each of the copies of the instrument of dissolution under the heading "Signature of Member", on page 2, and insert your vote allocation . . . If you do not agree to the Fund winding-up, do not sign the Instrument of Dissolution, merely send it back, with an indication of the sender, to the Acting Secretary at the address shown overleaf; in either event, please treat this matter as urgent and return the form as soon as possible. The assets of the Fund stand today at approximately £87,000 in value; the purchase of annuities will cost approximately £35,000, leaving a cash balance of £52,000. £40,000 will be required to purchase entry into the Thames Valley Benevolent Fund and the remaining assets will be transferred to the Bucks Constabulary Benevolent Fund for the benefit of any of the members of the former Bucks Constabulary for so long as any survive, which could be for another 60 to 70 years hence.'

And then, of course, there was attached to that letter, and this is what the people signed, represented by the fifth defendant, an instrument of dissolution, which contained, as head 5:

'The funds and property of the Society shall be appropriated and divided in the following manner after the payment of all debts and the expenses of dissolution: (1)

Purchase of annuities of 16s. per week for all widows and 2s. per week for children below the age of sixteen years. (2) Grant to the Thames Valley Constabulary Benevolent Fund of the sum of £40,000, the balance remaining after paying all expenses to be donated to the Bucks Constabulary Benevolent Fund.'

Counsel for the fifth defendant has submitted, and in my view has submitted correctly, that it is not a fair reading of that document, coupled with the instrument of dissolution, that people who signed it were directing the trustees to deal in any way with their beneficial interests. What they were told was that there had been an annual general meeting at which various matters had happened, including a resolution that the assets be realised to purchase annuities for all present beneficiaries and others to be transferred to the Thames Valley Benevolent Fund, to purchase the right of entry into that fund for all present and future beneficiaries, and anybody, I think, reading that and then looking at para 5 of the instrument of dissolution might very well have come to the conclusion, 'Well, that is what the annual general meeting decided, resolution 5 is just carrying that out. I want the fund to be distributed; I may have voted in favour of resolution 6, I may not have voted in favour of it, but I am quite content that the fund be wound up and its assets be applied properly. All right, I consent to the dissolution.' It must, I suppose, to some extent be a matter of impression, but I would judge that many people will have signed that instrument of dissolution on the basis of the information which they were given, and quite correctly given, in the letter, merely on the basis that, whatever their personal views as to the way in which the fund ought to be distributed, they were quite content that the fund should come to an end, and that distribution should take place in accordance with the wishes expressed at the annual general meeting, in accordance with resolutions there passed, whether they themselves really agreed with that or not.

Further, as counsel for the fifth defendant pointed out, this is really an odd situation. Nobody has suggested that proceedings should be taken against the trustee for a breach of trust. If such proceedings were taken, then any trustee might possibly be entitled to claim some form of indemnity or to impound the beneficial interests of the class which counsel represents. But at the moment, as she points out, it is purely a question of construction. We know that the £40,000 ought not to have been paid, as it was, to the Thames Valley Constabulary Benevolent Fund, but, even assuming that in properly constituted proceedings it would be possible to persuade the court that that was a sufficient consent to a breach of trust to bring the doctrine of impounding of beneficial interests into play, which in any event is an equitable, and, hence, highly discretionary, remedy, that is by no means the same thing as saying that, on its face, that is a direction to the trustees to deal with the individual beneficial interests of the persons who signed that form of dissolution. Plainly, in my judgment, it is not, and, therefore, for those reasons, I propose to answer the fourth question in the sense that the surplus funds and property ought to be distributed amongst the members, and the estates of members who have died since the fund was dissolved, in equal shares.

Question 4 answered in sense 4(a).

Solicitors: *Sharpe Pritchard & Co*, agents for *Boyle & Ormerod*, Aylesbury (for the plaintiff and the third and fifth defendants); *Treasury Solicitor*.

Jacqueline Metcalfe Barrister.

Practice Direction

EMPLOYMENT APPEAL TRIBUNAL

Employment Appeal Tribunal – Practice – Appeals – Listing of appeals.

Paragraph 10.A of the Practice Direction[1] dated 3rd March 1978 is revoked.
As from the date hereof the following paragraph is substituted.

A. *England and Wales*—(a) When the respondent's answer has been received and a copy served on the appellant, the case will be put in the list of cases for hearing. At the beginning of each calendar month a list will be prepared of cases to be heard on specified dates in the next following calendar month. That list will also include a number of cases which are liable to be taken in each specified week of the relevant month. The parties or their representatives will be notified as soon as the list is prepared. When cases in the list with specified dates are settled or withdrawn cases warned for the relevant week will be substituted and the parties notified as soon as possible. (b) A party finding that the date which has been given causes serious difficulties may apply to the listing officer before the 15th of the month in which the case first appears in the list. No change will be made unless the listing officer agrees, but every reasonable effort will be made to accommodate parties in difficulties. Changes after the 15th of the month in which the list first appears will not be made other than on application to the President of the Employment Appeal Tribunal; arrangements for the making of such an application should be made through the listing officer. (c) Other cases may be put in the list by the listing officer with the consent of the parties at shorter notice, eg where other cases have been settled or withdrawn or where it appears that they will take less time than originally estimated. Parties who wish their cases to be taken as soon as possible and at short notice should notify the listing officer. (d) Each week an up-to-date list for the following week will be prepared including any changes which have been made (in particular specifying cases which by then have been given fixed dates). (e) The monthly list and the weekly list will appear in the daily cause list and will also be displayed in room 6 at the Royal Courts of Justice and at 4 St James's Square, London SW1. It is important that parties or their advisers should inspect the weekly list as well as the monthly list. (f) If cases are settled or to be withdrawn notice should be given at once to the listing officer so that other cases may be given fixed dates.

22nd February 1979   SLYNN J

1   [1978] 2 All ER 293, [1978] 1 WLR 573

Re Blue Jeans Sales Ltd

CHANCERY DIVISION
OLIVER J
26th, 29th JUNE 1978

Company – Winding-up – Possession of property – Landlord of property leased to company applying to Companies Court for possession order against liquidator – Company having no defence to claim – Third parties in possession of property – Whether order for possession should be made in winding-up proceedings or leave given to commence separate action for possession – Whether making of order for possession likely to cause administrative inconvenience in winding-up proceedings – RSC Ord 45, r 3(a).

The landlord of premises which were leased to a company in liquidation under a winding-up order made in the Companies Court applied to that court for an order for possession of the premises against the liquidator. Possession was sought on the ground that forfeiture of the lease had been incurred by the non-payment of rent, and it was not disputed that the company were in arrears for a substantial amount of rent. The company had sublet the premises and third parties were in occupation of them. The registrar of the Companies Court refused to make an order for possession in the winding-up proceedings on the ground that the order might adversely affect the third parties who had no locus standi to be heard in the winding-up proceedings. However, the registrar gave the landlord leave to commence possession proceedings against the liquidator in the Queen's Bench Division. The landlord moved to vary the registrar's order, seeking an immediate order for possession. The liquidator contended that an order for possession in the winding-up proceedings would cause administrative inconvenience, and in particular the file in the proceedings would have to remain open even when the winding-up was completed in case the landlord wished to apply to the registrar for leave to issue a writ of possession to enforce the order.

Held – Because the company had no defence to the landlord's claim the court would make an order for possession against the liquidator in the winding-up proceedings even though third parties were in possession of the premises, for their rights would be protected under RSC Ord 45, r 3[a], whereby the registrar could not give the landlord leave to issue a writ of possession enforcing the order until notice to them had been given enabling them to apply for relief from forfeiture. Furthermore, no inconvenience would be caused by making the order in the winding-up proceedings because any application for relief from forfeiture by the third parties would have to be by proceedings separate from the winding-up. On completion of the winding-up, the registrar would not be required to keep open the file merely because the landlord might make an application to him for leave to issue a writ of possession (see p 644 *h* to p 645 *a* and *c* to *e* and *j*, p 646 *f* and p 647 *c* to *e*, post).

General Share and Trust Co v Wetley Brick and Pottery Co (1882) 20 Ch D 260 applied.

Notes
For proceedings against a company after a winding-up order, see 7 Halsbury's Laws (4th Edn) para 1365.

Case referred to in judgments
General Share and Trust Co v Wetley Brick and Pottery Co (1882) 20 Ch D 260, sub nom *Re Wetley Brick and Pottery Co* 30 WR 445, CA, 10 Digest (Reissue) 1111, 6842.

Case also cited
Centrifugal Butter Co Ltd, Re [1913] 1 Ch 188.

---

a   Rule 3, so far as material, is set out at p 645 *a b*, post

Motion

On 7th November 1977 an order for the winding-up of Blue Jeans Sales Ltd was made by the Companies Court. By a summons dated 22nd May 1978 MEPC Ltd ('the applicant') applied (i) for an order for possession of premises known as bays 6, 17a, 18a, 19a and 20a at 101 Farm Lane, Walham Green, Hammersmith, which they had leased to Blue Jeans Sales Ltd, or alternatively (ii) for leave to commence an action in the Queen's Bench Division against Blue Jeans Sales Ltd for possession of the premises. By an order dated 7th June 1978 Mr Registrar Dearbergh refused an order for possession but gave the applicant leave to commence an action in the Queen's Bench Division. By notice of motion dated 9th June 1978 the applicant moved that the order of Mr Registrar Dearbergh be varied to provide that the applicant be granted an order for possession of the premises. The facts are set out in the judgment of 26th June

David Neuburger for the applicant.
John Cone for the liquidator.

26th June. **OLIVER J.** This is a motion to vary an order Mr Registrar Dearbergh has made on 7th June 1978, whereby he gave leave under s 231 of the Companies Act 1948 to the applicant, who is the landlord of some premises let to a company in liquidation, to proceed under s 231 in the Queen's Bench Division for possession of the premises.

The ground on which possession is sought is that a forfeiture has been incurred for, inter alia, non-payment of rent. The facts as they appear from the note of the registrar, and I do not think that this is in dispute, are that there was a substantial sum of something over £2,800 arrears of rent due at the date of the commencement of the winding-up. There is now due something over £10,000 in rent. Subsidiary matters urged by the applicant, which is a company called MEPC Ltd, are that the premises have been sublet in breach of covenant and that they are being used for a purpose which was not one which was authorised by the lease. But the primary claim appears to be based on arrears of rent and it is common ground that that rent has not been paid.

The facts are that the company was ordered to be wound up on 7th November 1977 on a petition which had been presented the previous month, on 5th October, and the respondent to the summons, Mr Gilmore, who was the liquidator of the company, was appointed to that office by order of 15th February 1978. The landlord applicant served notice under s 146 of the Law of Property Act 1925 on 21st April 1978 and had previously, in December, served on the liquidator a notice under s 323(4) of the Companies Act 1948 requiring him to decide whether or not to disclaim. That notice has expired and no disclaimer had taken place. This summons was issued on 22nd May 1978.

The company had issued a debenture or debentures (I am not quite sure which) which, as I understand it, was or were in the usual form and, prior to the winding-up, a receiver had been appointed and is so acting.

When the matter came before the registrar, he acceded to the applicant's request for leave to commence proceedings. The applicant thereupon made application for an immediate order for possession basing itself on *General Share and Trust Co v Wetley Brick and Pottery Co*[1]. That was a case where some mines had been demised to the company, a receiver had been appointed by debenture holders, rent was in arrear and the landlord took out a summons for leave to disclaim or re-enter, but before the return date an order was made for the winding-up of the company. The summons was then amended by entitling it in the winding-up as well as in the action. Hall V-C held that, as the landlord was a creditor, leave could not be given to him to disclaim and that the claim to re-enter ought to be left to be tried in an action. The Court of Appeal held that the right of re-entry had accrued on the making of the winding-up order and that the title of the landlord to re-enter being clear, the court ought to order possession to be given to him and ought not to put

---

1   (1882) 20 Ch D 260

him to the useless expense of bringing an action to which there was no defence. The judgment of Jessel MR was in these terms, so far as relevant[1]:

> 'Under the terms of the proviso he was clearly entitled to re-enter, and could only be kept out of possession by the unlawful act of the tenant. The Vice-Chancellor thought that he ought not to be allowed to re-enter without establishing his right by an action. I see no reason for putting him to an action. I have often said both here and at the Rolls, that when in a winding-up a landlord comes to the Court asking for the possession of property which is under the control of the Court, and the claim is one against which the liquidator would have no defence, the right course is to order the liquidator to give up possession. It would be a cruel hardship to put the applicant to the expense of bringing an action when the Court can see that there is nothing to be tried. He might lose his costs, as he might be proceeding against the liquidator of a company with no assets. No question arises here as to the construction of the proviso for re-entry so far as regards non-payment of rent.'

On the basis of that case, the applicant applied to the registrar for an immediate order for possession. The registrar rejected that claim on this ground: the jurisdiction exercised by the court in that case was one which was appropriate where the company was in occupation of the premises and nobody else but the company through its liquidator could have any interest. What he said was that in a case where only the liquidator is in occupation, and the company would have no defence to an action for forfeiture, this court could only direct the liquidator to give up possession. But an unrestricted order for possession against the liquidator, where there were others in occupation and which it was sought to enforce against them under RSC Ord 45, r 3, would affect those people in occupation who might be trespassers or who might have some right they could assert but who would not have been heard on the making of the order and would not have any locus standi to be heard in the winding-up proceedings. If an order is made in this court requiring a liquidator to give up possession in a case where there are other persons who might be affected, it is subject to an implied or express qualification which restricts its effect to the liquidator alone. This may be of some assistance to the landlord and such orders have on occasion been made but it does not remove the need for further proceedings against other persons in occupation. Therefore, he said that his decision followed the practice which rightly or wrongly had been applied by the registrar in such cases for a considerable time. He thought that the *General Share and Trust Co* case[2] was decided before the right of the tenant for relief against forfeiture was as extensive as it is now. For those reasons, he rejected the landlord's application.

Counsel for the applicant submits that there is really no justification for declining to apply, in this case, the same rule as was applied by the Court of Appeal in the *General Share and Trust Co* case[2]. Here, he says, leaving aside any question of misuse of the premises or of unlawful sublettings, there is no dispute that the rent is in arrear and the premises being apparently of a capital value of less than the arrears of rent, there is no reason why the forfeiture should not take place immediately or why the landlord should be put to the expense of an action in the Queen's Bench Division when an order for possession could equally well be made now.

Counsel for the liquidator takes as his first and, indeed, his primary point (I am not sure indeed that it is not his only point) that the summons in this case is directed to the wrong persons, because, he says, there being a receiver acting, the receiver being the agent of the company under the debenture, the receiver ought to have been made a respondent to the summons; and the receiver has not been made a respondent to the summons. The receiver is the person who is actually in control of the premises and the liquidator is not. Therefore, no order ought to be made on this summons.

I will deal with that point first because, of course, if it is well founded, it really concludes the question against counsel for the applicant's contention. Counsel for the applicant has drawn my attention to the fact that in the *General Share and Trust Co* case[1] the receiver there appointed by the debenture holders had been made a party and that, in his judgment (right at the end of it) Jessel MR said[2]:

'As to the costs of the receiver, it was irregular to make him a party. He ought not to have been served unless a case of personal misconduct was made against him, and no such case is alleged. It is true he applied against the landlord for an order to commit, and this application against him is a sort of retort courteous, but that does not justify it. The Appellant must pay the receiver's costs below and here.'

So, counsel for the applicant starts, so he claims, from a position of high authority but he does not rest on that alone. As he points out, the claim here is a claim for forfeiture of the lease. The lessee is the company. The company is in liquidation and the appropriate party is the liquidator. The receiver, it is true, may be in actual control of the premises but the receiver is the agent of the company and, if an order is made against the company, then no doubt it can be enforced against whoever is in occupation whether that occupant be the receiver, as agent, or the receiver, as trespasser, or any other person under any other title.

Secondly, he says that the receiver, if he is indeed the person in possession, is in the same position as any other person in possession. It is not essential when seeking to forfeit a lease to join every person who happens to be in physical occupation of the premises. It may be necessary to join such persons when it comes to enforcing any order for possession made pursuant to the forfeiture of the lease but that is a different matter altogether. The company, as counsel for the applicant points out, is the tenant, always has been the tenant and remains the tenant. Therefore, the appropriate person against whom the order ought to be made is the company.

I am bound to say that I think that those submissions are well founded. It does not seem to me that the receiver is a necessary party to this summons at this stage even if (which seems to me to be open to doubt) his position as agent for the company was not determined by the liquidation.

I therefore reject that contention and I turn now to the main point on which the registrar based his decision, namely, that since it was known that there were other people who were in occupation of the premises, it would not be right that an order should be made in these proceedings. I am not sure that I see why it should be necessary for an action to which there can be no defence so far as the company is concerned (an action for forfeiture) should have to proceed in the Queen's Bench Division simply because there are other persons who are in occupation of the premises. It seems to me, for instance, that if an action for forfeiture had been commenced against the company prior to the commencement of the liquidation, that is a proceeding which under r 44 of the Companies (Winding-up) Rules 1949[3] would be transferred to the Companies Court and would proceed in the Companies Court. I see no reason why an order for possession should not be made in a case where proceedings have not in fact been commenced at the commencement of the liquidation, if an application is made for leave to commence such proceedings, and if it appears clear that there is no defence to the proceedings.

The substance of the registrar's decision is that an order for possession is going to affect other people. Of course that is right, but it does not seem to me that that is a matter which should influence the court in making the order for possession. The order for possession in itself does nothing but result in the termination of the lease, which is the object of the applicant's exercise. It cannot, of course, be enforced by a writ of possession except in accordance with the provisions of RSC Ord 45, r 3, to which the registrar referred. That provides that a writ of possession to enforce a judgment or order for the giving of

---

1   (1882) 20 Ch D 260

2   20 Ch D 260 at 267

3   SI 1949 No 330

possession of any land shall not be issued without the leave of the court except where the judgment or order was given or made in a mortgage action to which RSC Ord 88 applies, which is not this case. Paragraph (3) of RSC Ord 45, r 3, provides:

'Such leave shall not be granted unless it is shown—(a) that every person in actual possession of the whole or any part of the land has received such notice of the proceedings as appears to the Court sufficient to enable him to apply to the Court for any relief to which he may be entitled . . .'

Under the Companies (Winding-up) Rules 1949, r 4(3), it is provided that in every cause or matter within the jurisdiction of the judge, whether by virtue of the Act or by transfer or otherwise, the registrar shall in addition to his powers and duties under the rules have all the powers and duties of a master or registrar of the court. The master, of course, has power to issue a writ of possession or to grant leave for the writ of possession to issue and, I apprehend, so has the registrar. I can see no reason why the rights of any person who is in actual occupation (and that would include, of course, the receiver if the receiver wishes to make any application in relation to the premises) should not be properly safeguarded in the way in which RSC Ord 45, r 3, envisages, namely, by such persons being given notice and applying if necessary in the winding-up for such relief as they may be entitled to or may claim to be entitled to.

I therefore would not take the same restricted view as the registrar has taken in this case. I think that there is no defence vis-à-vis the landlord to the claim against the company for forfeiture of the lease and I would make the order for possession for which the applicant asks. Of course, the consequences of that would be that if the landlord wishes to enforce the order he must apply for a writ of possession and any third party rights can then be dealt with if, on being given notice of the order, application is made for the enforcement or recognition of third party claims.

[Oliver J requested the matter to be restored before him for further argument.]

29th June. **OLIVER J.** This is a further hearing of the matter which came before me on 26th June and in which, contrary to the decision which had been arrived at by Mr Registrar Dearbergh, I made an order for the possession of certain premises of which the company, Blue Jeans Sales Ltd, was the tenant. That has been restored before me for further argument at my request because, after the hearing the other day, it occurred to me that there might be some inconvenience in the company proceedings if matters were to be litigated which involved questions arising between persons who were not strictly parties to the liquidation at all, namely the landlord and other persons who were in possession of the demised premises and who might wish to claim relief.

I can see that, if it were the fact that an order for possession made in the winding-up, because the company had no defence, would have the result that there might have to be tried in the liquidation and before the registrar all sorts of questions arising between the landlord and third parties, that would be a very inconvenient matter and one which, as a matter of discretion, might persuade the court that the order which the registrar was inclined to make, namely simply to give the landlord leave to proceed in the Queen's Bench Division (or, I suppose, the Chancery Division if he wanted to) under s 231 of the Companies Act 1948, was the right order.

I have heard argument from counsel on this point and I am very grateful for it because it has served, I think, to clear my mind a little bit. It appears to me that the consequences which I considered might possibly ensue are really, in my judgment, illusory. The position, I think, is this. Mr Registrar Dearbergh was very much influenced by the fact that the order for possession might affect third parties. I think myself that that fear is really unfounded. It has been pointed out that the order for possession merely has the effect, in a case where the company has no conceivable defence, of forfeiting the lease. It does not, of course, in itself confer possession on the applicant and it does not disturb the occupation or possession of third parties or affect them at this stage. The point at which the rights of third parties may come into question is the point at which the order is sought to be enforced by the issue of a writ of possession.

Under RSC Ord 45, r 3, an order for possession of land may be enforced by a writ of possession. There are other means of enforcement which do not apply to this sort of order so I need not consider them. Effectively, the only means of enforcing the order which the court has made is by the issue of a writ of possession and it is provided in RSC Ord 45, r 3(2), that a writ of possession to enforce a judgment or order for the giving of possession of any land shall not be issued without the leave of the court except where the judgment or order was given or made in a mortgage action to which RSC Ord 88 applies, which is not this case. RSC Ord 45, r 3(3), provides:

'Such leave shall not be granted unless it is shown—(a) that every person in actual possession of the whole or any part of the land has received such notice of the proceedings as appears to the Court sufficient to enable him to apply to the Court for any relief to which he may be entitled . . .'

After I considered the matter the other day, it occurred to me that, if it be the situation that when the landlord applies for the enforcement of the order of possession by the issue of a writ of possession, there is left an opportunity for third parties to apply to the Companies Court for relief from forfeiture, that would be an extremely inconvenient way of proceeding because it would mean that the registrar would be trying, in effect, proceedings between third parties which really had nothing whatever to do with the company, the company being no longer concerned in the matter because the order for possession had been made against it. So far as it is concerned, the lease has been forfeited. But I am satisfied that that is not in fact the position. The only right that the third party, whether he be a mortgagee or a sublessee, has to claim relief from forfeiture, (and that is really what all this is about) is the right which is conferred by s 146 of the Law of Property Act 1925 which enables such a person to apply for relief in the action of the landlord, if any, or otherwise by action of his own.

It is, I think, clear that a winding-up proceeding (and ex hypothesi the order here is made in the winding-up) is not an 'action' and therefore this is not a case where the sub-tenant or mortgagee could apply for relief in the landlord's summons in the winding-up. It is a case where, if relief is sought to be granted at all, it has to be applied for by a separate proceeding. That proceeding would be something taking place altogether outside the liquidation and therefore the registrar would not, as I see it, be concerned with the matter at all.

I am left with the question of whether there is any residual inconvenience which ought to dictate that I should make some other order than the order which I made the other day. I do not think that there is. It seems to me that as a matter of elementary justice to the landlord, it is right that, there being no possible defence by the company, he should have his order for possession. If he wishes to enforce that order, he will, of course, have to give notice to persons in occupation of the premises and give them the requisite opportunity of making any application for relief which they may be advised to make; applications which no doubt they would make by action either in the Queen's Bench Division or in the Chancery Division.

If no such application is made, then the landlord can apply to the registrar for leave to issue the writ of possession and the matter can be concluded without his being put to the additional expense of instituting proceedings in the Queen's Bench Division or in the Chancery Division himself and a considerable burden will be removed from him. If the sub-tenant or a mortgagee does take proceedings against the landlord for relief, then presumably the landlord will not make an application for the writ of possession to issue unless and until those proceedings have been concluded and any claim for relief has been refused because, if a claim for relief is granted, the matter becomes academic.

The objection which has been urged by counsel for the liquidator to this proceeding, is this. I think it can be summarised in this way. Whether the matter be dealt with by the registrar himself (that is the matter of the enforcement of the order for possession by the grant of leave to issue a writ of possession) or whether it be dealt with by a master of the Chancery Division to whom the matter is transferred under RSC Ord 4, r 9 (assuming that to be possible, which I rather think it is, since the Companies (Winding-up) Rules 1949 give the registrar the powers of a master), whichever of those two applies, the matter remains a matter proceeding in the Companies Court. As the matter cannot be transferred out of the Companies Court, one must hypothesise that an application may be made in some other division of the court against the landlord for relief and, therefore, there may at some stage in the future be an application made to the registrar for leave to issue a writ of possession. The file, it is claimed, must therefore remain open because of the possibility of such an application being made. It is said that the consequence of that is that the liquidator would be greatly embarrassed because, as long as the file remains open, he will have to continue to call meetings and file returns because the affairs of the company cannot be completely wound up and the dissolution of the company will thus be delayed until such time as the proceedings for relief have been determined and until such time as the landlord chooses to make an application for enforcement of the order for possession.

I can readily see that may cause some inconvenience if it be right. But I am bound to say that I cannot at the moment see why the fact that the landlord, who is, ex hypothesi, involved in some proceedings in some other division, does not seek at this stage to apply for leave to issue a writ of possession should cause the dissolution by a completion of the winding-up of the company (which in the normal way is simply carried out by striking the company off the register after the liquidator has achieved his discharge) to be delayed. It simply does not seem to me that the two are connected. If no application for the enforcement of the order has been made at the time when the liquidator has filed his final accounts and completed the affairs of the company, I can see no reason at all why the registrar need keep the file open simply because an application may be made to him. Counsel for the liquidator's hypothesis is that once the company has been dissolved, no further application can thereafter be made in the winding-up proceedings for the enforcement of the order for possession. That may be right; I express no view about it. But if it is right, then the misfortune is not, as I see it, that of the registrar, who is perfectly entitled to close the file. It is the misfortune of the landlord who has not applied in time for the enforcement of the order for possession which he has obtained. It may be necessary for him, if counsel's hypothesis is correct, to apply for another order for possession in other proceedings. That is a matter, as it seems to me, of choice for the landlord. Therefore, as it seems to me, the argument that the order which I have made is likely to cause administrative inconvenience and embarrassment to the liquidator is one which has really no foundation.

I have to apologise to counsel for bringing them back to argue at some length on a matter which possibly I ought to have raised on the original hearing. I can only express my gratitude to them for having argued the matter before me but, having heard it argued, I see no reason to depart from the order which I pronounced the other day and that order can proceed.

Order for possession.

Solicitors: *Blok Woodford* (for the applicant); *Arram Fairfield & Co* (for the liquidator).

Evelyn Budd Barrister.

Edwards (Inspector of Taxes) v Clinch

CHANCERY DIVISION

WALTON J

22nd, 29th NOVEMBER 1978

Income tax – Emoluments from office or employment – Office – Inspector appointed to hold a public local inquiry – Whether inspector holding an 'office' – Whether inspector's remuneration taxable under Sch E, Case I – Income and Corporation Taxes Act 1970, s 181(1).

The taxpayer was one of a panel of some 60 persons invited by the Department of the Environment from time to time to act as inspectors at public local inquiries for the Secretary of State for the Environment. The taxpayer would be contacted by an official of the department, informed of the location and date of the inquiry and the daily fee payable, and invited to undertake the inquiry. The taxpayer could then either accept or refuse the invitation. If he accepted, the taxpayer was sent the relevant papers together with an authority in writing, signed on behalf of the Secretary of State, appointing him under the Acquisition of Land (Authorisation Procedure) Act 1946 to hold the particular inquiry. The taxpayer was solely responsible for the conduct and procedure at the inquiry, subject to the rules governing tribunals and inquiries. The Crown claimed that the taxpayer's position was a public office capable of being held by persons in succession and therefore an 'office' within the meaning of s 181(1)[a] of the Income and Corporation Taxes Act 1970, and accordingly the emoluments therefrom were chargeable to tax under Case I of Sch E. The taxpayer appealed contending that, in the discharge of his duties as an inspector, he did not hold an 'office' within Case I of Sch E and that in the circumstances he was assessable only under Case II of Sch D in respect of fees received from holding inquiries. The General Commissioners upheld the taxpayer's contention and allowed his appeal. The Crown appealed.

Held – For the purposes of s 181(1) of the 1970 Act, an inspector at public local inquiries held a series of offices to which he was appointed from time to time by the persons having the power of appointment to such offices, and accordingly the taxpayer was liable to tax under Case I of Sch E in respect of his remuneration as an inspector. The appeal would therefore be allowed (see p 655 *f* and p 656 *f*, post).

Notes

For office or employment, see 23 Halsbury's Laws (4th Edn) paras 647–648, and for cases on the subject, see 28(1) Digest (Reissue) 320–323, 337, 338, 1130–1147, 1219–1220, 1227.

For the Income and Corporation Taxes Act 1970, s 181, see 33 Halsbury's Statutes (3rd Edn) 255.

For 1974–75 and subsequent years of assessment, s 181(1) of the 1970 Act has been amended by s 21(1) and (9) of the Finance Act 1974.

Cases referred to in judgment

Attorney-General v Eyres [1909] 1 KB 723, 78 LJKB 348, 100 LT 396, 21 Digest (Repl) 94, 440.

Attorney-General v Lancashire and Yorkshire Railway Co (1864) 2 H & C 792, 4 New Rep 23, 33 LJ Ex 163, 10 LT 95, 10 Jur NS 705, 159 ER 327, 28(1) Digest (Reissue) 320, 1131.

Dale v Inland Revenue Comrs [1953] 2 All ER 671, [1954] AC 11, [1953] 3 WLR 448, 34 Tax Cas 468, 32 ATC 294, [1953] TR 269, 46 R & IT 513, HL, 28(1) Digest (Reissue) 583, 2163.

---

a   Section 181(1), so far as material, provides: 'The Schedule referred to as Schedule E is as follows:—
SCHEDULE E   1. Tax under this Schedule shall be charged in respect of any office or employment on emoluments therefrom . . .'

Great Western Railway Co v Bater (Surveyor of Taxes) [1920] 3 KB 266, 8 Tax Cas 231; *affd*
[1921] 2 KB 128, 8 Tax Cas 231, CA; *rvsd* [1922] 2 AC 1, 8 Tax Cas 231, HL, 28(1) Digest
(Reissue) 320, *1132*.
Inland Revenue Comrs v Brander & Cruickshank [1971] 1 All ER 36, [1971] 1 WLR 212, 46
Tax Cas 574, [1970] TR 353, HL, 28(1) Digest (Reissue) 46, *193*.
McMillan v Guest (Inspector of Taxes) [1942] 1 All ER 606, [1942] AC 561, 24 Tax Cas 190,
111 LJKB 398, 167 LT 329, HL, 28(1) Digest (Reissue) 337, *1219*.
Mitchell (Inspector of Taxes) v Ross [1961] 3 All ER 49, [1962] AC 813, [1961] 3 WLR 411,
40 Tax Cas 11, [1961] TR 191, 40 ATC 199, HL, 28(1) Digest (Reissue) 321, *1138*.

Case stated

1. At a meeting of the Commissioners for the General Purposes of the Income Tax for the
Division of Rochford held at the Court House, Victoria Avenue, Southend-on-Sea, on 25th
March 1977, Frank Howard Clinch ('the taxpayer') appealed against assessments for 1973–
74 in the sum of £6,678 and for 1974–75 in the sum of £11,579 made on him under Case
I of Sch E of the Income and Corporation Taxes Act 1970, in respect of certain emoluments.

2. The question for determination was whether certain sums which the Department of
the Environment paid to the taxpayer were assessable to tax under Sch E or under Sch D
Case II.

3. The following facts were proved or admitted: (a) During the years which were the
subject of the assessments the taxpayer was one of a panel of some 60 persons whom the
Department of the Environment invited from time to time to act as inspectors to hold
public local inquiries in respect of matters for which the Secretary of State for the
Environment was responsible. (b) The duties of such an inspector were to hold an
independent inquiry and to make a report thereon in writing to the Secretary of State.
(c) The procedure, as far as the taxpayer was concerned, was that when it became necessary
to hold such a public local inquiry, he would be contacted by telephone by a departmental
official who would inform him of the location and date of the inquiry, and the daily fee
payable, and would invite the taxpayer to undertake the inquiry. The taxpayer then had
complete discretion whether to accept or refuse the invitation. (d) The taxpayer was solely
remunerated by such daily fees according to the length of the inquiry, and received no
retainer or salary. Payment was made by the department only in response to a fee account
submitted by the taxpayer. He did, however, receive travelling and subsistence allowances
on Civil Service scales. No statement of 'terms of employment' under the Contracts of
Employment Act 1963 was ever served on the taxpayer, and no question of redundancy
payments arose on the completion of an inquiry. (e) On acceptance of the invitation, the
taxpayer would have forwarded to him the papers relevant to the inquiry together with an
authority in writing, signed on behalf of the Secretary of State, appointing him to hold the
particular inquiry. (f) Thereafter the taxpayer held an independent public inquiry without
direction or guidance from the Secretary of State, and always announced his independent
status publicly at the commencement of the inquiry. (g) The taxpayer was solely
responsible for the conduct and procedure at such an inquiry, subject to the rules governing
tribunals and inquiries. (h) If the taxpayer became ill, or had some urgent business to
attend to, during the progress of the inquiry, he could ask to be released from his
engagement. The department, if it consented to his release, would then find some other
inspector to conclude the inquiry. (i) The taxpayer stamped his own insurance card as a
self-employed person. (j) Prior to the two years under appeal the taxpayer had been
assessed under Sch D in respect of fees received for holding such public inquiries.

[Paragraph 4 listed the documents proved or admitted before the commissioners.]

5. It was contended by the taxpayer: (a) that in the discharge of such duties as an
inspector holding a public local inquiry he did not hold office or employment within the
meaning of Case I of Sch E; (b) that the holding of each inquiry was an 'ad hoc' appointment
of indeterminate length; (c) that he was a free agent, able to accept or refuse an invitation
from the department to hold an inquiry, and was not employed; and (d) that in all the

circumstances he should have been assessed under Sch D in respect of fees received for holding such inquiries.

6. It was contended by the Crown: (a) that whenever an inspector held such an inquiry he was carrying out a public function; (b) that his position was a public office which, on the evidence, was capable of being held by persons in succession; (c) that the office subsisted from the date when the inspector was appointed to the date when the report of the inquiry was delivered to the Secretary of State; (d) that each such office was a separate office within the meaning of s 181(1) of the 1970 Act; and (e) accordingly, that the emoluments from such offices were chargeable to income tax under Sch E and that the taxpayer was correctly assessed under that schedule.

[Paragraph 7 listed the cases[1] cited to the commissioners.]

8. The commissioners who heard the appeal were of the opinion that the circumstances of the taxpayer's discharge of the duties of an inspector holding a public local inquiry did not amount to the holding of an office within the meaning of Case I of Sch E as the appointment was merely a transient, indeterminate, once-only execution of a task for which he was peculiarly qualified, the nearest analogy to which was a barrister or solicitor conducting a case for a client. Similarly the commissioners felt that the execution of such a task could not amount to employment within the meaning of Case I as the taxpayer was a free agent. Accordingly the commissioners allowed the appeal, holding that the taxpayer was incorrectly assessed under Sch E on the sums in dispute, and determined the assessments in the following figures: 1973–74 £4,871; 1974–75 £4,651.

9. The Crown thereupon expressed dissatisfaction with the determination as being erroneous in point of law, and subsequently required the commissioners to state a case for the opinion of the High Court pursuant to s 56 of the Taxes Management Act 1970.

10. The question of law for the opinion of the court was whether the commissioners' decision was erroneous in point of law.

The Solicitor-General (Peter Archer QC) and *Brian Davenport* for the Crown.
The taxpayer appeared in person.

Cur adv vult

29th November. **WALTON J** read the following judgment: The taxpayer, who is basically a distinguished chartered civil engineer, was during the tax years 1973–74 and 1974–75, and I think still is, a member of a panel of some 60 persons whom the Department of the Environment invited from time to time to act as inspectors to hold public local inquiries in respect of matters for which the Secretary of State for the Environment was responsible. It was accepted at the hearing by both the Crown and the taxpayer that the relevant statutory provisions governing such appointments are those contained in the Acquisition of Land (Authorisation Procedure) Act 1946, which by s 5(1) provides as follows:

'For the purposes of the execution of his powers and duties under this Act, a Minister may cause to be held such public local inquiries as are directed by this Act and such other public local inquiries as he may think fit.'

Schedule 1 to that Act deals in Part I with purchases by local authorities and in Part II with purchases by Ministers, and provides the procedure for authorisation. After providing for notices of the intended compulsory purchases to be served on interested persons in various ways in order that objection may be taken thereto, para 4(2) of Sch 1 provides as follows:

---

1   *Dale v Inland Revenue Cmrs* [1953] 2 All ER 671, [1954] AC 11, 34 Tax Cas 468, HL; *Inland Revenue Comrs v Brander & Cruickshank* [1971] 1 All ER 36, [1971] 1 WLR 212, 46 Tax Cas 574, HL; *McMillan v Guest (Inspector of Taxes)* [1942] 1 All ER 606, [1942] AC 561, 24 Tax Cas 190, HL; *Mitchell (Inspector of Taxes) v Ross* [1961] 3 All ER 49, [1962] AC 813, 40 Tax Cas 11, HL

a   'If any objection duly made as aforesaid is not withdrawn, the confirming authority shall, before confirming the order, either cause a public local inquiry to be held or afford to any person by whom any objection has been duly made as aforesaid and not withdrawn an opportunity of appearing before and being heard by a person appointed by the confirming authority for the purpose, and, after considering the objection and the report of the person who held the inquiry or the person appointed as aforesaid, may confirm the order either with or without modifications.'

b   Part II of Sch 1 deals with the question of purchases by Ministers in substantially the same manner, with some necessary alterations. In such cases, however, the Compulsory Purchase by Ministers (Inquiries Procedure) Rules 1967[1], made under the provisions of s 7A of the Tribunals and Inquiries Act 1958, prescribe the procedure to be followed at the public local inquiries in such cases. I do not think that I need read any of the procedure so prescribed, save to note that these rules preserve what would be the position apart *c* therefrom; namely that, except as otherwise specifically provided, the procedure at the inquiry is to be such as the appointed person shall in his discretion determine.

It is of course of the utmost importance that 'the appointed person' (whom I shall call 'the inspector') should not only be, but should be seen to be, absolutely impartial. One is only too conscious of the fact that there has been, if there is not still, a widespread, though erroneous, impression abroad to the effect that inspectors are merely appointed for the *d* purpose of rubber-stamping the Minister's or department's decision, and that they are simply puppets in the hands of such Ministers or departments. Indeed, so widespread (though, let me once again emphasise, mistakenly so) is this impression that in a recent White Paper, Report on the Review of Highway Inquiry Procedures[2], it is stated as follows:

e   'The Inspectorate. Inquiries are held by persons appointed by the Secretaries of State. This has given rise to some criticism that they might be inclined to favour the Department of Transport's proposals. In fact, the appointments are made from a panel of highways inquiries Inspectors whose names are approved by the Lord Chancellor; but in order to meet the criticism the Secretaries of State will in future, in excercising their statutory obligations, ask the Lord Chancellor to nominate a particular individual considered by him to be suitable for a particular inquiry.'

f   I can now take the peculiar facts of the present case from the case stated. The following are all proved or admitted facts:

g   '(c) The procedure, as far as [the taxpayer] was concerned, was that when it became necessary to hold such a public local inquiry, he would be contacted by telephone by a Department official who would inform him of the location and date of the inquiry, and the daily fee payable, and would invite [the taxpayer] to undertake the inquiry. [The taxpayer] then has complete discretion whether to accept or refuse the invitation. (d) [The taxpayer] was solely remunerated by such daily fees according to the length of the inquiry, and received no retainer or salary. Payment was made by the Department only in response to a fee account submitted by [the taxpayer]. He did, however, receive travelling and subsistence allowances on Civil Service scales. No *h* statement of "terms of employment" under the Contracts of Employment Act 1963, was ever served on [the taxpayer], and no question of redundancy payments arose on the completion of an inquiry. (e) On acceptance of the invitation, [the taxpayer] would have forwarded to him the papers relevant to the inquiry together with an authority in writing, signed on behalf of the Secretary of State, appointing him to hold the particular inquiry. (f) Thereafter [the taxpayer] held an independent public *j* inquiry without direction or guidance from the Secretary of State, and always announced his independent status publicly at the commencement of the inquiry.

---

1   SI 1967 No 720
2   Cmnd 7133 (April 1978), para 27

(g) [The taxpayer] was solely responsible for the conduct and procedure at such an inquiry, subject to the Rules governing Tribunals and Inquiries. (h) If [the taxpayer] became ill, or had some urgent business to attend to, during the progress of the inquiry, he could ask to be released from his engagement. The Department, if it consented to his release, would then find some other Inspector to conclude the inquiry. (i) [The taxpayer] stamped his own insurance card as a self-employed person. (j) Prior to the two years under appeal [the taxpayer] had been assessed under Schedule D in respect of fees received for holding such public inquiries.'

Apparently there has been a change in the Revenue practice in such matters, and among the taxpayer's minor grievances (although, of course, in no way bearing directly on the merits of the present dispute) is that he was not notified in any way of the change of practice, or the proposed change of practice, prior to suddenly finding himself subjected to the provisions of s 204 of the Income and Corporation Taxes Act 1970 and the regulations made thereunder. When the PAYE deductions were accordingly made, the taxpayer challenged them and took his case to the General Commissioners. They found in his favour, and from their decision the Crown now appeals. I wish to make it perfectly clear, irrespective of the outcome of the present appeal, that if the facts are as the taxpayer has stated them to be (and I have no reason to doubt his word in the slightest) then the Revenue authorities have behaved in an extremely insensitive manner, and are to be censured accordingly.

Now what has caused the change of Revenue practice is that they are now of the opinion that, when acting as an inspector, the taxpayer has been holding an office within the meaning of s 181 of the 1970 Act, and thus falls under Sch E, as distinct from carrying on a profession or vocation falling within Case II of Sch D, s 109(2) of that Act.

The taxpayer's arguments before the General Commissioners are set out in the case stated as follows:

'a. That in the discharge of such duties as an Inspector holding a public local inquiry he did not hold office or employment within the meaning of Case I of Sch E. b. That the holding of each inquiry was an "ad hoc" appointment of indeterminate length. c. That he was a free agent—able to accept or refuse an invitation from the Ministry to hold an inquiry, and was not employed. d. That in all the circumstances he should have been assessed under Sch D in respect of fees received for holding such inquiries';

and he repeated these very persuasively before me. But before I come to deal specifically with these arguments and the reply of the Crown thereto, it was quite obvious from the whole tenor of the taxpayer's address to me that the real nub of the matter, so far as he is concerned, is essentially this: that he is afraid that, if the decision should go against him and it should be held that he is indeed holding an office within the meaning of s 181, in some manner his independence will thereby be compromised.

This I wish emphatically to refute. A moment's thought will suffice that no man's independence is threatened by the income tax case under which he happens to be taxed, as distinct from the amount of tax which may be extracted! He remains as independent quoad the outside world both in fact and in law no matter what schedule may be used to tax him. Nor do I think that in the eyes of the outside world the holder of an office is any more (or less) identified with the person who appointed him than is an appointed person identified with the person who appointed him. Indeed, the status of a person who may on one view be said to have been appointed to an office and on another view merely to be carrying on his own trade, profession or vocation is in both cases exactly and precisely the same. He is bound by precisely the same statutory constraints, subject to the same statutory duties and entitled to the same statutory privileges in both cases. It is only the label which is different. There is no essential change of status whatsoever. Were it not for the tax consequences, it would simply be like Mr Jourdain discovering for the first time late in life that he had been talking prose all his life without realising it. Therefore, I am certain that the taxpayer's fears in this direction are groundless.

a What, then, is meant by the word 'office' in s 181? There is some slight guidance to be found in some of the cases, to which I must shortly refer. The earliest in point of date is *Great Western Railway Co v Bater (Surveyor of Taxes)*[1]. The question there was whether a £130 per annum clerk in the employment of the Great Western Railway held 'public office or employment'. Rowlatt J, had he not been constrained by authority to a different view, would have found that he did not. He said[2]:

b 'Now it is argued, and to my mind argued most forcibly, that that shows that what those who use the language of the Act of 1842 meant, when they spoke of an office or an employment, was an office or employment which was a subsisting, permanent, substantive position, which had an existence independent from the person who filled it, which went on and was filled in succession by successive holders, and if you merely had a man who was engaged on whatever terms, to do duties which were assigned to him, his employment to do those duties did not create an office to which those duties *c* were attached. He merely was employed to do certain things and that is an end of it; and if there was no office or employment existing in the case as a thing, the so-called office or employment was merely an aggregate of the activities of the particular man for the time being. And I think myself that that is sound. I am not going to decide that, because I think I ought not to in the state of the authorities, but my own view is that the people in 1842 who used this language meant by an office a substantive *d* thing that existed apart from the holder. If I thought I was at liberty to take that view I should decide in favour of the Appellants, but I do not think I ought to give effect to that view because I think it is really contrary to what was proceeded upon in substance in the *Lancashire and Yorkshire* case[3] in 1864 and one ought not lightly to depart, of course, from a course of business proceeded upon in matters of this kind.'

e However, the House of Lords by a majority reversed this decision, and Lord Atkinson expressly approved this passage from Rowlatt J's judgment.

The next case is *McMillan v Guest*[4], where a director of the well-known company, A Wander Ltd, was held to hold a public office within the meaning of Sch E, basically because the position was subject to statutory regulation under the Companies Acts. The passage from Rowlatt J's judgment to which I have already referred was cited with approval *f* by Lord Atkin in the House of Lords.

There followed *Dale v Inland Revenue Comrs*[5], where executors and trustees under a will which provided that £1,000 a year (free of tax) should be paid to each of them so long as they acted as such and did not receive remuneration from certain other sources held offices of profit for the purposes of the taxing statutes. Lord Normand delivered the leading judgment, and he said this[6]:

g 'The words "of profit", I have no hesitation in saying, qualify the word "office". The first point to consider is whether trusteeship is within the ordinary sense of the word an "office", and on this I can only say that "office" is an apt word to describe a trustee's position, or any position in which services are due by the holder and in which the holder has no employer. In *A.-G. v. Eyres*[7] CHANNELL, J., held that a trustee is "the holder of an office" within the meaning of s. 2(1) of the Finance Act, 1894. The word *h* "office" is used both in s. 14(3) of the Finance Act, 1948, and in s. 2(1) of the Finance Act, 1894, in its ordinary sense, uncontrolled by any special context, and I agree with CHANNELL, J., in thinking that it includes trusteeship. If the trustee is given an annuity

---

j 1 [1920] 3 KB 266, 8 Tax Cas 231
     2 8 Tax Cas 231 at 235; cf [1920] 3 KB 266 at 274
     3 *Attorney-General v Lancashire and Yorkshire Railway Co* (1884) 2 H & C 792, 159 ER 327
     4 [1942] 1 All ER 606, [1942] AC 561, 24 Tax Cas 190
     5 [1953] 2 All ER 671, [1954] AC 11, 34 Tax Cas 468
     6 [1953] 2 All ER 671 at 673, [1954] AC 11 at 26, 34 Tax Cas 468 at 490
     7 [1909] 1 KB 723

under a will on condition that he continues to act as trustee, I cannot doubt that he holds an office of profit. The phrase is not a term of art, and there is again no context which prevents it from being understood in its ordinary sense. To my mind, a remunerated office is an office of profit,'

and virtually all their Lordships expressed complete agreement with Lord Normand.

In *Mitchell (Inspector of Taxes) v Ross*[1] a part-time consultant under the national health service was held to hold an office as he was an instrument of the Minister for the carrying out of the general scheme of the National Health Act 1946. Finally, in *Inland Revenue Comrs v Brander & Cruickshank*[2] it was held that a firm of law agents carrying on business as registrars of companies held offices within Sch E.

This is all the guidance which is available from the authorities. From the Oxford English Dictionary, for the word 'office' is, after all, an ordinary English word, though usable in many different ways, one can take the following definitions: 'A position or place to which certain duties are attached, especially one of a more or less public character; a position of trust, authority, or service under constituted authority; a place in the administration of government, the public service, the direction of a corporation, company, society, etc.'

Putting all this together, is the conclusion that a person appointed to conduct an inquiry under the Acquisition of Land (Authorisation Procedure) Act 1946 holds an office, or not? I do not think that there would be the slightest doubt about the position save for two matters to which I must allude in more detail. The factors which in my view would otherwise make such conclusion inevitable are: (1) That the inspector has no employer. It is of course quite true that the person who pays him, whoever that may be, has to deduct tax in accordance with the PAYE system if the inspector is assessable under Sch E, and that that person is, for the purposes of the regulations (see Income Tax (Employment) Regulations 1973[3], reg 2(1)), called the employer. However, apart from this artificial use of the word 'employer', an inspector has no employer. Provided that he keeps within the statutory guidelines, nobody can tell him what to do or how to do it. (2) That the person who conducts the inquiry is the person appointed, the inspector, and not the taxpayer considered as a person. Without the appointment having first been made, his acts would be wholly nugatory. (3) That the duty placed on the inspector was one which was placed by statute. Of course, he need not accept office but, having accepted office, the duties attached to it were statutory. (4) That in the event of the person originally appointed not for any reason carrying out the duties placed on him, the only method of procedure (apart from abandoning the proposed enquiry altogether) would be to appoint another inspector.

As I say, a combination of these facts appears to my mind to point irresistibly to the conclusion that the appointed person holds an office. And when, in addition to that, one has the circumstance that his remuneration, through whatever channel it is paid, is obviously paid out of public funds, it becomes clear that he is in fact holding a public office.

However, the taxpayer, in his able, moderate and persuasive argument, took two particular points. First, that, in complete contradistinction to the description of an office given by Rowlatt J in the passage I have cited above, the so-called 'office' here was of merely temporary nature: it was the reverse of permanent, in that once his report had been delivered he was functus officio and that was an end of that inquiry. Secondly, that in all the cases which I have summarised above the person found to be holding an office had enjoyed a steady remuneration therefrom, whereas an inspector was paid by means of fees, calculated so as to reflect the time which had been spent on the discharge of his duties under the appointment.

I feel the force of the taxpayer's first point, but I am unpersuaded by it. I do not think it is a proper use of authority to wrench a statement such as that made by Rowlatt J out of context. The context in which he was making that statement was in relation to who might

1   [1961] 3 All ER 49, [1962] AC 813, 40 Tax Cas 11
2   [1971] 1 All ER 36, [1971] 1 WLR 212, 46 Tax Cas 574
3   SI 1973 No 334

conceivably be, and who might not conceivably be, the holder of a public office in a railway company. When one is considering that kind of case, and this is the only kind of case which has fallen to be considered by the courts so far, it is natural to dwell on the contrast of permanence and impermanence. One can scarcely believe that somebody holding what turns out to be a temporary job on the railway is holding a public office therein; and the natural contrast is with those offices which are of their own nature fairly permanent, such as station-masters and the like.

However, in my judgment there is nothing essentially permanent about an office. It all depends on the duties of the office. The Solicitor-General instanced an imaginary person appointed by statute to act as supervising officer of the forthcoming Scottish referendum. There could be no question but that the position would be temporary, and also, I should consider, no doubt but that it would constitute an office (and a public office at that) within s 181. In other words, whilst the permanency of the duties to be discharged may well, in a suitable case, form an apt guide as to whether the person discharging them is or is not holding an office, this test is wholly inapplicable to a case where the office is confined to the discharge of one (or a few) specific duties which, in the very nature of such duties, will be discharged within a finite space of time.

The taxpayer's second point is based on the remuneration which he receives, which is based on the fee notes which he renders. He says, and says correctly, that in none of the other cases to which I have already referred in which a person has been found to hold an office has the remuneration been by way of fees, professional fees. Be that so, I cannot conclude that the method of calculation of remuneration has any real bearing on the nature of the function performed by the recipient. But if there is anything in this point at all, I think it is the other way round. In a marginal case I can conceive it might well be decisive that the person in question was in receipt of a salary, thus making it apparent that he was a person who had an employer who paid him his salary, as distinct from a person who received remuneration by way of a scale of fees, which, in so far as it indicates anything, indicates that he does not necessarily have an employer.

So I come to the conclusion that in his work as an inspector the taxpayer has been holding, for the purposes of the 1970 Act, a series of offices, offices which are indeed public offices, and to which he has from time to time been appointed by the persons having the power of appointment to such offices. I think that this also coincides with popular understanding. It is not the taxpayer, the distinguished chartered civil engineer, who presents his report at the end of the inquiry: it is the inspector appointed for that purpose, the holder of an office, and not the person himself.

However, this is by no means the end of the analysis, because the Solicitor-General posed this question: on the facts of the present case as found by the General Commissioners, what other conclusion is open, seeing that it has not been found as a fact that the taxpayer was at the relevant time carrying on any other profession of which the holding of such inquiries might be said to have formed part? There is obviously no profession which consists exclusively of carrying out inquiries, and, as no other profession is suggested, there can be no other conclusion. I think this is probably a fair enough argument as matters now stand on the case stated, but if I had thought that the appeal fell to be decided on so narrow and technical a ground I should undoubtedly (unless the Crown had then and there agreed to accept as a further fact that the taxpayer was carrying on a separate profession as a civil engineer) have remitted the case to the commissioners to find further facts.

So I do not think that this point is decisive of the appeal in any way, but I think it does high-light the crucial point. The taxpayer conducts an enquiry not because he is a civil engineer but because he has been appointed to do so; and such appointments are by no means confined to civil engineers. Other professions may be asked to supply inspectors, including, now, the Bar. And whatever the practice may be as to the sensible restriction of members of the panel to professional persons, some facet of whose normal work would doubtless assist them in their task, there is no necessary restriction of the membership to any particular professions. Inspectorship is therefore a matter which, if it is to be regarded as an aspect of a profession, falls within many professions. This cannot, I think, be correct. The taxpayer suggested that there was an analogy with the services rendered by a barrister for a client, but there is here no analogy whatsoever as the aim of a barrister is, *a* if he can, consistently with the etiquette of the Bar and all other hurdles in this path, to produce a particular result for a particular person or group of persons. This is totally different from the duties of an inspector. If a closer analogy is required, it is surely to be found in trusteeship, seeing that trustees are commonly drawn from many professions and from none, and where, as we know, it is quite clear that they hold an office. Trustees, of course, owe duties to many persons, but they may even owe duties to persons yet unborn, *b* and they may not consciously place the interests of any one of such persons above the others. This is much the same situation as that in which the inspector finds himself.

I would finally, in deference to the taxpayer's arguments, deal with one or two minor points which he sought to make but which do not, I think, have any real bearing on the matters in issue. As I have already indicated, his main worry in all this matter has not been to avoid the payment of any tax at all but to assert and maintain his complete *c* independence. His fear is that if he is holding an office he will in some way be tarred with the brush of the department conducting the enquiry. As I have already indicated, his fears are groundless. One of the reasons why I have found he is holding an office is precisely because he does not have, in the strict sense, an employer, whereas I think that, if he was in fact exercising his profession, he must have a client, and that client could only be the department. *d*

Born out of these worries, he emphasised to me that his employment card was stamped on the basis that he was a self-employed man. Since the taxpayer has a separate profession in any case, I cannot see why this situation should not continue. Nor, indeed, assuming that it does not, can it be on the basis that he is, whilst acting as an inspector, actually employed. Of course, for this purpose it is conceivable that he might be deemed to be employed, but this would be merely a statutory fiction. *e*

Similarly, he submitted that he had no contract of service and was never issued with terms of service under the Contracts of Employment Act 1963. This appears to me to be a confirmation of, rather than any detraction from, the proposition that he is not employed and holds an office, rather than the reverse.

I am very conscious, of course, that I am differing from the views of the General Commissioners, but the point at issue is to some extent a novel one and is undoubtedly a *f* difficult one, and the light shed by authority is but fitful. I think, however, I have perceived where the path lies, and I propose to follow it by allowing the appeal of the Crown.

Appeal allowed. No order for costs.

g

Solicitors: *Solicitor of Inland Revenue.*

Rengan Krishnan Esq   Barrister.

China National Foreign Trade Transportation Corporation v Evlogia Shipping Co SA of Panama

The Mihalios Xilas

COURT OF APPEAL, CIVIL DIVISION

LORD DENNING MR, GEOFFREY LANE AND EVELEIGH LJJ

15th, 16th, 18th, 19th MAY, 5th JULY 1978

Shipping – Time charterparty – Withdrawal of vessel for non-payment of hire – Waiver of right to withdraw – Underpayment of hire – Underpayment in time – Acceptance of underpayment – Whether waiver of owner's right to withdraw vessel in event of failure to pay full hire.

By a Baltime form charterparty the charterers hired a vessel for a period of eight to ten months at the charterers' option. Clause 6 of the charterparty provided that the owners had the right to withdraw the vessel from the service of the charterers 'in default of payment'. Clause 39 provided that 'Payment of hire to be made within seven working days from the time of the vessel's delivery and within seven working days from the date of every subsequent month' in London to the owners' bank for the credit of their agents 'without discount every calendar month in advance, except for the last month's hire to be estimated and paid in advance, less bunker cost and Owners' disbursements and other items of Owners' liability up to such time as vessel is expected to be redelivered'. The vessel was delivered to the charterers on 13th July 1973. On 5th March 1974 the owners' agents sent the charterers' agents an account for $US119,759·37 for the advance hire for the ninth month (beginning 13th March) which, under cl 39, was payable by 22nd March. On 13th March the vessel was in Vancouver preparing to load a cargo for carriage to a port in China where she was to be redelivered. On 19th March the charterers' agents sent the owners' agents a credit note for the ninth month's hire, setting out deductions from the hire, totalling $US31,354·96, and leaving a balance of $US88,404·41 to be credited to the owners. They did not indicate how the deductions had been arrived at. On 20th March the owners' agents informed the charterers' agents that the deductions were not acceptable but did not instruct the bank to refuse to accept payment. On 21st March the $US88,404·41 was transferred to the account of the owners' agents. On 22nd March the owners' agents were supplied with details of the deductions from which it appeared that the charterers had estimated that the vessel would be redelivered in the ninth month and had made the deductions allowed by cl 39 for the last month accordingly. The owners took the view, which was found by the umpire to be correct, that the charterparty would extend into the tenth month and that the charterers were therefore not entitled to make the deductions. Nonetheless they requested further details of some of the items. On 25th March the owners' agents informed the charterers' agents that if full details of the deductions, together with vouchers supporting them, were not given by noon on 26th March the vessel would be withdrawn. No further details or vouchers were sent and no further payments were made. During the early afternoon of 26th March the owners withdrew the vessel, claiming that the charterers' payment was an underpayment and constituted a default in the payment of the hire, within cl 6. The owners did not repay the hire paid in advance in respect of the period after the withdrawal. The charterers claimed damages against the owners for the wrongful withdrawal of the vessel, contending that by accepting the underpayment and by failing to return the hire in respect of the period after withdrawal the owners had waived their right to withdraw or were precluded from exercising it. The dispute was referred to arbitration and the umpire made an award in favour of the charterers but stated it in the form of a special case, the question of law for the opinion of the court being whether on the facts found and on the true construction of the charterparty the owners were in breach of the charterparty in withdrawing the vessel from the charterers' service. The judge held[a] that the owners could not be regarded as having waived their right of withdrawal and upheld an alternative award in favour of the owners. The charterers appealed.

Held – (i) Where, under a charterparty, a payment less deductions had been made in advance and there was a dispute as to the right to make those deductions, the owners had to elect within a reasonable time whether to accept the advance payment and allow the charterers to continue to use the vessel for the unexpired time covered by the payment or to refuse to accept the payment and exercise their right to withdraw the vessel. What the owners could not do was keep the advance payment while at the same time depriving the charterers of the use of the vessel for the unexpired portion of the charterparty (see p 665 d to f, p 666 b to g, p 670 c to f and p 674 e f, post). *Mardorf Peach & Co Ltd v Attica Sea Carriers Corpn of Liberia, The Laconia* [1977] 1 All ER 545 applied.

(ii) (Geoffrey Lane LJ dissenting) The owners, by their conduct between 22nd March (when they knew from the information supplied to them on that date that the charterers were in default in respect of the ninth month's hire) and the afternoon of 26th March, had indicated to the charterers that they had elected to treat the charterparty as continuing. It followed that their withdrawal of the vessel was wrongful, and accordingly the appeal would be allowed and the umpire's award restored (see p 662 j to p 663 b, p 667 e f and h to p 668 a, p 673 d to g and j to p 674 c and f and h j, post).

Decision of Kerr J [1976] 3 All ER 865 reversed.

Notes

For withdrawal of a ship for non-payment of hire, see 35 Halsbury's Laws (3rd Edn) 281–284, para 423, and for cases on the subject, see 41 Digest (Repl) 229, 532–539.

Cases referred to in judgments

Bridge v Campbell Discount Co Ltd [1962] 1 All ER 385, [1962] AC 600, [1962] 2 WLR 439, HL, Digest (Cont Vol A) 648, 39a.

Brimnes, The, Tenax Steamship Co Ltd v The Brimnes (Owners) [1973] 1 All ER 769, [1973] 1 WLR 386, [1972] 2 Lloyd's Rep 465; affd [1974] 3 All ER 88, [1975] QB 929, [1974] 3 WLR 613, [1974] 2 Lloyd's Rep 241, CA, Digest (Cont Vol D) 52, 298a.

Clough v London and North Western Railway Co (1871) LR 7 Exch 26, [1861–73] All ER Rep 646, 41 LJ Ex 17, 25 LT 708, 21 Digest (Repl) 440, 1479.

Fibrosa Spolka Akcyjna v Fairbairn Lawson Combe Barbour Ltd [1942] 2 All ER 122, [1943] AC 32, 111 LJKB 433, 167 LT 101, HL, 12 Digest (Reissue) 495, 3479.

French Marine v Compagnie Napolitaine d'Éclairage et de Chauffage par le Gaz [1921] 2 AC 494, [1921] All ER Rep 726, 90 LJKB 1068, 125 LT 833, 15 Asp MLC 358, 27 Com Cas 69, HL, 41 Digest (Repl) 234, 567.

Gilbert-Ash (Northern) Ltd v Modern Engineering (Bristol) Ltd [1973] 3 All ER 195, [1974] AC 689, [1973] 3 WLR 421, 72 LGR 1, HL, Digest (Cont Vol D) 86, 419d.

Hughes v Metropolitan Railway Co (1877) 2 App Cas 439, [1874–80] All ER Rep 187, 46 LJQB 583, 36 LT 932, 42 JP 421, HL, 21 Digest (Repl) 392, 1221.

Mardorf Peach & Co Ltd v Attica Sea Carriers Corpn of Liberia, The Laconia [1977] 1 All ER 545, [1977] AC 850, [1977] 2 WLR 286, [1977] 1 Lloyd's Rep 315, HL; rvsg [1976] 2 All ER 249, [1976] QB 835, [1976] 2 WLR 668, [1976] 1 Lloyd's Rep 395, CA.

Matthews v Smallwood [1910] 1 Ch 777, [1908–10] All ER Rep 536, 79 LJ Ch 322, 102 LT 288, 31(2) Digest (Reissue) 843, 6964.

Oceanic Freighters Corpn v mv Libyaville Reederei und Schiffahrts GmbH, The Libyaville [1975] 1 Lloyd's Rep 537.

Scarf v Jardine (1882) 7 App Cas 345, [1881–5] All ER Rep 651, 51 LJQB 612, 47 LT 258, 4 Digest (Reissue) 490, 4257.

---

a   [1976] 3 All ER 865

Stockloser v Johnson [1954] 1 All ER 630, [1954] 1 QB 476, [1954] 2 WLR 439, CA, 20 Digest (Repl) 548, 2565.

Tankexpress (A/S) v Compagnie Financière Belge des Petroles SA [1948] 2 All ER 939, [1949] AC 76, [1949] LJR 170, 82 Ll L Rep 43, HL, 41 Digest (Repl) 221, 482.

Timber Shipping Co SA v London & Overseas Freighters Ltd, The London Explorer [1971] 2 All ER 599, [1972] AC 1, [1971] 2 WLR 1360, [1971] 1 Lloyd's Rep 523, HL, Digest (Cont Vol D) 818, 481a.

Tonnelier v Smith (1897) 77 LT 277, 8 Asp MLC 327, 2 Com Cas 258, CA, 41 Digest (Repl) 222, 483.

United Australia Ltd v Barclays Bank Ltd [1940] 4 All ER 20, [1941] AC 1, 109 LJKB 919, 164 LT 139, 46 Com Cas 1, HL, 3 Digest (Repl) 224, 542.

Wehner v Dene Steam Shipping Co [1905] 2 KB 92, 74 LJKB 550, 10 Com Cas 139, 41 Digest (Repl) 277, 948.

Cases also cited

Allen v Roblas [1969] 3 All ER 154, [1969] 1 WLR 1193, CA.

Alma Shipping Corpn of Monrovia v Mantovani, The Dione [1975] 1 Lloyd's Rep 115, CA.

Cehave NV v Bremer Handelgesellschaft mbH, The Hansa Nord [1975] 3 All ER 739, [1976] QB 44, CA.

Central Estates (Belgravia) Ltd v Woolgar (No 2) [1972] 3 All ER 610, [1972] 1 WLR 1048, CA.

Central London Property Trust Ltd v High Trees House Ltd [1956] 1 All ER 256n, [1947] KB 130.

Efploia Shipping Corpn Ltd v Canadian Transport Co Ltd, The Pantanassa [1958] 2 Lloyd's Rep 449.

Esso Petroleum Co Ltd v Mardon [1976] 2 All ER 5, [1976] QB 801, CA.

Federal Commerce and Navigation Co Ltd v Molena Alpha Inc, The Nanfri, The Benfri, The Lorfri [1978] 3 All ER 1066, [1978] 3 WLR 309, CA.

Kammins Ballrooms Co Ltd v Zenith Investments (Torquay) Ltd [1970] 2 All ER 871, [1971] AC 850, HL.

Langford (Owners) v Canadian Forwarding and Export Co (1907) 96 LT 559, 10 Asp MLC 414, PC.

Maredelanto Compania Naviera SA v Bergbau-Handel GmbH, The Mihalis Angelos [1970] 3 All ER 125, [1971] 1 QB 164, CA.

Panchaud Frères SA v Etablissements General Grain Co [1970] 1 Lloyd's Rep 53, CA.

Reiss v Woolf [1952] 2 All ER 112, [1952] 2 QB 557, CA.

Rickards (Charles) Ltd v Oppenheim [1950] 1 All ER 420, [1950] 1 KB 616, CA.

Sanday (Samuel) & Co v Keighley, Maxted & Co (1922) 91 LJKB 624, 27 Com Cas 296, CA.

Segal Securities Ltd v Thoseby [1963] 1 All ER 500, [1963] 1 QB 887.

Smyth (Ross T) & Co Ltd v Bailey, Son & Co [1940] 3 All ER 60, 164 LT 102, HL.

Tropwood AG v Trade Enterprises Ltd, The Tropwind [1977] 1 Lloyd's Rep 397.

Woodhouse AC Israel Cocoa Ltd SA v Nigerian Produce Marketing Co Ltd [1972] 2 All ER 271, [1972] AC 741, HL.

Wulfsberg & Co v Weardale (Owners) (1916) 85 LJKB 1717, 115 LT 146, CA.

Appeal

By a Baltime form charterparty dated 16th June 1973 the appellants, China National Foreign Trade Transportation Corpn ('the charterers'), hired from the respondents, Evlogia Shipping Co SA of Panama ('the owners'), the vessel Mihalios Xilas for a period of eight to ten months at the charterers' option. The vessel was delivered by the owners to the charterers on 13th July 1973. On 5th March 1974 the owners' agents, Marathon Shipping Co Ltd ('Marathon'), sent to the charterers' agents, Lambert Brothers Shipbroking Ltd ('Lamberts'), an account in respect of hire due in advance for the ninth month of the charter period from 13th March to 13th April 1974. The charterers wrongfully treated the ninth month as the last month of the charter period and accordingly made certain deductions from the owners' account. On 21st March the reduced amount was transferred by Lamberts' bank to Marathon's bank for their account and was accepted by that bank. On 26th March Marathon withdrew the vessel from the charterers' service but did not return the hire payment. The charterers claimed, inter alia, that the owners had wrongfully withdrawn the vessel. In accordance with the charterparty the parties appointed arbitrators who, having failed to agree, appointed Frank E Rehder Esq as umpire. On the withdrawal claim the umpire found that the charterers had wrongfully treated the ninth month as the last month of the charter period. He also found that the hire payment for the ninth month, although made in time, was an underpayment and that under the terms of the charterparty the charterers were in default of payment, but that the owners by accepting and/or failing to return the hire in respect of the period after the withdrawal had waived their right to withdraw and/or were precluded from exercising that right. At the request of the owners and with the agreement of the arbitrators the umpire stated his award in respect of the withdrawal claim in the form of a special case for the decision of the High Court. The question of law for the opinion of the court was whether on the facts found and on the true construction of the charterparty the owners were in breach of the charterparty in withdrawing the vessel from the charterers' service. On 2nd July 1976 Kerr J[1] answered the question of law 'in the negative' and upheld the alternative award in the special case in which the charterers' claim was dismissed. The charterers appealed. The facts are set out in the judgments of Lord Denning MR and Geoffrey Lane LJ.

Kenneth Rokison QC and *Martin Moore-Bick* for the charterers.
A E Diamond QC and *Bruce Coles* for the owners.

Cur adv vult

5th July. The following judgments were read.

LORD DENNING MR. In June 1973 the owners of the Greek vessel 'Mihalios Xilas' let her on a time charter to the China National Foreign Trade Transportation Corpn. It was no doubt a nationalised corporation of China. The time charter was 'for a period of 8/10 months in charterers' option'. She was delivered on 13th July 1973. So the charterers were at liberty to redeliver the vessel at any time between 13th March 1974 (the end of the eighth month) and 13th May 1974 (the end of the tenth month), plus any margin needed for a legitimate last voyage. The charterers were to pay hire monthly in advance in external sterling in London. In default of payment, the owners were to have the right of withdrawing the vessel from the service of the charterers.

The vessel made several trips across the Pacific between China and USA. Each month the charterers paid the monthly hire in advance; but the practice was for them to deduct any disbursements which had been made by them on account of the owners, provided that they were supported by vouchers supporting them. No deductions were permitted in practice unless supported by documentary evidence in the shape of vouchers.

No trouble arose until the ninth month, which began on 13th March 1974. The total hire payable in advance for that month was $US119,759·37. But the charterers made deductions of $US31,354·96. So they only paid net $US88,404·41. That is about 75% of the whole. They paid it in advance in due time, but the owners disputed the deductions. They said that they were inadmissible. On that account the owners claimed that the charterers were 'in default of payment'. On 26th March 1974 the shipowners withdrew the vessel from the charterers' service.

This left the charterers in a sorry plight. The vessel was then in Vancouver. On her previous voyage she had been to the Gulf of Mexico and had discharged cargo at Galveston

---

1   [1976] 3 All ER 865

and New Orleans. She had called in at Cristobel. She had gone up to Vancouver to load cargo for her final voyage to China. She was being scaled and cleaned at Vancouver. She had taken on fuel in her bunkers in large quantity. She was nearly ready to load cargo for China when the owners withdrew her from the service of the charterers. By this time the market had risen. The charterers had to hire a substitute vessel to carry the cargo to China. The shipowners no doubt employed the Mihalios Xilas at the high market rates.

The charterers claimed that the withdrawal was wrongful and claimed damages for wrongful withdrawal. The matter went to arbitration in London. The two arbitrators disagreed. The umpire found in favour of the charterers and awarded them nearly $US420,000. As to part of that sum, $US260,000, he stated a case for the opinion of the courts. The judge[1] decided in favour of the owners. The charterers appeal to this court.

I must now turn to the details on which the case depends.

The material clauses

Clause 6:

> 'The Charterers to pay as hire: $U.S.6·60 . . . per ton on vessel's actual deadweight per Calendar month commencing [from the time the vessel is delivered and placed at the disposal of the charterers] until her re-delivery to the owners.
>
> *In default of payment the Owners to have the right of withdrawing the vessel from the service of the Charterers*, without noting any protest *and without interference by any court or any other formality whatsoever* and without prejudice to any claim the Owners may otherwise have on the Charterers under the Charter.' (Emphasis mine.)

Clause 39:

> 'Payment of hire to be made within seven working days from the time of her delivery and within seven working days from the date of every subsequent month in cash in external sterling in London to Williams and Glyns Bank Limited, 22 St. Mary Axe, London E.C.3, for the credit of Marathon Shipping Co. Ltd., London, without discount every calendar month in advance, *except for the last month's hire to be estimated and paid in advance, less bunker cost and Owners' disbursements and other items of Owners' liability up to such time as vessel is expected to be redelivered.*' (Emphasis mine.)

There were several clauses by which hire paid in advance was to be refunded or adjusted, e g on being requisitioned, or when off-hire, but there was no provision for it being refunded or adjusted in case of *withdrawal*. The charterers' London agents were Lamberts. The owners' London agents were Marathon.

The ninth payment

The ninth month commenced on 13th March 1974. Allowing for two non-working days, the 'seven working days' expired on 22nd March 1974. Within that time, on Thursday, 21st March 1974, Lamberts duly paid the sum of $US88,404·41 to Williams & Glyns Bank Ltd for the credit of Marathon; and this was accepted by the bank and placed to Marathon's credit. This was the ninth month's hire in advance, less a deduction of $US31,354·96.

The deduction made by the charterers

When making that payment, the charterers' London agents informed the owners' London agents that the deduction of $US31,354·96 was a figure that the London agents had received from China. At that date they did not have the details. These details were coming by mail from their principals in Peking. These were received by the charterers' agents in London on the morning of Friday 22nd March 1974, and immediately telephoned to the owners' London agents and confirmed by a letter collected by hand at noon on the

---

1   [1976] 3 All ER 865

same day. These details were supported by vouchers, except for three items which were
stated to be 'estimates'. They were as follows:

Estimated advance at Galveston	$9,500·00
Estimated advance at New Orleans	$4,000·00
Estimated bunkers and disbursements on redelivery	$18,000·00
	$31,500·00

The estimates were erroneous

These estimates were erroneous, in these respects:

(i) The charterers deducted $US4,000 and $US9,500 for estimated disbursements at
Galveston and New Orleans. These deductions were not admissible at that stage because
they were not supported by vouchers; but the estimates were extremely accurate and were
supported later by vouchers for $US4,110·34 and $US9,403·17, which were in the post. So
the deductions were premature, but otherwise perfectly valid.

(ii) The charterers deducted $US18,000 for 'estimated bunkers and disbursements on
redelivery'. This deduction was not admissible at that stage, because the ninth month was
not, as it turned out, the 'last month'. It was also excessive, because there was a clause in the
charterparty which required the vessel to be redelivered with 200/350 tons fuel oil and
40/60 tons diesel oil, at the price of £8 and £10 respectively. That cost would only come
to about $US10,000, and even allowing something for estimated owners' disbursements,
the estimated deduction of $US18,000 was not reasonable but was excessive. The umpire
so found.

The knowledge of the owners

As soon as the owners' London agents on 20th March 1974 received the short payment
they knew that it was short, and that the charterers were 'in default', or at any rate would
be. Nevertheless they accepted the short payment. On Friday morning, 22nd March
1974, they received the details and knew at once that the deductions were not admissible.
It was apparent to them that the charterers were treating the ninth month as the last month
of the charterparty and were making deductions in accordance with the provisions of cl
39. The umpire found that on receipt of the information contained in the letter of 22nd
March, the owners' London agents—

'were, or should reasonably have been aware, that charterers expected to redeliver
the vessel during or at the end of the 9th month of the Charter and were treating the
9th month as the final month of the charter.'

But the owners knew that the vessel was already committed by the charterers to a voyage
from Vancouver to China and that her commitments were such that she could not be
redelivered by the end of the ninth month (13th April 1974) but probably only redelivered
towards the end of April 1974. The umpire found:

'Mr. Dempster [of Marathon, the owners' London agents] considered that
Charterers' deduction for *estimated* bunkers remaining on board on redelivery and
Owners' disbursements up to the time of redelivery were unjustified; and in
Marathon's view the vessel could *not* be redelivered at or before the end of the 9th
month.'

The owners' delay

Despite that knowledge, the owners did not at once withdraw the vessel. As soon as the
short payment was offered on Wednesday, 20th March 1974, they accepted it. As soon as
details were given on Friday 22nd March 1974, they retained the payment. If they were
to withdraw the vessel on the ground that the ninth month was not the last month, they

ought to have withdrawn the vessel straightaway; but they did not do so. On Monday 25th March 1974 they gave an ultimatum to the charterers, in this form:

'If full details of the deductions are not given by noon of 26th March, together with vouchers supporting them, the owners will withdraw the vessel.'

That was an impossible request because the details were only 'estimates'. The charterers could not give any such vouchers. So in the early afternoon of Tuesday 26th March the owners withdrew the vessel from the charterers' service.

The retention of the money

Now here is an important point. When the owners withdrew the vessel, they took her over as she was, lying at Vancouver, with a large quantity of bunkers, all ready to load cargo; and they also retained the full sum that had been paid to them for hire in advance. The charterers had paid $US88,404·41 in advance for the month beginning on 13th March 1974 to 13th April 1974. At the time of withdrawal, only $US19,619·81 had been used up, leaving the sum of $US68,784·60 hire paid in advance and unearned. Yet the owners retained the whole of that sum. They held on to it although they had not earned it. They did not refund it or offer to refund it. This was a point which proved decisive with the umpire. He held that 'by accepting and/or failing to return the hire in respect of the period after withdrawal, owners waived their right to withdraw and/or from exercising the same.'

The effect of the withdrawal

In order to see whether the withdrawal was valid, it is instructive to consider the effect of it, if valid. A 'withdrawal' by the owners is not the same as 'redelivery' by the charterers. If the owners validly withdrew the vessel owing to default by the charterers, they would take her over as she was and as things then stood. I do not see any ground on which the charterers could claim the return of the hire paid in advance and unearned ($US68,784·60), or the cost of bunkers and water on board on withdrawal ($US52,728·63); or the other sums the charterers had already paid out. There is no provision in the charterparty for such amounts to be refunded to the charterers; and there is no ground for implying any term that they should be refunded. This must have been the view of the owners in this case; because they did not refund these amounts, nor did they offer to do so. It is in accord with the decision of the House of Lords in *French Marine v Compagnie Napolitaine d'Éclairage et de Chauffage par le Gaz*[1]. The majority of the House of Lords held that, under a time charter, when payment was made in advance for the month beginning 10th August 1919—and during that month, after six days, on 16th August 1919, the adventure was frustrated—the charterer could not recover the hire paid for the 25 days in advance and unearned. The same result seems to me to apply when owners withdraw the ship because of the default of the charterers. Lord Sumner said[2]:

'Payment means payment. Without some provision, expressed or necessarily to be implied from the expressions used, there is no right to repayment except such as the law gives. Here there was no total failure of consideration but a partial failure only, for which in law no pro rata repayment could be claimed. The right to repayment, in the events which happened, has to be found in the charter, and the fact that, in one form of words or another, the charter provides for repayment in certain named events, is good ground for saying that in other events repayment is not provided for.'

Every word of Lord Sumner applies to this case. There was here no total failure of consideration but only partial. The charter provided for repayment in certain named events but not in the case of withdrawal. Lord Dunedin[3] said likewise, and so did Lord

1   [1921] 2 AC 494, [1921] All ER Rep 726
2   [1921] 2 AC 494 at 517, [1921] All ER Rep 726 at 736
3   [1921] 2 AC 494 at 514, [1921] All ER Rep 726 at 735

Parmoor[1]. Later on, in *Fibrosa Spolka Ackcyjna v Fairbairn Lawson Combe Barbour Ltd*[2], this reasoning was accepted by Lord Atkin, Lord Wright, Lord Roche and Lord Porter. They held that just as freight paid in advance under a voyage charterparty cannot be recovered, so also hire paid in advance under a time charterparty cannot be recovered. If this is so, when the charterer is not in default at all (as in frustration), it must certainly be so when he is in default under a withdrawal clause. See also *Stockloser v Johnson*[3].

This conclusion exposes the highly penal nature of the withdrawal clause, at any rate, in a case like the present, where the charterer has paid a large sum (75%) of hire in advance. No such case has ever appeared before in our books. In *Mardorf Peach & Co Ltd v Attica Sea Carriers Corpn of Liberia, The Laconia*[4], Lord Wilberforce expressly reserved his opinion as to 'a case of punctual but insufficient payment'. Take this very case. The charterers deducted the sums of $US9,500 and $US4,000 for advances at Galveston and New Orleans, deductions which were perfectly good except for the fact that the vouchers were delayed in the post. This premature deduction would be remedied automatically on the next month's payment. Yet, because they were made prematurely, the owners claimed a right to withdraw the vessel, and did withdraw it. Similarly with the deduction for estimated bunkers of $US18,000, which was made prematurely and was excessive. But it could be remedied in the next month's payment.

Those facts expose the harshness of the penalty. It was utterly disproportionate to the offence. Just think of it. There was the vessel at Vancouver being made ready for her final voyage to China. She was being scaled and cleaned. She was taking on large quantities of fuel into her bunkers. She was about to start loading cargo. The charterers had entered into commitments with shippers and others. They had paid much of the hire in advance. Yet this was all set at nought by the withdrawal. The owners took to themselves the hire paid in advance without offering to refund it. They took to themselves the fuel in her bunkers without paying for it. They used the vessel for their own profit, no doubt, at high market rates. They put the charterers in a disastrous quandary, only to be avoided by hiring a substitute vessel at great expense.

Penalty and forfeiture clauses in general

It is just such a situation against which the judges have ever sought to relieve; and they have not been intimidated by stipulations (like that here) excluding the courts from interfering. Whenever a creditor stipulates for a penalty or forfeiture in case of non-payment, and prays in aid the strict letter of the law to enforce it, then the judges both at common law and in equity, and in civil law, have used every means at their disposal to mitigate the rigour of it. The books are full of illustrations. Need I mention the forfeit which the moneylender sought to enforce against the Merchant of Venice? More to the point, however, are the penalties or forfeitures sought to be exacted by mortgagees or lessors or hire-purchase companies, construction companies, or bondholders of all kinds. Although by the strict letter of the deed of contract, the creditor is entitled to his penalty or his forfeit, nevertheless by one means or another the judges have stopped him from exacting it: such as by giving the debtor an equity of redemption, or equitable relief against forfeiture; or by holding that the creditor has waived the forfeiture or is estopped in some way or other from enforcing it; or has elected to take a course inconsistent with its enforcement; or by giving a narrow construction to the clause, limiting its application; or by holding the clause to be invalid on the very ground that the penalty is out of all proportion to the damages; and so forth: see *Bridge v Campbell Discount Co Ltd*[5] and *Gilbert-Ash (Norton) Ltd v Modern Engineering (Bristol) Ltd*[6].

---

1   [1921] 2 AC 494 at 523, [1921] All ER Rep 726 at 739
2   [1942] 2 All ER 122 at 132, 140–141, 142, 145, [1943] AC 32 at 54, 71, 74, 79–80
3   [1954] 1 All ER 630, [1954] 1 QB 476
4   [1977] 1 All ER 545 at 552, [1977] AC 850 at 872
5   [1962] 1 All ER 385 at 399–400, [1962] AC 600 at 629–631, per Lord Denning
6   [1973] 3 All ER 195 at 199, 204, 210, [1974] AC 689 at 698, 703, 711

The withdrawal clause

a   The withdrawal clause is a new species of clause within this genus. It is only within the last few years that the courts have had to encounter it. And the courts have had to discover the principles appropriate to such a clause, which are different in several respects from other penalty or forfeiture clauses, as Lord Wilberforce observed in *The Laconia*[1].

Hitherto the only cases that have occurred are where the charterer pays nothing at all by the due date, but afterwards tenders the full sum; and the shipowner refuses to accept it.

b   Such cases occurred recently when the market rose rapidly to great heights. I described them in *The Laconia*[2]. The shipowners used to watch out for the slightest delay on the part of the charterer. As soon as the hire was overdue and unpaid, the shipowner would cry 'snap' and withdraw the vessel from the service of the charter. He would direct his bankers not to accept any late payment, because he knew that, once he accepted it, he would be held to have waived the default. The principle underlying the modern cases is the principle of

c   election between inconsistent courses, such as was stated in *United Australia Ltd v Barclays Bank Ltd*[3] by Lord Atkin:

'. . . if a man is entitled to one of two inconsistent rights, it is fitting that when, with full knowledge, he has done an unequivocal act showing that he has chosen the one, he cannot afterwards pursue the other, which, after the first choice, is by reason of the inconsistency, no longer his to choose.'

d   The shipowner has one of these two courses open to him: *either* to withdraw the vessel *or* to allow the charterer to continue to have the use of it. As soon as the shipowner knows of the default of the charterers, he must make up his mind which course to take. It would be most unjust for him to allow the charterers to go on loading the ship or taking on bunkers, with a sword hanging over their heads, which would render it all useless (cf the

e   principle in *Hughes v Metropolitan Railway Co*[4], per Lord Cairns). Accordingly, it has been said by Lord Wilberforce that the shipowner should make up his mind 'in a short time— viz. the shortest time necessary to hear of the default and issue instructions'. If he delays for any length of time, he will be held to have waived the default: see *The Laconia*[5], per Lord Wilberforce. And of course, if payment is tendered, he must make up his mind at once whether to accept it or reject it; because, once he accepts it, he will be held to have waived

f   the default; or, in other words, to have elected to allow the charter to continue.

No case has arisen before like the present one, where the charterers have paid a substantial sum in advance, for the future use of the vessel, and the shipowner steps in and deprives them of the future use for which they have paid.

To meet such a case, I would suggest two ways of mitigating the rigour of it. The first is by a process of construction. The courts should construe a withdrawal clause sensibly.

g   They should not apply it in any circumstances which are not plainly covered by the words. It has sometimes been supposed that a charterer is 'in default of payment' unless he pays up in full on the nail, not a dollar too short and not a minute too late. I cannot accept this suggestion. Nor do I think that the speeches in *Tankexpress (A/S) v Compagnie Financière Belge des Petroles SA*[6] warrant it. It certainly does not apply in cases where the charterer is by the contract, or in equity, or in practice, entitled to make a deduction from hire. He is

h   not to be held in default by reason of an erroneous estimate honestly made on reasonable grounds; or an excessive deduction due to an arithmetical error; or a premature deduction due to a delay in the post; any more than he is to be held to be 'in default' if he pays by the accepted method and it is delayed, as in *Tankexpress (A/S) v Compagnie Financière Belge des*

j   1   [1977] 1 All ER 545 at 550, [1977] AC 850 at 869–870
    2   [1976] 2 All ER 249 at 256–257, [1976] QB 835 at 848–849
    3   [1940] 4 All ER 20 at 37, [1941] AC 1 at 30
    4   (1877) 2 App Cas 439 at 448, [1874–80] All ER Rep 187 at 191
    5   [1977] 1 All ER 545 at 552, [1977] AC 850 at 872
    6   [1948] 2 All ER 939, [1949] AC 76

Petroles SA[1], per Lord Wright. In short, this penalty clause only applied to a clear and substantial default by the charterer. By so construing the clause, a charterer who makes an innocent mistake is saved from a penalty which is out of all proportion to his offence; the shipowner is not exposed to the temptation of acting unjustly, nor does he run the risk of heavy damages if his withdrawal is wrongful. Neither side makes an innocent mistake at his peril. A solution is found which is 'appropriate to a commercial relationship', such as we sought in *The Laconia*[2]. As matter of construction, I would hold that these deductions by the charterers, if honestly made, on reasonable grounds, did not put them 'in default of payment', even though afterwards said to be erroneous. There is difficulty in applying it here because of the umpire's finding that the estimate was not reasonable.

The second way of mitigating the rigour is by the principle of election between two inconsistent courses. In this way I assume that the words 'in default of payment' mean 'in default of full payment on the nail', so that any shortfall, even by so little as one-fourth or less, and any delay, even by a minute or two, by howsoever so innocent a mistake, gives rise to a right of withdrawal. In that case I am of opinion that the shipowner, when short payment is tendered, is put to his election. There are two courses open to him which are quite inconsistent one with the other. On the one hand, he can accept the payment in advance, in which case he is taking it for the future 24 or more days covered by it, and he cannot withdraw the vessel during that time. On the other hand, he can refuse to accept the payment and withdraw the vessel at once. But he cannot do both of these things together. He cannot pocket the money for the future use of the vessel, and, at the same time, deprive the charterers of the future use of it.

But then the question arises: suppose that, when the payment is tendered, with a shortfall, the charterer says that he is deducting one-fourth, claiming that he is entitled to make the deduction, and the shipowner disputes the deduction. It seems to me that, in this case also, when the payment is tendered, the shipowner must make his election then and there whether to accept the short payment or not. He knows the one material fact, which puts him to his election: he knows that there is a shortfall. If he accepts payment in advance for the future 24 days' use of the vessel, he cannot thereafter deprive the charterers of the future use of the vessel for that time.

It may be said, however, that the shipowner should be given a reasonable time so as to ascertain whether the deduction is justified or not. So be it. Even so, as soon as a reasonable time has expired, he must then at any rate make his election. He must make his election between these two inconsistent courses: *either* to withdraw the vessel at once and *at the same time refund* any money received for the outstanding future use of the vessel: *or* to allow the charterer to continue to use the vessel for the outstanding period for which he has paid. The one thing which he cannot lawfully do is to pocket the money for the future use of the vessel and, at the same time, deprive the charterer of the future use of it.

In support of this line of thought, I would cite passages from some recent judgments. The first is by Brandon J in *The Brimnes*[3]:

> 'I think that the common sense view of the matter is that the acceptance of the advance payment for the whole month is an unequivocal act inconsistent with withdrawing the ship during that month for cause already known.'

The second is by Edmund Davies LJ[4] in the same case:

> '... further relevant factors might well be that, in addition to accepting, the shipowners insisted on *retaining* the full month's hire ... I am at present far from satisfied that the shipowners were entitled to act as they did, and that it might well

1 [1948] 2 All ER 939 at 948, [1949] AC 76 at 97
2 [1976] 2 All ER 249 at 256–257, [1976] QB 835 at 848–849
3 [1973] 1 All ER 769 at 794, [1973] 1 WLR 386 at 412–413
4 [1974] 3 All ER 88 at 104, [1975] QB 929 at 955

a turn out that (had the point been taken against them) their retention of the whole sum, with full knowledge of why it was being paid, constituted a waiver of their right to rely on the failure to pay punctually as a ground for withdrawing the vessel.'

The third is by Cairns LJ[1] in the same case:

b 'It is contended for the shipowners that hire for the whole of the month of April could be accepted by them without waiving the right of withdrawal because some hire would accrue (for the use of the ship up to withdrawal) and they were entitled to receive the whole month's hire and later to account to the charterers for any overpayment. I do not think this can be right. It would mean that the shipowners could retain the money without comment for most of the month and then elect to withdraw and have the matter adjusted in accounts.'

c Finally, there is this passage by Mocatta J in *The Libyaville*[2]:

'In my judgment, however, what they accepted was paid and received as hire and once having been accepted as such the right to withdraw the vessel under cl. 5 for short payment was lost.'

d It seems to me that, in each of those passages, the judges are applying the doctrine of election between two inconsistent courses.

The umpire's decision
The umpire clearly applied the principle of election. He gave the shipowner a reasonable time to see whether the deductions were justified or not, and held that it was reasonable for
e him to take until the early afternoon of 26th March 1976. So up to that point he held everything in favour of the shipowner. But when it came to the crunch, he held against the shipowner, because at that crucial moment there were still several days to run for which the charterers had already paid hire in advance, and the shipowner had accepted it. The shipowner then did something he was not entitled to do. He pocketed the money and deprived the charterer of the use of the vessel for those future days. If he sought to
f withdraw, he ought at least to have refunded the hire for those days. It came to $US68,784·60. By holding on to it, he elected to treat the charterparty as continuing for those extra days. He cannot be permitted to say at the same time that he could withdraw the vessel from use for those days.

The judge's view
g The judge made a close analysis of the doctrine of waiver, and held that it did not apply in this case. He said[3]:

'. . . there was no waiver up to the point of withdrawal. The owners then withdrew the vessel and undoubtedly became obliged to repay the unearned balance of advance hire to the charterers.'

h It is at that point that I differ from him. If the withdrawal was valid, I can see no obligation on the owners to repay the unearned balance of hire. Nor did they do so. They pocketed it, and at the same time deprived the charterers of the use of the vessel. That they were not entitled to do. The charterers are, indeed, entitled to be repaid the unearned balance of advance hire, but only as damages for wrongful withdrawal. And not
j otherwise. That is what the umpire did. He awarded the charterers the hire paid in

1 [1974] 3 All ER 88 at 117, [1975] QB 929 at 972
2 [1975] 1 Lloyd's Rep 537 at 554
3 [1976] 3 All ER 865 at 879

advance and unearned ($US68,784·68), the bunkers and water on board at withdrawal ($US52,728·63), and other items. And, in addition, he awarded them the extra cost of the substitute vessel ($US248,647·73). That was, I think, right. In so doing, he reflected the good sense of commercial men in the City of London. I would, therefore, allow the appeal to this court, and restore the award of the umpire.

GEOFFREY LANE LJ. This appeal arises out of a charterparty dated 16th June 1973 by which the charterers hired from the owners the vessel Mihalios Xilas. The material terms of the Baltime form charter in this case are as follows:
Clause 1:

'The Owners let and the Charterers hire the Vessel for a period of 8/10 months in Charterers' option from the time the Vessel is delivered and placed at the disposal of the Charterers . . .'

Clause 6:

'The Charterers to pay as hire $U.S. 6.60 (Six Dollars and Sixty Cents) per ton on vessel's actual deadweight per Calendar month, commencing in accordance with clause 1 until her re-delivery to the Owners. In default of payment the Owners to have the right of withdrawing the Vessel from the service of the Charterers, without noting any protest and without interference by any Court or any other formality whatsoever and without prejudice to any claim the Owners may otherwise have on the Charterers under the Charter.'

Clause 7:

'. . . The Charterers to give the Owners not less than 20 days' approximate and ten days' notice at which port and on about which day the Vessel will be re-delivered.'

Clause 39:

'Payment of hire to be made within seven working days from . . . the date of every subsequent month in cash in external sterling in London to Williams and Glyns Bank Limited, 22 St. Mary Axe, London E.C.3, for the credit of Marathon Shipping Co. Ltd., London, without discount every calendar month in advance, except for the last month's hire to be estimated and paid in advance, less bunker cost and Owners' disbursements and other items of Owners' liability up to such time as vessel is expected to be redelivered.'

There are two questions for decision. First, was there a 'default' within the terms of cl 6 on the part of the charterers? Secondly, if so, did the owners waive their rights under cl 6 to withdraw the vessel from the service of the charterers?

First, was there a default? The charterers' submission is that there was no default of payment for the purposes of cl 6 if they genuinely, albeit wrongly and unreasonably, believed that the ninth month was the last month and therefore made deductions under the terms of cl 39. The problem is perhaps somewhat unreal. It is difficult (though not impossible) to imagine circumstances in which the charterers could form an estimate which no reasonable person could form and yet form it bona fide. Neither the umpire nor the judge had to face that problem, because the enquiry before them proceeded simply on the question of fact: 'was the estimate unreasonable?' and no one sought to argue the question of bona fides. Since the umpire found it was unreasonable it was unnecessary to go further.

The facts on which this part of the appeal is based are as follows. By the terms of cl 39, the ninth month's hire became due on 13th March 1974 and was then payable within seven working days. It was agreed that the last day for payment was Friday 22nd March.

a On 13th March the vessel was in Vancouver preparing to load a cargo of grain for carriage to a port in China where it was the intention to redeliver. The charterers took the view that the voyage together with the time necessary for loading and unloading could be completed and the vessel redelivered within the ninth month. The owners' view was that this was impossible. The umpire concluded that the owners' opinion was correct and that the charterers' belief was in the circumstances unreasonable. The importance of the point

b is clear. It is only in the last month that the charterers are entitled to make deductions. Thus if it is not truly the last month of the hire, and if the charterers have made deductions, then the amount they have paid will be less than is due, whereupon the owners' powers of withdrawal will arise.

Where so much turns on the charterers' estimate it would as I see it make the agreement commercially unworkable if the owners had to decide whether or not the charterers'

c estimate had been arrived at honestly or not. There would be little or no information available to them on which to base a decision, save their own view as to whether the estimate was one which could reasonably be held by any intelligent charterer. For that simple reason it seems to me that the 'last month's hire' in cl 39 means the hire for the month which is on reasonable grounds estimated by the charterers to be the last month. The charterers were correct in their decision not to contend otherwise before the umpire

d or judge. The law is correctly stated in Scrutton on Charterparties[1] as follows:

'WHERE a time charter is for a stated period, the date for redelivery should be regarded as an approximate date only, unless there is a clear agreement to the contrary. In the absence of such an agreement, the charterer commits no breach if he redelivers the ship after the stipulated date, provided he does so within a reasonable time . . . The charterer will, however, be in breach if: (1) He sends the ship on a voyage

e which he does not reasonably expect to finish within a reasonable time after the stated period . . .'

The bona fides or otherwise of the charterers is immaterial. The only question is whether their expectation of completing the voyage within the requisite time was reasonable. The umpire has found that it was not and that is the end of the matter.

f There remains the difficult question of waiver. The timetable of events was as follows: on 5th March 1974 the owners' agents, Marathon Shipping Co Ltd, sent to Lambert Brothers Shipbroking Limited, the charterers' agents, an account for the ninth month's hire due in advance, that month beginning on 13th March. The sum requested was $US119,759·37, the correct figure. On 19th March Lamberts wrote to Marathon enclosing a credit note for the ninth month's hire setting out deductions from the hire of some

g $US31,000 and leaving a balance of only $US88,404·41 for the owners. No particulars of the deductions were given. The credit note and its accompanying letter were received by Marathon on 20th March. They informed the owners of the proposed deductions and telephoned Lamberts and told them that the deductions were not acceptable. Lamberts promised to obtain details from the charterers and in fact sent a telex on 21st March, making the necessary enquiries.

h On Thursday 21st March, a day before the deadline, the sum of $US88,404·41 was transferred to Marathon's account and was accepted by the bank, no instructions to the contrary having been given. On Friday 22nd March, Lamberts telephoned to Marathon and gave them some details of the deductions which were confirmed by letter collected by Marathon at about midday on the same day. One of the items was 'Est. bunkers & Disbsts on redelivery $US18,000'. During the afternoon of that day Marathon again spoke to

j Lamberts asking for further details of some of the items and disputing (correctly, as events turned out) the charterers' estimate of the redelivery date and their right to make deductions in respect of owners' disbursements and bunkers remaining on board to

---

1 (18th Edn, 1974), p 357

redelivery. They also pointed out that no notice of delivery had been received. The
umpire found that on the receipt of this letter Marathon were or should reasonably have **a**
been aware that the charterers expected to redeliver the vessel during or at the end of the
ninth month of the charter and were treating that month as the final month. On the
following Monday, 25th March, Marathon again asked for further details of the deductions
and a little later, having consulted the owners, spoke to a director of Lamberts and told him
that if full details of the deductions were not given by noon on Tuesday 26th March,
together with vouchers supporting them, the vessel would be withdrawn. No further **b**
details or vouchers were sent. No further payments were made. During the early
afternoon of 26th March the owners withdrew the vessel from the charterers' service.
There is no dispute that the vital period for consideration as far as waiver is concerned is
from 22nd March, when Marathon were or should have been aware that the charterers
were treating the ninth month as the final month of the charter, until 26th March when
the vessel was withdrawn.   **c**

The doctrine of waiver is especially applicable to the lessor's rights reserved to him in
most leases to determine the lease on a breach by the lessee of any of the covenants by him
to be performed. The principles applicable to waiver by a shipowner are much the same
as those applicable to a lessee[1]:

> 'The exercise of such a power of forfeiture is a matter of election in the lessor. It is **d**
> in his election either to avoid or not to avoid the lease. An election, however, once
> made and expressed cannot be retracted . . . and once the lessor . . . elects not to avoid
> the lease, he cannot thereafter treat it as determined and seek to re-enter: *Clough* v.
> *London and North Western Railway Co.*[2] . . . If a lessor has knowledge of a breach giving
> rise to a power of forfeiture, any unequivocal act on his part which recognises the lease
> as having continued in existence subsequent to the breach, will operate as a waiver of **e**
> the forfeiture. Thus acceptance of rent falling due after the breach operates as a
> waiver, for by such acceptance the lessor recognises the lease as having continued in
> existence up to the time the rent fell due.'

If therefore the owners of a vessel have knowledge of a breach of the terms of the charter **f**
giving them the right to withdraw the vessel, any unequivocal act on their part which
recognises the charter as having continued in existence after they had knowledge of the
breach will serve to extinguish their right to withdraw. The actual intention of the owners
seems to be immaterial: *Scarf v Jardine*[3], per Lord Blackburn:

> '. . . whether he intended it or not, if he has done an unequivocal act—I mean an act **g**
> which would be justifiable if he had elected one way and would not be justifiable if
> he had elected the other way—the fact of his having done that unequivocal act to the
> knowledge of the persons concerned is an election.'

What acts were done by the lessor or owner is of course a question of fact. Whether these **h**
acts amounted to an unequivocal recognition of the continuance of the lease or charter
despite the breach is a question of law: see *Matthews v Smallwood*[4] per Parker J:

> 'It is also, I think, reasonably clear upon the cases that whether the act, coupled with
> the knowledge, constitutes a waiver is a question which the law decides, and therefore **j**

1 Smith's Leading Cases (13th Edn, 1929), p 39
2 (1871) LR 7 Exch 26 at 34
3 (1882) 7 App Cas 345 at 361, [1881–5] All ER Rep 651 at 658
4 [1910] 1 Ch 777 at 786, [1908–10] All ER Rep 536 at 542

it is not open to a lessor who has knowledge of the breach to say "I will treat the
a   tenancy as existing, and I will receive the rent, or I will take advantage of my power
as landlord to distrain; but I tell you that all I shall do will be without prejudice to my
right to re-enter, which I intend to reserve". That is a position which he is not entitled
to take up.'

Accordingly one must first examine the umpire's findings of fact to see the basis on
which the decision of law is to be founded. They are as follows. The owners had
b   knowledge of the breach on 22nd March. They withdrew the vessel on 26th March. The
owners made no attempt to repay to the charterers hire paid in advance which related to
the period after the vessel had been withdrawn. The owners could have repaid unearned
hire to the charterers immediately prior to or after withdrawing the vessel. The owners
were entitled to a reasonable time within which to ascertain whether the amounts
comprising the deductions were correct and the time from 21st March until noon on 26th
c   March was a reasonable time. The owners were entitled to a reasonable time after noon on
26th March within which to consider the question of the acceptance of the hire and the
exercise of their right to withdraw. The decision by the owners to withdraw the vessel in
the early afternoon of 26th March was made within a reasonable time.

Those being the umpire's findings, one may well enquire what is the unequivocal act on
the part of the owners from which the law will not allow them to resile. It cannot be the
d   acceptance of hire money from the charterers. This is not the simple case of payment
made after the due date, acceptance of which will in most cases operate as a waiver. This
is the payment of an inadequate amount before the due date. It is the inadequate amount
which is the potential breach. The charterers had the opportunity before time expired of
remedying that breach by paying the balance. Therefore the acceptance of the money was
not an election.

e   What did the owners do thereafter which could be construed as a waiver? The only
matter suggested by the umpire was their failure to return the hire in respect of the period
after withdrawal. I find it difficult to see how their inaction can be described as an
unequivocal act, an act which would not be justifiable if they had elected to withdraw the
ship. In the speech of Lord Blackburn in *Scarf v Jardine*[1] appear these words:

f   '... where a party in his own mind has thought that he would choose one of the
two remedies, even though he has written it down on a memorandum or has
indicated it in some other way, that alone will not bind him; but so soon as he has not
only determined to follow one of his remedies but has communicated it to the other
side in such a way as to lead the opposite party to believe that he has made that choice,
he has completed his election and can go no further. . .'

g   The first 'communication' made by the owner in the present case was the notice of
withdrawal and there can have been no doubt in the charterers' minds that that was the
choice the owners had made. Given the fact, as the umpire has found, that the owners
were entitled to hold their hand until the moment when the withdrawal was
communicated, I can see nothing in the facts which would justify a conclusion in law that
the right to withdraw had been waived. The only unequivocal act by the owners was the
h   withdrawal of the ship.

I am unable to agree that there is no ground on which the charterers can claim back any
overpayment in respect of hire. This was a point which was not argued on the appeal, but
it seems to me that, apart from any other possible grounds (as to which see Scrutton on
Charterparties[2] and *Tonnelier v Smith*[3]) an obligation on the owners to repay in these
j   circumstances should clearly be implied. If at the time the contract was being negotiated
someone had asked the owners and charterers what was to happen in the events which we

1   (1882) 7 App Cas 345 at 360–361, [1881–5] All ER Rep 651 at 658
2   (18th Edn, 1974), p 359
3   (1897) 77 LT 277

now know did happen, there is no doubt they would both have replied, 'We shall have to settle up outstanding financial matters between us and (inter alia) the owners will have to repay any unearned freight.' It does not seem to me that much assistance can be derived from the 'frustration' cases.

Finally, if I may say so, there is a danger in giving too much weight to the misfortunes of the charterers. We are here concerned not with a lessee, a mortgagor or a borrower who may be at a bargaining disadvantage vis-à-vis the lessor, mortgagee or moneylender, but with two powerful commercial concerns perfectly capable of looking after themselves. If the withdrawal clause was unfair or too stringent the charterers were under no obligation to agree to it. Since they did agree to it, they are bound by it; and it is not an occasion on which the court should exercise a benevolent paternalism to mitigate the plainly expressed rigours of the agreement. The owners, indeed both parties, are entitled to know the extent of their rights and obligations without having to face the peril of a court rewriting the charterparty for them in terms which they would probably never have agreed.

The judge was in my mind correct in his reasoning and in his conclusions and I would dismiss the appeal.

EVELEIGH LJ. From the statement of the facts in the judgment of Lord Denning MR it will be seen that the most important dates are as follows:

(a) Due date for payment in advance: 22nd March. (b) Date of actual payment of the monthly sum less deductions: 21st March. (c) Date of owners' knowledge that charterers were treating the ninth month as the final month of the charter: 22nd March (at the latest). (d) Date when owners considered deductions for estimated bunkers and owners' disbursements unjustified: 22nd March. (e) Date of owners' belief that the vessel could not be redelivered at or before the end of the ninth month: 22nd March. (f) Request for further details of deductions (first communication): 25th March. (g) Date of owners' ultimatum 'If full details of the deductions are not given by noon of 26th March, together with vouchers supporting them, the owners will withdraw the vessel' (second communication): 25th March. (h) Date of withdrawal of the vessel: 26th March.

If the charterers were wrong and this could not be the last month the position in my judgment is as follows: (1) A breach of an obligation to pay an intermediate month's hire was known to have occurred on 22nd March. (2) The owners knew that the deductions made could only possibly be justified if this was the last month. Indeed during the afternoon of 22nd March they disputed the charterers' right to make any deductions on the basis of estimates. (3) Therefore the owners had all the necessary material on which to decide whether or not to withdraw on the basis of a failure to pay for an intermediate month. (4) A reasonable time within which to decide was considerably less than by 26th March (which was found to be a reasonable time only on the basis that further details were necessary). (5) Further details were only necessary or relevant if the owners contemplated withdrawal on the basis that there had been an underpayment for the last month. (6) Consequently the owners were indicating an election not to treat the payment as a breach of payment for an intermediate month. (7) The owners' right of withdrawal after 23rd March or after the 25th at the very latest must be based on a right of withdrawal for underpayment in the last month.

I therefore must consider whether any such right existed under the charter. The deductions in respect of owners' accounts at New Orleans and Galveston were correct. The estimate of $US18,000 for value of bunkers remaining on board on redelivery and owners' disbursements up to the time of redelivery was not reasonable. The owners were therefore being deprived of the difference between $US18,000 and whatever a reasonable deduction would have been. The resulting amount in relation to the total hire would be small. That is the position on the facts of the present case. In these cases generally mistaken estimates could produce underpayments or overpayments large or small and the true position could only be ascertained after redelivery of the vessel. Thus the existence of the right of withdrawal in such a situation would produce in my view great uncertainty and

confusion. Neither party would really know his position and a decision would be in the
nature of a gamble. I cannot believe that the parties intended to agree to a term that would
have this effect. If a forfeiture clause is to be invoked it must be shown by the party relying
on it that the clause clearly applies. Clause 39 gives the charterers the right to estimate for
the last month. In the present case the charterers did estimate. I see nothing to indicate
an intention that the charterers should be in danger of forfeiture if they made a mistaken
estimate. The owners' position is fully protected. If the vessel is redelivered outside the
permitted time the owner can recover the charter rate of hire or the market rate whichever
is the greater: see *Timber Shipping Co SA v London & Overseas Freighters Ltd, The London
Explorer*.[1] Further, the estimation permitted to the charterers in cl 39 is in relation to
items incurred up to such time as the vessel is *expected* to be redelivered. Thus another
element of uncertainty, the expected date, is introduced into the calculations.

Clause 1 of the charter indicates that the period of hire is '8/10 months in charterers'
option'. It would be a perilously limited power to exercise if by so doing the charterers ran
the risk of withdrawal and all its consequences as the result of innocent miscalculation. I
therefore do not think that the clause has any application to a disputed last month
payment.

The position therefore is that the charter gave the owners the right to withdraw the
vessel if for any month other than the last month there was an underpayment. There was
an underpayment because deductions were made which could only lawfully be made in
the last month. I have to accept the finding that the ninth month was not the last
month. This assertion indeed was the very basis of the owners' complaint that the sum
paid was not enough. Consequently on 22nd March there was a default in payment
known to the owners which gave them a right to withdraw. Nothing happened thereafter
to provide further ground on which to exercise the right of withdrawal. No further
information was forthcoming which could be said to confirm the owners' belief that there
was an underpayment.

The owners are therefore unable to say that they needed time to verify the facts in case
the charterers should justify the deductions after all. Nor could they say that they were
offering the charterers some form of compromise before putting into effect the final
forfeiture because the demand they were making was for details and vouchers, which a
moment's thought would tell anyone could not exist, because the deductions included
future estimates. The right of withdrawal which the owners sought to exercise on 26th
March could only be that which existed on 22nd March. They had at that date all the
necessary material to make up their minds as is quite clear when one appreciates that they
were in no stronger position on 26th March.

After 21st March therefore the owners were engaged in checking details which were not
relevant to an underpayment unless the last month of hire had arrived. The sole question
is whether in behaving as they did on 22nd March until 26th March they lost their right
of withdrawal. In *Mardorf Peach & Co Ltd v Attica Sea Carriers Corpn of Liberia, The Laconia*[2]
Lord Wilberforce said:

'The result of my conclusions on these two points leaves the matter as follows . . .
2. The owners must within a reasonable time after the default give notice of
withdrawal to the charterers. What is a reasonable time—essentially a matter for
arbitrators to find—depends on the circumstances. In some, indeed many cases, it
will be a short time—viz the shortest time reasonably necessary to enable the
shipowner to hear of the default and issue instructions.'

In my opinion the effect of the arbitrators' finding is that a reasonable time had in fact
expired when the owners sought to exercise their right of withdrawal. They had, as I have
said, all the necessary material on 22nd March and the information they sought thereafter

---

1   [1971] 2 All ER 599, [1972] AC 1
2   [1977] 1 All ER 545 at 552, [1977] AC 850 at 872

was not relevant to a decision whether or not to withdraw on the basis of an underpayment for an intermediate month.

Lord Wilberforce[1] continued:

'3. The owners may be held to have waived the default (inter alia) if when a late payment is tendered, they chose to accept it as if it were timeous, or if they do not within a reasonable time give notice that they have rejected it.'

The short payment in the present case is in my opinion on the same footing as a late payment. It was not a proper payment. They chose to retain it and ask for details when they knew it could never be a proper intermediate month's payment, ie they knew that whatever details were given could not reconcile the payment with a proper one for an intermediate month. In so doing they chose to accept that payment for what it was, ie a last month estimate. They were not bound to acknowledge the correctness of the amount of any last month payment. They were perfectly entitled to check the details and then at the end of the hire when all uncertainties were resolved to arrive at a final state of accounts between themselves and the charterers. The number of days' hire would then be known, all deductions would be known whether or not the vessel had been redelivered at a date outside the permitted period for a last voyage so as to attract the appropriate difference if any in the owners' favour between the charter rate and the market rate.

However, if the shipowner withdraws the ship, he cannot recover any hire for the period after the withdrawal even though withdrawal takes place in the middle of a period for which hire is payable in advance: see *Wehner v Dene Steam Shipping Co*[2]. He may perhaps claim damages depending on the facts of the particular case. Consequently after withdrawal the owners would have had no right to retain the whole of the sum which they in fact held. Some of it might have been due to them but quite clearly, seeing that a month's hire had been taken as the basis of the calculation, the whole sum exceeded that which would be due to them if the vessel was withdrawn.

On 22nd March the owners had the following choices: (1) to reject the payment and exercise the right of withdrawal; and (2) to retain the money as paid for the last month and rely on the final settlement of accounts to produce the final and possibly greater figure. There is here a case of election between the two alternative courses of action. It seems to me that the retention of the money coupled with the demand for further details plus the fact that it was a matter of days rather than hours before they decided to withdraw indicate that the owners had elected for the second choice.

I do not say that the retention of money is of itself an election, even though there may be no right to keep it. Even after withdrawal there may be grounds for retaining the money. There may be other matters against which the money can be put. There may be difficulties in arranging return of the money and withdrawal of the ship simultaneously. Moreover I would find it difficult to say that a withdrawal which appeared lawful could be rendered nugatory because of a failure thereafter to return the money within a reasonable time. Each case must depend on its own facts. In the present case I think that the owners must be taken to have indicated their choice to retain the money as payment of hire, which, because it was an estimate, would have to be adjusted.

I do not think it necessary to go into such questions as to whether consideration is necessary to support waiver, or whether detriment is necessary to support election, or to what extent reliance on the representation is necessary to support estoppel. In my opinion the rules arrived at by Lord Wilberforce can be based on an implied term in the contract that the right of withdrawal must be exercised reasonably. In any event the activity of the charterers, referred to in Lord Denning MR's judgment, constituted sufficient detriment to provide support, if support is needed, for election. The expenses which they incurred would have been even far less if they had been informed earlier of the owners' intention

1 [1977] 1 All ER 545 at 552, [1977] AC 850 at 872
2 [1905] 2 KB 92

to withdraw. It follows that I do not base my judgment on an application of the principles
a of relief against forfeiture.

I agree that the appeal should be allowed.

Appeal allowed. Award of umpire restored. Leave to appeal to the House of Lords granted.

Solicitors: *Richards, Butler & Co* (for the charterers); *Holman, Fenwick & Willan* (for the
b owners).

Sumra Green Barrister.

R v Secretary of State for the Home
c   # Department, ex parte Iqbal

QUEEN'S BENCH DIVISION
LORD WIDGERY CJ, BOREHAM AND DRAKE JJ
24th APRIL, 23rd MAY 1978

d *Habeas corpus – Return to writ – Enquiry into truth of facts set out in return – Mistake in return*
– Return not justifying detention on its face – Whether applicant entitled to be released because of
defect in return – Whether court entitled to enquire further to see whether in fact detention justified
– Habeas Corpus Act 1816, s 3 – RSC Ord 54, r 7 (1).

Following enquiries by the immigration authorities the applicant was taken into custody
e as an illegal immigrant under a detention order issued by an immigration officer pursuant
to para 16(2)[a] of Sch 2 to the Immigration Act 1971. By mistake the order stated that the
applicant was to be held 'pending his further examination under the Act' instead of for the
reason appropriate for detention under para 16(2), namely 'pending the completion of
arrangements for dealing with him under the Act'. At the time the order was issued the
immigration authorities' enquiries had finished and the examination of the applicant was
f complete. The applicant, who maintained that he was a lawful entrant, applied for a writ
of habeas corpus contending, inter alia, that the immigration officer had no right to detain
him for the reason stated in the order. It was contended on behalf of the Secretary of State
that (i) by stating that the applicant was to be held under para 16(2) the order had properly
stated the reason for the applicant's detention and the incorrect reason stated in the order
was unnecessary and (ii) in any event, if the reason for the detention stated in the order was
g wrong the court was entitled to enquire further to see whether the detention was justified.

Held (Boreham J dissenting) – When on a return to an application for habeas corpus the
person having custody of the applicant produced as justification for the detention a
document which, though valid on its face, was subsequently found to contain some
material error, the court was entitled, as part of its enquiry under s 3[b] of the Habeas Corpus
h Act 1816 into the truth of the facts stated in the return, to go behind the wording on the
face of the return and see whether there were in fact good grounds for the detention of the
applicant and was not restricted to merely examining the reasons for the detention given
in the return. Since the immigration officer had in fact had valid grounds to authorise the
applicant's detention, and since the applicant had suffered no injustice or prejudice by the
error, the application would be dismissed (see p 684 *b c* and *e* to *h*, post).

j _____

a   Paragraph 16(2), so far as material, provides: 'A person . . . may be detained under the authority of
     an immigration officer pending the giving of directions and pending his removal in pursuance of
     any directions given.'
b   Section 3, so far as material, is set out at p 678 *e f*, post

Per Boreham and Drake JJ. It is doubtful whether a return to an application for habeas corpus which merely specifies that the applicant is being detained under a particular section of the 1971 Act is sufficient, having regard to the requirement in RSC Ord 54, r 7(1)[c], that the return 'must state all the causes of the detainer of the person restrained' (see p 679 *b c* and p 683 *c d*, post).

Notes

For the detention of persons liable to examination and removal, see 4 Halsbury's Laws (4th Edn) para 1009.

For deportation of non-patrials, see ibid paras 1011, 1015.

For the Immigration Act 1971, Sch 2, para 16, see 41 Halsbury's Statutes (3rd Edn) 67.

For the Habeas Corpus Act 1816, s 3, see 8 ibid 889.

Cases referred to in judgments

Christie v Leachinsky [1947] 1 All ER 567, [1947] AC 573, [1947] LJR 757, 176 LT 443, 111 JP 224, 45 LGR 201, HL, 14(1) Digest (Reissue) 206, *1491*.

Greene v Secretary of State for Home Affairs [1941] 3 All ER 388, [1942] AC 284, 111 LJKB 24, 166 LT 24, HL, 17 Digest (Reissue) 467, *29*.

Middlesex Sherriff's Case (1840) 11 Ad & El 273, 3 State Tr NS 1239, 113 ER 419, sub nom *Stockdale v Hansard* 3 Per & Dav 349, 4 Jur 70, sub nom *R v Evans and Wheelton* 8 Dowl 451, 9 LJQB 82, 16 Digest (Repl) 302, *763*.

R v Secretary of State for the Home Department, ex parte Hussain [1978] 2 All ER 423, [1978] 1 WLR 700, DC and CA.

Motion and appeal

By a notice of motion dated 7th February 1978 the applicant, Shahid Iqbal, applied for an order directing the issue of a writ of habeas corpus ad subjiciendum to the governor of HM Prison, Winson Green, Birmingham and the Secretary of State for the Home Department for the release of the applicant on the ground, inter alia, that the detention order issued under para 16 of Sch 2 to the Immigration Act 1971 under which the applicant had been detained since 28th January was invalid. The motion was heard by the Divisional Court on 24th April. On the same day a new detention order was served on the applicant but this was not brought to the notice of the Divisional Court. The court delivered judgment on 23rd May and the applicant appealed to the Court of Appeal on grounds other than the alleged invalidity of the detention order issued in January 1978. The case is reported solely on the question of the validity of the detention order, although the Court of Appeal decision is appended as a note. The facts are set out in the judgment of Boreham J.

Sibghat Kadri for the applicant.
Michael Kennedy for the Secretary of State.

Cur adv vult

23rd May. The following judgments were read.

BOREHAM J (delivering the first judgment at the invitation of Lord Widgery CJ). Counsel moves on behalf of the applicant for a writ of habeas corpus directed to the governor of HM Prison, Winson Green, to secure the applicant's release.

The matter arises in this way. On 28th January 1978 the applicant was taken into custody as an illegal immigrant pursuant to the written authority of one of Her Majesty's immigration officers. The applicant's case is that he was born in Pakistan on 20th September 1950, the son of Ghulam Sarwar Khan, that he arrived with his father at Heathrow on 1st October 1964, having travelled from Pakistan on his father's passport, that he and his father were then granted unconditional leave to enter the United Kingdom and that, save for two visits to Pakistan, when he travelled on his own passport and on his

---

c   Rule 7 is set out at p 684 *d e*, post

return from which he was given leave to enter for an indefinite period, he has lived and

a worked in this country ever since. Entries in the passports confirm the granting of leave on three occasions. He contends that he is a lawful entrant.

For the Secretary of State it is contended that the applicant is not the person he pretends to be, that he is not the son of Ghulam Khan, that he did not enter the United Kingdom before 1969 or 1970 and that the documents produced by Ghulam Khan on 1st October 1964 do not relate to the applicant. He is therefore an illegal immigrant.

b The central issue therefore is one of identity and, therefore, one of fact.

Counsel has taken two points on the applicant's behalf: (1) that, although the written authority for the applicant's detention is valid in law on its face, it is invalid in fact; (2) that the applicant is the son of Ghulam Khan, that he entered the country lawfully in 1964 and was given unconditional leave to stay and is therefore entitled to remain.

In either event it is said that the applicant's detention is unlawful. It is convenient to

c deal with the second point first.

The applicant's evidence of his own identity and of the circumstances of his arrival in this country in 1964 is supported by the affidavits of Ghulam Khan (his alleged father) and of Arshad Mahmood and Shahid Mahmood Aktar, two of Ghulam Khan's sons. There is evidence by three other deponents, each of whom say that they recognise the photograph of the applicant as that of a youth who was resident in Birmingham prior to 1970. Prima

d facie this appears to constitute a powerful body of evidence.

The immigration authorities have made enquiries. They have interviewed, amongst others, the applicant and the deponents referred to above and the persons in whose house the applicant alleges that he lived for most of the period from December 1964 until 1969. These interviews have revealed discrepancies and lacunae which together suggest that the applicant is not the person he says he is and that he was not where he says he was

e prior to 1970. For instance, when first interviewed in November 1977 the applicant failed to include Arshad Mahmood as a member of Ghuam Khan's family; when this omission was pointed out to him he said that he had never heard of Arshad Mahmood. The applicant has been unable to produce any documentary evidence of his presence in the United Kingdom prior to 1970 and he lacked knowledge of the pre-decimal currency. When the persons with whom the applicant says he lived between 1964 and 1969 were

f interviewed, they were sure that no one by the name of Shahid Iqbal had lived at the address during that period. At a later interview one of them said that he had seen the applicant on two or three occasions between 1964 and 1969 and blamed his prior failure to recall the applicant on a faulty memory and the fact that he had been sleepy when interviewed.

The evidence of the three witnesses who purported to recognise the applicant's photo as

g that of a youth resident in Birmingham prior to 1970 was considered by the Secretary of State, who concluded that they were mistaken.

Counsel concedes that we cannot retry the questions of fact. He accepts that we must be guided by the principles laid down by the Court of Appeal in *R v Secretary of State for the Home Department, ex parte Hussain*[1]. Those principles are to be found in a short extract from the judgment of Geoffrey Lane LJ quoting with approval the approach laid down by

h Lord Widgery CJ[2] in the Divisional Court:

> 'Questions of fact in these matters are ultimately questions of fact for the Secretary of State. There are limits to the extent to which this court can go and, as I see it, our obligation at the moment is to be satisfied that the Home Office approach to the problem is one taken in good faith. Further, we have to decide whether there is or is not adequate evidence here to justify the sort of conclusion which the Secretary of
>
> *j* State has reached.'

In the present case there is nothing to impugn the good faith of the Secretary of State.

---

1 [1978] 2 All ER 423, [1978] 1 WLR 700
2 [1978] 2 All ER 423 at 426, [1978] 1 WLR 700 at 703

As to the merits, there was evidence both for and against the applicant. It was for the Secretary of State to weigh that evidence. He has done so. He has concluded that the applicant is not the son of Ghulam Khan and that he entered the country illegally. I think there was ample evidence to justify those conclusions. Counsel for the applicant's second point fails.

His first point has more substance; it is that the written authority by virtue of which the applicant is detained is invalid.

The document in question is in standard form. It is headed 'Immigration Act 1971' and stamped thereunder 'Detention Order'. It purports to have been issued, as doubtless it was, for HM Immigration Office, Birmingham Airport. Below this, in the space provided for the purpose, is entered the applicant's name. It continues: 'The above-named is a person whose detention I have authorised under paragraph 16 of Schedule 2 to the Immigration Act 1971. I accordingly request you to receive the said person', and then follow two alternatives. The first: 'pending his further examination under the Act'; both counsel accept that this would be appropriate for detention ordered under para 16(1). The second: 'pending the completion of arrangements for dealing with him under the Act'; it is agreed that this would be appropriate for detention under para 16(2).

Each alternative is marked with an asterisk denoting that it should be deleted as appropriate. On the order in question the immigration officer has deleted the second alternative.

There are other matters in the order which are irrelevant for present purposes. After signature by the immigration officer the order is addressed to the governor of Her Majesty's Prison at Winson Green.

Counsel for the applicant conceded that the order is apparently complete and valid in law on its face. At one time this would have been conclusive against him. By the Habeas Corpus Act 1816 the court was given specific power in a civil matter to enquire into the facts. The material part of s 3 provides:

'In all cases provided for by this Act, although the return to any writ of habeas corpus shall be good and sufficient in law, it shall be lawful for the justice or baron, before whom such writ may be returnable, to proceed to examine into the truth of the facts set forth in *such a return* by affidavit or by affirmation . . .' (Emphasis mine.)

Section 4 further provides:

'The like proceedings may be had in the court for controverting the truth of the return to any such writ of habeas corpus awarded as aforesaid, although such writ shall be awarded by the said court itself, or be returnable therein.'

Our duty therefore is to enquire into the truth of the facts set out in the return of which the important part is the detention order.

In this case the enquiry has been brief, for counsel for the Secretary of State concedes that at the time the detention order was made the examination of the applicant was complete and it was no longer lawful to detain him 'pending his further examination under the Act'. It would however have been lawful to detain him 'pending the completion of arrangements to deal with him under the Act'. In other words the immigration officer had deleted what were the appropriate words and had allowed the inappropriate to remain.

Counsel for the applicant contends that that concludes the matter in the applicant's favour. He says, look at it how you will, there are two alternatives. Either: (a) the immigration officer had no power to make the order he did and therefore the order was invalid and the detention unlawful; or (b) in any event, the examination having been completed, there cannot be any right now to detain 'pending further examination under the Act'.

The reply of counsel for the Secretary of State is that: (i) the detention order was and is valid. It is expressed to be made under the provisions of para 16 of Sch 2 to the 1971 Act. So it is. The contention is that this is sufficient to validate the order that no complaint could have been made if the order had stopped with the words 'I accordingly request you

to receive the said person'; and that what follows in the order is unnecessary and should be
a disregarded; (ii) if the first argument is unacceptable, nevertheless the detention is lawful,
notwithstanding the defective order, because the true and valid reason for the detention is
to be found in the affidavit showing cause.

Neither counsel has referred the court to any authority on what is an interesting, but not
easy, problem. Nor am I aware of any authority.

I doubt whether there is any real basis for the Secretary of State's arguments as to the
b validity of the detention order. RSC Ord 54, r 7, requires the return to state all the causes
of the detainer of the person restrained. The detention order is the essential part of the
return and I doubt if an order, which simply states that detention was authorised under
para 16 of Sch 2 to the 1971 Act, without giving further particulars justifying such
detention, could be said to comply with the rule.

But even assuming that a detention order in such general terms would suffice, the
c question remains whether, if particulars are given which fail to justify the detention, they
can now be disregarded as unnecessary. I think not, and for a number of reasons.

First, in accordance with the provisions of s 3 of the Habeas Corpus Act 1816, the court
may, and I think should, examine the facts set out in the return.

Secondly, and apart from the statute, there is authority for the propositions that in
habeas corpus proceedings the court may examine any grounds given for the detention,
d notwithstanding that it was unnecessary to give them. In the *Middlesex Sheriff's Case*[1] the
important question was whether in habeas corpus proceedings a warrant directed by the
speaker of the House of Commons to the serjeant-at-arms committing the sheriff for
contempt of the House was bad because it omitted to state the grounds on which contempt
had been found. In his judgment Littledale J[2], in a passage quoted with approval by Lord
Maugham in *Greene v Secretary of State for Home Affairs*[3], said this: 'If the warrant declares
e the grounds of adjudication, this court, in many cases, will examine into their validity; but,
if it does not, we cannot go into such an inquiry.'

Finally, I find helpful and adopt the approach stated by Professor de Smith in The
Judicial Review of Administrative Action[4]:

> 'A ... distinction is drawn between superior and inferior courts. A superior court
> and a body such as the House of Commons which is analogous to a superior court, can
> *f* validly commit under a warrant which does not set out the facts giving it jurisdiction;
> though if it does set out the facts and they disclose lack of any legal justification for
> commitment habeas corpus may properly issue. Inferior courts ought to recite the
> facts giving them jurisdiction to commit.'

I would add that what applies to inferior courts should apply a fortiori to executive
g officers.

Professor de Smith compares the approach in habeas corpus proceedings with the
approach of this court in proceedings for certiorari to quash a speaking order. If the order
states no ground or justification and is complete and valid on its face it may not be
impugned. If however a ground or justification is given, albeit unnecessarily, which fails
to justify the order, then the order may be quashed. I find this an acceptable and helpful
h analogy.

Applying these principles to the present case it seems to me clear that the words in the
detention order 'pending his further examination under the Act' were intended to justify
the applicant's detention under para 16 of Sch 2. Even if the argument that they were
unnecessary is correct, their validity should be and has been examined. It is admitted that
they did not justify the detention. They purported to be the sole justification. Thus it
j follows that the applicant's detention was not justified by the terms of the order which

---

1   (1840) 11 Ad & El 273, 113 ER 419
2   11 Ad & El 273 at 293, 113 ER 419 at 426
3   [1941] 3 All ER 388 at 394, [1942] AC 284 at 295
4   3rd Edn (1973), p 525

purported to authorise it. This is no mere technicality. The order is one which has deprived the applicant of his liberty. It is the authority under which he has been detained. It is the prison governor's sole authority for detaining him. It appears to be valid on its face, but when the facts are examined it is shown that what purports to be the sole justification for the detention cannot be sustained. I think this is a fundamental error which invalidates the detention order.

It remains to consider counsel's second point for the Secretary of State, namely that notwithstanding the defective or invalid detention order the applicant's detention is lawful because there was in fact a valid justification for it as is shown by the affidavit showing cause. That there was in fact a valid justification is not disputed. Nevertheless, I find the argument unattractive. If it is correct it reduces the detention order to the level of a 'mere scrap of paper'. That however does not necessarily dispose of the argument.

The question is this: can an admittedly valid justification now be relied on in substitution for the invalid justification in the detention order?

In the absence of direct authority there comes to mind the analogous situation of the constable exercising his powers of arrest without warrant. It is now well settled that a constable must not only act within his legal powers, he must also make known to the person detained the reason or justification for the arrest. If he gives a reason which is invalid he cannot justify the arrest by the fact that he had a valid reason which he kept to himself (*Christie v Leachinsky*[1]).

I find this sort of approach acceptable in the case of an executive officer ordering the detention of an individual; perhaps even more acceptable because he, unlike the constable, may order detention for a substantial period without the intervention of any judicial authority.

Moreover, I can think of no good reason for allowing an executive officer to order the detention of an individual unless the true and lawful justification for the detention is stated in the detention order. It seems no more reasonable to allow one, who has given an invalid justification in the detention order, to justify the detention by asserting, albeit that he asserts truly, that he had a valid justification which was not disclosed. So far as I am aware, there is no authority which impels or even encourages such an approach. Indeed such authority as I have discovered tends to the contrary. In *Christie v Leachinsky*[2] Lord Simonds expressed himself thus:

'... the liberty of the subject and the convenience of the police or any other executive authority are not to be weighed in the scales against each other. This case will have served a useful purpose if it enables your Lordships once more to proclaim that a man is not to be deprived of his liberty except in due course and process of law.'

Bearing in mind the facts and issues in that case, I take those final words to mean that not only must the detention be justified in law but the proper procedures must be followed. One of the proper procedures in that case was for the constable to inform the detainee of the true and valid reason for his arrest. It had not been done. In my view one of the proper procedures in the present case was the making of a true and valid detention order. This has not been done.

I have come to the conclusion that the Secretary of State should not now be allowed to rely on a justification for the applicant's detention which is different from that which was relied on in the detention order and in the return. It is said that the true justification for the applicant's detention now appears from the affidavit showing cause and so it does. No doubt the affidavit proves the foundation or basis on which the detention order rests. It certainly explains the circumstances in which the detention order came to be made. But to allow it to be used as counsel for the Secretary of State now suggests is to substitute it for the detention order. This, in my judgment, goes too far. It is the detention order which is the prison governor's authority to detain the applicant and which is his sole justification

1 [1947] 1 All ER 567, [1947] AC 573
2 [1947] 1 All ER 567 at 576, [1947] AC 573 at 595

for that detention in his return in these proceedings. It seems to me that a true and valid
a detention order is essential if the detention is to be justified.

I am encouraged in this strict approach by the provisions made by the Rules of the
Supreme Court for the amendment and substitution of the return. RSC Ord 54, r 7(2),
provides: 'The return may be amended, or another return substituted therefor, by leave of
the Court or judge before whom the writ is returnable.'

I see no reason why a fresh and valid detention order should not have been served on the
b prison governor and application then made to substitute a fresh return. In fact no fresh
order has been served and no application has been made to amend the return or substitute
another. The proper procedures have not been followed and no attempt has been made to
put right that which it is admitted is wrong.

In these circumstances it ought not to avail the Secretary of State to say that a valid
detention order could have been drawn up, that there is a valid justification for such an
c order and thus no injustice has been done. If the detention order could have been put right
it should have been put right. The applicant should not remain in custody unless it be
under the authority of a valid detention order. In my judgment, for the reasons I have
attempted to give, the detention order is not valid.

Accordingly I would grant the relief which the applicant now seeks.

d **DRAKE J.** This is a motion on behalf of one Shahid Iqbal for a writ of habeas corpus to
release from Her Majesty's Prison at Winson Green the applicant who is at present detained
there. The authority for the applicant's detention there is said to be para 16 of Sch 2 to the
Immigration Act 1971; but a complication arises, as I shall explain later, because the
authority was originally stated to arise under para 16(1), whereas it should have been
claimed that it arises under para 16(2) of Sch 2.

e Counsel, who moves on behalf of the applicant, relies on two separate grounds in
support of the application.

The first ground relates to the complication I have just referred to, in that there was an
error in the document issued by an immigration officer under the authority of which the
applicant was detained by the governor of Her Majesty's Prison at Winson Green.

The second ground alleges that the applicant was not validly detained because an
f examination of the facts shows that the applicant is entitled to enter and remain in the
United Kingdom.

I think it convenient to deal first with this second ground, which requires a review of the
facts of this particular case, and which is a ground very commonly relied on by applicants
in proceedings similar to these.

The principles on which this court deals with applications such as this, when it is alleged
g that the facts do not support the conclusion reached by the Secretary of State for the Home
Department, are clearly laid down in *R v Secretary of State for the Home Department, ex parte
Hussain*[1]. In that case the Court of Appeal approved as correct the approach which had been
formulated by Lord Widgery CJ in the same case when it was before this court, when he
said[2]:

h 'Questions of fact in these matters are ultimately questions of fact for the Secretary
of State. There are limits to the extent to which this court can go and, as I see it, our
obligation at the moment is to be satisfied that the Home Office approach to the
problem is one taken in good faith. Further, we have to decide whether there is or is
not adequate evidence here to justify the sort of conclusion which the Secretary of
State has reached.'

j In the present case I am quite satisfied that there was ample evidence on which the
Secretary of State could properly reach the decision he came to, and no suggestion has been
made that he acted other than in good faith.

---

1   [1978] 2 All ER 423, [1978] 1 WLR 700
2   [1978] 2 All ER 423 at 426, [1978] 1 WLR 700 at 703

The applicant contends that he is the son of one Ghulam Sarwar Khan ('Mr Khan') and that he is entitled to enter and remain in the United Kingdom as a member of Mr Khan's family. The Secretary of State has refused the applicant permission to stay here and has denied his right to stay here on the ground that he has been guilty of deception and is not in fact the son of Mr Khan.

The applicant relies on a number of affidavits filed on his behalf and sworn by various people who in one way or another support his case. But enquiries carried out on behalf of the Home Office, including oral examination of the applicant and of Mr Khan and others by immigration officers, have revealed important flaws in the applicant's case.

He says he was born in Pakistan and first came to this country, accompanying his father, Mr Khan, in October 1964. He says that he lived and had casual employment in this country from 1964 until 1973 when he returned to Pakistan on holiday and became engaged to be married. He says he returned to England in November 1973 and remained here until November 1974 when he went back to Pakistan and was married; and that he finally came back here on 1st May 1975 and thereafter lived and worked in the Birmingham area until January 1978 when he was detained by immigration officers.

When he was first interviewed by an immigration officer he failed to mention the existence of one Arshad Mahmood, a son of Mr Khan, and therefore, if his own story is correct, one of his brothers. Furthermore when the immigration officer asked him if he knew Arshad Mahmood the applicant denied all knowledge of his existence.

The applicant told the immigration officer that he had no children, whereas Mr Khan had told the officer that the applicant did have one child. The applicant was unable to produce any documentary evidence whatsoever to support his claim that he had been in England prior to 1970, and he had no knowledge at all of the pre-decimal, pre-1971 English currency. When an immigration officer interviewed the man and wife with whom the applicant said he had lived for a period of about four years from 1966 until 1970, both of these people emphatically denied any knowledge of the applicant. They later explained that this denial was due to a misunderstanding, but this explanation did not convince the immigration officer.

For these and for other subsidiary reasons set out in an affidavit filed on behalf of the Secretary of State, I think there was ample evidence on which the Secretary of State could properly reach the decision he came to, namely that the applicant is not in truth the son of Mr Khan. Accordingly, in so far as the application is based on this ground, in my judgment it fails.

The remaining ground relied on by the applicant raises an interesting point of law and one which, so far as I am aware, is not directly covered by any decision of the court. We were not referred to any authorities by counsel on either side. As I have said, it relates to an error in the document under which the applicant has been detained in prison.

The document in question is a standard Home Office form used by immigration officers to authorise the detention of persons under the 1971 Act. It is headed 'H.O. Form IS 91', 'Immigration Act 1971' and is stamped 'Detention Order'. There is a space for the insertion of the name of the person to be detained in which, in this case, has been written the name of the applicant, and then follows the printed part of the form which reads: 'The above-named is a person whose detention I have authorised under paragraph 16 of Schedule 2 to the Immigration Act 1971.' Then follow the words: 'I accordingly request you to receive the said person', and then underneath are set out on separate lines what are clearly alternatives, firstly, 'pending his further examination under the Act', and, secondly 'pending the completion of arrangements for dealing with him under the Act'.

There is a further reference to the possible charging for the cost of detention and any escort, which is irrelevant to the present case, and then a space for a signature by and above the printed words 'Immigration Officer'.

The form ends with the wording: 'To the Chief Constable of', and a blank to be filled in, if appropriate, and the alternative 'To the Governor HM Prison', and a space, filled in, in this case 'Winson Green'.

The alternative wording requesting the person to whom the form is sent to receive the detainee, either 'pending his further examination under the Act' (which would be a detention under sub-para (1) of para 16 of Sch 2 to the Act) or 'pending the completion of arrangements dealing with him under the Act' (which would be a detention under sub-para (2) of para 16) are each accompanied by a request that they be deleted as appropriate.

In the present case the immigration officer deleted the second of these alternatives and left in the first one, 'pending his further examination under the Act'.

We do not know why he did this, but it was conceded at the outset of this hearing that the deletion was in error. The examination of the applicant had in fact been completed, and the immigration officer intended to request his detention 'pending the completion of arrangements for dealing with him under the Act', that is to say under the provisions of para 16(2).

It is certainly arguable that the alternative wording on the Home Office form is surplusage, in that it would suffice for the immigration officer to authorise detention simply 'under paragraph 16 of Schedule 2' to the 1971 Act, without condescending to the particulars of whether such detention is authorised under para 16(1) or para 16(2). I am not wholly convinced that this is correct having regard to the requirement under RSC Ord 54, r 7, that the return to a writ of habeas corpus ad subjiciendum '. . . must state all the causes of the detainer of the person restrained'. If in fact the return would be valid if it merely stated that the detention was authorised under para 16 of Sch 2, it would lend some weight to the further argument that an error in the further particulars, unnecessarily given, cannot be regarded as being as serious as a failure to state the *main* provision under which the applicant was detained.

Be that as it may, the document with which we are concerned did state the particular sub-paragraph under which the applicant was detained and it has been argued on his behalf that that error in the document vitiates it to the extent that the detention, whilst it could have been justified 'pending the completion of arrangements for dealing with' the applicant, is unlawful and that habeas corpus should therefore be granted to the applicant as of right.

For the Secretary of State it is said, as I understand the argument of counsel, that the document does properly state the reason for the applicant's detention, as being under para 16 of Sch 2 to the 1971 Act; and that the error of the immigration officer in deleting the wrong wording, which in effect gives further particulars of the reason for detention, does not render the whole document a nullity, and that provided the court is satisfied that the applicant was in fact detained on good grounds the detailed wording of the document is not material.

If I have properly understood the argument of counsel on behalf of the Secretary of State, then I am far from happy with such an approach. The document, which is relied on as the return to this application, is the authority under which a man has been deprived of his liberty; and it ought to be regarded as of very great importance and should be completed with care. If, as may be inevitable, some mistake is at some time made in the completion of such a document, then when the error is discovered it should be rectified immediately, or a fresh document, properly compiled, issued in its stead. That has not been done in this case and I think the omission unfortunate and wrong.

But it does not in my view conclude the matter against the Secretary of State; and leaves open the question which may be stated thus: 'When the person having custody of an applicant produces, as the justification for his detention, a document which, though valid on its face, is subsequently found to contain some material error, is the court entitled to enquire further to determine whether there were in fact good grounds on which the applicant was detained, or is the applicant entitled as of right to be released on the ground of the defect in the document which authorised his detention?'

Long ago the return to the writ of habeas corpus was all important. It was the beginning and the ending of the matter, and the court acted solely on the reasons for detention stated on the face of the return. If the reason shown was bad the person detained was entitled to be released; if the reason was good he was not entitled to habeas corpus, although it may have been open to him to pursue some other remedy, such as certiorari, under which the court would go behind the return and enquire into the evidence on which the detention was said to be justified.

But since the Habeas Corpus Act 1816 the court is empowered to enquire into the truth of the facts stated in the return. Indeed that is precisely the procedure relied on by applicants in the majority of applications which come before this court; and it is under that procedure that the applicant in the present case has sought to persuade this court to hold that, irrespective of what is stated on the return, there was in fact no sufficient evidence on which the Secretary of State should have reached his conclusion as to the true identity of the applicant.

Since the court is empowered to go behind the mere wording on the face of the return and enquire into the true facts, why should it not do so if and when, as in the present case, it is discovered that some mistake has been made in the wording of the document? In my judgment, the overriding function of the court is to see that no injustice is done to the person detained; and in order to see that justice is done the court should enquire into the true facts and not be hampered by the wording of the return.

I think it can be said that this is a situation in which the court should look to the substance rather than to the form, subject always to the overriding consideration that justice should be done.

I am strengthened in this view by the provisions of RSC Ord 54, r 7, which expressly provides as follows:

'(1) The return to a writ of habeas corpus ad subjiciendum must be indorsed on or annexed to the writ and must state all the causes of the detainer of the person restrained.
'(2) The return may be amended, or another return substituted therefor, by leave of the Court or judge before whom the writ is returnable.'

Since the return may be amended, or another return substituted by leave of the court, it does not seem to me to be right to hold that the court is bound to regard a return as bad when, as in the present case, the enquiry into the facts has shown, as in my judgment is the case, that the immigration officer did have valid grounds on which to authorise the detention of the applicant. Had the error been in some way prejudicial to the applicant, for example, by misleading him and causing him to take some step or omit to take some step by which his position or the presentation of his case to remain in this country had been harmed, then I think different considerations would arise. In the present case no such prejudice to the applicant has been suggested, and in my judgment no injustice is done to him by this court declining to grant his application on the ground of the error made when the immigration officer signed the authorisation for his detention.

I would therefore dismiss this application.

LORD WIDGERY CJ. I also would dismiss this application for the reasons just given by Drake J. The court has been required to examine the facts behind the return and this discloses a lawful power of detention under para 16 of Sch 2 to the Immigration Act 1971. I cannot see any difference in the nature and effect of the detention, according to whether it occurs after the completion of immigration enquiries or before such enquiries are concluded. Even where the liberty of the subject is involved, the court should strive not to be hamstrung by pointless technicalities.

Application dismissed.

Solicitors: *Sharpe, Pritchard & Co*, agents for *Taylor Hall-Wright & Co*, Birmingham (for the applicant); *Treasury Solicitor*.

Lea Josse Barrister.

Note

20th December. The following judgments in the Court of Appeal were delivered.

ROSKILL LJ (delivering the first judgment at the invitation of Megaw LJ). This is an appeal from an order of the Divisional Court on 23rd May 1978, dismissing an application made by counsel on behalf of the appellant, Shahid Iqbal, for a writ of habeas corpus. The appeal comes before this court in unusual circumstances. The appellant in this court, the applicant in the Divisional Court, was detained by the order of an immigration officer acting on behalf of the Secretary of State for the Home Department dated 28th January 1978. That order had been made on a common form printed form. After setting out the name of the applicant the subject of the detention order, it reads thus: 'The above-named is a person whose detention I have authorised under paragraph 16 of Schedule 2 to the Immigration Act 1971. I accordingly request you to receive the said person.' Then follow three alternatives, each of which has an asterisk; and at the bottom it says 'Delete as appropriate'. The first is: 'pending his further examination under the Act'; the second is, 'pending the completion of arrangements for dealing with him under the Act'; and the third is, 'The cost of detention and any escort should be charged to [blank]'.

The immigration officer, in filling up that form, by a regrettable mistake struck out the last two of those alternatives but left in the first, which was, of course, factually wrong, since the examination in question had already been completed. That was the ground on which application was made to the Divisional Court after leave to move had been given. When the matter came before the Divisional Court there was a difference of view, and that difference is reflected in the reserved judgments given on 23rd May 1978, Lord Widgery CJ and Drake J taking one view, in favour of the Secretary of State, and accepting the argument advanced on his behalf that this error did not vitiate the order. Boreham J, in a dissenting judgment, would have decided the matter in favour of the applicant and given leave for the issue of the writ.

It happened, though the Divisional Court seems not to have been told of this until after the reserved judgments were given, that on the very day the argument took place, and no doubt in order to prevent any further argument, a fresh detention order was made. This was properly made out on a similar form and signed by the immigration officer. It reads thus:

> 'The above-named is a person whose detention I have authorised under paragraph 16 of Schedule 2 to the Immigration Act 1971. I accordingly request you to receive the said person ... pending the completion of arrangements for dealing with him under the Act. The cost of detention and any escort should be charged to Home Office.'

The alternative 'pending his further examination under the Act' was this time properly struck through. As I have said, that document was not before the Divisional Court.

When this appeal was called on counsel for the Secretary of State sought leave to put in a fresh affidavit, from the deputy governor of Winson Green prison, exhibiting that further order. He also sought leave to amend the return to the writ, as there is power in the court to allow under RSC Ord 54, r 7(2). As to the latter of those two applications counsel for the applicant, for whose argument I am grateful, objected on the ground that the effect of granting that leave would be to amend the return retrospectively and that might adversely effect the legal rights of the applicant in relation to a possible claim for false imprisonment. I express no view whether that is right or wrong, but it is a possible view, and, being a possible view, we ought not to allow something which might retrospectively adversely affect rights of that kind. Faced with that objection, counsel for the Secretary of State withdrew that part of his application. But counsel for the applicant for his part did not object to our receiving the affidavit; and that we have done. It is, therefore, perfectly clear that, even if the appeal succeeded and counsel for the applicant were able to satisfy us that Boreham J were right and the Lord Widgery CJ and Drake J were wrong, a writ of habeas corpus could not properly issue because there is now in force, and has been in force since 24th April, a perfectly valid order detaining this applicant in Winson Green prison, where he still is.

Faced with that, counsel for the applicant, very properly if I may say so, said that he could not argue the first of the two grounds in his notice of appeal, which was that Boreham J's dissenting judgment was right. He had two further grounds of appeal, though they cover the same point. They raise the question of onus of proof. Counsel for the applicant frankly told us that his purpose in raising those grounds in this court was in the hope that we might be persuaded to give leave to go to the House of Lords, so that the House of Lords might consider the correctness or otherwise of two recent decisions of this court: *R v Secretary of State for the Home Department, ex parte Hussain*[1] and *R v Secretary of State for the Home Department, ex parte Choudhary*[2]. Counsel for the applicant conceded, rightly in my view, that he could not argue this point in this court. He advanced this ingenious argument, to which I hope I do no injustice by putting it in this way. He said that it may be that where there is a question whether or not someone who first comes into the country lawfully as a visitor, goes out again, and then returns and makes a false statement to the immigration officer, the burden of proof will be on the applicant to show that the Secretary of State's order was unlawful. But, he argued, where there is, as here, what he called a disputed identity case, the onus is or at least should be the other way round and it should be for the Secretary of State to justify the making of his order by showing that the person against whom the order is made is not the person whom the detainee claims to be. That point, as I have said, is not open for argument in this court. On any view it seems to me that counsel for the applicant might be in difficulty because in these proceedings he cannot assail the order of 24th April. But he contended that if he were allowed to take this matter further, the Secretary of State might then be willing to withdraw the order of 24th April on the hypothesis that it had been made placing the onus of proof the wrong way round. It seems to me that in this case it is impossible for us to do anything other than to dismiss this appeal.

BROWNE LJ. I agree.

MEGAW LJ. I also agree.

Appeal dismissed. Leave to appeal to House of Lords refused.

---

1 [1978] 2 All ER 423, [1978] 1 WLR 700
2 [1978] 3 All ER 790, [1978] 1 WLR 1177

R v Secretary of State for the Home Department, ex parte Ram

QUEEN'S BENCH DIVISION

LORD WIDGERY CJ, MAY AND TUDOR EVANS JJ

27th JULY 1978

Immigration – Detention – Illegal entrant – Entry in breach of immigration laws – Immigration officer mistakenly giving entrant leave to enter and stay indefinitely – Passport so stamped – Entrant not obtaining leave by fraud or misrepresentation – Entrant subsequently detained as illegal entrant – Whether entrant entitled to rely on stamp in passport – Whether immigration officer acting within his authority in giving indefinite leave to person not entitled to such leave – Immigration Act 1971, s 4.

The applicant arrived in the United Kingdom on an Indian passport on 27th February 1977. At the airport he was given leave by the immigration officer to enter and remain for an indefinite period and his passport was stamped to that effect. The immigration officer had power under s 4[a] of the Immigration Act 1971 'to give or refuse leave to enter the United Kingdom'. The officer was, however, mistaken in thinking that the applicant was entitled to indefinite leave to remain and in stamping the applicant's passport as he did. On 16th July 1978 the applicant was detained as an illegal immigrant. He applied for a writ of habeas corpus contending that, having regard to the stamp on his passport, he was a legal entrant. It was contended on behalf of the Secretary of State that, although the indefinite leave to enter and remain had been given to the applicant by mistake and not through any fraud or misrepresentation, nevertheless the immigration officer had no authority to stamp the passport as he did and therefore the applicant was an illegal immigrant.

Held – When giving the applicant indefinite leave to remain and stamping his passport to that effect the immigration officer had been acting within his powers under s 4 of the 1971 Act and in the absence of any fraud or dishonesty on the part of the applicant it could not be said that the immigration officer had no authority to act as he had. Since there were therefore no reasonable grounds on which the Secretary of State could have decided that the applicant was in the United Kingdom illegally, the applicant was entitled to a writ of habeas corpus (see p 692 b to h and p 693 c d, post).

Dictum of Geoffrey Lane LJ in *R v Secretary of State for the Home Department, ex parte Hussain* [1978] 2 All ER at 429 applied.

R v Secretary of State for the Home Department, ex parte Choudhary [1978] 3 All ER 790 distinguished.

Notes

For illegal entry into the United Kingdom, see 4 Halsbury's Laws (4th Edn) paras 976, 1027.

For powers of the Secretary of State and immigration officers, see ibid paras 1003–1010.

For the Immigration Act 1971, s 4, see 41 Halsbury's Statutes (3rd Edn) 22.

Cases referred to in judgments

R v Secretary of State for the Home Department, ex parte Badaike [1977] The Times 4th May, DC.

R v Secretary of State for the Home Department, ex parte Choudhary [1978] 3 All ER 790, [1978] 1 WLR 1177, CA.

---

[a]   Section 4, so far as material, is set out at p 689 j, post

R v Secretary of State for the Home Department, ex parte Hussain [1978] 2 All ER 423, [1978] 1 WLR 700, DC and CA.

R v Secretary of State for the Home Department, ex parte Nasir Ali [1978] Court of Appeal Transcript 421, CA.

Motion

The applicant, Tirath Ram, applied for an order directing the issue of a writ of habeas corpus ad subjiciendum to the Secretary of State for the Home Department to instruct the governor of H M Prison, Winson Green, Birmingham, to release the applicant from his detention pursuant to an order of an immigration officer issued under para 16(2) of Sch 2 to the Immigration Act 1971. The facts are set out in the judgment of May J.

Alan Campbell QC and *G Yazdani* for the applicant.
Robert Owen for the Secretary of State.

MAY J delivered the first judgment at the invitation of Lord Widgery CJ. In these proceedings counsel moves on behalf of one Tirath Ram, at present in custody in Winson Green prison in Birmingham, for the issue of a writ of habeas corpus directed to the immigration officer at Birmingham Airport and to the governor of the prison to release the applicant from detention. The grounds on which the applicant seeks this relief are, in brief, that he has leave to enter and remain in the United Kingdom. This is an unusual case and similar facts have not arisen in any previous decided case.

The applicant is a citizen of the Republic of India, and was born in October 1942. He first came to the United Kingdom on 1st September 1970, having been issued with the appropriate visa by the entry certificate officer at Delhi.

Between then and 1974 the applicant was in the United Kingdom either anticipating working in the Indian High Commission or as an appellant to the Home Office for permission to remain for various purposes in this country. Ultimately, on 26th January 1974 he left the United Kingdom for Canada.

On 1st November 1974 he came back to Heathrow Airport from Canada and, in so far as the evidence before this court is concerned, tendered his Indian passport openly and without any misrepresentation to the immigration officer on duty at Heathrow. The latter asked him various questions and then stamped the applicant's passport with the stamp that can be seen on the copy of the passport, which is one of the documents before the court, to the effect that the applicant was given leave to enter the United Kingdom for an indefinite period.

On that occasion the applicant told the immigration officer that he was returning to the United Kingdom to attend a wedding. In those circumstances, in so far as the general immigration provisions are concerned, and particularly the Rules for Control on Entry[1], the category, if categories strictly there be, of entrant under which the applicant then fell would have been that of visitor. As such, in the normal course, he would have been granted leave to enter not for the indefinite period stated in the stamp in the passport, but for a limited period to cover the purpose of his visit.

Counsel on the applicant's behalf, I think, accepts that the fact that his client's passport was then stamped with leave to enter for an indefinite period was a genuine mistake on the part of the relevant immigration officer, a mistake however in no way induced by any fraud or dishonesty on the part of the applicant.

Having entered in November 1974 in that way, a fortnight later the applicant left England for Canada. He has since returned on three separate occasions: on 31st July 1976, on 26th November 1976 and ultimately on 27th February 1977. When seeking entry in February 1977, the applicant again openly and without any misrepresentation presented

---

1 Statement of Immigration Rules for Control on Entry: Commonwealth Citizens (H of C Paper (1972–73) No 79)

his passport to the immigration officer, and, as one can see, on this occasion from the stamp in his passport, he was again given leave to enter the United Kingdom and remain here for an indefinite period.

In order to get one matter out of the way at the start, it is, I think, well settled that when this applicant left the United Kingdom on 14th November 1974 the leave to enter that he had been given on the 1st of that month lapsed, and he was not thereafter entitled to rely on it. Accordingly, if and in so far as he is legally within the United Kingdom at the present time, he must rely, and does rely, on the leave which was given to him on 22nd February 1977.

Again, as with the leave given in 1974, counsel for the applicant accepts that the 1977 leave was also given to him for an indefinite period by a genuine and honest mistake on the part of the relevant immigration officer, but once more there is no evidence before this court that that leave was obtained by this applicant by any fraud or other dishonesty.

In the course of the years the applicant has invested in a business in Smethwick in the West Midlands, and it seems that between February 1977 and 16th June 1978 he was principally attending to that business, considering himself lawfully in the United Kingdom pursuant to the leave stamped in his passport to which I have referred.

On 16th June 1978, however, two immigration officers called at his home and asked him to accompany them to Birmingham Airport; he was there interviewed and consequently transferred to Winson Green prison where, as I have indicated, he now is.

It is in those circumstances, and relying on the leave stamped in his passport, that this applicant contends that his detention is unlawful and that he should have the relief for which he asks. As I have said, this is the first case in which facts of this kind have occurred, and indeed cases such as the present case are likely to be very infrequent. The mistakes which I have outlined, as such they were on the evidence presently before the court, occur only very rarely indeed. Be that as it may, it is appropriate, first, to outline the statutory provisions regulating the immigration of persons such as the applicant.

He is not patrial and consequently must obtain leave to enter the United Kingdom pursuant to the provisions of s 1(2) of the Immigration Act 1971. That provides:

'Those not having that right may live, work and settle in the United Kingdom by permission and subject to such regulation and control of their entry into, stay in and departure from the United Kingdom as is imposed by this Act . . .'

By s 3 of the 1971 Act in sub-s (1) it is provided:

'Except as otherwise provided by or under this Act, where a person is not patrial—(a) he shall not enter the United Kingdom unless given leave to do so in accordance with this Act; (b) he may be given leave to enter the United Kingdom (or, when already there, leave to remain in the United Kingdom) either for a limited or for an indefinite period . . .'

Then sub-s (2) of s 3 provides:

'The Secretary of State shall from time to time (and as soon as may be) lay before Parliament statements of the rules, or of any changes in the rules, laid down as to the practice to be followed in the administration of this Act for regulating the entry into and stay in the United Kingdom of persons required by this Act to have leave to enter . . .'

It is pursuant to that provision that the Statement of Immigration Rules for Control on Entry: Commonwealth Citizens has been made by the Secretary of State.

Then s 4 of the 1971 Act provides:

'(1) The power under this Act to give or refuse leave to enter the United Kingdom shall be exercised by immigration officers, and the power to give leave to remain in the United Kingdom, or to vary any leave under section 3(3)(a) (whether as regards duration or conditions), shall be exercised by the Secretary of State . . .'

Then in s 33(1) of the 1971 Act an 'entrant' is defined as meaning—

'. . . a person entering or seeking to enter the United Kingdom, and "illegal entrant" means a person unlawfully entering or seeking to enter in breach of a deportation order or of the immigration laws, and includes also a person who has so entered.'

I then turn to the relevant rules to which I have just referred. Paragraph 7 provides: 'Leave to enter will normally be given for a limited period.' The provisions with regard to visitors are in Part II. The subsequent rules deal with different categories of potential entrants into the United Kingdom. Ultimately para 55 is in these terms:

'A passenger who does not qualify for admission under the foregoing provisions of these rules is to be refused leave to enter. In addition, the Immigration Officer has power (subject to the restrictions contained in the next paragraph) to refuse leave to enter on any of the grounds set out in *paragraphs 59–63* below.'

Returning to the 1971 Act itself and to Sch 2, the power to detain is given by para 16. It is not contended that the power to detain this applicant is exercisable under para 16(1) of Sch 2, but it is contended that that power is exercisable under sub-para (2), which reads:

'A person in respect of whom directions may be given under any of paragraphs 8 to 14 above may be detained under the authority of an immigration officer pending the giving of directions and pending his removal in pursuance of any directions given.'

If one turns to paras 8 to 10 inclusive, which are the only relevant rules in so far as the present case is concerned, briefly one can see that directions may be given, and thus under para 16(2) detention may be made only in respect of a person who is an illegal entrant. Thus crystallised is the issue, as I see it, in the present case.

Counsel on the applicant's behalf contends that he is a legal entrant, an entrant with leave having regard to the stamp on his passport.

On behalf of the Secretary of State it is contended that this applicant is an illegal entrant, and it is so contended on this basis. Unless an entrant can first bring himself within one of the categories of potential entrant within the immigration rules, and unless the length of the leave which is then given to that category of entrant is that normally contemplated by the relevant rule for that category, then the immigration officer, even in the absence of any fraud or dishonesty on the part of the entrant, has, it is submitted, no authority to stamp a passport otherwise than in accordance with that category and with the duration of leave normally appropriate to it. Consequently, mistake though it was, though induced by no dishonesty, the stamp in the passport was thus put there by the immigration officer without authority and gave the applicant in the present case no leave to enter. He is, consequently, an illegal entrant and is thus subject to detention and directions for removal under paras 16 and 8 to 10 inclusive of Sch 2 to the 1971 Act.

Counsel seeks to support this contention on behalf of the Secretary of State by reference to two decisions of the Court of Appeal earlier this year, the first is *R v Secretary of State for the Home Department, ex parte Choudhary*[1] and the second is *R v Secretary of State for the Home Department, ex parte Nasir Ali*[2], each of them immigration cases such as the present.

In order to illustrate and, as counsel for the Secretary of State submits, substantiate the contention put forward, I need only refer to a brief passage from *Choudhary's case*[3] where Lord Denning MR said:

'Mr Choudhary was clearly an illegal entrant. When he came back in 1973 he was an illegal entrant. He was not settled here. The immigration officer had no authority to stamp on his passport the words "Indefinite leave to enter" as he did. That want of

---

1 [1978] 3 All ER 790, [1978] 1 WLR 1177
2 [1978] Court of Appeal Transcript 421
3 [1978] 3 All ER 790 at 793, [1978] 1 WLR 1177 at 1181

authority in the immigration officer is a complete answer to Mr Choudhary's claim.'

Similarly in *Nasir Ali's* case[1] Lord Denning MR again said this:

'A similar situation has been considered in at least two other cases: and it seems to me that it has been established (at least in this court) that, if the man is not lawfully settled here, the immigration officer has no authority to stamp the words "Indefinite leave to enter" on to the passport. So it is not necessary to go into what was said at the airport. If he was an illegal entrant, the immigration officer had no authority to stamp those words on.'

In my judgment, however, both those two cases are distinguishable from the present case because in each of them there was fraud, there were untruths told by the would-be entrant to the relevant immigration officers leading them to believe that each of the two in fact was a person entitled to return to settle within the United Kingdom. In *Choudhary's* case[2] it is apparent from the first page of the judgment that, having lost his passport which would have made the situation perfectly clear had it been presented to the immigration officer, and having obtained a new passport, the applicant must have given answers to the immigration officer which were untrue leading the latter to accept that he was entitled to re-enter and settle. It was in those circumstances that Lord Denning MR, as I think, held that the immigration officer had no authority so to stamp the passport.

Similarly, *Nasir Ali's* case[1], was that of a man who did not take advantage of what has been called the 1973 amnesty. When he was interviewed and interrogated on a subsequent occasion he again told untruths to the relevant authorities, and had no right to re-enter to settle as one of the categories under the immigration rules.

In the present case, however, as I have indicated, the applicant has been guilty of no fraud or dishonesty in so far as the evidence before this court is concerned. Counsel does not contend otherwise. The applicant relies solely on a mistake made by the immigration officer and on the leave consequently stamped in his passport.

To see where that takes one I refer also to another case which was decided in the Court of Appeal in fact three days after *Choudhary's* case[2], *R v Secretary of State for the Home Department, ex parte Hussain*[3]. It is from the judgment of Geoffrey Lane LJ in that case, and from a particular dictum in it, that in my experience the present approach of this court to applications such as this for orders of habeas corpus in respect of allegedly illegal entrants stems.

In that case the Court of Appeal had to consider not merely the decision of this court in *Hussain's* case[3], but also a slightly earlier case, *R v Secretary of State for the Home Department, ex parte Badaike*[4], in which the leading judgment was given by Peter Pain J.

In his judgment in *Hussain's* case[5], Geoffrey Lane LJ said in relation to this type of application:

'The true view, as I see it, is this. If, on the evidence taken as a whole, the Secretary of State has grounds, and reasonable grounds, for coming to the conclusion that the applicant is here illegally, in contravention of the terms of the 1971 Act, this court will not interfere. Put into the terms of the present case, was the indefinite permission given by the immigration officer at Dover in May 1974 a proper exercise of discretion by which the Secretary of State is bound, or was it a decision brought about by deception, misrepresentation or fraud of the applicant? If it was, then the applicant cannot rely on it and the Secretary of State was entitled to act as he did and this appeal would fail.'

1   [1978] Court of Appeal Transcript 421
2   [1978] 3 All ER 790, [1978] 1 WLR 1177
3   [1978] 2 All ER 423, [1978] 1 WLR 700
4   [1977] The Times, 4th May
5   [1978] 2 All ER 423 at 429, [1978] 1 WLR 700 at 707

Further, in *Badaike's* case[1], Lord Widgery CJ said: 'In my judgment, in the absence of any suggestion that the immigration officer was misled by the applicant, it suffices to shift the onus on him if he could prove those facts', that is to say, if he could prove that he was given proper leave to enter.

In my judgment, if one puts aside the four cases to which I have referred and seeks to apply the principle contained in the dictum of Geoffrey Lane LJ, the situation is this. Where the Secretary of State detains an allegedly illegal immigrant under the powers given to him by the 1971 Act, and that decision is challenged by the entrant, this court merely looks to see whether on the evidence taken as a whole a reasonable Secretary of State, acting on the information available to the court and to the Secretary of State, could have acted as he did in ordering the detention that he did. But I think it also follows from the judgments, particularly those in *Hussain's* case[2] and that of Lord Widgery CJ, in *Badaike's* case[1], that where the allegedly illegal immigrant does put forward an explanation of his entry into the country which is consistent with him being lawfully there, then the onus, if it be such, shifts, and one has to see what the overall situation is.

In my opinion the contention that an entrant can only be a lawful entrant if he comes within one of the categories in the immigration rules and if, further, he is only allowed in for the usual period appropriate to that type of entrant, but that if by a mistake the immigration officer gives leave to enter otherwise than within those categories, or for that period, then the immigration officer had no authority to do so, is a contention which, where an entrant is prima facie lawful and his entry is not induced by any fraud or dishonesty, goes too far and is one which, for my part, I am not prepared to accept.

As I have said, *Choudhary's* case[3] and *Nasir Ali's* case[4] were each cases in which the immigration officer was misled and thus had no authority to allow the particular entrant in as that particular type of entrant for that particular period. This case, on the evidence presently before the court, is, in my judgment, different. As I see this case on the facts which I have outlined and the law to which I have briefly referred , the power of granting or refusing leave to enter has to be exercised by immigration officers under s 4 of the 1971 Act. The leave that the applicant was given to enter on 27th February 1977 was given by an immigration officer, purporting to exercise the powers given to him under s 4 of that Act on the true facts of the case.

There is no evidence before the court other than that contained in the affidavits of the applicant, and consequently this is not a case in which, in my view, looking at the evidence taken as a whole the Secretary of State has any reasonable grounds for coming to the conclusion that this applicant is here illegally. He is here pursuant to a leave stamped in his passport, to the grant of which he contributed in no way by any fraud or dishonesty on his part. I do not think that it can be said that in the circumstances of the present case the immigration officer had no authority to put that stamp in the passport, or that in consequence the Secretary of State had any power under para 16(2) to detain or, under paras 8 to 10 of Sch 2, to give directions for the removal of this particular applicant.

In my judgment, for the reasons which I have sought to give, on the facts of the present case I would grant the relief sought.

TUDOR EVANS J. I agree and I have nothing to add.

LORD WIDGERY CJ. I have found this case a little more difficult than May and Tudor Evans JJ, and it is quite clear if one looks at the judgment in *Badaike's* case[1] that at that time

---

1   [1977] The Times, 4th May
2   [1978] 2 All ER 423, [1978] 1 WLR 700
3   [1978] 3 All ER 790, [1978] 1 WLR 1177
4   [1978] Court of Appeal Transcript 421

I took the view, expressed by May J, that a mere mistake on the part of the immigration officer could not give rise to a vitiation of the permission unless it was induced by fraud of some kind. I said in the last paragraph of my judgment:

'Of course it may be that the immigration officer was mistaken. It may be that he misread the passport or something in it. It may be he would not have given leave to enter if he had appreciated the true position. But I do not see why a mistake of that kind in the mind of the immigration officer, even if proved, would be fatal to the claim in this case.'

Since I gave that judgment there are two decisions of the Court of Appeal to which reference has been made which clearly contemplate the possibility that there is a new and further principle here, namely that if the immigration officer had no authority to grant the particular permission which was granted that vitiates the permission and renders the leave void.

I would like to wait for another day to consider in greater detail how that doctrine should be included in this fast developing branch of the law. But I am content to say that, despite some doubts, I do not wish to take a different form of view from May and Tudor Evans JJ, and I agree also that, subject to the other matters counsel for the Secretary of State wants to raise, the writ of habeas corpus should go in this case.

Writ of habeas corpus granted.

Solicitors: *Haynes Duffell, Arnold & Co*, Birmingham (for the applicant): *Treasury Solicitor*.

Lea Josse Barrister.

R v Rogers

SUPREME COURT TAXING OFFICE
MASTER MATTHEWS
28th APRIL, 23rd MAY 1978

Legal aid – Taxation of costs – Criminal proceedings – Crown Court – Work undertaken and disbursements incurred by solicitor prior to assignment to client under legal aid order – Claim by solicitor for payment in respect of that work and those disbursements – Whether payment could be authorised for work undertaken and disbursements incurred before grant of legal aid order – Legal Aid Act 1974, s 28(7).

In August 1976 R was arrested and charged with illegally importing cannabis. He applied three times to the magistrates' court for a legal aid order. Each application was refused. On 23rd September he was committed for trial at the Crown Court. He applied to that court for a legal aid order and was informed on 21st October that the court would only grant him such an order if he deposited £50 towards any contribution order which the court might make at the conclusion of the proceedings. His solicitors were already working on his case and, after he paid the £50 deposit in mid-November, the court issued a legal aid order under s 28(7)[a] of the Legal Aid Act 1974 assigning them to him as his solicitors. At his trial, on 31st January 1977, he pleaded guilty and was sentenced to a term of imprisonment. His solicitors submitted their bill of costs for taxation and included in it a claim for the work which they had undertaken and the disbursements which they had

---

a Section 28(7) provides: 'Where a person is committed to or appears before the Crown Court for trial or sentence, or appears or is brought before the Crown Court to be dealt with, the court which commits him or the Crown Court may order that he shall be given legal aid for the purpose of the trial or other proceedings before the Crown Court.'

incurred in respect of R's case between the date of his committal and the issue of the legal aid order. The Crown Court taxing authority held that in the circumstances it ought not to allow those sums. The solicitors appealed, contending that a legal aid order operated retrospectively and that the taxing authority was bound to allow such costs and disbursements.

Held – On the true construction of the 1974 Act payment could be made only for the legal aid given to a legally assisted person under s 28(7) after a solicitor had been assigned to him by the Crown Court. It followed that no payment could be authorised for the work undertaken and the disbursements incurred by R's solicitors prior to the issue of the legal aid order. Accordingly the appeal would be dismissed (see p 697 *f* and p 700 *e*, post).

R v Tullett [1976] 2 All ER 1032 considered.

Notes

For legal aid in the Crown Court, see 11 Halsbury's Laws (4th Edn) paras 755, 757.

For the Legal Aid Act 1974, s 28, see 44 Halsbury's Statutes (3rd Edn) 127.

Cases referred to in judgment

Greenwood v Sketcher [1951] 1 All ER 750, CA, 50 Digest (Repl) 489, *1718*.

Hatch v Hatch [1951] WN 235, DC.

Lacey v W Silk & Son Ltd [1951] 2 All ER 128, 50 Digest (Repl) 489, *1716*.

Mills v Mills [1963] 2 All ER 237, [1963] P 329, [1963] 2 WLR 831, CA, 50 Digest (Repl) 494, *1752*.

R v Tullett [1976] 2 All ER 1032, [1976] 1 WLR 241, 140 JP 502, 62 Cr App R 225, 14(1) Digest (Reissue) 241, *1727*.

S v S (unassisted party's costs) [1978] 1 All ER 934, [1978] 1 WLR 11, CA.

Wallace v Freeman Heating Co Ltd [1955] 1 All ER 418, [1953] 1 WLR 172, 50 Digest (Repl) 498, *1769*.

Ward v Mills [1953] 2 All ER 398, [1953] 1 WLR 917, CA, 50 Digest (Repl) 489, *1720*.

Review of taxation

A firm of solicitors, Saunders and Ware (now Saunders & Co), applied for a review of the taxation by the taxing authority of the Crown Court at Middlesex Guildhall of their costs in respect of work undertaken and disbursements incurred by them when acting for an accused, Hone Rogers, in criminal proceedings. The facts are set out in the master's decision, which is reported with his permission.

William Birtles for the solicitors.
Harry Woolf as amicus curiae.

23rd May. **MASTER MATTHEWS** delivered the following decision: The accused was charged with importing cannabis, pleaded guilty, was sent to prison for 18 months and was recommended for deportation.

Having considered the notice of appeal dated 16th August 1977, the solicitors' representations and the taxing authority's reasons for its decision and having heard counsel on behalf of the solicitors and counsel instructed by the Treasury Solicitor as amicus curiae I have dismissed this appeal for the following reasons.

This appeal raises a single point of principle, namely whether the issue of a legal aid order by a Crown Court under s 28(7) of the Legal Aid Act 1974 permits or requires the payment of costs and disbursements to a solicitor assigned under that order for work undertaken prior to the date on which it was issued. There is no specific provision which deals with this point in unequivocal terms and the only authority is a decision of his Honour Judge Rubin sitting as a judge in the Inner London Crown Court in *R v Tullett*[1].

---

1 [1976] 2 All ER 1032, [1976] 1 WLR 241

As this point of principle has far reaching consequences I requested the assistance of an amicus curiae and the Attorney-General requested the Treasury Solicitor to instruct counsel who appeared to assist me. The appellant solicitors were represented by counsel.

The facts of this case were briefly as follows. The accused, Hone Rogers, a New Zealand citizen, was arrested at Heathrow Airport on 18th August 1976 and charged with the importation of 68 kilograms of cannabis resin and an additional 286 grams of liquid cannabis to which a value of £70,000 was attributed. It appears that three applications were made to the magistrates' court for the grant of a legal aid order but each was refused.

After Rogers was committed for trial at the Middlesex Crown Court on 23rd September 1976 a further application for legal aid was made to that court and on 21st October 1976 the court wrote to the accused in Pentonville Prison on Form 5142 in the following terms:

'The Court has considered your application for legal aid. Your application for legal aid will be refused unless you first deposit £50 on account of any contribution order that the court may make at the conclusion of the proceedings. The sum must be paid to the Crown Court forthwith. On receipt of the deposit a legal aid order will be made and confirmation sent to you.'

The deposit of £50 was not paid forthwith and on 11th November 1976 the solicitors wrote to the accused saying that he should 'attend to this without delay as [counsel's] Clerk will not be in a position to send him to Court unless either the case is legally aided or his brief fee is paid privately'. The accused replied by letter on 16th November asking that his cheque book be obtained from the prosecutor. The deposit was paid shortly thereafter and the legal aid order under s 28(7) of the 1974 Act was issued on 26th November 1976 assigning Messrs Saunders & Ware as the legally assisted person's solicitors.

In the meantime a letter dated 11th October 1976 had been received by Messrs Saunders & Ware from solicitors in New Zealand, whom the mother of the accused had consulted, saying that she was not in a position to stand as surety in the sum of £10,000 'but if necessary she would be willing to assist towards the costs of appearing and defending her son at the trial'.

On 18th October the solicitors replied saying:

'As to our fees we have been put in funds by a friend of Hone Rogers, and whilst these funds will not cover the actual costs of a trial, we have applied to the Court for legal aid and are hopeful that this will be granted. It appears that a contribution from Mrs. Rogers will be unnecessary, but if the position proves otherwise, we will write to you again.'

I am assured by the solicitors that the payment to which they referred related solely to their fees for the committal proceedings in the magistrates' court and that they have received no payment for their work in the Crown Court.

Although an earlier trial had been expected the case came into court on 31st January 1977 when Rogers pleaded guilty to both counts and was sent to prison for 18 months with a recommendation for his deportation.

When the solicitors submitted their bill of costs for taxation they included a claim for work which they had undertaken and disbursements they had incurred between the committal on 23rd September 1976 and the issue of a legal aid order on 26th November 1976. The taxing authority disallowed both the costs and disbursements attributable to that period.

In informal correspondence prior to the lodging of a formal objection under reg 8 of the Legal Aid in Criminal Proceedings (Fees and Expenses) Regulations 1968[1] the solicitors had cited the decision in R v Tullett[2] and the taxing authority had stated that the decision was not binding on him as it was a decision of a Crown Court judge.

---

1 SI 1968 No 1230
2 [1976] 2 All ER 1032, [1976] 1 WLR 241

Their formal objections under reg 8 on the point now at issue was in the following terms: 'The taxing authority erred in law in disallowing these items as the effect of the legal aid order is retrospective unless items have already been reimbursed.' In his formal reasons under reg 9(1) the taxing authority stated as follows:

'. . . the most substantial issue concerns the disallowance of sums totalling £178·50 on page 1 of the bill and £22 on page 2 of the bill as well as proportioned reductions under letters and telephone calls for work done by the solicitor prior to the granting of legal aid . . . I have looked at *Tullett's* case[1] and it appears to me that the Court (i.e. the Judge of the Court of trial) or the taxing officer has a discretion to consider the circumstances of the case whether any fees or costs incurred prior to the granting of the legal aid order should be allowed under the taxation of the costs due under the order. I cannot accept the impression gained from the solicitors' objections that it is mandatory for me to allow these items. In this present case legal aid was clearly refused on the 21st October 1976 unless a specific condition was observed and had the matter rested there legal aid would never have been granted. The solicitor himself was aware in his brief to counsel that legal aid had been refused on 3 occasions and even continued to work on this matter before the 18th October 1976 i.e. when the application was received by the Crown Court. After over one month had passed by the condition set by the Crown Court, namely the down payment of £50, was met [and] the legal aid order was then promptly granted. There is therefore a considerable difference between this case and *Tullett's* case[1]. In the case report of *Tullett*[1] the Judge at the outset mentioned the fact that Tullett had completed the form of application for legal aid which was not submitted by the solicitors to the Magistrates' Court. In the instant case applications had been refused and one was refused by the Crown Court. In *Tullett's* case[1] the solicitors might well have been under the impression that legal aid was granted but in this case the solicitors knew the opposite and in spite of knowing that no legal aid order had been given incurred considerable costs. I come therefore to the conclusion that the circumstances of this case do not provide me with sufficient evidence to justify back dating the allowance of costs to the solicitor beyond that when the legal aid was granted and I would have no power to allow costs prior to that when the Court had clearly refused to grant legal aid.'

For the sake of clarity I have calculated that the sums disallowed under this head were profit costs of £224 and disbursements of £16·32.

At the outset of the hearing before me it was accepted by both counsel that the decision in *R v Tullett*[1], although having considerable persuasive effect, was not binding on me and it was therefore my duty to consider and construe the relevant statutory provisions anew. It was also accepted that I was concerned to consider only one aspect of the decision in *R v Tullett*[1], namely whether the costs of a solicitor could be allowed on taxation for work undertaken by him prior to the issue of a legal aid order. I was not concerned with the principal point decided by that case, namely whether the Crown Court had power to issue a legal aid order at any time up to the final conclusion of the trial. Counsel for the solicitors correctly pointed out however that any construction of the statutory provisions relevant to the payment of costs must accommodate those cases in which a legal aid order is issued not at the beginning but during the course of or even at the end of the proceedings in the Crown Court.

Provision for legal aid in criminal proceedings is contained in Part II of the Legal Aid Act 1974 and the subordinate legislation made thereunder whilst provision for legal aid in civil

---

1   [1976] 2 All ER 1032, [1976] 1 WLR 241

cases is made under Part I of that Act and by separate sets of regulations. While assistance may be gained from considering Part I it is common ground that the question in this case falls to be decided on a proper construction of the language used in Part II.

After a number of provisions were drawn to my attention by counsel I came to the conclusion that the answer to the question must lie in the terms of ss 28(12), 30(1) and 37(1) and (2), and that any conclusion drawn from a construction of those sections must be tested against all the other relevant provisions and compared with any parallel provisions in Part I of the Act. Section 28(12) provides:

'In the following provisions of this Part of this Act "legal aid order" means an order made under any provision of this section and "legally assisted person" means a person to whom legal aid is ordered to be given by such an order.'

Section 30(1) provides:

'For the purposes of this Part of this Act legal aid, in relation to any proceedings to which a person is a party, shall be taken, subject to the following provisions of this section, as consisting of representation by a solicitor and counsel assigned by the court, including advice on the preparation of that person's case for those proceedings.'

Section 37(1) provides:

'Where a legal aid order has been made for the giving of aid to a legally assisted person, the costs of the legal aid given to him shall be paid—(a) in the case of proceedings in a magistrates' court, out of the legal aid fund; (b) in the case of any proceedings not falling within paragraph (a) above, by the Secretary of State.'

Section 37(2) provides:

'Subject to regulations under section 39 below, the costs of legal aid ordered to be given to a legally assisted person for the purpose of any proceedings shall include sums on account of the fees payable to any counsel or solicitor assigned to him and disbursements reasonably incurred by any such solicitor for or in connection with those proceedings.'

It appears to me that the meaning of these provisions taken together may be summarised as permitting payment of the costs of the legal aid given to a legally assisted person which consists of representation by a solicitor assigned by the court and consequently that no payment may be made for work undertaken before the solicitor was assigned.

Having reached that conclusion it is then necessary for me to consider whether it is invalidated by the reasoning in *R v Tullett*[1] or by any of the other relevant statutory provisions or by any anomalies which it produces in the practice of criminal legal aid.

Section 39 empowers the Secretary of State to make such regulations as appear to him necessary or desirable for giving effect to Part II of the 1974 Act and for preventing abuses thereof, and two sets of regulations have been made, namely the Legal Aid in Criminal Proceedings (General) Regulations 1968[2] ('the general regulations') and the Legal Aid in Criminal Proceedings (Fees and Expenses) Regulations 1968 ('the fees and expenses regulations').

Regulation 8 of the general regulations provides:

'. . . any person in respect of whom a legal aid order is made, entitling him to the services of a solicitor, may select any solicitor who is willing to act, and such solicitor shall be assigned to him.'

Regulation 9 provides:

1   [1976] 2 All ER 1032, [1976] 1 WLR 241
2   SI 1968 No 1231

'Where a legal aid order is made in respect of the services of solicitor and counsel, the solicitor may instruct any counsel who is willing to act: Provided that in the case of the Court of Appeal or the House of Lords, counsel may be assigned by the court . . .'

In any case in which a solicitor is assigned by a legal aid order it does not appear that counsel is assigned but is chosen by the solicitor and a strict interpretation of ss 30(1) and 37(2) would therefore lead to the conclusion that no payment could in such circumstances be made to counsel instructed by a solicitor. This interpretation would be so plainly contrary to the intention and purpose of the Act that it is untenable and is indicative in my view of imprecise drafting of those regulations. It does not invalidate the conclusion to which I have already come on the construction of the relevant sections.

Regulation 1 of the fees and expenses regulations provides as follows: 'Fees and expenses payable to a solicitor or counsel assigned to a legally assisted person shall be taxed by a taxing authority . . .' Subject to the discrepancy to which I have already referred the use of the word 'assigned' appears to support my construction.

Counsel as amicus curiae drew attention to sub-ss (8) and (9) of s 30 which provide that where under s 28 the Criminal Division of the Court of Appeal under sub-s (8) or the Courts-Martial Appeal Court under sub-s (9) order that legal aid be given 'for the purpose of an appeal and any proceedings preliminary or incidental thereto' they may under s 30(8) without prejudice to the definition of 'legal aid' in s 30(1) order that the legal aid may—

'. . . consist in the first instance of advice, by counsel or a solicitor assigned by the court, on the question whether there appear to be reasonable grounds of appeal and assistance by that solicitor in the preparation of an application for leave to appeal or in the giving of a notice of appeal.'

This gives those courts the power to issue a legal aid order to cover work done prior to the commencement of the appeal and consequently authorises the payment of costs for that work to a solicitor or counsel assigned by that order.

But s 30(9) goes further and empowers those courts, if they think fit, to—

'include provision that the legal aid ordered to be given shall be deemed to include the like advice and assistance previously given by counsel or a solicitor not then assigned by the court.'

This is a specific provision which permits those appellate courts to make the effect of a legal aid order retrospective so as to authorise payment to solicitor and counsel for work done by them before they were assigned under a legal aid order.

Counsel for the solicitors argued that this is a specific power given to the Court of Appeal to authorise payment to a solicitor and counsel who acted privately for the accused in the court below but who were not assigned by the Court of Appeal when it issued a legal aid order. Counsel as amicus curiae on the other hand submitted that such a provision would be otiose if as a general principle a legal aid order had retrospective effect and I prefer his contention particularly as the phrase used is 'not then assigned'.

He pointed out that Part I of the 1974 Act implies that the grant of legal aid could have no retrospective effect (see s 14(5)) and that there was a long line of authorities which decided that a civil aid certificate or any authority issued by a local committee or an area committee could not have any retrospective effect (see *Greenwood v Sketcher*[1], *Hatch v Hatch*[2], *Lacey v Silk*[3], *Ward v Mills*[4] and *Wallace v Freeman Heating Co Ltd*[5]). More recently the Court of Appeal in *S v S (unassisted party's costs)*[6] held that no costs could be allowed for any work

1   [1951] 1 All ER 750
2   [1951] WN 235
3   [1951] 2 All ER 128
4   [1953] 2 All ER 398, [1953] 1 WLR 917
5   [1955] 1 All ER 418, [1953] 1 WLR 172
6   [1978] 1 All ER 934, [1978] 1 WLR 11

undertaken before the date of the issue of a civil aid certificate. He argued that, if Part II
of the 1974 Act was intended to make similar provision, one would have expected the
draftsman to make a parallel provision but it was common ground that he had not done so.

It was also submitted on behalf of the solicitors that s 28(7) provides that the power of
the Crown Court is to order that legal aid be given 'for the purpose of the trial', and that
s 29(1) provides that the court shall grant legal aid where it appears to be desirable to do so
in the interest of justice, and by sub-s (6) that 'any doubt shall be resolved' in favour of
granting legal aid.

Counsel contrasted the position in respect of legal aid under Part I of the 1974 Act where
the Court of Appeal in *Mills v Mills*[1] held that a civil aid certificate could be issued to cover
part only of an action, cause or matter but that case had no application to Part II of the Act
where a legal aid order covered all the cases without restriction. Although there is a
specific power given to the Court of Appeal by reg 12 of the general regulations to 'specify
the stage of the proceedings at which the legal aid shall commence' no such power is given
to the Crown Court. The judge in *R v Tullett*[2] held that the theme which runs through s 28
'is that the power vested in a court to make an order for legal aid arises when the court
becomes seised of the proceeding and continues so long as it remains so seised'.

He also argued that if there is a power to grant legal aid at the end of the trial then if the
legal aid is not retrospective that power would have no effect. He conceded however that
another anomaly would arise where the accused did not nominate under reg 8 of the
general regulations the solicitor who had acted for him prior to the issue of that order and
a new solicitor was assigned to him by the court. He accepted that in such circumstances
the original solicitor could not claim any costs under s 37(2).

The general contention for the solicitors was that in a criminal case the accused has no
choice in the matter: he must appear in court to answer the charges against him and if the
case is to be properly prepared in time for the trial a solicitor cannot necessarily postpone
his work until a legal aid order is issued. A conscientious solicitor would not, unless the
order was retrospective, be able to recover the cost of the work undertaken promptly whilst
a solicitor who postponed preparation until after the issue of an order would be able to
charge for it. The language used by Parliament in this section, he submitted, did not
specifically prohibit payment of the costs which a solicitor had incurred before he was
assigned and the provisions should therefore be interpreted liberally.

Counsel as amicus curiae argued that as a civil aid certificate issued under Part I of the
1974 Act in a civil case was not retrospective then the draftsman of Part II would have made
such a fundamental distinction plain. The fact that there was no such provision indicates
that none was intended. He further argued that there is normally no need to make a legal
aid order retrospective as there are adequate overlapping provisions contained in s 30(5) to
(10). He suggested that to hold that a legal aid order should have retrospective effect was
inconsistent with the statutory framework and the practice in criminal legal aid cases. In
particular when a court considers an application for legal aid it is considering the position,
including the applicant's means at the time. Where the initial application is refused and
a later application submitted the applicant's position may well have changed and it would
be wrong if the subsequent grant should have the effect of overruling the original refusal.

In this particular case the reason for the original refusal was the failure of the accused to
pay a contribution of £50 which the court ordered him to pay under s 29(3). If a person
of substantial means refused to make a payment but on a fresh application could show that
he no longer had means, legal aid would be granted. The payment out of public funds to
his solicitor and counsel of the costs incurred during the intervening period would be
plainly against the policy of the 1974 Act.

Another anomaly would arise from the provisions of s 36(1), which provides that where
an order for costs is made in favour of a legally assisted person those costs must be paid
either to the magistrates' court or to the Secretary of State; yet s 36(2) provides that 'if the

1   [1963] 2 All ER 237, [1963] P 329
2   [1976] 2 All ER 1032 at 1034, [1976] 1 WLR 241 at 243

total contribution made by a legally assisted person is more than the difference between the costs incurred on his behalf and the sums due' under an order made in his favour the excess shall be repaid to him. The result in a case where the accused has already paid a part of his solicitors' costs would mean that there was no power to reimburse him from the costs recovered in respect of the period prior to the issue of the legal aid order. In his contention 'proceedings' plainly means the part of the proceedings after the issue of the legal aid order.

Counsel for the solicitors relied on the decision in *R v Tullett*[1] but counsel as amicus curiae contended that insufficient importance was attached in that case to the word 'assigned' wherever it was used and that the use of that word in s 30(9) which permitted payment to be made to a solicitor and counsel 'not then assigned' emphasised the significance of that word.

Counsel as amicus curiae also suggested that the word 'payable' in s 37(2) leads to a further anomaly in that in every case where a solicitor had acted privately for an accused prior to the issue of a legal aid order and who rendered a bill to his client for that work a failure by the client to pay that bill would transfer the costs to public funds. Further difficulty would arise if a payment on account of costs had been made by the client but no bill had been rendered for the work.

I have considered the judgment in *R v Tullett*[1] most carefully and having given due weight to the reasons given by the judge, but having had the benefit of detailed argument I am persuaded that the conclusion at which I have arrived on the principal sections of Part II of the 1974 Act is not inconsistent with any of the remaining statutory provisions and that the anomalies flowing from that conclusion do not outweigh the anomalies consequent on the opposite view.

I repeat that in my judgment on their plain meaning the relevant sections on which I rely permit payment to be made only for the legal aid which consists of work undertaken and disbursements incurred on behalf of a legally assisted person by a solicitor after he has been assigned by a legal aid order issued under s 28(7) of the 1974 Act and that no payment may be authorised for costs or disbursements incurred prior thereto. With considerable diffidence therefore I hold that this appeal must be dismissed.

Should the appellant solicitors be minded to appeal my decision to the High Court I certify under the proviso to reg 10 of the fees and expenses regulations that a point of principle of general importance arises in this case.

Finally a request was made to me by both counsel that this decision, in the event of there being no such appeal, should be made available for publication in the law reports.

I accede to their request and they are accordingly at liberty to take appropriate steps to that end.

Appeal dismissed.

Solicitors: *Saunders & Ware*; *Treasury Solicitor*.

Christine Ivamy   Barrister.

---

1   [1976] 2 All ER 1032, [1976] 1 WLR 241

R v Hull Prison Board of Visitors, ex parte St Germain and others
R v Wandsworth Prison Board of Visitors, ex parte Rosa

COURT OF APPEAL, CIVIL DIVISION

MEGAW, SHAW AND WALLER LJJ

25th, 26th 27th, 28th, 31st JULY, 3rd OCTOBER 1978

Certiorari – Jurisdiction – Prison board of visitors – Exercise of disciplinary powers – Whether certiorari can lie against prison board of visitors when sitting as disciplinary body.

Criminal Law – Appeal – Criminal cause or matter – Decision of Divisional Court – Appeal to House of Lords – Appeal against refusal of certiorari against prison board of visitors sitting as disciplinary body – Whether appeal in a 'criminal cause or matter' – Whether appeal lying only to House of Lords – Supreme Court of Judicature (Consolidation) Act 1925, s 31(1)(a) – Administration of Justice Act 1960, s 1(1).

Rioting took place at a prison at which five of the applicants were imprisoned. As a result the board of visitors pursuant to their powers under the Prison Act 1952 and the rules made thereunder heard charges against the five applicants, who had been involved in the rioting. The board imposed various disciplinary penalties against the applicants, including loss of remission. The applicants applied to the Divisional Court for orders of certiorari to quash the board's decisions contending that the board had failed to observe the rules of natural justice. The Divisional Court[a] refused their applications on the ground that although the board of visitors when sitting as a disciplinary body were performing a judicial and not an administrative function, certiorari did not lie because the board had been sitting as a closed body dealing with private and domestic disciplinary matters. The applicants appealed to the Court of Appeal. At the hearing of the appeal the question arose whether the applicants' appeals against the decision of the Divisional Court were appeals from the High Court in a 'criminal cause or matter', within s 31(1)(a) of the Supreme Court of Judicature (Consolidation) Act 1925, and whether, therefore, under s 1(1)(a) of the Administration of Justice Act 1960, appeal lay only to the House of Lords.

Held – (i) The Court of Appeal had jurisdiction to entertain the appeals because the disciplinary proceedings brought against the applicants were not penal proceedings for the infraction of an offence against public law and order and the board of visitors were not a court claiming criminal jurisdiction. The appeals were not therefore appeals in a 'criminal cause or matter' for the purposes of s 31(1)(a) of the 1925 Act (see p 706 c d, p 714 c d and f g, p 715 c and g h, p 719 c and p 721 e f, post); dicta of Viscount Cave in *Re Clifford and O'Sullivan* [1921] 2 AC at 580 and of Viscount Simon LC and of Lord Wright in *Amand v Secretary of State for Home Affairs* [1942] 2 All ER at 385 and 388 applied; *Amand v Secretary of State for Home Affairs* [1942] 2 All ER 381 distinguished.

(ii) The courts were the ultimate custodians of the rights and liberties of the subject whatever his status and however attenuated those rights and liberties were as the result of some punitive or other process, unless Parliament by statute decreed otherwise. There was no rule of law that the courts were to abdicate jurisdiction merely because the proceedings under review were of an internal disciplinary character and, having regard to the fact that under the Prison Act 1952 a prisoner remained invested with residuary rights regarding the nature and conduct of his incarceration despite the deprivation of his general liberty, the Divisional Court had been in error in refusing to accept jurisdiction (see p 707 d, p 710

___

a [1978] 2 All ER 198

f and *h*, p 712 *a*, p 716 *h* to p 717 *c*, p 719 *c* and p 723 *h* to p 724 *a*, post); *R v Metropolitan Police Comr, ex parte Parker* [1953] 2 All ER 717 and decision of Divisional Court of the Queen's Bench Division in *Ex parte Fry* [1954] 2 All ER 118 disapproved.

(iii) Whether certiorari could lie against the disciplinary decisions of a prison board of visitors was a matter to be decided according to public policy and established principles. A board of visitors when sitting to hear disciplinary charges were not imposing summary discipline as part of the day-to-day administration of the prison but were instead an independent body standing between the prison governor and the staff which could only punish the prisoner after a formalised enquiry and/or hearing. In doing so they were exercising a judicial function and their decisions were therefore subject to control by the courts by certiorari in appropriate cases. Although in form remission of sentence may have been the grant of a privilege, loss of remission was in fact a punishment or deprivation affecting the rights of the subject; and, although under r 7 of the Prison Rules 1964 a prisoner could petition the Secretary of State to remit or mitigate a disciplinary award, there was no provision for a formal appeal to the Secretary of State. There were accordingly no reasons why certiorari could not be granted against the disciplinary decisions of a board of visitors. The appeals would therefore be allowed (see p 708 *a*, p 711 *a* to *c e* and *j* to p 712 *a*, p 713 *f*, p 717 *e* to *h*, p 718 *g h*, p 719 *a* to *c*, p 723 *h*, p 724 *c* to *f* and p 725 *a b* and *j*, post).

Per Megaw and Waller LJJ. Although proceedings of boards of visitors in respect of offences against discipline are subject to judicial review by the courts, such interference will only be justified if there has been some failure to act fairly, having regard to all relevant circumstances, and such unfairness can reasonably be regarded as having caused a substantial, as distinct from a trivial or merely technical, injustice which is capable of remedy. Moreover the requirements of natural justice are not necessarily identical in all spheres (see p 713 *d e* and p 719 *c*, post).

Semble. Certiorari does not lie against a disciplinary decision of a prison governor (see p 711 *b c*, p 713 *b c*, p 718 *e*, p 719 *c* and p 722 *g*, post).

Decision of the Divisional Court of the Queen's Bench Division [1978] 2 All ER 198 reversed.

Notes

For right and mode of appeal from a decision of the Divisional Court, see 11 Halsbury's Laws (4th Edn) paras 1505–1506.

For bodies amenable to orders of certiorari, see 1 ibid paras 148–152, and for cases on the jurisdiction to grant certioriari, see 16 Digest (Repl) 471–485, 2905–3038.

For the Prison Act 1952, see 25 Halsbury's Statutes (3rd Edn) 828.

For the Supreme Court of Judicature (Consolidation) Act 1925, s 31, see 7 ibid 590.

For the Administration of Justice Act 1960, s 1, see 8 ibid 489.

For the Prison Rules 1964, see 18 Halsbury's Statutory Instruments (3rd Reissue) 13.

Cases referred to in judgments

Amand v Secretary of State for Home Affairs [1942] 2 All ER 381, [1943] AC 147, 111 LJKB 657, 167 LT 177, HL; *affg* [1942] 1 All ER 480, [1942] 2 KB 26, 111 LJKB 349, 166 LT 292, CA, 16 Digest (Repl) 308, 843.

Becker v Home Office [1972] 2 All ER 676, [1972] 2 QB 407, [1972] 2 WLR 1193, CA, Digest (Cont Vol D) 729, 33*b*.

Buckoke v Greater London Council [1971] 2 All ER 254, [1971] Ch 655, [1971] 2 WLR 760, 135 JP 321, 69 LGR 210, [1971] RTR 131, CA; *affg* [1970] 2 All ER 193, [1971] Ch 655, [1970] 1 WLR 1092, Digest (Cont Vol D) 739, 666*a*.

Clifford and O'Sullivan, Re [1921] 2 AC 570, 90 LJPC 244, 126 LT 97, 27 Cox CC 120, HL, 16 Digest (Repl) 433, 2364.

Cooper v Wilson [1937] 2 All ER 726, [1937] 2 KB 309, 106 LJKB 728, 157 LT 290, 101 JP 349, 35 LGR 436, CA, 37 Digest (Repl) 194, 31.

Daemar v Hall (13th February 1978) unreported, Supreme Court of New Zealand.

Fraser v Mudge [1975] 3 All ER 78, [1975] 1 WLR 1132, 130 JP 674, CA, Digest (Cont Vol D) 730, 33*c*.

Fry, Ex parte [1954] 2 All ER 118, [1954] 1 WLR 730, 118 JP 313, 52 LGR 320, DC and CA, 16 Digest (Repl) 489, 3115.

Kiss v United Kingdom (16th December 1976) unreported, Application 6224/73, European Commission of Human Rights.

Martineau and Butters v Matsqui Institution Inmate Disciplinary Board (1977) 74 DLR (3d) 1; *affg* (1976) 31 CCC (2d) 39.

R v Criminal Injuries Compensation Board, ex parte Lain [1967] 2 All ER 770, [1967] 2 QB 864, [1967] 3 WLR 348, DC, Digest (Cont Vol C) 282, 2557c.

R v Electricity Comrs, ex parte London Electricity Joint Committee Co (1920) Ltd [1924] 1 KB 171, [1923] All ER Rep 150, 93 LJKB 390, 130 LT 164, 88 JP 13, 21 LGR 719, CA, 16 Digest (Repl) 433, 2381.

R v Fletcher (1876) 2 QBD 43, 46 LJMC 4, 35 LT 538, 41 JP 310, 13 Cox CC 358, CA, 16 Digest (Repl) 530, 3701.

R v Gaming Board for Great Britain, ex parte Benaim [1970] 2 All ER 528, [1970] 2 QB 417, [1970] 2 WLR 1009, 134 JP 513, CA, Digest (Cont Vol C) 397, 352Aa.

R v Garrett, ex parte Sharf [1917] 2 KB 99, 86 LJKB 894, 116 LT 398, 81 JP 145, 25 Cox CC 627, CA, 16 Digest (Repl) 441, 2484.

R v Hogan, R v Tompkins [1960] 3 All ER 149, [1960] 2 QB 513, [1960] 3 WLR 426, 124 JP 457, 44 Cr App R 255, CCA, 14(1) Digest (Reissue) 444, 3802.

R v Institutional Head of Beaver Creek Correctional Camp, ex parte MacCaud [1969] 1 OR 373, [1969] 1 CCC 37, 2 DLR (3d) 545, 5 CR(NS) 317, Digest (Cont Vol C) 807, *5b.

R v Metropolitan Police Comr, ex parte Parker [1953] 2 All ER 717, [1953] 1 WLR 1150, 117 JP 440, DC, 16 Digest (Repl) 461, 2811.

Ridge v Baldwin [1963] 2 All ER 66, [1964] AC 40, [1962] 2 WLR 935, 127 JP 295, 61 LGR 369, HL, 37 Digest (Repl) 195, 32.

Cases also cited

Anisminic Ltd v Foreign Compensation Commission [1969] 1 All ER 208, [1969] 2 AC 147, HL.

Attorney-General v British Broadcasting Corpn [1978] 2 All ER 731, [1978] 1 WLR 477, DC.

Glynn v Keele University [1971] 2 All ER 89, [1971] 1 WLR 487.

Leary v National Union of Vehicle Builders [1970] 2 All ER 713, [1971] Ch 34.

London Borough of Hounslow v Twickenham Garden Developments Ltd [1970] 3 All ER 326, [1971] 1 Ch 233.

M'Donald v Lanarkshire Fire Brigade Joint Committee, Earl v Same, O'Hare v Same 1959 SC 141, 1959 SLT 309.

Maynard v Osmond [1977] 1 All ER 64, [1977] QB 240.

R v Metropolitan Police Comr, ex parte Blackburn [1968] 1 All ER 763, [1968] 2 QB 118, CA.

R v Secretary of State for the Home Department, ex parte Hosenball [1977] 3 All ER 452, [1977] 1 WLR 766, CA.

R v Secretary of State for War, ex parte Martyn [1949] 1 All ER 242, DC.

R v Visiting Justice at Her Majesty's Prison, Pentridge, ex parte Walker [1975] VR 883.

Savundra, Re [1973] 3 All ER 406, [1973] 1 WLR 1147n, DC.

Stevenson v United Road Transport Union [1977] 2 All ER 941, CA.

Stratton v Holden [1977] WAR 97.

Wolff v McDonnell (1974) 418 US 539.

X v United Kingdom (17th July 1974) unreported, Application 5916/72, European Commission of Human Rights.

Appeals and motion

The applicants, Ronald St Germain, Michael Reed, Keith Saxton, Kenneth Anderson and Peter Rajah, appealed against the decision of the Divisional Court[1] (Lord Widgery CJ,

---

1 [1978] 2 All ER 198, [1978] QB 678

Cumming-Bruce LJ and Park J) dated 6th December 1977 refusing their applications for orders of certiorari to bring up and quash decisions of the Board of Visitors of Hull Prison *a* in respect of awards made by the board under the Prison Rules 1964 in respect of alleged offences against discipline arising out of a riot at Her Majesty's Prison, Hull, which took place on 2nd September 1976. The applicants had alleged, inter alia, that the board of visitors had failed to comply with the rules of natural justice.

The applicant, Raymond Rosa, pursuant to leave of the Court of Appeal given on 4th October 1977, moved the Court of Appeal for an order of certiorari to remove into the *b* Court of Appeal for the purpose of its being quashed a finding of the Board of Visitors of Wandsworth Prison dated 20th January 1977 that the applicant was guilty of certain offences against discipline, on the ground that the board in arriving at that finding had not complied with the principles of natural justice.

The five appeals and the motion were by consent heard together since they raised the same issue, ie whether proceedings of boards of visitors established under the Prison Act *c* 1952 and the rules made thereunder which resulted in awards in respect of offences against discipline under the rules were subject to judicial review by way of certiorari.

At the outset of the hearing of the appeal the further issue was raised whether, assuming certiorari did lie, the five appeals were against a decision of the Divisional Court in a 'criminal cause or matter' within s 31(1)(a) of the Supreme Court of Judicature (Consolidation) Act 1925 with the consequence that under s 1(1)(a) of the Administration *d* of Justice Act 1960 an appeal lay only to the House of Lords. The facts are set out in the judgment of Megaw LJ.

Andrew Collins for the applicant St Germain.
Michael Beloff for the applicants Reed, Saxton, Anderson, Rajah and Rosa.
Philip Otton QC and *Harry Woolf* for the boards of visitors.   *e*

Cur adv vult

3rd October. The following judgments were read.

MEGAW LJ. At the end of August and the beginning of September 1976 rioting took place in Her Majesty's Prison, Hull. As a result, disciplinary proceedings were taken in *f* respect of 180 prisoners. Seven prisoners who had thus been dealt with applied to the Divisional Court of the Queen's Bench Division for leave to move for orders of certiorari to quash the awards made by the board of visitors of Hull Prison in their respective cases. The court granted leave ex parte, but thereafter, on an inter partes hearing, by judgments[1] delivered on 6th December 1977, refused the applications, holding that the remedy of certiorari did not lie in respect of awards made by boards of visitors in respect of alleged *g* offences against discipline under the Prison Rules 1964[2]. Five of those applicants, namely Ronald St Germain, Michael Reed, Keith Saxton, Kenneth Anderson and Peter Rajah, appeal from that decision to this court. A sixth case raising the same issue is also before us, having come by a different route. That is the application of Raymond Rosa by way of original motion to this court, by leave granted on 4th October 1977, for leave to move for an order of certiorari. In Rosa's case, the respondents are the board of visitors of Her *h* Majesty's Prison, Wandsworth. That case is not concerned with the Hull Prison riots but with events in Wandsworth Prison in January 1977.

All six cases have by consent been heard together, since they all raise one and the same single issue. That issue is an issue of law. It is whether the proceedings of boards of visitors established under the Prison Act 1952 and the Prison Rules 1964 made by statutory instrument thereunder, where those proceedings result in awards in respect of offences against discipline under the rules, are subject to judicial review. Counsel for the applicants *i*

---

1 [1978] 2 All ER 198, [1978] QB 678
2 SI 1964 No 388

submitted that such proceedings are 'subject to judicial review, at any rate where the
a allegations are of breaches of the procedure laid down in the Prison Rules and/or the rules
of fairness and natural justice'. I quote those words, to which I shall return at the end of
my judgment, from the opening submissions of counsel who appeared on behalf of five of
the applicants, that is, all except the applicant St Germain.

The Divisional Court, holding that as a matter of jurisdiction certiorari did not lie,
therefore did not investigate the allegations in any of these cases as to the alleged breaches
b of the required procedure or of natural justice in the proceedings of the boards of
visitors. Neither are we concerned to investigate those matters. We were told that the
allegations on which the applications are founded include allegations that the applicants
were not allowed by the boards of visitors concerned to cross-examine witnesses or to call
witnesses whom they desired to call in order to seek to establish that they, the applicants,
had not in fact committed the disciplinary offences with which they were charged.
c Since these appeals come before us by way of a preliminary issue of law, we are, as I see
it, obliged to consider the preliminary issue on the hypothesis that there might be
established, if and when the facts come to be examined, some failure to act fairly which
could properly be regarded as having caused injustice in one or more of these cases. That
is, of course, hypothetical only.

It follows that, assuming that we have jurisdiction to hear these appeals, we do not have
d to decide, and we do not have material on which we could begin to decide, whether in any
of these cases, if the Divisional Court does have jurisdiction, the discretion which it would
then have should be exercised by it in any particular way. That, as I understand it, is
common ground before us.

Let me give an example to illustrate what that means in practical terms. One of the
arguments for the boards of visitors which I shall consider later is that certiorari does not
e lie, at least at this stage, because there is provision in the Prison Rules 1964 for what is, it
is claimed, in effect an appeal by the prisoner to the Secretary of State from an award of the
board of visitors. Let it be assumed for the moment that the existence of that provision
does not have the effect of excluding jurisdiction to grant certiorari in respect of the
award. It may, nevertheless, still be of relevance as affecting the exercise of the discretion,
whether because of the mere existence of another possible remedy, or because it may
f emerge that a sufficient remedy has in fact been provided. But, for the purpose of the
preliminary issue of law, going solely to the question of jurisdiction, we should not make
any such assumption.

I have, a little earlier, used the precautionary words, 'assuming that we have jurisdiction
to hear these appeals'. That was a question which I felt bound to raise at an early stage of
counsel's submissions. Section 31(1)(a) of the Supreme Court of Judicature (Consolidation)
g Act 1925 provides that no appeal shall lie to this court from any judgment of the High
Court in any criminal cause or matter. Section 1(1) of the Administration of Justice Act
1960 provides for an appeal to the House of Lords, subject to the conditions set out in that
section, from a decision of the Divisional Court of the Queen's Bench Division in a criminal
cause or matter. If the decision of the Divisional Court in these cases now before us is
properly to be regarded as being in a criminal cause or matter, then this court has no
h jurisdiction to entertain the five appeals, and the grant of leave to the sixth prisoner, Rosa,
would have been by inadvertence.

In *Amand v Secretary of State for Home Affairs*[1] it was held that this court had been right
in holding that it had no jurisdiction to entertain an appeal from a refusal by the Divisional
Court of Amand's application for habeas corpus. He had been brought before the chief
metropolitan magistrate in order that he might be handed over to the Netherlands military
police, apparently so that he might be brought before some Netherlands military court or
j tribunal under Netherlands law as being a deserter or an absentee without leave from the
Netherlands forces. It was held by the House of Lords that the question whether it was a
'criminal cause or matter' depended on the nature and character of the proceeding in which

---

1   [1942] 2 All ER 381, [1943] AC 147

habeas corpus (or in the present cases, certiorari) is sought. If the matter be one, the direct outcome of which may be trial of the applicant and his possible punishment for an alleged offence by a court or tribunal (in that case, a foreign court or tribunal) claiming jurisdiction to impose punishment for the offence, then the 'matter' is 'criminal'. The result in that case was that no appeal lay. In the present case, if that authority governs, the appeals, if any, would be to the House of Lords, direct, under the 1960 Act: not to this court.

Counsel for all the parties before us submitted that the judgment from which the appeals are brought is not 'in a criminal cause or matter', that *Amand's* case[1] does not apply, and that this court has jurisdiction. Reference was made to *Fraser v Mudge*[2], where this court refused an ex parte application on behalf of a prisoner (the application having been refused earlier the same day by the judge in chambers) for an injunction to restrain a board of visitors from enquiring into a charge of an offence against discipline until the prisoner should be represented by counsel. The court held that the holding of the proceedings without Fraser being represented by counsel was not an infringement of natural justice. The question of jurisdiction by reference to 'criminal cause or matter' was not raised in this ex parte application. The decision is therefore not relevant as an authority on this question of jurisdiction. I do not find any assistance on this question from *Cooper v Wilson*[3].

In the end I have been persuaded by the views of Shaw and Waller LJJ, aided by the fact that counsel for all the parties urge that the judgment appealed from is not a 'criminal cause or matter'. Because in the rules the offences are specifically described as 'offences against discipline', they can be treated as other than 'offences against the public law'. Therefore, *Amand's* case[1] can properly be distinguished.

This special significance in the phrase 'offences against discipline' is, I think, of relevance to the issue of law which, having jurisdiction, we thus have to decide. The question which we are considering arises out of a special, as it were 'private law', code of discipline, related to a particular and limited class of persons, and in respect of which special considerations apply. Thus the warning signals are hoisted against any ready and uncritical assumption that principles which apply generally in other spheres can, or ought necessarily to, be applied in this sphere, without, at least, regard to possible modifications.

It is desirable to set out in some detail the provisions of the Prison Act 1952 and of the Prison Rules 1964 which may be relevant, whether as general background or by reference to particular submissions. I take first the Prison Act 1952. Section 1 provides that all powers and jurisdiction in relation to prisons and prisoners which were before the Prison Act 1877 exercisable by any other authority shall be exercisable by the Secretary of State, that is, the Home Secretary.

Section 4 enacts that the Secretary of State shall have the general superintendence of prisons, and that officers of the Secretary of State duly authorised shall visit all prisons and examine, amongst other things, the treatment and conduct of prisoners and shall ensure that the provisions of the Act and of any rules made thereunder are duly complied with.

Section 6(2) makes provision for the appointment for every prison of a board of visitors of whom not less than two shall be justices of the peace. By sub-s (3) it is provided that rules made under s 47 of the 1952 Act shall prescribe the functions of boards of visitors—

'and shall among other things require members to pay frequent visits to the prison and hear any complaints which may be made by the prisoners and report to the Secretary of State any matter which they consider it expedient to report; and any member of a board of visitors may at any time enter the prison and have free access to it and to every prisoner.'

Section 47(1) reads:

'The Secretary of State may make rules for the regulation and management of

1   [1942] 2 All ER 381, [1943] AC 147
2   [1975] 3 All ER 78, [1975] 1 WLR 1132
3   [1937] 2 All ER 726, [1937] 2 KB 309

prisons . . . and for the . . . discipline and control of persons required to be detained therein.'

Section 47(2) says:

> 'Rules made under this section shall make provision for ensuring that a person who is charged with any offence under the rules shall be given a proper opportunity of presenting his case.'

Section 52 provides that any power of the Secretary of State to make rules shall be exercisable by statutory instrument and that any statutory instrument shall be laid before Parliament.

I turn now to the Prison Rules 1964, which were made under s 47 of the 1952 Act. They have subsequently been amended. I shall refer to the rules as amended.

Rules 4 and 5 provide for privileges and for remission of sentence. Strictly, remission is a privilege. Though this was stressed in argument for the boards of visitors, I do not think anything turns on it in this case. The rules, before their amendment in 1968[1], included corporal punishment as a possible award. An award of loss of remission is also properly to be regarded as a punishment, even though the prisoner may have no legal right to the remission, and may have no legal remedy for a failure to grant the remission.

Rule 47 provides: 'A prisoner shall be guilty of an offence against discipline if he . . .', and then are set out 21 items, each of which is such an offence. They include, but are not confined to, acts which would also be offences against the ordinary criminal law. Examples are: (1) mutiny; (2) doing gross personal violence to any officer; (4) any assault; (5) escape from prison; (6) absenting himself from any place where he is required to be; (11) wilful damage to any part of the prison or any property; (12) making any false or malicious allegation against an officer; (16) repeatedly making groundless complaints; (17) idleness, carelessness or negligence at work, or refusal to work; (20) in any way offending against good order and discipline.

Rule 48 provides that where a prisoner is to be charged with an offence against discipline, the charge shall be laid as soon as possible; and that every charge shall be enquired into, in the first instance, by the governor.

Rule 49 reads:

> '(1) Where a prisoner is charged with an offence against discipline, he shall be informed of the charge as soon as possible, and, in every case, before it is inquired into by the governor.
> (2) At any inquiry into a charge against a prisoner he shall be given a full opportunity of hearing what is alleged against him and of presenting his own case.'

Rule 49(2) thus gives effect to the mandatory provision of s 47(2) of the 1952 Act.

At this stage, I leave the rules, temporarily, in order to refer to Form 1145. This is a printed form which, we were told, is handed to prisoners when they are to appear before a board of visitors on an 'adjudication'. That word comes from r 48. It means the determination of a charge of an offence against discipline. Form 1145 is not, as I understand it, a form which has statutory authority; but no doubt it has the approval of the Secretary of State. It sets out in simple language the procedure which the prisoner can expect to be followed when he appears before the board of visitors. It shows that the prisoner will be asked whether he pleads guilty or not guilty to the charge; that there will then be evidence of witnesses in support of the charge; that he may question such witnesses; that after the evidence against him he may make his defence to the charge, or, if he had pleaded guilty, offer an explanation. Then para 7 of the form reads:

> 'If you want to call witnesses ask the Chairman for permission to do so. Tell him

---

1   SI 1968 No 440, r 1 and Sch

who they are and what you think their evidence will prove. If the Board think that the witnesses may be able to give useful evidence, they will hear them.'

This, to my mind, points to a judicial proceeding.

I return to the Prison Rules 1964. Rule 50 deals with governor's awards. It sets out under heads (*a*) to (*h*) 'awards', which include a caution, stoppage of earnings up to 28 days, 'cellular confinement' not exceeding three days, and forfeiture of remission for up to 28 days.

Rule 51 deals with 'graver offences', and in that context brings in the board of visitors. Paragraph (1) provides that where a prisoner is charged with escaping or attempting to escape, assaulting an officer, or doing personal violence to any person not an officer the governor shall inform the Secretary of State, and, unless otherwise directed by him, refer the charge to the board of visitors. (This, it was suggested, gives the Secretary of State the opportunity to decide whether the charge should be brought before the ordinary criminal courts.) Paragraph (2) provides that where a prisoner is charged with any serious or repeated offence against discipline, for which the awards which the governor can make appear insufficient, the governor may, after investigation, refer the charge to the board of visitors. Paragraph (3) provides that where such a charge is referred, the chairman of the board shall summon 'a special meeting' at which not more than five nor less than two members shall be present. Paragraph (4) says that the board so constituted shall enquire into the charge, and, if they find the offence proved, shall make one or more of the eight specified awards. Those awards include a caution, stoppage of earnings not exceeding 56 days, and forfeiture of remission of a period not exceeding 180 days.

It will be seen that the offences against discipline with which a board of visitors will be required to deal are at least likely to be substantially more serious than the offences with which the governor can deal, and that the punishments which the board of visitors can award are very much more severe.

Rule 52 is concerned with 'especially grave offences', that is, mutiny or incitement to mutiny, or doing gross personal violence to an officer. Again, the governor is required to inform the Secretary of State, and, unless otherwise directed, to refer the charge to the board of visitors. In such a case, the 'special meeting' must consist of not more than five nor less than three members, of whom at least two must be justices of the peace. If the board find the offence proved, they shall make one of the awards listed in r 51(4), though in such a case the forfeiture of remission awarded may exceed 180 days.

Rule 56 deals with remission and mitigation of awards. It provides by para (1) that the Secretary of State may remit a disciplinary award or mitigate it either by reducing it or by substituting a less severe award. Paragraph (2) provides that, subject to any directions by the Secretary of State, the governor may remit or mitigate any award made by a governor, and the board of visitors may remit or mitigate any disciplinary award (including, presumably, an award made by a governor).

A prisoner can always submit a petition to the Secretary of State. He must (r 7) be informed by the governor of the proper method of petitioning. This would include the right, or at any rate the opportunity, of making complaint to the Secretary of State as to any injustice which he might wish to claim had occurred in proceedings in connection with an alleged offence against discipline. This, it is suggested, provides, in effect, for an appeal to the Secretary of State. I shall return later to the submission which was made for the boards of visitors by reference to this provision.

Counsel for the boards of visitors referred us to rr 88 to 97, which deal with the constitution of boards of visitors, their proceedings, their general and particular duties, their obligation to visit the prison frequently, and their duty to make an annual report to the Secretary of State. I do not think it necessary to cite the detail of those rules. Counsel for the boards of visitors was clearly justified in his submission that the board of visitors have many other statutory functions and duties in respect of the prison and prisoners therein, over and above their functions in relation to charges of offences against discipline. His submission on that aspect was that the board of visitors are an integral part of the administration of a prison; their role is administrative; and, although they have what he describes as quasi-judicial functions, those functions do not alter their administrative role in relation to the management of the prison. Their administrative functions, he contends, are such that the courts should not interfere with any of the decisions or procedures arising out of the exercise of their powers.

This submission, along with two others, was raised in this court by a respondents' notice. I shall refer to it again later in that context.

The leading judgment in the Divisional Court was delivered by Lord Widgery CJ. He held[1], and I respectfully agree, that 'the act which the board of visitors perform under this jurisdiction is a judicial act'. Therefore I do not find it relevant to consider the difficult and debatable questions as to the borderline between judicial and administrative acts or as to the effect on the right to judicial review according as the act is to be classified as judicial or administrative.

Lord Widgery CJ then considered the speech of Lord Reid in *Ridge v Baldwin*[2], accepting that that was where the modern approach to certiorari is to be found. Lord Reid had cited the much-quoted passage from the judgment of Atkin LJ in *R v Electricity Comrs, ex parte London Electricity Joint Committee (1920) Ltd*[3] as follows:

'. . . the operation of the writs [of prohibition and certiorari] has extended to control the proceedings of bodies which do not claim to be, and would not be recognized as, Courts of Justice. Wherever any body of persons having legal authority to determine questions affecting the rights of subjects, and having the duty to act judicially, act in excess of their legal authority, they are subject to the controlling jurisdiction of the King's Bench Division exercised in those writs.'

Lord Widgery CJ, as I have said, accepted that in this context the board of visitors had a duty to act judicially. He then cited a passage from the judgment of Lord Parker CJ in *R v Criminal Injuries Compensation Board, ex parte Lain*[4]. The paragraph, set out in full, is as follows:

'The position as I see it is that the exact limits of the ancient remedy by way of certiorari have never been, and ought not to be, specifically defined. They have varied from time to time, being extended to meet changing conditions. At one time the writ only went to an inferior court. Later its ambit was extended to statutory tribunals determining a lis inter partes. Later again it extended to cases where there was no lis in the strict sense of the word, but where immediate or subsequent rights of a citizen were affected. The only constant limits throughout were that the body concerned was under a duty to act judicially and that it was performing a public duty. Private or domestic tribunals have always been outside the scope of certiorari since their authority is derived solely from contract, that is from the agreement of the parties concerned.'

The concluding words of that paragraph make it clear that Lord Parker CJ's exception of 'private or domestic tribunals' was related to the agreement of the parties, a factor which, of course, does not apply in the present case.

Lord Widgery CJ commented[5]: '. . . if one wanted encouragement to extend the scope of certiorari, one could hardly find a more powerful phrase' to constitute that encouragement . . .' He then went on to ask: 'What is to be said on the other side?' The answer which the board of visitors had given, and which Lord Widgery CJ, Cumming-

---

1   [1978] 2 All ER 198 at 202, [1978] QB 678 at 689
2   [1963] 2 All ER 66 at 77, [1964] AC 40 at 74
3   [1924] 1 KB 171 at 205, [1923] All ER Rep 150 at 161
4   [1967] 2 All ER 770 at 778, [1967] 2 QB 864 at 882
5   [1978] 2 All ER 198 at 203, [1978] QB 678 at 690

Bruce LJ and Park J in the Divisional Court accepted, was that there was an exception to the general rule as to the scope of certiorari, which prevents it from going, even though the circumstances otherwise appear entirely suitable and appropriate for it. Lord Widgery CJ said[1]:

'That exception is where the order under challenge is an order made in private, disciplinary proceedings where there is some closed body, and a body which enjoys its own form of discipline and its own rules, and where there is a power to impose sanctions within the scope of those rules donated as part of the formation of the body itself. If one gets that situation, it is possible, in my judgment, on the authorities to say that certiorari will not go even though in other respects the case is suitable for it.'

The principal authority which, as he himself said, moved Lord Widgery CJ was a decision of the Divisional Court, presided over by Lord Goddard CJ, in *Ex parte Fry*[2]. With all respect, I think that the criticism made before us of the judgment of Lord Goddard CJ in that case is well founded, at least as regards dicta therein. Though the decision in *Ex parte Fry*[2] was upheld by this court, that approval was expressed to be on the basis of another ground than that given by the Divisional Court, namely, that in any event the exercise of the discretion to grant the remedy would not be appropriate on the facts of the case. It is right also to emphasise that the decision of the Divisional Court in *Ex parte Fry*[2], so far as it dealt with the question of jurisdiction, as distinct from discretion, appears to have been, at least partly, founded on an earlier decision of that court, *R v Metropolitan Police Comr, ex parte Parker*[3]. In my view, it would be unsafe to treat that decision as still being good law, having regard both to what was said in the speeches in *Ridge v Baldwin*[4] and the observations of Lord Denning MR, in a judgment concurred in by Lord Wilberforce and Phillimore LJ, in *R v Gaming Board for Great Britain, ex parte Benaim*[5]. So far as *Ex parte Fry*[2] itself is concerned, its authority, in relation to the question of jurisdiction, is at any rate rendered doubtful by the observations of Lord Denning MR, obiter, in *Buckoke v Greater London Council*[6].

Nevertheless, it is in my view open to this court, particularly in the light of the very special nature of these 'private law' proceedings as to offences against discipline in prisons, to consider as a matter of public policy whether or not in principle certiorari should be allowed to go in respect of awards of boards of visitors. It is for the courts, subject to overriding statutory provisions, to say where the limits lie. There is no authority binding on this court which either requires us to accept or prevents us from accepting that the present cases fall inside or outside those limits.

Lord Widgery CJ would, as I read his judgment, have held that the awards of boards of visitors may be subject to judicial review, but for his view that, if this were to be accepted as regards boards of visitors, it would have to be accepted also as regards awards by governors. If I had thought that that consequence followed, I should have agreed with the decision of the Divisional Court. But, with great respect, in my judgement that consequence does not follow.

Counsel for the applicants both submitted, though not as their primary argument, that a valid distinction could be drawn between awards by the governor and awards by the board of visitors. I think that is right. It is at that point, and for that reason, that I would, respectfully, part company from the Divisional Court in deciding this issue of law. I would hold that judicial review of awards of boards of visitors in respect of offences against discipline is in principle available by way of certiorari.

---

1 [1978] 2 All ER 198 at 204, [1978] QB 678 at 690
2 [1954] 2 All ER 118, [1954] 1 WLR 730
3 [1953] 2 All ER 717, [1953] 1 WLR 1150
4 [1963] 2 All ER 66, [1964] AC 40
5 [1970] 2 All ER 528 at 533, [1970] 2 QB 417 at 430
6 [1971] 2 All ER 254 at 259, [1971] Ch 655 at 669

To my mind, contrary to the submission put forward by the boards of visitors in their respondents' notice, while the board of visitors have numerous other functions connected with the administration of the prison, their function in acting as a judicial tribunal in adjudicating on charges of offences against discipline, and in making awards consequent on findings of guilt, is properly regarded as a separate and independent function, different in character from their other functions. It is materially different, in my judgment, from the function of the governor in dealing with alleged offences against discipline. While the governor hears charges and makes awards, his position in so doing corresponds to that of the commanding officer in military discipline or the schoolmaster in school discipline. His powers of summary discipline are not only of a limited and summary nature but they are also intimately connected with his functions of day-to-day administration. To my mind, both good sense and the practical requirements of public policy make it undesirable that his exercise of that part of his administrative duties should be made subject to certiorari. But the same does not apply to the adjudications and awards of boards of visitors who, to quote from the alternative submission on this part of the case of counsel for five of the applicants, 'are enjoined to mete out punishment only after a formalised enquiry and/or hearing'. It may be difficult to define the distinction as a strict matter of logic. But I think that, as a matter of the proper practical application of the law in the general interest, not forgetting the legitimate interest of prisoners, that is where the line should be drawn, in respect of this 'private law' disciplinary machinery. I think that, after giving full weight to all that has been said and done over recent years affecting the extension of the scope of the remedy of certiorari, there is nothing in existing law which requires us to decline to draw that line of distinction.

I have reached my conclusion on the issues before us after considering the additional grounds set out in the respondents' notice. The first of these, already mentioned, is that the true role of the board of visitors, viewed as a whole, is administrative. Whatever the consequence might be if that were correct, I do not think it arises here, for, in my view, the judicial functions of the board of visitors should be treated as separate from, and independent of, their other functions. The second submission is put thus: 'The decisions of the board of visitors are subject to review on petition to the Home Secretary.' (This arises from r 56 of the Prison Rules 1964.) 'In so far as that remedy has not been exercised, the courts should not intervene.'

That proposition was amplified in the written summary of submissions which counsel for the boards of visitors helpfully put before us, as follows:

> 'Certiorari has always been regarded as a residual remedy, and where a statutory remedy has been provided the courts are reluctant to interfere with the immediate determination. Therefore, if the remedy of certiorari were to be available at any stage of disciplinary proceedings that stage should be after the matter had been considered by the Secretary of State, in relation to his determination. The consequences are twofold: (i) Either as a matter of law or as a matter of discretion courts will not interfere until the prisoner has exhausted his "right" of petition to the Secretary of State. (ii) If the court were to intervene, it would intervene in relation to the Secretary of State's determination, looking, in so far as it is appropriate to do so, to what happened before the board of visitors in order to assess whether that had any effect on the Secretary of State's determination.'

I say nothing further than I have already said earlier as to the relevance of this consideration in the exercise of the discretion of the Divisional Court. That is not a matter before us on these appeals, among which I include Rosa's case. In so far as it is put forward as a matter of law, affecting the jurisdiction of the Divisional Court to grant certiorari, I might have been disposed to take a different view, if there had been in the Act or rules some formal provision for an appeal to the Secretary of State and a requirement for him to make a determination thereon, perhaps corresponding to the Secretary of State's 'decision letter' in the different sphere of appeals under the Town and Country Planning Act 1971. But, as it is, I do not think that the existence of r 56 precludes, as a matter of law, the prisoner's right to claim, or the court's discretion to grant, the remedy of certiorari on review of the proceedings of the board of visitors in their judicial capacity.

The third submission in the respondents' notice is this: 'The awards of the board of visitors do not affect any right of the prisoners concerned. The award can do more than interfere with the prisoner's expectation of having a privilege conferred on him.' I have already expressed the view that the awards which a board of visitors make are properly to be regarded as punishments.

Having reached my conclusions on the issue before us, I am glad to find that they conform with the views expressed by McMullin J of the Supreme Court of New Zealand in his judgment, in *Daemar v Hall*[1]. I find that authority the most helpful and persuasive of a number of cases which were cited to us from Commonwealth and United States jurisdictions. The judge made a careful and very lucid review of relevant authorities in the English courts and in other jurisdictions, and of views expressed by the learned authors of well-known textbooks. Of course, any decision in another jurisdiction has to be treated with care, among other reasons because the provisions of statutes and rules are inevitably different. Thus, in *Daemar v Hall*[1] it does not appear what, if any, were the rules relating to the disciplinary powers of the governor of the prison in New Zealand law. Nevertheless, I respectfully agree with McMullin J's approach, reasoning and conclusions.

First, McMullin J, rightly as I think, puts on one side the substantial number of decided cases which relate to attempted actions for damages brought by prisoners for alleged breaches of prison rules. He accepts, and counsel for the applicants in these present appeals accept, that the Prison Rules 1964 do not confer on a prisoner any rights which may be enforced by an action for damages on the ground that any statutory duty was owed to him. That is the subject-matter of the observations of Lord Denning MR in *Becker v Home Office*[2], quoted by Lord Widgery CJ[3]:

> 'If the courts were to entertain actions by disgruntled prisoners, the governor's life would be made intolerable. The discipline of the prison would be undermined. The Prison Rules are regulatory directions only. Even if they are not observed, they do not give rise to a cause of action.'

But, though accepting that that is the law regarding actions by prisoners, McMullin J went on to hold, again rightly as I think, that this does not lead to the conclusion that there does not exist a discretion in the court to make a judicial review of allegations of breaches of procedural rules amounting to infringement of natural justice. 'The walls of the prison', he says, 'are no bar to the use of the prerogative writ of certiorari in such a case'.

McMullin J goes on, however, to make these, to my mind, extremely pertinent observations:

> 'There must, of course, be many cases in which the power of prison officers to discipline inmates can never be the subject of review. The very nature of a prison institution will require that "on the spot" decisions be made by prison officers, the effect of which will be to impose some restrictions and possibly punishments on inmates. I do not intend by this judgment to suggest that the power of those officers will be in any way curbed. If it were otherwise the day-to-day running of a prison institution might be jeopardised and the life of prison officers made a nightmare. Interference with that kind of day-to-day activity would be as unthinkable as interference by the civil courts with the actions of a non-commissioned officer on a parade ground. I think it was of actions of this kind that Jackett CJ was speaking in *Martineau's* case[4] when he said: "In my view, disciplinary decisions in the course of

1   (13th February 1978) unreported
2   [1972] 2 All ER 676 at 682, [1972] 2 QB 407 at 418
3   [1978] 2 All ER 198 at 205, [1978] QB 678 at 692
4   *Martineau and Butters v Matsqui Institution Inmate Disciplinary Board* (1976) 31 CCC (2d) 39 at 51–52

a   managing organised units of people such as armies or police forces or in the course of managing institutions such as penal institutions are, whether or not such decisions are of a routine or penal nature, an integral part of the management operation".'

(*Martineau's* case[1] is a case decided by the Supreme Court of Canada.)

Relating the observations of McMullin J to the particular question before us, I should regard the governor's investigations and awards under the Prison Rules 1964 as being within the category of what the learned judge describes as 'on the spot' decisions; and I b would extend the 'unthinkability' (or, at any rate, undesirability) of interference by the civil courts with the actions of a non-commissioned officer on the parade ground to the actions of a commanding officer exercising powers of summary discipline. That, in my opinion, corresponds to the position of the governor in respect of prison discipline. To that extent, at least, I would not dissent from the dictum of Lord Goddard CJ in *Ex parte Fry*[2] relating to the commanding officer's 'power to deal with certain disciplinary offences in the c orderly room'.

I referred early in this judgment to the submission of counsel that proceedings of boards of visitors in respect of offences against discipline are 'subject to judicial review, at any rate where the allegations are of breaches of the procedure laid down in the Prison Rules and/or rules of fairness and natural justice'. I think that is too widely stated. It is certainly not any d breach of any procedural rule which would justify or require interference by the courts. Such interference, in my judgment, would only be required, and would only be justified, if there were some failure to act fairly, having regard to all relevant circumstances, and such unfairness could reasonably be regarded as having caused a substantial, as distinct from a trivial or merely technical, injustice which was capable of remedy. Moreover, it would be fallacious to assume as appears frequently to be assumed, that the requirements of natural justice in one sphere are necessarily identical in a different sphere. One small e example of that, as between prison discipline before a board of visitors and ordinary criminal proceedings in the sphere of public law, is offered by the decision of this court in *Fraser v Mudge*[3], previously cited. That sort of question, however, if it should arise in these cases, would be a matter for consideration by the Divisional Court.

I would accordingly allow the appeals, as well as Rosa's application. As I understand it, f it is agreed that the consequence is that all the cases before us will fall to be remitted to the Divisional Court, for hearing as applications inter partes for leave to move for judicial review under the provisions of the recently amended RSC Ord 53[4].

Any question as to the form of the orders can be considered after Shaw and Waller LJJ have delivered their judgments.

g   **SHAW LJ.** The history which brings these appeals to this court has been recounted in detail in the judgment of Megaw LJ. For the purposes of the judgment I am about to give no further elaboration is necessary. I therefore address myself exclusively to the matters of law which emerge from that history.

The fundamental specific question that arises is whether or not the High Court has jurisdiction to review the proceedings of a board of visitors in the exercise of their h disciplinary powers conferred by the Prison Act 1952 and defined by the Prison Rules 1964. A Divisional Court of the Queen's Bench Division presided over by Lord Widgery CJ renounced such jurisdiction. The applicants contend that it was wrong so to do. The basis of this contention is that the proceedings which have been described constitute an activity of a judicial or quasi-judicial character. If this proposition is well founded, those proceedings fall within the ambit of the supervisory jurisdiction of the High Court. It

j

1   (1977) 74 DLR (3d) 1, *affg* 31 CCC (2d) 39
2   [1954] 2 All ER 118 at 119, [1954] 1 WLR 730 at 733
3   [1975] 3 All ER 78, [1975] 1 WLR 1132
4   Substituted by RSC (Amendment No 3) 1977 (SI 1977 No 1955)

would follow that certiorari might go to a board of visitors when acting in the context of their disciplinary function if a case is made out on the merits.   a

As the Divisional Court did not accept jurisdiction, it heard no argument on the merits, and this court is in no way concerned with them. The cardinal issue is whether or not the High Court is endowed with jurisdiction. Indeed this was the sole issue raised by these appeals. However, at the outset of the hearing Megaw LJ raised the incidental but critical question as to whether this court had jurisdiction to entertain the present appeals. The answer to this question depends on the nature of the disciplinary proceedings leading to   b and involving the adjudication of a board of visitors. If those proceedings constitute 'a criminal cause or matter' an appeal from the High Court lies only to the House of Lords. This would follow from the provisions of s 31(1)(a) of the Supreme Court of Judicature (Consolidation) Act 1925 and of s 1(1) of the Administration of Justice Act 1960.

In my judgment the proceedings with which these appeals are concerned do not fall within the concept of 'a criminal cause or matter'. It is no doubt true that such proceedings   c possess some of the attributes of such a cause or matter. Thus there are involved the elements of accusation, enquiry and adjudication as well as possible consequences of a punitive character. What is absent is the essential characteristic of a criminal cause or matter, namely, that it is a penal proceeding for the infraction of a requirement relating to the enforcement and preservation of public law and order. An act or course of conduct which is of a criminal character may also, in a particular environment, be a breach of   d domestic discipline. The nature of any proceedings which ensue is not inexorably determined by the fact that their subject-matter is criminal and their outcome punitive. It is necessary to take account also of their context and their overall objective.

What is the effect of these considerations in regard to the proceedings giving rise to the present appeals? It is manifest that some of the offences set out in r 47 of the Prison Rules 1964 coincide with crimes under the general or public law, and that they could be dealt   e with as such in a court exercising criminal jurisdiction. It is true also that the consequence to a prisoner may be a deprivation of some privilege which in a broad sense corresponds to a penalty or punishment. However, as I have said, the combination of these factors does not serve to transform what is essentially a domestic disciplinary proceeding into a criminal cause or matter. Such a proceeding does not purport to deal with misconduct in its relation to the public law or the public interest albeit that the particular misconduct may have an   f impact on both. It is a proceeding designed and pursued with the limited objective of maintaining order within the confines of a prison, and it is in that narrow context that its character falls to be determined.

There is the further consideration, if need be, that some of the offences set out in r 47 do not amount to criminal offences under the general law. They could not be the subject-matter of a criminal prosecution. It would be illogical and anomalous to regard proceedings   g arising from them as constituting a criminal cause or matter.

I would, therefore, hold that the present appeals are competent and justiciable by this court. It is right to add that counsel for the boards of visitors did not contend to the contrary.

The speeches of their Lordships in *Amand v Secretary of State for Home Affairs*[1] seem to me to support this view notwithstanding that the proceedings there considered had their   h origin in an alleged breach of Dutch military law. It was not simply contended for the appellant that this fell to be regarded as a disciplinary rather than as a criminal offence. The argument advanced on behalf of the appellant was that if he was handed over to the Dutch military authorities it was not a necessary sequel that he would be tried by a court-martial at all (Mr G O Slade, arguendo[2]). He might be dealt with in some other way. This consideration, it was submitted, prevented the proceedings against the appellant at the   j stage which the matter had reached when it came before the courts of this country from

---

1   [1942] 2 All ER 381, [1943] AC 147
2   [1943] AC 147 at 151

having the character of a criminal cause or matter. It is this argument of which Viscount
a Simon LC disposed when he said[1]:

> 'It is the nature and character of the proceeding in which *habeas corpus* is sought
> which provide the test. If the matter is one the direct outcome of which may be trial
> of the applicant and his possible punishment for an alleged offence by a court
> claiming jurisdiction to do so, the matter is criminal . . . I agree with GODDARD, L.J.[2],
b that it would be unduly pedantic to require formal proof that a Netherlands conscript
> deserting or absent without leave from his unit in time of war is liable to be charged
> with an offence against the military law of his country. The proceedings in the
> present case are for the direct purpose of handing the appellant over so that he may be
> dealt with on these charges. Whether they are hereafter withdrawn or disproved does
> not affect the criminal character of the matter in the least . . .'

c What emerges from these passages is that to stamp proceedings as being of a criminal
nature there must be in contemplation the possibility of trial by a *court* for some offence.
So also in the speech of Lord Wright[3] one finds the statement:

> '. . . if the cause or matter is one which, if carried to its conclusion, might result in
> the conviction of the person charged and in a sentence of some punishment such as
d imprisonment or fine, it is "a criminal cause or matter".'

The use of the word 'conviction' involves the concept of a court exercising criminal
jurisdiction and not that of a tribunal administering a domestic disciplinary code.
In his speech Lord Porter said[4]:

> 'It was argued, however, that, although an Englishman might be in jeopardy from
e an English court-martial, yet there was no evidence as to the Netherlands law in the
> matter, and that an absentee without leave, at any rate if he had a reasonable excuse,
> might be subject to discipline but not guilty of any crime. The answer is, I think, to
> be found in the words of GODDARD, L.J., . . . when he says[2]: "We do not think that this
> court is bound to require proof that a soldier deserting or being absent without leave
f from his unit in time of war is guilty of an offence against the military law of his
> country" . . . [The] appellant was put in jeopardy of having a criminal charge preferred
> against him before a judicial tribunal claiming jurisdiction to impose punishment for
> the offence . . . [It] is not necessary that the charge must be preferred or must be about
> to be preferred before such a court".'

In this passage the theme is reiterated. There must be at least the prospect that a judicial
g tribunal will try a criminal charge in order to give rise to a criminal cause or matter. A
court-martial is such a tribunal and offences against military law may be tried as crimes.
In the present cases there was no judicial tribunal: emphatically there was none before
which an offender was liable to be *convicted* of a criminal offence and punished for such an
offence.
It is time to turn to the primary question. Counsel for five of the applicants in his
h opening of the appeal stated it in these terms:

> 'Are the proceedings of a board of visitors under the Prison Act 1952 and the Prison
> Rules made thereunder subject to judicial review where it is asserted that there have
> been violations of the procedures laid down in those rules or of the principles of
> natural justice?'

j

1 [1942] 2 All ER 381 at 385, [1943] AC 147 at 156–157
2 [1942] 1 All ER 480 at 483, [1942] 2 KB 26 at 31
3 [1942] 2 All ER 381 at 388, [1943] AC 147 at 162
4 [1942] 2 All ER 381 at 390, [1943] AC 147 at 165–166

Section 47 of the Prison Act 1952 deals with what the rubric describes as rules for the management of prisons and other institutions. Subsection (1) reads:

'The Secretary of State may make rules for the regulation and management of prisons, remand centres, detention centres and Borstal institutions respectively, and for the classification, treatment, employment, discipline and control of persons required to be detained therein.'

Thus part of the subject-matter of the rules which the Home Secretary is empowered to make is discipline and control of persons detained in one or other of the institutions named. Generally speaking the maintenance of discipline and the exercise of control is a matter of domestic administration. It is in essence an executive function. In its discharge a prison governor is responsible ultimately to the Secretary of State in whom s 1 of the 1952 Act vests 'all powers and jurisdiction in relation to prisons and prisoners which before the Prison Act 1877 was exercisable by any other authority'. The administrative structure includes Prison Commissioners whose function it is to assist the Secretary of State in regard to the management of prisons (s 2) and boards of visitors (s 6) whose functions are prescribed by rules made under s 47 of the Prison Act 1952. The Secretary of State is answerable only to Parliament for ministerial acts done by him in pursuance of his powers in this regard.

In the scheme envisaged by the 1952 Act and shaped by those rules, the courts have no defined place and no direct or immediate function. Judicial intervention in the domestic management of a prison would generally be not merely irrelevant but also intrusive and impolitic. Prisoners are subject to a special regimen and have a special status. Nonetheless they are not entirely denuded of all the fundamental rights and liberties which are inherent in our constitution. Thus r 2(1) of the Prison Rules 1964 provides:

'Order and discipline shall be maintained with firmness but with no more restriction than is required for safe custody and well ordered community life.'

Rule 7(1) states:

'Every prisoner shall be provided ... with information ... about those provisions of these Rules and other matters which it is necessary that he should know ... and the proper method of making complaints and of petitioning the Secretary of State.'

Returning to the Prison Act 1952 itself, s 47(2) enacts:

'Rules made under this section shall make provision for ensuring that a person who is charged with any offence under the rules shall be given a proper opportunity of presenting his case.'

This primary requirement of the Act is reflected in r 49(2), which provides:

'At any inquiry into a charge against a prisoner he shall be given a full opportunity of hearing what is alleged against him and of presenting his own case.'

Thus despite the deprivation of his general liberty, a prisoner remains invested with residuary rights appertaining to the nature and conduct of his incarceration.

Now the rights of a citizen, however circumscribed by a penal sentence or otherwise, must always be the concern of the courts unless their jurisdiction is clearly excluded by some statutory provision. The courts are in general the ultimate custodians of the rights and liberties of the subject whatever his status and however attenuated those rights and liberties may be as the result of some punitive or other process. Although r 7(1) impliedly enables a prisoner to petition the Secretary of State in respect of some grievance or deprivation, there is nowhere in the 1952 Act or the rules made under it any indication that such rights, however attenuated, as he may still possess are not cognisable in a court of law. Once it is acknowledged that such rights exist the courts have function and jurisdiction. It is irrelevant that the Secretary of State may afford redress where the rules have been infringed or their application has been irregular or unduly harsh. An essential

characteristic of the right of a subject is that it carries with it a right of recourse to the courts
a unless some statute decrees otherwise. What should be the nature and measure of the relief
accorded must be a matter for the courts. Public policy or expediency as well as merits
may well be factors to consider and they may influence the answer to any application for
relief; but to deny jurisdiction on the ground of expediency seems to me, with all respect
to the views expressed in the judgment of Lord Widgery CJ in the Divisional Court, to be
tantamount to abdicating a primary function of the judiciary. It is true that some
b authority for this attitude is to be found in the judgment of Lord Goddard CJ in *Ex parte
Fry*[1]; but when that judgment was considered by the Court of Appeal[1] it was upheld on the
exercise of discretion and not on the issue of jurisdiction. In my view the Divisional Court
erred in that case in so far as it held that it was without jurisdiction. Neither principle nor
policy would serve to deprive the courts of jurisdiction to supervise the conduct of a
proceeding of a judicial or quasi-judicial character the outcome of which might effect the
c rights or liberties or status of a subject. It is unnecessary to look further than the speech of
Lord Reid in *Ridge v Baldwin*[2] for an exposition of contemporary legal principle in regard
to the forms of relief based on the old prerogative writs. Apart from statute or specific
contract there can be no external fetters on the exercise by the court of its jurisdiction to
control the proceedings of bodies or individuals who have the power to deal with the rights
or liberties or status of a subject. In my view the only necessary restraint on the exercise
d of this supervisory and salutary jurisdiction is an internal one, namely the discretion of the
court from whom relief is sought. This appears to be the philosophical approach which
emerges from the opinions expressed by their Lordships in *Ridge's* case[3] and which had
been earlier stated in the judgment of Atkin LJ in *R v Electricity Comrs, ex parte London
Electricity Joint Committee Co*[4].

If, therefore, it is recognised, as it was by Lord Widgery CJ in his judgment, that a board
e of visitors is required to act judicially in the discharge of its disciplinary function, it must
follow that the supervisory jurisdiction of the High Court is at once alerted. The
proceedings of a board in this context, involving, as they do, a charge, a hearing and an
adjudication, and affecting as they may the rights or liberties or status of a prisoner, are the
very subject-matter of the controlling or corrective jurisdiction of the High Court. It may
be inexpedient or perhaps stultifying in relation to prison discipline that recourse to the
f courts should be available to a prisoner who advances some capricious complaint as to
the manner in which he has been disciplined. There are no finite limits to the extent of the
jurisdiction of the High Court in this regard. The practical limits are to be sought
in the exercise of the power to grant relief which is always a matter of discretion.

Indeed all the arguments advanced in opposing these appeals appeared to me to go to
discretion and not jurisdiction. The opportunity for a prisoner to seek from the Secretary
g of State redress for a grievance (rr 7 and 56) does not amount to a right of appeal for review
of an unwarranted decision by a board of visitors or a prison governor. The fact that such
means of possible redress has not been pursued before application is made to the court may
in some cases be regarded as a discretionary obstacle to the grant relief by the courts; but
it cannot be an absolute bar.

If the adjudication of a board has been irregularly or unfairly arrived at, no ultimate
h prejudice may result, and this may be apparent at the first glimpse which the High Court
is afforded of the matter of complaint. It is readily understandable that discipline in a
prison may be weakened if its exercise can be challenged in the courts; but until Parliament
chooses to enact that the proceedings of a board of visitors in its disciplinary function,
however conducted, shall be free from supervision or control by the High Court, the scope
of its inherent jurisdiction must, in my view, include such proceedings. I do not for my
j part find it easy, if at all possible, to distinguish between disciplinary proceedings conducted

1   [1954] 2 All ER 118, [1954] 1 WLR 730
2   [1963] 2 All ER 66 at 77, [1964] AC 40 at 74
3   [1963] 2 All ER 66, [1964] AC 40
4   [1924] 1 KB 171, [1923] All ER Rep 150

by a board of visitors and those carried out by a prison governor. In each case the subject-matter may be the same; the relevant fundamental regulations are common to both forms of proceeding. The powers of a governor as to the award he can make (which really means the punishment he can impose) are more restricted than those of a board of visitors in a corresponding situation; but the essential nature of the proceedings as defined by the Prison Rules is the same. So, in nature if not in degree, are the consequences to a prisoner.

I do not overlook the observations of Lord Denning MR in *Becker v Home Office*[1] in a passage already referred to by Megaw LJ in his judgment. However, disgruntled prisoners may have serious grounds for complaint of some award which is not only peremptory but also arbitrary. I repeat what I have already indicated that the High Court may in any but the most blatant case refuse leave at the outset if there has been no prior recourse to the Secretary of State.

I would refer to the judgment of the Ontario Court of Appeal in *R v Institutional Head of Beaver Creek Correctional Camp, ex parte MacCaud*[2] and quote the passage which reads:

'... in a matter in which he is required to act judicially the institutional head [and, I interpose parenthetically, the prison governor] shall observe the basic principles of fundamental justice ... [This] requires [that] the inmate affected be fully informed of the disciplinary offence he is alleged to have committed, that he be given a fair opportunity to present his case and the evidence relevant to the matters he is called upon to face and that the decision of the institutional head be arrived at judicially, upon the material properly before him ... It is only where the action of the institutional head does not affect the rights of the inmate as a person, or his statutory rights as an inmate, that the institutional head is not answerable to the Court for the propriety of his procedures and the legality of his decision.'

However, this court is not called on to decide how a disciplinary decision of the governor of a prison would stand in regard to certiorari. It is relevant to consider it only because Lord Widgery CJ concluded that certiorari would not go to a board of visitors because he equated their position in relation to disciplinary proceedings with that of a prison governor. The next step in his judgment was that the disciplinary acts of a prison governor could not be judicially reviewed without disrupting if not destroying the whole system of discipline within prisons. This theme was a substantial element in the argument advanced on behalf of the boards of visitors. In my judgment that argument is effectively disposed of by a passage in another judgment from a court of the Commonwealth. It occurs in the judgment of McMullin J, sitting in the Supreme Court of New Zealand in *Daemar v Hall*[3]:

'I am of the view that where a statute or regulation clearly indicate that disciplinary proceedings are to be conducted by a judicial officer following judicial procedures closely allied to those which would be followed by a court sitting outside a prison institution, the Supreme Court has power to review the decision of the visiting justice if he acts outside the powers conferred upon him. The walls of a prison are no bar to the use of the prerogative writ of certiorari in such a case. If on an examination of all the circumstances the Supreme Court finds that the case of the applicant is unmeritorious, the court will exercise its discretion against him. If the case is meritorious, the discretion can be exercised in his favour.'

There follows a reference to the judgment of Lord Goddard CJ in *Ex parte Fry*[4]. It reads:

'As Professor Wade[5] has said, "The danger of Lord Goddard's doctrine ... is that the court would deny jurisdiction altogether, so that the good and bad cases would be

1   [1972] 2 All ER 676 at 682, [1972] 2 QB 407 at 418
2   (1968) 2 DLR (3d) 545 at 553–554
3   (13th February 1978) unreported
4   [1954] 2 All ER 118, [1954] 1 WLR 730
5   Administrative Law (3rd Edn, 1971), p 200; see now (4th Edn, 1977), p 441

rejected indiscriminately". In view of the decision which I have reached on the basis

of the plain words of the statute and the regulations, I do not need to consider whether there has been a breach of natural justice. There can be no substitute for the plain words of the statute and regulations.'

By substituting for 'judicial officer' the phrase 'board of visitors acting in their disciplinary function' and reading references to 'statute and regulations' as pertaining to the relevant provisions of the Prison Act 1952 and the Prison Rules 1964, the answer to the

b present appeals is, in my view, accurately stated.

I would reiterate what I said at the outset in regard to merits. This court has not heard, and does not need to hear, argument in relation to them. They must be considered and determined by the Divisional Court. In arriving at the view I have reached, I express no view, for I have formed none, as to the ultimate outcome of the applications of the respective appellants.

c I would allow the appeals.

WALLER LJ. Save that I would reserve a final decision on whether or not certiorari would lie against the governor of a prison until it arises, I agree with the judgment of Megaw LJ. As we are differing from the Divisional Court I will, however, set out in my own words my reasons for doing so.

d In 1976 there was a riot at Hull Prison as a result of which very considerable damage was done. Part of the riot included a number of prisoners climbing on to the roof. 180 prisoners were dealt with by the board of visitors, consisting of two magistrates and one other prison visitor, in the late autumn of 1976. This court is concerned with five of those prisoners who have made allegations that they were not allowed to cross-examine and not allowed to call witnesses as alibi witnesses when appearing before the board of visitors.

e There is also before us a sixth case, Rosa, as already described by Megaw LJ. The Divisional Court ruled that the order of certiorari did not run against the board of visitors, and appeal is made to this court to decide whether or not there can be judicial review of proceedings before a board of visitors. This court is not concerned with the merits of the applications at all.

It is not necessary to set out the awards which were made in each of the cases. It is

f sufficient to say that in the most serious case, that of Saxton, he was ordered to lose 720 days' remission, an award which was later reduced by the Secretary of State to 600 days.

The constitution and duties of boards of visitors are set out in Part IV of the Prison Rules 1964, made under s 6 of the Prison Act 1952. The general duties are set out in r 94 and the particular duties in r 95. They have to satisfy themselves as to the state of the prison premises, the administration of the prison and the treatment of prisoners. They have to

g direct the attention of the governor to matters calling for his attention and report to the Secretary of State any matter which they consider expedient to report. They have to inform the Secretary of State of any abuse. In particular they have to hear complaints from prisoners, have to arrange for the food to be inspected, etc. In addition to all these matters they have a part to play in the discipline of the prison.

I next deal with discipline. Rule 2 deals with the maintenance of order and discipline

h and in particular says that order and discipline shall be maintained with firmness but with no more restriction than is required for safe custody and well ordered community life (r 2(1)). Rules 44, 45 and 46 deal with the use of force by an officer, temporary confinement by the governor, and restraints which the governor may order and the safeguards there are on the exercise of his powers. Then come the offences against discipline in r 47. There are there set out 21 offences against discipline ranging from inciting mutiny to failing to

j return to prison when the prisoner should have done so after temporary release. Rule 48 deals with disciplinary charges; and r 49 deals with the rights of prisoners charged and para (2) says:

'At an enquiry into a charge against a prisoner he shall be given a full opportunity of hearing what is alleged against him and of presenting his own case.'

This rule is in effect carrying out the provisions of s 47(2) of the Prison Act 1952, which says:

> 'Rules made under this section shall make provision for ensuring that a person who is charged with any offence under the rules shall be given a proper opportunity of presenting his case.'

There then follow rr 50, 51 and 52. Rule 50 deals with governors' awards and sets out the minor matters which are dealt with by the governor. For example, his power to order a forfeiture of remission is limited to 28 days. Rule 51 deals with graver offences such as escaping or assaulting an officer, and there the governor has the power to dismiss the charge but otherwise has to refer the facts to the Secretary of State and refer the charge to the board of visitors. The board of visitors when dealing with such a charge have greater powers, for example they can order remission to be forfeited for a period not exceeding 180 days. Then r 52 deals with especially grave offences where the board of visitors may exceed the 180 days. Finally I should mention r 56(1), which reads:

> 'The Secretary of State may remit a disciplinary award or mitigate it either by reducing it or by substituting another award which is in his opinion less severe.'

It is relevant in dealing with this rule to draw attention also to r 7(1), which requires information in writing to be provided to every prisoner which includes 'the proper method of making complaints and of petitioning the Secretary of State'. Although the rules do not say so, the method of drawing the Secretary of State's attention to a complaint against the board of visitors' award would be by petition.

At the outset of the case the question of whether or not this was a criminal cause or matter within s 31(1)(a) of the Supreme Court of Judicature (Consolidation) Act 1925 was raised as going to the jurisdiction of the court. If it was a criminal cause or matter there would be no appeal to the Court of Appeal. The meaning of the phrase has been considered in a number of cases and I refer to two of them. In *Re Clifford and O'Sullivan*[1] Viscount Cave said:

> '... but in order that a matter may be a criminal cause or matter it must, I think, fulfil two conditions which are connoted by and implied in the word "criminal". It must involve the consideration of some charge of crime, that is to say, of an offence against the public law (Imperial Dictionary, tit. "Crime" and "Criminal"); and that charge must be preferred or be about to be preferred before some Court or judicial tribunal having or claiming jurisdiction to impose punishment for the offence or alleged offence. If these conditions are fulfilled, the matter may be criminal, even though it is held that no crime has been committed, or that the tribunal has no jurisdiction to deal with it (see *Reg.* v. *Fletcher*[2], per Amphlett J.A., and *Rex* v. *Garrett*[3], per Bankes L.J.), but there must be at least a charge of crime (in the wide sense of the word) and a claim to criminal jurisdiction.'

That was a case concerning a special military court set up by the Royal Prerogative in Ireland in 1920.

In *Amand v Secretary of State for Home Affairs*[4] the question was whether an application for a writ of habeas corpus was a criminal cause or matter. The applicant was Dutch. Had he been English, Viscount Simon LC regarded it as plain that it would be a criminal cause or matter because s 154(3) of the Army Act, with which the case was concerned, read as follows:

> 'Where a person is brought before a court of summary jurisdiction charged with being a deserter or absentee without leave under this Act, such court may deal with

1 [1921] 2 AC 570 at 580
2 (1876) 2 QBD 43 at 47
3 [1917] 2 KB 99 at 105
4 [1942] 2 All ER 381, [1943] AC 147

the case in like manner as if such person were brought before the court charged with
a an indictable offence, or in Scotland an offence.'

Viscount Simon LC said[1]:

'It will be observed that these decisions[2], which I accept as correct, involve the view
that the matter in respect of which the accused is in custody may be "criminal"
although he is not charged with a breach of our own criminal law; and (in the case of
b the Fugitive Offenders Act, 1881) although the offence would not necessarily be a
crime at all if committed here. It is the nature and character of the proceeding in
which *habeas corpus* is sought which provide the test. If the matter is one the direct
outcome of which may be trial of the applicant and his possible punishment for an
alleged offence by a court claiming jurisdiction to do so, the matter is criminal.'

c And Lord Wright, in the same case, said[3]:

'The principle which I deduce from the authorities which I have cited and the other
relevant authorities which I have considered is that, if the cause or matter is one
which, if carried to its conclusion, might result in the conviction of the person
charged and in a sentence of some punishment, such as imprisonment or fine, it is a
"criminal cause or matter". The person charged is thus put in jeopardy. Every order
d made in such a cause or matter by an English court, is an order in a criminal cause or
matter, even though the order, taken by itself, is neutral in character and might
equally have been made [in] a cause or matter which is not criminal.'

In the present case each matter was dealt with as an offence against discipline and not as
a criminal offence. Each was not a 'charge of crime, that is to say, of an offence against
public law' (to quote Viscount Cave in *Re Clifford and O'Sullivan*[4]). Nor was it an English
e court. The board of visitors is not a court claiming criminal jurisdiction, and a finding by
a board of visitors could not be the foundation of a plea of autrefois acquit or convict if a
charge of a criminal offence is later made and tried on indictment (see *R v Hogan, R v
Tompkins*[5]). In my opinion these matters do not come within the definition of a criminal
cause or matter. They are neither criminal charges nor are they before a court of criminal
f jurisdiction.

I next come to the substantial question which arises in this appeal, namely, does the writ
of certiorari run against a board of visitors when considering charges of offences against
prison discipline. There is no direct authority on this question, which therefore, has to be
considered on general principles bearing in mind the requirements of public policy.

In all matters of discipline, whether the governor is deciding or whether the decision is
that of the board of visitors, there is an overriding obligation to give the prisoner 'a full
g opportunity of hearing what is alleged against him and of presenting his own case' (r 49 of
the Prison Rules 1964). This rule was made 'for *ensuring*' that he has a 'proper opportunity
of presenting his case' (s 47(2) of the Prison Act 1952). The Act and the rules made
thereunder require a fair hearing and in effect impose in statutory form rules approaching
those of natural justice.

Rule 56 empowers the Secretary of State to remit or mitigate an award but it is only by
h petition to the Secretary of State that a prisoner can ask for an award to be remitted or
mitigated. There is no specific right of appeal, but r 7 requires each prisoner to be
informed of the proper method of petitioning the Secretary of State, and the governor has
to ensure that each prisoner knows of this right within 24 hours of his admission to prison.

---

j 1 [1942] 2 All ER 381 at 385, [1943] AC 147 at 156
    2 *Ex parte Woodhall* (1888) 20 QBD 832 and *R v Brixton Prison (Governor), ex parte Savarkar* [1910] 2
       KB 1056
    3 [1942] 2 All ER 381 at 388, [1943] AC 147 at 162
    4 [1921] 2 AC 570 at 580
    5 [1960] 3 All ER 149, [1960] 2 QB 513

The Divisional Court decided that certiorari did not lie. Lord Widgery CJ, following *Ex parte Fry*[1], after quoting the words of Lord Goddard CJ, said[2]:

> 'The principle there that domestic discipline in the form of a disciplinary body is something for the officer charged with the duty of maintaining discipline and not something for the courts is a principle which, in my judgment, we should adhere to and not allow to be wasted away. It is in no way inconsistent with the general approach to certiorari. It sets aside these particular situations of disciplinary bodies and would, and does, in my judgment, open the way to refusing certiorari when an order of such a disciplinary body is under review.'

Lord Widgery CJ then went on[2]:

> 'At first I thought this was a principle which would apply only to the governor. I saw the governor equated with the commanding officer of the regiment in Lord Goddard CJ's judgment, and it was not until the argument had progressed some way that it seemed to me right that we should include in this principle the board of visitors. The reason why I think it is right to include them is because I think that when they are sitting as a disciplinary body they are part of the disciplinary machinery of the prison. I reject entirely any suggestion that the governor's decision should be the subject of certiorari and I cannot see myself how, if the governor is left out, the board of visitors can be put in.'

In my opinion the judgment of Lord Goddard CJ in *Ex parte Fry*[1] is of doubtful authority for the proposition that certiorari will not lie in disciplinary proceedings against a fire officer. I say this partly because, on appeal, the Court of Appeal upheld the Divisional Court's decision but based its view as a matter of discretion. Further, in *Buckoke v Greater London Council*[3] Lord Denning MR said:

> 'Plowman J[4] devoted a considerable part of his judgment to *Ex parte Fry*[1], but that case was not canvassed before us. It does not warrant the proposition that the rules of natural justice do not apply to disciplinary bodies. They must act fairly just the same as anyone else; and are just as subject to control by the courts. If the firemen's disciplinary tribunal were to hold an order to be a lawful order, when it was not, I am sure that the court could interfere; or, if it proceeded contrary to the rules of natural justice in a matter of serious import, so also the courts could interfere.'

Nevertheless I find it difficult to visualise any circumstances in which certiorari would lie against the governor. His decisions are an intimate part of the disciplinary system of the prison. At the lowest level discipline is maintained in accordance with r 2. It is the face-to-face discipline which is maintained by the prison officer on the landing, in the prison yard or in the prison workshops. Example and leadership are required, and such firmness as may be necessary. It is only when this level of control fails in some way that the governor is brought into the picture. Rule 47 sets out 21 specific offences against discipline of varying degrees of seriousness. Every charge has first to be enquired into not later than the next day after it is laid (other than a Sunday or public holiday) (see r 48(4)) and no doubt in the majority of the less serious offences is disposed of. I agree with the passage from the judgment of Lord Widgery CJ[2] which I have already quoted in which he emphasises the importance of the officer charged with maintaining discipline not being interfered with by the courts.

1   [1954] 2 All ER 118, [1954] 1 WLR 730
2   [1978] 2 All ER 198 at 204, [1978] QB 678 at 691
3   [1971] 2 All ER 254 at 259, [1971] Ch 655 at 669
4   [1970] 2 All ER 193 at 195–197, [1971] Ch 655 at 660–662

a The important question that we have to consider, however, is whether this principle extends to boards of visitors. Whereas the governor's maximum power is to award forfeiture of remission not exceeding 28 days (I do not set out the other powers which he has) the board of visitors can award forfeiture of 180 days for graver offences and more for especially grave offences. Furthermore the board of visitors may not hear the case for some time. In the present instances, for example, the hearings took place over a period of some two months, starting some two months after the events. Again, whereas the governor is intimately concerned with the day-to-day discipline of the prison, the board of visitors have

b a multiplicity of duties in many respects standing between the prisoner and the governor in ways which I have already set out. It is only a comparatively small part of their duties to hear charges, and only a small proportion of charges ever reach the board of visitors. We were told that the 1977 statistics show that only 4·7% of all the adjudications in the prison system were by boards of visitors.

c Two questions arise. Firstly, do the rules of natural justice apply to proceedings before boards of visitors, and secondly, are there nevertheless reasons why certiorari should not lie? I must first refer to *Ridge v Baldwin*[1], where Lord Reid said:

'The appellant's case is that in proceeding under the Act of 1882[2] the watch committee were bound to observe what are commonly called the principles of natural justice, that before attempting to reach any decision they were bound to inform him

d of the grounds on which they proposed to act and to give him a fair opportunity of being heard in his own defence ... It appears to me that one reason why the authorities on natural justice have been found difficult to reconcile is that insufficient attention has been paid to the great difference between various kinds of cases in which it has been sought to apply the principle.'

e And later[3] is the passage quoted in the judgment of Lord Widgery CJ. I agree with Lord Widgery CJ when he says[4]: 'Hence, as I say, I approach this on the footing that the board of visitors have a judicial task to perform and proceeded to perform it.' Furthermore, in *R v Criminal Injuries Compensation Board, ex parte Lain*[5] Lord Parker CJ says:

'The position as I see it is that the exact limits of the ancient remedy by way of certiorari had never been and ought not to be specifically defined. They have varied

f from time to time, being extended to meet changing conditions. At one time the writ only went to an inferior court. Later its ambit was extended to statutory tribunals determining a lis inter partes. Later again it extended to cases where there was no lis in the strict sense of the word but where immediate or subsequent rights of a citizen were affected. The only constant limits throughout were that the body concerned was under a duty to act judicially and that it was performing a public

g duty. Private or domestic tribunals have always been outside the scope of certiorari since their authority is derived solely from contract, that is from the agreement of the parties concerned.'

The board of visitors is not a private or domestic tribunal and their authority is not derived solely from contract.

In my judgment the rules of natural justice do apply to hearings before boards of visitors

h and certiorari would lie unless there are compelling reasons to the contrary. The possible reasons which have emerged in argument are as follows.

(1) That the prisoners have no legally enforceable rights. This argument is based on the submission that there is no right to remission on the ground of good behaviour because r 5(1) of the Prison Rules 1964 simply says that a prisoner 'may ... be granted remission'.

j But it was common ground between the parties that a prisoner is credited with his full

1   [1963] 2 All ER 66 at 71, [1964] AC 40 at 64–65
2   The Municipal Corporations Act 1882
3   [1963] 2 All ER 66 at 77, [1964] AC 40 at 74–75
4   [1978] 2 All ER 198 at 203, [1978] QB 678 at 690
5   [1967] 2 All ER 770 at 778, cf [1967] 2 QB 864 at 882

remission when he arrives in prison after sentence and he is told then his earliest date of release. Whether it is a right or a privilege a prisoner can expect to be released on that date unless he is ordered to forfeit some remission. Lord Reid[1] quoted deprivation 'of rights or privileges' as being of equal importance, and I respectfully agree with him. Whether remission is a right or a privilege is in my opinion immaterial. It is only necessary to consider the case of Saxton, who was ordered to forfeit 720 days. As a result he would have to serve nearly two years beyond his earliest date of release. It was a very substantial privilege which he had lost.

(2) That the board of visitors is an integral part of the disciplinary system of the prison. It is not possible to divide up arithmetically the time spent on various duties by the members of the board of visitors but consideration of rr 94 and 95 leads to the conclusion that apart from discipline the duty of boards of visitors is to hold the balance between the governor and the prisoner. The member of the board of visitors hears complaints, he looks at the state of the premises and the treatment of the prisoner. He is relatively independent of the governor. Does his position alter when the board of visitors sits to hear charges? For myself I cannot see why it should. When especially grave offences are being considered the rules (r 52(2)) provides that at least two members should be justices of the peace. I would expect the board to be independent in their judgment although, of course, the members would be assisted by their local knowledge of the prison concerned. Although counsel for the boards of visitors argues the contrary, support for this view comes from the United Kingdom Government case before the European Commission of Human Rights, *Kiss v United Kingdom*[2]:

> 'The Government conclude that the proceedings against the applicant were of a purely disciplinary nature to which the provisions of art. 6[3] need not have applied. In any event, the Government submit that the applicant had a full and fair hearing of his case before the Board of Visitors which is an impartial and independent authority.'

In my judgment there is nothing in the board's position in relation to the disciplinary system of the prison to make it other than an independent body which, when dealing with charges, has the duty of acting judicially. I therefore see no reason in this respect for saying that certiorari should not run.

(3) It was also submitted that the board of visitors was an administrative body. It follows from what I have said above that while many of the functions are administrative, indeed probably most of them are administrative, I am quite satisfied that when sitting as a board of visitors dealing with disciplinary matters the duties of the board were judicial.

(4) That certiorari is a residual remedy and therefore no right exists until the prisoner has exhausted his right of appeal to the Secretary of State. It was further submitted that then the court would consider the Secretary of State's determination only referring to the board of visitors' determination so far as necessary. It must first be remarked that the prisoner is nowhere in the Prison Rules 1964 given a right of appeal. No rule says so. He is informed when he is received into prison that he can petition the Secretary of State; but that is all. Furthermore, even when he does petition the Secretary of State there is no power in the Secretary of State to quash the finding of guilt (see r 56). In one of the present cases (Rosa) it is submitted that the finding of guilt cannot be expunged even though the whole of the forfeiture has been remitted by the Secretary of State. It is not necessary to decide whether this submission is correct; it is sufficient to assume that it may be. It is difficult to see how certiorari could be addressed to the Secretary of State with any valuable result, because there is no laid-down procedure before him. He probably looks at the record, makes enquiries and comes to a decision. Furthermore, there is no formal record of his decision. We were told that the decision is communicated orally by the governor to the

---

1 [1963] 2 All ER 66 at 77, [1964] AC 40 at 75
2 (16th December 1976)
3 Convention for the Protection of Human Rights and Fundamental Freedoms (TS 71 (1953) Cmd 8969)

prisoner who is summoned before him for the purpose. In my judgment the writ would
always go to the board of visitors whether or not the case had been to the Secretary of State,
and the fact of having been to the Secretary of State would be no bar (see for example *Ridge
v Baldwin*[1]). In all probability the Divisional Court would be very unlikely to grant
certiorari if the applicant had not been to the Secretary of State, but that does not mean that
there would be no right to make such grant.

(5) Finally it is argued that there are reasons of public policy which make it undesirable
to allow the writ to run. I do not find these arguments convincing. They fall under five
main heads:

(i) The possibility of many applications including applications for relief by way of
prohibition and/or mandamus. I realise that when dealing with prisoners living in a
prison world there is the risk of a number of unmeritorious applications for judicial
review. This is a risk which must always be accepted so long as there is a possibility of a
meritorious application. I would regard the possibility of an application in the nature of
prohibition or mandamus as so remote as to be ignored; and I would expect a successful
application for certiorari to be only a remote possibility in any event. The fact that there
are no precedents for such applications is a possible indication that there will not be a flood
of applications. But even if there were, that would not be a ground for refusing the
remedy, because there might in a particular case be a possibility of real injustice.

(ii) It is argued that some internal reports may have consequences as serious as awards by
boards of visitors. There are many administrative decisions made within prisons which
would not be capable of review and which would have as serious consequences to the
prisoner as some findings of a board of visitors. Section 12 of the Prison Act 1952 allows
the Secretary of State to confine 'in any prison' and to remove from one prison to
another. Prisoners may be categorised A, B or C, and the consequences in conditions may
be very different, for example the difference between a top-security prison and an open
prison. A prisoner may be segregated under r 43. This would be an administrative
decision with serious consequences but one which could not be reviewed by a court. I do
not find this consideration as pointing against the review of board of visitors' decisions.
The possibility of such a review I would expect to be rare and probably only in cases of
especial gravity.

(iii) It is argued that the possibility of judicial review would have an adverse effect on
morale and discipline. The contrary argument which was made was that morale would be
improved with the knowledge that the finding could in certain cases be reviewed by the
courts. My own view is that the possible granting of certiorari would be unlikely to have
any effect on the morale or discipline of prisons in either way. It would be as likely to
improve morale as to make no difference at all.

(iv) It is suggested that the inevitable delay of judicial review would cause difficulties.
One of these difficulties, it was argued, was that there was a possibility that a sentence
might be completed before the hearing of judicial review had taken place. In my opinion
this is a very remote possibility indeed and one which should not affect the decision in the
instant case.

(v) I have left until last the suggestion that it is difficult to distinguish between the
governor and the board of visitors because it is a matter which I have already briefly
considered. I do not find the distinction difficult to make. The governor is an essential
part of the organisation of discipline in the prison. Discipline is his responsibility at all
times. He is at the head of the disciplinary pyramid, and being at the head there is a greater
degree of formality. His position is strictly comparable with the commanding officer of
a service unit. Boards of visitors hold the balance between the governor and the internal
discipline of the prison and the prisoner himself and, when sitting, can be regarded as 'an
impartial and independent authority'.

In my opinion, therefore, it is open to an applicant to apply for judicial review of an
award by the board of visitors. I say nothing whatever about the merits of any of these

1   [1963] 2 All ER 66, [1964] AC 40

applications but merely arrive at this conclusion on the hypothesis that some of their grounds may be true. Without expressing any such opinion I would allow this appeal.   *a*

Appeals of St Germain, Rajah, Reed, Saxton and Anderson allowed. Application by Rosa allowed. All applications remitted accordingly to the Divisional Court of the Queen's Bench Division for hearing and determination. Leave to appeal to House of Lords refused.

Solicitors: *George E Baker & Co*, Guildford (for the applicant St Germain); *Sharpe Pritchard*   *b* *& Co*, agents for *Philip Hamer & Co*, Hull (for the applicant Reed); *Bindman & Partners* (for the applicant Saxton); *Douglas-Mann & Co*, agents for *Patterson, Glenton & Stracey-Donald Harvey & Co*, South Shields (for the applicant Anderson); *Hilary Kitchen* (for the applicant Rajah); *Neilson & Co* (for the applicant Rosa); *Treasury Solicitor*.

Mary Rose Plummer   Barrister.   *c*

Midland Bank Trust Co Ltd and another v Green and others (No 2)

CHANCERY DIVISION
OLIVER J
27th JUNE 1978

d

Pleading – Amendment – Amendment at trial or hearing – Defence – Defence struck out for failure to comply with order for discovery – Judgment in default of defence entered against defendant as   *e* *personal representative – Enquiry into damages ordered – Application by personal representative before enquiry held to serve a defence pleading plene administravit – Whether jurisdiction to give leave – RSC Ord 24, r 17, Ord 35, r 2.*

A son commenced an action against his father claiming damages for breach of an option to convey land. The father died and under an order to carry on the proceedings his   *f* executrix became the defendant to the action but due to inadvertence she did not plead in her defence the usual executor's plea of plene administravit or plene administravit praeter. The executrix was ordered to give discovery of documents in connection with the action, but she failed to comply with that order. The son died, and on the application of the plaintiffs (the son's personal representatives), and after hearing the solicitors on both sides, the executrix's defence to the action was struck out under RSC Ord 24, r 16[a].   *g* Thereafter the action proceeded undefended and at the hearing judgment was entered against the executrix in default of defence, an enquiry into damages was ordered and costs were awarded against the executrix. Evidence filed on the summons for the enquiry into damages showed that the total of the damages claimed and the costs was some £100,000 but that the assets of the father's estate in the hands of the executrix consisted only of some £9,000. Since the executrix had not pleaded plene administravit praeter, she was   *h* personally liable for the balance of the damages and costs if the plaintiffs sought to enforce the judgment for damages. The executrix therefore applied for leave to serve a defence pleading plene administravit praeter.

Held – When judgment in an action had been given and all that remained to be done was to hold an enquiry into the damages, the court did not have jurisdiction under RSC Ord 24,   *j* r 17[b] to revoke a previous order made under Ord 24, r 16 striking out the defence and to make a further order allowing a defence to be served in order to plead plene administravit

---

a   Rule 16, so far as material, is set out at p 734 *b*, post
b   Rule 17 is set out at p 734 *c*, post

a or plene administravit praeter because, as judgment had been given, the subsequent order would not be one made 'at . . . the trial of' the cause or matter in connection with which the previous order was made, within r 17, even though an enquiry into damages was outstanding. The court's jurisdiction under RSC Ord 20, r 5 to permit the amendment of pleadings even after judgment did not apply because there was no defence on the record that could be amended, and it would not be an appropriate use of RSC Ord 35, r 2[c] to set aside the order giving judgment merely to enable a defendant to plead plene administravit *b* or plene administravit praeter. Furthermore, once judgment had been given, the court's inherent jurisdiction did not extend to allowing a party whose defence had been struck out for failure to comply with an order for discovery, and who was therefore in contempt, to serve a defence. It followed that the application would be dismissed (see p 733 *j* to p 734 *a*, p 735 *e* to *g* and *j* to p 736 *c*, post).

c   *Haigh v Haigh* (1885) 31 Ch D 478 applied.
   The Duke of Buccleuch [1892] P 201 distinguished.

Notes

For when leave to amend pleadings will be allowed, see 30 Halsbury's Laws (3rd Edn) 33–36, paras 71–73, and for cases on the subject, see 50 Digest (Repl) 126–127, 1093–1098.

d   For the pleas of plene administravit and plene administravit praeter, see 17 Halsbury's Laws (4th Edn) para 1580, and for cases on the subject, see 24 Digest (Repl) 796–799, 7857–7892.

Cases referred to in judgment

Attorney-General v Birmingham Corpn (1880) 15 Ch D 423, 43 LT 77, CA, 50 Digest (Repl) 126, 1093.
Dictator, The [1892] P 64, 304 [1891–4] All ER Rep 360, 61 LJP 73, 67 LT 563, 7 Asp MLC *e*   251, 50 Digest (Repl) 276, 226.
Duke of Buccleuch, The [1892] P 201, 61 LJP 57, 67 LT 739, 7 Asp MLC 294, CA, 1 Digest (Repl) 205, 922.
Haigh v Haigh (1885) 31 Ch D 478, 55 LJ Ch 190, 53 LT 863, 50 Digest (Repl) 161, 1392.
Heard v Borgwardt [1883] WN 173, 50 Digest (Repl) 464, 1592.
Keith v Butcher (1884) 25 Ch D 750, 53 LJ Ch 640, 50 LT 203, 50 Digest (Repl) 126, 1094.
f   *Long v Crossley* (1879) 13 Ch D 388, 39 LJ Ch 168, 41 LT 793, 50 Digest (Repl) 459, 1545.
Phillips v Homfray (1883) 24 Ch D 439, 52 LJ Ch 833, 49 LT 5, CA; *on appeal* sub nom
   Phillips v Fothergill (1886) 11 App Cas 466, HL, 24 Digest (Repl) 688, 6731.
Walcott v Lyons (1885) 29 Ch D 594, 54 LJ Ch 847, 52 LT 399, CA, 50 Digest (Repl) 456, 1513.

Application

g   The plaintiff, Thomas Geoffrey Green, brought an action claiming, inter alia, damages for conspiracy against the defendant Walter Stanley Green. On Walter Stanley Green's death, his personal representative, Mrs Beryl Rosalie Kemp, carried on the action as a defendant by an order to carry on the proceedings dated 19th January 1973. The plaintiff also died and, by an order dated 16th November 1973, his personal representatives, the Midland Bank Ltd and Margaret Ann Green, carried on the action as the plaintiffs. Mrs Kemp failed *h* to comply with an order for discovery of documents, and on 7th October 1975 her defence to the action was struck out in consequence of that failure. On 21st October 1977 the plaintiffs obtained judgment against Mrs Kemp as Walter Stanley Green's executrix, in default of defence, and an enquiry into damages was ordered and an order for costs made against Mrs Kemp. By an order dated 20th April 1978 the damages and costs were to be levied on the real and personal estate of Walter Stanley Green in her hands, and if no *j*   sufficient assets of the estate were in her hands, the costs were to be levied on her personal goods, chattels and property. By a summons dated 9th June 1978 Mrs Kemp applied for an order that notwithstanding the order of 7th October 1975 striking out her defence, she should be at liberty to serve a defence pleading plene administravit praeter, namely that

c   Rule 2 is set out at p 735 *h*, post

she had fully administered Walter Stanley Green's estate except for assets to the value of £9,070·54 in her hands, and had no assets of the estate in excess of that value to satisfy the plaintiffs' claim for damages. The facts are set out in the judgment.

James Munby (who was not instructed in the matter until February 1978) for Mrs Kemp.
Jonathan Parker for the plaintiffs.

OLIVER J. This is a very curious and unusual application made in circumstances in which, I am bound to say, I have the very greatest sympathy with Mrs Kemp, the defendant.

It arises out of an action which was tried by me[1] last October, an action in which the original plaintiff, Mr Thomas Geoffrey Green, was seeking against his late father, Mr Walter Stanley Green, and against the estate of his late mother, Mrs Evelyne Green, the following relief: as against his mother, he was seeking an order for specific performance of an option agreement into which he had entered with his father, that agreement having been frustrated by the father's transfer to the mother, of the land, the subject matter of the option, and as against his father, damages.

His father died after the commencement of the action and his personal representative, Mrs Kemp, became a defendant to the action by an order to carry on made on 19th January 1973. Subsequently Mr Thomas Geoffrey Green died and the Midland Bank Trust Co Ltd and his widow, Mrs Margaret Ann Green, became his personal representatives. There was a further order to carry on between the personal representatives of the plaintiff and Mr Robert Derek Green (the personal representative of Mrs Evelyne Green) and Mrs Kemp on 16th November 1973.

That action came on for trial, as I have said, and judgment was given in these circumstances. On 24th January 1974 an order was made against Mrs Kemp, as personal representative of the late Walter Stanley Green, for discovery. The order was that:

'[Mrs Kemp] do on or before 21st March 1974 or subsequently within 4 days after service . . . make and serve on the Plaintiffs and on the Defendant Robert Derek Green a list of documents which are or have been in her possession custody or power relating to the matters in question in this Action and accounting therefor.'

That order was not complied with and, on 2nd July 1975, the plaintiffs took out a summons to have her defence struck out. On 7th October 1975 an order was made which was expressed to be, and there is no doubt about it that it was, 'upon hearing' the solicitors for the plaintiffs and for Mrs Kemp, and it was recited that it appeared that Mrs Kemp had not complied with the order of 24th January 1974 and that:

'[Mrs] Kemp by her Solicitors not opposing this Order save as to costs IT IS ORDERED that the Defence of [Mrs] Kemp be struck out.'

From there on, as against the estate of the late Walter Green, the action proceeded undefended. Mrs Kemp took no part in the hearing. At the hearing of the action, which occupied the time of the court for some four or five days, I came to the conclusion that the plaintiffs' claim, so far as it related to specific performance against the estate of the original plaintiff's mother, could not succeed. An alternative claim against that estate for damages likewise could not succeed because there was a time limitation which operated in favour of the estate. Accordingly, I made an order which was in the following terms so far as is material to the present application:

'. . . that this Action do as against the Defendant Robert Derek Green (the surviving Executor of the . . . Testatrix Evelyne Green) . . . stand dismissed with costs . . . AND . . . upon this action as against the Defendant [Mrs] Kemp joined in this Action by virtue of the above-mentioned Order to carry-on proceedings dated 19th January 1973 as the Executrix of the said Will of the former now deceased Defendant Walter

---

1   *Midland Bank Trust Co Ltd v Green* [1978] 3 All ER 555

Stanley Green deceased IT IS ORDERED that the following Inquiry be made, that is to say An Inquiry what damages have been sustained by the estate of the said Thomas Geoffrey Green by reason of the execution of a Conveyance in or about August 1967 pursuant to an agreement or an arrangement made between the Defendant Walter Stanley Green and the said Evelyne Green.'

Then there was an order for costs also against Mrs Kemp, down to and including the day of the order dated 7th October 1975.

There was also an order that, subject as hereinafter appearing, Mrs Kemp, as the executrix of the former deceased defendant Walter Stanley Green—

'. . . do within one month of the Master's certificate to be made upon the said Inquiry, pay to the Plaintiffs the amount of the said damages thereby certified to be due from the estate of the said former now deceased Defendant Walter Stanley Green to the Estate of the said former now deceased original Plaintiff Thomas Geoffrey Green and do pay to the Plaintiffs the amount of all the said costs so as to be taxed as against her when so taxed as aforesaid . . .'

Then there was the limitation which is incorporated in orders against personal representatives:

'. . . the said damages and costs to be levied of the real and personal estate within the meaning of the Administration of Estates Act 1925 of the said Walter Stanley Green deceased at the time of his death which come to the hands of the Defendant [Mrs] Kemp as such Executrix of his said Will as aforesaid to be administered if she has or shall hereafter have so much thereof in her hands to be administered.'

The action in which this order was made was an action which had been commenced in 1970. There had been a previous action by Thomas Geoffrey Green against his father; that was an action started in 1968, the reference to the record of which is G3540. Mrs Kemp had been substituted as a defendant in that action but had never appeared. I think that was done in December 1973.

Subsequent to the order which I have referred to made in the 1970 action, the reference to the record of which is G334 (ie the specific performance action), on 20th April 1978, a further order was made, in action G3540, against Mrs Kemp, in default of appearance, for damages to be assessed for breach of contract.

A summons to proceed with the enquiry ordered in action G334 has been issued. The estate of the testator, Walter Stanley Green, was sworn for probate at a little over £9,000. The affidavit evidence so far filed in support of the summons on the enquiry as to damages indicates that the plaintiffs' claim for the damages and costs, whether well-founded or not (at this stage it is not for me to say), is of the order of £100,000 so that there is, as between the amount of the estate and the amount of damages now claimed, a very extensive shortfall. It has now come to the notice of Mrs Kemp, or rather, it has been brought to her notice in unmistakable fashion, that she has, as a result of the judgment which has been entered, incurred a personal liability for the damages and costs except to the extent that she has assets in her hands to meet them, she having failed to plead in either the action G334 or the action G3540, plene administravit or plene administravit praeter. She is thus now precluded from raising, in any subsequent action based on the judgment, the deficiency of assets in her hands.

The principles are not in doubt. I take the principle from Williams and Mortimer on Executors, Administrators and Probate[1] where it is said that:

'If a personal representative has not assets to satisfy the debt, upon which an action is brought against him, he must take care to plead *plene administravit* or *plene administravit praeter*, etc. For it seems that, even under the present system of pleading, if a personal representative fails to plead that he has fully administered the assets, or

---

1   (1970) p 1008

that with the exception of certain assets he has fully administered, and judgment, whether by default or otherwise, is given for the plaintiff, this amounts to a conclusive admission that he has assets to satisfy such judgment.'

It is said that[1]:

'Whenever the action against an executor or administrator can only be supported against him in that character, and he pleads any plea which admits that he has acted as such (except a release to himself), the judgment against him must be that the plaintiff do recover the debt and costs to be levied out of the assets of the testator, if the defendant have so much; but if not, then the costs out of the defendant's own goods. So where the executor pleads *plene administravit*, and it is found against him, the judgment is *de bonis testatoris, et si non,* etc., then the costs *de bonis propriis.*'

Under the heading of 'Judgment by default is admission of assets', it is said that[2]:

'If a personal representative allows judgment by default to go against him, this is an admission of assets, but it does not justify a judgment *de bonis propriis* against him, for no such judgment can be entered unless a *devastavit* is proved or is alleged and remains unanswered. The judgment in default against an executor is therefore in form *de bonis testatoris* as regards the debt and costs, and as to the costs only, *et si non de bonis propriis.* But after a return of *nulla bona testatoris* the plaintiff may bring a second action for the debt, for such a return raises a presumption of *devastavit.* The presumption may, however, be rebutted if an explanation is forthcoming. If the presumption is not rebutted, the defendant is estopped by the first judgment from denying assets; and judgment in the second action, if the defendant again makes default, will then be *de bonis testatoris et si non de bonis propriis* as to both debt and costs.'

I have also been referred to the passage in Atkins' Court Forms[3] where the principle is set out and it is said that:

'If in these circumstances the plaintiff does not obtain satisfaction of his judgment out of the assets of the estate, he may proceed personally against the defendant. In order to enable him to do so he must first sue out a writ of *fieri facias de bonis testatoris.* The sheriff will then make a return to the writ, and if the return is of *nulla bona* the presumption of a *devastavit* is raised and the plaintiff can bring a second action against the defendant alleging a *devastavit.* In this second action the defendant cannot re-open the question of the existence of assets, but inasmuch as the return of *nulla bona* only raises a presumption of a *devastavit,* it is open to him to prove that there were goods of the deceased that the sheriff might have taken in execution, and that these were pointed out to him; it is also open to him to show that there is a satisfactory explanation for the disappearance of the assets, as, for example, the appointment of a receiver in an administration action between the date of the judgment and the issue of the *fieri facias.*'

So there is the principle set out; a personal representative who is sued as such for damages and fails to plead either plene administravit or plene administravit praeter may find himself, if the plaintiff cannot satisfy the judgment out of the testator's estate in the hands of the personal representative, personally liable for the balance.

In this application, Mrs Kemp seeks an order that notwithstanding the order made on 7th October 1975 whereby it was ordered, inter alia, that her defence be struck out, she may be at liberty now to serve a defence or alternatively an amended defence in this action, inter alia, in the following terms:

'The Defendant [Mrs] Kemp has fully administered all the estate and effects of the

1   Williams and Mortimer on Executors, Administrators and Probate (1970), p 1022
2   Ibid, p 1026
3   2 Court Forms (2nd Edn) p 56

above-named Walter Stanley Green deceased (hereinafter called the Deceased) which
have ever come to her hands to be administered except estate and effects to the value
of £9,070·54 (being the value of all the estate of the Deceased shown in an Inland
Revenue affidavit made by the Defendant [Mrs] Kemp and the Defendant [Mrs]
Kemp had not at the beginning of this action nor has she had since nor has she now
any such estate or effects except the said estate and effects of the value aforesaid and the
Defendant [Mrs] Kemp accordingly does not admit assets of the Deceased sufficient to
satisfy the Plaintiffs' claims if established in an amount exceeding the value aforesaid.'

I should mention that at the same time as that summons came before the master (it was,
I think, on the plaintiffs' summons to proceed under the enquiry), an informal application
was made in similar terms in relation to the action G3540. On that application, the master,
on an undertaking by Mrs Kemp's counsel to enter an appearance forthwith and to issue a
pro forma summons to set aside the default judgment dated 20th April 1978, and within
seven days to serve a defence limited to plene administravit praeter, ordered the judgment
in action G3540 to be set aside, the costs of obtaining the judgment and of that application
to be paid by Mrs Kemp in any event. That matter has been adjourned to me at the request
of the plaintiffs to come on with the present application on which the master did not feel
it appropriate to make any order, he taking the view (and I think rightly) that it was an
application which, judgment having been given in the action, ought to be made to the
judge who tried the action.

Both matters are now before me and the fact of the matter is that Mrs Kemp now finds
herself in the extremely difficult position of having delivered a defence in one action which
has been struck out and delivered no defence in the other action, having pleaded plene
administravit praeter in neither action, and being personally liable for any balance over and
above the estate in her hands if the plaintiffs seek to enforce any judgment for damages
which they may recover as a result of the enquiry.

Counsel for Mrs Kemp approaches the application in three stages. He first submits that
if this were merely a question of amending an existing defence, there would be ample
jurisdiction in the court under RSC Ord 20, r 5 to give leave to amend and to give leave to
amend by raising the plea which he now seeks to raise. It is worth bearing in mind the
terms of the relevant rule:

'Subject to Order 15, rules 6, 7 and 8 and the following provisions of this rule, the
Court may at any stage of the proceedings allow the plaintiff to amend his writ or any
party to amend his pleading on such terms as to costs or otherwise as may be just and
in such manner (if any) as it may direct.'

Counsel for Mrs Kemp has drawn my attention to two cases: *The Dictator*[1] and, in particular,
The Duke of Buccleuch[2] where the Court of Appeal had to consider whether after judgment
had been given for damages to be assessed in an Admiralty action an amendment could be
made by substituting a new party. The judgment of Jeune J at first instance is, I think,
instructive; he says[3]:

'Two arguments, but really, I think, converging to one, were presented. It was said
that a plaintiff who has a cause of action cannot be substituted for one who has none,
and reliance was placed on the decision in *Walcott v. Lyons*[4]; but it will be observed
that in that case the Court of Appeal would apparently have allowed the substitution
if the terms they imposed had been acceded to; and in the case of *Long v. Crossley*[5], a
plaintiff with a right was clearly substituted for a plaintiff with none. Indeed, the
provisions of [RSC Ord 16] rule 2 making a bonâ fide mistake a condition seem to

1 [1892] P 64, [1891–4] All ER Rep 360
2 [1892] P 201
3 [1892] P 201 at 207–208
4 (1885) 25 Ch D 594
5 (1879) 13 Ch D 388

include and almost to point to the person whose name was erroneously brought forward having no right in himself. I think, however, that this argument was really put forward only in combination with the argument founded on the proposition that the addition or substitution of a party cannot be made after a final judgment. No doubt such a proposition is perfectly true,'

and he refers to a case in the Chancery Division, *Attorney-General v Birmingham Corpn*[1], where it was held that after final decree, one defendant could not be substituted for another, and to *Keith v Butcher*[2] which shows 'that, for this purpose, in the Chancery Division, final decree means the actual drawing up and entering of the final decree'. He continues[3]:

'But this case is in the Admiralty Division, and what has to be considered is, what do the words "at any stage of the proceedings" in [RSC Ord 16] rule 11, or "determination of the matter" in [Ord 16] rule 2, mean, when applied to proceedings for collision before that division? The question of real importance in such cases is so clearly what was the conduct of persons on board each ship, or, to put it in another way, which ship is liable to the other ship, her cargo and crew, and the personalities of the owners of the ship and cargo are generally so immaterial till it comes to payment and receipt of the damages, that often, if not usually, in practice the names of the owners of ship and cargo do not appear in the pleadings, and seldom, if ever, is any question of the ownership of ship or cargo raised at the hearing. The result is, that really the only question determined by the decree is the fixing of the liability; the amount of damages and the persons to receive them are questions left to be determined by the registrar and merchants. I think that the fact that the damages remained to be assessed rendered the decree of the judge at the hearing no final judgment.'

Quoting from the judgment of Bowen LJ in *Phillips v Homfray*[4], he read this passage[5]:

'The inquiries, whatever the form of language in which they are directed, are an assessment of damages, and until they have been completed the action is still undetermined. [He then went on:] It would appear, therefore, that both in the Queen's Bench and Chancery Divisions a judgment is not to be considered as terminating the action whilst damages remain to be assessed. But in the Admiralty Division the matter does not rest only on assessment of damages. The title of the plaintiffs remains after the decree open to question, and it appears to me that the counsel for the *Duke of Buccleuch* are in the dilemma that if the decree is final Mr. Funck may be regarded as owner of the cargo, or if he is not so to be regarded, the decree is not final.'

At the end of his judgment he says this[6]:

'Reliance is placed on rule 12 [and I interpolate that r 12 provided that any application to add or strike out or substitute a plaintiff or defendant might be made to the court or a judge at any time before trial by motion or summons or at the trial of the action in a summary manner], as shewing that no application to add or substitute a party can be made after the trial, an argument which no doubt commended itself to the mind of Field, J., in *Heard v. Borgwardt*[7], as supporting the decision in *Attorney General v. Corporation of Birmingham*[1], which he was following. But I do not think that rule militates against the view I have expressed. If the word

1   (1880) 15 Ch D 423
2   (1884) 25 Ch D 750
3   [1892] P 201 at 208
4   (1883) 24 Ch D 439 at 466
5   [1892] P 201 at 209
6   [1892] P 201 at 210
7   [1883] WN 173

"trial" does not include a reference to the registrar and merchants, as I think it does, then the mode of application is left unprovided for in the case where the trial within the meaning of rule 12 does not terminate every stage of the proceedings within the meaning of rule 11.'

That decision was upheld in the Court of Appeal, Lord Esher MR observing that the application was within the very words of the two rules and going on[1]:

'But it is said that a judge cannot do that after the decree fixing the liability. That was an argument against the very words of the rule, which said "at any stage". The decree fixing the liability in the Admiralty Court is not a final judgment. The proceedings are not over. If there were no other judgment to be signed, the proceedings are not over, for the matter has to be sent to registrar and merchants. I take it that there would be, if necessary, another decree after the registrar and merchants had found what the amount would be.'

Fry LJ said[2]:

'I base my decision upon the words "at any stage of the proceedings". It has been argued that the rules do not apply after final judgment. They apply, in my opinion, as long as anything remains to be done in the case. In this case there remains the assessment of damages.'

That, I think, clearly establishes a general jurisdiction in the court to give leave to amend pleadings even after judgment. As I read the decision, it is not restricted in any way to Admiralty proceedings.

Indeed, counsel who appears for the plaintiffs, accepts that the court has jurisdiction to allow the amendment to pleadings after judgment but he says, and I think possibly says with some force, that this is a matter of discretion; it is not a power which ought to be utilised generally but is restricted to cases where the amendment which is sought to be made has some connection with the remaining relief to be determined in the action. Amendments, he says, will be allowed only if they relate to matters left to be decided. The cases do not seem to cover a situation like the present where what is sought to be raised is not a matter which relates to the enquiries as to damages. That has been ordered; it is to go on. It relates to something quite different; something outside the enquiry, that is to say, the extent to which a judgment in the proceedings can be enforced. It is a matter which, of course, raises issues which really have nothing whatever to do with the enquiry; issues which could have been determined on the trial of the action but which it is now sought to raise at a very late stage and which may lead to a great deal of additional cost and expense.

However, I think that the law as regards the consequences of a failure to plead plene administravit bear very hardly on a personal representative, particularly in a case where, as I am informed is the case here, the default was due to inadvertence. If the matter were simply one of giving leave to amend, I think that I should be inclined to exercise the jurisdiction, which counsel for the plaintiffs agrees that I have, to give leave to amend, even after judgment, to enable that plea to be raised although I should be inclined, I think, to impose on any leave that I gave some very severe terms as to costs in order to protect the position of the plaintiffs who now find themselves, if leave to amend were appropriate and were given, faced with issues which could have been tried before but which are now appearing for the first time. But, of course, the establishment of a jurisdiction in the court to give leave to amend an existing pleading is only the first step in counsel for Mrs Kemp's battle.

His real difficulty is that here there is no defence on the record at all; there is nothing which can be amended. Here he is faced with a situation where the defence was struck out and was struck out without any opposition on the part of the defendant Mrs Kemp, and,

1 [1892] P 201 at 211
2 [1892] P 201 at 212

indeed, struck out because she was in breach of an order of the court and was, I think there can be no doubt about it, in contempt of court.

Counsel for Mrs Kemp relies on the provisions of RSC Ord 24, r 17. Order 24, r 16 is the order which provides that the court may order the defence to be struck out if a party fails to comply with an order for discovery. It also underlines the contemptuous nature of such a default because in para (2) it is provided:

'If any party against whom an order for discovery or production of documents is made fails to comply with it, then, without prejudice to paragraph (1), he shall be liable to committal.'

Counsel for Mrs Kemp relies on RSC Ord 24, r 17 which provides:

'Any order made under this Order (including an order made on appeal) may, on sufficient cause being shown, be revoked or varied by a subsequent order or direction of the Court made or given at or before the trial of the cause or matter in connection with which the original order was made.'

He relies on the judgment of Jeune J in *The Duke of Buccleuch*[1] to which I have referred as indicating that the trial is still not concluded and that, therefore, RSC Ord 24, r 17 still leaves it open to me to revoke the order previously made and to restore the defence so that it can then be amended.

As regards this argument, there seems to me to be a number of answers. Counsel for the plaintiffs has referred me to *Haigh v Haigh*[2] which is really not altogether a dissimilar case. The defendant to an action disobeyed an order to produce documents for inspection; her defence was struck out and judgment given against her in default of defence. There was evidence that her solicitor had explained to her the effect of the order for production and the consequence of disobeying it and the court refused to set aside the judgment on any terms. Pearson J in that case said this[3]:

'I have no hesitation in saying that I have the strongest disinclination, as I believe every other Judge has, that any case should be decided otherwise than upon its merits. But this order was introduced to prevent plaintiffs and defendants from delaying causes by their negligence or wilfulness. So great was my anxiety to relieve this lady from the consequence of her wrong-headedness if, by any possibility, I could on proper terms, that I hesitated to refuse to make the order asked for, and I have looked into all the cases I could find on the subject to see what the practice of the Court has been on this order. And I can find no case in the books where it has been applied, where a man knowingly and wilfully has allowed judgment to go by default.'

After reviewing the cases, he said this[4]:

'It seems to me that there is no case which has gone to shew that this rule can be acted upon where the party who seeks to put it in force has, with full knowledge and wilfully, allowed judgment to go by default. Therefore I must refuse the application, and, I am afraid, with costs.'

Counsel for Mrs Kemp seeks to distinguish that on the ground that, in that case, there was a deliberate act because the consequences had been explained by the solicitor. I see the force of that but, at the same time, I find myself in some difficulty here because the solicitors in the instant case on behalf of Mrs Kemp appear, without actually consenting, not to have opposed any order. She was represented at the hearing and the fact of the matter is that she was in contempt and remains in contempt because she never complied with the order for discovery.

1 [1892] P 201
2 (1885) 31 Ch D 478
3 31 Ch D 478 at 482
4 31 Ch D 478 at 484

The difficulty, I feel, is in entertaining now, supposing I have jurisdiction to do so under RSC Ord 24, r 17 (a matter which I will consider in a moment) such an application by a party who is in contempt. Counsel for Mrs Kemp says that the rule that the court does not entertain applications by parties in contempt may need to be qualified where the party is herself being pursued by the other party to the litigation. She must be allowed to defend herself. That, I think, may have some force in ordinary circumstances but, here, this is not a case where Mrs Kemp is capable of purging the contempt. The fact of the matter is that the discovery was sought in connection with the action for specific performance and for damages against not only the estate which she represents but also the estate of her mother. I do not know what discovery might have yielded. I do not know whether discovery might not have cast a different light on the application by the plaintiffs for specific performance.

The plaintiffs continued the action, fought it to judgment without the benefit of discovery which was ordered but which Mrs Kemp failed to give and it really seems a little too late for her to turn round now and ask to be excused from the consequences of failing to give that discovery when she can no longer usefully give it.

If and in so far as the matter rests purely on discretion, I think that I should in any event have some reservations about making an order as counsel asks me to under RSC Ord 24, r 17.

Having said that, I turn now to the consideration of whether in any event I have jurisdiction to do so. Because of the limitation in the terms of RSC Ord 24, r 17, the order made pursuant to Ord 24, r 16 may, on sufficient cause being shown, be revoked or varied by a subsequent order or direction of the court made or given at or before the trial of the cause or matter in connection with which the original order was made. I think those words 'the trial of the cause or matter in connection with which the original order was made', have to be read together. The original order was made in connection with the trial of the proceedings for specific performance and damages against the two estates. That trial has taken place; an order has been made. All that remains to be done is the holding of the enquiry as to damages. Even if I were persuaded which, as I have indicated, I do not think that I am, that this is a case in which I ought, had I got a discretion, to exercise it in Mrs Kemp's favour, I do not think that on the true construction of that order I have got any jurisdiction to do so. There is nothing, I think, in the rules of court which enables a judge after judgment in the action to restore a defence which was not there or to permit a party to deliver a defence.

It is said that, possibly, the time for delivery of a defence could be extended because the rules provide that the time for serving a defence can be extended but, again, I do not see how that general discretion can be properly exercised in a case where there has already been a defence but that defence has been struck out.

Counsel for Mrs Kemp draws my attention to the provisions of RSC Ord 35, r 2. That provides:

'(1) Any judgment, order or verdict obtained where one party does not appear at the trial may be set aside by the Court, on the application of that party, on such terms as it thinks just.

'(2) An application under this rule must be made within 7 days after the trial.'

Although there is a discretion, of course, under RSC Ord 3, r 5 to extend that period.

Here again, it does not seem to me that that is an appropriate relief to seek in this case where all that is sought to be done is to deliver a defence raising a plea of plene administravit praeter. It is not suggested, at any rate on this application (although counsel for Mrs Kemp, I think quite rightly, wants to reserve his position as to the future), that the order itself could be resisted. The only effect of the application which counsel seeks to make is, I think, that I would be invited to set aside the order that was made simply for so long as it takes to serve a defence raising a plea of plene administravit praeter for the purposes of defending any proceedings for subsequent enforcement of the judgment and then to restore the order that had been previously made after that defence had been served. I do not think that that would be an appropriate use of RSC Ord 35, r 2.

Finally, I am left with counsel's final submission for Mrs Kemp which is an appeal to the court's inherent jurisdiction. Again, I am bound to say that no authority has been produced which satisfies me that the court has got any inherent jurisdiction, once a judgment in an action has been given, to permit a party whose defence has been struck out for failure to comply with an order for discovery in that action to serve a defence. The inherent jurisdiction, which is frequently resorted to in applications to strike out, is, I think, a jurisdiction in the court to regulate its own process to this extent, that it will not permit its procedure or rules to be abused. But I know of no inherent jurisdiction which would enable me to permit a party who has failed to defend and failed to defend in circumstances where she was and remains in contempt of court now to deliver a defence after judgment has been given against her.

I think, therefore, that although I have very great sympathy with Mrs Kemp in the position in which she finds herself and although, as her counsel has pointed out, it was said as long ago as the 18th century that the rule relating to plene administravit (or rather the failure to plead it) bore very hardly on personal representatives and although it might, I think, be looked at by those interested in law reform, I do not think that I can assist in this case by giving her the relief which she seeks in the action G334.

Counsel for the plaintiffs says that the two actions go hand in hand and that if that is the view that I take, as I do, on action G334, then I ought similarly to take the same course in relation to action G3540 and to refuse the relief which the master was prepared to accord.

I do not take that view. Counsel for the plaintiffs submits that I must look at the litigation as a whole but I think not. I think that in relation to the action G3540, there is no reason why I should not take the same course as that which the master thought it appropriate to take, a course which I think would certainly be taken in any action where a default judgment had been entered and where application was made timeously after the judgment had been entered. The course which the master himself was prepared to take was that, on the various undertakings which counsel was prepared to offer, the default judgment should be set aside.

I propose, therefore, on that action to make the same order as the master was prepared to make.

Orders accordingly.

Solicitors: *Lee, Bolton & Lee* (for Mrs Kemp); *Sidney Torrance & Co*, agents for *J Levi & Co*, Leeds (for the plaintiffs)

Evelyn M C Budd   Barrister.

Tilling and another v Whiteman

HOUSE OF LORDS

LORD WILBERFORCE, LORD DIPLOCK, LORD SALMON, LORD FRASER OF TULLYBELTON AND LORD SCARMAN

31st JANUARY, 8th MARCH 1979

Rent restriction – Possession – House required by landlord for own use – Claim by joint owners – House required for occupation as residence for only one owner – Whether both joint owners constituting 'the owner-occupier' – Whether necessary that house should be required as residence for both joint owners – Whether court having jurisdiction to grant possession if house required for only one joint owner – Rent Act 1968, Sch 3, Part II, Case 10.

The plaintiffs, who were unrelated, were the joint owners of a dwelling-house which the first plaintiff occupied as her residence. The plaintiffs then let the house to the defendant on a regulated tenancy for a period of two years. The tenancy agreement contained a notice to the defendant that 'the Landlord may recover possession of the premises under the provisions of Case 10ᵃ of Part II of Schedule 3 to the Rent Act 1968'. The notice was signed by both plaintiffs and the defendant signed an acknowledgment of its receipt. On the expiry of the term the defendant remained in occupation of the house and the plaintiffs commenced proceedings in the county court to recover possession under Case 10 on the ground that the house was now required as a residence by the first plaintiff. On a preliminary point the judge held that since the house was required as a residence for only one of the plaintiffs, it was not required 'for the owner-occupier', within Case 10, and therefore the plaintiffs were not entitled to recover possession. The first plaintiff appealed to the Court of Appealᵇ which dismissed the appeal. The first plaintiff appealed to the House of Lords.

Held (Lord Fraser of Tulleybelton dissenting) – The policy of Parliament in enacting Case 10 of Part II of Sch 3 to the 1968 Act was to encourage, at a time of serious shortage of residential accommodation, owners of dwelling-houses who had to leave them temporarily to let their premises during their absence by safeguarding their right to regain possession. Having regard to that policy, on the true construction of Case 10 one of two joint owners of a dwelling-house who together let it in such circumstances was entitled to recover possession as 'the owner-occupier' notwithstanding that the house was not required as a residence for both joint owners, since the emphasis in Case 10 was on occupation and residence and not on ownership, and the term 'owner-occupier' was merely shorthand for 'a person who occupied the house as his residence and let it' to the tenant. Since the plaintiff was such a person she would be entitled to recover possession if she could prove that she in fact required the house as a residence. The appeal would therefore be allowed (see p 739 c to h, p 740 b and d, p 741 d to h, p 742 d to f, p 743 c and p 744 e, post).

McIntyre v Hardcastle [1948] 1 All ER 696 distinguished.

Per Lord Wilberforce, Lord Diplock, Lord Salmon and Lord Scarman. Because of the difficulties caused to appellate courts and the increase in costs and length of proceedings, the practice in lower courts of allowing preliminary points of law to be decided on hypothetical facts ought to be confined to cases where the facts are complicated and the legal issues short and easily decided, or to exceptional cases (see p 738 j, to p 739 a, p 740 d, p 743 d and p 744 e f, post).

Decision of the Court of Appeal [1978] 3 All ER 1103 reversed.

Notes

For orders for possession where a dwelling-house is required by an owner-occupier for own use as residence, see Supplement to 23 Halsbury's Laws (3rd Edn) para 1607A.

For the Rent Act 1968, Sch 3, Part II, Case 10, see 18 Halsbury's Statutes (3rd Edn) 908.

---

a Case 10 is set out at p 738 *e f*, post

b [1978] 3 All ER 1103

As from 29th August 1977 Sch 3, Part II, Case 10 to the 1968 Act has been replaced by Sch 15, Part II, Case 11, to the Rent Act 1977

Case referred to in opinions

McIntyre v Hardcastle [1948] 1 All ER 696, [1948] 2 KB 82, [1948] LJR 1249, CA, 31(2) Digest (Reissue) 1092, 8516.

Appeal

The first plaintiff, Mrs Ethel Irene Elizabeth Tilling, appealed against a decision of the Court of Appeal[1] (Stephenson and Shaw LJJ, Eveleigh LJ dissenting) dated 22nd March 1978 dismissing her appeal against an order of his Honour Judge Sumner QC made at the Dover County Court on 3rd May 1977 whereby he dismissed a claim commenced in the Canterbury County Court by the first plaintiff and the second plaintiff, Miss Gertrude Louise May Dossett, against the defendant, Miss Josephine Whiteman, for possession of premises known as St Leonard's, The Street, Staple, Canterbury, Kent, under Case 10 of Part II of Sch 3 to the Rent Act 1968. The facts are set out in the opinion of Lord Wilberforce.

Ronald Bernstein QC and *Christopher Sumner* for Mrs Tilling.
Miss Whiteman appeared in person.

Their Lordships took time for consideration.

8th March. The following opinions were delivered.

LORD WILBERFORCE. My Lords, this appeal arises under Case 10 of Part II of Sch 3 to the Rent Act 1968, which reads as follows:

'Where a person who occupied the dwelling-house as his residence (in this Case referred to as "the owner-occupier") let it on a regulated tenancy and—(a) not later than the relevant date the landlord gave notice in writing to the tenant that possession might be recovered under this Case, and (b) the dwelling-house has not, since 8th December 1965, been let by the owner-occupier on a protected tenancy with respect to which the condition mentioned in paragraph (a) above was not satisfied, and (c) the court is satisfied that the dwelling-house is required as a residence for the owner-occupier or any member of his family who resided with the owner-occupier when he last occupied the dwelling-house as a residence.'

If these conditions are satisfied, s 10 of the 1968 Act requires an order for possession to be made. The appellant, Mrs Tilling, owns a small house in Canterbury jointly with Miss Dossett. She claims to have been in occupation of it immediately before 19th February 1975. On that date the joint owners let it to the respondent, Miss Whiteman, for two years. The tenancy agreement contained a clause whereby Miss Whiteman agreed to yield up the premises at the end of the tenancy. There was a statement, signed by the joint owners, addressed to Miss Whiteman that under the Rent Acts 1968 and 1974 '... the Landlord [sic] may recover possession of the premises under the provisions of Case 10'.

Miss Whiteman did not yield up possession as she had agreed, so the owners brought proceedings in the Canterbury County Court for possession and other relief. Pleadings were exchanged, and the case came on for trial in May 1977 with both sides legally represented. The judge took what has turned out to be an unfortunate course. Instead of finding the facts, which should have presented no difficulty and taken little time, he allowed a preliminary point of law to be taken, whether Case 10 applies to a case where there are joint owners one only of which requires the house as a residence. So the case has reached this House on hypothetical facts, the correctness of which remain to be tried. I, with others of your Lordships, have often protested against the practice of allowing

1   [1978] 3 All ER 1103, [1978] 3 WLR 137

preliminary points to be taken, since this course frequently adds to the difficulties of courts of appeal and tends to increase the cost and time of legal proceedings. If this practice cannot be confined to cases where the facts are complicated and the legal issue short and easily decided, cases outside this guiding principle should at least be exceptional.

My Lords, the legal issue in the present case is not an easy one. Case 10, and s 10 of the 1968 Act on which it is based, say nothing about joint owners, or joint occupiers. To read, or not to read, the singular expressions 'person' and 'landlord' as including the plural, gives rise to difficulties, as the judgments below well demonstrate. In my opinion our task must be to attribute that reasonably admissible meaning to the language which will best carry out what appears to be the legislative intention.

The two alternative views are clearly and forcefully set out in the judgments of the Court of Appeal. The first is that, for an order for possession to be made, the house must be required for the residence of both co-owners. This commended itself to Stephenson and Shaw LJJ. There is no doubt that a powerful case can be made for it on the language used, and some further support may be derived from the Court of Appeal decision in *McIntyre v Hardcastle*[1], decided on what became Case 8 in the same schedule.

The second alternative is that there is no such requirement, and that each of the three conditions stated in Case 10 are on the agreed or assumed facts satisfied in the present case. First, Mrs Tilling occupied the dwelling-house as her residence. Secondly, she let it on a regulated tenancy. Third, she requires it as a residence for herself. On these facts, the court must make an order for possession. This was the opinion of Eveleigh LJ.

My Lords, I propose to do little more than to say that, having to the best of my ability compared the weight of these rival arguments, and having carefully considered Miss Whiteman's printed case, I have come to the conclusion that on balance, the judgment of Eveleigh LJ is to be preferred. The arguments in its favour are so clearly stated in his judgment that nothing would be gained, and something might be lost, by my restating them in my own language. I will only add two observations.

First, the purpose of this piece of legislation, added to the bulky corpus of rent legislation in 1965, was to induce occupiers of dwelling-houses, who for some temporary reason desired, or had, to reside elsewhere for a time, to make their premises available for letting to others, on the basis that on their return they would be able, without dispute, to regain possession. (In cases within Case 10 an order for possession is mandatory.) The emphasis is on occupation: the person concerned must have occupied the dwelling-house as his residence, and must require it as his residence, or that of a member of his family who resided with him when he last resided there. As compared with this emphasis on occupation and residence, ownership plays a subsidiary part. It enters into the matter only because of the inherent fact that the dwelling-house is let, and letting is effected by a landlord. But Case 10, and the policy behind it, is not, if I may personalise, interested in the landlord: he is not, as such, the key figure: that is the 'owner-occupier'. This consideration, to my mind, provides justification for avoiding a strict interpretation of the words 'let it on a regulated tenancy', the words which mainly, if not wholly, support the argument that one of two or more joint owners cannot satisfy the Case unless they both also require to reside in the house. I find it therefore possible to say that Mrs Tilling, being at the time the occupier, when she decided to go to live elsewhere for a time, let her house on a regulated tenancy, even though, for the letting to be effective, Miss Dossett had to join in. This interpretation might, to a conveyancer, appear loose, but it is one which might easily appear in common parlance. For the reasons I have given I do not think that the strict conveyancing meaning is intended to be imposed.

Secondly, as regards *McIntyre v Hardcastle*[1] the wording in Case 8 (which has a separate and much longer history, being derived through the Rent and Mortgage Interest Restrictions (Amendment) Act 1933 from that of the Increase of Rent and Mortgage Interest (Restrictions) Act 1920 is (relevantly) 'where the dwelling-house is reasonably required by the landlord for occupation as a residence for (a) himself . . .' Here there is an

---

1 [1948] 1 All ER 696, [1948] 2 KB 82

identity between the person who has let the house and the person who requires it. There must then be great strength in the argument that if for one purpose the plural is deemed to be included in the singular, so it must for the other: plural landlords must require the house for themselves, not for one of them. This was the argument accepted by the Court of Appeal in *McIntyre's* case[1]. But assuming the correctness of this (and I agree that the question remains open in this House), the argument under Case 10 is different. There is no imposed identity between occupier and landlord: there may be a plurality of landlords, but only one occupier, and it may be possible to say that one of these landlords has let. I find therefore no necessity, or indeed attraction, in following the earlier case.

I would allow the appeal and remit the case to Dover County Court to decide the case on the basis that Case 10 applies to the agreed or assumed facts. As to the costs, while I have sympathy with Miss Whiteman as regards the burden which our expensive legal system places on litigants with small resources, I have to bear in mind that, for whatever reason, she did not pursue an application for legal aid in the Court of Appeal, or make an application in this House. Apart from the legal aid fund there is no other fund of public money out of which the costs she is liable to pay can be provided. I can see no alternative to an order that she must pay the appellant's costs in this House and in the Court of Appeal.

LORD DIPLOCK. My Lords, I have had the advantage of reading in draft form the speech prepared by my noble and learned friend, Lord Wilberforce. For the reasons that he gives I agree that the appeal should be allowed.

LORD SALMON. My Lords, two elderly ladies, Mrs Tilling and Miss Dossett, who are not related to each other, jointly own a cottage in the village of Staple, near Canterbury. Miss Dossett had once resided in the cottage with her friend Mrs Tilling, but some time prior to the tenancy to which I shall presently refer, she went to live in Oxfordshire where she has ever since continued to reside. Mrs Tilling was still living in the cottage immediately prior to 19th February 1975. The learned county court judge found it to be an agreed fact that both these ladies had occupied the cottage as their residence, 'Mrs Tilling immediately before the tenancy, Miss Dossett some time earlier'.

By an agreement in writing dated 19th February 1975, Mrs Tilling and Miss Dossett, as joint owners of the cottage, let it furnished on a regulated tenancy to Miss Whiteman for a period of two years from 21st February 1975 at a weekly rent of £12·50. At the foot of this agreement the following notice appears:

'To the tenant . . . J. Whiteman. TAKE NOTICE under the Rent Acts 1968 and 1974 that the Landlord may recover possession of the premises under the provisions of Case 10 of Part II of Schedule 3 to the Rent Act 1968. DATED this 19th day of February 1975.'

This notice was signed by both plaintiffs and beneath it there was an acknowledgment of its receipt signed by Miss Whiteman. Miss Whiteman however failed to deliver up possession of the cottage at the expiration of the two year term and still continues to reside there. On 4th March 1977 Mrs Tilling and Miss Dossett began proceedings in the Canterbury County Court against Miss Whiteman for possession of the cottage and mesne profits. Paragraph 4 of particulars of claim stated that the cottage which was jointly owned by the plaintiffs had formerly been occupied by the plaintiffs as their residence and is now required as a residence for the first plaintiff.

The case for the defendant was that, the cottage being required as a residence for only one but not for both of the plaintiffs, their claim for possession must fail. This defence succeeded in the county court. The first plaintiff, who is legally aided, appealed from that decision but her appeal was dismissed by a majority in the Court of Appeal. The first plaintiff now appeals to your Lordships' House against the decision of the Court of Appeal.

1 [1948] 1 All ER 696, [1948] 2 KB 82

The result of this appeal turns entirely on the true construction to be placed on Case 10
a in Part II of Sch 3 to the Rent Act 1968.

Part II is headed 'cases in which Court must order possession where dwelling-house
subject to regulated tenancy'. This heading derives from s 10(2) of the 1968 Act which, so
far as relevant, reads as follows:

> 'If . . . the landlord would be entitled to recover possession of a dwelling-house
> *b* which is for the time being let on or subject to a regulated tenancy, the court shall
> make an order for possession if the circumstances of the case are as specified in any of
> the Cases in Part II of Schedule 3 to this Act.'

Case 10 reads as follows:

> 'Where a person who occupied the dwelling-house as his residence (in this Case
> *c* referred to as "the owner-occupier") let it on a regulated tenancy and—(a) not later
> than the relevant date the landlord gave notice in writing to the tenant that possession
> might be recovered under this Case, and (b) the dwelling-house has not, since 8th
> December 1965, been let by the owner-occupier on a protected tenancy with respect
> to which the condition mentioned in paragraph (a) above was not satisfied, and (c) the
> court is satisfied that the dwelling-house is required as a residence for the owner-
> *d* occupier or any member of his family who resided with the owner-occupier when he
> last occupied the dwelling-house as a residence.'

In my opinion, it is plain from the opening words of Case 10 that the words 'the owner-
occupier' are only a kind of shorthand for the words 'a person who occupied the dwelling-
house as his residence [and] let it on a regulated tenancy'. Accordingly, the latter words can
properly be substituted for the former words where they appear in para (c) of Case 10. This
e would, no doubt, make the language of para (c) rather clumsy and may well explain why
the shorthand version was introduced.

Mrs Tilling is, in my view, indubitably a person who occupied the dwelling-house as her
residence and let it on a regulated tenancy. I entirely agree with Eveleigh LJ when he
says[1]:

> *f* 'The fact that two people do a thing together does not, in my understanding of the
> English language, prevent either one claiming that he himself did it. The argument
> to the contrary entails reading into the 1968 Act words something like "on his own".'

The majority of the Court of Appeal placed some reliance on the use of the words 'the
landlord' in para (a) of Case 10. I will assume that these words may be read as 'the
g landlords' when, as in the present case, there is more than one landlord. This, however,
does not, in my view, assist Miss Whiteman. Paragraph (a) was complied with since the
notice to the tenant was, in fact, signed by both plaintiffs. It follows, therefore, that (1) Mrs
Tilling is a person who occupied the dwelling-house as her residence and let it on a
regulated tenancy, (2) the necessary notice referred to in para (a) was duly served,
(3) the regulated tenancy expired on 21st February 1977, and (4) Mrs Tilling may well
h satisfy the county court that she requires the dwelling-house as a residence for herself.
Accordingly, on what I regard as the true interpretation of Case 10, all its conditions may
have been complied with.

The majority of the Court of Appeal in rejecting the above interpretation of Case 10
placed great reliance on McIntyre v Hardcastle[2]. In that case, two sisters sought possession
under Sch I to the Rent and Mortgage Interest Restrictions (Amendment) Act 1933 of a
j house they owned jointly on the ground that the house was required as a residence for one
of them only. The court held that that schedule did not entitle them to recover possession
because the house was not required as a residence for both of them.

---

1   [1978] 3 All ER 1103 at 1111–1112, [1978] 3 WLR 137 at 148
2   [1948] 1 All ER 696, [1948] 2 KB 82

Case 8 in Part I of Sch 3 to the 1968 Act[1] strongly resembles Sch I to the 1933 Act. I shall not recite it as it is fully set out in the judgment of Stephenson LJ. I am afraid that I cannot agree that there is any similarity between the language of Case 8 and that of Case 10. Indeed not only the language but also the object of these two cases are, in my view, strikingly dissimilar. Accordingly it seems to me that the decision in McIntyre v Hardcastle[2] as to the true interpretation of Sch I to the 1933 Act (substantially reproduced in Case 8) is of no assistance in interpreting the language of Case 10. It is not necessary for me to say any more about that decision; and I shall refrain from doing so. Although Case 10 cannot be described as a model of clarity, I am satisfied that the true interpretation of its language is that which I have stated.

Whilst I agree with Stephenson LJ that Case 10 is capable of more than one interpretation I cannot, however, agree that the interpretation which I favour is likely to lead to any serious difficulty on the ground that the joint owners are likely to disagree on whether the dwelling-house should be occupied by the tenant or one of the owners. In the present case, for example, if Miss Dossett had considered that the dwelling-house should be occupied by Miss Whiteman rather than by Mrs Tilling after the tenancy expired, it is unlikely that she would have signed the notice under para (a) which she and Mrs Tilling served on Miss Whiteman. I recognise that it is possible that Miss Dossett might later have changed her mind and become hostile to Mrs Tilling. But I do not understand how this possibility can affect what I regard as the true interpretation of Case 10 or even suggest that this construction can be contrary to the policy of the 1968 Act.

On the contrary, if the construction of Case 10 is to be affected by the policy which caused its introduction, that policy, in my view, strongly supports the construction of Case 10 which I favour. At the time when the 1968 Act was passed, there existed and had for many years existed, a serious shortage of residential accommodation. There were many cases of persons in occupation of homes which they owned jointly who, for one reason or another, had to leave them temporarily, sometimes for considerable periods; they would have liked to let them during their absence, but refrained from doing so for fear of losing them for ever to their tenants. Accordingly, many homes remained unoccupied, which would otherwise have been let to persons urgently in need of them. Case 10 was in my view designed to safeguard persons who occupied their homes against the danger of losing them should they let them during their absence; and accordingly enabled more living accommodation to become available to the public than would otherwise have been the case.

I think, therefore, the construction of Case 10 which I favour is in accordance with the policy of the 1968 Act and with the public good. I am afraid that I cannot accept the other construction which could lead to absurd and unjust results. Suppose, for example, a husband and wife who are co-owners of their home have to live abroad for say two years on account of the husband's business activities. They then let their home for those two years and comply with all the provisions of Case 10. Unfortunately, the husband falls in love with another woman and his wife divorces him. They, however, remain comparatively friendly, and the husband is willing for his wife to live in their former matrimonial home. The tenancy has expired but the tenant refuses to leave. An action is brought by both the co-owners for possession. The defence is that the action cannot succeed because the house is required as a residence for one only of the co-owners. If the majority decision of the Court of Appeal is correct, the action would fail.

Take another example. Three sisters are living in a house. Two of them are co-owners

---

1 Case 8 provides: 'Where the dwelling-house is reasonably required by the landlord for occupation as a residence for—(a) himself, or (b) any son or daughter of his over eighteen years of age, or (c) his father or mother, or (d) if the dwelling-house is let on or subject to a regulated tenancy, the father or mother of his wife or husband, and the landlord did not become landlord by purchasing the dwelling-house or any interest therein after 23rd March 1965 or, if the dwelling-house is let on or subject to a controlled tenancy, after 7th November 1956.'

2 [1948] 1 All ER 696, [1948] 2 KB 82

of the house. The third has no legal or equitable title to it. The two co-owners and their sister leave the house to live abroad temporarily, the house is let for say two years and all the provisions of Case 10 are complied with. Both the co-owners then get married and decide to live abroad. The third sister returns to England. She is a member of the family of both the co-owners and resided with them when last they occupied the house as a residence. The tenant is sued for possession by the two co-owners on the ground that the house is required as a residence for their sister. There could be no defence to the action and the co-owners' sister would be enabled to reside in the house. Suppose, however, that the first co-owner's sister and the third sister had married and decided to live abroad whilst the second sister who was a co-owner returned to England and an action for possession was brought on the ground that the house was required as a residence for her. The action would fail because it could not succeed unless the house was required as a residence for both the co-owners. Yet an action to enable the house to be occupied by the sister who had no legal or equitable title to it would have succeeded. This does not seem to me to make any sense at all. But it is the inevitable result of what might happen unless the construction of Case 10 which I favour is correct.

For the reasons I have stated, I would allow the appeal and remit the case to the county court for the learned judge to decide the few issues of simple fact which, most unfortunately, he did not dispose of before making his findings on the points of law. I would order with reluctance that the costs in this House and in the Court of Appeal be paid by Miss Whiteman. There is, I think, no other course which your Lordships can take. I am extremely disturbed that such a heavy financial burden should fall on Miss Whiteman's shoulders, particularly as it would have been avoided had she obtained legal aid; it may be that the Law Society will wish to consider whether there are any circumstances which might justify the order as to costs not being enforced.

LORD FRASER OF TULLYBELTON. My Lords, I regret that I am unable to agree with the view of my noble and learned friends with whom I heard the argument in this appeal. I can, therefore, have little confidence in my own view, but I shall express it as briefly as possible.

The appeal raises a question of construing words in Case 10, which is in Part II of Sch 3 to the Rent Act 1968. Part II is headed 'Cases in which court must order possession where dwelling-house subject to regulated tenancy'. Case 10 begins by describing the class of person for the benefit of whom, or whose family, it will operate if the other conditions are satisfied. The person has to be qualified in two ways: (1) he must have 'occupied the dwelling-house as his residence' and (2) he must have 'let it on a regulated tenancy'. The same person is referred to throughout, and he must have both occupied and let the house. His dual character is appropriately recognised in the statutory description of him as 'the owner-occupier'. The present case proceeds on an agreed statement of facts, which shows that (and I paraphrase): (1) the house is jointly owned by two ladies, Mrs Tilling, the appellant, and Miss Dossett, who are not related; (2) it was occupied by both of them, though only the appellant was occupying it immediately before it was let to the respondent; (3) it was let to the respondent under a lease to which the joint owners were one party, described in the lease as 'the landlord'; (4) it is now required as a residence for only one of the joint owners, the appellant.

In these circumstances it seems to me that the 'person' who let the house was the composite person consisting of both joint owners. Neither owner separately let the house. It may be that one of them could have let the house without the concurrence of the other, so far as the rest of the world is concerned, but that is not what happened. It follows that the only person who falls within the statutory description of 'the owner-occupier' is the composite person, and as the house is not required as a residence for that person, the claim for the appellant alone must fail. Like Stephenson and Shaw LJJ I can see no acceptable answer to that simple argument. With all respect to those who think otherwise, I do not regard it as right or possible to read the word 'let' in the first clause of Case 10 as if it meant 'concurred in letting'. Even if one joint owner could truthfully say in casual conversation that she had let the house, a matter on which I feel serious doubt, it does not follow that the statute, which is expressed in precise language, can be read in the same way. The singular 'person' can, of course, be read as including the plural: see the Interpretation Act 1889. If it is read as meaning the plural here, then so also must 'the owner-occupier' be read in the plural, with the result that para (c) of Case 10 will only apply where the house is required by both owner-occupiers or a member of their joint family as a residence.

Some support for my view is found in McIntyre v Hardcastle[1], though that is not directly in point as it was dealing with what later became Case 8 of Sch 3 to the 1968 Act, where the wording differs materially from the wording of Case 10. Nevertheless, I would adopt the words of Tucker LJ, where he said[2]:

> 'I do not think that the legislature really contemplated this situation at all when this paragraph was framed, and, therefore, I feel driven to interpret it merely in the light of the actual language used.'

That is what I have tried to do.

I do not find any assistance in the policy of s 10 of the 1968 Act, which is the section authorising Sch 3. No doubt s 10 is intended to benefit owners, and to increase the supply of houses for letting, but it is an exception to the main policy of Part II of the Act, which evidently is to give security of tenure to tenants. The question is what are the limits of the exception, and the answer must, I think, be found simply in the words used by Parliament. I would only add that, on the facts as known to me, it appears that the merits of the present dispute are on the side of the appellant rather than of the respondent, but that cannot justify straining the words of the 1968 Act in her favour.

I would refuse the appeal.

LORD SCARMAN. My Lords, I have had the advantage of reading in draft the speech delivered by my noble and learned friend, Lord Wilberforce. I agree with it. I would allow this appeal for the reasons given by Eveleigh LJ in his dissenting judgment. I also agree that the appellant should have her costs before this House and in the Court of Appeal.

The case presents two disturbing features. First, the decision in the county court was on a preliminary point of law. Had an extra half hour or so been used to hear the evidence, one of two consequences would have ensued. Either Mrs Tilling would have been believed when she said she required the house as a residence, or she would not. If the latter, that would have been the end of the case. If the former, your Lordships' decision allowing the appeal would now be final. As it is, the case has to go back to the county court to be tried. Preliminary points of law are too often treacherous short cuts. Their price can be, as here, delay, anxiety and expense. Secondly, it is a tragedy that Miss Whiteman, who has appeared in person before this House because of the expense of legal representation, was not legally aided. She had an eminently arguable case and, if legally aided, would have been protected against the burden of costs which under our law falls on the unsuccessful litigant. Perhaps she was above the very modest limits set to eligibility for legal aid. But there are indications that she chose not to apply. I wonder whether she fully understood the protection offered a litigant by legal aid. Surely those who helped her with advice (and she did have advisers, legal and lay, at various times) might have persuaded her. Perhaps they tried and failed. But the result, whatever its cause, is a financial disaster for her.

Appeal allowed. Order appealed from reversed and cause remitted to Dover County Court for a decision on the basis that Case 10 of Part II of Sch 3 to the Rent Act 1968 applied to the assumed facts.

Solicitors: *Williamson & Barnes* (for the appellant).

Mary Rose Plummer   Barrister.

---

1   [1948] 1 All ER 696, [1948] 2 KB 82
2   [1948] 1 All ER 696 at 699, [1948] 2 KB 82 at 90

a

Attorney-General v Leveller Magazine Ltd and others

HOUSE OF LORDS

LORD DIPLOCK, VISCOUNT DILHORNE, LORD EDMUND-DAVIES, LORD RUSSELL OF KILLOWEN AND LORD SCARMAN

b 28th, 29th, 30th NOVEMBER 1978, 1st FEBRUARY 1979

Contempt of court – Witness – Disclosure of identity – Justices in committal proceedings allowing witness to conceal his identity – Ruling given for reasons of national security – No formal direction or order by justices – Evidence elicited from witness in cross-examination enabling his identity to be ascertained without difficulty – No objection by prosecution to evidence – Newspapers publishing witness's name after committal proceedings – Whether publication of witness's name contempt of
c *court.*

During committal proceedings to commit three defendants for trial for offences under the Official Secrets Acts 1911 to 1939 the Crown requested that the identity of a witness, Colonel B, should be suppressed because disclosure of his identity would be injurious to national security. The justices, having been advised by their clerk that they could not give
d directions binding on the public preventing information about the proceedings from being published outside the court, ruled that Colonel B could write down his name which was then to be disclosed only to the court and defence counsel, and that the witness was to be referred to at the hearing in their court only as 'Colonel B'. Colonel B then gave his evidence in open court, in the course of which he gave the name and number of the army unit to which he belonged and referred to the fact that his posting to that unit was recorded in a particular issue of an army magazine available to the public. This evidence, which
e made it possible for Colonel B's identity to be discovered, was given without objection by the Crown and without application being made for the court to sit in camera. Shortly after the committal proceedings had ended the appellants published Colonel B's name in their journals. The Attorney-General applied to commit the appellants for contempt of court on the ground that they had deliberately flouted a direction of the justices prohibiting any
f attempt to disclose Colonel B's identity. There being some doubt as to whether the justices had made such a direction, the Attorney-General applied for leave to amend his grounds to allege that the actions of the appellants tended and was calculated to prejudice the due administration of justice and that they had deliberately flouted the procedure of the justices. The Divisional Court[a] refused leave but went on to find the appellants guilty of contempt because although there had not been a formal direction or order there had been a ruling intended to be mandatory within the court and the appellants' flouting of that
g ruling outside the court had frustrated it. The appellants were fined a total of £1,200. They appealed to the House of Lords.

Held – The appeals would be allowed for the following reasons—

(1) The appellants had not been guilty of contempt in disregarding the justices' ruling, because—

h (i) (per Lord Diplock, Viscount Dilhorne, Lord Edmund-Davies and Lord Scarman) In exercising its control over the conduct of proceedings being heard before it, a court was entitled to derogate from the principle of open justice by sitting in private or permitting a witness not to disclose his name when giving evidence if it was necessary to do so in the due administration of justice, and where a court adopted the latter procedure and took steps to preserve the anonymity of a witness, an attempt to frustrate the actions of the court
j by publishing his identity was capable of being a contempt if it interfered with the due administration of justice, but in the absence of such interference merely running counter to a direction of the court was not of itself enough to make the publication a contempt of the court (see p 750 *b* to *d*, p 751 *e f*, p 755 *f*, p 756 *b* to *e*, p 761 *b c* and *h*, p 764 *h* to

a [1978] 3 All ER 731

p 765 *a*, p 766 *d* to *g* and p 768 *c*, post); *R v Socialist Worker Printers and Publishers Ltd* [1975] 1 All ER 142 approved.

a

(ii) (per Lord Diplock, Lord Edmund-Davies and Lord Scarman; Lord Russell contra) However, having regard to the fact that interference with the administration of justice was a criminal offence, there had to be a clear direction or order restricting publication since it was not contempt to ignore an unexpressed wish of, or a mere request by, the court not to publish, and (per Lord Scarman) the direction or order must be made only if it is reasonably necessary and, further, the offence had to be committed beyond reasonable doubt (see *b* p 751 *b*, p 752 *f g*, p 759 *b c*, p 763 *h j*, p 764 *e f*, p 765 *a*, p 767 *j* to p 768 *c*, post).

(iii) (per Lord Diplock and Lord Scarman; Viscount Dilhorne, Lord Edmund-Davies and Lord Russell contra) Furthermore, the court was required to make clear what restrictions were intended to be imposed on publishing outside the court and whether those restrictions were precatory only or would be enforced by contempt proceedings if breached, unless (per Lord Diplock) the object of making the ruling was so obvious that no explicit warning was *c* required (see p 751 *c* and *h*, p 752 *h*, p 755 *b*, p 762 *c* and *h j*, p 764 *f* and p 768 *c d*, post).

(iv) Since (per Lord Diplock, Lord Edmund-Davies and Lord Scarman; Lord Russell contra) the nature and object of the justices' ruling was not clear, and (per Lord Diplock) the justices had not given a warning that publication of anything likely to lead to the identification of Colonel B would frustrate their ruling, and (per Lord Scarman) it was not apparent that the justices had made their ruling to protect the administration of justice, the *d* appellants had not been in contempt in disregarding the ruling (see p 751 *j* to p 752 *a*, p 759 *f* to *h*, p 763 *e* to *g*, p 764 *f*, p 767 *g h* and p 768 *d*, post).

(2) (per Viscount Dilhorne, Lord Edmund-Davies and Lord Scarman) The Divisional Court had been wrong to proceed on the basis that the appellants had flouted the justices' intention when the Attorney-General had moved to commit the appellants on the different basis that an explicit direction had been given, since the appellants were entitled to know *e* with reasonable precision the charge they had to meet, and (per Lord Edmund-Davies) in any event the justices' ruling was indeterminate as to their intention (see p 754 *c d*, p 758 *a* to *c*, p 759 *a b* and *e* to *g* and p 767 *g*, post).

(3) (per Lord Diplock, Viscount Dilhorne and Lord Russell) It was not, in the circumstances, a contempt to publish what could be deduced from evidence given in open court which was freely reportable, and since the identity of Colonel B could be discovered *f* from such evidence it was not a contempt to publish his name (see p 752 *b* to *e*, p 754 *b c* and *h* to p 755 *a*, p 756 *d* and p 764 *c* to *g*, post).

Per Lord Diplock, Viscount Dilhorne and Lord Edmund-Davies. Whenever a court makes a ruling in the interests of the due administration of justice involving a departure from the ordinary mode of conduct of proceedings in open court, it is desirable that the court should explain the result that the ruling is designed to achieve and what kind of *g* information about the proceedings would, if published, tend to frustrate that result and would accordingly expose the publisher to the risk of proceedings for contempt (see p 751 *g h*, p 752 *h j*, p 755 *b c* and p 762 *b c*, post).

Per Viscount Dilhorne and Lord Edmund-Davies; Lord Russell contra; Lord Diplock leaving the matter open. A court does not have power to make an order directed to and binding on the public ipso jure as to what might lawfully be published outside the *h* courtroom (see p 751 *d e*, p 754 *d* to *g* and p 761 *a* to *c* and *g*, post); *Taylor v Attorney-General* [1975] 2 NZLR 675 distinguished.

Per Lord Scarman. In the absence of statutory authority, a court has no power to sit in private or permit a witness not to disclose his name when giving evidence merely because it believes that to sit in public would prejudice national security (see p 766 *d*, post).

Decision of the Divisional Court of the Queen's Bench Division [1978] 3 All ER 731 *j* reversed.

Notes

For contempts outside the court, see 9 Halsbury's Laws (4th Edn) paras 7–14, and for cases on criminal contempt, see 16 Digest (Repl) 17–45, 102–396.

Cases referred to in opinions

a   *Attorney-General v Butterworth* [1962] 3 All ER 326, sub nom *Re Attorney-General's Application* [1963] 1 QB 696, LR 3 RP 327, [1962] 3 WLR 819, CA, Digest (Cont Vol A) 454, 395*a*.

Attorney-General v Times Newspapers Ltd [1973] 3 All ER 54, [1974] AC 273, [1973] 3 WLR 298, HL, Digest (Cont Vol D) 254, 204*c*.

Delbert-Evans v Davies and Watson [1945] 2 All ER 167, 173 LT 289, sub nom *R v Davies, ex*
b   *parte Delbert-Evans* [1945] KB 435, 114 LJKB 417, DC, 16 Digest (Repl) 25, 195.

F (a minor) (publication of information), Re [1977] 1 All ER 114, [1977] Fam 58, [1976] 3 WLR 813, CA.

Johnson v Grant 1923 SC 789, 16 Digest (Repl) 18,* 68.

R v Blumenfeld, ex parte Tupper (1912) 28 TLR 308, 16 Digest (Repl) 31, 263.

R v Border Television Ltd, ex parte Attorney-General, R v Newcastle Chronicle and Journal Ltd,
c   *ex parte Attorney-General* [1978] The Times, 18th January, DC.

R v Lewes Prison (Governor), ex parte Doyle [1917] 2 KB 254, 86 LJKB 1514, 116 LT 407, 81 JP 173, 25 Cox CC 635, 16 Digest (Repl) 146, 281.

R v Socialist Worker Printers and Publishers Ltd, ex parte Attorney-General [1975] 1 All ER 142, [1975] QB 637, [1974] 3 WLR 801, DC, Digest (Cont Vol D) 255, 394*b*.

Scott v Scott [1913] AC 417, [1911–13] All ER Rep 1, 82 LJP 74, 109 LT 1, HL, 16 Digest
d   (Repl) 40, 339.

Taylor v Attorney-General [1975] 2 NZLR 675.

Thomas (PA) & Co v Mould [1968] 1 All ER 963, [1968] 2 QB 913, [1968] 2 WLR 737, 28 (2) Digest (Reissue) 1143, 1455.

Appeals

e   By notices of motion the Attorney-General applied for orders under RSC Ord 52, r 9, and for orders of committal against Leveller Magazine Ltd, publishers of the magazine Leveller, and David Anthony Clark, Russell David Southwood, David Nigel Mitchell Thomas, Philip John Kelly and Timothy Reginald Gopsill, producers of the Leveller, issues no 11 dated January 1978 and no 13 dated March 1978, against Peace News Ltd, publishers of the periodical Peace News, and Alison de Reybekill, Helen Linton, Christopher Jones, Michael
f   Holderness and Albert Beale, producers of Peace News issued on 16th December 1977, and against the National Union of Journalists, publishers of the periodical Journalist, for contempt of court in deliberately disclosing the identity of one Colonel B, a witness in committal proceedings when the examining justices had ruled that the witness should be referred to in court as Colonel B and not by his real name which should be written down and disclosed only to the court, the defendants and their counsel. On 19th May 1978 the
g   Divisional Court of the Queen's Bench Division[1] (Lord Widgery CJ, Croom-Johnson and Stocker JJ) held that the respondents to the motions had been guilty of criminal contempt of court and refused them leave to appeal to the House of Lords. The National Union of Journalists, Timothy Reginald Gopsill, Philip John Kelly and David Anthony Clark, Peace News Ltd, Alison de Reybekill, Helen Linton, Christopher Jones, Michael Holderness and Albert Beale appealed to the House of Lords pursuant to leave granted by the House on 6th
h   July 1978. The facts are set out in the opinion of Lord Diplock.

John Melville Williams QC and *John Hendy* for the National Union of Journalists.
Stephen Sedley for the appellants other than the National Union of Journalists.
Lord Rawlinson QC, Harry Woolf and *Rodger Bell* for the Attorney-General.

j   Their Lordships took time for consideration.

1st February. The following opinions were delivered.

LORD DIPLOCK. My Lords, in November 1977 three defendants, two of whom were journalists, had been charged with offences under the Official Secrets Acts 1911 to 1939. *a* Committal proceedings against them were being heard before the Tottenham magistrates' court acting as examining justices. The proceedings extended over a considerable number of days. On the first day, on the application of counsel for the prosecution, some of the evidence was heard in camera pursuant to s 8(4) of the Official Secrets Act 1920. On the third day, 10th November, counsel for the prosecution made an application that the next witness whom he proposed to call should, for his own security and for reasons of national *b* safety, be referred to as 'Colonel A' and that his name should not be disclosed to anyone. The magistrates, on the advice of their clerk, ruled correctly but with expressed reluctance, that this would not be possible and that although the witness should be referred to as 'Colonel A', his name would have to be written down and disclosed to the court and to the defendants and their counsel. The prosecution decided not to call that witness and the proceedings were adjourned. *c*

The hearing was resumed four days later on 14th November. The prosecution called, instead of Colonel A, another witness. Counsel for the prosecution applied for him to be referred to as 'Colonel B' and that his name be written down and shown only to the court, the defendants and their counsel. This was said to be necessary for reasons of national safety; risk to Colonel B's own security was not relied on. Counsel for the defendants raised no objection to the course proposed; the magistrates assented to it and the witness then *d* gave evidence in open court. He was throughout referred to as 'Colonel B'; his real name was never mentioned. For the purposes of the proceedings for contempt of court with which the Divisional Court and now your Lordships have been concerned, it must be taken, although initially there was conflicting evidence as to this, that the magistrates gave no express ruling or direction other than that the witness was to be referred to in court as 'Colonel B' and not by his real name and that his real name was to be written down and *e* disclosed only to the court, the defendants and their counsel.

In the course of the cross-examination of Colonel B questions were put the effect of which was to elicit from him (1) the official name and number of the army unit to which he belonged and (2) the fact that his posting to it was recorded in a particular issue of Wire, the magazine of the Royal Corps of Signals which is obtainable by the public. These answers enabled his identity to be discovered by anyone who cared to follow up this simple *f* clue. The line of questioning which elicited this information was pursued without objection from counsel for the prosecution, the witness or the magistrates; and the answers which made his identity so easy to discover were included in the colonel's deposition read out to him in open court before he signed it.

In the issue of Peace News for 18th November these two pieces of information about Colonel B elicited in open court were published; and in the issue for 16th December the *g* name of Colonel B was disclosed and an account was given of his military career. In the January and March 1978 issues of another magazine, the Leveller, the name of Colonel B was published. Finally in the issues of Journalist for March and April 1978 published by the National Union of Journalists Colonel B was again identified by name.

All this occurred before the trial of the defendants at the Central Criminal Court began.

On 22nd March 1978 the Attorney-General brought in the Divisional Court proceedings *h* for contempt of court against Peace Magazine Ltd and Leveller Magazine Ltd and persons responsible for the publication in those periodicals of the articles which published the real name of Colonel B; and on 18th April he brought similar proceedings against the National Union of Journalists in respect of the articles appearing in the Journalist. In each of these proceedings the statement filed pursuant to RSC Ord 52, r 2, contained an allegation that at the committal proceedings in Tottenham magistrates' court on 14th November 1977 *j* not only had the magistrates permitted Colonel B not to disclose his identity but their chairman had also given an express direction in open court that no attempt should be made to disclose the identity of Colonel B. Before the three motions, which were heard together, came on for hearing, an affidavit by the clerk to the Tottenham magistrates was filed, denying that any such explicit direction had been given by the chairman of the magistrates

and stating that the reason why such a direction was not given was because he had advised
the magistrates that they had no power to do so. In view of this evidence the hearing of the
a motions proceeded on the basis that no explicit direction had been given to those present
at the hearing that no attempt should be made to disclose the identity of Colonel B, and
that what had happened at the committal proceedings in relation to the witness being
referred to only as Colonel B was as I have already stated it.

My Lords, it is not disputed that the disclosure of Colonel B's identity by the appellants
b was part of a campaign of protest against the Official Secrets Acts. It was designed, no
doubt, to ridicule the notion that national safety needed to be protected by suppression of
the colonel's name. The only question for your Lordships is whether in doing what they
did the appellants were guilty of contempt of court.

The Divisional Court found contempt of court established against all appellants but
made orders only against the National Union of Journalists and the two companies. The
National Union of Journalists was fined £200, Peace Magazine Ltd and Leveller Magazine
c Ltd were each fined £500. Against these orders these appeals are now brought to this
House.

In the judgment of the Divisional Court delivered by Lord Widgery CJ it is pointed out
that contempt of court can take many forms. The publication by the appellants of the
witness's identity after the magistrates had ruled that he should be referred to in their court
d only as 'Colonel B' was held by the Divisional Court to fall into a class said to be exemplified
in *Attorney-General v Butterworth*[1] and *R v Socialist Worker Printers and Publishers Ltd, ex parte
Attorney-General*[2] and variously described in the course of the judgment as 'a deliberate
flouting of the court's authority', 'a flouting (or deliberate disregard) outside the court of
the court's ruling', a 'deliberate intention of frustrating the arrangement which the court
had made to preserve Colonel B's anonymity' and finally a 'deliberate flouting of the court's
e intention'. I do not think that any of these ways of describing what the appellants did is
sufficiently precise to lead inexorably to the conclusion that what they did amounted to
contempt of court. Closer analysis is needed.

The only 'ruling' that the magistrates had in fact given was that the witness should be
referred to *at the hearing in their court* as 'Colonel B' and that his name must be written down
and shown to the court, the defendants and their counsel but to no one else. That it was
f also the only ruling that they intended to give is apparent from the fact that they had been
advised by their clerk that it was the only ruling that they had power to give, however
much they might have preferred to give a wider one. None of the appellants committed
any breach of this ruling. What they did, and did deliberately, outside the court and after
the conclusion of Colonel B's evidence in the committal proceedings, was to take steps to
ensure that this anonymity was not preserved.

My Lords, although criminal contempts of court may take a variety of forms they all
g share a common characteristic: they involve an interference with the due administration
of justice, either in a particular case or more generally as a continuing process. It is justice
itself that is flouted by contempt of court, not the individual court or judge who is
attempting to administer it.

Of those contempts that can be committed outside the courtroom the most familiar
h consist of publishing, in connection with legal proceedings that are pending or imminent,
comment or information that has a tendency to pervert the course of justice, either in those
proceedings or by deterring other people from having recourse to courts of justice in the
future for the vindication of their lawful rights or for the enforcement of the criminal
law. In determining whether what is published has such a tendency a distinction must be
drawn between reporting what actually occurred at the hearing of the proceedings and
j publishing other kinds of comment or information; for prima facie the interests of justice
are served by its being administered in the full light of publicity.

As a general rule the English system of administering justice does require that it be done

---

1   [1962] 3 All ER 326, [1963] 1 QB 696
2   [1975] 1 All ER 142, [1975] QB 637

in public: *Scott v Scott*[1]. If the way that courts behave cannot be hidden from the public ear and eye this provides a safeguard against judicial arbitrariness or idiosyncrasy and maintains the public confidence in the administration of justice. The application of this principle of open justice has two aspects: as respects proceedings in the court itself it requires that they should be held in open court to which the Press and public are admitted and that, in criminal cases at any rate, all evidence communicated to the court is communicated publicly. As respects the publication to a wider public of fair and accurate reports of proceedings that have taken place in court the principle requires that nothing should be done to discourage this.

However, since the purpose of the general rule is to serve the ends of justice it may be necessary to depart from it where the nature or circumstances of the particular proceeding are such that the application of the general rule in its entirety would frustrate or render impracticable the administration of justice or would damage some other public interest for whose protection Parliament has made some statutory derogation from the rule. Apart from statutory exceptions, however, where a court in the exercise of its inherent power to control the conduct of proceedings before it departs in any way from the general rule, the departure is justified to the extent and to no more than the extent that the court reasonably believes it to be necessary in order to serve the ends of justice. A familiar instance of this is provided by the 'trial within a trial' as to the admissibility of a confession in a criminal prosecution. The due administration of justice requires that the jury should be unaware of what was the evidence adduced at the trial within a trial until after they have reached their verdict; but no greater derogation from the general rule as to the public nature of all proceedings at a criminal trial is justified than is necessary to ensure this. So far as proceedings in the courtroom are concerned the trial within a trial is held in open court in the presence of the Press and public but in the absence of the jury. So far as publishing those proceedings outside the court is concerned any report of them which might come to the knowledge of the jury must be withheld until after they have reached their verdict; but it may be published after that. Only premature publication would constitute contempt of court.

In the instant case the only statutory provisions that have any relevance are s 8(4) of the Official Secrets Act 1920 and s 12(1)(c) of the Administration of Justice Act 1960. Both deal with the giving of evidence before a court sitting in camera. They do not apply to the evidence given by Colonel B in the instant case. Their relevance is thus peripheral and I can dispose of them shortly.

Section 8(4) of the Official Secrets Act 1920 applies to prosecutions under that Act and the Official Secrets Act 1911. It empowers but it does not compel a court to sit to hear evidence in private if the Crown applies for this on the ground that national safety would be prejudiced by its publication. Section 12(1) of the Administration of Justice Act 1960 defines and limits the circumstances in which the publication of information relating to proceedings before any court sitting in private is of itself contempt of court. The circumstances defined in s 12(1)(c) is 'where the court sits in private for reasons of national security during that part of the proceedings about which the information in question is published'. So to report evidence in camera in a prosecution under the Official Secrets Acts would be contempt of court.

In the instant case the magistrates would have had power to sit in camera to hear the whole or part of the evidence of Colonel B if this had been requested by the prosecution; and although they would not have been bound to accede to such a request it would naturally and properly have carried great weight with them. So would the absence of any such request. Without it the magistrates, in my opinion, would have had no reasonable ground for believing that so drastic a derogation from the general principle of open justice as is involved in hearing evidence in a criminal case in camera was necessary in the interests of the due administration of justice.

In substitution for hearing Colonel B's evidence in camera which it could have asked for,

---

1   [1913] AC 417, [1911–13] All ER Rep 1

the prosecution was content to treat a much less drastic derogation from the principle of
a open justice as adequate to protect the interests of national security. The witness's evidence
was to be given in open court in the normal way except that he was to be referred to by the
pseudonym of 'Colonel B' and evidence as to his real name and address was to be written
down and disclosed only to the court, the defendants and their legal representatives.

I do not doubt that, applying their minds to the matter that it was their duty to consider
the interests of the due administration of justice, the magistrates had power to accede to
b this proposal for the very reason that it would involve less derogation from the general
principle of open justice than would result from the Crown being driven to have recourse
to the statutory procedure for hearing evidence in camera under s 8(4) of the Official
Secrets Act 1920; but in adopting this particular device which on the face of it related only
to how proceedings within the courtroom were to be conducted it behoved the magistrates
to make it clear what restrictions, if any, were intended by them to be imposed on
c publishing outside the courtroom information relating to those proceedings and whether
such restrictions were to be precatory only or enforceable by the sanction of proceedings for
contempt of court.

My Lords, in the argument before this House little attempt was made to analyse the
juristic basis on which a court can make a 'ruling', 'order' or 'direction' (call it what you
will) relating to proceedings taking place before it, which has the effect in law of restricting
d what may be done outside the courtroom by members of the public who are not engaged
in those proceedings as parties or their legal representatives or as witnesses. The Court of
Appeal of New Zealand in *Taylor v Attorney-General*[1] was clearly of opinion that a court had
power to make an explicit order directed to and binding on the public ipso jure as to what
might lawfully be published outside the courtroom in relation to proceedings held before
it. For my part I am prepared to leave this as an open question in the instant case. It may
e be that a 'ruling' by the court as to the conduct of proceedings can have binding effect as
such within the courtroom only, so that breach of it is not ipso facto a contempt of court
unless it is committed there. Nevertheless where (1) the reason for a ruling which involves
departing in some measure from the general principle of open justice within the courtroom
is that the departure is necessary in the interests of the due administration of justice and
(2) it would be apparent to anyone who was aware of the ruling that the result which the
f ruling is designed to achieve would be frustrated by a particular kind of act done outside
the courtroom, the doing of such an act with knowledge of the ruling and of its purpose
may constitute a contempt of court, not because it is a breach of the ruling but because it
interferes with the due administration of justice.

So it does not seem to me to matter greatly in the instant case whether or not the
magistrates were rightly advised that they had in law no power to give directions which
would be binding as such on members of the public as to what information relating to the
g proceedings taking place before them might be published outside the courtroom. What
was incumbent on them was to make it clear to anyone present at, or reading an accurate
report of, the proceedings, what in the interests of the due administration of justice, was
the result that was intended by them to be achieved by the limited derogation from the
principle of open justice within the courtroom which they had authorised, and what kind
h of information derived from what happened in the courtroom would if it were published
frustrate that result.

There may be many cases in which the result intended to be achieved by a ruling by the
court as to what is to be done in court is so obvious as to speak for itself; it calls for no
explicit statement. Sending the jury out of court during a trial within a trial is an example
of this; so may be the common ruling in prosecutions for blackmail that a victim called as
j a witness be referred to in court by a pseudonym: see *R v Socialist Worker Printers and
Publishers Ltd*[2]; but, in the absence of any explicit statement by the Tottenham magistrates
at the conclusion of the colonel's evidence that the purpose of their ruling would be

---

1   [1975] 2 NZLR 695
2   [1975] 1 All ER 142, [1975] QB 637

frustrated if anything were published outside the courtroom that would be likely to lead to the identification of Colonel B as the person who had given evidence in the case, I do not *a* think that the instant case falls into this class.

The ruling that the witness was to be referred in court only as 'Colonel B' was given before any of his evidence had been heard and at that stage of the proceedings it might be an obvious inference that the effect intended by the magistrates to be achieved by their ruling was to prevent his identity being publicly disclosed. As I have already pointed out however the evidence that he gave in open court in cross-examination did in effect disclose *b* his identity to anyone prepared to take the trouble to consult a particular issue (specified in the evidence) of a magazine that was on sale to the public. This evidence was elicited without any protest from counsel for the prosecution; no application was made that this part of the evidence should be heard in camera; no suggestion, let alone request, was made to members of the Press present in court that it should not be reported; and once it was reported the witness's anonymity was blown. *c*

In these circumstances whatever may have been the effect intended to be achieved by the magistrates at the time of their initial ruling, this, as it seems to me, had been abandoned with the acquiescence of counsel for the Crown, by the time that Colonel B's evidence was over. I see no grounds on which a person present at or reading a report of the proceedings was bound to infer that to publish that part of the colonel's evidence in open court that disclosed his identity would interfere with the due administration of justice so as to *d* constitute a contempt of court. Indeed the natural inference is to the contrary and it may not be without significance that no proceedings were brought against Peace News in respect of the issue of 18th November in which this evidence was published, without actually stating what would be found to be the colonel's name if the particular issue of Wire were consulted. But if there was no reason to suppose that publication of this evidence would interfere with the due administration of justice, how could it reasonably be supposed *e* that to take the final step of publishing the name itself made all the difference?

My Lords, I would allow these appeals on the ground that in the particular and peculiar circumstances of this case the disclosure of Colonel B's identity as a witness involved no interference with the due administration of justice and was not a contempt of court.

The difficulty that has arisen, as my noble and learned friends, Viscount Dilhorne and Lord Edmund-Davies, point out, is because the proceedings were launched on the basis *f* that at the conclusion of Colonel B's evidence the chairman of the examining magistrates 'had stressed that no attempt should be made to disclose the identity of Colonel B'. At the hearing, however, the proceedings, if persisted in had to be conducted on the basis that no such explicit statement had been made. So everything was left to implication except the actual ruling as to how the witness was to be referred to in court and as to the persons to whom alone his real name and identity were to be disclosed. *g*

My Lords, in cases where courts, in the interests of the due administration of justice, have departed in some measure from the general principle of open justice no one ought to be exposed to penal sanctions for criminal contempt of court for failing to draw an inference or recognise an implication as to what it is permissible to publish about those proceedings unless the inference or implication is so obvious or so familiar that it may be said to speak for itself. *h*

Difficulties such as those that have arisen in the instant case could be avoided in future if the court, whenever in the interests of due administration of justice it made a ruling which involved some departure from the ordinary mode of conduct of proceedings in open court, were to explain the result that the ruling was designed to achieve and what kind of information about the proceedings would, if published, tend to frustrate that result and would, accordingly, expose the publisher to risk of proceedings for contempt of court. *j*

VISCOUNT DILHORNE. My Lords, the question to be determined in this appeal is whether the appellants were, as the Divisional Court held, guilty of contempt of court in publishing in Peace News, the Leveller and the Journalist, respectively, the identity of Colonel B.

In the statements dated 17th March and 17th April 1978, filed pursuant to the rules of
court in support of the Attorney-General's motions and which stated the grounds for the
motions, it was alleged that they had revealed his identity after he had been referred to as
'Colonel B' in the committal proceedings and—

'(b) The said "Colonel B" had properly been permitted not to disclose his identity
when giving evidence to the said Magistrates, [the Chairman directing in open Court
that no attempt should be made to disclose the identity of "Colonel B"].

'(c) [The appellants were at all material times well aware that the aforesaid direction
had been given.]

'(d) The said disclosure of the identity of "Colonel B" tended and was calculated to
prejudice the due administration of justice; it was intended to [flout the aforesaid
direction and] make it difficult for witnesses in the position of "Colonel B" to give
evidence in open Court.'

The motions were supported by an affidavit sworn by Miss Anne Butler, a member of
the Director of Public Prosecutions' Office. In it she said that at the conclusion of the
hearing on 14th November 1977 the chairman of the magistrates had 'stressed that no
attempt should be made to disclose the identity of Colonel B'. In this, according to Mr
Pratt, the clerk to the magistrates, she was mistaken. In an affidavit sworn by him on 27th
April 1978 he said that he had no recollection of that being said and in fact did not agree
that it had happened. Paragraphs 3 and 4 of his affidavit read as follows:

'3. The Official Secrets Act provides for exclusion of all or part of the public and, in
fact, the public were excluded during the playing of the tape but I am not aware of
any other provision relevant to these proceedings enabling an Order to be made such
as is referred to or implied in Anne Butler's Affidavit and that was the reason why the
Magistrates did not make any Order such as she refers to—because I advised them that
they had no power to do so.

'4. I am not aware of any provision enabling my Court to purport to impose
any restriction on anything said in Court in the presence of the public in the
proceedings . . .'

At the hearing of the motions, the contention that the appellants had published Colonel
B's name in breach of a direction given by the chairman was abandoned and the Crown
sought leave to amend the statement filed by the deletion of the words which I have
enclosed in square brackets. Leave to do so was refused.

Breach of the chairman's direction was clearly the main plank in the Crown's case when
the proceedings were initiated. Abandonment of that contention meant that the Crown
was consequently limited to establishing that the appellants had been guilty of contempt
in publishing Colonel B's name after he 'had properly been permitted not to disclose his
identity when giving evidence'.

That they had done so after he had been given that permission was not in dispute. The
question is whether, in all the circumstances of the case, that amounted to a contempt.

From his deposition it appears that, at the commencement of his cross-examination,
Colonel B gave the following evidence:

'I have been with the Ministry of Defence for some three years. I left earlier this
month. My posting was Colonel, General Staff, in the Defence Intelligence Staff. The
Defence Intelligence number is D.I.24 Army. I realise that it may have been published
in various publications but I am now aware it was published in "Wire" December
1974–January 1975.'

Wire is the Royal Signals Magazine. Among the appointments listed in this issue was
that of Colonel H A Johnstone MBE as 'Col: G D S D I (Army) 11.74'.

I do not know to what issue in the case the questions which elicited this information
about Colonel B's career were directed. I assume that they were relevant to some issue. We
were not told that any objection was made to them and it does not appear that any

application was made for the hearing of his evidence in camera once the line the cross-examination was taking became apparent. However relevant the questions may have been, the answers given in open court made it possible, for anyone who wished to do so, to find out who Colonel B was. He had only to look at that issue of *Wire*. In the issue of the *Leveller* of 13th March 1978 it was said that these answers given in open court enabled that paper and *Peace News* to 'deduce his identity'.

Unless the magistrates had power to prohibit and had prohibited it, the publication of this evidence could not be a contempt of court. It was not suggested that there had been any such prohibition or that the magistrates had power to impose one. If publication of the evidence could not be a contempt of court, was it a contempt to publish what could be deduced from that evidence, namely the identity of Colonel B? In my opinion the answer is in the negative unless the magistrates had power to prohibit and had prohibited any attempt being made to ascertain his identity and the publication of his identity. The abandonment of the Crown's allegation that the chairman had given the direction alleged meant that it could not be contended that the publication of his identity by the appellants was in breach of a prohibition.

It follows that in my opinion the appellants were not guilty of contempt in disclosing his identity and on this ground I would allow these appeals.

If the magistrates had power to direct and had directed that Colonel B's name should not be published and such a direction was operative not only within but outside the court, then the case might be different. In *R v Socialist Worker Printers and Publishers Ltd*[1] the Crown did not contend that the court had any power to make orders affecting the Press or other media in their conduct outside the court and in the present case the Crown, rightly in my opinion, did not contend that examining magistrates had any such power. In *Taylor v Attorney-General*[2] where the judge in a trial for offences under the Official Secrets Act of New Zealand made an order 'prohibiting the publication of anything that may lead to the identification of officers of the New Zealand Security Service' the Court of Appeal of New Zealand held that he had power to make that order and that it operated outside the court. It is not necessary to express an opinion on whether that case was rightly decided. It suffices for me to say that in my opinion the courts of this country have no such power, except when expressly given by statute. Although in *Scott v Scott*[3] Viscount Haldane LC expressed the view that in exceptional cases publication of what had occurred in camera might be prohibited for a time or altogether, that view was not endorsed by those sitting with him, Earl Loreburn saying[4] that the court did not possess any such power and Lord Shaw of Dunfermline[5] regarding its exercise as not only 'an encroachment upon and suppression of private right, but the gradual invasion and undermining of constitutional security'.

As there is no statutory provision which gives to a court power to make an order applying to all members of the public prohibiting the publication of information which might lead to the identification of a witness such as Colonel B, it follows that in my opinion the advice given by Mr Pratt to his Bench was right and that if the chairman had given any such direction it would not have operated to convert conduct which otherwise did not constitute a contempt into one.

Were it not for the evidence given by Colonel B in open court from which his identity could be ascertained without difficulty, I would have been in favour of dismissing these appeals. It must have been clear to all in court and to all who learnt what had happened in court that the object sought to be achieved by the justices allowing Colonel B to write down his name was the preservation of his anonymity. Knowing that but believing that concealment of his name was not necessary in the national interest, the appellants disclosed

1 [1975] 1 All ER 142, [1975] QB 637
2 [1975] 2 NZLR 675
3 [1913] AC 417 at 438, [1911–13] All ER Rep 1 at 10
4 [1913] AC 417 at 448, [1911–13] All ER Rep 1 at 15
5 [1913] AC 417 at 476, [1911–13] All ER Rep 1 at 30

his identity. But the effect of what the magistrates had permitted to be done was destroyed
a by Colonel B's evidence in open court, which, as I have said, made it possible for anyone
who wished to do so to find out who he was.

If he had not given that evidence, then the appellants would have frustrated the object
which the magistrates by their ruling sought to achieve. True it is that no warning was
given that anyone who published his name might be proceeded against for contempt of
court. In *R v Border Television Ltd, ex parte Attorney-General* and *R v Newcastle Chronicle and*
b *Journal Ltd, ex parte Attorney-General*[1] heard together by the Divisional Court on 17th
January 1978 it was held that in those cases no warning was necessary. While I do not
think that it was strictly necessary for the magistrates to give such a warning in this case,
I think it very desirable that in future cases where a court takes the course that the
magistrates took in this case a warning that publication of the witness's identity might lead
to proceedings for contempt should be given. Such a warning will make it clear that it is
c not just a request not to publish that is being made, a request usually made when the
identity of a person is inadvertently disclosed and one that is usually complied with.

In the *Newcastle Journal* case[1] the fact that the defendant at a trial had pleaded guilty to
four counts in an indictment was published during the course of her trial on the remaining
16 counts in that indictment. In the *Border Television* case[1] there had been publication of
what had happened in the course of a trial within a trial when the jury had been sent out
d so that they should not hear what was discussed. Each publication was held to be a
contempt of court.

For conduct which frustrates what a court has done to be a contempt of court, the action
taken by the court must be within its powers and the question which has troubled me is
whether in this case the magistrates had jurisdiction to allow Colonel B to conceal his
identity when the application was made on the ground that to reveal it would prejudice
e national safety. Section 8(4) of the Official Secrets Act 1920 gives a court power to sit in
camera if it appears that the publication of any evidence or statement would be prejudicial
to national safety. This subsection does not require the application for a sitting in camera
to be supported by evidence and in my opinion a court is entitled in the exercise of its
discretion to make an order under it excluding the public in the light of the information
given to it and the reasons advanced for taking that course. But the terms of that
f subsection cannot in my opinion be construed as giving power during a sitting in open
court to permit or to direct that a witness's identity should not be disclosed.

Proceedings in the courts of this country are normally conducted in public. The courts
have, however, inherent jurisdiction to sit in camera if that is necessary for the due
administration of justice: see *Scott v Scott*[2], *R v Lewes Prison (Governor), ex parte Doyle*[3] per
Lord Reading CJ and *Attorney-General v Times Newspapers Ltd*[4] per Lord Reid. In *Scott v
g Scott*[5] Earl Loreburn said:

'. . . in all cases where the public has been excluded with admitted propriety, the
underlying principle, as it seems to me, is that the administration of justice would be
rendered impracticable by their presence, whether because the case could not be
effectively tried, or the parties entitled to justice would be reasonably deterred from
seeking it at the hands of the Court . . .'

h It cannot be said that disclosure of Colonel B's name would have rendered the trial of the
three accused impracticable, nor is it in my opinion the case that its disclosure would have
reasonably deterred the Crown from instituting proceedings for offences under the Official
Secrets Acts which ought in the national interest to be brought. The likely result if the
magistrates had refused the application made by the Crown would have been an application

1 [1978] The Times, 18th January
2 [1913] AC 417, [1911–13] All ER Rep 1
3 [1917] 2 KB 254 at 271
4 [1973] 3 All ER 54 at 60, [1974] AC 273 at 294
5 [1913] AC 417 at 446, [1911–13] All ER Rep 1 at 14

that the court should sit in camera for his name to be given, the rest of his evidence being given in open court, and the likely consequence in future cases that there would be more applications for sittings in camera. So in the present case the administration of justice was not rendered impracticable on either of the two grounds mentioned by Lord Loreburn. Nor do I think that it can be said that the writing down of Colonel B's name involved less derogation from the open administration of justice than the giving of his name in camera with the rest of his evidence being given in open court.

If the criteria which apply in relation to the exercise of the court's inherent jurisdiction to sit in camera apply in relation to allowing or directing a witness to write down his name, then I do not think that those criteria are satisfied in this case. But I have come to the conclusion that they do not apply. Judges and justices have a wide measure of control over the conduct of proceedings in their courts. On occasions for a variety of reasons witnesses are allowed to write down a piece of evidence instead of giving it orally and I know of a number of occasions when in Official Secrets Acts cases witnesses have been allowed to conceal their identity. In my opinion it is within the jurisdiction of the court to allow this in the exercise of control over the conduct of the proceedings just as a judge is entitled to send a jury out in the course of a trial and to have a trial within a trial. In cases where a court permits this and takes every step within its power, short of sitting in camera, to preserve the anonymity of a witness, a person who seeks to frustrate what the court has done may well be guilty of contempt. The giving of evidence in open court by the unnamed witness from which his identity can be deduced is not likely to occur often and it was the giving of that evidence which frustrated the magistrates' efforts to conceal Colonel B's identity. As I have said it is only because that happened in this case that I think that the appeals should be allowed.

In my opinion *R v Socialist Worker Printers and Publishers Ltd*[1] was rightly decided. In that case there was a deliberate attempt to frustrate the effect of the court's direction that the names of the persons who alleged that they had been blackmailed should not be disclosed. The giving of that direction was a proper exercise by the court of its jurisdiction to control the conduct of the proceedings. It is generally, if not invariably, recognised that the disclosure of the identity of witnesses alleged to have been blackmailed is likely to deter others blackmailed from seeking the protection of the courts.

In the course of the argument s 12(1) of the Administration of Justice Act 1960 was referred to. As that subsection deals only with the publication of information relating to proceedings in private, it has not, in my opinion, any relevance to this case.

For the reasons I have stated I would allow these appeals with costs here and in the Divisional Court.

LORD EDMUND-DAVIES. My Lords, it is manifest that this appeal is of considerable public importance. The salient facts have been related in the speech of my noble and learned friend, Lord Diplock, and I shall not repeat them. Although I regard the proper outcome of these benighted proceedings as clear, the hearing in your Lordships' House has ranged over such a wide area that I do not propose to restrict myself simply to indicating how they should be disposed of. There has been much discussion of many aspects of the confused and confusing law relating to what, as the noble and learned Lord, Lord Cross of Chelsea, complained in *Attorney-General v Times Newspapers Ltd*[2], is still unfortunately called 'contempt of court', which were not touched on when that appeal was heard in your Lordships' House. Though not strictly necessary for present purposes, in these circumstances it would, as I believe, be unfortunate if we withheld such views as we have formed regarding them, and I do not propose to do so. This seems all the more desirable in view of the fact that it was only 18 years ago that, for the first time, a general right of appeal in cases of civil or criminal contempt of court was created (see the Administration

---

1   [1975] 1 All ER 142, [1975] QB 637
2   [1973] 3 All ER 54 at 83, [1974] AC 273 at 322

of Justice Act 1960, s 13) and there has been comparatively little judicial comment on the
topic meanwhile.

'The phrase "contempt of court" does not in the least describe the true nature of the
class of offence with which we are here concerned ... The offence consists in
interfering with the administration of the law; in impeding and perverting the course
of justice ... It is not the dignity of the court which is offended—a petty and
misleading view of the issues involved—it is the fundamental supremacy of the law
which is challenged.'

(*Johnson v Grant*[1] per Lord President Clyde). When contempt is alleged the courts have for
generations found themselves called on to tread a judicial tightrope, for, as Phillimore J put
it in *R v Blumenfeld*[2]:

'The court had to reconcile two things—namely, the right of free speech and the
public advantage that a knave should be exposed, and the right of an individual suitor
to have his case fairly tried. The only way in which the court could save both was to
refuse an unlimited extension of either right. It became, then, a question of degree.'

This dilemma most frequently arises in relation to Press and other reports of court
proceedings, for the public interest inherent in their being fairly and accurately reported
is of great constitutional importance and should never lead to punitive action unless,
despite their factual accuracy, they nevertheless threaten or prejudice the due administration
of justice.

It is of paramount importance to examine at the outset the statement filed pursuant to
RSC Ord 52, r 2, in support of the present proceedings for contempt brought against
Leveller Magazine Ltd, Peace News Ltd, the National Union of Journalists and various
individuals. Taking as a typical example that filed on 17th April 1978, in relation to the
Journalist, we find the following assertions:

'(b) The said "Colonel B" had properly been permitted not to disclose his identity
when giving evidence by the said Magistrates, the Chairman directing in open Court
that no attempt should be made to disclose the identity of "Colonel B".
'(c) The said National Union of Journalists was at all material times well aware that
the aforesaid direction had been given.
'(d) The said disclosure of the identity of "Colonel B" tended and was calculated to
prejudice the due administration of justice; it was intended to flout the aforesaid
direction and make it difficult for witnesses in the position of "Colonel B" to give
evidence in open Court.'

The basis of these assertions unquestionably was the earlier affidavit of a Miss Butler, a
member of the Director of Public Prosecutions' staff, that, the examining magistrates
having ruled that Colonel B's name should be written down and shown only to the court,
defence counsel and the defendants, on the Crown's contention that disclosure would not
be in the interests of national security:

'At the conclusion of the proceedings on that day the Chairman of the Justices
reminded the Court of his earlier ruling *and stressed that no attempt should be made to
disclose the identity of "Colonel B"*.'

The words which I have italicised undoubtedly constituted the 'direction' relied on by the
Attorney-General in his motion to commit. But before it was heard, Mr Pratt, the clerk to
the justices, swore an affidavit in which he said:

'The Official Secrets Act provides for exclusion of all or part of the public ... but I
am not aware of any other provision relevant to these proceedings enabling an order
to be made such as is referred to or implied in Anne Butler's Affidavit, and that was

1   1923 SC 789 at 790
2   (1912) 28 TLR 308 at 311

the reason why the Magistrates did not make any Order such as she refers to—because I advised them that they had no power to do so.'　　　　　　　　　　　　　　　　**a**

Confronted by this latter affidavit, during the hearing of the motion counsel for the Attorney-General sought leave to amend his grounds by substituting the word 'procedure' for the word 'direction' in paras (c) and (d) of the Attorney-General's statement. But the Divisional Court refused leave to amend. As I see it, it follows that the whole proceedings thereafter must be regarded as having taken place on the basis that a committal was sought on the single ground (a) that the magistrates had given a direction that no attempt must be **b** made to disclose the identity of Colonel B, and (b) that deliberate publication of his identity by the appellants sprang from their determination to disregard that direction. That, and that alone, was the case which the appellants were called on to meet. And, whatever view one may hold of their behaviour generally, in my judgment it is irrefutable that the appellants destroyed that case. Or perhaps it would be more accurate to say that it had already been destroyed by affidavit, for at no time during the hearing did the Attorney- **c** General contend that the magistrates had in fact given the direction deposed to by Miss Butler. Yet the Divisional Court seemingly attached no importance to this decisive fact. What Lord Widgery CJ said was[1]:

'Central to all the [appellants'] arguments was the contention that this type of contempt requires a direction or mandatory order of a court and breach of that order, **d** whereas here it is said that there was no order against disclosure, but merely a request.'

After considering the challenge to Miss Butler's evidence, he continued[2]:

'In view of that conflict of evidence, counsel for the Attorney-General has not sought to rely on any disregard of such a statement, but relies on the earlier ruling in conformity with which it is said "Colonel B" gave his evidence. Indeed, if the **e** chairman of the justices did say what Miss Butler says he said, its direct authority would only have gone to those within the court. The relevant ruling for present purposes was when the court gave permission for Colonel B to write down his name, in accordance with the same decision it had made for Colonel A. It is the authority of that ruling which is for consideration. If it was an effective ruling, a later so-called "direction" would have added nothing to it, and consequently can be ignored.'　　**f**

A little later, dealing with the power of a court to allow a witness to write down his name, to order a witness to leave the court, and so on, Lord Widgery CJ added[3]:

'They are matters on which the court gives a ruling or a decision. The court may add something which can be called a formal direction, but no such formality is **g** required. All such rulings are given (and only purported to be given) to those in court and not outside it. A flouting in court of the court's ruling will be a contempt. Equally a flouting (or deliberate disregard) outside the court will be a contempt if it frustrates the court's ruling . . . The fact that the justices' ruling had no direct effect outside the court does not prevent the publications here in question from being a contempt if they were made with the deliberate intention of frustrating the **h** arrangement which the court had made to preserve Colonel B's anonymity. It is this element of flouting the court which is the real basis of the contempt here alleged. It can be sustained without proof that something like a direction or a specific order of the court has been breached.'

Yet a little later, he added[4]:　　　　　　　　　　　　　　　　　　　　　　　　　　　**j**

1　[1978] 3 All ER 731 at 735, [1978] 3 WLR 395 at 400
2　[1978] 3 All ER 731 at 735, [1978] 3 WLR 395 at 400–401
3　[1978] 3 All ER 731 at 736, [1978] 3 WLR 395 at 401–402
4　[1978] 3 All ER 731 at 737, [1978] 3 WLR 395 at 402

'The contempt here relied on is the deliberate flouting of the court's intention. The public has an interest in having the courts protected from such treatment and that is the public interest on which the Attorney-General relies.'

My Lords, I have to repeat with the greatest respect that the Attorney-General had moved to commit the appellants on an entirely different basis and on that basis alone. That basis having in effect been abandoned by the Attorney-General in my judgment it was not open to the Divisional Court (and particularly after refusing to allow him to amend his grounds of application) to entertain an entirely different case on which to commit the appellants for criminal contempt.

This is no mere judicial quibble. Persons charged with criminal misconduct are entitled to know with reasonable precision the basis of the charge. If proceedings such as the present were tried on indictment and the statement of the charge 'Criminal contempt', it would be impermissible to present a case wholly different from that outlined in the particulars of the charge and then to urge that the departure was immaterial, since the new misconduct relied on was, like the old, simply another variety of criminal contempt.

Nor, my Lords, would it be acceptable were the Attorney-General to urge, in effect, that no injustice has here been done, since the *wishes* of the court were clear and the determination of the appellants to flout or disregard those wishes equally clear. Counsel for the appellants other than the National Union of Journalists rightly observed that, if no direction was in fact given, thinking cannot have made it so, and the appellants were correct in thinking that by publishing they were breaching no ruling of the court. I have to say respectfully that I am made uneasy by the view expressed by Lord Widgery CJ that[1] 'the deliberate flouting of the court's *intention*' is sufficient to constitute criminal contempt, for as O'Connor J said in *P A Thomas & Co v Mould*[2]: '. . . where parties seek to invoke the power of the court to commit people to prison and deprive them of their liberty, there has got to be quite clear certainty about it.' In the absence of any such ruling as that deposed to by Miss Butler, but denied by the clerk of the court, was it the unmistakable intention of the magistrates in the present case that no one should behave as these appellants later did, particularly when those magistrates were specifically advised by their clerk that they had no power to make any order restricting the publication outside their court of Colonel B's identity? In such circumstances 'intention' and 'preference' seem indistinguishable. The latter would have been manifested by the expression of a mere request that no such publication should take place, and when the magistrates elected to discontinue sitting in camera and thereafter did no more than rule that in their court the name of the witness should be written down their 'intention' regarding what must or must not be done outside court was, in my judgment, indeterminable. Indeed, it was ex hypothesi non-existent, since they had been advised that they could in no way control such conduct. They might well have *preferred* that no publication of Colonel B's name should take place anywhere or at any time, but it is going too far to say that they had manifested an intention to do all they could to guard against it by ruling as they did. 'No man should be condemned by an implication', observed my noble and learned friend, Lord Diplock, in the course of counsel's submissions. Condemnation is even more objectionable when the implication underlying the court's conduct is a matter of reasonable conjecture by reasonable people, and I have already indicated why I consider that such omission was fatal in the circumstances and should lead to these appeals being allowed.

I should add that I am for a like reason not wholly satisfied about the ratio decidendi of the Divisional Court in *R v Socialist Worker Printers and Publishers Ltd*[3] in contempt proceedings following on a blackmail prosecution in which the trial judge had directed that the victims who gave evidence should be referred to in court by letters, notwithstanding

---

1   [1978] 3 All ER 731 at 737, [1978] 3 WLR 395 at 402
2   [1968] 1 All ER 963 at 967, [1968] 2 QB 913 at 923
3   [1975] 1 All ER 142, [1975] QB 637

which the defendants proceeded to publish their names. I have ascertained that the ipsissima verba of the statement filed by the Attorney-General pursuant to RSC Ord 52, r 2,   *a* were that—

> '. . . the said witnesses be referred to by letters . . . the said publication tended and was calculated to prejudice the due administration of justice by causing victims of blackmail to fear publicly and thus deter them from coming forward in aid of legal proceedings or from seeking the protection of the law and/or by holding up to public obloquy witnesses who had given evidence in criminal proceedings.'   *b*

One of the two grounds on which the Divisional Court granted the application to commit was (in the words of Lord Widgery CJ[1]) '. . . that by publishing the names of these two witnesses in defiance of the judge's directions the respondents were committing a blatant affront to the authority of the court'. If there was any 'direction' it was at best implicit. And it should be observed that no publication of the victims' names took place until the   *c* judge was about to sum up, and there was accordingly no question of the administration of justice in *that* case being prejudiced by their being deterred from giving evidence for the prosecution. So the basis of the decision seems to be that publication was objectionable on the *general* ground that in any and every blackmail case the administration of justice in future prosecutions will be interfered with if victims' names are published. But, while many (and perhaps most) would accept this, is it necessarily so? I certainly recall one   *d* eminent judge (now retired) who in such cases scrutinised with very great care counsel's request that the victims should remain anonymous and emphatically rejected the idea that in every such case the administration of justice would automatically be prejudiced by publication. Counsel for two of the appellants in the present case submitted that it does not follow that everything done which had the effect of deterring possible witnesses necessarily constitutes a contempt, the proper test being whether it is a *prohibited* act   *e* calculated to deter. The time may yet come when this House will be called on to adjudicate on the point.

Neither in *R v Socialist Worker Printers and Publishers Ltd*[2] nor in the instant case did the court give any direction against publication purporting to operate outside the courtroom. It has to be said that hitherto the view seems to have been widely accepted that no such power exists. Thus, in the *Socialist Worker* case[3] the present Attorney-General submitted: *f*

> 'The trial judge did not give any express direction about revealing the names of the witnesses in the press. Indeed, he had no power to make orders affecting the press or other media in their conduct outside the court.'

He nevertheless added[3]:

> 'The direction could only protect the witnesses effectively if their names were not   *g* revealed subsequently. Hence the direction was concerned with publication outside as well as inside the court.'

Defence counsel likewise submitted that[4]: 'A trial judge has no power to order the Press not to publish matters elicited at an open trial.'

In the present appeal, again, appellants and respondents alike concurred in submitting   *h* that (as, indeed, Lord Widgery CJ had himself observed[5]) the magistrates' court had no power to direct that there should be no publication in the Press or by any other means of the identity of the 'Colonel B' who had given evidence before them. Counsel for the Attorney-General told your Lordships in terms that the court could not direct the outside

                                                           j

1   [1975] 1 All ER 142 at 148, [1975] QB 637 at 469
2   [1975] 1 All ER 142, [1975] QB 637
3   [1975] QB 637 at 639
4   [1975] QB 637 at 640
5   [1978] 3 All ER 731 at 735, [1978] 3 WLR 395 at 400–401

world, but added that its ruling nevertheless extended outside its walls. For myself I found
a this difficult to follow, particularly as no illustrations were forthcoming of what learned
counsel had in mind. After considerable reflection I have come to the conclusion that a
court has no power to pronounce to the public at large such a prohibition against
publication that all disobedience to it would automatically constitute a contempt. It is
beyond doubt that a court has a wide inherent jurisdiction to control its own procedure.
In certain circumstances it may decide to sit wholly or in part in camera. Or witnesses may
b be ordered to withdraw, 'lest they trim their evidence by hearing the evidence of others'
(as Earl Loreburn put it in *Scott v Scott*[1]). Or part of a criminal trial may be ordered to take
place in the absence of the jury, such as during the hearing of legal submissions or during
a 'trial within a trial' regarding the admissibility of an alleged confession. Or the court may
direct that throughout the hearing in open court certain witnesses are to be referred to by
letter or number only. But it does not follow that were a person (and even one with
c knowledge of the procedure which had been adopted) thereafter to make public that which
had been wholly or partially concealed he would ipso facto be guilty of contempt. Nothing
illustrates this more clearly than the hearing of evidence in camera, '. . . it being plain that
inherent jurisdiction exists in any court which enables it to exclude the public where it
becomes necessary in order to administer justice': *R v Lewes Prison (Governor), ex parte
Doyle*[2] per Viscount Reading CJ. It might be thought that disclosure of that which had
d been divulged only in secret would in all cases constitute the clearest example of
contempt. Thus we find Oliver J saying in *R v Davies, ex parte Delbert-Evans*[3]:

> '. . . everything the public has a right to know about a trial . . . *that is to say,
> everything that has taken place in open court*, may be published, and beyond that there is
> no need or *right* to go.' (The italics are mine.)

e But *Scott v Scott*[4] has long established that this is not so. And the Administration of Justice
Act 1960 provides in terms by s 12(1) that 'The publication of information relating to
proceedings before any court sitting in private shall not of itself be contempt of court
except in the following cases . . .' Five types of proceedings are then set out, ending with
'(e) where the court (having power to do so) expressly prohibits the publication of all
information relating to the proceedings or of information of the description which is
f published'. Section 12(4) provides: 'Nothing in this section shall be construed as implying
that any publication is punishable as contempt of court which would not be so punishable
apart from this section.' I am in respectful agreement with Scarman LJ (as he then was)
who said in *Re F (a minor)*[5] that this last obscure subsection '. . . was enacted to ensure that
no one would in future be found guilty of contempt who would not also under the pre-
existing law have been found guilty'. And what appears certain is that at common law the
g fact that a court sat wholly or partly in camera, and even where in such circumstances the
court gave a direction prohibiting publication of information relating to what had been
said or done behind closed doors, publication thereafter did not of itself and in every case
necessarily mean that there had been contempt of court.
   For that to arise something more than disobedience of the court's direction needs to be
established. That something more is that the publication must be of such a nature as to
h threaten the administration of justice either in the particular case in relation to which the
prohibition was pronounced or in relation to cases which may be brought in the future.
So the liability to be committed for contempt in relation to publication of the kind with
which this House is presently concerned must depend on all the circumstances in which
the publication complained of took place.
   It may be objected that, in an area where the boundaries of the law should be defined

j

1   [1913] AC 417 at 446, [1911–13] All ER Rep 1 at 14
2   [1917] 2 KB 254 at 271
3   [1945] 1 KB 435 at 446, cf [1945] 2 All ER 167 at 175
4   [1913] AC 417, [1911–13] All ER Rep 1
5   [1977] 1 All ER 114 at 131, [1977] Fam 58 at 99

with precision, such a situation confronts those engaged in the public dissemination of information with perils which cannot always be foreseen or reasonably safeguarded *a* against. To retort that this has always been so affords no comfort, but intelligent anticipation of what would be fair and what would be unfair can go a long way to ease the burden of the disseminators. They would themselves be in all probability the first to resist court 'directions' as to what they may or may not publish, and I have already expressed my disbelief in their general validity. But the Press and others could, as I believe, be helped *b* were a court when sitting in public to draw express attention to any procedural decisions it had come to and implemented during the hearing, to explain that they were aimed at ensuring the due and fair administration of justice, and to indicate that any who by publishing material or otherwise acting in a manner calculated to prejudice that aim would run the risk of contempt proceedings being instituted against them. Farther than that, in my judgment, the court cannot go. As far as that they could, as I believe, with advantage go. The public and the Press would thereby be relieved of the burden of *c* divining what was the court's 'intention', for this would have been made clear and it would be up to them to decide whether they would respect it or frustrate it. Even so, ignoring the warning by disobedience or otherwise would not of itself necessarily establish a case of contempt. But the knowledge that the warning had been given should prove at least a guide to possible consequences and would render it impossible for the person responsible for publication to urge (as was done in R v Socialist Worker Printers and Publishers Ltd[1]) that *d* he was under the impression that the court had merely *requested* that there be no disclosure of certain specified matters, or that, as the editor of the Journalist said in the present case, '. . . my understanding was that [Colonel B] had been permitted to write his name down rather than give it in evidence, but that there was no direct [intimation] . . . that his name should not be published'.

Were such intimation as I have in mind given by the court, the possible plea of a *e* publisher that he had no knowledge of it would be of little moment. In such cases as the instant one, we are concerned not with improper publication by a private individual (as to whom nothing presently arises) but with people controlling or connected with powerful organs of publicity who, for reasons of their own (one of which may be no more than the desire to boost sales), decide to take the course of defiant dissemination of matter which ought to be kept confidential. It is incumbent on such people to ascertain what had *f* happened in court. They have the means of doing this, and they cannot be heard to complain that they were ignorant of what has taken place. Perhaps the time has come when heed should be paid to the view expressed in the (Phillimore) Report of the Committee on Contempt of Court[2], in reference to the *Socialist-Worker* case[3], that:

> 'We incline to the view that the important question of what the press may publish concerning proceedings in open court should no longer be left to judicial requests *g* (which may be disregarded) nor to judicial directions (which, if given, may have doubtful legal authority) but that legislation . . . should provide for these specific circumstances in which a court shall be empowered to prohibit, in the public interest, the publication of names or of other matters arising at a trial.'

Although it should be unnecessary, perhaps I ought to add that nothing I have said *h* should be regarded as implying that there can be no committal for contempt unless there has been some sort of warning against publication. While, for the reasons I have indicated, it would be wise to warn, the court is under no obligation to do so. And there will remain cases where a court could not reasonably have considered a warning even desirable, such as where the later conduct complained of should not have been contemplated as likely to occur. R v Newcastle Chronicle and Journal Ltd[4] is an example of such a case. There the *j*

1   [1975] 1 All ER 142 at 145, [1975] QB 637 at 646
2   (1974) Cmnd 5794, p 60, n 72
3   [1975] 1 All ER 142, [1975] QB 637
4   [1978] The Times, 18th January

Divisional Court rightly held contempt proved where, during the course of a trial on an
indictment containing 20 counts for dishonesty, a newspaper reported that on arraignment
on the first day the defendant had pleaded guilty to four of the counts and that the trial was
proceeding only on the remaining 16. Lord Widgery CJ rightly commented:

'It is to be observed that the learned trial judge gave no sort of warning to
representatives of the press in his court that the evidence would contain matter which
should not be reported. I do not think that there is any obligation on the judge to give
a warning to the press, or indeed to anybody else, when the matter complained of and
relied on is so elementary and well understood as this one ... Certainly it does not
seem to me to be an unfair burden on the newspaper reporter to say that he ought to
know (and, knowing, ought to practise in his profession) that any reference to
additional offences committed by the accused is something which ought to be kept
out of the jury's ears *unless* there is some clear exception which covers the matter.'

My Lords, I said at the outset that I should digress, and I fear I have done so at some
length, but I comfort myself by the reflection that I am not alone among your Lordships
in this respect. Let me now return to the matter in hand and say that, for the reason earlier
indicated, I hold that all these appeals should be allowed.

LORD RUSSELL OF KILLOWEN. My Lords, I propose to state briefly my conclusions
on the questions relevant to this case. From what happened in connection with the
deposition of Colonel B, and from the opening sentence of that deposition itself, it was clear
that the examining magistrates decided that his identity should have strictly limited
publication. Contempt of court in its essentials consists in interference with the due
administration of justice. It is true that in this case the application by the Crown to which
the magistrates acceded was based on the suggestion that revelation of the witness's
identity would be inimical to national safety, and no specific mention appears to have been
made of the requirements of the due administration of justice. But this was a prosecution
under the Official Secrets Acts. In my opinion it really goes without saying that behind the
application (and the decision) lay considerations of the due administration of justice. In the
first place an alternative to the via media adopted would be an application that Colonel B's
evidence be taken in camera; and in principle the less that evidence is taken in camera the
better for the due administration of justice, a point with which journalists certainly no less
than others would agree. In the second place, a decision on anonymity (the via media)
would obviously, and for the same reasons, be highly desirable in the interest of the due
administration of justice as a continuing process in future in such cases. In the third place
it appears to me that the furtherance of the due administration of justice was the only
ground to support the decision of the magistrates.

I arrive therefore at the conclusion that it should have been apparent to the appellants,
from the very form of the deposition of Colonel B, that the magistrates had arrived at a
decision on his anonymity designed to promote not merely national safety but the due
administration of justice. (Incidentally I reject entirely the specious suggestion that there
was here merely a polite request to the Press not to publish the identity.)

I do not, my Lords, regard as of any relevance the question whether the magistrates had
any power or authority directly to forbid all publication of Colonel B's identity. The field
in which contempt of court, or as I prefer to describe it improper interference with the due
administration of justice, may be committed is not circumscribed by the terms of an order
enforceable against the accused. I find no problem in the concept that a decision or
direction may have no immediate aim and no direct enforceability beyond the deciding
and directing court, but yet may have such effect in connection with contempt of court.
Merely to state, as is the law, that in general contempt of court is the improper interference
with the due administration of justice is to state that it need not involve disobedience to an
order binding on the alleged contemnor.

Where then, in the light of these principles, stands the present case? I dismiss at once the
fact, which I am prepared to assume, that the *motive* which induced the appellants to

publish the identity of Colonel B was that they considered the Crown's view that its revelation would endanger national safety to be nonsense. Their motive is irrelevant to guilt if they intended to do that which amounted in law to interference with the due administration of justice and therefore contempt.

It is at this stage that I feel great concern with this case. There can be no doubt that the publication in toto of Colonel B's deposition was permissible without contempt of court. In it was to be found a reference to a particular edition of the Royal Corps of Signals publication Wire in which Colonel B admitted in his deposition that his name in association with his stated then current posting was to be found. (I believe that the reference to the particular edition was due to a question by the clerk to the magistrates and not to cross-examining counsel.) This edition of Wire was available to the public, including anyone who read a report of the deposition, which of course was freely reportable; no doubt it was also deposited in the British Museum. No objection was raised by the prosecution to this part of the deposition, nor by the magistrates.

The position therefore was that, notwithstanding the decision of the magistrates designed to preserve the anonymity of Colonel B, his deposition itself revealed at one simple remove, his identity. Publication in full of his deposition, given as it was in open court, could not have been a contempt. It would have told the world (if interested) where to look for Colonel B's identity. Would it have transgressed the limits of the permissible if the publication of the deposition had been accompanied by a republication of the stated edition of Wire, or the relevant extracts from it? I do not think so. The substance of the magistrates' decision would not have been breached. The gaff was already blown by the deposition, to the publication of which no objection could be taken.

For these reasons, which depend entirely on the totally revealing content of Colonel B's deposition, I would allow these appeals. I see no sufficient justification for holding that the direct short cut to breach of the decided anonymity of Colonel B is to be regarded in the particular circumstances of this case as a contempt of court.

If, my Lords, I may summarise. (1) The decision of the examining magistrates should have been recognised by the appellants as one designed to preserve the anonymity of Colonel B. (2) That decision should be taken as made in the interests of the due administration of justice, both in that case and in the due administration of justice as a continuing process. (3) No specific warning of a risk of contempt of court by ignoring the decision should be necessary to found such a charge, though it might be useful. (4) There was no justification for thinking that this decision involved merely a request. (5) But for the substantially self-identifying content of Colonel B's legitimately reportable deposition I would have been for dismissal of these appeals. (6) Because, and only because, the properly reportable deposition of Colonel B really in itself revealed his identity, without protest from either magistrates or prosecution, I would allow these appeals, with costs here and below.

LORD SCARMAN. My Lords, when an application is made to commit for contempt of court a journalist or editor for the publication of information relating to the proceedings of a court, freedom of speech and the public nature of justice are at once put at risk. The general rule of our law is clear. No one shall be punished for publishing such information unless it can be established to the satisfaction of the court to whom the application is made that the publication constitutes an interference with the administration of justice either in the particular case to which the publication relates or generally. Parliament clearly had the general rule in mind when in 1960 it enacted that even the publication of information relating to proceedings before any court sitting in private shall not of itself be contempt of court save in specified exceptional cases: see s 12(1) of the Administration of Justice Act 1960.

The law does not treat any, or every, interference with the course or administration of justice as a contempt. The common law rule which was affirmed by this House in *Scott v Scott*[1] is that the interference must be such as to render impracticable the administration of

1 [1913] AC 417, [1911–13] All ER Rep 1

justice or to frustrate the attainment of justice either in the particular case or generally. Further, since such interference is a criminal offence, the court to whom the application to commit is made must be satisfied beyond reasonable doubt that the interference is of such a character. If the court is not sure, the application must be dismissed.

Three questions arise for consideration in this appeal. (1) Did the examining justices have power to sit in private to take the evidence of the witness described in court as 'Colonel B'? (2) Did they have the power, without going into private session, to require evidence as to the identity of the witness to be written down and not to be mentioned in open court? (3) If either of the first two questions be answered in the affirmative, was it a contempt of court to publish information relating to the identity of the witness?

Since the history of the case is fully set out in the speech of my noble and learned friend, Lord Diplock, I propose to refer only to those facts which I consider to be critical.

This is an appeal from an order of the Divisional Court of the Queen's Bench Division (Lord Widgery CJ presiding). The court found, on the application of the Attorney-General, that the criminal offence of a contempt of court had been established against the appellants. The alleged offence consisted of publication in three newspapers, Peace News, the Leveller and the Journalist, of the true name of a witness who, using the pseudonym 'Colonel B', had given evidence for the prosecution in committal proceedings against three men accused of offences under the Official Secrets Acts. His identity was not disclosed in those proceedings, though he gave his evidence orally in open court. The examining justices had ruled that his name should be written down and shown to the defence but not mentioned in court. The justices gave no direction prohibiting publication of the name, since they were advised by their clerk that they had no power to do so. In finding the contempt established the Divisional Court held that it consisted of a flouting of the authority of the court in that the appellants, with notice of the proceedings and the ruling, had caused the witness's name to be published in the three newspapers. The court, accepting that a contempt could not be shown unless the publications frustrated a decision of the court, the object of which was to avert the risk of interference with the administration of justice either in the particular case or generally, found that this was the object of the ruling and that the appellants' publication had frustrated it. In adopting this criterion for determining a contempt of court, the Divisional Court followed the decision of the Court of Appeal in *Attorney-General v Butterworth*[1], where, however, the facts were very different.

The powers of the court—the first question

The committal proceedings being in respect of offences alleged under the Official Secrets Acts, the examining justices had power to exclude the public from any part of the hearing, if, on the application of the prosecution, they thought a public hearing prejudicial to national safety: see s 8(4) of the Official Secrets Act 1920. They had exercised this power in respect of certain tape-recordings, but they did not use it (though it was open to them to do so) in respect of Colonel B's evidence. The public were not excluded when he gave evidence. The subsection, therefore, does not apply. The only relevance of the subsection is that it indicates that Parliament considered it necessary to augment, in official secrets cases, whatever common law powers a court had to sit in private by one the exercise of which would not be dependent on the court's assessment of the danger of publicity to the administration of justice. The exercise of this power would, of course, enable contempt proceedings to be brought, if there was publication of the matter kept private: see s 12(1)(c) of the Administration of Justice Act 1960.

Examining justices also have the power to sit in private if the 'ends of justice' appear to them to require it: see s 6(1) of the Criminal Justice Act 1967. As they chose to sit in public, this statutory power cannot be invoked to support their ruling.

Examining justices also have the common law power, which belongs to all courts, to sit in private in the exceptional cases specified in *Scott v Scott*[2].

1   [1962] 3 All ER 326, [1963] 1 QB 696
2   [1913] AC 417, [1911–13] All ER Rep 1

In *Scott v Scott*[1] your Lordship's House affirmed the general rule of the common law that justice must be administered in public. Certain exceptions were, however, recognised. The interest of national security was not one of them; indeed, it was not mentioned in any of the speeches. The House was divided as to whether protection of the administration of justice from interference was an exception. A majority held that it was, though their respective formulations of the exception differed markedly in emphasis. Earl Loreburn[2] held the underlying principle to be that the public were to be excluded if 'the administration of justice would be rendered impracticable by their presence'. Viscount Haldane LC[3] thought that—

> 'to justify an order for hearing in camera it must be *shewn* [my emphasis] that the paramount object of securing that justice is done would really be rendered doubtful of attainment if the order were not made.'

Lord Halsbury[4] (maxime dubitans) agreed with Viscount Haldane LC, while also, in effect, agreeing with Lord Shaw of Dunfermline[5] who thought the ground put forward by Viscount Haldane LC was 'very dangerous ground'.

While paying heed to the dangers of extending this sensitive branch of the law by judicial decision, I think it plain that the basis of the modern law is as Viscount Haldane LC declared it was. It follows: (1) that, in the absence of express statutory provision (eg s 8(4) of the Official Secrets Act 1920), a court cannot sit in private merely because it believes that to sit in public would be prejudicial to national safety, (2) that, if the factor of national safety appears to endanger the due administration of justice, eg by deterring the Crown from prosecuting in cases where it should do so, a court may sit in private, (3) that there must be material (not necessarily formally adduced evidence) made known to the court on which it can reasonably reach its conclusion.

'The device'—the second question

In the present case the justices, instead of sitting in private, adopted the device of allowing a piece of evidence to be written down and requiring it not to be mentioned in open court. If they took this course in the interest of justice, they adopted what Lord Widgery CJ described as a convenient device: for it achieved a result, ie no mention of the name in open court, which otherwise would only be achieved by the court going into camera. In other words, it was a substitute for sitting in private. I agree with Lord Widgery CJ in believing this device to be a valuable and proper extension of the common law power to sit in private, and to be available where the court would have power at common law to sit in private but chooses not to do so. I think *R v Socialist Worker Printers and Publishers Ltd*[6] (a blackmail case) was correctly decided.

Was it a contempt of court?—the third question

I turn now to the third question.

The law of contempt of court has been, throughout its history, bedevilled by technicalities. One of them was raised in this appeal. Can a court make an order, or give a ruling, which is binding on persons who are neither witnesses nor parties in the proceedings before the court? It is a misconception of the nature of the criminal offence of contempt to regard it as being an offence because it is the breach of a binding order. The offence is interference, with knowledge of the court's proceedings, with the course or administration of justice: see *Re F (a minor)*[7]. It was for this reason, no doubt, that Lord Widgery CJ in this case stressed the element of 'flouting' the authority of the court. Though I would not have chosen the word, I think it does reflect the essence of the offence,

1　[1913] AC 417, [1911–13] All ER Rep 1
2　[1913] AC 417 at 446, [1911–13] All ER Rep 1 at 14
3　[1913] AC 417 at 439, [1911–13] All ER Rep 1 at 10
4　[1913] AC 417 at 442, [1911–13] All ER Rep 1 at 12
5　[1913] AC 417 at 485, [1911–13] All ER Rep 1 at 34
6　[1975] 1 All ER 142, [1975] QB 637
7　[1977] 1 All ER 114, [1977] Fam 58

namely that the conduct complained of, in this case the publication, must be a deliberate
a frustration of the effort of the court to project justice from interference.

In the present case the examining justices took a course which was a substitute for sitting
in private. If, as I think, the device is an acceptable extension of the common law power
of a court to control its proceedings by sitting in private, where necessary, in the court's
judgment, to protect the administration of justice from interference, s 12(1) of the
Administration of Justice Act 1960 is relevant. For the principle governing contempt of
b court when a court sits in private must also govern the situation where the common law
device is used in substitute for private session. The subsection is in these terms:

> 'The publication of information relating to proceedings before any court sitting in
> private shall not of itself be contempt of court except in the following cases, that is to
> say—(a) where the proceedings relate to the wardship or adoption of an infant or
> wholly or mainly to the guardianship, custody, maintenance or upbringing of an
c > infant, or rights of access to an infant; (b) where the proceedings are brought under
> Part VIII of the Mental Health Act, 1959, or under any provision of that Act
> authorising an application or reference to be made to a Mental Health Review
> Tribunal or to a county court; (c) where the court sits in private for reasons of national
> security during that part of the proceedings about which the information in question
> is published; (d) where the information relates to a secret process, discovery or
d > invention which is in issue in the proceedings; (e) where the court (having power to
> do so) expressly prohibits the publication of all information relating to the proceedings
> or of information of the description which is published.'

The subsection confers no new powers on the court. It leaves the common law and
statutory powers of sitting in private exactly as they were. Paragraphs (a), (b), (d) and (e)
e add nothing to the common law. It would be strange if the exception stated in para (c)
should prove alone to have made a fundamental modification in the law. I do not so
interpret it. It provides for the case where at common law or by statute the court may sit
in private for reasons of national security. The statutory power which the justices had
under s 8(4) of the 1920 Act is not relevant, because the justices chose not to sit in
private. The common law power is relevant, because the device employed was within the
f inherent power of the court at common law.

But, since the common law power to sit in private arises only if the administration of
justice be threatened, the third question becomes one of fact. What was the reason for the
justices' ruling? If it was to avert an interference with the administration of justice, was
there material on which the ruling could reasonably be based? The third question cannot
therefore be answered without considering the facts. Here I find myself in a state of doubt.
g I do not think that the Attorney-General has discharged the burden of proof on him.
Uncertainty surrounds, and continues to surround, the ruling made by the justices and its
object. First, one cannot be sure that they took into account all the matters to which it was
their duty to have regard if they were giving notice in open court that to protect the
administration of justice the name of the witness was not to be published. The justices
clearly had regard to national security; but did they understand that, in exercising their
h common law power, the national security risk must be shown also to be a risk to the
administration of justice and assess the degree of the latter risk? Did they address
themselves to that question at all? It cannot be said with any certainty that they did, or that
the Crown adduced any material, by way of evidence or otherwise, to show that the
national security issue was such that publication of the colonel's name would endanger the
due administration of justice.

j Secondly, there was, and remains, considerable doubt as to the nature of the 'ruling'.
Was it a decision, an indication, or only a request? As all know, who have experience of the
forensic process in this country, courts frequently allow a witness to write down his name
or address or to give some other specified evidence (eg a medical or welfare report) in
writing and make it clear that they do not wish the matter to be mentioned in open
court. A court may do so only to save a witness or a party from distress or pain, eg in a

personal injury or matrimonial case.   On the other hand, a court may, as the Attorney-General contends in this case, have in mind that publication outside as well as inside the court is to be prevented as an interference with the administration of justice.   Unless the ruling in this case is to be interpreted as a decision taken to prevent interference with the administration of justice, the publication of information as to Colonel B's identity would be no contempt.   If, on its proper interpretation, the 'ruling' was no more than an indication or request, publication would be no contempt.   It is only if the ruling must be read as a prohibition of publication in the interests of the administration of justice, ie as falling within para (e) of s 12(1) of the 1960 Act, that the appellants can, in my judgment, be found guilty of contempt.   After a careful study of the case and listening to full argument, I remain unsure as to the nature and object of the ruling.

I would summarise my conclusions thus.   If a court is satisfied that for the protection of the administration of justice from interference it is necessary to order that evidence either be heard in private or be written down and not given in open court, it may so order.   Such an order or ruling may be the foundation of contempt proceedings against any person who, with knowledge of the order, frustrates its purpose by publishing the evidence kept private or information leading to its exposure.   The order or ruling must be clear and can be made only if it appears to the court reasonably necessary.   There must be material (not necessarily evidence) made known to the court on which it could reasonably reach its conclusion, and those who are alleged to be in contempt must be shown to have known, or to have had a proper opportunity of knowing, of the existence of the order (see Re F (a minor)[1]).

Neither the Crown nor the examining justices made clear what they were seeking to do or on what grounds the court was being asked, and decided, to act.   That certainty which the criminal law requires before a man can be convicted of a criminal offence is lacking. I would, therefore, allow the appeals.

Appeals allowed.

Solicitors: *Vizards* (for the National Union of Journalists); *Seifert Sedley & Co* (for the appellants other than the National Union of Journalists); *Director of Public Prosecutions.*

Mary Rose Plummer   Barrister.

---

1   [1977] 1 All ER 114, [1977] Fam 58

Au Pui-kuen v Attorney-General of Hong Kong

PRIVY COUNCIL

LORD DIPLOCK, LORD SIMON OF GLAISDALE, LORD SALMON, LORD EDMUND-DAVIES AND LORD KEITH OF KINKEL

3rd, 4th OCTOBER, 4th DECEMBER 1978

Criminal law – Trial – Retrial – Order for retrial – Power of appeal court – Retrial for murder ordered by Hong Kong Court of Appeal – Whether court required to be satisfied of probability of conviction on retrial – Hong Kong Criminal Procedure Ordinance, s 83E(1).

Criminal law – Appeal – Oral decision – Written reasons for decision stated to be given later – Duty of court regarding written reasons.

The appellant was convicted in Hong Kong of murder and appealed against his conviction to the Hong Kong Court of Appeal. That court allowed the appeal on the ground of the trial judge's erroneous direction on self defence, and quashed the conviction. In the exercise of the discretion under s 83E(1)[a]of the Hong Kong Criminal Procedure Ordinance to order a retrial 'in the interests of justice', the court ordered a retrial by an oral order not supported by subsequent written reasons. The appellant appealed against the order for a retrial to the Judicial Committee of the Privy Council contending, inter alia, that the court had erred in law in holding that it was not required to be satisfied that conviction would be probable on the retrial.

Held – It was implicit in the judicial character of an unqualified power to order a new trial, such as the power under s 83E(1), that it should be exercised judicially, ie in the interests of justice, and the express reference in s 83E(1) to the interests of justice did no more than state that implicit requirement. The interests of justice included the interests of the public that persons guilty of serious crimes should be brought to justice, as well as the interests of the prosecutor and the accused. It was not a condition precedent to the exercise of a discretion to order a new trial that the court should have reached the conclusion that conviction was probable on the retrial, and it was sufficient if the court were of the opinion, on a proper consideration of the evidence, that conviction might result on the retrial. Since the material before the Board could not justify an inference that the Court of Appeal in exercising its discretion had taken into consideration matters to which it should not have had regard or had failed to take into consideration matters to which it should have had regard, there were no grounds to justify interference with the court's order for a retrial. The appeal would therefore be dismissed (see p 771 *j* to p 772 *a*, p 773 *e f* and p 774 *b c*, post).

Per Curiam. If a court proposes to provide written reasons later for its oral decision, it should announce in open court that such is its intention; the written reasons should be 'handed down' to the parties or otherwise formally communicated to them, and if they relate to proceedings in open court should be made available for public inspection (see p 771 *d e*, post).

Notes

For venire de novo and retrial, see 11 Halsbury's Laws (4th Edn) paras 667, 668.

Cases referred to in judgment

Alpin v R [1976] Hong Kong LR 1028.
Burks v United States (1978) 98 S Ct 2141
Greene v Massey (1978) 98 S Ct 2151
Ng Yuk Kin v R (1955) 39 Hong Kong LR 49

---

[a]   Section 83E(1) is set out at p 771 *g*, post

Appeal

This was an appeal by Au Pui-kuen from an oral order of the Court of Appeal of Hong Kong (Huggins and Pickering JJA, Briggs CJ dissenting) dated 17th February 1977 affirming that court's previous order of 21st January 1977 quashing the appellant's conviction of murder by the High Court of Hong Kong on 30th September 1976 before Li J and a jury, and ordering a retrial. The facts are set out in the judgment of the Board.

M H Jackson-Lipkin QC and *Lucille Fung* (both of the Hong Kong Bar) and *David Ross* for the appellant.

W A *Macpherson* QC and *Thomas Gall* (of the Hong Kong Bar) for the Crown.

LORD DIPLOCK. This is an appeal from an order of the Court of Appeal of Hong Kong dated 17th February 1977 whereby it allowed the appeal of the appellant Au Pui-kuen against his conviction of murder and (by a majority) exercised its discretion under s 83E(1) of the Criminal Procedure Ordinance to order that the appellant be retried.

The respondent, the Attorney-General of Hong Kong, does not contest that part of the Court of Appeal's order which quashed the appellant's conviction. He is concerned only to uphold the order for a new trial. As their Lordships have reached the conclusion that they would not be justified in advising Her Majesty that the order of the Court of Appeal ought to be interfered with, their Lordships will refrain from saying any more about the evidence adduced in the previous trial of the appellant than is necessary for a proper understanding of the circumstances in which his conviction came to be quashed.

The appellant was a detective constable in the Royal Hong Kong Police Force. On 9th January 1976 at a time when he was not on duty he got into a dispute with three young men in a public street. This developed into a fight between the appellant and the three young men. It took place in the presence of a number of eye-witnesses, and in the course of it the appellant drew his revolver and fired three shots. One shot killed Lai Hon-shing, one of the three young men with whom he had been struggling; another shot injured a bystander.

A coroner's inquiry into the death of Lai Hon-shing was held between 2nd February and 20th May 1976 at which the appellant gave evidence. The coroner's jury of three brought in a verdict of 'excusable homicide'. Nevertheless, pursuant to leave granted by the Chief Justice, an indictment against the appellant was filed in the High Court based on the evidence called at the inquest. It charged the appellant on two counts: one of the murder of Lai Hon-shing, and one (in respect of the second shot) of shooting with intent to do grievous bodily harm.

The trial, before Li J and a jury of seven, took place between 20th and 30th September 1976. The jury returned a verdict of guilty on the murder count and not guilty on the other count.

The appellant applied to the Court of Appeal for leave to appeal against his conviction. Numerous grounds of appeal were filed. The first four of these alleged misdirections of the learned judge on the law relating to such matters as self-defence and the defence available to a police officer who kills in the legal exercise of his duty. At the hearing of the application on 21st January 1977 these objections to the summing-up in point of law were argued first; the Court of Appeal held that the judge's direction as to self-defence was erroneous in law. The president (Briggs CJ) stated that the application for leave to appeal would be granted, the appeal allowed and the conviction quashed. He then invited submissions on the question of retrial. After hearing brief arguments by counsel, Briggs CJ announced that (by a majority) the court would order a new trial.

Counsel for the appellant on reflection considered that he had not sufficiently developed his arguments against a new trial. On 3rd February 1977 he applied for a further hearing on this question. At the hearing of the application two points were argued. The first was whether the Court of Appeal had become functus officio. This was decided in favour of the appellant because, although the order for a new trial had been pronounced orally at the conclusion of the hearing on 21st January 1977, it had not yet been drawn up and served on the trial judge.   The second point argued was whether counsel for the appellant should

a   be granted an opportunity of addressing the court further on what he submitted was the
weak and unsatisfactory nature of the evidence adduced by the prosecution at the trial.
Submissions were made as to the importance which an appellate court in exercising its
discretion to order a new trial ought to attach to the strength of the evidence that had been
adduced by the prosecution at the previous trial.

In the course of the argument Briggs CJ indicated that, having already read the transcript

b   of the whole of the evidence given at the trial, he was of opinion that it was not sufficient
to justify a conviction.   At the conclusion of the argument and a short retirement he
announced that a further hearing would be granted.   Neither he nor the other members
of the court (Huggins and Pickering JJA) gave oral reasons at the hearing for the court's
decision to allow a further hearing; but at some time later, following what appears to be a
long-established practice in Hong Kong, a document bearing the date 3rd February 1977,

c   described as a 'Judgment' and purporting to be delivered by Huggins JA, was placed in the
court file and a copy of it was supplied to the librarian of the Supreme Court Library for
filing there.   It gives reasons for the Court of Appeal's decision on 3rd February 1977 to
allow a further hearing on the question whether a new trial should be ordered; but the
contents of the document were never read out in open court, nor were the parties supplied
with copies or even informed of its existence, which in fact they only discovered by chance.

d   Their Lordships appreciate that, particularly in criminal cases, it may be desirable, in
order to avoid delay, that a court should announce its decision orally at the conclusion of
the hearing and state that reasons for the decision will be rendered in writing later.   This
is a common practice in criminal appeals and an analogous procedure is often adopted by
this Board.   It is, however, in their Lordships' view, important if the court proposes to
provide written reasons for its decision later (1) that it should announce in open court that

e   such is its intention: (2) that the written reasons when prepared should be 'handed down'
to the parties or otherwise formally communicated to them; and, if they relate to
proceedings that have taken place in open court, (3) that the written reasons should be
available for public inspection.   In so far as the current practice in Hong Kong departs from
any of these three requirements it ought, in their Lordships' view, to be changed.

The further hearing ordered on 3rd February 1977 took place on 16th and 17th

f   February 1977, when counsel addressed the court on discrepancies in the accounts given by
various eye-witnesses of and participants in the fracas in the course of which Lai Hon-shing
was shot dead by the appellant.   At the conclusion of this hearing Briggs CJ announced that
by a majority (Huggins and Pickering JJA) the court had decided to order a new trial.   It
is against this order that appeal is brought by special leave to Her Majesty in Council.

Their Lordships have already indicated that the power of the Court of Appeal of Hong

g   Kong to order an appellant in a criminal appeal to be retried is a discretionary power.   It is
conferred in the broadest terms by s 83E(1) of the Criminal Procedure Ordinance:

'Where the Court of Appeal allows an appeal against conviction and it appears to the
Court of Appeal that the interests of justice so require, it may order the appellant to
be retried.'

h   The power to order a retrial when a conviction is quashed owes its origin not to the
common law of England but to the Indian Code of Criminal Procedure more than a 100
years ago.   A similar power, not always conferred by identical words, has subsequently
been incorporated in the criminal procedure codes of many other Commonwealth
jurisdictions.   In some, as was the case in Hong Kong before 1972, the power to order a new
trial is unqualified by any explicit reference to the requirements of justice; in some 'shall

j   order' is substituted for 'may order' which appears in the Hong Kong Ordinance.   In their
Lordships' view these minor verbal differences are of no significance.   The power to order
a new trial must always be exercised judicially.   Any criminal trial is to some degree an
ordeal for the accused; it goes without saying that no judge exercising his discretion
judicially would require a person who has undergone this ordeal once to endure it for a
second time unless the interests of justice required it.   So the amendment to the Hong

Kong Criminal Procedure Ordinance which inserted the express reference to the interests of justice did no more than state what had always been implicit in the judicial character of the unqualified power to order a new trial conferred by the Indian Criminal Procedure Code and the pre-amendment terms of the Hong Kong Criminal Procedure Ordinance. The pre-amendment terms of the Hong Kong Ordinance were, in their Lordships' view, rightly construed in *Ng Yuk Kin v R*[1] as authorising the ordering of a new trial only in cases where the interests of justice so required.

The discretion whether or not to exercise the power to order a new trial in any particular case is confided to the Court of Appeal of Hong Kong and not to their Lordships' Board. To exercise it judicially may involve the court in considering and balancing a number of factors some of which may weigh in favour of a new trial and some may weigh against it. The interests of justice are not confined to the interests of the prosecutor and the accused in the particular case. They include the interests of the public in Hong Kong that those persons who are guilty of serious crimes should be brought to justice and should not escape it merely because of a technical blunder by the judge in the conduct of the trial or his summing-up to the jury.

It would not, in their Lordships' view, be helpful to attempt a catalogue of the various factors which the Court of Appeal should take into consideration in determining how to exercise their discretion, still less to make any suggestion as to the relative weight to be given to them. The factors that are relevant and their relative importance may vary greatly as between one case and another. These are matters which call for the exercise of the collective sense of justice and common sense of the members of the Court of Appeal of Hong Kong, who are familiar, as their Lordships are not, with local conditions. Their Lordships would not interfere with that court's exercise of its discretion in such a matter unless they were satisfied that it must have reached its decision as to whether or not to order a new trial by taking into consideration matters to which it ought not to have had regard or by failing to take into consideration matters to which it should have had regard, and that in consequence a substantial injustice had been done.

In the instant case, their Lordships do not know all the factors that the majority of the Court of Appeal took into account in reaching their decision of 17th February 1977 that there should be a new trial; for neither at that time nor thereafter have they given their reasons for it. If a new trial is to be ordered it is often the case that in the interests of justice at the fresh trial, the less said by the Court of Appeal, the better. In the absence of disclosed reasons their Lordships can infer that the Court of Appeal took into account the matters urged on them by counsel for the appellant and repeated at the hearing before their Lordships.

Two of these matters can be disposed of briefly. The first was that the first trial was both preceded and accompanied by virulent publicity prejudicial to the appellant and that the second trial might attract a similar publicity campaign against him. In their Lordships' view the weight to be attached to this factor was pre-eminently a matter for a Hong Kong court. So was the weight to be attached to the second matter relied on, viz that a new trial would, in effect, inflict a third ordeal on the appellant since before the first trial he had appeared as a witness at the coroner's inquiry.

A third matter, which could not be relied on before the Court of Appeal, was the lapse of time between the date of the killing in January 1976 and any new trial which could now take place. Their Lordships are informed that if the Court of Appeal's order of 17th February 1977 had not been appealed against the retrial could have been heard within a couple of months, viz by April 1977. Any delay beyond that date is of the appellant's own making and no specific ground has been advanced to show that it will operate to his disadvantage on a retrial.

The principal ground on which it was argued before their Lordships that a new trial was not required in the interests of justice, was that the Court of Appeal had erred in law in

---

1   (1955) 39 Hong Kong LR 49

holding that it was not a condition precedent to any exercise of their discretion in favour
of ordering a new trial that they should be satisfied that it was *probable* that a fresh jury
properly directed by the judge would convict the appellant on the evidence adduced at the
previous trial. This argument had been addressed to and considered by the Court of
Appeal at the hearing on 3rd February 1977. It is referred to in the so-called judgment of
Huggins JA bearing that date and subsequently placed in the court file; so the view of the
Court of Appeal on it is a matter of knowledge and not merely a matter of inference.

The strength of the evidence adduced against the accused in the previous trial is clearly
one of the factors to be taken into consideration in determining whether or not to order a
new trial. At the one extreme it may be so tenuous that a verdict of guilty on that evidence
would be set aside as unsafe or unsatisfactory under s 83(1)(*a*) of the Criminal Procedure
Ordinance. In such a case the Court of Appeal would be exercising its discretion
unjudicially if it ordered a new trial; for under the adversary system of criminal procedure
which is followed in common law jurisdictions it would be contrary to the interests of
justice to allow a new trial so as to give the prosecution a second chance to get its tackle in
order by adducing additional evidence. In the United States of America where new trials
in criminal cases are a commonplace a similar principle has recently been held by the
Supreme Court of the United States to be applicable in both federal and state courts: see
Burks v United States[1] and *Greene v Massey*[2]

At the other extreme the evidence at the previous trial may have been so strong that any
reasonable jury if properly directed would have convicted the accused and that no
miscarriage of justice had actually occurred. In such a case instead of quashing the
conviction and ordering a new trial the appropriate course would be to dismiss the appeal
under the proviso to s 83(1).

Between these two extremes, however, there lies a whole gradation in the apparent
credibility and cogency of the evidence that has been adduced at the trial rendered abortive
by some technical blunder of the judge. The strength or weakness of the evidence is a
factor to be taken into account but it is only one among what may be many other factors;
and if the Court of Appeal are of opinion that on a proper consideration of the evidence by
the jury a conviction might result it is not a necessary condition precedent to the exercise
of their discretion in favour of ordering a new trial that they should have gone further and
reached the conclusion that a conviction on the retrial was probable.

In the so-called judgment of Huggins JA this question was dealt with thus:

'The true principle is that the court will *not* order a new trial where a conviction is
improbable or where a conviction will, assuming the same evidence is given, be
unsafe or unsatisfactory. In any other case the court will consider the strength of the
evidence as just one of the factors relevant to the determination of what are the
interests of justice. It is a factor which in some cases may assume greater importance
than in others.'

In their Lordships' view this states the matter correctly, although in one respect it may
be too favourable to the accused. If by the reference to a conviction being 'improbable' is
meant no more than that the court believes that an acquittal is more likely than a
conviction, there may be cases where this belief does not in itself provide a conclusive
reason for not ordering a new trial. As was pointed out by Gould ACJ in *Ng Yuk Kin v R*[3],
which was a case of rape, there may be cases where—

'It is in the interest of the public, the complainant, and the appellant himself that
the question of guilt or otherwise be determined finally by the verdict of a Jury, and
not left as something which must remain undecided by reason of a defect in legal
machinery.'

---

1   (1978) 98 S Ct 2141
2   98 S Ct 2151
3   (1955) 39 Hong Kong LR 49 at 60

Their Lordships refer to this because there had been dicta in previous cases in the Court of Appeal of Hong Kong some of which lent colour to the view that the court ought to be **a** satisfied that there is a strong probability of conviction on the re-trial. The latest of these was in *Aplin v R*[1] where it was said 'in considering the issue of retrial a question of paramount importance is the prospect of a further successful prosecution'. The 'paramountcy' here claimed for the factor of the likelihood of a conviction on the retrial was rightly rejected in the so-called 'judgment' in the instant case.

In their Lordships' view there is nothing in the material before them that could justify **b** the inference that in exercising their discretion the majority of the Court of Appeal took into consideration any matters to which they should not have had regard or failed to take into consideration any matters to which they should have had regard. Their Lordships accordingly can see no ground on which they would be justified in interfering with the court's order that the appellant be retried.

Their Lordships will humbly advise Her Majesty that the appeal be dismissed.   **c**

Appeal dismissed.

Solicitors: *Stephenson Harwood* (for the appellant); *Charles Russell & Co* (for the Crown).

Mary Rose Plummer Barrister. **d**

Pickett v British Rail Engineering Ltd
British Rail Engineering Ltd v Pickett   **e**

HOUSE OF LORDS

LORD WILBERFORCE, LORD SALMON, LORD EDMUND-DAVIES, LORD RUSSELL OF KILLOWEN AND LORD SCARMAN

12th, 13th, 14th, 15th JUNE, 2nd NOVEMBER 1978

Damages – Personal injury – Loss of future earnings – Shortened expectation of life – Plaintiff's life **f**
expectancy diminished as a result of defendant's negligence – Plaintiff bringing action in own lifetime – Whether damages for loss of future earnings restricted to period of likely survival – Whether damages for loss of future earnings should include whole period of plaintiff's pre-accident expectancy of earning life – Whether interest on damages can be awarded if damages have been increased to allow for inflation.

g

The plaintiff developed a lung disease as a result of inhaling asbestos dust while working in the defendant's workshops from 1949 to 1974. The symptoms first manifested themselves in 1974, and in 1975 he brought an action against the defendant claiming damages for personal injuries. The defendant admitted liability but contested the quantum of damages. At the date of the trial in October 1976 the plaintiff was aged 53 and married with two children. He had an excellent health record and but for his exposure to **h** asbestos dust could have expected to have been employed until the normal retiring age of 65. The plaintiff's lung disease had, however, shortened his life expectancy to one year. The trial judge awarded the plaintiff damages under various heads, including £7,000 general damages for pain and suffering and loss of amenities, interest on that sum at 9% per annum from the date of service of the writ to the date of the trial amounting to £787·50, and £1,502·88 for loss of earnings which he could have expected to earn during his **j** shortened life expectancy. The plaintiff appealed to the Court of Appeal, but before the appeal was heard he died and his widow was substituted as plaintiff. The Court of Appeal increased the award of general damages to £10,000 but refused to allow any interest on

1   [1976] Hong Kong LR 1028 at 1039

that increased sum on the ground that as damages were now normally subject to increase
to take account of inflation there was no occasion to award interest as well. Following
authority, the court left undisturbed the award for loss of future earnings, holding that
damages in respect of loss of earnings beyond the period of likely survival were not
recoverable. The plaintiff appealed to the House of Lords against the court's refusal to
award any sum for loss of earnings beyond the survival period or to award interest on the
general damages. The defendant cross-appealed against the increase of the general damages
to £10,000.

Held – (i) (Lord Russell of Killowen dissenting) Where the plaintiff's life expectancy was
diminished as the result of the defendant's negligence, the plaintiff's future earnings were
an asset of value of which he had been deprived and which could be assessed in money
terms, and were not merely an intangible expectation or prospect to be disregarded in the
assessment of damages, since what he had been deprived of was the money over and above
that which he would have spent on himself and which he would have been free to dispose
of as he wished, and not merely something which was of no value to him if he was not
there to use it. Thus, if the plaintiff brought an action in his own lifetime, then, on the
assumption that if he was successful his dependants would not in law have a cause of action
under the Fatal Accidents Act 1976 after his death, and in accordance with the principle
that a plaintiff was entitled to be compensated for the loss of anything having a money
value, his loss of future earnings were to be assessed as a separate head of damage and not
merely included as an element in the assessment of damages for loss of expectation of
life. The damages awarded to a plaintiff whose life expectancy was diminished were
therefore to include damages for economic loss resulting from his diminished earning
capacity for the whole period of the plaintiff's pre-accident expectancy of earning life and
not merely the period of his likely survival. Those damages were to be assessed objectively,
disregarding loss of financial expectations which were too remote or unpredictable and
speculative, and after deducting the plaintiff's own living expenses which he would have
expended during the 'lost years', since they would not have formed part of his estate.
Because the trial judge and the Court of Appeal had both restricted damages for loss of
future earnings to the plaintiff's period of likely survival the plaintiff's appeal would be
allowed on this point (see p 780 f to h, p 781 d to f, p 782 a and h to p 783 a, p 784 a to f,
p 791 f g, p 792 e to g, p 795 b, p 796 g, p 797 a to d and p 798 b and e f, post); *Phillips v
London and South Western Railway Co* (1879) 5 QBD 78 and *Skelton v Collins* (1966) 115 CLR
94 applied; *Harris v Bright's Asphalt Contractors Ltd* [1953] 1 All ER 395 and *Oliver v Ashman*
[1961] 3 All ER 323 overruled; dictum of Viscount Simon LC in *Benham v Gambling* [1941]
1 All ER at 13 explained.

(ii) The trial judge's assessment of the general damages at £7,000 was not so grossly
insufficient as to lead to the conclusion that some error must have taken place. On the
contrary since he had correctly apprehended the facts and adopted the correct approach in
law his award ought not to have been interfered with by the Court of Appeal. The
defendant's cross-appeal would therefore be allowed and the trial judge's award restored
(see p 782 e, p 788 e f, p 792 g to p 793 a, p 795 a b and p 799 e f, post).

(iii) An award of interest on general damages was given to compensate a plaintiff for
being deprived of the use of the damages until judgment, whereas the award of an increase
in damages for inflation was designed to preserve the real value of the damages to the
plaintiff, and the Court of Appeal had been wrong to confuse the purpose of the two awards
and disallow the award of interest. The plaintiff's appeal on this point would therefore be
allowed and the trial judge's award of interest restored (see p 782 c d, p 788 e f, p 793 d to
g, p 795 a b and p 800 b to g, post); dictum of Lord Denning MR in *Cookson v Knowles* [1977]
2 All ER at 823 disapproved.

Notes

For interest payable on damages, see 12 Halsbury's Laws (4th Edn) para 1204.
For measure of damages for non pecuniary loss in personal injury actions, see ibid paras
1146–1151. For damages for lost years, see ibid para 1154.

Cases referred to in opinions

Admiralty Comrs v Owners of Steamship Amerika [1917] AC 38, [1916–17] All ER Rep 177,
　86 LJP 58, sub nom *The Amerika* 116 LT 34, 13 Asp MLC 558, HL, 36 (1) Digest (Reissue)
　340, *1356*.

Benham v Gambling [1941] 1 All ER 7, [1941] AC 157, 110 LJKB 49, 164 LT 290, HL; *rvsg*
　[1940] 1 All ER 275, CA, 36 (1) Digest (Reissue) 383, *1544*.

Chaplin v Hicks [1911] 2 KB 786, [1911–13] All ER Rep 224, 80 LJKB 1292, 105 LT 285, CA,
　17 Digest (Reissue) 100, *106*.

Cookson v Knowles [1977] 2 All ER 820, [1977] QB 913, [1977] 3 WLR 279, [1977] 2 Lloyd's
　Rep 412, CA; *affd* [1978] 2 All ER 604, [1978] 2 WLR 978, HL.

Davies v Powell Duffryn Associated Collieries Ltd [1942] 1 All ER 657, [1942] AC 601, 111
　LJKB 418, 167 LT 74, HL, 36(1) Digest (Reissue) 368, *1484*.

Flint v Lovell [1935] 1 KB 354, [1934] All ER Rep 200, 104 LJKB 199, 152 LT 231, CA, 36(1)
　Digest (Reissue) 317, *1276*.

Griffiths v Kerkmayer (1977) 15 ALR 387, 51 ALJR 792, HC of Aust.

Harris v Bright's Asphalt Contractors Ltd [1953] 1 All ER 395, [1953] 1 QB 617, [1953] 1
　WLR 341, 51 LGR 296, 36(1) Digest (Reissue) 41, *131*.

Jefford v Gee [1970] 1 All ER 1202, [1970] 2 QB 130, [1970] 2 WLR 702, [1970] 1 Lloyd's
　Rep 107, CA, Digest (Cont Vol C) 709, *182a*.

Livingstone v Rawyards Coal Co (1880) 5 App Cas 25, 42 LT 334, 44 JP 392, HL, 17 Digest
　(Reissue) 89, *38*.

McCann v Sheppard [1973] 2 All ER 881, [1973] 1 WLR 540, CA, 17 Digest (Reissue) 98, *99*.

Murray v Shuter, N & S Coaches and National Coal Board [1972] 1 Lloyd's Rep 6, CA, Digest
　(Cont Vol D) 1060, *2763a*.

Murray v Shuter [1975] 3 All ER 375, [1976] 1 QB 972, [1975] 3 WLR 597, [1975] 2 Lloyd's
　Rep 470, CA, Digest (Cont Vol D) 718, *1491a*.

Oliver v Ashman [1961] 3 All ER 323, [1962] 2 QB 210, [1961] 3 WLR 669, CA; *affg* [1960]
　3 All ER 677, [1961] 1 QB 337, [1960] 3 WLR 924, 36(1) Digest (Reissue) 313, *1267*.

Phillips v London and South Western Railway Co (1879) 5 QBD 78, 41 LT 121, 43 JP 749, CA;
　affg 4 QBD 406, 48 LJQB 693, 40 LT 813, 17 Digest (Reissue) 221, *932*.

Pope v D Murphy & Son Ltd [1960] 2 All ER 873, [1961] 1 QB 222, [1960] 2 WLR 861, 36(1)
　Digest (Reissue) 317, *1279*.

Read v Great Eastern Railway Co (1868) LR 3 QB 555, 9 B & S 714, 37 LJQB 278, 18 LT 822,
　33 JP 199, 36(1) Digest (Reissue) 354, *1419*.

Reid v Lanarkshire Traction Co 1934 SC 79.

Roach v Yates [1937] 3 All ER 442, [1938] 1 KB 256, 107 LJKB 170, CA, 36(1) Digest
　(Reissue) 317, *1277*.

Rose v Ford [1937] 3 All ER 359, [1937] AC 826, 106 LJKB 576, 157 LT 174, HL, 36(1)
　Digest (Reissue) 382, *1530*.

Skelton v Collins (1966) 115 CLR 94, [1966] ALR 449, HC of Aust.

West (H) & Son Ltd v Shephard [1963] 2 All ER 625, [1964] AC 326, [1963] 2 WLR 1359,
　HL, 36(1) Digest (Reissue) 314, *1269*.

Williams v Mersey Docks and Harbour Board [1905] 1 KB 804, 74 LJKB 481, 92 LT 444, 69
　JP 196, 3 LGR 529, CA, 36(1) Digest (Reissue) 345, *1379*.

Wise v Kaye [1962] 1 All ER 257, [1962] 1 QB 638, [1962] 2 WLR 96, CA, 36(1) Digest
　(Reissue) 313, *1268*.

Appeal and cross-appeal

The plaintiff, Joan Kathleen Pickett, the widow of Ralph Henry Pickett deceased and the
administratrix of his estate, appealed against an order of the Court of Appeal (Lord
Denning MR, Lawton and Goff LJJ) dated 14th November 1977 allowing an appeal by the
plaintiff against an order of Stephen Brown J dated 12th October 1976 and ordering that
damages of £14,947·64 awarded in respect of personal injuries sustained by the deceased
as a result of exposure to asbestos dust in his employment with the defendant, British Rail
Engineering Ltd, between 1949 and 1974, be increased to £17,410·14. The damages

awarded was the total of various sums awarded under different heads. In particular the
a Court of Appeal confirmed the order of the trial judge that there should be awarded the
sum of £1,508·88 in respect of loss of future earnings and increased the award of general
damages for pain, suffering and loss of amenities from £7,000 to £10,000 but ordered that
no interest should be awarded on that sum. The plaintiff appealed against the award of
£1,508·88 for loss of future earnings and also against the refusal of the Court of Appeal to
award interest on the general damages. The defendant cross-appealed against the increase
b of general damages by the Court of Appeal from £7,000 to £10,000. The appeals were
conjoined by order of the House of Lords dated 5th April 1978. The deceased died on 15th
March 1977 pending the hearing of his appeal to the Court of Appeal and an order to carry
on the proceedings was made in favour of his widow as administratrix of his estate. The
facts are set out in the opinion of Lord Wilberforce.

c *Peter Weitzman QC* and *A G McDuff* for the plaintiff.
Michael Lewis QC and *Geoffrey Nice* for the defendant.

Their Lordships took time for consideration.

d 2nd November. The following opinions were delivered.

LORD WILBERFORCE. My Lords, this appeal raises three questions as to the amount
of damages which ought to have been awarded to Mr Ralph Henry Pickett ('the deceased')
against his employer, the defendant, for negligence and/or breach of statutory duty.
e   From 1949 to 1974 Mr Pickett was working for the defendant in the construction of the
bodies of railway coaches, which work involved contact with asbestos dust. In 1974 he
developed symptoms which proved to be of mesothelioma of the lung, of which he later
died.
    On 14th July 1975 he issued a writ against the defendant claiming damages for personal
injuries or physical harm. The defendant admitted liability but contested the issue of
f quantum of damages. The case came for trial before Stephen Brown J who on 12th
October 1976 awarded damages under various heads. Those in issue in this appeal were
three: (i) £7,000 by way of general damages in respect of pain, suffering and loss of
amenities, (ii) £787·50 as interest on the £7,000 at 9% from the service of the writ, (iii)
£1,508·88 as a net sum in respect of loss of earnings (this sum was based on a finding that
the deceased's expectation of life had been reduced to one year from the date of trial, and
g the loss of earnings related to that period, ie the period of likely survival). The judge also
awarded £500 for loss of expectation of life, and the total for which he gave judgment was
£14,947·64.
    Mr Pickett appealed to the Court of Appeal against this judgment, but before the appeal
was heard he died. An order to carry on the proceedings was made in favour of his widow
as administratrix of his estate. The appeal was heard in November 1977. The Court of
h Appeal did not award any sum for loss of earnings beyond the survival period but increased
the general damages award to £10,000, without interest.
    The widow now appeals to this House contending that a much larger amount ought to
have been awarded in respect of loss of future earnings. She also claims that interest should
be awarded on the general damages. The defendant appeals against the award of £10,000
general damages.
j   In 1974, when his symptoms became acute, the deceased was a man of 51 with an
excellent physical record. He was a champion cyclist of Olympic standard, he kept himself
very fit and was a non-smoker. He was leading an active life and cycled to work every
day. He had a wife and two children. There was medical evidence at the trial as to his
condition and prospects, which put his then expectation of life at one year: this the judge
accepted. There can be no doubt that but for his exposure to asbestos dust in his

employment he could have looked forward to a normal period of continued employment up to retiring age. That exposure, for which the defendant accepts liability, has resulted in this period being shortened to one year. It seems, therefore, strange and unjust that his claim for loss of earnings should be limited to that one year (the survival period) and that he should recover nothing in respect of the years of which he has been deprived (the lost years). But this is the result of authority binding on the judge and the Court of Appeal, *Oliver v̇ Ashman*[1]. The present is, in effect, an appeal against that decision.

Oliver v Ashman[1] is part of a complex of law which has developed piecemeal and which is neither logical nor consistent. Judges do their best to make do with it but from time to time cases appear, like the present, which do not appeal to a sense of justice. I shall not review in any detail the state of the authorities for this was admirably done by Holroyd Pearce LJ in *Oliver v Ashman*[1]. The main strands in the law as it then stood were: (1) the Law Reform (Miscellaneous Provisions) Act 1934 abolished the old rule actio personalis moritur cum persona and provided for the survival of causes of action in tort for the benefit of the victim's estate; (2) the decision of this House in *Rose v Ford*[2] that a claim for loss of expectation of life survived under the 1934 Act, and was not a claim for damages based on the death of a person and so barred at common law (cf *Admiralty Comrs v Owners of Steamship Amerika*[3]); (3) the decision of this House in *Benham v Gamblin*[4] that damages for loss of expectation of life could only be given up to a conventional figure, then fixed at £200; (4) the Fatal Accidents Acts under which proceedings may be brought for the benefit of dependants to recover the loss caused to those dependants by the death of the breadwinner; the amount of this loss is related to the probable future earnings which would have been made by the deceased during 'lost years'.

This creates a difficulty. It is assumed in the present case, and the assumption is supported by authority, that if an action for damages is brought by the victim during his lifetime, and either proceeds to judgment or is settled, further proceedings cannot be brought after his death under the Fatal Accidents Acts. If this assumption is correct, it provides a basis, in logic and justice, for allowing the victim to recover for earnings lost during his lost years.

This assumption is based on the wording of s 1 of the 1846 Act (now s 1 of the Fatal Accidents Act 1976) and is not supported by any decision of this House. It cannot however be challenged in this appeal, since there is before us no claim under the Fatal Accident Acts. I think, therefore, that we must for present purposes act on the basis that it is well founded, and that if the present claim, in respect of earnings during the lost years, fails it will not be possible for a fresh action to be brought by the deceased's dependants in relation to them.

With this background, *Oliver v Ashman*[1] may now be considered. I shall deal with it on authority and on principle.

It is clear from the judgment of Holroyd Pearce LJ that he considered that, apart from the decision in *Benham v Gambling*[4], there was, at the least, a case for giving damages in respect of the lost years. Thus he said[5]:

> 'On one view of the matter there is no loss of earnings when a man dies prematurely. He is no longer there to earn them, since he has died before they could be earned. He has merely lost the prospect of some years of life which is a complex of pleasure and pain, of good and ill, of profits and losses. On the other view, he has, in addition to losing a prospect of the years of life, lost the income he would have earned, and the profits that would have been his had he lived.'

1   [1961] 3 All ER 323, [1962] 2 QB 210
2   [1937] 3 All ER 359, [1937] AC 826
3   [1917] AC 38, [1916–17] All ER Rep 177
4   [1941] 1 All ER 7, [1941] AC 157
5   [1961] 3 All ER 323 at 330, [1962] 2 QB 210 at 228

He then proceeded to examine *Benham v Gambling*[1] and reached the conclusion that it was
a binding authority in favour of the first view. The critical passage in the speech of
Viscount Simon LC was that containing these words[2]:

'Of course, no regard must be had to financial losses or gains during the period of
which the victim has been deprived. The damages are in respect of loss of life, not of
loss of future pecuniary prospects.'

My Lords, if more recent periods in the House exemplify excessive multiplication of
speeches, there are instances, of which this must certainly be one, where a single speech
may generate uncertainty. How far was Viscount Simon LC intending to go? Was he
intending to lay down a principle 'in clear and careful terms' of general application? Or are
his words to be related to the case then before this House? These and other perplexities
might well have been resolved if any of the five (sic)[3] other learned Lords had expressed his
views in his own words. It is, of course, the function of this House to lay down general
rules, to reduce the partialities of previous decisions to some simple universal, but even
after the most comprehensive of arguments there remain aspects of a legal problem which
were not in view when the decision is reached. *Benham v Gambling*[1] was a case of a small
child (2½ years old) almost instantly killed. The claim was for loss of expectation of life.
There was no claim for loss of future earnings. Claims for loss of expectation of life,
validated by *Flint v Lovell*[4], and held to survive in *Rose v Ford*[5], had begun to proliferate, and
sums of differing amounts, some quite large, had begun to be awarded. The judge in
Benham v Gambling[1] had awarded £1,200. There was a clear need to bring order into this
situation and the solution, to fix a conventional sum, was adapted to this need. The quoted
words of Viscount Simon LC can well be understood as expressing no more than a principle
for assessing damages under this particular heading of life expectation and as saying no
more than that there was not inherent in a claim for such damages any claim for pecuniary
loss arising from the loss of earnings.

Apart from these general considerations, such references as can be made to the argument
point both ways. There was a reference to the speech of Lord Roche in *Rose v Ford*[5] and to
the judgment of Lord Blackburn in the Inner House in *Reid v Lanarkshire Traction Co*[6]. It
was said that in each of these cases passages can be found to support the proposition that loss
of earnings can only be recovered as an element in the loss of expectation of life. But these
passages, in particular the opinion of Lord Wark as Lord Ordinary in *Reid's* case[7], were
neither reported as relied on in argument nor taken up in the speech of Viscount Simon
LC. So I do not find here any support for the argument that his Lordship was dealing with
loss of earnings in any way. Secondly, as the reporter mentions in a parenthesis[8], mention
was made in argument of the then recent Court of Appeal case of *Roach v Yates*[9]. The
headnote[10] in that case describes it as deciding that damages for earnings during the lost
years *can* be recovered. Whether that headnote is wholly accurate or not, it is inconceivable
that Viscount Simon LC would have made no mention of the case if, as is contended, he
was laying down a rule to govern the assessment of damages for loss of earnings in the
future. If he was, he must have expressed disagreement with it.

The conclusion must be (and to my mind it is clear) that *Benham v Gambling*[1] was no

---

1   [1941] 1 All ER 7, [1941] AC 157
2   [1941] 1 All ER 7 at 13, [1941] AC 157 at 167
3   Lord Roche appears as one of the appellate committee in [1941] 1 All ER 7, 110 LJKB 49 and 164
    LT 290 but not in [1941] AC 157
4   [1935] 1 KB 354, [1934] All ER Rep 200
5   [1937] 3 All ER 359, [1937] AC 826
6   1934 SC 79 at 84
7   1934 SC 79 at 80
8   [1941] AC 157 at 159
9   [1937] 3 All ER 442, [1938] 1 KB 256
10 [1938] 1 KB 256

authority compelling the decision in *Oliver v Ashman*[1]. It was not dealing with, and Viscount Simon LC did not have in mind, a claim by a living person for earnings during the lost years. Once this is established, the two views stated by Holroyd Pearce LJ remain open, and on them the existing balance of authority was slightly the other way (see *Phillips v London and South West Railway Co*[2], *Roach v Yates*[3], *Pope v D Murphy & Son Ltd*[4]; *Harris v Bright's Asphalt Contractors Ltd*[5] contra).

As to principle, the passage which best summarises the underlying reasons for the decision in *Oliver v Ashman*[6] is the following:

'. . . what has been lost by the person assumed to be dead is the opportunity to enjoy what he would have earned, whether by spending it or saving it. Earnings themselves strike me as being of no significance without reference to the way in which they are used. To inquire what would have been the value to a person in the position of this plaintiff of any earnings which he might have made after the date when ex hypothesi he will be dead strikes me as a hopeless task.'

Or as Holroyd Pearce LJ put it[7]: 'What is lost is an expectation, not the thing itself.'

My Lords, I think that these are instinctual sentences, not logical propositions or syllogisms, none the worse for that because we are not in the field of pure logic. It may not be unfair to paraphrase them as saying: 'Nothing is of value except to a man who is there to spend or save it. The plaintiff will not be there when these earnings hypothetically accrue: so they have no value to him.' Perhaps there are additional strands, one which indeed Willmer LJ had earlier made explicit, that the whole process of assessment is too speculative for the courts to undertake; another that the only loss is a subjective one, an emotion of distress. But if so I would disagree with them. Assumptions, chances, hypotheses enter into most assessments, and juries had, we must suppose, no difficulties with them; the judicial approach, however less robust, can manage too. And to say that what calls for compensation is injured feelings does not provide an answer to the vital question which is whether, in addition to this subjective element, there is something objective which has been lost.

But is the main line of reasoning acceptable? Does it not ignore the fact that a particular man, in good health, and sound earning, has in these two things an asset of present value quite separate and distinct from the expectation of life which every man possesses? Compare him with a man in poor health and out of a job. Is he not, and not only in the immediate present, a richer man? Is he not entitled to say, at one moment I am a man with existing capability to earn well for 14 years, the next moment I can only earn less well for one year? And why should he be compensated only for the immediate reduction in his earnings and not for the loss of the whole period for which he has been deprived of his ability to earn them? To the argument that 'they are of no value because you will not be there to enjoy them' can he not reply, 'Yes they are; what is of value to me is not only my opportunity to spend them enjoyably, but to use such part of them as I do not need for my dependants, or for other persons or causes which I wish to support. If I cannot do this, I have been deprived of something on which a value, a present value, can be placed'?

I do not think that the problem can be solved by describing what has been lost as an 'opportunity' or a 'prospect' or an 'expectation'. Indeed these words are invoked both ways, by the Lords Justices as denying a right to recover (on grounds of remoteness, intangibility or speculation), by those supporting the appellant's argument as demonstrating the loss of some real asset of true value. The fact is that the law sometimes allows damages to be given

---

1   [1961] 3 All ER 323, [1962] 2 QB 210
2   (1879) 5 QBD 78; *affg* 4 QBD 406
3   [1937] 3 All ER 442, [1938] 1 KB 256
4   [1960] 2 All ER 873, [1961] 1 QBD 222
5   [1953] 1 All ER 395, [1953] 1 QB 617
6   [1961] 3 All ER 323 at 338, [1962] 2 QB 210 at 240, per Willmer LJ
7   [1961] 3 All ER 323 at 332, [1962] 2 QB 210 at 230

for the loss of things so described (e g *Chaplin v Hicks*[1]), sometimes it does not. It always has
to answer a question which in the end can hardly be more accurately framed than as: 'Is the
a loss of this something for which the claimant should and reasonably can be compensated?'

The defendant, in an impressive argument, urged on us that the real loss in such cases
as the present was to the victim's dependants and that the right way in which to compensate
them was to change the law (by statute; judicially it would be impossible) so as to enable
the dependants to recover their loss independently of any action by the victim. There is
b much force in this, and no doubt the law could be changed in this way. But I think that
the argument fails because it does not take account, as in an action for damages account
must be taken, of the interest of the victim. Future earnings are of value to him in order
that he may satisfy legitimate desires, but these may not correspond with the allocation
which the law makes of money recovered by dependants on account of his loss. He may
wish to benefit some dependants more than, or to the exclusion of, others; this (subject to
c family inheritance legislation) he is entitled to do. He may not have dependants, but he
may have others, or causes, whom he would wish to benefit, for whom he might even
regard himself as working. One cannot make a distinction, for the purposes of assessing
damages, between men in different family situations.

There is another argument, in the opposite sense; that which appealed to Streatfeild J in
Pope v D Murphy & Son Ltd[2]. Why, he asked, should the tortfeasor benefit from the fact
d that as well as reducing his victim's earning capacity he has shortened his victim's life?
Good advocacy but unsound principle, for damages are to compensate the victim not to
reflect what the wrongdoer ought to pay.

My Lords, in the case of the adult wage earner with or without dependants who sues for
damages during his lifetime, I am convinced that a rule which enables the 'lost years' to be
taken account of comes closer to the ordinary man's expectations than one which limits his
e interest to his shortened span of life. The interest which such a man has in the earnings he
might hope to make over a normal life, if not saleable in a market, has a value which can
be assessed. A man who receives that assessed value would surely consider himself and be
considered compensated; a man denied it would not. And I do not think that to act in this
way creates insoluble problems of assessment in other cases. In that of a young child (cf
Benham v Gambling[3]) neither present nor future earnings could enter into the matter; in the
f more difficult case of adolescents just embarking on the process of earning (cf *Skelton v
Collins*[4]) the value of 'lost' earnings might be real but would probably be assessable as small.

There will remain some difficulties. In cases, probably the normal, where a man's actual
dependants coincide with those for whom he provides out of the damages he receives,
whatever they obtain by inheritance will simply be set off against their own claim. If on
the other hand this coincidence is lacking, there might be duplication of recovery. To that
g extent injustice may be caused to the wrongdoer. But if there is a choice between taking
a view of the law which mitigates a clear and recognised injustice in cases of normal
occurrence, at the cost of the possibility in fewer cases of excess payments being made, or
leaving the law as it is, I think that our duty is clear. We should carry the judicial process
of seeking a just principle as far as we can, confident that a wise legislator will correct
resultant anomalies.

h My Lords, I have reached the conclusion which I would recommend so far without
reference to *Skelton v Collins*[4] in which the High Court of Australia, refusing to follow *Oliver
v Ashman*[5], achieved the same result. The value of this authority is twofold: first in
recommending by reference to authority (per Taylor J) and in principle (per Windeyer J)
the preferable solution, and, secondly, in demonstrating that this can properly be reached
by judicial process. The judgments, further, bring out an important ingredient, which I

j

---

1   [1911] 2 KB 786, [1911–13] All ER Rep 224
2   [1960] 2 All ER 873, [1961] 1 QB 222
3   [1941] 1 All ER 7, [1941] AC 157
4   (1966) 115 CLR 94
5   [1961] 3 All ER 323, [1962] 2 QB 210

would accept, namely that the amount to be recovered in respect of earnings in the 'lost' years should be that amount after deduction of an estimated sum to represent the victim's *a* probable living expenses during those years. I think that this is right because the basis, in principle, for recovery lies in the interest which he has in making provision for dependants and others, and this he would do out of his surplus. There is the additional merit of bringing awards under this head into line with what could be recovered under the Fatal Accidents Acts. *Skelton v Collins*[1] has been followed and applied recently by the High Court of Australia in *Griffiths v Kerkmayer*[2]. *b*

I would allow the appeal on this point and remit the action to the Queen's Bench Division for damages to be assessed accordingly. We are not called on in this appeal to lay down any rules as to the manner in which such damages should be calculated; this must be left to the courts to work out in conformity with established principles.

I shall deal briefly with the other issues. As to interest on damages, I would restore the decision of the judge. This was varied by the Court of Appeal on the theory that as *c* damages are now normally subject to increase to take account of inflation, there is no occasion to award interest as well. I find this argument, with respect, fallacious. Increase for inflation is designed to preserve the 'real' value of money, interest to compensate for being kept out of that 'real' value. The one has no relation to the other. If the damages claimed remained, nominally, the same, because there was no inflation, interest would normally be given. The same should follow if the damages remain in real terms the *d* same. Apart from the inflation argument no reason was suggested for interfering with the exercise of the judge's discretion.

As to the general damages, I would also restore the judgment of the trial judge. He gave this matter most careful attention and the Court of Appeal were unable to find that he erred in principle in any way. It is important that judges' assessments should not be disturbed unless such error can be shown, or unless the amount is so grossly excessive or *e* insufficient as to lead to the conclusion that some such error must have taken place.

If the appeal and cross-appeal are disposed of as I have suggested, the plaintiff should have the costs of the appeal in this House and the defendant the costs of the cross-appeal.

LORD SALMON. My Lords, the relevant facts have been fully and lucidly set out by my noble and learned friend, Lord Wilberforce. They raise only one point of law which is of *f* great public importance; I shall confine myself to examining that point alone. I propose to do so first by considering the principles involved and then the authorities.

Suppose a plaintiff who is 50 years old and earning a good living with a reasonable expectation of continuing to do so until he reaches 65 years of age. As a result of the defendant's negligence, he has contracted a disease or suffered injuries which cut down his expectation of life to, say, five years and prevent him from earning any remuneration *g* during that period. Are the damages to which he is entitled confined to compensation for the loss of the remuneration he would probably have earned during those five years, or do they include compensation for the loss of the remuneration which, but for the defendant's negligence, he would probably have earned for a further ten years, ie for the rest of what would have been his working life? In my opinion, there is no reason based either on justice or logic for supporting the view that he, and therefore his estate, is entitled to no *h* damages in respect of the money he has been deprived from earning during these ten years.

Suppose that, in the case I have postulated, the plaintiff's action for damages for negligence came to trial two years after he first became incapacitated. He would obviously be entitled to compensation for the remuneration he had lost in those two years. He would also, in my opinion, be entitled to a lump sum to compensate him for the undoubted loss of remuneration which, but for the defendant's negligence, he would probably have *j* earned in the next 13 years, ie up to the date when he would have reached retiring age. I do not accept that there can be any justification for limiting this compensation to

1   (1966) 115 CLR 94
2   (1977) 51 ALR 387

compensation for the earnings he would have lost in the three years immediately following
a the trial, and awarding him nothing in respect of the remuneration he would, but for the
defendant's negligence, have lost during the next ten years, commonly known in cases
such as these as the 'lost years'.

In most cases of this kind, the plaintiff, whether or not he knows he is likely to die as a
result of the defendant's negligence, will bring his case to court or settle it as soon as
possible because he is in urgent need of that part of the damages to which he is entitled, so
b that he may support himself and his family during his life. There can be no sensible reason
why by doing so he should forfeit the balance of the damages attributable to the loss of
remuneration caused by the defendant's negligence.

Although the point has never been considered by your Lordships' House, it is generally
assumed that should the plaintiff accept a sum in settlement of his claim or obtain
judgment for damages in respect of the defendant's negligence, his dependants will have
c no cause of action under the Fatal Accidents Acts after his death. This assumption is
supported by strong authority: see *Read v Great Eastern Railway Co*[1], *Williams v Mersey
Docks and Harbour Board*[2] and *Murray v Shuter*[3]. No point about the correctness of this
assumption arises for decision in this appeal and therefore I express no concluded opinion
about it. I think, however, that the assumption which has held the field for upwards of
100 years is probably correct and that, for present purposes, it must be accepted. In the
d overwhelming majority of cases a man works not only for his personal enjoyment but also
to provide for the present and future needs of his dependants. It follows that it would be
grossly unjust to the plaintiff and his dependants were the law to deprive him from
recovering any damages for the loss of remuneration which the defendant's negligence has
prevented him from earning during the 'lost years'. There is, in my view, no principle of
the common law that requires such an injustice to be perpetrated.

e When the Fatal Accidents Acts 1846 to 1908 were passed, it is, in my view, difficult to
believe that it could have occurred to Parliament that the common law could possibly be
as stated, many years later, by the Court of Appeal in *Oliver v Ashman*[4]. The clear intention
of Parliament in passing those Acts appears to have been to deal with the all too frequent
cases in which, as a result of someone else's negligence, a man suffered injuries which
incapacitated him from earning and caused his death before he could obtain any damages
f from the tortfeasor to compensate him for the loss of the money he would have earned but
for the tort. The policy of the Acts was, in my opinion, clearly to put that man's
dependants, as far as possible, in the same financial position as they would have been in if
the breadwinner had lived long enough to obtain judgment against the tortfeasor. In my
opinion, Parliament correctly assumed that, had the deceased lived, he would have
recovered judgment for a lump sum by way of damages as compensation for the money
g he would have earned but for the tortfeasor's negligence, and that these damages would
have included the money which the deceased would have earned during 'the lost years'.
Otherwise, Parliament would, surely, have made it plain that no judgment in favour of the
deceased or settlement of his claim could bar a claim by his dependants under the Fatal
Accidents Acts; I certainly do not think Parliament would have used the language which
it did use in s 1 of those Acts.

h The common law does not award a plaintiff annual payments in respect of the money he
would have earned during the rest of his life had it not been for the defendant's
negligence. It awards him a lump sum by way of damages to compensate him for all the
money he has probably been prevented from earning because of the defendant's
negligence. The common law takes many factors into account in assessing those damages,
eg that the lump sum awarded will yield interest in the future, that the plaintiff might
j have lost his job in any event, that he might have been incapacitated or killed in some other

1   (1868) LR 3 QB 555
2   [1905] 1 KB 804
3   [1972] 1 Lloyd's Rep 6 at 7
4   [1961] 3 All ER 323, [1962] 2 QB 210

way, so that the defendant's negligence may not necessarily have been the cause of his loss of earnings.

One of the factors which, however, the common law does not, in my view, take into account for the purpose of reducing damages is that some of the earnings, lost as a result of the defendant's negligence, would have been earned in the 'lost years'. Damages for the loss of earnings during the 'lost years' should be assessed justly and with moderation. There can be no question of these damages being fixed at any conventional figure because damages for pecuniary loss, unlike damages for pain and suffering, can be naturally measured in money. The amount awarded will depend on the facts of each particular case. They may vary greatly from case to case. At one end of the scale, the claim may be made on behalf of a young child or his estate. In such a case, the lost earnings are so unpredictable and speculative that only a minimal sum could properly be awarded. At the other end of the scale, the claim may be made by a man in the prime of life or, if he dies, on behalf of his estate; if he has been in good employment for years with every prospect of continuing to earn a good living until he reaches the age of retirement, after all the relevant factors have been taken into account, the damages recoverable from the defendant are likely to be substantial. The amount will, of course, vary, sometimes greatly, according to the particular facts of the case under consideration.

I recognise that there is a comparatively small minority of cases in which a man whose life, and therefore his capacity to earn, is cut short, dies intestate with no dependants or has made a will excluding dependants, leaving all his money to others or to charity. Subject to the family inheritance legislation, a man may do what he likes with his own. Certainly, the law can make no distinction between the plaintiff who looks after dependants and the plaintiff who does not, in assessing the damages recoverable to compensate the plaintiff for the money he would have earned during the 'lost years' but for the defendant's negligence. On his death those damages will pass to whosoever benefits under his will or on an intestacy.

I think that in assessing those damages, there should be deducted the plaintiff's own living expenses which he would have expended during the 'lost years' because these clearly can never constitute any part of his estate. The assessment of these living expenses may, no doubt, sometimes present difficulties, but certainly no difficulties which would be insuperable for the courts to resolve, as they always have done in assessing dependancy under the Fatal Accidents Acts.

I now turn to the authorities. The first reported case in which the assessment of damages for loss of future earnings was discussed in relation to a plaintiff who faced a speedy death as a result of the defendant's negligence was *Phillips v London and South Western Railway Co*[1]. The plaintiff, Phillips, was a consultant physician. After reciting a passage from the trial judge's summing-up, James LJ said[2]:

'That comes to this, you are to consider what his income would probably have been, how long that income would probably have lasted, and you are to take into consideration all the other contingencies to which a practice is liable. I do not know how otherwise the case could be put.'

Brett and Cotton LJJ agreed with that judgment. I am not at all surprised that it never occurred to that distinguished court that the 'lost years' should be ignored in assessing damages for loss of earnings, nor that it did not occur to Serjeant Ballantine, who appeared for the defendants. In my opinion, to ignore the 'lost years' would be to ignore the long established principles of the common law in relation to the assessment of damages.

The next relevant case was *Roach v Yates*[3]. The judgments in that case were given ex tempore. I confess that I find it difficult to discover anything from the judgment of

---

1   (1879) 5 QBD 78
2   5 QBD 78 at 87
3   [1937] 3 All ER 442, [1938] 1 KB 256

a Greer LJ except that he and his brethren had agreed that the damages of £2,742 awarded by the trial judge were far too low and should be increased to £6,542. The reasons on which Greer LJ based that conclusion are obscure. He did, however, refer to the judgment in *Phillips v London and South Western Railway Co*[1] without disagreeing with it. On the other hand, Slesser LJ did make plain the grounds on which he based his conclusions. He said[2]:

b 'Speaking for myself . . . I think the proper way of approaching the problem is that which was followed in *Phillips v. London & South Western Ry. Co.*[1], the leading case on this matter—namely, first to consider what sum he [the plaintiff] would have been likely to make during his normal life if he had not met with the accident.'

c MacKinnon LJ's judgment consists only of the enigmatic words 'I agree'. It is by no means plain whether he agreed with the reasons given by Slesser LJ who had indicated, in giving those reasons, that he was speaking for himself, or whether MacKinnon LJ was agreeing only that the damages should be raised to £6,542. Although I agree with the reasons given by Slesser LJ, I think that it is doubtful whether the headnote[3] was correct in saying that those reasons were the reasons on which the whole court based its judgment.

d I now turn to *Harris v Bright's Asphalt Contractors Ltd*[4]. This is the first case in this country in which it was argued and indeed decided that (a) damages for the loss of earnings for the 'lost years' is nil, and (b) 'the only relevance of earning which would have been earned after death is that they are an element for consideration in assessing damages for loss of expectation of life, in the sense that a person earning a reasonable livelihood is more likely to have an enjoyable life'[5]. Slade J who gave that judgment attempted, I think unsuccessfully, to explain away what had been said in *Phillips v London and South Western Railway Co*[1] and *Roach v Yates*[6]. It is interesting to note that although counsel for the defendants and third parties had relied[7] on *Benham v Gambling*[8], Slade J apparently considered, correctly in my view, that *Benham v Gambling*[8] had so little to do with the point in issue that it was not worth even mentioning in his judgment. Nor was he able to cite any other authority in support of his decision.

f In *Pope v D Murphy & Son Ltd*[9], Streatfeild J refused to follow Slade J's judgment in *Harris v Bright's Asphalt Contractors Ltd*[4] and decided the issue on damages in favour of the plaintiff, relying on what had been said in the Court of Appeal in the earlier cases to which I have referred.

Then came *Oliver v Ashman*[10]. The plaintiff was a young boy who, when 20 months old, had suffered injuries as a result of the defendant's negligence which turned him into a low grade mental defective and reduced his expectation of life from 60 years to 30 years. He g claimed damages not only for loss of expectation of life, pain, suffering, loss of amenities and the expenses incurred in taking care of him, but also for the loss of what he might have earned but for the accident. Lord Parker CJ[11], who tried the case at first instance, followed the decision in *Pope v D Murphy & Co Ltd*[9] and awarded him a lump sum of £11,000. The

---

h

1   (1879) 5 QBD 78
2   [1938] 1 KB 256 at 268, cf [1937] 3 All ER 442 at 447
3   [1938] 1 KB 256
4   [1953] 1 All ER 395, [1953] 1 QB 617
5   [1953] 1 QB 617 at 634, cf [1953] 1 All ER 395 at 402
j   6   [1937] 3 All ER 442, [1938] 1 KB 256
7   [1953] 1 QB 617 at 624 and 625
8   [1941] 1 All ER 7, [1941] AC 157
9   [1960] 2 All ER 873, [1961] 1 QB 222
10 [1961] 3 All ER 323, [1962] 2 QB 210
11 [1960] 3 All ER 677, [1961] 1 QB 337

plaintiff appealed on the ground that that award was too low. The defendant cross-appealed on the ground that the award was too high. The Court of Appeal[1] overruled *Pope v D Murphy & Co Ltd*[2] and held that *Harris v Bright's Asphalt Contractors Ltd*[3] had been correctly decided. Nevertheless they did not reduce the award because they concluded, quite rightly in my view, that in the case of a child of such tender years the amount of the earnings which he might have lost was so speculative and unpredictable that the sum in the award attributable to that element must have been minimal and could therefore be disregarded.

In considering whether loss of earnings during the 'lost years' could ever be taken into account in assessing damages, Holroyd Pearce LJ said[4]:

'On one view of the matter there is no loss of earnings when a man dies prematurely. He is no longer there to earn them, since he has died before they could be earned. He has merely lost the prospect of some years of life which is a complex of pleasure and pain, of good and ill, of profits and losses. On the other view, he has in addition to losing a prospect of the years of life, lost the income which he would have earned, and the profits which would have been his had he lived.'

Holroyd Pearce LJ came down in favour of the first view because he concluded that he was bound to do so by the decision of your Lordships' House in *Benham v Gambling*[5]. So did Willmer and Pearson LJJ. I cannot agree with that conclusion. In *Benham v Gambling*[5] the plaintiff was the father and administrator of the estate of his infant child who was 2½ years old and who was so badly injured by the negligent driving of the defendant that he died on the day of the accident. Not surprisingly, no claim was made for damages in respect of the earnings that this infant might have lost because such damages could only have been minimal; and accordingly no argument was addressed to this House on the issue raised on the present appeal. The claim was confined solely to damages for the loss of expectation of life. The trial judge assessed those damages at £1,200. The Court of Appeal[6], by a majority, refused to reduce that amount on the defendant's appeal. The defendant then successfully appealed to your Lordships' House.

Accordingly, the decision in *Benham v Gambling*[5] does not touch the issue now before this House. Indeed Viscount Simon LC who made the only speech in *Benham v Gambling*[7] (with whom all the other noble and learned Lords agreed) said:

'The present appeal raises the problem of the assessment of damage for loss of expectation of life before this House for the first time, and it is, indeed, the only issue with which we are now concerned.'

He then went on, carefully, to explain all the factors to be taken into account in assessing those damages and to stress the necessity for moderation, which he perhaps emphasised by reducing the damages, in the circumstances of that case, to £200. Two sentences which concluded a paragraph towards the end of that speech were fastened on by the Court of Appeal in *Oliver v Ashman*[8] and indeed constituted the cornerstone of their judgment. The sentences read as follows[9]:

'Of course, no regard must be had to financial losses or gains during the period of which the victim has been deprived. The damages are in respect of loss of life, not of loss of future pecuniary interests.'

1 [1961] 3 All ER 323, [1962] 2 QB 210
2 [1960] 2 All ER 873, [1961] 1 QB 222
3 [1953] 1 All ER 395, [1953] 1 QB 617
4 [1961] 3 All ER 323 at 330, [1962] 2 QB 210 at 228
5 [1941] 1 All ER 7, [1941] AC 157
6 [1940] 1 All ER 275
7 [1941] 1 All ER 7 at 9, [1941] AC 157 at 162
8 [1961] 3 All ER 323 at 331, [1962] 2 QB 210 at 229
9 [1941] 1 All ER 7 at 13, [1941] AC 157 at 167

Those sentences exactly fitted the facts of that case because no claim in respect of pecuniary loss was being made. As Viscount Simon LC himself acknowledged, the only issue with which the House was then concerned was the assessment of damages for loss of expectation of life.

Holroyd Pearce and Willmer LJJ considered that what I call the two excised sentences in Viscount Simon LC's speech must have been intended to apply to cases in which damages for loss of earnings during the 'lost years' are being claimed, because the speech by Lord Roche in *Rose v Ford*[1] and the judgment in *Reid v Lanarkshire Traction Co*[2] had been cited in the argument in *Benham v Gambling*[3]. I would point out that *Rose v Ford*[1] was itself a case solely concerned with a claim for damages for loss of expectation of life. No damages for pecuniary loss were claimed on behalf of the deceased's estate. Lord Roche alone did, however, make some obiter observations which might have been of some help to the defendant in *Oliver v Ashman*[4]. According to the report of the argument in *Benham v Gambling*[5], that, however, was not the passage in Lord Roche's speech which was cited to this House. Similarly, it is true that in *Reid v Lanarkshire Traction Co*[2], Lord Wark, the Lord Ordinary, made some observations which would also have helped the defendant in *Oliver v Ashman*[4]; but again, according to the report of *Benham v Gambling*[6], that judgment was not cited in argument. What was cited was a passage from Lord Blackburn's judgment in the Inner House which had nothing to do with claims for pecuniary loss.

I hardly think that the excised sentences were intended to apply to cases in which there was a claim for damages in respect of loss of earnings during the 'lost years'. If they had been, it seems as incredible to me as it does to my noble and learned friend, Lord Wilberforce, that Viscount Simon LC would not have disapproved *Roach v Yates*[7], and I think also *Phillips v London and South Western Railway Co*[8].

My Lords, in my opinion, *Benham v Gambling*[3] illustrates how unfortunate it may sometimes be to have only one speech, however excellent, to explain the decision of the appellate committee. I have little doubt that if any other of the noble and learned Lords concerned in that case had also delivered a speech, there would have been no misunderstanding about the meaning of what I have described as the two excised sentences in Viscount Simon LC's speech. I agree with the view often expressed by Lord Reid that if there is only one speech it is apt to be construed as a statute, which is not how a speech ought to be treated. If, however, there are a number of speeches, the general principles which it is the function of this House to lay down will be distilled from them. I am not, of course, suggesting that there are not sometimes circumstances in which, for instance, one section in a statute has to be construed, and one speech may accordingly be appropriate.

Before leaving *Oliver v Ashman*[4], I should like to refer to the passage in the judgment of Pearson LJ which reads as follows[9]:

'In my view the conclusion, shortly stated, is that the conventional sum in the region of £200 which is to be awarded for loss of expectation of life should be regarded as covering all the elements of it—e.g., joys and sorrows, work and leisure, earning and spending or saving money, marriage and parenthood and providing for dependants—and should be regarded as excluding any additional assessment for any of those elements.'

1 [1937] 3 All ER 359, [1937] AC 826
2 1934 SC 79
3 [1941] 1 All ER 7, [1941] AC 157
4 [1961] 3 All ER 323, [1962] 2 QB 210
5 [1941] AC 157 at 159
6 [1941] AC 157
7 [1937] 3 All ER 442, [1938] 1 KB 256
8 (1879) 5 QBD 78
9 [1961] 3 All ER 323 at 341, [1962] 2 QB 210 at 245

I say nothing about the exiguous amount of the damages with which the present appeal is not concerned. I do not, however, agree with the rest of that passage unless one exludes from it the words 'earning and spending or saving money ... and providing for dependants'. These words seem to me to conflict with the two sentences in Viscount Simon LC's speech in *Benham v Gambling*[1] to which I have already referred and with which I agree.

I am reinforced in the opinion I have formed by the judgments of Kitto, Taylor, Menzies, Windeyer and Owen JJ in *Skelton v Collins*[2]. I will cite only the judgment of Windeyer J[3]:

> 'The next rule that, as I see the matter, flows from the principle of compensation is that anything having a money value which the plaintiff has lost should be made good in money. This applies to that element in damages for personal injuries which is commonly called "loss of earnings". The destruction or diminution of a man's capacity to earn money can be made good in money. It can be measured by having regard to the money that he might have been able to earn had the capacity not been destroyed or diminished ... what is to be compensated for is the destruction or diminution of something having a monetary equivalent ... I cannot see that damages that flow from the destruction or diminution of his capacity [to earn money] are any the less when the period during which the capacity might have been exercised is curtailed because the tort cut short his expected span of life. We should not, I think, follow the English decisions in which in assessing the loss of earnings the "lost years" are not taken into account.'

The only English decisions to which the High Court of Australia can have been referring in relation to the 'lost years' were the decisions of Slade J in *Harris v Bright's Asphalt Contractors Ltd*[4] and of the Court of Appeal in *Oliver v Ashman*[5]. My Lords, I have already stated my reasons for holding that both those decisions were wrong and should be overruled.

I entirely agree with what my noble and learned friend, Lord Wilberforce, has said about the issues relating to (a) the interest on the general damages and (b) the amount of the general damages for pain and suffering and the like to which I cannot add anything.

I would, therefore, allow the appeal and cross-appeal and remit the action to the Queen's Bench Division to assess the damages in relation to the plaintiff's loss of earnings during the 'lost years'.

LORD EDMUND-DAVIES. My Lords, in the autumn of 1976 Stephen Brown J had before him a claim for damages for negligence brought by a workman against his employers. For many years Mr Pickett had worked in contact with asbestos dust and, as a result, he developed mesothelioma of the lung, a condition which first exhibited symptoms in 1974. In the following year he instituted these proceedings and, at the time of the hearing, he was a married man of 53 with a wife and two children. Until 51 years of age he had been very fit, and was leading a most active life. Liability was admitted by the employers, and the one issue arising in this appeal relates to the award of general damages. This was compounded for the greater part by the sum of £7,000 for pain, suffering and loss of amenities. The judge also awarded interest at 9% on the £7,000, calculated from the date of service of the writ to the date of trial.

Mr Pickett died on 15th March 1977, less than four months after he had obtained judgment, and his widow and administratrix was substituted as plaintiff for the purpose of appealing from that decision. The Court of Appeal increased the award for pain and

---

1 [1941] 1 All ER 7 at 13, [1941] AC 157 at 167
2 (1966) 115 CLR 94
3 115 CLR 94 at 129
4 [1953] 1 All ER 395, [1953] 1 QB 617
5 [1961] 3 All ER 323, [1962] 2 QB 210

suffering from £7,000 to £10,000, and the compensation for shortened expectation of life
(as to which no question arises) from £500 to £750, but ordered that no interest should be
awarded on the general damages.

Three questions now arise for determination. These are: (1) Is it right that in calculating
an award for loss of future earnings, it should be restricted to the sum which the injured
plaintiff would have earned (but for the accident) during what remains of his shortened
life, or should he be further compensated by reference to what he could reasonably have
been expected to earn during such working life as would in all probability been left to him
had it not been cut down by the defendant's negligence? In short, is he also entitled to be
compensated for what have conveniently been called the 'lost years'? (2) Should the Court
of Appeal have increased the general damages? (3) Was the Court of Appeal right in
depriving the plaintiff of interest on the general damages? I proceed to deal with these
questions in turn.

(1) Damages for the lost years

The question has long been debated; indeed, ever since *Oliver v Ashman*[1]. Before
considering that case in any detail, it should be stressed that the decision proceeded on the
basis that the Court of Appeal was there bound by what Viscount Simon LC had said in the
House of Lords in *Benham v Gambling*[2]: see, for example, the judgment of Holroyd Pearce
LJ[3] and that of Willmer LJ[4]. But, my Lords, in reality that was not so. It is true that in
Benham v Gambling[5] Viscount Simon LC did say at one stage:

'Of course, no regard must be had to financial losses or gains during the period of
which the victim has been deprived. The damages are in respect of loss of life, not of
loss of future pecuniary prospects.'

But the claim there being considered was what sum should be awarded to the estate of a
child of 2½ who died the day after he was injured. Ever since the decision in *Rose v Ford*[6],
the awards for shortened expectation of life had varied enormously, and it is clear from the
submissions of learned counsel in *Benham v Gambling*[7] that guidance only on that matter
was there being sought. This was stated in terms by Viscount Simon LC, who added[8]
'. . . and it is indeed the only issue with which we are now concerned'. Notwithstanding
its citation by Upjohn LJ in *Wise v Kaye*[9] as authority for the contrary proposition that 'a
dead man's estate . . . cannot . . . claim for loss of future pecuniary prospects', in my
judgment the proper conclusion is that, as Lord Morris of Borth-y-Gest said in *H West &
Son Ltd v Shephard*[10]:

'The guidance given in *Benham v. Gambling*[2] was, I consider, solely designed and
intended to apply to the assessment of damages in respect of the rather special "head"
of damages for loss of expectation of life.'

There being thus no decision compelling the Court of Appeal in *Oliver v Ashman*[1] to reject
a claim for damages for the 'lost years', what guidance was to be found in the earlier
cases? James LJ said in *Phillips v London and South Western Railway Co*[11] of a physician
injured in a railway accident:

---

1   [1961] 3 All ER 323, [1962] 2 QB 210
2   [1941] 1 All ER 7, [1941] AC 157
3   [1961] 3 All ER 323 at 330 et seq, [1962] 2 QB 210 at 228 et seq
4   [1961] 3 All ER 323 at 337, [1962] 2 QB 210 at 238
5   [1941] 1 All ER 7 at 13, [1941] AC 157 at 167
6   [1937] 3 All ER 359, [1937] AC 826
7   [1941] AC 157
8   [1941] AC 157 at 162
9   [1962] 1 All ER 257 at 268, [1962] 1 QB 638 at 659
10 (1963) 2 All ER 625 at 632, [1964] AC 326 at 348
11 (1879) 5 QBD 78 at 87

'. . . you are to consider what his income would probably have been, *how long that income would probably have lasted,* and you have to take into consideration all the other contingencies to which a practice is liable.' (The italics are mine.)

In *Roach v Yates*[1] Slesser LJ took a similar view regarding a claim made by a plaintiff of 33. He said[2]:

'Criticism has been made of the suggestion that one method of estimating his loss [of wages] is to consider what he would have earned during his life. Speaking for myself, I see no justification for approaching that problem by starting with the assumption that he would have lived only so long as the accident has now allowed him to live. I think the proper way of approaching the problem is that which was followed in *Phillips* v. *London and South Western Ry. Co.*[3], the leading case on this matter—namely, first to consider what sum he would have been likely to make during his normal life if he had not met with his accident.'

It is said that it is not clear whether Greer LJ was of the same view, but MacKinnon LJ agreed with both judgments, and it is difficult to regard as other than accurate the headnote which attributes to all three members of the Court the view expressed by Slesser LJ. But in *Harris v Bright's Asphalt Contractors Ltd*[4] Slade J doubted that this was so, and held that no compensation could be awarded for earnings during the 'lost years' to a plaintiff of 37 whose expectation of life had been reduced to two years. He said[5]:

'. . . I cannot think it right that I should give damages for loss of earnings for a period during which ex hypothesi he is not alive to earn them . . . In my judgment, therefore, the only relevance of earnings which would have been earned after death is that they are an element for consideration in assessing damages for loss of expectation of life, in the sense that a person earning a reasonable livelihood is more likely to have an enjoyable life.'

The whole field of decisions was again surveyed by Streatfeild J in *Pope v D Murphy & Son Ltd*[6] and led him to say, in arriving at the opposite conclusion[7]:

'In my view, the proper approach to this question of loss of earning capacity is to compensate the plaintiff, who is alive now, for what he has in fact lost. What he has lost is the prospect of earning whatever it was he did earn from his business over the period of time which he might otherwise, apart from the accident, have reasonably expected to earn it.'

And so we come to *Oliver v Ashman*[8], where a boy aged 20 months was injured by an accident which it was estimated had halved his reasonable expectation of living another 60 years. Lord Parker CJ[9] followed *Pope v D Murphy & Son Ltd*[6] by taking as a separate head of damage the earnings which would have accrued to the plaintiff during the period by which life had been shortened. But this was reversed in the Court of Appeal[8], although Holroyd Pearce LJ accepted that the earlier authorities were in accord with *Pope's* case[6]. He

1   [1937] 3 All ER 442, [1938] 1 KB 256
2   [1938] 1 KB 256 at 268, cf [1937] 3 All ER 442 at 447
3   (1879) 5 QBD 78
4   [1953] 1 All ER 395, [1953] 1 QB 617
5   [1953] 1 QB 617 at 633–634, cf [1953] 1 All ER 395 at 402
6   [1960] 2 All ER 873, [1961] 1 QB 222
7   [1960] 2 All ER 873 at 878, [1961] 1 QB 222 at 231
8   [1961] 3 All ER 323, [1962] 2 QB 210
9   [1960] 3 All ER 677, [1961] 1 QB 337

summarised the nature of the conflict between that case and *Harris v Bright's Asphalt Contractors Ltd*[1] in this way[2]:

'On one view of the matter there is no loss of earnings when a man dies prematurely. He is no longer there to earn them, since he has died before they could be earned. He has merely lost the prospect of some years of life which is a complex of pleasure and pain, of good and ill, of profits and losses. On the other view, he has in addition to losing a prospect of the years of life, lost the income that he would have earned, and the profits that would have been his had he lived.'

Holroyd Pearce LJ then examined *Benham v Gambling*[3] in detail, and concluded[4]:

'In my judgment, therefore, the matter is concluded in this court by *Benham* v. *Gambling*[3] and the decision of Slade, J., in *Harris* v. *Bright's Asphalt Contractors, Ltd.*[1] was correct.'

But, as I have already sought to show, the House of Lords had *not* concluded the matter, and it would have been sounder to say that the point had been disposed of in *Roach v Yates*[5] by the Court of Appeal itself in favour of the plaintiff. Willmer LJ[6] was, with respect, similarly mistaken about the effect of *Benham v Gambling*[3]. Pearson LJ, after a wider citation of authorities, said[7]:

'In my view the conclusion, shortly stated, is that the conventional sum in the region of £200 which is to be awarded for loss of expectation of life should be regarded as covering all the elements of it—e.g., joys and sorrows, work and leisure, earnings and spending or saving money, marriage and parenthood and providing for dependants—and should be regarded as excluding any additional assessment for any of those elements.'

My Lords, I am unable to accept that conclusion. I prefer not to complicate the problem by considering the impact on dependants of an award to a living plaintiff whose life has been shortened, as to which see s 1(1) of the Fatal Accidents Act 1976, *Murray v Shuter*[8] and *McCann v Sheppard*[9], for our present consideration relates solely to the personal entitlement of an injured party to recover damages for the 'lost years', regardless both of whether he has dependants and of whether or not he would (if he has any) make provision for them out of any compensation awarded to him or his estate. With respect, it appears to me simply not right to say that, when a man's working life and his natural life are each shortened by the wrongful act of another, he must be regarded as having lost nothing by the deprivation of the prospect of future earnings for some period extending beyond the anticipated date of his premature death. In the Australian case of *Skelton v Collins*[10], Taylor J referred to 'the anomaly that would arise if *Oliver* v. *Ashman*[11] is taken to have been correctly decided', adding:

'An incapacitated plaintiff whose life expectation has not been diminished would be entitled to the full measure of the economic loss arising from his lost or diminished capacity. But an incapacitated plaintiff whose life expectancy has been diminished would not.'

1 [1953] 1 All ER 395, [1953] 1 QB 617
2 [1961] 3 All ER 323 at 330, [1962] 2 QB 210 at 228
3 [1941] 1 All ER 7, [1941] AC 157
4 [1961] 3 All ER 323 at 331–332, [1962] 2 QB 210 at 230
5 [1937] 3 All ER 442, [1938] 1 KB 256
6 *Oliver v Ashman* [1961] 3 All ER 323 at 337, [1962] 2 QB 210 at 238
7 [1961] 3 All ER 323 at 341, [1962] 2 QB 210 at 245
8 [1975] 3 All ER 375, [1976] 1 QB 972
9 [1973] 2 All ER 881, [1973] 1 WLR 540
10 (1966) 115 CLR 94 at 121
11 [1961] 3 All ER 323, [1962] 2 QB 210

And Windeyer J[1] speaking of 'the principle of compensation ... that anything having a money value which the plaintiff has lost should be made good in money', continued:

> 'This applies to that element in damages for personal injuries which is commonly called "loss of earnings"... The plaintiff could, if he had not been injured, have sold his labour and his skill or the fruits of his labour and his skill. I cannot see that damages that flow from the destruction or diminution of his capacity to do so are any the less when the period during which the capacity might have been exercised is curtailed because the tort cut short his expected span of life.'

My Lords, neither can I see why this should be so. In my judgment, Holroyd Pearce LJ was in error in saying in *Oliver v Ashman*[2]:

> 'When the [variegated tapestry of life] is severed there is but one sum recoverable in respect of that severance. What is lost is an expectation, not the thing itself. The House of Lords have laid down that on an objective and artificial valuation, the sum which the loss of expectation is to be assessed must be a moderate one on the scale indicated in *Benham v. Gambling*[3].'

In the present case Goff LJ expressed the view that *Oliver v Ashman*[4] 'does seem ... to work a grave injustice', and I regard it as wrongly decided. It follows that the judgment of the trial judge and the Court of Appeal on this first question, based as they were on that case, should now be reversed.

This House lacks the material to enable it to estimate what would be proper compensation for the 'lost years', and the task will have to be remitted to the Queen's Bench Division for determination. It is likely to prove a task of some difficulty, though (contrary to the view expressed by Willmer LJ in *Oliver v Ashman*[5]) the lost earnings are not 'far too speculative to be capable of assessment by any court of law'. The only guidance I can proffer is that, in reaching their final figure, the court should make what it regards as a suitable deduction for the total sum which Mr Pickett would have been likely to expend on himself during the 'lost years'. This calculation, too, is by no means free from difficulty, but a similar task has to be performed regularly in cases brought under the Fatal Accidents Act. And in Scotland the court is required, in such cases as the present, to 'have regard to any diminution ... by virtue of expenses which in the opinion of the court the pursuer ... would reasonable have incurred ... by way of living expenses' (see the Damages (Scotland) Act 1976, s 9(2)(c)). For, macabre though it be to say so, it does not seem right that, in respect of those years when ex hypothesi the injured plaintiff's personal expenses will be nil, he should recover more than that which would have remained at his disposal after such expenses had been discharged.

(2) General Damages

My Lords, I am unable to adopt the view of the Court of Appeal that the experienced trial judge erred in any way in assessing the general damages at £7,000. They do not criticise his general approach; indeed, Lawton LJ said expressly '... it is manifest that he approached the matter of the assessment of damages on the right lines'. What is suggested is that he committed errors (a) by failing to take sufficiently into account the distress caused to Mr Pickett by the realisation 'that his dependants would be left without him to care for them' and (b) by starting at too low a figure and then failing to allow sufficiently for inflation.

I have to say that I see no signs of the trial judge having failed in these or any other respects. It may be that £7,000 would be regarded by some judges as on the low side, but even so, in my judgment, it did not merit interference. I would therefore allow the

1   (1966) 115 CLR 94 at 129
2   [1961] 3 All ER 323 at 332, [1962] 2 QB 210 at 230
3   [1941] 1 All ER 7, [1941] AC 157
4   [1961] 3 All ER 323, [1962] 2 QB 210
5   [1961] 3 All ER 323 at 338, [1962] 2 QB 210 at 240

a defendant's cross-appeal against the decision of the Court of Appeal to increase this head of damages to £10,000 and restore the £7,000 awarded.

(3) *Interest on General Damages*

Although it was seemingly agreed by both sides before the trial judge that the sum of £7,000 was to carry interest at 9% from the date of service of the writ (amounting to £787·50), the Court of Appeal ordered that no interest was to be payable on the increased sum of £10,000. We have no record of what led to this variation in the trial judge's order,

b but we were told that it sprang from the Court of Appeal decision in *Cookson v Knowles*[1], where Lord Denning MR said:

'In *Jefford v Gee*[2], in 1970, we said that, in personal injury cases, when a lump sum is awarded for pain and suffering and loss of amenities, interest should run "from the date of service of the writ to the date of trial". At that time inflation did not stare us

c in the face. We had not in mind continuing inflation and its effect on awards. It is obvious now that that guideline should be changed. The courts invariably assess the lump sum on the "scale" for figures current at the date of trial, which is much higher than the figure current at the date of the injury or at the date of the writ. The plaintiff thus stands to gain by the delay in bringing the case to trial. He ought not to gain still more by having interest from the date of service of the writ.'

d My Lords, I have to say with great respect that the fallacy inherent in the passage quoted is in thinking that a plaintiff who, owing to inflation, gets a bigger award than he would have secured had the case been disposed of earlier is better off in real terms. But in fact the bigger award is made simply to put the plaintiff in the same financial position as he would have been had judgment followed immediately on service of the writ. The reality is that the plaintiff in this case had been kept out of £7,000 until the date of judgment, and there

e is no reason why he should be deprived of the £787 interest awarded by the trial judge for the 15-month period between writ and judgment simply because a lesser sum than £7,000 might or would have been awarded had the case come on earlier. Furthermore, the suggestion that the defendant is prejudiced overlooks the fact that he has meanwhile had the use of the money.

My Lords, in the result, I would allow the plaintiff's appeal in respect of points (1) and

f (3) and the defendant's cross-appeal in respect of point (2). I am in agreement regarding the proposed order as to costs.

LORD RUSSELL OF KILLOWEN. My Lords, on two of the three questions in this case, those touching interest and the increase in damages by the Court of Appeal from £7,000 to £10,000 I am in agreement, and need not repeat the reasons given for what is

g proposed.

The third question, touching the 'lost years' I have found very difficult.

We are not directly concerned on that question with either the Law Reform (Miscellaneous Provisions) Act 1934 or the Fatal Accidents Act 1976. The deceased plaintiff survived to trial and judgment; the appeal is by his personal representative as representing his estate and does not need the 1934 Act to support it, the cause of action having merged

h in the judgment.

The problem is this. Was the plaintiff at the time of judgment entitled to damages on the ground that as a result of the wrong done to him his life has been shortened and that he will not in consequence receive financial benefits which would in the ordinary course of events have come to him during those lost years?

I may say at once that I do not regard what was said in *Benham v Gambling*[3] in this House

j as throwing any light on this problem. That case was dealing only with a head of damages for loss of expectation of life which, as was there stressed, is not a question of deprivation

---

1   [1977] 2 All ER 820 at 823, [1977] QB 913 at 921
2   [1970] 1 All ER 1202 at 1212, [1970] 2 QB 130 at 151
3   [1941] 1 All ER 7, [1941] AC 157

of financial benefits at all. The problem has, as your Lordships have pointed out, been touched on in a number of cases, but its solution is at large for this House.

I have stated the problem without confining it to earnings in the lost years. Suppose a plaintiff injured tortiously in a motoring accident, aged 25 at trial, with a resultant life expectation then of only one year. Suppose him to be life tenant of substantial settled funds. If the lost years are to be brought into assessment of damages presumably allowance must be made for that part of the life interest which he would have received but will not receive. So also if he had a reversionary interest contingent on surviving a life in being then aged 60: he will have been deprived of the probability of the funds coming to him during the lost years. Again he might at the trial be shown to be the sole beneficiary under the will of a rich relation whose age made it probable that the testator would die during the lost years, and whose testimony at the trial was that he had no intention of altering his will. In such cases presumably an allowance in damages would require to be made for the lost, and may be valuable, spes successionis, unless the testator was an ancestor of the plaintiff and the plaintiff was likely to have children surviving him (see s 32 of the Wills Act 1837).

I refer to these possible situations in order to suggest that the problems which exist even in the field of earnings in the lost years may in a given case be far more difficult of solution, once there is introduced into the field of damages allowance for financial 'loss' of that which death ex hypothesi forestalls. Damages are compensatory not punitive, so that it is no valid argument that a wrongdoer should not benefit by inducing early death rather than a full lifetime of pain and suffering; that must happen anyway, e g when an infant is killed outright.

It has been said that if in a case such as this damages are not to be awarded in respect of benefits that would have accrued to the plaintiff in the lost years it introduces an anomaly, since if the claim were under the Fatal Accidents Act by dependants their claim would extend into the lost years. But this so called anomaly arises from the particular nature of such a claim, which is by living people in respect of their living periods, which is expressly based on what they have lost by a death. It is not a claim by a dead person. I do not accept the suggestion that Parliament in enacting the Fatal Accidents Acts must have assumed a live plaintiff's claim for the lost years.

It has, my Lords, correctly been remarked that though in the instant case the plaintiff had dependants who (it was assumed) were barred from a Fatal Accidents Act claim by the judgment, the question of the lost years must be answered in the same way in a case of a plaintiff without dependants. But the solution proposed, involving as it does deduction from lost years' earnings of the plaintiff's living expenses, appears to me to attempt to splice two quite separate types of claim: a claim by dependants for dependency and a claim by the plaintiff himself. If a plaintiff is to be entitled to claim in respect of lost years' earnings, why should his claim be reduced by what, no doubt enjoyably, he would have spent on himself? Why should he be limited to that which he would have given away either inter vivos or by will or intestacy? The answer is I suppose that being dead he has no living expenses. But this, in the current phrase, is where we came in. I find it difficult in point of principle to accept as part of compensatory damages a sum based on that for which, had he lived longer, he would ex hypothesi have had no use save to give it away. The comment that the law is not concerned with what a plaintiff does with the damages to which he is entitled is of course sound, but it assumes entitlement to the damages, which is the very question.

My Lords, these problems have been debated by the Law Commission[1]. An attempt to solve them has been made for Scotland by the Damages (Scotland) Act 1976. My own opinion is that the solution is a matter whose complications are more suited for legislation than judicial decision by this House in the manner proposed.

Your Lordships being unanimously of opinion on this problem to the contrary, I have not felt it necessary to argue the point in great detail.

---

1 Report on Personal Injury Litigation—Assessment of Damages (1973) Law Com 56

In the result I would allow the appeals on the questions of interest and quantum of
a damages (£7,000 or £10,000) and dismiss the appeal on the lost years point.
In the circumstances of your Lordships' decision I agree with the order for remission
proposed and for costs.

LORD SCARMAN. My Lords, I agree with the speeches of my noble and learned
friends, Lord Wilberforce, Lord Salmon and Lord Edmund-Davies. My excuse for
b burdening your Lordships with a speech must be that, as my noble and learned friend,
Lord Wilberforce, has remarked, in some cases a single speech may generate uncertainty.
I would add a comment: one justification (there are others) for several speeches in your
Lordships's House supporting the same conclusion is that they can show that there are
more ways than one of journeying to the same end. They can shed light, and diminish the
possibility of misunderstanding.
c   Mr Pickett, who was the plaintiff in the action, claimed damages from the defendant,
British Rail Engineering Ltd, his employer, for serious personal injury sustained in the
course of his employment. The defendant admits liability. The issue between the parties
is as to the amount of damages which the judge at trial ought to have awarded Mr Pickett,
a living plaintiff.
    Mr Pickett, a married man with two children, was aged 53 at the time of trial, which was
d on 11th and 12th October 1976. His wife was then 47 years old. He first realised he was
ill when he became short of breath in the spring of 1974. In the words of the trial judge,
'he was then 51 years of age, a very fit man who was a non-smoker, a cyclist of great
accomplishment, for he had been a champion cyclist of apparently Olympic standard, and
he was still leading a most active life in March 1974, cycling to work each day'.
    Medical treatment and investigations culminating in an operation in January 1975
e revealed a malignant tumour which covered the whole of his right lung and could not be
wholly removed. It was caused by asbestos dust inhaled over the years while he was
working in the defendant's workshops. On the basis of the medical reports with which he
was provided the trial judge found that at the date of trial Mr Pickett's expectation of life
was one year. In fact, he died five months later, on 15th March 1977. But for his injury,
Mr Pickett could have expected to work until normal retiring age (ie 65) and to enjoy
f thereafter a period of retirement.
    The judge's task was to assess the damages to be paid to a living plaintiff, aged 53, whose
life expectancy had been shortened to one year. He awarded a total of £14,947·64
damages. This total included: (1) £7,000, general damages for pain, suffering, and loss of
amenities; (2) £787·50, interest on the award of these general damages from date of service
of writ (18th July 1975) to date of trial; (3) £1,508·88 damages for loss of the earnings
g which he could have expected to earn during his shortened life expectancy; (4) £500
damages for loss of expectation of life. Mr Pickett appealed but before the appeal could be
heard he had died. His widow, as administratrix of his estate, obtained an order to carry
on the proceedings, and the appeal was heard in November 1977. The Court of Appeal
increased the award of general damages to £10,000; but refused to allow interest on this
award. Following *Oliver v Ashman*[1], the court left undisturbed the award for loss of future
h earnings. It increased to £750 the award for loss of expectation of life. The plaintiff now
appeals against the refusal of interest on the general damages and against the sum awarded
for loss of future earnings. The defendant appeals against the increase by the Court of
Appeal in the award of general damages.
    First, some general observations.
    The recent development of the judicial practice of 'itemising damages', though as a
j matter of history closely linked with the need to differentiate between heads of damage for
the purpose of calculating interest on damages, has, my Lords, helped towards a juster
assessment of the capital element in damages for personal injuries. For it ensures that

---

1   [1961] 3 All ER 323, [1962] 2 QB 210

pecuniary loss and non-pecuniary loss will be assessed separately. As the Law Commission has shown in its report[1], the assessment of damages for non-pecuniary loss is a very *a* different matter from assessment of damages for pecuniary loss. There is no way of measuring in money pain, suffering, loss of amenities, loss of expectation of life. All that the court can do is to make an award of fair compensation. Inevitably this means a flexible judicial tariff, which judges will use as a starting-point in each individual case, but never in itself as decisive of any case. The judge, inheriting the function of the jury, must make an assessment which in the particular case he thinks fair; and, if his assessment be based on *b* correct principle and a correct understanding of the facts, it is not to be challenged, unless it can be demonstrated to be wholly erroneous: *Davies v Powell Duffryn Associated Collieries Ltd*[2].

But, when a judge is assessing damages for pecuniary loss, the principle of full compensation can properly be applied. Indeed, anything else would be inconsistent with the general rule which Lord Blackburn[3] has formulated in these words: *c*

> '. . . that, where any injury is to be compensated by damages, in settling the sum of money to be given . . . you should as nearly as possible get at that sum of money which will put the party who has been injured, or who has suffered, in the same position as he would have been in if he had not sustained the wrong.'

Though arithmetical precision is not always possible, though in estimating future pecuniary loss a judge must make certain assumptions (based on the evidence) and certain *d* adjustments, he is seeking to estimate a financial compensation for a financial loss. It makes sense in this context to speak of full compensation as the object of the law. It is on this basis, my Lords, that I approach the three questions raised in this appeal, with which I propose to deal in this order: (1) damages for loss of future earnings, (2) damages for pain, suffering and loss of amenities, (3) interest on the damages for pain and suffering.

e

(1) Damages for loss of future earnings

In *Oliver v Ashman*[4], the Court of Appeal decided that in an action for damages for personal injuries, whether brought by a living plaintiff or on behalf of the estate of a dead plaintiff, damages for loss of earnings are limited in the first case to the period of shortened expectation of life, and, in the second, to the shortened period of life. Under the *Oliver v Ashman*[4] rule no claim for loss of earnings can be made in respect of the period the plaintiff *f* could have expected to live, had his life expectation not been shortened by the accident giving rise to his claim. He cannot recover in respect of the earnings he could have expected during the 'lost years'.

My noble and learned friends, Lord Wilberforce, Lord Salmon and Lord Edmund-Davies, have analysed the case law which lies behind this decision. I agree with them in thinking that the decision was based on a misconception of what this House had decided *g* in *Benham v Gambling*[5]. The relevant line of authority is not that which culminated in *Benham v Gambling*[5] but that which had begun with *Phillips v London and South Western Railway Co*[6] and culminated in *Roach v Yates*[7]. If, therefore, attention be directed only to the authorities, I think it may be said that *Oliver v Ashman*[4] was wrongly decided, and that the court in that case should have followed its own decision in *Roach v Yates*[7].

Your Lordships' House is, however, concerned with the principle of the matter. The *h* principle has been exhaustively discussed in the Australian case of *Skelton v Collins*[8].

---

1   Report on Personal Injury Litigation—Assessment of Damages (1973) Law Com 56
2   [1942] 1 All ER 657, [1942] AC 601
3   *Livingstone v Rawyards Coal Co* (1880) 5 App Cas 25 at 39
4   [1961] 3 All ER 323, [1962] 2 QB 210
5   [1941] 1 All ER 7, [1941] AC 157
6   (1879) 5 QBD 78
7   [1937] 3 All ER 442, [1938] 1 KB 256
8   (1966) 115 CLR 94

Windeyer J[1] found it in 'the general principle that damages are compensatory'. He
thought it flowed from that principle 'that anything having a money value which the
a plaintiff has lost should be made good in money'. He went on: 'The destruction or
diminution of a man's capacity to earn money can be made good in money.' And he
concluded by saying:

'I cannot see that damages that flow from the destruction or diminution of his
capacity [to earn] are any the less when the period during which the capacity might
b have been exercised is curtailed because the tort cut short his expected span of life.'

The same point was made by Streatfeild J in *Pope v D Murphy & Son Ltd*[2]:

'What he has lost is the prospect of earning whatever it was he did earn from his
business over the period of time that he might otherwise, apart from the accident,
have reasonably expected to earn it.'

c I would add that this line of reasoning is consistent with Lord Blackburn's formulation of
the general principle of the law, to which I have already referred: see *Livingstone v Rawyards
Coal Co*[3].

Principle would appear, therefore, to suggest that a plaintiff ought to be entitled to
damages for the loss of earnings he could have reasonably expected to have earned during
the 'lost years'. But it has been submitted by the respondent that such a rule, if it be
d thought socially desirable, requires to be implemented by legislation. It is argued that a
judicial graft would entail objectionable consequences, consequences which legislation
alone can obviate.

There is force in this submission. The major objections are these. First, the plaintiff
may have no dependants. Secondly, even if he has dependants, he may have chosen to
make a will depriving them of support from his estate. In either event, there would be a
e windfall for strangers at the expense of the defendant. Thirdly, the plaintiff may be so
young (in *Oliver v Ashman*[4] he was a boy aged 20 months at the time of the accident) that
it is absurd that he should be compensated for future loss of earnings. Fourthly (a point
which has weighed with my noble and learned friend, Lord Russell of Killowen), if
damages are recoverable for the loss of the prospect of earnings during the lost years, must
it not follow that they are also recoverable for loss of other reasonable expectations, e g a life
f interest or an inheritance? Fifthly, what does compensation mean when it is assessed in
respect of a period after death? Sixthly, as my noble and learned friend, Lord Wilberforce,
has pointed out, there is a risk of double recovery in some cases, i e of both the estate and
the dependants recovering damages for the expected earnings of the lost years.

The law is not concerned with how a plaintiff spends the damages awarded to him. The
first two objections can, therefore, be said to be irrelevant. The second objection is,
g however, really too serious to be thus summarily rejected. The social justification for
reversing the rule in *Oliver v Ashman*[4] is that it imposes hardship on dependants. But this
justification is undermined if a plaintiff, having recovered damages for his lost future
earnings, can thereafter exclude by will his dependants from any share of his estate. To this
objection the law provides an answer: his estate will be subject to the right of dependants
for whom no or no sufficient provision has been made to apply for provision under the
h Inheritance (Provision for Family and Dependants) Act 1975.

The third objection will be taken care of in the ordinary course of litigation: a measurable
and not too remote loss has to be proved before it can enter into the assessment of damages.

The fourth 'objectionable consequence' does not seem to me objectionable. I agree with
the Law Commission[5] where they say:

j
_____

1   (1966) 115 CLR 94 at 129
2   [1960] 2 All ER 873 at 878, [1961] 1 QB 222 at 231
3   (1880) 5 App Cas 25 at 39
4   [1961] 3 All ER 323, [1962] 2 QB 210
5   (1973) Law Com 56, para 90

'There seems to be no justification in principle for discrimination between deprivation of earning capacity and deprivation of the capacity otherwise to receive economic benefits. The loss must be regarded as a loss of the plaintiff; and it is a loss caused by the tort even though it relates to moneys which the injured person will not receive because of his premature death. No question of the remoteness of damage arises other than the application of the ordinary foreseeability test.'

For myself, as at present advised (for the point does not arise for decision and has not been argued), I would allow a plaintiff to recover damages for the loss of his financial expectations during the lost years provided always the loss was not too remote.

There is, it has to be confessed, no completely satisfying answer to the fifth objection. But it does not, I suggest, make it unjust that such damages should be awarded. The plaintiff has lost the earnings and the opportunity, which, while he was living, he valued, of employing them as he would have thought best. Whether a man's ambition be to build up a fortune, to provide for his family, or to spend his money on good causes or merely a pleasurable existence, loss of the means to do so is a genuine financial loss. The logical and philosophical difficulties of compensating a man for a loss arising after his death emerge only if one treats the loss as a non-pecuniary loss, which to some extent it is. But it is also a pecuniary loss: the money would have been his to deal with as he chose, had he lived.

The sixth objection appears to me unavoidable, though further argument and analysis in a case in which the point arose for decision might lead to a judicial solution which was satisfactory. But I suspect that the point will need legislation. However, if one must choose between a law which in some cases will deprive dependants of their dependency through the chances of life and litigation and a law which, in avoiding such a deprival, will entail in some cases both the estate and the dependants recovering damages in respect of the lost years, I find the latter to be the lesser evil.

I conclude, therefore, that damages for loss of future earnings (and future expectations) during the lost years are recoverable, where the facts are such that the loss is not too remote to be measurable. But I think, for the reasons given by Lord Wilberforce, Lord Salmon and Lord Edmund-Davies, that a plaintiff (or his estate) should not recover more than that which would have remained at his disposal after meeting his own living expenses.

(2) *Damages for pain, suffering, and loss of amenities*

The Court of Appeal thought that the sum (£7,000) awarded by the judge was too low, and substituted a figure of £10,000. Lord Denning MR said:

'Although I well appreciate the care which the judge gave to this case, it seems to me that there is one feature which the judge did not take into account sufficiently, and that is the distress which Mr Pickett must have suffered knowing that his widow and dependants would be left without him to care for them. I think we ought to take this distress into account. Taking it into account, it seems to me that we can properly increase the figure given by the judge to the sum of £10,000. This seems itself all too little; but, as I have said, with the law as it now stands, I do not think it is open to the court to increase it further because no compensation is at the moment available for loss of earnings during the "lost years".'

My Lords, I have to say that I think that in this passage Lord Denning MR was influenced (understandably, if I may respectfully say so) by the pitifully small sum available to the plaintiff as damages for loss of future earnings under the law which bound the judge and the Court of Appeal. The distress suffered by Mr Pickett knowing that his widow and children would be left without him to care for them was an element in his suffering for which I agree Mr Pickett was entitled to fair compensation. But it would be bad law if this element of non-pecuniary damage should be used to make good in whole or in part the loss of earnings during the 'lost years', which under the law as it stood when this case was before the Court of Appeal were not recoverable as damages. I am far from being persuaded that the judge failed to take into account this element of Mr Pickett's suffering. Lord Denning MR in the passage which I have quoted paid his tribute to the care which the judge gave

the case. Lawton LJ hesitated before differing from the judge. He said: 'My reason for
having some hesitation is that it is manifest that he approached the matter of the assessment
of damages on the right lines.' I respectfully agree. In the course of an eloquent passage
in his judgment describing Mr Pickett's pain and suffering, the trial judge said:

> 'He has, according to his evidence, no precise knowledge of what the future holds
> for him, but he must be aware—I am certain that he is aware—that it is a very limited
> future. It may be that he will become aware of the position so far as the future is
> concerned. Although he has been kept out of court, it is unfortunately impossible to
> guarantee that that fact will not be communicated to him in some way. I am satisfied
> that it is right that the court should bear in mind the possibility; indeed, I would rate
> it as a probability.'

And he summed it all up when he said that he had endeavoured to take into account 'all the
features of the tragic situation in which Mr Pickett finds himself'. It is not possible,
therefore, to fault the judge's approach to the assessment of general damages.

It is not the function of an appellate court to substitute its opinion for that of the trial
judge. Lord Wright stated the general principle in a well-known passage in his speech in
Davies v Powell Duffryn Associated Collieries Ltd[1]:

> 'In effect the court, before it interferes with an award of damages, should be
> satisfied that the judge has acted on a wrong principle of law, or has misapprehended
> the facts, or has for these or other reasons made a wholly erroneous estimate of the
> damage suffered. It is not enough that there is a balance of opinion or preference.
> The scale must go down heavily against the figure attacked if the appellate court is to
> interfere, whether on the ground of excess or insufficiency.'

The trial judge correctly apprehended the facts, and adopted the correct approach in law.
Though to some the award of £7,000 may seem low, it is not so low as to support the
inference that the judge's estimate was wholly erroneous. In a task as imprecise and
immeasurable as the award of damages for non-pecuniary loss, a preference for £10,000
over £7,000 is a matter of opinion, but not by itself evidence of error. I would, therefore,
allow the cross-appeal and restore the judge's award of £7,000 general damages.

(3) Interest

In *Cookson v Knowles*[2] your Lordships' House has recently reviewed the guidelines for the
exercise of the court's discretion in awarding interest on damages in fatal accident cases.
The House expressly left open the question of interest on damages for non-pecuniary loss
in a personal injury action. My noble and learned friend, Lord Diplock, concluded his
speech with these words[3]:

> 'The question of damages for non-economic loss which bulks large in personal
> injury actions, however, does not arise in the instant case. It has not been argued
> before your Lordships and I refrain from expressing any view about it.'

When, however, that case was in the Court of Appeal[4], the court did deal, obiter, with
interest on damages for non-pecuniary loss awarded to a living plaintiff in a personal injury
case. Lord Denning MR, delivering the judgment of the court, said[5]:

> 'In *Jefford v Gee*,[6] in 1970, we said that, in personal injury cases, when a lump sum
> is awarded for pain and suffering and loss of amenities, interest should run "from the
> date of service of the writ to the date of trial". At that time inflation did not stare us
> in the face. We had not in mind continuing inflation and its effect on awards. It is

j 1   [1942] 1 All ER 657 at 664–665, [1942] AC 601 at 617
     2   [1978] 2 All ER 604, [1978] 2 WLR 978
     3   [1978] 2 All ER 604 at 612, [1978] 2 WLR 978 at 987–988
     4   [1977] 2 All ER 820, [1977] QB 913
     5   [1977] 2 All ER 820 at 823, [1977] QB 913 at 921
     6   [1970] 1 All ER 1202, [1970] 2 QB 130

obvious now that that guideline should be changed. The courts invariably assess the lump sum on the "scale" for figures current at the date of the trial, which is much higher than the figure current at the date of the injury or at the date of the writ. The plaintiff thus stands to gain by the delay in bringing the case to trial. He ought not to gain still more by having interest from the date of service of the writ. We would alter the guideline, therefore, by suggesting that no interest should be awarded on the lump sum awarded at the trial for pain and suffering and loss of amenities.'

In the instant case the Court of Appeal has followed its dictum, disallowing the interest granted by the judge on the damages for pain and suffering. My Lords, I believe the reasoning of the Court of Appeal to be unsound on this point. It is based on a fallacy; and is inconsistent with the statute.

First, the fallacy. It is assumed that because the award of damages made at trial is greater, in monetary terms, than it would have been, had damages been assessed at date of service of writ, the award is greater in terms of real value. There is here a complete non sequitur. The cash awarded is more, because the value of cash, i e its purchasing power, has diminished. In theory the higher award at trial has the same purchasing power as the lower award which would have been made at the date of the service of the writ; in truth, of course, judicial awards of damages follow, but rarely keep pace with, inflation so that in all probability the sum awarded at trial is less, in terms of real value, than would have been awarded at the earlier date. In theory, therefore, and to some extent in practice, inflation is taken care of by increasing the number of money units in the award so that the real value of the loss is met. The loss, for which interest is given, is quite distinct, and not covered by this increase. It is the loss which is suffered by being kept out of money to which one is entitled.

Secondly, the statute. Section 22 of the Administration of Justice Act 1969, amending s 3 of the Law Reform (Miscellaneous Provisions) Act 1934, provides that the court *shall* (my emphasis) exercise its power to award interest on damages, or on such part of the damages as the court considers appropriate, 'unless the court is satisfied that there are special reasons why no interest should be given in respect of those damages'. Such is the general rule laid down by the statute, which does, however, confer on the court a discretion as to the period for which interest is given and also permits differing rates. Nothing can be clearer than the duty placed on the court to give interest in the absence of special reasons for giving none. Inflation is an economic and financial condition of general application in our society. Its impact on this plaintiff has been neither more nor less than on everybody else; there is nothing special about it.

For these reasons I think the Court of Appeal erred in refusing to allow interest on the award of damages for non-pecuniary loss. I would reinstate the judge's award.

In conclusion, I agree that the appeal and cross-appeal should both be allowed and that the order proposed by my noble and learned friend, Lord Wilberforce, should be made. I also agree with the order as to costs which he has proposed.

Appeal and cross-appeal allowed.

Solicitors: *John L Williams* (for the plaintiff); *Evan Harding* (for the defendant).

Mary Rose Plummer   Barrister.

a # B v B (matrimonial proceedings: discovery)

FAMILY DIVISION
DUNN J
14th, 15th, 16th, 17th, 20th, 21st MARCH 1978

b *Divorce – Financial provision – Discovery – Disclosure and production of documents in proceedings for financial provision – Documents belonging to company of which husband director and controlling shareholder – Documents relating to husband's entertainment and travel expenses and amounts expended on family – Whether company documents in husband's 'custody' or 'power' – Whether jurisdiction to order disclosure of documents – Whether production of disclosed documents should be ordered – RSC Ord 24, r 7(1).*

c The husband had a controlling interest in, and was a director of, a private company ('the company') by virtue of his shareholding in another private company, a holding company. Members of his family held the majority of the remaining shares in the holding company. There were six other directors of the company. The wife applied in a divorce suit pending between herself and the husband for financial provision for herself and the *d* children of the marriage and for a transfer of property order. The wife alleged that there were discrepancies in the audited accounts of the company, and wished to see company documents relating to the husband's expenditure on entertainment and travel. The husband applied to the court for the right to occupy the matrimonial home under s 1 of the Matrimonial Homes Act 1967 and in those proceedings the registrar made an order for discovery against him (which the parties accepted was also applicable in the wife's *e* application for financial provision) requiring the husband to disclose and produce for inspection documents of the company relating to his personal expenditure on entertainment, travel etc, and expenditure on goods for his family, whether incurred in his own name or in the name of the company. Bills relating to the husband's expenditure on entertainment and travel were sent to him at the company's offices where he scrutinised them and gave instructions to have them paid. Further, by cl 17 of the order for discovery, *f* the husband was required to produce, inter alia, all the account books, private ledgers, paid cheques, cheque stubs, documents and vouchers of the company in relation to all bills and expenses incurred by him or the company and paid by or charged to the company, and records of all moneys received by the company in the course of trading over a specified period. The husband appealed against the order on the ground that the registrar had no jurisidiction to make it because it involved discovery and production of documents of the company, which was not a party to the proceedings between the husband and wife. *g* Alternatively he contended that the registrar should have exercised his discretion against making the order.

Held – (1) Under RSC Ord 24, r 7(1)[a], the court had a discretion to order disclosure of particular documents specified or described in the application of the party seeking *h* discovery which were in the possession, custody or power of the other party to the suit. Accordingly, company documents which were relevant to the matters in issue in the litigation, although in the legal possession of the company, might be required to be disclosed by a director of the company who was a party to the suit if they were or had been in his actual physical possession, even though he held them merely as servant or agent of the company, since in that circumstance they were or had been in his custody.

j _____

a Rule 7(1), so far as material, provides: '. . . the Court may at any time, on the application of any party to a cause or matter, make an order requiring any other party to make an affidavit stating whether any document specified or described in the application or any class of document so specified or described is, or has at any time been, in his possession, custody or power, and if not then in his possession, custody or power when he parted with it and what has become of it.'

Furthermore, even where the relevant company documents had never been in his custody, he might be required to disclose them because they were within his power, in the sense that he had an enforceable right to inspect them or to obtain possession or control of them. Whether company documents were within a director's power was a question of fact depending on his shareholding, whether the minority shareholders were adverse to him, the constitution of the board of directors and whether they objected to disclosure of the documents. Documents would not be within his power merely because he had a right under s 12[b] of the Companies Act 1976 to inspect them; but where the company was the director's alter ego, so that he had unfettered control of its affairs, company documents would be within his power (see p 806 *d e*, p 807 *a b* and *d* to *h*, p 809 *a b* and *e* and p 811 *c* to *e*, post); *Alfred Crompton Amusement Machines Ltd v Customs and Excise Comrs (No 2)* [1973] 2 All ER 1169 applied.

(ii) Where disclosure was ordered of relevant company documents in the custody or power of a husband who was a director of the company, the court's discretion under RSC Ord 24 whether to order production of them should be exercised by balancing the relevance and importance of the documents and the hardship likely to be caused to the wife by their non-production against any prejudice likely to be caused to the husband or to third parties, such as other directors and shareholders, if an order for production was made. However, it was not the court's practice to order production of company documents where the board of directors of the company objected on affidavit to production, provided that the objection was not contrived to frustrate the court's powers (see p 810 *h j* and p 811 *e f*, post).

(iii) Although, in an application by a wife for financial provision, disclosure of the audited accounts of a company of which the husband was shareholder would in most cases be sufficient disclosure, together with full disclosure of the husband's financial records, there were cases where the court would go behind the company accounts and order discovery of specific company documents. The documents relating to the husband's entertainment and travel expenses and his expenditure on his family were relevant to the applications which were before the court, and since those documents had been in the husband's custody, they should be disclosed and, subject to any objection to their production, produced for inspection. However, the documents specified in cl 17 of the order did not appear to be relevant to the matters in issue, nor could it be said that the company was the husband's alter ego so as to confer power on him to produce those documents. Accordingly cl 17, save for certain provisions, would be deleted from the order (see p 810 *c d*, p 812 *b* to *f* and *h* and p 813 *a*, post).

Notes

For documents in the possession, custody or power of a party, see 13 Halsbury's Laws (4th Edn) para 39, and for cases on the subject, see 18 Digest (Reissue) 49–52, 346–366.

For the obligation to produce documents for inspection, and for documents protected from production, see 13 Halsbury's Laws (4th Edn) paras 56, 69, and for cases on the subject, see 18 Digest (Reissue) 70–72, 490–505.

Cases referred to in judgment

Bovill v Cowan (1870) LR 5 Ch App 495, 39 LJ Ch 768, 22 LT 503, 18 Digest (Reissue) 55, 390.

Carew v Carew [1891] P 360, 61 LJP 24, 65 LT 167, 18 Digest (Reissue) 73, 511.

Chantry Martin & Co v Martin [1953] 2 All ER 691, [1953] 2 QB 286, CA, 18 Digest (Reissue) 148, 1184.

Crompton (Alfred) Amusement Machines Ltd v Customs and Excise Comrs (No 2) [1973] 2 All ER 1169, [1974] AC 405, [1973] 3 WLR 268, HL, 18 Digest (Reissue) 102, 756.

Dallas v Dallas (1960) 24 DLR (2d) 746, 18 Digest (Reissue) 162, *637.

Hadley v McDougall (1872) LR 7 Ch App 312, 41 LJ Ch 504, 26 LT 379, 18 Digest (Reissue) 91, 673.

---

b　Section 12, so far as material, is set out at p 807 *e*, post.

Kettlewell v Barstow (1872) LR 7 Ch App 686, 41 LJ Ch 718, 27 LT 258, 18 Digest (Reissue)
a 94,704.

London and Yorkshire Bank Ltd v Cooper (1885) 15 QBD 473, 54 LJQB 495, CA, 18 Digest
(Reissue) 74, 517.

Nelson (James) & Sons Ltd v Nelson Line (Liverpool) Ltd [1906] 2 KB 217, 75 LJKB 895, 95 LT
180, 10 Asp MLC 265, 11 Com Cas 228, CA, 18 Digest (Reissue) 94, 704.

Norwich Pharmacal Co v Customs and Excise Comrs [1973] 2 All ER 943, [1974] AC 133,
b [1973] 3 WLR 164, [1974] RPC 101, HL, 18 Digest (Reissue) 8, 23.

O'Donnell v O'Donnell [1975] 2 All ER 993, sub nom *O'D v O'D* [1976] Fam 83, [1975] 3
WLR 308, CA, Digest (Cont Vol D) 429, 6962Af.

Povey v Povey [1970] 3 All ER 612, [1972] Fam 40, [1971] 2 WLR 381, DC, 27(2) Digest
(Reissue) 770, 6146.

Rattenberry v Monro (1910) 103 LT 560, 18 Digest (Reissue) 50, 351.

c *Reid v Langlois* (1849) 1 Mac & G 627; 2 H & Tw 59, 19 LJ Ch 337, 41 ER 1408, 18 Digest
(Reissue) 115, 872.

Skoye v Bailey [1971] 1 WWR 144, 18 Digest (Reissue) 51, *187.

Swanston v Lishman (1881) 45 LT 360, 4 Asp MLC 450, CA, 18 Digest (Reissue) 13, 54.

Taylor v Rundell (1841) Cr & Ph 104, 41 ER 429, LC, 18 Digest (Reissue) 50, 356.

Williams v Ingram (1900) 16 TLR 451, CA; affg 16 TLR 434, 18 Digest (Reissue) 147, 1183.

d
Cases also cited
Proctor v Smiles (1886) 55 LJQB 527, CA.
Salomon v Salomon and Co Ltd [1897] AC 22, [1895–9] All ER Rep 33, HL.
Ward v Marshall (1887) 3 TLR 578.

e **Appeal**
In proceedings by the husband under s 1 of the Matrimonial Homes Act 1967, Mr
Registrar Kenworthy, by an order dated 9th December 1977, ordered the husband to
disclose and produce: by cl 3 of the order, inter alia, bills, invoices, receipts, credit card
accounts, receipts and other vouchers relating to entertainment, air fares, holidays, hotels,
restaurants, night clubs and other places of entertainment and all other activities, and all
f other expenses incurred by the husband, whether in his own name or in the name of a
company ('the operating company'), in which he had a controlling interest, for himself or
his wife or children or other persons for the past two years; by cl 4 of the order, documents
relating to the purchase of clothing, furs, jewellery, furniture, pictures etc whether paid for
by the husband or by the operating company; by cl 11, bills, invoices and receipts from
suppliers of food and alcoholic liquor for the use of the husband's family, whether paid for
g by him or by the operating company; and by cl 17 all books of account, private ledgers,
paid cheques, cheque stubs, documents and vouchers of the operating company for three
years from 1st April 1974 in relation to all bills and expenses incurred by the husband on
his behalf and/or on behalf of the operating company and paid by and/or charged to the
company, and records of all receipt of moneys by the company in the course of trading and
the disposal thereof for the same period. Clause 17 also ordered the husband to account for
h all documents relating to any Swiss bank account or bank account abroad in his name or
in the name of any nominee or over which he had power to operate alone or jointly with
any other person, firm, company, trust or trustee. The husband appealed against the
registrar's order, seeking to delete from cll 3, 4 and 11 reference to the operating company,
and to delete cl 17 from the order. The facts are set out in the judgment.

j *Jack Hames QC, Edward Cazalet* and *David Ritchie* for the husband.
Geoffrey M Rutter, solicitor, for the wife.

DUNN J. This is an appeal by a husband against part of an order for discovery which was
made by Mr Registrar Kenworthy on 9th December 1977. The appeal raises important

questions as to the law and practice relating to discovery in financial proceedings in the
Family Division, and at the request of the parties I am giving judgment in open court.   *a*

The parts of the order against which the husband appeals are those which refer to
documents of a private company of which the husband is chairman and managing
director. I shall call that company the 'operating company': 75% of the shares of the
operating company are held by another private company which I shall call the 'holding
company', of which the husband is the owner of 51% of the registered share capital. The
majority of the remaining shares of the holding company are held by members of the   *b*
husband's family. The remaining 25% of the shares in the operating company are held by
a public company which I shall call the 'public company'. The effect of the shareholdings
is that the husband, through the holding company, has a controlling interest in the
operating company. There are six other directors of the operating company in addition to
the husband, of whom two are nominees of the public company. Three of the other four
directors hold shares in the holding company.   *c*

The husband, before the order was made, had already given discovery of certain
documents relating to his own income tax returns and private bank accounts. The order
made by the registrar ordered him to disclose and produce documents relating to his own
personal expenditure and that of his family, whether made by himself or by the operating
company, and also contained a clause, cl 17, requiring him to produce all the books of
account, private ledgers, paid cheques, cheque stubs, documents and vouchers of the   *d*
operating company in relation to all bills and expenses incurred by the husband or the
company, and paid by or charged to the company, and records of all receipts of moneys by
the operating company in the course of its trading over the period from 1st April 1974.
The effect of that clause is to enable the wife through accountants to carry out an audit of
the books of the operating company from 1st April 1974.

It is said on her behalf that, for reasons which were accepted by the registrar, such an   *e*
audit is necessary to enable the court to dispose fairly of the issues between the parties. It
is said on behalf of the husband that the registrar had no jurisdiction to make such an
order, involving as it does, not only discovery but also production of company documents,
the operating company not being a party to the proceedings between the husband and
wife. Alternatively, it is said on behalf of the husband that in the exercise of his discretion
the registrar should not have made the order.   *f*

Although the order for discovery was made in proceedings by the husband under s 1 of
the Matrimonial Homes Act 1967, there are also before the court applications by the wife
in the pending divorce suit for financial provision for herself and the two children of the
family, and for transfer of property. It is accepted by both parties before me that the order
is applicable to those proceedings as well as to the proceedings under s 1 of the 1967 Act.
It follows that all documents relating to the income, earning capacity, property, and other   *g*
financial resources of the husband are relevant documents, as are documents relating to his
financial needs, obligations and responsibilities, to the standard of living enjoyed by the
family before the breakdown of the marriage, and to the contributions made by the
husband to the welfare of the family, and, indeed, all matters referred to in s 25 of the
Matrimonial Causes Act 1973.

By r 77(5) of the Matrimonial Causes Rules 1977[1], the registrar may at any stage of the   *h*
proceedings order the discovery and production of any document and require any further
affidavits. It was accepted on behalf of the wife that that rule gives the registrar no greater
powers in relation to discovery than those contained in RSC Ord 24, which, with
modifications, is applicable to defended divorce suits by reason of r 28 of the 1977 rules.
RSC Ord 24 is also applicable to proceedings under s 1 of the Matrimonial Homes Act 1967,
since they are proceedings commenced by originating summons, and RSC Ord 24 applies   *j*
to all such proceedings. RSC Ord 24, as is well known, places on the parties to a suit the
obligation to make discovery of all documents which are or have been in their possession,
custody or power, relating to matters in question in the proceedings. In the first instance,

1   SI 1977 No 344

discovery must be made without any order of the court. The court may make an order
a either for general discovery or discovery of specific documents or classes of documents.
The court may also make an order for the production of documents for inspection by the
other party or by the court, but all these types of order are discretionary. The rules provide
that the court shall refuse to make such an order if and in so far as it is of the opinion that
discovery is not necessary either for disposing fairly of the proceedings or for saving costs
or is premature.

b   Although in practice it will often be convenient to deal with discovery in one piece, it
is important to remember that under the terms of the rules discovery proceeds by stages,
and different considerations may apply at each stage. The order in this case was an order
under RSC Ord 24, r 7, for the discovery by the husband of specific classes of documents
and for their production for inspection by the wife's solicitors. Before any question of
discretion arises, however, the court has no jurisdiction to make an order for discovery or
c production unless, firstly, the person against whom discovery is sought is a party to the
suit, secondly, the documents are in his possession, custody or power, and, thirdly, the
documents relate to matters in question in the proceedings. These requirements must be
satisfied before discovery is ordered even if hardship is thereby caused to one party to the
suit: see *James Nelson & Son Ltd v Nelson Line (Liverpool) Ltd*[1].

    As to the first requirement, it is well established that, save in exceptional cases, and in
d cases falling within RSC Ord 24, r 7A, which does not apply to the Family Division, no
discovery can be obtained against a person not party to the proceedings. A person cannot
be made a party to the proceedings solely for the purpose of obtaining discovery against
him, except in exceptional circumstances. The exceptional circumstances are where a
person without incurring any personal liability has become involved in the tortious acts of
another, so that he comes under a duty to assist one injured by those acts by giving him full
e information by way of discovery and disclosing the identity of the wrongdoers: see
Norwich Pharmacal Co v Customs and Excise Comrs[2].

    It is not suggested in this case that the wife could take proceedings against the operating
company in reliance on that principle. In the course of his speech in *Norwich Pharmacal Co
v Customs and Excise Comrs*[3] Lord Reid reaffirmed 'the mere witness rule', and stated in it
these terms:

f   'It has been clear at least since the time of Lord Hardwicke that information cannot
        be obtained by discovery from a person who will in due course be compellable to give
        that information either by oral testimony as a witness or on a subpoena duces tecum.'

If the wife cannot obtain the documents she requires on discovery, she may be able to apply
under RSC Ord 38 for leave, since these proceedings are in chambers, to issue a subpoena
g duces tecum against the secretary or other officers of the company to produce relevant
documents.

    The person to be considered is therefore the husband, the party to the suit, and the next
and vital question in the case is: are these documents which were ordered to be produced
documents which are or have been in the possession, custody or power of the husband? For
this purpose 'possession' means, the right to the possession of a document. 'Custody' means
h the actual, physical or corporeal holding of a document regardless of the right to its
possession, for example, a holding of a document by a party as servant or agent of the true
owner. 'Power' means, an enforceable right to inspect the document or to obtain possession
or control of the document from the person who ordinarily has it in fact. The requirements
of the rules are disjunctive in their operation, so far as possession, custody and power are
concerned.

j   Many authorities have been cited to me as to the application of the rule and of these
definitions most of them relate to the old Chancery practice before that was stated in rules

1   [1906] 2 KB 217.
2   [1973] 2 All ER 943, [1974] AC 133
3   [1973] 2 All ER 943 at 947, [1974] AC 133 at 174

of court, or to the rules of court before 1964 when the word 'custody' was added to the words 'possession or power'. Before 1964 the word 'possession' was held to mean 'corporeal possession pursuant to legal possession', but 'corporeal possession' is now embraced by the word 'custody'. In the Supreme Court Practice 1976[1] there is a note, 'Production and Inspection'. It is in the following terms:

'Until 1962, there was a distinction between the obligation to give discovery (i.e., to disclose the existence of documents) and the obligation to produce disclosed documents for inspection. A party was (and still is) obliged to disclose the existence of documents in his possession, etc., even though his possession may not be exclusive or may be only physical custody, e.g., as a servant; the obligation to produce documents was narrower and extended only to documents in the sole legal possession of the party giving discovery... Under the present rules the obligation to give inspection extends prima facie to all documents to which the obligation to give discovery extends... But the Court has a discretion whether to order inspection, and it may be that, in the exercise of such discretion, it will have regard to any prejudice to persons having a right to the documents in question. Moreover, the Court will not make an order either for discovery or inspection which is premature or not necessary for disposing fairly of the cause of matter or for saving costs...'

The terms of that note were expressly approved by Lord Cross of Chelsea in *Alfred Crompton Amusement Machines Ltd v Customs and Excise Comrs (No 2)*[2] and three others of their Lordships agreed with the speech of Lord Cross. It follows, therefore, that a person has the obligation to disclose all relevant documents which are or have been in his custody or power, even if he is not the owner or sole owner of them; and prima facie he is obliged to produce all such documents for the inspection of the other party. If he objects to production the court has a discretion whether or not to order production. In exercising its discretion the court will take into account all the circumstances of the case including any prejudice to persons having any right or interest in the document in question. The party against whom an order for production is sought should state on affidavit the nature and the interest of any person not a party to the action: see *Bovill v Cowan*[3]. He should also state whether or not he has tried to obtain consent to the production and why consent has been refused: see *Taylor v Rundell*[4]. If the court should refuse production on the ground of joint possession, it may allow an interrogatory as to the contents of the document: see *Rattenbury v Monro*[5] and *Swanston v Lishman*[6]. Cases such as *Hadley v McDougall*[7], *Kettlewell v Barstow*[8], *Reid v Langlois*[9] and *Chantrey Martin & Co v Martin*[10], on this point, are all examples of the old rule of Chancery practice incorporated into the Rules of the Supreme Court before 1964, whereby production would not be ordered of documents of which a party was not the sole owner.

As I have said, this is now a matter for discretion; though, in exercising that discretion, the court would no doubt have regard to the words of James LJ in *Kettlewell v Barstow*[11]:

'... the Court will not order the Defendants to do what they have no power to do; but it is no ground for resisting production that a person not before the Court has an interest in the documents.'

1   (1976), vol 1, p 399, para 24/2/4; see now 1979 edition, vol 1, p 405, para 24/2/4
2   [1973] 2 All ER 1169 at 1180–1181, [1974] AC 405 at 429
3   (1870) LR 5 Ch App 495
4   (1841) Cr & Ph 104, 41 ER 429
5   (1910) 103 LT 560
6   (1881) 45 LT 360
7   (1872) LR 7 Ch App 312
8   (1872) LR 7 Ch App 686
9   (1849) 1 Mac & G 627
10 [1953] 2 All ER 691, [1953] 2 QB 286
11 LR 7 Ch App 686 at 693

How do these general principles apply to the director of a company in relation to
_a_ company documents, that is to documents which are in the possession of the company in
the sense that the company has the sole legal right to their possession? If they are or have
been in the custody or physical possession of the director, even if he only held them or
holds them as servant or agent of the company, or in his capacity as an officer of the
company, then they must be disclosed. Whether such documents are or have been in his
custody is a question of fact in each case. It is a matter for the discretion of the court
_b_ whether they should be produced: see _Skoye v Bailey_[1] and _Williams v Ingram_[2].

It is interesting to observe that as long ago as 1900, when _Williams v Ingram_[2] was decided,
Lord Alverstone MR said that it was well worth consideration whether the power of the
court was sufficient with regard to the production before trial of documents in the
possession of third parties, but as matters then stood, his Lordship was satisfied that the
decision of Byrne J[3], at first instance, was right. As the law and practice then stood, said
_c_ Lord Alverstone MR, it was impossible to compel production of the documents in
question. If any alteration was to be made in the practice, it could only be done by a new
rule, if that were possible, or by fresh legislation. In refusing production of books of a
company, in the absence of consent by the company to their production, Byrne J made it
clear that the objection was a genuine one and that he was not satisfied that there was any
contrivance to defeat the powers of the court such as would justify him in making an order
_d_ of the kind there asked for.

It is plain from those cases that before 1964 it was not the practice of the court to order
production of such documents if the board of directors objected to its production on
affidavit, but the court must be satisfied that the objection was not contrived. But what of
relevant company documents which are not and never have been in the custody of the
director who is a party to the proceedings to which the company is not a party? Are such
_e_ documents within the power of the director? Section 12(1) of the Companies Act 1976
provides that 'Every company shall cause accounting records to be kept . . .', and sub-s (6)
provides that such records 'shall be kept at the registered office of the company or at such
other place as the directors of the company think fit and shall at all times be open to
inspection by the officers of the company'. But the right to inspect, under the provisions
of that section, is a right vested in a director in his capacity as a director or officer of the
_f_ company; he is in a fiduciary relationship with the company; he owes duties to the
company and to its shareholders. Without the consent of the company he has no right to
inspect documents, much less to take copies of them or remove them from the premises
of the company for his own purposes unconnected with the business of the company.
Because, in his capacity as a director, he has the right to inspect the company documents,
it does not follow that in his personal capacity he has an enforceable right to inspect or to
_g_ obtain possession or control of them so that the documents can be said to be in his power.
It is a question of fact in each case whether or not a director has such an enforceable right;
much will depend on the share structure of the company. In cases of a one man company,
where the director owns all or substantially all the shares and any minority shareholders are
not adverse to him, then the inference may be drawn that the company, although a
separate legal entity, does not control him but he controls the company in such manner as
_h_ to make it his other person or alter ego. In such a case, where the director controls the
company and nominates the other directors, all the documents of the company are within
his power in the sense that in truth and in fact he is able to obtain control of them.

There is no English authority which has been cited to me to support this proposition
but, as a result of the searches of the wife's solicitors, a Canadian case of _Dallas v Dallas_[4] was
cited to me. _Dallas v Dallas_[4] is a decision of the Court of Appeal of British Columbia. It was
_j_ an action between husband and wife for a declaration, the wife being the plaintiff, that they

1   [1971] 1 WWR 144
2   (1900) 16 TLR 451
3   (1900) 16 TLR 434
4   (1960) 24 DLR (2d) 746

were joint owners of his shares in a limited company. The wife sought discovery of the documents of the company. She contended that the documents were in the husband's office and in his possession and that, therefore, he should be required to produce them. The husband contended that the documents, while in his possession, were nevertheless the property of the company and, therefore, the company had the right to prevent his producing them, and he had no authority from the company to produce them. In giving judgment, Sheppard JA set out the shareholding of the company, which showed that of 1,200,003 shares the husband was the registered owner of 1,198,999, the wife of one share, and their 16 year old son 1,000 shares; and there were three qualifying shares issued to three directors. Sheppard JA said[1]:

'It is therefore evident that the defendant controls the company, elects the directorate, and also has provided the qualifying shares for three of the four directors. The defendant and those three nominees are the Board of Directors. The company holds oil leases which were acquired from funds obtained by the defendant from a joint bank account of the plaintiff and defendant. The plaintiff in contending that she is entitled to one-half of whatever interest the defendant has in the company, seeks to make the defendant produce the company documents so that she may ascertain what is his interest, and possibly obtain evidence which will enable her to trace the funds from their joint bank account. The documents being in the defendant's office, and therefore in his possession, are *prima facie* within his control: *London & Yorkshire Bank Ltd.* v. *Cooper*[2], *per* Brett M.R.: "It has been argued that the documents are not in his control; but if they are in his possession, they are *prima facie* under his control." The defendant contends, however, that he has the mere custody and that the company, which is not a party to the action, has control, and therefore he, the defendant, should not be required to produce those documents as he has no authority from the company to do so and as the company may prevent his so doing. The question is whether the defendant's control is such that his production of the documents should be excused. As a shareholder he controls the company subject to any restraint by the minority, but in this instance the minority interest is not important. One share is held by his wife who can offer no objection to her obtaining inspection by production of the documents; the remaining outstanding shares are not adverse to the defendant. The defendant's mind is the directing and controlling mind of the company and of the board of directors. Again, the defendant has provided funds whereby the company acquired oil leases and some of those moneys at least came from the joint bank account. It is evident that the company does not control him but that he controls the company in such manner as to make it his "other person".'

Then reference was made to certain English cases, which were distinguished. The judgment concludes[3]:

'In the case at bar the defendant has possession and there are no minority shareholders in whose interest the company might assert control over the documents. On the appeal no argument was directed to the question whether all the documents were relevant. Hence it should be understood that the defendant's obligation to produce should be limited to those documents relevant to issues in this action . . .'

The appeal was allowed and the order for production of relevant documents was made. That case seems to be entirely in line with the various principles which have been followed by the English courts over the years, and I follow it and adopt it.

At the other end of the scale there is the case where the director who is involved in

---

1   (1960) 24 DLR (2d) 746 at 747
2   (1885) 15 QBD 473 at 474
3   24 DLR (2d) 746 at 748

litigation cannot be said to control the company at all. The documents of such a company
a would not be in the power of the director without the consent of the board of directors.
Then there are cases, of which this case is an example, falling somewhere between the
two. In such cases the court will consider the extent of the shareholding of the husband,
whether it amounts to control of the company, whether the minority shareholders are
adverse to him, how the board of directors is constituted and whether there is any objection
by the board to disclosure of any documents sought.

b   It was submitted on behalf of the wife that because the board in this case has consented
to disclosure of certain company documents the court is entitled to draw the inference that
other documents, to the disclosure of which the board has objected, are in the power of the
husband. It was said that the board cannot pick and choose, and cannot approbate and
reprobate. I do not accept that submission as a proposition of law. Every document or
class of documents must be looked at separately, and because disclosure of certain classes of
c documents is not objected to, it does not follow that other classes of documents the
disclosure of which is objected to, are within the power of the husband. In any event it has
been made clear that in this case the objection in point of law extends to all documents in
the possession of the company, although an ex gratia offer to disclose certain documents has
been made. It was also submitted on behalf of the wife that the court was entitled to look
at the way in which the husband had used the resources of the company for his private
d purposes over the years; and to the extent to which his business life and his personal life
were intermingled it was submitted that, if the evidence showed that the husband had
lived off the company in the sense that the company had met all or substantially all his
private expenditure in cash and kind, that was an additional fact from which it could be
inferred that the husband in truth and in fact controlled the company and that the
documents of the company were in his power. I am not prepared to say that as a matter
e of law these factors are irrelevant, but the court will, however, consider them against the
background of the share structure of the company, the constitution of the board, and other
matters to which I have referred.

   The third requirement before an order for discovery can be made is that the documents
should be relevant to the matters in issue between the parties. It is a feature of financial
proceedings in the Family Division that very wide ranging issues are involved. In *O'Donnell*
f v *O'Donnell*[1] Ormrod LJ said this:

   'In approaching a case like the present, the first stage should be to make as reliable
   an estimate as possible of the husband's current financial position and future
   prospects. In making this assessment the court is concerned with the reality of the
   husband's resources, using that word in a broad sense to include not only what he is
   shown to have but also what could reasonably be made available to him if he so
g   wished. Much will depend on the interpretation of accounts, balance sheets and so
   on, which will require in many cases the expert guidance of accountants. It will
   rarely be possible to arrive at arithmetically exact figures. The court must penetrate
   through the balance sheets and profit and loss accounts to the underlying realities,
   bearing in mind that prudent financial management and skilled presentation of
   accounts are unlikely to overstate the husband's real resources, and, on the other side,
h   that there may be a great difference between wealth on paper and true wealth.
   Valuations may overstate or understate the results of realisation of assets, many of
   which may not be realisable within the immediate or foreseeable future.'

   It is another feature of such proceedings that one party, usually the wife, is in a situation
quite different from that of ordinary litigants. In general terms, she may know more than
j anyone else about the husband's financial position; she will know at first hand of the
standard of living of the family during the marriage; she will know about the furnishings
and equipment of the matrimonial home, and of the physical possessions of the husband,
and perhaps the approximate amount of cash kept in the house. She may also know, from

---

1   [1975] 2 All ER 993 at 996–997, [1976] Fam 83 at 90

conversations with the husband in the privacy of the matrimonial home, the general
sources of his wealth and how he is able to maintain the standard of living that he does.
But she is unlikely to know the details of such sources or precise figures, and it is for this
reason that discovery now plays such an important part in financial proceedings in the
Family Division.

Applications for such discovery cannot be described as 'fishing' for information, as they
might be in other divisions. The wife is entitled to go 'fishing' in the Family Division
within the limits of the law and practice.

It is said on behalf of the husband, and this is indeed the fact, that if the court decides
that the husband has not made a full disclosure of all relevant documents the court will
accept the evidence of the wife and draw adverse inferences against the husband. It is said
that that is the real sanction against non-disclosure by a husband. It is true that this has
been the practice ever since the days of the ecclesiastical courts, but it may result in
injustice to one or both parties and it is no substitute for full discovery of all documents
relating to the financial resources of the parties. The wife normally puts the husband to
proof of his financial resources, and it is then for the husband to make full disclosure,
including disclosure of all documents relating thereto. If his initial discovery is manifestly
incomplete the wife may apply for further discovery. In many, perhaps most, cases
audited accounts of companies of which the husband is a shareholder will be sufficient, together with full disclosure of all the husband's personal financial records. But there are
cases when the court will go behind company accounts and order discovery of company
books and documents, if it has the power within the law and within the rules to do so. It
is not usual, however, for the court to take this course unless there is evidence before it
from accountants or other experts that the published accounts of the company cannot be
relied on.

In cases in which it is alleged that the husband has the handling of very large sums of
cash, the court should consider whether it is likely that there would be records of such
sums in the company's books, before making any order against the company. It may be
that in cases of that kind the court will be more concerned with evidence as to the standard
of living of the husband, and of the expenditure actually made by him, than of evidence
of company records and books.

I turn now to consider the question of the discretion of the court. Assuming that the
court has jurisdiction to order discovery and decides to do so, then it is a matter for
discretion whether or not to order production. If there is no jurisdiction to order discovery
no question of discretion can arise. The various meanings of 'discretion' are set out by Sir
Jocelyn Simon P in *Povey v Povey*[1]. So far as the discretion to order production of company
documents is concerned, the court will have regard to all the circumstances. The discretion
must be exercised judicially, holding the balance evenly between the parties and any third
person affected by discovery. The court will not have discretion to order production unless
the documents are either in the custody of the husband or in his power, in the sense which
I have already described; and, in considering whether company documents are in the
power of the husband, the court will already have considered any objections by the board
of directors to their production. In considering the exercise of discretion the court will
balance the relevance and importance of the documents, and the hardship to the wife likely
to be caused by non-production, against any prejudice likely to be caused to the husband
and any other directors or shareholders of the company if an order for production is made;
and the court will not order production unless it is of opinion that the order is necessary
either for fairly disposing of the matter or for saving costs.

The confidentiality of documents is of itself no ground for refusing production. It may
be relevant to the existence of one of the accepted heads of privilege: see *Alfred Crompton
Amusement Machines Ltd v Customs and Excise Comrs (No 2)*[2], by Lord Cross. In that context

---

1   [1970] 3 All ER 612 at 617–618, [1972] Fam 40 at 48
2   [1973] 2 All ER 1169 at 1180, [1974] AC 405 at 429

there is an implied undertaking by a party who obtains production of documents against
a any improper disclosure.

Assuming that the court has no jurisdiction to make the order for discovery sought, it
is not powerless: it can give leave to issue a subpoena duces tecum under RSC Ord 38, r 14,
against the secretary of the company for production of relevant documents: see *Carew v
Carew*[1]; or the court can make an order for the production of documents under RSC Ord
38, r 13, which is incorporated into the Matrimonial Causes Rules by r 3 of the Matrimonial
b Causes Rules 1977. Although RSC Ord 38, r 13, is in quite general terms, it appears from
the notes in the Supreme Court Practice[2] that the rule does not enable an order to be made
for the inspection of documents in the hands of persons not parties. On the other hand, it
also appears from the notes[3] that if it is proved to the satisfaction of the court that a banking
account nominally that of a person not a party is really that of a party, or that the party is
so closely connected with it that items in it would be evidence against him at the trial, then
c the court in its discretion may order inspection before the trial.

I will conclude this part of my judgment by summarising my conclusions as to the law.
(1) A party to a suit must disclose all the documents in his possession, custody or power
which are relevant to the matters in issue. The court has a discretion whether or not to
order him to make such disclosure, and also has a discretion whether or not to order him
to produce the documents for inspection by the other party or the court. (2) The documents
d of a company are in the legal possession of the company. If they are or have been in the
actual physical possession of a director who is a party to litigation they must be disclosed
by that director, if relevant to the litigation, even though he holds them as servant or agent
of the company in his capacity as an officer of the company. (3) Whether or not documents
of a company are in the power of a director who is a party to the litigation is a question of
fact in each case. 'Power' in this context means 'the enforceable right to inspect or obtain
e possession or control of the document'. If the company is the alter ego of such a director
so that he has unfettered control of the company's affairs, he must disclose and produce all
relevant documents in the possession of the company. (4) Where relevant documents in
the possession of a company are disclosed by a director as being in his custody or power, the
court has a discretion whether or not to order production of them. (5) The discretion is a
judicial discretion, and in exercising it the court will have regard to all the circumstances.
f The court will balance the relevance and importance of the documents and the hardship
likely to be caused to the wife by non-production against any prejudice to the husband and
third parties likely to be caused by production. It has not hitherto been the practice of the
court to order production of company documents to which the board of directors objects
on affidavit, provided that the court is satisfied that the objection is not contrived for the
purpose of frustrating the powers of the court. The court will not in the exercise of its
g discretion order parties to do that which they have no power to do. The court will not
order production unless it is satisfied that production is necessary either for disposing fairly
of the issues between the parties or for saving costs.

[His Lordship continued his judgment in chambers. The following extract from that
part of his judgment is published with his Lordship's permission:] It is said that by reason
of discrepancies in the company's accounts the wife does not accept the audited accounts of
h the company, and does not trust the auditors to produce certified figures of the husband's
expenditure. It is said, in these circumstances, that it is necessary for accountants on her
behalf to see not only the receipts and any other documents relating to the expenditure but
also to see the company's books in order to ascertain to whom the various items of
expenditure were charged.

It is said on behalf of the husband that the books and documents of the company would

j ───

1   [1891] P 360
2   Supreme Court Practice 1976, vol 1, p 578, para 38/13/1; see now 1979 edition, vol 1, p 599, para
    38/13/1
3   Supreme Court Practice 1976, vol 1, p 579, para 38/13/3; see now 1979 edition, vol 1, p 600, para
    38/13/3

neither confirm nor deny the wife's allegations, especially in regard to the large sums of cash, because, if they had been improperly obtained, they would not have passed through **a** the books.

I am not satisfied that at this stage the documents referred to in cl 17 are relevant to the matters in dispute. I think that having regard to the allegations by the wife the court at the hearing is likely to be more interested in the actual standard of living and expenditure of the husband over the years than in books and records of the company which may well not show cash expenditure. But I accept that the various documents referred to in cll 3, 4 and **b** 11 are relevant to the matters in issue. All those documents are in the possession of the company; they are not in the possession of the husband in the sense that I have used it in this judgment. The husband has, however, given some evidence as to how those documents were dealt with. He said this in his affidavit of 22nd April 1977: 'The mechanics of the financing of my expenditure is that the restaurant or night club will send the bill to the office, where it will be scrutinised by me, and I will give instructions to have **c** it paid.' I take it that that procedure refers to all documents relating to the expenditure and payments referred to in cll 3, 4 and 11 of the order. Those documents are documents, in my judgment, which are or have been in the custody of the husband and, therefore, he must disclose them. The company have offered limited disclosure of those documents, but they have taken the position that they shall be the judges of which documents are or are not relevant. The registrar refused to accept that position. I deal with it in this way, which I **d** believe to be the way that the law requires it to be dealt with, namely that the documents must be disclosed; and if any objection is made to their production that objection can be made on affidavit after the documents have been properly disclosed. The registrar will then be able to consider the objections to production as they are made in respect of the individual classes of documents, and will also have the power to order their production, or the production of some of them, to the court, so that he can make up his mind whether or **e** not they are documents which are relevant and which therefore should be produced, or not. In deciding whether the document is to be produced for inspection by the wife, he will of course have regard to the various matters of discretion to which I have referred earlier in this judgment. If that course is adopted, then the production of the documents to the wife will be regulated by the court and not by the company; but the documents must be disclosed as being in the custody of the husband. **f**

So far as cl 17 is concerned, I have already expressed the view that at this stage I am not satisfied that those documents are relevant, save in so far as they include documents under cll 3, 4 and 11 which I have already dealt with. I would add this: considering all the evidence in the case and applying to it the principles which I have enunciated, I cannot say that the operating company is the alter ego of the husband, so that he can control it to the extent that he can require production of those documents. Clause 17 must therefore be **g** deleted from the order, save for the provision relating to the Swiss bank accounts. So far as the Swiss bank accounts are concerned, it seems to me that documents relating to any Swiss bank account which the husband has a mandate to operate alone or jointly with any other person or persons are documents which are in his custody or power, and they must therefore be disclosed. If there is any objection to production of any of those documents, then that objection must be made on affidavit by any person who claims to have a joint **h** interest in the document. That also is a matter which will be dealt with by the registrar in the discretion of the court.

The documents referred to in cl 12 of the order, namely the documents in the action between the holding company and the public company, are not in my judgment documents within the custody or power of the husband; cl 12 must therefore be deleted from the order. **j**

Finally, I deal with the second part of the order, which is an order requiring the husband to file an affidavit setting out particulars of visits abroad, and particulars of motor cars owned by the company. These matters do not fall within the considerations affecting discovery, to which I have referred at some length, and I see no reason why the husband should not file a further affidavit in the terms ordered by the registrar. That affidavit must a   be filed within 21 days, and the affidavit will be in the form originally ordered by the registrar.

To the extent which I have stated, therefore, this appeal will be allowed.

Appeal allowed in part. Leave to appeal.

b   *4th December. An application by the wife to stand the appeal out of the list generally was, by consent, granted, pending determination whether the discovery she sought had now been given by the husband.*

Solicitors: *Theodore Goddard & Co* (for the husband); *S Rutter & Co* (for the wife).

Georgina Chambers   Barrister.

c

Practice Direction

FAMILY DIVISION

d   *Family Division – Appeal – Appeal from registrar – Notes of evidence and registrar's judgment.*

This direction is issued by the President with the concurrence of the Lord Chancellor.

1. As from 12th March 1979 on entering an appeal to a judge from a judgment, order or decision of a registrar exercising Family Division jurisdiction in the High Court or in the county court the following procedure will apply.

e   2. When the appellant is represented by a solicitor, he shall—(a) at the time of entering the appeal, certify (if this is the case) that it has been agreed with the solicitor for the respondent that nothing in any oral evidence taken before the registrar is relevant to any issue arising on the appeal, and that no notes of evidence will be lodged, and (b) unless otherwise directed, and subject as aforesaid, lodge prior to the hearing of the appeal a copy

f   of the registrar's notes of evidence and judgment (if any) or a copy of any such notes as have been prepared and agreed by the parties' legal advisers and approved by the registrar.

3. Where the appellant is acting in person, he should lodge a copy of any notes of evidence and judgment that are available to him. If none are available the respondent's solicitor (if any) shall, after service of the notice of the appeal, comply with the obligations imposed by para 2(a) and (b) above as if he were acting for the appellant and inform the appellant of the lodging of such notes and (if so requested) supply to him a copy thereof on

g   payment of the usual copying charges.

4. Where both parties to the appeal are acting in person, the registrar shall, where possible, make a note for the assistance of the judge hearing the appeal and shall, prior to the hearing, furnish each party with a copy of that note or certify that no note can be made.

R L BAYNE-POWELL
Senior Registrar.

h   26th February 1979

Zarczynska v Levy

a

EMPLOYMENT APPEAL TRIBUNAL
KILNER BROWN J, MR T H GOFF AND MR B L MACKIE
21st SEPTEMBER, 20th OCTOBER 1978

Race relations – Unlawful discrimination – Discrimination against complainant personally – Less favourable treatment – Barmaid instructed not to serve coloured people – Barmaid dismissed for ***b*** *refusing to obey instruction – Barmaid making complaint to industrial tribunal – Whether barmaid discriminated against personally on racial grounds – Whether industrial tribunal had jurisdiction to hear barmaid's complaint – Race Relations Act 1976, ss 1(1)(a), 30, 63(3)(b).*

A publican ('the employer') who did not wish to have coloured people as customers instructed his barmaids that they were not to serve coloured people. One of the barmaids ***c*** ('the employee') disagreed with the instruction because it was unreasonable and unlawful and her employment was terminated forthwith. The employee made a complaint to an industrial tribunal under the Race Relations Act 1976 alleging that she had been unfairly dismissed and victimised. The tribunal held that they had no jurisdiction to hear the complaint because the employee had not been personally discriminated against on racial grounds, and since the discrimination related to an instruction to do something which was ***d*** unlawful under the 1976 Act it fell within s 30[a] of that Act and accordingly, under s 63(3)(b)[b] of that Act, could only be dealt with in the county court on the application of the Commission for Racial Equality. The employee appealed, contending that she had been discriminated against personally because she had been treated less favourably than the other barmaids on racial grounds, within s 1(1)(a)[c] of the 1976 Act and was entitled to a personal remedy in addition to any proceedings the commission might bring against the ***e*** employer in the county court under s 63(3)(b).

Held – Applying a purposive construction to the 1976 Act, s 1 stated a general principle which was not restricted or limited by subsequent provisions in the Act providing remedies for particular breaches of the general principle, since Parliament if it had considered the employee's situation would not have intended the injustice which resulted from a strict ***f*** interpretation. It followed that s 63(3)(b) of the 1976 Act did not exclude a complaint to an industrial tribunal by an employee who had, for the purposes of s 1(1)(a), been treated less favourably on racial grounds, and since the employee had been treated less favourably on racial grounds than barmaids who obeyed the unlawful instruction, the industrial tribunal had erred in law in refusing to hear her complaint. The appeal would therefore be allowed (see p 817 *f* to *h* and p 818 *a* to *c*, post).

Dicta of Lord Denning MR and Stephenson LJ in *Race Relations Board v Applin* [1973] 2 ***g*** All ER at 1196 and 1199 and of Lord Denning MR in *Nothman v London Borough of Barnet* [1978] 1 All ER at 1246 applied.

Notes

For the meaning of unlawful discrimination, see 4 Halsbury's Laws (4th Edn) para 1035. ***h***
For the Race Relations Act 1976, ss 1, 30, 63, see 46 Halsbury's Statutes (3rd Edn) 395, 418, 441.

---

a   Section 30 is set out at p 815 *h*, post
b   Section 63, so far as material, provides:
     '(1) Proceedings in respect of a contravention of section 29, 30 and 31 shall be brought only by ***j***
     the Commission in accordance with the following provisions of this section.
     '(2) The proceedings shall be—(a) an application for a decision whether the alleged contravention occurred . . .
     '(3) An application under subsection (2)(a) shall be made—(a) in a case based on any provision of Part II, to an industrial tribunal; and (b) in any other case, to a designated county court . . .'
c   Section 1, so far as material, is set out at p 816 *a*, post

Cases referred to in judgments

a *Nothman v London Borough of Barnet* [1978] 1 All ER 1243, [1978] 1 WLR 220, [1978] ICR 336, 76 LGR 617, CA; *affd* p 142, *ante*, [1979] 1 WLR 67, HL.

Race Relations Board v Applin [1973] 2 All ER 1190, [1973] QB 815, [1973] 2 WLR 895, CA; *affd* sub nom *Applin v Race Relations Board* [1974] 2 All ER 73, [1975] AC 259, [1974] 2 WLR 541, 138 JP 522, 72 LGR 479, HL, 2 Digest (Reissue) 371, 1786.

Stock v Frank Jones (Tipton) Ltd [1978] 1 All ER 948, [1978] 1 WLR 231, [1978] ICR 347, HL.

b

Appeal

Krystine Zarczynska ('the employee') appealed against the decision of an industrial tribunal (chairman G V Kenyon Esq) sitting in London on 3rd February 1978 rejecting her complaint under s 54 of the Race Relations Act 1976 against her employer, Peter Levy ('the employer'), that she had been discriminated against and unfairly dismissed within s 4(2)(c)

c of the Act.

Duncan Pratt for the employee.
Ernst Horridge for the employer.

Cur adv vult

d 20th October.   **KILNER BROWN J** read the following judgment of the appeal tribunal: On 8th July 1977 Miss Zarczynska ('the employee') obtained employment as a part-time barmaid at a public house where Mr Peter Levy ('the employer') was the licensee. The employer and his wife did not want coloured people as customers and they instructed the barman and the barmaids that they were not to serve them. On 25th August the employee was told that she must not serve some black customers; she insisted that this was not a reasonable or lawful instruction and her employment came to an abrupt end. Whether she

e resigned or was dismissed is immaterial because, if it was an order in breach of the law, the conduct of the employer would be in breach of the contract of employment, entitling her to walk out. The employee reported the matter and the Commission for Racial Equality has taken up the case. The commission has begun proceedings against the employer in the county court under s 30 of the Race Relations Act 1976. If they succeed, they will obtain

f a declaration that the licensee has given instructions to his employees which are in contravention of the 1976 Act and which discriminate against customers on racial grounds.

But what good is this to the unfortunate and righteous employee? She has lost her job because she tried to uphold the law. She made an application to an industrial tribunal in London North alleging that she was unfairly dismissed and victimised under the 1976 Act. Her case was heard on 3rd February 1978 and the industrial tribunal unanimously

g but reluctantly decided that they had no jurisdiction to hear the application. From that decision she now appeals. The industrial tribunal correctly came to the decision that as she had not been employed for sufficient length of time she could not bring what might be called the 'ordinary' proceedings alleging unfair dismissal. The only available complaint had therefore to be brought within the provisions of the 1976 Act. The industrial tribunal came to the conclusion that the facts fell squarely within the provisions of s 30 and that the

h scope of that section coupled with ss 54 and 63 was exclusive of all other remedies in any other context and that no remedy was available to the applicant. Section 30 reads as follows:

'It is unlawful for a person—(a) who has authority over another person; or (b) in accordance with whose wishes that other person is accustomed to act, to instruct him to do any act which is unlawful by virtue of Part II or Part III or procure or attempt

j to procure the doing by him of any such act.'

The industrial tribunal said that on the facts as set out in the employee's complaint this section applied to the situation. No one disputes that. On behalf of the employee it is submitted that the tribunal were wrong in law to conclude that on these facts no remedy was available to the employee herself and that the tribunal fell into error in ruling that because she had not been personally discriminated against on racial grounds she could not rely on other provisions of the 1976 Act. In order to appreciate the argument it is necessary *a* to consider all sections of the 1976 Act which may conceivably be relevant. It is convenient to begin with s 1(1)(*a*). That provides: 'A person discriminates against another in any circumstances relevant for the purposes of any provision of this Act if—(*a*) on racial grounds he treats that other less favourably than he treats or would treat other persons . . .'

Pausing there, the critical question which arises in this case is whether the words used can be construed or, in order to do justice, ought to be construed so as to cover the case of *b* a person who has been dismissed because an unlawful order was given on racial grounds in contravention of s 30. It is appropriate next to move on to s 2(1)(*d*) which reads:

> 'A person ("the discriminator") discriminates against another person ("the person victimised") in any circumstances relevant for the purposes of any provision of this Act if he treats the person victimised less favourably than in those circumstances he treats or would treat other persons, and does so by reason that the person victimised *c* has . . . (*d*) alleged that the discriminator or any other person has committed an act which (whether or not the allegation so states) would amount to a contravention of this Act . . .'

We proceed to that part of the 1976 Act entitled Part II and consider s 4(2)(*c*). That reads as follows: *d*

> 'It is unlawful for a person, in the case of a person employed by him at an establishment in Great Britain, to discriminate against that employee . . . (*c*) by dismissing him, or subjecting him to any other detriment.'

It has taken us a long period of acute concentration to disentangle the conceivably relevant passages from an accumulation of complicated terminology. We pause again, this *e* time to sympathise with the busy members of an industrial tribunal who are expected to embark on this sort of intellectual exercise and to admire the celerity with which they wielded the executioner's axe to dispose of this lady's case. That they were able to do so is on account of the lucidity with which Parliament has phrased ss 54 and 63 of the 1976 Act. After emerging from the gloom of the forest of difficulty, the light is blinding in its clarity. It provides that a complaint may be made by any person to an industrial tribunal *f* where the respondent to the application has committed an act of discrimination against the complainant which is unlawful by virtue of Part II of the 1976 Act. On the other hand s 63 provides that a breach of s 30, that is the giving of an order in breach of the 1976 Act, can only be dealt with in the county court in proceedings brought by the Commission for Racial Equality. The industrial tribunal decided, as has already been indicated, that this was a s 30 case and that as there was no breach of Part II of the 1976 Act alleging a *g* discrimination on racial grounds against the employee personally she was not entitled to make a complaint to an industrial tribunal and therefore they had no jurisdiction.

The industrial tribunal did not like the situation in which they found themselves. We are equally unhappy and consider it most unjust that this lady should be deprived of any opportunity to obtain compensation for losing her job because she tried to uphold the law which forbids discrimination on racial grounds. It is not easy for us to discover any error *h* of law. But can nothing be done? Can the Court of Appeal help us? We think it does. We turn first to the Court of Appeal decision in *Race Relations Board v Applin*[1]. It is not exactly in point because it largely concerned the question as to whether or not there were provisions of services to a section of the public; but there are passages in the judgment of Lord Denning MR and Stephenson LJ which afford us help and guidance even though they may be strictly obiter dicta. Thus Lord Denning MR[2] dealt with the application of the *j* words in s 1(1) of the Race Relations Act 1968 which are very similar to the words used in the 1976 Act, viz: '. . . a person discriminates against another if on the grounds of

---

1 [1973] 2 All ER 1190, [1973] QB 815
2 [1973] 2 All ER 1190 at 1196, [1973] QB 815 at 828

colour . . . he treats that other . . . less favourably than he treats . . . other persons.' Taking the example of two white women coming into a public house with coloured men and who might be barred against entry by the innkeeper, Lord Denning MR concluded that the innkeeper would be discriminating against the women on grounds of colour. Stephenson LJ[1] added that if it were necessary for the purposes of his judgment he would agree with and decide as Lord Denning MR that A can discriminate against B on the grounds of C's colour, race or ethnic origin. Can it not be said in the instant case that in dismissing the one barmaid because she wanted to serve some coloured men, and not dismissing a barmaid who was prepared to apply the embargo, the licensee treated the one less favourably than the other on racial grounds? We recognise that s 1(1) of the 1976 Act has to be read in conjunction with the other provisions to which reference has been made and that a broad approach to s 1(1) may be prevented or delimited by the effect of other provisions. If we could say, however, that such other provisions are explanatory of or provide remedies for instances of breach of the general principle then the general principle would not be restricted. This might involve reading into s 1 the purposive intent of Parliament to make it a section which overrides subsequent sections which might otherwise be deemed to limit the provisions of that section. If this is not done the strict interpretation of the relevant sections taken as a whole may well create an absurd or unjust situation which Parliament would not have intended if they had contemplated its possibility. What guidance does Lord Denning MR give us? In *Notham v London Borough of Barnet*[2] he said:

'Whenever the strict interpretation of a statute gives rise to an absurd and unjust situation, the judges can and should use their good sense to remedy it—by reading words in, if necessary—so as to do what Parliament would have done had they had the situation in mind.'

In other cases we have uttered words of caution to industrial tribunals to avoid rewriting Acts of Parliament to suit their understanding of what Parliament really intended. We apply these words of caution to ourselves and remind ourselves of the unanimous opinions of their Lordships in the House of Lords in *Stock v Frank Jones (Tipton) Ltd*[3]. Inferior tribunals must be very careful before indulging in speculation about the purposive intent of an Act of Parliament. In the instant case the industrial tribunal were right to shrink from such an exercise. Can we embark on it and ought we to do so? Is there a point of law? That is easily answered. Interpretation of statutory provisions is a point of law. Did the industrial tribunal err on a point of law? The answer is, No, unless they ignored the purposive intent of Parliament and erred in their interpretation of s 1(1)(a). Did they ignore the purposive intent of Parliament? That question can only be answered if we assume the right to speculate on the purpose of the 1976 Act. This is not a case where we are called on to pronounce on the meaning of individual words or phrases but to look at the general intention of Parliament. Lord Wensleydale's 'golden rule'[4] permitted the judiciary to modify the natural and ordinary meaning of words if they produced an injustice which Parliament never contemplated. We are of opinion here that if Parliament had had pre-knowledge of this unfortunate lady's predicament they would have made clear that the great civilised principle on which the 1976 Act was based was one which overrode all apparent limitations expressed in other sections which had the effect of denying justice to someone who was victimised. We have hesitated long before taking this course, because we may be pre-empting the right and the duty of the Court of Appeal to pronounce on this matter. The phraseology of the judicial member of this appeal tribunal was characterised

1   [1973] 2 All ER 1190 at 1199, [1973] QB 815 at 831
2   [1978] 1 All ER 1243 at 1246, [1978] 1 WLR 220 at 228
3   [1978] 1 All ER 948, [1978] 1 WLR 231
4   See *Caledonian Railway Co v North British Railway Co* (1881) 6 App Cas 114 at 131 per Lord Blackburn

as that of an out-of-date grammarian by Lord Denning MR in *Notham v London Borough of Barnet*[1]. In the instant case he is prepared to be a contemporary pragmatist and assume most respectfully that the Court of Appeal would find in favour of this lady's argument if we were to reject it. The Commission for Racial Equality stand firmly behind her and would fight her case to the bitter end. So, with the active encouragement of the lay members the judicial member is prepared to hold and to advise that this appeal should be allowed.

It is allowed on the basis that the industrial tribunal erred in finding that there was no contravention of Parts I and II of the 1976 Act. Further, there should be read into s 54 words to the effect that the said jurisdiction shall be exercised in addition to the jurisdiction provided for in s 63 of the 1976 Act.

We unanimously conclude that the decision of the industrial tribunal should be set aside and declare that there is jurisdiction to hear and determine the employee's application in so far as she claims compensation for victimisation.

Appeal allowed.

Solicitors: *Bindman & Partners* (for the employee); *Charkham, Marcus & Co* (for the employer).

Salim H J Merali Esq   Barrister.

Practice Direction

QUEEN'S BENCH DIVISION

Practice – Personal injuries action – Experts' reports – Agreed reports – Reports to be lodged with proper officer after agreement or setting down for trial – RSC Ord 34, r 3.

1. In personal injury actions it would be of great convenience and assistance to the trial judge to have the opportunity before the trial to read the reports of the experts, both medical and other experts, which have been agreed between the parties.

2. Accordingly, in personal injury actions, a copy of the reports of the medical and other experts which have been agreed between the parties must be lodged by the plaintiff with the proper officer (as defined in RSC Ord 34, r 3(5)) at the place where the action has been set down for trial, within 14 days after such reports have been agreed or as soon after setting down as is practicable.

3. These reports will be placed by the proper officer with the documents required to be lodged with him when setting an action down for trial under RSC Ord 34, r 3, and they will accompany such documents for the use of the trial judge.

4. Each such report should state on the face of it the name of the party on whose behalf the expert has given that report and the date on which it was given.

Sir Jack I H Jacob QC
Senior Master of the Supreme Court.

15th February 1979

---

1   [1978] 1 All ER 1243 at 1246, [1978] 1 WLR 220 at 228

Allen and another v Greenwood and another

COURT OF APPEAL, CIVIL DIVISION
BUCKLEY, ORR AND GOFF LJJ
12th, 13th, 16th OCTOBER 1978

Easement – Light – Degree of light acquired by prescriptive right – Ordinary amount of light – Obstruction of sunlight to greenhouse – Greenhouse illuminated sufficiently for working in but not for growing plants – Light required for ordinary use of greenhouse to grow plants – Right to light acquired by prescription – Whether high degree of light required for greenhouse 'ordinary' light for that purpose – Whether right to exceptional degree of light acquired by prescription — Whether right to light restricted to amount of light required for illumination – Whether right to direct sunlight able to be acquired by prescription – Prescription Act 1832, s 3.

The plaintiffs occupied a residential property consisting of a house and garden. In the garden there was a greenhouse some 16 feet long built alongside the boundary with the neighbouring property and which had been used for the ordinary purposes of a greenhouse for at least the previous 20 years. The defendants, who owned the neighbouring property, erected a fence on the boundary some six inches from the greenhouse and then parked a caravan next to the fence alongside the greenhouse. The effect of the fence and the caravan was to exclude direct sunlight from half the greenhouse and seriously interfere with the plaintiffs' use of it to grow tomatoes and pot plants, although the greenhouse still received sufficient ordinary light to work in. The plaintiffs sought injunctions restraining the defendants from obstructing the light to the greenhouse. They contended that the access and use of light to and for the greenhouse having been enjoyed for 20 years without interruption they therefore had an absolute and indefeasible right to that light under s 3[a] of the Prescription Act 1832. The judge dismissed the action on the ground that a greenhouse was a building which required special light and as there was no evidence that the defendants knew of the precise purpose being made of the greenhouse there was no nuisance provided they did not prevent it being used for the ordinary purposes of a room in a house. On appeal the defendants contended that if the plaintiffs had obtained a prescriptive right to light it was a right to the amount of light required for the purposes of ordinary illumination and not a right to the direct rays of the sun.

Held – The appeal would be allowed for the following reasons—

(i) The amount of light to which an occupier was entitled by virtue of a prescriptive right to light acquired under s 3 of the 1832 Act was to be measured according to the nature of the building and the purposes for which it was normally used. Since the normal use of a greenhouse required a high degree of light, the plaintiffs had acquired, as part of their prescriptive right to ordinary light, the right to that degree of light and the benefits of light including the rays of the sun required to grow plants in the greenhouse and not just the amount of light required for illumination (see p 824 *e f*, p 825 *c* to *e*, p 827 *f g*, p 828 *b c* and *e* to *j* and p 829 *a* and *c d* and p 831 *d*, post); *Colls v Home and Colonial Stores Ltd* [1904–7] All ER Rep 5 applied.

(ii) Alternatively, a right to an exceptional or extraordinary amount of light for a particular purpose could be acquired by prescriptive right provided it was enjoyed for the full period of 20 years to the knowledge of the servient owners, and, since the defendants must have known how the greenhouse was being used, the plaintiffs had acquired a right to an exceptionally high degree of light by known enjoyment of that degree of light over 20 years. Because the defendants were blocking the light to the greenhouse, the plaintiffs were accordingly entitled to the injunctions sought (see p 825 *g*, p 826 *d* to *f*, p 827 *g*, p 828 *b* to *d*, p 829 *d e*, p 830 *h* to p 831 *d*, post); dicta of Malins V-C in *Lanfranchi v Mackenzie* (1867) LR 4 Eq at 430 applied; dicta of Lord Davey in *Colls v Home and Colonial Stores Ltd*

---
a   Section 3 is set out at p 821 d, post

[1904–7] All ER Rep at 19 and of Bray J in *Ambler v Gordon* [1905] 1 KB at 424 not followed.
Per Goff and Orr LJJ. In the case of solar heating it may be possible and right to separate *a*
heat or some other property of the sun from its light. That was an entirely open question
to be left for decision when it arises (see p 828 *a* and *c*, post).

Notes
For the extent of an easement of light, and extraordinary user, see 14 Halsbury's Laws (4th
Edn) paras 213, 214, 218, and for cases on the subject, see 19 Digest (Repl) 146–154, 952– *b*
1007.
For the Prescription Act 1832, s 3, see 9 Halsbury's Statutes (3rd Edn) 554.

Cases referred to in judgment
Ambler v Gordon [1905] 1 KB 417, 74 LJKB 185, 92 LT 96, 19 Digest (Repl) 153, *1004.*
City of London Brewery Co v Tennant (1873) LR 9 Ch App 212, 43 LJ Ch 457, 29 LT 755, 38 *c*
JP 468, 19 Digest (Repl) 85, *502.*
Clifford v Holt [1899] 1 Ch 698, 68 LJ Ch 332, 80 LT 48, 63 JP 22, 19 Digest (Repl) 139, 897.
Colls v Home and Colonial Stores Ltd [1904] AC 179, [1904–7] All ER Rep 5, 73 LJ Ch 484, 90
LT 687, HL, 19 Digest (Repl) 135, 872.
Hortons' Estate Ltd v Beattie Ltd [1927] 1 Ch 75, 96 LJ Ch 15, 136 LT 218, 19 Digest (Repl)
151, 983. *d*
Kelk v Pearson (1871) LR 6 Ch App 809, 24 LT 890, 36 JP 196, 19 Digest (Repl) 138, 887.
Lanfranchi v Mackenzie (1867) LR 4 Eq 421, 36 LJ Ch 518, 16 LT 114, 31 JP 627, 19 Digest
(Repl) 153, 998.
Lazarus v Artistic Photographic Co [1897] 2 Ch 214, 66 LJ Ch 522, 76 LT 457, 19 Digest
(Repl) 153, *1001.*
Ough v King [1967] 3 All ER 859, [1967] 1 WLR 1547, 19 P & CR 40, CA, Digest (Cont Vol *e*
C) 305, 986a.
Semon (Charles) & Co v Bradford Corp [1922] 2 Ch 737, 91 LJ Ch 602, 127 LT 800, 19 Digest
(Repl) 150, 982.
Warren v Brown [1900] 2 QB 722, 69 LJQB 842, 83 LT 318; *rvsd* [1902] 1 KB 15, 71 LJKB
12, 85 LT 444, CA, 19 Digest (Repl) 150, 977.

Cases also cited *f*
Browne v Flower [1911] 1 Ch 219, [1908–10] All ER Rep 545.
News of the World Ltd v Allen Fairhead & Sons Ltd [1931] 2 Ch 402, [1931] All ER Rep 630.
Phipps v Pears [1964] 2 All ER 35, [1965] 1 QB 76, CA.

Appeal *g*
The plaintiffs, Hubert Allen and his wife Marjorie Allen, who were the owners of a house
and residential property at 13 Wood Top Avenue, Bansford, Rochdale, appealed from the
decision dated 6th October 1977 of Blackett-Ord V-C sitting in the Chancery Division of
the High Court of Justice at Manchester, refusing to grant the plaintiffs prohibitive and
mandatory injunctions to restrain the defendants, Tyrell Sandiford Greenwood and his
wife Lilian Alice Greenwood, the owners of the house and property at 15 Wood Top *h*
Avenue from obstructing the light to the greenhouse situated in the garden of the
plaintiffs' house. The facts are set out in the judgment of Goff LJ.

H E Francis QC and *A W Simpson* for the plaintiffs.
Paul V Baker QC and *B C Maddocks* for the defendants.

GOFF LJ delivered the first judgment at the invitation of Buckley LJ. This is an appeal *j*
from an order of Blackett-Ord V-C dated 6th October 1977, whereby he refused relief by
way of prohibitive and mandatory injunctions in respect of the alleged obstruction of light
to the plaintiffs' greenhouse and dismissed the action.
The plaintiffs, who are husband and wife, have occupied their home since September

a 1954, first as tenants and since December 1974 as owners in fee simple. As the photographs show, it is a pleasant detached house with a spacious garden.

The defendants, who are also a married couple, are owners in fee simple of a comparable house and property to the south, which they purchased in 1966 and which they have occupied ever since. The level of the plaintiffs' garden is some 26 or 28 inches lower than that of the defendants' and the defendants' land is supported by a low retaining wall commencing a little to the east of the greenhouse, with a low brick-built pillar.

b The plaintiffs' greenhouse is of the following agreed dimensions. It is 16 feet long, 9 feet 6 inches wide, 6 feet 9 inches to the eaves, and then it has a pitched roof with the ridge 3 feet above that. It is built right up against the retaining wall. In fact that wall forms one of its walls. Two of the other three are built up to, or perhaps bonded into, the retaining wall to form a level support, and the glazed structure rises directly above these four walls. So on the south side the frame of the glass is actually resting on, or secured to, the retaining wall itself. That wall belongs wholly to the plaintiffs; it is not a party wall.

c It is clear that the greenhouse was built soon after the erection of the plaintiffs' house some time between 1939 and 1941, and user of it for the ordinary purposes of a greenhouse for at least 20 years next before action brought was duly proved. The plaintiffs complain of an infringement of a prescriptive right to light to their greenhouse, founding their claim on s 3 of the Prescription Act 1832, which is in these terms:

d 'When the access and use of light to and for any dwelling house, workshop, or other building shall have been actually enjoyed therewith for the full period of twenty years without interruption, the right thereto shall be deemed absolute and indefeasible, any local usage or custom to the contrary notwithstanding, unless it shall appear that the same was enjoyed by some consent or agreement expressly made or given for that purpose by deed or writing.'

e There was in this case no such consent.

Prior to 1969 there were certain buildings or structures on the defendants' land, in addition of course to their house. There was an air raid shelter a little to the west of the greenhouse, and a shed to the east of the greenhouse. After the war the air raid shelter was put to use as a coal bunker. Mr Allen, one of the plaintiffs, gave evidence at the trial. He *f* was cross-examined, suggesting that these buildings or structures had obstructed the light to the greenhouse, but there was an open space of some 20 feet between the air raid shelter and the garden shed, and it became clear that those structures did not cause any obstruction and that line was not pursued.

In that year, 1969, the defendants caused the air raid shelter, or coal bunker, and the garden shed to be removed. For a time they had a car port to the west of their garage, that *g* is, further away from the greenhouse, and that did not cause any obstruction. At this time they also had a wall built across their land from the pillar to the house, and laid out the part of their property to the east of that wall as a patio, leaving an open tarmac space in front of the greenhouse. So there was still no obstruction. Indeed, there was no trouble of any kind until May 1974, when the defendants applied for planning permission to erect a two-storey extension at the rear of their house. Notice of that application was given to the *h* plaintiffs by the borough planning officer. Mr Allen inspected the plans and formed the view that such an extension would interfere with the access of light to the greenhouse and to his sitting room. He, therefore, instructed solicitors, who wrote to Mr Greenwood on 7th August 1974, saying:

j 'Mr Allen has inspected the deposited plans and finds that if the proposed extension is carried out it will cause a serious diminution of the access of light to our client's greenhouse and some diminution of light to his sitting-room. The buildings on our clients' land have been erected long enough to have acquired a right to light and therefore, we trust that you will not proceed with the extension in such a way as to infringe the rights of our clients. Mr Allen has felt it necessary to lodge a formal objection to your application. We trust that it will not be necessary for our clients to take any further steps to enforce their rights and we shall be glad to hear from you that the matter can be amicably disposed of.'

There was no reply to that letter, but shortly afterwards the defendants started to park their caravan immediately alongside the greenhouse. Prior to that it had been parked to the west of the old car port, that is, between the car port and the road, where, of course, it was not an obstruction to the greenhouse.

On 28th August the defendants put in posts, or supports, for a fence very close to the greenhouse. That fence, which is close-boarded and creosoted, was finished by 1st September from a point at the east end of the greenhouse nearly, but not quite, up to the west end. The fence was built to a height which, having regard to the difference in level of the two properties, brought it about 18 inches above the eaves.

The plaintiffs' solicitors wrote a further letter on 6th September in the following terms:

'Further to our letter of the 7th August 1974 we are now informed that you have erected a boarded fence on the boundary of your property adjacent to that of our client's the top of which in part by reason of the difference of levels extends 9′ above the level upon which our client's greenhouse stands and is at a distance of approximately 5″ from it. This fence naturally interferes very seriously indeed with the access of light to the greenhouse. We have already pointed out to you that our client has acquired a right to light by prescription in view of the fact that the greenhouse has occupied its present position for a period considerably in excess of 20 years. Unless therefore the fence in its present form is removed our client will institute proceedings for an Order to enforce its removal without delay. We must therefore request you to advise us within the next 7 days that this will be done.'

On receipt of that letter the fence, so far as it was immediately opposite the greenhouse, was dismantled but the caravan was then again placed alongside the greenhouse. Between October 1974 and 5th February 1975 the fence was restored and extended right to the west end of the greenhouse and approximately 5½ feet beyond. When first restored it came only up to eave level, but it was later raised to 18 inches above, when the plaintiffs' gardener placed boxes of seeds and young plants at about eave level to get as near to the light as possible to prevent them from getting drawn up.

The position, therefore, when the action commenced was, and it still is, that there is this fence from the east end of the greenhouse to a point some 5 feet 6 inches beyond it on the west, only about 6 inches away from the glass, with the caravan parked close up to the fence.

It was clear from Mr Allen's evidence that the greenhouse had been used at all material times in the ordinary normal way in which such an appurtenance would be used in a private garden. He was asked: 'What use, since 1954 when you went into occupation of the house, have you made of the greenhouse?' and he answered: 'I have invariably grown tomatoes during the summer. We have raised our own plants from seed.' Then Blackett-Ord V-C asked: 'Do you mean tomato plants?' and Mr Allen answered:

'Tomato plants. Sometimes we have bought tomato plants; sometimes we have raised them from seed. Then we have geraniums, and we raise cuttings and so forth. Indeed, we are accustomed also to grow pot plants for the purpose not only of being able to see them in the greenhouse, but also when required to be able to take them inside the house. My wife is fond of plants and flowers inside the house, and I am myself for that matter. Of course, the greenhouse has served a useful purpose in that sense.'

Then counsel went on:

'Q. You have mentioned so far tomatoes, geraniums and house plants? A. Yes.
'Q. Do you raise any plants other than tomatoes from seeds? A. Oh, yes, a whole range of biannual type bedding plants that one raises from seed in the spring.
'Q. What sort of plants? A. Stocks, antirrhinums, various kinds of marigold, zinnias, violets, pansy, the red ones that are rather tender; that sort of plant, you see.'

He also gave evidence of the disastrous effect of the obstructions, which is well illustrated by a number of photographs, and he said this when asked in a question:

'Q. Some things do not like too much light? A. I can put ferns there, but it is no use trying to grow flowers there; so, in effect, I am in difficulty now cultivating flowers in pots in that greenhouse, which I was able to do earlier, prior to the existence of the fence. It used to be nice to walk into the greenhouse and see flowers, and also it used to supply the house with flowering plants.
'Q. What about seedlings? A. We are able to grow some, but we are still somewhat deprived, because we cannot; we used to erect a temporary bench at the southerly side to put the seed trays on before they germinated, and just for a short time after germination. There is no point in that now. Virtually speaking, the southern half of my greenhouse is useless for what were previously its normal functions. In respect of my seedlings, when I grow them I have to bring them towards the centre of the greenhouse more than would have been necessary. The result is that there is a greater depth between the seed pans and the glazing, and there is a greater tendency for them to be drawn, and be less sturdy plants.'

And then Blackett-Ord V-C summed up his evidence by saying: 'What it boils down to is that you say that half of your greenhouse is really very little use?', to which Mr Allen replied: 'Yes.'

He was cross-examined, but the cross-examination did not shake him, and Blackett-Ord V-C found as follows:

'. . . the result, of course, is totally to exclude all sunlight from the south except to a small extent when the sun is high, and roughly half of the greenhouse gets no sun at all . . . I accept the evidence of Mr Allen, which was very fairly given, that the use of the greenhouse for the purposes for which he was expected to use it, namely growing tomatoes and pot plants, has been seriously interfered with . . . there is, of course, plenty of light left in the greenhouse for actually carrying out any operations. If you want to pick the tomatoes, or pot plants, or indeed if you want to get away from the family and read a book, there is plenty of light for those purposes in the greenhouse . . . Here, of course, the structure was obviously a greenhouse, but there is no evidence that the owners of the servient tenement, the successive owners, knew the precise use which was being made of it. Some plants require more light than others . . . There is ample light left in the greenhouse, I find, for everything except the special purpose of growing certain plants.'

It is to be observed that he did not say that there was anything special about the plants; nor indeed was there. So the ratio decidendi of Blackett-Ord V-C's decision is that a greenhouse is a building which by its nature requires special light and there is no nuisance, although that purpose be defeated, so long as there is enough light to work in the place, though the work be rendered useless or seriously less effective, so long as there is sufficient light to use it as if it were a living room in a house, and not a greenhouse; at all events, unless the servient owners have some particularly detailed knowledge of the user, which Blackett-Ord V-C described as 'precise'.

Such being the facts, the first question which arises is whether a greenhouse is a 'building' within the meaning of s 3 of the 1832 Act, and *Clifford v Holt*[1] is an express decision that it is. The defendants reserved the right to argue in this court that it was not, but they have not done so and I proceed on the basis that it is. Also, a greenhouse is not to be regarded simply as a garden under glass, but as a building with apertures, namely the glass roof and sides: see Gale on Easements[2].

Accordingly, the plaintiffs submit that they had, by the time they commenced their action, acquired a right of light to the greenhouse, and they say 'The law will protect the

---

1   [1899] 1 Ch 698
2   14th Edn (1972), p 239

dominant owner in the enjoyment of so much light as, according to the ordinary notions of mankind, he reasonably requires for all ordinary purposes for which the building is a adapted', and further that the evidence shows, as it does, that the user throughout the 20 years has been the normal and ordinary use of a greenhouse in a private garden. Therefore, they submit, they are entitled to such light as is reasonably required for the continuation of that use, as being light required for the ordinary use of that type of building. Alternatively, they say that as they have in fact so used the greenhouse for the full period of 20 years, they are entitled to such light as is required for the normal use of the b greenhouse, even though that use should be regarded as one which calls for a specially high degree of light.

The defendants, on the other hand, say that the plaintiffs are, at the least, claiming a specially high degree of light, which they cannot have because, it is submitted, one can only prescribe for light which is required for ordinary residence, or ordinary business, in the tenement in question; and they say that ordinary business means a business requiring c an ordinary amount of light, not necessarily to be measured by the business in fact being carried on there or the business for which the tenement is adapted.

But their objection goes much deeper than that, for they say that in any event one can only prescribe a right to light, whether ordinary or special in degree, for purposes of illumination, not a right to the direct rays of the sun, or to heat, or to other beneficial properties from the sun's rays. In effect they submit that the plaintiffs are out of court d because of Blackett-Ord V-C's finding, which I have read, as to the amount of light remaining in the greenhouse. They argue that the plaintiffs are not claiming light for human purposes or activities, but for its beneficial effect on the plants or, looking at it another way, for the purpose of carrying out some chemical process. By analogy with a factory or workshop they submit that there is no actionable wrong if there be enough light to enable the workman to see what he is doing, even if he is carrying out some process e which itself requires light, and there is insufficient to make it work.

The starting point for the resolution of these contending arguments must be in *Colls v Home and Colonial Stores Ltd*[1], which does, as it seems to me, establish the basic principle that the measure of the light to which right is acquired, of which it has to be seen whether there is such diminution as to cause a nuisance, is the light required for the beneficial use of the building for any ordinary purpose for which it is adapted. f

I think this emerges clearly from the speech of Lord Davey, with which Lord Robertson agreed, and from that of Lord Lindley. Lord Davey[2] approved a passage from the judgment of James LJ in *Kelk v Pearson*[3], which is in these terms:

'... I am of opinion that the statute has in no degree whatever altered the pre-existing law as to the nature and extent of this right. The nature and extent of the right before that statute was to have that amount of light through the windows of a g house which was sufficient, according to the ordinary notions of mankind, for the comfortable use and enjoyment of that house as a dwelling-house, if it were a dwelling-house, [and now come the important words] or for the beneficial use and occupation of the house, if it were a warehouse, a shop, or other place of business. That was the extent of the easement—a right to prevent your neighbour from building upon his land so as to obstruct the access of sufficient light and air, to such h an extent as to render the house substantially less comfortable and enjoyable.'

Lord Lindley approved a similar passage in the case of *City of London Brewery Co v Tennant*[4], and Lord Lindley said[5]:

1   [1904] AC 179, [1904–7] All ER Rep 5
2   [1904] AC 179 at 198–199, [1904–7] All ER Rep 5 at 17
3   (1871) LR 6 Ch App 809 at 811
4   (1873) LR 9 Ch App 212
5   [1904] AC 179 at 208, [1904–7] All ER Rep 5 at 21–22

'That doctrine, as stated in *City of London Brewery Co. v. Tennant*[1] is that generally speaking an owner of ancient lights is entitled to sufficient light according to the ordinary notions of mankind for the comfortable use and enjoyment of his house as a dwelling-house, if it is a dwelling-house, or for the beneficial use and occupation of the house if it is a warehouse, a shop, or other place of business. The expressions "the ordinary notions of mankind," "comfortable use and enjoyment," and "beneficial use and occupation" introduce elements of uncertainty; but similar uncertainty has always existed and exists still in all cases of nuisance, and in this country an obstruction of light has commonly been regarded as a nuisance, although the right to light has been regarded as a peculiar kind of easement.'

Those passages do, in my judgment, tie the measure of the light to the nature of the building and the purposes for which it is normally adapted.

Counsel for the defendants relied considerably on a dictum of Bray J in *Ambler v Gordon*[2] where he said: 'I think that the word "ordinary" is used solely with reference to light, and an ordinary user or ordinary business means a user or business which in fact requires only an ordinary amount of light', and he submits that there is only one standard, which does not vary with the type of building. That case, of course, is not binding on us, and I confess for my own part that I do not wholly understand the conception of 'an ordinary amount of light' in the abstract. It seems that what is ordinary must depend on the nature of the building and to what it is ordinarily adapted. If, therefore, the building be, as it is in this case, a greenhouse, the normal use of which requires a high degree of light, then it seems to me that that degree is ordinary light. Therefore, subject to the defendants' argument, to which I shall refer as the overriding argument, and which I shall consider later in this judgment, that the light of which the plaintiffs have been deprived is not, on the findings, required for illumination but for the process of raising and growing plants, I would hold that, in the case of a greenhouse, light required for its normal use is ordinary and is, therefore, acquired under the 1832 Act by 20 years' enjoyment.

But lest I be wrong on that, I turn to consider, still subject to the overriding argument, whether, assuming it is a specially high degree of light, the right to it is acquired by 20 years' user to the knowledge of the servient owners.

Blackett-Ord V-C said that *Ambler v Gordon*[3] is 'a clear decision that no claim of right by prescription for an extraordinary amount of light lies when the servient owner is unaware of the use being made of the dominant tenement'. That I accept and apply, but Blackett-Ord V-C went on, as I have already read, to say that there was no evidence that the owners of the servient tenement knew the precise use which was being made of it.

In my judgment, however, with all respect, that was an error. It is an irresistible inference from the photographs that the defendants and their predecessors, owners successively of the defendants' house, must have been fully aware at all times of the way in which the greenhouse was being used. As Buckley LJ said in argument, the contrary is inconceivable. There is no suggestion in this case that the greenhouse is now, or ever has been, used for any exotic purposes.

The problem, therefore, is whether a right to a specially high degree of light can be acquired by known enjoyment of that specially high degree for the full period of 20 years. Strangely enough, there is no decision on this question, although there are conflicting dicta.

The first is that of Malins V-C in *Lanfranchi v Mackenzie*[4] where he said:

'I intend to decide this case on broad general principles, and my view of the law is this, that if there be a particular user, and the quantity of light claimed for that is such as would not belong to the ordinary occupations of life, a person who claims that

---

1   (1873) LR 9 Ch App 212
2   [1905] 1 KB 417 at 422
3   [1905] 1 KB 417
4   (1867) LR 4 Eq 421 at 430

extraordinary quantity of light cannot establish his right to it unless he can shew that   *a*
he has been in the enjoyment of it for twenty years. If a man cannot establish a right
within twenty years to an ordinary quantity of light, how can he establish in a less
period the right to an extraordinary quantity? All he can establish is the right to the
quantity of light he would be entitled to for ordinary purposes. If he has been in the
enjoyment of an extraordinary user for twenty years, that would establish the right
against all persons who had reasonable knowledge of it.'

Lord Davey, however, threw some doubt on that in *Colls v Home and Colonial Stores Ltd*[1]   *b*
where he said:

'If the plaintiffs had intended to claim and rely on a special easement of that
description, it was for them to state their claim and prove the facts to support it. It is
unnecessary to say, therefore, whether such a claim would be good in law. Malins
V.-C. thought it could be sustained if the special user was had with the knowledge of   *c*
the owner of the servient tenement. I will only say that I see some difficulties in the
way, and reserve my opinion.'

In *Ambler v Gordon*[2] Bray J went further and specifically disagreed with Malins V-C,
saying: 'I am, however, prepared to go further, and to hold that even twenty years'
enjoyment to the knowledge of the servient tenement will not give a larger right.'
With all respect to Lord Davey, who after all merely reserved his opinion, and to Bray J,   *d*
I would adopt Malin V-C's dictum. It is clear that a right to a greater degree of light than
such as is normally obtained by prescription could be the subject of a valid grant, and in my
judgment, therefore, it is capable of being acquired by prescription. That being so,
provided it is enjoyed for the full period of 20 years to the knowledge of the servient
owners, I fail to see any ground on which it should be held not to have been acquired by   *e*
prescription.
Of course, where the operation which needs special light is carried on indoors it may be
very difficult in fact to prove sufficiently precise knowledge, but here the user was
completely obvious. Blackett-Ord V-C decided this point against the plaintiffs, as I have
already observed, on the ground that there was no evidence that the owners of the servient
tenement knew the precise use which was being made of the greenhouse, but, with all   *f*
respect to him, in my judgment the evidence was amply sufficient to prove knowledge,
and sufficient knowledge.
In my opinion, therefore, the crux of this case at the end of the day is the overriding
argument, which I must now consider.
The defendants argue on this as follows. (1) In *Colls v Home and Colonial Stores Ltd*[3] the
House of Lords was seeking to limit, or restrict, the extent of the right to light, so as to
prevent undue restrictions on the development or improvement of surrounding land or   *g*
buildings, and the court should be very chary of any extension of the right. (2) Although
the standards prescribed by the speeches in *Colls'* case[3] are expressed in terms susceptible of
a wider interpretation, in their context they must be taken as referring to illumination
only. (3) In all cases, at least since *Colls's*[3], the right to light has been tested or measured in
terms of illumination only. They refer, for example, to Mr Waldram's calculations and the
theory of the 'grumble point' (see *Charles Semon & Co v Bradford Corpn*[4]) and to *Hortons'*   *h*
Estate Ltd v James Beattie Ltd[5], where the question was whether the extent of the right to
light should vary according to locality, and Russell J said[6]: 'The human eye requires as
much light for comfortable reading and sewing in Darlington Street, Wolverhampton, as

---

1   [1904] AC 179 at 203–204, [1904–7] All ER Rep 5 at 19
2   [1905] 1 KB 417 at 424
3   [1904] AC 179, [1904–7] All ER Rep 5
4   [1922] 2 Ch 737
5   [1927] 1 Ch 75
6   [1927] 1 Ch 75 at 78

j

in Mayfair.' Junior counsel for the defendants, in his supporting argument, referred also
a to *Warren v Brown*[1], where the test was stated to be 'All ordinary purposes of inhabitancy
or business', and to the test applied by this court in *Ough v King*[2]: 'Ordinary notions of
contemporary mankind.' These, however, I think, are at best neutral and possibly tell the
other way, since a greenhouse is perfectly normal and ordinary in private gardens. So far
as the last case is concerned, however, junior counsel relied on the fact that this court
approved of the county court judge having had a view, which again, he suggests, points to
b illumination as the test, though that I take leave to doubt. (4) In no case since *Colls's*[3] has
the right to light been established, save on the basis of what is required for illumination.
That is true, but in *Lazarus v Artistic Photographic Co*[4] Kekewich J expressly extended the
right to light for photography, which is not simply illumination but extra light required
to effect a chemical process. That case was wrongly decided, because he held that such a
right could be acquired though the special light required for the purpose had been enjoyed
c for part only of the 20 years, but nevertheless it has, I think, some value as a negation of the
defendants' argument. Moreover, in *Colls's* case[5] itself Lord Davey instanced a photographic
studio. True, he was there saying that one could not increase the burden on the servient
tenement by changing over to such user within the 20 years, but at least he clearly
envisaged a claim to light for such a purpose as a possibility. (5) A distinction must be
drawn between the heat and other properties of the sun and the light which emanates from
d it, and the defendants say that, having regard to Blackett-Ord V-C's findings, the only
complaint that the plaintiffs can have is loss of heat or radiant properties, and they postulate
the example of a swimming pool, part of which is fortuitously warmed by sunlight
coming through a south window. They say, and I have no doubt rightly, that the owners
could have no cause of action against one who, whilst leaving fully adequate light for the
complete enjoyment of the swimming pool, so shaded the sun as to deprive it of this
e chance warmth. That, I think, is a very different case from the present. (6) In reality or in
substance the injury here is not deprivation of light, but of heat or other energising
properties of the sun and it is the plant life and not the human beings who are deprived.

I do not think this last point is in any case wholly accurate, as plants need light as well
as heat, but it seems to me, with all respect to Blackett-Ord V-C and to counsel, to lead to
an absurd conclusion. It cannot, I think, be right to say that there is no nuisance because
f one can see to go in and out of a greenhouse and to pot plants which will not flourish, and
to pick fruit which cannot properly be developed and ripened, still less because one can see
to read a book.

The plaintiffs answer all this simply by submitting that they are entitled, by virtue of
their prescriptive right to light, to all the benefits of the light, including the rays of the
sun. Warmth, they say, is an inseparable product of daylight, and they stress the absurd
g conclusion which I have already mentioned, to which the contrary argument inevitably
leads. This reply commends itself to me, and I adopt it.

So the overriding argument, in my judgment, does not prevail, and for the reasons I
have already given the plaintiffs are right, both on their primary and their alternative case,
and I would allow this appeal.

Subject to any observations of Buckley and Orr LJJ or of counsel, I would grant an
h injunction on the following lines: restraining the defendants by themselves, their servants,
contractors, workmen or otherwise from continuing to keep the caravan and fence in such
a position on the defendants' property as to obstruct or diminish the access of light to the
southerly and south-easterly walls and glass roof of the said greenhouse to such an extent
as to cause a nuisance. Secondly, a mandatory order that the defendants do forthwith

j
---
1   [1900] 2 QB 722 at 725
2   [1967] 3 All ER 859, [1967] 1 WLR 1547
3   [1904] AC 179, [1904–7] All ER Rep 5
4   [1897] 2 Ch 214
5   [1904] AC 179 at 203, [1904–7] All ER Rep 5 at 19

remove the said caravan and fence from such a position as so to obstruct or diminish the access of light to the said southerly and south-easterly glass walls and glass roof of the said   *a* greenhouse.

I desire, however, to add one important safeguarding proviso to this judgment. On other facts, particularly where one has solar heating (although that may not arise for some years) it may be possible and right to separate the heat, or some other property of the sun, from its light, and in such a case a different result might be reached. I leave that entirely open for decision when it arises. My judgment in this case is based on the fact that this was   *b* a perfectly ordinary greenhouse, being used in a perfectly normal and ordinary manner, which user has, by the defendants' acts, been rendered substantially less beneficial than it was throughout the period of upwards of 20 years before action brought, and if necessary on the fact that all this was known to the respondents and their predecessors for the whole of the relevant time.

c

ORR LJ. I agree that this appeal should be allowed for the reasons given by Goff LJ, and I too would reserve for a case in which they require a decision the problems which may arise in relation to solar heating.

BUCKLEY LJ. I entirely agree with the judgment which has been delivered by Goff LJ; I only add some observations of my own, first, because we are differing from Blackett-Ord   *d* V-C and secondly because this is a point which has not hitherto been directly covered by authority and it is one which may have a fairly wide application, for the number of domestic greenhouses in this country must be very large.

It is unnecessary for me to recapitulate the facts or restate the nature of the argument which has been presented to us; those matters have already been fully covered by Goff LJ in the judgment which he has delivered.   *e*

The authority which must now be regarded as the leading case on this topic is undoubtedly the decision of the House of Lords in *Colls v Home and Colonial Stores Ltd*[1], from which I think the following formulation of the principle can be distilled: the amount of light to which a dominant owner is entitled under a prescriptive claim is sufficient light, according to ordinary notions, for the comfortable or beneficial use of the building in question, again according to ordinary notions, for such purposes as would constitute   *f* normal uses of a building of its particular character. If the building be a dwelling-house, the measure must be related to reasonable standards of comfort as a dwelling-house. If it be a warehouse, a shop or a factory, the measure must be related to reasonable standards of comfort or beneficial use (for comfort may not be the most appropriate test in the case of such a building) as a warehouse, a shop or a factory as the case may be. These may very probably differ from the standards which would apply to a dwelling-house. If the building   *g* be a greenhouse, the measure must in my opinion be related to its reasonably satisfactory use as a greenhouse.

In the present case the plaintiffs have not used their greenhouse otherwise than for such purposes as a domestic greenhouse would normally be used for, purposes for which domestic greenhouses have been used for many generations. Accordingly, no question arises of their claiming an amount of light which would be extraordinary for a   *h* greenhouse. It is true that the satisfactory use of a greenhouse may require a freer access of light than a room in a dwelling-house, just as the comfortable use of a dwelling-house may require more light than the satisfactory use of a warehouse; but this, in my view, is of no significance. It would be in my judgment, and with deference to those who have suggested otherwise, be ridiculous to say that a greenhouse had enough light because a man could read a newspaper there with reasonable comfort. A north light may be very   *j* good for an artist's studio and may do very well for a sitting room in a dwelling-house, but may be quite inadequate for a greenhouse.

1   [1904] AC 179, [1904–7] All ER Rep 5

Counsel for the defendants have developed an interesting and ingenious argument to
a the effect that all reported cases on easements of light relate exclusively to the use of light
for purposes of illumination, whereas, as they say, in a greenhouse light is used not merely
for illumination but for its chemical effects on the plants in the greenhouse. It is true that
we have been referred to only one case relating to a greenhouse, *Clifford v Holt*[1], in which
Kekewich J held that a greenhouse was a building for the purposes of the Prescription Act
1832. It had been in existence for more than 25 years. It was not suggested in that case
b that the use of the light in a greenhouse had any special characteristic which might exclude
it from ordinary considerations applying to easements of light, although it was argued that
a greenhouse was not ejusdem generis with a dwelling-house or workshop. Of course,
where illumination has been the sole or predominant significance of the light, it is natural
that no reference has been made to other possible aspects of its enjoyment. It seems to me
that in the case of a dwelling-house it might well be argued (I do not say with what degree
c of success, for this must depend on expert evidence) that adequate light was important not
only for illumination but also for health and hygiene. I feel unable to accept this argument
of the defendants' counsel. In my judgment it involves an unjustified and undesirable
qualification of the principle which, as I have indicated, has in my view been established
by the authority of *Colls v Home and Colonial Stores Ltd*[2].
Prescription, in accordance with that principle, is not dependant on actual use but on
d enjoyment for the prescriptive period of the ability to enjoy the measure of light indicated
by the formula. So it is not dependent on the servient owner's knowing what actual use
the dominant owner is making of the building. This is not inconsistent with the dominant
owner's obtaining by prescription a right to an extraordinary amount of light requisite for
a particular use of the dominant tenement if the servient owner has throughout the
prescriptive period been aware that the dominant owner has throughout that period been
e using the dominant tenement in that way, provided, no doubt, that the enjoyment of light
for that particular use has not been permissive.
If, contrary to my primary view, a right to the access of such light to a domestic
greenhouse as is necessary for successful cultivation of the kinds of plants normally
cultivated in such a greenhouse is not capable of being acquired by prescription as a right
to an ordinary amount of light, can it be acquired as an extraordinary amount of light? I
f feel no doubt that such a right could be acquired by express grant. Why, I ask, should such
a right not be acquired by a presumed grant or by prescription? There appears to be no
decisive authority on the point.
In *Lanfranchi v Mackenzie*[3], Malins V-C expressed the view, obiter, that 20 years' use for
a special purpose would establish a claim to an extraordinary amount of light against all
who had knowledge of such use. In *Colls v Home and Colonial Stores Ltd*[2], Lord Davey
g approved the decision in *Lanfranchi v Mackenzie*[4], but reserved his opinion on prescription
to an extraordinary amount of light. Lord Lindley said[5]:

'The decision in *Kelk v. Pearson*[6] has a far-reaching effect. If there is no absolute
right to all the light which comes to a given window, no action will lie for an
obstruction of that light unless the obstruction amounts to a nuisance. If there is no
right of action, a fortiori there is no right to an injunction to prevent a permanent
h diminution of light unless it amounts to a nuisance. But, in considering what is an
actionable nuisance, regard is had, not to special circumstances which cause something
to be an annoyance to a particular person, but to the habits and requirements of

---

j 1   [1899] 1 Ch 698
2   [1904] AC 179, [1904–7] All ER Rep 5
3   (1867) LR 4 Eq 421 at 430
4   LR 4 Eq 421
5   [1904] AC 179 at 209, [1904–7] All ER Rep 5 at 22
6   (1867) LR 6 Ch App 809

ordinary people, and it is by no means to be taken for granted that a person who wants an extraordinary amount of light for a particular business can maintain an action for a diminution of light if only his special requirements are interfered with.'

That seems to me to be a carefully guarded statement on the part of Lord Lindley.

After *Lanfranchi v Mackenzie*[1], but before *Colls v Home and Colonial Stores Ltd*[2], Kekewich J had held in *Lazarus v Artistic Photographic Co*[3] that a photographer was entitled to protection of an extraordinary amount of light for his business, although he had not enjoyed it for as much as 20 years. That decision could not now, I think, be upheld, because of lack of enjoyment of the extraordinary amount of light for a sufficient period. In *Warren v Brown*[4], Wright J had to consider a case in which a building had been used for a purpose requiring an extraordinary amount of light for less than the statutory prescriptive period. He held that the plaintiff was not entitled to protection of an extraordinary amount of light in those circumstances.

In *Ambler v Gordon*[5], decided after the decision of the House of Lords in *Colls v Home and Colonial Stores Ltd*[2], Bray J had to deal with office premises which seem to have been suitable for any normal kind of office use, but had in fact been used in part by an architect as a drawing office and in part by a cloth merchant for examining and matching cloth, both uses which required exceptionally good light. There was no evidence that the occupiers of the servient tenements were aware of these special uses. Bray J said[6]:

'First, what is meant by the expressions which are to be found in this special case and in the judgments in *Colls' Case*[2]—"ordinary user," or "ordinary business," or "ordinary purposes"? I think that the word "ordinary" is used solely with reference to light, and an ordinary user or ordinary business means a user or business which in fact requires only an ordinary amount of light.'

With regard to that citation I would associate myself with what Goff LJ has said in the judgment that he has just delivered. Bray J said[7]: 'I am, however, prepared to go further, and to hold that even twenty years' enjoyment to the knowledge of the servient tenement will not give a larger right.' That observation was obiter, but was supported by reference to a passage in Lord Davey's speech in *Colls v Home and Colonial Stores Ltd*[8], in which Lord Davey had said:

'If the actual user is not the test where the use falls below the standard of what may reasonably be required for the ordinary uses of inhabitancy and business, why (it may be asked) should it be made a test where the use has been of a special or extraordinary character in excess of that standard?'

But it must be borne in mind that Lord Davey expressly reserved his opinion on that point in the course of his speech.

We have been referred to no other relevant authority or observation. Accordingly there is, I think, no decision directly in point.

In the case of an easement of way, the extent of the use to which a claim can be established, whether on foot only or with animals or vehicles, depends, whether under the doctrine of lost grant or prescription, on the nature of the user which has been enjoyed as of right for a sufficient period. By analogous reasoning it seems to me that the same principle should apply to an easement of light. If in any case it could be shown that a use

1 (1867) LR 4 Eq 421
2 [1904] AC 179, [1904–7] All ER Rep 5
3 [1897] 2 Ch 214
4 [1900] 2 QB 722
5 [1905] 1 KB 417
6 [1905] 1 KB 417 at 421–422
7 [1905] 1 KB 417 at 424
8 [1904] AC 179 at 203, [1904–7] All ER Rep 5 at 19

of the dominant tenement for a period and in circumstances justifying the implication of
a a lost grant has been such as to make an exceptional amount of light necessary for the
particular use to which the tenement has been put, I can see no reason why a lost grant of
such an exceptional amount of light should not be presumed. If in any case it can be
shown that there has been such a use of the dominant tenement for 20 years or upwards
before action brought, I see no reason why a prescriptive right should not be obtained in
respect of the dominant tenement to such an exceptional amount of light as may be
b necessary to the satisfactory enjoyment of that use; but the use, to demonstrate a claim as
of right to the exceptional amount of light, must be one which, according to ordinary
notions, reasonably requires such an exceptional amount of light and must be known at all
material times to the occupier of the servient tenement. Whether the use must be
continuous thoughout the period is not a question which arises in the present case, for it
is not disputed that in this case the greenhouse has been used by the occupiers of the
c plaintiffs' house as an ordinary domestic greenhouse throughout the 20 year period.

Accordingly, I agree with Goff LJ that if the plaintiffs' claim is not good on the basis of
the ordinary use of light for a building of the character of a greenhouse, it succeeds as a
claim to an extraordinary amount of light enjoyed as of right to the knowledge of the
occupiers from time to time of the defendants' house, throughout the period of upwards
of 20 years before action brought.

d For these reasons, in addition to all the reasons which have been developed by Goff LJ in
his judgment, I would allow this appeal.

Appeal allowed. Leave to appeal to House of Lords refused.

Solicitors: *Blackhurst, Parker & Yates,* Lancaster (for the plaintiffs); *Brierley & Hudson,*
e Rochdale (for the defendants).

J H Fazan Esq   Barrister.

f # Practice Direction

FAMILY DIVISION

Divorce – Consent applications – Divorce Registry – Procedure – Periodical payments direct to
child.

g
Where a consent summons or notice of application seeks an order which includes agreed
terms for periodical payments direct to a child in excess of the amounts qualifying for the
time being as 'small maintenance payments' under s 65 of the Income and Corporation
Taxes Act 1970, it is no longer necessary for the solicitor to certify whether the child is or
is not living with the party who will be making the payments under the proposed terms.

h Paragraph 2 of the Registrar's Direction of 22nd December 1975[1] is accordingly hereby
cancelled.

R L BAYNE-POWELL
5th March 1979   Senior Registrar.

1   [1976] 1 All ER 272, [1976] 1 WLR 74

Re Green (a bankrupt), ex parte Official Receiver v Cutting and others

CHANCERY DIVISION
WALTON J
26th, 27th JUNE, 4th JULY 1978

Bankruptcy – Effect on antecedent transactions – Protection of bona fide transactions made without notice – Attachment of earnings order made against judgment debtor – Money deducted by employer from judgment debtor's earnings and paid into court – Money not distributed to creditors by court – Receiving order made against judgment debtor – Whether attachment of earnings order constituting assignment to creditors of money deducted by employer – Whether payment into court constituting protected transaction – Bankruptcy Act 1914, s 45 – Attachment of Earnings Act 1971, s 13(1).

On 21st June 1977 a consolidated attachment of earnings order was made, under the Attachment of Earnings Act 1971, against the debtor in favour of four judgment creditors, requiring the debtor's employer to make the specified deductions from his earnings and pay them into court monthly. Under s 13(1)[a] of the 1971 Act, sums paid under an attachment of earnings order were to be dealt with as if they had been paid by the debtor to satisfy the relevant judgment. In the case of a consolidated order, it was the practice of the county court to accumulate the sums paid in until it had sufficient money to declare a dividend. In accordance with the order, the debtor's employer made the required monthly payments into court on 1st July, 5th August, 5th September and 3rd October. The court accumulated the money and no distribution had been made when, on 3rd October, a receiving order was made against the debtor, founded on an act of bankruptcy committed on 1st July. On 17th October the debtor was adjudicated bankrupt. The Official Receiver, relying on ss 18, 37 and 38 of the Bankruptcy Act 1914, applied for a declaration that the money held by the court to the credit of the judgment creditors belonged to the debtor's estate and should be paid to the Official Receiver as his trustee in bankruptcy. The judgment creditors contended that the undistributed money belonged to them because the making of an attachment of earnings order created an assignment of the money deducted by an employer, and conferred on a judgment creditor in whose favour the order was made a proprietary interest in the money so deducted from the date of the order. The Official Receiver submitted that no assignment was created by the order and that a judgment creditor did not obtain any proprietary interest in the money deducted by an employer until the money was paid out to him.

Held – An order made under the 1971 Act did not effect an assignment to the judgment creditor of the moneys to which the order referred, but directly the money deducted by the employer was paid into court it was held to the order of the judgment creditor. Since on the facts the judgment creditors had no notice of any act of bankruptcy when the payments into court were made on 5th August and 5th September, those transactions were protected by s 45[b] of the 1914 Act and those payments, together with that made before the act of bankruptcy on 1st July, belonged to the judgment creditors. The last payment in, on 3rd

---

a   Section 13(1) is set out at p 837 g to j, post

b   Section 45, so far as material, provides: '. . . nothing in this Act shall invalidate, in the case of a bankruptcy—(a) Any payment by the bankrupt to any of his creditors . . . Provided that both the following conditions are complied with, namely—(i) that the payment . . . [or] assignment . . . takes place before the date of the receiving order; and (ii) that the person (other than the debtor) to . . . whom the payment . . . [or] assignment . . . was made . . . has not at the time of the payment . . . [or] assignment . . . notice of any available act of bankruptcy committed by the bankrupt before that time.'

a
October, belonged to the Official Receiver as the debtor's trustee because it was not made before the date of the receiving order (see p 835 g, p 843 h j, p 844 e to h, p 845 b to g and p 846 a to e, post).

Notes

For transactions before receiving order and protected transactions within the period of relation back, see 3 Halsbury's Laws (4th Edn) paras 379, 662.

b
For the Attachment of Earnings Act 1971, s 13, see 41 Halsbury's Statutes (3rd Edn) 804.
For the Bankruptcy Act 1914, ss 18, 37, 38, 45, see 3 Halsbury's Statutes (3rd Edn) 60, 87, 97.

Cases referred to in judgment

Collins, Re, [1925] Ch 556, [1925] All ER Rep 215, 95 LJ Ch 55, 133 LT 479, [1925] B & CR
c   90, 5 Digest (Reissue) 827, 6940.
De Marney, Re, Official Receiver v Salaman [1943] 1 All ER 275, [1943] Ch 126, 112 LJ Ch
125, 168 LT 217, 5 Digest (Reissue) 748, 6395.
Jones, Re, ex parte Nichols (1883) 22 Ch D 782, [1881–5] All ER Rep 170, 52 LJ Ch 635, 48
LT 492, CA, 5 Digest (Reissue) 747, 6393.
King v Michael Faraday and Partners Ltd [1939] 2 All ER 478, [1939] 2 KB 753, 108 LJKB
d   589, 160 LT 484, 4 Digest (Reissue) 407, 3586.
Lewis v Madocks (1803) 8 Ves 150, 32 ER 310; *subsequent proceedings* (1810) 17 Ves 48, 34 ER
19, LC, 40 Digest (Repl) 537, 482.
Pollard (H E) Re, ex parte S R Pollard [1903] 2 KB 41, 72 LJKB 509, 88 LT 652, 10 Mans 152,
CA, 5 Digest (Reissue) 875, 7268.
Tailby v Official Receiver (1888) 13 App Cas 523, [1886–90] All ER Rep 486, 58 LJQB 75, 60
e   LT 162, HL, 5 Digest (Reissue) 747, 6391.
Wilmot v Alton [1896] 2 QB 254, 65 LJQB 669; *affd* [1897] 1 QB 17, [1895–9] All ER Rep
188, 66 LJQB 42, 75 LT 447, 4 Mans 17, CA, 5 Digest (Reissue) 747, 6389.

Cases also cited

f
Combined Weighing and Advertising Machine Co, Re, (1890) 43 Ch D 99, [1886–90] All ER Rep
1044, CA.
Curran v Newpark Cinemas Ltd [1951] 1 All ER 295, CA.
Curtoys, Re, ex parte Pillers (1881) 17 Ch D 653, [1881–5] All ER Rep 723, CA.
Ford, Re, ex parte the trustee [1900] 2 QB 211.
George v Tompson's Trustee [1949] 1 All ER 554, [1949] Ch 322.
g
Gordon, Re, ex parte Navalchand [1897] 2 QB 516.
O'Shea's Settlement, Re, Courage v O'Shea [1895] 1 Ch 325, [1891–4] All ER Rep 935, CA.
Overseas Aviation Engineering (GB) Ltd, Re, [1962] 3 All ER 12, [1963] Ch 24, CA.
Roberts, Re, [1900] 1 QB 122, CA.
Wild v Southwood [1897] 1 QB 317, [1895–9] All ER Rep 1193.

h
Special case stated

The Official Receiver applied to the Ipswich County Court for (1) a declaration that the sum of £102·35 held by that court to the credit of the respondents, Frederick Forby Cutting, David Henry Johnson, D B Warehouses Ltd, and Ipswich Co-operative Society Ltd, pursuant to attachment of earnings orders culminating in Attachment of Earnings Order No 11 of 1977, was, and had at all times, been the property of the Official Receiver as
j trustee of Bernard John Green, a bankrupt, pursuant to ss 18, 37 and 38 of the Bankruptcy Act 1914; and (2) an order that the £102·35 be paid out to the Official Receiver. During the proceedings, his Honour Judge David Stinson was requested to state a special case for the opinion of the High Court, pursuant to s 100(3) of the Bankruptcy Act 1914. The terms of the special case are set out in the judgment.

Edward Evans-Lombe QC for the Official Receiver.
Simon Mortimore for the third and fourth respondents.
The first and second respondents were not represented.

a

Cur adv vult

b

4th July. **WALTON J** read the following judgment: This matter is a case stated by his
Honour Judge David Stinson in the Ipswich County Court for the opinion of the High
Court, pursuant to s 100(3) of the Bankruptcy Act 1914, raising a question of law as to the
application of the Attachment of Earnings Act 1971.

The facts are admirably summarised in the case stated, and I cannot do better than read
it as it stands:

c

'1. On 2nd March 1973, under the provisions of the Attachments of Earnings Act
1971, and the rules applicable . . . an Attachment of Earnings Order D.409 was made
against Bernard John Green at the request of a Creditor, Frederick Forby Cutting, in
the total sum of £184, payable at the rate of £1·00 a week. 2. Mr Cutting then
applied for another Attachment of Earnings on a later judgment, and on 18th
February 1975 the Attachment of Earnings Order referred to above was discharged.
Three actions between the parties were consolidated, and a New Attachment of
Earnings Order, G46, was made. The total judgment debt of £602·29 was to be paid
at the rate of £4 a week for 3 months and then £5 a week. By County Court Order
25 rule 83 the employer, although making weekly deductions, was to account to the
Court at monthly intervals. 3. On 2nd March 1977 an Attachment of Earnings
Order J40 was made in respect of a judgment debt due to D B Warehouses Limited.
£42·91 was to be paid by weekly deductions of £0·75 payable monthly. 4. On 20th
April 1977 an Attachment of Earnings Order J110 was made in respect of a judgment
debt of £61·47 due to David Henry Johnson. The weekly deduction was £1 payable
monthly. 5. On 21st June 1977, Ipswich Co-operative Society Limited, a judgment
creditor for £29·12 applied for consolidation of that debt with the existing orders,
under S. 17 of the Act and Order 25 rule 90. 6. On 21st June 1977 a Consolidated
Attachment of Earnings Order Number 11 of 1977 was issued. The four creditors
were:—F F CUTTING, D B WAREHOUSES LIMITED, D H JOHNSON, IPSWICH CO-OPERATIVE
SOCIETY LIMITED, the total amount due was £581·49, the weekly deductions, by the
employer, were £6·75 payable to the Court monthly. 7. S. 13(1) of the Act provides
that sums paid in under an Attachment of Earnings Order shall be dealt with as if they
had been paid by the debtor to satisfy the relevant adjudication. 8. Prior to 21st June
1977 money received under the Orders would be credited to the particular action and
paid out to the judgment creditor on the first payment day after receipt. 9. Once a
Consolidated Order has been made, County Court Order 25 rule 90(9) authorises the
Registrar to apply money received under such an order by dividing it among the
creditors included in the Order in proportion to the amounts payable "and for that
purpose dividends may from time to time" be declared and distributed among the
creditors entitled thereto. 10. It is the practice at Ipswich County Court to accumulate
sufficient money to declare a minimum dividend of 10 pence in the pound. 11. Each
monthly instalment received by the Court consists of the sum of individual deductions
made by the Employer during the preceding 4–5 weeks. 12. By 3rd October 1977
the sum of £107·75 had accumulated in the account of the Consolidated Attachment
of Earnings Order Number 11 of 1977. The four creditors listed in paragraph 7 were
the only persons entitled to share in any money credited to that account unless and
until the Court made any alteration to the terms of the Order. 13. The dates and
amount of payments received by the Court to 3rd October 1977 under the
Consolidated Order are:—

d

e

f

g

h

j

'1977
 1st July   £20·00
 5th August   £33·75
 5th September   £27·00
 3rd October   £22·00

                     £107·75

'As at 3rd October 1977, no distribution had been made. 14. On 3rd June 1977 a Bankruptcy Notice was issued in the Ipswich County Court against B J Green, at the request of Home Insulation Limited, a judgment creditor for £268·92. It was served on 24th June 1977. 15. On 18th August 1977 a Bankruptcy Petition was issued in the Ipswich County Court, founded on non compliance with the Bankruptcy Notice. 16. On 3rd October 1977 a Receiving Order was made against Bernard John Green and on the 17th October 1977 the debtor was adjudged bankrupt. The Official Receiver is the trustee. 17. It is the contention of the Official Receiver in Bankruptcy, relying on Ss 18, 37 and 38 of the Bankruptcy Act 1914, that the money at present in Court belongs to the Bankrupt's Estate and should be paid out to the Official Receiver. 18. It is contended by the Creditors listed in the Consolidated Attachment of Earnings Order that the money in Court, although undistributed, belongs to them and should be dealt with accordingly. 19. High Court is asked to decide which of the rival contentions is correct in law.'

The first question which arises is: what is the precise effect of the making of an order for the attachment of earnings under the 1971 Act? One possibility is that it creates an assignment of the moneys deducted by the employer pursuant to the order under the Act, vesting a proprietary interest in the moneys so deducted in the judgment creditor in whose favour the order is made from the date of the order. This is the view favoured by counsel who appeared on behalf of the third and fourth respondents, the first two respondents being unrepresented. The other view is that no assignment is created by the order, and that the first time that the judgment creditor obtains any proprietary interest in the moneys deducted by the employer is when those moneys are paid out to him. The corollary is that as regards any moneys which have not been so paid out to the judgment creditor at the date to which the trustee's title under s 37 of the Bankruptcy Act 1914 relates back will vest in the trustee. It will be observed that in the present case the relevant act of bankruptcy was failure to comply with a bankruptcy notice dated 3rd June but served on 24th June 1977. The act of bankruptcy was therefore committed at the last moment of 1st July, but at some time earlier during that day the first of the four payments referred to in para 13 of the case stated had been made, and obviously the moneys had actually been deducted even earlier. In these circumstances counsel for the Official Receiver did not press any claim to these moneys.

The first enquiry therefore is, what does the 1971 Act itself say about attachment orders? This is to be found in the following provisions of the Act as amended.

Section 1 provides:

'(1) The High Court may make an attachment of earnings order to secure payments under a High Court maintenance order.

'(2) A county court may make an attachment of earnings order to secure—(a) payments under a High Court or a county court maintenance order: (b) the payment of a judgment debt, other than a debt of less than £5 or such other sum as may be prescribed by county court rules; or (c) payments under an administration order . . . [Then sub-s (3) deals with the magistrates' court.]

'(4) The following provisions of this Act apply, except where otherwise stated, to attachment of earnings orders made, or to be made, by any court.

'(5) Any power conferred by this Act to make an attachment of earnings order includes a power to make such an order to secure the discharge of liabilities arising before the coming into force of this Act.'   *a*

Section 2 provides:

'... (*d*) "the relevant adjudication", in relation to any payment secured or to be secured by an attachment of earnings order, means the conviction, judgment, order or other adjudication from which there arises the liability to make the payment; and (*e*) "the debtor", in relation to an attachment of earnings order, or to proceedings in *b* which a court has power to make an attachment of earnings order, or to proceedings arising out of such an order, means the person by whom payment is required by the relevant adjudication to be made.'

Section 3 provides:

'(1) The following persons may apply for an attachment of earnings order:—(*a*) the person to whom payment under the relevant adjudication is required to be made *c* (whether directly or through an officer of any court)...

'(3) For an attachment of earnings order to be made on the application of any person other than the debtor it must appear to the court that the debtor has failed to make one or more payments required by the relevant adjudication...'

Section 6 provides: *d*

'(1) An attachment of earnings order shall be an order directed to a person who appears to the court to have the debtor in his employment and shall operate as an instruction to that person—(*a*) to make periodical deductions from the debtor's earnings in accordance with Part I of Schedule 3 to this Act; and (*b*) at such times as the order may require, or as the court may allow, to pay the amounts deducted to the collecting officer of the court, as specified in the order.   *e*

'(2) For the purposes of this Act, the relationship of employer and employee shall be treated as subsisting between two persons if one of them, as a principal and not as a servant or agent, pays to the other any sums defined as earnings by section 24 of this Act.

'(3) An attachment of earnings order shall contain prescribed particulars enabling the debtor to be identified by the employer.   *f*

'(4) Except where it is made to secure maintenance payments, the order shall specify the whole amount payable under the relevant adjudication (or so much of that amount as remains unpaid), including any relevant costs.

'(5) The order shall specify—(*a*) the normal deduction rate, that is to say, the rate (expressed as a sum of money per week, month or other period) at which the court thinks it reasonable for the debtor's earnings to be applied to meeting his liability *g* under the relevant adjudication; and (*b*) the protected earnings rate, that is to say the rate (so expressed) below which, having regard to the debtor's resources and needs, the court thinks it reasonable that the earnings actually paid to him should not be reduced...

'(7) For the purposes of an attachment of earnings order, the collecting officer of the court shall be (subject to later variation of the order under section 9 of this *h* Act)... (*b*) in the case of an order made by a county court, the appropriate officer of that court...

'(8) In subsection (7) above "appropriate officer" means an officer designated by the Lord Chancellor.'

Section 7 provides: *j*

'(1) Where an attachment of earnings order has been made, the employer shall, if he has been served with the order, comply with it; but he shall be under no liability for non-compliance before seven days have elapsed since the service.

'(2) Where a person is served with an attachment of earnings order directed to him and he has not the debtor in his employment, or the debtor subsequently ceases to be in his employment, he shall (in either case), within ten days from the date of service or, as the case may be, the cesser, give notice of that fact to the court.

'(3) Part II of Schedule 3 to this Act shall have effect with respect to the priority to be accorded as between two or more attachment of earnings orders directed to a person in respect of the same debtor.' (We are not in fact here concerned with priority.)

Section 8 provides:

'(2) Where a county court has made an attachment of earnings order to secure the payment of a judgment debt—(a) no order or warrant of commitment shall be issued in consequence of any proceedings for the enforcement of the debt begun before the making of the attachment of earnings order; and (b) so long as the order is in force, no execution for the recovery of the debt shall issue against any property of the debtor without the leave of the county court . . .

'(4) An attachment of earnings order made to secure the payment of a judgment debt shall cease to have effect on the making of an order of commitment or the issue of a warrant of commitment for the enforcement of the debt . . .'

Section 9 provides:

'(1) The court may make an order discharging or varying an attachment of earnings order.

'(2) Where an order is varied, the employer shall, if he has been served with notice of the variation, comply with the order as varied; but he shall be under no liability for non-compliance before seven days have elapsed since the service.

'(3) Rules of court may make provision—(a) as to the circumstances in which an attachment of earnings order may be varied or discharged by the court of its own motion; (b) in the case of an attachment of earnings order made by a magistrates' court . . . [and that does not apply.]

'(4) Where an attachment of earnings order has been made and the person to whom it is directed ceases to have the debtor in his employment, the order shall lapse (except as respects deduction from earnings paid after the cesser and payment to the collecting officer of amounts deducted at any time) and be of no effect unless and until the court again directs it to a person (whether the same as before or another) who appears to the court to have the debtor in his employment.

'(5) The lapse of an order under subsection (4) above shall not prevent its being treated as remaining in force for other purposes . . .'

Section 13 provides:

'(1) Subject to subsection (3) below, the collecting officer to whom a person makes payments in compliance with an attachment of earnings order shall, after deducting such court fees, if any, in respect of proceedings for or arising out of the order, as are deductible from those payments, deal with the sums paid in the same way as he would if they had been paid by the debtor to satisfy the relevant adjudication.

'(2) Any sums paid to the collecting officer under an attachment of earnings order made to secure maintenance payments . . . [and that does not apply.]

'(3) Where a county court makes an attachment of earnings order to secure the payment of a judgment debt and also, under section 4(1) of this Act, orders the debtor to furnish to the court a list of all his creditors, sums paid to the collecting officer in compliance with the attachment of earnings order shall not be dealt with by him as mentioned in subsection (1) above, but shall be retained by him pending the decision of the court whether or not to make an administration order and shall then be dealt with by him as the court may direct.'

Section 17 provides:

'(1) The powers of a county court under sections 1 and 3 of this Act shall include power to make an attachment of earnings order to secure the payment of any number of judgment debts; and the powers of the magistrates' court . . . [and that does not apply.]   *a*

'(2) An attachment of earnings order made by virtue of this section shall be known as a consolidated attachment order.

'(3) The power to make a consolidated attachment order shall be exercised subject to and in accordance with rules of court; and rules made for the purposes of this section may provide—(a) for the transfer from one court to another—(i) of an   *b* attachment of earnings order . . .' [and various other ancillary reliefs which are not relevant.]

Section 23 provides:

'(2) Subject to this section, a person commits an offence if—(a) being required by section 7(1) or 9(2) of this Act to comply with an attachment of earnings order, he fails   *c* to do so . . .

'(3) Where a person commits an offence under subsection (2) above in relation to proceedings in, or to an attachment of earnings order made by, the High Court or a county court, he shall be liable on summary conviction to a fine of not more than £25 or he may be ordered by a judge of the High Court or the county court judge (as the case may be) to pay a fine of not more than £25 or, in the case of an offence   *d* specified in subsection (4) below, to be imprisoned for not more than fourteen days; and where a person commits an offence under subsection (2) otherwise than as mentioned above in this subsection, he shall be liable on summary conviction to a fine of not more than £25 . . .

'(6) Where a person is convicted or dealt with for an offence under subsection (2)(a), the court may order him to pay, to whoever is the collecting officer of the court for   *e* the purposes of the attachment of earnings order in question, any sums deducted by that person from the debtor's earnings and not already paid to the collecting officer.'

The relevant rules are CCR Ord 25, rr 77–94. The form of the order is prescribed by r 86(1) and Form 405. I observe in passing that that form, applicable to judgment debts, does not, as does Form 407, applicable to maintenance, include, as it should do under   *f* s 6(5)(b) of the 1971 Act, details of the protected earnings rate.

Rule 89 deals with variation and discharge of the order by the court of its own motion, and sub-r (7) thereof reads as follows:

'Where it appears to the court that a receiving order or an order of adjudication in bankruptcy has been made against a person in respect of whom an attachment of earnings order is in force to secure the payment of a judgment debt, the court may   *g* discharge the attachment of earnings order.'

Finally, it is to be noticed that in the county court the normal manner in which a judgment debt is discharged is by payment into court, pursuant to the County Courts Act 1959, s 99(3), although as the proviso to that subsection makes clear, where no instalment order is made, the court may, if it thinks fit, make an order for direct payment to the judgment creditor. The effect of the normal method of payment is made clear by Ord 24,   *h* r 14(1): 'A person liable to pay money under a judgment or order may at any time pay money into court in reduction of the amount payable by him.' And r 15 provides:

'Where any payment into court is made under a judgment or order, the registrar shall, where the payment (a) exceeds £3; or (b) increases the amount remaining in court paid under the judgment or order from a sum not exceeding £3 to a sum exceeding £3; or (c) is for the whole amount or the balance due under the judgment   *j* or order . . . give notice in Form 142 to the person entitled to the money, unless, in a case to which paragraph (a), (b) or (c) applies, the money is to be paid out pursuant to County Court Funds Rules without any demand or request to the person entitled thereto.'

Form 142 is, so far as material, in the following terms: 'I HEREBY GIVE YOU NOTICE that the

a sum of £   stands to your credit in the books of the Court having been paid under the
judgment (*or* order) in this action.' And finally on this aspect of the matter I need only
refer to the County Court Funds Rules 1965[1], r 10(1), which deals with 'suitors' money', ie
money payable to one or other of the parties after the determination of the action, and is
in these terms: 'A party entitled to money in court or his solicitor may, at his own risk as
regards safe transit, request the registrar to transmit the money by post.'

b   I now revert to the main question, namely: is the effect of the 1971 Act on an order made
thereunder to effect an assignment of the moneys to which it refers to the judgment
creditor, or not? This is, eventually, a question of the true construction of that Act, and as
to that counsel for the Official Receiver pointed out, and pointed out correctly, that from
first to last it does not use the word assignment. I think that whilst this is undoubtedly
true, and is a point to be borne in mind, it is not conclusive if, on a fair construction of all

c its provisions, that is what it does, indeed, effect. Counsel, however, produced a series of
reasons why the order under the Act could not possibly have the effect of an assignment,
and with these pre-emptive reasons I must first of all deal. His main one was that where,
as in the present case, there was, at the date of the order, no existing debt due to the
bankrupt from his employer, and that debt would only come into existence if the bankrupt
did work for his employer so to earn it, there could not, in law, be a valid assignment of

d that future debt. That appeared to me then and indeed still appears to me to be a
submission wholly inconsistent with the decision of the House of Lords in *Tailby v Official
Receiver*[2], and I need only quote from the speech of Lord Watson[3]:

'The rule of equity which applies to the assignment of future choses in action is, as
I understand it, a very simple one. Choses in action do not come within the scope of

e   the Bills of Sale Acts, and though not yet existing, may nevertheless be the subject of
present assignment. As soon as they come into existence, assignees who have given
valuable consideration will, if the new chose in action is in the disposal of their
assignor, take precisely the same right and interest as if it had actually belonged to
him, or had been within his disposition and control at the time when the assignment
was made. There is but one condition which must be fulfilled in order to make the

f   assignee's right to a future chose in action, which is, that, on its coming into existence,
it shall answer the description in the assignment, or, in other words, that it shall be
capable of being identified as the thing, or as one of the very things assigned. When
there is no uncertainty as to its identification, the beneficial interest will immediately
vest in the assignee. Mere difficulty in ascertaining all the things which are included
in a general assignment, whether in esse or in posse, will not affect the assignee's right

g   to those things which are capable of ascertainment or are identified. Lord Eldon said
in *Lewis* v. *Madocks*[4]: "If the Courts find a solid subject of personal property they
would attach it rather than render the contract nugatory." In the case of book debts,
as in the case of choses in action generally, intimation of the assignee's right must be
made to the debtor or obligee in order to make it complete.'

h   Of course, as we are here dealing with the effect of a statute, no question as to
consideration can arise. But counsel for the Official Receiver did not merely rely on a
general submission, he backed up that submission with a series of decided cases, to which
I must now refer. The first one is *Re Jones, ex parte Nichols*[5]. The headnote reads as
follows[6]:

j 1   SI 1965 No 1500
   2   (1888) 13 App Cas 523, [1886–90] All ER Rep 486
   3   13 App Cas 523 at 533–534, [1886–90] All ER Rep 486 at 491
   4   (1803) 8 Ves 150 at 157
   5   (1883) 22 Ch D 782, [1881–5] All ER Rep 170
   6   22 Ch D 782

'An assignment by a trader of the future receipts of his business, even if made for value, is, as regards receipts accruing after the commencement of his subsequent bankruptcy, inoperative as against the title of the trustee in the bankruptcy.' *a*

In my view, the reason for this undeniably correct decision is contained in a very few sentences in the judgment of Jessel MR[1]:

'Then it is said that the Respondents are claiming under a mortgage or assignment made to them by the bankrupts before the bankruptcy. The answer to that is, that by *b* no assignment or charge can a bankrupt give a good title as against his trustee to profits of his business accruing after the commencement of the bankruptcy. The bankrupt cannot as against the trustee assign these profits; they are not his property. It was an accident in the present case that the business was carried on at all after the filing of the petition, but, being so carried on, it was carried on *ex relatione* by the trustee for the benefit of the bankrupts' estate.' *c*

In other words, on the bankruptcy, the business vested in the trustee, and as the profits in question were profits of that business, they passed to the trustee unaffected by any prior mortgage by the debtor. When and as the profits arose, they were profits of a business vested in the trustee and no longer vested in the debtor.

The next case cited in order of date was *Wilmot v Alton*[2]. The headnote reads[3]: *d*

'A trader, who carried on the business of a theatrical costumier, contracted with a company to supply dresses for a ballet and keep them in repair for the sum of 40l. a week for twelve weeks commencing from a certain date. She subsequently charged her right and interest under the contract in favour of the plaintiff as security for an advance made by him. The dresses were duly supplied to the company under the contract, but before any moneys became payable under it the trader became *e* bankrupt:—*Held*, affirming the judgment of [Lord Russell of Killowen CJ], that the charge in favour of the plaintiff gave no title as against the defendants, the trustees in bankruptcy, to moneys which might become due under the contract after the bankruptcy.'

Lord Esher MR said[4]: *f*

'In my opinion the true construction of the contract is that she would be entitled to be paid at the end of each week, if during the week she had done all that was required, or had been ready and willing to do all that might have been required under the contract. Therefore, to entitle her to payment of the moneys payable under the contract, she had to perform onerous conditions during the whole of the period mentioned. During the period contemplated by the contract she became bankrupt. *g* The effect of that was that she could no longer fulfil the contract. The trustee in bankruptcy in such a case may, if he thinks it for the benefit of the estate, carry on the business and the contract; but he is not obliged to do so. He would have a right to say that he would not have anything to do with the contract. If the trustee in this case had done so, no moneys not already accrued due under the contract could after that become payable to anyone under it. After the bankruptcy therefore no money would *h* have become payable under the contract, unless the trustee had elected to go on with it, and to perform the conditions which by the terms of it were to be performed by the bankrupt. If he did go on with the contract, then in consideration of his doing so week by week the sums of money payable under the contract would become due. Therefore the case stands thus. At the moment of the bankruptcy, there is, as regards sums to become payable in futuro under the contract, no debt due. There are *j*

---

1 (1883) 22 Ch D 782 at 786, [1881–5] All ER Rep 170 at 172
2 [1897] 1 QB 17, [1895–9] All ER Rep 188
3 [1897] 1 QB 17
4 [1897] 1 QB 17 at 20–21, cf [1895–9] All ER Rep 188 at 190

a   amounts which may or may not become due according as the conditions of the contract are or are not fulfilled. In order to earn those amounts, the conditions of the contract must be fulfilled, and their fulfilment depends upon the question whether the trustee in bankruptcy will go on with the contract or not.'

I think that this is fully in line with the interpretation I have placed on *Re Jones*[1]. But, lest there be any doubt, one may refer to the terms of the judgment which the Court of Appeal were affirming, a judgment incidentally, which Rigby LJ said he was simply following.

b   Lord Russell of Killowen CJ said[2]:

'But her right to receive moneys under that contract lasted only so long as she was not a bankrupt. The moment she became a bankrupt she ceased to have any rights under the contract to enforce. The contract ceased to be hers, and, together with the right to receive moneys under it, became vested in the trustees. There was

c   consequently no right of hers upon which the indenture of charge could operate at the time when it was sought to make that charge effective. The moneys in question represent the earnings arising from the hire of goods subsequently to July 13, at which date the goods, and the contract relating to them, by relation back of the trustees' title, became the property of the trustees.'

d   The next case is *Re Collins*[3]. The headnote reads[4]:

'For some years before his bankruptcy a surveyor and assessment specialist with a staff of clerks had entered into contracts with clients for personal service in the latter capacity. Under these contracts he had to value his clients' properties for rating purposes and give expert evidence on their appeals, his remuneration being a percentage of the reduction of their assessments when obtained. He mortgaged these

e   contracts and the sums to become due on completion thereof to a mortgagee, who by special arrangement with the mortgagor gave no notice to the clients so as not to imperil the mortgagor's business position, the mortgagor being allowed to collect the fees when due in his own name and hand them over to the mortgagee. At the date of the mortgagor's bankruptcy, some fees (a) were due on completed contracts, but some fees (b) were still unearned. The trustee employed the bankrupt and some of his

f   staff to carry out the uncompleted contracts and earn fees (b):—*Held*, that though the work to be done under contracts required a certain amount of technical skill on which the bankrupt's clients relied, it was nevertheless part of the bankrupt's business, so that the fees (a) due at the date of the bankruptcy were due to him "in the course of his trade or business" and being in his order and disposition by the consent of the mortgagee belonged to the trustee under s 38(c) of the Bankruptcy Act, 1914 . . . *Held*

g   also that the mortgage of fees (b) earned since the bankruptcy was inoperative against the trustee. *Ex parte Nichols*[5] and *Wilmot v. Alton*[6] applied.'

This is of course interesting because the whole argument there was that the fees in question were not the earnings of a business, but the personal earnings of the bankrupt. It was never suggested by the experienced counsel who argued the case for the trustee that this made no difference to their client's claim. Nor did Astbury J think that it was immaterial. He said[7]:

h   'That is decisive of this question, except as to one point taken by the mortgagee, if that point is sound. He says that this is not a case of a trader carrying on a business

---

j   1   (1883) 22 Ch D 782, [1881–5] All ER Rep 170
     2   [1896] 2 QB 254 at 259
     3   [1925] Ch 556, [1925] All ER Rep 215
     4   [1925] Ch 556
     5   *Re Jones, ex parte Nichols* (1883) 22 Ch D 782, [1881–5] All ER Rep 170
     6   [1897] 1 QB 17, [1895–9] All ER Rep 188
     7   [1925] Ch 556 at 563–564, [1925] All ER Rep 215 at 219

within the meaning of these authorities, but a case where moneys may become payable in the future under certain contracts made in reliance upon the bankrupt's personal skill and personal work. There are two answers to that: In the first place it *a* is perfectly plain that the bankrupt in the present case carried on a business. It is quite true there was a certain amount of technical skill involved in the carrying on of this business, but it was nevertheless a business carried on by him for the purpose of gain, he and a staff of clerks doing the necessary work: secondly, having regard to that fact, the authorities I have referred to completely cover the point. I was told, I have no *b* doubt accurately, that there is no reported case quite similar to the present, but for the reasons I have given, the order and disposition clause covers the first set of cases I have mentioned, and the ratio decidendi in *Ex parte Nichols*[1] and *Wilmot v. Alton*[2] covers the second.'

So the learned judge there accepted the analysis of the authorities which appeals to me, and also recognised that if the earnings had been purely personal earnings, and not those of a *c* business, the decision might well have been the other way. *King v Michael Faraday and Partners Ltd*[3] went off on another point, but, admittedly purely by way of dicta, Atkinson J said[4]:

'The next point which was made was this. It was argued that a man cannot charge his personal earnings to be made during a bankruptcy, because such earnings become, so it was said, due not merely to the debtor, but also to the trustee in cases like *Re Jones*, *d* *Ex p. Nichols*[1] and *Wilmot v. Alton*[2] and that class of case, upon which reliance was placed. If those cases are analysed, it will be seen that in all of them the earnings in dispute were made, not by the bankrupt, but by the trustee. If a trustee permits a debtor to carry on his business, he carries it on as agent for the trustee, and it is true to say that the earnings are really the earnings of the trustee, and not of the debtor. In this case, however, the debtor is carrying on under a personal agreement. He is not *e* carrying on in any sense as agent for the trustee. At any rate, so far as I am concerned, I am not prepared to hold that a man cannot before bankruptcy charge his personal earnings under a personal agreement over and above what is required for the maintenance of himself and his family so as to give a good title against his trustee. Therefore, I think that the argument based on *Re Jones, Ex p. Nichols*[1] fails as well.'

However, there were other matters there. Again, this is fully in line with the analysis I *f* would myself make of the cases. The last case under this head is *Re De Marney*[5], a decision of that great equity lawyer Farwell J. The headnote reads[6]:

'An assignment by a member of a profession of his future earnings is, as regards receipts accruing after the commencement of his subsequent bankruptcy, inoperative as against his trustee in bankruptcy.'

Farwell J said[7]:
g

'The question is whether, having regard to the terms of the deed of assignment, the trustee in bankruptcy is entitled to be paid the moneys earned by the debtor since the date of the adjudication. If this was a charge on the future profits of a business, there would be no doubt that the trustee in bankruptcy would be entitled to them. It is said, however, that as this is a charge on the future professional earnings of the debtor, *h* different considerations arise. I have considered with care the cases which were cited

1   (1883) 22 Ch D 782, [1881–5] All ER Rep 170
2   [1897] 1 QB 17, [1895–9] All ER Rep 188
3   [1939] 2 All ER 478, [1939] 2 KB 753
4   [1939] 2 All ER 478 at 484, [1939] 2 KB 753 at 760
5   [1943] 1 All ER 275, [1943] Ch 126
6   [1943] Ch 126
7   [1943] Ch 126 at 127, cf [1943] 1 All ER 275 at 276

j

to me, and I am quite unable to find sufficient justification for saying that the principle applicable to the profits of a business does not apply to the present case. Accordingly, the trustee in bankruptcy is entitled to the relief which he seeks.'

It is extremely unfortunate that the learned judge's attention was not called to Atkinson J's dictum; and it is also quite impossible from the report to gather why he was quite unable to distinguish between the profits of a business, the profit making apparatus of which vests in the trustee under s 38 of the 1914 Act, and the personal earnings of the bankrupt himself, dependent on the skill and knowledge of his own hands and brain, and nothing else, which do not so vest. It may, of course, be that on the facts of that case (which are but sparsely stated in the reports) there was something more to the bankrupt's earnings as an actor than his mere skill: his livelihood may have, for example, depended on properties which did indeed vest in the trustee. That would put a completely different complexion on the case. But, taking it as it stands, I am unfortunately wholly unable to reconcile it with *Tailby's* case[1], and I must follow that decision of the House of Lords in preference to it.

I must therefore conclude, from this review of the authorities, that there is nothing intrinsically impossible in a bankrupt making a mortgage or assignment of his future earnings which will hold good as against his trustee in bankruptcy, provided that such earnings are the fruit of his own skill and knowledge, and not in truth the earnings of a business which has indeed vested in the trustee.

Logically the next point taken by counsel for the Official Receiver was that, since there is undoubtedly a power in the court to revoke an attachment order under s 9 of the 1971 Act, the alleged 'assignment' is not an absolute one, and therefore cannot be an assignment. I entirely failed to follow this submission, as it is by no means a necessary concomitant of an assignment that it should be absolute: in equity, an assignment by way of mortage is one of the commonest creatures alive. Of course, an assignment under s 136 of the Law of Property Act 1925 has to be absolute; but that is rather a different matter. I see no reason why an assignment in equity (and of course hence a fortiori one effected by statute) of a running series of payments should not be terminable in certain events. In the present case, assuming an assignment, there will be termination when the debt is paid in full (which cannot, of course, be predicated in advance, as in some weeks a debtor may not earn more than the protected amount, or earn less than the amount of deduction stated in the order) and also termination earlier if the court so directs. Of course, if, on such termination by the court, there could be a revesting of moneys already paid to the collecting officer, it would be obvious that there had been no assignment thereof in the first place; but there is no suggestion in the Act that a discharge of the order is to have any retrospective effect of that nature.

Coming more nearly to the question of the true construction of the Act, counsel for the Official Receiver submitted that there could be no change of proprietorial interest in the moneys deducted and paid over by the employer unless the collecting officer was constituted a trustee for the judgment creditor, and he submitted that he was clearly not so constituted. I would agree that he is not so constituted, but it appears quite clear to me that, taking the whole of the relevant parts of the Act and County Court Rules dealing with payment into court, and the County Court Funds Rules, that the true position is closely analogous to that of a customer and his bank. True it is that the court is constituted the banker of the judgment creditor whether or not he would wish it, but Form 142 and the Funds Rules makes it crystal clear that, from the moment of the moneys being paid to the collecting officer they are held as the moneys of the judgment creditor. In my judgment, the fact that the collecting officer is not constituted a trustee is nihil ad rem: from the moment of payment in the moneys are the moneys of the judgment creditor and of nobody else.

So I first of all dismiss all the alleged considerations which would suggest that the Act

1   (1888) 13 App Cas 523, [1886–90] All ER Rep 486

could not have effected a valid assignment of the appropriate slice of the bankrupt's future earnings to the judgment creditor, and turn to the Act itself. Does it, on its true construction, effect such an assignment or not? But for one important matter I should have answered unhesitatingly in the affirmative. The whole shape of the Act is to transfer to the judgment creditor such a slice of the debtor's earnings, such slice being ascertained on quite certain principles, as will discharge the creditor's debt. And the machinery provided is such that although payment is not to be made directly to the judgment creditor, the moneys are in effect to be paid to a secure banker on his account. There are thus all the indicia of an assignment.

However, before one can come to the conclusion that there is an assignment, one must look to that side of the coin which becomes apparent if the employer does not comply with his obligations under the Act. If there has been a true assignment, then there must have been a passing of the beneficial interest in the appropriate slice of the debtor's earnings when he earned them, and thus, by whatever machinery this is effected, the situation must be at the end of the day that those moneys find their way to the judgment creditor.

This, however, is where the theory of assignment breaks down. It will be recalled that it is under s 7(1) of the 1971 Act that the employer is bound to make the deductions set out in the order, with a seven day grace period. What happens if he does not do so? Naturally, he commits an offence (see s 23(2)(*a*)). And this offence is punishable by a fine (see sub-s (3)). But what happens as regards the moneys which the employer ought to have deducted? This is dealt with in s 23(6), which reads as follows:

> 'Where a person is convicted or dealt with for an offence under subsection (2)(*a*), the court may order him to pay, to whoever is the collecting officer of the court for the purposes of the attachment of earnings order in question, any sums deducted by that person from the debtor's earnings and not already paid to the collecting officer.'

Now it will be seen that there is no obligation on the court even to make the employer pay over sums which he has deducted and not yet paid over; the matter is discretionary. And I think the inference from this is irresistible that no such order for payment over can be made in respect of sums which ought to have been, but have not in fact been, deducted by the employer.

Given that position, can one properly hold that there has been an assignment of these moneys to the judgment creditors? I think not. It is surely of the essence of an assignment that the moneys assigned inevitably find their way into the hands of the assignee. I think that the channels by which that happens are irrelevant, and, of course, there may well be a valid assignment where in fact the assignee finds himself in the last resort with merely an action against somebody for the sum in question without any certainty that the action will prove fruitful. But if, as under the Act, there is no certainty that moneys which are actually available to answer the order must inevitably find their way into the pocket of the judgment creditor in cash, or by way of a judgment debt against some third party other than the debtor, it appears to me that no assignment of these moneys has been effected.

This is, of course, an extremely narrow, although in my judgment unanswerable, ground on which to base the conclusion that the Act does not effect an assignment. I would also point out that this conclusion necessarily involves, as will be seen, that the effectiveness of an attachment order under the 1971 Act ceases at some point in the bankruptcy (which as will be seen I place at the date of the receiving order). And yet, CCR Ord 25, r 89(7), obviously proceeds on the assumption that an attachment order may validly continue even after the debtor has been adjudicated bankrupt. Such a conclusion (unless restricted solely to orders made in respect of maintenance, and even, indeed, further) can, I think, only be based on the supposition that the order does indeed create a valid assignment. This consideration has troubled me considerably, although in the ultimate analysis I have felt unable to give it much weight. Naturally, however, this circumstance undermines to some extent my confidence in the conclusion to which I have come, and it is for this reason that I have dealt fully with counsel for the Official Receiver's wider propositions.

Where does this leave the matter? I do not think it is possible to bring the position
a under s 40 of the Bankruptcy Act 1914, since the phrase used in sub-s (1) thereof 'attached
any debt due to him' clearly refers in the first instance to garnishee proceedings, and it is
well established that in such proceedings the 'debt' in question has to be debitum in
praesenti, even although solvendum in futuro. That is not the case with earnings under a
contract of employment, which are not earned unless and until the services have been
rendered. Accordingly, I think it is impossible to bring attachment of earnings orders
b within the scope of s 40.

It therefore appears to me that, at the end of the day, the applicable provisions are those
to be found in s 45 of the 1914 Act which protects bona fide transactions without notice.
Nothing in the 1914 Act, so that section provides, is to invalidate, in the case of a
bankruptcy, any payment by the bankrupt to any of his creditors provided that (i) the
payment takes place before the date of the receiving order and, (ii) the judgment creditor
c had not at the time of the payment notice of any available act of bankruptcy committed by
the bankrupt before that time.

Counsel for the Official Receiver submitted that this section did not apply at all, because
there was in the present case no payment by the bankrupt. I do not think it is possible to
take that view. The payment made to the collecting officer is a payment made on behalf
of the debtor by the employer out of moneys which would otherwise belong to the debtor,
d and is a payment made, as is made perfectly plain by s 13 of the 1971 Act, on behalf of the
debtor in satisfaction of the debtor's debts. I see no difficulty in regarding all payments
made to the collecting officer as payments made on behalf of the debtor even though such
agent acting on his behalf has an unwilling principal.

I should perhaps explain here, that in my view the operation of an attachment of
earnings order under the 1971 Act is completely different from the operation of an
e ordinary garnishee order. Under such an order the garnishee pays the debt which he owes
to the garnishor in discharge of his own liability to the judgment debtor. Under an
attachment of earnings order, the employer first of all satisfies his liability to the judgment
debtor completely, although in two parts, (i) by retaining the amount stated in the order,
and (ii) by payment of the balance to the judgment debtor. Therefore, the moneys which
he pays to the collecting officer are not his own moneys, paid in discharge of his own
f liability to the judgment debtor; they are, on the contrary, moneys of the judgment
debtor, in the sense that the judgment debtor is entitled to the full amount of the beneficial
interest in such moneys. Hence, when the employer pays the collecting officer, what he
is doing is to pay moneys to which the judgment debtor is entitled, in the sense I have
already indicated, to a banker for the judgment creditor. It appears to me that it is
therefore perfectly correct to describe this operation as payment by the judgment debtor
g albeit by a statutorily constituted agent pro hac vice.

Once this is out of the way, the whole question here is what is to be taken as the date of
the payment by the bankrupt to the creditor. Is it the date (i) when the employer deducts
the sums he is obliged to deduct from the earnings of the bankrupt; (ii) when the employer
pays those moneys into court; or (iii) when the court pays out those moneys to the
judgment creditor?

h In my judgment, I must reject the first of these dates because, for the reasons already
discussed when considering the question of an assignment, there can be no certainty that
these moneys will, in fact, ever reach the judgment creditor. I may add here that the Act,
by reason of this fact, poses some difficult problems; in whom is the title to moneys which
the employer, having deducted quite properly in accordance with the terms of the order,
fails to pay over, if he is not ordered to pay them into court? However, that is one problem
j I am fortunately not concerned with.

The last date has this to be said for it, that it appears naturally to coincide with the
provisions of s 13(2) of the 1971 Act dealing with payments made under orders securing
maintenance payments, where it is provided:

'Any sums paid to the collecting officer . . . shall, when paid to the person entitled
to receive those payments, be deemed to be payments made by the debtor . . .'

This is, however, a special provision relating to such orders, and cannot, in my judgment, affect the fact that, as already noted, from the moment of the payment in of the moneys *a* they are held (subject to the possible payment of court fees) to the order of the judgment creditor. The fact that to suit the convenience of the administration of the court moneys do not go out as fast as they come in is, in my judgment, nihil ad rem. The moneys from the moment of payment in belong to the judgment creditor just as much as if those moneys had been paid into his bank. It is a pure matter of accident when those moneys do, in fact, reach him, but money standing to the credit of the judgment creditor in the books *b* of the court are in all respects to be equated with moneys in his hands: see *Re H E Pollard, ex parte S R Pollard*[1].

There is only one final observation that I would wish to make, merely to indicate that I have not overlooked the point. Of course, in the present case, although I have consistently spoken of the matter as if the cases concerned a single attachment order, in fact in the present case what is in issue is a consolidated order in favour of several judgment creditors. *c* It was, however, accepted on all hands that the principles applicable to a single order were the same as those applicable to a consolidated order.

There being no suggestion that any of the four respondent judgment creditors had notice, either themselves or through any agent, when the payments into court were made on 5th August and 5th September, of any act of bankruptcy, it appears to me that these payments are transactions protected by s 45 of the 1914 Act, and accordingly the first three *d* payments here in question are the creditors' moneys.

The last payment in with which I am concerned was made on the same day as the receiving order; the payment therefore did not take place before the date of the receiving order, and therefore it appears to me that as regards these moneys the Official Receiver succeeds.

I was informed at the commencement of the hearing that this is something in the nature *e* of a test case, designed to obtain a decision as to the true nature of orders under the 1971 Act, and that in consequence the Department of Trade proposed, very properly indeed, to pay the costs of all parties. I am therefore relieved from the necessity of considering what would otherwise have been the proper order under the circumstances that neither the Official Receiver nor respondents has wholly succeeded.

Order accordingly.   *f*

Solicitors: *Treasury Solicitor*; *Ellison & Co*, Colchester (for the third and fourth respondents).

Jacqueline Metcalfe Barrister.

Procedure Direction   *g*

HOUSE OF LORDS

House of Lords – Costs – Petition for leave to appeal – Leave to brief counsel obtained – Agent's charge for preparing brief.

h

The Appeal Committee have determined that, where leave to brief counsel before them has been obtained pursuant to Direction no 8[2], agents will be permitted to make a charge for preparing counsel's brief.

Item (xvi) on p 6 of the Forms of Bills of Costs applicable to Judicial Taxations in the House of Lords[3] will be amended accordingly.

| | PETER HENDERSON | *j* |
| 7th December 1978 | Clerk of the Parliaments. | |

---

1   [1903] 2 KB 41
2   Form of Appeal, Directions as to Procedure and Standing Orders (the Blue Book, 1977), p 10
3   The Green Book (1977)

Imperial Metal Industries (Kynoch) Ltd v Amalgamated Union of Engineering Workers

COURT OF APPEAL, CIVIL DIVISION

STEPHENSON, ROSKILL AND GEOFFREY LANE LJJ

10th, 11th, 12th JULY 1978

Arbitration – Arbitrator – Definition – Government supply contract incorporating Fair Wages Resolution of House of Commons – Contract providing that any question whether Fair Wages Resolution was being observed to be referred by Minister to independent tribunal for decision – Minister referring question to Central Arbitration Committee – One party to reference not a party to contract – Whether Central Arbitration Committee acting as arbitrator in deciding question.

In 1976 the employers entered into a contract with the Ministry of Defence to supply it with a large quantity of ammunition. Clause 17 of the contract incorporated the Fair Wages Resolution of the House of Commons dated 14th October 1946, which stated, inter alia, that persons in the employers' position were required, in the execution of the contract, to observe and fulfil certain obligations specified in the resolution. Clause 17(3) provided for any question whether the requirements of the resolution were being observed to be referred by the Secretary of State for Employment to an independent tribunal for decision. The contract also contained an arbitration clause (cl 23) which provided that all disputes, differences or questions arising between the parties to the contract with respect to any matter or thing arising out of or relating to the contract, except to the extent to which special provision for arbitration was made elsewhere in the contract, should be referred to arbitration in accordance with the Arbitration Act 1950. A trade union complained that the conditions of the Fair Wages Resolution were not being observed by the employers in respect of certain training instructors and pursuant to cl 17(3) of the contract the Secretary of State referred the matter to the Central Arbitration Committee as an independent tribunal. The president of the committee nominated three of its members to deal with the matter. The employers asked them to state a special case for the opinion of the High Court. They refused and the employers applied by summons for an order under s 21[a] of the Arbitration Act 1950 requiring them to do so. The judge dismissed their application on the ground that the 'arbitration' was not of the kind that fell within the 1950 Act and so no special case could be stated. The employers appealed contending (i) that there was an arbitration agreement within s 32[b] of the 1950 Act; (ii) that, even if there was not, the court could nonetheless order a special case to be stated because s 21 gave it power to do so whenever there was a 'reference' irrespective of whether that reference arose under an arbitration agreement as defined in s 32.

Held – The appeal would be dismissed for the following reasons—

(i) (per Roskill and Stephenson LJJ) In determining the matter submitted to them by the Secretary of State under cl 17(3), the members of the committee were not acting as arbitrators but were merely ascertaining for him whether a particular state of affairs, alleged by the union to be a fact, existed (see p 855 c to e and p 859 f, post); *R v Industrial Court, ex parte ASSET* [1964] 3 All ER 130 explained.

(ii) Even if they were acting as arbitrators, they were not doing so pursuant to an arbitration agreement as defined in s 32 of the 1950 Act. For there to be a submission to arbitration within s 32 there not only had to be an agreement between the parties to submit disputes to arbitration but also the arbitration itself had to be between the parties to the agreement about a matter which they had agreed to refer to arbitration, and in the present case the union was not a party to the contract (see p 856 c to f and p 859 g, post).

---

a   Section 21, so far as material, is set out at p 857 f, post

b   Section 32 is set out at p 855 g, post

(iii) Furthermore, where there was no arbitration agreement within s 32, the court had no power to order a special case to be stated because, on the true construction of the 1950 **a** Act, the word 'reference' in s 21 meant a reference arising out of an arbitration agreement as defined in s 32 (see p 858 *e f*, p 859 *e* and *g* to p 860 *a*, post).

Notes

For arbitration agreements, see 2 Halsbury's Laws (4th Edn) para 509, and for the power of the High Court to direct an arbitrator to state a special case, see ibid para 599.   **b**
    For the Arbitration Act 1950, ss 21, 32, see 2 Halsbury's Statutes (3rd Edn) 450, 459.

Cases referred to in judgments

Arenson v Casson, Beckman, Rutley & Co [1975] 3 All ER 901, [1977] AC 405, [1975] 3 WLR 815; sub nom *Arenson v Arenson and Casson, Beckman, Rutley & Co* [1976] 1 Lloyd's Rep 179, HL, Digest (Cont Vol D) 1016, 26a.   **c**
British Broadcasting Corpn v Association of Cinematograph Television and Allied Technicians (ACTAT) (1966) 1 KIR 773, Digest (Cont Vol B) 699, 36a.
R v Industrial Court, ex parte ASSET [1964] 3 All ER 130, [1965] 1 QB 377 [1964] 3 WLR 680, DC, 45 Digest (Repl) 385, 36.
Racal Communications Ltd v Pay Board [1974] 3 All ER 263, [1974] 1 WLR 1149, [1974] ICR 590, [1974] IRLR 209, Digest (Cont Vol D) 660, 671f.   **d**
Sutcliffe v Thackrah [1974] 1 All ER 859, [1974] AC 727, [1974] 2 WLR 295, [1974] 1 Lloyd's Rep 318, HL, Digest (Cont Vol D) 87, 481a.

Appeal

This was an appeal by the plaintiffs, Imperial Metal Industries (Kynoch) Ltd, against an **e** order of Slynn J made on 3rd June 1977 dismissing an application by the plaintiffs for an order directing the second defendants, N Singleton, P Turner and G L Dennis ('the committee') (to whom a question raised by the first defendants, the Amalgamated Union of Engineering Workers (Technical Administrative and Supervisory Section) ('the union'), during the working out of a contract between the plaintiffs and the Ministry of Defence had been referred for decision by the Secretary of State for Employment pursuant to cl **f** 17(3) of that contract) to state a special case for the decision of the High Court under s 21(1) of the Arbitration Act 1950. The facts are set out in the judgment of Roskill LJ.

Peter Crawford QC and *Michael E Collins* for the plaintiffs.
Jeffrey Burke for the union.   **g**
Peter Scott for the committee.

ROSKILL LJ delivered the first judgment at the invitation of Stephenson LJ. This is an appeal from an order of Slynn J dated 3rd June 1977. The judge in, if I may say so, a characteristically lucid judgment which he delivered without reserving it because of the **h** alleged urgency of the matter, refused to order two gentlemen and one lady, being members of the Central Arbitration Committee, to state a special case for the decision of the court under s 21 of the Arbitration Act 1950. Those two gentlemen and the one lady are the second respondents to the originating summons which was taken out by the applicants to the summons, Imperial Metal Industries Ltd ('the plaintiffs') in order to obtain that order. The other respondents to that summons were the Amalgamated Union of **j** Engineering Workers.
    On 5th January 1977 the Secretary of State for Employment had made a reference to the Central Arbitration Committee of a question which, in his view, had arisen in respect of certain training instructors employed by the plaintiffs whether (and I quote from the terms of reference)—

'. . . at the factory, workshop or place occupied or used by him [the company is there referred to as the contractor] for the execution of the contract the conditions of the Fair Wages Resolution are being observed by the Contractor. Those who are concerned with the said question are the Contractor and the Amalgamated Union of Engineering Workers (Technical Administrative and Supervisory Section). The said question has not otherwise been disposed of and, accordingly, the Secretary of State for Employment hereby refers the same for decision to the Central Arbitration Committee, as an independent tribunal, pursuant to Clause 3 of the Fair Wages Resolution.'

On 25th March 1977 the hearing of that reference took place in Birmingham before the two gentlemen and the lady I have mentioned. Those three had been nominated, we have been told, by the president of the Central Arbitration Committee. They had not been nominated by the Secretary of State. The plaintiffs were represented by junior counsel at that hearing, and he, no doubt on instructions, asked the committee for a special case to be stated under the Arbitration Act 1950.

The committee considered that application, they no doubt, as appears from the documents, took advice, and subsequently a letter was written in which they made it plain that they were not prepared to state such a special case. Indeed, so far as one can gather from the papers, although there have been a large number of previous references of this kind, no one hitherto has ever thought of suggesting to the committee that a special case should be stated under that statute. Accordingly the plaintiffs took out the summons I have mentioned.

The problem has arisen because of the incorporation of the Fair Wages Resolution of the House of Commons dated 14th October 1946, which appears as clause 17 of the Standard Conditions of Government Contracts for Stores Purchases into a contract dated 20th August 1976 entered into by the plaintiffs with the Ministry of Defence for the supply by the plaintiffs to that department of a huge quantity (running into tens of millions of units) of ball ammunition. A copy of the contracting letter will be found in the bundle of correspondence. It is dated 20th August 1976. That letter incorporates terms and conditions known as DEFCON 112P. I need not refer to that in detail. The incorporation is as follows: 'Conditions of Contract. The Contract is subject to :—DEFCON 112P (Edn. 6/75).' That, then, brings in the standard conditions; and, as I have said, cl 17, to which I will come back, is the Fair Wages Resolution of the House of Commons dated 14th October 1946.

Clause 22 provides: 'The Contract shall be considered as a contract made in England and subject to English Law.' Clause 23, which is of importance, bears the rubric 'Arbitration (English Law)' (there is a parallel arbitration clause if the contract is governed by Scots law):

'Where Condition No. 22 forms part of the Contract [pausing there, it does] then, except as provided by Condition No. 50, all disputes, differences or questions between the parties to the Contract with respect to any matter or thing arising out of or relating to the contract, other than a matter or thing as to which the decision of the Authority is under the contract to be final and conclusive and except to the extent to which special provision for arbitration is made elsewhere in the contract, shall be referred to the arbitration of two persons, one to be appointed by the Authority and one by the contractor, or their Umpire, in accordance with the provisions of the Arbitration Act, 1950, or any statutory modification or re-enactment thereof.'

That, subject to one or two special provisions, is a common form arbitration clause providing for a reference of disputes arising out of or relating to this contract to be referred to two arbitrators and an umpire. Clauses 50, 51 and 52 do not require reading, but each is a clause which makes provision for certain questions to be determined in the event of dispute by a body called a review board, and quite plainly each of them is a special provision within the exception I have just read from cl 23.

The Fair Wages Resolution clause repeats verbatim the House of Commons resolution, but for clarity I ought to read the whole of cl 17 of the contract:

'17. *Fair Wages, &c.*—The Contractor shall, in the execution of the contract, observe and fulfil the obligations upon contractors specified in the Fair Wages Resolution passed by the House of Commons on the 14th October, 1946, namely:—

'"1. (*a*) The contractor shall pay rates of wages and observe hours and conditions of labour not less favourable than those established for the trade or industry in the district where the work is carried out by machinery or negotiation or arbitration to which the parties are organisations of employers and trade unions representative respectively of substantial proportions of the employers and workers engaged in the trade or industry in the district. (*b*) In the absence of any rates of wages, hours or conditions of labour so established the contractor shall pay rates of wages and observe hours and conditions of labour which are not less favourable than the general level of wages, hours and conditions observed by other employers whose general circumstances in the trade or industry in which the contractor is engaged are similar.

'"2. The contractor shall in respect of all persons employed by him (whether in execution of the contract or otherwise) in every factory, workshop or place occupied or used by him for the execution of the contract comply with the general conditions required by this Resolution. Before a contractor is placed upon a Department's list of firms to be invited to tender, the Department shall obtain from him an assurance that to the best of his knowledge and belief he has complied with the general conditions required by this Resolution for at least the previous three months."'

Then follows cl 3, which is the all-important provision:

'3. In the event of any question arising as to whether the requirements of this Resolution are being observed, the question shall, if not otherwise disposed of, be referred by the Minister of Labour and National Service to an independent Tribunal for decision.'

Pausing there, the submission on behalf of the plaintiffs is that that is a submission to arbitration within the Arbitration Act 1950, and that accordingly this is an appropriate case in which the court has the power, which it should exercise, to order the second respondents to state a case under that section for the decision of the court.

Although counsel for the plaintiffs, in his reply this morning, sought to argue otherwise, as Lane LJ, pointed out, cl 3 is, if one views this clause critically as a matter of drafting, in a somewhat illogical position, because it appears in the middle of the resolution, immediately following two obligations which are imposed on the contractors in cl 1 and 2 which I have just read but before three more obligations in 4, 5 and 6, which I will now read:

'4. The contractor shall recognise the freedom of his workpeople to be members of Trade Unions.

'5. The contractor shall at all times during the continuance of a contract display, for the information of his workpeople, in every factory, workshop or place occupied or used by him for the execution of the contract a copy of this Resolution.

'6. The contractor shall be responsible for the observance of this Resolution by sub-contractors employed in the execution of the contract, and shall if required notify the Department of the names and addresses of all such sub-contractors.'

There follows a note: 'Copies of the Resolution for display in factories, etc., in accordance with paragraph 5 thereof may be purchased from H.M. Stationery Office.'

During the working out of this contract for the supply to the Ministry of Defence by the plaintiffs of this large quantity of ball ammunition a question did arise in respect of the training instructors, the question being that which I have already read from the terms of reference and the plaintiffs thereupon asserted that this question involved a question of law or, at least, a question of mixed law and fact which was a suitable subject-matter for the statement of a special case. That was the question raised and decided before Slynn J.

When one looks at the terms of reference, at what follows, that being a letter from the Department of Employment to the Secretary of the Central Arbitration Committee, one observes that the parties in dispute, according to the secretary, are the claimant (that is the union), and the employer (that is the plaintiffs, Imperial Metal Industries (Kynoch) Ltd.) The Ministry of Defence, who were parties to the contract, are not parties to this reference, although they are described in this letter as 'The other body concerned'. But they are not a party to the dispute, and never have been. I regard this as a matter of great importance, as did the judge, Slynn J. It is a striking fact, as counsel for the committee pointed out yesterday afternoon, and as, indeed, is mentioned by the judge in his judgment, that any question which may arise in connection with the Fair Wages Resolution can be raised by anyone. Such a question does not have to be raised by a party to the contract; it can be, as it was here, raised by the union in furtherance of what the union believe to be the interests of their members, certain employees of the plaintiffs. It could have been raised by a stranger; it could have been raised by anyone. And one might well have the position, as the judge envisaged in his judgment, where the two parties to the contract both took the view that there was no breach of the Fair Wages Resolution but that some outsider, such as a union, took the view that there had; and that, notwithstanding the views of the parties to the contract, would, in my view, be a perfectly fit matter for the Minister, now the Secretary of State, if he thought fit, to refer to an independent tribunal.

Now the Secretary of State, as I have already said, referred this question, which is defined with precision in the terms of reference, to the Central Arbitration Committee. I have mentioned that body more than once without saying who they are. That body came into existence under the Employment Protection Act 1975. As is now well known Part I of that Act, beginning with s 1, sets out what is described in the Act as 'Machinery for Promoting the Improvement of Industrial Relations', and s 1 creates the Advisory, Conciliation and Arbitration Service 'in this Act referred to as "the Service"', a body now popularly known by its initial letters, namely ACAS. Section 3 bears the rubric 'Arbitration' and reads:

'Where a trade dispute exists or is apprehended the Service may, at the request of one or more parties to the dispute and with the consent of all the parties to the dispute, refer all or any of the matters to which the dispute relates for settlement to the arbitration of—(a) one or more persons appointed by the Service for that purpose (not being an officer or servant of the Service); or (b) the Central Arbitration Committee constituted under section 10 below.'

Section 3(5) provides that Part I of the Arbitration Act 1950 shall not apply to an arbitration under that section. The present proceedings, of course, were not proceedings under that section. The committee is set up by s 10, which provides: 'There shall be a body to be known as the Central Arbitration Committee, in this Act referred to as the "Committee"', and it is common ground, it was before the learned judge, and has been in this court, that this committee is the statutory successor of the former Industrial Court, which was set up as long ago as 1919 to deal with disputes which arose in the aftermath of the First World War.

Under the Employment Protection Act 1975 certain statutory functions are conferred on the Central Arbitration Committee. Those are referred to in Part I of the 1975 Act, and are in Sch 1 to that Act.

I need not refer to those statutory provisions, for it is common ground that when the Secretary of State referred this particular question to these three individuals he was not inviting or requiring the committee to perform any statutory function. In the view of the Secretary of State this body was an 'independent tribunal' suitable for dealing with the question which had arisen, and his powers under para 3 of cl 17 of the House of Commons resolution are to refer the question to an independent tribunal for decision.

Before the judge, and again in this court, the plaintiffs relied greatly on what has become known as the *ASSET* case, *R v Industrial Court, ex parte ASSET*[1], which were the initial letters of the Association of Supervisory Staffs, Executives and Technicians, who were the body concerned in that case seeking relief by way of an order of mandamus against the then Industrial Court enjoining them to hear and determine the particular industrial dispute which had then arisen. The matter came before the Divisional Court. I shall have to refer to the judgment of Lord Parker CJ in more detail hereafter. Suffice it to say, for present purposes, that the effect of the decision, so far as presently relevant, is accurately set out in the headnote[2]:

'(2) That the reference to the industrial court of March 2, 1964, was a reference to private arbitrators and not a statutory reference under the Industrial Courts Act, 1919, and, accordingly, the industrial court's jurisdiction was not confined by the terms of the Act... (5) That, as the order of mandamus could not go to private arbitrators, the court had no jurisdiction to order the industrial court acting as an arbitral tribunal to hear and determine the reference made to it by the Ministry of Labour.'

Founding on that decision the plaintiffs argued before Slynn J and in this court that since, as the Divisional Court held in the *ASSET* case[1], the committee were acting as private arbitrators, it was appropriate that they should be ordered to state a case under the Arbitration Act 1950. Further reliance was placed on a passage in a judgment of Megaw J in *British Broadcasting Corpn v Association of Cinematograph, Television and Allied Technicians*[3], known for short as ACTAT. Megaw J, in a passage, the only passage I need read from this case, said[4]:

'Of course, it may well be that, after the determination of the Industrial Court of that matter, there may be further skirmishes or battles in this war to which I have referred, whether by way of requiring a case to be stated by the Industrial Court as arbitrator or by attacking its awards on grounds of error of law, or whatever it may be.'

The judge undoubtedly envisaged the possibility that the Industrial Court, as it was in those days, might be required to state a case under the Arbitration Act 1950. But that, in my judgment, as in Slynn J's, was not a decision by Megaw J that that court could be so ordered. He was no more than canvassing a possibility. And, of course, he, like Slynn J in the present case, was bound by the decision of the Divisional Court in the *ASSET* case[1]. We are not; and counsel for the committee has invited us to say that whether or not the *ASSET* case[1] was correctly decided, the underlying reasoning, and in particular the conclusion, that the Industrial Court were acting as private arbitrators in a private capacity was, with the utmost respect to a most strongly constituted Divisional Court, erroneous. That court consisted of Lord Parker, then Lord Chief Justice, Winn J and the present Lord Chief Justice, then Widgery J. I shall return to the *ASSET* case[1] later.

Although Slynn J dealt with a number of other points in his judgment it seemed clear to each of us, on reading the papers, that unless the plaintiffs could satisfy us that the judge reached a wrong conclusion on the issues which arise under the Arbitration Act 1950 no other point arose or necessarily arose for decision. We therefore invited counsel for the plaintiffs to deal with that point first. He has done so, and that is the point to which the arguments by all counsel have been directed.

Counsel for the plaintiffs repeated in this court his submission that there was here an arbitration agreement within s 32 of the 1950 Act; but he added in this court what was

1   [1964] 3 All ER 130, [1965] 1 QB 377
2   [1965] 1 QB 377 at 378
3   (1966) 1 KIR 773
4   1 KIR 773 at 780

claimed by both counsel for the committee and counsel for the union to be a new
submission, namely that even if there were not an arbitration agreement within the
a definition of that phrase in s 32 of the 1950 Act nonetheless there was, on the true
construction of s 21 of the 1950 Act, power in the court to order a special case since there
was, as he contended, a reference, and that was enough to entitle the court, if it thought fit,
to order the committee to state a case whether or not there was an arbitration agreement
as defined in s 32.

b Counsel for the plaintiffs claimed that this point had been raised below. It is not
necessary to go into the controversy whether or not that is right. There is no reference in
the judge's judgment to this point, nor is there any express reference to it in the notice of
appeal. But neither counsel for the committee nor counsel for the union raised objection
to this point being raised in this court, whether or not it was raised below. We have
allowed it to be argued, for it is a point of some general importance, and accordingly I shall
c deal with both points in due course.

But when counsel for the committee rose to address us yesterday afternoon he invited us
to approach the whole question of the possible applicability of the Arbitration Act 1950
and whether or not a special case could be ordered or be stated on a much broader basis than
had counsel for the plaintiffs. He contended, as I have already indicated, that the reasoning
of the Divisional Court in the ASSET case[1] was wrong, even though (and he made no
d admission one way or the other) the Divisional Court were right in the result in saying that
the prerogative order sought should not issue.

The submission that appears to have been urged by the then Attorney-General, Sir John
Hobson QC, and accepted by the Divisional Court, was that the minister's reference in that
case was a reference to the Industrial Court to act as private arbitrators. That submission
appears in the very full report of his argument and that of Mr Peter Webster, who were
e appearing for the Minister of Labour. I accept counsel's submission for the committee
yesterday afternoon that some importance attaches to the fact that in those proceedings the
Industrial Court was not represented. The Attorney-General and Mr Webster were
appearing, not for the Industrial Court but for the Minister of Labour, and it by no means
follows, in matters of this kind, that the interests of the Industrial Court (or, in the present
case, the CAC) and of the Minister in that case (or now the Secretary of State) were or are
f identical. Of course, the Secretary of State appoints the Central Arbitration Committee;
but counsel for the committee rightly pointed out that that body derives its importance
from the fact that it is an independent body, independent from the Department of
Employment, and its views may not therefore coincide with those of its appointor. It is by
no means certain, to my mind, that if the Industrial Court had been represented before the
Divisional Court their submissions would have been identical with those of the then
g Attorney-General for the then Minister of Labour.

When one looks at the report of the arguments of Mr Peter Pain who was appearing for
the union and of the Attorney-General and of the argument by counsel on behalf of the
company on the other side the whole case appears to have been argued on the basis that a
reference to an independent tribunal under cl 17(3) was a reference to arbitration, and that
the issue to be decided was whether or not that reference to arbitration was a reference to
h the Industrial Court in what was described as its public capacity, so that a prerogative order
would lie, or in its private capacity, so that its members should be treated as arbitrators
within the purview of the Arbitration Act 1950. But so far as I can see from the report of
the arguments and the judgment of Lord Parker CJ, the Divisional Court was never invited
to approach the construction of cl 17(3) in the way in which we have been invited to
approach it by counsel for the Central Arbitration Committee. And, of course, while this
j decision in the ASSET case[1] is entitled to the greatest respect, having regard to the
constitution of the court, it does not bind this court, and it does now appear that the
matters argued before us were not argued before that court.

---

1   [1964] 3 All ER 130, [1965] 1 QB 377

The history of the Fair Wages Resolution was canvassed by Griffiths J in *Racal Communications v Pay Board*[1]. I shall not lengthen this judgment by quoting Griffiths J's judgment, which sets out the history of the Fair Wages Resolution, going well back into the last century, but of which the most recent version is that appearing in cl 17 of the Standard Conditions applicable to the present contract.

I think counsel for the committee is right when he says that the Fair Wages Resolution is an expression of opinion (to use his phrase) of the House of Commons directed to the government of the day, and no doubt to future governments, how government contracts should be allotted. The House, as the supreme legislative authority, was directing the government's attention to the fact that government contracts should be allotted to those contractors who were willing to accept the obligations imposed by the resolution. I accept counsel's submission for the committee that, properly understood, the resolution falls into two parts. First, it requires the government to impose certain obligations on contractors as a condition of those contractors being allotted contracts; no doubt a contractor who is unwilling to accept these obligations is unlikely to find himself on the list of possible contractors. Secondly, the resolution seeks to establish, and in my judgment does establish, supervisory machinery in order that the responsible minister, in those days the Minister of Labour and National Service, today the Secretary of State for Employment, can ensure, in the manner prescribed, that the terms of the resolution are complied with by contractors. I have already indicated that if one looks at the resolution with a critical draftsman's eye, para 3 of the Fair Wages Resolution is not in its correct place; but it is important to observe, as was pointed out yesterday, that whereas paras 1, 2, 4, 5 and 6 of the resolution all start with the words 'The contractor shall', the critical paragraph, para 3, does not contain those words. It begins with the words 'In the event of any question arising', and then goes on 'as to whether the requirements of this Resolution are being observed, the question shall, if not otherwise disposed of, be referred by the Minister . . . to an independent Tribunal for decision'.

Counsel for the plaintiffs argued that that 'reference' in para 3 of the Fair Wages Resolution is a 'special provision for arbitration' 'made elsewhere in the contract' within cl 23, which I have already read. I am afraid I cannot accept that submission. It may or may not be a provision for arbitration, I will consider that in a moment, but I am quite unable to see that it is 'a special provision' within cl 23, or that cl 23 refers to cl 17(3). That paragraph is providing *extra*-contractual machinery for investigation, report, and maybe advice, in the event of a complaint by someone, by no means, as I have said, necessarily a party to the contract in which the provision is contained, of alleged non-compliance with the resolution, the purpose of the enquiry being to enable the minister to secure in whatever way he thinks right, compliance with the report or advice which he receives if he thinks it proper to act on it. It is to be observed that the final words of para 3 are 'to an independent Tribunal for decision'.

Counsel for the committee said that these submissions were not advanced in the *ASSET* case[2]. If the submissions be right, one naturally asks what means there are of control of the Central Arbitration Committee by the courts when it is carrying out functions referred to it under cl 17(3)? Counsel for the committee invited us not to deal with this question because it does not directly arise for decision in this case. I propose to adopt that course. Taking the view that I do that cl 17(3) is not a clause providing for reference to arbitration and not an arbitration agreement under s 32 of the Arbitration Act 1950 it is not necessary to consider what, if any, remedies may be available to someone who wishes to complain of a decision of the Central Arbitration Committee. There are a number of possibilities. Counsel did not submit that the committee took the view that no remedies would be available. But that is not a matter which arises for decision, and it must await decision until it does.

---

1   [1974] 3 All ER 263, [1974] 1 WLR 1149
2   [1964] 3 All ER 130, [1965] 1 QB 377

The question we do have to consider is whether the Divisional Court was right in the
a ASSET case[1] in the passage when Lord Parker CJ said: 'As I have already said, it [that is, the
Industrial Court] is not acting as a court in accordance with the Act which set it up; it is
only acting as an arbitral tribunal.' Pausing there for a moment, I agree it is not acting as
a court in accordance with the Act which set it up, but whether it can be said to be acting
as an arbitral tribunal must depend, I think, on what meaning one gives to that latter
phrase. Lord Parker CJ went on[1]:

b
'In these circumstances it seems to me clear that on general principles mandamus
cannot go to a private arbitrator. [With respect, I agree. He continued:] The remedy
of the parties in such a case, if there is thought to be an excess of jurisdiction, is I think
to proceed in an appropriate case for an injunction, or to get a declaration of the court
that he has no jurisdiction, or to await the award and have it set aside, or, indeed, still
further when sued on the award to set up lack of jurisdiction ...'

c
I do not find it necessary to consider, as I have already said, what is the appropriate
remedy, but where I do most respectfully differ from the Divisional Court is in its
conclusion that the Central Arbitration Committee today, or the Industrial Court then, can
be said to be equated with private arbitrators in the sense in which that phrase is used in
what one might call an ordinary submission to arbitration under, for example, a
d commercial contract.
There is here no mutuality. There is here no decision inter partes of legal rights under
this contract. All there is is machinery provided, through the incorporation of the House
of Commons resolution into this contract, for the minister referring a question, not
necessarily arising, and in this case not arising, between the parties to this contract to an
extra-statutory body for decision. For my part I do not think it right to describe this as a
e private reference to arbitration. With all respect to the Divisional Court, it seems to me to
have none of the characteristics of such a reference to arbitration.
If that is right then the question we have to decide is answered. As I say, it was not open
to Slynn J, who was bound by the decision in the ASSET case[2], to reach that conclusion by
this route.
But lest I be wrong in this conclusion and the reasoning underlying the decision in the
f ASSET case[2] is right (contrary to my view) I have to consider the rest of the argument and
the ground on which Slynn J decided this case against the plaintiffs.
The first question is whether there was here a submission to arbitration within s 32 of
the Arbitration Act 1950. Section 32 defines an arbitration agreement thus:

'In this Part of this Act, unless the context otherwise requires, the expression
"arbitration agreement" means a written agreement to submit present or future
g differences to arbitration, whether an arbitrator is named therein or not.'

In answer to my Lord, counsel for the plaintiffs accepted that the learned judge had
correctly summarised his arguments (which he repeated in this court) as he set them out
as follows:

h
'The basis of counsel for the plaintiffs' submission was this: he accepts that there
must be, for the Arbitration Act to apply, an agreement to submit disputes to
arbitration. He says that once there is such an agreement to submit differences or
questions (I do not think there is any difference between them) it does not matter that
the differences are not differences between the parties to the contract; the differences
and questions can arise between other persons, can be raised by other persons; and it
is not necessary that there should be any dispute between the parties to the agreement
j to refer. In his submission condition 17 of the conditions is a clause which provides

---

1   [1964] 3 All ER 130 at 136, [1965] 1 QB 377 at 389
2   [1964] 3 All ER 130, [1965] 1 QB 377

contractually that there shall be arbitration; two conclusions flow from that. Firstly, the Secretary of State has power to refer, and in so doing he is doing nothing different *a* in passing to this particular tribunal from what the President of the Law Society does in nominating an arbitrator. Secondly, the company are bound by the result: the Ministry of Defence is entitled to participate but he is not obliged to do so. In essence what flows from condition 17 is that there is an arbitration proceeding of a judicial kind. That proceeding is created by the contract and arises out of the contractual provision. He says that it does not change the identity of the process that the matters *b* raised have not been raised in the first instance by one of the parties, or that the dispute does not rise between them.'

The judge then sets out counsel's argument for the committee and he states his conclusion:

'In my judgment counsel for the committee in this submission is right. What one has to find for the Act to apply is that there is an arbitration agreement between two *c* or more parties to submit differences to arbitration; the arbitration must be between parties to that agreement; and it must be as to a matter which they have agreed to refer to arbitration. If those conditions are not satisfied then, it seems to me, that there is not an arbitration for the purpose of the 1950 Act. That is the conclusion to which I myself have come without turning to the two authorities on which counsel for the plaintiffs relies. It seems to me, looking at it without those authorities, that *d* here the union and the company are involved in "an arbitration", a difference which may have arisen out of the contract, but they were not both parties to the agreement to refer, and the parties to the agreement to refer are not both the parties to the dispute . . . If, out of that, the only people who take part in the proceedings before the tribunal are the company and the union, or the third person, it does not seem to me that that is an arbitration which qualifies for the purposes of the 1950 Act.' *e*

If I may, I would adopt verbatim the whole of that passage in the judge's judgment. I could not hope to improve on its clarity and succinctness. In my judgment it is manifestly right, as a matter of the construction of the contract and other documents. I see no answer to it, and I am afraid that counsel for the plaintiffs has wholly failed to persuade me that the judge, in that respect, was guilty of any error. *f*

I do not find it necessary to refer to two recent decisions of the House of Lords, *Sutcliffe v Thackrah*[1] and *Arenson v Casson, Beckman, Rutley & Co*[2]. I do not think that those decisions of their Lordships' House assist in the solution of the problem before us.

That leaves what for ease of reference I will call the 'new' point. Can the High Court, when there is no arbitration agreement within s 32, order an arbitrator or an umpire to state a special case under s 21? We have not got the benefit of the judge's view on this point *g* because, as I have said, it is not clear that this point was argued before him. This point, so far as counsel has been able to discover, has never previously been raised, either during the currency of the Common Law Procedure Act 1854 or of the Arbitration Act 1889, or of the Arbitration Act 1934 or, until this case, of the Arbitration Act 1950. But in the current edition of Russell on Arbitration[3], for which Mr Anthony Walton QC is responsible, this passage appears: *h*

'On the other hand, the court's power to remit or set aside the award, to order a case to be stated and to hear the stated case, and to remove an arbitrator or umpire for misconduct or delay, would seem to be independent of the existence of an "arbitration agreement".'

There is no authority cited for that proposition, and counsel has told us, and I have *j*

---

1   [1974] 1 All ER 859, 1 [1974] AC 727
2   [1975] 3 All ER 901, [1977] AC 405
3   The Law of Arbitration (18th Edn, 1970), p 47

verified this, that this passage first appears in the 15th edition of Russell[1]. It does not
a appear in the 14th edition of Russell[2] or in any earlier edition of that book.

The 1950 Act, as its short title shows, is a consolidating Act. It is described as an Act to
consolidate the Arbitration Acts 1889 and 1934. When one looks at the repeal section,
s 44(3) repealed the 1889 Act, the Arbitration Clauses (Protocol) Act 1924, the Arbitration
Act 1934 and also the Arbitration (Foreign Awards) Act 1930. Thus a clean sweep was
made of the whole earlier arbitration code, and a consolidated code was enacted in the 1950
b Act. We were invited by counsel for the plaintiffs to look at the earlier legislation, and we
have done so, though for my part I doubt whether it is legitimate, in construing a
consolidating Act, to look back at the earlier legislation which the consolidating Act
replaces, particularly in circumstances where it is plain that the consolidating Act uses
different language from that of the original legislation.

It is common knowledge that the 1889 Act replaced the Common Law Procedure Act
c 1854 in the relevant respects. It is also common knowledge that the Arbitration Act 1934
followed the report of a committee, over which the late MacKinnon LJ presided, appointed
to remedy the defects which by then were apparent in the many disputes that arose after
the First World War in the 1920s and 1930s and which revealed the inadequacy of the 1889
Act. Certain amendments were made in important respects to the provisions for stating
special cases.

d When the draftsman of the 1950 Act was faced with the formidable task of producing
a consolidating Act he could not borrow verbatim the language of the earlier legislation.
He was faced with what is always a notoriously difficult task for Parliamentary draftsmen,
the problem of not going outside the previous legislation and yet, at the same time, trying
to make good the deficiencies of language and drafting in that legislation which had been
revealed. It is, of course, notorious (if I may use the word without offence) that there are
e certain defects of drafting in the 1950 Act. It is not a matter for criticism; it is a matter for
sympathy in the difficult task with which the draftsman, whoever he was, was faced. But
what is argued is that whatever may be the effect of the first 18 sections of the 1950 Act,
when one comes to consider ss 19, 20, 21, 22 and 23 there is in those five sections no
reference to an arbitration agreement. Indeed, not only is there no reference in s 21 to an
arbitration agreement but, it is said, the only relevant phrase there is 'the reference'; if one
f looks at s 21(1)(a) one finds the phrase 'any question of law arising in the course of the
reference', and in s 21(2): 'A special case with respect to an interim award or with respect
to a question of law arising in the course of a reference may be stated, or may be directed
by the High Court to be stated, notwithstanding that proceedings under the reference are
still pending.' It is argued that although the other sections, 1 to 18 inclusive, and apparently
24 to 34 inclusive, do refer to and apply only to cases where there has been an arbitration
g agreement as defined, nonetheless these sections from 19 to 23 inclusive and in particular
s 21 empower the court to act in the manner therein provided when there is a 'reference',
irrespective of whether that 'reference' arises pursuant to an arbitration agreement as
defined.

This is a question of the construction of this statute. It has to be observed that, in order
to give effect to this suggested construction, one has to jump about and pick and choose
h between these various sections, making selections in order to give effect to counsel's
argument for the plaintiffs.

It is necessary to have two things well in mind. First, as I have said, the 1950 Act is a
consolidating Act establishing a code for arbitration proceedings and for the control by the
court of arbitration proceedings, although some common law powers do undoubtedly
remain in the courts to control arbitration proceedings. Secondly, one has to construe
j statutes as a whole having regard to their content. All these provisions appear in Part I of
the Act, from s 1 to s 34. It seems to me to be quite illegitimate to jump about from one

1   (1952), p 32
2   (1949)

section to another and say: 'That section is of unlimited application, that section is only of limited application', when Part I as a whole is dealing with arbitration agreements as defined. It is true that the statute does not start by saying: 'This Act only applies to arbitration agreements as defined', but equally it has been said on the other side: 'Nor does the Act start by saying, "The following sections only apply where there is an arbitration agreement as defined".'

Counsel have taken us through all the sections in Part I of the Act, and I hope I shall not be thought unappreciative of their arguments if I do not engage in the same exercise. It seems to me plain that the earlier sections, that is, ss 1 to 18, are dealing with, and only with, arbitration agreements, and that they have no application save in the case of an arbitration under an arbitration agreement as defined. When one looks, for example, at s 4, s 4(1), which is still in force, provides:

'If any party to an arbitration agreement . . . commences any legal proceedings in any court against any other party to the agreement [note the words 'the agreement', meaning 'the arbitration agreement'] or any person claiming through or under him, in respect of any matter agreed to be referred . . .'

In sub-s (2) one finds the same phraseology, although that subsection has recently been replaced by s 1 of the Arbitration Act 1975. That section, s 1(1) of the Arbitration Act 1975, uses the same language: 'If any party to an arbitration agreement to which this section applies . . . commences any legal proceedings in any court against any other party to the agreement . . . in respect of any matter agreed to be referred', and goes on to make provision for a stay. That gives a clear clue to what Parliament meant, in other sections of the Act, by 'a reference'. The phrase 'a reference' simply means a reference arising out of an arbitration agreement, and I think it is plain that there is a reference, within the meaning of this Act, whenever there is a dispute which is referred to arbitration under an arbitration agreement. I find it impossible to construe the word 'reference' in s 21(1) as meaning that, in any proceedings which can be called a reference, irrespective of whether it is reference of a dispute arising under an arbitration agreement, the court has power to order a special case to be stated. I therefore think it is impossible to construe this section otherwise than as restricted to references under arbitration agreements, as defined.

I reach that conclusion simply as a matter of the construction of this statute. We were urged to look at the earlier legislation. I have done so with hesitation. With all respect to counsel for the plaintiffs, I think the earlier legislation, so far from reinforcing his submissions, militates very strongly against them. He drew our attention to the provisions of s 7 and s 19 of the Arbitration Act 1889, and he pointed out that in s 19, the old consultative case section, the language is: 'Any referee, arbitrator, or umpire may at any stage of the proceedings under a reference'. He said there you get the same width of language, differing from the language of the other sections which speak of 'submissions' or 'references under submissions'.

As my Lord pointed out, when one looks at the Arbitration Act 1889 one finds that its provisions fall under three heads. The first head, which covers ss 1 to 12 inclusive, speaks of 'References by Consent out of Court'. The second, that is, ss 13 to 17, speaks of 'References under Order of Court'. Then follow ss 18 to 30, and that is headed 'General'. Therefore it seems to me plain that those general provisions, which include the provisions of s 19, are referring to both the antecedent sections of the Act dealing with references by consent out of court and references under order of the court.

When I go to the 1934 Act, I do not find any different pointers in that statute.

If my view of the earlier legislation be right, then for counsel for the plaintiffs to succeed on the construction of the 1950 Act involves that the draftsman, in his consolidating Act, had introduced a change in the law from that enacted in 1889 and 1934. That can happen, but it would have been a legislative accident if it had, and for my part I should require different and much stronger language in a consolidating Act (even if I could get any help from the earlier legislation) before I would be prepared to construe that consolidating Act as altering the law from what it had been before. I am afraid, therefore, with all respect to the present and past editors of Russell[1], the next edition will have, if my judgment be right,

a   to contain an amendment.

Finally, and I can deal with this shortly, it is said on behalf of the plaintiffs that there was here an arbitration agreement by conduct by their appearing and taking part in the proceedings before the Central Arbitration Committee. I do not think that that can possibly be said to be a submission to arbitration of any kind. What is referred must be determined by the terms of reference from the Secretary of State, and not by what may

b   have happened thereafter.

It was also sought to be said, I thought a little faintly, by counsel for the plaintiffs, that there was a reference between the parties under cl 23 of the contract whether or not there had been a breach of contract by the plaintiffs. I do not think that the reference to the Central Arbitration Committee can possibly, by any stretch of imagination, be said to be a reference of any question whether or not there has been any breach of contract by the

c   appellants. It seems to me to be a reference of, and only of, the question specified in the terms of reference which I have already read.

For those reasons, which I am afraid I have given at rather great length, I would dismiss this appeal.

GEOFFREY LANE LJ. I agree that the appeal fails. The matter was accurately and

d   concisely dealt with by Slynn J in the course of his judgment in the passage Roskill LJ has just read. With those words of the judge I respectfully agree. They seem to me to conclude the matter in favour of the defendants here, irrespective of whether the decision of the Divisional Court in *R v Industrial Court, ex parte ASSET*[2] in 1965 was correct or not, as to which I prefer to express no view.

I agree with Roskill LJ, and for the reasons expressed by him, that the Arbitration Act

e   1950, and in particular s 21 of that Act, does not apply to an arbitration which is not within the ambit of s 32 of the Act.

I would accordingly dismiss the appeal.

STEPHENSON LJ. I agree. I accept counsel's argument for the committee that, in deciding the question submitted by the Secretary of State, the committee, or its three

f   members, are not acting as arbitrators or making an award binding on the plaintiffs or the Ministry of Defence or affecting the rights and obligations of the union or the Secretary of State, but finding for him whether a particular state of affairs alleged to be a fact by the union is a fact. Accordingly if this finding of fact involves a question of law the committee or its three members cannot be directed to state that question in the form of a special case.

There is another reason why they cannot. If they were arbitrators at all they would not

g   be arbitrators appointed by or by virtue of an arbitration agreement as defined by s 32 of the Arbitration Act 1950. In my judgment arbitrators so appointed are the only arbitrators with which Part I of the Act deals: see s 1. The arbitrator who may be required to state a case under s 21(1) is not described as so appointed, but that is because it goes without saying that he is so appointed. In section after section 'arbitration agreement' is mentioned, and where it is not it is taken for granted. So 'reference' is mentioned, sometimes expressed to

h   be under an arbitration agreement, sometimes not, because it is assumed to be so without unnecessary repetition. The parties to an arbitration agreement come and go throughout Part I, without raising any inference that it is others who are being considered in their absence. This, to my mind, is the natural interpretation of the language of the 1950 Act, read as a whole, for the reasons given by Roskill LJ, as both counsel for the committee and counsel for the union have contended. I am not persuaded by counsel for the plaintiffs'

j   argument that every omission of the qualifying description is deliberate and expresses a legislative intention to widen the scope of a statute which puts the qualification in the opening words of its first section and is consolidating enactments which permit even less

---

1   The Law of Arbitration
2   [1964] 3 All ER 130, [1965] 1 QB 377

easily the inclusion of oral agreements to refer disputes to arbitration or to accept the
arbitrament of persons to whom disputes have been referred by others.

    a

    I agree that the appeal fails because there is here no reference to arbitration under the Act
or at all, even if our decision throws doubt on what was said and decided by the Divisional
Court in the *ASSET* case[1], to which Roskill LJ has referred.

Appeal dismissed.

    b

Solicitors: *B J W Winterbotham* (for the plaintiffs); *Robin Thompson & Partners*, Birmingham
(for the union); *Treasury Solicitor.*

L I Zysman Esq   Barrister.

    c

Rolfe Lubell & Co (a firm) v Keith and another

QUEEN'S BENCH DIVISION
KILNER-BROWN J
23rd, 24th, 27th NOVEMBER, 8th DECEMBER 1978

    d

*Bill of exchange – Indorsement – Indorsement on behalf of company – Indorser also acceptor of bill
– Signature as acceptor in same form as signature as indorser – Signature followed by words 'for
and on behalf of company' – Whether indorsement in personal or representative capacity – Whether
evidence admissible to show parties' intended indorsement to be in personal capacity – Bills of*
Exchange Act 1882, s 26(1).

    e

A company, which became an unsatisfactory payer, needed some goods for its business.
The plaintiffs agreed to supply the goods if bills of exchange drawn in payment were
personally indorsed by two officers of the company. That condition was made orally to
and understood by the first defendant, a director of the company. The first defendant then
told the second defendant, the company secretary, what was required, but there was no
evidence that the second defendant understood that his personal indorsement was
required. When the bills were accepted by the defendants the second defendant applied a
rubber stamp to the back of them with the words 'For and on behalf of [the company]'
and dotted lines and the descriptions 'Director' and 'Secretary' where the signatures were to
appear, and signed in the space designated for the company secretary. The first defendant
signed in the space designated for the director. Subsequently the bills were dishonoured.
The plaintiffs brought an action against the defendants claiming the amount of the bills
from the defendants as indorsers of the bills on the ground that they had indorsed them in
their personal capacities. The plaintiffs later discontinued the action against the second
defendant. The plaintiffs contended that, as the first defendant's signature as indorser was
in the same form as his signature as acceptor, validity could be given to the indorsements
only by construing them as having been made by the first defendant in a different capacity
from that in which he had accepted the bills, ie as having been made in his personal
capacity, and that evidence was admissible to show that it was the parties' intention that the
first defendant should indorse the bills in his personal capacity. The first defendant, in
reliance on the first part of s 26(1)[a] of the Bills of Exchange Act 1882, contended that, as the
words added to his signature as indorser indicated that he had signed in his representative
capacity as director, he was not personally liable on the bills, and that evidence was not

    f

    g

    h

    j

---

1   [1964] 3 All ER 130, [1965] 1 QB 377

a Section 26 is set out at p 862 *c* to *e*, post

admissible to give a different meaning to his signature from the meaning unambiguously
a expressed by the form of it.

Held – Where a dispute arose as to the capacity in which an indorser had indorsed a bill of
exchange evidence was admissible to resolve any ambiguity that might arise. Since there
was evidence that the first defendant had agreed to indorse the bills in his personal capacity
the words 'For and on behalf of [the company]' and 'Director' in the indorsements were to
b be ignored as being contrary to that clear agreement, and it followed that he was personally
liable on the bills (see p 863 *b c* and *e* and p 864 *a b* and *e*, post).

Per Curiam. Since an indorsement on a bill of exchange amounts to a warrant that the
bill will be honoured and in certain circumstances transfers liability from the acceptor to
the indorser, an indorsement is to be construed as binding someone other than the
acceptor, and where a bill is indorsed by the acceptor in the same capacity in which he
c accepted the bill the indorsement is meaningless because it purports to transfer liability
from the acceptor to himself (see p 863 *a* to *d*, post).

Notes
For liability on a bill of exchange of a person signing as agent or in a representative
capacity, see 4 Halsbury's Laws (4th Edn) paras 376–378, and for cases on the subject, see
d 6 Digest (Reissue) 105–106, 794–802.
For the Bills of Exchange Act 1882, s 26, see 3 Halsbury's Statutes (3rd Edn) 203.

Cases referred to in judgment
Chapman v Smethurst [1909] 1 KB 927, 78 LJKB 654, 100 LT 465, 14 Com Cas 94, 16 Mans
171, CA, 1 Digest (Repl) 746, 2869.
e *Elliott v Bax-Ironside* [1925] 2 KB 301, [1925] All ER Rep 209, 94 LJKB 807, 133 LT 624, CA,
6 Digest (Reissue) 105, 797.
Macdonald v Whitfield (1883) 8 App Cas 733, 52 LJPC 70, 49 LT 446, PC, 6 Digest (Reissue)
288, 2110.
Steele v M'Kinlay (1880) 5 App Cas 754, 43 LT 358, HL, 6 Digest (Reissue) 11, 24.
Yeoman Credit Ltd v Gregory [1963] 1 All ER 245, [1963] 1 WLR 343, 6 Digest (Reissue) 203,
f 1385.

Action
By a specially indorsed writ issued on 28th February 1977, as amended on 11th May 1978,
the plaintiffs, Rolfe Lubell & Co (a firm), claimed against the defendants, H Keith and F W
Greenwood, the managing director and secretary respectively of Grafton Manquest Ltd
g ('the company'), as indorsers of two bills of exchange, the amount of the bills totalling
£6,441·98 and interest thereon. Subsequently the plaintiffs discontinued the action as
against the second defendant, Mr Greenwood. The first defendant, Mr Keith, by his
defence denied indebtedness to the plaintiffs on the ground that the bills were signed and
indorsed by him as director of the company and not in his personal capacity, and that it was
not intended that he should indorse them in his personal capacity. The facts are set out in
h the judgment.

Frederick Reynold for the plaintiffs.
Norman Primost for the first defendant.

Cur adv vult

j 8th December. **KILNER-BROWN J** read the following judgment: In this action the
plaintiffs claim remains against the first defendant only, they having discontinued the
action against the second defendant. It raises an interesting and, surprisingly, a novel issue
under two bills of exchange.
The plaintiffs were and are the holders of two bills, one for £3,200 and one for

£3,241·98. These were two of three drawn in favour of the plaintiffs on 17th November 1976 and accepted by a company named Grafton Manquest Ltd ('the company') of whom *a* the first defendant was managing director and the second defendant company secretary. All three bills were indorsed on the back by both defendants. The first bill was honoured on the due date, but the other two were dishonoured and no payment has been made thereunder. The plaintiffs' case is that the bills were indorsed by the defendants in their personal capacity. The first defendant's case is that the indorsement was in his capacity as a director of and for and on behalf of the company. The indorsement takes the form of the *b* signatures of the two defendants in a rubber stamped 'box' which has the stamped words 'For and on behalf of Grafton Manquest Limited', and where the written signatures appear, there are dotted lines and the description 'Director' and 'Secretary'. Obviously at first sight these signatures appear to be written in an official capacity and representative of the company. Section 26(1) of the Bills of Exchange Act 1882 is clear and explicit. It reads:

'Where a person signs a bill as drawer, indorser, or acceptor, and adds words to his *c* signature, indicating that he signs for and on behalf of a principal, or in a representative character, he is not personally liable thereon; but the mere addition to his signature of words describing him as an agent or as filling a representative character, does not exempt him from personal liability.'

The case for the first defendant is that the first part of the subsection is applicable. On the *d* other hand it is submitted as part of the argument on behalf of the plaintiffs that on the facts of this case the first defendant is caught by the words of sub-s (2), which reads:

'In determining whether a signature on a bill is that of the principal or that of the agent by whose hand it is written, the construction most favourable to the validity of the instrument shall be adopted.'

e

In addition to the effect of s 26(1) the first defendant further relies on the proposition that words which are clearly set out speak for themselves and as a general rule admit of no evidence which seeks to establish that they were intended to mean something different from their natural and obvious meaning.

There are a number of authorities which deal with signatures on bills of exchange. I have been referred to several but none is exactly in point or even germane to the critical *f* issue. The earliest of these cases and the one most strongly relied on by the first defendant is *Steele v M'Kinlay*[1]. As to this authority it is to be observed that it was a decision before the passing of the Bills of Exchange Act 1882; it appears to some extent to be in conflict with decisions of the Court of Appeal given after the codification of the law and in any event can be distinguished on the facts from the instant case. Other authorities I have been asked to consider and bear in mind were *Macdonald v Whitfield*[2], a Privy Council case in which Lord *g* Watson used words, relied on in *Yeoman Credit Ltd v Gregory*[3], hereinafter referred to, and which lend powerful support for the plaintiffs' argument; *Chapman v Smethurst*[4] which decided that oral evidence was not admissible when construing the effect of a signature on a promissory note in the context of acceptance; *Elliott v Bax Ironside*[5] which is a decision concerned *not* with the words 'per pro' but a descriptive status as contemplated by the second part of s 26(1) of the Bills of Exchange Act 1882; *Yeoman Credit Ltd v Gregory*[3] which *h* was a case where extrinsic evidence was admitted but was concerned with the validity of a second indorsement where one was clearly made in a personal capacity.

These authorities are useful by way of analogous comparisons, but the diligent researches of counsel have failed to discover any case which deals directly with the problems now

j

---

1   (1880) 5 App Cas 754
2   (1883) 8 App Cas 733
3   [1963] 1 All ER 245, [1963] 1 WLR 343
4   [1909] 1 KB 927
5   [1925] 2 KB 301, [1925] All ER Rep 209

under consideration. In the instant case the form of signature as acceptors on the face of the bill and as indorser on the back of the bill is precisely the same. The two defendants signed for and on behalf of the company and made the company liable on the bill as acceptor. By signing in similar form on the back of the bill they produced what counsel for the plaintiffs described as a mercantile nonsense. An indorsement on the back of a bill amounts to a warrant that the bill will be honoured and imposes in certain circumstances a transfer of liability to the indorser. No one can transfer liability from himself to himself. The only way in which validity can be given to this indorsement is by construing it to bind someone other than the acceptor. As soon therefore as it becomes obvious that the indorsement as worded is meaningless and of no value there is a patent ambiguity which allows evidence to be admitted to give effect to the intentions of the parties. The first defendant disputes this. It is submitted that no evidence can be admitted to give a different meaning to words which have an accepted meaning and which seeks to prove a different relationship between the parties than that which is unambiguously expressed. I agree with and accept the submission on behalf of the plaintiffs and reject that put forward on behalf of the defendant. I therefore admit the evidence.

I turn now to the factual situation. The plaintiffs are a firm who supply cloth for manufacture and making up. The company were customers, and became unsatisfactory payers by the beginning of 1976. Ultimately the company was put in the hands of a receiver in January 1977. Mr Lubell, the active partner of the plaintiffs, arranged for the drawing of a bill of exchange in March 1976, but he was not satisfied with the financial stability of the company and called for and obtained the personal indorsement on the back of the bill of one of the directors, Mr Keith junior, the son of the first defendant. That bill was duly presented and met. By November there was over £9,000 owing to the plaintiffs, a cheque had bounced and Mr Lubell thought that the only latitude he could extend if he forbore to sue was to repeat the process and obtain three bills of exchange to which again he wanted the personal indorsement of officers of the company. He had an interview with the first defendant. I accept Mr Lubell's evidence to the effect that he made it quite clear that he wanted personal indorsement by officers of the company, and this time he wanted two signatures. Mr Keith (the first defendant) deposed in evidence that he did not appreciate that personal liability by indorsement was being required. I regret that I cannot accept this. The first defendant agreed that he was desperately anxious for the company to continue trading and to avoid the devastating consequences of proceedings being taken against the company. In my view he believed that if the company could avoid such a disaster somehow or other the money could be found from company resources to honour the bill, as indeed was the case on the first bill. In the end things turned out to be worse than he expected. Even if Mr Lubell did not make it crystal clear in his evidence that the first defendant specifically said in terms that he agreed to accept personal liability, his conduct demonstrated that he knew what was required and he took steps to perform that to which he impliedly agreed. In Mr Lubell's presence he telephoned the second defendant, told him what was proposed and that the signatures of two officers were required by way of indorsement on the back of three bills of exchange. The second defendant, Mr Greenwood, the company secretary, told me that he did not understand that his personal indorsement was required, and this may well be so. He was getting an abbreviated and second-hand account of an agreement reached in his absence by Mr Lubell and the first defendant. In the circumstances the plaintiffs have acted very properly by discontinuing the action against the second defendant. He could not understand what good the signatures of two officers of the company would be by way of indorsement, but he vaguely remembered something being said by the first defendant to the effect that it might be better for clearing with the bank if they were indorsed on the back. So when the three bills were sent to him he applied the rubber stamp to the back and signed in the space designated for the company secretary. They went back to the first defendant who signed in the space designated for a director. Mr Lubell told me frankly and honestly that he must have seen the words which were rubber stamped, but it made no impact and he paid no attention to them. Indeed it has not been argued that Mr Lubell waived his requirement or impliedly varied the agreement. The first of the three bills due in December was honoured; the next two due in January and February were dishonoured. The company *a* was in the hands of the receiver, and so the plaintiffs now claim against the indorser, the first defendant. On the evidence I find as a fact that the first defendant agreed personally to indorse the bills; that his signature is evidence of that agreement and consequently a valid indorsement in a personal capacity and that he is personally liable on the two bills which were dishonoured on presentation. It follows that in my judgment the words 'for and on behalf of the company' are of no significance in so far as the relationship between *b* the plaintiffs and the first defendant are concerned; they do not vary or amend a clear agreement personally to indorse and thereby to warrant and assume liability for the default of the company. The signature is the relevant and significant act.

If I had not been so convinced I would have had to consider the further or alternative claim which was for an order of rectification requiring the deletion of the words 'for and on behalf of the company'. The plaintiffs would have had to show that there was either a *c* common mistake or a unilateral mistake. In view of Mr Lubell's evidence that he never applied his mind to the presence of the words rubber stamped along with the signatures, paid no attention to them and rightly, as I find, considered them of no significance because the first defendant had agreed to indorse personally, it would be difficult to establish a common mistake. The problem about a unilateral mistake would be that in the light of certain Court of Appeal decisions the plaintiffs would have to go so far as to establish a *d* degree of sharp practice on the part of the first defendant. I do not consider that any such suggestion ought to be made. In my view the first defendant paid no more attention to the words 'for and on behalf of the company' than did Mr Lubell. I do not therefore make an order for rectification. In view of my assessment of the evidence given and the conclusions pursuant thereto, such an order becomes unnecessary and the plaintiffs succeed in their claim on the merits and in law. There must therefore be judgment for the plaintiffs *e* against the remaining defendant Mr Keith.

Judgment for the plaintiffs.

Solicitors: *Osmond Gaunt & Rose* (for the plaintiffs); *Barry Posner, Pentol & Co* (for the first defendant).   *f*

K Mydeen Esq Barrister.

Miles v Miles

COURT OF APPEAL, CIVIL DIVISION

ORMROD, WALLER AND BRANDON LJJ

3rd, 23rd NOVEMBER 1978

Husband and wife – Maintenance – Attachment of earnings – Husband in receipt of pension – Fire service pension payable for past services and not for disability – Husband retiring on account of disability and receiving ill-health pension – Amount of pension depending solely on length of service – Husband in arrears with maintenance payments to wife – Application by wife for attachment of earnings order to secure maintenance payments – Whether husband's pension 'earnings' – Whether court entitled to make attachment of earnings order on pension – Attachment of Earnings Act 1971, s 24(2)(d) – Firemen's Pension Scheme Order 1973 (SI 1973 No 966), arts 12, 14, Sch 1.

M, a married man, was employed by the fire service as a fireman. In 1971 his marriage was dissolved and he was ordered to pay his wife maintenance for herself and their son. On 31st December 1972, when he was aged 52 and had been with the fire service for 28½ years, he had to retire prematurely because he had osteo-arthritis and had become permanently disabled by it. By the Firemen's Pension Scheme Order 1973 a fireman of M's age who retired after that length of service was entitled, under art 12(1)[a] of that order, to an ordinary pension calculated in accordance with Part I[b] of Sch 1 to that order by reference to the length of pensionable service. If, however, he was permanently disabled and retired on that account he was entitled, under art 14[c] of the 1973 order, to an ill-health pension calculated in accordance with Part III[d] of Sch 1 to the 1973 order also by reference to the length of his pensionable service but at a higher rate. M was paid a pension under art 14 and Sch 1, Part III. In 1977 he was in arrears with his maintenance payments. His wife applied under the Attachment of Earnings Act 1971 for an attachment of earnings order to secure those payments. M contended that the court had no power to make such an order because his pension was paid in respect of a disability and s 24(2)(d)[e] of the 1971 Act provided that pensions payable in respect of disablement or disability were not earnings in respect of which an attachment of earnings order could be made.

Held – M's pension was not a 'pension . . . payable in respect of disablement or disability', within s 24(2)(d) of the 1971 Act, because the amount of his pension was calculated solely by reference to the length of his pensionable service and took no account of the extent or degree of his disablement. It was, like a fireman's ordinary pension under art 12(1) of the 1973 order, a pension payable in respect of past services and as such it came within the definition of 'earnings' in s 24(1)(b) of the 1971 Act. It followed that the court had jurisdiction to make an attachment of earnings order on it (see p 868 h j and p 869 d e, post).

Notes

For the law relating to attachment of earnings orders generally, see 17 Halsbury's Laws (4th Edn) para 546.

For the Attachment of Earnings Act 1971, s 24, see 41 Halsbury's Statutes (3rd Edn) 816.

Appeal

This was an appeal by Gordon Henry Miles against an order of the Divisional Court of the Family Division (Sir George Baker P, Purchas and Wood JJ) made on 17th July 1978,

---

a   Article 12(1), so far as material, is set out at p 867 *d*, post

b   Part I, so far as material, is set out at p 867 *f*, post

c   Article 14, so far as material, is set out at p 867 *e*, post

d   Part III, so far as material, is set out at p 867 *g* to p 868 *a*, post

e   Section 24, so far as material, is set out at p 866 *j* to p 867 *a*, post

dismissing his appeal by way of case stated by the justices for the petty sessional division of Taunton Deane in the county of Somerset after ruling that the justices had power, on an application by the respondent, Joan Elsie Miles, to make an attachment of earnings order under s 1(3) of the Attachment of Earnings Act 1971 on the pension he received under the Firemen's Pension Scheme Order 1973. The facts are set out in the judgment of the court.

Peter Hunt for Mr Miles.
Harry Woolf as amicus curiae.
Mrs Miles did not appear.

Cur adv vult

23rd November. **BRANDON LJ** read the following judgment of the court: This appeal relates to proceedings between Mrs Joan Elsie Miles and Mr Gordon Henry Miles, who were formerly married and whose marriage was dissolved in or about 1971.

By an order of the Taunton County Court made on 10th October 1971 and registered in the Weston-super-Mare Magistrates' Court on 14th December 1971, for payment to be made through the Taunton Deane Magistrates' Court, as subsequently varied, it was ordered that Mr Miles should pay to Mrs Miles maintenance at the rate of £11 per week for herself and £5 per week for a child of the family, Richard.

By 18th January 1977 there were arrears of £563·51 under the maintenance order just mentioned, and on that date the Taunton Deane Magistrates' Court, on the application of Mrs Miles, made an attachment of earnings order against Mr Miles to secure the payments due under the former order. The attachment of earnings order was directed to the Somerset County Council, by whom Mr Miles is paid a pension as a retired member of the Somerset Fire Brigade. It ordered that authority to make deductions from Mr Miles' pension at the normal rate of £18 a week and specified the protected earnings rate as £22 a week. The figure of £18 a week was made up of £16 a week in respect of current payments under the maintenance order and £2 in respect of arrears.

At the hearing of Mrs Miles' application for an attachment of earnings order before the Taunton Deane Magistrates' Court it was contended for Mr Miles that the court had no power to make such an order in respect of his pension. The justices rejected that contention and made the order to which we have referred. Pursuant to notice of appeal dated 24th February 1977, Mr Miles appealed by way of case stated against the decision of the justices to a Divisional Court of the Family Division. On 17th July 1978 that court by a majority (Sir George Baker P and Wood J, Purchas J dissenting) dismissed the appeal. Mr Miles now appeals, pursuant to leave granted by this court, against that decision of the Divisional Court.

Mr Miles was born on 11th July 1920. He retired from the Somerset Fire Brigade on 31st December 1972, after 28½ years' service. He was then permanently disabled due to osteo-arthritis in both hips and his retirement was on account of that disablement. On his retirement he became entitled to be paid a pension by the Somerset County Council under the Firemen's Pension Scheme Order 1973[1] ('the order'), which came into force on 1st July 1973 with retrospective effect as from 1st April 1972.

The power of the justices to make an attachment of earnings order is governed by the Attachment of Earnings Act 1971 ('the Act'). The Act only gives power to make such orders in respect of 'earnings' as defined in s 24. That section provides, so far as material:

'(1) For the purposes of this Act, but subject to the following subsection, "earnings" are any sums payable to a person . . . (b) by way of pension (including an annuity in respect of past services, whether or not rendered to the person paying the annuity . . .).'

1   SI 1973 No 966

a
'(2) the following shall not be treated as earnings ... (d) pension or allowances payable in respect of disablement or disability.'

The effect of these provisions is that pensions in general, including those in respect of past services by whomsoever paid, are earnings for the purposes of the Act, so that an order attaching them can be made, but that one particular kind of pension is not to be treated as earnings for those purposes, namely a pension in respect of disablement or disability. It

b
follows that the question for decision in this case is whether the pension payable to Mr Miles following his retirement on account of permanent disablement at the end of 1972 is a pension in respect of disablement or disability within the meaning of s 24(2)(d) of the Act or not. If it is, the justices had no power to make an attachment order in respect of it; if it is not, they had such power. It is, therefore, necessary to consider the true nature of Mr Miles' pension, and for this purpose to examine the order under which it is payable to him.

c
The material provisions of the pension scheme created by the order are to be found in Part II of Appendix 2 to it. That part is headed 'Awards on Retirement of Regular Firemen' and contains ten articles numbered 12 to 21.

Article 12 (1), which is headed 'Fireman's ordinary pension', provides:

d
'Every regular fireman who has attained the age of 50 years and retires, being entitled to reckon at least 25 years' pensionable service, shall be entitled to a fireman's ordinary pension of an amount calculated in accordance with Part I of Schedule 1 ...'

Article 14, which is headed 'Fireman's ill-health award', provides:

e
'(1) Every regular fireman who is permanently disabled and retires on that account shall be entitled to an ill-health award as hereinafter provided.
'(2) In the case of a fireman—(a) who is entitled to reckon at least 5 years' pensionable service; or (b) whose infirmity of mind or body is occasioned by a qualifying injury, the award under paragraph (1) shall be an ill-health pension calculated in accordance with Part III of Schedule 1 ...'

f
Part I of Sch 1, referred to in art 12(1) above, provides:

'Fireman's Ordinary Pension: ... an ordinary pension shall be of an amount equal to 30 sixtieths of the fireman's average pensionable pay, with the addition, subject to a maximum of 40 sixtieths, of a sixtieth for each completed half year by which his pensionable service exceeds 25 years.'

g
Part III of Sch 1, referred to in art 14(2) above, provides:

'Fireman's Ill-Health Pension: 1. ... the amount of the ill-health pension shall be determined in accordance with paragraph 2, 3 or 4 as the case may require.
'2. Where the fireman has not completed 5 years' pensionable service, the amount of the pension shall not be less than a sixtieth of his average pensionable pay, and,

h
subject as aforesaid, shall be equal to a sixtieth of his average pensionable pay for each completed year of pensionable service.
'3. Where the fireman has completed 5 years' but less than 11 years' pensionable service, subject to paragraph 5, the amount of the pension shall be equal to 2 sixtieths of his average pensionable pay for each completed year of pensionable service.
'4. Where the fireman has completed at least 11 years' pensionable service, the

j
amount of the pension shall be not less than 20 sixtieths of his average pensionable pay and, subject as aforesaid and to paragraph 5, shall be equal to 7 sixtieths of his average pay with the addition—(a) of a sixtieth for each year of pensionable service up to 20 years, and (b) of a sixtieth for each completed half year by which his pensionable service exceeds 20 years.

'5. In the case of a fireman who, had he continued to serve until he could be required to retire on account of age, would have become entitled to an ordinary ... pension, a pension calculated in accordance with paragraph 3 or 4 shall not exceed the pension to which he would have become so entitled calculated, however, by reference to the average pensionable pay by reference to which the ill-health pension is calculated.'

The effect of those provisions in the case of Mr Miles is this. If he had retired on 31st December 1972, otherwise than on account of permanent disablement, he would have been entitled to be paid an ordinary fireman's pension under art 12(1). That pension would have amounted, under Part I of Sch 1, to $\frac{28}{60}$ of his average pensionable pay, with the addition of $\frac{1}{60}$ for each completed half year by which his pensionable service exceeded 25 years. Since his pensionable service exceeded 25 years by seven completed half years, this addition would have been $\frac{7}{60}$, making $\frac{35}{60}$ in all.

In the events which occurred, however, namely that Mr Miles was permanently disabled and retired on 31st December on that account, he became entitled to an ill-health pension under art 14. The amount of that pension, if calculated solely on the basis set out in para 4 of Part III of Sch 1 and without regard to para 5, would have been $\frac{7}{60}$ of his average pensionable pay with the addition of (a) $\frac{1}{60}$ for each completed year of service up to 20 years, that is to say, $\frac{20}{60}$, and (b) $\frac{1}{60}$ for each completed half year by which his pensionable service exceeded 20 years, that is to say, $\frac{17}{60}$, making $\frac{44}{60}$ in all. The effect of para 5 of Part III of Sch 1, however, was to reduce his entitlement to a maximum of $\frac{43}{60}$.

In the result, because Mr Miles retired on account of permanent disablement, he became entitled to an ill-health pension equal to $\frac{43}{60}$ of his average pensionable pay; whereas, if he had retired otherwise than on that account, he would have become entitled to an ordinary pension equal to $\frac{35}{60}$ of his average pensionable pay.

On behalf of Mr Miles it was contended before this court, as it had been contended previously before the justices and the Divisional Court, that the ill-health pension to which he was entitled, on the basis which we have explained, under art 14 of Part II of Appendix 2 to the order was a pension payable in respect of disablement or disability within s 24(2)(d) of the Act, and that it did not, therefore, constitute earnings for the purposes of the Act. The contrary view, that it was not such a pension, but came within s 24(1)(b) of the Act, was put forward by counsel who appeared before us instructed by the Treasury Solicitor and to whom we are much indebted for his assistance.

The point is in essence a short one, although we appreciate that it is by no means an easy one. In approaching it, it is, in our view, necessary to recognise and have regard to the distinction between two concepts. The first concept, which appears in both s 24(1)(b) and s 24(2)(d) of the Act, but is not to be found in art 14(1) or (2) of Part II to Appendix 2 to the order, is that of a pension payable in respect of something, past services generally in the case of s 24(1)(b) and disablement or disability in the case of s 24(2)(d). The second concept, which appears in art 14(1) of Part II of Appendix 2 to the order, but is not to be found in s 24(1)(b) or s 24(2)(d) of the Act, is that of retirement on account of something, namely permanent disablement.

If the distinction between these two concepts is recognised and regard had to it, the situation seems to us to be this. Mr Miles' retirement was on account of his disablement and he became entitled to his pension on such retirement. The amount of the pension, however, was calculated solely by reference to the length of his pensionable service, and in no way by reference to the extent or degree of his disablement. In these circumstances the pension is not, on a true view of the matter, a pension payable in respect of disablement; it is, on the contrary, like a fireman's ordinary pension under art 12(1), a pension payable in respect of past services.

While we have expressed that opinion in relation to a case in which, because of Mr Miles' long service, the pension falls to be calculated on the basis set out in para 4 of Part III of Sch 1, we should be of the same opinion in relation to a case in which, because the length of

service concerned was shorter, the amount of the pension fell to be calculated on one or
a other of the two different bases set out in paras 2 or 3.

In considering this matter comparison can, we think, usefully be made with firemen's
injury awards payable under art 15 of Part II of Appendix 2 to the order, which comprise
both a gratuity and an injury pension calculated in accordance with Part V of Sch 1. That
part of that schedule provides:

b '2. An injury pension shall be calculated by reference to the person's degree of
disablement, his average pensionable pay and the number of his completed years
of service and ... shall be the amount specified as appropriate to his degree of
disablement in columns (3), (4), (5) or (6) of the following Table, whichever is
applicable to his completed years of pensionable service.'

There follows a table, which specifies the amount of the injury pension payable as a
c percentage of average pensionable pay, and makes the degree of disablement one of the two
factors (the other being the length of pensionable service) in the determination of that
percentage.

It is not necessary in this case to decide whether an injury pension payable under art 15
is a pension in respect of disablement or disability within s 24(2)(*d*) of the Act, or a pension
in respect of past services within s 24(1)(*b*), or partly the one and partly the other. We can,
d however, see strong grounds for holding that, having regard to the basis on which its
amount is calculated, it should be regarded as being, in whole or at least in part, a pension
in respect of disablement or disability within s 24(2)(*d*).

So far, however, as an ill-health pension under art 14 is concerned, our opinion is that
which we have already indicated, namely that, since its amount depends wholly on length
of pensionable service and in no way on degree of disablement, it is not a pension in respect
e of disablement or disability within s 24(2)(*d*), but a pension in respect of past services
within s 24(1)(*b*).

For the reasons which we have given we have reached the same conclusion as the
majority in the Divisional Court and, subject to one small qualification, would dismiss the
appeal. That qualification relates to the description of the pension in the justices' order.
It is there described as a 'medical' pension. Having regard to the terms of art 14(1) of Part
f II of Appendix 2 to the order, it should have been described as an 'ill-health' pension, and
the justices' order should in this minor respect be varied accordingly.

Appeal dismissed.

Solicitors: *Morgan & Lamplugh,* Hastings (for Mr Miles); *Treasury Solicitor.*

Avtar S Virdi Esq Barrister.

Re a debtor (No 2 of 1977), ex parte the debtor v Goacher

<small>a</small>

CHANCERY DIVISION
WALTON AND FOX JJ
21st NOVEMBER, 19th DECEMBER 1977

<small>b</small>

Bankruptcy – Receiving order – Jurisdiction to make order – Bankruptcy notice based on judgment debt of £1,418 – Bankruptcy petition filed – Execution levied by judgment creditor – £1,400 paid by judgment debtor to sheriff in respect of money owed to two creditors – £1,329 appropriated to judgment creditor – Debtor contending that court could not make order because judgment debt reduced below £200 – Whether payment by judgment debtor to sheriff satisfying judgment creditor's claim – Bankruptcy Act 1914, ss 4(1)(a), 41.

<small>c</small>

On 22nd March 1977 a creditor ('the judgment creditor') obtained judgment against the debtor for a sum which, together with costs, amounted to £1,417·95. On 13th April he served on the debtor a bankruptcy notice based on that debt. The debtor did not comply with the notice, so on 26th April the judgment creditor filed a bankruptcy petition, which was served on the debtor the following day. The hearing of the petition was fixed for 31st May. Meanwhile the judgment creditor had levied execution and on 23rd May the debtor paid £1,400 to the sheriff. The sheriff had a number of other writs of execution to execute against the debtor and he appropriated £70·63 towards the claim of a prior creditor and the balance of £1,329·37 to the satisfaction of the judgment creditor's debt. At the hearing of the petition on 31st May the registrar, after being informed that the debtor had paid £1,400 to the sheriff and that there was another judgment creditor for a sum of over £1,000 who had not been paid, made a receiving order. The debtor applied for rescission of the receiving order on the ground that the registrar had no jurisdiction to make it because s 4(1)(a)[d] of the Bankruptcy Act 1914 provided that the minimum sum on which a creditor's petition could be founded was £200 and the debt owed to the judgment creditor had been reduced to £88·58 prior to the making of the order. He contended that the payment to the sheriff constituted payment to the judgment creditor; that it was immaterial that, by virtue of s 41[b] of the 1914 Act, the sheriff had to retain the money for 14 days; and that, if s 41 caused the money to be paid to the Official Receiver or the trustee in bankruptcy, it would do so by way of divesting from the judgment creditor the previously vested interest which he had in the money.

<small>d</small>

<small>e</small>

<small>f</small>

<small>g</small>

Held – The payment by the debtor to the sheriff did not satisfy the judgment creditor's claim. That claim could only be satisfied when the judgment creditor was in a position to maintain an action against the sheriff for money had and received in respect of the sum in question. Since, on a true analysis of the situation, he could maintain such an action only if all the conditions precedent necessary to constitute his right to the money had been fulfilled, ie if the 14 day period prescribed by s 41 had expired without the stated events having taken place, he could not, on 31st May, be described as having a vested interest in the money liable to be divested. It followed that the registrar had jurisdiction to make the receiving order and the application would be dismissed (see p 874 *d* to *f* and *h* to p 875 *a* and *d* and p 876 *h*, post).

<small>h</small>

Re William Hockley Ltd [1962] 2 All ER 111 distinguished.

<small>j</small>

<small>a</small>   Section 4(1), as amended, so far as material, provides: 'A creditor shall not be entitled to present a bankruptcy petition against a debtor unless—(a) the debt owing by the debtor to the petitioning creditor . . . amounts to two hundred pounds . . .'
<small>b</small>   Section 41 is set out at p 873 *c* to *f*, post

Notes

a For rescission of receiving orders, see 3 Halsbury's Laws (4th Edn) paras 417–422, and for cases on the subject of appeals from and applications to rescind or set aside receiving orders, see 4 Digest (Reissue) 184–189, *1631–1687*.

For sheriff's duties under execution, see 3 Halsbury's Laws (4th Edn) paras 889–893, and for cases on the subject, see 5 Digest (Reissue) 878–885, *7271–7318*.

For the Bankruptcy Act 1914, ss 4 and 41, see 3 Halsbury's Statutes (3rd Edn) 44, 92.

b Section 4(1)(*a*) of the 1914 Act was amended by the Insolvency Act 1976, s 1(1), Sch 1. For s 1 of, and Sch 1 to, the 1976 Act, see 46 ibid 154, 163.

Cases referred to in judgment

Benson, a debtor, Re, The debtor v Rubinstein Nash & Co [1971] Court of Appeal Transcript 94.

Cohen (a bankrupt), Re, ex parte the bankrupt v Inland Revenue Comrs [1950] 2 All ER 36, CA,
c   4 Digest (Reissue) 188, *1674*.

Gentry, Re [1910] 1 KB 825, 79 LJKB 585, DC, 4 Digest (Reissue) 148, *1302*.

Greer, Re, Napper v Fanshawe [1895] 2 Ch 217, 64 LJ Ch 620, 72 LT 865, 59 JP 441, 2 Mans 350, 13 R 598, 5 Digest (Reissue) 878, *7271*.

Hockley (William) Ltd, Re [1962] 2 All ER 111, [1962] 1 WLR 555, 10 Digest (Reissue) 932, *5435*.

d *Hooper v Lane* (1857) 6 HL Cas 443, 27 LJQB 75, 30 LTOS 33, 3 Jur NS 1026, 10 ER 1368, HL, 41 Digest (Repl) 84, *86*.

Morland v Pellatt (1828) 8 B & C 722, 3 Man & Ry KB 411, 7 LJOS KB 54, 108 ER 1211, 5 Digest (Reissue) 891, *7368*.

Rook v Wilmot (1590) Cro Eliz 209, 78 ER 465, 21 Digest (Repl) 560, *560*.

Taylor v Baker (1677) Freem KB 453, 3 Keb 788, 2 Mod Rep 214, 89 ER 338, 21 Digest
e   (Repl) 621, *1068*.

Case also cited

Debtor (No 39 of 1974), Re a, ex parte OKill v Gething [1977] 3 All ER 489, [1977] 1 WLR 1308, DC.

f **Appeal**

This was an appeal by the debtor against an order of Mr Registrar Gray, made in Scarborough County Court on 9th June 1977, dismissing an application by the debtor for rescission of a receiving order made on 31st May 1977 on the petition of the respondent, Alfred Lawrence Goacher ('the judgment creditor'). The facts are set out in the judgment of the court.

g
E C Evans-Lombe for the debtor.
J W Secker, solicitor, for the judgment creditor.
J E Friend, the Official Receiver, in person.

Cur adv vult

h

19th December. **WALTON J** read the following judgment of the court: On 22nd March 1977 the respondent ('the judgment creditor') obtained a judgment in the Scarborough District Registry of the High Court against the appellant ('the debtor') in a sum which, together with the costs, amounted to £1,417·95. On 13th April 1977 the judgment
j creditor served a bankruptcy notice based on this debt on the debtor. The debtor did not comply with such notice, and on 26th April the judgment creditor filed a bankruptcy petition which was served on the debtor the following day. On 31st May a receiving order was made on this petition.

However, in the meantime the judgment creditor had levied execution and on 23rd May the debtor paid a sum of £1,400 to the sheriff, who had a number of other writs of

execution against the debtor to execute as well. He accordingly appropriated a small sum
towards the claim of a prior creditor, and appropriated the remaining £1,329·37 to the
satisfaction of the judgment creditor's judgment debt. Before the registrar made the
receiving order he was correctly informed of the payment to the sheriff's officer, and also
of the fact that there was another judgment creditor, R J Shingler & Co Ltd, for a sum of
over £1,000 who had not been paid.

On 9th June 1977 an application was made to the registrar for rescission of the receiving
order. The grounds of such application were:

'(1) The debt having been reduced below £200·00 prior to the date of the hearing
the court had no jurisdiction to make a Receiving Order. (2) The Debtor did not
receive a copy of the Petition and had no knowledge of the hearing date and was
therefore not represented at that hearing. (3) The Debtor's goods have been seized by
the Sheriff's Officer under Writ of fi. fa. (issued by the Creditor) prior to the issue of
the Bankruptcy Notice.'

So far as the first ground is concerned, there are no disputes as to the facts. If the
payment to the sheriff of the sum of £1,329·37 is to be regarded as a payment to the
judgment creditor, the judgment creditor's debt was reduced to the sum of £88·58, a sum
less than £200. The significance of this figure is that it is now the minimum sum for a
creditor's petition, pursuant to s 4(1)(a) of the Bankruptcy Act 1914, as amended by s 1(1)
of and Sch 1 to the Insolvency Act 1976, which provisions were in force at all relevant
times.

So far as the second ground is concerned, this is a pure question of fact, on which direct
oral evidence was given by the debtor and the process server. Suffice it to say that it was
the process server who was believed. This point accordingly disappeared.

So far as the third ground is concerned, it appears from the registrar's notes of the
hearing on 9th June that evidence was given that the debtor had entered into a walking
possession agreement with the sheriff's officer, but no evidence was given as to when this
had happened. Accordingly there was no hard evidence to support this ground. The
registrar accordingly dismissed the application for rescission. From that dismissal the
debtor appeals to this court, the grounds of the appeal being stated as follows:

'1. That the debt having been reduced below £200 prior to the making of the
Receiving Order on the 31st day of May 1977 the Court had no jurisdiction to make
the said Receiving Order. 2. The said [debtor] did not receive a copy of the Petition
and had no knowledge of the hearing on the 31st day of May 1977 and was therefore
not represented at that hearing.'

It is quite extraordinary to find the second ground repeated, when it was a pure question
of fact which had been decided adversely to the debtor by the registrar, there being ample
evidence on which the registrar could come to this conclusion; indeed counsel for the
debtor did not waste his breath on it. He was, however, inclined to ask for leave to add the
original third ground to the notice of appeal, but we saw no reason to give such leave.

The notice of appeal is dated 22nd June 1977. On 23rd August 1977 a fresh application
was made to the registrar, this time for rescission of the receiving order on the basis that the
debtor could pay all his debts in full. We do not think we need deal further with this
application, because it was withdrawn on 6th September.

Now although the present appeal is in form an appeal against the registrar's refusal to
rescind the receiving order, it is, in substance, an appeal against the making of the receiving
order itself. In these circumstances, it was accepted by counsel for the debtor following
Re Cohen (a bankrupt), ex parte the bankrupt v Inland Revenue Comrs[1], that this court will not
exercise its jurisdiction to review the position unless adequate grounds are shown which
would make it proper to hear an appeal out of time. We shall therefore consider first the
strict legal position and secondly the factors affecting any exercise of the court's discretion
to extend the time for appeal.

---

1 [1950] 2 All ER 36

What was the sum owing to the judgment creditor on 31st May? Counsel for the debtor put the matter very simply and attractively. He said that the sheriff was the agent of the judgment creditor to accept payments made to him, citing Halsbury's Laws of England[1], which reads as follows:

'Payment To Sheriff. The sheriff has authority from the judgment creditor to receive the amount to be levied, and can give a discharge. If payment or tender is made, he must withdraw from possession, and if no payment is made, he must, after the seizure, proceed at once to prepare for sale.'

He cited the two cases therein referred to, namely *Rook v Wilmot*[2] and *Taylor v Baker*[3]. However, on examination those two cases did not appear to establish the precise proposition for which they were cited. But, on the basis of agency, he said that payment to the sheriff was payment to the judgment creditor, so that the effect of the provisions of the Bankruptcy Act 1914, s 41, were divesting provisions which, if they came into operation, would divest from the judgment creditor an already vested interest. That section reads:

'(1) Where any goods of a debtor are taken in execution, and before the sale thereof, or the completion of the execution by the receipt or recovery of the full amount of the levy, a notice is served on the sheriff that a receiving order has been made against the debtor, the sheriff shall, on request, deliver the goods and any money seized or received in part satisfaction of the execution to the official receiver, but the costs of the execution shall be a first charge on the goods or money so delivered, and the official receiver or trustee may sell the goods, or an adequate part thereof, for the purpose of satisfying the charge.

'(2) Where, under an execution in respect of a judgment for a sum exceeding twenty pounds the goods of a debtor are sold or money is paid in order to avoid sale, the sheriff shall deduct his costs of the execution from the proceeds of sale or the money paid, and retain the balance for fourteen days, and, if within that time notice is served on him of a bankruptcy petition having been presented by or against the debtor, and a receiving order is made against the debtor thereon or on any other petition of which the sheriff has notice, the sheriff shall pay the balance to the official receiver or, as the case may be, to the trustee, who shall be entitled to retain it as against the execution creditor.'

Accordingly, counsel submitted that when the debtor made the payment of £1,400 to the sheriff, the sheriff accepted £1,329·37 of that payment as agent for the judgment creditor who was thereby paid in full, and that it was quite immaterial that the sheriff was unable to pay the money over to the judgment creditor because of the provisions of s 41; and that if those provisions finally resulted in the moneys having to be paid to the Official Receiver or trustee, they would take effect by way of divesting from the judgment creditor the previously vested interest which he had in those moneys.

There are, undoubtedly, expressions of opinion to be found in the cases to the effect that the effect of s 41, or its precursors, do, indeed, have this divesting effect. See, for example, the dictum of Chitty J in *Re Greer, Napper v Fanshawe*[4]:

'The result of the authorities, apart from that enactment, is that the sheriff holds the money to the use of the judgment creditor, and is liable to be sued in an action for money had and received. For that proposition it is sufficient to cite the case of *Morland v. Pellatt*[5]. By the enactment referred to the sheriff is directed to retain the money for fourteen days; and in the event of bankruptcy supervening the execution creditor loses his right to the money. The effect is to place a temporary embargo or

---

1   17 Halsbury's Laws (4th Edn) para 492
2   (1590) Cro Eliz 209, 78 ER 465
3   (1677) Freem KB 453, 89 ER 338
4   [1895] 2 Ch 217 at 221
5   (1829) 8 B & C 722, 108 ER 1211

stop on the money. If more technical language is requisite, I say the execution
creditor's right to the money is vested, but liable to be divested. His right to the *a*
money is not a contingent right.'

That was recently approved and applied by Pennycuick J in *Re William Hockley Ltd*[1].
Indeed, the facts of that case bear a very considerable likeness to the facts of the present case,
and we shall take them from the headnote, which reads as follows[2]:

> 'A company against which a judgment creditor had issued execution paid the *b*
> sheriff on Feb. 6, 1962, a sum sufficient to discharge the judgment debt and costs, but
> did not inform the judgment creditor of the payment. On Feb. 7, 1962, the judgment
> creditor presented a petition for winding-up the company. On Feb. 9, 1962, the
> petitioning creditor's solicitors received a letter, written on Feb. 7, 1962, from the
> sheriff informing them that the amount due had been recovered and that a cheque
> would be sent to them on Feb. 21, 1962, which was the end of the fourteen days' *c*
> period prescribed by s. 326(2) of the Companies Act, 1948. On the question of the
> liability for the costs of the petition, *Held*: a contingent creditor of a company within
> s. 224(1) of the Companies Act, 1948, was a person towards whom under an existing
> obligation the company would or might become subject to a present liability on the
> happening of some future event or at a future date ... the petitioning creditor was
> not, on Feb. 7, 1962, such a person, because the judgment had been extinguished *d*
> by payment, and accordingly the petitioning creditor must pay the costs of the
> petition ...'

However, we find this analysis an unsatisfactory one. There can be no possible doubt,
and indeed it was so accepted by Pennycuick J in the latter case[1], that the remedy of the
judgment creditor to recover moneys so paid to the sheriff is by means of an action for *e*
money had and received: see *Morland v Pellatt*[3]. We find the concept of moneys which can
only be recovered in this manner as possibly 'vested but liable to be divested' wholly
inappropriate. If the worst came to the worst, and the judgment creditor had to sue to
recover such moneys, he could only do so, as we see it, when all the conditions precedent
necessary to constitute his right to the money had been fulfilled, that is to say, when the 14
day period had expired without the stated events having taken place. If, for example in *Re*
William Hockley Ltd[1], one could imagine that the petitioning creditor, having managed to *f*
issue a writ and commence RSC Ord 14 proceedings forthwith, had come before a master
on 8th February and asked for summary judgment, can there be any question but that his
application would have been equally summarily dismissed? For, in truth, the sheriff in
such a situation is not simply an agent for the judgment creditor; he has much wider
responsibilities, which now include duties towards the official receiver or trustee in *g*
bankruptcy. Compare what was said by Lord Cranworth LC in *Hooper v Lane*[4]:

> 'But the answer is, that the sheriff, though for some purposes an agent of the party
> who puts the writ into his hands, is not a mere agent. He is a public functionary,
> having indeed duties to perform towards those who set him in motion analogous, in
> many respects, to those of an agent towards his principal; but he has also duties *h*
> towards others, and particularly towards those against whom the writs in his hands
> are directed.'

We therefore conclude that payment by the judgment debtor to the sheriff does not
satisfy the claim of the execution creditor, which claim is only satisfied when the judgment

j

1　[1962] 2 All ER 111, [1962] 1 WLR 555
2　[1962] 2 All ER 111
3　(1828) 8 B & C 722, 108 ER 1211
4　(1857) 6 H L Cas 443 at 549-550, 10 ER 1368 at 1410

creditor is in a position to maintain an action against the sheriff for money had and
received in respect of the sum in question. It is, we think, possible to distinguish *Re*
a
William Hockley Ltd[1] on its own facts, since in that case the winding-up petition was only
presented after the payment to the sheriff had been made, so that at the date of payment
there was no pending petition, whereas in the present case there was in fact the creditor's
petition pending at the time the payment was made, but we would regard such a distinction
as unsatisfactory. We have no doubt whatsoever that the decision in that case was correct
b on its own facts, because there were no other creditors supporting or opposing the petition,
so that on dismissal of the petition the creditor became indisputably entitled to the moneys
in the hands of the sheriff; but we do not feel able to adopt the reasoning by which that
result was reached.

There is, however, one special distinction between a winding-up petition and a
bankruptcy petition in relation to the duty of the creditor to accept payment off of his
c debt. A creditor who has knowledge of an available act of bankruptcy is always fully
justified in refusing to accept payment off of his debt, and proceeding to present a
bankruptcy petition: see *Re Gentry*[2] in the Court of Appeal. By parity of reasoning, we see
no reason why a creditor in the position of the judgment creditor in the present case should
not say that he elects to proceed with his petition and thus (in effect) waive the benefit of
the execution which he otherwise might probably have enjoyed for the benefit of all
d creditors.

We therefore reach the conclusion that, as a matter of law, the sole remaining ground of
appeal in the notice of appeal is not made out. But we do not desire to leave the matter
there, and we proceed to consider what the position would be if we are wrong in this view
so that if we were to give leave to appeal out of time the appeal would necessarily succeed.

What consequences follow? On the above basis we think we cannot do better than
e consider the various points listed by Cairns LJ in *Re Benson*[3] in the Court of Appeal as
matters which the court should consider on an application for leave to appeal out of time,
namely, (1) whether there is reasonable excuse for the delay, (2) whether there is any
substance in the proposed appeal, (3) whether the applicant will obtain any real benefit if
the appeal succeeds, (4) whether it would be a hardship or an injustice to other parties if the
application were granted, and (5) whether the applicant's conduct has been such as to
f forfeit any claim to favourable consideration of the exercise of the court's discretion.

As we have indicated already, we now start with item (2) presumed in the appellant's
favour. As regards item (1), no excuse has been given for any delay, but in any event that
delay has not in itself been very great, and we would not wish to found anything on the
delay that has taken place. Item (3) is a very different matter. It is not possible for us to be
certain as to the debtor's debts, because no advertisement has taken place so far pursuant to
various orders of the court. But we can say with tolerable certainty that they are not less
g than £10,819·28. This includes one very substantial debt to R J Shingler & Co Ltd in
respect of rent and other matters of which the debtor must have known, but which he did
not disclose in his statement of affairs. There are also other now known but undisclosed
debts.

Now the position is that the debtor is hopelessly insolvent, and his assets are unlikely to
h amount to 50p in the £ of his debts, unless a sum of £6,500 can be raised from the sale of
a fish and chip business owned by the debtor jointly with his wife, or possibly by one or
other of them alone, but which his wife says she is willing to let him have. There has been
a contract of sale entered into for this business on the 22nd August 1977 at a price of
£6,500. It is blindingly obvious that no purchaser is going to pay for the goodwill of a
business of this nature unless he is assured of a tenancy of the premises, and cl 3 of the
j agreement provides accordingly:

---

1   [1962] 2 All ER 111, [1962] 1 WLR 555
2   [1910] 1 KB 825
3   [1971] Court of Appeal Transcript 94

'The Vendors shall endeavour to obtain from the Landlord of the said shop and premises an Assignment of the existing tenancy agreement or alternatively a new *a* lease in the Purchaser's favour on such terms as may be agreed between the Landlord and the Purchaser.'

Clause 5 reads:

'On the completion of the purchase the Vendors shall further deliver up to the Purchaser possession of the shop and premises aforesaid upon which the said business *b* is carried on.'

Now the substantial undisclosed debt to which we have already referred is one which partly in respect of a claim for rent in respect of the very premises at which this business is carried on. And there is at present pending in the Scarborough County Court an application by the debtor for a new tenancy under the provisions of the 1954 Act, and on the application of the debtor those proceedings stand adjourned.   *c*

From all this, it appears to us that the prospects of the sale ever being completed are remote in the extreme. The agreement itself provides for completion on 1st October, and we were offered no information whatsoever as to why the sale had not been completed. The bankruptcy proceedings themselves do not stand in the way, as the registrar gave a direction that the sale could be completed on certain terms relating to the safeguarding of the proceeds of sale. Be that as it may, in the absence of any explanation as to what is *d* happening in relation to such sale, we feel that we must entirely discount the likely receipt of the £6,500.

Accordingly, we think that the debtor would gain no lasting benefit whatsoever from the appeal being allowed. Per contra, we think it would be unfortunate if the appeal were allowed, in that the landlord of the fish and chip premises served a bankruptcy notice on 29th April 1977 and, but for the actual present proceedings, would have presented a *e* petition based thereon. We do not think that the creditors should be exposed to the possibility of the debtor dealing with his assets whilst a fresh notice is being served and taking effect.

But even if all the other matters were in the debtor's favour, we consider that his conduct as a whole is such that he has completely forfeited any claim to favourable consideration of the exercise of the court's discretion. In the first place, he has not disclosed his debts fully *f* in the statement of affairs. We therefore have no means of knowing what his true position really is, although it is clearly bad. Secondly, he asserted that he was never served with a copy of the petition, and was on this point disbelieved by the registrar. Thirdly, as the official receiver has reported, he has failed to keep proper books of account; he has traded with knowledge of his insolvency (and here it must be borne in mind additionally that according to the debtor he is not strictly entitled to any share in the fish and chip business *g* at all) and he has been adjudged bankrupt on a previous occasion.

Looking at the matter in the round, therefore, we are clearly of opinion that even if the appeal were bound to succeed, we would not have thought that this was a proper case in which to give leave to appeal out of time. We therefore dismiss this appeal.

Appeal dismissed.   *h*

Solicitors: *Bedwells*, Scarborough (for the debtor); *Cook, Fowler & Outhet*, Scarborough (for the judgment creditor).

Jacqueline Metcalfe   Barrister.

Ferguson v The Queen

PRIVY COUNCIL

VISCOUNT DILHORNE, LORD EDMUND-DAVIES, LORD FRASER OF TULLYBELTON, LORD SCARMAN AND SIR ROBIN COOKE

12th JULY, 5th OCTOBER 1978

Criminal law – Trial – Direction to jury – Standard of proof – Direction on what amounts to reasonable doubt – Judge directing jury that reasonable doubt could be kind of doubt affecting person in the conduct of important affairs – Judge also repeatedly emphasising to jury importance of being sure of accused's guilt – Whether misdirection – Whether use of formula in directing jury desirable.

Criminal law – Appeal – No miscarriage of justice – Murder – Application of proviso – Error of law by Court of Appeal in applying proviso – Whether appropriate for Judicial Committee of Privy Council to exercise discretion under proviso – Whether direction on identification safe – West Indies Associated States Supreme Court (Grenada) Act 1971 (Grenada), s 41(1) proviso.

Shortly after 9.15 pm on 6th April 1974 the deceased, who was driving a lorry accompanied by his wife and two other women, reached a bridge which was blocked by heaps of stones. His wife remained in the lorry while he and the two other women got out to remove the stones. The wife had with her a bag containing $200. Whilst she was sitting in the lorry a man leapt from behind the bridge, pointed a gun at her and demanded all the money she had. She handed him the bag. He demanded more money. At that point one of the other women noticed what was happening and called to the deceased who was at the far end of the bridge. As he came running towards the wife the man fired at him, shouting 'Don't come any closer'. The deceased kept on running, with his hands in the air, and when he was only six feet away the man fired another shot which killed him. The next day the appellant was charged with the deceased's murder. At the trial the wife was the only witness who identified the appellant as the killer and her evidence was not corroborated. Moreover, on the night of the killing the wife did not identify the killer as a person she knew whereas at the trial she gave evidence that she had known the appellant for some six years, and described the clothing he wore on the night of the killing. The defence was an alibi. The trial judge did not leave the issue of manslaughter to the jury since he took the view that the only proper verdict was murder or an acquittal. The judge's direction to the jury contained a misdirection on the necessary intent to establish murder. Further, in directing the jury on the standard of proof required from the prosecution he told them that, if they entertained the kind of doubt about the appellant's guilt 'which might affect the mind of a person in the conduct of important affairs', the burden on the prosecution of proving guilt beyond reasonable doubt would not be discharged; however, thereafter the judge repeatedly emphasised to the jury the importance of being sure of the appellant's guilt. On the issue of identification the judge reminded the jury that the wife was the only witness to identify the appellant as the killer, and of the facts which might lead them to doubt her reliability on that issue, and said that if they believed her and disbelieved the appellant and his witness they must convict. The jury returned a verdict of guilty of murder. The appellant appealed to the Court of Appeal of Grenada on the grounds of the unsatisfactory nature of the evidence on identity, and of the misdirection as to intent. The Crown conceded the misdirection on intent, but invited the court to apply the proviso to s 41(1)[a] of the West Indies Associated States Supreme Court (Grenada) Act 1971 and to dismiss the appeal on the ground that there had been no miscarriage of justice. The court applied the proviso and dismissed the appeal holding that, as a verdict of murder was the only reasonable verdict on the evidence, there had been no miscarriage of justice.

The appellant appealed against conviction to the Judicial Committee of the Privy Council

---

a   Section 41 is set out at p 880 c to e, post

contending that the proviso should not be applied because (i) the issue of manslaughter
should have been left to the jury, (ii) the evidence of identification was unsafe and the
direction on that issue inadequate, (iii) the direction on the standard of proof, that a
reasonable doubt could be such a doubt as might affect a person in the conduct of
important affairs, was a misdirection because it might have led the jury to apply a lower
standard than being satisfied of guilt beyond reasonable doubt, (iv) the court were in error
when applying the proviso to s 41 in asking themselves not whether the verdict was unsafe
or unsatisfactory but whether there was evidence on which a reasonable jury could convict,
and (v) as the Court of Appeal had erred in applying the proviso, the Board itself should
consider whether the proviso was applicable in all the circumstances.

Held – The appeal would be dismissed for the following reasons—
    (i) Since the judge had used words which clearly conveyed to the jury that they must feel
sure of the appellant's guilt and had repeatedly emphasised that requirement, there was no
misdirection on the standard of proof (see p 882 b, post); *Walters v The Queen* [1969] 2 AC
26 applied.
    (ii) The Court of Appeal were in error in their approach in applying the proviso to s 41
of the 1971 Act since what they were required to ask themselves was whether the verdict
was unsafe or unsatisfactory and not whether there was evidence on which a reasonable
jury could convict. Although only very rarely would the Board consider it appropriate itself
to exercise the discretion conferred on the Court of Appeal by the proviso to s 41, in the
unusual circumstance that the court had erred in applying the proviso, the Board would
consider whether it would itself apply the proviso. In all the circumstances no miscarriage
of justice had occurred because (a) there was no evidence on which a verdict of
manslaughter could have been returned and the judge had been right not to leave that issue
to the jury, (b) there was no misdirection as to the standard of proof, and (c) it had been safe
to convict on the identification evidence since the judge had fully and fairly summed up
the evidence on that issue and the jury were fully alerted to the difficulties in that part of
the Crown's case. Accordingly, the Board would apply the proviso and dismiss the appeal
(see p 881 b, p 882 c to e and p 883 b to d, post).
    Per Curiam. While the law does not require use of a particular formula in directing a
jury on the standard of proof, as a general rule a judge would be wise to adopt one; in
general it is safe and sufficient to use the time-honoured formula of directing the jury that
they must be satisfied beyond reasonable doubt (see p 881 h to p 882 a, post).

Notes
For directions on the burden of proof, see 11 Halsbury's Laws (4th Edn) para 298.
    For application of the proviso to s 2(1) of the Criminal Appeal Act 1968, see ibid para
649.
    For unsafe or unsatisfactory verdict, see ibid para 650.
    Section 41 of the West Indies Associated States Supreme Court (Grenada) Act 1971
(Grenada) corresponds with s 2 of the Criminal Appeal Act 1968. For s 2 of the 1968 Act,
see 8 Halsbury's Statutes (3rd Edn) 690.

Cases referred to in judgment
Bullard v R [1961] 3 All ER 470n, [1957] AC 635, [1957] 3 WLR 656, 121 JP 576, 42 Cr App
    R 1, PC, 14(2) Digest (Reissue) 818, 7055.
Dawson v The Queen (1961) 106 CLR 1, 35 ALJR 360, HC of Aust.
R v Turnbull [1976] 3 All ER 549, [1977] QB 224, [1976] 3 WLR 445, 140 JP 648, 63 Cr App
    R 132, CA, 14(2) Digest (Reissue) 489, 4038.
Walters v The Queen [1969] 2 AC 26, [1969] 2 WLR 60, 31 WIR 354, PC, 14(2) Digest
    (Reissue) 811, 6982.

Appeal

a This was an appeal by Charles Ferguson, by special leave granted on 21st December 1977, against the judgment and order of the Court of Appeal of Grenada (Maurice Davis CJ, St Bernard and Peterkin JJA) dated 28th May 1976 whereby the appellant's appeal against conviction of murder and sentence of death in the High Court of Justice (Criminal), at St George's Grenada Assizes (Nedd J and a jury) on 4th November 1975, was dismissed. The facts are set out in the judgment of the Board.

b

Nigel Murray and Lloyd L Noel (of the Grenada Bar) for the appellant.
Jeffrey Thomas QC and David Ashby for the Crown.

LORD SCARMAN. Shortly after 9.15 pm on 6th April 1974 the late Roy Donald was driving a pick-up lorry towards the River Antoine bridge, La Poterie, Grenada. He was *c* accompanied by his wife Louise, his sister-in-law Linette Rock, Angela Drakes and a small child. Louise Donald had with her a bag containing $200 and some other items of property. They found the bridge blocked by heaps of stones set in three places, at each end and in the middle of the bridge. Roy Donald stopped and, leaving the headlights on, went to the far end of the bridge to remove the stones there. Angela Drakes went to the nearest heap, and Linette Rock to the one in the middle. Louise Donald remained in the vehicle. *d* A man suddenly leaped from behind the bridge and advanced towards Louise Donald, pointing a gun at her. He told her to remain where she was and ordered her to give him 'all the money you made today'. She handed him the bag, saying: 'Here it is.' He replied: 'This is not all, it has more.' She then said: 'Take the money and leave us alone.'

At this moment Linette Rock saw what was going on. She called out, 'Roy'. As he came running towards his wife, the man fired a shot, crying out: 'Don't come any closer.' But *e* Roy Donald kept on coming, hands in air, and shouting: 'Kill me if you want to kill me.' The man fired a second shot, at a range of about six feet. The bullet entered Roy Donald's chest and penetrated the heart, killing him.

The appellant was arrested the next day and charged with the murder of Roy Donald. He was tried and convicted at the October 1974 assizes. His defence, which he supported by himself giving evidence, was an alibi. The trial judge directed the jury that the burden *f* was on him to disprove the prosecution's case by establishing his alibi to their satisfaction. He appealed. It came on for hearing at the end of May 1975. Faced with this fundamental misdirection, the Court of Appeal quashed the conviction and ordered a new trial.

The new trial was before Nedd J and a jury in October and November 1975. The appellant was again convicted of murder. His appeal against conviction was dismissed on 28th May 1976. He was granted special leave to appeal to Her Majesty in Council on 21st *g* December 1977.

Nothing new emerged at the retrial. There was really no dispute as to how Roy Donald came to his death. The critical issue was the identity of the killer. He was identified by Louise Donald, but by no other witness on whom reliance could be put. The defence was, as before, an alibi, but this time the appellant did not give evidence. He did call a witness, and he made a statement from the dock. The summing-up on the facts was full and fair, *h* as indeed counsel admitted in the Court of Appeal, where in effect only two points were taken. They were: (1) that the evidence of identity was so unsatisfactory as to render the conviction unsafe; (2) that the judge misdirected the jury as to the intent necessary to establish the crime of murder.

Counsel did not suggest there had been any misdirection on the issue of identity, though counsel for the appellant has submitted before their Lordships' Board that it was inadequate *j* by the standard now set by the English Court of Appeal in *R v Turnbull*[1]. The Court of Appeal rejected the first ground of appeal, holding 'that there was sufficient evidence on which a reasonable jury could have come to the conclusion that the man who shot the deceased Donald was the appellant'.

1　[1976] 3 All ER 549, [1977] QB 224

The second ground, misdirection as to the intent necessary to establish the crime of murder, the Court of Appeal held to be a valid criticism of the summing-up. Section 242 of the Criminal Code, Chapter 76, of the Laws of Grenada provides (so far as is material): 'Whoever intentionally causes the death of another person by any unlawful harm is guilty of murder . . .' The judge directed the jury that—

> 'The prosecution must prove that the accused intentionally did an act which caused harm to the deceased Roy Donald; that that harm was unlawful and resulted in the death of Roy Donald.'

The Crown conceded that this was a misdirection but submitted that no injustice was done and invited the Court of Appeal to apply the proviso to s 41(1) of the West Indies Associated States Supreme Court (Grenada) Act 1971, and to dismiss the appeal. Section 41, as amended, is in substantially the same terms as s 2(1) of the English Criminal Appeal Act 1968. It is as follows:

> '(1) The Court of Appeal on any such appeal against conviction shall, subject as hereinafter provided, allow the appeal if it thinks that the verdict of the jury should be set aside on the ground that it is unsafe or unsatisfactory or that the judgment of the Court before whom the Appellant was convicted should be set aside on the ground of a wrong decision of any question of law or that there was a material irregularity in the course of the trial and in any other case shall dismiss the appeal: Provided that the Court of Appeal may, notwithstanding that it is of the opinion that the point raised in the appeal might be decided in favour of the appellant, dismiss the appeal if it considers that no miscarriage of justice has actually occurred.
> '(2) Subject to the provisions of this Act the Court of Appeal shall, if it allows an appeal against conviction, quash the conviction, and direct a judgment and verdict of acquittal to be entered, or, if the interests of justice so require, order a new trial.'

The Court of Appeal decided to apply the proviso, but not before they had considered the question (not raised in the notice of appeal) whether the judge was right in his refusing to leave to the jury the possibility of their returning a verdict of manslaughter. The court concluded that the judge was right. They held he was abundantly justified when he said to the jury: 'You convict of murder or acquit.'

At the end of the day the Court of Appeal summarised their view of the case in these words:

> 'In the present case the defence of the appellant was an alibi and the jury by their verdict showed that they were satisfied of his identity. The verdict of guilty of murder was the only proper verdict on the evidence in the case and despite the misdirection in law to the jury the appellant, in our opinion, has suffered no injustice and we find that no miscarriage of justice has actually occurred. This court will apply the proviso to s 41(1) of the West Indies Associated States Supreme Court (Grenada) Act 1971 and dismiss the appeal.'

Counsel for the appellant, to whom their Lordships' Board is indebted for a most helpful and cogent argument, has submitted that the Court of Appeal was wrong to apply the proviso in the circumstances of this case. In support of the submission he made the following points: (1) that manslaughter, as a possible alternative verdict, should have been left to the jury; (2) that the direction on the issue of identity was inadequate; (3) that the evidence of identification was unsafe; (4) that the Court of Appeal, when dealing with the submission that the verdict was unsafe and unsatisfactory, adopted an approach which was wrong in law in that they asked themselves not whether the verdict was unsafe and unsatisfactory but whether there was evidence on which a reasonable jury could convict; (5) that the trial judge's direction as to the standard of proof was incorrect in law. Counsel for the appellant went on to submit that the verdict was unsafe and that on a proper consideration of the points raised in the Court of Appeal and before their Lordships' Board it was not possible to say that no miscarriage of justice had actually occurred.

a   In their Lordships' view, if the contention that manslaughter ought to have been left to the jury is made good, the conviction must be quashed. For there could then be no question of applying the proviso. As Lord Tucker said in *Bullard v R*[1]:

> 'Every man on trial for murder has the right to have the issue of manslaughter left to the jury if there is any evidence on which such a verdict can be given. To deprive him of this right must of necessity constitute a grave miscarriage of justice and it is idle to speculate what verdict the jury would have reached.'

b   Counsel for the appellants took us carefully through the evidence in an endeavour to establish the possibility of manslaughter. But their Lordships were totally unconvinced. The circumstances of the shooting were such that, if the jury were satisfied by the evidence of identity, the only proper verdict was one of murder. There was no evidence on which a verdict of manslaughter could have been returned.

c   It is convenient, at this stage, to deal with counsel for the appellant's final point, that the judge's direction as to standard of proof was incorrect. The direction was ample (counsel for the appellant really says 'too ample') and repeated five times in the course of the summing-up, twice at the beginning, once in the middle, and twice at the end. The jury must have known what the judge required of them. One passage from the summing-up suffices for a true understanding of counsel for the appellant's criticism. The judge said:

d   '... it is required to satisfy you beyond reasonable doubt—to satisfy you beyond reasonable doubt that from the evidence before you—all the evidence, whether it be from the prosecution or from the defence—that the accused is guilty of murder, as I have explained murder to you. If you entertain the kind of doubt, which might affect the mind of a person in the conduct of important affairs, then you entertain a reasonable doubt which is the kind of doubt which the prosecution must remove in

e   order to secure a conviction. The burden of thus proving the accused guilty rests on the prosecution and remains there from the beginning to the end of the case, even when, as in this case, the accused has pleaded an alibi. The prosecution must satisfy you that the accused's plea of alibi cannot, in the light of the evidence before you, stand the light of day, or hold water, or, if you prefer more dignified language, be entertained. Once you entertain that reasonable doubt, it must be resolved in favour

f   of the accused, and he must be acquitted.'

It is submitted that the judge encouraged 'too subjective' an approach by telling the jury that the doubt must be such as 'might affect the mind of a person in the conduct of important affairs'.

g   Their Lordships were told and accepted that in certain Commonwealth jurisdictions some judges avoid this formulation. It is criticised as being unhelpful and possibly dangerous, in that questions arising in the conduct of important affairs often have little resemblance to the issues in a criminal trial and individual jurors may well decide such questions by applying standards lower than satisfaction beyond reasonable doubt and analogous, if to anything, to the civil standard of the balance of probabilities. In *Walters v The Queen*[2] their Lordships had to consider a direction almost identical in part with that

h   in this case. Delivering the judgment in that case (which was not an appeal, but an application for special leave to appeal) Lord Diplock pointed out that a distinction between 'objective' and 'subjective' tests is not apt in this context. The Board expressed the view in that case that the formula used in summing-up does not matter so long as it is made clear to the jury, whatever words are used, that they must not return a verdict against a defendant unless they are sure of his guilt. Their Lordships' Board agree with these

j   comments, with one reservation. Though the law requires no particular formula, judges are wise, as a general rule, to adopt one.

---

1   [1961] 3 All ER 470 at 471, [1957] AC 635 at 644
2   [1969] 2 AC 26

The time-honoured formula is that the jury must be satisfied beyond reasonable doubt. As Dixon CJ said in *Dawson v The Queen*[1], attempts to substitute other expressions have never prospered. It is generally sufficient and safe to direct a jury that they must be satisfied beyond reasonable doubt so that they feel sure of the defendant's guilt. Nevertheless, other words will suffice, so long as the message is clear. In the present case, the jury could have been under no illusion. The importance of being sure was repeatedly emphasised. The judge thrust it home when, abandoning the language of the law for homely metaphors with which the jury would have been well familiar, he said that the prosecution had to satisfy them that the accused's alibi could not 'stand the light of day, or hold water, or, if you prefer more dignified language, be entertained'. In their Lordships' opinion there is nothing in counsel for the appellant's point on standard of proof.

Their Lordships turn next to the point that the Court of Appeal erred in law when they asked themselves not whether the verdict was unsafe and unsatisfactory but whether there was evidence on which a reasonable jury could convict. In the light of the terms of the amended s 41 of the 1971 Act, the point is a good one. The Court of Appeal overlooked the new wording which, following on that of the English Criminal Appeal Act 1968, s 2(1), has introduced the modern criterion, is the verdict unsafe or unsatisfactory? The use which counsel for the appellant's seeks to make before their Lordships' Board of this error by the Court of Appeal, is that he submits that this Board has itself to consider whether in all the circumstances the proviso ought to be applied. In the unusual circumstances of this case their Lordships accept the submission, while recognising that only very rarely would they think it appropriate to exercise the discretion which the statute confers on the Court of Appeal.

The application of the proviso is justified only if the court considers 'that no miscarriage of justice has actually occurred'. One is, therefore, driven back to a consideration of the trial and the summing-up. The criticisms that manslaughter should have been left to the jury and that the judge erred in his direction as to standard of proof having been rejected, the fundamental issue arises: was it safe to convict on the identification evidence? If there be any reasonable doubt as to the identity of the killer, their Lordships could not say that no miscarriage of justice had actually occurred.

Though the judge did not direct the jury in the terms now approved in *R v Turnbull*[2], he left the jury in no doubt as to the state of the evidence and their duty. There was only one witness who recognised the appellant as the killer, Louise Donald. He reminded them of this fact and of the facts which might lead the jury to doubt the reliability of her identification, and concluded: 'If you believe Louise Donald, after considering Dr Gibbs' evidence, and disbelieve the accused and his witness, you must convict.' In their Lordships' view there is nothing in the way in which the judge dealt with the issue of identity to suggest that the jury were not fully alert to the difficulties in this part of the Crown's case.

But that is not the end of the matter. Before the proviso is applied, the court (in this exceptional case, the Board) must consider that no miscarriage of justice has actually occurred. It is necessary, therefore, to examine Louise Donald's evidence with care. First, her evidence was uncorroborated by either her sister, Linette Rock, or Angela Drakes. Secondly, according to the evidence, she told no one on the night of the killing that she had recognised the killer. Thirdly, Dr Gibbs, who conducted the post mortem, swore an affidavit in May 1975 (ie after the first trial and shortly before the first appeal) in which he said that at about 10.30 pm on 6th April 1974 he was at the hospital when he heard Louise Donald, in answer to the question repeatedly put to her as to whether she knew who shot her husband, as repeatedly respond: 'All I know is that it was a tall man, fair complexion, wearing a coat, and a hat drawn over his face.' When questioned at the second trial, Dr Gibbs said he did not hear Mrs Donald speak these words. He said it had occurred to him that he might have been confusing her with her sister, who was also at the hospital that night.

---

1   (1961) 106 CLR 1 at 18
2   [1976] 3 All ER 549, [1977] QB 224

a Louise Donald, under cross-examination, said she saw Dr Gibbs that night, but did not recall that she told anyone that night it was the appellant who shot her husband or that anyone asked her if she recognised the person who shot her husband.

Clearly the jury must have accepted Dr Gibbs' explanation of his affidavit. The question therefore is as to the inherent strength of Louise Donald's identification. She must also have been accepted as truthful. But was she reliable, or was there the possibility that she was mistaken? She conversed with the killer; he was close enough to take her bag from b her; he pushed a gun at her. She recognised him as a man she had known for some five or six years. She described his dress (including, significantly, not a hat but a cap).

Their Lordships have considered anxiously all the evidence as to identification. It was summed up fully and fairly; the evidence of Dr Gibbs was put to the jury in its correct context, ie as capable of throwing doubt on Louise Donald's reliability. The whole emphasis of the summing-up as to the facts was as favourable to the appellant as it could c be. Their Lordships are in no doubt that the jury reached a true verdict. No miscarriage of justice has occurred at the end of this protracted and unhappy case, involving as it has done two trials, two appeals, and requiring (a most exceptional feature) their Lordships' Board to consider whether or not to apply the proviso. Accordingly, their Lordships will report to Her Majesty that the appeal should be dismissed.

d *Appeal dismissed.*

Solicitors: *Seifert Sedley & Co* (for the appellant); *Osmond Gaunt & Rose* (for the Crown).

Mary Rose Plummer   Barrister.

e

Johnson and another v Agnew

HOUSE OF LORDS

LORD WILBERFORCE, LORD SALMON, LORD FRASER OF TULLYBELTON, LORD KEITH OF KINKEL AND
f LORD SCARMAN

11th, 12th, 13th DECEMBER 1978, 8th MARCH 1979

Sale of land – Damages for breach of contract – Damages in substitution for specific performance – Damages at common law for repudiation of contract – Purchaser failing to complete in time – Vendor choosing to pursue remedy of specific performance – Specific performance rendered g impossible – Land sold by mortgagees because vendor defaulting on mortgages – Purchaser's failure to complete preventing vendor from redeeming mortgages and being able to convey land to purchaser – Whether vendor entitled to seek alternative remedy of common law damages for repudiation of contract – Whether damages to be assessed at date when remedy of specific performance aborted.

h By a contract dated 1st November 1973 the vendors agreed to sell a house and some grazing land to the purchaser. The properties were mortgaged under separate mortgages. The purchase price exceeded the amount required to pay off the mortgages and also a bank loan obtained by the vendors for the purchase of another property. The contract fixed the completion date as 6th December. The purchaser paid part of the deposit and accepted the vendors' title, but did not complete on that date. On 21st December the vendors served on j the purchaser a notice making time of the essence of the contract and fixing 21st January 1974 as the final date by which completion was to take place. The purchaser failed to complete, and on 8th March the vendors commenced an action against her, claiming specific performance and damages in addition to, or in lieu of, specific performance, and alternatively, a declaration that the vendors were no longer bound to perform the contract, and further relief. On 20th May the vendors issued a summons under RSC Ord 86 for

summary judgment for specific performance. An order for specific performance of the
contract was made on 27th June, but it was not drawn up and entered until 26th
November. By then the mortgagees of the house had obtained an order for possession. On
7th March 1975 the mortgagees of the grazing land also obtained an order for possession.
On 3rd April they contracted to sell the land and on 20th June the mortgagees of the house
contracted to sell the house. Completion of both sales by the mortgagees took place in
July. Thus the vendors, who had taken no action to enforce the order for specific
performance, were not in a position to convey the properties to the purchaser after 3rd
April. On 5th November they applied by motion (i) for an order that the purchaser should
pay the balance of the purchase price and for an enquiry as to damages, or (ii) alternatively,
for a declaration that they were entitled to treat the contract as repudiated by the purchaser
and an enquiry as to damages. The judge dismissed the motion. The vendors appealed,
seeking an order for payment of the balance of the purchase price, or, alternatively,
damages at common law for breach of contract, and in the further alternative damages in
lieu of specific performance under the Chancery Amendment Act 1858. They contended
that their election, on 20th May, to proceed for the remedy of specific performance was not
irrevocable and that on obtaining an order for specific performance which subsequently
became incapable of being worked out they were entitled to claim the alternative remedy
of damages for repudiation of the contract. The purchaser contended that the election to
proceed for specific performance was irrevocable and, furthermore, in the circumstances
it would be inequitable to award the vendors damages under the 1858 Act because the non-
completion of the contract was caused by the mortgagees obtaining orders for possession
of the properties due to the vendors failing to pay the sums due under the mortgages. The
Court of Appeal[a] held (i) that, as the vendors were no longer able to perform their
obligations under the contract to convey the properties, it would be wrong to compel the
purchaser to pay the balance of the purchase price, and so the vendors could not obtain
relief under the order for specific performance; (ii) that where a vendor elected to pursue
the remedy of specific performance and obtained an order, he could not, if it became
impossible to enforce the order, revert to the position before the election and claim the
alternative remedy of repudiation of the contract and damages therefor; (iii) but where, as
in the present case, an order for specific performance was no longer capable of being
worked out, damages in lieu of specific performance could be awarded by the court under
the equitable jurisdiction created by the 1858 Act. The court allowed the appeal on the
ground that it would be equitable to allow the vendors damages in lieu of specific
performance because it was the purchaser and not the vendors who had rendered specific
performance impossible, and ordered the damages to be assessed as at 26th November 1974
(i e the date of entry of the order for specific performance) and discharged the order for
specific performance. On appeal by the purchaser,

Held – (i) A vendor who sought specific performance merely elected for a course which
might or might not lead to the implementation of the contract: he was not electing for an
eternal or unconditional affirmation of the contract but simply for the contract to be
continued under the court's control. If he obtained an order for specific performance and
it became impossible to enforce it, he then had the right to ask the court to discharge the
order and terminate the contract. On such an application he could be awarded damages at
common law for breach of contract since the contract was not rescinded ab initio but
remained in existence until it was terminated by the court. The court, however, would not
make an order discharging the decree of specific performance and terminating the contract
if to do so would be unjust, in the circumstances then existing, to the other party. On the
facts, the non-completion, and ultimate impossibility of completion, of the contract was
the fault of the purchaser and the vendors were entitled not only to an order discharging
the specific performance order and terminating the contract, but also to damages at

common law for breach of contract (see p 890 *b c e f*, p 894 *a* to *g*, p 895 *c* to *f* and p 897 *b*

a to *e*, post); dicta of Lord Porter in *Heyman v Darwins Ltd* [1942] 1 All ER at 360–361 and of Greene MR in *Austins of East Ham Ltd v Macey* [1941] Ch at 341 applied; *McKenna v Richey* [1950] VLR 360 and dicta of Dixon J in *McDonald v Dennys Lascelles Ltd* (1933) 48 CLR at 476–477 and of Dixon CJ in *Holland v Wiltshire* (1954) 90 CLR at 416 adopted; *Henty v Schröder* (1879) 12 Ch D 666, *Hutchings v Humphreys* (1885) 54 LJ Ch 650, *Jackson v De Kadich* [1904] WN 168, *Barber v Wolfe* [1945] 1 All ER 399 and *Capital and Suburban*

b *Properties Ltd v Swycher* [1976] 1 All ER 881 overruled; *Horsler v Zorro* [1975] 1 All ER 584 overruled in part.

(ii) The fact that the vendors were entitled to recover damages at common law did not affect the measure of damages, because damages awarded under the 1858 Act were assessed in the same manner as damages at common law (see p 895 *h* to p 896 *a d* and p 897 *b* to *e*, post); *Ferguson v Wilson* (1866) LR 2 Ch App 77, *Rock Portland Cement Co v Wilson* (1882) 48

c LT 386, *Wroth v Tyler* [1973] 1 All ER 897, *Horsler v Zorro* [1975] 1 All ER 584 and *Malhotra v Choudhury* p 186, ante, considered.

(iii) The date at which the damages should be assessed should be fixed not at 26th November 1974 but at 3rd April 1975 (ie the first date on which the mortgagees contracted to sell part of the property) as the vendors had acted reasonably in pursuing the remedy of specific performance and that was the date at which the remedy became aborted. It

d followed that the appeal would be dismissed subject to the variation of the order of the Court of Appeal by the substitution of 3rd April 1975 for 26th November 1974 as the date by reference to which the damages should be assessed (see p 896 *e* to p 897 *e*, post); *Ogle v Earl Vane* (1868) LR 3 QB 272, *Hickman v Haynes* (1875) LR 10 CP 598 and *Radford v De Froberville* [1978] 1 All ER 33 considered.

Decision of Court of Appeal [1978] 3 All ER 314 varied.

e

Notes

For remedies under an uncompleted contract, see 34 Halsbury's Laws (3rd Edn) 320–334, paras 543–566, and for cases on the subject, see 40 Digest (Repl) 239–240, *1989–2016*.

For the Chancery Amendment Act 1858, s 2, see 25 Halsbury's Statutes (3rd Edn) 703.

f
Cases referred to in opinions

Austins of East Ham Ltd v Macey [1941] Ch 338, 110 LJ Ch 159, 165 LT 47, CA, 40 Digest (Repl) 240, *2014*.

Barber v Wolfe [1945] 1 All ER 399, [1945] Ch 187, 114, LJ Ch 149, 172 LT 384, CA, 40 Digest (Repl) 240, *2016*.

g *Barker (John) & Co Ltd v Littman* [1941] 2 All ER 537, [1941] Ch 405, 111 LJ Ch 123, 165 LT 340, CA, 40 Digest (Repl) 240, *2015*.

Boston Deep Sea Fishing & Ice Co Ltd v Ansell (1888) 39 Ch D 339, [1886–90] All ER Rep 65, 59 LT 345, CA, 1 Digest (Repl) 551, *1726*.

Buckland v Farmer & Moody (a firm) [1978] 3 All ER 929, [1979] 1 WLR 221, CA.

Capital and Suburban Properties Ltd v Swycher [1976] 1 All ER 881, [1976] Ch 319, [1976] 2

h WLR 822, CA.

Clough v London & North Western Railway Co (1871) LR 7 Exch 26, [1861–73] All ER Rep 646, 41 LJ Ex 17, 25 LT 708, Ex Ch, 39 Digest (Repl) 652, *1566*.

Ferguson v Wilson (1866) LR 2 Ch App 77, 36 LJ Ch 67, 15 LT 230, 30 JP 788, LJJ, 44 Digest (Repl) 152, *1325*.

Grant v Dawkins [1973] 3 All ER 897, [1973] 1 WLR 1406, 27 P & CR 158, Digest (Cont Vol

j D) 856, *837b*.

Hall v Burnell [1911] 2 Ch 551, [1911–13] All ER Rep 631, 81 LJ Ch 46, 105 LT 409, 40 Digest (Repl) 245, *2057*.

Henty v Schröder (1879) 12 Ch D 666, 48 LJ Ch 792, 40 Digest (Repl) 239, *1994*.

Heyman v Darwins Ltd [1942] 1 All ER 337, [1942] AC 356, 166 LT 306, HL, 2 Digest (Repl) 492, *435*.

Hickman v Haynes (1875) LR 10 CP 598, 44 LJCP 358, 32 LT 873, 39 Digest (Repl) 799, 2687.

Holland v Wiltshire (1954) 90 CLR 409.

Horsler v Zorro [1975] 1 All ER 584, [1975] Ch 302, [1975] 2 WLR 183, 29 P & CR 180, Digest (Cont Vol D) 803, 2016a.

Hutchings v Humphreys (1885) 54 LJ Ch 650, 52 LT 690, 40 Digest (Repl) 239, 1995.

Hythe Corpn v East (1866) LR 1 Eq 620, 35 LJ Ch 257, 13 LT 788, 44 Digest (Repl) 152, 1330.

Jackson v De Kadich [1904] WN 168.

Leeds Industrial Co-operative Society Ltd v Slack [1924] AC 851, [1924] All ER Rep 259, 93 LJ Ch 436, 131 LT 710, HL, 30 Digest (Reissue) 257, 631.

Malhotra v Choudhury p 186, ante, [1978] 3 WLR 825, CA.

Mayson v Clouet [1924] AC 980, 93 LJPC 237, 131 LT 645, PC, 40 Digest (Repl) 261, 2201.

McDonald v Dennys Lascelles Ltd (1933) 48 CLR 457, [1933] ALR 381, 40 Digest (Repl) 261, *1179.

McKenna v Richey [1950] VLR 360.

Morel Brothers & Co Ltd v Earl of Westmoreland [1904] AC 11, [1900–3] All ER Rep 397, 73 LJKB 93, 89 LT 702, HL, 1 Digest (Repl) 673, 2376.

Moschi v Lep Air Services Ltd [1972] 2 All ER 393, [1973] AC 331, [1972] 2 WLR 1175, HL; *affg* sub nom *Lep Air Services Ltd v Rolloswin Investments Ltd* [1971] 3 All ER 45, [1971] 1 WLR 934, CA, Digest (Cont Vol D) 368, 625a.

Ogle v Earl Vane (1868) LR 3 QB 272, 9 B & S 182, 37 LJQB 77, Ex Ch; *affg* LR 2 QB 275, 36 LJQB 175, 39 Digest (Repl) 819, 2815.

Radford v De Froberville [1978] 1 All ER 33, [1977] 1 WLR 1262.

Rock Portland Cement Co v Wilson (1882) 52 LJ Ch 214, 48 LT 386, 44 Digest (Repl) 152, 1331.

Scarf v Jardine (1882) 7 App Cas 345, [1881–5] All ER Rep 651, 51 LJQB 612, 47 LT 258, HL, 21 Digest (Repl) 299, 633.

Sudagar Singh v Nazeer [1978] 3 All ER 817, [1978] 3 WLR 785.

Sweet v Meredith (1863) 4 Giff 207, 32 LJ Ch 147, 7 LT 664, 666 ER 680, 40 Digest (Repl) 239, 1990.

United Australia Ltd v Barclays Bank Ltd [1940] 4 All ER 20, [1941] AC 1, 109 LJKB 919, 164 LT 139, 46 Com Cas 1, HL, 3 Digest (Repl) 224, 542.

Watson v Cox (1873) LR 15 Eq 219, 42 LJ Ch 279, 27 LT 814, 40 Digest (Repl) 239, 1992.

Wood (Harold) Brick Co Ltd v Ferris [1935] 1 KB 613; *on appeal* [1935] 2 KB 198, 104 LJKB 533, 153 LT 241, CA, 40 Digest (Repl) 279, 2327.

Wroth v Tyler [1973] 1 All ER 897, [1974] Ch 30, [1973] 2 WLR 405, 25 P & CR 138, Digest (Cont Vol D) 855, 837a.

Appeal

By a writ dated 8th March 1974 Michael Charles Johnson and Renee Marie Johnson ('the vendors') brought an action against Adeline Agnew ('the purchaser') claiming (i) specific performance of a written agreement ('the agreement') dated 1st November 1973 for the sale and purchase of freehold property at Wooburn Common, Hitcham, Buckinghamshire, comprising premises known as Sheepcote Grange and Sheepcote Cottage and lands in the vicinity thereof; (ii) all necessary and consequential accounts, directions and enquiries; (iii) damages for breach of contract in lieu of or in addition to specific performance; and (iv) a declaration that the vendors were entitled to a lien on the property for the unpaid balance of the purchase money and interest payable under the agreement; alternatively (v) a declaration that by reason of the purchaser's breaches of the agreement the vendors were no longer bound to perform the sale of the property to her; (vi) a declaration that the deposit due under the agreement had been forfeited to the vendors; (vii) a declaration that the vendors were entitled to resell the property and recover any loss on the resale from the purchaser; and (viii) payment of £8,700 being the balance of the deposit. On 27th June

1974, on the vendors' application by summons, Master Dyson ordered that the agreement

a should be specifically performed. By notice of motion dated 5th November 1976 and amended on 26th January 1977, the vendors applied, inter alia, for (i) an order that the purchaser should pay to the vendors the balance of the purchase price and interest less the rents and profits received by the vendors since 6th December 1973; and (ii) an order that there should be an enquiry whether the vendors had suffered damage since 27th June 1974 by reason of the purchaser's failure to complete the agreement; alternatively (iii) a

b declaration that the vendors were entitled to treat the agreement as repudiated by the purchaser (iv) an order that the deposit of £3,000 paid by the purchaser be forfeited to the vendors; and (v) an order for an enquiry as to the damage sustained by the vendors by reason of such repudiation. On 25th February 1977 Megarry V-C dismissed the vendors' motion. The vendors appealed seeking, inter alia, an order in the terms of paras (i) and (ii) of the motion; alternatively an order in the terms of para (ii) of the motion; and in the further alternative an order in the terms of paras (iii) to (v) of the motion. On 13th

c December 1977 the Court of Appeal[1] (Buckley, Goff LJJ and Sir David Cairns) (i) ordered that the order of 25th February 1977 be discharged; (ii) declared that in view of the circumstances in which the purchaser had failed to complete her part of the agreement and on the vendors electing to have the order for specific performance discharged and to treat the agreement as having been repudiated by the purchaser, it was just and equitable to

d award the vendors damages in lieu of specific performance under the jurisdiction originally conferred on the court by the Chancery Amendment Act 1858; (iii) directed that the order for specific performance of the agreement be discharged; (iv) declared that the vendors and the purchaser were no longer bound specifically to perform the agreement; (v) ordered the following enquiries to be made (a) an enquiry as to what damages had been sustained by the vendors by reason of the failure of the purchaser to perform the agreement specifically

e according to its terms, such damages to be assessed by reference to the difference between £117,000 (being the purchase price payable under the agreement) and the value of the property as at 26th November 1974 (being the date of entry of the order for specific performance) but not to exceed the difference between the purchase price and the aggregate of the sum of £3,000 (being the portion of the deposit paid by the defendant as purchaser under the agreement) and the proceeds of the sales by the mortgagees of the several parts

f of the property to the extent to which such proceeds discharged indebtedness of the vendors; (b) an enquiry as to the amount of rents and profits of the property received by the vendors or by any other person or persons by their order or for the use of the vendors since 6th December 1973 (being the date of the sale); (vi) ordered that what should be found due on enquiry (b) should be deducted from what should be found due under enquiry (a) and the balance certified; and the court was to add to the certified balance interest on the sum

g of £114,000 (being the unpaid balance of the purchase price under the agreement) at the rate of 17% per annum from 6th December 1973 to 26th November 1974; (vii) ordered (but without prejudice nevertheless to the general powers of the court as to the award of interest in respect of any subsequent period or periods) that the vendors were not to be allowed any interest in respect of the period from 26th November 1974 down to and including 13th May 1977; and (viii) ordered that the purchaser should pay to the vendors

h the amount of the certified balance together with interest to be added thereto as aforesaid and the interest (if any) awarded under the general powers of the court. The purchaser appealed. The facts are set out in the opinion of Lord Wilberforce.

J H Hames QC and *James Denniston* for the purchaser.
Peter Millett QC and *Dirik Jackson* for the vendors.

j 8th March. The following opinions were delivered.

---

1 [1978] 3 All ER 314, [1978] Ch 176

LORD WILBERFORCE. My Lords, this appeal arises in a vendors' action for specific performance of a contract for the sale of land, the appellant being the purchaser and the *a* vendors the respondents. The factual situation is commonplace, indeed routine. An owner of land contracts to sell it to a purchaser; the purchaser fails to complete the contract; the vendor goes to the court and obtains an order that the contract be specifically performed; the purchaser still does not complete; the vendor goes back to the court and asks for the order for specific performance to be dissolved, for the contract to be terminated or 'rescinded', and for an order for damages. One would think that the law as to so typical *b* a set of facts would be both simple and clear. It is no credit to our law that it is neither. Learned judges in the Chancery Division and in the Court of Appeal have had great difficulty in formulating a rule and have been obliged to reach differing conclusions. That this is so is due partly to the mystification which has been allowed to characterise contracts for the sale of land, as contrasted with other contracts, partly to an accumulated debris of decisions and textbook pronouncements which has brought semantic confusion and *c* misunderstandings into an area capable of being governed by principle. I hope that this may be an opportunity for a little simplification.

I must state the facts in some detail because the sequence of events may be important. I repeat however that such additional elements as appear in the relevant history do not take the present case away from the normal. Many sellers of one property commit themselves concurrently to buying another; indeed to do so is often the main reason for the sale. *d* Many sellers of property have incumbrances on that property. The law should be able to accommodate such matters without indigestion.

The contract for sale was dated 1st November 1973. The property sold was called Sheepcote Grange, Wooburn Common, Bucks; it consisted of the grange itself and some grazing land. On the grange there was a first legal charge to a building society for £15,600 and two other charges. On the grazing land there was a first legal charge to a finance *e* company for £6,000 and a second legal charge to a bank. The purchase price under the contract was £117,000 and so was ample to pay off the charges and to leave the vendors with money to buy another property. In fact on 1st November 1973 they contracted to buy one for £34,000, and raised the purchase money by loan from a bank. If the first contract had been completed according to its terms, no difficulty would have arisen; the bank loan would have been discharged from the purchase price. *f*

The contract was made by reference to the Law Society's General Conditions of Sale (1973 Edn) and provided for completion on 6th December 1973. A deposit of 10% was to be paid but the purchaser only paid £3,000. Before 6th December 1973 the purchaser had accepted the vendors' title (this of course disclosed the existence of the mortgages) and a form of conveyance was agreed. However the purchaser did not complete on that date. On 21st December 1973 the vendors' solicitors served a notice, under condition 19 of the *g* conditions of sale, making time of the essence of the contract and fixing 21st January 1974 as the final date by which completion was to take place. The purchaser failed to complete on that date. On 8th March 1974 the vendors issued a writ claiming specific performance and damages in lieu of or in addition thereto and alternatively a declaration that the vendors were no longer bound to perform the contract and further relief. On 20th May 1974 the vendors issued a summons under RSC Ord 86 for summary judgment for specific *h* performance, and the order sought was made in the usual form on 27th June 1974. It was not however drawn up and entered until 26th November 1974.

Meanwhile action was taken by the vendors' mortgagees. The building society obtained an order for possession of the grange on 22nd August 1974, they sold it on 20th June 1975 and completion took place on 18th July 1975. The finance company obtained an order for possession of the grazing land on 7th March 1975, they sold it on 3rd April 1975 and *j* completion took place on 11th July 1975. Thus by 3rd April 1975 specific performance of the contract for sale had become impossible. The vendors took no action on the order for specific performance until 5th November 1976 when they issued a notice of motion seeking (i) an order that the purchaser should pay the balance of the purchase price and an enquiry as to damages or (ii) alternatively a declaration that they were entitled to treat the

contract as repudiated by the purchaser and to forfeit the deposit and an enquiry as to
damages.

On 25th February 1977 Megarry V-C dismissed the motion. He rejected the first claim
on the ground that, as specific performance was no longer possible, it would be unjust to
order payment of the full purchase price. The second claim was not pressed, on the ground
that it was precluded by authority (ie *Capital and Suburban Properties Ltd v Swycher*[1]).

The vendors appealed to the Court of Appeal[2] who again rejected each alternative; they
followed the previous decision in *Swycher's* case[1]. However they held that the vendors
could recover damages under the Chancery Amendment Act 1858 (Lord Cairns's Act),
which enables the court to award damages in addition to or in substitution for specific
performance. They accordingly made an order discharging the order for specific
performance and an order for an enquiry as to damages. They fixed the date on which
damages should be assessed as 26th November 1974, being the date of entry of the order
for specific performance. The purchaser is now appealing against this order.

In this situation it is possible to state at least some uncontroversial propositions of law.
First, in a contract for the sale of land, after time has been made, or has become, of the
essence of the contract, if the purchaser fails to complete, the vendor can *either* treat the
purchaser as having repudiated the contract, accept the repudiation, and proceed to claim
damages for breach of the contract, both parties being discharged from further performance
of the contract; *or* he may seek from the court an order for specific performance with
damages for any loss arising from delay in performance. (Similar remedies are of course
available to purchasers against vendors.) This is simply the ordinary law of contract
applied to contracts capable of specific performance. Secondly, the vendor may proceed by
action for the above remedies (viz specific performance or damages) in the alternative. At
the trial he will however have to elect which remedy to pursue. Thirdly, if the vendor
treats the purchaser as having repudiated the contract and accepts the repudiation, he
cannot thereafter seek specific performance. This follows from the fact that, the purchaser
having repudiated the contract and his repudiation having been accepted, both parties are
discharged from further performance.

At this point it is important to dissipate a fertile source of confusion and to make clear
that although the vendor is sometimes referred to in the above situation as 'rescinding' the
contract, this so-called 'rescission' it quite different from rescission ab initio, such as may
arise for example in cases of mistake, fraud or lack of consent. In those cases, the contract
is treated in law as never having come into existence. (Cases of a contractual right to
rescind may fall under this principle but are not relevant to the present discussion.) In the
case of an accepted repudiatory breach the contract has come into existence but has been
put an end to or discharged. Whatever contrary indications may be disinterred from old
authorities, it is now quite clear, under the general law of contract, that acceptance of a
repudiatory breach does not bring about 'rescission ab initio'. I need only quote one
passage to establish these propositions. In *Heyman v Darwins Ltd*[3] Lord Porter said:

> 'To say that the contract is rescinded or has come to an end or has ceased to exist
> may in individual cases convey the truth with sufficient accuracy, but the fuller
> expression that the injured party is thereby absolved from future performance of his
> obligations under the contract is a more exact description of the position. Strictly
> speaking, to say that, upon acceptance of the renunciation of a contract, the contract
> is rescinded is incorrect. In such a case the injured party may accept the renunciation
> as a breach going to the root of the whole of the consideration. By that acceptance he
> is discharged from further performance and may bring an action for damages, but the
> contract itself is not rescinded.'

1   [1976] 1 All ER 881, [1976] Ch 319
2   [1978] 3 All ER 314, [1978] Ch 176
3   [1942] 1 All ER 337 at 360–361, [1942] AC 356 at 399

See also *Boston Deep Sea Fishing & Ice Co Ltd v Ansell*[1] per Bowen LJ, *Mayson v Clouet*[2] per Lord Dunedin and *Moschi v Lep Air Services Ltd*[3] per Lord Reid and Lord Diplock. I can see no *a* reason, and no logical reason has ever been given, why any different result should follow as regards contracts for the sale of land, but a doctrine to this effect has infiltrated into that part of the law with unfortunate results. I shall return to this point when considering *Henty v Schröder*[4] and cases which have followed it down to *Barber v Wolfe*[5] and *Horsler v Zorro*[6].

Fourthly, if an order for specific performance is sought and is made, the contract *b* remains in effect and is not merged in the judgment for specific performance. This is clear law, best illustrated by the judgment of Greene MR in *Austins of East Ham Ltd v Macey*[7], in a passage which deals both with this point and with that next following. It repays quotation in full:

> 'The contract is still there. Until it is got rid of, it remains as a blot on the title, and the position of the vendor, where the purchaser has made default, is that he is entitled, *c* not to annul the contract by aid of the court, but to obtain the normal remedy of a party to a contract which the other party has repudiated. He cannot, in the circumstances, treat it as repudiated except by order of the court and the effect of obtaining such an order is that the contract, which until then existed, is brought to an end. The real position, in my judgment, is that, so far from proceeding to the enforcement of an order for specific performance, the vendor, in such circumstances *d* is choosing a remedy which is alternative to the remedy of proceeding under the order for specific performance. He could attempt to enforce that order and could levy an execution which might prove completely fruitless. Instead of doing that, he elects to ask the court to put an end to the contract, and that is an alternative to an order for enforcing specific performance.'

e

Fifthly, if the order for specific performance is not complied with by the purchaser, the vendor may *either* apply to the court for enforcement of the order, *or* may apply to the court to dissolve the order and ask the court to put an end to the contract. This proposition is as stated in *Austins of East Ham Ltd v Macey*[8] (and see also *Sudagar Singh v Nazeer*[9] per Megarry V-C) and is in my opinion undoubted law, both on principle and authority. It follows, indeed, automatically from the facts that the contract remains in force after the *f* order for specific performance and that the purchaser has committed a breach of it of a repudiatory character which he has not remedied, or as Megarry V-C put it[9], that he is refusing to complete.

These propositions being, as I think they are, uncontrovertible, there only remains the question whether, if the vendor takes the latter course, ie of applying to the court to put an end to the contract, he is entitled to recover damages for breach of the contract. On *g* principle one may ask 'Why ever not?' If, as is clear, the vendor is entitled (after and notwithstanding that an order for specific performance has been made) if the purchaser still does not complete the contract, to ask the court to permit him to accept the purchaser's repudiation and to declare the contract to be terminated, why, if the court accedes to this, should there not follow the ordinary consequences, undoubted under the general law of contract, that on such acceptance and termination the vendor may recover damages for *h* breach of contract?

1　(1888) 39 Ch D 339 at 365, [1886–90] All ER Rep 65 at 73–74
2　[1924] AC 980 at 985
3　[1972] 2 All ER 393 at 399, 403, [1973] AC 331 at 345, 350
4　(1879) 12 Ch D 666
5　[1945] 1 All ER 399, [1945] Ch 187
6　[1975] 1 All ER 584, [1975] Ch 302
7　[1941] Ch 338 at 341
8　[1941] Ch 338
9　[1978] 3 All ER 817 at 821, [1978] 3 WLR 785 at 790

I now consider the arguments which are said to support the negative answer.

a The principal authority lies in *Henty v Schröder*[1] in which Jessel MR is briefly reported as having laid down that a vendor 'could not at the same time obtain an order to have the agreement rescinded and claim damages against the defendant for breach of the agreement'. The unsatisfactory nature of this statement has often been remarked on. It is unsupported by reasons, and is only reported in oratio obliqua. It is in direct conflict with previous authorities: *Sweet v Meredith*[2] and, *Watson v Cox*[3]; yet no reason is given why these

b authorities are not followed, nor is it said that they are overruled. If it were not for the great authority of Jessel MR, I can hardly believe that so fragile and insecure a foundation for the law would ever have survived. Explanations have been canvassed: that Jessel MR was confusing discharge of a contract by accepted repudiation with rescission ab initio, a desperate hypothesis; that (much more plausibly) the statement was procedural in character, the emphasis being on 'at the same time'; there was indeed authority that, at that

c time, in order to obtain damages a separate bill had to be filed (see *Hythe Corpn v East*[4]). But it is not profitable to pursue these; the authority, weak as it is, is there and has been followed; it is necessary to see what strength it has gained in the process.

At first instance, it has been followed usually uncritically. In *Hutchings v Humphreys*[5] it was followed by North J but on a misapprehension as to what was ordered in *Watson v Cox*[5]. In *Jackson v De Kadich*[6], if contrary to sound practice this report is citable at all,

d Farwell J (logically enough, if *Henty v Schröder*[7] was right) appears to have decided that a vendor who did not proceed with an order for specific performance could not forfeit the purchaser's deposit, but in *Hall v Burnell*[8] Eve J took a different view. In *Harold Wood Brick Co Ltd v Ferris*[9] Swift J treated *Henty v Schröder*[7] as depending on Chancery procedure at the time (1879). In recent times it has been treated as good law in *Barber v Wolfe*[10] and *Horsler v Zorro*[11], but in each of these cases the judgment is discoloured by the erroneous conception

e of rescission ab initio as a remedy for breach of contract[12]. *Horsler v Zorro*[11] was itself firmly doubted, for this reason, by Goff LJ in *Buckland v Farmer & Moody (a firm)*[13], in a passage with which I respectfully agree. Finally, *Henty v Schröder*[7] was endorsed by the Court of Appeal in *Capital and Suburban Properties Ltd v Swycher*[14], but on a new basis which I shall shortly consider, and in the present case.

Textbook authority in general supports the decision. Fry on Specific Performance[15]

f mentions the proposition with lack of enthusiasm, but the main pillars in this case are Mr Cyprian Williams's books on The Contract of Sale of Land and on Vendor and Purchaser. In the former work[16] he firmly commits himself to the theory of rescission plus restitutio in integrum as remedies for breach of the contract. In the latter, a well-known book of reference on conveyancing matters, he equally firmly denies a right to damages. I refer to the fourth edition where the learned author writes[17]:

g

---

1 (1879) 12 Ch D 666 at 667
2 (1863) 4 Giff 207
3 (1873) LR 15 Eq 219; more fully in 42 LJ Ch 279
4 (1866) LR 1 Eq 620
5 (1885) 54 LJ Ch 650
h 6 [1904] WN 168
7 12 Ch D 666
8 [1911] 2 Ch 551, [1911–13] All ER Rep 631
9 [1935] 1 KB 613; *on appeal* [1935] 2 KB 198
10 [1945] 1 All ER 399, [1945] Ch 187
11 [1975] 1 All ER 584, [1975] Ch 302
12 See *Barber v Wolfe* [1945] 1 All ER 399 at 400, [1945] Ch 187 at 189; *Horsler v Zorro* [1975] 1 All
j ER 584 at 589–590, 591, [1975] Ch 302 at 309, 311
13 [1978] 3 All ER 929 at 943, [1979] 1 WLR 221 at 237
14 [1976] 1 All ER 881, [1976] Ch 319
15 6th Edn (1921), p 548
16 (1930), p 121
17 (1936), vol 2, pp 1025–1026

'And if he obtains an order for specific performance of the contract, that will be a
bar to his recovering damages for the breach; for in equity the plaintiff suing on a
breach of contract was required, as a rule, to elect which remedy he would pursue;
and a man entitled to alternative remedies is barred, after judgment on the one, from
asserting the other.'

See also an earlier passage[1].

My Lords, this passage is almost a perfect illustration of the dangers, well perceived by
our predecessors but tending to be neglected in modern times, of placing reliance on
textbook authority for an analysis of judicial decisions. It is on the face of it a jumble of
unclear propositions not logically related to each other. It is 'supported' by footnote
references to cases (two of this House and one of the Privy Council) which are not explained
or analysed. It would be tedious to go through them in detail, but I am satisfied that, with
the exception of the reference to *Henty v Schröder*[2], they fail to support the text; it is enough
to mention that the decisions cited of this House are *Scarf v Jardine*[3], a case of choosing
between two inconsistent *rights* (see *United Australia Ltd v Barclays Bank Ltd*[4] per Lord
Atkin), and *Morel Brothers & Co Ltd v Earl of Westmorland*[5], an instance of the rule that after
suing an agent, and obtaining judgment, you cannot sue the principal. Neither of these
cases in any way bears on such as the present.

The state of authority then, so far as English law is concerned, is that, starting from a
judgment in which no reasons are given, and which may rest on any one of several
foundations, of which one is unsound and another obsolete, a wavering chain of precedent
has been built up, relying on that foundation, which is itself unsound. Systems based on
precedent unfortunately often develop in this way and it is sometimes the case that the
resultant doctrine becomes too firmly cemented to be dislodged.

This is however the first time that this House has had to consider the right of an innocent
party to a contract for the sale of land to damages on the contract being put an end to by
accepted repudiation, and I think that we have the duty to take a fresh look. I should
certainly be reluctant to invite your Lordships to endorse a line of authority so weak and
unconvincing in principle. Fortunately there is support for a more attractive and logical
approach from another bastion of the common law whose courts have adopted a robuster
attitude. I quote first from a judgment of Dixon J[6] which with typical clarity sets out the
principle, this, be it observed, in a case concerned with a contract for the sale of land:

'When a party to a simple contract, upon a breach by the other contracting party of
a condition of the contract, elects to treat the contract as no longer binding upon him,
the contract is not rescinded as from the beginning. Both parties are discharged from
the further performance of the contract, but rights are not divested or discharged
which have already been unconditionally acquired. Rights and obligations which
arise from the partial execution of the contract and causes of action which have
accrued from its breach alike continue unaffected. When a contract is rescinded
because of matters which affect its formation, as in the case of fraud, the parties are to
be rehabilitated and restored, so far as may be, to the position they occupied before the
contract was made. But when a contract, which is not void or voidable at law, or
liable to be set aside in equity, is dissolved at the election of one party because the
other has not observed an essential condition or has committed a breach going to its
root, the contract is determined so far as it is executory only and the party in default
is liable for damages for its breach.'

---

1   4th Edn (1936), vol 2, p 1004
2   (1879) 12 Ch D 666
3   (1882) 7 App Cas 345
4   [1940] 4 All ER 20 at 37–38, [1941] AC 1 at 30
5   [1904] AC 11
6   *McDonald v Dennys Lascelles Ltd* (1933) 48 CLR 457 at 476–477

Closer to the present case, in *Holland v Wiltshire*[1] the High Court of Australia was directly
a concerned with a question of damages for breach of contract for the sale of land. The
purchaser having failed to complete, the vendor claimed damages. Dixon CJ said[2]:

'The proper conclusion is that the vendor proceeded not under the contractual
provision but on the footing that the purchasers had discharged him from the
obligations of the contract. It follows that he is entitled to sue for unliquidated
damages. Some suggestion was made for the defendants appellants that once the
b contract was treated by the vendor as discharged he could not recover for breach. This
notion, however, is based on a confusion with rescission for some invalidating cause.
It is quite inconsistent with principle and has long since been dissipated. It is enough
to refer to the note upon the subject in Mr. *Voumard's Sale of Land in Victoria*[3].'

Voumard's Sale of Land[4], in a judicially approved passage, is explicit that damages can be
c recovered.

Then, in *McKenna v Richey*[5], a case very similar to the present, it was decided by O'Bryan
J in the Supreme Court of Victoria that, after an order for specific performance had been
made, which in the event could not be carried into effect, even though this was by reason
of delay on the part of the plaintiff, the plaintiff could still come to the court and ask for
damages on the basis of an accepted repudiation. The following passage is illuminating[6]:

d 'The apparent inconsistency of a plaintiff suing for specific performance and for
common law damages in the alternative arises from the fact that, in order to avoid
circuity of action, there is vested in one Court jurisdiction to grant either form of
relief. The plaintiff, in effect, is saying: "I don't accept your repudiation of the
contract but am willing to perform my part of the contract and insist upon your
performing your part—but if I cannot successfully insist on your performing your
e part, I will accept the repudiation and ask for damages." Until the defendant's
repudiation is accepted the contract remains on foot, with all the possible consequences
of that fact. But if, from first to last, the defendant continues unwilling to perform
her part of the contract, then, if for any reason the contract cannot be specifically
enforced, the plaintiff may, in my opinion, turn round and say: "Very well, I cannot
have specific performance; I will now ask for my alternative remedy of damages at
f common law." This, in my opinion, is equally applicable both before and after decree
whether the reason for the refusal or the failure of the decree of specific performance
is due to inability of the defendant to give any title to the property sold, or to the
conduct of the plaintiff which makes it inequitable for the contract to be specifically
enforced.'

g Later[7] the judge said of the case:

'It is an appropriate case for a Court of Equity to say: "As a matter of discretion, this
contract should not now be enforced specifically, but, in lieu of the decree for specific
performance, the Court will award the plaintiff such damages as have been suffered
by her in consequence of the defendant's breach. That is the best justice that can be
done in this case."'

h The judge in his judgment fully discusses and analyses the English cases but nevertheless
reaches this view.

---

1 (1954) 90 CLR 409
2 90 CLR 409 at 416
3 (1939) p 499
4 Ibid p 508
5 [1950] VLR 360
6 [1950] VLR 360 at 372
7 [1950] VLR 360 at 376

My Lords, I am happy to follow the latter case. In my opinion *Henty v Schröder*[1] cannot stand against the powerful tide of logical objection and judicial reasoning. It should no longer be regarded as of authority; the cases following it should be overruled. In particular *Barber v Wolfe*[2] and *Horsler v Zorro*[3] cannot stand so far as they are based on the theory of 'rescission ab initio' which has no application to the termination of a contract on accepted repudiation.

The second basis for denying damages in such cases as the present is that which underlies the judgment of the Court of Appeal in *Swycher's* case[4]. This is really a rationalisation of *Henty v Schröder*[1] the weakness of which case the court well perceived. The main argument there accepted was that by deciding to seek the remedy of specific performance the vendor (or purchaser) has made an election which either is irrevocable or which becomes so when the order for specific performance is made. A second limb of this argument (but in reality a different argument) is that the vendor (or purchaser) has adequate remedies under the order for specific performance so that there is no need, or equitable ground, for allowing him to change his ground and ask for damages.

In my opinion, the argument based on irrevocable election, strongly pressed by the appellant's counsel in the present appeal, is unsound. Election, though the subject of much learning and refinement, is in the end a doctrine based on simple considerations of common sense and equity. It is easy to see that a party who has chosen to put an end to a contract by accepting the other party's repudiation cannot afterwards seek specific performance. This is simply because the contract has gone, what is dead is dead. But it is no more difficult to agree that a party, who has chosen to seek specific performance, may quite well thereafter, if specific performance fails to be realised, say, 'Very well, then, the contract should be regarded as terminated.' It is quite consistent with a decision provisionally to keep alive, to say, 'Well, this is no use—let us now end the contract's life.' A vendor who seeks (and gets) specific performance is merely electing for a course which may or may not lead to implementation of the contract; what he elects for is not eternal and unconditional affirmation, but a continuance of the contract under control of the court which control involves the power, in certain events, to terminate it. If he makes an election at all, he does so when he decides not to proceed under the order for specific performance, but to ask the court to terminate the contract (see the judgment of Greene MR in *Austins of East Ham Ltd v Macey*[5]). The fact is that the election argument proves too much. If it were correct it would deny the vendor not just the right to damages, but the right to 'rescind' the contract, but there is no doubt that this right exists; what is in question is only the right, on 'rescission', to claim damages.

The authority most relied on to support this argument is in the end the passage already quoted from Williams on Vendor and Purchaser[6]; I have commented on this[7]. The cases cited relate to different situations where an election might well be regarded as creating a new situation from which subsequent departure would be impossible. Cases relating to acceptance of defective goods, or to waiver or enforcement of forfeiture, or to a decision to sue one set of parties rather than another (*Scarf v Jardine*[8]) or to a case of fraud, to be asserted or waived (*Clough v London & North Western Railway Co*[9]), are examples, and there are many others, where an election creates, or recognises, a situation from which consequences flow and when the election is irrevocable. But this is clearly not such a case, or the right to 'rescind' after an order for specific performance would not have been recognised.

1   (1879) 12 Ch D 666
2   [1945] 1 All ER 399, [1945] Ch 187
3   [1975] 1 All ER 584, [1975] Ch 302
4   [1976] 1 All ER 881, [1976] Ch 319
5   [1941] Ch 338 at 341
6   4th Edn (1936), vol 2, pp 1025–1026
7   See p 892, ante
8   (1882) 7 App Cas 345, [1881–5] All ER Rep 651
9   (1871) LR 7 Ex 26

So far as regards the subsidiary argument, it is equally the case that it proves too much,
a for if correct it would result in a denial of the undoubted power to 'rescind'. Moreover the
argument is itself refuted by the action taken by the Court of Appeal itself, for after
allowing the vendors to rescind they awarded damages under Lord Cairns's Act. So clearly
there was nothing inappropriate or unnecessary in granting the vendors 'rescission' and
damages. As Goff LJ[1] pointed out it was not possible to leave the vendors to 'work out' the
decree for specific performance; their only remedy (if any) must lie in an award of
b damages.

In my respectful opinion therefore, *Swycher's* case[2], whether it should be regarded as
resting on *Henty v Schröder*[3] or on an independent argument based on election, was
wrongly decided in so far as it denied a right to contractual damages and should so far be
overruled. The vendors should have been entitled, on discharge of the contract, on
grounds of normal and accepted principle, to damages appropriate for a breach of contract.
c There is one final point, on this part of the case, on which I should make a brief
observation. Once the matter has been placed in the hands of a court of equity, or one
exercising equity jurisdiction, the subsequent control of the matter will be exercised
according to equitable principles. The court would not make an order dissolving the
decree of specific performance and terminating the contract (with recovery of damages) if
to do so would be unjust, in the circumstances then existing, to the other party, in this case
d to the purchaser. (To this extent, in describing the vendor's right to an order as ex debito
justitiae Clauson LJ may have put the case rather too strongly in *John Barker & Co Ltd v
Littman*[4].) This is why there was, in the Court of Appeal, rightly, a relevant and substantial
argument, repeated in this House, that the non-completion of the contract was due to the
default of the vendors; if this had been made good, the court could properly have refused
them the relief sought. But the Court of Appeal came to the conclusion that this non-
e completion, and the ultimate impossibility of completion, was the fault of the purchaser.
I agree with their conclusion and their reasons on this point and shall not repeat or add to
them.

It is now necessary to deal with questions relating to the measure of damages. The Court
of Appeal, while denying the vendors' right to damages at common law, granted damages
under Lord Cairns's Act. Since on the view which I take, damages can be recovered at
f common law, two relevant questions now arise: (1) whether Lord Cairns's Act provides a
different measure of damages from the common law? If so, the respondents would be in
a position to claim the more favourable basis to them; and (2) if the measure of damages
is the same, on what basis they should be calculated?

Since the decision of this House, by a majority, in *Leeds Industrial Co-operative Society Ltd
v Slack*[5], it is clear that the jurisdiction to award damages in accordance with s 2 of Lord
g Cairns's Act (accepted by the House as surviving the repeal of the Act) may arise in some
cases in which damages could not be recovered at common law; examples of this would be
damages in lieu of a quia timet injunction and damages for breach of a restrictive covenant
to which the defendant was not a party. To this extent the Act created a power to award
damages which did not exist before at common law. But apart from these, and similar
cases where damages could not be claimed at all at common law, there is sound authority
h for the proposition that the Act does not provide for the assessment of damages on any new
basis. The wording of s 2 that damages 'may be assessed in such manner as the court shall
direct' does not so suggest, but clearly refers only to procedure.

j

1   [1978] 3 All ER 314 at 329, [1978] Ch 176 at 199
2   [1976] 1 All ER 881, [1976] Ch 319
3   (1879) 12 Ch D 666
4   [1941] 2 All ER 537 at 541, [1941] Ch 405 at 412
5   [1924] AC 851, [1924] All ER Rep 259

In *Ferguson v Wilson*[1] Turner LJ, sitting in a court which included Cairns LJ himself, expressed the clear opinion that the purpose of the Act was to enable a court of equity to **a** grant those damages which another court might give; a similar opinion was strongly expressed by Kay J in *Rock Portland Cement Co v Wilson*[2], and Fry on Specific Performance[3] is of the same opinion. In *Wroth v Tyler*[4] however, Megarry J, relying on the words 'in lieu of specific performance', reached the view that damages under the Act should be assessed as on the date when specific performance could have been ordered, in that case as at the date of the judgment of the court. This case was followed in *Grant v Dawkins*[5]. If this **b** establishes a different basis from that applicable at common law, I could not agree with it, but in *Horsler v Zorro*[6], Megarry J went so far as to indicate his view that there is no inflexible rule that common law damages must be assessed as at the date of the breach. Furthermore, in *Malhotra v Choudhury*[7] the Court of Appeal expressly decided that, in a case where damages are given in substitution for an order for specific performance, both equity and the common law would award damages on the same basis, in that case as on the date **c** of judgment. On the balance of these authorities and also on principle, I find in the Act no warrant for the court awarding damages differently from common law damages, but the question is left open on what date such damages, however awarded, ought to be assessed.

The general principle for the assessment of damages is compensatory, ie that the innocent party is to be placed, so far as money can do so, in the same position as if the contract had been performed. Where the contract is one of sale, this principle normally **d** leads to assessment of damages as at the date of the breach, a principle recognised and embodied in s 51 of the Sale of Goods Act 1893. But this is not an absolute rule; if to follow it would give rise to injustice, the court has power to fix such other date as may be appropriate in the circumstances.

In cases where a breach of a contract for sale has occurred, and the innocent party reasonably continues to try to have the contract completed, it would to me appear more **e** logical and just rather than tie him to the date of the original breach, to assess damages as at the date when (otherwise than by his default) the contract is lost. Support for this approach is to be found in the cases. In *Ogle v Earl Vane*[8] the date was fixed by reference to the time when the innocent party, acting reasonably, went into the market; in *Hickman v Haynes*[9] at a reasonable time after the last request of the defendants (the buyers) to withhold delivery. In *Radford v de Froberville*[10], where the defendant had covenanted to **f** build a wall, damages were held measurable as at the date of the hearing rather than at the date of the defendant's breach, unless the plaintiff ought reasonably to have mitigated the breach at an earlier date.

In the present case if it is accepted, as I would accept, that the vendors acted reasonably in pursuing the remedy of specific performance, the date on which that remedy became aborted (not by the vendors' fault) should logically be fixed as the date on which damages **g** should be assessed. Choice of this date would be in accordance both with common law principle, as indicated in the authorities I have mentioned, and with the wording of the Act 'in substitution for ... specific performance'. The date which emerges from this is 3rd April 1975, the first date on which mortgagees contracted to sell a portion of the property. I would vary the order of the Court of Appeal by substituting this date for that fixed by them, viz 26th November 1974. The same date (3rd April 1975) should be used for the **h**

1   (1866) LR 2 Ch App 77 at 88
2   (1882) 48 LT 386
3   6th Edn (1921), p 602
4   [1973] 1 All ER 897, [1974] Ch 30
5   [1973] 3 All ER 897, [1973] 1 WLR 1406
6   [1975] 1 All ER 584 at 596, [1975] Ch 302 at 316
7   Page 186, ante
8   (1867) LR 2 QB 275; *affd* LR 3 QB 272
9   (1875) LR 10 CP 598
10 [1978] 1 All ER 33, [1977] 1 WLR 1262

purpose of limiting the respondents' right to interest on damages. Subject to these
a modifications I would dismiss the appeal.

LORD SALMON. My Lords, I have had the advantage of reading in draft the speech
prepared by my noble and learned friend Lord Wilberforce. I agree with it, and for the
reasons which he gives I also would dismiss the appeal, subject to the variation of the order
of the Court of Appeal which he has proposed.

b
LORD FRASER OF TULLYBELTON. My Lords, I have had the great benefit of
reading in draft the speech prepared by my noble and learned friend, Lord Wilberforce.
I entirely agree with it and, for the reasons given by him, I also would dismiss this appeal,
subject to the alteration of date which he has proposed.

c **LORD KEITH OF KINKEL.** My Lords, I have had the great benefit of reading in draft
the speech of my noble and learned friend Lord Wilberforce. I agree entirely with the
reasoning and conclusions therein contained, and that the appeal should accordingly be
dismissed subject to variation, in the manner which he proposed, of the order of the Court
of Appeal.

d **LORD SCARMAN.** My Lords, I have had the advantage of reading in draft the speech
of my noble and learned friend Lord Wilberforce. I agree entirely with his reasoning and
conclusions. I agree that the appeal should be dismissed, subject to the variation proposed
by Lord Wilberforce in the order of the Court of Appeal.

Appeal dismissed subject to variation of order of Court of Appeal by the substitution of 3rd April
e *1975 for 26th November 1974 as the date by reference to which damages should be assessed.*

Solicitors: *Bircham & Co* (for the purchaser); *Ward Bowie* (for the vendors).

Christine Ivamy   Barrister.

R v Lemon
R v Gay News Ltd

HOUSE OF LORDS

LORD DIPLOCK, VISCOUNT DILHORNE, LORD EDMUND-DAVIES, LORD RUSSELL OF KILLOWEN AND LORD SCARMAN

20th, 21st, 22nd, 23rd, 27th NOVEMBER 1978, 21st FEBRUARY 1979

Criminal law – Blasphemy – Blasphemous libel – Ingredients of offence – Intent – Attack on Christianity – Poem describing acts of sodomy and fellatio with body of Christ – Whether subjective intent to attack Christianity required to be proved.

The appellants, the editor and publishers of a newspaper for homosexuals, published in the newspaper a poem accompanied by a drawing illustrating its subject-matter which purported to describe in explicit detail acts of sodomy and fellatio with the body of Christ immediately after His death and to ascribe to Him during His lifetime promiscuous homosexual practices with the Apostles and with other men. The appellants were charged with the offence of blasphemous libel. The particulars of the offence alleged that the appellants unlawfully and wickedly published or caused to be published a blasphemous libel concerning the Christian religion, namely 'an obscene poem and illustration vilifying Christ in His life and in His crucifixion'. The trial judge directed the jury that in order to secure the conviction of the appellants for publishing a blasphemous libel it was sufficient if they took the view that the publication complained of vilified Christ in His life and crucifixion and that it was not necessary for the Crown to prove an intention other than an intention to publish that which in the jury's view was a blasphemous libel. The appellants were convicted. They appealed to the Court of Appeal contending that a subjective intent on the part of the appellants to shock and arouse resentment among Christians had to be proved by the prosecution and that the judge had misdirected the jury. The Court of Appeal[a] dismissed their appeal and they appealed to the House of Lords.

Held (Lord Diplock and Lord Edmund-Davies dissenting) – In order to secure a conviction for the offence of publishing a blasphemous libel it was sufficient, for the purpose of establishing mens rea, for the prosecution to prove an intention to publish material which was in fact blasphemous and it was not necessary for them to prove further that the defendants intended to blaspheme. Accordingly the appeals would be dismissed (see p 911 *d* to *g*, p 921 *d* to *f* and p 927 *f* to p 928 *a*, post).

R v Shipley (1784) 21 St Tr 847, *R v Hetherington* (1841) 4 St Tr NS 563, *R v Bradlaugh* (1883) 15 Cox CC 217 and *R v Ramsay and Foote* (1883) 15 Cox CC 231 considered.

Per Curiam. A blasphemous libel is material calculated to outrage and insult a Christian's religious feelings (see p 900 *g h*, p 906 *f g*, p 912 *d e*, p 920 *g h*, p 922 *b c*, p 924 *a* to p 925 *b* and p 927 *f* to p 928 *a*, post).

Per Lord Edmund-Davies and Lord Scarman. It was not an essential ingredient of the crime of blasphemy that the publication must tend to lead to a breach of the peace (see p 920 *f* and p 925 *b c*, post).

Decision of the Court of Appeal, Criminal Division [1978] 3 All ER 175 affirmed.

Notes

For blasphemous libel, see 11 Halsbury's Laws (4th Edn) para 1009, and for cases on the subject, see 15 Digest (Reissue) 1016–1018, 8799–8831.

Cases referred to in opinions

Bowman v Secular Society Ltd [1917] AC 406, [1916–17] All ER Rep 1, 86 LJ Ch 568, 117 LT 161, HL, 15 Digest (Reissue) 1017, 8830.

---

a [1978] 3 All ER 175

Director of Public Prosecutions v Beard [1920] AC 479, [1920] All ER Rep 21, 14 Cr App R
  158, sub nom *R v Beard* 89 LJKB 437, 84 JP 129, 122 LT 625, 26 Cox CC 573, HL, 15
  Digest (Reissue) 1137, 9621.
Director of Public Prosecutions v Majewski [1976] 2 All ER 142, [1977] AC 443, [1976] 2 WLR
  623, 140 JP 315, 62 Cr App R 262, HL, 14(1) Digest (Reissue) 54, 258.
Director of Public Prosecutions v Morgan [1975] 2 All ER 347, [1976] AC 182, [1975] 2 WLR
  913, 139 JP 76, 61 Cr App R 136, HL, 15 Digest (Reissue) 1212, 10,398.
Director of Public Prosecutions v Smith [1960] 3 All ER 161, [1961] AC 290, [1960] 3 WLR
  546, 124 JP 473, 44 Cr App R 261, HL, 15 Digest (Reissue) 1133, 9569.
Hyam v Director of Public Prosecutions [1974] 2 All ER 141, [1975] AC 55, [1974] 2 WLR 607,
  138 JP 374, 59 Cr App R 91, 15 Digest (Reissue) 1111, 9338.
Lim Chin Aik v R [1963] 1 All ER 223, [1963] AC 160, [1963] 2 WLR 42, PC, 2 Digest
  (Reissue) 194, *839.
Parmiter v Coupland (1840) 6 M & W 105, 9 LJ Ex 202, 4 Jur 701, 151 ER 340, 32 Digest
  (Repl) 84, 1063.
R v Aldred (1909) 74 JP 55, 22 Cox CC 1, 15 Digest (Reissue) 896, 7714.
R v Bedford (1713) Gilb 297, 93 ER 334 (cited in 5 Bac Abr (7th Edn, 1832) 200, 2 Stra at
  789).
R v Boulter (1908) 72 JP 188, 15 Digest (Reissue) 1017, 8828.
R v Bradlaugh (1883) 15 Cox CC 217, 15 Digest (Reissue) 1017, 8825.
R v Burdett (1821) 4 B & Ald 95, 314, 1 State Tr NS 1, 106 ER 873, 953, 15 Digest (Reissue)
  897, 7726.
R v Burns (1886) 2 TLR 510, 16 Cox CC 355, 15 Digest (Reissue) 894, 7696.
R v Carlile (Mary Ann) (1821) 1 State Tr NS 1033, 15 Digest (Reissue) 1016, 8807.
R v Carlile (Richard) (1819) 1 State Tr NS 1387; subsequent proceedings 3 B & Ald 161, 106
  ER 621, 15 Digest (Reissue) 1016, 8801.
R v Caunt (17th November 1947) unreported, Liverpool Assizes.
R v Dixon (1814) 3 M & S 11, 105 ER 516, NP, 14(2) Digest (Reissue) 484, 3992.
R v Gott (1922) 16 Cr App R 87, CCA, 15 Digest (Reissue) 1017, 8816.
R v Harvey and Chapman (1823) 2 B & C 257, 2 State Tr NS 1, 3 Dow & Ry KB 464, [1814–
  23] All ER Rep 658, 2 LJOSKB 4, 107 ER 379, 15 Digest (Reissue) 894, 7692.
R v Hetherington (1841) 4 State Tr NS 563, 5 JP 496, 5 Jur 529, 15 Digest (Reissue) 1016,
  8809.
R v Hicklin (1868) LR 3 QB 360, 37 LJMC 89, 16 WR 801, 11 Cox CC 19, sub nom *R v
  Wolverhampton Recorder, Re Scott v Wolverhampton Justices* 18 LT 395, 32 JP 533, 15
  Digest (Reissue) 1035, 8972.
R v Holbrook (1878) 4 QBD 42, 48 LJQB 113, 39 LT 536, 43 JP 38, 27 WR 313, 14 Cox CC
  185, DC, 14(1) Digest (Reissue) 26, 85.
R v Holyoake (1842) 4 State Tr NS 1381, 15 Digest (Reissue) 1017, 8812; see also 'The Trial
  of George Jacob Holyoake on an Indictment for Blasphemy', published by Thomas
  Paterson, 1842.
R v Hone (1817) The Three Trials of William Hone (London, 1818), Blake Odgers on Libel
  and Slander (5th Edn, 482) 15 Digest (Reissue) 1018, 8831.
R v Keach (1665) 6 State Tr 701, 15 Digest (Reissue) 896, 7721.
R v Moxon (1841) 4 State Tr NS 693, 2 Town St Tr 356, 15 Digest (Reissue) 1016, 8810.
R v Pooley (1857) 8 State Tr NS 1089, 15 Digest (Reissue) 1017, 8813.
R v Ramsay and Foote (1883) 48 LT 733, 15 Cox CC 231, Cab & El 126, 15 Digest (Reissue)
  1017, 8827.
R v Shipley (1784) 4 Doug KB 73, 21 State Tr 847, 99 ER 774, sub nom *R v St Asaph (Dean)*,
  3 Term Rep 428n, 32 Digest (Repl) 82, 1049.
R v Taylor (1676) 1 Vent 293, 3 Keb 607, 621, 86 ER 189, 15 Digest (Reissue) 1016, 8799.
R v Woolston (1729) 1 Barn KB 162, 266, Fitz-G 64, 2 Stra 834, 94 ER 112, 181, 15 Digest
  (Reissue) 1017, 8822.
Sweet v Parsley [1969] 1 All ER 347, [1970] AC 132, [1969] 2 WLR 470, 133 JP 188, 53 Cr
  App R 221, HL, 15 Digest (Reissue) 1084, 9179.

Sydlyes Case (1663) 1 Keb 620, 83 ER 1146, sub nom *R v Sidney* 1 Sid 168, 15 Digest
(Reissue) 1031, 8942.

Woolmington v Director of Public Prosecutions [1935] AC 462, [1935] All ER Rep 1, 104 LJKB
433, 153 LT 232, 25 Cr App R 72, 30 Cox CC 234, HL, 14(2) Digest (Reissue) 474, 3919.

Appeals

On 11th July 1977 at the Central Criminal Court, before his Honour Judge Alan King-
Hamilton QC and a jury, the appellants, Denis Lemon and Gay News Ltd, were convicted
of blasphemous libel, in a private criminal prosecution brought by the respondent, Mary
Whitehouse. On 12th July Mr Lemon was sentenced to nine months' imprisonment
suspended for 18 months, fined £500 and ordered to pay one-fifth of the costs of the
prosecution and was also ordered to contribute a maximum of £434 towards his legal aid
costs. Gay News Ltd were fined £1,000, to be paid within three months, and ordered to
pay four-fifths of the prosecution costs. Both appellants appealed against conviction on the
grounds, inter alia, that the trial judge erred in law (1) in ruling that intention, ie an
intention to attack the Christian religion and/or to insult or outrage Christian sympathisers
and/or believers, and/or to provoke a breach of the peace, was not a necessary element of the
offence of blasphemous libel and (2) in ruling that an attack on Christ or the Christian
religion was not a necessary element of the offence of blasphemy. Both appellants also
applied for leave to appeal against sentence. On 17th March 1978 the Court of Appeal,
Criminal Division[1] (Roskill, Eveleigh LJJ and Stocker J) dismissed their appeals, refused
them leave to appeal but certified that a point of law of general public importance was
involved in the decision. The appellants appealed to the House of Lords pursuant to leave
of the House granted on 17th May 1978. On 24th May the appeals were consolidated. The
facts are set out in the opinion of Lord Diplock.

Louis Blom-Cooper QC and *Geoffrey Robertson* for the appellant Lemon.
Geoffrey Robertson for the appellant Gay News Ltd.
John Smyth and *Jeremy Maurice* for the Crown.

Their Lordships took time for consideration.

21st February. The following opinions were delivered.

LORD DIPLOCK. My Lords, the appellants are the editor and publishers of a newspaper
called Gay News. As its name suggests its readership consists mainly of homosexuals
though it is on sale to the general public at some bookstalls. In an issue of Gay News
published in June 1976 there appeared a poem by a Professor James Kirkup entitled 'The
Love that Dares to Speak its Name' and accompanied by a drawing illustrating its subject-
matter. The poem purports to describe in explicit detail acts of sodomy and fellatio with
the body of Christ immediately after His death and to ascribe to Him during His lifetime
promiscuous homosexual practices with the Apostles and with other men.

The issue in this appeal is not whether the words and drawing are blasphemous. The
jury, though only by a majority of ten to two, have found them to be so. As expressed in
the charge against them they 'vilify Christ in His life and in His crucifixion', and do so in
terms that are likely to arouse a sense of outrage among those who believe in or respect the
Christian faith and are not homosexuals and probably among many of them that are. The
only question in this appeal is whether in 1976 the mental element or mens rea in the
common law offence of blasphemy is satisfied by proof only of an intention to publish
material which in the opinion of the jury is likely to shock and arouse resentment among
believing Christians or whether the prosecution must go further and prove that the
accused in publishing the material in fact intended to produce that effect on believers, or
(what comes to the same thing in criminal law) although aware of the likelihood that such

---

1   [1978] 3 All ER 175, [1979] QB 10

a effect might be produced, did not care whether it was or not, so long as the publication
   achieved some other purpose that constituted his motive for publishing it. Wherever I
   speak hereafter of 'intention' I use the expression as a term of art in that extended sense.
       At the trial the judge in a carefully considered ruling given after lengthy argument held
   that the offence was one of strict liability. The ruling made irrelevant (and therefore
   inadmissible) any evidence by Mr Lemon, the editor of Gay News, about his own intentions
   in publishing the poem and drawing; accordingly he did not go into the witness box and
b no other evidence was called on behalf of the accused. The judge summed up to the jury
   in masterly fashion and in accordance with his ruling; the jury by a majority verdict
   convicted both appellants.
       The convictions were upheld by the Court of Appeal[1], who certified that the following
   point of law of general public importance was involved in their decision to dismiss the
   appeals:

c   'Was the learned trial judge correct (as the Court of Appeal held) first in ruling and
       then in directing the jury that in order to secure the conviction of the appellants for
       publishing a blasphemous libel (1) it was sufficient if the jury took the view that the
       publication complained of vilified Christ in His life and crucifixion and (2) it was not
       necessary for the Crown to establish any further intention on the part of the appellants
       beyond an intention to publish that which in the jury's view was a blasphemous
d   libel?'

       My Lords, the offence of publishing a blasphemous libel has a long and at times
   inglorious history in the common law. For more than 50 years before the prosecution in
   the instant case was launched the offence seemed to have become obsolete, the last previous
   trial for it having taken place in 1922[2]. Originally the offence was cognisable only in the
e ecclesiastical courts. Its history from the 17th century when jurisdiction over it was first
   assumed by the courts of common law until its apparent disappearance from the criminal
   calendar after 1922 is traced in fascinating detail in G D Nokes's work, A History of the
   Crime of Blasphemy, published in 1928 and now out of print. A shorter historical account
   is to be found in Lord Sumner's famous speech in Bowman v Secular Society Ltd[3], but none
   of the speeches in that case touches at all on the question of intention. The judgment of the
f Court of Appeal in the instant case contains a valuable historical survey of most of the
   relevant cases with special reference to the intention of the publisher in publishing the
   blasphemous matter. In this House, too, the speeches to be delivered by my noble and
   learned friends, Viscount Dilhorne and Lord Edmund-Davies, will each incorporate a
   critical analysis of the varying terms in which judicial pronouncements on mens rea in
   blasphemous and seditious libel were expressed as the 19th century progressed. My own
g complete agreement with Lord Edmund-Davies's analysis relieves me of the task of
   attempting what would be no more than a paraphrase of it; but, since it leads to a
   conclusion as to the state of the law on this topic by the time the century ended which is
   diametrically opposed to that reached by Viscount Dilhorne (with which my noble and
   learned friend, Lord Scarman, also concurs) I feel bound to concede that by the beginning
   of the present century the law as to the mental elements in the offence of blasphemous libel
h was still uncertain. The task of this House in the instant appeal is to give to it certainty
   now, and to do so in a form that will not be inconsistent with the way in which the general
   law as to the mental element in criminal offences has developed since then.
       Two things emerge clearly from the earlier history. First that between the 17th century
   and the last quarter of the 19th, when Sir James Fitzjames Stephen published his History
   of the Criminal Law of England[4] the characteristics of the substantive offence of

j _____

   1 [1978] 3 All ER 175, [1979] QB 10
   2 R v Gott (1922) 16 Cr App R 87
   3 [1917] AC 406 at 454 et seq, [1916–17] All ER Rep 1 at 25 et seq
   4 (1883)

blasphemous libel had undergone progressive changes; and secondly, that, as Stephen reluctantly acknowledges in his chapter on seditious offences[1], those changes (which he *a* personally regretted) were largely shaped by the procedural changes in the trial of prosecutions for all forms of criminal libel resulting from Fox's Libel Act 1792 and by the passing of Lord Campbell's Libel Act 1843.

In the post-Restoration politics of 17th and 18th century England, Church and state were thought to stand or fall together. To cast doubt on the doctrines of the established church or to deny the truth of the Christian faith on which it was founded was to attack the *b* fabric of society itself; so blasphemous and seditious libel were criminal offences that went hand in hand. Both were originally what would now be described as offences of strict liability. To constitute the offence of blasphemous libel it was enough for the prosecution to prove that the accused, or someone for whose acts the law of libel held him to be criminally responsible, had published matter which (in trials held before Fox's Libel Act) the judge ruled, or (in trials held after that) the jury found, to be blasphemous, whether the *c* accused knew it to be so or not. Furthermore, criminal libel in its four manifestations, seditious, blasphemous, obscene and defamatory, was unique among common law offences, in imputing to any person who carried on the business of publisher or bookseller, vicarious criminal liability for acts of publication done by persons in his employment even though these were done without his authority, consent or knowledge. Since in practice prosecutions were brought against publishers and booksellers rather than against authors, *d* so long as this remained the law, as it did until the passing of s 7 of Lord Campbell's Libel Act in 1843, it could not logically be reconciled with the notion that the accused's own actual intention was a relevant element in the offence.

The severity of the law of blasphemous libel had, however, been somewhat mitigated before 1843 by judicial rulings not as to the mens rea but as to the actus reus of the offence. To publish opinions denying the truth of doctrines of the established Church or *e* even of Christianity itself was no longer held to amount to the offence of blasphemous libel so long as such opinions were expressed in temperate language and not in terms of offence, insult or ridicule: see *R v Hetherington*[2]. This introduces into the concept of the actus reus, in addition to the act of publication itself, the effect that the material published is likely to have on the minds of those to whom it is published.

At a period when an accused could not give evidence in his own defence and his *f* intention to produce a particular result by his acts, where this was an ingredient of the offence, was ascertained by applying the presumption that a man intends the natural consequences of his acts, the distinction was often blurred between the *tendency* of the published words to produce a particular effect on those to whom they were published and the *intention* of the publisher to produce that effect. So that one finds F L Holt in his textbook on The Law of Libel[3] published in 1816 defining blasphemous libel as requiring *g* the publication to be made 'with an *intent* to subvert man's faith in God, or to impair his reverence of him' and during the 20 years before Lord Campbell's Libel Act in 1843 one also finds in reported summings-up of various judges occasional references to the *intention* of the accused.

The abolition in 1843 of vicarious criminal liability for blasphemous libel and the growing influence of Starkie's textbook on the law of criminal libel[4] opened the way for a *h* further development in the definition of the crime of blasphemous libel; but this time in its mental element or mens rea which was brought into closer harmony with the changed concept of the actus reus. Starkie was one of the Criminal Law Commissioners during the 1840s and became Downing Professor of Law at Cambridge. He adopted F L Holt's

j

---

1   Vol 2, ch 24, p 298
2   (1841) 4 State Tr NS 563
3   2nd Edn (1816), ch 2, p 64
4   Law of Slander and Libel

definition and elaborated it in a paragraph[1] later to be adopted as an accurate statement of
a the law by Lord Coleridge CJ in *R v Ramsay and Foote*[2]:

> 'The law visits not the honest errors, but the malice of mankind. A wilful intention
> to pervert, insult, and mislead others, by means of licentious and contumelious abuse
> applied to sacred subjects, or by wilful misrepresentations or wilful sophistry,
> calculated to mislead the ignorant and unwary is the criterion and test of guilt. A
> *b* malicious and mischievous intention, or what is equivalent to such an intention, in
> law, as well as morals—a state of apathy and indifference to the interests of society—
> is the broad boundary between right and wrong.'

The language in which this statement is expressed is perhaps more that of the advocate
of law reform than of the draftsman of a criminal code. The reference to misleading others
is probably outdated in this more sceptical and agnostic age unless what misleads is
c couched in terms that are likely to shock and arouse resentment among believing
Christians. Nevertheless, the statement clearly requires intent on the part of the accused
himself to produce the described effect on those to whom the blasphemous matter is
published and so removes blasphemous libel from the special category of offences in which
mens rea as to one of the elements of the actus reus is *not* a necessary constituent of the
offence.

d Although Stephen continued to resist in his writings what he described as this 'milder
view of the law' accepted by Lord Coleridge CJ, it appears to have been adopted by judges
in summing up in subsequent prosecutions for blasphemous libel which, after 1883,
became very rare. The industry of G D Nokes[3] enabled him to identify only five between
1883 and 1922. In the only one in which the summing-up is reported in a legal journal,
R v Boulter[4], Phillimore J read to the jury the first part of the passage from Starkie referring
e to wilful intention that I have cited above. In *R v Gott*[5] the summing-up is reported only
in The Freethinker for 8th January 1922. Avory J is there recorded as being less specific in
his citation from Lord Coleridge CJ, but refers to the necessity for the words to be
'calculated and *intended* to insult the feelings and the deepest religious convictions . . . of
persons amongst whom we live'.

I accept that, on the state of the authorities, it is still open to this House to approve the
f stricter view of the law preferred by Stephen to the milder view adopted by Lord Coleridge
CJ in his summing-up in *R v Ramsay and Foote*[6]; but there are, as it seems to me, compelling
reasons why we should not. The paucity of subsequent prosecutions for blasphemous libel
does not enable one to point to any judicial developments in the legal concept of the mens
rea required in this particular offence; but this does not necessarily mean that the law of
blasphemous libel, now the offence has been revived after a lapse of fifty years, should be
g treated as having been immune from those significant changes in the general concept of
mens rea in criminal law that have occurred in the last hundred years. All of these in my
opinion point to the propriety of your Lordships adopting the milder view that the offence
today is no longer one of strict liability, but is one requiring proof of what was called in
Director of Public Prosecutions v Beard[7], a 'specific intention', namely, to shock and arouse
resentment among those who believe in or respect the Christian faith.

h The first great change that influenced the general concept of mens rea after 1883 was
procedural, the passing of the Criminal Evidence Act 1898, which enabled the accused to
testify as a witness in his own defence. Prior to this his actual intention could only be

j 1 4th Edn (1876) pp 599–600
    2 (1883) 15 Cox CC 231 at 236
    3 A History of the Crime of Blasphemy (1928)
    4 (1908) 72 JP 188
    5 (1922) 16 Cr App R 87
    6 15 Cox CC 231
    7 [1920] AC 479, [1920] All ER Rep 21

ascertained as a matter of inference from what he was proved to have done and the circumstances in which he did it; and juries were instructed to apply what was referred to *a* as the 'presumption' that a man intends the natural consequence of his own acts. In the case of blasphemous libel if the jury found that words published by the accused, looked at objectively, had the tendency to produce the effect that it was the policy of the law to prevent, eg to shock and arouse resentment among believing Christians, then the application of the presumption was sufficient to convert this objective tendency into the actual intention of the accused. So the milder view of the law adopted by Lord Coleridge *b* CJ in 1883 might have had little practical effect if there had been any further prosecutions before the passing of the Criminal Evidence Act 1898.

Although this Act enabled the accused to give direct evidence of his own intention and thus added to the available material on which the jury's finding as to the accused's intention could be based, the presumption that a man intends the natural consequences of his own acts survived as a true presumption at least until the decision of this House in *c* *Woolmington v Director of Public Prosecutions*[1], that is to say, it was an inference that the jury was bound to draw unless the accused overcame the evidential burden of proving facts of a kind regarded by the law as being sufficient to rebut it.

This presumption, which was of general application to offences in which the intention of the accused to produce a particular proscribed result formed an essential element in the mens rea, has had a chequered history since 1898, both before and after *Woolmington*[1]. *d* Discussion of it is mainly to be found in cases of homicide. There were two schools of thought among the judges as to how the presumption could be rebutted. The stricter school applied what has come to be known as the 'objective test'. It took the view that if the result proscribed were foreseeable by a reasonable man as being a likely consequence of his act, the presumption that the accused intended that result could only be rebutted by proof that he was insane or, in charges of murder brought after the passing of the *e* Homicide Act 1957, that he suffered from some abnormality of mind. The onus of proving insanity or abnormality of mind lay on the accused. The milder school which predominated 20 years ago, when I myself was trying criminal cases, applied the 'subjective test'. It treated the presumption, prior to *Woolmington*[1], as having the effect of casting on the accused the evidential burden of proving that he had *not* intended the natural consequences of his act. After *Woolmington*[1] the evidential burden cast on the accused was *f* the lesser one of inducing doubt in the jury's mind as to whether such was his intention. These competing views as to the nature and effect of the presumption and the authorities in support of each of them, are cited in the judgments of the Court of Criminal Appeal and of this House in *Director of Public Prosecutions v Smith*[2]. In the Court of Criminal Appeal the milder 'subjective test' prevailed; in this House the stricter 'objective test' triumphed.

If the law as expounded by this House in *Smith*[2] had remained unchanged and had been *g* treated as applicable beyond the field of homicide to other crimes which required a specific intention, which during the next six years trial judges showed a uniform reluctance to do, blasphemous libel might well have reverted to what in effect would be an offence of strict liability. But Parliament stepped in to reinstate the milder view of the presumption by enacting s 8 of the Criminal Justice Act 1967:

> 'A court or jury, in determining whether a person has committed an offence,—(a) *h* shall not be bound in law to infer that he intended or foresaw a result of his actions by reason only of its being a natural and probable consequence of those actions; but (b) shall decide whether he did intend or foresee that result by reference to all the evidence, drawing such inferences from the evidence as appear proper in the circumstances.'

j

This is now the law that your Lordships must apply. It throws no light on the question whether an intention to produce a particular effect on those to whom the blasphemous

1   [1935] AC 462, [1935] All ER Rep 1
2   [1960] 3 All ER 161, [1961] AC 290

matter is published is an essential element in the offence of blasphemous libel; but, if it is,
a the section makes the 'subjective test' of the accused's intention applicable, and the evidence
of the actual publisher as to what he intended or foresaw as the result of the publication
becomes relevant and admissible to rebut the inference as to his intention that the jury
might otherwise draw from what they themselves, as representing the reasonable man,
considered would be the likely effect of what was published on those who saw and read it.

My Lords, if your Lordships were to hold that Lord Coleridge CJ and those judges who
b preceded and followed him in directing juries that the accused's intention to shock and
arouse resentment among believing Christians was a necessary element in the offence of
blasphemous libel were wrong in doing so, this would effectively exclude that particular
offence from the benefit of Parliament's general substitution of the subjective for the
objective test in applying the presumption that a man intends the natural consequences of
his acts; and blasphemous libel would revert to the exceptional category of crimes of strict
c liability from which, on what is, to say the least, a plausible analysis of the contemporaneous
authorities, it appeared to have escaped nearly a century ago. This would, in my view, be
a retrograde step which could not be justified by any considerations of public policy.

The usual justification for creating by statute a criminal offence of strict liability, in
which the prosecution need not prove mens rea as to one of the elements of the actus reus,
is the threat that the actus reus of the offence poses to public health, public safety, public
d morals or public order. The very fact that there have been no prosecutions for blasphemous
libel for more than fifty years is sufficient to dispose of any suggestion that in modern
times a judicial decision to include this common law offence in this exceptional class of
offences of strict liability could be justified on grounds of public morals or public order.

The fear that, by retaining as a necessary element of the mens rea of the offence the
intention of the publisher to shock and arouse resentment among believing Christians,
e those who are morally blameworthy will be unjustly acquitted appears to me to manifest
a judicial distrust of the jury's capability of appreciating the meaning which in English
criminal law is ascribed to the expression 'intention' of the accused. When Stephen was
writing in 1883, he did not then regard it as settled law that, where intention to produce
a particular result was a necessary element of an offence, no distinction is to be drawn in
law between the state of mind of one who does an act because he desires it to produce that
f particular result and the state of mind of one who, when he does the act, is aware that it is
likely to produce that result but is prepared to take the risk that it may do so, in order to
achieve some other purpose which provided his motive for doing what he did. It is by now
well-settled law that both states of mind constitute 'intention' in the sense in which that
expression is used in the definition of a crime whether at common law or in a statute. Any
doubts on this matter were finally laid to rest by the decision of this House in *Hyam v
g* *Director of Public Prosecutions*[1].

Stephen, who deprecated this development of the criminal law as leading to a legal
fiction, did not hesitate to express his own distrust of the jury's ability or willingness to
distinguish between intention and motive. In writing of seditious libel he says[2]:

> 'A jury can hardly be expected to convict a man whose motives they approve and
> sympathize with, merely because they regard his intention with disapproval. An
h > intention to produce disaffection is illegal, but the motive for such an intention may
> be one with which the jury would strongly sympathize, and in such a case it would
> be hard even to make them understand that an acquittal would be against their oath.'

It had been just such judicial distrust of the reliability of juries that had led to the rule
of procedure in the 18th century that was eventually abolished by Fox's Libel Act. Dare I
j suggest that it was just such distrust that led to the decision of this House in *Director of
Public Prosecutions v Smith*[3] as to the legal nature of the presumption that a man intends the

---

1   [1974] 2 All ER 41, [1975] AC 55
2   History of the Criminal Law of England (1883), vol 2, ch 24, pp 360–361
3   [1960] 3 All ER 161, [1961] AC 290

natural consequences of his acts that was reversed by the Criminal Justice Act 1967? If juries through sympathy do occasionally acquit a defendant whom the judge, applying the law strictly, would have convicted, it may be that that is one of the things that juries are for.

My own feeling of outrage at the blasphemous material with which the instant appeal is concerned makes it seem to me improbable that if Mr Lemon had been permitted to give evidence of his intentions the jury would have been left in any doubt that whatever his motives in publishing them may have been he knew full well that the poem and accompanying drawing were likely to shock and arouse resentment among believing Christians and indeed many unbelievers. Nevertheless, Mr Lemon was entitled to his opportunity of sowing the seeds of doubt in the jury's mind. By the judge's ruling he was denied this opportunity. For this reason, if the decision had lain with me, I would have allowed the appeal.

VISCOUNT DILHORNE. My Lords, the appellants, Denis Lemon and Gay News Ltd, were tried at the Central Criminal Court on an indictment which contained the following count:

> 'Statement of Offence
> 'Blasphemous Libel.

> 'Particulars of Offence
> 'Gay News Limited and Denis Lemon on a day or days unknown between the 1st day of May and 30th day of June 1976 unlawfully and wickedly published or caused to be published in a newspaper called Gay News No. 96 a blasphemous libel concerning the Christian religion namely an obscene poem and illustration vilifying Christ in His life and in His crucifixion.'

After a trial which lasted for seven days they were found guilty by a majority verdict of ten to two. They appealed to the Court of Appeal (Criminal Division) on a number of grounds. Their appeal against conviction was dismissed and they now appeal with the leave of this House, the Court of Appeal having certified that a point of law of general public importance was involved, namely the question:

> 'Was the learned trial Judge correct (as the Court of Appeal held) first in ruling and then in directing the jury that in order to secure the conviction of the appellants for publishing a blasphemous libel (1) it was sufficient if the jury took the view that the publication complained of vilified Christ in His life and crucifixion and (2) it was not necessary for the Crown to establish any further intention on the part of the appellants beyond an intention to publish that which in the jury's view was a blasphemous libel?'

By their verdict the jury showed that they were satisfied that the publication complained of, a poem by a Professor James Kirkup and a drawing published alongside it, vilified Christ in His life and crucifixion and were blasphemous. That finding has not been challenged in this appeal, nor could it have been with the slightest prospect of success.

Gay News Ltd publish a newspaper for homosexuals called Gay News of which Denis Lemon is the editor. He holds the majority of the shares in that company. The jury's conclusion that they published the poem and the drawing was not challenged.

The only question to be decided in this appeal is what mens rea has to be established to justify conviction of the offence of publishing a blasphemous libel. The choice does not, in my opinion, lie between regarding the offence as one of strict liability or as one involving mens rea, for, as was said by Stephen in 1883 in his History of the Criminal Law of England[1]:

> 'It is undoubtedly true that the definition of libel, like the definitions of nearly all other crimes, contains a mental element the existence of which must be found by a

---

1   Vol 2, ch 24, p 351

a jury before a defendant can be convicted, but the important question is, What is that
mental element? What is the intention which makes the act of publishing criminal?
Is it the mere intention to publish written blame, or is it an intention to produce by
such a publication some particular evil effect?'

He said[1] that he knew of no authority for saying that the presence of any specific
intention other than the intent to publish was necessary before Fox's Libel Act 1792.
b During the course of the proceedings in Parliament on the Bill which became that Act, a
number of questions were put to the judges[2]. In their answer to one of them they said[3]:

'The crime consists in publishing a libel. A criminal intention in the writer is no
part of the definition of libel at the common law. "He who scattereth firebrands,
arrows, and death," which, if not a definition, is a very intelligible description of a
libel, is eâ ratione criminal; it is not incumbent on the prosecutor to prove his intent,
c and on his part he shall not be heard to say, "Am I not in sport?"'

In the Dean of St Asaph case[4] Erskine had argued that it had to be proved that the dean
had had a seditious intent. That argument was rejected in that case as it was by the judges
in their answer to Parliament. Prior to 1792 on a charge of publishing a seditious libel, the
only questions left to the jury were (1) did the matter published bear the meaning ascribed
to it in the indictment or information and (2) was it published by the defendant? It was
d for the judges to rule whether the matter published, bearing the sense ascribed to it, was
seditious, that being regarded as a question of law (see R v Shipley[4]). I do not doubt that the
same procedure was followed when the charge was of publishing any other form of
criminal libel.

It thus appears that prior to 1792 the specific intent of the accused was not an ingredient
of the offence. Why was that? It is, I think, only explicable on the ground that the evil
e sought to be prevented by treating the publication of a libel as a criminal offence was the
dissemination of libels. The mischief lay in the scattering of firebrands in the form of
libels, and, if what was published was held to be seditious, the person who published it or
was responsible for its publication was guilty. It mattered not, if what had been published
was seditious, that he had no seditious intent (see R v Shipley[4]).

The next question for consideration is, was the definition of a criminal libel altered later,
f either by Fox's Libel Act 1792 or in the course of the development of the common law, so
that on a charge of publishing a seditious or a blasphemous libel proof that the defendant
had a seditious or blasphemous intent, as the case might be, was essential to establish guilt?

Fox's Libel Act was 'An Act to remove Doubts respecting the Functions of Juries in Cases
of Libel'. Its preamble stated that doubts had arisen whether on a trial 'for the making or
publishing any libel' the jury could give their verdict 'upon the whole matter put in issue'
g and its first section provided that they might do so and that they should not be directed to
find a defendant guilty merely on proof of publication by him and of the sense ascribed to
the matter published in the indictment or information.

Parke B in Parmiter v Coupland[5] said that the Act was declaratory and put prosecutions
for libel on the same footing as other criminal cases. While the Act allowed a trial judge
h to tell the jury his opinion of the publication, after 1792 it was for the jury to decide what
its character was.

I can see nothing in this Act 'to remove Doubts respecting the Functions of Juries' to
justify the conclusion that it made a change in the definition of the offence of publishing
a criminal libel. It does not mention intent, and if it had been the desire of Parliament to
give statutory authority to the argument of Erskine in R v Shipley[4] and to reject the opinion

j ──────────────────────────────

1 Ibid, p 353
2 See 22 State Tr 296–297
3 22 State Tr 300–301; Stephen's History of the Criminal Law of England (1883), vol 2, ch 24, p 344
4 R v Shipley (1783) 21 State Tr 847
5 (1840) 6 M & W 105

of the judges as to the ingredients of the offence, I regard it as inconceivable that the Act
would have taken the form it did. Stephen[1], however, regarded it as having enlarged 'the
old definition of a seditious libel by the addition of a reference to the specific intentions of
the libeller—to the purpose for which he wrote', and said that the Act assumed that the
specific intentions of the defendant were material. I must confess my inability to find in
the Act any basis for either conclusion. Professor Holdsworth in his History of English
Law[2] recognised that the view that 'the crime was not so much the intentional publication
of matter bearing the seditious or defamatory meaning . . . as its publication with a
seditious or malicious intent' began to appear in the 18th century. He did not attribute
this to Fox's Libel Act but to the practice of filling indictments 'with averments of every
sort of bad intention on the part of the defendant', averments which in Stephen's opinion
were surplusage.

The conclusion to which I come is that if any change in the definition of the offence
occurred after 1792 it did not result from Fox's Libel Act.

Stephen[3] also asserted that since that Act the law had ever since been administered on the
supposition that the specific intentions of the defendant were material. My examination
of the cases since 1792 leads me to think that that is not so and Professor Holdsworth[4] said
that the view that the publication had to be with a seditious or malicious intent was 'not
finally got rid of till the nineteenth century'. I infer from what he said that he thought that
that view was erroneous.

It was not until 1967 by the Criminal Justice Act, s 8, that it was enacted that a court or
jury should not be bound in law to infer that an accused intended or foresaw a result of his
actions by reason only of its being a natural and probable result of those actions but that
whether he intended or foresaw that result had to be decided by reference to all the
evidence drawing such inferences from the evidence as appeared proper. If the conclusion
was reached that a particular publication was blasphemous and it was proved that the
defendant had published it, it could be presumed under the old law that he had done so
with intent to blaspheme. In many cases it may be that the existence of such an intent was
undeniable but the fact that a man might be presumed to have such an intent or had that
intent does not in my opinion lead to the conclusion that the existence of such an intent
was an essential element in the crime, though it may account for a reference being made
in some cases in the course of a summing-up to the accused's intent (see, for instance, R v
Hone[5], R v Richard Carlile[6], R v Moxon[7], R v Holyoake[8]).

In this appeal we are not, as I see it, concerned with how such an intent is to be
established or its existence rebutted but whether it is an element in the offence. So with
great respect to my noble and learned friend, Lord Diplock, I do not think that the terms
of the Criminal Evidence Act 1898 and of s 8 of the Criminal Justice Act 1967 have any
relevance to the question to be decided. If in a prosecution for the publication of a
blasphemous libel the accused's intent to blaspheme has to be proved, the 1898 Act enables
him to give evidence that he had no such intent and the 1967 Act gives guidance as to the
proof of such an intent.

What I regard as of great significance is that in none of what I regard as the leading cases
on the publication of a blasphemous libel is there to be found any direction to the jury
telling them that it had to be proved that the defendant intended to blaspheme, and I have
not found in any decided case any criticism of the omission to do so.

In R v Mary Ann Carlile[9], in an intervention, Best J told the defendant that he would be

1   History of the Criminal Law of England (1883), vol 2, ch 24, p 359
2   2nd Edn (1937), vol 8, p 342
3   History of the Criminal Law of England (1883), vol 2, ch 24, p 359
4   History of English Law (2nd Edn, 1937), vol 8, p 342
5   (1817) The Three Trials of William Hone (London, 1818)
6   (1819) 1 State Tr NS 1387
7   (1841) 4 State Tr NS 693
8   (1842) 4 State Tr NS 1381
9   (1821) 1 State Tr NS 1033

happy to hear anything that she might urge to show that the publication was not a
a blasphemous libel and that she was not the publisher. It is not without significance that
he said nothing about her intent particularly in view of the fact that in *R v Richard Carlile*[1],
tried only a short time before, the direction to the jury had referred to the accused's intent.
   A case of more importance is *R v Hetherington*[2]. Hetherington was prosecuted for
publishing a blasphemous libel, it being alleged that such a libel had been sold from his
shop by his employee. He was convicted. It was not suggested that it had to be shown that
b he had any blasphemous intent, nor, it is to be noted, that the employee had any such
intent. It sufficed to show that what was published was a blasphemous libel and that he
was responsible for its publication. This vicarious criminal liability is wholly inconsistent
with an intent to engage in blasphemy being regarded at that time as an ingredient of the
offence.
   Two years later Parliament changed the law, not by enacting that proof of such an intent
c was necessary for a conviction but by s 7 of Lord Campbell's Libel Act 1843 providing that,
on a trial for the publication of a libel where the publication was by the act of a person other
than the defendant but with his authority, it was competent for the defendant to prove that
the publication was made without his authority, consent or knowledge, and that the
publication did not arise from want of care or caution on his part. As Stephen observes[3] by
virtue of this Act the 'negligent publication of a libel by a bookseller who is ignorant of its
d contents' suffices to render him guilty and the fact that he may be found guilty if negligent
is wholly inconsistent with the existence of any necessity to show that he intended to
blaspheme. Again it may be noted that the intention of the person actually responsible for
the publication was not relevant. If proof of such an intent was and is necessary, this Act
did not serve any useful purpose.
   I now come to the first of the two cases which I regard as the leading cases in this field.
e Prior to *R v Bradlaugh*[4] there had been very considerable controversy about what constituted
blasphemy. In the 18th century and before it appears to have been thought that any attack
or criticism, no matter how reasonably expressed, on the fundamental principles of the
Christian religion and any discussion hostile to the inspiration and perfect purity of the
Scriptures was against the law. That was Stephen's view[5] but in this case it was rejected by
Lord Coleridge CJ[6] who told the jury that he thought the law had been accurately stated in
f Starkie on Slander and Libel[7] in the following terms:

> 'The wilful intention to insult and mislead others by means of licentious and
> contumelious abuse offered to sacred subjects, or by wilful misrepresentations or
> wilful sophistry, calculated to mislead the ignorant and unwary, is the criterion and
> test of guilt. A malicious and mischievous intention, or what is equivalent to such an
> intention, in law, as well as morals—a state of apathy and indifference to the interests
g > of society—is the broad boundary between right and wrong.'

   At first sight the citation of this passage by Lord Coleridge CJ might appear to give
support to the view that such an intent on the part of the accused had to be proved but it
is to be noted that Lord Coleridge CJ began his summing-up by telling the jury that there
were two questions to be considered, first, whether the publications in question were
blasphemous libels and, secondly, whether, assuming them to be so, Mr Bradlaugh was
h guilty of publishing them. He did not at any time tell the jury that they had to consider
Mr Bradlaugh's intent, an astonishing omission if he regarded it necessary to prove that he
had a blasphemous intent, and the passage he cited from Starkie was cited by him as
providing the test for determining whether or not the publication itself was blasphemous.

---

1   (1819) 1 State Tr NS 1387
j 2   (1841) 4 State Tr NS 563
3   History of the Criminal Law of England (1883), vol 2, ch 24, pp 361–362
4   (1883) 15 Cox CC 217
5   History of the Criminal Law of England (1883), vol 2, ch 24, pp 473 et seq
6   15 Cox CC 217 at 226
7   4th Edn (1876), p 599

This, to my mind, is shown beyond doubt by the fact that, after citing Starkie, he said[1]:

> 'That I apprehend to be a correct statement of the law, and if you think the broad *a* boundary between right and wrong that is laid down in the passage, has been overpast in the articles which are the subject-matter of this indictment, then it will be your duty to answer the first question . . . against the defendant.'

And by his saying at the end of his summing-up[2]:

> 'It is a question, first of all, whether these things are not in any point of view *b* blasphemous libels, whether they are not calculated and intended to insult the feelings and the deepest religious convictions of the great majority of the persons amongst whom we live; and if so they are not to be tolerated any more than any other nuisance is tolerated. We must not do things that are outrages to the general feeling of propriety among the persons amongst whom we live. That is the first thing. Then the second thing is: Is Mr. Bradlaugh made out to have joined in the publication of *c* these?'

'To say that the crime lies in the manner and not in the matter appears to me an attempt to evade and explain away a law which has no doubt ceased to be in harmony with the temper of the times' was Stephen's view[3], but since 1883 it has been accepted that it is the manner in which they are expressed that may constitute views expressed in a publication *d* a blasphemous libel and this passage from Starkie has been relied on as providing the test for determining whether the publication exceeds that which is permissible. It is the intention revealed by the publication that may lead to its being held to be blasphemous. There was nothing in Lord Coleridge CJ's summing-up to support the view that there was a third question for the jury to consider, namely the intent of the accused.

This case was followed by *R v Ramsay and Foote*[4], a case greatly relied on by the *e* appellants, a case of great importance and also tried by Lord Coleridge CJ. Again he told the jury that there were two questions for them to consider[5]:

> 'First, are these publications in themselves blasphemous libels? Secondly, if they are so, is the publication of them traced home to the defendants so that you can find them guilty?'
f

He went on to say[5]: 'The great point still remains, are these articles within the meaning of the law blasphemous libels?'

Again he cited the passage from Starkie, not as indicating that it must be shown that the accused had an intention to blaspheme but as providing the test for determining whether the articles exceeded the permissible bounds. Again Lord Coleridge CJ gave no direction to the jury as to the intent of the accused, an omission which I regard as of great *g* significance.

Lord Coleridge CJ's approach in this case was followed by Phillimore J in *R v Boulter*[6].

While it may be that the development of the law as to seditious libel has now taken a different course, in *R v Aldred*[7], in the course of his summing-up on a charge of publishing a seditious libel, Coleridge J told the jury that the accused could not plead the innocence of his motive as a defence to the charge, telling them that— *h*

> 'The test is not either the truth of the language or the innocence of the motive with which he published it, but the test is this: was the language used calculated, or was it not, to promote public disorder or physical force or violence in a matter of State?'

---

1   (1883) 15 Cox CC 217 at 226
2   15 Cox CC 217 at 230–231
3   History of the Criminal Law of England (1883), vol 2, ch 25, p 475
4   (1883) 48 LT 733, 15 Cox CC 231
5   48 LT 733 at 734; cf 15 Cox CC 231 at 233
6   (1908) 72 JP 188
7   (1909) 22 Cox CC 1 at 3

j

and[1] if the language was calculated to promote public disorder—

a
    'then, whatever his motives, whatever his intentions, there would be evidence on which a jury might, on which I should think a jury ought, and on which a jury would decide that he was guilty of a seditious publication.'

This direction was not followed in *R v Caunt*[2] a seditious libel case tried in 1947. The transcript of that case shows that counsel agreed that a man published a seditious libel if he did so with a seditious intent and Birkett J so directed the jury.

b
It is not necessary in this appeal to decide whether Birkett J's direction was right or unduly favourable to the accused and whether *R v Aldred*[3] was rightly decided for we are only concerned with blasphemous libel.

The last case to which I need refer is *R v Gott*[4]. Avory J in his summing-up[5] cited the passage I have cited from the end of Lord Coleridge CJ's summing-up in *R v Bradlaugh*[6].

c
He did not tell the jury that it was necessary to prove that the defendant had a blasphemous intent. He said nothing about the accused's intent. The case went to appeal but his omission to do so was not a ground of appeal or the subject of adverse comment by the Court of Criminal Appeal.

In the light of the authorities to which I have referred and for the reasons I have stated, I am unable to reach the conclusion that the ingredients of the offence of publishing a

d
blasphemous libel have changed since 1792. Indeed, it would, I think, be surprising if they had. If it be accepted, as I think it must, that that which it is sought to prevent is the publication of blasphemous libels, the harm is done by their intentional publication, whether or not the publisher intended to blaspheme. To hold that it must be proved that he had that intent appears to me to be going some way to making the accused judge in his own cause. If Mr Lemon had testified that he did not regard the poem and drawing as

e
blasphemous, that he had no intention to blaspheme, and it might be, that his intention was to promote the love and affection of some homosexuals for Our Lord, the jury properly directed would surely have been told that unless satisfied beyond reasonable doubt that he intended to blaspheme they should acquit, no matter how blasphemous they thought the publication. Whether or not they would have done so on such evidence is a matter of speculation on which views may differ.

f
The question we have to decide is a pure question of law and my conclusions thereon do not, I hope, evince any distrust of juries. The question here is what is the proper direction to give to them, not how they might act on such a direction; and distrust, which I do not have, of the way a jury might act, does not enter into it.

My Lords, for the reasons I have stated in my opinion the question certified should be answered in the affirmative. Guilt of the offence of publishing a blasphemous libel does

g
not depend on the accused having an intent to blaspheme but on proof that the publication was intentional (or, in the case of a bookseller, negligent (Lord Campbell's Libel Act 1843)) and that the matter published was blasphemous.

I would dismiss these appeals.

LORD EDMUND-DAVIES. My Lords, in June 1976 there appeared in an issue of Gay

h
News, a newspaper published seemingly for male homosexuals in the main, a poem entitled 'The Love that Dares to Speak its Name' and an accompanying drawing. The nature of the poem is sufficiently indicated by Roskill LJ who said in the Court of Appeal[7] that it 'purports to describe in explicit detail acts of sodomy and fellatio with the body of

---

j
  1 (1909) 22 Cox CC 1 at 4
  2 (17th November 1947), unreported
  3 22 Cox CC 1
  4 (1922) 16 Cr App R 87
  5 Reported only in The Freethinker, 8th January 1922, p 28
  6 (1883) 15 Cox CC 217 at 230–231
  7 [1978] 3 All ER 175 at 177, [1979] QB 10 at 12

Christ immediately after the moment of His death'. The publishers of the newspaper were
Gay News Ltd, its editor Mr Lemon. The publication led to their indictment for *a*
blasphemous libel, the particulars of the charge being that they had—

> 'unlawfully and wickedly published or caused to be published in a newspaper called
> Gay News No. 96 a blasphemous libel concerning the Christian religion, namely an
> obscene poem and illustration vilifying Christ in His life and in His crucifixion.'

Before his Honour Judge King-Hamilton QC and a jury they were, by a majority verdict, *b*
both convicted and sentenced.

The Court of Appeal upheld both convictions and, while refusing leave to appeal,
certified in the following terms that a point of law of general public importance was
involved:

> 'Was the learned trial judge correct (as the Court of Appeal held) first in ruling and
> then in directing the jury that in order to secure the conviction of the appellants for *c*
> publishing a blasphemous libel (1) it was sufficient if the jury took the view that the
> publication complained of vilified Christ in His life and crucifixion, and (2) it was not
> necessary for the Crown to establish any further intention on the part of the appellants
> beyond an intention to publish that which in the jury's view was a blasphemous
> libel?'
>
> *d*

By your Lordships' leave, the defendants now appeal to this House.

By far the principal contest during the hearing of this appeal was that which gave rise to
the certified question. The actus reus of the offence charged was said to be that the
published poem and illustration vilified Christ, and in the course of a summing-up which,
apart from its treatment of the contested matter of intent, has rightly been regarded as a
model of its kind, the learned judge correctly directed the jury on the matter of obscenity *e*
and vilification. By their verdict they found that the publication, objectively considered,
was in fact blasphemous. It followed that, as Roskill LJ emphasised[1], any quashing of the
convictions—

> 'would not in any way involve overturning the conclusions implicit in the jury's
> verdict of guilty that the allegedly offending poem and drawing was obscene in the
> ordinary meaning of that word, or that it "vilified Christ in His life and crucifixion" *f*
> in the ordinary meaning of that phrase.'

But was that enough to justify the verdicts of guilty? The Court of Appeal thought it
was, despite the strong contrary submission of defendants' counsel. Now, although the
certified question of law related solely to mens rea, it cannot be answered without regard
being had to the actus reus of blasphemous libel. Nor should one overlook the fact that *g*
seditious libel, blasphemous libel, obscene libel and defamatory libel all had their common
origin in the Star Chamber, which (in the words of Mr J R Spencer[2]), '. . . regarded with the
deepest suspicion the printed word in general, and anything which looked like criticism of
the established institutions of Church or State in particular'. It was on the abolition of the
Star Chamber in 1641 that the Court of King's Bench inherited its criminal jurisdiction,
and shortly after the Restoration tried the dramatist Sir Charles Sedley[3] for indecency and *h*
blasphemy. For centuries thereafter[4]—

> '. . . a published attack on a high state official . . . might be prosecuted as either a
> seditious or a defamatory libel, and an attack on the Church or its doctrine might be
> prosecuted as either a blasphemous or a seditious libel. What the attack in question
> was called seems to have depended largely on the taste in vituperative epithet of the
> man who drafted the indictment or information. (Thus in one case a man was *j*

---

1   [1978] 3 All ER 175 at 179, [1979] QB 10 at 14
2   [1977] Crim LR 383
3   (1663) 1 Keb 620, 1 Sid 168; see 17 State Tr 155, Pepys's Diary, 1st July 1663
4   [1977] Crim LR 383 at 384

a prosecuted for seditious rather than blasphemous libel when he published a book
contrary to the teaching of the Church of England: *Keach*[1].)'

As to the actus reus, at first all open expressions of a disbelief in Christianity were
punishable, the Bench repeatedly laying down the plain principle that the public
importance of the Christian religion was so great that no-one was to be allowed to deny its
truth, just as in *R v Bedford*[2] a man was convicted of the kindred offence of seditious libel
simply for discussing, civilly and gravely and 'without any reflection whatever upon any
b part of the then existing Government', the respective advantages of hereditary and elective
monarchies. As late as 1841 the Commissioners on Criminal Law[3] reported that 'The law
distinctly forbids *all* denial of the Christian religion', but nevertheless added that in actual
practice '. . . the course has been to withhold the application of the penal law unless
insulting language is used'. These last words mark the second stage in the development of
the actus reus of blasphemy, and echo the ruling of Lord Denman a year earlier in *R v*
c *Hetherington*[4], that criminality lies 'not altogether on the matter of opinion, but is in a great
degree a question as to the tone and style and spirit'.

My Lords, during the long years when the actus reus of blasphemy was constituted by
the mere denial (however decently expressed) of the basic tenets of Christianity or, later,
the couching of that denial in scurrilous language, there was no necessity to explore the
intention of the accused, for his words were regarded as revealing in themselves what that
d intention was. And that was so, notwithstanding the fact that indictments for blasphemy
habitually contained assertions regarding the defendant's intention. Let me illustrate.
One finds in Archbold's Pleading and Evidence in Criminal Cases[5] an indictment charging
that the accused—

e 'wickedly and profanely devising and intending to bring the Holy Scriptures and
the Christian religion into disbelief and contempt among the people of this Kingdom
. . . unlawfully and wickedly did compose, print and publish . . . a certain scandalous,
impious, blasphemous and profane libel . . .'

The appended note gives a cross-reference to an indictment for seditious libel, and,
notwithstanding an allegation in the latter[6] of 'intending to stir up and excite discontents
and seditions amongst His Majesty's subjects', the author observed[7]:
f

'And whether the defendant really intended, by his publication, to alienate the
affections of the people from the government is . . . immaterial; if the publication be
calculated to have that effect, it is a seditious libel. *R. v. Burdett*[8]; *R. v. Harvey and*
Chapman[9].'

Such an assertion in such a book affords a good illustration of the laxity of language
g employed, certainly up to Lord Campbell's Libel Act 1843. And it is worthwhile
considering at some little length the two cases cited in support of the author's proposition
that seditious libel was regarded, in effect, as a crime of strict liability, in order to determine
whether in reality they did anything of the sort. In my judgment, they were, if anything,
authorities for the directly contrary proposition. Thus, in *R v Burdett*[10] Best J directed the
jury regarding an allegedly seditious libel:
h

1   (1665) 6 State Tr 701
2   (1713) Gilb 297; see 5 Bac Abr (7th Edn, 1832), p 200
3   Sixth Report of the Commissioners on Criminal Law (3rd May 1841)
4   (1841) 4 State Tr NS 563 at 590
j 5   7th Edn (1838), p 501
6   Ibid, p 492
7   Ibid, pp 493–494
8   (1821) 4 B & Ald 95
9   (1823) 2 B & C 257
10 4 B & Ald 95 at 120

'. . . that the question, whether it was published with the intention alleged in the information, was peculiarly for their consideration; but I added, that the intention *a* was to be collected from the paper itself, unless the import of the paper were explained by the mode of publication, or any other circumstances. I added, that if it appeared that the contents of the paper were likely to excite sedition and disaffection, the defendant must be presumed to intend that which his act was likely to produce. I told them further, that if they should be of opinion that such was the intention of the defendant, then it was my duty to declare that, in my opinion, such a paper, *b* published with such an intent, was a libel; leaving it, however, to them . . . to find whether it was a libel or not.'

Now that direction (later upheld[1] by a full court of four judges on a motion for a new trial) in no sense brushed aside as irrelevant the intention of the accused publisher. On the contrary, it stressed the importance of his intention, while at the same time instructing the *c* jury, in effect, that (as Lord Ellenborough CJ had recently said in *R v Dixon*[2]), it is a 'universal principle, that when a man is charged with doing an act, of which the probable consequence may be highly injurious, the intention is an inference of law resulting from doing the act . . .' A similar comment can properly be made regarding the second case cited by Archbold[3], *R v Harvey and Chapman*[4], where the proprietor, printer and publisher *d* of a newspaper were charged in relation to a statement that they had good authority for asserting that King George IV laboured under mental infirmity. The defendants admitted that it was false to say that they had good authority for making the assertion, but urged that they nevertheless believed it to be true, in the light of widely prevalent rumours. Having directed the jury that, in his opinion, the publication was a libel calculated to vilify His Majesty, Abbott CJ added[5] (as Fox's Libel Act 1792 required him to do): 'But you have a right to exercise your own judgment upon the publication, and I invite you so to do.' After *e* a retirement, the jury returned and asked for the Lord Chief Justice's opinion whether or not it was necessary that there should be a malicious intention to constitute a libel. They were thereupon told[6]:

'The man who publishes slanderous matter, in its nature calculated to defame and vilify another, must be presumed to have intended to do that which the publication *f* is calculated to bring about, *unless he can shew the contrary*; and it is for him to shew the contrary.'

Subsequently, on the hearing of an unsuccessful motion for a new trial on the ground of misdirection, Bayley and Best JJ, made similar observations[7] in upholding Abbott CJ's direction. *g*

My Lords, the admirable survey of many of the decided cases (but not including the two last-mentioned) contained in the Court of Appeal judgment delivered by Roskill LJ fortunately renders it unnecessary to go through them again. But of that thought-provoking judgment I have to say respectfully that the one-sentence reference[8] to the presumption as to intending natural consequences pays inadequate attention to the great importance of that concept in evaluating many of the decided cases, and one which goes far *h* to explain the frequent absence of a clear direction regarding the necessity of proving a subjective intention, a point to which the Court of Appeal attached much weight. Another

---

1   (1821) 4 B & Ald 314
2   (1814) 3 M & S 11 at 15
3   Pleading and Evidence in Criminal Cases (7th Edn, 1838), p 494   *j*
4   (1823) 2 B & C 257
5   2 B & C 257 at 258
6   2 B & C 257 at 259
7   2 B & C 257 at 261, 268
8   [1978] 3 All ER 175 at 187, [1979] QB 10 at 25

insufficiently appreciated factor, as it appears to me, is that until Lord Campbell's Libel Act
a 1843 there existed what Lord Coleridge CJ described in *R v Bradlaugh*[1] as—

> '. . . the anomaly that whereas in no other case in the criminal law was a man
> responsible for the act of the agent unless he had authorised the particular act, yet it
> had been held that in the case of a libel a man might be criminally responsible for the
> act of an agent to whom he had given only a general authority.'

b   The full vigour of this doctrine of vicarious responsibility was reduced by s 7 of the 1843
Act, and the significant impact of the statutory change was described by Lush J in *R v
Holbrook*[2] in the following terms:

> 'The effect of it read by the light of previous decisions, and read so as to make it
> remedial, must be that an authority from the proprietor of a newspaper to the editor
> to publish what is libellous is no longer to be, as it formerly was, a presumption of law,
c > but a question of fact. Before the Act the only question of fact was whether the
> defendant authorized the publication of the paper; now, it is whether he authorized
> the publication of the libel . . . But when he has proved that the literary department
> was intrusted entirely to an editor, the question what was the extent of the authority
> which that employment involved is to be tried upon the principle which is applicable
> to all other questions of authority. And I think the jury ought to be told, in this as in
d > every other case, that criminal intention is not to be presumed, but is to be proved,
> and that, in the absence of any evidence to the contrary, a person who employs
> another to do a lawful act is to be taken to authorize him to do it in a lawful and not
> in an unlawful manner.'

This passage, expressly approved of five years later by Lord Coleridge CJ in *R v Bradlaugh*[3],
e indicated that the change was thus a considerable one. Mr Richard Buxton has shown in
a valuable article[4], to which I desire to acknowledge my indebtedness, that it is essential to
have it in mind in considering such pre-1843 cases as *R v Hetherington*[5], which the Court of
Appeal regarded as important, and in particular that they stressed[6] that Lord Denman CJ[7]
had directed the jury that:

> 'The question before you and the only question for you to decide is a matter of fact
f > and of opinion. Aye or no, is this in your opinion a blasphemous publication and has
> the defendant in point of fact issued it knowingly and wilfully? If these questions are
> answered in the affirmative it is the duty of the jury to pronounce a verdict
> accordingly.'

But what needs to be remembered is that, when Hetherington was tried in 1840, not
g only was he incompetent to testify as to his intention, or, indeed, as to anything else, but
he was liable to be convicted even had he lacked all knowledge that he had even published
a blasphemy, and it would accordingly have been idle to investigate his intention in
publishing. And as many of the reported cases of blasphemous libel up to that time
involved publishers rather than authors, Mr Buxton rightly comments[8] that—

> '. . . the special "publisher" rule was likely to restrict any general statements [by
h > judges] that might otherwise have been made about the mental element in
> blasphemy. The surprising thing, in fact, is that references to intention are found
> even in these unpromising circumstances. And with the abolition of the special rule

---

1   (1883) 15 Cox CC 217 at 227–228
2   (1878) 4 QBD 42 at 50–51
j 3   15 Cox CC 217 at 228
4   [1978] Crim LR 673
5   (1841) 4 State Tr NS 563
6   [1978] 3 All ER 175 at 189, [1979] QB 10 at 27
7   4 State Tr NS 563 at 593
8   [1978] Crim LR 673 at 676

for publishers in 1843 circumstances became more propitious for a restatement of the
elements of blasphemy in terms of subjective responsibility.'   *a*

I have already referred to two pre-1843 cases where, so far from intention being brushed
aside as irrelevant, the jury were directed that they could and should deal with it on the
basis of the presumption as to probable consequences. And in 1812 Mr Starkie (later
Downing Professor of Law at Cambridge, one of the Criminal Law Commissioners both
in 1833 and 1845, and co-draftsman with Lord Campbell of the Libel Act 1843) declared   *b*
in his highly esteemed textbook on the law of libel[1] that, 'The law visits not the honest
errors, but the malice of mankind' and (as Professor Courtney Kenny later wrote in 1922[2])
'urged that the penalties of blasphemy should be limited to cases where the offender
intended either to insult sacred subjects by contumelious language or to mislead his readers
by wilful misrepresentation'. Fourteen years after the 1843 Act, Coleridge J accepted in *R
v Pooley*[3] the following definition of the offence of blasphemy contained in Stephen's Digest
of the Criminal Law[4]:   *c*

> 'Every publication ... which contains matter relating to God, Jesus Christ, the
> Bible, or the Book of Common Prayer, and *intended* to wound the feelings of mankind,
> or to excite contempt and hatred against the Church by law established or to promote
> immorality.' (Italics supplied.)

But the Court of Appeal would presumably have held that the only mental element there   *d*
being referred to was the defendant's decision to publish the words complained of. That
was seemingly the view they took of the two important cases on blasphemous libel
consecutively decided by Lord Coleridge CJ in 1883.

My noble and learned friend, Viscount Dilhorne, has emphasised that in the first of these
(*R v Bradlaugh*[5]) Lord Coleridge CJ directed the jury in these words: *e*

> 'The question really and substantially raised is one and only one, whether Mr.
> Bradlaugh published these libels. Of course, the two questions are legally raised: first,
> whether the publications which are the subject matter of indictment are or are not
> blasphemous libels; the second is whether, assuming they are so, Mr. Bradlaugh is
> guilty of publishing them so as to be amenable to the criminal law?'

Lord Coleridge CJ used similar words when directing the jury a few days later in the second *f*
trial, that of *R v Ramsay and Foote*[6], and my noble and learned friend considers it astonishing
that in these two passages there should be no reference to the defendant's intent if it be the
law that intent is in truth an essential ingredient in blasphemous libel. My Lords, my
submission is that, when the reports of the two cases are considered in their entirety, the
inescapable conclusion is that such was indeed Lord Coleridge CJ's view of the law.

Addressing himself to his first question in *R v Bradlaugh*[7], Lord Coleridge said: 'To the *g*
law on that subject laid down by Mr. Starkie (and read by Sir H Giffard) [for the Crown] I
entirely assent.' To what *was* he assenting? He made this clear beyond doubt by saying[8]:

> 'The law has been laid down, in my judgment, with perfect accuracy in the passage
> read from the work of Mr. Starkie[9]—"The wilful intention to insult and mislead

h

---

1   The Law of Slander and Libel (1st Edn, 1812), p 590
2   (1922) 1 CLJ 127 at 136
3   (1857) 8 State Tr NS 1089
4   5th Edn (1894), art 179, p 125; 9th Edn (1950), art 214, p 163   *j*
5   (1883) 15 Cox CC 217 at 225
6   (1883) 15 Cox CC 231 at 233
7   15 Cox CC 217 at 225
8   15 Cox CC 217 at 226
9   Law of Slander and Libel (4th Edn, 1876), pp 599–600

a others by means of licentious and contumelious abuse offered to sacred subjects, or by wilful misrepresentations or wilful sophistry, calculated to mislead the ignorant and unwary, is the criterion and test of guilt. A malicious and mischievous intention, or what is equivalent to such an intention, in law, as well as morals—a state of apathy and indifference to the interests of society—is the broad boundary between right and wrong".'

b And, by way of applying the law as laid down by Starkie, Lord Coleridge CJ concluded[1]:

'It is a question, first of all, whether these things are not in any point of view blasphemous libels, *whether they are not calculated and intended to insult the feelings and the deepest religious convictions of the great majority of the persons amongst whom we live*; and if so they are not to be tolerated any more than any other nuisance is tolerated.' (Italics supplied.)

c Turning now to *R v Ramsay and Foote*[2], after asking the question, 'Are these passages *within the meaning of the law* blasphemous libels?', Lord Coleridge CJ directed the jury in clear terms that 'to asperse the truth of Christianity cannot per se be sufficient to sustain a criminal prosecution for blasphemy'. What, then, did he consider was further required? For answer, he again turned to what he described as one of 'the best books of authority' (Starkie on Libel) and quoted a passage from the 4th edition[3] dealing with '. . . the splendid d advantages which result to religion and truth from the exertions of free and unfettered minds', which continued with these words[4]: 'It is the *mischievous* abuse of this state of intellectual liberty which calls for penal censure. The law visits not the honest errors but the malice of mankind.'

There then followed those words which Lord Coleridge CJ had quoted a few days earlier in *R v Bradlaugh*[5], beginning with 'The wilful intention to insult and mislead others . . .' e And the matter was not left to rest even there, for in the final passage of his summing-up, he said[6]:

'The defendant Foote has admitted that these publications were intended to be attacks on Christianity and on the Hebrew Scriptures, and he has cited a number of passages from approved writers which he says are to the same effect . . . But no one can f fail to see the difference between the works which have been quoted and the language used in the publications now before us; and I am obliged to say that it is a difference not only in degree, but in kind and nature. There is a grave and earnest tone, a reverent—perhaps I might even say a religious—spirit about the very attacks on Christianity itself which we find in the authors referred to, *which shows that what they aimed at was not insult to the opinions of the majority of mankind nor to Christianity itself; but* g *real, quiet, earnest pursuit of truth.*' (Italics supplied.)

The passages quoted from Starkie and their setting in the direction to the jury, both in *R v Bradlaugh*[7] and in *R v Ramsay and Foote*[8], surely went beyond mere consideration of the language of controversy. They made clear that the proper answer to the first question posed by Lord Coleridge CJ in each of the two cases depended not merely on the words used but on the state of mind of the person using them. In other words, what was his h 'aim'? Yet the Court of Appeal concluded[9] that:

---

1 (1883) 15 Cox CC 217 at 230
2 (1883) 15 Cox CC 231 at 234–235
3 (1876), pp 599–600
4 15 Cox CC 231 at 236
5 15 Cox CC 217 at 226
6 15 Cox CC 231 at 238–239
7 15 Cox CC 217
8 15 Cox CC 231
9 [1978] 3 All ER 175 at 189, [1979] QB 10 at 27

'Intent in the sense for which the appellants have contended was not a live issue in *R v Ramsay and Foote*[1], for Foote . . . had admitted his intention. It is, we think, a legitimate comment that since this was the position in that case, the passages in Starkie on Libel[2] . . . approved by Lord Coleridge CJ cannot have been thought by the Lord Chief Justice to have borne the meaning contended for by the appellants.'

But, as to this, the *only* admission was that the publications complained of 'were intended to be attacks on Christianity and on the Hebrew Scriptures'[3]. And Mr Buxton has rightly observed[4]:

'But Lord Coleridge thought that simply to attack Christianity did *not* constitute the *actus reus* of blasphemy. It therefore cannot be assumed that Foote, by admitting what he did, thereby also admitted an intent to blaspheme, as defined by Lord Coleridge.'

In my judgment, accordingly, the intention of the defendants in publishing was assuredly a live issue in both trials, and Lord Coleridge CJ made it clear that such was his view of the law.

Between *R v Ramsay and Foote*[1] and *R v Gott*[5] there were very few blasphemy prosecutions, and none thereafter until the present trial. Of the intervening cases, the direction of Phillimore J in *R v Boulter*[6] is, despite the misleadingly emphatic headnote, equivocal as to the necessity for intention, and the same is true of Avory J's direction in *R v Gott*[7] itself. But it was the latter decision which sparked off Professor Kenny's survey of the relevant law, which led him to the conclusion that[8]—

'in criminal proceedings, guilt can only arise where the offensive matter was published with full knowledge of its contents and with readiness to offend. "Wilful intention", as Professor Starkie said, "is the criterion and test of guilt."'

My Lords, we have seen that sedition and blasphemy were in origin twin types of criminal libel, the latter consisting in its earliest stage as *any* attack on the Christian Church, as part of the state, and Hale CJ declaring in *R v Taylor*[9] that 'Christianity is parcel of the laws of England'. I understood the respondent to these appeals to accept that, in relation to *sedition*, the intention of the defendant is an essential ingredient, and such cases as *R v Burns*[10] and *R v Caunt*[11] proceeded on that basis. It would be inexplicable were intention relevant in the one case but not in the other. *R v Burns*[12] is also important as illustrating the lessening respect paid, as the 19th century progressed, to the presumption as to intention, Cave J saying[13]:

'In order to make out the offence of speaking seditious words there must be a criminal intent upon the part of the accused, they must be words spoken with a seditious intent; and, although it is a good working rule to say that a man must be taken to intend the natural consequences of his acts, and it is very proper to ask a jury to infer, if there is nothing to show the contrary, that he did intend the natural

1   (1883) 15 Cox CC 231
2   4th Edn (1876), pp 599–600
3   15 Cox CC 231 at 238
4   [1978] Crim LR 673 at 680
5   (1922) 16 Cr App R 87
6   (1908) 72 JP 188
7   The Freethinker, 8th January 1922, at p 28
8   The Evolution of the Law of Blasphemy (1922) 1 CLJ 127 at 140
9   (1676) 1 Vent 293
10 (1886) 16 Cox CC 355 at 360
11 (17th November 1947), unreported
12 16 Cox CC 355
13 16 Cox CC 355 at 364

a   consequences of his acts, yet, if it is shown from other circumstances that he did not actually intend them, I do not see how you can ask a jury to act upon what has then become a legal fiction.'

My Lords, allow me to summarise. This appeal raises the questions whether it is sufficient for conviction that the defendants intended to *publish* the blasphemous words for which they were indicted, as the learned trial judge held. Or was it necessary that they should have also known of their offensive character and have intended to offend, or *b*   alternatively that they published with reckless indifference to the consequences of publication? Different answers to these questions were called for at different stages in the evolution of the law of blasphemy. In the earliest stage it was clearly a crime of strict liability and consisted merely of any attack on the Christian church and its tenets. In the second stage the original harshness of the law was ameliorated, and the attack was not punishable unless expressed in intemperate or scurrilous language. In the third stage *c*   opinions were mixed. Some judges held that the subjective intention of author or publisher was irrelevant, others that it was of the greatest materiality. The stricter view was explicable on several grounds:

(1) By reason of the presumption of intention as to the probable consequences of one's actions, which, though increasingly unpopular, was not finally eliminated until s 8 of the Criminal Justice Act 1967 was enacted.

d   (2) By reason of the fact that, as until Fox's Libel Act 1792 it was for the judge (and not the jury) to decide whether a publication was blasphemous, he was relieved of any necessity for directing the jury as to intention. In the view of Stephen[1]:

'The effect of the Libel Act . . . was to embody in the definition of the crime of seditious libel the existence of some kind of bad intention on the part of the offender *e*   . . . And a seditious libel might since the passing of that Act be defined (in general terms) as blame of public men, laws or institutions, published with an illegal intention on the part of the publisher.'

And, as G D Nokes pointed out[2], '. . . there is no distinction in the Act between seditious and blasphemous libels'.

f   (3) By reason of the doctrine of vicarious responsibility, earlier discussed, which subsisted in an unqualified form until Lord Campbell's Libel Act 1843.

(4) By reason of the fact that, until the Criminal Evidence Act 1898, persons accused of blasphemy were incompetent to give evidence on their own behalf.

The preponderance of authority was nevertheless increasingly and markedly in favour of the view that intention to blaspheme must be established if conviction was to ensue. In my judgment, such is now indeed the law and any 20th century cases in conflict with it, *g*   such as *R v Aldred*[3], should be regarded as wrongly decided.

Something should, however, be said about certain practical difficulties suggested by the Court of Appeal in the way of adopting this final view of the law. They asked[4]:

'If subjective intention were a necessary ingredient in this offence, whose intention has to be proved? Is it the intention of anyone concerned in the publication, or only *h*   the intention of the accused? If it is only his, could it be a defence that his only intention when putting the offending matter into circulation was to make money, or to inform the world of the writings of another? If it be the intention of the author that matters, then the fate of the publisher might depend, at least in the case of a dead writer, on an intention difficult to ascertain save from the language of that which was known to have been written or spoken in the past.'

j   My Lords, these are, with respect, imagined difficulties, and the answers to such

---

1   History of the Criminal Law of England (1883), vol 2, ch 24, pp 358–359
2   A History of the Crime of Blasphemy (1928), p 80
3   (1909) 22 Cox CC 1
4   [1978] 3 All ER 175 at 190, [1979] QB 10 at 27–28

questions are, I think, clear. The subjective intention to blaspheme or recklessness as to the blasphemous effect of the words published must be brought home in turn to each person *a* charged. If he be the author, the all-important question is what was his state of mind in supplying the material for publication; if he be the editor or publisher of the words of another, as to their state of mind in playing their respective roles in the act of publishing. And it would be nihil ad rem that one or all of them were motivated by, for example, the desire to make money or to make known the blasphemous words of another.

My Lords, even were the reported cases so divided in their effect as to render it *b* impossible to say that the necessity of a subjective intention to blaspheme has hitherto been decisively established over the years, I should urge that this House, being free in such circumstances to declare what the law is, should now hold that such is indeed the law. My noble and learned friend, Lord Diplock, has rightly observed that s 8 of the Criminal Justice Act 1967 is concerned simply with how intention is to be proved *when intention is of relevance*, and says nothing about *when* intention is to be proved. Such indeed was the view *c* I expressed in *Director of Public Prosecutions v Majewski*[1], and I adhere to it. But the section is nevertheless of significance in relation to the present proceedings in its manifestation of conformity with the increasing tendency in our law to move away from strict liability in relation both to statutory offences (see *Sweet v Parsley*[2]) and to common law crimes (see *Lim Chin Aik v R*[3] and *Director of Public Prosecutions v Morgan*[4]). For in truth it is with strict liability that we are concerned in this appeal, for '. . . an offence is regarded—and properly *d* regarded—as one of strict liability if no *mens rea* need be proved as to a single element in the *actus reus*'[5].

There are those who dislike this tendency. But to treat as irrelevant the state of mind of a person charged with blasphemy would be to take a backward step in the evolution of a humane code. Unfortunately, despite the exemplary care taken by the learned trial judge, lacking as he did the prolonged and patient probing into the law of which this House has *e* had the benefit, I am afraid that that is what has happened in this case. Accordingly, despite my strong feelings of revulsion over this deplorable publication, I find myself most reluctantly compelled to answer the certified question in the negative and to hold that these appeals against conviction should be allowed.

For the sake of completeness, and so as to show that I have not overlooked the point, I should add that I am at one with the Court of Appeal in upholding as 'faultless' the learned *f* judge's outright rejection of a further submission for some of the appellants that, in order to justify a conviction for blasphemous libel, the publication, when objectively considered, must tend to lead to a breach of the peace.

LORD RUSSELL OF KILLOWEN. My Lords, it must be made at the outset absolutely clear that it is accepted by the appellants that the publication of blasphemous libel is still *g* a criminal offence: it is no part of your Lordships' function in this case to hold the contrary. Moreover, if the only ingredient of the offence is the knowing publication of matter which will in fact shock and outrage the feelings of ordinary Christians it must equally be made clear that, as the jury found, this publication was a blasphemous libel. It is not for your Lordships to agree or disagree with that finding; though speaking for myself as an ordinary Christian, I found the publication quite appallingly shocking and outrageous. *h*

There is in this case one question only: whether an intention in the publisher to shock and outrage, or an indifference to a recognised possibility that it will do so, is a necessary ingredient of the offence. If it be such an ingredient, then the refusal of the trial judge to allow Mr Lemon to give evidence of his subjective intention was an error in law; and however much one may doubt, as I do, that Mr Lemon would have been able to persuade

j

---

1 [1976] 2 All ER 142 at 170, [1977] AC 443 at 497
2 [1969] 1 All ER 349, especially at 350 and 362, [1970] AC 132, especially at 149 and 163
3 [1963] 1 All ER 223 at 227, [1963] AC 160 at 172
4 [1975] 2 All ER 347 at 358, [1976] AC 182 at 210
5 Smith and Hogan, Criminal Law (4th Edn, 1978), p 79

a jury that he did not think that the publication was likely to shock and outrage, yet if the
direction was thus erroneous in law I would not consider the conviction should be
supported under the proviso.

   It should be noted that the only evidence which could be said to be erroneously excluded
was that of Mr Lemon's state of mind. Of this only he could speak. 'Expert' evidence
would surely have been irrelevant, on any footing. I do not doubt that he had a *motive* in
making this publication which seemed to him to justify it, supposedly (though I am
guessing) that those of his usual readers who were active or passive homosexuals should not
feel that they were for that reason excluded from the fellowship of Christianity. But,
whether intention is or is not an ingredient of the offence, motive is certainly not a defence.

   So I return to the question of intent. The authorities embrace an abundance of
apparently contradictory or ambivalent comments. There is no authority in your
Lordships' House on the point. The question is open for decision. I do not, with all respect
to the speech of my noble and learned friend, Lord Diplock, consider that the question is
whether this is an offence of strict liability. It is necessary that the editor or publisher
should be aware of that which he publishes. Indeed that was the function of Lord
Campbell's Act[1], which assumed the law to be that an intention in the accused to blaspheme
was not an ingredient of the offence, since it removed by statute a vicarious liability for an
act of publication done by another without authority.

   Why then should this House, faced with a deliberate publication of that which a jury
with every justification has held to be a blasphemous libel, consider that it should be for the
prosecution to prove, presumably beyond reasonable doubt, that the accused recognised
and intended it to be such or regarded it as immaterial whether it was? I see no ground for
that. It does not to my mind make sense: and I consider that sense should retain a function
in our criminal law. The reason why the law considers that the publication of a
blasphemous libel is an offence is that the law considers that such publication should not
take place. And if it takes place, and the publication is deliberate, I see no justification for
holding that there is no offence when the publisher is incapable for some reason particular
to himself of agreeing with a jury on the true nature of the publication.

   Accordingly, I would answer the certified question of law in the affirmative and dismiss
the appeal, and order the respondent's costs to be paid out of public funds.

LORD SCARMAN. My Lords, I do not subscribe to the view that the common law
offence of blasphemous libel serves no useful purpose in the modern law. On the contrary,
I think there is a case for legislation extending it to protect the religious beliefs and feelings
of non-Christians. The offence belongs to a group of criminal offences designed to
safeguard the internal tranquillity of the kingdom. In an increasingly plural society such
as that of modern Britain it is necessary not only to respect the differing religious beliefs,
feelings and practices of all but also to protect them from scurrility, vilification, ridicule
and contempt. Professor Kenny, in his brilliant article[2] on 'The Evolution of the Law of
Blasphemy', gives two quotations which are very relevant to British society today. When
the Home Secretary was pressed to remit the sentence on Gott after the dismissal of his
appeal[3], he wrote:

   'The common law does not interfere with the free expression of *bona fide* opinion.
   But it prohibits, and renders punishable as a misdemeanour, the use of coarse and
   scurrilous ridicule on subjects which are sacred to most people in this country. Mr.
   Shortt could not support any proposal for an alteration of the common law which

---

1   Libel Act 1843
2   (1922) 1 CLJ 127
3   *R v Gott* (1922) 16 Cr App R 87

would permit such outrages on the feelings of others as those of which Gott was found
to be guilty.'   *a*

When nearly a century earlier Lord Macaulay protested in Parliament against the way
the blasphemy laws were then administered, he added[1]: 'If I were a judge in India, I should
have no scruple about punishing a Christian who should pollute a mosque.'

When Macaulay became a legislator in India, he saw to it that the law protected the
religious feelings of all. In those days India was a plural society; today the United Kingdom   *b*
is also.

I have permitted myself these general observations at the outset of my opinion because,
my Lords, they determine my approach to this appeal. I will not lend my voice to a view
of the law relating to blasphemous libel which would render it a dead letter, or diminish
its efficacy to protect religious feelings from outrage and insult. My criticism of the
common law offence of blasphemy is not that it exists but that it is not sufficiently   *c*
comprehensive. It is shackled by the chains of history.

While in my judgment it is not open to your Lordships' House, even under the Lord
Chancellor's policy announcement of 26th July 1966[2], to extend the law beyond the limits
recognised by the House in *Bowman v Secular Society Ltd*[3], or to make by judicial decision
the comprehensive reform of the law which I believe to be beneficial, this appeal does offer
your Lordships the opportunity of stating the existing law in a form conducive to the social   *d*
conditions of the late 20th century rather than to those of the 17th, 18th or even the 19th
century. This is, my Lords, no mere opportunity: it is a duty. As Lord Sumner said in his
historic speech in *Bowman v Secular Society Ltd*[4]:

> 'The words, as well as the acts, which tend to endanger society differ from time to
> time in proportion as society is stable or insecure in fact, or is believed by its
> reasonable members to be open to assault. In the present day meetings or processions   *e*
> are held lawful which a hundred and fifty years ago would have been deemed
> seditious, and this is not because the law is weaker or has changed, but because, the
> times having changed, society is stronger than before. In the present day reasonable
> men do not apprehend the dissolution or the downfall of society because religion is
> publicly assailed by methods not scandalous. Whether it is possible that in the future
> irreligious attacks, designed to undermine fundamental institutions of our society,   *f*
> may come to be criminal in themselves, as constituting a public danger, is a matter
> that does not arise. The fact that opinion grounded on experience has moved one way
> does not in law preclude the possibility of its moving on fresh experience in the other;
> nor does it bind succeeding generations, when conditions have again changed. After
> all, the question whether a given opinion is a danger to society is a question of the
> times and is a question of fact. I desire to say nothing that would limit the right of   *g*
> society to protect itself by process of law from the dangers of the moment, whatever
> that right may be, but only to say that, experience having proved dangers once
> thought real to be now negligible, and dangers once very possibly imminent to have
> now passed away, there is nothing in the general rules as to blasphemy and irreligion,
> as known to the law, which prevents us from varying their application to the
> particular circumstances of our time in accordance with that experience.'   *h*

The point of law certified by the Court of Appeal as of general public importance on
which the House gave leave to appeal is in these terms:

j

---

1   (1922) 1 CLJ at 135; Speeches, p 116
2   *Note* [1966] 3 All ER 77, [1966] 1 WLR 1234
3   [1917] AC 406, [1916–17] All ER Rep 1
4   [1917] AC 406 at 466–467, [1916–17] All ER Rep 1 at 32

'Was the learned trial judge correct (as the Court of Appeal held) first in ruling and
a   then in directing the jury that in order to secure the conviction of the appellants for
publishing a blasphemous libel: (1) it was sufficient if the jury took the view that the
publication complained of vilified Christ in His life and crucifixion and (2) it was not
necessary for the Crown to establish any further intention on the part of the appellants
beyond an intention to publish that which in the jury's view was a blasphemous
libel?'

b   The appellants' case is that it was necessary for the Crown to establish a further specific
intention, and their counsel formulated the intention as follows: '. . . the intention to
attack the Christian religion so violently or scurrilously as to insult the adherents of the
Christian religion to such an extent that a breach of the peace is likely.'
The Crown led no evidence to prove any intention other than the intention to publish
the words complained of; and the judge directed the jury in effect that any such evidence
c   would be irrelevant. If, therefore, the appellants are correct in law that an intention
beyond that of publication must be proved, it matters not whether their counsel have
accurately formulated the specific intention required: their convictions must be quashed.
The appellants Gay News Ltd publish a newspaper for homosexuals called Gay News.
The appellant Mr Lemon is its editor. An issue of the paper, published in 1976, contained
a poem entitled 'The Love that Dares to speak its Name' written by Professor James
d   Kirkup. The poem was printed with an illustration of the crucifixion featuring the body
of Christ in the embrace of a Roman centurion. The appellants were indicted for the
offence of blasphemous libel. They were tried in July 1977 at the Central Criminal Court
before his Honour Judge King-Hamilton QC and a jury. After a masterly summing-up
(for such it was, whether or not correct on the question of intention), the jury by a majority
found both appellants guilty. On appeal, the Court of Appeal upheld the convictions.
e   In a judgment (delivered by Roskill LJ) remarkable for its learning and historical
research the Court of Appeal reached the conclusion that for a defendant to be guilty of
publishing a blasphemous libel it was not necessary for the Crown to prove an intent other
than an intent to publish the words of which complaint is made. It is enough, the court
held, to prove that the defendant intended to publish that which offends.
In your Lordships' House it was recognised that no challenge could effectually be made
f   against the finding of the jury that the poem and illustration were blasphemous. Equally
it has to be recognised that no intention to insult or outrage has been established by the
modern criteria of English law. No doubt because the judge ruled that any intention other
than an intention to publish was irrelevant, Mr Lemon did not give evidence. Had he
given evidence, I have little doubt that he would have said, and truly said, that he had no
intention to shock Christian believers but that he published the poem not to offend
g   Christians but to comfort practising homosexuals by encouraging them to feel that there
was room for them in the Christian religion. I am prepared to assume the honesty and
sincerity of his motives.
The actus reus of the offence of blasphemy consists of the publication of words spoken
or written. In the 17th century words challenging or questioning the doctrines of the
established church were regarded as blasphemy: for 'Christianity is parcel of the laws of
h   England; and therefore to reproach the Christian religion is to speak in subversion of the
law', as Hale CJ put it in R v Taylor[1]. His view was accepted in 1729 in R v Woolston[2],
though Raymond CJ did add[3]: '. . . we do not meddle with any differences in opinion and
. . . we interpose only when the very root of Christianity is struck at . . .'
Nevertheless in almost all the reported cases (including Taylor[1] and Woolston[2]) the words

j

1   (1676) 1 Vent 293
2   (1729) 1 Barn KB 162, Fitz-G 64, 2 Stra 834
3   Fitz-G 64 at 66

complained of were scurrilous, insulting or offensive; indeed Keble[1] reports Hale CJ as saying expressly that 'contumelious reproaches of the established religion are punishable *a* here'. And in one famous case, that of *R v Shipley*[2], in which there was no element of scurrility, the defendant was ultimately acquitted.

The watershed between the old and the modern law comes with the cases of *R v Hetherington*[3] and *R v Ramsay and Foote*[4]. Lord Denman CJ's summing-up in *Hetherington's* case[5] contains the remarkable passage quoted by the Court of Appeal in this case. Its importance is such that I make no apology for quoting it again: *b*

'Now, gentlemen, upon the question whether it is blasphemous or not I have this general observation to make, which I have often heard from Lord Tenterden in cases of this description, namely, that the question is not altogether a matter of opinion, but that it must be, in a great degree, a question as to the tone, and style, and spirit, in which such enquiries are conducted. Because, a difference of opinion may subsist, not only as between different sects of Christians, but also with regard to the great doctrines *c* of Christianity itself; and I have heard that great judge declare, that even discussions upon that subject may be by no means a matter of criminal prosecution, but, if they be carried on in a sober and temperate and decent style, even those discussions may be tolerated, and may take place without criminality attaching to them: but that, if the tone and spirit is that of offence, and insult, and ridicule, which leaves the judgment *d* really not free to act, and, therefore, cannot be truly called an appeal to the judgment, but an appeal to the wild and improper feelings of the human mind, more particularly in the younger part of the community, in that case the jury will hardly feel it possible to say that such opinions, so expressed, do not deserve the character which is affixed to them in this indictment. With that general observation, I leave the question of libel to you. Is it, or is it not, a blasphemous libel which the defendant appears to have *e* published in his shop?'

In *R v Ramsay and Foote*[6] Lord Coleridge CJ finally dispelled any further possibility of a mere denial of the truth of the Christian religion being treated as a blasphemous libel. The 'attack' on Christianity or the Scriptures must be, he directed the jury, 'calculated to outrage the feelings of the general body of the community'.

Since *Ramsay and Foote's* case[4], the modern law has been settled and in 1917 received the *f* accolade of this House's approval. 'What the law censures or resists is not the mere expression of anti-Christian opinion', said Lord Sumner in *Bowman v Secular Society Ltd*[7]. The words must constitute, as it is put by Odgers on Libel and Slander[8], an interference with our religious feelings, creating a sense of insult and outrage 'by wanton and unnecessary profanity'.

This is an appropriate moment to mention two points made on behalf of the appellants, *g* albeit in the context of the intention to be proved. It was said that to constitute a blasphemous libel the words must contain an *attack* (emphasis supplied) on religion and must tend to provoke a breach of the peace, and that the accused must so intend. The plausibility of the first point derives from the undoubted fact that, as a matter of history, most of the reported cases are of attacks on the doctrines, practice or beliefs of the Christian religion. Since *Hetherington's* case[3] it has been clear, however, that the attack is irrelevant: *h*

---

1 (1676) 3 Keb 607; cf 1 Vent 293
2 (1784) 21 State Tr 847
3 (1841) 4 State Tr NS 563
4 (1883) 15 Cox CC 231
5 4 State Tr NS 563 at 590–591
6 15 Cox CC 231 at 232
7 [1917] AC 406 at 460, [1916–17] All ER Rep 1 at 28
8 6th Edn (1929), p 404

what does matter is the manner in which 'the feelings of the general body of the
a community' have been treated. If the words are an outrage on such feelings, the opinion
or argument they are used to advance or destroy is of no moment. In the present case, had
the argument for acceptance and welcome of homosexuals within the loving fold of the
Christian faith been advanced 'in a sober and temperate style', there could have been no
criminal offence committed. But the jury (with every justification) rejected this view of
the poem and drawing.

b   The trial judge and the Court of Appeal effectually dealt with the second point. I would
only add that it is a jejune exercise to speculate whether an outraged Christian would feel
provoked by the words and illustration in this case to commit a breach of peace. I hope,
and happen to believe, that most, true to their Christian principles, would not allow
themsevles to be so provoked. The true test is whether the words are calculated to outrage
and insult the Christian's religious feelings; and in the modern law the phrase 'a tendency
c to cause a breach of peace' is really a reference to that test. The use of the phrase is no more
than a minor contribution to the discussion of the subject. It does remind us that we are
in the field where the law seeks to safeguard public order and tranquillity.

What, then, is the mens rea required by law to constitute the crime? No one has
suggested that blasphemy is a crime of strict liability. The issue is as to the nature of the
intention which has to be proved. As Eveleigh LJ[1] is reported to have put it in argument
d in this case, must the appellants have had an intention to offend in the manner complained
of, or is it enough that he or they intended to publish that which offends? *Bowman's case*[2]
throws no light on the point. The history of the law is obscure and confused. The point
is, therefore, open for your Lordships' decision as a matter of principle. And in deciding
the point your Lordships are not saying what the law was in the past or ought to be in the
future but what is required of it in the conditions of today's society. As Lord Sumner said
e in *Bowman's case*[3]:

'The fact that opinion grounded on experience has moved one way does not in law
preclude the possibility of its moving on fresh experience in the other; nor does it
bind succeeding generations, when conditions have again changed.'

The history of the law affords little guidance for a number of reasons. First, the nature
f of an indictment was, until the reforms in criminal procedure of the last hundred years,
more an exercise in an advocate's skill in vituperation than a temperate formulation of the
legal ingredients of the offence charged. Secondly, it was not until the enactment of the
Criminal Evidence Act 1898 that an accused could give evidence in his own behalf. He
was not, therefore, always heard in his own defence, and his intention had to be gathered
from the words he had used. (One may mention, in passing, that persons accused of
g blasphemy very often defended themselves and so enabled the jury to form a view as to
their intention. Richard Carlile at his trial[4] read to the jury the whole of Paine's Age of
Reason.) Thirdly, it was not until the enactment of s 8 of the Criminal Justice Act 1967
that courts finally put away the notion that a man must be presumed to have intended the
natural consequences of his acts.

The combined influence of these three factors was to obscure the distinction between the
h meaning and effect of the words and the intention of the accused. The words, as interpreted
and understood (by the judge before Fox's Libel Act 1792 and by the jury after that Act)
were the best, perhaps the only, indication of the accused's intention. And the high
rhetoric to be found in the indictment charging the accused with devising and intending

j

---

1   [1978] 3 All ER 175 at 180, [1979] QB 10 at 16
2   [1917] AC 406, [1916–17] All ER Rep 1
3   [1917] AC 406 at 467, [1916] All ER Rep 1 at 32
4   *R v Richard Carlile* (1819) 1 State Tr NS 1387

('machinans et intendens', in the old cases) all manner of wickedness and evil against the
Church and state was not traversable at trial. Indeed the more outrageous the rhetoric of
the indictment the more likely I suspect it was that the crime being charged was one of
'strict liability'. Certainly poor Taylor in his case[1] got nowhere with the defence that he did
not mean the words in the sense 'they ordinarily bear'.

My Lords, I agree with the historical analysis of the case law to be found in the judgment
of the Court of Appeal and in the speech of my noble and learned friend, Viscount
Dilhorne. Lord Denman CJ stated the law correctly as it was in his time when, in *R v
Hetherington*[2], he told the jury that the only question for them to decide was a matter of fact
and of opinion: 'Aye or no, is this in your opinion a blasphemous publication, and has the
defendant . . . issued it knowingly and wilfully?' In context his adverb 'wilfully' meant no
more than 'deliberately'. As F L Holt commented in his work on The Law of Libel[3]:
'Malice, in legal understanding, implies no more than wilfulness', and the first enquiry of
a court is to see if there is present the mark of a voluntary act. He then quotes the advice
of the judges to the House of Lords on 27th April 1792[4]:

> 'The crime consists in publishing a libel . . . He who scatters firebrands, arrows and
> death (which, if not an accurate definition, is a very intelligible description of a libel),
> is *eâ ratione* criminal.—It is not incumbent in the prosecutor to prove his intent; and,
> on his part, he shall not be heard to say, "Am I not in sport?"'

Was the law changed by the famous summing-up of Lord Coleridge CJ in *R v Ramsay
and Foote*[5]? For the reasons given by the Court of Appeal and developed by my noble and
learned friend, Viscount Dilhorne, I do not think it was. There was never any doubt, or
issue, in that case as to the accused's intention. Lord Coleridge CJ drew on the passage in
Professor Starkie's famous work to explain not the mens rea but the nature of the actus reus
of blasphemy. Mens rea not being an issue in the case, I do not think it legitimate to read
the direction as an authority on the nature of the mens rea required to establish the offence.

Neither Lord Denman CJ (*Hetherington's* case[6]) nor Stephen (Digest of the Criminal Law[7]
and Draft Code of the Criminal Law[8]) nor the subsequent case law supports Starkie's view[9]
quoted by Lord Coleridge CJ in *Ramsay and Foote's* case[10] that a 'wilful intention to pervert,
insult, and mislead others . . . is the criterion and test of guilt'. Indeed, if Starkie's view of
the law on this point were correct, it is inconceivable that Avory J could have summed up
in *R v Gott*[11] as he did or that the Court of Criminal Appeal[12] could have affirmed him, as
they did. Your Lordships have had the opportunity of seeing the full report of the
summing-up in *Gott's* case[11] published in the issue of The Freethinker of 8th January
1922. The whole weight of the summing-up was directed to the question: were the words
complained of 'anything more than vilification and ridicule of the Christian religion and
of the Scriptures'?

For these reasons I am of the opinion that historically the law has required no more than
an intention to publish words found by the jury to be blasphemous. Yet I recognise that
another view, such as that developed by my noble and learned friend, Lord Edmund-

---

1   *R v Taylor* (1676) 1 Vent 293
2   (1841) 4 State Tr NS 563 at 593
3   2nd Edn (1816), p 47
4   Ibid, p 48
5   (1883) 15 Cox CC 231
6   4 State Tr NS 563
7   7th Edn (1926), art 231, p 160
8   Report of the Royal Commission on the Law Relating to Indictable Offences (C 2345 (1879)),
    Appendix, s 141
9   Law of Slander and Libel (4th Edn, 1876), pp 599–600
10 15 Cox CC 231 at 236
11 The Freethinker, 8th January 1922, at p 28
12 (1922) 16 Cr App R 87

a   Davies, has great persuasive force. Indeed, it has the formidable support of my noble and learned friend, Lord Diplock.

The issue is, therefore, one of legal policy in the society of today. There is some force in the lawyer's conceptual argument that in the matter of mens rea all four species of criminal libel (seditious, blasphemous, obscene and defamatory) should be the same. It is said that an intention to stir up sedition is necessary to constitute the crime of seditious libel. I am not sure that it is or ought to be: contrast *R v Aldred*[1] with Birkett J's direction in *R v*
b   *Caunt*[2]. Prior to the enactment of the Obscene Publications Act 1959 it was not necessary to establish an intention to deprave and corrupt in order to prove an obscene libel: *R v Hicklin*[3]. At worst, the common law may be said to have become fragmented in this area of public order offences; at best, it may be said (as I believe to be true) to be moving towards a position in which people, who know what they are doing, will be criminally liable if the words they choose to publish are such as to cause grave offence to the religious feelings of
c   some of their fellow citizens or are such as to tend to deprave and corrupt persons who are likely to read them.

The movement of the law is illustrated by recent statutes. The Obscene Publications Act 1959 focuses attention on the words or article published, not the intention of the author or publisher. The test of obscenity depends on the article itself. Section 5 of the Public Order Act 1936 has been significantly amended by the addition of a new section, s 5A. The Race
d   Relations Act 1976, s 70(2), by providing that s 5A be added, has made it unnecessary to prove an intention to provoke a breach of the peace in order to secure a conviction for incitement to racial hatred. All this makes legal sense in a plural society which recognises the human rights and fundamental freedoms of the European Convention[4]. Article 9 provides that every one has the right to freedom of religion, and the right to manifest his religion in worship, teaching, practice and observance. By necessary implication the article
e   imposes a duty on all of us to refrain from insulting or outraging the religious feelings of others. Article 10 provides that every one shall have the right to freedom of expression. The exericise of this freedom 'carries with it duties and responsibilities' and may be subject to such restrictions as are prescribed by law and are necessary 'for the prevention of disorder or crime, for the protection of health or morals, for the protection of the reputations or rights of others'. It would be intolerable if by allowing an author or publisher to plead the
f   excellence of his motives and the right of free speech he could evade the penalties of the law even though his words were blasphemous in the sense of constituting an outrage on the religious feelings of his fellow's citizens. This is no way forward for a successful plural society. Accordingly, the test of obscenity by concentrating attention on the words complained of is, in my judgment, equally valuable as a test of blasphemy. The character of the words published matters, but not the motive of the author or publisher.

g   For these reasons as well as for those developed in the speeches of my noble and learned friends, Viscount Dilhorne and Lord Russell of Killowen, with both of which I agree, I would dismiss these appeals. In my judgment the modern law of blasphemy is correctly formulated in art 214 of Stephen's Digest of the Criminal Law[5]:

h   'Every publication is said to be blasphemous which contains any contemptuous, reviling, scurrilous or ludicrous matter relating to God, Jesus Christ, or the Bible, or the formularies of the Church of England as by law established. It is not blasphemous to speak or publish opinions hostile to the Christian religion, or to deny the existence of God, if the publication is couched in decent and temperate language. The test to

---

j   1   (1909) 22 Cox CC 1
    2   (17th November 1947), unreported
    3   (1868) LR 3 QB 360
    4   Convention for the Protection of Human Rights and Fundamental Freedoms (Rome, 4th November 1950); TS 71 (1953); Cmd 8969
    5   (9th Edn, 1950)

be applied is as to the manner in which the doctrines are advocated and not as to the substance of the doctrines themselves. Everyone who publishes any blasphemous document is guilty of the [offence] of publishing a blasphemous libel. Everyone who speaks blasphemous words is guilty of the [offence] of blasphemy.'

Appeals dismissed.

Solicitors: *Offenbach & Co* (for the appellants); *Robbins, Olivey & Lake* (for the Crown).

Mary Rose Plummer   Barrister.

Ravenseft Properties Ltd v Davstone (Holdings) Ltd

QUEEN'S BENCH DIVISION
FORBES J
23rd, 24th, 25th, 26th, 30th OCTOBER 1978

Landlord and tenant – Repair – Construction of covenant – Covenant 'to repair' – Covenant to repay landlord cost of repairs – Inherent defect – Building constructed of concrete frame and stone claddings – Expansion joints omitted from structure – Not standard practice to include expansion joints at date of erection – Cladding becoming loose and in danger of falling due mainly to lack of expansion joints but also because of defective workmanship in tying in stones – Landlord executing remedial works by removing cladding and reinstating it with expansion joints and proper ties – Whether tenant liable to repay cost of inserting expansion joints – Whether repair caused by inherent defect in premises falling within covenants to repair or pay for repairs.

A building erected between 1958 and 1960, consisting of a 16-storey block of maisonettes, was constructed of a reinforced concrete frame with stone claddings. Expansion joints were omitted from the structure because at the date of erection it was not standard practice to include them in such a structure since it was not then realised that the expansion rates of the concrete frame and the stone cladding were different. In 1966 the tenant took an underlease of the building. The underlease contained covenants by the tenant 'to repair' the building including the walls, and to repay to the landlord costs incurred in executing works to remedy, inter alia, want of reparation. In 1973 part of the stone cladding on the building became loose and in danger of falling because of bowing of the stones caused principally by the defect in design of lack of expansion joints, but also because of defective workmanship in failing properly to tie in the stones. In view of the urgency of securing the cladding the landlord executed the necessary remedial works removing the cladding and reinstating it with expansion joints (which by that date, 1973, it was standard practice to insert) and proper ties. The total cost of the work was £55,000 of which only £5,000 was attributable to the work of inserting the joints. The cost of erecting the building in 1973 would have exceeded £3 million. The landlord brought an action against the tenant claiming repayment of the whole of the cost of the works carried out, under the covenants to repair and to repay the cost of repairs executed by the landlord. The tenant denied liability for the cost of inserting the joints on the grounds that it was caused by an inherent defect in the demised premises and repairs resulting from an inherent defect could not fall within the ambit of a covenant to repair; alternatively he contended that the tenant was not bound to pay for that part of the repairs which remedied an inherent defect.

Held – There was no doctrine that want of repair due to an inherent defect in the demised premises could not fall within the ambit of a covenant to repair. It was a question of degree whether that which the tenant was asked to do, or pay for, could properly be described as repair so as to fall within a covenant to repair, or whether it involved giving back to the landlord a wholly different thing from that demised in which case the work would not fall within a covenant to repair or pay for repairs. The insertion of the joints did not amount to changing the character of the building so as to take that work out of the ambit of the covenant to repair or the covenant to pay for repairs, for the joints formed a trivial part only of the whole building, and the cost of inserting them was trivial compared to the value of the building. It followed that the landlord was entitled to repayment of the whole of the cost of the works executed (see p 937 *d* to *h* and p 938 *e*, post).

Dictum of Lord Esher MR in *Lister v Lane and Nesham* [1891–4] All ER Rep at 390, *Lurcott v Wakely and Wheeler* [1911–13] All ER Rep 41, *Pembery v Lamdin* [1940] 2 All ER 434, *Sotheby v Grundy* [1947] 2 All ER 761 and *Brew Brothers Ltd v Snax (Ross) Ltd* [1970] 1 All ER 587 applied.

Collins v Flynn [1963] 2 All ER 1068 doubted.

Notes

For the construction of covenants to repair, see 23 Halsbury's Laws (3rd Edn) 578–580, paras 1254–1255 and for cases on the subject, see 31(2) Digest (Reissue) 599–601, 617–619, 4877–4893, 5020–5040.

Cases referred to in judgment

Brew Brothers Ltd v Snax (Ross) Ltd [1970] 1 All ER 587, [1970] 1 QB 612, [1969] 3 WLR 657, 20 P & CR 829, CA, 31(2) Digest (Reissue) 615, 5001.

Calthorpe v McOscar [1924] 1 KB 716, [1923] All ER Rep 198, 93 LJKB 273, 130 LT 691, 32(2) Digest (Reissue) 618, 5037.

Collins v Flynn [1963] 2 All ER 1068, 31(2) Digest (Reissue) 616, 5011.

Lister v Lane and Nesham [1893] 2 QB 212, [1891–4] All ER Rep 388, 62 LJQB 583, 69 LT 176, 57 JP 725, 31(2) Digest (Reissue) 617, 5027.

Lurcott v Wakeley and Wheeler [1911] 1 KB 905, [1911–13] All ER Rep 41, 80 LJKB 713, 104 LT 290, 31(2) Digest (Reissue) 623, 5088.

Pembery v Lamdin [1940] 2 All ER 434, CA, 31(2) Digest (Reissue) 600, 4888.

Proudfoot v Hart (1890) 25 QBD 42, [1886–90] All ER Rep 782, 59 LJQB 389, 63 LT 171, 55 JP 20, 31(2) Digest 618, 5034.

Sotheby v Grundy [1947] 2 All ER 761, 38 Digest (Repl) 256, 649.

Soward v Leggatt (1836) 7 C & P 613, 173 ER 269 NP, 31(2) Digest (Reissue) 620, 5060.

Wright v Lawson (1903) 68 JP 34, CA, 31(2) Digest (Reissue) 618, 5040.

Case also cited

Morcom v Campbell-Johnson [1955] 3 All ER 264, [1956] 1 QB 106, CA.

Action

By a writ and statement of claim issued on 30th July 1975 the plaintiffs, Ravenseft Properties Ltd, the leasehold owners of premises comprising two blocks of flats and premises known as Campden Hill Towers and Campden Hill Flats, Notting Hill Gate, London, claimed against the defendants, Davstone (Holdings) Ltd, the lessees of the premises, a declaration that the defendants were liable to repay the plaintiffs on demand the cost (including any surveyor's or other professional fees incurred) of the repairs and works carried out by the plaintiffs to repair and make good defects, decays and want of repair in the premises, the sum of £29,982·89 as part of the cost of the repairs and works executed by the plaintiffs, and further or other relief. The facts are set out in the judgment.

Ronald Bernstein QC and *Stanley Burnton* for the plaintiffs.
John Stuart Colyer QC and *Kim Lewison* for the defendants.

Cur adv vult

30th October. **FORBES J** read the following judgment: In this case, the plaintiffs sue the defendants substantially on repairing covenants in a lease in which the plaintiffs are the landlords and the defendants, tenants. The building is part of a complex at Notting Hill Gate in London. The part of the building with which we are concerned, is firstly a 16-storey block of maisonettes, and secondly, a four-storey block of flats, those buildings being known as Campden Hill Towers and Campden Hill Flats respectively. Campden Hill Flats plays only a subordinate part in this matter and I shall concentrate very largely on Campden Hill Towers. That building is a modern, rectangular structure made with a reinforced concrete frame. It looks, if I may be excused the analogy, like nothing more than a set of pigeon-holes, or perhaps to use a marine analogy, a flag locker, and the square section pigeon-holes each contain one maisonette on two floors. The edges of the pigeon-holes, if I may pursue the analogy, are veneered with a cladding of Portland stone. This stone is about 3 inches thick and 8 inches wide and runs upwards along each of the vertical divisions and horizontally along each of the horizontal ones. At the edges of the structure there are slightly wider bands of stone running vertically. The same treatment occurs on both the eastern and the western elevation. The building was built between 1958 and a   1960 and it was let in 1960 to a predecessor of the defendants by a predecessor of the plaintiffs.

In 1973 the stones in the cladding on the eastern elevation were observed to be loose and in some danger of falling, and emergency measures were taken to secure the more dangerous of the stones. The plaintiffs notified the defendants of this situation and called on them to carry out the necessary work to repair and secure the stone work. The defendants, while agreeing that the work was necessary, disputed any liability to pay for it
b   under the repairing covenants. The plaintiffs thought, quite rightly, that the matter was urgent, and the plaintiffs and the defendants accordingly agreed that the plaintiffs should give the orders and assume the primary liability for the remedial work necessary and leave the question of the liability of the defendants over for later determination. The work was put in hand. Initially I think the defendants paid half of the earlier bills but later stopped paying, and the sum in dispute is now claimed by the plaintiffs in this action.

c   I do not think it is necessary to go into great detail about the cause of the difficulty which arose with the stone. The main concrete frame and the stone cladding have different co-efficients of expansion. The result was that in certain sections some of the stones were being bowed away from the concrete frame. The potential danger can be realised if it is understood that if the stone cladding is pinned or fixed in some way to the main frame at 10 foot intervals, 100th of an inch of difference in the extent of expansion in 10 feet will
d   result in a bowing of one inch in the centre of that part of the stone work. There were three stones to each floor, six that is to each maisonette, and every third stone was what has been called a 'booted' stone; that is it was, in section, L-shaped, with the projection of the L running back into a channel or piece cut out of the main frame, so that the booted stone was held in that position. The stones, including the booted stones, were intended to be tied back into the main frame by metal straps of some kind, but in fact, many of the ties were
e   either not there or misapplied in the eastern elevation. Besides the ordinary shrinkage of the frame which occurs over the first few years after construction with a concrete framed building of this kind, there are also other movements which take place in a concrete frame structure during the life of the building and it will be seen, therefore, that a difference in expansion coefficient between the cladding and the frame is likely to cause difficulties where the ends of the stones abut on to the horizontal cladding, where in effect they will
f   be prevented from movement in a vertical direction. In this case the bowing of the stones was principally due to lack of expansion joints but there was a subsidiary cause of failure and that was the omission to tie in the stones properly. As I understand the evidence, if the stones had been tied in properly, any individual stones would have been unlikely to fall, despite the movement of the frame relative to them. The movement would, however, possibly or probably cause cracking and chipping of the stones with, of course, an attendant
g   degree of danger of the fall of smaller pieces of stone, but not the whole stones themselves. When a full inspection was made of the building and the very large number of untied stones were found in the eastern elevation, it was decided that the only safe way of dealing with that was to take down all the stone cladding on this elevation and replace it with proper ties, but also with expansion joints. I should mention here that the top three storeys of the building were slightly out of plumb. The frame was leaning backwards
h   slightly and the stones were set plumb, so that the distance between the back of the stones and the front of the frame increased a little in the top three or four storeys. The expansion joints were effected by cutting off half an inch from the top of each stone which lay under a booted stone, in other words, every third stone on the elevation, and filling the gap with a plastic expansion absorbing material. On the western elevation and on Campden Hill Flats the symptoms were not so severe. Nevertheless in view of the potential danger, two
j   out of each lift of three stones were pinned to the frame by inserting metal dowels through the stones into the frame at a downward angle, and once again the top half inch of every third stone was removed and an expansion joint placed in the gap. It was not necessary however, as I understand the evidence, on the western elevation of Campden Hill Towers and on Campden Hill Flats, to remove the cladding stones in order to carry out this remedial work.

Throughout the work the defendants' surveyors joined in the inspection of the work from time to time with the plaintiffs' consulting engineers and at no time was there any *a* suggestion that the work being done was unnecessary, though, of course, the defendants maintained their argument that they were not liable under the repairing covenants.

The necessity for placing expansion joints in a construction of this kind was not realised by architects or structural engineers at the time the building was constructed and it was not engineering practice at that time to include expansion joints when a construction of this type was being carried out. It was only in 1961, when the publication of the Building *b* Research Station's Annual Report for 1960 pointed out the difficulty and danger, that the problem was recognised, and that report suggested sensible remedies. By 1973–74 when this remedial work was carried out it could be said to have become standard practice in constructing a building in this way to include expansion joints of this type.

I should turn now to the repairing covenants in the lease. It is, in fact, an underlease, but I do not think I need bother at all about the headlease. There are three subclauses to which *c* I need refer and only three. They appear in cl 5 of the underlease, which is the main clause concerned with the tenants' covenants. Sub-clause 6, to repair, reads in this way:

> 'When where and so often as occasion shall require well and sufficiently to repair renew rebuild uphold support sustain maintain pave purge scour cleanse glaze empty amend and keep the premises and every part thereof (including all fixtures and additions thereto) and all floors walls columns roofs canopies lifts and escalators *d* (including all motors and machinery therefor) shafts stairways fences pavements forecourts drains sewers ducts flues conduits wires cables gutters soil and other pipes tanks cisterns pumps and other water and sanitary apparatus thereon with all needful and necessary amendments whatsoever (damage by any of the insured risks excepted so long as the Lessor's policy or policies of insurance in respect thereof shall not have become vitiated or payment of the policy moneys be refused in whole or in part in *e* consequence of some act or default of the Lessee) and to keep all water pipes and water fittings in the premises protected from frost and to be responsible in all respects for all damage caused to the premises or to the said buildings or any part thereof or to the neighbouring property or to the respective owners or occupiers thereof through the bursting overflowing or stopping up of such pipes and fittings occasioned by or *f* through the neglect of the Lessee or its servants or agents.'

I have read that in full to indicate that it is one of those clauses in which the ingenuity of the draughtsman has been given full rein in an attempt to cover every conceivable eventuality. Then we pass to sub-cl 11:

> 'To permit the Superior Lessors and the Lessor at all reasonable times during the said term to enter upon the premises and every part thereof to view the state and *g* condition of the same and to take any measurements plans or sections thereof and of all defects decays and wants of reparation there found to give to the Lessee notice in writing in manner hereinafter prescribed.'

And sub-cl 12:

> 'Within three months next after every such notice as aforesaid (or immediately in *h* case of urgency) well and sufficiently to repair and make good all such defects decays and wants of reparation to the premises at the Lessee's own cost absolutely Provided Always that if the Lessee shall fail to comply with the requirements of any such notice as aforesaid it shall be lawful for the Lessor (but without prejudice to the right of re-entry hereinafter contained) to enter upon the premises at any time after the expiration of such three months or immediately in case of urgency and execute such *j* repairs and works and the cost thereof (including any surveyors' or other professional fees incurred) shall be repaid by the Lessee to the Lessor on demand.'

In addition to those three covenants, and sub-cll 6 and 12 are specifically pleaded in the statement of claim as giving rise to causes of action, there was also an agreement between

the parties to which I have already very briefly referred, namely that the work should be
a done and that there should be an argument, if necessary, about the cost of it later. Now
that is pleaded in para 10 of the statement of claim in these terms:

> 'Further on or about 24th January 1974 it was agreed inter alia between the
> Plaintiffs and the Defendants by their agents that the work of repairing and making
> good the said defects, decays and wants of reparation should be carried out as a matter
> of urgency by the Plaintiffs' contractors, and that the cost of such works should be paid
b > by the Defendants if they were liable for the same under the terms of the said
> Underlease. The works of repair and making good were commenced pursuant to the
> said agreement.'

Now that paragraph is admitted in the defence so that it seems to me it is quite
unnecessary for me to look further than at the allegation as set out in the statement of claim
and admitted in the defence. There is correspondence of around that period which
c supports that paragraph but I do not think it is necessary, in view of the admission on the
pleadings, to advert to that further.

Now despite somewhat lengthy cross-examination of the plaintiffs' witnesses, there is
here no dispute on fact and the defendants called no evidence. In these circumstances the
plaintiffs, the landlords, claim to be reimbursed by the defendants, the tenants, for the cost
of the work carried out and they put their claim under three headings. First, under the
d repairing covenant, cl 5(6); secondly under the covenant to pay the cost of repairs carried
out by the plaintiffs under cl 5(12); and thirdly under the agreement of 24th January
1974. In fact, both counsel agree that the agreement adds nothing new as it merely
requires the defendants to pay what is due under either cl 5(6) or cl 5(12).

The defence is two-fold. Counsel for the defendants says first, there is in that branch of
landlord and tenant law concerned with repairing covenants, a doctrine of inherent defect
e which is applicable to such covenants to repair. This is that where wants of reparation arise
which are caused by some inherent defect in the premises demised, the results of the
inherent defect can never fall within the ambit of a covenant to repair.

Secondly he says that if that proposition is wrong the covenantor is still not bound to pay
for any works which, in fact, remedy the inherent defect.

f The plaintiffs answer that broadly in this way. Counsel says there is no such thing as a
doctrine of inherent defect. The question is simply this, 'is what the tenant is asked to do
fairly represented by the word "repair"?' and this question is to be judged as a matter of
degree in each case.

The leading cases on the matter have been referred to by both counsel and I need only,
I think, list them at this stage and then consider at any rate some of them in a little more
detail later. They are *Proudfoot v Hart*[1], *Lister v Lane and Nesham*[2], *Wright v Lawson*[3], *Lurcott*
g *v Wakely and Wheeler*[4], *Calthorpe v McOscar*[5], *Pembery v Lamdin*[6], *Sotheby v Grundy*[7], *Collins
v Flynn*[8] and *Brew Brothers Ltd v Snax (Ross) Ltd*[9]. All these cases are, I think, very well
known and I do not intend to recite the facts or the judgments in detail, though there are
one or two matters which will have to be considered more carefully. Of these cases it
seems that it is unnecessary to consider further *Proudfoot v Hart*[1] and *Calthorpe v
McOscar*[5]. They are concerned with questions of the standard of repair required under a
h repairing covenant rather than what is included in the term 'repair'.

---

1 (1890) 25 QBD 42, [1886–90] All ER Rep 782
2 [1893] 2 QB 212, [1891–4] All ER Rep 388
j 3 (1903) 68 JP 34
4 [1911] 1 KB 905, [1911–13] All ER Rep 41
5 [1924] 1 KB 716, [1923] All ER Rep 198
6 [1940] 2 All ER 434
7 [1947] 2 All ER 761
8 [1963] 2 All ER 1068
9 [1970] 1 All ER 587, [1970] 1 QB 612

One should start with *Lister v Lane and Nesham*[1] and the frequently quoted passage from the judgment of Lord Esher MR: a

> '... if a tenant takes a house which is of such a kind that by its own inherent nature it will in course of time fall into a particular condition, the effects of that result are not within the tenant's covenant to repair. However large the words of the covenant may be, a covenant to repair a house is not a covenant to give a different thing from that which the tenant took when he entered into the covenant. He has to repair that thing which he took; he is not obliged to make a new and different thing, and, moreover, the result of the nature and condition of the house itself, the result of time upon that state of things, is not a breach of the covenant to repair.'

From this passage and the case in general, counsel for the defendants derives this proposition. If it can be shown that any want of reparation has been caused by an inherent defect, then that want of reparation is not within the ambit of a covenant to repair. Inherent defect he defines as an omission of something in the original design. A defect in the quality of workmanship or materials is not, he says, an inherent defect. The want of reparation in that case, counsel says, was the failure to reconstruct the wall by providing the whole house with under-pinned foundations, and that want of reparation was directly due to the omission of proper foundations in the original construction.

I started with *Lister's* case[1] and the well-known passage from Lord Esher MR's judgment, but counsel for the defendants says that *Lister's* case[2] itself was founded on *Soward v Leggatt*[3], and it is necessary to look briefly at that case. There the floor joists were repaired by laying them on bricks rather than on mud, as the original floor joists had been laid, and counsel for the defendants seeks to found an argument on that, that any work to a building which involves a different method of construction must be regarded as giving to the landlord a different thing from that which the tenant took. But such a broad proposition cannot, I think, survive close consideration of the later case of *Lurcott v Wakely and Wheeler*[4]. It should be remembered that in that case the court was dealing with the rebuilding of the eastern external wall of a house in Hatton Garden and that what had happened was that the premises had been certified as being in a dangerous state by the district surveyor and that later in compliance with a demolition order, under the London Building Acts 1894 and 1898, the plaintiff had taken down the wall to the level of the ground floor, and then in compliance with a further notice by the district surveyor, had pulled down the remaining wall and rebuilt it with concrete foundations and damp courses in accordance with the requirements of the 1894 Act. The question was whether the tenant was liable under the repairing covenant for this work and it is clear that the wall originally lacked concrete foundations and damp courses, and that the insertion of these features in the rebuilt wall was the result of statutory notices by the local authority. Both Cozens-Hardy MR and Buckley LJ regarded the matter as a question of degree rather than as one of method of construction, and clearly the method of construction was wholly different. In any event, counsel's first point for the defendants depends on causation, and *Soward v Leggatt*[3] was not concerned with direct causation but turned on whether the work was an improvement or not, which is counsel's second rather than his first point.

Turning to *Wright v Lawson*[5] counsel for the defendants explains that in the same way as he explained *Lister's* case[2]. There, he says, the want of reparation complained of by the landlord was the failure to provide a bay window supported on pillars but this failure in turn was directly due to the absence of sufficient stability in the house to support a cantilever bay window. Counsel accepts that the only case in which this doctrine of

1   [1893] 2 QB 212 at 216–217, [1891–4] All ER Rep 388 at 390
2   [1893] 2 QB 212, [1891–4] All ER Rep 388
3   (1836) 7 C & P 613
4   [1911] 1 KB 905, [1911–13] All ER Rep 41
5   (1903) 68 JP 34

inherent defect was argued was *Collins v Flynn*[1]. It is necessary therefore to look at that case,
a but before doing so one should, I think, look at *Sotheby v Grundy*[2] because in *Collins v Flynn*[1]
Sir Brett Cloutman QC deals with *Lister's case*[3] and *Sotheby's case*[2] in a sense together.

Now the facts in *Sotheby's case*[2] were not unimportant. The house which was the
demised premises in that case was found in 1944 to have bulged and fractured walls and
the house was condemned as a dangerous structure and demolished by the council.
Expenses incurred by the council were recovered from the landlord who sought to recover
b them from the tenant as damages for breach of a repairing covenant, so the case itself was
not directly concerned with work of repair but with the cost of demolition due to failure
to repair. The evidence showed that in fact the house was built, in defiance of the
requirements of the Metropolitan Building Act 1855, entirely without footings, or in some
places, on defective footings and in consequence, and because of the defective footings,
there was every likelihood that the house would, in fact, fall into the dangerous state into
c which it did fall. 'That very wise and experienced judge' (as Sachs LJ in *Brew Brothers Ltd
v Snax (Ross) Ltd*[4] called him) Lynskey J, found that the wants of reparation were caused by
what he called[5] 'the inherent nature of the defect in the premises' but nevertheless felt it
incumbent on him to consider as a matter of degree whether the finding that the tenant
was liable for the works required would be asking the tenant to give the landlord something
different in kind from that which had been demised. This is clearly to reject, or overlook,
d any argument that a want of reparation caused by inherent defect could not in any
circumstances be within the ambit of the repairing covenant.

Now looking at *Collins v Flynn*[6], Sir Brett Cloutman deals with these points:

'The last case that is really in point is *Sotheby v. Grundy*[2]. This was the case of the
condemned house, built in or about 1861, the main walls having been built either
e without footings or defective footings. The foundation had settled and this could
have been avoided only by under-pinning and substituting a new foundation. On the
authority of LORD ESHER's judgment in *Lister v. Lane and Nesham*[3], it was held that the
tenant was not liable for the cost of demolition. The expenses were incurred because
of the inherent nature in the defect of the premises, and, therefore, did not come
within the terms of the repairing covenant. Plainly the doctrine of liability for the
f defects in a subsidiary part could have nothing to do with that case. The case, as it
seems to me, was on all fours with *Lister v. Lane and Nesham*[3]. Oddly enough, LYNSKEY,
J., does introduce it, in what I think is an obiter passage. He said[7]: "It may be that the
inherent nature of the building may result in its partial collapse. One can visualise
the floor of a building collapsing owing to defective joists having been put in. I do not
think *Lister v. Lane*[3] would be applicable to such a case. In those circumstances, in my
g opinion, the damage would fall within the ambit of the covenant to repair, but as I
say, it must be a question of degree in each particular case".'

Sir Brett Cloutman went on to talk about what he described as 'obiter joists', referred to also
in *Lister's case*[3] and *Lurcott's case*[8]. Then he said[9]:
h

---

i 1 [1963] 2 All ER 1068
2 [1947] 2 All ER 761
· 3 [1893] 2 QB 212, [1891–4] All ER Rep 388
j 4 [1970] 1 All ER 587 at 603, [1970] 1 QB 612 at 640
5 [1947] 2 All ER 761 at 762
6 [1963] 2 All ER 1068 at 1073
7 [1947] 2 All ER 761 at 761–762
8 [1911] 1 KB 905, [1911–13] All ER Rep 41
9 [1963] 2 All ER 1068 at 1074

'I now come to the crucial point. Do the words "repair" and "renew" import a
liability to rebuild with newly designed foundations and footings the pier supporting   *a*
the girder which in turn carries a great part of the rear wall and a part of the side wall
in addition? This is manifestly a most important improvement, which, if executed
by the tenant, would involve him in rendering up the premises in different condition
from that in which they were demised, and on the authority of LORD ESHER, M.R., in
Lister v. *Lane and Nesham*[1], I do not think that the tenant is under any such
obligation. Furthermore, although a suggestion of liability for removal of an inherent   *b*
defect in a subsidiary part seems to have been touched on in *Sotheby* v. *Grundy*[2], I do
not think that the obiter remarks of LYNSKEY, J., as to defective joists have any bearing
on the present case.'

In these passages it seems to me that Sir Brett Cloutman misdirects himself on the ratio
of *Sotheby's* case[2]. The question of whether the inherent nature of the building might   *c*
result in its partial collapse was not obiter at all. It was part of the ratio in this sense that,
treating the question as a matter of degree, a partial collapse, in the view of Lynskey J,
would have been of a degree which brought it within the tenant's covenant to repair,
whereas a total collapse would put it outside. As, therefore, it was not a matter of part only,
but of putting in new foundations in the entire building, Lynskey J found it was not   *d*
within the ambit of the covenant. Insofar as he appears to be misdirecting himself on the
ratio of *Sotheby*[2], the persuasive authority of Sir Brett Cloutman's judgment in *Collins*[3] must
be considerably eroded.

The only remaining cases in the list are *Pembery v Lamdin*[4] and *Brew Brothers Ltd v Snax
(Ross) Ltd*[5].

Now *Pembery*[4] was clearly a case of inherent defect but the court did not there decide that
the plaintiff failed because there existed a doctrine such as that put forward by counsel for   *e*
the defendants. One can, I think, epitomise Slesser LJ's judgment in that case in this
way. The plaintiff failed because her argument, if correct, would have involved ordering
the defendant to give her a different thing from that which was demised. This is clearly,
in my view, a decision arrived at by considering the question as one of degree. *Brew
Brothers Ltd v Snax (Ross) Ltd*[5], though a case where the defect was not inherent (see Harman   *f*
LJ, arguendo[6]), was nevertheless a case where at any rate a doctrine of inherent defect such
as that suggested by counsel for the defendants was put forward in argument by the
landlord[7], and countered by the tenants[6]. But both Sachs LJ[8] and Phillimore LJ[9] appear to
indicate that, whether or not the cause of any want of reparation is an inherent defect, the
question must still be regarded as one of degree in each case.

This necessarily brief review of authorities indicates quite clearly to my mind that apart
from *Collins v Flynn*[3], which I consider of doubtful authority, the explanation of the ratio   *g*
in *Lister's* case[1] as giving the tenant a complete defence, if the cause of the want of
reparation is an inherent defect, has never been adopted by any court, but on the contrary,
in *Pembery v Lamdin*[4] and *Sotheby v Grundy*[2], the court, when dealing with wants of
reparation caused by inherent defect, chose to treat the matter as one of degree, and in *Brew*

h

---

1   [1893] 2 QB 212, [1891–4] All ER Rep 388
2   [1947] 2 All ER 761
3   [1963] 2 All ER 1068
4   [1940] 2 All ER 434   *j*
5   [1970] 1 All ER 587, [1970] 1 QB 612
6   [1970] 1 QB 612 at 622
7   [1970] 1 QB 612 at 618
8   [1970] 1 All ER 587 at 602–603, [1970] 1 QB 612 at 640
9   [1970] 1 All ER 587 at 607, [1970] 1 QB 612 at 646

Brothers[1] the court effectively said that every case, whatever the causation, must be treated

a   as one of degree.

I find myself, therefore, unable to accept counsel's contention for the defendants that a doctrine such as he enunciates has any place in the law of landlord and tenant. The true test is, as the cases show, that it is always a question of degree whether that which the tenant is being asked to do can properly be described as repair, or whether on the contrary it would involve giving back to the landlord a wholly different thing from that which he

b   demised.

In deciding this question, the proportion which the cost of the disputed work bears to the value or cost of the whole premises, may sometimes be helpful as a guide. In this case the figures have not been finally worked out in complete detail. I have, however, the evidence of Mr Clark, the contracts manager for Stone Firms Ltd, the contractors who actually carried out the work. He was not himself responsible for any of the work as he

c   joined that company after the work was completed. He is, however, familiar with that company's methods of charging and so on, and he has studied the drawings and the analysed quotations produced by the company. From these he has been able to give me, not a detailed and accurate costing, but a reliable, broad, estimate of the cost of that part of the remedial work relating solely to the insertion of expansion joints. It is, as he said, an indication of the order of magnitude of the cost. Although cross-examined by counsel for

d   the defendants, no rebutting evidence was called and I accept Mr Clark's estimate that the cost would have been in the region of £5,000. The total cost of the remedial works was around £55,000, the balance of £50,000 being for re-fixing the stones and other ancillary works which was not, as I find, necessary to cure any defect of design, but to remedy what was originally defective workmanship. For comparison, the cost of building a structure of this kind in 1973 would have been in the region of £3 million, or rather more. I find

e   myself wholly unable to accept that the cost of inserting these joints could possibly be regarded as a substantial part of the cost of the repairs, much less a substantial part of the value or cost of the building. Counsel for the defendants urges me not to consider cost and that may, perhaps, in some circumstances, be right. He argues that the result of carrying out this improvement is to give back to the landlord a safe building instead of a dangerous one and this means the premises now are of a wholly different character. Further, he

f   argues that because they are of a wholly different character, the work on expansion joints, the work necessary to cure the inherent defect, is an improvement of a character which transforms the nature of the premises demised, and, therefore, cannot fall within the ambit of the covenant to repair. I cannot accept this. The expansion joints form but a trivial part of this whole building and looking at it as a question of degree, I do not consider that they amount to such a change in the character of the building as to take them out of the ambit

g   of the covenant to repair.

I pass to counsel's second point for the defendants, namely that the tenant is not liable under the repair covenant for that part of any work of repair necessary to remedy an inherent defect. Again it seems to me that this must be a question of degree.

In *Lurcott v Wakely and Wheeler*[2] the wall was defective in the sense that it had no proper footings or damp course. When it was rebuilt, concrete footings and damp course were

h   provided. The court nevertheless found the tenant liable for the whole cost of the work including these improvements. Counsel for the defendants seeks to distinguish that case because he says that in *Lurcott*[2], the improvements were necessary to comply with the requirements of the statute. Here there was no such requirement and the expansion joints were included merely as a matter of moral duty.

It is quite clear to me from the evidence of both Mr Sculley and Dr Michael, the two

j   expert structural engineers who gave evidence, and the only evidence I have on this point,

---

1   [1970] 1 All ER 587, [1970] 1 QB 612
2   [1911] 1 KB 905, [1911–13] All ER Rep 41

that no competent professional engineer would have permitted the remedial work to be done without the inclusion of these expansion joints. By this time it was proper engineering practice to see that such expansion joints were included, and it would have been dangerous not to include them. In no realistic sense, therefore, could it be said that there was any other possible way of reinstating this cladding than by providing the expansion joints which were, in fact, provided. It seems to me to matter not whether that state of affairs is caused by the necessary sanction of statutory notices or by the realistic fact that as a matter of professional expertise no responsible engineer would have allowed a re-building which did not include such expansion joints to be carried out. I find myself, therefore, bound to follow the guidance given by Cozens-Hardy MR in *Lurcott's* case[1]:

> 'It seems to me we should be narrowing in a most dangerous way the limit and extent of these covenants if we did not hold that the defendants were liable under covenants framed as these are to make good the cost of repairing this wall *in the only sense in which it can be repaired*, namely, by rebuilding it according to the requirements of the county council.' (Emphasis mine.)

Because of the view I have formed, I have not thought it necessary to consider certain further submissions by counsel for the plaintiffs. These were based on the special words used in the covenants in the underlease. I have already mentioned the plethora of words used to describe the obligations of the tenant in cl 5(6). In cl 5 (11) and (12), there are very many fewer words, but they include the important word, 'defects'. The view I have formed is, of course, relative to the use of the word 'repair', and that by itself seems to me to be sufficient to render the defendants, the tenants, liable for the whole cost of remedial works. It is not, therefore, necessary to pursue the question of whether, if it had not been so, other words used would have been sufficient to fix the tenant with liability.

I accordingly consider that the plaintiffs are entitled to judgment for the proper cost of the entire works in this case.

Judgment for the plaintiffs.

Solicitors: *Forsyte Kerman & Phillips* (for the plaintiffs); *Thornton Lynne & Lawson* (for the defendants).

K Mydeen Esq   Barrister.

---

1   [1911] 1 KB 905 at 914, [1911–13] All ER Rep 41 at 44

Wong Kam-ming v The Queen

PRIVY COUNCIL

LORD DIPLOCK, LORD HAILSHAM OF ST MARYLEBONE, LORD SALMON, LORD EDMUND-DAVIES AND LORD KEITH OF KINKEL

17th, 18th, 19th OCTOBER, 20th DECEMBER 1978

Criminal evidence – Admissions and confessions – Answers and statements to police – Issue as to admissibility – Whether on voire dire prosecution entitled to cross-examine accused as to truth of confession – Whether prosecution entitled on trial of general issue to adduce evidence of and cross-examine accused as to evidence given on voire dire.

An indictment charged the appellant and five other men with murder at a massage parlour. The only evidence implicating the appellant was a signed statement he had given to the police in which he admitted that he had been present at the material time at the parlour, that at one stage he had had a knife in his hand and that he had 'chopped' someone at the parlour. At the commencement of the trial counsel for the appellant challenged the admissibility of the statement on the ground that it was not made voluntarily. The trial judge dealt with that issue of admissibility on the voire dire on which the appellant gave evidence as to the circumstances in which the statement was made, and was then cross-examined on the contents of the statement to establish their truth. Shorthand-writers took down the cross-examination. The trial judge ruled that the statement was inadmissible. When trial of the general issue was resumed the Crown sought to establish the appellant's presence at the parlour by calling the shorthand-writers to produce extracts from the transcript of the cross-examination on the voire dire. The judge allowed the Crown to adduce that evidence in support of its case, and also allowed the Crown to cross-examine the appellant on his evidence-in-chief on the general issue by reference to the extracts from his cross-examination on the voire dire. In his summing-up the trial judge told the jury that the answers in cross-examination on the voire dire indicated that the appellant was present at the parlour. The appellant was convicted of murder. His appeal against conviction was dismissed by the Court of Appeal of Hong Kong. He appealed to the Judicial Committee of the Privy Council contending that, on the voire dire, cross-examination as to the truth of his statement ought not to have been permitted, but that, if it was permissible, the Crown was not entitled at the trial of the general issue to adduce evidence of his testimony on the voire dire or to cross-examine him on that evidence.

Held – The appeal would be allowed, and the conviction quashed, for the following reasons—

(i) (Lord Hailsham of St Marylebone dissenting) On a voire dire as to the admissibility of an extra-judicial statement by an accused the prosecution was not entitled to cross-examine the accused as to the truth of the statement, for the sole issue on the voire dire was whether the statement had been made voluntarily, and whether it was true was not relevant to that issue. It followed that the Crown's cross-examination of the appellant on the voire dire was a substantial irregularity in the trial (see p 943 *c f g* and p 946 *c d*, post); *R v Hammond* [1941] 3 All ER 318 overruled.

(ii) Furthermore, whether the accused's statement was excluded or admitted on the voire dire, the Crown was not entitled as part of its case on the general issue to adduce evidence of the testimony given by the accused on the voire dire. Accordingly, the calling of the shorthand-writers to give evidence of what the appellant had said on the voire dire, and his cross-examination on the general issue were also substantial irregularities in the trial (see p 944 *d* to *g*, p 945 *c*, p 946 *c* to *f*, p 947 *d e* and p 949 *f*, post); *R v Treacy* [1944] 2 All ER 229 applied.

Per Curiam. Where a statement is admitted as voluntary on the voire dire and the accused in giving evidence on the general issue gives evidence as to the reliability of the admissions in the statement, and in so doing departs materially from his testimony on the

voire dire, cross-examination on the discrepancies between his testimony on the voire dire
and his evidence on the general issue is permissible, for then his statements in evidence on
the voire dire stand on the same basis as, for example, evidence given by the accused in a   *a*
previous trial where the jury have disagreed (see p 945 *f* to p 946 *b*, p 947 *a* to *e* and p 949
f, post).

Notes

For the duty of the trial judge in relation to admissibility of confessions, and for use of facts   *b*
discovered as a result of an inadmissible statement, see 11 Halsbury's Laws (4th Edn) paras
413, 418.

Cases referred to in judgment

Chan Wai-keung v R [1967] 1 All ER 948, sub nom *Chan Wei Keung v R* [1967] 2 AC 160,
   [1967] 2 WLR 552, 51 Cr App R 257, PC, 14(2) Digest (Reissue) 551, 4509.   *c*
Chitambala v R [1961] R & N 166.
DeClercq v R [1968] SCR 902, 70 DLR (2d) 530, [1969] 1 CCC 197, 14(2) Digest (Reissue)
   571, *3607.
Director of Public Prosecutions v Ping Lin [1975] 3 All ER 175, [1976] AC 574, [1975] 3 WLR
   419, 139 JP 651, 62 Cr App R 14, HL, 14(2) Digest (Reissue) 564, 4596.
Ibrahim v R [1914] AC 599, [1914–15] All ER Rep 874, 83 LJPC 185, 111 LT 20, 24 Cox CC   *d*
   174, PC, 14(2) Digest (Reissue) 562, 4583.
Li Kim-hung v R [1969] Hong Kong LR 84.
Ng Chun-Kwan v R [1974] Hong Kong LR 319.
R v Hammond [1941] 3 All ER 318, 166 LT 135, 106 JP 35, 40 LGR 1, 28 Cr App R 84, CCA,
   14(2) Digest (Reissue) 469, 3911.
R v Hnedish (1958) 26 WWR 685, 29 CR 347, 14(2) Digest (Reissue) 554, *3400.   *e*
R v Treacy [1944] 2 All ER 229, 30 Cr App R 93, CCA, 14(2) Digest (Reissue) 550, 4505.
R v Wright [1969] SASR 256.

Appeal

This was an appeal in forma pauperis, by special leave of the Judicial Committee granted
on 1st March 1978, by Wong Kam-ming against the judgment of the Court of Appeal of   *f*
Hong Kong (Briggs CJ and Huggins JA, McMullin J dissenting) dated 12th July 1977
whereby the appellant's appeal against his conviction by the Supreme Court of Hong Kong
(before Commissioner Garcia and a jury) on 1st October 1976 for murder and on two
counts of wounding with intent to do grievous bodily harm was dismissed. The facts are
set out in the majority judgment of the Board.

Charles Fletcher-Cooke QC, William Glossop and *George Warr* for the appellant.   *g*
John Marriage QC and *Daniel Marash* (Crown Counsel, Hong Kong) for the Crown.

LORD EDMUND-DAVIES. This is an appeal by special leave granted by this Board
from a judgment of the Court of Appeal of Hong Kong, dismissing the appeal of Wong
Kam-ming against his conviction in October 1976 of murder by the Supreme Court   *h*
(Commissioner Garcia and a jury). The indictment charged the appellant and five other
males on counts of murdering one man and of maliciously wounding two others. The case
for the Crown was that the accused men were part of a gang who went to a massage parlour
in Kowloon and there fatally attacked the manager and wounded others in retaliation for
an earlier attack on one of their number. Four of the accused were acquitted on all charges,
while the other two (including the present appellant) were convicted on each.   *j*
    When the trial opened, the only evidence implicating the appellant consisted of a signed
statement which he had given to the police. In this he admitted being one of those present
in the massage parlour, that at one stage he had a knife in his hand and that he had
'chopped' one of those present. Defending counsel having intimated to the court that he
challenged the admissibility of this statement on the ground that it was not voluntary,

before the Crown opened its case the judge (in the absence of the jury) proceeded to deal
with the issue of admissibility on the voire dire. After two police witnesses had testified to
its making, the appellant gave evidence that he was never cautioned, that he was questioned
at length while in custody, that he was grabbed by the shirt and shaken, that an inducement
was offered that if he confessed his 'sworn brother' would not be arrested and that he had
been forced to copy out and sign a statement drafted by the police. Under cross-examination
he was asked a series of questions based on the detailed contents of the statement, and
directed at establishing its truth. At this stage it is sufficient to say that, at the conclusion
of the voire dire, the trial judge excluded the statement.

This ruling placed the Crown in dire difficulty, for it is common ground that without
it they could not establish even that the appellant was present in the massage parlour at any
material time. Finding themselves in that situation, they resorted to a course of action
which none of their Lordships had hitherto ever heard of. Prosecuting counsel indicated
to the trial judge (in the absence of the jury) that he proposed to establish, by reference to
what had transpired in the voire dire, that the appellant had, 'in circumstances where there
is no question of involuntariness, admitted he was present and involved in the incident
with which we are concerned'. As authority for submitting that he should be allowed to
prove such admission by calling the shorthand-writer present during the voire dire he cited
R v Wright[1], to which reference must later be made. Defending counsel's objection was
overruled, the trial judge holding that *R v Wright*[1] was good law, and expressly refusing to
exercise in favour of the appellant any discretion he might have to exclude the proffered
new evidence. Two shorthand-writers were then called to produce extracts from their
transcripts of what the appellant had said during the voire dire, and this despite a renewed
objection by defending counsel.

A submission of 'No case' was likewise overruled, the trial judge saying: 'The main point
here is presence at the scene at the relevant time.' Defending counsel thereupon called the
appellant. Following his evidence-in-chief, he was closely cross-examined by reference to
the shorthand transcript of what he had said on the voire dire, prosecuting counsel
repeatedly pointing out discrepancies and observing at one stage: '*That* is extraordinarily
different from the evidence you have given *this* time.' And in the course of summing-up
the judge told the jury that the appellant—

> '... in certain proceedings held on 25th and 26th August this year gave answers to
> certain questions put to him in cross-examination by [Crown counsel], and such
> answers indicate that he was present in the premises of the music parlour[2] on the
> night of 28th December 1975. A copy of those questions and answers is also in your
> hands.'

Following on these proceedings which, it will be seen, had taken several unusual turns,
the jury, as already indicated, convicted the appellant on all three charges, and he was
sentenced to death on the murder charge. The conduct of the trial has been attacked in
several respects, and these were conveniently summarised by counsel for the appellant in
framing the following questions: 1. During the cross-examination of an accused in the
voire dire as to the admissibility of his challenged statement, may questions be put as·to its
truth? 2. If 'Yes', has the court a discretion to exclude such cross-examination, and (if so)
was it properly exercised in the present case? 3. Where, although the confession is held
inadmissible, the answers to questions 1 and 2 are nevertheless in favour of the Crown, is
the prosecution permitted, on resumption of the trial of the main issue, to adduce evidence
of what the accused said during the voire dire? 4. If 'Yes', is there a discretion to exclude
such evidence, and (if so) was it properly exercised here? 5. Even though it be held that the
answer to question 3 is 'No', may the accused nevertheless be cross-examined on what he
said during the voire dire? Their Lordships proceed to consider these questions.

---

1   [1969] SASR 256
2   The music parlour was on the floor below the massage parlour; both establishments were owned
    by the same proprietor, and employees from one establishment could be called to the other

Questions 1 and 2: relevance of truth of extra-judicial statements

In *R v Hammond*[1] prosecuting counsel was held entitled to ask the accused, when cross-examining him during the voire dire, whether a police statement which the accused alleged had been extorted by gross maltreatment was in fact true, and elicited the answer that it was. Upholding the propriety of putting the question, Humphreys J said in the Court of Criminal Appeal[2]:

'In our view, [the question] clearly was not inadmissible. It was a perfectly natural question to put to a person, and it was relevant to the issue of whether the story which he was then telling of being attacked and ill-used by the police was true or false . . . it surely must be admissible, and in our view it is admissible, because it went to the credit of the person who was giving evidence. If a man says, "I was forced to tell the story. I was made to say this, that and the other", it must be relevant to know whether he was made to tell the truth, or whether he was made to say a number of things which were untrue. In other words, in our view, the contents of the statement which he admittedly made and signed were relevant to the question of how he came to make and sign that statement, and, therefore, the questions which were put were properly put.'

Although much criticised, that decision has frequently been followed in England and Wales and in many other jurisdictions, though it would serve little purpose to refer to more than a few of the many decisions cited by learned counsel. Mention must, however, be made to *DeClercq v R*[3], a majority decision of the Supreme Court of Canada following *R v Hammond*[1], where Martland J said[4]:

'. . . it does not follow that the truth or falsity of the statement must be irrelevant . . . An accused person, who alleged that he had been forced to admit responsibility for a crime committed by another, could properly testify that the statement obtained from him was false. Similarly, where the Judge conducting the voire dire was in some doubt on the evidence as to whether the accused had willingly made a statement, or whether, as he contended, he had done so because of pressure exerted by a person in authority, the admitted truth or the alleged falsity of the statement could be a relevant factor in deciding whether or not he would accept the evidence of the accused regarding such pressure.'

Their Lordships were told by learned counsel that in England and Wales it has become common practice for prosecuting counsel to ask the accused in the voire dire whether his challenged statement was in fact true. It is difficult to understand why this practice is permitted, and impossible to justify it by claiming that in some unspecified way it goes to 'credit'. As McMullin J said in his dissenting judgment in the instant case:

'. . . I cannot see that the answer to this question has any material relevance even to the issue of credibility. Where the answer to the question "Is this confession the truth?" is "No" the inquiry is no further advanced. The credibility of the defendant in relation to the alleged improprieties can scarcely be enhanced or impaired by an answer which favours his own interests in opposing the admission of the statement. On its own, demeanour apart, it is neutral.'

The cogency of these observations may be respectfully contrasted with those of Huggins JA who said, in delivering the majority judgment:

'Although questions may be put to the defendant as to the truth of his extrajudicial confession that does not make the truth or falsehood of that confession relevant to the

---

1   [1941] 3 All ER 318
2   [1941] 3 All ER 318 at 321
3   (1968) 70 DLR (2d) 530
4   70 DLR (2d) 530 at 537

issue of voluntariness: what is relevant—because it goes to the credibility of the defendant—is that the defendant asserts that the extrajudicial confession is true or false.'

But the basis of this assertion is unclear. If the accused denies the truth of the confession or some self-incriminating admission contained in it, the question whether his denial is itself true or false cannot be ascertained until after the voire dire is over and the accused's guilt or innocence has been determined by the jury, an issue which the judge has no jurisdiction to decide. If, on the other hand, the accused made a self-incriminating admission that the statement is true, than, as one critic has expressed it, 'If the confession is true, this presumably shows that the accused tends to tell the truth, which suggests that he is telling the truth in saying the police were violent'[1].

The sole object of the voire dire was to determine the voluntariness of the alleged confession in accordance with principles long established by such cases as *Ibrahim v R*[2]. This was emphasised by this Board in *Chan Wai-Keung v R*[3], while the startling consequences of adopting the *Hammond*[4] approach were well illustrated in the Canadian case of *R v Hnedish*[5], where Hall CJ said:

'Having regard to all the implications involved in accepting the full impact of the *Hammond*[4] decision which can, I think, be summarized by saying that regardless of how much physical or mental torture or abuse has been inflicted on an accused to coerce him into telling what is true, the confession is admitted because it is in fact true regardless of how it is obtained, I cannot believe that the *Hammond*[4] decision does reflect the final judicial reasoning of the English courts . . . I do not see how under the guise of "credibility" the court can transmute what is initially an inquiry as to the "admissibility" of the confession into an inquisition of an accused. That would be repugnant to our accepted standards and principles of justice; it would invite and encourage brutality in the handling of persons suspected of having committed offences.'

It is right to point out that learned counsel for the Crown did not seek to submit that the prosecution could in *every* case properly cross-examine the accused during the voire dire regarding the truth of his challenged statement. Indeed, he went so far as to concede that in many cases it would be wrong to do anything of the sort. But he was unable to formulate an acceptable test of its propriety, and their Lordships have been driven to the conclusion that none exists. In other words, in their Lordships' view, *R v Hammond*[4] was wrongly decided, and any decisions in Hong Kong which purported to follow it should be treated as overruled. The answer to question 1 is therefore 'No', and it follows that question 2 does not fall to be considered.

Questions 3 and 4

Their Lordships turn to questions 3 and 4. As part of its case on the main issue, may the prosecution lead evidence regarding the testimony given by the accused on the voire dire? As already related, the trial judge originally thought that this question required a negative answer, but he was led to change his mind by the decision in *R v Wright*[6], where the Supreme Court of South Australia held that the Crown was entitled to lead such evidence, subject to the discretion of the trial judge to disallow it. But the weight of judicial authority is against such a conclusion. The earliest relevant decision appears to be that of the Federal Supreme Court of Southern Rhodesia in *Chitambala v R*[7], where Clayden ACJ said:

1 Heydon: Cases and Materials on Evidence (1975), p 181
2 [1914] AC 599, [1914–15] All ER Rep 874
3 [1967] 1 All ER 948, [1967] 2 AC 160
4 [1941] 3 All ER 318
5 (1958) 26 WWR 685 at 688
6 [1969] SASR 256
7 [1961] R & N 166 at 169

'In any criminal trial the accused has the right to elect not to give evidence at the
conclusion of the Crown case. To regard evidence given by him on the question of   *a*
admissibility as evidence in the trial itself would mean either that he must be
deprived of that right if he wishes properly to contest the admissibility of a statement,
or that, to preserve that right, he must abandon another right in a fair trial, the right
to prevent inadmissible statements being led in evidence against him ... To me it
seems clear that deprivation of rights in this manner, and the changing of a trial of
admissibility into a full investigation of the merits, cannot be part of a fair criminal   *b*
trial.'

This decision was followed in Hong Kong in *Li Kim-hung v R*[1] and in *Ng Chun-kwan v
R*[2] In the latter McMullin J (who dissented in the instant case) said, in giving the
judgment of the Full Court[3]:

'... what the accused says on the voire dire may not be used as substantive evidence   *c*
against him or his co-accused ... In this respect evidence on the voire dire is
distinguishable from an extra-judicial confession and the basis for the distinction lies
in the accused's right to remain silent upon the trial of the general issue even though
he has elected to give evidence on the voire dire.'

d

Yet in the instant appeal counsel for the Crown felt constrained to submit that, even
were the trial judge to exclude a confession on the ground that torture had been used to
extort it, any damaging statements made by the accused on the voire dire could nevertheless
properly be adduced as part of the prosecution's case. Boldness could go no further.

Fortunately for justice, their Lordships have concluded that, where the confession has
been excluded, the argument against ever admitting such evidence as part of the Crown   *e*
case must prevail. But what if the confession is held *admissible*? In such circumstances, it
is unlikely that the prosecution will need to do more than rely on the confession itself.
Nevertheless, in principle should they be prevented from proving in addition any
admission made by the accused on the voire dire? This question has exercised their
Lordships a great deal, but even in the circumstances predicated it is preferable to maintain
a clear distinction between the issue of voluntariness, which is alone relevant to the voire   *f*
dire, and the issue of guilt falling to be decided in the main trial. To blur this distinction
can lead, as has already been shown, to unfortunate consequences, and their Lordships have
therefore concluded that the same exclusion of evidence regarding the voire·dire
proceedings from the main trial must be observed, regardless of whether the challenged
confession be excluded or admitted.

It follows that question 3 must be answered in the negative, and question 4 accordingly   *g*
does not arise.

Question 5

Question 5 remains for consideration by their Lordships. Notwithstanding the answer
to question 3, in the event of the accused giving evidence in the main trial, may he be cross-
examined in respect of statements made by him during that voire dire? In the instant case   *h*
the majority of the court held that he could, and McMullin J (who dissented) had earlier
been of the same view, having said in *Ng Chun-kwan v R*[3]:

'The only way in which evidence of an admission made by the accused on the voire
dire may be adduced in evidence is by way of rebuttal if he gives evidence on the
general issue and if that evidence is inconsistent with what he has said on the voire   *j*

---

1   [1969] Hong Kong LR 84
2   [1974] Hong Kong LR 319
3   [1974] Hong Kong LR 319 at 328

a   dire ... we cannot see any warrant for the contention ... that everything which transpires in the course of a voire dire is to be regarded as having acquired an indefeasible immunity from all further resort for any purpose whatsoever.'

The problem is best approached in stages. In *R v Treacy*[1], where the accused's answers under police interrogation were held inadmissible, it was held that he could not be cross-examined to elicit that he had in fact given those answers, Humphrey J saying[2]:

b   'In our view, a statement made by a prisoner under arrest is either admissible or it is not admissible. If it is admissible, the proper course for the prosecution is to prove it ... If it is not admissible, nothing more ought to be heard of it, and it is a complete mistake to think that a document can be made admissible in evidence which is otherwise inadmissible simply because it is put to a person in cross-examination.'

c   In their Lordships' judgment, *R v Treacy*[1] was undoubtedly correct in prohibiting cross-examination as to the *contents* of confessions which the court has ruled inadmissible. But what if during the voire dire the accused has made self-incriminating statements not strictly related to the confession itself but which nevertheless have relevance to the issue of guilt or innocence of the charge preferred? May the accused be cross-examined so as to elicit those matters? In the light of their Lordships' earlier conclusion that the Crown may not adduce as part of its case evidence of what the accused said during a voire dire *d*   culminating in the exclusion of an impugned confession, can a different approach here be permitted from that condemned in *R v Treacy*[1]?

Subject to what was said to be the court's discretion to exclude it in proper circumstances, counsel for the Crown submitted that it can be, citing in support s 13 of the Hong Kong Evidence Ordinance, which was based on the familiar provision in s 4 of the Criminal Procedure Act 1865 of the United Kingdom, relating to the confrontation of a witness with *e*   his previous inconsistent statements. But these statutory provisions have no relevance if the earlier statements cannot be put in evidence. And, having already concluded that the voire dire statements of the accused are not admissible during the presentation of the prosecution's case, their Lordships find it impossible in principle to distinguish between such cross-examination of the accused on the basis of the voire dire as was permitted in the instant case by the trial judge and upheld by the majority of the Court of Appeal and that *f*   cross-examination based on the contents of an excluded confession, which, it is common ground, was rightly condemned in *R v Treacy*[1].

But what if the voire dire resulted in the impugned confession being *admitted*, and the accused later elects to give evidence? If he then testifies to matters relating, for example, to the *reliability* of the confession (as opposed to its *voluntariness*, which ex hypothesi, is no longer in issue) and in so doing gives answers which are markedly different from his *g*   testimony given during the voire dire, may he be cross-examined so as to establish that at the earlier stage of the trial he had told a different story? Great injustice could well result from the exclusion of such cross-examination, and their Lordships can see no justification in legal principle or on any other ground which renders it impermissible. As has already been observed, an accused seeking to challenge the admissibility of a confession may for all practical purposes be *obliged* to testify in the voire dire if his challenge is to have any chance *h*   of succeeding, and his evidence is then (or certainly should be) restricted strictly to the issue of admissibility of the confession. But the situation is quite different where, the confession having been *admitted* despite his challenge, the accused later elects to give evidence during the main trial and, in doing so, departs materially from the testimony he gave in the voire dire. Having so chosen to testify, why should the discrepancies not be elicited and demonstrated by cross-examination? In their Lordships' view, his earlier statements made *j*   in the voire dire provide as acceptable a basis for this cross-examination to that end as any

1   [1944] 2 All ER 229
2   [1944] 2 All ER 229 at 236

other earlier statements made by him, including, of course, his confession which, though
challenged, had been ruled admissible. Indeed, for such purposes and in such *a*
circumstances, his voire dire statements stand on no different basis than, for example, the
sworn testimony given by an accused in a previous trial where the jury had disagreed.

No doubt the trial judge has a discretion and, indeed, a duty to ensure that the right of
the prosecution to cross-examine or rebut is not used in a manner unfair or oppressive to
the accused, and no doubt the judge is under an obligation to see to it that any statutory
provisions bearing on the situation (such as those earlier referred to) are strictly complied *b*
with. But, subject thereto, their Lordships hold that cross-examination in the circumstances
predicated which is directed to testing the credibility of the accused by establishing the
inconsistencies in his evidence is wholly permissible.

In the instant case, however, the challenged confession was excluded. It therefore
follows that in the judgment of their Lordships no less than three substantial irregularities
occurred in the trial: (1) in the voire dire the accused was cross-examined with a view to *c*
establishing that is extra-judicial statement was true; (2) in the trial proper, the Crown was
permitted to call as part of its case evidence regarding answers given by the accused during
the voire dire; and (3) the accused was permitted to be cross-examined so as to demonstrate
that what he had said in chief was inconsistent with his statement in the voire dire.

As a result, evidence was wrongly placed before the jury that the appellant was one of
those present in the massage parlour at the material time and that he had then been in *d*
possession of a weapon. But for that evidence, it is common ground that the submission
of 'No case' made by defending counsel must have succeeded.

It follows that their Lordships will humbly advise Her Majesty that this appeal should
be allowed and the conviction quashed.

Dissenting opinion by **LORD HAILSHAM OF ST MARYLEBONE.** I regret that for *e*
the reasons which follow there is a substantial portion of the advice of the majority in this
case from which I must respectfully record my dissent.

I wish to begin, however, by making it plain that I entirely endorse the result
proposed. This is because I entirely agree with the proposed answer to the third of the
questions posed by counsel for the appellant and referred to in the advice of the majority,
and this is sufficient to dispose of the whole appeal. I also agree with both parts of the *f*
proposed answer to the fifth question. Once a statement has been excluded I consider that,
to adapt the words of Humphreys J in R v Treacy[1], nothing more should be heard of the
voire dire unless it gives rise to a prosecution for perjury.

I have stated elsewhere[2] that the rule, common to the law of Hong Kong and that of
England, relating to the admissibility of extra-judicial confessions is in many ways
unsatisfactory, but any civilised system of criminal jurisprudence must accord to the *g*
judiciary some means of excluding confessions or admissions obtained by improper
methods. This is not only because of the potential unreliability of such statements, but
also, and perhaps mainly, because in a civilised society it is vital that persons in custody or
charged with offences should not be subjected to ill treatment or improper pressure in
order to extract confessions. It is therefore of very great importance that the courts should
continue to insist that before extra-judicial statements can be admitted in evidence the *h*
prosecution must be made to prove beyond reasonable doubt that the statement was not
obtained in a manner which should be reprobated and was therefore in the truest sense
voluntary. For this reason it is necessary that the accused should be able and feel free either
by his own testimony or by other means to challenge the voluntary character of the
tendered statement. If, as happened in the instant appeal, the prosecution were to be
permitted to introduce into the trial the evidence of the accused given in the course of the *j*
voire dire when the statement to which it relates has been excluded whether in order to
supplement the evidence otherwise available as part of the prosecution case, or by way of

1 [1944] 2 All ER 229
2 *Director of Public Prosecutions v Ping Lin* [1975] 3 All ER 175, [1976] AC 574

cross-examination of the accused, the important principles of public policy to which I have
a referred would certainly become eroded, possibly even to vanishing point.

I also agree with the opinion of the majority that when and if the statement has been
admitted as voluntary and the prosecution attempt to cross-examine an accused on
discrepancies between his sworn testimony on the voire dire and his evidence on the
general issue at the trial, rather different considerations apply. By the time that evidence
is given the statement will have been admitted on the ground that the prosecution has
b succeeded in establishing to the satisfaction of the judge beyond reasonable doubt that it
was properly obtained, and the whole evidence relating to the statement will have to be
rehearsed once more, this time in front of the jury (where there is one) in order that they
may form a conclusion not as to its admissibility but as to the reliability of the admissions
made. It seems to me that in those circumstances the statements on oath made by the
defendant on the voire dire as material for cross-examination do not, from the point of
c view of public policy, stand in any other situation than any other statements made by him,
including the statement which has been admitted. For this purpose the true analogy is the
position of his sworn testimony in a previous trial where the jury have disagreed. No
doubt the trial judge has a discretion to see that the right of the prosecution to cross-
examine or rebut is not used in a manner unfair or oppressive to the accused, and no doubt
the judge is under a strict obligation to see that any statutory provisions (for instance those
d in the Criminal Evidence Act 1898 or its Hong Kong equivalent) are rigorously complied
with. But, in my view, once the substantive statement is admitted on the voire dire, the
fewer the artificial rules limiting the admissibility of evidence which may be logically
probative the better. I therefore agree with both parts of the advice tendered by the
majority to the fifth of the questions propounded by counsel in argument.

The reservations I feel about the opinion of the majority in this case are therefore
e confined to the views they express in relation to questions 1 and 2. In order to avoid
prejudice to the accused the voire dire normally takes place in the absence of a jury. It is
therefore a trial on an issue of fact before a judge alone. It is open to the accused
(presumably under the provisions of the Criminal Evidence Act 1898 or its Hong Kong
equivalent) to give evidence and there are limits imposed by that Act or the equivalent
Ordinance on what may be asked him in cross-examination. Subject to these limitations,
f and to any other general rules of evidence (such as those relating to hearsay) it seems to me
that the only general limitations on what may be asked or tendered ought to be relevant
to the issue to be tried, as in any other case in which an issue of fact is to be tried by a judge
alone, and as to this, subject to appeal, the judge is himself the arbiter on the same
principles as in any other case in which he is the judge of fact. It appears to be the opinion
of the majority that it is possible to say a priori that in no circumstances is the truth or
g falsity of the alleged confession relevant to the question at issue on the voire dire or
admissible as to credibility of either the prosecution or defence witness. I disagree.

It is common ground that the question at issue on the voire dire is the voluntary
character of the statement. This is the factum probandum, and, since the burden is on the
prosecution, the prosecution evidence is taken before that of the defence. The voire dire
may take place, as in the instant appeal, at the beginning of the trial, when all that is known
h of the facts must be derived from the depositions, or from counsel's opening. More
frequently, however, the voire dire takes place at a later stage in the trial when the
prosecution tenders the evidence, usually of the police, in support of the voluntary character
of the statement. By that time many facts are known and much of the evidence has been
heard. I can conceive of many cases in which it is of the essence of the defence case on the
voire dire that the confession, whose voluntary character is in issue, is in whole or in part
j untrue, and, it may be, contrary to admitted fact. If the defence can succeed in establishing
this or even raising a serious question about it either as the result of cross-examining the
prosecution witnesses or by evidence led by the defence itself, serious doubt can be raised
as to the voluntary nature of the confession. How can it be said, counsel for the defence
might wish to argue, that the accused can have provided so much inaccurate information
to his own detriment, unless he was forced to do so by some improper means? If the

defence can be allowed to make the point, which seems to me to be a valid one, it must be
open to the prosecution to cross-examine on it when it is the turn of the defence witnesses *a*
to be scrutinised.

It must be remembered that it is frequently the case that the alleged confession is not
always, as in the instant appeal, a written statement copied out in the writing of the
accused, though the point can arise even in such a case. Often, perhaps more often, the
statement in question may have been oral, and the case on the voire dire for the defence
may be that it was obtained only after a long period in custody, perhaps without rest, food, *b*
or drink, as the result of a long and harassing interrogation at which either no caution was
administered or improper pressures were brought to bear. In such circumstances it seems
to me inevitable that the truth or otherwise of what is alleged to have been said, and what
was actually said in response to what questions or the accuracy of what is alleged to have
been copied down in the police notebooks (and the questions though logically separate are
often difficult to separate in practice), must be investigated in order to establish, or cast *c*
doubt on, the voluntary character of the confession. I am the first to deprecate what
counsel for the Crown, who has a wide experience of current practice at the Central
Criminal Court and elsewhere, admitted without justifying to be a growing habit of
counsel for the prosecution, namely to begin his cross-examination on the voire dire in
every case with a question directed to the truth or otherwise of the confession.

Though I tend to regard the use made in the advice of the majority of the passage in *d*
Heydon on Evidence[1], as an example of the fallacy known as ignorantia elenchi, I agree
with them that it is no answer when the admissibility of an alleged confession has been
challenged on the grounds that it was improperly obtained, that it was a confession of the
truth and not the reverse. But counsel for the prosecution may be entitled to know the
exact limits of the case he has to meet. Has he to answer the suggestion that the confession
is more likely to be involuntary because it was so contrary to fact? Can he himself rely on *e*
the argument that it is inconceivable that a detailed albeit admittedly truthful confession
of a really serious crime, as for instance murder, was elicited as the result of a relatively
trivial inducement such for instance as being allowed to see a close relative for a short time?

I am wholly unable to see that these are not questions and arguments which can in
particular cases have a bearing on the voluntary or involuntary character of statements
tendered in evidence by the prosecution and therefore, in suitable cases, investigated at the *f*
voire dire. Disputes not infrequently occur on the voire dire not merely as to the facta
probanda but as to what was said and at what stage (eg before or after a caution) and,
though a voire dire is not required at all when the defence case is that no statement of any
sort was made, the more usual situation at the voire dire is that what is in dispute between
the parties is not merely whether what was said was voluntary (the factum probandum on
the voire dire) or whether anything was said (a question for the jury, and not the judge) but *g*
exactly what was said and in what circumstances and at what point of time, and as the
result of what inducement if any (facta probantia or reprobantia, but not probanda). For
these questions, which must be investigated before a judge admits a statement on the voire
dire, it seems to me impossible to say a priori that every question of the truth or falsity of
the statements must be excluded, and although I agree that in the ultimate resort the
questions will be for the jury if the statement is admitted, the judge may often be in a *h*
position when he is compelled to form an opinion as to the relative reliability of rival
versions of what took place in order to form an opinion as to whether what was said was
said voluntarily or as the consequence of inducement. An example of another kind is
where the prosecution case is that a statement was originally volunteered orally and
subsequently signed voluntarily by the accused, and the case for the accused is that the
statement was concocted by the police, written down by the police and then signed by the *j*
accused under improper pressures. In this case the prosecution may wish to say that details
in the alleged concoction could only have come from the accused and were accurate facts

---

1 Heydon: Cases and Materials on Evidence (1975), p 181

not otherwise known at the time, and the accused may wish to point to inaccuracies in the
a statement as pointing to concoctions.

In each case, although not directly affecting the allegation of signature under pressure,
the accuracy or otherwise of the contents of the confession must be open to some enquiry
on the voire dire. Obviously the judge must be allowed a discretion in the matter. He
must not permit counsel to pursue the matter of the truth or falsity of items in a confession
for an ulterior reason or in an oppressive manner, or at undue length, but I am not able to
b say a priori that all must necessarily be irrelevant. I am somewhat fortified in this view by
the reflection that if the voire dire is decided in favour of the prosecution, almost all of the
evidence given is repeated at the trial of the general issue, where the factum probandum
is guilt or innocence and not the voluntary or involuntary character of the statement
admitted. Contrary, I believe, to what is suggested at one point in the majority opinion,
the jury are absolutely free to form their one view of the circumstances in which the
c statement was obtained irrespective of the opinion of the judge (as to which in theory at
least they are wholly ignorant) in order to form their own opinion as to the facts relied on
by the prosecution or the defence on the general issue. Though the judge has found the
confession to be voluntary, and therefore admissible, the jury is perfectly entitled to act on
the contrary belief and therefore to disregard it as unreliable. It is of course not logically
necessary that the converse of this position is also true, namely that the judge can be
d assisted by his view of the truth or otherwise of the material contained in an alleged
statement in order to determine whether the statement is wholly voluntary or not. In
many cases no doubt (*R v Hammond*[1] was one) the judge will be wholly uninfluenced in his
decision by whether the confession contained accurate or inaccurate material and in such
a case either the question is improper or the answer irrelevant. But I am not prepared to
say a priori that in all cases it must always be so. In my opinion questions of relevance or
e otherwise can only seldom be decided a priori, as in my view the opinion of the majority
purports to do, but are far better left to the logical faculties of the trial judge in the context
of the concrete case which he has to try.

For these reasons I would give different answers to questions 1 and 2 to those proposed
by the majority. I agree with their answers to questions 3 and 4 and to both aspects of
question 5 and that the appeal must in consequence be allowed.

f
Appeal allowed.

Solicitors: *Hatchett, Jones & Kidgell* (for the appellant); *Charles Russell & Co* (for the Crown).

Mary Rose Plummer   Barrister.

g
1 [1941] 3 All ER 318

London Borough of Enfield v Local Government Boundary Commission for England and another

a

COURT OF APPEAL, CIVIL DIVISION

LORD DENNING MR, EVELEIGH LJ AND SIR DAVID CAIRNS

27th JULY 1978

b

Local government – Electoral arrangements – Proposal for change of arrangements – Objection by local authority – Commission required to observe rules laid down for considering electoral arrangements – Failure to observe rule to achieve electoral equality between wards – Commission rejecting scheme based on electoral equality and adopting scheme not based on electoral equality – Scheme adopted by commission in interests of effective and convenient local government – Whether proposals valid – Whether commission required to comply with rules – Whether interests of effective and convenient local government an overriding consideration – Local Government Act 1972, s 47(1), Sch 11, para 3(2)(a).

c

The Local Government Boundary Commission for England ('the commission'), in making proposals under s 47(1)[a] of the Local Government Act 1972 for changes in the electoral arrangements of a local authority, were required by s 78(2)[b] of the Act to comply, so far as reasonably practicable, with the rules set out in Sch 11 to the Act. In making proposals for electoral changes in a London borough the commission adopted a scheme put forward by a local political party that there should be 66 councillors and 33 wards in the borough, and rejected the scheme put forward by the borough council for 70 councillors and 35 wards. The council's scheme was reasonably practicable, and provided, as nearly as possible, for electoral equality, ie equal weight for each vote throughout the borough, whereas the scheme adopted by the commission did not provide for electoral equality to that degree. The council applied for a declaration that the commission's proposals were invalid because it had failed to comply with the rule, in para 3(2)(a)[c] of Sch 11, that the proposed electoral arrangements should provide 'as nearly as may be' for electoral equality. The judge[d] granted the declaration on the ground that the rule in para 3(2)(a) was mandatory and the failure to comply with it invalidated the proposals. The commission appealed.

d

e

f

Held – The rules in Sch 11 were subsidiary to the overriding provision in s 47(1) of the 1972 Act that the proposed changes should appear to the commission to be desirable in the interests of effective and convenient local government. Reading the commission's proposals as a whole, they had taken the broad view that it was in the interests of effective and convenient local government to have 66 councillors and 33 wards, that being the best way of dealing with the borough; and by virtue of s 47(1) they had been entitled to take that view in making the proposals. Accordingly, the proposals would be upheld and the appeal allowed (see p 953 e to p 954 c, post).

Decision of Bristow J [1978] 2 All ER 1073 reversed.

g

h

Notes

For changes in English local government areas, see Supplement to 24 Halsbury's Laws (3rd Edn) para 778A.

For the Local Government Act 1972, s 47 and Sch 11, para 3, see 42 Halsbury's Statutes (3rd Edn) 887, 1147.

j

---

a   Section 47(1), so far as material, is set out at p 951 *j*, post
b   Section 78(2) is set out at p 952 *b c*, post
c   Paragraph 3(2), so far as material, is set out at p 952 *d*, post
d   [1978] 2 All ER 1073

Appeal

a This was an appeal by the first defendants, the Local Government Boundary Commission for England ('the commission'), against the decision of Bristow J[1] dated 25th January 1978 granting the plaintiffs, the London Borough of Enfield ('the borough'), a declaration that the commission in considering the electoral arrangements for the borough failed to comply with s 78 of and Sch 11 to the Local Government Act 1972, and that the report and proposals submitted by the commission to the second defendant, the Secretary of State for *b* the Home Department, were invalid. The grounds of the appeal were that the judge misdirected himself in law (i) in not taking into account that s 47(1) of the 1972 Act required the commission to make proposals to the Secretary of State for effecting changes 'appearing to the Commission desirable in the interests of effective and convenient local government' and that a scheme which was ideal regarding electoral equality might nevertheless appear to the commission to be undesirable, (ii) in regarding Sch 11 to the *c* 1972 Act as requiring the commission to adopt a scheme, irrespective of other relevant considerations, because it got as near as could be got to the ideal of electoral equality, ie one vote of equal strength for each voter, (iii) in comparing in respect of electoral equality the commission's proposals and the borough's scheme instead of considering whether the commission's proposals complied with the rules in Sch 11 as far as was reasonably practicable, and (iv) in giving too restrictive an interpretation to the words 'as nearly as may *d* be' in para 3(2)(a) of Sch 11. The facts are set out in the judgment of Lord Denning MR.

Michael Mann QC and *Harry Woolf* for the commission and the Secretary of State.
Michael Howard for the borough.

LORD DENNING MR. By the Local Government Act 1972 our whole system of local *e* government was reorganised. The areas were changed. The councils were changed. There were new electoral arrangements. And so forth. In order to effect the changes there was established under the Act a commission, called the English Commission, to make proposals to the Secretary of State for the Home Department for effecting the changes. The question in this case is about the changes proposed for the London Borough of Enfield ('the borough'). The English Commission invited the then council of Enfield to submit a *f* scheme for the new wards and the new number of councillors, and so forth, for the borough. In addition, the English Commission invited other interested parties to submit schemes. In particular, the local political parties were invited to submit schemes. All did so.

I will come to the end first. The commission recommended to the Secretary of State that there should be 33 wards, each electing two councillors: so the total number of councillors *g* would be 66 in all. The commission's recommendations have been challenged by the council of Enfield. They say that the proper number should be 35 wards, two councillors in each, making 70 councillors in all. So strongly does the council of the borough feel about this matter that they have brought the question before the courts. They say that 70 councillors, 35 wards, is the correct number consistent with the rules laid down by Parliament, and that the commission, in recommending 66 councillors and 33 wards, did *h* not follow the rules. The judge below, Bristow J[1], held in favour of the borough. The commission now appeal to this court.

The point depends on the provisions of the 1972 Act. Section 47(1) of the Act reads:

'... the English Commission may in consequence of a review conducted by them ... make proposals to the Secretary of State for effecting changes appearing to the Commission desirable in the interests of effective and convenient local *j* government.'

That is their aim and object.

---

1   [1978] 2 All ER 1073

The section then goes on to specify the various means by which the changes may be effected. These include such things as the alteration of electoral areas, the constitution of a new London boroughs and 'a change of electoral arrangements for any local government area'.

We are here concerned with a change of electoral arrangements for the Borough of Enfield. Section 78(1) gives a definition of 'electoral arrangements' which shows that they are concerned with the number of councillors, the number of wards, the boundaries of wards, the number of councillors for each ward, and so on. Section 78(2) says, and this is important:

> 'In considering the electoral arrangements for local government areas for the purposes of this Part of this Act, the Secretary of State, each of the Commissions and every district council shall so far as is reasonably practicable comply with the rules set out in Schedule 11 to this Act.'

This sends us to Sch 11. In para 3(2) it says that when the commission considers the electoral arrangements for a London borough (like Enfield) they are to comply with this rule:

> '(a) the ratio of the number of local government electors to the number of councillors to be elected shall be, [this is imperative] as nearly as may be, the same in every ward of the district or borough.'

That sounds very complicated. But what it means is 'one man one vote of equal weight'. Each person in the whole area of Enfield is to have equal weight given to his vote 'as nearly as may be'. Take a particular ward where there are 6,000 electors and there are two councillors for that ward: each elector's vote is of certain weight. But if you have an adjoining ward of 8,000 people voting for two councillors, then obviously each of those 8,000 electors has less weight for his vote than the 6,000; whereas if there are only 4,000 electors in the next ward for two councillors, each of those 4,000 would have a greater weight for his vote. That result is undesirable. 'As nearly as may be' mathematically means that in making the electoral arrangements for the borough each man in any one ward should have an equal weight for his vote as the man in the next ward or any other ward.

Then para 3(3) says:

> 'Subject to sub-paragraph (2) above, in considering the electoral arrangements . . . regard shall be had to—(a) the desirability of fixing boundaries which are and will remain easily identifiable [that means the lines of the wards have to be drawn quite reasonably]; and (b) any local ties which would be broken by the fixing of any particular boundary.'

There it is.

No doubt in applying the rules the principal consideration is the mathematical one: 'as nearly as may be' one man one vote of equal weight. Such are the provisions of the statute.

Now I turn to see how far the commission have obeyed the rules or have not obeyed them. The commission had before them many proposals. When they first considered the schemes of all the various parties they adopted a scheme put forward by the local Liberal Party. That scheme proposed that there should be 66 councillors and 33 wards. They rejected the council's proposal of 70 councillors and 35 wards.

Later on, revisions were made in the proposed boundaries between wards and so forth. The matter was referred to an assistant commissioner. The assistant commissioner was independent of the commission. He was a Mr Slocombe who had come, we are told, from Welwyn Garden City. He went into the matter. He considered the proper number of councillors. He had before him the guidelines which said that the number of councillors should be between 50 and 70 for the London boroughs. Mr Slocombe said:

'I have given all proper weight to the council's views and evidence [these were in favour of 70 councillors and 35 wards] but am quite firmly of the opinion that their proposals should not be approved. There is a solid weight of evidence against 70. I consider that the maximum figure in the guidelines should be used sparingly, and I think it is too many for Enfield. I cannot believe that the committee structure cannot quickly be adapted to a council of 66, which is only about a 5 per cent reduction. My view is that 66 is the right number and this figure forms the basis of most of the other schemes prepared by the political parties.'

So he rejected the council's proposal of 70 councillors and came down in favour of 66.

He recognised though that in so doing he was departing to some extent from the ideal of 'one man one vote of equal weight'. Figures were put before him (and shown to us) that if you take 35 wards with two councillors each you will get a more equal representation than you will with the proposal of 33 wards and two councillors each. In other words, to get equality 'as nearly as may be', 70 councillors would be better than 66. Mr Slocombe recognised that. He said: 'The council's scheme cannot be faulted on an electoral ratio basis —in this respect it is almost perfect.' That is the underlying reasoning of the judge's judgment below. He thought that the overriding consideration for the commission was the rule in Sch 11, para 3(2)(a), which I will repeat again: '. . . the ratio of the number of local government electors to the number of councillors to be elected shall be, as nearly as may be, the same in every ward of the district or borough.'

If there were no overriding clauses, I think the borough would be right. The words 'as nearly as may be' apply to a mathematical test.

But there are some overriding clauses. First, there is s 78(2) which says that 'the Commission and every district council shall so far as is reasonably practicable comply with the rules'. That is not sufficient to carry the day here. It was reasonably practicable to have 70 councillors, and not 66.

Next, however, there are the words at the beginning of s 47: '. . . changes appearing to the Commission desirable in the interests of effective and convenient local government.' These words seem to me to be overriding words which the commission must apply in the whole of their consideration. Remember, they are a completely independent commission. They are independent of any political party. It is important that they should be. They must do what is desirable in the interests of effective and convenient local government. All the other rules are subsidiary to overriding considerations. As I read their recommendations, that is the method they adopted. They said:

'We considered our draft proposals in the light of the comments which we had received and of the report of the assistant commissioner. We concluded that the recommendations of the assistant commissioner should be accepted and we modified our draft proposals in accordance with those recommendations. We then formulated our final proposals.'

It seems to me, reading the whole of their recommendations together, that they took the broad view that in the interests of effective and convenient local government, the right number of councillors for Enfield should be 66, divided into 33 wards, that being the best way of dealing with Enfield. That is what they thought was 'desirable' in accordance with s 47(1). I think they were entitled to take that view.

I only differ from the judge in this. It seems to me that he gave too much weight to the particular rules of the schedule, whereas I think greater weight should be given to the opening words of s 47.

I would, therefore, allow the appeal and uphold the report of the commission.

EVELEIGH LJ. I agree. The role of the commission is to make proposals as indicated by s 47(1) of the 1972 Act; and in considering what proposals they will make for achieving sufficient and convenient local government they must comply with s 78 in so far as electoral arrangements may come within their contemplated proposals. That section requires the commission, so far as is reasonably practicable, to comply with the rules. 'As far as reasonably practicable' in my view does not mean 'possible in practice'. It permits a *a* balancing of relevant considerations which may well conflict one with another; and one and by no means the least of those considerations will be efficient and convenient local government. Section 78 does not require that the proposals put forward shall comply with the rules. It requires the commission and others concerned to comply with the rules so far as is reasonably practicable when considering the electoral arrangements—when considering them and not when making their proposals.   *b*

I agree with Lord Denning MR's interpretation of the phrase 'as nearly as may be' and with the conclusion that he has reached that this appeal should be allowed.

SIR DAVID CAIRNS. The court has listened to such excellent arguments on both sides in the course of the hearing of this appeal that my mind has swayed from one side to the other. In the end I am persuaded that the view which has been taken by Lord Denning MR *c* and Eveleigh LJ is the right one for the reasons they have given, and I have nothing to add.

Appeal allowed. Leave to appeal to the House of Lords.

Solicitors: *Treasury Solicitor*; *Wilfred D Day*, Enfield (for the borough).

d

Gavin Gore-Andrews Esq Barrister.

R v Wheatley   *e*

COURT OF APPEAL, CRIMINAL DIVISION
LORD WIDGERY CJ, BRIDGE LJ AND WIEN J
30th OCTOBER 1978

Explosives – Offence – Knowingly possessing explosive substance under suspicious circumstances *f* *– Explosive substance – Whether 'explosive substance' to be construed by reference to definition in Explosives Act 1875 – Explosive Substances Act 1883, s 4(1).*

The appellant was charged with unlawful possession of an explosive substance, namely a metal pipe bomb filled with fire-dampened sodium chlorate mixed with sugar, contrary to s 4[a] of the Explosive Substances Act 1883. The expert evidence for the Crown contended *g* that those materials were capable of producing an explosive effect and were explosive substances, while expert evidence for the appellant contended that they would produce only a pyrotechnic effect and were not explosive substances. The trial judge held that the words 'explosive substance' in s 4 of the 1883 Act were to be construed by reference to the definition of 'explosive' in s 3(1)[b] of the Explosives Act 1875, which included any substance used with a view to producing a 'pyrotechnic effect'. He therefore directed the jury that *h* the materials were explosive substances and withdrew that issue from them. The appellant was convicted. He appealed against conviction on the ground that the judge had erred in law in his construction of 'explosive substance' and ought to have left to the jury the issue whether the materials were explosive substances within s 4 of the 1883 Act.

Held – Having regard to the long title of the 1883 Act which was 'An Act to amend the *j* Law relating to Explosive Substances', that Act was intended to amend, inter alia, the 1875

---

a   Section 4, so far as material, is set out at p 956 *d g*, post
b   Section 3(1) is set out at p 956 *f g*, post

a Act, and both Acts were in pari materia, having regard to the nature of their provisions and their respective short and long titles. It followed that what was an explosive substance within s 4 of the 1883 Act was to be determined by applying the definition of 'explosive' in s 3(1) of the 1875 Act and the judge had accordingly correctly directed the jury. The appeal would therefore be dismissed (see p 956 j and p 957 c g, post).

Notes

For possessing explosive substances, see 11 Halsbury's Laws (4th Edn) para 1208.

For the Explosives Act 1875, s 3, see 13 Halsbury's Statutes (3rd Edn) 160.

For the Explosive Substances Act 1883, s 4, see 8 ibid 221.

Cases cited

Attorney-General v HRH Prince Ernest Augustus of Hanover [1957] 1 All ER 49, [1957] AC
c   436, HL.

Powell v Cleland [1947] 2 All ER 672, [1948] 1 KB 262, CA.

Appeal

The appellant was tried at the Central Criminal Court (Judge Gwyn Morris QC and a jury) on an indictment containing four counts charging unlawfully putting a destructive
d substance at a place with intent to do grievous bodily harm, contrary to s 29 of the Offences against the Person Act 1861 (count 1), doing an act with intent to cause by an explosive substance an explosion likely to endanger life or injure property, contrary to s 3(*a*) of the Explosive Substances Act 1883 (count 2), making an explosive substance with intent to endanger life or injure property, contrary to s 3(*b*) of the 1883 Act (count 3), and knowingly possessing explosive substances, contrary to s 4(1) of the 1883 Act (count 4). The judge
e directed the jury that there was no defence to count 4, and on 2nd August 1977 the appellant was convicted on that count, but acquitted on counts 1, 2 and 3. He appealed against the conviction on the grounds, inter alia, that the judge had erred in law in construing the words 'explosive substance' in s 4(1) of the 1883 Act by reference to the definition of 'explosive' in the Explosives Act 1875, and ought to have left to the jury the issue whether the materials found in his possession were explosive substances. The facts
f are set out in the judgment of the court.

David Altaras for the appellant.
Timothy Cassel for the Crown.

BRIDGE LJ delivered the following judgment of the court: This appellant, on the 2nd
g August 1977, having been tried on an indictment charging him with four offences under the Explosive Substances Act 1883, was convicted of the least serious of those, one offence of unlawful possession of an explosive substance contrary to s 4 of the Act, and was sentenced to two years' imprisonment suspended for two years. He now appeals against his conviction by leave of the single judge.

The short point which the appeal raises is one of pure construction of the statute, and in
h those circumstances it is unnecessary to indicate more than the barest outline of the facts. The appellant had been on bad terms with his brother-in-law, and on 2nd August 1976 the brother-in-law discovered what was described as a small pipe bomb attached to the exhaust pipe of his motor vehicle. He removed it and contacted the police. The following day police officers went to the appellant's house and found in his car another pipe bomb, a metal pipe apparently intended for making another bomb, and in a tin found at his house
j a quantity of fire-dampened sodium chlorate. The substance with which each of the pipe bombs were filled was also fire-dampened sodium chlorate mixed with sugar. The count under s 4 of the 1883 Act related to the pipe bomb found in the appellant's car, a metal pipe and the tin with the fire-dampened sodium chlorate.

In the end, the sole issue which arose relating to that count was whether those materials constituted an explosive substance on the true construction of s 4 of the 1883 Act. Expert evidence had been led on both sides, the Crown's expert contending that, as a matter of language and as a matter of scientific fact in any event, the fire-dampened sodium chlorate-sugar mixture used in the pipe bombs was capable of producing an explosive effect; the expert on the other side contended that it would produce no explosive effect but only what he called a 'pyrotechnic effect'.

It has never been in dispute that, if the phrase 'explosive substance' in the 1883 Act has its ordinary English meaning and is to be construed without assistance from any statutory definition, the evidence in this case raised an issue for the jury which should have been left to them. In fact, the judge withdrew the issue from the jury. Having heard submissions on the true construction of the statute, he came to the conclusion that the 1883 Act should be construed in the light of the definition of 'explosive' in the Explosives Act 1875. Having regard to the terms of that definition, he held that on any view the evidence could only lead to the conclusion that the materials here in question were explosive substances.

It is common ground that, if he was right to adopt and apply the definition of 'explosive' derived from the 1875 Act, he reached the right conclusion in applying that definition to the facts in this case, so that the only issue for us is whether it is correct to construe the phrase 'explosive substance' in the 1883 Act in the light of and in the application of the definition of 'explosive' derived from the 1875 Act.

I should start from the 1883 Act and first read the section which creates the offence of which this appellant was convicted. It is s 4, which provides:

'(1) Any person who makes or knowingly has in his possession or under his control any explosive substance, under such circumstances as to give rise to a reasonable suspicion that he is not making it or does not have it in his possession or under his control for a lawful object, shall, unless he can show that he made it or had it in his possession or under his control for a lawful object, be . . . liable to [imprisonment] for a term not exceeding fourteen years . . . and the explosive substance shall be forfeited . . .'

That is the section falling to be construed, and the starting point in considering the issue raised in this appeal is the 1875 Act and the definition of 'explosive' which is there found. Section 3 provides:

'This Act shall apply to gunpowder and other explosives as defined by this section. The term "explosive" in this Act—(1) Means gunpowder, nitro-glycerine, dynamite, gun-cotton, blasting powders, fulminate of mercury or of other metals, coloured fires, and every other substance, whether similar to those above mentioned or not, used or manufactured with a view to produce a practical effect by explosion or a pyrotechnic effect; and (2) Includes fog-signals, fireworks, fuzes, rockets, percussion caps, detonators, cartridges, ammunition of all descriptions, and every adaptation or preparation of an explosive as above defined.'

This definition is found in an Act the short title of which is the Explosives Act 1875, but the long title of which reads as follows: 'An Act to amend the Law with respect to manufacturing, keeping, selling, carrying, and importing Gunpowder, Nitro-glycerine, and other Explosive Substances'. It is, as counsel for the appellant has rightly pointed out to us, an Act whose primary function is to regulate and control lawful operations undertaken by those who are concerned in manufacturing, keeping, selling, carrying and importing explosive substances. It is at the same time a statute which creates a number of criminal offences in relation to the handling of explosive substances.

The 1883 Act, in which the section creating the offence here is found, has the short title the Explosives Substances Act 1883, and the long title: 'An Act to amend the Law relating to Explosive Substances'. At an early stage in the argument the question was raised what law is intended to be amended by the 1883 Act. Counsel for the appellant submitted to us that the law to be amended was to be found in certain sections of the Malicious Damage Act 1861 and the Offences against the Person Act 1861. It seems to this court that, on the face of it, the law relating to explosive substances which the 1883 Act was intended to amend must include the Explosives Act 1875.

In the 1883 Act there is a definition of 'explosive substance'. It reads as follows:

a
'9. (1) . . . The expression "explosive substance" shall be deemed to include any materials for making any explosive substance; also any apparatus, machine, implement, or materials used, or intended to be used, or adapted for causing, or aiding in causing, any explosion in or with any explosive substance; also any part of any such apparatus, machine, or implement . . .'

b
It will be seen at once when one reads that definition that it is what one might call an expansive definition. Whatever an explosive substance means, this definition extends the meaning to materials which would otherwise not be within the primary connotation of the phrase. This definition, by contrast with the definition of 'explosive' in the 1875 Act, provides no indication of the primary meaning of what is meant by an 'explosive substance'.

Looking at the two statutes, at the nature of the provisions which they both contain, and
c
in particular at the short and long titles of both statutes, it appears to this court that clearly they are in pari materia, and that conclusion alone would seem to us to be sufficient to justify the conclusion which the judge reached that the definition of the word 'explosive' found in the 1875 Act is available to be adopted and applied under the provisions of the 1883 Act.

But if that conclusion were in any way in doubt, it is, in our judgment, put beyond
d
doubt by the express provisions of s 8 of the 1883 Act which is in these terms:

'(1) Sections seventy-three, seventy-four, seventy-five, eighty-nine, and ninety-six of the Explosives Act, 1875 (which sections relate to the search for, seizure and detention of explosive substances, and the forfeiture thereof, and the disposal of explosive substances seized or forfeited), shall apply in like manner as if a crime or forfeiture under this Act were an offence or forfeiture under the Explosives Act, 1875 . . .'

e
Here is Parliament in terms providing that certain powers in relation to explosive substances under the 1875 Act shall be applied for the purposes of the 1883 Act. That, as it seems to us, shows Parliament assuming of necessity that what is an explosive substance essentially under the one Act will be the same as under the other. It is true that the extended meaning of 'explosive substance' under s 9 of the 1883 Act, as counsel for the appellant has pointed out, would not necessarily be available and applicable under the 1875 Act, but the converse, in our judgment, really does not follow. It would make a nonsense of any attempt to apply s 8 of the 1883 Act if one had to say that the concept of 'explosive' as defined in the 1875 Act did not apply for the purposes of the 1883 Act, and one had to apply under the 1883 Act a very much narrower, layman's concept of what an 'explosive' is.

g
For those reasons we reach the conclusion that the judge here in the ruling which he gave on submissions made to him in the course of the trial reached the right conclusion, and on the evidence he was right to withdraw this issue from the jury and to tell the jury that the substances to which count 4 of the indictment related were explosive substances.

Accordingly, the appeal against conviction is dismissed.

h   *Appeal dismissed.*

Solicitors: *Registrar of Criminal Appeals*; *Director of Public Prosecutions*.

Lea Josse   Barrister.

Practice Direction

a

SUPREME COURT TAXING OFFICE

Costs – Taxation – Bill of costs – Simplified procedure – RSC Ord 62, App 2 (as amended by RSC (Amendment) 1979).

b

As from 24th April 1979 and until further direction the practice notes hereto annexed will apply to all bills lodged for taxation in the Supreme Court Taxing Office.

E J T Matthews
29th January 1979   Chief Master.

The Masters' Practice Notes 1979   c

1. The amendment to RSC Ord 62, App 2, provided for by the Rules of the Supreme Court (Amendment) 1979[1], and these practice notes will apply with effect from 24th April 1979 to all taxations governed by RSC Ord 62 other than matrimonial causes as defined by s 50 of the Matrimonial Causes Act 1973. These notes are intended to supplement and not to supersede the existing practice.

d

2. The new App 2 is designed to simplify the process of drawing, reading and taxing a contentious bill of costs and thereby to reduce the time and expense of the taxation procedure. It has been constructed by merging items which are similar in nature and by abandoning other items which are either obsolete or which ought properly to be considered as part of a solicitor's normal overhead cost and as such provided for in his expense rate. (The table set out in Sch 1 hereto shows how the items in the former appendix have been assimilated to the items in the new appendix or abolished.)

e

3. In addition to this general simplification a new procedure has been provided in the block allowance prescribed in Part II, item 5, which will apply to all actions for personal injury and may, if the party entitled to the costs so elects, apply to any other action subject, in either case, to a direction to the contrary made by the taxing officer.

4. The new appendix will apply, subject to the transitional provisions included in Ord 62, to all bills lodged after the appointed day no matter (save as provided in Ord 62, r 32(1)) when the work was done so that it will not usually be necessary to divide bills into separate parts for work done before and after that day. However it will still be necessary to divide bills into parts, as at present, to show separately work done before and after the introduction of VAT and before and after the issue of a civil aid certificate. If therefore a block allowance is included in a divided bill it must be apportioned between the several parts but the total allowed by the taxing officer will not exceed the amount which would have been allowed if the bill had not been divided.

f

g

5. The object of this new procedure is to simplify and hasten taxation and the block allowance is intended to provide a reasonable allowance for the items in Part I taken as a whole but if an action for personal injury is of such unusual weight that the block allowance would be wholly inappropriate an application should be made, for leave to deliver an extended bill. Conversely it will not be appropriate in an action other than one for personal injury to elect to insert a block allowance and then on taxation to seek to apply under r 32(2) for a large increase over the permitted maximum: if the case warrants substantial Part I charges beyond the maximum, the new procedure should not be chosen.

h

6. Where in an action for personal injury it is desired for proper reasons to avoid the use of the block allowance, the party entitled to the costs should apply for leave to the taxing officer to whom the taxation has been referred. In general, this application may be made ex parte and before the bill is drawn, by letter setting out the grounds, although the taxing officer may require the applicant to attend before him before giving his decision. The

j

---

1   SI 1979 No 35

a lodging of a bill in extended form will in itself be accepted as an application for leave but it must be emphasised that there is no right of election in personal injury cases, and should leave be refused no extra costs will on taxation be allowed for drawing the rejected bill. The granting of leave is a matter for the taxing officer in the exercise of his discretion in any particular case, but for the general guidance of the profession it is anticipated that leave will be granted only where it is clearly shown that there are unusual circumstances which would make the use of the block allowance wholly inappropriate or unfair.

b 7. In cases other than personal injury cases, the lodging of a bill which includes a block allowance will in general be taken as a sufficient election but, since the taxing officer may, of his own motion, refuse to accept the election with or without affording the elector the right to be heard, a preliminary application may if so desired be made to him ex parte by letter in cases in which there is real doubt or difficulty.

8. In cases to which Part II applies, the bill is to be drawn in the form prescribed in Sch
c 2 hereto. In order to facilitate taxation the bill, or each part as the case may be, is to be prefaced by a chronological table setting out all the main events in the action in the relevant part of it. No profit costs allowances should be included for any of these events which fall within the scope of items comprised in Part II. Where the events in question relate to attendances covered by Part III the profit costs allowances should be set out against each such event in this part of the bill. Where any such event has occasioned a
d disbursement the amount claimed should be inserted alongside that event. It will be noted that, to conform with the normal practice on taxation, item 10 has been placed after all items other than item 12 (costs of taxation) including attendance at the trial or hearing. This practice should also be followed in bills in which the block allowance is not used, which will otherwise be drawn with the several items in chronological order in the same manner as prior to the amendment to the rules.

e 9. Part I, item 3. A charge for preparing instructions to counsel to settle a document under item 3(*d*) will be allowed as a separate charge only where there is no charge allowable for preparing the document in question under item 1, 2 or 3(*a*), (*b*) or (*c*). Preparation of proofs of evidence should be charged under item 10 and not under this item. In cases to which a Part II block allowance does not apply, copy documents required to be exhibited to an affidavit should be charged under item 4 and the collating time under item
f 10(*a*)(ix). There will no longer be a separate charge for marking exhibits. The reference to 'additional copies' in the note to item 3 does not include any allowance for copies made for the use of the solicitor, his agent and his client or for counsel to settle.

10. Part III. Attendance in court or at chambers should appear with a note of the time engaged and, in the case of summonses, of what order for costs was made. Similarly, attendances on counsel in conference or consultation should have the time noted.
g 11. There will no longer be a separate profit charge for service of any process. Where, however, a solicitor makes use of a process server, that process server's charges should be shown as a disbursement. Where another solicitor is instructed solely to serve process his charge should be included as such a disbursement.

12. Accounts must accompany the bill for all payments claimed (other than court fees
h or minor out-of-pocket disbursements) whether or not these payments have later to be vouched. In the case of professional fees (other than fees to counsel or to medical experts) over £25, the account must be accompanied by details showing the work done and the computation of the charge. Where fees claimed are substantial, copies of the accounts should be annexed to the copy bill served on the paying party.

13. Where allowable travelling expenses are claimed they should be shown as a
j disbursement and details supplied. Local travelling expenses claimed by a solicitor will not be allowed. The definition of 'local' is a matter for the discretion of the taxing officer and in district registry cases enquiry should be made of the taxing officer concerned. While no absolute rule can be laid down, as a matter of guidance, in cases proceeding in the High Court in London, 'local' will, in general, be taken to mean within a radius of ten miles from the Royal Courts of Justice.

14. Conduct money paid to witnesses who attend a trial or hearing should be shown as part of the expenses claimed at the trial or hearing and not included in the bill at the date of the service of a subpoena.

15. Part IV, item 10. This item should conveniently be prefaced by a brief narrative indicating the issues, the status of the fee-earners concerned and the expense rates claimed. It is stressed that this statement should be short and succinct: the assessment of an allowance which depends partly on an arithmetical computation and partly on a judgment of value is not assisted by prolixity, which may lead to a reduction in the amount allowed for taxation. The narrative should be followed by a statement in two parts: (i) setting out a breakdown of the work done in relation to the relevant sub-paragraphs of item 10(a), and (ii) a statement in relation to care and conduct under item 10(b) referring to the relevant factors set out in Part VII (formerly Part X) relied on. The amount claimed for care and conduct should be expressed as a separate monetary amount as well as a percentage of the work figure. Telephone calls will be allowed as a time charge if, but only if, they stand in place of an attendance whereby material progress has been made and the time has been recorded or can otherwise be established. A notional conversion into a time charge of letters and routine telephone calls will not be accepted.

16. Charges as between a principal solicitor and a solicitor agent will continue to be dealt with on the established principle that such charges form, where appropriate, part of the principal solicitor's profit costs. Where these charges relate to the items comprised in Parts I, II or III they should be included in their chronological order. Where they relate to work done under Part IV, item 10, para (xi), they may either be included in the principal solicitor's item 10 or they may be shown as a separate item properly detailed following afterwards. Solicitors are reminded however that agency charges for advising the principal how to proceed are not recoverable inter partes.

17. Item 12. No narrative will be required for this item but on taxation the party entitled to the costs must justify the amount claimed.

18. When bills are lodged for taxation they should be supported by the relevant papers arranged in the order set out below. This requirement will be strictly applied in the Supreme Court Taxing Office and failure to observe it may result in the bill being refused or the allowance for taxation reduced. This practice may however vary in district registries and where necessary guidance should be sought from the taxing officer concerned:

(i) The bill of costs.
(ii) A bundle comprising all civil aid certificates and amendments thereto, notices of discharge or revocation and specific legal aid authorities. Copies of the offer and acceptance of a civil aid certificate will no longer be accepted in place of a copy of the actual certificate.
(iii) A certificate of times or a copy of the associate's certificate unless the relevant information is included in the judgment or order or the parties have agreed the times.
(iv) A bundle comprising counsel's fee notes and accounts for other disbursements.
(v) One complete set of pleadings arranged in chronological order. Where one is available a bound copy is to be preferred. To this set should be annexed any interlocutory summonses and lists of documents.
(vi) Cases to counsel to advise with his advices; opinions and instructions to counsel to settle documents and briefs to counsel with enclosures, all arranged in chronological order.
(vii) Reports and opinions of medical and other experts arranged in chronological order.
(viii) The solicitor's correspondence and attendance notes. Files should be left intact and not for the purpose of taxation divided into different sections to relate to different portions of the bill.
(ix) Any additional papers should be bundled and so labelled.

1. Assimilation of App 2 items

After April 1979	*Prior to April 1979*
Item	Items
1	1, 2, 3, 4(*b*), 6(*a*), (*b*).
2	5, 13, 14(*a*), (*b*), 15, 40 (part), 41.
3	6(*c*), 7, 8, 9, 10, 11, 12(*a*), (*b*), 16, 22(*a*), (*b*), (*c*), 25(*a*), (*b*), (*c*), 28, 30 (part), 72, 73 (part), 74, 75, 76, 77, 78, 79.
4	82(*a*), (*b*).
5	No corresponding item.
6	19, 20(*a*), (*b*), 21, 32, 33(*a*), 34.
7	29.
8	33(*b*), (*c*).
9	61, 62, 63, 64, 65, 66, 67, 68, 69, 70, 71.
10	23, 24(*a*), (*b*), 26(*a*)–(*j*), 27(*a*)–(*j*), 30 (part), 40 (part), 41, 52, 53, 54, 56, 57, 60, 73 (part), 80, 81, 84, 86, 87, 98, 99, 100.
11	90, 91, 92, 93(*a*), (*b*), 94, 95, 96(*a*), (*b*), 97.
12	36, 37, 38, 39.

2. Items in App 2 prior to April 1979 for which no item is provided in the appendix from April 1979: 4(*a*), 17, 18, 31, 35, 42(*a*), (*b*), 43, 44, 45(*a*), (*b*), 46, 47, 48, 49, 50(*a*), (*b*), (*c*), (*d*), 51, 55, 58, 59, 83, 85, 88(*a*), (*b*) and 89(*a*), (*b*).

SCHEDULE 2

In the High Court of Justice
Queen's Bench Division

Plaintiff's costs of action commenced by writ of summons

Item no		VAT	Disbursements	Profit costs
3(*d*)	[*Date*] Instructions to counsel To advise Paid counsel's fee			—
	[*Date*] Letter before action			—
3(*a*)	[*Date*] Order for service out of jurisdiction Paid oath and exhibit	£1·40		—
1(*a*)	[*Date*] Writ of summons. Paid	£25·00		—
3(*a*)	[*Date*] Substituted service Paid oath and exhibit	£1·40		— —
1(*c*)	[*Date*] Concurrent writ of summons			—

Item no		VAT	Disbursements	Profit costs
3(c)	[Date] Affidavit of service Paid oath and exhibit	£1·40		—
1(c)	[Date] Renewal of writ of summons			
6	[Date] Attending defendants Application for security			£2–£17
9	[Date] Attending to pay money into court			[Discretionary]
3(d)	[Date] Instructions to counsel to settle statement of claim Paid counsel to settle			—
6	[Date] Attending defendants Summons for time			£2 £17

3(d)	[Date]
	Instructions to counsel to settle
	   further and better particulars of
	   statement of claim
	Paid counsel to settle
				—

	[Date] Defence and counterclaim delivered			—

3(d)	[Date]
	Instructions to counsel to advise and
	   to settle request for particulars of
	   defence and counterclaim
	Paid counsel to advise
	Paid counsel to settle request
				—

	[Date] Particulars delivered			—

3(d)	[Date]
	Instructions to counsel to advise on
	   particulars and to settle reply and
	   defence to counterclaim
	Paid counsel to advise
	Paid counsel to settle reply and
	   defence
				—
				
				—

	[Date] Summons for leave to amend defence			—
3(d)	[Date] Brief to counsel Paid counsel's fee			—
7	Attending conference [for each half hour or part]			£4·00
6	[Date] Attending summons			£2–£17

Item no		VAT	Disbursements	Profit costs
	[*Date*] Amended defence delivered			—
3(*d*)	[*Date*] Instructions to counsel to settle amended statement of claim Paid counsel to settle			—
3(*b*) 3(*b*)	[*Date*] Plaintiff's list of documents Affidavit verifying Paid oath and exhibit	£1·40		— —
	[*Date*] Defendant's list of documents			—
3(*d*)	[*Date*] Instructions to counsel to advise on evidence and to settle interrogatories Paid counsel's fee to advise Paid counsel's fee to settle			—
2	[*Date*] Summons for directions			—
3(*d*)	[*Date*] Brief to counsel Paid counsel's fee			—
7	[*Date*] Attending conference [*for each half hour or part*]			£4·00
6	[*Date*] Attending summons			£2–£17
3(*b*)	[*Date*] Interrogatories delivered			—
	[*Date*] Answer to interrogatories delivered			—
	[*Date*] Action set down Paid	£15·00		—
	[*Date*] Defendant paid money into court			—
3(*d*)	[*Date*] Instructions to counsel to advise thereon Paid counsel's fee			—
3(*d*)	[*Date*] Brief on application to vary date fixed for trial Paid counsel's fee			—
6	[*Date*] Attending application			£2–£17

Item no		VAT	Disbursements	Profit costs
2	[*Date*] Summons for examination of witness [*Date*] Attending application			£2–£17
3(d) 7	[*Date*] Brief on examination Paid counsel's fee Attending conference [*for each half hour or part*]			— £4·00
6	[*Date*] Attending examination			£2–£17
3(d) 4	[*Date*] Preparing brief for hearing Copy documents prepared throughout			— —
	[*Date*] Brief delivered Paid fee			—
7	[*Date*] Attending conference [*for each half hour or part*]			£4·00
8	[*Date*] Attending hearing			£5–£21
9	[*Date*] Drawing request for payment by post			[*Discretionary*]
6	[*Date*] Drawing judgment and attending to enter			£2–£17
5	BLOCK ALLOWANCE			£20–£100
10	INSTRUCTIONS FOR TRIAL OR HEARING			[*Discretionary*]
	PAID WITNESSES			
12A	[*Date*] TAXATION PROCEDURE			[*Discretionary*]

a
Butler Machine Tool Co Ltd v Ex-Cell-O Corporation (England) Ltd

COURT OF APPEAL, CIVIL DIVISION

LORD DENNING MR, LAWTON AND BRIDGE LJJ

25th APRIL 1977

b   *Contract – Offer and acceptance – Counter-offer – Terms and conditions on which contract made – Seller offering to sell subject to terms and conditions which were to prevail over buyer's terms – Buyer offering to buy subject to own terms and conditions – Seller acknowledging receipt of buyer's order – Whether buyer's order a counter-offer – Whether seller's acknowledgment of receipt of buyer's order an acceptance of a counter-offer – Whether contract concluded on buyer's or seller's terms.*

c   On 23rd May 1969, in response to an enquiry by the buyers, the sellers made a quotation offering to sell a machine tool to the buyers for £75,535, delivery to be in ten months time. The offer was stated to be subject to certain terms and conditions which 'shall prevail over any terms and conditions in the Buyer's order'. The conditions included a price variation clause providing for the goods to be charged at the price ruling on the date of delivery. On 27th May the buyers replied by placing an order for the machine. The order was stated to

d   be subject to certain terms and conditions, which were materially different from those put forward by the sellers and which, in particular, made no provision for a variation in price. At the foot of the buyers' order there was a tear-off acknowledgment of receipt of the order stating that 'We accept your order on the Terms and Conditions stated thereon'. On 5th June the sellers completed and signed the acknowledgment and returned it to the buyers with a letter stating that the buyers' order was being entered in accordance with the

e   sellers' quotation of 23rd May. When the sellers came to deliver the machine they claimed that the price had increased by £2,892. The buyers refused to pay the increase in price and the sellers brought an action claiming that they were entitled to increase the price under the price variation clause contained in their offer. The buyers contended that the contract had been concluded on the buyers' rather than the sellers' terms and was therefore a fixed-price contract. The judge upheld the sellers' claim on the ground that the contract had been

f   concluded on the basis that the sellers' terms were to prevail since they had stipulated that in the opening offer and all subsequent negotiations had been subject to that. The buyers appealed.

Held – The appeal would be allowed for the following reasons—

(i) Applying the doctrine of offer and acceptance, the buyers' order of 27th May was a

g   counter-offer which destroyed the offer made in the sellers' quotation of 23rd May. The sellers by completing and returning the acknowledgment of the order on 5th June, which was stated to be on the buyers' terms and conditions, had accepted the counter-offer on the buyers' terms and could not therefore claim to increase the price under the price variation clause contained in their own offer. The sellers' letter of 5th June with its reference to the quotation of 23rd May was irrelevant as it merely referred to the price and identity of the

h   machine and did not operate to incorporate the sellers' terms back into the contract (see p 967 j to p 968 b, p 969 c and h, p 970 a to c and p 971 c to h, post); *Hyde v Wrench* (1840) 3 Beav 334 applied.

(ii) (per Lord Denning MR) The documents comprised in a 'battle of forms' were to be considered as a whole to discover the consensus of the parties by reasonable implication if the conflicting terms and conditions of both parties were irreconcilable, and on that basis

j   the acknowledgment of the order of 5th June was the decisive document since it made it clear that the contract was to be on the buyers' and not the sellers' terms (see p 968 d e and p 969 a to c, post); *Brogden v Metropolitan Railway Co* (1877) 2 App Cas 666 applied.

Notes

For counter-offers, see 9 Halsbury's Laws (4th Edn) para 258, and for difficulties which may

arise when each party purports to contract on his own standard conditions, see ibid para
285. For cases on offer, and the communication and termination of offer generally, see 12   **a**
Digest (Reissue) 60, 70–71, 313, 357–361.

Cases referred to in judgments

British Road Services Ltd v Arthur V Crutchley & Co Ltd [1968] 1 All ER 811, [1968] 1 Lloyd's
  Rep 271, CA, 3 Digest (Reissue) 444, 2993.

Brogden v Metropolitan Railway Co (1877) 2 App Cas 666, HL, 12 Digest (Reissue) 60, 313.   **b**

Hyde v Wrench (1840) 3 Beav 334, 4 Jur 1106, 49 ER 132, 12 Digest (Reissue) 71, 360.

New Zealand Shipping Co Ltd v AM Satterthwaite & Co Ltd [1974] 1 All ER 1015, [1975] AC
  154, [1974] 2 WLR 865, [1974] 1 Lloyd's Rep 534, [1974] 1 NZLR 505, PC, Digest Cont
  Vol D) 114, *99a.

Trollope & Colls Ltd and Holland & Hannen and Cubitts Ltd, trading as Nuclear Civil Constructors
  (a firm) v Atomic Power Constructions Ltd [1962] 3 All ER 1035, [1963] 1 WLR 333, Digest   **c**
  (Cont Vol A) 72, 22a.

Cases also cited

Davies (A) & Co (Shopfitters) Ltd v William Old Ltd (1969) 67 LGR 395.

Stevenson v McLean (1880) 5 QBD 346, 49 LJQB 401.

Appeal   **d**

The appellants, Ex-Cell-O Corpn (England) Ltd ('the buyers'), appealed against the
judgment of Thesiger J given on 12th February 1976 in the Queen's Bench Division at
Leeds ordering the buyers to pay the respondents, Butler Machine Tool Co Ltd ('the
sellers'), damages of £2,892 and interest of £1,410 being the amount claimed by the sellers
in respect of the increase in price of a 'Butler' double column plano-miller machine tool
sold by the sellers to the buyers under a contract of sale which, the sellers alleged, provided   **e**
for the goods to be charged at the price ruling at the date of delivery. The grounds of
appeal were, inter alia, that the judge was wrong in law in holding that the conditions of
sale set out in the sellers' quotation and which included the price variation clause formed
part of the contract between the buyers and the sellers. The facts are set out in the
judgment of Lord Denning MR.

  f

John Griffiths QC and *Rex Tedd* for the buyers.
Lionel Scott for the sellers.

LORD DENNING MR. This case is a 'battle of forms'. The suppliers of a machine,
Butler Machine Tool Co Ltd ('the sellers'), on 23rd May 1969 quoted a price for a machine
tool of £75,535. Delivery was to be given in ten months. On the back of the quotation   **g**
there were terms and conditions. One of them was a price variation clause. It provided for
an increase in the price if there was an increase in the costs and so forth. The machine tool
was not delivered until November 1970. By that time costs had increased so much that the
sellers claimed an additional sum of £2,892 as due to them under the price variation clause.

The buyers, Ex-Cell-O Corpn, rejected the excess charge. They relied on their own
terms and conditions. They said: 'We did not accept the sellers' quotation as it was. We   **h**
gave an order for the self-same machine at the self-same price, but on the back of our order
we had our own terms and conditions. Our terms and conditions did not contain any price
variation clause.'

The judge held that the price variation clause in the sellers' form continued through the
whole dealing and so the sellers were entitled to rely on it. He was clearly influenced by
a passage in the 24th edition of Anson's Law of Contract[1], of which the editor is Professor   **j**
Guest; and also by a passage in Treitel's The Law of Contract[2]. The judge said that the
sellers did all that was necessary and reasonable to bring the price variation clause to the

---

1 (1975), pp 37–38
2 4th Edn (1975), p 15

notice of the buyers. He thought that the buyers would not 'browse over the conditions'
a of the sellers, and then, by printed words in their (the buyers') document, trap the sellers
into a fixed price contract.

I am afraid that I cannot agree with the suggestion that the buyers 'trapped' the sellers
in any way. Neither party called any oral evidence before the judge. The case was decided
on the documents alone. I propose therefore to go through them.

On 23rd May 1969 the sellers offered to deliver one 'Butler' double column plano-miller
b for the total price of £75,535, 'DELIVERY: 10 months (Subject to confirmation at time of
ordering) Other terms and conditions are on the reverse of this quotation'. On the back
there were 16 conditions in small print starting with this general condition:

> 'All orders are accepted only upon and subject to the terms set out in our quotation
> and the following conditions. These terms and conditions shall prevail over any
> terms and conditions in the Buyer's order.'

c
Clause 3 was the price variation clause. It said:

> '. . . Prices are based on present day costs of manufacture and design and having
> regard to the delivery quoted and uncertainty as to the cost of labour, materials etc.
> during the period of manufacture, we regret that we have no alternative but to make
> it a condition of acceptance of order that goods will be charged at prices ruling upon
d > date of delivery.'

The buyers, Ex-Cell-O, replied on 27th May 1969 giving an order in these words: 'Please
supply on terms and conditions as below and overleaf.' Below there was a list of the goods
ordered, but there were differences from the quotation of the sellers in these respects: (i)
there was an additional item for the cost of installation, £3,100; (ii) there was a different
e delivery date: instead of 10 months, it was 10 to 11 months. Overleaf there were different
terms as to the cost of carriage, in that it was to be paid to the delivery address of the buyers;
whereas the sellers' terms were ex warehouse. There were different terms as to the right
to cancel for late delivery. The buyers in their conditions reserved the right to cancel if
delivery was not made by the agreed date, whereas the sellers in their conditions said that
cancellation of order due to late delivery would not be accepted.
f On the foot of the buyers' order there was a tear-off slip:

> 'ACKNOWLEDGEMENT: Please sign and return to EX-CELL-O CORP. (England) LTD. We
> accept your order on the Terms and Conditions stated thereon—and undertake to
> deliver by . . . Date . . . Signed . . .'

In that slip the delivery date and signature were left blank ready to be filled in by the sellers.
g On 5th June 1969 the sellers wrote this letter to the buyers:

> 'We have pleasure in acknowledging receipt of your official order dated 27th May
> covering the supply of one 'Butler' Double Column Plano-Miller . . . This is being
> entered in accordance with our revised quotation of 23rd May for delivery in 10/11
> months, ie March/April, 1970. We return herewith, duly completed, your
> acknowledgement of order form.'
h
They enclosed the acknowledgment form duly filled in with the delivery date, March/April
1970, and signed by the Butler Machine Tool Co Ltd.

No doubt a contract was then concluded. But on what terms? The sellers rely on their
general conditions and on their last letter which said 'in accordance with our revised
quotation of 23rd May' (which had on the back the price variation clause). The buyers rely
j on the acknowledgment signed by the sellers which accepted the buyers' order 'on the
terms and conditions stated thereon' (which did not include a price variation clause).

If those documents are analysed in our traditional method, the result would seem to me
to be this: the quotation of 23rd May 1969 was an offer by the sellers to the buyers
containing the terms and conditions on the back. The order of 27th May 1969 purported
to be an acceptance of that offer in that it was for the same machine at the same price, but

it contained such additions as to cost of installation, date of delivery and so forth, that it was
in law a rejection of the offer and constituted a counter-offer. That is clear from *Hyde v*
Wrench[1]. As Megaw J said in *Trollope & Colls Ltd v Atomic Power Constructions Ltd*[2]: '... the
counter-offer kills the original offer.' The letter of the sellers of 5th June 1969 was an
acceptance of that counter-offer, as is shown by the acknowledgment which the sellers
signed and returned to the buyers. The reference to the quotation of 23rd May 1969
referred only to the price and identity of the machine.

To go on with the facts of the case. The important thing is that the sellers did not keep
the contractual date of delivery which was March/April 1970. The machine was ready
about September 1970 but by that time the buyers' production schedule had to be re-
arranged as they could not accept delivery until November 1970. Meanwhile the sellers
had invoked the price increase clause. They sought to charge the buyers an increase due to
the rise in costs between 27th May 1969 (when the order was given) and 1st April 1970
(when the machine ought to have been delivered). It came to £2,892. The buyers rejected
the claim. The judge held that the sellers were entitled to the sum of £2,892 under the
price variation clause. He did not apply the traditional method of analysis by way of offer
and counter-offer. He said that in the quotation of 23rd May 1969 'one finds the price
variation clause appearing under a most emphatic heading stating that it is a term or
condition that is to prevail'. So he held that it did prevail.

I have much sympathy with the judge's approach to this case. In many of these cases our
traditional analysis of offer, counter-offer, rejection, acceptance and so forth is out-of-date.
This was observed by Lord Wilberforce in *New Zealand Shipping Co Ltd v A M*
Satterthwaite[3]. The better way is to look at all the documents passing between the parties
and glean from them, or from the conduct of the parties, whether they have reached
agreement on all material points, even though there may be differences between the forms
and conditions printed on the back of them. As Lord Cairns LC said in *Brogden v*
Metropolitan Railway Co[4]:

> ... 'there may be a *consensus* between the parties far short of a complete mode of
> expressing it, and that *consensus* may be discovered from letters or from other
> documents of an imperfect and incomplete description.'

Applying this guide, it will be found that in most cases when there is a 'battle of forms'
there is a contract as soon as the last of the forms is sent and received without objection
being taken to it. That is well observed in Benjamin on Sale[5]. The difficulty is to decide
which form, or which part of which form, is a term or condition of the contract. In some
cases the battle is won by the man who fires the last shot. He is the man who puts forward
the latest term and conditions: and, if they are not objected to by the other party, he may
be taken to have agreed to them. Such was *British Road Services Ltd v Arthur V Crutchley*
& Co Ltd[6] per Lord Pearson; and the illustration given by Professor Guest in Anson's Law
of Contract[7] where he says that 'the terms of the contract consist of the terms of the offer
subject to the modifications contained in the acceptance'. That may however go too far.
In some cases, however, the battle is won by the man who gets the blow in first. If he offers
to sell at a named price on the terms and conditions stated on the back and the buyer orders
the goods purporting to accept the offer on an order form with his own different terms and
conditions on the back, then, if the difference is so material that it would affect the price,
the buyer ought not to be allowed to take advantage of the difference unless he draws it
specifically to the attention of the seller. There are yet other cases where the battle depends
on the shots fired on both sides. There is a concluded contract but the forms vary. The

1   (1840) 3 Beav 334
2   [1962] 3 All ER 1035 at 1038, [1963] 1 WLR 333 at 337
3   [1974] 1 All ER 1015 at 1019–1020, [1975] AC 154 at 167
4   (1877) 2 App Cas 666 at 672
5   Benjamin on the Sale of Goods (9th Edn, 1974), pp 84–85
6   [1968] 1 All ER 811 at 816–817, [1968] 1 Lloyd's Rep 271 at 281–282
7   24th Edn (1975), pp 37–38

a terms and conditions of both parties are to be construed together. If they can be reconciled so as to give a harmonious result, all well and good. If differences are irreconcilable, so that they are mutually contradictory, then the conflicting terms may have to be scrapped and replaced by a reasonable implication.

b In the present case the judge thought that the sellers in their original quotation got their blow in first; especially by the provision that 'These terms and conditions shall prevail over any terms and conditions in the Buyer's order'. It was so emphatic that the price variation clause continued through all the subsequent dealings and that the buyer must be taken to have agreed to it. I can understand that point of view. But I think that the documents have to be considered as a whole. And, as a matter of construction, I think the acknowledgment of 5th June 1969 is the decisive document. It makes it clear that the contract was on the buyers' terms and not on the sellers' terms: and the buyers' terms did not include a price variation clause.

c I would therefore allow the appeal and enter judgment for the buyers.

LAWTON LJ. The modern commercial practice of making quotations and placing orders with conditions attached, usually in small print, is indeed likely, as in this case, to produce a battle of forms. The problem is how should that battle be conducted? The view taken by the judge was that the battle should extend over a wide area and the court should d do its best to look into the minds of the parties and make certain assumptions. In my judgment, the battle has to be conducted in accordance with set rules. It is a battle more on classical 18th century lines when convention decided who had the right to open fire first rather than in accordance with the modern concept of attrition.

The rules relating to a battle of this kind have been known for the past 130-odd years. They were set out by the then Master of the Rolls, Lord Langdale, in *Hyde v Wrench*[1], and e Lord Denning MR has already referred to them; and, if anyone should have thought they were obsolescent, Megaw J in *Trollope & Colls Ltd v Atomic Power Constructions Ltd*[2] called attention to the facts that those rules are still in force.

When those rules are applied to this case, in my judgment, the answer is obvious. The sellers started by making an offer. That was in their quotation. The small print was headed by the following words:

f 'GENERAL. All orders are accepted only upon and subject to the terms set out in our quotation and the following conditions. These terms and conditions shall prevail over any terms and conditions in the Buyer's order.'

That offer was not accepted. The buyers were only prepared to have one of these very expensive machines on their own terms. Their terms had very material differences in g them from the terms put forward by the sellers. They could not be reconciled in any way. In the language of art 7 of the Uniform Law on the Formation of Contracts for the International Sale of Goods[3] they did materially alter the terms set out in the offer made by the sellers.

As I understand *Hyde v Wrench*[1] and the cases which have followed, the consequence of placing the order in that way, if I may adopt Megaw J's words[4], was 'to kill the quotation'. h It follows that the court has to look at what happened after the buyers made their counter-offer. By letter dated 4th June 1969 the sellers' acknowledged receipt of the counter-offer, and they went on in this way: 'Details of this order have been passed to our Halifax works for attention and a formal acknowledgement of order will follow in due course.' That is clearly a reference to the printed tear-off slip which was at the bottom of the buyers'

j

1 (1840) 3 Beav 334
2 [1962] 3 All ER 1035, [1963] 1 WLR 333
3 See Uniform Laws on International Sales Act 1967, s 2, Sch 2, art 7(2)
4 *Trollope & Colls Ltd v Atomic Power Constructions Ltd* [1962] 3 All ER 1035 at 1038, [1963] 1 WLR 333 at 337

counter-offer. By letter dated 5th June 1969 the sales office manager at the sellers' Halifax factory completed that tear-off slip and sent it back to the buyers.

It is true, as counsel for the sellers has reminded us, that the return of that printed slip was accompanied by a letter which had this sentence in it: 'This is being entered in accordance with our revised quotation of 23rd May for delivery in 10/11 months.' I agree with Lord Denning MR that, in a business sense, that refers to the quotation as to the price and the identity of the machine, and it does not bring into the contract the small print conditions on the back of the quotation. Those small print conditions had disappeared from the story. That was when the contract was made. At that date it was a fixed price contract without a price escalation clause.

As I pointed out in the course of argument to counsel for the sellers, if the letter of 5th June which accompanied the form acknowledging the terms which the buyers had specified had amounted to a counter-offer, then in my judgment the parties never were ad idem. It cannot be said that the buyers accepted the counter-offer by reason of the fact that ultimately they took physical delivery of the machine. By the time they took physical delivery of the machine, they had made it clear by correspondence that they were not accepting that there was any price escalation clause in any contract which they had made with the plaintiffs.

I agree with Lord Denning MR that this appeal should be allowed.

BRIDGE LJ. Schedule 2 to the Uniform Laws on International Sales Act 1967 is headed 'The Uniform Law on the Formation of Contracts for the International Sale of Goods'. To the limited extent that that schedule is already in force in the law of this country, it would not in any event be applicable to the contract which is the subject of this appeal because that was not a contract of international sale of goods as defined in that statute.

We have heard, nevertheless, an interesting discussion on the question of the extent to which the terms of art 7 of Sch 2 are mirrored in the common law of England today. No difficulty arises about para 1 of the article, which provides:

'An acceptance containing additions, limitations or other modifications shall be a rejection of the offer and shall constitute a counter-offer.'

But para 2 of the article is in these terms:

'However, a reply to an offer which purports to be an acceptance but which contains additional or different terms which do not materially alter the terms of the offer shall constitute an acceptance unless the offeror promptly objects to the discrepancy; if he does not so object, the terms of the contract shall be the terms of the offer with the modifications contained in the acceptance.'

For my part, I consider it both unnecessary and undesirable to express any opinion on the question whether there is any difference between the principle expressed in that para 2 and the principle which would prevail in the common law of England today without reference to that paragraph, but it was presumably a principle analogous to that expressed in para 2 of art 7 which the editor of the 24th edition of Anson's Law of Contract[1], Professor Guest, had in mind in the passage from that work which was quoted in the judgment of Lord Denning MR. On any view, that passage goes a good deal further than the principle expressed in art 7 of Sch 2 to the 1967 Act, and I entirely agree with Lord Denning MR that it goes too far.

But, when one turns from those interesting and abstruse areas of the law to the plain facts of this case, this case is nothing like the kind of case with which either the makers of the convention which embodied art 7 of Sch 2 or the editor of the 24th edition of Anson had in mind in the passages referred to, because this is a case which on its facts is plainly governed by what I may call the classical doctrine that a counter-offer amounts to a rejection of an offer and puts an end to the effect of the offer.

1   (1975) pp 37–38

The first offer between the parties here was the seller's quotation dated 23rd May 1969.
a The conditions of sale in the small print on the back of that document, as well as embodying the price variation clause, to which reference has been made in the judgments already delivered, embodied a number of other important conditions. There was a condition providing that orders should in no circumstances be cancelled without the written consent of the sellers and should only be cancelled on terms which indemnified the sellers against loss. There was a condition that the sellers should not be liable for any loss
b or damage from delay however caused. There was a condition purporting to limit the sellers' liability for damage due to defective workmanship or materials in the goods sold. And there was a condition providing that the buyers should be responsible for the cost of delivery.

When one turns from that document to the buyers' order of 27th May 1969, it is perfectly clear not only that that order was a counter-offer but that it did not purport in any
c way to be an acceptance of the terms of the sellers' offer dated 23rd May. In addition, when one compares the terms and conditions of the buyers' offer, it is clear that they are in fact contrary in a number of vitally important respects to the conditions of sale in the sellers' offer. Amongst the buyers' proposed conditions are conditions that the price of the goods shall include the cost of delivery to the buyers' premises, that the buyers shall be entitled to cancel for any delay in delivery, and a condition giving the buyers a right to reject if on
d inspection the goods are found to be faulty in any respect.

The position then was, when the sellers received the buyers' offer of 27th May, that that was an offer open to them to accept or reject. They replied in two letters dated 4th and 5th June respectively. The letter of 4th June was an informal acknowledgment of the order, and the letter of 5th June enclosed the formal acknowledgment, as Lord Denning MR and Lawton LJ have said, embodied in the printed tear-off slip taken from the order itself and
e including the perfectly clear and unambiguous sentence: 'We accept your order on the Terms and Conditions stated thereon.' On the face of it, at that moment of time, there was a complete contract in existence, and the parties were ad idem as to the terms of the contract embodied in the buyers' order.

Counsel for the sellers has struggled manfully to say that the contract concluded on those terms and conditions was in some way overruled or varied by the references in the two
f letters dated 4th and 5th June to the quotation of 23rd May 1969. The first refers to the machinery being as quoted on 23rd May. The second letter says that the order has been entered in accordance with the quotation of 23rd May. I agree with Lord Denning MR and Lawton LJ that that language has no other effect than to identify the machinery and to refer to the prices quoted on 23rd May. But on any view, at its highest, the language is equivocal and wholly ineffective to override the plain and unequivocal terms of the printed
g acknowledgment of order which was enclosed with the letter of 5th June. Even if that were not so and if counsel for the sellers could show that the sellers' acknowledgment of the order was itself a further counter-offer, I suspect that he would be in considerable difficulties in showing that any later circumstance amounted to an acceptance of that counter-offer in the terms of the original quotation of 23rd May by the buyers. But I do not consider that question further because I am content to rest on the view that there is
h nothing in the letter of 5th June which overrides the plain effect of the acceptance of the order on the terms and conditions stated thereon.

I too would allow the appeal and enter judgment for the buyers.

Appeal allowed. Leave to appeal to the House of Lords refused.

j Solicitors: *Tringhams*, agents for *Harvey Ingram*, Leicester (for the buyers); *Wood, Nash and Winter's*, agents for *Wilkinson, Woodward & Ludlam*, Halifax (for the sellers).

Sumra Green   Barrister.

Gibson v Manchester City Council   a

HOUSE OF LORDS

LORD DIPLOCK, LORD EDMUND-DAVIES, LORD FRASER OF TULLYBELTON, LORD RUSSELL OF KILLOWEN AND LORD KEITH OF KINKEL

24th JANUARY, 8th MARCH 1979

Contract – Offer and acceptance – Offer – Sale of land – Council informing tenant of council house b
that council 'may be prepared to sell' house to him – Tenant invited 'to make a formal application
to buy' – Tenant completing and returning application to purchase – Council later refusing to
proceed with application following change of policy – Whether council had made an offer to sell to
tenant – Whether parties had concluded a binding contract.

In September 1970 a city council adopted a policy of selling council houses to its tenants.   c
The respondent who was renting a council house applied on a printed form supplied by the
council for details of the price of the house and mortgage terms available from the
council. On 10th February 1971 the city treasurer wrote to the respondent that the council
'may be prepared to sell the house to you at the purchase price of £2,725 less 20% = £2,180
(freehold)'. The letter then gave details of the mortgage likely to be made available to the
respondent and went on: 'If you would like to make formal application to buy your   d
Council house please complete the enclosed application form and return it to me as soon
as possible.' The application form was headed 'Application to buy a council house' and
concluded with a statement: 'I . . . now wish to purchase my Council house. The above
answers [ie the answers in the application form] are correct and I agree that they shall be
the basis of the arrangements regarding the purchase . . .' The respondent completed the
application form except for the purchase price and returned it to the council on 5th   e
March. On 18th March the respondent wrote to the council: 'I would be obliged if you
will carry on with the purchase as per my application already in your possession.' Before
contracts were prepared and exchanged there was a change in control of the council
following the local government elections in May 1971 and on 7th July the council resolved
to discontinue the scheme for the sale of council houses forthwith and to proceed only with
those sales where there had been an exchange of contracts. On 27th July the council wrote   f
to the respondent to advise him that the council was unable to proceed further with his
application to purchase. The respondent brought an action alleging that there was a
binding contract for the sale of the house constituted by an offer contained in the city
treasurer's letter of 10th February 1971 and his acceptance of it by the return of the
application form on 5th March and his letter of 18th March, and claiming specific
performance of the contract. The county court judge and, on appeal, the Court of Appeal[a]   g
held that there was a concluded contract for the sale of the house by the council and
ordered specific performance. The council appealed.

Held – The parties had not concluded a binding contract because the council had never
made an offer capable of acceptance, since the statements in the city treasurer's letter of
10th February that the council 'may be prepared to sell' and inviting the respondent 'to   h
make formal application to buy' were not an offer to sell but merely an invitation to
treat. The respondent was therefore not entitled to specific performance and accordingly
the appeal would be allowed (see p 974 f g, p 975 h j, p 976 e and g, p 978 g h, p 980 e f and
h j and p 981 a, post).

Decision of the Court of Appeal, Civil Division [1978] 2 All ER 583 reversed.

Notes   j

For the formation of contracts for the sale of land, see 34 Halsbury's Laws (3rd Edn) 205,
para 342, and for cases on the subject, see 40 Digest (Repl) 11–14, 1–38.

---

a   [1978] 2 All ER 583

Cases referred to in opinions

a *Brogden v Metropolitan Railway Co* (1877) 2 App Cas 666, HL, 12 Digest (Reissue) 60, 313.

Clarke v Earl of Dunraven, The Satanita [1897] AC 59, 66 LJP 1, 75 LT 337, 8 Asp MLC 190, HL, 12 Digest (Reissue) 85, 436.

Hyde v Wrench (1840) 3 Beav 334, 4 Jur 1106, 49 ER 132, 12 Digest (Reissue) 71, 360.

Stevenson v McLean (1880) 5 QBD 346, 49 LJQB 701, 42 LT 897, 12 Digest (Reissue) 71, 363.

Storer v Manchester City Council [1974] 3 All ER 824, [1974] 1 WLR 1403, 73 LGR 1, CA,
b   Digest (Cont Vol D) 793, 26a.

Appeal

This was an appeal by the defendants, Manchester City Council, against a decision of the Court of Appeal[1] (Lord Denning MR and Ormrod LJ, Geoffrey Lane LJ dissenting), affirming an order made by his Honour Judge Bailey, sitting in the Manchester County *c* Court on 15th December 1976, whereby he ordered specific performance of a contract for the sale by the council to the plaintiff, Robert Gibson, of the freehold interest in a dwelling-house known as 174 Charlestown Road, Blackley, Manchester, owned by the council. The facts are set out in the opinion of Lord Diplock.

H E Francis QC and *A W Simpson* for the council.
d *George Carman QC* and *Bruce Caulfield* for Mr Gibson.

Their Lordships took time for consideration.

8th March. The following opinions were delivered.

e **LORD DIPLOCK.** My Lords, this is an action for specific performance of what is claimed to be a contract for the sale of land. The only question in the appeal is of a kind with which the courts are very familiar. It is whether in the correspondence between the parties there can be found a legally enforceable contract for the sale by the Manchester Corporation to Mr Gibson of the dwelling-house of which he was the occupying tenant at the relevant time in 1971. That question is one that, in my view, can be answered by *f* applying to the particular documents relied on by Mr Gibson as constituting the contract, well settled, indeed elementary, principles of English law. This being so, it is not the sort of case in which leave would have been likely to be granted to appeal to your Lordships' House, but for the fact that it is a test case. The two documents principally relied on by Mr Gibson were in standard forms used by the council in dealing with applications from tenants of council houses to purchase the freehold of their homes under a scheme that had *g* been adopted by the council during a period when it was under Conservative Party control. Political control passed to the Labour Party as a result of the local government elections held in May 1971. The scheme was then abandoned. It was decided that no more council houses should be sold to any tenant with whom a legally binding contract of sale had not already been concluded. At the date of this decision there were a considerable number of tenants, running into hundreds, whose applications to purchase the houses *h* which they occupied had reached substantially the same stage as that of Mr Gibson. The two documents in the same standard form as those on which he principally relies had passed between each one of them and the council. So their rights too are likely to depend on the result of this appeal.

My Lords, the contract of which specific performance is sought to be enforced is a contract for the sale of land. It is thus subject to the requirements as to writing laid down *j* in s 40 of the Law of Property Act 1925; but nothing turns on this since the only contract that is alleged is one made by letters and accompanying documents passing between the parties. The outcome of this appeal depends on their true construction.

In the Manchester County Court where the action started, the case was pleaded in the

---

1   [1978] 2 All ER 583, [1978] 1 WLR 520

conventional way. The particulars of claim alleged an offer in writing by the council to sell
the freehold interest in the house to Mr Gibson at a price of £2,180 and an acceptance in   *a*
writing of that offer by Mr Gibson. The judge (his Honour Judge Bailey) followed the
same conventional approach to the question that fell to be decided. He looked to see
whether there was an offer of sale and an acceptance. He held that, on their true
construction, the documents relied on as such in the particulars of claim did amount to an
offer and an acceptance respectively and so consituted a legally enforceable contract. He
ordered specific performance of an open contract for the sale to Mr Gibson of the freehold   *b*
interest in the house at the price of £2,180.

The council's appeal against this judgment was dismissed by a majority of the Court of
Appeal[1] (Lord Denning MR and Ormrod LJ); Geoffrey Lane LJ dissented. Lord Denning
MR rejected what I have described as the conventional approach of looking to see whether
on the true construction of the documents relied on there can be discerned an offer and
acceptance. One ought, he said, to 'look at the correspondence as a whole and at the   *c*
conduct of the parties and see therefrom whether the parties have come to an agreement
on everything that was material'. This approach, which in referring to the conduct of the
parties where there is no allegation of part performance appears to me to overlook the
provisions of s 40 of the Law of Property Act 1925, led him however to the conclusion that
there should be imported into the agreement to be specifically performed additional
conditions, against use except as a private dwelling-house and against advertising and a   *d*
restriction not to sell or lease the property for five years. These are conditions which would
not be implied by law in an open contract for the sale of land. The reason for so varying
the county court judge's order was that clauses in these terms were included in the standard
form of 'Agreement for Sale of a Council House' which, as appears from the earlier case of
Storer v Manchester City Council[2], was entered into by the council and council tenants whose
applications to purchase the freehold of their council house reached the stage at which   *e*
contracts were exchanged. There was, however, no reference to this standard form of
agreement in any of the documents said to constitute the contract relied on in the instant
case, nor was there any evidence that Mr Gibson had knowledge of its terms at or before the
time that the alleged contract was concluded.

Ormrod LJ, who agreed with Lord Denning MR, adopted a similar approach but he did
also deal briefly with the construction of the document relied on by Mr Gibson as an   *f*
unconditional offer of sale by the council. On this he came to the same conclusion as the
county court judge.

Geoffrey Lane LJ in a dissenting judgment, which for my part I find convincing,
adopted the conventional approach. He found that on the true construction of the
documents relied on as constituting the contract, there never was an offer by the council
acceptance of which by Mr Gibson was capable in law of constituting a legally enforceable   *g*
contract. It was but a step in the negotiations for a contract which, owing to the change in
the political complexion of the council, never reached fruition.

My Lords, there may be certain types of contract, though I think they are exceptional,
which do not fit easily into the normal analysis of a contract as being constituted by offer
and acceptance; but a contract alleged to have been made by an exchange of correspondence
between the parties in which the successive communications other than the first are in   *h*
reply to one another is not one of these. I can see no reason in the instant case for departing
from the conventional approach of looking at the handful of documents relied on as
constituting the contract sued on and seeing whether on their true construction there is to
be found in them a contractual offer by the council to sell the house to Mr Gibson and an
acceptance of that offer by Mr Gibson. I venture to think that it was by departing from this
conventional approach that the majority of the Court of Appeal was led into error.   *j*

The genesis of the relevant negotiations in the instant case is a form filled in by Mr
Gibson on 28th November 1970 enquiring what would be the price of buying his council

---

1   [1978] 2 All ER 583, [1978] 1 WLR 520
2   [1974] 3 All ER 824, [1974] 1 WLR 1403

house at 174 Charlestown Road, Blackley, and expressing his interest in obtaining a
a mortgage from the council. The form was a detachable part of a brochure which had been
circulated by the council to tenants who had previously expressed an interest in buying
their houses. It contained details of a new scheme for selling council houses that had been
recently adopted by the council. The scheme provided for a sale at market value less a
discount dependent on the length of time the purchaser had been a council tenant. This,
in the case of Mr Gibson, would have amounted to 20%. The scheme also provided for the
b provision by the council of advances on mortgage which might amount to as much as the
whole of the purchase price.

    As a result of that enquiry Mr Gibson's house was inspected by the council's valuer and
on 10th February 1971 the letter which is relied on by Mr Gibson as the offer by the council
to sell the house to him was sent from the city treasurer's department. It was in the
following terms:

c   'Dear Sir,

'Purchase of Council House

'Your Reference Number 82463 03

    'I refer to your request for details of the cost of buying your Council house. *The
Corporation may be prepared to sell the house to you at the purchase price of £2,725 less
20% = £2,180 (freehold).*

d

'Maximum mortgage the Corporation may grant:

                                  £2,177 repayable over 20 years.

'Annual fire insurance premium: £2·45

'Monthly Repayment charge calculated by:—

    '(i) flat rate repayment method: £19·02

e

'If you wish to pay off some of the purchase price at the start and therefore require a
mortgage for less than the amount quoted above, the monthly instalment will
change; in these circumstances, I will supply new figures on request. The above
repayment figures apply so long as the interest rate charged on home loans is 8½%.
f The interest rate will be subject to variation by the Corporation after giving not less
than three months' written notice, and if it changes, there will be an adjustment to the
monthly instalment payable. This letter should not be regarded as firm offer of a
mortgage.

    *'If you would like to make formal application to buy your Council house, please complete the
enclosed application form and return it to me as soon as possible.*

'Yours faithfully,

'(Sgd) H. R. Page

'City Treasurer

g

'Mr. Robert Gibson.'

    My Lords, the words I have italicised seem to me, as they seemed to Geoffrey Lane LJ,
h to make it quite impossible to construe this letter as a contractual offer capable of being
converted into a legally enforceable open contract for the sale of land by Mr Gibson's
written acceptance of it. The words 'may be prepared to sell' are fatal to this; so is the
invitation, not, be it noted, to accept the offer, but 'to make formal application to buy' on
the enclosed application form. It is, to quote Geoffrey Lane LJ, a letter setting out the
financial terms on which it may be the council would be prepared to consider a sale and
j purchase in due course.

    Both Ormrod LJ and the county court judge, in reaching the conclusion that this letter
was a firm offer to sell the freehold interest in the house for £2,180, attached importance
to the fact that the second paragraph, dealing with the financial details of the mortgage of
which Mr Gibson had asked for particulars, stated expressly, 'This letter should not be
regarded as a firm offer of a mortgage'. The necessary implication from this, it is suggested,

is that the first paragraph of the letter *is* to be regarded as a firm offer to sell despite the fact that this is plainly inconsistent with the express language of that paragraph. My Lords, *a* with great respect, this surely must be fallacious. If the final sentence had been omitted the wording of the second paragraph, unlike that of the first, with its use of the indicative mood in such expressions as 'the interest rate *will* change', might have been understood by council tenants to whom it was addressed as indicating a firm offer of a mortgage of the amount and on the terms for repayment stated if the council were prepared to sell the house at the stated price. But, whether or not this be the explanation of the presence of the *b* last sentence in the second paragraph, it cannot possibly affect the plain meaning of the words used in the first paragraph.

Mr Gibson did fill in the application form enclosed with this letter. It was in three sections: section A headed 'Application to buy a council house', section B 'Application for a loan to buy a council house', and section C 'Certificate to be completed by all applicants'. He left blank the space for the purchase price in section A and sent the form to the council *c* on 5th March 1971 with a covering letter in which he requested the council either to undertake at their own expense to carry out repairs to the tarmac path forming part of the premises or to make a deduction from the purchase price to cover the cost of repairs. The letter also intimated that Mr Gibson would like to make a down payment of £500 towards the purchase price instead of borrowing the whole amount on mortgage. In reply to the request made in this letter the council, by letter of 12th March 1971, said that the condition *d* of the property had been taken into consideration in fixing the purchase price and that repairs to the tarmac by the council could not be authorised at this stage. This letter was acknowledged by Mr Gibson by his letter to the council of 18th March 1971 in which he asked the council to 'carry on with the purchase as per my application already in your possession'.

My Lords, the application form and letter of 18th March 1971 were relied on by Mr *e* Gibson as an unconditional acceptance of the council's offer to sell the house; but this cannot be so unless there was a contractual offer by the council available for acceptance, and, for the reason already given I am of opinion that there was none. It is unnecessary to consider whether the application form and Mr Gibson's letters of 5th and 18th March 1971 are capable of amounting to a contractual offer by him to purchase the freehold interest in the house at a price of £2,180 on the terms of an open contract, for there is no suggestion *f* that, even if it were, it was ever accepted by the council. Nor would it ever have been even if there had been no change in the political control of the council, as the policy of the council before the change required the incorporation in all agreements for sale of council houses to tenants of the conditions referred by Lord Denning MR in his judgment and other conditions inconsistent with an open contract.

I therefore feel compelled to allow the appeal. One can sympathise with Mr Gibson's *g* disappointment on finding that his expectations that he would be able to buy his council house at 20% below its market value in the autumn of 1970 cannot be realised. Whether one thinks this makes it a hard case perhaps depends on the political views that one holds about council housing policy. But hard cases offer a strong temptation to let them have their proverbial consequences. It is a temptation that the judicial mind must be vigilant to resist.   *h*

LORD EDMUND-DAVIES. My Lords, this is a hard case, and we all know where hard cases can take a judge. It is also a test case, some 350 others being in a like situation to the respondent. Mr Gibson had been employed by the Manchester City Corporation for 16 years and, since March 1959, tenant of their dwelling-house, 174 Charlestown Road, Blackley. As long ago as July 1968 he had intimated to the council his desire to buy his *j* home, and to that end he had completed and sent them in the following December the form of application to purchase with which they supplied him. Events moved slowly, and in June 1970 Mr Gibson enquired when he might have a decision on his application and whether he might meanwhile be permitted to make certain improvements, including the repair of paths. It was in September 1970 that the council resolved to sell the freeholds of

their dwellings and not (as hitherto) merely leasehold interests. In October 1970, their
a housing manager wrote to Mr Gibson apologising for the delay and regretting that 'it is not
possible to indicate how long it will be before I will be able to give you the opportunity of
purchasing your house', adding that in due course the property would be valued and the
applicant informed of the result. In the following month, the council circulated those
tenants who, like Mr Gibson, had already expressed their desire to purchase their homes,
and enclosed a brochure entitled 'Full details of how you can buy your council house'. This
b began: 'The City Council are prepared to sell freehold ... any Council house ... to the
tenant of that house, providing he has been in occupation of it for at least one year', at
market value less a discount to be calculated according to the length of his occupation.
Particulars were also given about mortgage facilities.

Mr Gibson filled in and submitted to the council a form attached to the brochure and
beginning, 'Dear Sir, Please inform me of the price of buying my Council house'. The
c reply thereto, dated 10th February 1971 and signed by the city treasurer, is important as
it was the tenant's case that this consituted an offer by the council to sell. I set out its
material parts:

'Purchase of Council House

. . .

'I refer to your request for details of the cost of buying your Council house. The
d Corporation may be prepared to sell the house to you at the purchase price of £2,725
less 20% = £2,180 (freehold).

'The details which you requested about a Corporation mortgage are as follows:—

'Maximum mortgage the Corporation may grant: £2,177 repayable over 20
years ...

'This letter should not be regarded as a firm offer of a mortgage.

e 'If you would like to make formal application to buy your Council house, please
complete the enclosed application form and return it to me as soon as possible.'

The form itself, which Mr Gibson completed on 3rd March 1971, was headed:
'Application to buy a Council house and application for a mortgage'. He left the purchase
price blank, but filled in the particulars required in relation to his application for a loan.
f And he signed the certificate at the end of the form, which was worded in this way:

'I have read the explanatory leaflet [ie the brochure] on how to buy my Council
house and your letter stating the costs involved, and now wish to purchase my
Council house. The above answers are correct and I agree that they shall be the basis
of the arrangements regarding the purchase and, if appropriate, the loan between
myself and the Manchester Corporation.'

g Mr Gibson sent off that form under cover of a letter dated 5th March 1971, the opening
paragraph of which read:

'With reference to enclosed application for purchase of above property. Before the
transaction is finalised I would appreciate your comments on the following. [There
followed a complaint that, although the council's "direct works" department had
h undertaken to repair Mr Gibson's tarmac paths, nothing had been done.] I would
therefore like your assurance that Direct Works will not exclude these premises when
re-surfacing or re-laying starts, or alternatively would you deduct an amount of
money from the purchase price and I will undertake the repairs myself. Whichever
decision you arrive at I would like to make an initial cash payment of £500—so I
would be obliged if you will let me have the figures to allow for the deposit
j mentioned. I have left the purchase price blank on the application form until I hear
from you.'

On 12th March the housing manager retorted that, as the general condition of the property
had been taken into account in arriving at the price of £2,180, he could not authorise
repairing the paths. On 18th March Mr Gibson replied by a letter which was said to

constitute his acceptance of the council's alleged offer to sell and which read in this way:

> 'Reference your letter of March 12th ... In view of your remarks I would be *a*
> obliged if you will carry on with the purchase as per my application already in your
> possession.'

The council did not reply to that letter. In May 1971 the political control of the council changed hands and the scheme to sell off council houses was suspended. In July 1971 it was formally discontinued.

My Lords, it was on the basis of the foregoing documents and correspondence that Mr *b*
Gibson instituted proceedings in the county court in September 1974 for specific performance of what he, in effect, submitted was an open contract whereby the council had agreed to sell to him the freehold of his dwelling for £2,180. It was pleaded that the council had so offered by their letter of 10th February 1971 and the accompanying application form, the acceptance (as I understand) being conveyed by Mr Gibson's *c*
completing and returning that form and later 'unconditionally accepted the said offer by letter to the defendants dated 18th March 1971'. Reliance was also sought to be laid on an internal memorandum passing between two of the council's departments which was said to constitute an admission by the council that they had (presumably by *that* date) sold the freehold to Mr Gibson. It is convenient to mention also at this stage that both in the county court and in the Court of Appeal the plaintiff relied further on the fact that during 1971 *d*
the town clerk, in the course of a letter he sent a city councillor who had espoused Mr Gibson's case, had written regarding the treasurer's letter of 10th February 1971:

> 'Mr. Gibson accepted this offer, but before the papers could be passed to me for
> preparation of the formal contract the local elections intervened. Since then no more
> contracts have been prepared, pending a formal decision being taken by the present
> Council regarding the policy to be adopted in relation to the sale of Council houses . . .' *e*

It is, however, right to observe that, later in his same letter, the town clerk wrote of the unwisdom of Mr Gibson's having carried out certain alterations 'before there was a binding contract in existence', although these words may, or may not, have been intended to refer to the absence of any 'formal contract', a fact to which the writer also adverted.

The pleaded defence was simple: the council had made no offer; alternatively, if they *f*
had, Mr Gibson had not accepted it; the internal memorandum constituted no admission; and there was non-compliance with s 40 of the Law of Property Act 1925. None of these pleas found favour with the learned county court judge, who ordered specific performance.

The appeal was dismissed in extempore judgments delivered by Lord Denning MR and Ormrod LJ, with Geoffrey Lane LJ dissenting. The majority upheld the pleaded case of offer and acceptance, whereas Geoffrey Lane LJ held that it failed in limine as it was *g*
impossible to regard the council's letter of 10th February 1971 as an offer to sell. I agree with him, and for the reasons he gave. These are to be found in the reports below[1] and there would be no advantage in my repeating them. There was at best no more than an invitation by the council to tenants to apply to be allowed to purchase freeholds. I am not, however, with Geoffrey Lane LJ in treating Mr Gibson's letter of 5th March 1971 (regarding non-repair of his tarmac paths) as a counter-offer which had the effect of destroying an offer *h*
to sell, if the council had made one. On the contrary, I read it as merely exploratory of the possibility of a reduction in price in the eventuality indicated. In other words, this case is like *Stevenson v McLean*[2] and unlike *Hyde v Wrench*[3]. But that point is of no practical importance in this appeal, for, even had there been an offer, I hold that counsel for the council was right in submitting that there followed no acceptance, but nothing more than an application to buy at an unstated price, coupled with an application for a loan. *j*

The offer and acceptance approach obviously presenting certain difficulties, the majority

---

1   [1978] 2 All ER 583 at 591–592, [1978] 1 WLR 520 at 529–530
2   (1880) 5 QBD 346
3   (1840) 3 Beav 334

held in the Court of Appeal that it was not the only one, and it is undoubted that, as Cheshire and Fifoot observed[1]—

a

'. . . there are cases where the courts will certainly hold that there is a contract even though it is difficult or impossible to analyse the transaction in terms of offer and acceptance (see e.g. *Clarke v. Earl Dunraven*[2]) . . .'

Lord Denning MR said[3] that in such cases—

b

'You should look at the correspondence as a whole and at the conduct of the parties and see therefrom whether the parties have come to an agreement on everything that was material. If by their correspondence and their conduct you can see an agreement on all material terms, which was intended thenceforward to be binding, then there is a binding contract in law even though all the formalities have not been gone

c

through. For that proposition I would refer to *Brogden v Metropolitan Railway Co*[4].'

On that alternative basis, Lord Denning MR concluded that the parties had in truth contractually bound themselves. His first ground for so concluding was the nature of the correspondence between the parties, and I have already indicated why, for my part, I hold that of itself this disclosed the making of no contract. His second ground was that, in the

d belief that a contract to sell would emerge, Mr Gibson did much work in repairing and improving his house and premises. But no evidence was called as to when such work had been done, and it appears from the correspondence that, although as far back as June 1970 Mr Gibson had enquired whether he might proceed to improve the property, '. . . to the mutual benefit of the City and myself until such time as my case comes up for consideration', the council's reply in the following October gave no encouragement to the

e tenant to execute any improvements, and concluded, 'If at any time you decide to withdraw your application I should be obliged if you would let me know'. It is therefore impossible to conclude that improvements were executed on the basis that the council had already committed themselves to sell. Nor, with respect to Lord Denning MR, can it be material that, entirely unknown to Mr Gibson, the council at one stage took 174 Charlestown Road off the list of houses being maintained by them and put it on the list of 'pending sales', for

f that action had been taken in February 1971 in relation to all cases where the direct works department had been notified that sales were 'proceeding'. And it has to be observed that this alteration in the list was effected a month earlier than the time when, according to Mr Gibson's pleaded case, he accepted the council's 'offer' to sell. And, finally, the town clerk's letter to the city councillor already referred to cannot in my judgment have relevance to the matter of consensus ad idem. I have already sought to show that, read as a whole, its

g wording is equivocal; and, even were it clear, the proper question is not whether the town clerk considered that a contract had been concluded but whether this was so in fact and in law.

My Lords, there are further difficulties in Mr Gibson's way. It is common ground that, had the council not altered its policy, the parties would in the ordinary way have entered into a standard 'Agreement for Sale of a Council House', such as that concluded in *Storer v*

h *Manchester City Council*[5]. That agreement contained a provision that—

'Deeds of Conveyance or Transfer and Mortgage to be in the Corporation's standard forms including conditions against use except as a private dwelling-house and against advertising and a restriction not to sell or lease the property for five years.'

j

1   Law of Contract (9th Edn, 1976), p 26
2   [1897] AC 59
3   [1978] 2 All ER 583 at 586, [1978] 1 WLR 520 at 523
4   (1877) 2 App Cas 666
5   [1974] 3 All ER 824, [1974] 1 WLR 1403

But in the instant case no such agreement was ever prepared or referred to, and it is not suggested that Mr Gibson ever had knowledge of any special conditions, and still less that *a* he assented to them. And as these special conditions are not such as may be implied in an open contract for the sale of land, their introduction would create, from his point of view, the difficulty of non-compliance with s 40 of the Law of Property Act 1925 and therefore unenforceability. I am accordingly in respectful disagreement with Lord Denning MR, who concluded that[1]—

b

'. . . such a clause is to be imported into the correspondence; or alternatively, when granting specific performance, the court in its discretion should include such a clause. The order should be for specific performance of an agreement for the sale of a council house containing the clauses in the form in general use in Manchester. It is a contract for sale on the terms of the usual agreement for selling a council house.'

c

In the result, the alternative approach adopted in the Court of Appeal did not in my judgment avail the plaintiff.

My Lords, although this appeal could, as I have indicated, have been disposed of with considerable brevity, I have dealt with it at some length. This I have thought it right to do for three reasons. First, out of respect for the Court of Appeal, from whose majority judgment I am differing. Secondly, because this is indeed a hard case for Mr Gibson, who *d* had long wanted to buy his house and had every reason to think he would shortly be doing so on distinctly advantageous terms until the council's bombshell announcement. And, thirdly, because there are many tenants in a like situation and it is right that they should be fully informed why this appeal is being allowed. Sympathetic though one must be to Mr Gibson, for the reasons I have indicated I am forced to the conclusion that this House should uphold the dissenting judgment of Geoffrey Lane LJ and allow the appeal. *e*

LORD FRASER OF TULLYBELTON. My Lords, I have had the advantage of reading in draft the speeches prepared by my noble and learned friends, Lord Diplock and Lord Russell of Killowen. I agree with both of them and, for the reasons stated by them, I would allow this appeal. *f*

LORD RUSSELL OF KILLOWEN. My Lords, the allegation of Mr Gibson of a concluded contract for sale to him of his council house was quite simply based. He alleged an offer by the council to sell contained in the letter dated 10th February 1971 written by the city treasurer to him; he alleged acceptance by him of that offer to him by a combination of the application form and his letter dated 18th March 1971. Thus he said *g* was a contract for sale constituted, of which he claimed specific performance: a plain case of contract constituted by offer to sell capable of acceptance as such. I do not see the relevance to the case of general references to consensus in the judgments below. There was no oral evidence.

My Lords, I cannot bring myself to accept that a letter which says that the possible *h* vendor 'May be prepared to sell the house to you' can be regarded as an offer to sell capable of acceptance so as to constitute a contract. The language simply does not permit such a construction. Nor can the statement that the letter should not be regarded as a firm offer of a mortgage operate to turn into a firm offer to sell that which quite plainly it was not.

On that short ground I would allow the appeal and set aside the orders of the Court of Appeal and the county court judge, save as to costs having regard to the terms on which *j* leave to appeal was given by the Court of Appeal. For the same reasons there should be no order for costs in this House.

1   [1978] 2 All ER 583 at 588, [1978] 1 WLR 520 at 525

LORD KEITH OF KINKEL. My Lords, I have had the advantage of reading in draft
the speech of my noble and learned friend, Lord Diplock. I agree entirely with his
reasoning and conclusions, and accordingly I too would allow the appeal.

a

Appeal allowed.

Solicitors: *Sharpe Pritchard & Co* (for the council); *C M Alfille & Co,* agents for *Hargreaves*
b *& Co,* Manchester (for Mr Gibson).

Mary Rose Plummer   Barrister.

Re Tarling

c

QUEEN'S BENCH DIVISION
LORD WIDGERY CJ, GRIFFITHS AND GIBSON JJ
13th, 14th, 15th NOVEMBER, 14th DECEMBER 1978

Extradition – Habeas corpus – Fugitive – Renewal of application for habeas corpus – Grounds of
d *renewed application – Passage of time since offence – What constitutes fresh evidence – Whether*
grounds for discharge in statute grounds for purpose of renewed application for habeas corpus –
Whether applicant adducing fresh evidence – Whether applicant should be discharged under court's
general jurisdiction – Administration of Justice Act 1960, s 14(2) – Fugitive Offenders Act 1967,
s 8(3)(b).

e In December 1975 the Singapore government brought 17 charges against the applicant in
connection with his alleged activities as chairman of the board of directors of a company
in Singapore. The applicant resided in England. The Singapore government applied to
the United Kingdom government under the Fugitive Offenders Act 1967 for his arrest and
return to Singapore to be tried on the charges. Charges 12 to 16, which alleged wilful
failure to comply with the Singapore Companies Act, were the only charges which did not
f allege dishonesty. Committal proceedings held in England in January 1977 resulted in the
applicant's committal to custody for return to Singapore for trial on 15 of the charges,
including charges 12 to 16, on the ground that a prima facie case had been made out
against him. On 14th February 1977 the applicant applied to the Divisional Court for a
writ of habeas corpus for discharge from custody ('the first application'). The grounds of
that application relating to charges 12 to 16 were, inter alia, that it would be unjust and
oppressive, within s 8(3)(a)[a] of the 1967 Act, to return him by reason of the trivial nature
g of the offences, but on the first application the applicant did not rely, under s 8(3)(b), on the
passage of time since the alleged offences were committed. In July 1977 the Divisional
Court upheld the committals on charges 12 to 17 but dismissed the remaining charges.
The court refused leave to appeal to the House of Lords. On 13th October the Appeals
Committee of the House gave the applicant leave to appeal against committal on charge 17,
h and gave the Singapore government leave to appeal in respect of the charges dismissed by
the Divisional Court. The House gave judgment on the appeals in April 1978, allowing
the applicant's appeal and dismissing the appeal of the Singapore government. In the
result, the applicant remained committed in custody for return on charges 12 to 16. The
applicant then petitioned the Secretary of State to exercise his discretion under s 9 of the
1967 Act not to order his return. On 16th June the Secretary of State determined that it
j would not be unjust or oppressive to return him and issued his warrant under s 9 for the
applicant's return. On 23rd June the applicant applied a second time for habeas corpus in
respect of his committal in custody on charges 12 to 16 ('the second application'). The

---

a   Section 8(3), so far as material, is set out at p 985 *e*, post

grounds of the second application were (i) that it would be unjust and oppressive, within *a*
s 8(3)(*b*), to return him by reason of the total passage of time which had elapsed since the
offences were committed, including the passage of time which had elapsed since the first
application, because of the appeals to the House of Lords and the application to the
Secretary of State, (ii) that it would be unjust and oppressive, within s 8(3)(*a*), to return him
by reason of the triviality of the alleged offences (the applicant conceded that this was not
a new ground but contended that there was 'fresh evidence', within s 14(2)^b of the
Administration of Justice Act 1960, to support it, and furthermore, that it was part of the *b*
circumstances relevant to the new ground of passage of time under s 8(3)(*b*)), and (iii) that
the court was entitled to discharge him from detention under its general jurisdiction
because of the fresh evidence which was before the court. In support of the ground in
s 8(3)(*b*) (ie passage of time) the applicant contended that there was a presumption of
oppression by reason of the time which had elapsed from 1975 down to the date of the
second application in June 1978, which was accentuated by 'fresh evidence' of the lack of *c*
gravity of the offences, which involved no dishonesty, that the applicant had made no
personal gain from the offences, that under English law the offences were punishable by a
non-custodial sentence only, that he was not involved as a principal offender and that he
had never lived in Singapore. In support of the ground in s 8(3)(*a*) (triviality of the
offences) the applicant contended that a report of an inspector into the company's affairs
and evidence submitted to the inspector were 'fresh evidence'. The Secretary of State, *d*
supported by the Singapore government and the prison governor, contended that the
grounds for discharge in s 8(3) of the 1967 Act were not new grounds for the purpose of a
subsequent application for habeas corpus under s 14(2) of the 1960 Act, since the power to
discharge under s 8(3) was a power separate from the power to grant relief by habeas
corpus, and furthermore that the phrase 'on the same grounds' in s 14(2) referred to the
facts of the detention, and as the second application was made with reference to the same *e*
committal with which the first application was concerned, there were no new grounds,
within s 14(2) of the 1960 Act.

Held – (1) An applicant for habeas corpus was required to put forward on his initial
application the whole of the case then fairly available to him, and the doctrine of res
judicata, whereby it was an abuse of process to raise in subsequent proceedings matters *f*
which could have been litigated in earlier proceedings, applied to subsequent proceedings
for habeas corpus. Furthermore, to constitute 'fresh evidence' in support of a subsequent
application, within s 14(2) of the 1960 Act, the evidence must be not merely additional to
or different from that which was adduced before the court on the first application but
evidence which the applicant could not have, or could not reasonably have been expected
to, put forward on the first application (see p 987 *d* to *g*, post); *Johnson v Johnson* [1900] P 19,
R v Medical Appeal Tribunal (North Midland Region), ex parte Hubble [1959] 3 All ER 40 and *g*
Yat Tung Investment Co Ltd v Dao Heng Bank Ltd [1975] AC 581 applied.

(2) The reasons for discharge from custody listed in s 8(3) of the 1967 Act were 'grounds'
for the purpose of a renewed application for habeas corpus under s 14(2) of the 1960 Act
because—

(i) there was nothing in the 1967 Act which expressly or impliedly prohibited a renewed
application on those grounds. On the contrary, s 8(1) and (3) of the 1967 Act expressly *h*
provided that an application for relief under s 8 was to be made by application for habeas
corpus (see p 988 *j* to p 989 *a*, post);

(ii) an application for discharge from custody on a ground in s 8(3) was an 'application
for habeas corpus', within s 14(2) of the 1960 Act, and not merely the exercise of a statutory
power to mitigate a lawful detention separate and distinct from a habeas corpus application
(see p 988 *d* to *f*, post); *R v Governor of Brixton Prison, ex parte Savarkar* [1908–10] All ER *j*
Rep 603 distinguished;

(iii) the phrase 'on the same grounds' in s 14(2) of the 1960 Act was to be given its
ordinary meaning and was not limited to the facts of the detention, and a subsequent

---

b   Section 14(2), so far as material, is set out at p 986 *d*, post

application on a ground in s 8(3), where that ground had not been fairly available to the
a applicant on his first application, would therefore be an application made on a different
ground, within s 14(2) (see p 988 *b c*, post).

(3) The issuing of a warrant by the Secretary of State under s 9 of the 1967 Act did not
finally conclude the matter and did not, therefore, preclude a subsequent application for
habeas corpus, either under the court's general jurisdiction or under s 8(3) of the 1967 Act;
but the duty of an applicant to put forward his full case on his first application would
b ensure that only in exceptional circumstances would the court order an applicant's
discharge after a warrant for his return had been issued. It followed that the court had
jurisdiction to entertain the second application (see p 989 *b* to *d*, post).

(4) Although the applicant, in relying in the second application on the additional
passage of time since the first application, was relying on a new ground for the purpose of
s 14(2) of the 1960 Act, such new material as he had put forward in support of the second
c application did not qualify as fresh evidence, within s 14(2), because it had been either
before the court on the first application or fairly available to the applicant on that
application. Moreover, the material before the court did not establish that by reason of the
total passage of time since the alleged offences were committed it would be unjust or
oppressive to return the applicant, within s 8(3)(*b*) of the 1967 Act, for the total passage of
time was no more than that reasonably caused by the investigation and prosecution of
d complicated charges. Furthermore, the court would not exercise its general discretion to
discharge the applicant for there was no evidence that he would inevitably be acquitted by
a Singapore court, or that his committal for return had been wrong. It followed that the
second application would be dismissed (see p 989 *e f*, p 990 *h* to p 991 *b* and *f* and *j* to p 992
b, post); dictum of Lord Diplock in *Kakis v Government of Cyprus* [1978] 2 All ER at 638
applied.

e **Notes**

For renewal of an application for habeas corpus, see 11 Halsbury's Laws (4th Edn) para
1479, and for cases on the subject, see 16 Digest (Repl) 293–294, 645–650.

For application for habeas corpus by a person committed to custody to await return
under the Fugitive Offenders Act 1967, see 18 Halsbury's Law (4th Edn) para 271, and for
cases on the subject see 24 Digest (Repl) 1013–1015, 173–177.

f For the Administration of Justice Act 1960, s 14, see 7 Halsbury's Statutes (3rd Edn) 723.

For the Fugitive Offenders Act 1967, s 8, see 13 ibid, 293.

Cases referred to in judgment

Hastings, Re, (No 2) [1958] 3 All ER 625, [1959] 1 QB 358, [1958] 3 WLR 768, 123 JP 79,
43 Cr App R 47, 16 Digest (Repl) 293, 649.

g *Johnson v Johnson* [1900] P 19, 69 LJP 13, 81 LT 791, 64 JP 72, DC, 27(2) Digest (Reissue)
1020, 8144.

Kakis v Government of Cyprus [1978] 2 All ER 634, [1978] 1 WLR 779, HL.

R v Governor of Brixton Prison, ex parte Savarkar [1910] 2 KB 1056, [1908–10] All ER Rep
603, 80 LJKB 57, 103 LT 423, CA, 21 Digest (Repl) 241, 298.

R v Medical Appeal Tribunal (North Midland Region), ex parte Hubble [1959] 3 All ER 40,
h [1959] 2 QB 418, [1959] 3 WLR 456, CA, 34 Digest (Repl) 665, 4585.

Yat Tung Investment Co Ltd v Dao Heng Bank Ltd [1975] AC 581, [1975] 2 WLR 690, PC,
Digest (Cont Vol D) 311, *254a.

Cases also cited

Bouvy, Ex parte, (No 2) (1900) 18 NZLR 601.

j *Cobbett, Re* (1845) 5 LTOS 130.

Cox v Hakes (1890) 15 App Cas 506, HL.

Director of Public Prosecutions v Humphrys [1976] 2 All ER 497, [1977] AC 1, HL.

Hastings, Re, (No 3) [1959] 1 All ER 698, [1959] Ch 368, CA.

Hoystead v Comr of Taxation [1926] AC 155, [1925] All ER Rep 56, PC.

R v Brixton Prison Governor, ex parte Enahoro [1963] 2 All ER 477, [1963] 2 QB 455, DC.

R v Park (1961) 46 Cr App R 29, CCA.
R v Suddis (1801) 1 East 306, 102 ER 119.
Schtraks, Re [1962] 2 All ER 176, [1963] 1 QB 55, DC, sub nom Schtraks v Government of
Israel [1962] 3 All ER 529, [1964] AC 556, HL.
Union of India v Narang [1977] 2 All ER 348, [1978] AC 247, HL.

Application for habeas corpus

This was a renewed application for habeas corpus, dated 23rd July 1978, by Richard Charles
Tarling ('the applicant') to secure his discharge from custody in Pentonville prison where
he had been committed for return to Singapore under the Fugitive Offenders Act 1967,
pursuant to an order by the chief metropolitan magistrate (Kenneth Barraclough Esq)
made on 26th January 1977, for trial on, inter alia, five charges brought against him by the
Singapore government in respect of alleged offences under the Singapore Companies Act.
The grounds of the renewed application were (i) that by reason of the total passage of time
since the alleged offences were committed it was unjust and oppressive , within s 8(3)(b) of
the 1967 Act, to return him to Singapore; (ii) that it was unjust and oppressive, within
s 8(3)(a) of the 1967 Act, to return him by reason of the triviality of the offences; and (iii)
that the court was entitled to discharge him under its general jurisdiction. The applicant
contended that ground (i) was a fresh ground for the purpose of s 14(2) of the
Administration of Justice Act 1960, and that fresh evidence, within s 14(2), had been
adduced in support of the renewed application. The respondents to the application were
the Secretary of State for the Home Department, the Government of the Republic of
Singapore and the Governor of H M Prison at Pentonville. The facts are set out in the
judgment of the court.

Louis Blom-Cooper QC and *Michael Burton* for the applicant.
Harry Woolf and *Philip Havers* for the Secretary of State for the Home Department.
Alexander Irvine QC and *D Lloyd-Jones* for the Singapore government.
Colin Nicholls for the governor of Pentonville prison.

Cur adv vult

14th December. **GIBSON J** read the following judgment of the court: In this case the
applicant applies for a writ of habeas corpus. The purpose of the application is to seek his
discharge from an order of committal made on 26th January 1977 by the chief metropolitan
magistrate on an application by the Singapore government for the return to Singapore of
the applicant on five separate criminal charges. The applicant has been on bail.

The facts of the case can be briefly stated. In June 1971 Slater Walker Securities Ltd
('Slater Walker') acquired a 49·88% interest in Haw Par Brothers International Ltd ('Haw
Par'), a Singapore company. Executives of Slater Walker, including the applicant, were
appointed directors of Haw Par and of associated companies. In September 1971 the
applicant became chairman of the board of Haw Par. He never resided in Singapore but
made visits there in connection with his work as a director.

The five charges relate to alleged wilful failures to deal fully and properly in the accounts
of Haw Par with certain transactions relating to dealings in shares and to a specially formed
unit trust called Melbourne Unit Trust. By those transactions, which the directors of Haw
Par caused to be carried out, the directors intended to avoid revealing, as profits made in
one year, certain very large profits made by Haw Par on dealings in shares. The two sets
of accounts, to which the five charges relate, were prepared for the years ended 31st
December 1972 and 1973, and the applicant signed the chairman's statements for those sets
of accounts on 19th April 1973 and on 8th May 1974 respectively. The applicant ceased to
be a director of Haw Par in August 1974 and since June 1974 he has not been in Singapore.

In July 1975 the Singapore government became aware of the facts relevant to these five
charges and, because of those facts and other circumstances concerned with Haw Par,
inspectors were appointed under the Singapore Companies Act to investigate the affairs of
Haw Par.

In December 1975 the Attorney-General of the Republic of Singapore made the decision
to commence certain prosecutions with reference to the affairs of Haw Par including that
against the applicant. On 24th June 1976 the Singapore government applied to the United
Kingdom government for the arrest, and return to Singapore, of the applicant and Mr
Slater, both executives of Slater Walker, pursuant to the Fugitive Offenders Act 1967. On
6th October 1976 the Secretary of State gave his authority to proceed under s 5 of that Act.

The committal proceedings commenced on 5th January 1977 and lasted 13 days. There
were then 17 charges in all which the chief magistrate had to consider. He decided that the
evidence did not justify committing Mr Slater on any charge against him. As to the
charges against the applicant, he was committed on charges 1 to 4 and on charges 7 to
17. All the charges, other than the five charges numbered 12 to 16 which still survive
against the applicant, alleged against the applicant conspiracy with other persons and acts
of dishonesty with reference to the affairs of Haw Par and subsidiary companies.

The Singapore government applied to the Divisional Court to quash the decision of the
chief magistrate on the charges against Mr Slater. That application failed.

The applicant on 4th February 1977 applied to the Divisional Court (Shaw LJ, Nield and
Stocker JJ) for habeas corpus to secure his discharge on all the charges against him. His
application was based primarily on the ground that the evidence revealed no prima facie
case against him on any charge, and on the terms of s 8(3) of the Fugitive Offenders Act
1967 which provides, so far as is relevant to this case, that on any application for habeas
corpus by a person committed:

> '... the High Court ... may, without prejudice to any other jurisdiction of the
> court, order the person committed to be discharged from custody if it appears to the
> court that—(a) by reason of the trivial nature of the offence of which he is accused
> ... or, (b) by reason of the passage of time since he is alleged to have committed it
> ... or, (c) because the accusation against him is not made in good faith in the interests
> of justice, it would, having regard to all the circumstances, be unjust or oppressive to
> return him.'

This hearing before the Divisional Court also lasted some 13 days. Charges 7 to 10 were
abandoned by the Crown. The court found no valid ground for committal on charges 1
to 4 or on charge 11, but they upheld the decision of the chief magistrate on the surviving
five charges 12 to 16 and on charge 17. Judgment was given on 29th July 1977.

On that application the applicant had not relied on s 8(3)(b), passage of time, but he had
argued that charges 12 to 16 were so trivial that he should be discharged with reference to
them: that is the ground in s 8(3)(a).

On 13th October 1977 application was made by the applicant to the Appeal Committee
of the House of Lords. He was given leave to appeal on charge 17, which was the only
charge then remaining against him which alleged dishonesty on his part. Leave to appeal
on charges 12 to 16, which are the five surviving charges, was refused to him. Leave to
appeal was also granted to the Singapore government with reference to charges 1 to 4 and
to charge 11, all of which alleged dishonesty and on which the applicant had succeeded in
the Divisional Court.

The hearing before the Appellate Committee of the House of Lords continued from
25th January to 20th February 1978. Judgment was delivered on 19th April 1978. The
applicant's appeal succeeded: he was discharged from charge 17. The appeal of the
Singapore government failed. In the result, the applicant remained committed on charges
12 to 16, in respect of which the House of Lords had refused leave to appeal, and no charge
in which dishonesty was alleged remained effective against him.

The applicant then petitioned the Secretary of State. In short, the applicant was asking
the Secretary of State to exercise the discretion given to the Secretary of State by s 9 of the
1967 Act not to make an order for his return to Singapore although the Divisional Court
had dismissed his application to that court for discharge on those charges. That section (so
far as is relevant to this case) requires the Secretary of State not to make an order for the

return of any person under the Act if it appears to the Secretary of State, on the grounds set out in s 8(3) above, that it would be unjust or oppressive to return that person.

On 16th June 1978 the Secretary of State issued his warrant under s 9 of the 1967 Act ordering the return of the applicant to Singapore on charges 12 to 16. It had, accordingly, not appeared to the Secretary of State that it would be unjust or oppressive to return the applicant on any of the grounds set out in s 8(3) of the 1967 Act.

On 23rd June 1978 the applicant applied to this court for leave to apply for habeas corpus in respect of his committal on charges 12 to 16 and leave was given. The effective hearing of his application commenced on 13th November 1978.

The procedure laid down by the Fugitive Offenders Act 1967 was thus apparently completed on 16th June 1978 when, on the completion of the processes of appeal, the Secretary of State issued his warrant. The questions in this case have been whether the applicant has shown any ground on which he is entitled to start again that part of the procedure under the 1967 Act which allows application to this court for discharge on the statutory grounds; and, if he has shown any such ground, whether he has produced any evidence which has made it appear oppressive or unjust to return him.

The making of a second or successive application for habeas corpus is now controlled by the provisions of s 14(2) of the Administration of Justice Act 1960 which provides as follows:

'Notwithstanding anything in any enactment or rule of law, where a criminal or civil application for habeas corpus has been made by or in respect of any person, no such application shall again be made by or in respect of that person *on the same grounds*, whether to the same court or judge or to any other court or judge, unless fresh evidence is adduced in support of the application . . .'

It was accordingly an essential part of the applicant's application to the court to show that this, his second application, was not made 'on the same grounds' as those on which his first application was put forward, and, if he could not show that, to show that on this application he has adduced fresh evidence in support of it.

The main ground of application advanced by counsel for the applicant was under s 8(3)(b) of the 1967 Act, namely that 'by reason of the passage of time since he is alleged to have committed the offence . . . it would, having regard to all the circumstances, be unjust or oppressive to return him'. He contends that the time has now been extended from 29th July 1977, when the Divisional Court gave its decision on the first application, down to November 1978 when this court heard this application; and he contends that this passage of time has been caused by the prosecution of appeals, both by the applicant and by the Singapore government, on which the applicant has wholly succeeded. This further time has been spent, he says, in attempts by the Singapore government to secure his committal on charges which, as has been shown by the results of the appeals, should not have been put forward.

Reliance on injustice or oppression through passage of time is, therefore, a new or fresh ground in the sense that it has not been put forward before, and the additional passage of time, of course, has elapsed since the applicant made his first application.

The applicant has also claimed to rely again on the ground set out in s 8(3)(a) of the 1967 Act, namely triviality of the offences. He acknowledges that this is not a fresh ground, having been argued on the first application, but he says that this court could discharge him on that ground since it is now supported by fresh evidence. It is further said that the triviality of the offence is in any event part of the circumstances relevant to be considered with reference to the new s 8(3)(b) ground, namely injustice or oppression from passage of time.

Lastly, it has been submitted that, apart from reliance on the statutory grounds in s 8(3) of the 1967 Act, the applicant is entitled to be discharged under the court's general jurisdiction on the ground that, on the fresh evidence now submitted and new argument made, the applicant is bound in law to be acquitted on these five charges under the laws of Singapore. This point has not previously been put forward.

To these submissions, counsel for the Secretary of State, counsel for the Singapore
government, and counsel for the governor of Pentonville prison have replied with
a contentions to the effect that on the material before the court there is no jurisdiction to
make any order of discharge on this renewed application. These contentions have united
on some points and diverged on others. In addition, counsel for the Singapore government
has submitted that, if there is jurisdiction, there is no basis on the facts on which this court
should order the discharge of the applicant.

b In the view of this court, if the arguments on jurisdiction are all resolved in favour of the
applicant, there is on the evidence, for reasons which will be explained, no ground on
which this court can find it to be in any way unjust or oppressive for him to be returned
to Singapore on these five charges, and his application must therefore be rejected. It is,
accordingly, not necessary for the court to decide the questions as to jurisdiction which
have been raised. The points have, however, been fully argued and we will state the
c conclusions which we have reached on the submissions made.

Before dealing with the questions of jurisdiction it is to be noted that, on two important
principles, which bear on the position of an applicant for habeas corpus who seeks to make
a second application in respect of the same detention, there was no substantial dispute
between the parties in this case.

Firstly, it is clear to the court that an applicant for habeas corpus is required to put
d forward on his initial application the whole of the case which is then fairly available to
him. He is not free to advance an application on one ground, and to keep back a separate
ground of application as a basis for a second or renewed application to the court.

The true doctrine of estoppel known as res judicata does not apply to the decision of this
court on an application for habeas corpus: we refer to the words of Lord Parker CJ,
delivering the judgment of the court in *Re Hastings (No 2)*[1]. There is, however, a wider
e sense in which the doctrine of res judicata may be applicable, whereby it becomes an abuse
of process to raise in subsequent proceedings matters which could, and therefore should,
have been litigated in earlier proceedings: see the judgment of the Privy Council (Lord
Morris, Lord Cross and Lord Kilbrandon) in *Yat Tung Investment Co Ltd v Dao Heng Bank
Ltd*[2]. In our judgment, that principle is applicable to proceedings for habeas corpus,
whether under the 1967 Act or under the general jurisdiction of the court although, no
f doubt, the stringency of the application of the principle may be different in cases
concerning the liberty of the subject from that in cases concerning such matters as disputes
on property.

Secondly, it is also clear to the court that, in s 14(2) of the Administration of Justice Act
1960, in the phrase 'no such application shall again be made on the same grounds unless
fresh evidence is adduced in support of the application', the words 'fresh evidence' are used
g in that meaning which is well known and established in such contexts, namely not merely
evidence additional to or different from the evidence before the court on the first occasion,
but evidence which the applicant could not have put forward on the first application, or
which he could not then reasonably be expected to have put forward, see *Johnson v Johnson*[3]
and *R v Medical Appeal Tribunal (North Midland Region), ex parte Hubble*[4].

As to the arguments on jurisdiction, the first point was this. Counsel for the Secretary
h of State argued that those 'reasons' which are listed in s 8(3) of the 1967 Act, including
triviality and passage of time, are not 'grounds' for the purposes of s 14(2) of the 1960
Act. The court in ordering discharge under s 8(3) of the 1967 Act is not, so ran this
argument, granting relief by way of habeas corpus but is exercising a separate and distinct
statutory power, and the application for habeas corpus is no more than the procedure by
which the matter is brought before the court. Further, according to this argument, the
j phrase 'on the same grounds' in s 14(2) of the 1960 Act, refers to that detention which is the

1   [1958] 3 All ER 625 at 631, [1959] 1 QB 358 at 371
2   [1975] AC 681
3   [1900] P 19
4   [1959] 3 All ER 40, [1959] 2 QB 418

subject-matter of the application for habeas corpus, and not the reasons relied on in support of the application for discharge. On this argument, 'passage of time', under s 8(3)(*b*), *a* although not relied on, nor fairly available on the first application, cannot qualify as a new ground and, since the application is made with reference to the same committal, the application is made 'on the same grounds'.

For the Singapore government, counsel supported this argument: he submitted that the phrase 'on the same grounds' in s 14(2) of the 1960 Act was to be construed as a reference to the 'same complex of facts of the detention' in question. Counsel for the governor of *b* Pentonville prison also supported this argument.

We do not accept this submission. The phrase 'on the same grounds' in s 14(2) of the 1960 Act cannot have the limited and technical meaning which this submission would attach to it. The phrase should be given its ordinary meaning. The grounds of an application include those facts on which the court is asked to base the decision which the court is asked to make, namely that the detention is unlawful, or that in the exercise of its *c* discretion under the 1967 Act the applicant should be discharged from that detention. This construction of the phrase will not permit the process of return under the 1967 Act to be improperly prolonged because, as has been stated, the court would not permit an applicant to hold back, and not use, a ground of application which was fairly available to him on his initial application and then claim to put forward that ground on a second application.   *d*

We also reject the submission, which was made in support of the submission as to the meaning of the phrase 'on the same grounds', to the effect that, in ordering discharge under s 8(3) of the 1967 Act the court is not granting relief by way of habeas corpus. It was argued that the court, in ordering discharge under s 8(3), is merely exercising a separate and distinct statutory power to mitigate what is in fact a lawful detention, as opposed to ordering, in what was called a true habeas corpus application, discharge from unlawful *e* detention. Reference was made to *R v Governor of Brixton Prison, ex parte Savarkar*[1], a case under the Fugitive Offenders Act 1881, where the Court of Appeal drew a distinction between relief by habeas corpus and the relief which the court was empowered to give under the provisions of that Act which resembled s 8 of the 1967 Act. Whatever may have been the position under the 1881 Act, it is clear to us that the 1967 Act, by its express language, provides that an application to the court for relief under s 8 is to be made by *f* application for habeas corpus (see s 8(1) and (3)) and that, in enacting s 8 in those terms in 1967, with s 14 of the 1960 Act already on the statute book, Parliament intended an application for habeas corpus, on any ground set out in s 8 of the 1967 Act, to be regarded as an application for habeas corpus, on the grounds put forward in support of it, for the purposes of and within the meaning of s 14(2) of the 1960 Act.

We would add that, even if the decision of the Court of Appeal in *Savarkar's* case[1] were *g* to be applied to the provisions of the 1967 Act, so that an application to the court for discharge under s 8 of that Act is not to be regarded as an application for habeas corpus under s 14(2) of the 1960 Act, the procedural position would not, in our judgment, be different in any relevant respect. A person committed for return under the 1967 Act would still be able to make a second or successive application for discharge under s 8, provided that the ground on which he made his application for discharge under this *h* particular statutory power was not a ground which was fairly available to him on his initial application; and provided that, if he was applying on a ground on which he had applied before, the application was supported by fresh evidence. We reach that conclusion because we find nothing in the provisions of the 1967 Act which expressly or by necessary implication prohibits the making of such a further application and, since the 1967 Act by s 8 expressly directs that an application for the exercise of the special statutory power to *j* order discharge shall be made by the procedure of an application for habeas corpus, the

---

1 [1910] 2 KB 1056, [1908–10] All ER Rep 603

court must, in our judgment, apply all those attributes of that procedure which favour the
liberty of the subject.

a   We come now to the second point on jurisdiction. It turns on the fact that the Secretary
of State had, before this second application for habeas corpus was made, performed his
duties under s 9 of the 1967 Act and issued his warrant for the return of the applicant to
Singapore. Counsel for the Singapore government submitted that the issuing of the
warrant concluded the matter, so far as concerned both habeas corpus and the power of the
b   court to order discharge under the 1967 Act. He argued that the issuing of the warrant by
the Secretary of State could only be set aside or overridden if the court had material before
it on which it could properly quash that warrant by certiorari. This submission was
supported by counsel for the governor of Pentonville prison. It did not receive the support
of counsel for the Secretary of State.

We reject this submission also. The 1967 Act contains no express provision which
c   makes the issuing of the warrant by the Secretary of State final and conclusive in the sense
contended for, and we can see nothing in the 1967 Act which by necessary implication
could require that such finality be attributed to the issuing of the warrant.

The principles of law discussed above, including the duty of any applicant to put
forward his full case on his initial application, will ensure that it would be only in most
exceptional circumstances that the court would consider ordering the discharge of an
d   applicant after the Secretary of State has issued his warrant. It is, however, possible to think
of entirely exceptional circumstances in which the court, on new material, would be
compelled to order the discharge of the applicant under s 8(3) of the 1967 Act
notwithstanding the fact that the Secretary of State had previously issued his warrant under
s 9, and in our opinion the Act gives this court power to do so.

As to the facts of this application by the applicant, his second application with reference
e   to the same committal, it seems to the court that such new material as the applicant has put
forward on this application is not capable of qualifying as 'fresh evidence', according to the
proper meaning of those words, save for one circumstance only, and that is the time which
has passed since his first application to the court in February 1977. Further, in seeking to
rely on that passage of time, added to the time which had previously passed, the applicant
has applied to this court on grounds which, in our judgment, are not 'the same grounds'
f   as formed the basis of his first application. As has already been stated, however, this 'new
ground' does not on the facts before the court provide any basis for this court to order his
discharge.

The date to which the relevant lapse of time is to be considered is, in our view, the
commencement of the present application, that is June 1978. The court was referred to
Kakis v Republic of Cyprus[1] where the House of Lords considered s 8(3) of the 1967 Act.
g   Lord Diplock there said[2]:

> '. . . the passage of time to be considered is the time that passed between the date of
> the offence . . . and the date of the hearing in the Divisional Court . . . for that is the
> first occasion on which this ground for resisting extradition can be raised by the
> accused . . .'

h   Nothing in *Kakis v Republic of Cyprus*[1] turned on any lapse of time between the date of
the application to the Divisional Court and the date of the hearing. The date to be taken
in this case, in our view, as the 'first occasion' on which the applicant was able to raise the
further period of delay as a ground for resisting his return to Singapore was when he
applied the second time to this court. It is true that he could have made this application in
April 1978, instead of waiting until June when his petition to the Secretary of State had
j   been rejected, but in this case the distinction is of no importance.

Counsel for the applicant argued that the period of delay caused by the appeals to the
House of Lords should be regarded as delay for which the Singapore government was

---

1   [1978] 2 All ER 634, [1978] 1 WLR 779
2   [1978] 2 All ER 634 at 638, [1978] 1 WLR 779 at 782

responsible. It is wholly clear that the applicant was in no sense responsible for the further delay, but the Singapore government is not to be regarded, in our view, as in any way at fault for the time spent in the appeal. The charges alleging dishonesty have all been conclusively rejected, but the Singapore government was not acting unfairly in presenting to the courts of this country, for consideration under the 1967 Act, the charges which were advanced.

It was next contended that the period of three years, from the time in 1975 when the Singapore government knew of the facts of the alleged offences, down to June 1978 when the second application was presented, by itself gives rise to a presumption of oppression, and that certain features of this case accentuated that presumption. Those features were said to be the lack of gravity in the offences, which involve no dishonesty, the fact that the applicant has made no personal gain from the alleged offences, the fact that the alleged offences are punishable only by non-custodial sentences by English law and the fact that the applicant was not involved in the alleged offences as a principal offender.

It was added that the applicant had never lived in Singapore and that it was hard to make him return there to face such charges. The court was also asked to consider a contention that the applicant was led to believe, as a result of negotiations for settlement of certain civil claims, that he would not be prosecuted.

There is, in our judgment, nothing fresh in any sense in any of these features of the case. They were all in substance argued before the Divisional Court on the first application, or were fairly available to the applicant then. The alleged lack of gravity was then expressly advanced as triviality under s 8(3)(a) of the 1967 Act. References to the settlement of the civil proceedings, and to the fact that it was followed within days by the application by the Singapore government under the 1967 Act for the return of the applicant, were made in support of a contention, then made to the Divisional Court, that the application for return was not made bona fide but for an ulterior purpose. That contention was, of course, rejected and has not been repeated in this application.

We accept, however, that the features of the case to which counsel for the applicant referred are, in so far as they are established by the evidence, part of the circumstances in and by reference to which the new ground of lapse of time must be considered.

It was not submitted to the Divisional Court in February 1977 that the time which had then passed could be regarded as grounds for ordering discharge, and on behalf of the applicant on this application it has been asserted that that submission could not then possibly have been made.

The question, accordingly, is whether by reason of the additional lapse of time which was caused by the appeal to the House of Lords the total time which has now passed is such that it is unjust or oppressive to return the applicant to Singapore. In *Kakis v Government of Cyprus*[1] Lord Diplock, with reference to the provisions of s 8(3), said:

'"Unjust" I regard as directed primarily to the risk of prejudice to the accused in the conduct of the trial itself, "oppressive" as directed to hardship to the accused resulting from changes in his circumstances that have occurred during the period to be taken into consideration; but there is room for overlapping, and between them they would cover all cases where to return him would not be *fair*.'

It is clear that the passage of time has not in any way prejudiced the accused in the conduct of the trial on these charges. It has not been suggested to us that any such prejudice has occurred.

As to 'oppressiveness', the evidence has revealed nothing which in our opinion could be regarded as hardship to the applicant resulting from changes in his circumstances that have occurred during the period to be taken into consideration and which could be regarded as justifying his discharge.

We would add that, as to the general question of 'fairness', we are not able to find that the total passage of time has in any way, or from any point of view, made it unfair for the

---

1 [1978] 2 All ER 634 at 638, [1978] 1 WLR 779 at 782–783

applicant to be required to return to Singapore to face these charges. The applicant chose
a for commercial reasons to take part as a director in the business affairs of a Singapore
company and for that purpose to visit Singapore as frequently as was necessary. There has
been found to be a prima facie case that he was guilty of wilful failure to comply with the
provisions of the Singapore Companies Act with reference to that company. Since there
has been nothing dilatory or unfair in the investigation or prosecution of these alleged
offences by the Singapore government, there is nothing unfair in now ordering the
b applicant to return to Singapore to face those charges. The total passage of time has been
no more than that reasonably caused by the investigation and prosecution of charges which
arise on documents and transactions of intricate complication, and in the forming and
carrying out of those transactions the applicant appears to have played an active and
comprehending part.

As to the contention that the passage of time included a period, from 1975 to June 1976,
c when civil claims by Haw Par against Slater Walker were finally settled, during which, by
reason of those negotiations, a reasonable expectation was induced in the applicant that, if
the settlement was reached he would not be prosecuted, we are unable to accept that the
applicant could ever reasonably have held such expectation for the reason given.

The civil claims which were settled related to the diversion, to the Slater Walker
directors including the applicant, of about 10% of those shares on which Haw Par made the
d very large profits mentioned above. The applicant's share of the profit so diverted was said
to be about £176,000. The settlement included repayment in full by Slater Walker of the
full amount of profit on the diverted shares. It is common ground in this application that
no promise whatever, express or implied, was given on behalf of the Singapore government
in return for settlement of the civil claims.

The applicant may have hoped that, if the civil claims were settled, the attitude of the
e Singapore government might be affected by that fact, but, if he entertained such hopes, he
did not do so by reason of anything said or done by or on behalf of the Singapore
government, and the disappointment of those hopes, which occurred as long ago as
October 1976, cannot in any way be regarded as oppression resulting from any relevant
passage of time.

As to the submission that the applicant can rely again on the alleged injustice or
f oppression in returning him, by reason of the trivial nature of the offences charged in the
five surviving charges, we reject the submission that this ground of triviality is on this
application supported by anything that can properly be called 'fresh evidence' for the
purposes of s 14(2) of the 1960 Act.

The material which it was argued should be regarded as fresh evidence consisted of the
report of the inspector into the affairs of Haw Par, the statement of Arthur Young & Co to
g the inspector and the evidence on affidavit of Mr Morpeth and Mr Richardson as to
accountancy practice. The report of the inspector was a public document which was
available to the applicant at the date of the first application. The statement of Arthur
Young & Co, as a document referred to in the schedule to that report, was equally
available. Having looked at the documents it is plain to us that the material in them could
not have affected the view of the court as to 'triviality'.

h As to the affidavits of Mr Morpeth and Mr Richardson, this new evidence is expert
evidence as to accountancy practice and theory at the time of the alleged offences directed
to the acceptable methods of dealing with such profits as are referred to in charges 12 to
16. There is no apparent reason for regarding this evidence as 'fresh evidence': it was
plainly available at the time of the first application. This evidence in any event does not
cast any doubt whatever on the existence of a prima facie case on charges 12 to 16 or cause
j us to consider that the charges could be regarded as trivial.

There is finally the submission to the effect that, apart from the special statutory grounds
under s 8(3) and para (b) of the 1967 Act, the applicant should be discharged under the
court's general jurisdiction on the ground that, on the evidence and the new argument
made, the applicant is bound in law to be acquitted on charges 12 to 16 under the laws of
Singapore.

It is sufficient for us to say that the argument did not persuade us either that, on the evidence, the applicant must inevitably be acquitted in Singapore, or that the chief *a* magistrate was wrong in finding a prima facie case to support charges 12 to 16 by reference to English law. This new argument seems to us to be an argument to be addressed to the court in Singapore. Further, if this contention could support the applicant's application for habeas corpus it was in our judgment fairly open to the applicant when he made his first application to this court and is therefore not open to him now.

For all these reasons we can see no ground for thinking that it is either unjust or *b* oppressive to require the applicant to return to Singapore to face these charges and this application must be dismissed.

Application dismissed. Leave to appeal to the House of Lords refused.

Solicitors: *D J Freeman & Co* (for the applicant); *Treasury Solicitor*; *Charles Russell & Co* (for *c* the Singapore government); *Director of Public Prosecutions.*

N P Metcalfe Esq   Barrister.

End of Volume 1